T0252798

Static and Dynamic Neural Networks

Static and Dynamic Neural Networks

From Fundamentals to Advanced Theory

Madan M. Gupta, Liang Jin, and Noriyasu Homma

Foreword by Lotfi A. Zadeh

IEEE
IEEE PRESS

WILEY-
INTERSCIENCE

A JOHN WILEY & SONS, INC., PUBLICATION

Copyright © 2003 by John Wiley & Sons, Inc. All rights reserved.

Published by John Wiley & Sons, Inc., Hoboken, New Jersey.
Published simultaneously in Canada.

No part of this publication may be reproduced, stored in a retrieval system, or transmitted in any form or by any means, electronic, mechanical, photocopying, recording, scanning, or otherwise, except as permitted under Section 107 or 108 of the 1976 United States Copyright Act, without either the prior written permission of the Publisher, or authorization through payment of the appropriate per-copy fee to the Copyright Clearance Center, Inc., 222 Rosewood Drive, Danvers, MA 01923, 978-750-8400, fax 978-750-4470, or on the web at www.copyright.com. Requests to the Publisher for permission should be addressed to the Permissions Department, John Wiley & Sons, Inc., 111 River Street, Hoboken, NJ 07030, (201) 748-6011, fax (201) 748-6008, e-mail: permreq@wiley.com.

Limit of Liability/Disclaimer of Warranty: While the publisher and author have used their best efforts in preparing this book, they make no representations or warranties with respect to the accuracy or completeness of the contents of this book and specifically disclaim any implied warranties of merchantability or fitness for a particular purpose. No warranty may be created or extended by sales representatives or written sales materials. The advice and strategies contained herein may not be suitable for your situation. You should consult with a professional where appropriate. Neither the publisher nor author shall be liable for any loss of profit or any other commercial damages, including but not limited to special, incidental, consequential, or other damages.

For general information on our other products and services please contact our Customer Care Department within the U.S. at 877-762-2974, outside the U.S. at 317-572-3993 or fax 317-572-4002.

Wiley also publishes its books in a variety of electronic formats. Some content that appears in print, however, may not be available in electronic format.

Library of Congress Cataloging-in-Publication Data:

Static and Dynamic Neural Networks: From Fundamentals to Advanced Theory—
Madan M. Gupta, Liang Jin, and Noriyasu Homma

ISBN 978-0-471-21948-4

ॐ भूर्भुवः स्वः ।

तत्स वितुर्व रेण्यम ॥

भर्गो देवस्य धीमहि ।

धियो यो नः प्रचोदयात् ॥

॥ ॐ शान्ति शान्ति शान्तिः ॥

OM BHURBHUVAH SVAH !
TATSAVITUR VARENYAM !!
BHARGO DEVASYA DHIMAHI !
DHIYO YO NAH PRACHODAYATH !!
OM SHANTI ! SHANTI !! SHANTIHI !!!

(yajur-36-3, Rig Veda 3-62-10)

We meditate upon the Adorable Brilliance of that Divine Creator.
Who is the Giver of life, Remover of all sufferings, and Bestower of bliss.
We pray to Him to enlighten our minds and make our thoughts clear,
And inspire truth in our perception, process of thinking, and the way of our life.
Om Peace! Peace!! Peace!!!

全能の神への祈り
神は生命を与え　苦しみを取り除き　そして至福を授ける
神よ　我々の心に真実の光を照らし
知覚　思考　人生すべてを真理へと導きたまえ
そして　泰平の安らぎを

We dedicate this book to

Professor Lotfi A. Zadeh
(The father of fuzzy logic and soft computing)

and

Dr. Peter N. Nikiforuk
(Dean Emeritus, College of Engineering),
who jointly inspired the work reported in these pages;

and, also to

The research colleagues and students in this global village,
who have made countless contributions to the developing fields of
neural networks, soft computing and intelligent systems,
and, have inspired the authors to learn, explore and thrive in these areas.

Also, to

Suman Gupta, Shan Song, and Hideko Homma,
who have created a synergism in our homes
for quenching our thirst for learning more and more.

Madan M. Gupta
Liang Jin
Noriyasu Homma

Contents

Foreword: Lotfi A. Zadeh *xix*

Preface *xxiii*

Acknowledgments *xxvii*

PART I FOUNDATIONS OF NEURAL NETWORKS

1 Neural Systems: An Introduction **3**

1.1 Basics of Neuronal Morphology *4*
1.2 The Neuron *8*
1.3 Neurocomputational Systems: Some Perspectives *9*
1.4 Neuronal Learning *12*
1.5 Theory of Neuronal Approximations *13*
1.6 Fuzzy Neural Systems *14*
1.7 Applications of Neural Networks: Present and Future *15*
1.7.1 Neurovision Systems *15*
1.7.2 Neurocontrol Systems *16*
1.7.3 Neural Hardware Implementations *16*
1.7.4 Some Future Perspectives *17*
1.8 An Overview of the Book *17*

2 Biological Foundations of Neuronal Morphology **21**

2.1 Morphology of Biological Neurons *22*
2.1.1 Basic Neuronal Structure *22*

2.1.2 Neural Electrical Signals 25
2.2 Neural Information Processing 27
2.2.1 Neural Mathematical Operations 28
2.2.2 Sensorimotor Feedback Structure 30
2.2.3 Dynamic Characteristics 31
2.3 Human Memory Systems 32
2.3.1 Types of Human Memory 32
2.3.2 Features of Short-Term and Long-Term Memories 34
2.3.3 Content-Addressable and Associative Memory 35
2.4 Human Learning and Adaptation 36
2.4.1 Types of Human Learning 36
2.4.2 Supervised and Unsupervised Learning Mechanisms 38
2.5 Concluding Remarks 38
2.6 Some Biological Keywords 39
Problems 40

3 Neural Units: Concepts, Models, and Learning 43
3.1 Neurons and Threshold Logic: Some Basic Concepts 44
3.1.1 Some Basic Binary Logical Operations 45
3.1.2 Neural Models for Threshold Logics 47
3.2 Neural Threshold Logic Synthesis 51
3.2.1 Realization of Switching Function 51
3.3 Adaptation and Learning for Neural Threshold Elements 62
3.3.1 Concept of Parameter Adaptation 62
3.3.2 The Perceptron Rule of Adaptation 65
3.3.3 Mays Rule of Adaptation 68
3.4 Adaptive Linear Element (Adaline) 70
3.4.1 α-LMS (Least Mean Square) Algorithm 71
3.4.2 Mean Square Error Method 75
3.5 Adaline with Sigmoidal Functions 80
3.5.1 Nonlinear Sigmoidal Functions 80
3.5.2 Backpropagation for the Sigmoid Adaline 82
3.6 Networks with Multiple Neurons 84

3.6.1 A Simple Network with Three Neurons 85
3.6.2 Error Backpropagation Learning 88
3.7 Concluding Remarks 94
Problems 95

PART II STATIC NEURAL NETWORKS

4 Multilayered Feedforward Neural Networks (MFNNs) and Backpropagation Learning Algorithms 105
4.1 Two-Layered Neural Networks 107
4.1.1 Structure and Operation Equations 107
4.1.2 Generalized Delta Rule 112
4.1.3 Network with Linear Output Units 118
4.2 Example 4.1: XOR Neural Network 121
4.2.1 Network Model 121
4.2.2 Simulation Results 123
4.2.3 Geometric Explanation 127
4.3 Backpropagation (BP) Algorithms for MFNN 129
4.3.1 General Neural Structure for MFNNs 130
4.3.2 Extension of the Generalized Delta Rule to General MFNN Structures 135
4.4 Deriving BP Algorithm Using Variational Principle 140
4.4.1 Optimality Conditions 140
4.4.2 Weight Updating 142
4.4.3 Transforming the Parameter Space 143
4.5 Momentum BP Algorithm 144
4.5.1 Modified Increment Formulation 144
4.5.2 Effect of Momentum Term 146
4.6 A Summary of BP Learning Algorithm 149
4.6.1 Updating Procedure 149
4.6.2 Signal Propagation in MFNN Architecture 151
4.7 Some Issues in BP Learning Algorithm 155
4.7.1 Initial Values of Weights and Learning Rate 155
4.7.2 Number of Hidden Layers and Neurons 158
4.7.3 Local Minimum Problem 162

4.8 *Concluding Remarks* 163
Problems 164

5 Advanced Methods for Learning and Adaptation in MFNNs 171
5.1 *Different Error Measure Criteria* 172
5.1.1 *Error Distributions and L_p Norms* 173
5.1.2 *The Case of Generic L_p Norm* 175
5.2 *Complexities in Regularization* 177
5.2.1 *Weight Decay Approach* 179
5.2.2 *Weight Elimination Approach* 180
5.2.3 *Chauvin's Penalty Approach* 181
5.3 *Network Pruning through Sensitivity Calculations* 183
5.3.1 *First-Order Pruning Procedures* 183
5.3.2 *Second-Order Pruning Procedures* 186
5.4 *Evaluation of the Hessian Matrix* 191
5.4.1 *Diagonal Second-Order Derivatives* 192
5.4.2 *General Second-Order Derivative Formulations* 196
5.5 *Second-Order Optimization Learning Algorithms* 198
5.5.1 *Quasi-Newton Methods* 199
5.5.2 *Conjugate Gradient (CG) Methods for Learning* 200
5.6 *Linearized Recursive Estimation Learning Algorithms* 202
5.6.1 *Linearized Least Squares Learning (LLSL)* 202
5.6.2 *Decomposed Extended Kalman Filter (DEKF) Learning* 204
5.7 *Tapped Delay Line Neural Networks (TDLNNs)* 208
5.8 *Applications of TDLNNs for Adaptive Control Systems* 211
5.9 *Concluding Remarks* 215
Problems 215

6 Radial Basis Function Neural Networks 223
6.1 *Radial Basis Function Networks (RBFNs)* 224
6.1.1 *Basic Radial Basis Function Network Models* 224
6.1.2 *RBFNs and Interpolation Problem* 227
6.1.3 *Solving Overdetermined Equations* 232

6.2 Gaussian Radial Basis Function Neural Networks 235
6.2.1 Gaussian RBF Network Model 235
6.2.2 Gaussian RBF Networks as Universal Approximator 239
6.3 Learning Algorithms for Gaussian RBF Neural Networks 242
6.3.1 K-Means Clustering-Based Learning Procedures in Gaussian RBF Neural Network 242
6.3.2 Supervised (Gradient Descent) Parameter Learning in Gaussian Networks 245
6.4 Concluding Remarks 246
Problems 247

7 Function Approximation Using Feedforward Neural Networks 253
7.1 Stone–Weierstrass Theorem and its Feedforward Networks 254
7.1.1 Basic Definitions 255
7.1.2 Stone–Weierstrass Theorem and Approximation 256
7.1.3 Implications for Neural Networks 258
7.2 Trigonometric Function Neural Networks 260
7.3 MFNNs as Universal Approximators 266
7.3.1 Sketch Proof for Two-Layered Networks 267
7.3.2 Approximation Using General MFNNs 271
7.4 Kolmogorov's Theorem and Feedforward Networks 274
7.5 Higher-Order Neural Networks (HONNs) 279
7.6 Modified Polynomial Neural Networks 287
7.6.1 Sigma–Pi Neural Networks (S-PNNs) 287
7.6.2 Ridge Polynomial Neural Networks (RPNNs) 288
7.7 Concluding Remarks 291
Problems 292

PART III DYNAMIC NEURAL NETWORKS

8 Dynamic Neural Units (DNUs): Nonlinear Models and Dynamics **297**

8.1 Models of Dynamic Neural Units (DNUs) 298
8.1.1 A Generalized DNU Model 298
8.1.2 Some Typical DNU Structures 301
8.2 Models and Circuits of Isolated DNUs 307
8.2.1 An Isolated DNU 307
8.2.2 DNU Models: Some Extensions and Their Properties 308
8.3 Neuron with Excitatory and Inhibitory Dynamics 317
8.3.1 A General Model 317
8.3.2 Positive–Negative (PN) Neural Structure 320
8.3.3 Further Extension to the PN Neural Model 322
8.4 Neuron with Multiple Nonlinear Feedback 324
8.5 Dynamic Temporal Behavior of DNN 327
8.6 Nonlinear Analysis for DNUs 331
8.6.1 Equilibrium Points of a DNU 331
8.6.2 Stability of the DNU 333
8.6.3 Pitchfork Bifurcation in the DNU 334
8.7 Concluding Remarks 338
Problems 339

9 Continuous-Time Dynamic Neural Networks **345**

9.1 Dynamic Neural Network Structures: An Introduction 346
9.2 Hopfield Dynamic Neural Network (DNN) and Its Implementation 351
9.2.1 State Space Model of the Hopfield DNN 351
9.2.2 Output Variable Model of the Hopfield DNN 354
9.2.3 State Stability of Hopfield DNN 357
9.2.4 A General Form of Hopfield DNN 361
9.3 Hopfield Dynamic Neural Networks (DNNs) as Gradient-like Systems 363
9.4 Modifications of Hopfield Dynamic Neural Networks 369
9.4.1 Hopfield Dynamic Neural Networks with Triangular Weighting Matrix 369

9.4.2 *Hopfield Dynamic Neural Network with Infinite Gain (Hard Threshold Switch)* 372
9.4.3 *Some Restrictions on the Internal Neural States of the Hopfield DNN* 373
9.4.4 *Dynamic Neural Network with Saturation (DNN-S)* 374
9.4.5 *Dynamic Neural Network with Integrators* 378
9.5 *Other DNN Models* 380
9.5.1 *The Pineda Model of Dynamic Neural Networks* 380
9.5.2 *Cohen–Grossberg Model of Dynamic Neural Network* 382
9.6 *Conditions for Equilibrium Points in DNN* 384
9.6.1 *Conditions for Equilibrium Points of DNN-1* 384
9.6.2 *Conditions for Equilibrium Points of DNN-2* 386
9.7 *Concluding Remarks* 387
Problems 387

10 Learning and Adaptation in Dynamic Neural Networks 393
10.1 *Some Observation on Dynamic Neural Filter Behaviors* 395
10.2 *Temporal Learning Process I: Dynamic Backpropagation (DBP)* 398
10.2.1 *Dynamic Backpropagation for CT-DNU* 399
10.2.2 *Dynamic Backpropagation for DT-DNU* 403
10.2.3 *Comparison between Continuous and Discrete-Time Dynamic Backpropagation Approaches* 407
10.3 *Temporal Learning Process II: Dynamic Forward Propagation (DFP)* 411
10.3.1 *Continuous-Time Dynamic Forward Propagation (CT-DFP)* 411
10.3.2 *Discrete-Time Dynamic Forward Propagation (DT-DFP)* 414
10.4 *Dynamic Backpropagation (DBP) for Continuous-Time Dynamic Neural Networks (CT-DNNs)* 421
10.4.1 *General Representation of Network Models* 421
10.4.2 *DBP Learning Algorithms* 424

10.5 Concluding Remarks 431
Problems 432

11 Stability of Continuous-Time Dynamic Neural Networks 435

11.1 Local Asymptotic Stability 436
11.1.1 Lyapunov's First Method 437
11.1.2 Determination of Eigenvalue Position 440
11.1.3 Local Asymptotic Stability Conditions 443
11.2 Global Asymptotic Stability of Dynamic Neural Network 444
11.2.1 Lyapunov Function Method 444
11.2.2 Diagonal Lyapunov Function for DNNs 445
11.2.3 DNNs with Synapse-Dependent Functions 448
11.2.4 Some Examples 450
11.3 Local Exponential Stability of DNNs 452
11.3.1 Lyapunov Function Method for Exponential Stability 452
11.3.2 Local Exponential Stability Conditions for DNNs 453
11.4 Global Exponential Stability of DNNs 461
11.5 Concluding Remarks 464
Problems 464

12 Discrete-Time Dynamic Neural Networks and Their Stability 469

12.1 General Class of Discrete-Time Dynamic Neural Networks (DT-DNNs) 470
12.2 Lyapunov Stability of Discrete-Time Nonlinear Systems 474
12.2.1 Lyapunov's Second Method of Stability 474
12.2.2 Lyapunov's First Method 475
12.3 Stability Conditions for Discrete-Time DNNs 478
12.3.1 Global State Convergence for Symmetric Weight Matrix 479
12.3.2 Norm Stability Conditions 481
12.3.3 Diagonal Lyapunov Function Method 481
12.3.4 Examples 486

12.4 *More General Results on Globally Asymptotic Stability* 488
12.4.1 *Main Stability Results* 490
12.4.2 *Examples* 496
12.5 *Concluding Remarks* 500
Problems 500

PART IV SOME ADVANCED TOPICS IN NEURAL NETWORKS

13 Binary Neural Networks **509**
13.1 *Discrete-Time Two-State Systems* 510
13.1.1 *Basic Definitions* 510
13.1.2 *Lyapunov Function Method* 519
13.2 *Asynchronous Operating Hopfield Neural Network* 521
13.2.1 *State Operating Equations* 521
13.2.2 *State Convergence of Hopfield Neural Network with Zero-Diagonal Elements* 524
13.2.3 *State Convergence of Dynamic Neural Network with Nonnegative Diagonal Elements* 530
13.2.4 *Estimation of Transient Time* 534
13.3 *An Alternative Version of the Asynchronous Binary Neural Network* 539
13.3.1 *Binary State Updating* 539
13.3.2 *Formulations for Transient Time in Asynchronous Mode* 543
13.4 *Neural Network in Synchronous Mode of Operation* 547
13.4.1 *Neural Network with Symmetric Weight Matrix* 547
13.4.2 *Neural Network with Skew–Symmetric Weight Matrix* 556
13.4.3 *Estimation of Transient Time* 560
13.5 *Block Sequential Operation of the Hopfield Neural Network* 561
13.5.1 *State Updating with Ordered Partition* 561
13.5.2 *Guaranteed Convergence Results for Block Sequential Operation* 564

13.6 *Concluding Remarks* 571
Problems 572

14 Feedback Binary Associative Memories **579**
14.1 *Hebb's Neural Learning Mechanisms* 580
14.1.1 *Basis of Hebb's Learning Rule* 580
14.1.2 *Hebb's Learning Formulations* 582
14.1.3 *Convergence Considerations* 584
14.2 *Information Retrieval Process* 591
14.2.1 *The Hamming Distance (HD)* 591
14.2.2 *Self-Recall of Stored Patterns* 592
14.2.3 *Attractivity in Synchronous Mode* 597
14.3 *Nonorthogonal Fundamental Memories* 608
14.3.1 *Convergence for Nonorthogonal Patterns* 608
14.3.2 *Storage of Nonorthogonal Patterns* 613
14.4 *Other Learning Algorithms for Associative Memory* 618
14.4.1 *The Projection Learning Rule* 618
14.4.2 *A Generalized Learning Rule* 620
14.5 *Information Capacity of Binary Hopfield Neural Network* 624
14.6 *Concluding Remarks* 626
Problems 627

15 Fuzzy Sets and Fuzzy Neural Networks **633**
15.1 *Fuzzy Sets and Systems: An Overview* 636
15.1.1 *Some Preliminaries* 636
15.1.2 *Fuzzy Membership Functions (FMFs)* 639
15.1.3 *Fuzzy Systems* 641
15.2 *Building Fuzzy Neurons (FNs) Using Fuzzy Arithmetic and Fuzzy Logic Operations* 644
15.2.1 *Definition of Fuzzy Neurons* 645
15.2.2 *Utilization of* **T** *and* **S** *Operators* 647
15.3 *Learning and Adaptation for Fuzzy Neurons (FNs)* 652
15.3.1 *Updating Formulation* 652
15.3.2 *Calculations of Partial Derivatives* 654
15.4 *Regular Fuzzy Neural Networks (RFNNs)* 655

15.4.1 *Regular Fuzzy Neural Network (RFNN) Structures* 656
15.4.2 *Fuzzy Backpropagation (FBP) Learning* 657
15.4.3 *Some Limitations of Regular Fuzzy Neural Networks (RFNNs)* 658
15.5 *Hybrid Fuzzy Neural Networks (HFNNs)* 662
15.5.1 *Difference-Measure-Based Two-Layered HFNNs* 662
15.5.2 *Fuzzy Neurons and Hybrid Fuzzy Neural Networks (HFNNs)* 665
15.5.3 *Derivation of Backpropagation Algorithm for Hybrid Fuzzy Neural Networks* 667
15.5.4 *Summary of Fuzzy Backpropagation (FBP) Algorithm* 670
15.6 *Fuzzy Basis Function Networks (FBFNs)* 671
15.6.1 *Gaussian Networks versus Fuzzy Systems* 672
15.6.2 *Fuzzy Basis Function Networks (FBFNs) Are Universal Approximators* 677
15.7 *Concluding Remarks* 679
Problems 680

References and Bibliography **687**

Appendix A Current Bibliographic Sources on Neural Networks **711**

Index **715**

Foreword

It is very hard to write a book that qualifies to be viewed as a significant addition to the voluminous literature on neural network theory and its applications. Drs. Gupta, Jin, and Homma have succeeded in accomplishing this feat. They have authored a treatise that is superlative in all respects and links neural network theory to fuzzy set theory and fuzzy logic.

Although my work has not been in the mainstream of neural network theory and its applications, I have always been a close observer, going back to the pioneering papers of McCulloch and Pitts, and the work of Frank Rosenblatt. I had the privilege of knowing these major figures and was fascinated by the originality of their ideas and their sense of purpose and mission. The coup de grace of Minsky and Papert was an unfortunate event that braked the advancement of neural network theory for a number of years preceding publication of the path-breaking paper by Hopfield. It is this paper and the rediscovery of Paul Werbos' backpropagation algorithm by Rumelhart et al. that led to the ballistic ascent of neural-network-related research that we observe today.

The power of neural network theory derives in large measure from the fact that we possess the machinery for performing large volumes of computation at high speed, with high reliability and low cost. Without this machinery, neural network theory would be of academic interest. The stress on computational aspects of neural network theory is one of the many great strengths of "static and dynamic neural networks" (SDNNs). A particularly important contribution of SDNN is its coverage of the theory of dynamic neural networks and its applications.

Traditionally, science has been aimed at a better understanding of the world we live in, centering on mathematics and the natural sciences. But as we move further into the age of machine intelligence and automated reasoning, a major aim of science is becoming that of automation of tasks performed by humans, including speech understanding, decisionmaking, and pattern recognition and control.

To solve some of the complex problems that arise in these realms, we have to marshal all the resources that are at our disposal. It is this need that motivated the genesis of soft computing — a coalition of methodologies that are both complementary and synergistic — and that collectively provide a foundation for computational intelligence. Neural network theory is one of the principal members of the soft computing coalition — a coalition that includes, in addition, fuzzy logic, evolutionary computing, probabilistic computing, chaotic computing, and parts of machine learning theory. Within this coalition, the principal contribution of neural network theory is the machinery for learning, adaptation, and modeling of both static and dynamical systems.

One of the important contributions of SDNN is the chapter on fuzzy sets and fuzzy neural systems (Chapter 15), in which the authors present a compact exposition of fuzzy set theory and an insightful discussion of neurofuzzy systems and their applications. An important point that is stressed is that backpropagation is a gradient-based technique that applies to both neural and fuzzy systems. The same applies to the widely used methods employing radial basis functions.

Another important issue that is addressed is that of universal approximation. It is well known that both neural networks and fuzzy rule-based systems can serve as universal approximators. However, what is not widely recognized is that a nonlinear system, S, can be arbitrarily closely approximated by a neural network, N, or a fuzzy system, F, only if S is known, rather than merely given as a black box. The fact that S must be known rules out the possibility of asserting that N or F approximates to S to within a specified error, based on a finite number of exemplars drawn from the input and output functions.

An important aspect of the complementarity of neural network and fuzzy set theories relates to the fact that, in most applications, the point of departure in the construction of a fuzzy system for performing a specified task is the knowledge of how a human performs that task. This is not a necessity in the case of a neural network. On the other hand, it is difficult to construct a neural network with a capability to reason through the use of rules of inference, since such rules are a part of the machinery of fuzzy logic but not of neural network theory.

SDNN contains much that is hard to find in the existing literature. The quality of exposition is high and the coverage is thorough and up-to-date. The authors and the publisher, John Wiley and Sons, have produced a treatise that addresses, with high authority and high level of expertise, a wide variety of issues, problems, and techniques that relate in a basic way to the conception, design, and utilization of intelligent systems. They deserve our applause.

University of California, Berkeley *Lotfi A. Zadeh*

Preface

With the evolution of our complex technological society and the introduction of new notions and innovative theoretical tools in the field of intelligent systems, the field of neural networks is undergoing an enormous evolution. These evolving and innovative theoretical tools are centered around the theory of *soft computing*, a theory that embodies the theory from the fields of *neural networks, fuzzy logic, evolutionary computing, probabilistic computing*, and *genetic algorithms*. These tools of soft computing are providing some intelligence and robustness in the complex and uncertain systems similar to those seen in natural biological species.

Intelligence — the ability to learn, understand, and adapt — is the creation of nature, and it plays a key role in human actions and in the actions of many other biological species. Humans possess some robust attributes of learning and adaptation, and that's what makes them so intelligent. We humans react through the process of learning and adaptation on the information received through a widely distributed network of sensors and control mechanisms in our bodies. The *faculty of cognition* — which is found in our carbon-based computer, the brain — acquires information about the environment through various natural sensory mechanisms such as vision, hearing, touch, taste, and smell. Then the process of cognition, through its intricate neural networks — *the cognitive computing* — integrates this information and provides appropriate actions. The cognitive process then advances further toward some attributes such as learning, recollection, reasoning, and control.

The process of cognition takes place through a perplexing biological process — *the neural computing* — and this is the process of computation that makes a human an intelligent animal. (More or less all animals possess intelligence at various levels, but *humans fall into the category of the most intelligent species.*)

Human actions in this advancing technological world have been inspired by many intriguing phenomena occurring in the nature. We have been inspired to fly by birds, and then we have created flying machines that can fly almost in synchrony with the sun.

We are learning from the carbon-based cognitive computer — the brain — and now trying to induce the process of cognition and intelligence into robotic machines. One of our aims is to construct an autonomous robotic vehicle that can think and operate in uncertain and unstructured driving conditions. Robots in manufacturing, mining, agriculture, space and ocean exploration, and health sciences are just a few examples of challenging applications where humanistic attributes such as *cognition* and *intelligence* can play an important role. Also, in the fields of decisionmaking, such as health sciences, management, economics, politics, law, and administration, some of the mathematical tools evolving around the notion of neural networks, fuzzy logic, and, in general, soft computing may contribute to the strength of the decisionmaking field. We envision robots evolving into electromechanical systems — perhaps having some attributes of human cognition.

The human cognitive faculty — the carbon-based computer — has a vast network of processing cells called *neural networks*, and this science of neural networks has inspired many researchers in biological as well as nonbiological fields. This inspiration has generated keen interest among engineers, computer scientists, and mathematicians for developing some basic mathematical models of neurons, and to use the collective actions of these neural models to find the solutions to many practical problems. The concepts evolved in this realm have generated a new field of *neural networks*.

The idea for this textbook on neural networks was conceived during the classroom teachings and research discussions in the laboratory as well as at international scientific meetings. We are pleased to see that our several years of work is finally appearing in the form of this book. This book, of course, has gone through several phases of writings and rewritings over the last several years.

The contents of this book, entitled *Static and Dynamic Neural Networks: From Fundamentals to Advanced Theory*, follows a logical style providing the readers the basic concepts and then leading them to some advanced theory in the field of neural networks.

The mathematical models of a basic neuron, the elementary components used in the design of a neural network, are a fascinating blend of heuristic concepts and mathematical rigor. It has become a subject of large interdisciplinary areas of teaching and research, and these mathematical concepts have been successfully applied in finding some robust solutions for problems evolving in the many fields of science and technology. Our own studies have been in the fields of *neurocontrol systems, neurovision systems, robotic systems, neural chaotic systems, pattern recognition*, and *signal and image processing*.

In fact, since the early 1980s the field of neural networks has undergone the phases of exponential growth, generating many new theoretical concepts. At the same time, these theoretical tools have been applied successfully to the solution of many applied problems.

Over the years, through their teaching and research in this exponentially evolving field of neural networks, the authors have collected a large volume of ideas. Some of their works have appeared in the form of research publications, and this present volume represents only a small subset of this large set of ideas and studies.

The material in this volume is arranged in a pedagogical style, which, we do hope, will serve both the students and researchers in this evolving field of neural networks.

In designing the present book we strove to present a pedagogically sound volume that would be useful as a main text for graduate students, as well as provide some new directions to academic and industrial researchers. We cover some important topics in neural networks from very basic to advanced material with appropriate examples, problems, and reference material.

In order to keep the book to a manageable size, we have been selective in our coverage. Our first priority was to cover the central concepts of each topic in enough detail to make the material clear and coherent. Each chapter has been written so that it is relatively self-contained. The topics selected for this book were based on our experience in teaching and research.

This book contains 15 chapters, which are classified into the following four parts:

Part I: Foundations of Neural Networks
(Chapters 1–3)
Part II: Static Neural Networks
(Chapters 4–7)

Part III: Dynamic Neural Networks (Chapters 8–12)
Part IV: Some Advanced Topics in Neural Networks (Chapters 13–15)

Part I provides the basic material, but from Parts II, III, and IV, instructors may choose material to suit their class needs. Part IV deals with some advanced topics on neural networks involving *fuzzy sets* and *fuzzy neural networks* as well, which have become very important topics in terms of both the theory and applications.

Also, we append this book with two appendixes:

Appendix A: Current Bibliographic Sources on Neural Networks
Appendix B: Classified List of Bibliography on Neural Networks (`ftp://ftp.wiley.com/public/sci_tech_med/neural_networks/`)

Appendix A provides various sources from which a student or researcher can find the current work in the field. Appendix B gives an extensive list of references (over 1500) classified into various categories on the ftp site:
`ftp://ftp.wiley.com/public/sci_tech_med/neural_networks/`
that will provide the readers with the information on reference material from its inception (early 1940s) to recent works.

This book is written for graduate students and academic and industrial researchers working in this developing field of neural networks and intelligent systems. It provides some comprehensive views of the field, as well as its accomplishments and future potentials and perspectives.

We do hope that this book will provide new challenges to its readers, that it will generate curiosity for learning more in the field, and that it will arouse a desire to seek new theoretical tools and applications. We will consider our efforts successful if the study of neural networks through this book raises the level of curiosity and thirst of its readers.

University of Saskatchewan — *Madan M. Gupta*
GlobespanVirata, Inc. — *Liang Jin*
Tohoku University — *Noriyasu Homma*

Acknowledgments

The authors would like to express their appreciation and gratitude to many research colleagues and students from this international community who have inspired our thinking and, thereby, our research in these emerging field of fuzzy logic and neural networks. Indeed, we are pleased to see that the fruits of our teaching and research are finally appearing in the form of this textbook.

We wish to acknowledge the very constructive and positive feedback that we have received from the reviewers on the raw manuscript for this book. Their comments were very helpful in improving the contents of the book. Several of our students provided some very constructive feedback on the contents and organization of the book. We are grateful to Sanjeeva Kumar Redlapalli and Mubashshar Ahmed for helping us in the reorganization of the bibliography and in some proofreading of the text. We also acknowledge the great assistance of our graduate and undergraduate students at Tohoku University — Masao Sakai, Taiji Sugiyama, Misao Yano, and Yosuke Koyanaka — for helping us in making the diagrams and typing some of the manuscript.

Also the authors would like to thank John Wiley & Sons Inc. and its staff for providing valuable professional support during the various phases of the preparation of this book. Specifically we would like to acknowledge the following persons for their professional support: Philip Meyler (Former Editor), George Telecki (Associate Publisher), Val Moliere (Editor for the Wiley Interscience Division), Andrew Prince (Senior Managing Editor), Rosalyn

Farkas (Production Manager), Mike Rutkowski (Graphic Designer), Kirsten Rohstedt (Editorial Assistant), and many more who have helped us make this book possible.

Finally, we are very grateful to the University of Saskatchewan and our research colleagues and students in the College of Engineering for creating a warm teaching and intellectual research atmosphere for the nourishment of this book and many similar research projects and research publications over the years. Our gratitude is also extended to the staff of the Engineering Computer Centre and the Peter N. Nikiforuk Teaching and Learning Centre, in particular to Ian MacPhedren, Bruce Coates, Randy Hickson, and Mark Tomtene, for their continuous assistance that we received during the preparation of this manuscript.

We also acknowledge the very constructive help of our research assistant, Elizabeth Nikiforuk, who took on the challenging task of organizing and assembling the manuscript during the many phases of its preparation over the last several years.

University of Saskatchewan — *Madan M. Gupta*
GlobespanVirata, Inc. — *Liang Jin*
Tohoku University — *Noriyasu Homma*

December, 2002

Part I

FOUNDATIONS OF NEURAL NETWORKS

Chapter 1. Neural Systems: An Introduction

Chapter 2. Biological Foundations of Neuronal Morphology

Chapter 3. Neural Units: Concepts, Models, and Learning

1

Neural Systems: An Introduction

1.1 Basics of Neuronal Morphology

1.2 The Neuron

1.3 Neurocomputational Systems: Some Perspectives

1.4 Neuronal Learning

1.5 Theory of Neuronal Approximations

1.6 Fuzzy Neural Systems

1.7 Applications of Neural Networks: Present and Future

1.8 An Overview of the Book

The path that leads to scientific discovery often begins when one of us takes an adventurous step into the world of endless possibilities. Scientists intrigued by a mere glimpse of a subtle variation may uncover a clue or link, and from that fragment emerges an idea that has to be developed and worked into shape.

Humans have always dreamed of creating a portrait of themselves, a machine with humanlike attributes such as *locomotion, speech, vision, and cognition* (memory, learning, thinking, adaptation, and intelligence). Through our learning from biological processes and very creative actions, we have been able to realize some of our dreams. In today's technological society we have created machines that have some of the human attributes that emulate several humanlike functions with tremendous capabilities. Some examples of these humanlike functions are *human locomotion to transportation systems, human speech and vision to communications systems*, and *human low-level cognition to computing systems*. No doubt the machines that are an extension of human muscular power (cars, tractors, aircraft, trains, robots, etc.), have brought luxury to human life. But who provides control to these mighty machines — human intelligence, the human cognition.

The subject of intelligent systems today is in such an exciting state of research primarily because of the wealth of information that we researchers are able to extract from the carbon-based computer — the neuronal morphology of the brain, biological sensory systems such as vision, and the human cognition and decisionmaking processes that form the elements of soft computing.

1.1 BASICS OF NEURONAL MORPHOLOGY

Humans have been learning from nature. They have imitated birds and have created super flying machines. Now we are trying to imitate some of the attributes of cognitions and intelligence of the brain, and are striving for the creation of intelligent systems. Some of the recent work in the field of intelligent systems has led us to a strong belief that our efforts should focus on the understanding of neuropsychological principles and the development of new morphologies of intelligent control systems encompassing the various disciplines of system science (Amari and Arbib 1982, Amit 1989, Anderson 1988, Arbib 1987, Churchland 1988, Churchland and Sejnowski 1988, Hiramoto et al. 2000, Kohara et al. 2001, Pedrycz 1991a, Skarda and Freeman 1987).

At this stage, we give an analogy from the field of aviation. Until the Wright brothers invented the airplane, the basic scientific thinking had been to create a flying machine that, in a way, would mimic a bird. Most scientists of those days thought that the crucial component of flying was the flapping of wings. It took the genius of the Wright brothers to understand that, although wings were required to increase the buoyancy in the air, they also needed power from the propeller to make the flight possible. In the same way, although there is significant emphasis in the current scientific community on the understanding of the working of the human brain and developing the theory of soft computing that can mimic the human linguistic expressions, feelings, and functioning of the brain, there is a great danger in trying to mimic without a thorough understanding of the functions of this carbon-based cognitive computer and of human expression.

Figures 1.1a and 1.1b show an artificial flying machine with fixed wings that has evolved from the biological bird with flapping wings. Likewise, Figs. 1.1c–h show the evolution of the computing elements — the neuron, a neural network, and a cognitive computing system — that are in the process of evolving from their respective biological counterparts.

Thus, today's flying machines in many ways emulate the aerodynamic behavior of a flying bird, but they are not replicas of the natural bird. For many centuries we have attempted to understand the neuronal computing aspect of biological sensory and control mechanisms. This basic understanding, combined with the strength of the new computing technology (optical computing, molecular computing, etc.) and the thinking of the systems scientists, can create artificial sensory and intelligent control mechanisms. These concepts may also lead us in the development of a new type of computing machine: a cognitive computing machine.

Biological Systems | Artificial Systems

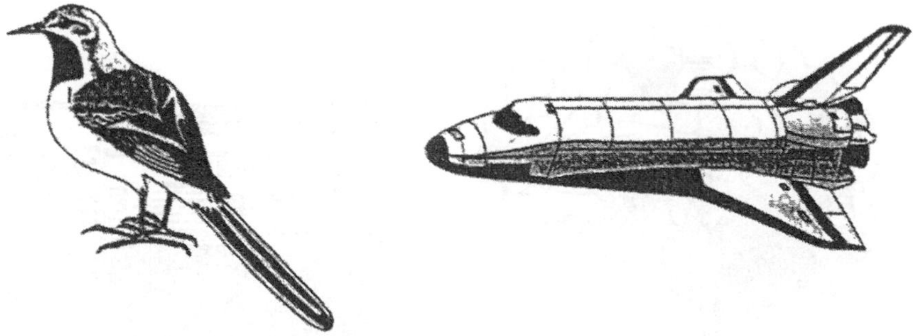

(a) Biological bird with flapping wings

(b) Flying machine fixed wings: an artificial flying bird

Figure 1.1 (Continued)

Biological Systems

Artificial Systems

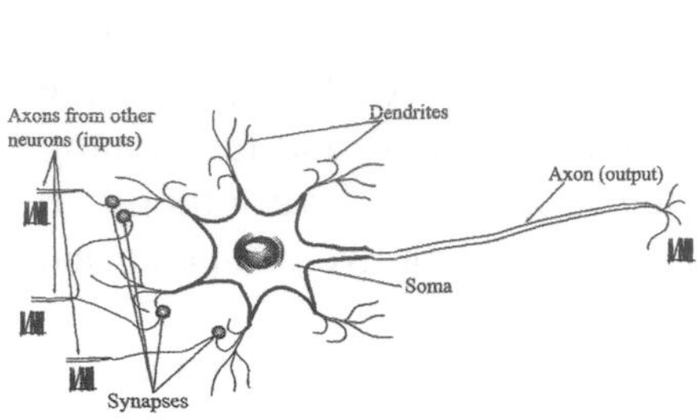

(c) Biological neuron: a biological computing processing element

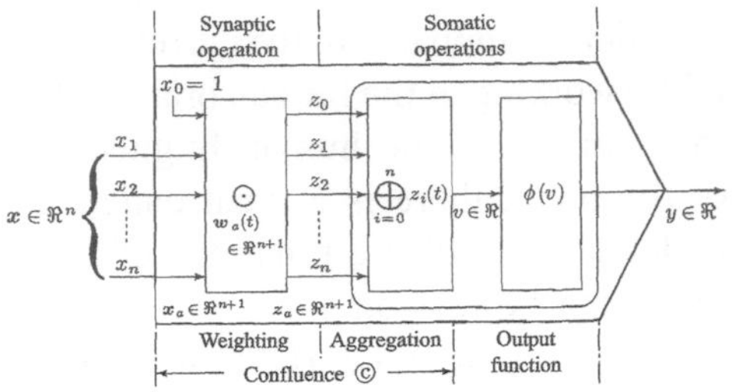

(d) Artificial neuron: an artificial computing processing element

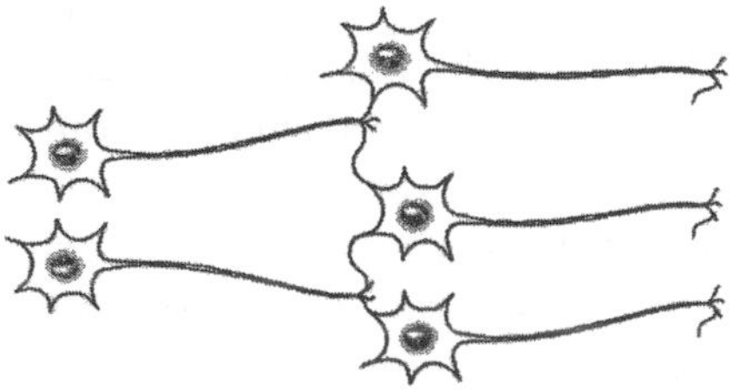

(e) Biological neural network

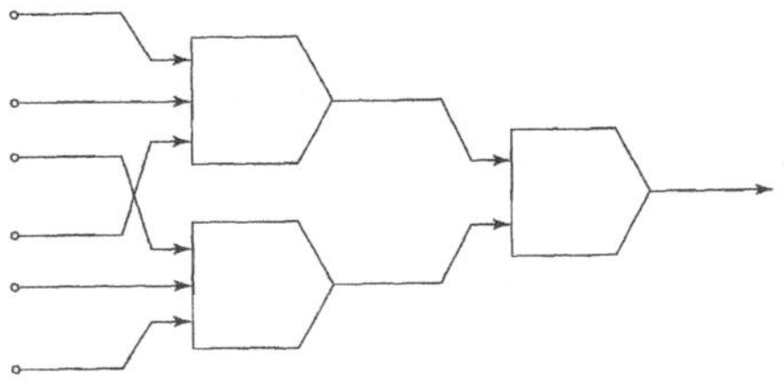

(f) Artificial neural network

(Morphological similarity between biological and artificial neural network)

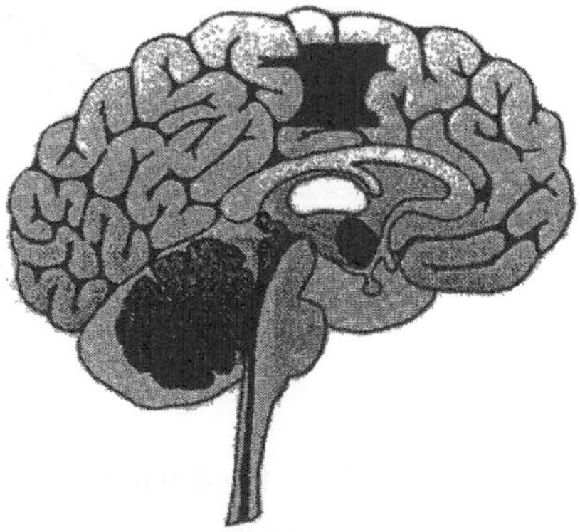

(g) Biological neural computing system: the cognitive faculty

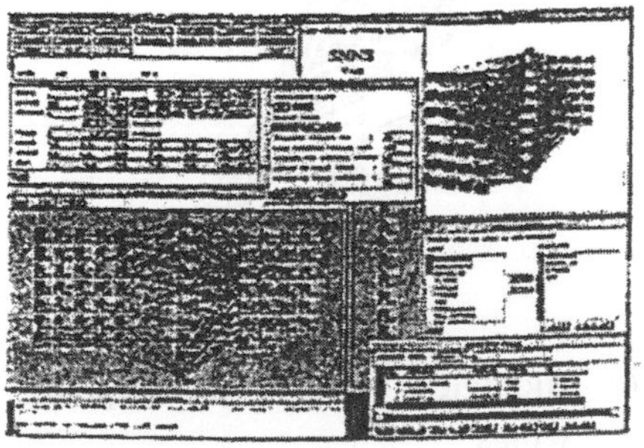

(h) Artificial neural computing: the cognitive computer

Figure 1.1 From biological to artificial systems.

Although it is very difficult, and often unwise to make predictions about the future, we nevertheless feel that further research in neurosensory systems (such as neurovision systems) and neurocontrol systems will be the key to the development of truly intelligent control systems and, in general, intelligent systems. We also believe that we are slowly progressing in that direction, and early in the twenty-first century, may be able to see versions of *intelligent systems*. To continue our analogy with aviation, most scientists in the nineteenth century did not believe that it was possible to have flying machines that were heavier than air, and a great deal of work was devoted to developing lighter-than-air flying machines, such as balloons and zeppelins. On the other hand, today we have heavy flying machines (airplanes) that are much faster and more versatile than biological birds. In the same way, it appears quite probable that, as our understanding of cognitive faculty improves, we may be able to develop intelligent control systems that may even surpass the human brain in some respects. In this (twenty-first) century, we can expect the evolution of intelligent robots that will be able to perform most routine household and industrial work (Fig. 1.2).

Now, we are moving into a new era of information systems, the systems for extracting some useful information from our working environment, and making use of it in our decisionmaking processes. Humans and machines in their decisionmaking process face two types of information: statistical and cognitive. Statistical information arises from the physical processes, while cognitive information originates from the human cognitive faculty.

New computing theories with a sound biological understanding are evolving. This new field of computing falls under the category of *neural and soft*

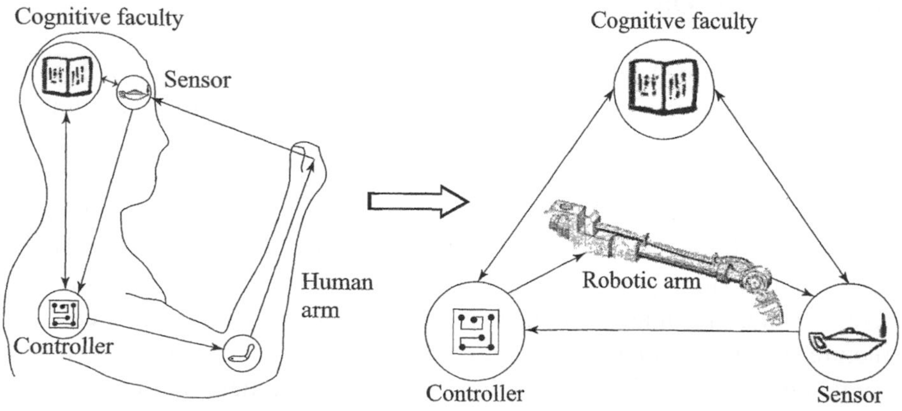

Figure 1.2 From human cognitive and control functions to robotics cognitive and control function: an intelligent robot.

computing systems. Some new computing technology is evolving under disciplines such as optical computing, optoelectronics, and molecular computing. This new technology seems to have the potential of surpassing the *micro-*, *nano-*, and *pico*technologies. Neural computing has also been proven (theoretically) to be able to supplement the enormous processing power of the von Neumann digital computer. Hopefully, these new computing methods, with the neural architecture as a basis, will be able to develop a thinking robotic machine, a low-level cognitive machine for which scientists have been striving for so long.

Today, we are in the process of designing neural-computing-based information processing systems using the biological neural system as a basis. The highly *parallel* processing and layered neuronal morphology with learning abilities of the human cognitive faculty — the brain — provide us with a new tool for designing a cognitive machine that can learn and recognize complicated patterns — like human faces and Japanese characters. The theory of fuzzy logic, the basis for soft computing, provides mathematical power for the emulation of the higher-order cognitive functions, the thought and perception processes. A marriage between these evolving disciplines, such as neural computing, genetic algorithms, and fuzzy logic, may provide a new class of computing systems — the neural fuzzy systems — for the emulation of higher-order cognitive power. The chaotic behavior inherent in biological systems, the heart and brain, for example, and the neuronal phenomena and the genetic algorithms are some of the other important subjects that promise to provide robustness to our neural computing systems (Honma et al. 1999, Skarda and Freeman 1987).

1.2 THE NEURON

Nature has developed a very complex neuronal morphology in biological species (Fig. 1.3). Biological neurons, over one hundred billion in number, in the central nervous systems (CNS) of humans play a very important role in the various complex sensory, control, affective, and cognitive aspects of information processing and decision making (Amari and Arbib 1982, Amit 1989, Anderson 1988, Gupta and Sinha 1995, Sinha et al. 1999, Zurada 1992). In neuronal information processing, there are a variety of complex mathematical operations and mapping functions that act in synergism in a parallel cascade structure forming a complex pattern of neuronal layers evolving into a sort of pyramidal pattern. The information flows from one neuronal layer to another in the forward direction with continuous feedback, and it evolves into a dynamic pyramidal structure. The structure is pyramidal in the sense of the extraction and convergence of information at each point in the forward

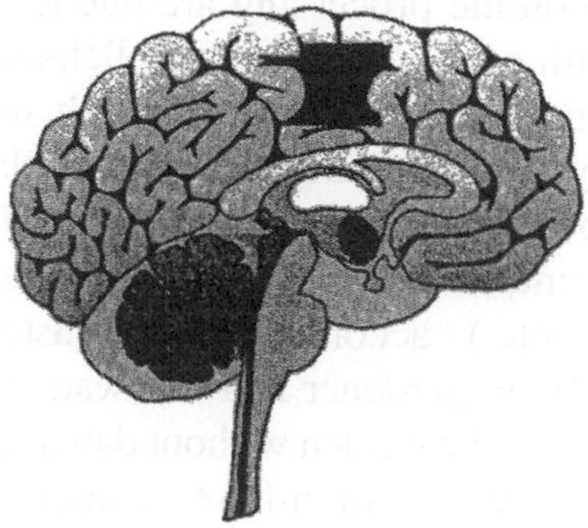

(a) Biological neural computing system: the cognitive faculty

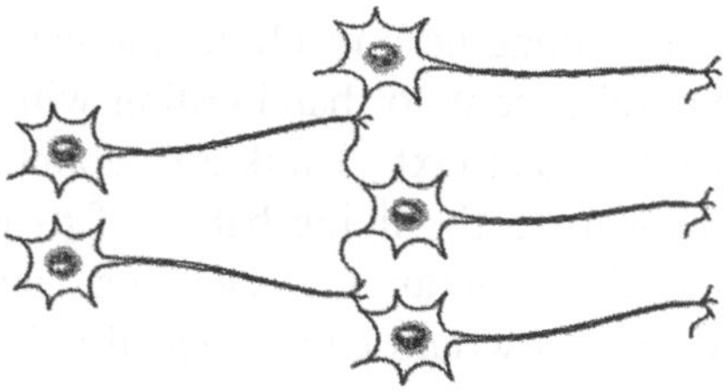

(b) Biological neural network

Figure 1.3 Biological computing process: the brain and its neural neural networks.

direction. A study of biological neuronal morphology provides not only a clue but also a challenge in the design of a realistic cognitive computing machine — an intelligent processor.

From the neurobiological as well as the neuralmathematical point of view, we identify two key neuronal elements in a biological neuron: *the synapse* and *the soma*. These two elements are responsible for providing neuronal attributes such as learning adaptation knowledge (storage or memory of past experience), aggregation, and nonlinear mapping operations on neuronal information (Fig. 1.3). Neuronal morphology is described in detail in Chapter 2.

1.3 NEUROCOMPUTATIONAL SYSTEMS: SOME PERSPECTIVES

Humans have always dreamed of creating a portrait of themselves — a machine that can walk, see, and think intelligently. The *neuron*, the basic information processing element in the central nervous systems (CNS), plays an important and diverse role in human sensory processing, locomotion, control, and cognition (thinking, learning, adaptation, perception, etc.).

The field of *neurocontrol*, has evolved since the early 1990s, particularly since over late 1990s, and the intent of the researchers working in this field is to create an intelligent machine with several levels of control, just as nature does in the control of various biological functions (Gupta and Sinha 1995).

It should be noted that biological neurons, each with a bandwidth of the order of about 400 Hz or so, possess some tremendous capacities and capabilities that are unrealizable even by the nano- and picosilicon-based technologies.

These capabilities for almost real-time and online processing are due to the layered nature of the network of neurons with a high degree of parallelism.

Just imagine a machine that can learn and recognize human speech with natural accents or handwriting with a fuzzy flow of characters and translate it into typed text. Think also about a computerized slaverobotic system that has learned the living habits of its master, and does all the household tasks (cooking, vacuuming, cleaning, gardening, etc.) according to its master's wishes. It would be wonderful to have a robotic gardener that can water the flowers and vegetables, and also prune and weed the garden without damaging the useful plants. Questions arise as to whether algorithm-based computing can do all the wonderful things that humans can do so easily. The human brain follows a nonalgorithmic approach with some wonderful attributes such as *genetics* and *learning*.

The carbon-based cognitive faculty — the brain — is a mysterious machine with a very complex neuronal morphology. All our actions and emotions are controlled by this mysterious organ. We perceive, think, see, and learn. We compose and recite poems and play musical instruments. We devise mechanisms for solving complex problems, we think about what we know, and we investigate new things. We enjoy the beauty of snow peaks and that of the blue sky. Some events make us happy and we laugh, others make us unhappy and we cry. Intuition tells us that the neuronal morphology of organs doing all these wonderful things must be very complex. Indeed, this brain is too complex to understand. It is wrong to call it a computer because, unlike a computer, it does things beyond simple numerical computations, such as cognition and perception. Nature has endowed the brain with a marvelous and a complex neuronal morphology that is beyond human comprehension. Yet we know that it is composed of a large number of nerve (neural) cells with a high degree of interconnectivity. There are over 10^{11} (one hundred billion) neural cells, and each neuron, on the average, receives information from about 10^4 neighboring neurons. Thus, there are typically over 10^{15} connections (synapses) in the brain. The anatomic morphology of these neurons and their connections are what make the brain so complex, and it is very precise in conducting the various cognitive tasks.

It is important to study a broad view of the biological neuronal morphology that forms the basis for our neurocontrol processes. Let us look at the neural mechanism in our own vision and control mechanisms. When we write and read these lines, the photonic energy emitting from these characters strikes the photoreceptors — 125 million rods and 5 million cones — in each retina. Complex biochemical reactions in the photoreceptors change the photonic energy into equivalent electrical impulses. The task of the retina and the rest of the brain is not only to coordinate the function of our hands (in writing) and eyes (in reading) but also to think and extract useful cognitive information from these lines. It would be wonderful if we could explain this neuronal computing phenomenon in our retina and brain. In spite of tremendous progress in neurophysiology, our knowledge about biological neuronal computing is shrouded by ignorance. However, since the early 1990s or so, scientists and engineers have embarked on creating a computational neural machine.

Although the subject of neurophysiology is relatively old, it was only around the early 1990s that we started thinking in terms of neural computational systems — a science for developing neural models for computational applications. Since 1985, the field has enjoyed an exponential growth, giving rise to a vast volume of literature in the form of books, scientific journals, and international scientific conferences and symposia sponsored by some major scientific societies. At the same time, the field of neural computing has generated tremendous commercial interests, which in turn have resulted in many major computer-oriented companies becoming involved in the development of neural hardwares and softwares. Interestingly, at the same time, they gave birth to many new commercial outfits around the globe.

The basic concepts of learning and adaptation in the field of control systems were introduced in the early 1960s, and several extensions and advances have been made since then. However, advances in the understanding of the physiology of biological control has spurred the interest of system scientists to explore the field of neurocontrol. Biology has certainly provided motivation to the field of neurocontrol, as it has to the field of neurovision. More recent mathematical models and the architectures of neurocontrol systems have generated many theoretical and industrial interests. Recent advances in static (memoryless) and dynamic (with memory) neural networks have created a profound impact on the field of neurocontrol. Now, researchers are moving toward the design of intelligent control systems using biological neurocontrol as a basis (Werbos 1974). This work deals with a diverse group of neurocontrol problems, such as the neural architecture for adaptation and control, introduction to the backpropagation algorithms, and identification and control problems for a general class of dynamic systems. There is an extensive list of recent research literature in the following fields:

(i) Learning and adaptation (Asari 2001, Bengio and Bengio 2000, Castro et al. 2000, Darken et al. 1992, Engelbrecht 2001, Gers et al. 2000, Gori et al. 2000, Jin et al. 1993b, Leung et al. 2001, Nadeau and Benjio 2000, Nishiyama and Suzuki 2001, Watanabe 2001, Yan and Miller 2000, Zeng and Yeung 2001);

(ii) Dynamic neural systems (Atiya and Parlos 2000, Bianchini et al. 2001a, 2001b, Chen 2001, Chen and Amari 2001a, 2001b, 2001c, Gers and Schmidhuber 2000, 2001, Homma et al. 2001, Jin and Gupta 1996a, 1999, Leistritz et al. 2001, Liang 2001a, 2001b, Liang and Wang 2000, Parlos et al. 2001, Rao et al. 2000, Sudharsanan and Sundareshan 1991b, Zhang and Jin 2000, Zhao and Macau 2001, Zhao et al. 2000);

(iii) Self-learning and control (Alahakoon et al. 2000, Heskes 2001, Kohonen et al. 2000, Pal et al. 2001, Vesanto and Alhoniemi 2000);

(iv) Adaptive filters and equalizers (Chen et al. 2000, 2001a, 2001b, Cristianini et al. 2000, Fu and Shortliffe 2000, Kewley et al. 2000, Konig 2000, Lee et al. 2000, Lin 2001, Lu 2000, Sebald and Bucklew 2000, Shin et al. 2000, Tipping 2000, Zhang et al. 2000).

1.4 NEURONAL LEARNING

Biological species have adopted strategies that are based on learning, adaptation, and self-organization in an uncertain environment. "Learning while functioning" is the most important attribute that makes these biological species so robust and flexible. It is natural, therefore, that we adopt a similar strategy in the design of intelligent systems.

Certainly, the process of neuronal learning and adaptation in biological species is enormously complex, and the progress made in the understanding of the neural network field through experimental observations in the fields such as neurophysiology and psychology during the twentieth century was limited and crude compared to the achievements in the physical sciences during the same period. Nevertheless, neurophysiological and psychological understanding of the biological process has provided a tremendous impetus to the emulation of certain neurological morphologies and their learning behavior through the fields of mathematics and system sciences. We have a long way to go before we can speak of understanding the principles of cognition (learning, thinking, reasoning, and perception) and, thus, of the field of cognitive computing to the degree that we understand the principles of the electrochemical, biochemical, and ionic behaviors of neuronal populations in biological species.

We have emphasized some of the difficulties in the understanding of neurophysiology. Still, biology has inspired the work of system scientists in the past, and at an accelerated pace more recently. There have been an exponentially increasing number of attempts to develop neuronal paradigms for application to problems such as machine vision and control systems. Indeed, the neuronal learning paradigms developed more recently, combined with the cognitive strength of the notion of graded membership, promise to provide robust solutions to problems in pattern recognition, decisionmaking, control of complex dynamic flexible structures in space, and, in general, intelligent robotic systems for applications to manufacturing and medical sciences.

1.5 THEORY OF NEURONAL APPROXIMATIONS

The theory of functions approximation is an important class of problems in both static and dynamic processes. We would like to approximate a given experimental curve by a class of polynomials, or a time evolution of a dynamic process by a difference or differential equation. We would also like to approximate a complex periodic or almost periodic phenomenon using Fourier analysis by a series of sinusoids. System identification, estimation of a signal from a noisy measurement, or forecasting stockmarkets using the past history and current economic trends are just a few examples that have baffled system scientists and economists.

The theory of neuronal approximations has captured the attention of neural scientists only recently. It was at the IEEE First International Conference of Neural Networks in 1987 held at San Diego when R. Hecht-Nielsen reiterated the theorem of Kolmogorov (1957) and made some comparisons with the attributes of neural networks. Kolmogorov's theorem states that one can express a continuous multivariable function, on a compact domain, in terms of sums and compositions of single variable functions. Furthermore, the number of single-variable functions required is finite. It implies that there are no nemesis functions that cannot be modeled (approximated) by neural networks.

Indeed, the parallel and layered morphology of the neural systems is responsible for solving a wider class of problems in fields such as system approximation (identification), control, learning, and adaptation (Gupta and Sinha 1995, Sinha et al. 1999). In this book, we have presented a representative chapter, Chapter 7, that deals with the theory of neuronal approximation. This chapter provides a mathematical foundation of neural approximations, and shows how layered networks can approximate given static and/or dynamic physical entities to a desired degree of accuracy (Jin et al. 1994a, 1995a). Such an approximation, in fact, forms the basis in problems dealing with pattern classification, system identification, control, robotics manipulator problems, and also in the design of neural filters and equalizers. Some recent works in these fields can be found in Aonishi and Kurata 2000, Azimi-Sadjadi et al. 2000, Bargiela 2000, Cabrelli et al. 2000, Chen and Wang 2001, Datta et al. 2000, Gabrys and Bargiela 2000, Girolami 2001, Franco and Cannas 2001, Hoppensteadt and Izhikevich 2000, Huang et al. 2000, Lehtokangas 2000,

Li and Lee 2001, Lim et al. 2000, Nabney 1999, Papadpopoulos et al. 2001, Simmon 2001, Simone and Moabito 2001, Yuan et al. 2000.

1.6 FUZZY NEURAL SYSTEMS

The faculty of cognition and perception in humans is very complex, but it possesses a very efficient mechanism for information processing and expression. "The weather is just beautiful for playing a game of golf" conveys a large amount of information in just a brief sentence. This is the attribute of graded membership in our natural language and thinking processes that makes our knowledge base and information processing abilities so efficient. This notion of graded membership due to Lotfi A. Zadeh has been adopted in the calculus of fuzzy logic. Now, this notion promises to provide some robust algorithms for intelligent robotic systems.

Human cognition, which embodies all our thinking and logic processes and our actions and decisions, is full of imprecision and uncertainties. The natural world in which we live is a world of imprecision. Imprecision arises from physical phenomena and is inherent in our cognitive process. The human brain has evolved around cognitive uncertainties, and through the process of learning, it is able to extract important information and make decisions. It is a robust and, to a large measure, a fault-tolerant system. A mystery, however, shrouds the working and mathematics of this cognitive process. This mystery has existed for years because of the lack of the right mathematical tools for understanding and modeling this mysterious cognitive process. Conventional mathematical tools and artificial logical tools are nothing but paradoxes even in simple human logical tasks. It was in the early 1960s when Professor Lotfi A. Zadeh pondered over these paradoxes and the mathematical models of human logic and reasoning. He carefully considered the relevance and validity of the precision of our decisions and binary logic (*yes* or *no*, *white* or *black*, *0* or *1*) under cognitive uncertainties.

Zadeh's earlier works, prior to the mid-1960s, were devoted to the use of "precise" mathematical tools in systems theory and decision processes. No doubt, this work made a great contribution to the field of controls and systems, but his seminal work on fuzzy logic, which appeared in a paper in 1965, renewed a widespread interest in the fields of systems, decision analysis, cognitive uncertainty, and modeling of human cognition (process of learning, thinking, reasoning, and adaptation). Since the publication of that work, a worldwide community of scholars and scientists have made many important contributions to the field, leading to some important commercial, industrial, and domestic applications. In growing numbers, investigators in a wide variety of fields — ranging from psychology, sociology, philosophy, and economics to natural sciences, engineering, and computer sciences — are exploring this new path (which seems to be very bright and promising) to the understanding of human reasoning and cognition. They are also developing novel methods for dealing with systems and processes that are too complex to be analyzed by conventional quantitative techniques (Gupta et al. 1979; Gupta and Yamakawa 1988a, 1988b; Gupta and Knopf 1994; Gupta and Rao 1994b; Gupta and Sinha 1995; Kauffman and Gupta 1985, 1988; Sinha et al. 1999; Zadeh 1965, 1968, 1972a, 1972b, 1973, 1984, 1986, 1994, 1996, 1997, 1999).

In retrospect, it is evident that the trend toward the use of fuzzy logic — a logic that is much closer in spirit to human cognition and language than conventional logical systems — could have been anticipated during the past century. What held back the development of fuzzy logic were the attitudes from the mechanistic era of the nineteenth century and, more recently, the habits of programmatic reasoning fostered by the rapidly widening use of digital machine computation.

Fuzzy logic rests on the notion that the key elements in human cognition are based not on precise numbers but on a class of numbers (objects) in which the transition from membership to nonmembership is gradual rather than abrupt.

These newly developing fields of fuzzy neural network and soft computing encompass features of the human brain: the cognitive aspects in fuzzy logic, and the learning and adaptation strengths of neural networks. This new field, combined with the genetic aspects of humans, promises to provide many theoretical and applied advances. Some recent achievements in this new field have been developed in Ding and Gupta 2000, Fujimori et al. 2001a, Gupta 2001, Mitra and Hayashi 2000, Musilek and Gupta 2000, Yang and Wang 2000, Yidliz 2001, Yidliz and Alpaydin 2000.

1.7 APPLICATIONS OF NEURAL NETWORKS: PRESENT AND FUTURE

1.7.1 Neurovision Systems

The emulation of biological vision and other functions of the human central nervous system (CNS) presents numerous challenges that are theoretical, algorithmic, technological, and implementational in nature. The processing power of biological vision lies in the large number of dynamic neurons that are linked by an enormous amount of synapses (interconnections). Currently available technology does not permit dense "biological-like" interconnections. However, since the early 1990s biology has motivated the design of neurovision systems, and many new computational architectures have evolved with some exciting applications (Gupta and Knopf 1994, Indiveri 2000, 2001a, 2001b, Indiveri et al. 2001, Itti and Koch 2001).

Biological neurons have inspired scientists to generalize the neuronal mathematical notion and the neurons' intricate connectivity within the central nervous system. This has further spurred the interest of engineers to develop new neural computing architectures and their hardware implementations.

1.7.2 Neurocontrol Systems

The subject of adaptive control systems, with various terms such as neoadaptive control systems, intelligent control systems, cognitive control systems, and neurocontrol systems, therefore, falls within the domain of control of complex industrial and robotic systems with reasoning, learning, and adaptive abilities.

Novel neural morphologies with learning and adaptive capabilities have infused new control power into the control of complex dynamic systems. Theoretical developments in the field are evolving, and many new applications are springing up (Gupta and Rao 1994a).

Mathematically formulated neural network elements, although biologically inspired, represent certain neural models, abstract or computational architectures, for some specific control tasks. In this book our objective is not to mimic the central nervous system, but to develop some motivations for solving specific problems facing the system scientists.

1.7.3 Neural Hardware Implementations

J. J. Hopfield and D. W. Tank provide a new conceptual framework and minimization principle for the understanding of computations in neural circuits (Hopfield and Tank 1986). The celebrated work of Hopfield and Tank consists of nonlinear graded responses organized into networks with effectively symmetric synaptic connections. This neural architecture attempts to retain certain important biological computational features. The authors show that certain complex optimization problems can be analyzed and understood without the need to follow the circuit dynamics in detail. The basic conceptual details provided by some leading researchers may lead to various other neuronal architectural morphologies.

Current computational models of neurons have somewhat merged in the silicon-based environment of analog very large-scale integration (VLSI) circuits. One typical network design utilizes transconductor amplifiers as the variable synaptic weights, both excitatory and inhibitory. The soma of this neuron can be constructed using operational amplifiers acting as compactors.

1.7.4 Some Future Perspectives

Progress in information-based technology has significantly broadened the capabilities and application of computers. Today's computers, however, are being used merely for the storage and processing of numerical data (hard uncertainty and hard information). Should we not reexamine the functions of these computing tools in view of the increasing interest in subjects such as knowledge-based systems, expert systems, and intelligent robotic systems, as well as for solving problems related to decision and control? Human mentation acts on cognitive information, and cognitive information is characterized using relative grades. Human mentation and cognition functions use fresh information (acquired from the environment by our natural sensors) together with the information (experience, knowledge base) stored in the biological memory.

Shannon's definition of "information" was based on certain physical measurements of random activities in physical systems, in particular, in communication channels. This definition was restricted, however, to a class of information arising from physical systems.

If we wish to emulate in a machine, some of the cognitive functions (learning, remembering, reasoning, intelligence, perceiving, etc.) of humans, we have to generalize the definition of information and develop new mathematical tools and hardware. These new mathematical tools and hardware must deal with the simulation and processing of cognitive information and soft logic. Many new notions, although still in primitive stages, are emerging around the mathematics of fuzzy neural logic and, it is hoped, we will be able to nurture some interesting studies in the not too distant future. Indeed, biological processes have much to offer to engineers, system scientists, and mathematicians for solving many practical problems of the world in which we live today (Homma and Gupta 2002a, McClelland and Rumelhart 1988, Skarda and Freeman 1987).

After we finish some initial studies on an intelligent machine, the next natural stage for us would be to embark on the design of a robotic machine that could play a game of pingpong with us with the same degree of emotion, enthusiasm, and pleasure that we receive when we are playing with our students, friends, and family members. Such studies would also, of course, need basic understanding of the theory of metaphysics.

1.8 AN OVERVIEW OF THE BOOK

This book on neural systems contains fifteen chapters which are divided into the following four parts:

Part I: Foundations of Neural Networks (Chapters 1 to 3)
Part II: Static Neural Networks (Chapters 4 to 7)
Part III: Dynamic Neural Networks (Chapters 8 to 12)
Part IV: Some Advanced Topics in Neural Networks (Chapters 13 to 15).

After this introductory chapter, in Chapter 2 of Part I, to understand some basic functions and architectural building blocks of the human brain from engineering and mathematical perspectives, we briefly introduce some topics on biological neural systems such as the morphology of biological neurons, neural signal processing, and human memory and learning systems. In Chapter 3, our discussion focuses on some basic and simple concepts, mathematical models, and adaptive processes of neural units, as they are the basic building blocks for complex neural network architectures. These chapters provide us with a foundation for further exploring architectures and adaptive learning process of neural networks.

In Part II of the book (Chapters 4–7), we study *static neural networks.* In Chapter 4, we first introduce the basic notion of two-layered static neural networks and their extension to multilayered feedforward neural networks (MFNNs). We then give an extensive discussion of learning and adaptation problems, including the backpropagation (BP) algorithms. In Chapter 5, to provide a more comprehensive viewpoint of the neural network structures and learning algorithms for MFNNs, some further problems associated with MFNNs are presented. We then introduce the concepts of radial basis function (RBF) neural networks and give some of its applications in Chapter 6. The universal approximation capability of feedforward neural networks is studied mainly using the Stone–Weierstrass theorem in Chapter 7, as the functional approximation capability of a feedforward neural network architecture is one of the most exciting properties of the neural structures and has potentials for applications to problems such as system identification, communication channel equalization, signal processing, control, and pattern recognition.

In Part III (Chapters 8–12), *dynamic neural networks* (DNNs) are studied. In Chapter 8, we explore various configurations of dynamic neural units (DNUs) and study some of their dynamic properties which will be useful in forming neural architectures. In Chapter 9, using some of these continuous-time dynamic neural units (CT-DNUs) with feedback connections, dynamic neural networks (DNNs) are introduced. In Chapter 10, learning algorithms for the dynamic neural units and for the dynamic neural networks are studied extensively. Some stability analysis approaches and stability results for a general class of continuous-time dynamic neural networks (CT-DNNs) are presented in Chapter 11, and the stability analysis is extended to the discrete-time dynamic neural networks in Chapter 12.

In Part IV (Chapters 13–15), some advanced topics are discussed. In Chapter 13, by using the dynamic system language, we present models of binary neural networks that are a class of neural networks with only two states in a discrete-time domain. In Chapter 14, feedback binary associative memories are studied using the binary neural networks architecture. In Chapter 15, we provide an overview of the basic principles, mathematical descriptions, and the state-of-the-art developments of fuzzy neural networks.

The book is appended with an extensive list of references and bibliographical material along with the bibliographical sources on neural networks and a classified list of bibliography on neural networks.

2

Biological Foundations of Neuronal Morphology

2.1 Morphology of Biological Neurons

2.2 Neural Information Processing

2.3 Human Memory Systems

2.4 Human Learning and Adaptation

2.5 Concluding Remarks

2.6 Some Biological Keywords

Problems

The most fundamental understanding of the human brain is that its nervous system is organized using a very large number of computational units called *neurons*. These neurons are located in functional constellations or assemblies and form complex connections through which the neurons communicate with each other. A neuron is an individual cell characterized by architectural features that represent rapid changes in voltage across its membrane as well as voltage changes in neighboring neurons (Churchland and Sejnowski 1992). There are over 10^{10} neurons forming a massively interconnected neural structure in the human brain. Biological neurons are involved in complex sensory, control, thinking, perceptive, and various other cognitive operations. Various complex cognitive mappings and mathematical processing functions can be identified in biological processes. Different mechanisms for explanation and classification of neurons on the basis of their neuronal morphology have been investigated. However, there is some commonly accepted knowledge of biological neurons, which forms a basis for developing various mathematical models of neurons.

The intellectual functions of the human brain, as well as its learning and memory capabilities, set humans apart from animals. It is learning and memory that make humans adaptive and intelligent for handling complex, uncertain, and time-varying real-world environments. In order to understand some basic functions and architectural building blocks of the human brain from engineering and mathematical perspectives, this chapter briefly introduces such topics of biological neural systems as the morphology of biological neurons, neural signal processing, and human memory and learning systems. This basic biological description of neuronal morphology will provide some inspiration for the development of new neural structures for engineering and science applications.

2.1 MORPHOLOGY OF BIOLOGICAL NEURONS

2.1.1 Basic Neuronal Structure

The basic building element of the central nervous system (CNS), including the brain, retina, and spinal cord, is the *neuron*. This biological cell receives and processes information and then communicates with various parts of the human body. A simplified schematic view of a biological neural process is shown in Fig. 2.1, and an ideal biological neuron is depicted in Fig. 2.2. The nerve cell body is called the *soma* and is surrounded by a thin plasma membrane filled with cytoplasm.

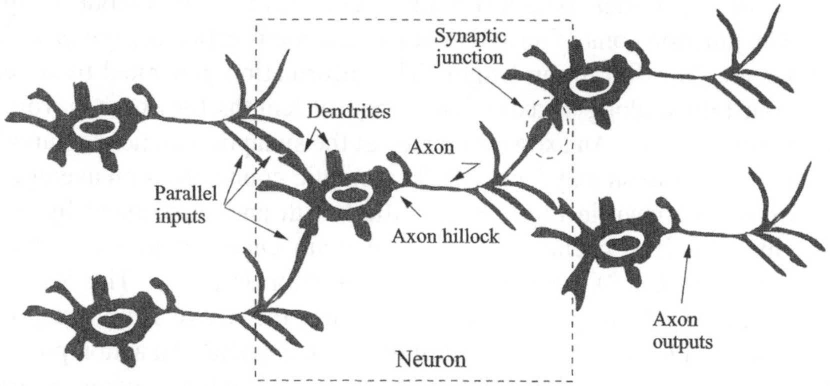

Figure 2.1 A schematic diagram of five interconnected neurons. Each neuron receives numerous parallel input signals through its dendrites and yields a single output that is transmitted to other neurons.

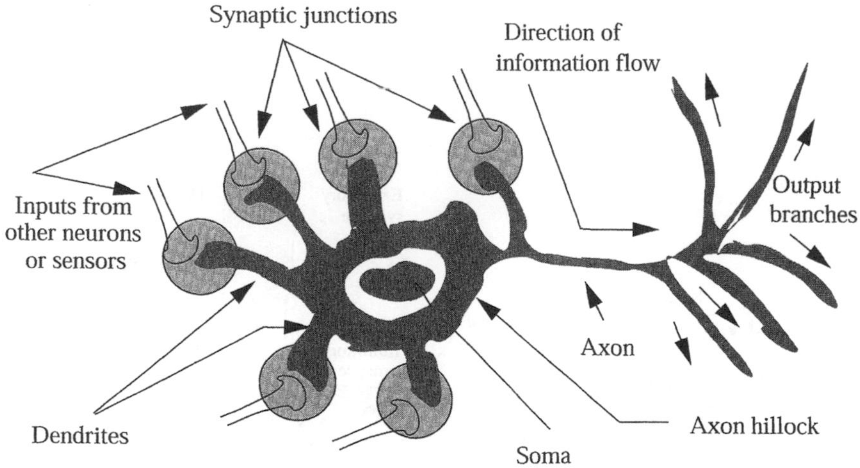

Figure 2.2 A schematic diagram of an ideal biological neuron. Each neuron receives multiple inputs through its dendrites and generates a single output along its axon.

The soma is approximately 30 μm in diameter. Within the soma is a cell nucleus. Each nerve cell receives many inputs (of the order of 10^4) through the *dendrites*, and after some processing generates a single output along its *axon*. The junction point of an axon with a dendrite is called the *synapse*. The dendrites are 200–300 μm in length. The information generated by a nerve cell is transmitted along its axon. The range of lengths for axons is from 50 μm to several meters. An axon terminates at the synaptic junctions of another neuron. A single axon may have 10,000 synaptic connections on average.

Neurons, as shown in Fig. 2.3, are filled with and surrounded by fluids containing dissolved chemical ions. The main chemical ions are sodium (Na^+), calcium (Ca^{2+}), potassium (K^+) and chloride (Cl^-). The Na^+ and K^+ ions are largely responsible for generating the active neural response, which is also called the *action potential* or *nerve impulse*. An action potential is defined by a sharp positive pulse followed by a slowly decaying electrical potential (Scott 1977). Figure 2.3(a) shows that the K^+ ions are concentrated mainly inside the cell of the neuron whereas, the Na^+ ions are concentrated outside the cell membrane. In the state of inactivity (rest), the interior of the neuron, the *protoplasm*, is negatively charged compared to the surrounding neural liquid. The action potential curve in Fig. 2.4 indicates that the neural resting potential of about -70 mV is supported by the action of the cell membrane, which is impenetrable for Na^+ ions, causing a deficiency of positive ions in the protoplasm (Müller and Reinhardt 1991).

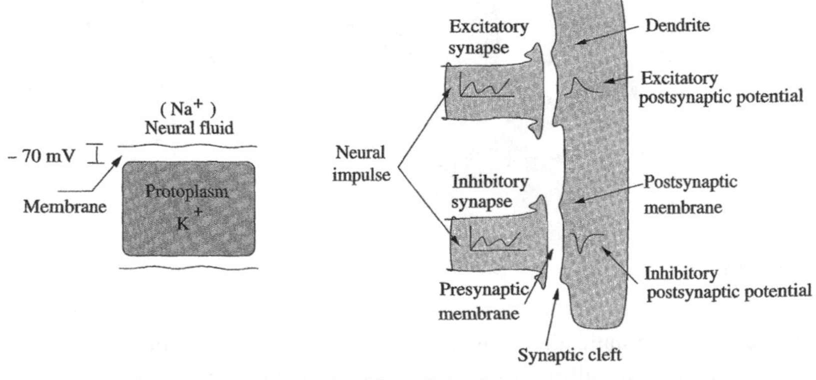

(a) Chemical structure of a neuron (b) Simplified structure of synapses

Figure 2.3 Simplified structures of a biological neuron.

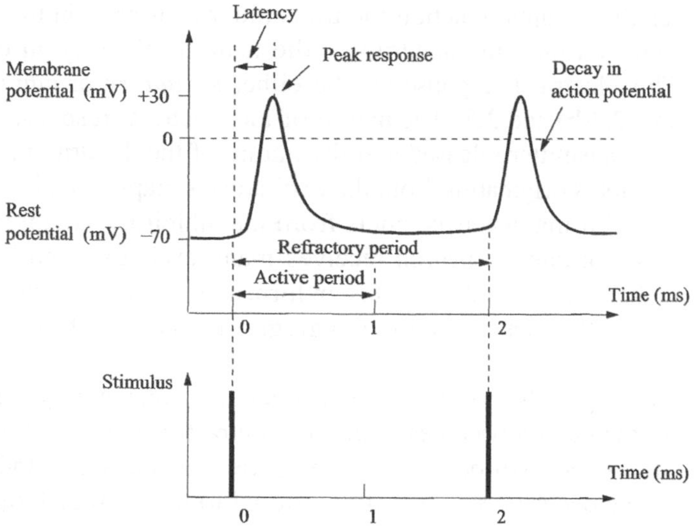

Figure 2.4 An idealized version of two successive action potentials.

2.1.2 Neural Electrical Signals

In biological neural processes, the dendrites appear to provide receptive surfaces for input signals to the neurons. They transmit these signals passively with no amplification to the soma, the main body of the neuron.

The soma carries out such mathematical operations on these synaptic signals as aggregation and nonlinear transformation, and yields a single action potential that is passed to the axon. In the axons these action potentials appear as a train of impulses, called *nerve impulses*, *nerve action potentials*, or simply *spikes*. The action potentials are propagated with no attenuation along the axon and its branches to target cells such as other neurons, muscles, or receptors.

The process of generating action potentials in either the neuron (where the processing of information takes place) or the axon (through which the transmission of information takes place) is due to the exchange of K^+ and Na^+ ions caused by a change in the permeability of the cell membrane. The axon of a neuron is connected to the dendrites of other neurons through a synaptic junction. This synaptic junction employs a chemical transmitter to convey a signal across the boundary of the junction. The action potentials conducted along the axon are converted by the synapses to a voltage signal in the dendrite.

A neuron is considered active if it is generating a sequence of action potentials. When the nerve impulse, in the form of action potentials along the axon, reaches the synaptic junction the transmitter substance in the synaptic vesicles is released onto the dendrite of the neuron, eliciting an electrical response. This electrical response can be either *excitatory* or *inhibitory*, as shown in Figs. 2.3(b) and 2.5. The nature of the electrical response depends on the type of transmitter released and the nature of the dendrite membrane. The dendritic inputs originating from the excitatory synapses tend to increase the rate of neural firing, whereas inputs from the inhibitory synapses tend to decrease this firing rate. A neuron receives many excitatory and inhibitory inputs from other neurons and generates, in turn, a series of electrical impulses with a frequency that depends on the aggregated behavior of the incoming signals.

Simply speaking, if the excitatory inputs become strong enough, the output impulse from the neuron becomes large. In contrast, if the inhibitory inputs are strong, the output will be small or completely suppressed. Indeed, the magnitude of the dendritic signal is proportional to the average frequency at which the pulses arrive at the synaptic junction. The synaptic junction usually occurs between the axons and dendrites, and it can also appear between axon and axon, between dendrite and dendrite, and even between axon and cell body.

A single neuron is capable of encoding stimulus signals into sequences of frequency-modulated electrical pulses as shown in Fig. 2.4. Two important properties of action potentials are directly related to the frequency encoding ability of the axon potential. The first property is the *latency* or *effective rise time*, which is defined as the time between the application of the stimulus and the peak of the resulting action potential. This response time decreases exponentially as the stimulus intensity increases. The second property, called the *refractory period*, represents the minimum time required for the axon to generate two consecutive action potential responses as shown in Fig. 2.4. In other words, the refractory period is the minimum time between the occurrence of two successive action potentials. The threshold for the second stimulus to fire a neuron depends on this refractory period that exists independent of

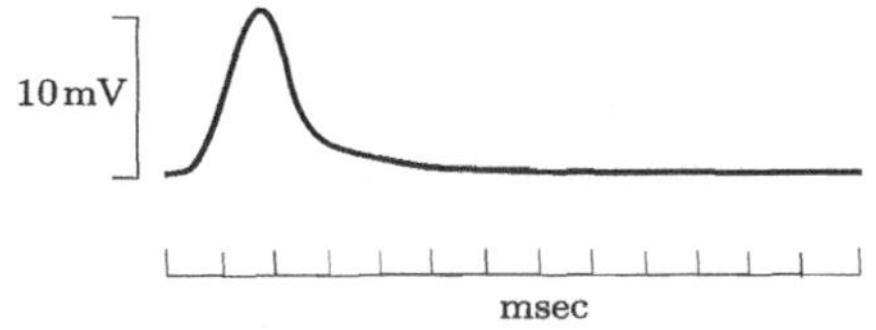

(a) Excitatory potential

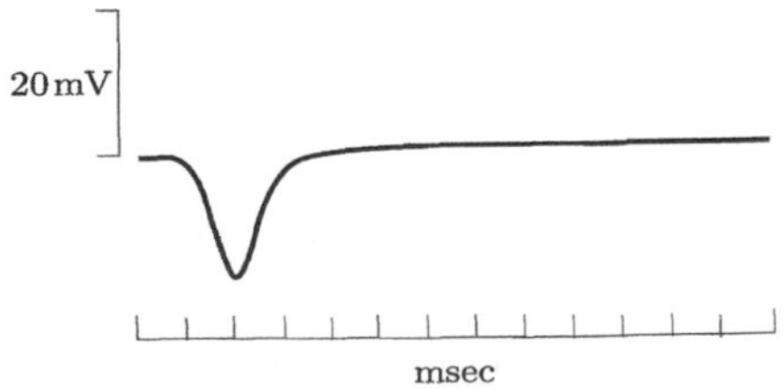

(b) Inhibitory potential

Figure 2.5 Postsynaptic potentials.

the strength of any new stimulus. There is also a deadzone period, called the *absolute refractory period.* During this period it is impossible to generate another output pulse. After the absolute refractory period has expired, the stimulus intensity threshold for the second pulse decreases exponentially as the refractory period increases. Therefore, from the preceding analysis it is postulated that if a constant stimulus of suprathreshold intensity is applied to an axon, both the latency and refractory periods will control the frequency of the output pulses. For example, a stimulus with a high intensity will yield a small refractory period and a faster rise time, thereby generating a higher frequency action potential.

In the following section, we briefly describe the activities of a neuron with respect to information processing.

2.2 NEURAL INFORMATION PROCESSING

The human brain has more than 10 billion neural cells, which have complicated interconnections, and these neurons constitute a large-scale signal processing and memory neural network. Indeed, the understanding of the neural mechanisms of the higher functions of the brain is very complex. In the conventional neurophysiological approach, one can obtain only some fragmentary knowledge of the neural processes and formulate only some mathematical models for various applications. The mathematical study of a single neural model and its various extensions is the first step in the design of a complex neural network for applications such as neural signal processing, pattern recognition, control of complex processes, neurovision systems, and other decisionmaking processes.

A simple neural model is presented in Fig. 2.6. In terms of information processing, an individual neuron with dendrites as multiple-input terminals and an axon as a single-output terminal may be considered a multiple-input/single-output (MISO) system. The processing functions of this MISO neural processor may be divided into the following four categories:

(i) Dendrites: They consist of a highly branching tree of fibers, and act as input points to the main body of the neuron. On average, there are 10^3–10^4 dendrites per neuron, which form receptive surfaces for input signals to the neurons.

(ii) Synapse: It is a storage area of the past experience (knowledge base). It provides long-term memory (LTM) to the past accumulated experience. It receives information from sensors and other neurons and provides outputs through the axons.

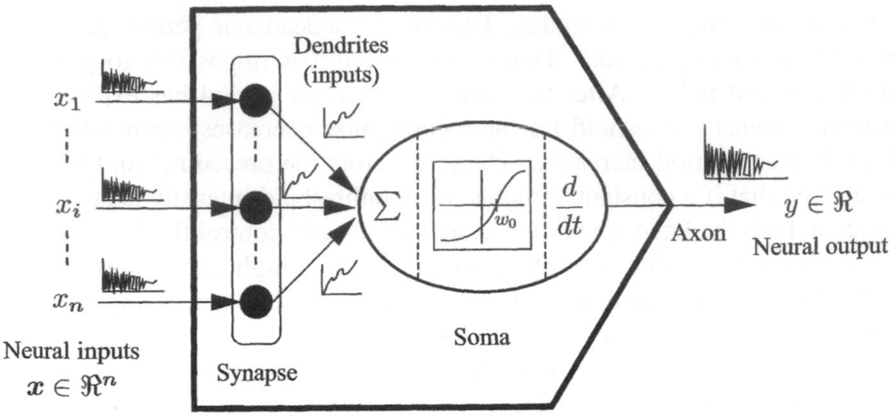

Figure 2.6 A simple neural model as a multiinput (dendrites) and single-output (axon) processor.

(iii) Soma: The neural cell body is called the *soma*. It is the large, round central neuronal body. It receives synaptic information and performs further processing of the information. Almost all the logical functions of the neuron are carried out in the soma.

(iv) Axon: The neural output line is called the *axon*. The output appears in the form of an action potential that is transmitted to other neurons for further processing.

The electrochemical activities at the synaptic junctions of the neurons exhibit a complex behavior because each neuron makes hundreds of interconnections with other neurons. Each neuron acts as a parallel processor because it receives action potentials in parallel from the neighboring neurons and then transmits pulses in parallel to other neighboring synapses. In terms of information processing, the synapse also performs a crude pulse frequency-to-voltage conversion as shown in Fig. 2.6.

2.2.1 Neural Mathematical Operations

In general, it can be argued that the role played by neurons in the brain reasoning processes is analogous to the role played by a logical switching element in a digital computer. However, this analogy is too simple. A neuron contains a sensitivity threshold, adjustable signal amplification or attenuation at each synapse, and an internal structure that allows incoming nerve signals to be integrated over both space and time. From a mathematical point of view, it may be concluded that the processing of information within a neuron involves the following two distinct mathematical operations:

(i) Synaptic operation: The strength (weight) of the synapse is a representation of the storage of knowledge and thus the memory for previous knowledge. The synaptic operation assigns a relative weight (significance) to each incoming signal according to the past experience (knowledge) stored in the synapse.

(ii) Somatic operation: The somatic operation provides various mathematical operations such as aggregation, thresholding, nonlinear activation, and dynamic processing to the synaptic inputs. If the weighted aggregation of the neural inputs exceeds a certain threshold, the soma will produce an output signal to its axon.

A simplified representation of the above neural operations for a typical neuron is shown in Fig. 2.7. A biological neuron deals with some interesting mathematical mapping properties because of its nonlinear operations combined with a thresholding in the soma. If neurons were only capable of carrying out linear operations, the complex human cognition and the robustness of neural systems would disappear.

Observations from both experimental and mathematical analysis have indicated that neural cells can transmit reliable information if they are sufficiently redundant in numbers. However, in general, a biological neuron is an unpredictable mechanism for processing information. Therefore, it is postulated that the collective activity generated by large numbers of locally redundant neurons is more significant than the activity generated by a single neuron.

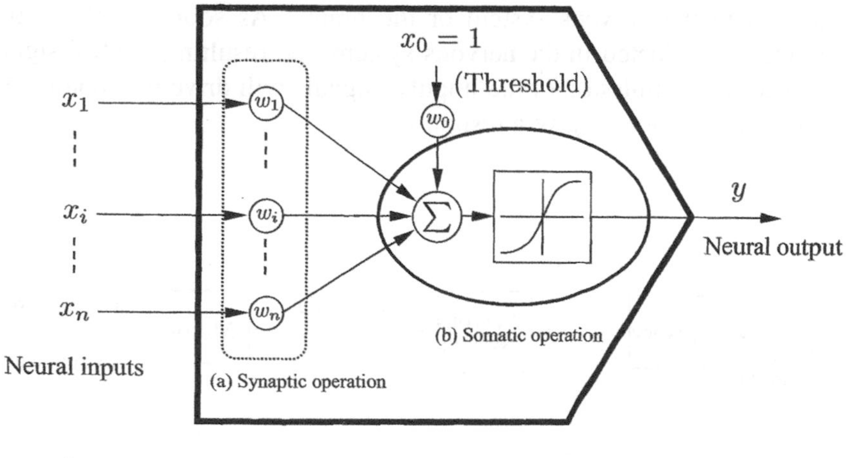

Figure 2.7 Simple model of a neuron showing (a) synaptic and (b) somatic operations.

2.2.2 Sensorimotor Feedback Structure

The nervous system consists of millions of neurons that form the basis for information processing units. Many neurons are packed together in layers, and the synaptic connections are very intricate in such a system. It is the interaction of many neurons that makes activities such as learning, recognition, decisionmaking, discrimination, and generalization possible. Most operations of the nervous system are complex. However, some examples of their neuronal behavior may be given. For example, the pain reflex is mediated by a neural sensorimotor mechanism. The sensory neurons detect a painful stimulus and transmit this message to the spinal cord. The information is passed to the motor neurons via a single set of synapses. The motor neurons transmit signals to muscles that move the body away from painful stimuli. The information is transmitted to the brain. However, the reflex process is simple in nature.

Sensors interface the real world to the brain, and from this point the information is passed through multiple levels of the nervous system. To carry out this information transformation from lower to higher levels of the brain, different levels of cerebral functions such as abstraction, conceptualization, and feature detection are involved. The nervous system can detect specific features while it deals with ambiguous information. These sensations may not be understood until they are processed by many layers in several areas of the brain. Information sensed by the eyes, ears, or touch is passed through many layers of nerves.

Using systems language, biological neural behavior may be considered as a sensorimotor scheme having the three functions, shown in Fig. 2.8. The three blocks have internal feedforward and feedback information exchange. The sensors receive stimulus inputs from the environment and transmit the information to the nervous system or the brain. As soon as information processing is conducted in the nervous system, the resulting control signals represented in the emission of the impulse signals will drive the motor, such as muscles and glands, to give a response.

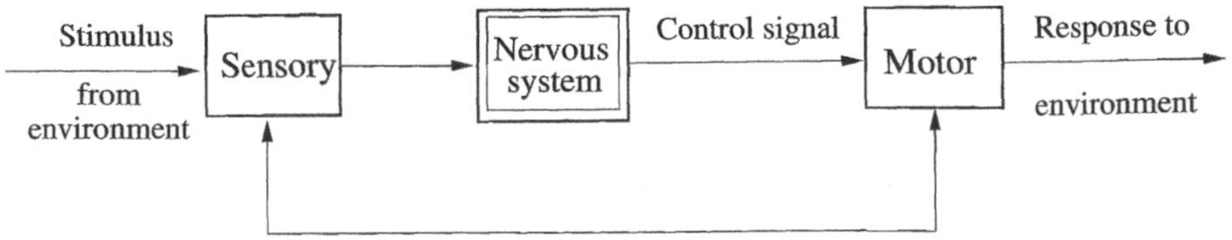

Figure 2.8 Three functions involved in a sensorimotor control structure.

2.2.3 Dynamic Characteristics

Several of the dynamic information processes that occur in biological neural systems are integrally linked to the morphology of these neural processes. These dynamic neural processors form the basis from which the higher-order properties of the neural systems emerge. Some of the important features of these dynamic neural information processes are briefly described now.

(i) *Distributed and parallel processing:* Neural information accessed by various biological sensors is distributed across multiple neurons. Further, neural information processes seem to involve the activation of multiple neurons that not only receive and transmit information in parallel but also incorporate parallelism and distributed updating mechanisms with an adaptive capability in order to learn, recognize, generalize, and discriminate. In fact, there are two sensory distribution systems in the brain; one is the specific sensorithalamocortical system, and the other is a nonspecific system used for attention and motivation. These structures verify the importance and plausibility of parallel distributed knowledge in the brain.

(ii) *Temporal encoding capability:* Stimulus information received by neurons is encoded as spike trains. A given axon will typically have a constant spiking amplitude, but its frequency of response will carry the information content. Usually the information is encoded in the form of frequency modulation and is stored in the brain as either short-term memory (STM) or long-term memory (LTM).

(iii) *The role of lateral inhibition:* Lateral inhibition introduces information exchange from neuron to neuron and affects a neuron blocking the action of another neuron. This inhibitive mechanism commonly exists, and may be prevalent throughout the nervous system. However, lateral inhibition is a mechanism of local neural interaction, and it gives rise to significant global properties. From an information perspective, lateral inhibition provides information on the changes of information. Thus, lateral inhibition may be viewed simultaneously as a biological principle and as a mathematical description of a biological neural system.

(iv) *Feedforward and feedback processing:* It appears that the brain uses circular or reverberatory loops for processing information. This looping occurs when one part of the brain processes an input and passes the information to another area and the new area processes and passes the information directly back to the originating location, or through other intermediate locations for further updating. In the end, the information is returned through the original brain area to reverberate again through the structures. This process obviously involves feedforward and feedback loops with some dynamic processing. This dynamic processing caused by feedback provides some robust characteristics in information processing.

2.3 HUMAN MEMORY SYSTEMS

One feature that distinguishes of humans from other animals is the immense amount of information that humans can learn and remember. Learning and memory are basic to human experience and constitute the basis of the brain function. Memory involves time-dependent processing relying on encoding and retrieval as well as storage of information. Simply speaking, memory is information stored in the brain as a result of sensory experience.

2.3.1 Types of Human Memory

One approach to the understanding of biological memory processes is to examine the differences that exist among memory mechanisms that deal with different time frames of the storage process. As illustrated in Fig. 2.9, human memory can be classified into three different categories: sensory memory, short-term memory, and long-term memory. However, it is not clear that different types of information to be stored must necessarily pass through all of these mechanisms, but much of it clearly does.

(i) Sensory memory (SM): The first stage of storage in memory is frequently referred to as *sensory memory* (SM). Incoming information from sensory elements is placed into this temporary storage for a brief period. The apparent function of sensory memory is to retain a record of the sensory

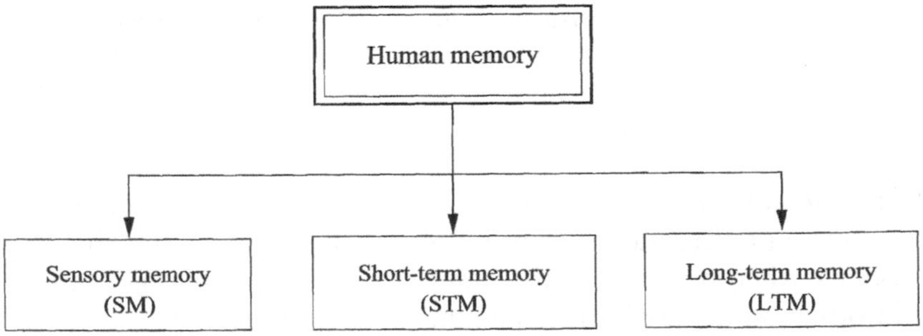

Figure 2.9 Three types of human memory.

events long enough for perceptual mechanisms. One distinguishing property of such memory is that the information spontaneously begins decaying with time; older images appear fainter, which explains the disappearing trail following the image. In addition to spontaneous decay with time, several other features distinguish sensory memory from other types of neural storage. The first is that all the information in the input is stored in sensory memory. The second important feature of sensory memory is that it is erasable.

(ii) Short-term memory (STM): All of the information in sensory memory is not lost after approximately half a second or so. Obviously, if a page full of characters is shown in a brief flash only, some of them will be remembered for a few seconds. Hence, this more persistent form of memory contains less information than sensory memory, but through an attentionlike process any item of information in the sensory memory may be transferred into it. This second state of the memory process is commonly called *short-term memory* (STM). Several seconds of the latest sensory information are sustained, presumably via reverberation around neural feedback loops. If the sensory information is deemed to be important, the store gate acts as a trigger and instructs the memory stacks to permanently store the information. Several facts about short-term memory can be established. Its capacity is relatively small. Also, the addition of new items erases old ones in a temporal sequence, so that adding new items causes the oldest to be dropped off the stack. As attention shifts to new items, the content of the short-term memory is continuously updated from the sensory memory.

(iii) Long-term memory (LTM): The third stage in the information storage sequence is usually referred to as *long-term memory* (LTM). Information items are expected to be stored permanently or for a relatively long time. In other words, long-term memory refers to the more or less permanent form of information storage in the brain. The capacity of a long-term memory is relatively large. Information seems to enter long-term memory as a result of repeated rehearsal of the contents of short-term memory. It may take many repetitions or activations of data in short-term memory to establish it in long-term memory; that is, the process of learning and memorizing. A loss of long-term memory is usually associated with the phenomenon of forgetting, which is a true loss of information from storage. It is almost universally assumed that long-term memory is defined in the nervous system in terms of variations in synaptic efficiency, and that biochemical changes

associated with learning and memory act primarily by mediating such changes in synaptic efficiency.

2.3.2 Features of Short-Term and Long-Term Memories

A hypothetical scheme of the human memory system is shown in Fig. 2.10. Sensory information enters a sensory memory, where it is held in detail for a brief period. Some of this information is transferred to short-term memory. Moreover, some of the information in short-term memory can be transferred to long-term memory, usually by rehearsing or repeating it. Other information from short-term memory is lost (forgotten). When a person remembers something, it is transferred from short-term memory into long-term memory. Short-term memory is roughly equivalent to consciousness or awareness. It should also be noted that in some books, sensory memory is considered as a special type of short-term memory because of its fast decaying feature.

In summary, some features of short-term memory processes versus long-term memory processes are compared in Table 2.1. A neural system comprised of the phase with rapid change dynamics would be particularly suitable for emulating short-term memory because of the rapidity of storage and access to storage of such a system. However, the neural system's dynamic process would not be suitable for long-term memory because of its vulnerability to disruptive forces and its relatively large energy demands for operation during the period of recycling. Comparatively, a long-term memory system is energy efficient, stable, and has a larger overall storage capacity.

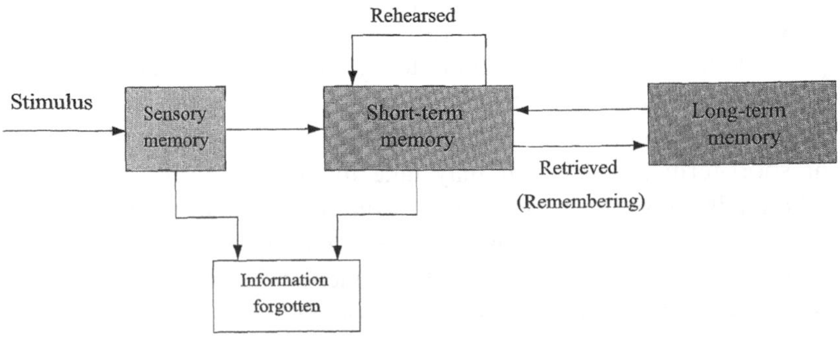

Figure 2.10 The process of information storage in the human memory system.

Table 2.1 Main features of short- and long-term memory

Advantages	Disadvantages
Short-term memory (STM)	
• Dynamic storage	• Low robustness: vulnerable to physical interruption, causing loss of information
• Easy and speedy access	• Small memory capacity
	• High energy requirement
Long-term memory (LTM)	
• Equilibrium storage	• Processing is more complicated
• Stable and robust	• Access is more difficult and slower
• Large storage capacity	• Time coupling between storage and processing
	• Erasing a stable memory is difficult

2.3.3 Content-Addressable and Associative Memory

In a conventional computer system, memory addresses are used to access the storage location of a particular byte of information. More recently, content-addressable or associative memory systems have appeared in which the underlying principle is the provision for data retrieval by a keyword that is associated with the desired information. The keyword is either an actual position of the information, or simply associated with the information in storage. It has been found that in this associative property of long-term memory, data is obtained by assembling as many stimuli as possible that were associated with the desired data at the time of its entry into the memory system.

As used, the term *associative* refers to the property of biological memories that allows them to return items similar to the one specifically addressed. This aspect is considered in more detail in later chapters of this book. In the brain, long-term memory appears to store information according to its semantic category relationship rather than in sequential order, as in short-term memory. Hence items that share some semantic-level properties will have similar pointers or retrieval keys for their access. One function of this type of memory system is the recognition of the final or intermediate goal states that are similar to those involved in a current problem and with which we have had some experience in the past. One may never have had to find a path to the present goal state before, but its representation in a memory recall operation may produce a similar past situation, which in turn has a remembered path for its reproduction. If it is sufficiently similar to the desired state, it may constitute a sufficient solution. If not, it may prove to be valuable intermediate information. Associative memories are thus fundamental not only to the operations that adapt the brain to real-world problems, but also in the design of the artificial neural memory systems.

2.4 HUMAN LEARNING AND ADAPTATION

One of the most remarkable features of the human brain is its ability to adaptively learn in response to knowledge, experience, and environment. The basis of this learning appears to be a network of interconnected adaptive elements by means of which transformation between inputs and outputs is performed. Learning can be defined as the acquisition of new information. In other words, learning is a process of memorizing new information. Adaptation implies that the element can change in a systematic manner and in so doing alter the transformation between input and output. In the brain, transmission within the neural system involves coded nerve impulses and other physical chemical processes that form reflections of sensory stimuli and incipient motor behavior.

Many biological aspects are associated with such learning processes, including (Harston 1990)

- Learning overlays hardwired connections
- Synaptic plasticity versus stability: a crucial design dilemma
- Synaptic modification, providing a basis for observable organism behavior

2.4.1 Types of Human Learning

Learning may also be considered as a change in behavior as a result of experience. Neuroscientists have so far studied three kinds of simple learning: (i) habituation, (ii) sensitization, and (iii) associative learning. These three types of learning are simple in the sense that they occur without the subject's awareness of a change in behavior. Simple learning is different from those kinds of human learning that are voluntary and that require, for example, the formation of concepts or the use of classifications.

(i) *Habituation:* Habituation takes place when a stimulus organism that has originally responded is presented so often that the organism stops responding to it. In *sensitization*, the opposite of habituation, the human learns to respond vigorously to a previous neural stimulus. Human adults manifest habituation all the time. Suppose that you have just moved into a house that is close to a highway with heavy traffic. For the first few nights, the sound of heavy traffic under your window keeps you awake all night. However, after a few days you manage to fall asleep with all that noise. You have habituated to the sound of the traffic.

(ii) *Sensitization:* This is also a very adaptive aspect of behavior. A sudden or painful stimulus increases the likelihood and strength of a variety of responses. If you hear a loud and unexpected sound, you immediately become alert and aroused. Your autonomic system becomes more active and you look around for the source of the sound, which might indicate danger. As soon as you find that the sound does not mean danger, you stop being sensitized to it.

(iii) *Associative learning:* Unlike habituation and sensitization, associative learning corresponds to a stimulus with a response to an event. Such learning occurs most readily when it has adaptive consequences. One form of associative learning, called *classical conditioning*, can be illustrated by Pavlov's experiment, in which a dog learned to associate the sound of a bell with food after repeated trials in which the bell always rang just before the food was provided (Pavlov 1993). Another form of associative learning, called *operant conditioning* or *instrumental learning*, is illustrated by an experiment. A hungry rat is given the opportunity to discover that a pellet of food is provided every time it presses a bar when a signal light is on, but no food is provided when the light is off. The rat quickly learns to press the bar only when the light is on. In classical conditioning the conditioned stimulus is always followed by the unconditioned stimulus regardless of the animal's response. In operant conditioning, reinforcement is provided only when the animal responds to the conditioning stimulus in the desired way.

2.4.2 Supervised and Unsupervised Learning Mechanisms

A learning process requires adaptation. In fact, the changes in function that distinguish complex learning from simpler forms of adaptation are the ones that require a process of adaptation of the parameters that are sensitive to the environment. They are also conducive to self-organization. The problem is to produce orderly adaptation that can deal with the production of specific outputs based on particular inputs. Then sensory perception, although still somewhat distorted by repeated transmissions, will be orderly rather than chaotic.

An important question is how neural adaptation might depend on contingencies, both intrinsic and extrinsic, for each neuron and maintain organization within a dynamic neural system of complex architecture. Two types of adaptation are found in human learning:

(i) Supervised learning: One type of learning is based on a preprogrammed response to a particular input. This type of adaptation, called *supervised learning*, will occur regardless of the remaining system state or other variables. The contingencies for its occurrence are preestablished and fixed in supervised learning.

(ii) Unsupervised learning: The other type of learning is *unsupervised learning* and admits further modification based on feedback of information concerning the effects of prior learning. This information may come, in part, from the adaptive element itself, providing an update of the local system state, or it may arise extrinsically from the environment. Feedback to elements within the system permits an evolutionary type of adaptation based on the past performance. In addition, it allows interaction between past and present events.

2.5 CONCLUDING REMARKS

The human brain is the most complex structure in biological processes. The highly parallel processing and layered morphology with learning and memory facilities of the human cognitive faculty — the brain — provides us with a new tool for designing an intelligent machine that can learn, recognize, and control complicated tasks. Two important discoveries in the nineteenth century have formed the foundation for the science of nervous systems (Churchland and Sejnowski 1992): (i) macroimages displayed by nervous systems depend on individual cells whose paradigm anatomic structures include both long axons for sending signals and treelike dendrites for receiving signals; and (ii) these cells are essentially electrical devices whose basic task is to transmit and receive signals by causing and responding to electric current. On the basis of these discoveries, the mysteries of the human brain could be understood more clearly.

This chapter has covered some basic knowledge of the human brain from a biological point of view. First, the morphology of a single neuron, which is a basic unit of the human neural structure, was reviewed to provide a preliminary understanding of the human brain. Then, an engineering treatment of human neural processing, such as neural electrical signal, and neural mathematical operations, was presented. Finally, the memory and learning capabilities of human beings were described.

2.6 SOME BIOLOGICAL KEYWORDS

For the sake of convenience, some of the biological terms used in the text are described below.

Action potential: The pulse of the electric potential that is generated across the membrane of a neuron (or an axon) following the application of a stimulus greater than the threshold value.

Axon: The output fiber of a neuron that carries the information in the form of action potentials to other neurons in the network.

Cortex: The layer of gray matter that covers most of the brain where much of the cognitive faculty is housed.

Dendrite: The input line of the neuron that carries a temporal summation of action potentials to the soma.

Excitatory neuron: A neuron that transmits an action potential that has an excitatory (positive) influence on the recipient neural cells.

Inhibitory neuron: A neuron that transmits an action potential that has an inhibitory (negative) influence on the recipient neural cells.

Lateral inhibition: The local spatial interaction where the neural activity generated by one neuron is suppressed by the activity of the neighboring neurons.

Long-term memory (LTM): The process of neural information retention by adaptation to the strength of the neural synaptic connections.

Neuron: The basic neural cell for processing biological information.

Neural population: An assembly of neurons that lie in close spatial proximity.

Neural state: A neuron is active if it is firing a sequence of action potentials.

Refractory period: The minimum time required for the soma to generate two consecutive action potentials.

Retina: The sensory transducer of the visual system: the layers of neurons at the back of the eye containing such basic cells as photoreceptors and retinal ganglion cells.

Short-term memory (STM): The process of neural information retention for a short period of time after the input stimulus is removed.

Soma: The body of a neuron that provides aggregation, thresholding, and nonlinear activation to the dendritic inputs.

Stimulus: A signal of biological significance usually defined as being capable of eliciting some response.

Synapse: The junction point between the axon (of a presynaptic neuron) and the dendrite (of a postsynaptic neuron). This acts as a memory (storage) of the past accumulated experience (knowledge).

Problems

2.1 Describe an idealized model of biological neurons.

2.2 Name the four main components of a neuron and explain the main functions of these components in the sense of neural information processing.

2.3 Describe an example of the human sensorimotor feedback structure.

2.4 Show a process when a short-term memory becomes the long-term memory.

2.5 Use a block diagram to show a recall procedure of a long-term memory in the human brain.

2.6 Elaborate on the following statements:

(a) "The human mind is the source of facts, fantasies, creativity, ideas, and feeling";

(b) "The phenomenal attributes of the brain such as learning, memory speech, and thought processes are associated with the cerebrum".

2.7 Although, they may look identical, the twin halves of the brain perform totally different functions. Provide a functional view of the two halves of the brain.

2.8 With every passing moment of our working lives, we experience new things, and store them in our memories. Memory creates a knowledge-base of our past experiences for our future reference. As a result of our past knowledge, we act in certain ways. In fact, learning influences every aspect of our lives. Describe briefly the anatomy of learning in the biological process.

2.9 "Reinforcement or a reward in a behavioral situation is a most effective way of learning." Explain it.

2.10 "Learning from our mistakes (supervised learning) is another aspect of learning." Explain it.

2.11 Memory involves the whole brain, but the most indispensable regions invade the hippocampi and the mammillary bodies. Memory can be classified into (i) short-term memory (STM) and (ii) long-term memory (LTM). STM possesses very limited capacity and is useful only for immediate recall, whereas LTM seems to have *unlimited* capacity. Discuss the neural aspects of STM and LTM and give some biological plausible models.

2.12 What is human intelligence? How to measure it? How does it compare with biological species? Comment also on the emulation of such intelligence for applications to robotic systems.

2.13 Discuss the neuronal morphology of biological neurons.

2.14 Give a brief description of the human central nervous systems (CNS). Use appropriate sketches.

2.15 Identify the various sensory and control regions in the cognitive faculty — the brain.

2.16 What aspects of the cognitive faculty can help system scientists in the development of the neural computing field?

2.17 Define the keywords: cognition, perception, learning, adaptation, memory, thinking, and thought processes.

2.18 What are the main features and attributes of biological neurons that *have* inspired and *can* inspire the field of neural computing?

2.19 In biology, a neuron is a basic information processing element (in sensory, control, and cognitive functions). The neuron has basically two mathematical operations: (i) *Synaptic* and (ii) *Somatic*.

(a) Discuss the action potential (which is the somatic operation) and its biochemical reactions (in terms of K^+ and Na^+ ions exchange);

(b) In neural action potential clearly identify the following: threshold, depolarization, repolarization, refractory period, bandwidth;

(c) How does the conductivity of the potassium and sodium ionic channels change during the various phases of the action potential?

2.20 The field of neural computing systems has been inspired by the strength of cognition (reasoning, perception, learning, adaptation, and control) that lies in the biological cognitive faculty — the brain, in particular, and the central nervous system (CNS), in general. The biological neuron is a basic computing element in CNS. Its response (excitation) is purely dependent on ionic currents. Describe a model of a biological neuron, its action potential, and how Na^+, K^+, and other ionic currents contribute towards its phases such as the polarization, depolarization, threshold, and refractory (forced inactive) periods, etc. (Kandel and Schwartz 1985, Nicholls et al. 2001).

3

Neural Units: Concepts, Models, and Learning

3.1 Neurons and Threshold Logic: Some Basic Concepts

3.2 Neural Threshold Logic Synthesis

3.3 Adaptation and Learning for Neural Threshold Elements

3.4 Adaptive Linear Element (Adaline)

3.5 Adaline with Sigmoidal Functions

3.6 Networks with Multiple Neurons

3.7 Concluding Remarks

Problems

Artificial neural networks, as models of specific biological computational structures, consist of distributed information processing units, and thus possess an inherent potential for parallel computation. The basis of an artificial neural network is that it has many interconnected processing units, called *neurons*, which form the layered configurations. Discussions appeared in the existing literature often considers the behavior of a single neuron as the basic computing unit for describing neural information processing operations. Each computing unit in the network is based on the concept of an *idealized* neuron. An *ideal* neuron is assumed to respond optimally to the applied inputs. Neural network is a collective set of such neural units, in which the individual neurons are connected through complex synaptic connections characterized by weight coefficients and every single neuron makes its contribution towards the computational properties of the whole system.

In nature, biological neurons are involved in various complex sensory, control, and cognitive aspects of mathematical and decision making processes as discussed in Chapter 2. Various complex mathematical mapping and processing functions can possibly be identified in biological processes. Studies on the mathematical models of neural units started at the time when the problem of the mathematical description of the human brain attracted the attention of researchers. The first formal model of the neuron was proposed as early as 1943 by McCulloch and Pitts. More recently, the development of adaptive methods offers an opportunity for emulating the *learning* function of biological neural processes. Some of such neural models were developed in the 1960s (Widrow 1962, Rosenblatt 1958). In general, as an information processor, an individual neuron performs an aggregation on its weighted inputs and yields an output through a nonlinear activation function with a threshold.

In this chapter, our discussion focuses on basic and simple concepts, mathematical models, and adaptive processes of neural units, as they are the basic building blocks for complex neural network architectures. The connections between the classic threshold logic and neural logic are analyzed first. Basic and well-known adaptive concepts, approaches, and equations are then introduced for some basic neural units. A simple three-neuron network is presented as a beginning for studying neural networks. The results studied in this chapter will lay a foundation for further exploring architectures and adaptive learning processes of neural networks.

3.1 NEURONS AND THRESHOLD LOGIC: SOME BASIC CONCEPTS

The reanalysis of threshold logic has attracted the attention of those interested in switching circuit and neural networks. As an important technique for the design of switching circuits, the threshold networks, were studied extensively in the 1960s. The usefulness of threshold logic in large scale digital systems and integrated circuits (IC) design is determined by the availability, cost, and capabilities of the basic building blocks, as well as by the existence of effective synthesis procedures. Stimulation response characteristics of the primitive neuron proposed by McCulloch and Pitts (1943) can be modeled with a threshold element. As a result, similarities exist between threshold networks and binary neural networks. Tracing the basic concepts of the threshold networks may help us understand the breakthrough of neural networks compared with the traditional logic circuit in terms of both structure and systems. Therefore, in this section we will use several examples for illustrating the basic concepts and similarities between basic binary logic operations and neural networks.

3.1.1 Some Basic Binary Logical Operations

3.1.1.1 Unipolar Binary Logic

A switching algebra is a binary algebraic system consisting of the unipolar set $\{0, 1\}$, two binary operations called *OR* and *AND*, and one uniary operation called *NOT*.

For a given unipolar set (x_1, x_2), $x_1, x_2 \in \{0, 1\}$, the binary logic operations are defined as follows:

(i) OR (logic sum) operation:

$$y = x_1 \; OR \; x_2 = x_1 + x_2 = x_1 \vee x_2 \tag{3.1}$$

(ii) AND (logic multiplication) operation:

$$y = x_1 \; AND \; x_2 = x_1 \cdot x_2 = x_1 \wedge x_2 \tag{3.2}$$

Table 3.1 **Truth table for *OR* operation:** $y = x_1 \; OR \; x_2$

x_1	x_2	$y = x_1 \; OR \; x_2$
0	0	0
0	1	1
1	0	1
1	1	1

Table 3.2 **Truth table for *AND* operation:** $y = x_1 \text{ AND } x_2$

x_1	x_2	$y = x_1 \text{ AND } x_2$
0	0	0
0	1	0
1	0	0
1	1	1

Table 3.3 **Truth table for *NOT* operation:** $y = \text{NOT } x_1$

x_1	$y = \text{NOT } x_1$
0	1
1	0

(iii) NOT (logic complementation) operation:

$$y = \text{NOT } x_1 = \overline{x}_1 = x_1' \tag{3.3}$$

3.1.1.2 Bipolar Binary Logic

Logic operations in Eqns. (3.1)–(3.3) are given for unipolar sets $\{0, 1\}$. These basic operations can be extended to the bipolar set $\{-1, 1\}$ as well.

For a unipolar set $\{0, 1\}$ and its equivalent bipolar, the conversion is defined as follows:

$$Bipolar = 2(unipolar) - 1 \tag{3.4}$$

(i) Bipolar binary OR, AND, and NOT logic operations:

These *OR*, *AND*, and *NOT* binary logic operations for the bipolar set x_1 and x_2 are defined as in Table 3.4.

Table 3.4 **Binary logic operation for bipolar sets**

x_1	x_2	$x_1 \text{ OR } x_2$	$x_1 \text{ AND } x_2$	$\text{NOT } x_1$
−1	−1	−1	−1	1
−1	1	1	−1	1
1	−1	1	−1	−1
1	1	1	1	−1

Table 3.5 **Truth table for *EXCLUSIVE-OR* (*XOR*) or *MODULO-2 addition***

x_1	x_2	x_1 *XOR* x_2
-1	-1	-1
-1	1	1
1	-1	1
1	1	-1

(ii) XOR (EXCLUSIVE–OR) operation:

Another binary operation on the set of switching elements is the *EXCLUSIVE–OR* or *XOR*, which is denoted by the symbol $\oplus$ and is defined as

$$\begin{aligned} x_1 \oplus x_2 &= (x_1 + x_2)(\overline{x}_1 + \overline{x}_2) \\ &= \overline{x}_1 x_2 + x_1 \overline{x}_2, \qquad x_1, x_2 \in \{-1, 1\} \end{aligned} \tag{3.5}$$

that is, $x_1 \oplus x_2 = 1$, if either x_1 or x_2 is 1, but not both. The *XOR* operation is also called the *modulo-2 addition* operation. This operation is illustrated in Table 3.5.

A *switching* function $f(x_1, x_2, \ldots, x_n)$ of n binary variables $x_1, x_2, \ldots, x_n$ is defined by assigning either -1 or 1 to the 2^n points $(x_1, x_2, \ldots, x_n)^T$ in the finite state space $\{-1, 1\}^n$. In particular, a *XOR* function of n binary variables $x_1, x_2, \ldots, x_n$, is defined as

$$\begin{aligned} f(x_1, x_2, \ldots, x_n) &= x_1 \oplus x_2 \oplus \cdots \oplus x_n \\ &= (x_1 \oplus x_2 \oplus \cdots) \oplus x_n \\ &= x_1 \oplus (x_2 \oplus \cdots) \oplus x_n \end{aligned} \tag{3.6}$$

This multivariable *XOR* function is also referred to as the odd *parity function* since it assigns the value 1 if and only if the number of the variables that have the value 1 is odd.

3.1.2 Neural Models for Threshold Logics

On the basis of the highly simplified considerations of the biological neural systems described in Chapter 2, the first formal mathematical description of a neural model for a threshold logic was provided by McCulloch and Pitts (1943). This model forms the basis of a neural network structure in contemporary neural computing.

In this section we will give a mathematical development of a neural model for a threshold circuit, first for unipolar binary inputs, $\boldsymbol{x} \in \{0, 1\}^n$, and then we will extend it to bipolar inputs, $\boldsymbol{x} \in \{-1, 1\}^n$.

3.1.2.1 Neural Threshold Logic for Unipolar Inputs, $x \in \{0,1\}^n$

A McCulloch–Pitts neural model is an element with n two-valued inputs $x_1, x_2, \ldots, x_n \in \{0,1\}$ and a single two-valued output $y \in \{0,1\}$. Its internal parameters are n two-valued weights $w_1, w_2, \ldots, w_n \in \{-1,1\}$, and a threshold $w_0 \in \Re$, where each weight w_i is associated with a particular input variable x_i. A positive weight $w_i = 1$ corresponds to an excitatory synapse, while a negative weight $w_i = -1$ implies that x_i is an inhibitory input.

Taking a refractory period as the unit of time, the neuron is assumed to be operating on a discrete-time scale $k = 1, 2, 3, \ldots$, and the firing rule of its output at time $(k + 1)$ is modeled as follows:

$$
y(k+1) = \begin{cases} 1, & \text{if} \quad \sum_{i=1}^{n} w_i x_i(k) \geq w_0 \\ \\ 0, & \text{if} \quad \sum_{i=1}^{n} w_i x_i(k) < w_0 \end{cases}
\tag{3.7}
$$

where the sum and product operations are the conventional arithmetic ones, and the sum, $\sum_i w_i x_i$, is called the *weighted sum* of the binary inputs. The firing rule given in Eqn. (3.7) indicates that the neuron fires an impulse along its axon at time $(k+1)$ if the weighted sum of its inputs at time k exceeds w_0, the threshold of the neuron. In a more compact vector form, introducing the input vector $x = [x_1, x_2, \ldots, x_n]^T$ and the weight vector $w = [w_1, w_2, \ldots, w_n]^T$, we can rewrite Eqn. (3.7) in a matrix form as

$$
y(k+1) = \begin{cases} 1, & \text{if} \quad w^T x(k) \geq w_0 \\ 0, & \text{if} \quad w^T x(k) < w_0 \end{cases}
\tag{3.8}
$$

Define a unipolar *step function* $g(v)$ as depicted in Fig. 3.1.

$$
g(v) = \begin{cases} 1, & \text{if} \quad v \geq 0 \\ 0, & \text{if} \quad v < 0 \end{cases}
\tag{3.9}
$$

$$
g(v) = \begin{cases} 1, & v \geq 0 \\ 0, & v < 0 \end{cases}
$$

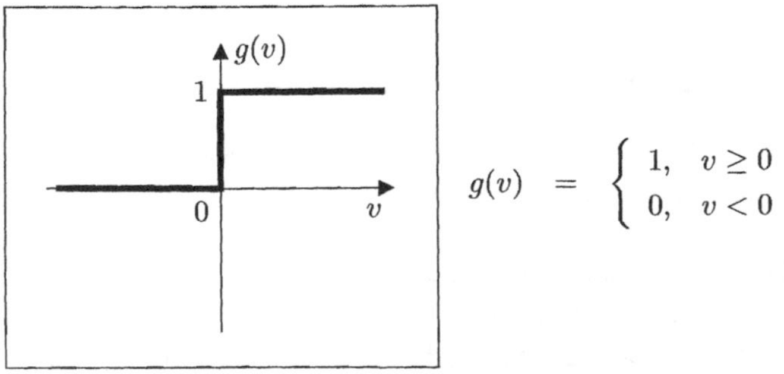

Figure 3.1   Unipolar step function, $g(v)$, for the unipolar binary $\{0,1\}$ convention.

Thus, Eqn. (3.8) can be rewritten as

$$y(k+1) = g\left(\sum_{i=1}^{n} w_i x_i - w_0\right) = g\left(\boldsymbol{w}^T\boldsymbol{x} - w_0\right) \tag{3.10}$$

3.1.2.2 Neural Threshold Logic for Bipolar Inputs, $x \in \{-1, 1\}^n$

Without loss of generality, we may redefine the n binary inputs $x_1, x_2, \ldots, x_n$ and binary output y by assigning either -1 or 1, where the bipolar binary $\{-1, 1\}$ convention is strictly equivalent to the unipolar binary $\{0, 1\}$ convention. Then, a modified version of this McCulloch–Pitts neuron may be represented as

$$y(k+1) = \begin{cases} 1, & \text{if} \quad \sum_{i=1}^{n} w_i x_i(k) \geq w_0 \\ -1, & \text{if} \quad \sum_{i=1}^{n} w_i x_i(k) < w_0 \end{cases}$$

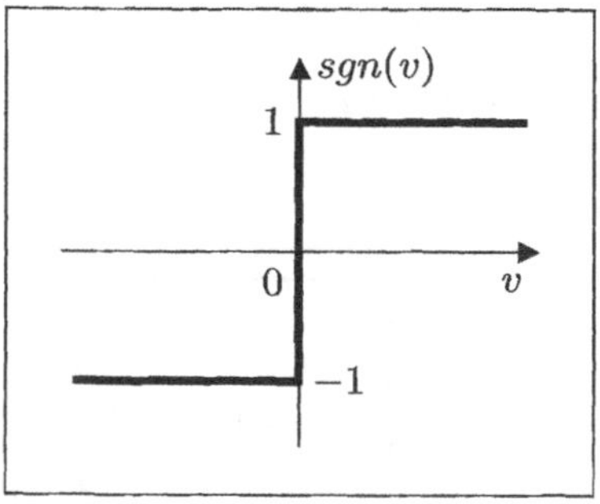

$$sgn(v) = \begin{cases} 1, & v \geq 0 \\ -1, & v < 0 \end{cases}$$

Figure 3.2 Signum function, $sgn(v)$, for the bipolar binary $\{-1, 1\}$ convention.

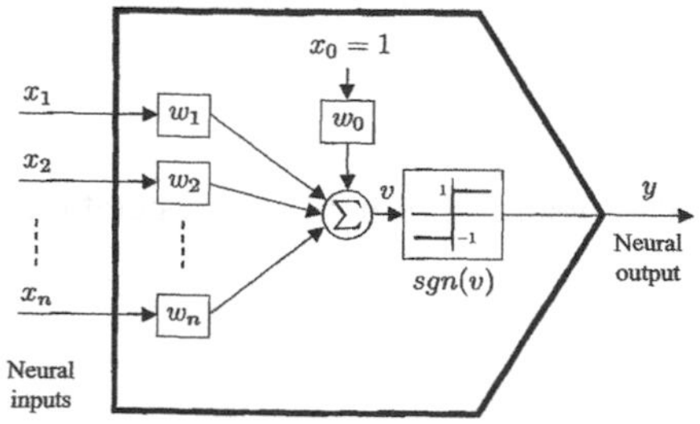

(a) Block diagram representation

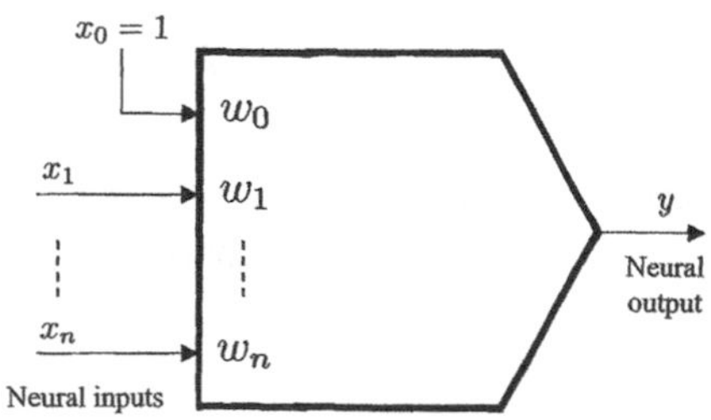

(b) Symbolic representation

Figure 3.3 A schematic representation of a neural threshold logic element.

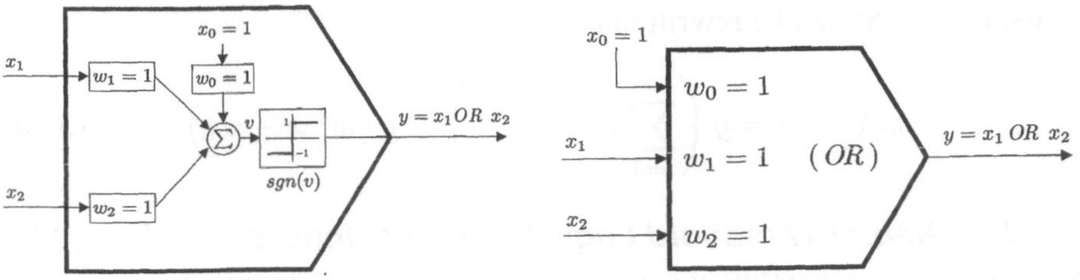

(i) Block diagram of logic *OR* (ii) Symbolic representation of logic *OR*

(a) *OR* logic gate, $y = x_1 OR\ x_2 = x_1 + x_2$.

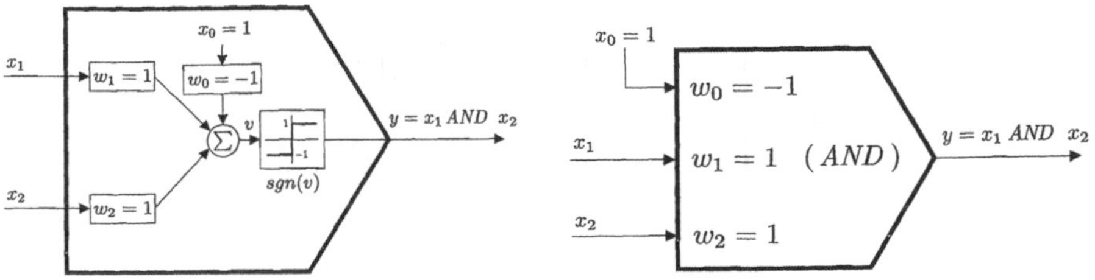

(i) Block diagram of logic *AND* (ii) Symbolic representation of logic *AND*

(b) *AND* logic gate, $y = x_1 AND\ x_2 = x_1 \cdot x_2$.

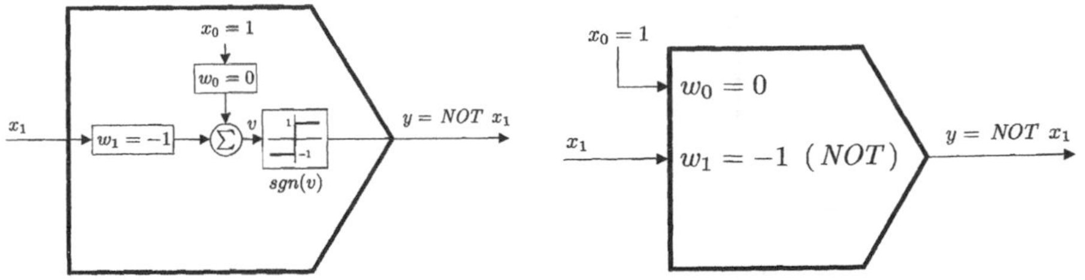

(i) Block diagram of logic *NOT* (ii) Symbolic representation of logic *NOT*

(c) *NOT* logic gate, $y = NOT\ x_1 = \overline{x}_1$.

Figure 3.4 Example 3.1: *OR*, *AND*, and *NOT* neural threshold logic operations for bipolar inputs, $x \in \{-1, 1\}$.

or

$$y(k+1) = sgn\left(\sum_{i=1}^{n} w_i x_i(k) - w_0\right) = sgn\left(\boldsymbol{w}^T \boldsymbol{x}(k) - w_0\right) \quad (3.11)$$

where the signum function $sgn(v)$, shown in Fig. 3.2, is defined as

$$sgn(v) = \begin{cases} 1, & \text{if} \quad v \geq 0 \\ -1, & \text{if} \quad v < 0 \end{cases} \quad (3.12)$$

The realization of this threshold neural logic unit can be achieved by introducing the notion of the augmented vectors of the neural inputs and weights, and is described in the next section.

The block diagrams and symbols representing this threshold neural logic are given in Fig. 3.3. The element, defined algebraically by the relation given in Eqn. (3.8), can be implemented using either the traditional resistor–transistor gates or the magnetic core schemes. Even if the threshold neural logic has a simple structure, it can be used to realize some logical operations such as *OR*, *AND*, and *NOT*, through an appropriate choice of the weights w_i, $i = 1, 2, \ldots, n$ and the threshold parameter w_0. Example 3.1 illustrates this operation. Since these neural logic gates can be used to build some type of computers, the computing potential of the neuron with some further extension may form a complex neural computing scheme that is capable of simulating any computing algorithm.

Example 3.1 The three main types of the logical operations, *OR*, *AND*, and *NOT*, may be implemented with threshold elements shown in Fig. 3.4. ■

3.2 NEURAL THRESHOLD LOGIC SYNTHESIS

3.2.1 Realization of Switching Function

In this section we present a procedure for synthesizing a neural threshold logic. In this procedure, the weights w_i are assigned an appropriate real value, positive, negative, or zero. Thus, the values of the weights $w_1, w_2, \ldots, w_n$ and that of the threshold w_0 may be a real, finite, positive, or negative number, and there exists a wide range of weights and threshold combinations that can realize a large class of switching functions. As to whether every switching function is realizable by only one threshold element, the answer is "No", as will be shown in the following examples.

3.2.1.1 Notion of Augmented Vector

In order to simplify the notion of threshold w_0 in the threshold neural logic circuit, we will introduce the notion of an augmented vector of synaptic weights $\boldsymbol{w}_a$ and an augmented vector of neural inputs $\boldsymbol{x}_a$ which is defined as follows:

$$\begin{aligned} \boldsymbol{w}_a &= [w_0, w_1, w_2, \ldots, w_n]^T \in \Re^{n+1} \\ &= \text{augmented vector of synaptic weights including the threshold weight } w_0 \\ \boldsymbol{x}_a &= [x_0, x_1, x_2, \ldots, x_n]^T \in \Re^{n+1}, \; x_0 = 1 \\ &= \text{augmented vector of neural inputs, where } x_0 = 1 \text{ accounts for the threshold (bias)} \end{aligned}$$

Thus, as illustrated in Fig. 3.5, we can write the neural signals using the notion of the augmented vectors as

$$\begin{aligned} v &= \boldsymbol{w}_a^T \boldsymbol{x}_a = \boldsymbol{x}_a^T \boldsymbol{w}_a \qquad (3.13) \\ &= < \boldsymbol{w}_a, \boldsymbol{x}_a > \text{(inner product of two vectors } \boldsymbol{w}_a \text{ and } \boldsymbol{x}_a) \end{aligned}$$

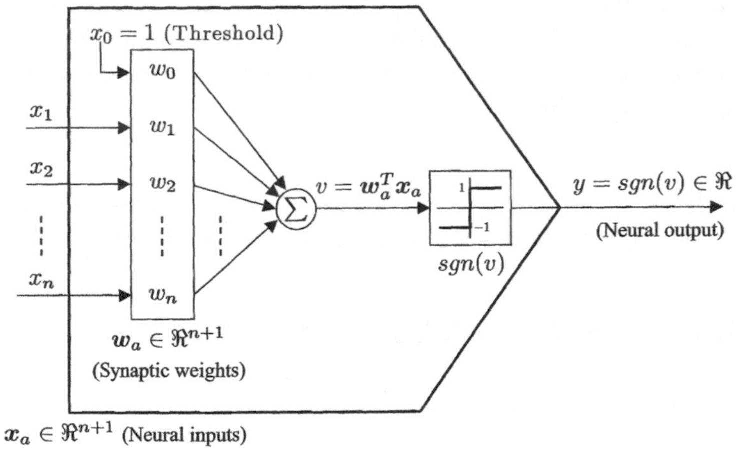

$$\begin{aligned} \boldsymbol{w}_a &= [w_0, w_1, w_2, \ldots, w_n]^T \in \Re^{n+1} \\ &\quad \text{(augmented vector of synaptic weights)} \\ \boldsymbol{x}_a &= [x_0, x_1, x_2, \ldots, x_n]^T \in \Re^{n+1}, \; x_0 = 1 \\ &\quad \text{(augmented vector of neural inputs)} \end{aligned}$$

Figure 3.5 A generalized threshold logic neural unit with augmented vectors $\boldsymbol{w}_a$ and $\boldsymbol{x}_a$.

and

$$y = sgn(v) = sgn\left(\boldsymbol{w}_a^T \boldsymbol{x}_a\right) \tag{3.14}$$

Example 3.2 In this example, for a given set of neural weights, we will attempt to synthesize the binary logic. Let us consider a three–neural–input threshold logic with the augmented neural input vector $\boldsymbol{x}_a = [x_0, x_1, x_2, x_3]^T \in \Re^4$, $x_0 = 1$ and augmented synaptic weight vector $\boldsymbol{w}_a = [-2, 2, 4, -1]^T \in \Re^4$. Using the symbols shown in Fig. 3.5, the output signals are given by

$$\begin{aligned} v = \boldsymbol{w}_a^T \boldsymbol{x}_a &= [-2, 2, 4, -1] \cdot [1, x_1, x_2, x_3]^T \\ &= -2 + 2x_1 + 4x_2 - x_3 \end{aligned}$$

and

$$y = sgn(v) = sgn\left(\boldsymbol{w}_a^T \boldsymbol{x}_a\right) \tag{3.15}$$

This neural threshold logic is shown in Fig. 3.6, and the corresponding truth table in Table 3.6.

Looking at the truth table (Table 3.6), it can be seen that this neuron forms the following binary logic:

$$\begin{aligned} y = sgn(v) &= \overline{x}_1 \, AND \, x_2 \, AND \, \overline{x}_3 \\ &\qquad OR \quad x_1 \, AND \, x_2 \, AND \, \overline{x}_3 \\ &\qquad OR \quad x_1 \, AND \, x_2 \, AND \, x_3 \\ &= x_2 \, AND \, [\, x_1 \, OR \, \overline{x}_1 \, AND \, \overline{x}_3 \,] \\ &= x_2 \, AND \, (x_1 \, OR \, \overline{x}_3) \\ &= x_2(x_1 + \overline{x}_3) \end{aligned}$$

■

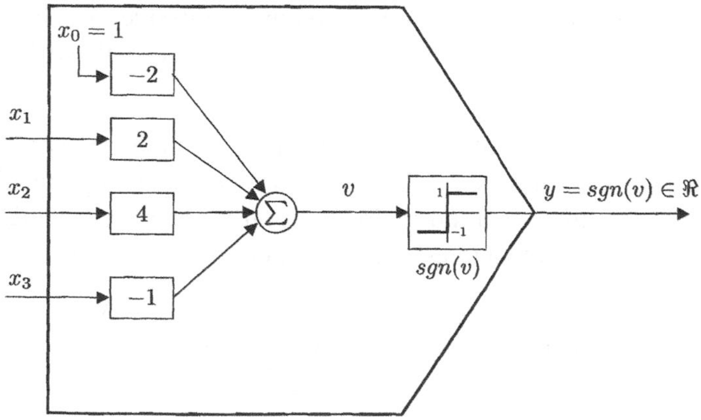

Figure 3.6 Example 3.2: a threshold neural logic for $y = x_2(x_1 + \overline{x}_3)$.

Table 3.6 **Truth table for Example 3.2**

Neural Inputs x_1	x_2	x_3	$v = \boldsymbol{w}_a^T \boldsymbol{x}_a = -2 + 2x_1 + 4x_2 - x_3$	$y = sgn(v) = sgn(\boldsymbol{w}_a^T \boldsymbol{x}_a)$
−1	−1	−1	−7	−1
−1	−1	1	−9	−1
−1	1	−1	1	1
−1	1	1	−1	−1
1	−1	−1	−3	−1
1	−1	1	−5	−1
1	1	−1	5	1
1	1	1	3	1

Example 3.3 Consider a switching function with the following form

$$y = f(x_1, x_2, x_3) = x_2(\overline{x}_1 + \overline{x}_3)$$

If it can be implemented by a neuron with weights w_1, w_2, and w_3, and a threshold w_0, the output of this element is -1 for both the input combinations $x_1x_2x_3$ and $\overline{x}_1\overline{x}_2\overline{x}_3$. Thus

$$w_1 + w_2 + w_3 < w_0$$

and

$$-w_1 - w_2 - w_3 < w_0$$

Clearly, the requirements in the above inequalities are conflicting, and no weights and threshold values can satisfy them. Consequently, the switching function $y = f(x_1, x_2, x_3) = x_2(\overline{x}_1 + \overline{x}_3)$ cannot be realized by a single threshold element. ■

A switching function that can be realized by a single threshold element is called a *threshold function*. That is, given a switching function $y = f(x_1, x_2, \ldots, x_n)$, there is a threshold function if there exist weight coefficients w_1, w_2, ..., w_n and a threshold w_0 such that

$$y = f(x_1, x_2, \ldots, x_n) = sgn\left(\sum_{j=1}^{n} w_j x_j + w_0\right) \tag{3.16}$$

A threshold function is also called a *linearly separable function* because of the following geometric interpretation. Consider an n-dimensional Euclidean space in which an arbitrary point is represented by $(x_1, x_2, \ldots, x_n)$. For continuous variables $(x_0, x_1, x_2, \ldots, x_n)$, $x_0 = 1$, the weighted sum of the neural inputs

$$v = \boldsymbol{w}_a^T \boldsymbol{x}_a = \sum_{i=0}^{n} w_i x_i = 0 \tag{3.17}$$

represents a hyperplane. All 2^n points of $\{-1, 1\}^n$ are divided into two sets by this hyperplane. By the definition of the threshold function $f(x_0, x_1, x_2, \ldots, x_n)$, all the *true* points of f that yield $f = 1$ are on one side of the hyperplane, and the *false* points of f that yield $f = -1$ are on the other side of the hyperplane. Thus, when f is a threshold function, there exists a hyperplane that separates the true points of f from the false points. If there exists no such a hyperplane, a given function is not a threshold function.

In illustrations given in Figs. 3.7 and 3.8, a threshold element with two binary inputs x_1 and $x_2 \in \{-1, 1\}$ is considered and all possible binary inputs to this element are represented using four dots in two-dimensional pattern space.

In this space, the components of the input pattern vectors lie along the coordinate axes. The straight line defined by setting the weighted sum of the inputs including the threshold

$$L: \; w_0 + w_1 x_1 + w_2 x_2 = 0$$

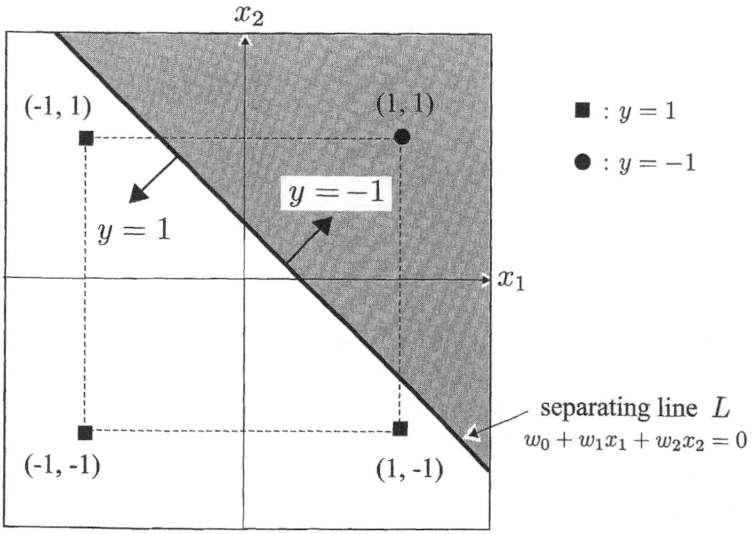

Figure 3.7 A two-dimensional example of pattern separation: separating line in pattern space. $L: w_0 + w_1 x_1 + w_2 x_2 = 0$.

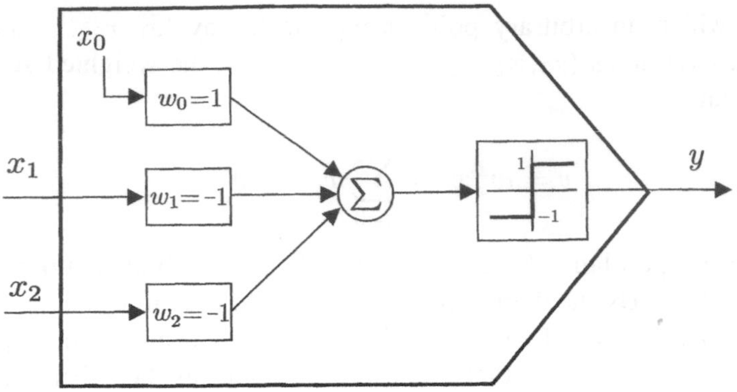

Figure 3.8 A two-dimensional example of pattern separation: threshold element w_0 with two inputs x_1, x_2, $\boldsymbol{w}_a = [-1, -1, 1]^T$, $y = sgn(1 - x_1 - x_2) = NOT[x_1 AND\ x_2] = [\overline{x}_1\, OR\, \overline{x}_2]$.

separates the input patterns into two categories. One side of this separating line corresponds to a positive output, while the opposite side of the separating line corresponds to a negative output. For the linearly separable functions sketched in Fig. 3.7, the binary patterns are divided into classes

$$
\begin{array}{lccc}
Upper\ side: & (1,1) & \longrightarrow & -1 \\
 & (-1,-1) & \longrightarrow & 1 \\
Lower\ side: & (-1,1) & \longrightarrow & 1 \\
 & (1,-1) & \longrightarrow & 1
\end{array}
$$

An example of functions that are not linearly separable is the two-input *XOR* function:

$$
\left\{
\begin{array}{ccc}
(-1,-1) & \longrightarrow & -1 \\
(-1,1) & \longrightarrow & 1 \\
(1,-1) & \longrightarrow & 1 \\
(1,1) & \longrightarrow & -1
\end{array}
\right.
$$

Since there is no straight line that can separate these patterns, we conclude that the *XOR* function is not a linearly separable function. Indeed, with three neural inputs (x_1, x_2, x_3) and one threshold x_0, the separating boundary is a two-dimensional plane; and with n neural inputs, the boundary is a $(n-1)$-dimensional hyperplane. On the other hand, if the threshold parameter is zero, the separating hyperplane is homogeneous and passes through the origin in the pattern space.

With n binary variables, since 2^n rows in the truth table yield 2^{2^n} combinations of output functions, there are a total number of 2^{2^n} possible logic functions. Deriving an exact expression for the number of threshold logic functions, which is denoted by $NTL(n)$, is a difficult task. However, the following expression for boundedness is wellknown (Muroga 1971):

$$2^{n(n-1)/2} < NTL(n) \leq 2\sum_{i=0}^{n}\binom{2^n-1}{i} < 2^{n^2} \tag{3.18}$$

This is a vanishingly small percentage of the total number of switching functions for a large n. For instance, when $n = 2$, then $NTL(2) \leq 16$; that is, the number of the two-variable threshold functions is less than 16! A principal goal in studying the threshold logic is the development of methods for the identification and realization of threshold functions.

A straightforward approach to the identification problem of threshold functions is to solve 2^n linear inequalities that may be easily derived from the truth table. From the input combinations for which $f = 1$, we obtain all the weighted sums that must exceed or be equal to the threshold w_0, and from the input combinations for which $f = -1$, all the weight sums must be less than w_0. If a solution of the inequalities described above exists, it provides the values for the weights and threshold. Otherwise, no solution exists, and it may be concluded that f is not a suitable threshold function.

3.2.1.2 Network Synthesis

If a given switching function is a threshold function, it can be realized by a single threshold element. If not, a threshold network which consists of more than one threshold elements can be used to realize the function. The input variables and output of a threshold network, denoted by x_i and y, respectively, belong to the binary set $\{-1, 1\}$.

Example 3.4 As discussed in Example 3.3, the switching function

$$y = f(x_1, x_2, x_3) = x_2(\overline{x}_1 + \overline{x}_3)$$

cannot be realized by a single neural unit, but it can be realized by a neural network with two neural elements, as shown in Fig. 3.9, where the intermediate variable z and the output y are formulated as follows:

$$z = \begin{cases} 1, & \text{if } -1 - x_1 + x_2 - x_3 \geq 0 \\ -1, & \text{if } -1 - x_1 + x_2 - x_3 < 0 \end{cases}$$

That is

$$z = sgn\left([-1, -1, 1, -1]\begin{bmatrix} 1 \\ x_1 \\ x_2 \\ x_3 \end{bmatrix}\right) \tag{3.19}$$

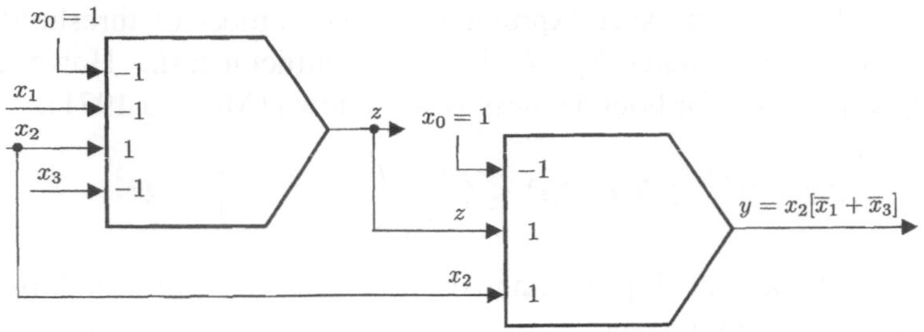

Figure 3.9 Example 3.4: a neural network that realizes the logic function $y = x_2(\overline{x}_1 + \overline{x}_3)$.

Table 3.7 **Truth table for Example 3.4,** $y = x_2[\bar{x}_1 + \bar{x}_3]$

Neural inputs			Intermediate variable	Neural output
x_1	x_2	x_3	$z = sgn(-1 - x_1 + x_2 - x_3)$	$y = sgn(-1 + z + x_2) = x_2[\overline{x}_1 + \overline{x}_3]$
−1	−1	−1	1	−1
−1	−1	1	−1	−1
−1	1	−1	1	1
−1	1	1	1	1
1	−1	−1	−1	−1
1	−1	1	−1	−1
1	1	−1	1	1
1	1	1	−1	−1

$$y = \begin{cases} 1, & \text{if } -1 + z + x_2 \geq 0 \\ -1, & \text{if } -1 + z + x_2 < 0 \end{cases}$$
$$= sgn\left([-1, 1, 1]\begin{bmatrix} 1 \\ z \\ x_2 \end{bmatrix}\right) \tag{3.20}$$

More compactly, the input-output relationship of the network may be given as follows:

$$y = sgn\left(-1 + sgn(-1 - x_1 + x_2 - x_3) + x_2\right)$$

The truth table is given in Table 3.7. ■

An effective approach to such a neural network synthesis is to develop a procedure for the decomposition of the non-threshold function into two or more terms, each of which will be a threshold function. Let Q be the minimum number of the terms which are the neural functions required to express the given function. Then any given switching function may be realized by a two-layered threshold network with at the most Q threshold elements. However, the number of neural elements in this network may not be minimized. Generally speaking, a switching function that is not a threshold function may be realized by a two-layered threshold network as shown in Fig. 3.10, where $layer$ 1 has m neural units while $layer$ 2 has only a single neural unit. The intermediate variables $z_1, z_2, \ldots, z_m$, which represent the outputs of the elements in $layer$ 1 may be computed by

$$z_i = sgn\left(\boldsymbol{w}_a^T \boldsymbol{x}_a\right)$$

that is,

$$z_i = \begin{cases} 1, & \text{if } \sum_{j=0}^{n} w_{ij}^1 x_j \geq 0 \\ -1, & \text{if } \sum_{j=0}^{n} w_{ij}^1 x_j < 0 \end{cases} \tag{3.21}$$

where w_{ij}^1 is the weight to the neural input x_i in the first layer. Then, the output that realizes a specified switching function may be obtained as follows:

$$y = sgn\left((\boldsymbol{w}_a^2)^T \boldsymbol{x}_a\right)$$

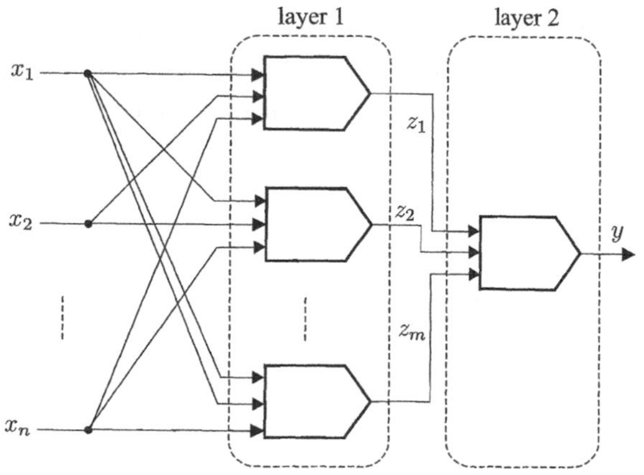

Figure 3.10 A two-layered neural network that may realize an arbitrary switching function.

that is,

$$y = \begin{cases} 1, & \text{if } \sum_{i=0}^{m} w_i^2 z_i \geq 0 \\ -1, & \text{if } \sum_{i=0}^{m} w_i^2 z_i < 0 \end{cases} \tag{3.22}$$

where w_i^2 is the weight of the neural element in the second layer associated with the intermediate variable z_i. Therefore, the input–output equation of the threshold network may be represented as

$$\begin{aligned} y &= sgn(\sum_{i=0}^{m} w_i^2 z_i) \\ &= sgn\left(\sum_{i=0}^{m} w_i^2 sgn(\sum_{j=0}^{n} w_{ij}^1 x_j)\right) \end{aligned} \tag{3.23}$$

It is a natural extension that, similar to the two-layered structure, a multilayered neural network structure may also be constructed to realize a switching function. It is worth noting that the realization of a switching function using the neural network is not unique. To obtain a desired realization, some additional requirements such as the minimum number of units or the minimum number of connections may be attached.

Example 3.5 (Problem of realization of *XOR* using a single neural unit) Consider a two-variable *XOR* function:

$$y = f(x_1, x_2) = x_1 \oplus x_2 = x_1\overline{x}_2 + \overline{x}_1 x_2, \qquad x_1 x_2 \in \{-1, 1\}$$

As shown previously, it is not a linearly separable function. In fact, if it can be realized by a single neural unit with weights w_0, w_1, and w_2, then the output of this element is 1 for the input combinations $x_1\overline{x}_2$ or $\overline{x}_1 x_2$, and -1 for the input combinations $x_1 x_2$, or $\overline{x}_1\overline{x}_2$. Therefore, we have

$$\begin{cases} w_1 \leq w_0 \\ w_2 \leq w_0 \end{cases}$$

and

$$\begin{aligned} w_1 + w_2 &< 0 \\ w_0 &< 0 \end{aligned}$$

Obviously, there is no such solution for w_0, w_1, and w_2 that satisfies these contradictory inequalities; that is, *the XOR function is not an ordinary threshold function that can be realized by a single neural unit.* ■

Example 3.6 (Realization of *XOR* using a two–layered neural network) As shown in Fig. 3.11, the *XOR* function of Example 3.5 can be realized using a neural network with three neural units.
In this case, one has

$$\begin{aligned} y = f(x_1, x_2) &= x_1 \oplus x_2 \\ &= sgn(1 - z_1 + z_2) \\ &= sgn\left(1 - sgn(1 - x_1 + x_2) + sgn(-1 - x_1 + x_2)\right) \end{aligned}$$

As shown in Fig. 3.12, in the $x_1 - x_2$ plane, the four binary patterns are separated using two discriminant lines which are defined by

$$\begin{aligned} L_1 : \quad & z_1 = 1 - x_1 + x_2 = 0 \\ L_2 : \quad & z_2 = -1 - x_1 + x_2 = 0 \end{aligned}$$

In the shaded region between the two lines L_1 and L_2, $y = -1$, while in the regions outside these two lines, $y = 1$. ■

The operation implemented in this neural network may be treated also as a static, nonlinear, and discontinuous mapping from the binary input space to the binary output space with preprogrammed weight parameters. No adaptive weight updating and real dynamics are involved in the network. Neural threshold logic is a unified theory of logic gates that is composed of the major subjects of conventional switching theory, whereas automata theory and formal-language theory apply respectively to computer organization and computer programming. Since the idea of the logical operation based on

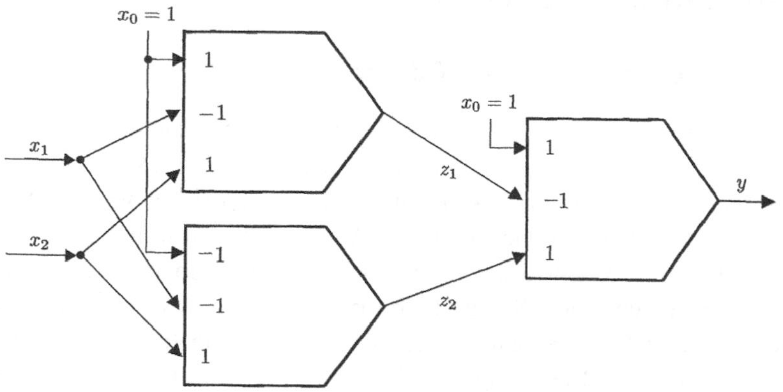

Figure 3.11 Example 3.6: a threshold network for *XOR* function $y = x_1 \oplus x_2 = sgn(1 - z_1 + z_2)$, $z_1 = sgn(1 - x_1 + x_2)$, $z_2 = sgn(-1 - x_1 + x_2)$.

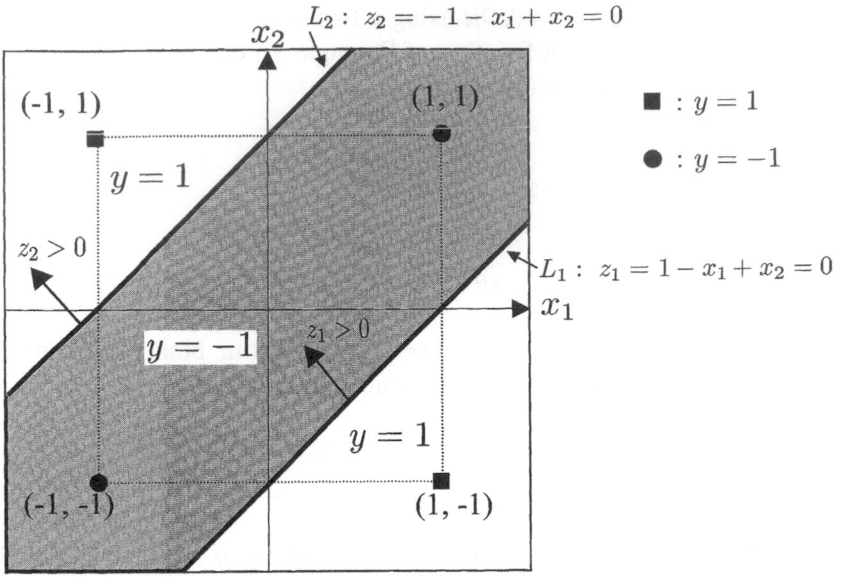

Figure 3.12 Example 3.6: two discriminant lines for *XOR* function $y = x_1 \oplus x_2$.

the threshold principle is simple and general, there are many other applications of threshold logic such as in the field of adaptive networks and pattern recognition.

3.3 ADAPTATION AND LEARNING FOR NEURAL THRESHOLD ELEMENTS

3.3.1 Concept of Parameter Adaptation

In the previous section it was pointed out that the basic neural threshold element can be used to realize some switching functions. An important task not yet discussed is how to design an effective algorithm for adapting the weights and threshold of the element. Linear programming may provide an alternative for solving a set of inequalities that can be derived from a given switching function. Since all the possible values of the function are represented in such a synthesis procedure at the same time, this algorithm might be characterized as being parallel in nature. In this case, a computer programmed to perform the procedure must have sufficient memory to store the entire switching function, either as a table of combinations or as a Boolean function.

In contrast to this, there are a number of procedures that can be characterized as iterative or sequential. That is, at any instant of time the procedure is presented with the value of the function for only the input combination, and there is no memory available to store the previously presented functional values. The necessary memory is needed to store the procedure's current estimate of the correct realization that consists of the values of the weights and the threshold. When the functional value for some particular input combination is presented, an error signal between this functional value and the current estimate can be obtained and fed back so that the procedure can change the current estimate of the realization, but can store no other information. The idea is that after each input combination has been presented a sufficient number of times, the procedure's estimate of the realization will converge to a correct one. This type of procedure is also called *adaptation* or *learning* because of its somewhat tenuous relation to certain processes in biological neurons.

Given a set of n-input variables $x_1, x_2, \ldots, x_n$, as shown in Fig. 3.13, an output of a *linear combiner* is simply defined as

$$s = \sum_{i=0}^{n} w_i x_i, \; x_0 = 1 \tag{3.24}$$

Defining the augmented vectors of neural inputs and neural weights, we obtain

$$\begin{aligned} \boldsymbol{x}_a &\triangleq [x_0, x_1, x_2, \ldots, x_n]^T \in \Re^{n+1} \\ &= [1, x_1, x_2, \ldots, x_n]^T \\ \boldsymbol{w}_a &\triangleq [w_0, w_1, w_2, \ldots, w_n]^T \in \Re^{n+1} \end{aligned}$$

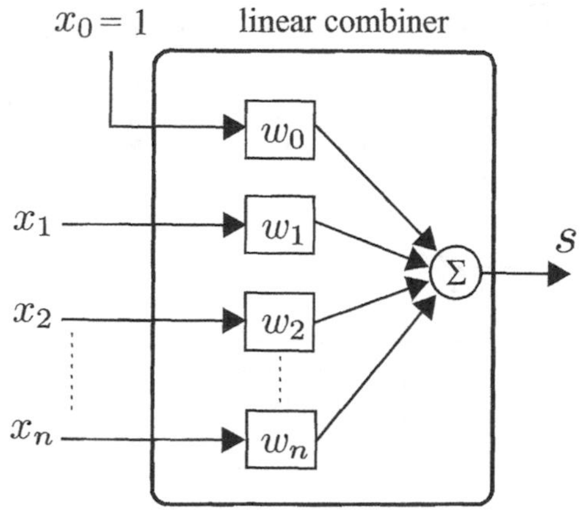

Figure 3.13 Block diagram of a linear combiner.

then, Eqn. (3.24) can be rewritten as

$$s = \boldsymbol{w}_a^T \boldsymbol{x}_a \tag{3.25}$$

Furthermore, given a switching function $f(x_1, x_2, \ldots, x_n)$, an adaptive process for a threshold element that may be considered as a linear combiner cascaded with a hard-limiter is schematically described in Fig. 3.14. The error signal between the known switching function and the output of the neural threshold element is given as

$$\begin{aligned} e &= d(k) - sgn(\boldsymbol{w}_a^T \boldsymbol{x}_a) \\ &= f(x_1, x_2, \ldots, x_n) - sgn(\boldsymbol{w}_a^T \boldsymbol{x}_a) \\ &= f(x_1, x_2, \ldots, x_n) - sgn\left(\sum_{i=0}^{n} w_i x_i\right) \end{aligned} \tag{3.26}$$

where $d(k) = f(x_1, x_2, \ldots, x_n)$ is the desired function of the variables x_i, $i = 1, \ldots, n$. The adaptive algorithm, which is a key issue in such a procedure of minimizing the error function, is discussed later.

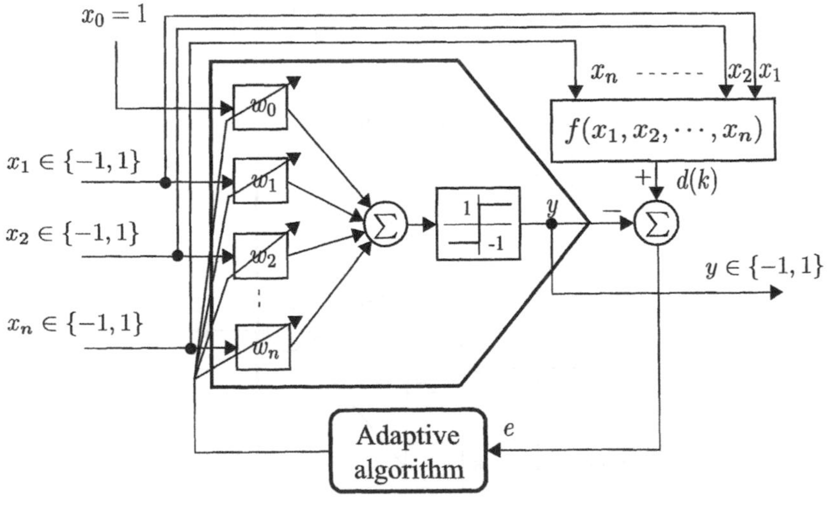

Figure 3.14 Schematic representation of an adaptive process for a neural threshold element.

3.3.2 The Perceptron Rule of Adaptation

Rosenblatt's binary perceptron learning rule for a threshold element was first presented in 1958 (Rosenblatt 1958). Given a desired response $d(k)$, the adaptive updating with the perceptron rule utilizes a "quantizer error" $e(k)$, defined to be the difference between the desired response and the output of the threshold element

$$\begin{aligned} e(k) &\triangleq d(k) - y(k) \\ &= d(k) - sgn(\boldsymbol{w}_a^T \boldsymbol{x}_a(k)) \end{aligned} \tag{3.27}$$

where there are only three possible values for $e(k)$:

$$e(k) = \begin{cases} 0, & \text{if} \quad d(k) = y(k) \\ 2, & \text{if} \quad d(k) = 1 \quad \text{and} \quad y(k) = -1 \\ -2, & \text{if} \quad d(k) = -1 \quad \text{and} \quad y(k) = 1 \end{cases}$$

As in the procedure used for α-LMS algorithm described in a later section, let $\boldsymbol{w}_a(k)$ be an estimate of the weight vector at time k. One may then rewrite the instantaneous error $e(k)$ as

$$e(k) = d(k) - sgn(\boldsymbol{w}_a^T(k)\boldsymbol{x}_a(k)) \tag{3.28}$$

For the fixed input $\boldsymbol{x}(k)$ and the desired response $d(k)$, the new instantaneous error associated with the updated weight parameters at the instant $(k+1)$ may be represented as

$$e(k+1) = d(k) - sgn(\boldsymbol{w}_a^T(k+1)\boldsymbol{x}_a(k)) \tag{3.29}$$

where

$$\boldsymbol{w}_a(k+1) = \boldsymbol{w}_a(k) + \Delta\boldsymbol{w}_a(k) \tag{3.30}$$

Our goal here is to find an updating rule to update the weight $\boldsymbol{w}_a(k)$ such that

$$e(k+1) \longrightarrow 0 \tag{3.31}$$

or

$$sgn(\boldsymbol{w}_a^T(k+1)\boldsymbol{x}_a(k)) \longrightarrow d(k) \tag{3.32}$$

In fact, if

$$e(k) = 2$$

or equivalently

$$d(k) = 1, \quad \text{and} \quad y(k) = sgn(\boldsymbol{w}_a^T(k)\boldsymbol{x}_a(k)) = -1$$

one may select

$$\Delta \boldsymbol{w}_a^T(k)\boldsymbol{x}_a(k) > 0 \tag{3.33}$$

such that

$$sgn(\boldsymbol{w}_a^T(k+1)\boldsymbol{x}_a(k)) = 1 \tag{3.34}$$

On the other hand, if

$$e(k) = -2$$

or equivalently

$$d(k) = -1 \quad \text{and} \quad y(k) = sgn(\boldsymbol{w}_a^T(k)\boldsymbol{x}_a(k)) = 1$$

one desires

$$\Delta \boldsymbol{w}_a^T(k)\boldsymbol{x}_a(k) < 0$$

which may cause

$$sgn(\boldsymbol{w}_a^T(k+1)\boldsymbol{x}_a(k)) = -1 \tag{3.35}$$

Thus, one wise choice of $\Delta \boldsymbol{w}_a(k)$ is

$$\Delta \boldsymbol{w}_a(k) = \alpha e(k)\boldsymbol{x}_a(k) \tag{3.36}$$

that is

$$\Delta w_i(k) = \alpha e(k) x_i(k), \qquad i = 0, 1, \ldots, n \tag{3.37}$$

and

$$\boldsymbol{w}_a(k+1) = \boldsymbol{w}_a(k) + \alpha e(k)\boldsymbol{x}_a(k) \tag{3.38}$$

where $\alpha > 0$ is a so-called learning rate.

From Eqn. (3.37), we may conclude that the change $\Delta w_i(k)$ is correlated with the input signal $x_i(k)$ and the error signal $e(k)$. If the correlation is zero; that is, $e(k)x_i(k) = 0$, then the change $\Delta w_i(k)$ is also zero. The block diagram of the preceding updating algorithm is given in Fig. 3.15.

For a threshold element with n inputs, the augmented input vector $\boldsymbol{x}_a = [1, \boldsymbol{x}^T]^T$ with $\boldsymbol{x} = [x_1, x_2, \ldots, x_n]^T \in \{-1, 1\}^n$ is repeatedly presented to the learning procedure described above so that all the weights are adapted during each cycle. Note that a threshold function can be realized by many threshold elements with different combinations of the weight values. The α-perceptron learning rule may converge to different solutions of weights with different choices of the initial weight values and the learning rate α. The perceptron rule stops adapting once the training binary patterns are correctly separated. There is no restraining force controlling the magnitude of the weights since the direction of the weight vector, and not its magnitude, determines the separating function. The perceptron rule has been proven to be capable of separating any linearly separable set of binary training patterns. However, for a set of training patterns that are not linearly separable, it does not lead to convergence.

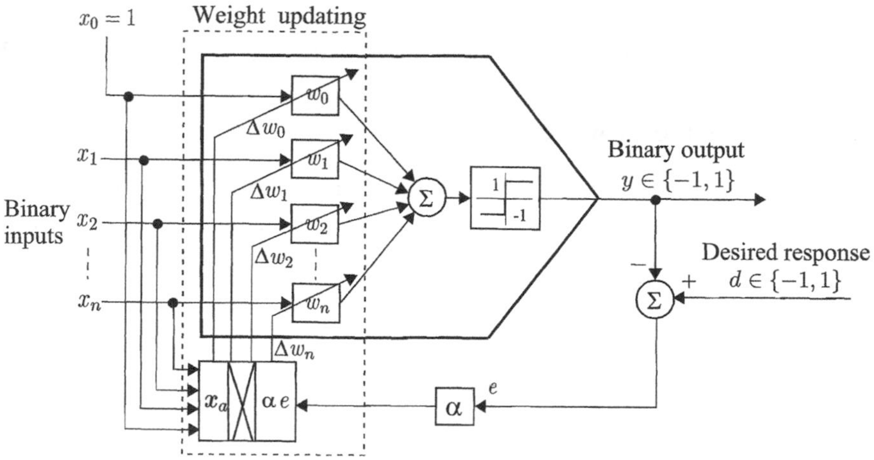

Figure 3.15 Neural threshold element with perceptron rule of adaptation.

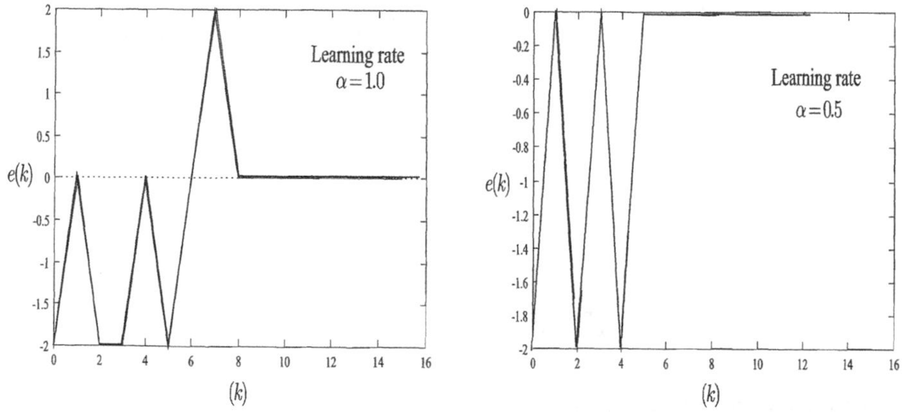

(a) $\alpha = 1.0$ (b) $\alpha = 0.5$

Figure 3.16 Example 3.7: the error curves for different learning rate α.

Example 3.7 We will again consider the neural threshold function given in Example 3.4 as follows:

$$y = f(x_1, x_2, x_3) = x_2(\overline{x}_1 + \overline{x}_3)$$

A threshold element with the weight parameters w_0, w_1, w_2, and w_3 is trained using the α-perceptron rule with two different values of the learning rate α: (a) $\alpha = 1$, and (b) $\alpha = 0.5$. The instantaneous learning errors for both learning rates, $\alpha = 1$ and $\alpha = 0.5$ are shown in Fig. 3.16. The initial values of the weights are selected as zero. With these initial conditions, the weights converge to

$$w_0 = -1.0, \quad w_1 = -1.0, \quad w_2 = 1.0, \quad w_3 = -1.0$$ ■

3.3.3 Mays Rule of Adaptation

The increment adaptation versions of the α-perceptron rule, as shown in Fig. 3.17, were studied by Mays (1963). The increment adaptation in its general form involves the use of a "dead zone" with a radius $\gamma \geq 0$ for the linear output

$$s(k) = \sum_{i=0}^{n} w_i x_i(k) \tag{3.39}$$

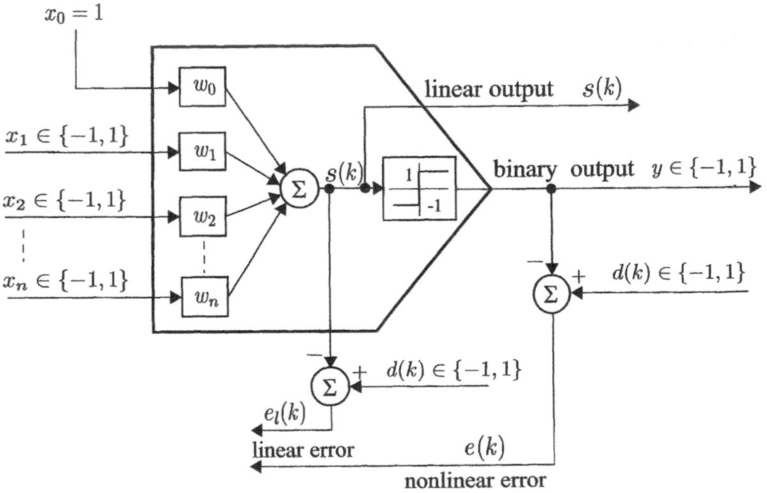

Figure 3.17 Mays rule of adaptation with linear output and linear error.

If the linear output $s(k)$ falls outside the dead zone γ, that is

$$|s(k)| \geq \gamma \tag{3.40}$$

then as in Eqn. (3.36), the adaptation follows a normalized variant of the *fixed-increment perceptron* rule with $\alpha/|\boldsymbol{x}_a|^2$ used in place of α. If the linear output falls within the dead zone, $|s(k)| < \gamma$, regardless of whether the output response $y(k)$ is correct or not, the weights are adapted by the normalized variant of the α-perceptron rule with $d/|\boldsymbol{x}_a|^2$ used in place of e. Mathematically, Mays incremental adaptation algorithm can be expressed as

$$\boldsymbol{w}_a(k+1) = \begin{cases} \boldsymbol{w}_a(k) + \alpha e(k) \frac{\boldsymbol{x}_a(k)}{|\boldsymbol{x}_a(k)|^2}, & \text{if } |s(k)| \geq \gamma \\ \boldsymbol{w}_a(k) + \alpha d(k) \frac{\boldsymbol{x}_a(k)}{|\boldsymbol{x}_a(k)|^2}, & \text{if } |s(k)| < \gamma \end{cases}$$

where $e(k)$ is the quantizer error at time k defined as

$$e(k) = d(k) - sgn(s(k))$$

and $d(k)$ is the desired response at time k.

It is obvious that if the radius of the dead zone is zero, that is, $\gamma = 0$, Mays incremental adaptation algorithm reduces to a normalized version of the perceptron rule. Mays other rule, called the *modified relaxation* algorithm, is designed using the error between the desired response and the linear output. This error, called the linear error $e_l(k)$, is

$$e_l(k) \triangleq d(k) - s(k) \tag{3.41}$$

However, the incremental adaptation rule changes the weights with increments that are seldom proportional to the linear error $e_l(k)$. If the neural output $y(k)$ is wrong, or if the linear output $s(k)$ falls within the dead zone, the adaptation algorithm employs the linear error $e_l(k)$. If the quantizer output $y(k)$ is correct and the linear output $s(k)$ falls outside the dead zone, the weights are not adapted. The weight updating rule for this algorithm, thus, can be written as

$$\boldsymbol{w}_a(k+1) = \begin{cases} \boldsymbol{w}_a(k), & \text{if } e(k) = 0 \text{ and } |s(k)| \geq \gamma \\ \boldsymbol{w}_a(k) + \alpha e(k) \frac{\boldsymbol{x}_a(k)}{|\boldsymbol{x}_a(k)|^2}, & \text{otherwise} \end{cases} \tag{3.42}$$

Mays proved that if the training patterns are linearly separable, both algorithms will always converge and separate the patterns in a finite number of steps. It was also shown that the use of the dead zone reduces the sensitivity to the weighted errors.

3.4 ADAPTIVE LINEAR ELEMENT (ADALINE)

The *ada*ptive *lin*ear *e*lement (Adaline), used as the basic building block in many feedforward neural networks, was first studied by Widrow and his colleagues in the 1960s. A simple adaptive linear combiner is shown in Fig. 3.18, where the output of the unit is a weighted sum of all the inputs. Usually, an Adaline consists of an adaptive linear combiner cascaded with a hard-limiting quantizer, which is used to produce a binary output $y = sgn(s)$. The threshold parameter, or bias weight w_0, which is always connected to a constant input $x_0 = 1$, effectively controls the threshold level of the quantizer.

To perform an adaptive process in the discrete-time domain, one assumes that this element receives an input pattern vector $\boldsymbol{x}(k) = [x_1(k), x_2(k), \ldots, x_n(k)]^T$, and a desired response $d(k)$, which may be a function of time k. The components of the input vector are weighted by a set of coefficients or weights denoted by the weight vector $\boldsymbol{w} = [w_1, w_2, \ldots, w_n]^T$ whose components may have either positive or negative values. Using the notation of the augmented vectors, a linear output at time k is then obtained by an inner product of the augmented input pattern vector and the augmented weight vector as follows:

$$s(k) = \sum_{i=0}^{n} w_i x_i(k) = \boldsymbol{w}_a^T \boldsymbol{x}_a(k) \tag{3.43}$$

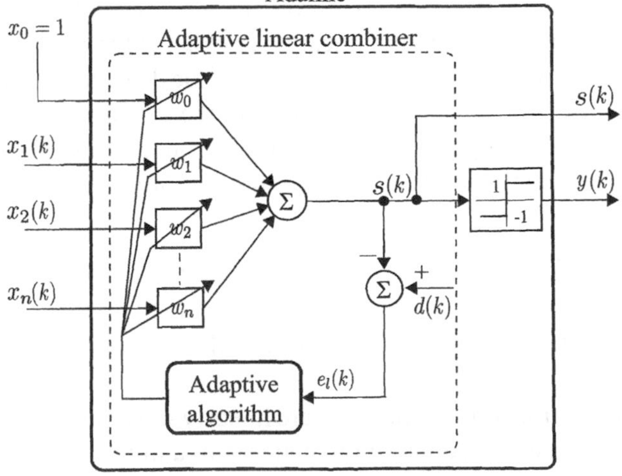

Figure 3.18 *Ada*ptive *lin*ear *e*lement (Adaline).

3.4.1 α-LMS (Least Mean Square) Algorithm

The α-LMS algorithm rule provides a simple and effective updating formulation for the weights of the linear combiner given in Fig. 3.18. This algorithm is derived using the *minimal disturbance principle* and was proposed by Widrow and Hoff (1960).

Let $\boldsymbol{w}_a(k) = [w_0(k), w_1(k), w_2(k), \ldots, w_n(k)]^T$ be an estimate of the augmented weight vector $\boldsymbol{w}_a$ at time k. The present linear error between the desired response $d(k)$ and the linear output $s(k)$ with the current estimates of the weights $\boldsymbol{w}_a(k)$ is defined as

$$e_l(k) \triangleq d(k) - \boldsymbol{w}_a^T(k)\boldsymbol{x}_a(k) \tag{3.44}$$

The next error is defined to be the difference between the desired response $d(k)$ and the linear output $s(k)$ with the next estimates of the weights $\boldsymbol{w}_a(k+1)$ as follows:

$$e_l(k+1) \triangleq d(k) - \boldsymbol{w}_a^T(k+1)\boldsymbol{x}_a(k) \tag{3.45}$$

It can be seen that at time k changing the weights yields a corresponding change in the error:

$$\begin{aligned} \Delta e_l(k) &\triangleq e_l(k+1) - e_l(k) \\ &= \boldsymbol{w}_a^T(k)\boldsymbol{x}_a(k) - \boldsymbol{w}_a^T(k+1)\boldsymbol{x}_a(k) \\ &= -\boldsymbol{x}_a^T(k)[\boldsymbol{w}_a(k+1) - \boldsymbol{w}_a(k)] \\ &= -\boldsymbol{x}_a^T(k)\Delta\boldsymbol{w}_a(k) \end{aligned} \tag{3.46}$$

The next task is to find an updating rule so that the error $e_l(k)$ will asymptotically converge to zero. To ensure the convergence of the error due to the weights updating, one may assume

$$e_l(k+1) = (1-\alpha)e_l(k) \tag{3.47}$$

that is

$$\Delta e_l(k) = -\alpha e_l(k) \tag{3.48}$$

where α is a constant that is chosen such that the error $e_l(k)$ is asymptotically stable:

$$\lim_{k \longrightarrow \infty} e_l(k) = 0 \tag{3.49}$$

Combining Eqns. (3.46) and (3.48), one obtains

$$-\boldsymbol{x}_a^T(k)\Delta\boldsymbol{w}_a(k) = -\alpha e_l(k) \tag{3.50}$$

Multiplying both sides of this equality by $\boldsymbol{x}_a(k)$ yields

$$-\Delta \boldsymbol{w}_a(k)(\boldsymbol{x}_a^T(k)\boldsymbol{x}_a(k)) = -\alpha e_l(k)\boldsymbol{x}_a(k) \tag{3.51}$$

Therefore, one finally obtains

$$\Delta \boldsymbol{w}_a(k) = \alpha \frac{e_l(k)\boldsymbol{x}_a(k)}{|\boldsymbol{x}_a(k)|^2}$$

and therefore

$$\begin{aligned} \boldsymbol{w}_a(k+1) &= \boldsymbol{w}_a(k) + \Delta \boldsymbol{w}_a(k) \\ &= \boldsymbol{w}_a(k) + \alpha \frac{e_l(k)\boldsymbol{x}_a(k)}{|\boldsymbol{x}_a(k)|^2} \end{aligned} \tag{3.52}$$

where

$$\Delta \boldsymbol{w}_a(k) = \alpha \frac{e_l(k)\boldsymbol{x}_a(k)}{|\boldsymbol{x}_a(k)|^2}$$

is an increment amount. Equation (3.52) is the Widrow–Hoff delta rule. Given an arbitrary initial $e_l(0)$, $e_l(k)$ may be represented as

$$\begin{aligned} e_l(k) &= (1-\alpha)e_l(k-1) \\ &= (1-\alpha)^2 e_l(k-2) \\ &\vdots \\ &= (1-\alpha)^k e_l(0) \end{aligned} \tag{3.53}$$

To ensure the convergence of $e_l(k)$, that is, the condition given by Eqn. (3.49) is satisfied, one implies that

$$|(1-\alpha)| < 1$$

that is

$$-1 < 1 - \alpha < 1 \tag{3.54}$$

Thus, the error is asymptotically stable if the constant α is chosen as

$$0 < \alpha < 2 \tag{3.55}$$

To avoid overcorrection, a practical range for α is

$$0.1 < \alpha < 1.0 \tag{3.56}$$

Unlike the α-perceptron rule for the adaptive neural threshold elements, the inputs to an Adaline may be either binary or analog patterns. An Adaline can be used for realizing threshold functions by appropriately adjusting the weights. Even if both the α-perceptron and α-LMS learning rules are derived from the error correction procedures and have very similar updating formulations, they have in fact quite different behavior (Widrow and Lehr 1990). The main difference between these two algorithms is that Rosenblatt's rule employs a quantized error $e = (d - sgn(s))$, while the α-LMS algorithm rule employs a linear error, $e_l = d - s$. This means that the α-perceptron algorithm involves a nonlinear function of the signals via the hard-limiting nonlinearity, whereas the α-LMS algorithm is essentially a linear process.

Example 3.8 In this simple simulation example, we consider an adaptive linear combiner with three binary inputs x_1, x_2, and $x_3 \in \{-1, 1\}$. Let the weights and threshold used for the simulation studies be

$$w_0 = -2, \quad , w_1 = 1, \quad w_2 = -1, \quad w_3 = 1$$

As shown in Table 3.8 in this case, there are eight possible inputs and eight corresponding outputs, which are obtained by $d = w_0 + w_1 x_1 + w_2 x_2 + w_3 x_3$.

Using the α-LMS learning algorithm, the input–output data pairs are repeatedly used for the learning algorithm until the weights and threshold converge to the correct values. The condition for terminating the learning algorithm is

Table 3.8 **The input and desired output pairs**

	Neural Inputs			Desired neural output
j	x_1	x_2	x_3	$d = -2 + x_1 - x_2 + x_3$
1	−1	−1	−1	−3
2	−1	−1	1	−1
3	−1	1	−1	−5
4	−1	1	1	−3
5	1	−1	−1	−1
6	1	−1	1	1
7	1	1	−1	−3
8	1	1	1	−1

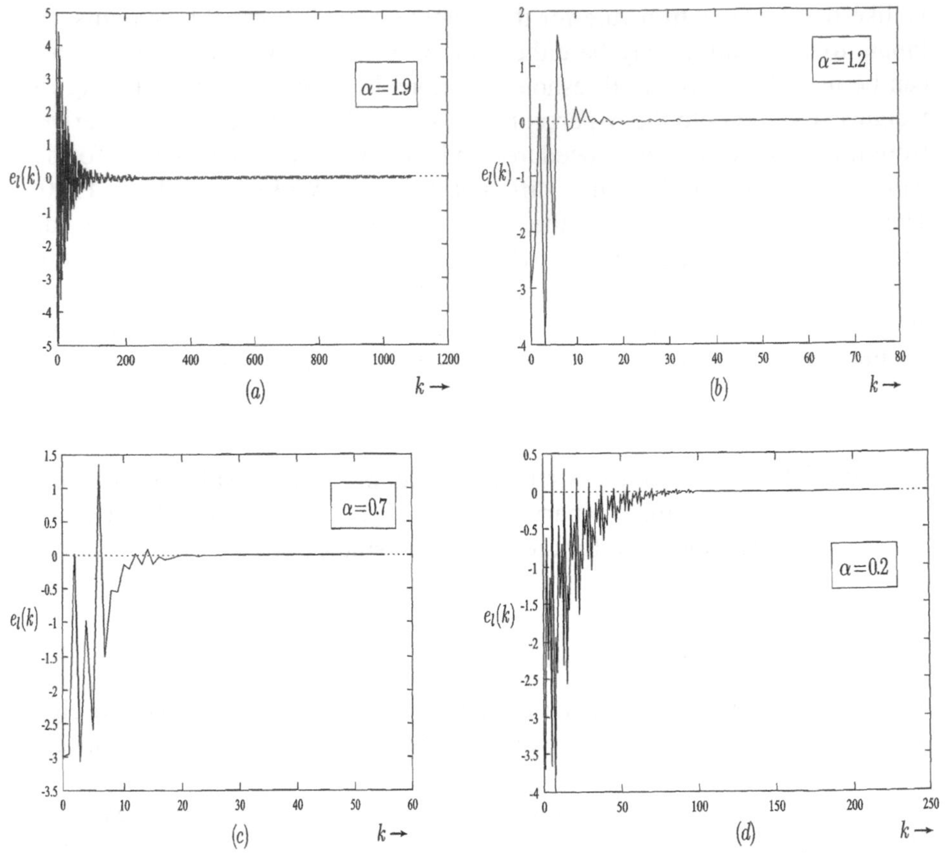

Figure 3.19 Example 3.8: the error curves for the different learning rates α: (a) $\alpha = 1.9$, (b) $\alpha = 1.2$, (c) $\alpha = 0.7$, and (d) $\alpha = 0.2$.

designed as

$$\sum_{j=1}^{8} \left| d(j) - \sum_{i=0}^{3} x_i(j) w_i(j) \right| \leq 0.0001$$

and the initial values of the unknown weight parameters are selected as 0.5. For the different choices of the learning rate α, the histories of the error $e_l(k)$ during the learning phases are given in Fig. 3.19 while the estimate of every parameter converges to the corresponding correct value with the absolute value error ≤ 0.0001. The simulation results indicate that the learning procedure has a better convergence speed with the choice of the learning rate α around 0.7. ∎

3.4.2 Mean Square Error Method

3.4.2.1 Non-iterative Formulation

As pointed out by Widrow and Lehr (1990), the concept of the mean square error may be used to determine a weight vector for a given input and the desired data patterns using either a non-iterative or an iterative algorithm. Without loss of generality, we assume that the input $\boldsymbol{x}(k)$ and the desired output $d(k)$ are drawn from a statistically stationary population. The square of the error between the output of the linear combiner and the desired output at time k may be expanded as follows:

$$\begin{aligned} e_l^2(k) &= (d(k) - \boldsymbol{x}_a^T(k)\boldsymbol{w}_a)^2 \\ &= d^2(k) - 2d(k)\boldsymbol{x}_a^T(k)\boldsymbol{w}_a + \boldsymbol{w}_a^T\boldsymbol{x}_a(k)\boldsymbol{x}_a^T(k)\boldsymbol{w}_a \end{aligned} \tag{3.57}$$

Since the linear combiner will produce an error $e_l(k)$ at every time k , the ensemble average of error square in Eqn. (3.57) yields

$$E[e_l^2(k)] = E[d^2(k)] - 2E[d(k)\boldsymbol{x}_a^T(k)]\boldsymbol{w}_a + \boldsymbol{w}_a^T E[\boldsymbol{x}_a(k)\boldsymbol{x}_a^T(k)]\boldsymbol{w}_a \tag{3.58}$$

The term on the left-hand side is called the *mean square error* (MSE). Let

$$\boldsymbol{p} \triangleq E[d(k)\boldsymbol{x}_a(k)] = E\begin{bmatrix} d(k) \\ d(k)x_1(k) \\ \vdots \\ d(k)x_n(k) \end{bmatrix}$$

which is the cross-correlation vector between the desired output $d(k)$ and the neural input vector $\boldsymbol{x}_a(k)$.

Similarly, define the input correlation matrix $\boldsymbol{R}$ as

$$\boldsymbol{R} \triangleq E[\boldsymbol{x}_a(k)\boldsymbol{x}_a^T(k)] = E\begin{bmatrix} 1 & x_1(k) & \dots & x_n(k) \\ x_1(k) & x_1(k)x_1(k) & \dots & x_1(k)x_n(k) \\ \vdots & \vdots & & \vdots \\ x_n(k) & x_n(k)x_1(k) & \dots & x_n(k)x_n(k) \end{bmatrix}$$

which is a real, symmetric, and positive definite matrix, or in rare cases, a positive semi-definite matrix. Thus, the expectation of the square error given in Eqn. (3.58) may be rewritten as

$$E[e_l^2(k)] = E[d^2(k)] - 2\boldsymbol{p}^T\boldsymbol{w}_a + \boldsymbol{w}_a^T\boldsymbol{R}\boldsymbol{w}_a \tag{3.59}$$

The gradient $\nabla_{\boldsymbol{w}_a}$ of the MSE function with respect to the weight vector $\boldsymbol{w}_a$ is obtained by differentiating Eqn. (3.59) as follows:

$$\nabla_{\boldsymbol{w}_a}(E[e_l^2(k)]) \triangleq \begin{bmatrix} \frac{\partial E[e_l^2(k)]}{\partial w_0} \\ \frac{\partial E[e_l^2(k)]}{\partial w_1} \\ \vdots \\ \frac{\partial E[e_l^2(k)]}{\partial w_n} \end{bmatrix} = -2\boldsymbol{p} + 2\boldsymbol{R}\boldsymbol{w}_a \tag{3.60}$$

This is a linear vector equation of the weight vector. The optimal weight vector $\boldsymbol{w}^*$, also called the *Wiener weight vector*, may be solved by setting the gradient to zero. Thus, the optimal weight is

$$\boldsymbol{w}_a^* = \boldsymbol{R}^{-1}\boldsymbol{p} \tag{3.61}$$

This solution involves a procedure for computing the inverse of the matrix $\boldsymbol{R}$. For very large number of inputs, this might be a very time-consuming task, even if some advanced matrix computational algorithms, such as singular-value decomposition (SVD), are being used to avoid a direct matrix inverse calculation. Moreover, an iterative gradient descent approach will be introduced to overcome this computing complexity.

Example 3.9 Reconsider the three-input linear combiner given in Example 3.8. From the input and desired output pairs, one may easily obtain

$$\boldsymbol{p} = \tfrac{1}{8}\sum_{j=1}^{8} d(j)\boldsymbol{x}_a^T(j) = \begin{bmatrix} -2 \\ 1 \\ -1 \\ 1 \end{bmatrix}$$

and

$$\boldsymbol{R} = \tfrac{1}{8}\sum_{j=1}^{8} \boldsymbol{x}_a(j)\boldsymbol{x}_a^T(j) = \begin{bmatrix} 1 & 0 & 0 & 0 \\ 0 & 1 & 0 & 0 \\ 0 & 0 & 1 & 0 \\ 0 & 0 & 0 & 1 \end{bmatrix}$$

Thus, the optimal weight vector is given by

$$\boldsymbol{w}_a^* = \boldsymbol{R}^{-1}\boldsymbol{p} = \begin{bmatrix} w_0^* \\ w_1^* \\ w_2^* \\ w_3^* \end{bmatrix} = \begin{bmatrix} -2 \\ 1 \\ -1 \\ 1 \end{bmatrix}$$

which is exactly equal to the desired weight vector. ■

3.4.2.2 μ-LMS (Least Mean Square) Algorithm

The μ-LMS may be developed from the conventional gradient descent method, where the searching optimal weight vector is performed in the weight space along the direction provided by the gradient of an instantaneous square error between the current output and the desired output. Since it is a quadratic function of the weights, this surface is convex and has a unique global minimum. Using Eqn. (3.57), an instantaneous gradient may be obtained based on the instantaneous linear error function as follows:

$$\nabla_{\boldsymbol{w}_a}\left(e_l^2(k)\right) \triangleq \frac{\partial e_l^2(k)}{\partial \boldsymbol{w}_a(k)} = \begin{bmatrix} \frac{\partial e_l^2(k)}{\partial w_0} \\ \frac{\partial e_l^2(k)}{\partial w_1} \\ \vdots \\ \frac{\partial e_l^2(k)}{\partial w_n} \end{bmatrix} = -2e_l(k)\boldsymbol{x}_a(k) \tag{3.62}$$

Thus, the gradient descent learning algorithm may be given as

$$\begin{aligned} \boldsymbol{w}_a(k+1) &= \boldsymbol{w}_a(k) - \mu\frac{\partial e_l^2(k)}{\partial \boldsymbol{w}_a(k)} \\ &= \boldsymbol{w}_a(k) + 2\mu e_l(k)\boldsymbol{x}_a(k) \\ &= \boldsymbol{w}_a(k) + \Delta w(k) \end{aligned} \tag{3.63}$$

This is Widrow's μ-LMS algorithm, where the learning rate $\mu > 0$ determines the convergence of the learning procedure. As pointed out by Widrow and Lehr (1990), if μ satisfies

$$0 < \mu < \frac{1}{trace[\boldsymbol{R}]} = \frac{1}{1 + \sum_{i=1}^{n} E[x_i^2(k)]} \tag{3.64}$$

the μ-LMS algorithm converges in the mean to $\boldsymbol{w}^*$, which is the optimal Wiener solution given by Eqn. (3.61).

A geometric representation of the μ-LMS rule is given in Fig. 3.20. According to Eqn. (3.63), $\boldsymbol{w}_a(k+1)$ equals $\boldsymbol{w}_a(k)$ added to the increment $\Delta\boldsymbol{w}_a(k)$, and $\Delta\boldsymbol{w}_a(k)$ is in parallel with the neural input pattern vector $\boldsymbol{x}_a(k)$. On the other hand, the change in error due to the change in the weight vector is equal to the negative inner product of $\boldsymbol{x}_a(k)$ and $\Delta\boldsymbol{w}_a(k)$. Since the μ-LMS algorithm selects $\Delta\boldsymbol{w}_a(k)$ to be collinear with $\boldsymbol{x}_a(k)$, the desired error correction is achieved with a weight change of suitable magnitude. When updating to respond properly to a new input pattern, the responses to the previous training patterns are, therefore, on the average minimally updated.

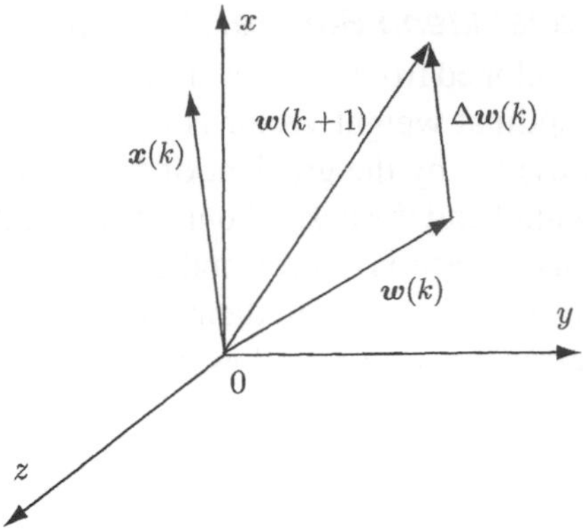

Figure 3.20 A geometric explanation of the α-LMS and μ-LMS learning algorithms.

When comparing the α-LMS and μ-LMS algorithms, it is of interest to understand that the α-LMS rule is a self-normalized version of the μ-LMS rule since the α-LMS rule may easily be rewritten as

$$\begin{aligned} \boldsymbol{w}_a(k+1) &= \boldsymbol{w}_a(k) + \alpha e_l(k) \frac{\boldsymbol{x}_a(k)}{|\boldsymbol{x}_a(k)|^2} \\ &= \boldsymbol{w}_a(k) + \alpha \left(\frac{d(k)}{|\boldsymbol{x}_a(k)|} - \boldsymbol{w}_a^T(k) \frac{\boldsymbol{x}_a(k)}{|\boldsymbol{x}_a(k)|} \right) \frac{\boldsymbol{x}_a(k)}{|\boldsymbol{x}_a(k)|} \\ &= \boldsymbol{w}_a(k) + \alpha \overline{e_l}(k) \overline{\boldsymbol{x}}_a(k) \end{aligned} \tag{3.65}$$

where

$$\begin{aligned} \overline{e_l}(k) &\triangleq \overline{d}(k) - \boldsymbol{w}_a^T(k) \overline{\boldsymbol{x}}_a(k) \\ \overline{d}(k) &\triangleq \frac{d(k)}{|\boldsymbol{x}_a(k)|} \\ \overline{\boldsymbol{x}_a}(k) &\triangleq \frac{\boldsymbol{x}_a(k)}{|\boldsymbol{x}_a(k)|} \end{aligned} \tag{3.66}$$

are, respectively, the normalized error, normalized desired response, and normalized input patterns. Equation (3.65) is the μ-LMS learning rule with 2μ replaced by α. Thus, the weight updating designed by the α-LMS rule is equivalent to that of the μ-LMS algorithm presented with a different training set, which is the normalized training set defined by Eqn. (3.66).

A continuous-time version of the above μ-LMS algorithm can easily be obtained by minimizing the error function

$$e_l^2(t) = (d(t) - \boldsymbol{x}_a^T(t)\boldsymbol{w}_a(t))^2 \tag{3.67}$$

which is an instantaneous estimate of the mean square error, and $\boldsymbol{w}_a(t)$ is an estimate of the augmented weight vector $\boldsymbol{w}_a$ at time t. Applying the gradient steepest-descent method yields

$$\begin{aligned} \frac{d\boldsymbol{w}(t)}{dt} &= -\mu \frac{\partial e_l^2(t)}{\partial \boldsymbol{w}(t)} = -2\mu \frac{\partial e_l(t)}{\partial \boldsymbol{w}(t)} \\ &= -2\mu e_l(t)\boldsymbol{x}_a(t) \end{aligned} \tag{3.68}$$

A block diagram of the implementation of the continuous-time μ-LMS algorithm using analog multipliers and integrators is given in Fig. 3.21.

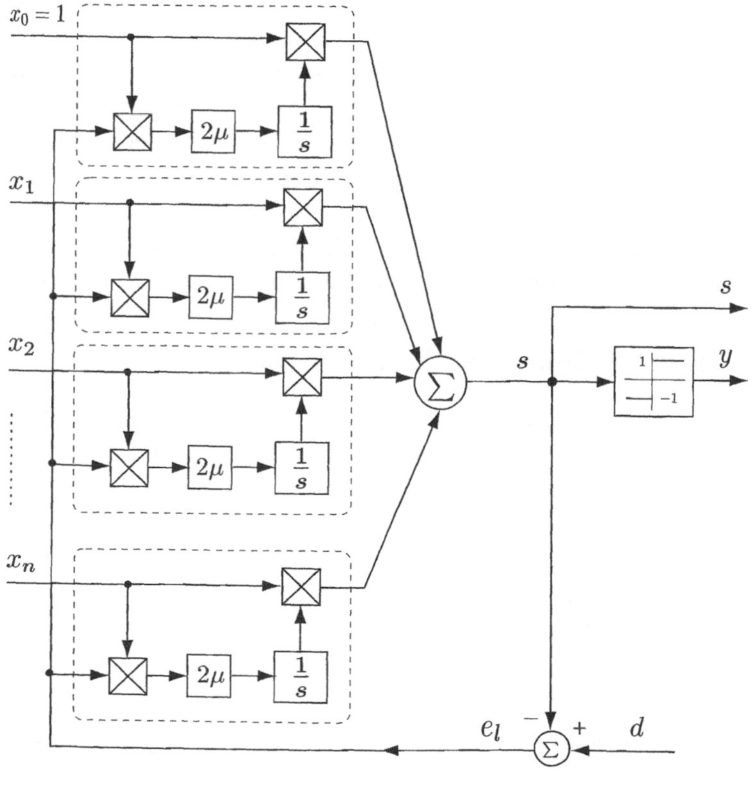

Figure 3.21 Block diagram of continuous-time μ-LMS algorithm.

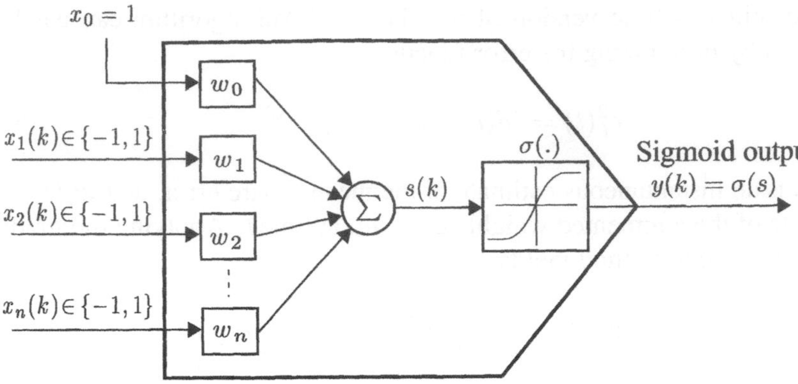

Figure 3.22 Block diagram of Adaline with sigmoidal function.

3.5 ADALINE WITH SIGMOIDAL FUNCTIONS

The Adaline elements considered so far use only the hard-limiting quantizer at their outputs. The input–output mapping of the hard–limiting quantizer is $y = sgn(s)$, as shown earlier, in Fig. 3.15. Since the early 1980s, other forms of nonlinear activation functions, such as the sigmoidal type, have come into use as shown in Fig. 3.22. Compared with the hard-limiting nonlinearity, these nonlinear functions not only retain saturation for output decision making but also provide differentiable input–output characteristics so that the adaptation procedure may be employed. In this section we describe the structure of Adaline by using a sigmoid in place of the signum, and then present some suitable adaptation algorithms associated with the sigmoidal functions used.

3.5.1 Nonlinear Sigmoidal Functions

The nonlinear neural activation function $\sigma(.)$ in the adaptive neural structures maps the neural state $x \in \Re^n$ to a bounded neural output space. In general, the neural output is in the range of $[0, 1]$ for unipolar signals, and $[-1, 1]$ for bipolar signals. Without loss of generality, we will assume that $\sigma(.) \in [-1, 1]$. For the continuous-time neural models, the nonlinear neural activation function $\sigma(.)$ may be chosen as a continuous and differentiable nonlinear sigmoidal function satisfying the following conditions:

(i) $\sigma(x) \longrightarrow \pm 1$ as $x \longrightarrow \pm\infty$;

(ii) $\sigma(x)$ is bounded with the upper bound 1 and the lower bound -1;

(iii) $\sigma(x) = 0$ at a unique point $x = 0$;

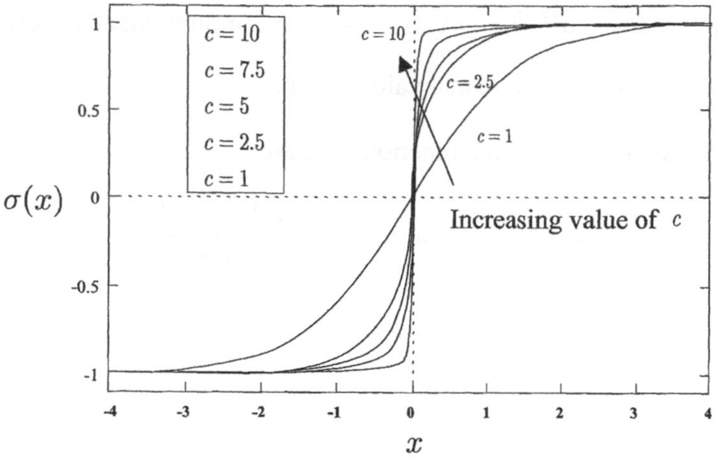

(a) $\sigma(x) = \tanh(cx)$

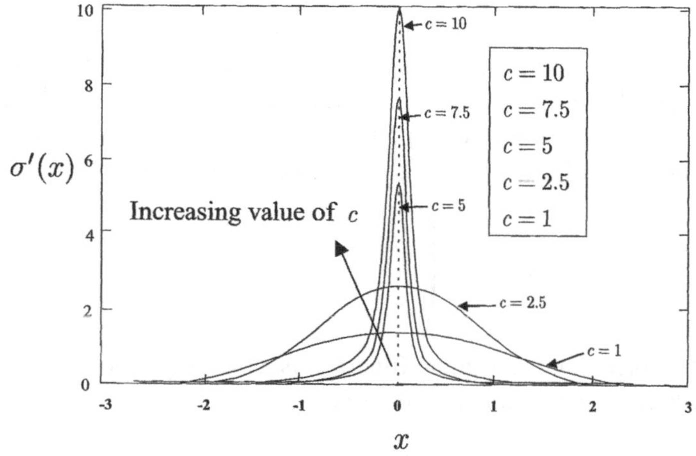

(b) $\sigma'(x) = c\,\mathrm{sech}^2(cx)$

Figure 3.23 A sigmoidal nonlinear neural activation function $\sigma(x) = \tanh(cx)$ and its derivative $\sigma'(x) = c\,\mathrm{sech}^2(cx)$ for various activation gain values c.

(iv) $\sigma'(x) > 0$ and $\sigma'(x) \longrightarrow 0$ as $x \longrightarrow \pm\infty$ (monotonically increasing);

(v) $\sigma'(x)$ has a global maximal value $c > 0$.

Typical examples of such a function $\sigma(.)$ are

$$\begin{aligned}
\sigma_1(x) &= \tanh(cx) = \frac{e^{cx} - e^{-cx}}{e^{cx} + e^{-cx}} \\
\sigma_2(x) &= \tanh\left(\frac{cx}{2}\right) = \frac{1 - e^{-cx}}{1 + e^{-cx}} \\
\sigma_3(x) &= \frac{2}{\pi}\tan^{-1}\left(\frac{\pi c}{2}x\right)
\end{aligned}$$

where $c > 0$ is a constant that determines the slope of $\sigma(x)$, the *activation gain*. The above described nonlinear activation functions are bounded, monotonic, and non-decreasing as shown in Fig. 3.23, and may be implemented by nonlinear operational amplifiers in analog hardware circuit systems.

A commonly used hard–limiting, the signum function, is defined by

$$sgn(x) = \begin{cases} 1, & x \geq 0 \\ -1, & x < 0 \end{cases}$$

It should be noted that the signum function is a limiting case of the sigmoidal function when the activation gain $c \to \infty$:

$$\lim_{c \to +\infty} \tanh(cx) = \lim_{c \to +\infty} \frac{e^{(cx)} - e^{-(cx)}}{e^{(cx)} + e^{-(cx)}} = sgn(x), \qquad x \neq 0$$

3.5.2 Backpropagation for the Sigmoid Adaline

The adaptive learning algorithm discussed in the previous section may be extended to the sigmoidal Adaline element, which incorporates a sigmoidal nonlinearity. We shall adapt Adaline with the objective of minimizing the mean square of the sigmoid error defined as

$$\begin{aligned}
e(k) &\triangleq d(k) - y(k) \\
&= d(k) - \sigma(s(k)) \\
&= d(k) - \sigma(\boldsymbol{w}_a^T \boldsymbol{x}_a(k))
\end{aligned} \tag{3.69}$$

An instantaneous gradient estimate obtained during presentation of the kth input vector $\boldsymbol{x}_a(k)$ is given by

$$\nabla_{\boldsymbol{w}_a}\left(e^2(k)\right) = \frac{\partial e^2(k)}{\partial \boldsymbol{w}_a(k)} = 2e(k)\frac{\partial e(k)}{\partial \boldsymbol{w}_a(k)} \tag{3.70}$$

Differentiating Eqn. (3.69) with respect to the augmented weight vector $\boldsymbol{w}_a$ yields

$$\frac{\partial e(k)}{\partial \boldsymbol{w}_a(k)} = -\frac{\partial \sigma(s(k))}{\partial \boldsymbol{w}_a(k)} = -\sigma'(s(k))\frac{\partial s(k)}{\partial \boldsymbol{w}_a(k)} \tag{3.71}$$

Note that, since

$$s(k) = \boldsymbol{x}_a^T(k)\boldsymbol{w}_a(k) \tag{3.72}$$

we have

$$\frac{\partial s(k)}{\partial \boldsymbol{w}_a(k)} = \boldsymbol{x}_a(k) \tag{3.73}$$

Substituting this result in Eqn. (3.71) gives

$$\frac{\partial e(k)}{\partial \boldsymbol{w}_a(k)} = -\sigma'(s(k))\boldsymbol{x}_a(k) \tag{3.74}$$

Inserting this into Eqn. (3.70) yields

$$\nabla_{\boldsymbol{w}_a}\left(e^2(k)\right) = -2e(k)\sigma'(s(k))\boldsymbol{x}_a(k) \tag{3.75}$$

Using this gradient estimate with the steepest–descent method provides a tool for minimizing the mean square error $e^2(k)$. Thus, the updating algorithm for the augmented weight vector is given by

$$\begin{aligned} \boldsymbol{w}_a(k+1) &= \boldsymbol{w}_a(k) - \mu\nabla_{\boldsymbol{w}_a}\left(e^2(k)\right) \\ &= \boldsymbol{w}_a(k) + 2\mu e(k)\sigma'(s(k))\boldsymbol{x}_a(k) \end{aligned} \tag{3.76}$$

This is the *backpropagation* (BP) algorithm for the sigmoid Adaline element. The representation by a block diagram of the updating process is given in Fig. 3.24. The term *backpropagation* makes more sense when the algorithm is developed in a layered network, which will be studied in a later chapter. Usually, the sigmoidal function is chosen to be the hyperbolic tangent function $\tanh(s)$. In this case, the derivative $\sigma'(s)$ is given by

$$\begin{aligned} \sigma'(s) &= \frac{\partial(\tanh(s))}{\partial s} \\ &= 1 - \tanh^2(s) = 1 - \sigma^2(s) \end{aligned} \tag{3.77}$$

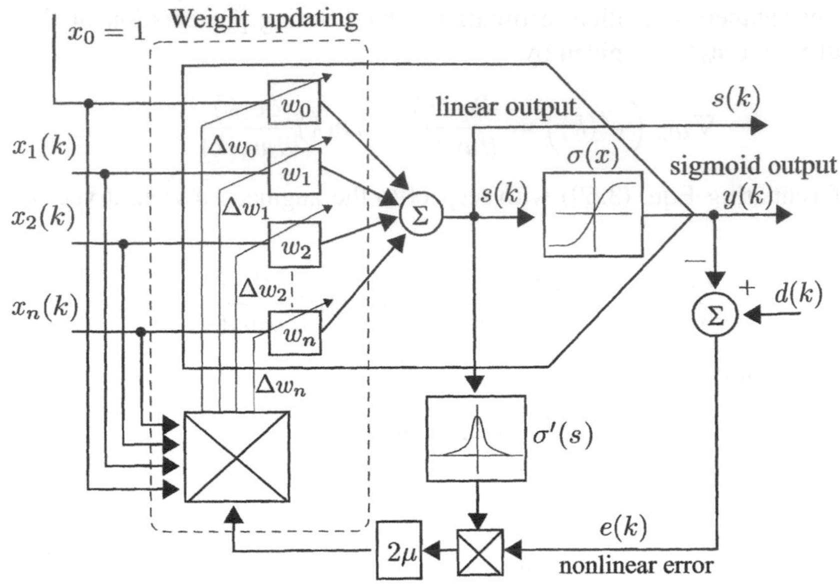

Figure 3.24 Schematic representation of the backpropagation algorithm for a sigmoid Adaline.

Thus, Eqn. (3.76) can equivalently be rewritten as

$$\boldsymbol{w}_a(k+1) = \boldsymbol{w}_a(k) + 2\mu e(k)(1 - y^2(k))\boldsymbol{x}_a(k) \tag{3.78}$$

The algorithm described above can be easily converted into a continuous-time version described by the following set of differential equations

$$\begin{aligned} \frac{d\boldsymbol{w}_a(t)}{dt} &= 2\mu e(t)\sigma'(s(t))\boldsymbol{x}_a(t) \\ &= 2\mu\sigma'(s(t))\left[e(t)\boldsymbol{x}_a(t)\right] \end{aligned} \tag{3.79}$$

The bracketed term [.] in Eqn. (3.79) provides a correlation between the error $e(t)$ and the neural input vector $\boldsymbol{x}_a(t)$ for a change in the weight $\boldsymbol{w}_a$. Thus, the change in the weight $w_i(k)$ is proportional to the strength of the correlation between the error $e(k)$ and the corresponding neural input x_i, $i = 0, 1, \ldots, n$.

3.6 NETWORKS WITH MULTIPLE NEURONS

As computational models of biological neurons, some adaptive units, such as adaptive threshold elements, Adaline, and sigmoid Adaline, were discussed previously. From the structural point of view, this type of units involves a linear combiner cascaded with a nonlinear activation function. As a computational element, it deals with a weighted linear summation for the input signals and a nonlinear operation on the output of the linear combiner. The former part of the computing conducts a synaptic operation, while the latter part performs a somatic operation. Because of the close similarity of these units to biologic neurons, these models of adaptive units are also called models of *computational neurons*, *artificial neurons*, or simply *neurons*. Accordingly a single unit of these structures would be a single neuron acting as a basic building block for more complex neural structures. In fact, a neural network structure of a great number of such single neural units may provide more powerful computation capability for solving science and engineering computing problems than could a single neuron. A simple example given earlier in this chapter is for a threshold network with multiple threshold elements that may be used to implement an arbitrary switching function, but a single threshold element can realize only a small class of switching functions, which are the threshold functions.

It is important to point out that since the hard-limiting nonlinearity used in McCulloch–Pitts neuron model can be considered, mathematically, as a special limiting case of a sigmoidal nonlinear function with an infinite activation gain, the neural models with a sigmoidal activation function may be employed as a general and useful neural structure. The differentiable property of the sigmoidal nonlinearity provides the possibility of applying some well-known mathematical tools such as optimization method, filtering, and recursive estimation method for the adaptation processes.

3.6.1 A Simple Network with Three Neurons

3.6.1.1 Structure and Basic Equations

As a beginning for studying the architectures and adaptive learning processes of neural networks, one exploits a simple two-layered neural network with only three neurons as shown in Fig. 3.25. The two neurons, termed $neuron(1, 1)$ and $neuron(1, 2)$, are located in the first neural layer, and another neuron, named $neuron(2, 1)$ is arranged in the second layer. The neurons in the first layer receive n inputs $x_1, x_2, \ldots, x_n \in \Re$ and produce two outputs $y_1^{(1)}$ and $y_2^{(1)}$, respectively. The outputs $y_1^{(1)}$ and $y_2^{(1)}$ of the first layer are applied as the inputs to the neuron in the second layer, and, finally, the single output $y_1^{(2)}$ of the network is generated directly from the neuron in the second layer. Since the neuron in the second layer delivers the final output, it is referred to as an output layer.

Let the weights associated with $neuron(1, 1)$, $neuron(1, 2)$, and $neuron(2, 1)$ be, respectively, given as

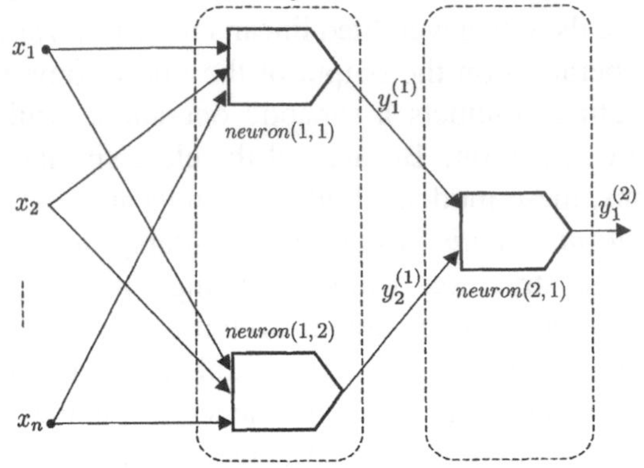

(a) Topological neural structure

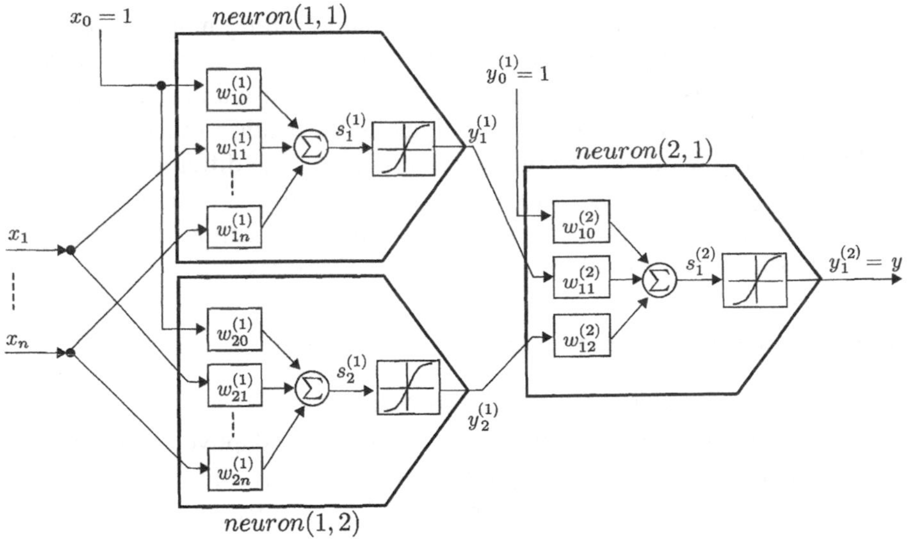

(b) A detailed diagram of two-layered neural network

Figure 3.25 A two-layered neural network with three neurons.

$$w_{11}^{(1)}, w_{12}^{(1)}, \ldots, w_{1n}^{(1)}$$
$$w_{21}^{(1)}, w_{22}^{(1)}, \ldots, w_{2n}^{(1)}$$
$$w_{11}^{(2)}, w_{12}^{(2)}$$

where $w_{ij}^{(1)}$ $(i = 1, 2; j = 1, 2, \ldots, n)$ represents the connection weight from the jth input to $neuron(1, i)$ and $w_{1j}^{(2)}$ is the weight from the $neuron(1, j)$ to $neuron(2, 1)$. The superscript here represents the number of the layer, the first subscript denotes the position of the neuron in the layer, and the second subscript represents the number of the input associated with the weight and applied to the neuron.

Furthermore, let $s_1^{(1)}$, $s_2^{(1)}$, and $s_1^{(2)}$ be the outputs of the linear combiners corresponding to $neuron(1, 1)$, $neuron(1, 2)$, and $neuron(2, 1)$. Then, the input–output equations of the three neurons may be obtained as follows

$$neuron(1,1): \quad \begin{cases} s_1^{(1)} = \sum_{i=0}^{n} w_{1i}^{(1)} x_i, & x_0 = 1 \\ y_1^{(1)} = \sigma(s_1^{(1)}) \end{cases} \tag{3.80}$$

$$neuron(1,2): \quad \begin{cases} s_2^{(1)} = \sum_{i=0}^{n} w_{2i}^{(1)} x_i, & x_0 = 1 \\ y_2^{(1)} = \sigma(s_2^{(1)}) \end{cases} \tag{3.81}$$

$$neuron(2,1): \quad \begin{cases} s_1^{(2)} = \sum_{j=0}^{2} w_{1j}^{(2)} y_j^{(1)}, & y_0^{(1)} = 1 \\ y_1^{(2)} = \sigma(s_1^{(2)}) \end{cases} \tag{3.82}$$

where $w_{10}^{(1)}$, $w_{20}^{(1)}$, and $w_{10}^{(2)}$ are the threshold corresponding to the $neuron(1, 1)$, $neuron(1, 2)$, and $neuron(2, 1)$, respectively, and $\sigma(.)$ is a bipolar sigmoidal function as discussed in Section 3.5.

3.6.1.2 Vector Expressions

The vector of the weights are expressed as

$$\boldsymbol{w}_1^{(1)} \triangleq [w_{11}^{(1)}, w_{12}^{(1)}, \ldots, w_{1n}^{(1)}]^T$$
$$\boldsymbol{w}_2^{(1)} \triangleq [w_{21}^{(1)}, w_{22}^{(1)}, \ldots, w_{2n}^{(1)}]^T$$
$$\boldsymbol{w}_1^{(2)} \triangleq [w_{11}^{(2)}, w_{12}^{(2)}]^T$$

Using the notion of the augmented neural input vector and weighting function, we write for the first layer

$$\begin{aligned}
\text{Augmented neural input vector: } & \boldsymbol{x}_a \triangleq [x_0, x_1, x_2, \ldots, x_n]^T, \quad x_0 = 1 \\
\text{Augmented weight vector: } & \boldsymbol{w}_{a1}^{(1)} \triangleq [w_{10}^{(1)}, w_{11}^{(1)}, \ldots, w_{1n}^{(1)}]^T \\
\text{Augmented weight vector: } & \boldsymbol{w}_{a2}^{(1)} \triangleq [w_{20}^{(1)}, w_{21}^{(1)}, \ldots, w_{2n}^{(1)}]^T
\end{aligned}$$

and, for the second layer $neuron(2, 1)$

$$\begin{aligned}
\text{Augmented neural input vector: } & \boldsymbol{y}_a^{(1)} \triangleq [y_0^{(1)}, y_1^{(1)}, y_2^{(1)}]^T, \quad y_0^{(1)} = 1 \\
\text{Augmented weight vector: } & \boldsymbol{w}_{a1}^{(2)} \triangleq [w_{10}^{(2)}, w_{11}^{(2)}, w_{12}^{(2)}]^T
\end{aligned}$$

Therefore, the formulations regarding $s_1^{(1)}$, $s_2^{(1)}$, and $s_1^{(2)}$ given in Eqns. (3.80)–(3.82) may be rewritten as

$$s_1^{(1)} = (\boldsymbol{w}_{a1}^{(1)})^T \boldsymbol{x}_a \tag{3.83}$$

$$s_2^{(1)} = (\boldsymbol{w}_{a2}^{(1)})^T \boldsymbol{x}_a \tag{3.84}$$

$$s_1^{(2)} = (\boldsymbol{w}_{a1}^{(2)})^T \boldsymbol{y}_a^{(1)} \tag{3.85}$$

$$\boldsymbol{y}_a^{(1)} = [y_0^{(1)}, \sigma(s_1^{(1)}), \sigma(s_2^{(1)})]^T \tag{3.86}$$

$$y_1^{(2)} = y = \sigma(s_1^{(2)}) \tag{3.87}$$

3.6.2 Error Backpropagation Learning

3.6.2.1 Squared Error Function

The adaptive learning process for a simple neural network like the one described in Fig. 3.25 can be summarized as follows. Given a known pattern sequence or desired response $d(k)$, design an adapting formulation for synaptic weights in the network such that the output of the network will approach $d(k)$ as closely as possible. As stated earlier, backpropagation derived using the gradient or steepest–descent method can be used to solve the problem. The details of this procedure are now given.

The instantaneous squared error between the desired response d and the output $y_1^{(2)}$ of the network at time k is

$$\begin{aligned}
e^2(k) &= \left(d(k) - y_1^{(2)}(k) \right)^2 \\
&= \left(d(k) - \sigma(s_1^{(2)}(k)) \right)^2
\end{aligned} \tag{3.88}$$

After the desired response $d(k)$ as a supervised function has been presented to the network, and the error of the output response has been calculated, the next step of the backpropagation algorithm involves finding the derivatives δs of the instantaneous squared error associated with each summing junction of the linear combiner in the network.

3.6.2.2 Error Partial Derivatives δs

Without loss of generality, the time variable k is omitted in the following derivations. The squared error derivatives associated with the neurons in the network are then defined as

$$\delta_1^{(1)} \triangleq -\frac{1}{2}\frac{\partial e^2}{\partial s_1^{(1)}} \tag{3.89}$$

$$\delta_2^{(1)} \triangleq -\frac{1}{2}\frac{\partial e^2}{\partial s_2^{(1)}} \tag{3.90}$$

$$\delta_1^{(2)} \triangleq -\frac{1}{2}\frac{\partial e^2}{\partial s_1^{(2)}} \tag{3.91}$$

Expanding the squared-error term e^2 on the right-hand side of Eqn. (3.89) by Eqn. (3.88) yields

$$\delta_1^{(2)} = -\frac{1}{2}\frac{\partial\left(d - y_1^{(2)}\right)^2}{\partial s_1^{(2)}} = -\frac{1}{2}\frac{\partial\left(d - \sigma(s_1^{(2)})\right)^2}{\partial s_1^{(2)}}$$

Noting that d and $s_1^{(2)}$ are independent yields

$$\begin{aligned} \delta_1^{(2)} &= \left(d - \sigma(s_1^{(2)})\right)\frac{\partial \sigma(s_1^{(2)})}{\partial s_1^{(2)}} \\ &= e_1^{(2)}\sigma'(s_1^{(2)}) \end{aligned} \tag{3.92}$$

where the error is defined by

$$e_1^{(2)} = e = (d - y_1^{(2)}) = y = d - \sigma(s_1^{(2)})$$

Developing the expressions for the squared error derivatives associated with the neurons in the first layer is not very difficult. By using the chain rule, one has

$$\delta_1^{(1)} = -\frac{1}{2}\frac{\partial e^2}{\partial s_1^{(1)}} = -\frac{1}{2}\frac{\partial e^2}{\partial s_1^{(2)}}\frac{\partial s_1^{(2)}}{\partial s_1^{(1)}} = \delta_1^{(2)}\frac{\partial s_1^{(2)}}{\partial s_1^{(1)}} \tag{3.93}$$

and

$$\delta_2^{(1)} = -\frac{1}{2}\frac{\partial e^2}{\partial s_2^{(1)}} = -\frac{1}{2}\frac{\partial e^2}{\partial s_1^{(2)}}\frac{\partial s_1^{(2)}}{\partial s_2^{(1)}} = \delta_1^{(2)}\frac{\partial s_1^{(2)}}{\partial s_2^{(1)}} \tag{3.94}$$

Expanding the output $s_1^{(2)}$ of the linear combiner associated with the $neuron(2,1)$ by Eqns. (3.80)–(3.82) gives

$$\begin{aligned}\frac{\partial s_1^{(2)}}{\partial s_1^{(1)}} &= \frac{\partial\left(w_{10}^{(2)} + w_{11}^{(2)}y_1^{(1)} + w_{12}^{(2)}y_2^{(1)}\right)}{\partial s_1^{(1)}} \\ &= \frac{\partial\left(w_{10}^{(2)} + w_{11}^{(2)}\sigma(s_1^{(1)}) + w_{12}^{(2)}\sigma(s_2^{(1)})\right)}{\partial s_1^{(1)}} \\ &= w_{11}^{(2)}\sigma'(s_1^{(1)})\end{aligned}$$

and

$$\begin{aligned}\frac{\partial s_1^{(2)}}{\partial s_2^{(1)}} &= \frac{\partial\left(w_{10}^{(2)} + w_{11}^{(2)}\sigma(s_1^{(1)}) + w_{12}^{(2)}\sigma(s_2^{(1)})\right)}{\partial s_1^{(2)}} \\ &= w_{12}^{(2)}\sigma'(s_2^{(1)})\end{aligned}$$

Substituting these results into the right-hand sides of Eqns. (3.90) and (3.91), respectively, yields

$$\delta_1^{(1)} = \delta_1^{(2)}w_{11}^{(2)}\sigma'(s_1^{(1)})$$

and

$$\delta_2^{(1)} = \delta_1^{(2)}w_{12}^{(2)}\sigma'(s_2^{(1)})$$

Now, let

$$e_1^{(1)} \triangleq \delta_1^{(2)}w_{11}^{(2)}$$

and

$$e_2^{(1)} \triangleq \delta_1^{(2)}w_{12}^{(2)}$$

which are linear functions of the network output error $e_1^{(2)}$ created in the output layer. They may thus be considered as output errors of the neurons in the first layer due to the backpropagation of the network output error $e_1^{(2)}$ with respect to the desired response d.

Accordingly, we have

$$\delta_1^{(1)} = e_1^{(1)}\sigma'(s_1^{(1)})$$

and

$$\delta_2^{(1)} = e_2^{(1)}\sigma'(s_2^{(1)})$$

It can be seen that a squared error derivative δ of the neuron is a product of its output error and the derivative of the sigmoid function with the output of its linear combiner as a variable.

3.6.2.3 Weight Updating Formulations

We have obtained the derivatives δ for each neuron in the network. The next step is to use these δ values to obtain the corresponding gradients. First, for the augmented weight vector $\boldsymbol{w}_{a1}^{(2)}$ associated with the $neuron(2,1)$, one has

$$\begin{aligned}\nabla_{\boldsymbol{w}_{a1}^{(2)}}\left(e^2\right) &= \frac{\partial e^2}{\partial \boldsymbol{w}_{a1}^{(2)}} \\ &= \frac{\partial e^2}{\partial s_1^{(2)}}\frac{\partial s_1^{(2)}}{\partial \boldsymbol{w}_{a1}^{(2)}} \\ &= -2\left(\frac{1}{2}\frac{\partial e^2}{\partial s_1^{(2)}}\right)\frac{\partial s_1^{(2)}}{\partial \boldsymbol{w}_{a1}^{(2)}} \\ &= -2\delta_1^{(2)}\frac{\partial s_1^{(2)}}{\partial \boldsymbol{w}_{a1}^{(2)}} \qquad (3.95)\end{aligned}$$

Indeed, from the output equation of the linear combiner involved in the $neuron(2,1)$, one has

$$s_1^{(2)} = (\boldsymbol{w}_{a1}^{(2)})^T \boldsymbol{y}_a^{(1)}$$

which implies

$$\frac{\partial s_1^{(2)}}{\partial \boldsymbol{w}_{a1}^{(2)}} = \boldsymbol{y}_a^{(1)}$$

Substituting this result into the right-hand side of Eqn. (3.95) gives

$$\nabla_{\boldsymbol{w}_{a1}^{(2)}}\left(e^2\right) = -2\delta_1(2)\boldsymbol{y}_a^{(1)} \qquad (3.96)$$

Next, the gradient vector associated with the augmented weight vectors of the neurons in the first layer is calculated.

$$\nabla_{\boldsymbol{w}_{a1}^{(1)}}\left(e^2\right) = \frac{\partial e^2}{\partial \boldsymbol{w}_{a1}^{(1)}} = \frac{\partial e^2}{\partial s_1^{(1)}}\frac{\partial s_1^{(1)}}{\partial \boldsymbol{w}_{a1}^{(1)}} + \frac{\partial e^2}{\partial s_2^{(1)}}\frac{\partial s_2^{(1)}}{\partial \boldsymbol{w}_{a1}^{(1)}}$$

Since the output $s_2^{(1)}$ is independent of the augmented weight vector $\boldsymbol{w}_{a1}^{(1)}$, one obtains

$$\nabla_{\boldsymbol{w}_{a1}^{(1)}}\left(e^2\right) = \frac{\partial e^2}{\partial \boldsymbol{w}_{a1}^{(1)}} = \frac{\partial e^2}{\partial s_1^{(1)}}\frac{\partial s_1^{(1)}}{\partial \boldsymbol{w}_{a1}^{(1)}} = -2\left(\frac{1}{2}\frac{\partial e^2}{\partial s_1^{(1)}}\right)\frac{\partial s_1^{(1)}}{\partial \boldsymbol{w}_{a1}^{(1)}} = -2\delta_1^{(1)}\frac{\partial s_1^{(1)}}{\partial \boldsymbol{w}_{a1}^{(1)}}$$

Indeed

$$s_1^{(1)} = (\boldsymbol{w}_{a1}^{(1)})^T \boldsymbol{x}_a$$

implies

$$\frac{\partial s_1^{(1)}}{\partial \boldsymbol{w}_{a1}^{(1)}} = \boldsymbol{x}_a$$

Hence, one finally obtains

$$\nabla_{\boldsymbol{w}_{a1}^{(1)}}\left(e^2\right) = -2\delta_1^{(1)}\boldsymbol{x}_a \tag{3.97}$$

Using the same procedure, one may derive the gradient vector associated with the augmented weight vector $\boldsymbol{w}_{a2}^{(1)}$ of the $neuron(1, 2)$. It is given by

$$\nabla_{\boldsymbol{w}_{a2}^{(1)}}\left(e^2\right) = -2\delta_2^{(1)}\boldsymbol{x}_a \tag{3.98}$$

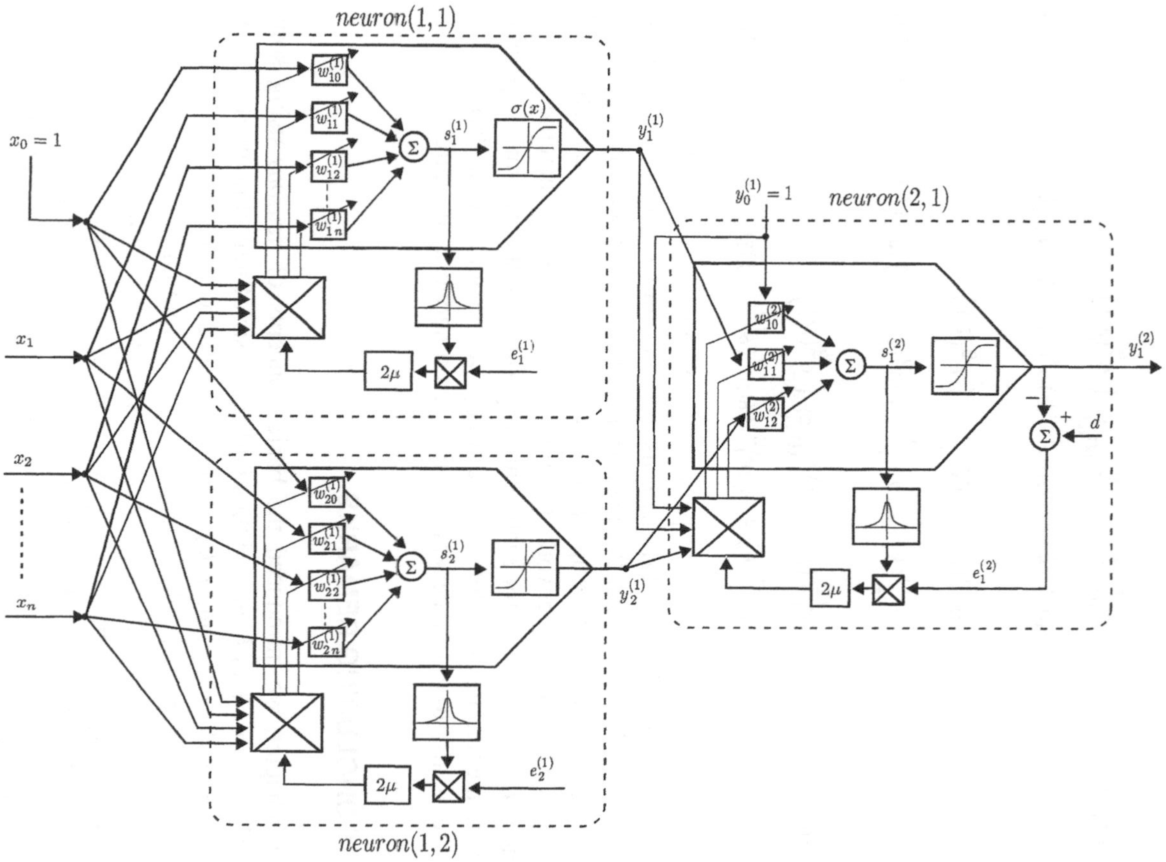

Figure 3.26 A two-layered neural network with parameter adaptation.

Using the method of steepest descent with instantaneous gradient, the formulations of the updated augmented weight vectors in the network are represented by

$$\begin{aligned} \boldsymbol{w}_{a1}^{(1)}(k+1) &= \boldsymbol{w}_{a1}^{(1)}(k) - \mu \nabla_{\boldsymbol{w}_{a1}^{(1)}} \left(e^2(k) \right) \\ &= \boldsymbol{w}_{a1}^{(1)}(k) + 2\mu e_1^{(1)}(k) \sigma'(s_1^{(1)}(k)) \boldsymbol{x}_a(k) \end{aligned} \tag{3.99}$$

$$\begin{aligned} \boldsymbol{w}_{a2}^{(1)}(k+1) &= \boldsymbol{w}_{a2}^{(1)}(k) - \mu \nabla_{\boldsymbol{w}_{a2}^{(1)}} \left(e^2(k) \right) \\ &= \boldsymbol{w}_{a2}^{(1)}(k) + 2\mu e_2^{(1)}(k) \sigma'(s_2^{(1)}(k)) \boldsymbol{x}_a(k) \end{aligned} \tag{3.100}$$

$$\begin{aligned} \boldsymbol{w}_{a1}^{(2)}(k+1) &= \boldsymbol{w}_{a1}^{(2)}(k) - \mu \nabla_{\boldsymbol{w}_{a1}^{(2)}} \left(e^2(k) \right) \\ &= \boldsymbol{w}_{a1}^{(2)}(k) + 2\mu e_1^{(2)}(k) \sigma'(s_1^{(2)}(k)) \boldsymbol{y}_a^{(1)}(k) \end{aligned} \tag{3.101}$$

where $\mu > 0$ is a learning rate parameter. Equations (3.99), (3.100), and (3.101) give the updating formulations for the augmented weight vectors of $neuron(1,1)$, $neuron(1,2)$, and $neuron(2,1)$, respectively. A block diagram representation of the updating scheme is given in Fig. 3.26. The result obtained for this simple network structure indicates that the increment of the augmented weight vector for each neuron involved in the network is parallel to its augmented input vector and is directly proportional to its derivative δ. This fact is also true for a general multi-layered network structure.

3.7 CONCLUDING REMARKS

In this chapter, we introduced the basic concepts of *neurons* using some examples of *threshold logic* and thus laid the basis of neural networks. Properties such as *learning* and *adaptation* associated with neural systems were examined in great detail with examples. The sigmoidal function used in the formulation of the neural output was also studied in detail. The well-known method of backpropagation learning was also briefly presented in this chapter.

Thus, in this chapter we have introduced some basic mathematical models and their learning and adaptation concepts. In the subsequent chapters these basic mathematical neural concepts will allow us to introduce more complex neural architectures for both static and dynamic neural networks. Therefore, with a good understanding of the materials provided in this chapter, we gain a basic theoretical foundation for this evolving field of neural networks.

Problems

3.1 Present a *static* model of a biological neuron in terms of *synaptic* and *somatic* operations. Can you identify some additional neuronal operations not discussed in this Chapter?

3.2 Present some generalizations of synaptic and somatic operations for a *static* neuron.

3.3 In Problems 3.1 and 3.2, we considered only the *static* neuronal model. Present a survey of dynamic models highlighting the characteristics of each model.

3.4 A synaptic operation is considered as a confluence operation between the past experience (knowledge, memory, ...), and fresh neural inputs. Present some models (with the logic behind each model) of the synaptic operations (See also Problems 3.1 and 3.2).

3.5 A somatic operation is considered as an aggregation of the dendritic inputs with a threshold and nonlinear mapping. Present some models of the somatic operation. Give the logic behind each model. (See also Problems 3.1, 3.2, and 3.4).

3.6 Develop the mathematics of a neuronal model combing appropriately the *synaptic* and *somatic* operations.

3.7 In Problem 3.6, we moved the threshold operation from the somatic to the synaptic operation. This necessitated the definitions of the *augmented* vector of neural inputs $\boldsymbol{x}_a(t) \in \Re^{n+1}$, and the *augmented* vector of synaptic weights, $\boldsymbol{w}_a(t) \in \Re^{n+1}$. Present the mathematics of this neural model

(a) Linear mapping operations for $\boldsymbol{x}_a(t) \in \Re^{n+1}$, to $v(t) \in \Re$;

(b) Nonlinear mapping operations from $v(t) \in \Re$, to $y(t) \in \Re$.

3.8 Consider a unipolar neural input vector $\boldsymbol{x}(t) \in \Re^n$ and a unipolar output vector $y(t) \in \Re$, $y(t) \in [0, 1]$.

(a) Present a set of possible candidates for the nonlinear mapping function $y(t) = \phi(v(t))$, where $\phi(.)$: $\Re^n \longrightarrow \Re$ is the linear mapping from $\boldsymbol{x}(t) \in \Re^n$ to $v(t) \in \Re$;

(b) Derive the sensitivity function for each $\phi(v)$ presented in **(a)**

$$\text{Sensitivity function:} \quad \frac{\partial \phi(v(t))}{\partial v} = \phi'(v)$$

3.9 As presented in Problems 3.1 and 3.2, the neuronal processing may be considered as a nonlinear mapping operation from *many* neural inputs to *one* neural output. Present a graphical explanation (supported by appropriate mathematics) of the mapping operation. (In biology, there are over 10^{11} neurons, and each neuron receives, on the average, about 10^4 neural inputs.)

3.10 Briefly describe a model of a single artificial static neuron. Clearly define the *synaptic* and *somatic* operations and their functions in the context of neural systems.

3.11 Given the unipolar signal: $\alpha \in [0, +\gamma], \gamma > 0$ and the bipolar signal: $\beta \in [-\gamma, +\gamma], \gamma > 0$, show that the relationship for converting unipolar to bipolar is

$$\text{(i)} \quad \beta = 2\alpha - \gamma$$

and for bipolar to unipolar

$$\text{(ii)} \quad \alpha = \frac{\beta + \gamma}{2}$$

Illustrate this conversion graphically.

3.12 Discuss the special mapping properties of the sigmoidal mapping functions: $y = \phi(v) = Sigmoid(g, v)$ with a gain g, for (i) unipolar signals, and (ii) bipolar signals.

3.13 The response $y(t) \in \Re$ of the single static neuron may be modeled as

$$y(t) = \phi(v(t)), \qquad v(t) = \boldsymbol{w}_a^T \boldsymbol{x}_a(t)$$

where $\boldsymbol{x}_a(t) \in \Re^{n+1}$: vector of augmented neural inputs,
$\boldsymbol{w}_a(t) \in \Re^{n+1}$: vector of augmented synaptic weights,
$\phi(v) \in \Re$: somatic nonlinearity (activation function), and
$v \in (-\infty, \infty)$.
Given a unipolar nonlinear function

$$y = \phi(v) = \frac{e^{gv}}{e^{gv} + e^{-gv}}, \quad y \in [0, 1], \quad g > 0$$

(a) Plot $\phi(v)$ and $s(v) = d\phi(v)/dv = \phi'(v)$, and show the effect of the neural somatic gain $g \in (0, \infty)$;

(b) Convert $\phi(v)$ into a bipolar neuronal nonlinear function (see Problems 3.11 and 3.12);

(c) Plot $\phi(v)$ and $\phi'(v)$, and show the effect of the somatic gain $g \in (0, \infty)$.

3.14 Make a table of the various possible unipolar and bipolar neuronal nonlinear (activation) functions giving the following information:

(a) Function $\phi(v)$ and the plot;
(b) $\phi'(v)$ and the plot;
(c) The effect of the somatic gain g.

3.15 Substantiate the following statement using the appropriate references. "Given a process (static or dynamic), one can approximate the behavior of the process with a degree of desired accuracy, using a multilayered neural network". (See also Chapter 7).

3.16 As presented in several earlier problems, the nonlinear mapping from $v(t) \in \Re$ to $y(t) = \phi(v(t)) \in \Re$ is an important neural somatic operation. Here, we present a set of possible candidates for such a mapping function $\phi(v)$.

(i) $y(t) = \phi(v) = sgn(v)$

(ii) $y(t) = \phi(v) = \exp(-gv)$, g: neural gain

(iii) $y(t) = \phi(v) = 1 - \exp(-gv)$

(iv) $y(t) = \phi(v) = [1 + \exp(-gv)]^{-1}$

(v) $y(t) = \phi(v) = \exp(-gv^2)$

(vi) $y(t) = \phi(v) = \dfrac{e^{gv} - e^{-gv}}{e^{gv} + e^{-gv}} = \tanh(gv)$

(vii) $y(t) = \phi(v) = \dfrac{1 - e^{-gv}}{1 + e^{-gv}}$

(viii) $y(t) = \phi(v) = \dfrac{v^n}{c + v^n}$

(ix) $y(t) = \phi(v) = \begin{cases} gv & \text{for } |v| < v_0 \\ gv_0 sign(v) & \text{for } |v| \geq v_0 \end{cases}$

(a) For each function $\phi(v)$, derive the sensitivity function $s(v) = \partial\phi(v)/\partial v = \phi'(v)$;

(b) Using the information about $\phi(v)$ and $s(v)$, present some discussions on the attributes of each function;

(c) List other possible candidates for such a nonlinear function not listed in this problem;

(d) Use "Mathematica", "Matlab", or other suitable software to obtain a graphical sketch of $\phi(v)$ and $s(v)$.

3.17 Consider a two-dimensional neural input $\boldsymbol{x}(t) = [x_1\ x_2]^T \in [0, 1]^2$. Design the appropriate neural logic circuits for the following logic operations:

(i) *OR*, (ii) *AND*, (iii) *NOT*, (iv) *NOR*, (v) *NAND*, and (vi) *EXCLUSIVE–OR* (*XOR*)

and draw appropriate sketches for the discriminant lines or surfaces.

3.18 Repeat Problem 3.17 for bipolar neural inputs $\boldsymbol{x}(t) = [x_1\ x_2]^T \in [-1, 1]^2$.

3.19 Repeat Problem 3.17 for bipolar neural inputs $\boldsymbol{x}(t) = [x_1\ x_2\ x_3]^T \in [-1, 1]^3$: (Three dimensional case).

3.20 In an aircraft, three sensors are used to monitor the state of the cargo door. The warning light is *on* if the majority of the sensors indicate an improper state (the door is open). Design a neural logic circuit for such an operation, and draw appropriate sketches for the discriminant lines or surfaces.

3.21 Show that for bipolar signals $\boldsymbol{x}(t) = [x_1\ x_2]^T \in [-1, 1]^2$, and draw appropriate sketches for the discriminant lines or surfaces.

(a) $x_1 \oplus x_2 = -sgn(x_1 \times x_2)$: *EXCLUSIVE–OR*

(b) $x_1 \circ x_2 = sgn(x_1 \times x_2)$: *EXCLUSIVE–NOR*

3.22 Using a neural model (with only -1 or 1 weights), derive the following n-variable logical functions

(a) *OR* function: $y = x_1 + x_2 + \cdots + x_n$;

(b) *AND* function: $y = x_1 x_2 \ldots x_n$;

(c) *Majority* function:

$$y = maj(x_1, x_2, \ldots, x_n) = \begin{cases} 1, & \text{if the majority of the } x_i = 1 \\ -1, & \text{otherwise} \end{cases}$$

3.23 Obtain a four-variable switching function $f(x_1, x_2, x_3, x_4)$ that cannot be realized using a single neural threshold unit.

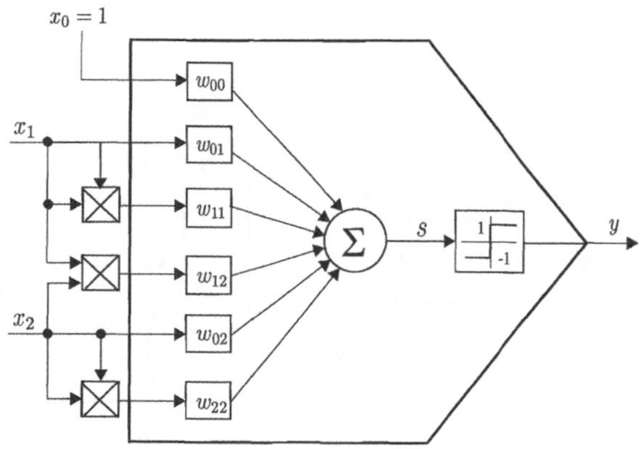

Figure 3.27 Problem 3.25: threshold element with linear and nonlinear inputs.

3.24 Design a neural threshold network for realizing the non-threshold function obtained in Problem 3.23.

3.25 Consider a two-variable neural unit with linear and nonlinear inputs shown in Fig. 3.27:

(a) Derive the input–output equation of this neural unit and express it in a matrix form;

(b) Show that this nonlinear neural unit is capable of separating any two-dimensional binary pattern;

(c) Draw the separating boundary in the pattern plane.

3.26 Solve the pattern separation problem for a *XOR* function

$$y = f(x_1, x_2) = x_1 \oplus x_2$$

using the nonlinear neural unit defined in Problem 3.25.

3.27 Given 2^n binary patterns $\boldsymbol{x} = [x_1, x_2, \ldots, x_n]^T \in \{-1, 1\}^n$, prove that the $(n+1) \times (n+1)$-dimensional matrix $\boldsymbol{R}$ defined by

$$\boldsymbol{R} \triangleq \frac{1}{2^n} \sum_{j=1}^{2^n} \boldsymbol{x}_a(j) \boldsymbol{x}_a^T(j)$$

is an identity matrix; that is

$$\boldsymbol{R} = \boldsymbol{I}$$

where $\boldsymbol{x}_a \triangleq [1, \boldsymbol{x}^T]^T$ is the augmented pattern vector.

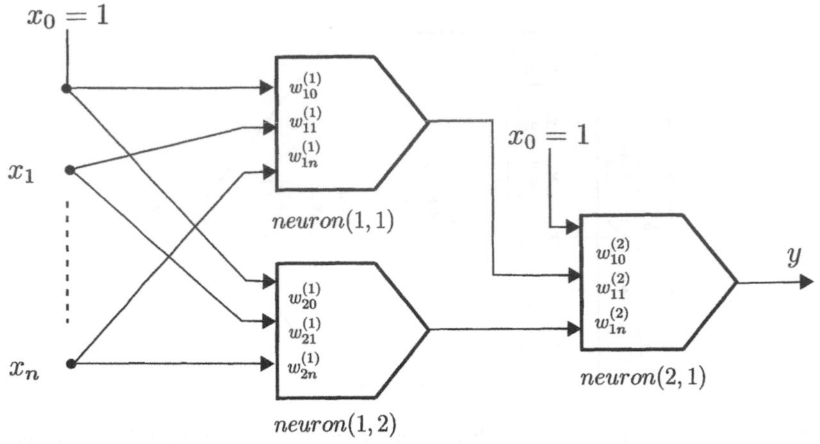

Figure 3.28 Problem 3.29: three-unit neural network.

3.28 Design a neural network for realizing the three-input *XOR* function

$$f(x_1, x_2, x_3) = x_1 \oplus x_2 \oplus x_3$$

3.29 Consider the three-unit neural network with n inputs as shown in Fig. 3.28:

(a) Obtain the input-output equation $y = f(x_1, x_2, \ldots, x_n)$;

(b) Design an adaptive learning algorithm for the weights updating using the error–correction method.

3.30 Obtain a simulation result for realizing the two-input *XOR* function

$$f(x_1, x_2) = x_1 \oplus x_2$$

using the algorithm developed in Problem 3.29.

3.31 Show the convergence of the backpropagation algorithm for the sigmoid Adaline using the mean-value theorem.

3.32 Consider a continuous-time sigmoid neural network with three inputs $x_1(t)$, $x_2(t)$ and $x_3(t)$, and the desired output given by

$$d(t) = \tanh(7 + 3x_1 + 4x_2 - 6x_3)$$

Let the initial weights be chosen randomly between the interval $[-1, 1]$. Train the network to approximate the desired response for the arbitrary inputs x_1, x_2, and $x_3 \in \Re$.

3.33 Show that the *hyperbolic tangent function* $f(x) = \tanh(x)$ satisfies the following properties:

(a) $f(x)$ is a *strictly increasing function*; that is, for $x_1 < x_2$, $f(x_1) < f(x_2)$;

(b) $f(x)$ is a *uniformly linear growing function*; that is, there exists a constant $\beta_1 > 0$ such that $|f(x)| \leq \beta_1 |x|$ for all $x \in \Re$.

3.34 A four-neuron network is given in Fig. 3.29, where $neuron(4)$ has a linear activation function; that is, the network has a linear output element:

(a) Give the input–output equation;

(b) Derive a backpropagation learning algorithm for the adaptation of the weights.

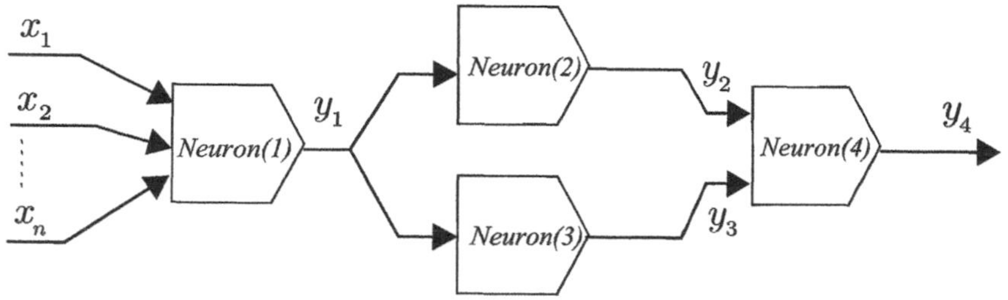

Figure 3.29 Problem 3.34: a feedforward neural network with four neurons.

Part II

STATIC NEURAL NETWORKS

Chapter 4. Multilayered Feedforward Neural Networks (MFNNs) and Backpropagation Learning Algorithms

Chapter 5. Advanced Methods for Learning and Adaptation in MFNNs

Chapter 6. Radial Basis Function Neural Networks

Chapter 7. Function Approximation Using Feedforward Neural Networks

4

Multilayered Feedforward Neural Networks (MFNNs) and Backpropagation Learning Algorithms

4.1 Two-Layered Neural Networks

4.2 Example 4.1: XOR Neural Network

4.3 Backpropagation (BP) Algorithms for MFNN

4.4 Deriving BP Algorithm Using Variational Principle

4.5 Momentum BP Algorithm

4.6 A Summary of BP Learning Algorithm

4.7 Some Issues in BP Learning Algorithm

4.8 Concluding Remarks

Problems

As a tool for scientific computing and engineering applications, the morphology of static multilayered feedforward neural networks (MFNNs) consists of many interconnected signal processing elements called *neurons*. These neurons form layered network configurations through only feedforward interlayered synaptic connections in terms of the neural signal flow. In general, an individual neuron aggregates its weighed inputs and yields outputs through a nonlinear activation function with a threshold. The MFNN is one of the main classes of static neural networks and it plays an important role in many types of problems such as system identification, control, channel equalization, and pattern recognition. Since the early 1990s, significant progress has been made on the principles, architectures, and applications of this type of neural networks, but many unresolved issues concerning these neural models still remain.

From the morphological point of view, a MFNN has only feedforward information transmission from the lower neural layers to the higher layers. On the other hand, a MFNN is a static neural model in the sense that its input–output relationship may be described by an algebraic nonlinear mapping function. The most widely used *static neural networks* are characterized by nonlinear equations that are memoryless; that is, their outputs are a function of only the current inputs. An obvious characteristic of a MFNN is its capability for implementing a nonlinear mapping from many neural inputs to many neural outputs. The backpropagation (BP) algorithm (Werbos 1974, Rumelhart and McClelland 1986, and Hecht-Nielsen 1989) is a basic and the most effective weight updating method of MFNNs for performing some specific computing tasks. The BP algorithm was originally developed using the gradient descent algorithm to train multilayered neural networks for performing desired tasks. Among supervised learning algorithms, the backpropagation algorithm is probably the most widely used algorithm. Since the original BP learning algorithm was developed, several extensions have evolved. The advantages of the BP learning algorithm include its parallel computational structure, its ability to store many more patterns than the number of network inputs, and its ability to acquire a complex nonlinear mapping.

In this chapter, we will first introduce the basic notion of two-layered static neural networks and their extension to multilayered feedforward neural networks (MFNNs). We will then give an extensive discussion of learning and adaptation problems including the backpropagation (BP) algorithms.

4.1 TWO-LAYERED NEURAL NETWORKS

4.1.1 Structure and Operation Equations

4.1.1.1 Mathematical Description

A generalization of the simple two-layered neural network with only three neural units, as addressed in the Chapter 3, to a two-layered network with multiple neurons can be achieved by adding a number of neurons to each neural layer. A general structure of a two-layered feedforward neural network is given in Fig. 4.1, where the first layer has p neurons denoted as $neuron(1,1)$, $neuron(1,2)$, . . ., $neuron(1,p)$, and the second layer has m neurons denoted as $neuron(2,1)$, $neuron(2,2)$, . . ., $neuron(2,m)$. In this text, we refer to the first layer as an *input* layer, and the second layer as an output layer, hence the name, a two-layered feedforward neural network.

Before we discuss the mathematical description of such a feedforward neural network, scripts that will be used as superscripts or subscripts in this section are defined as follows:

$$\begin{aligned} i &= 1, 2, \ldots, p \quad \text{(input layer)} \\ j &= 1, 2, \ldots, m \quad \text{(output layer)} \end{aligned}$$

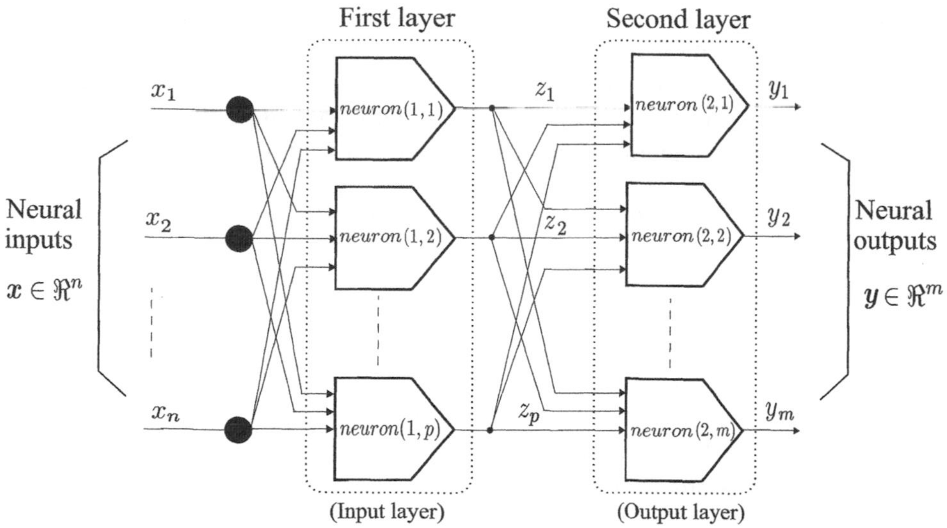

Figure 4.1 A two-layered feedforward neural network: p input neurons, and m output neurons:

Neural inputs: $\boldsymbol{x} = [x_1 \ \cdots \ x_i \ \cdots \ x_n]^T \in \Re^n$
Neural outputs: $\boldsymbol{y} = [y_1 \ \cdots \ y_i \ \cdots \ y_m]^T \in \Re^m$

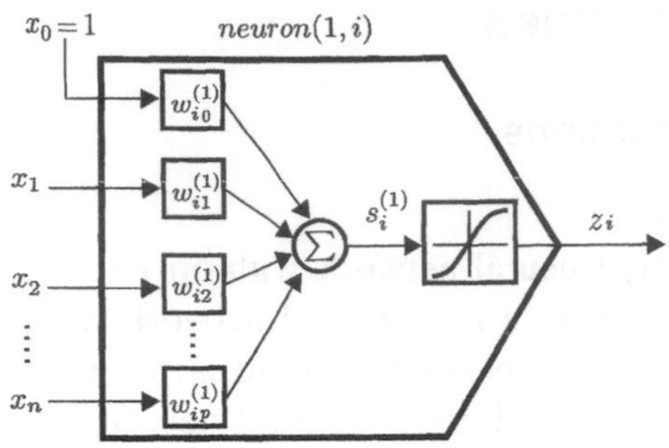

(a) $neuron(1, i)$, $(i = 1, 2, \ldots, p)$ in the input layer

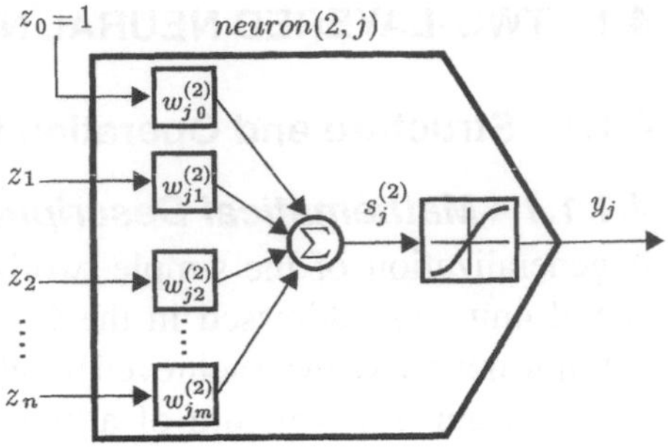

(b) $neuron(2, j)$, $(j = 1, 2, \ldots, m)$ in the output layer

Figure 4.2 Neurons in the input and output layers.

$$\begin{aligned} k &= 1, 2, \ldots, n \\ \ell &= 1, 2, \ldots, m \\ q &= 1, 2, \ldots, p \end{aligned}$$

The detailed structures of the input and output neurons are shown in Fig. 4.2. Let $neuron(1, i)$, $(i = 1, 2, \ldots, p)$ in the first layer receive n input signals x_1, x_2, ..., x_n; or a vector-valued signal $\boldsymbol{x} = [x_1 \ x_2 \ \cdots \ x_n]^T$, and deliver an output signal z_i, $(i = 1, 2, \ldots, p)$. The outputs of all the neurons in the input layer, represented by a p-dimensional vector $\boldsymbol{z} = [z_1 \ z_2 \ \cdots \ z_p]^T$, are fed forward to the neurons in the second layer. Finally, $neuron(2, j)$, $(j = 1, 2, \ldots, m)$ in the second layer generates an output signal y_j, $(j = 1, 2, \ldots, m)$, and the neural network has an output vector

$$\boldsymbol{y} = [y_1 \ y_2 \ \cdots \ y_m]^T \tag{4.1}$$

Let the weights corresponding to $neuron(1, i)$ in the first layer be $w_{i1}^{(1)}$, $w_{i2}^{(1)}$, ..., $w_{in}^{(1)}$, $(i = 1, 2, \ldots, p)$, and the weights corresponding to $neuron(2, j)$ in the second layer $w_{j1}^{(2)}$, $w_{j2}^{(2)}$, ..., $w_{jp}^{(2)}$, $(j = 1, 2, \ldots, m)$, where $w_{ik}^{(1)}$ is the connection weight from the kth input to the $neuron(1, i)$, and $w_{jq}^{(2)}$ is the connection weight from the input $neuron(1, q)$ to the output $neuron(2, j)$. The vector expressions for the above weights can be represented as

$$\boldsymbol{w}_i^{(1)} = [w_{i1}^{(1)} \ w_{i2}^{(1)} \ \cdots \ w_{in}^{(1)}]^T \in \Re^n, \quad i = 1, 2, \ldots, p \tag{4.2}$$

and

$$\boldsymbol{w}_j^{(2)} = [w_{j1}^{(2)} \ w_{j2}^{(2)} \ \cdots \ w_{jp}^{(2)}]^T \in \Re^p, \quad j = 1, 2, \ldots, m \tag{4.3}$$

where the superscript represents the number of the layer, the firstsubscript denotes the position of the neuron in the layer, and the secondsubscript represents the number of the input associated with the weight. The weights associated with the input and output layers may also be represented by the following weight matrices

$$\boldsymbol{W}^{(1)} = [\boldsymbol{w}_1^{(1)} \quad \boldsymbol{w}_2^{(1)} \quad \cdots \quad \boldsymbol{w}_p^{(1)}]^T = \begin{bmatrix} w_{11}^{(1)} & w_{12}^{(1)} & \cdots & w_{1n}^{(1)} \\ w_{21}^{(1)} & w_{22}^{(1)} & \cdots & w_{2n}^{(1)} \\ \vdots & \vdots & \ddots & \vdots \\ w_{p1}^{(1)} & w_{p2}^{(1)} & \cdots & w_{pn}^{(1)} \end{bmatrix} \tag{4.4}$$

(input layer)

and

$$\boldsymbol{W}^{(2)} = [\boldsymbol{w}_1^{(2)} \quad \boldsymbol{w}_2^{(2)} \quad \cdots \quad \boldsymbol{w}_m^{(2)}]^T = \begin{bmatrix} w_{11}^{(2)} & w_{12}^{(2)} & \cdots & w_{1p}^{(2)} \\ w_{21}^{(2)} & w_{22}^{(2)} & \cdots & w_{2p}^{(2)} \\ \vdots & \vdots & \ddots & \vdots \\ w_{m1}^{(2)} & w_{m2}^{(2)} & \cdots & w_{mp}^{(2)} \end{bmatrix} \tag{4.5}$$

(output layer)

where the ith row elements of $\boldsymbol{W}^{(1)}$ are obviously associated with $neuron(1, i)$ in the input layer, whereas the jth row of $\boldsymbol{W}^{(2)}$ corresponds to $neuron(2, j)$ in the output layer.

Furthermore, let $s_i^{(1)}$ and $s_j^{(2)}$ be, respectively, the outputs of the linear combiners of $neuron(1, i)$ and $neuron(2, j)$. Then, the input–output equations of the neurons in the network can also be expressed as

$$\begin{array}{c} neuron(1, i) \\ \text{(input layer)} \end{array} \quad \begin{cases} s_i^{(1)} = \sum_{k=0}^{n} w_{ik}^{(1)} x_k \\ z_i = \sigma(s_i^{(1)}) \\ i = 1, 2, \ldots, p \end{cases} \tag{4.6}$$

$$
\begin{array}{ll}
\begin{array}{c} neuron(2,j) \\ \text{(output layer)} \end{array} &
\left\{
\begin{array}{l}
s_j^{(2)} = \sum_{q=0}^{m} w_{jq}^{(2)} z_q \\
\\
y_j = \sigma(s_j^{(2)}) \\
\\
j = 1, 2, \ldots, m
\end{array}
\right.
\end{array}
\tag{4.7}
$$

where $\sigma(.)$ is a nonlinear activation function. These equations are also called the *transfer functions* of the neurons.

Using the augmented expressions of the neural inputs and weights by including the bias (threshold) as introduced in Chapter 3, we have

$$x_0 \equiv 1, \quad w_{i0}^{(1)}$$

and

$$z_0 \equiv 1, \quad w_{j0}^{(2)}$$

Then, the augmented versions of the input and weight vectors are defined as follows. For $neuron(1, i)$ in the input layer:

$$
\begin{array}{l}
\boldsymbol{x}_a \triangleq [x_0 \ x_1 \ x_2 \ \cdots \ x_n]^T \in \Re^{(n+1)}, \quad x_0 = 1 \\
\boldsymbol{w}_{ai}^{(1)} \triangleq [w_{i0}^{(1)} \ w_{i1}^{(1)} \ \cdots \ w_{in}^{(1)}]^T \in \Re^{(n+1)}, \quad i = 1, 2, \ldots, p
\end{array}
\tag{4.8}
$$

and for $neuron(2, j)$ in the output layer:

$$
\begin{array}{l}
\boldsymbol{z}_a \triangleq [z_0 \ z_1 \ z_2 \ \cdots \ z_p]^T \in \Re^{(p+1)}, \quad z_0 = 1 \\
\boldsymbol{w}_{aj}^{(2)} \triangleq [w_{j0}^{(2)} \ w_{j1}^{(2)} \ \cdots \ w_{jp}^{(2)}]^T \in \Re^{(p+1)}, \quad j = 1, 2, \ldots, m
\end{array}
\tag{4.9}
$$

Thus, the outputs of the linear combiners associated with $neuron(1, i)$ and $neuron(2, j)$ are given as

$$s_i^{(1)} = (\boldsymbol{w}_{ai}^{(1)})^T \boldsymbol{x}_a \tag{4.10}$$

and

$$s_j^{(2)} = (\boldsymbol{w}_{aj}^{(2)})^T \boldsymbol{z}_a \tag{4.11}$$

4.1.1.2 Nonlinear Neural Mapping

For an input vector signal $\boldsymbol{x} \in \Re^n$, the neural network produces a response signal $\boldsymbol{y} \in \Re^m$ through complex nonlinear operations. In fact, the neural network generates a nonlinear mapping process from the n-dimensional input signal space to the m-dimensional output signal space, where the output signal domain is usually designed as a desired task space for some specified applications. To obtain an analytical expression of the nonlinear mapping equation implemented by the neural network, we denote the augmented weights matrices as

$$\begin{aligned} \boldsymbol{W}_a^{(1)} &= [\boldsymbol{w}_{a1}^{(1)} \quad \boldsymbol{w}_{a2}^{(1)} \quad \cdots \quad \boldsymbol{w}_{ap}^{(1)}]^T \\ &= \begin{bmatrix} w_{10}^{(1)} & w_{11}^{(1)} & w_{12}^{(1)} & \cdots & w_{1n}^{(1)} \\ w_{20}^{(1)} & w_{21}^{(1)} & w_{22}^{(1)} & \cdots & w_{2n}^{(1)} \\ \vdots & \vdots & \vdots & \ddots & \vdots \\ w_{p0}^{(1)} & w_{p1}^{(1)} & w_{p2}^{(1)} & \cdots & w_{pn}^{(1)} \end{bmatrix} \in \Re^{p\times(n+1)} \end{aligned} \tag{4.12}$$

and

$$\begin{aligned} \boldsymbol{W}_a^{(2)} &= [\boldsymbol{w}_{a1}^{(2)} \quad \boldsymbol{w}_{a2}^{(2)} \quad \cdots \quad \boldsymbol{w}_{am}^{(2)}]^T \\ &= \begin{bmatrix} w_{10}^{(2)} & w_{11}^{(2)} & w_{12}^{(2)} & \cdots & w_{1p}^{(2)} \\ w_{20}^{(2)} & w_{21}^{(2)} & w_{22}^{(2)} & \cdots & w_{2p}^{(2)} \\ \vdots & \vdots & \vdots & \ddots & \vdots \\ w_{m0}^{(2)} & w_{m1}^{(2)} & w_{m2}^{(2)} & \cdots & w_{mp}^{(2)} \end{bmatrix} \in \Re^{m\times(p+1)} \end{aligned} \tag{4.13}$$

Furthermore, let

$$\boldsymbol{s}^{(1)} = \begin{bmatrix} s_1^{(1)} \\ s_2^{(1)} \\ \vdots \\ s_p^{(1)} \end{bmatrix}, \qquad \boldsymbol{s}^{(2)} = \begin{bmatrix} s_1^{(2)} \\ s_2^{(2)} \\ \vdots \\ s_m^{(2)} \end{bmatrix}$$

Thus, the input–output equations of a two-layered network may be rewritten in the following vector forms

$$\text{Input layer:} \qquad \begin{cases} \boldsymbol{s}^{(1)} = \boldsymbol{W}_a^{(1)} \boldsymbol{x}_a \\ \boldsymbol{z}_a = \boldsymbol{\sigma}_a(\boldsymbol{s}^{(1)}) \end{cases} \tag{4.14}$$

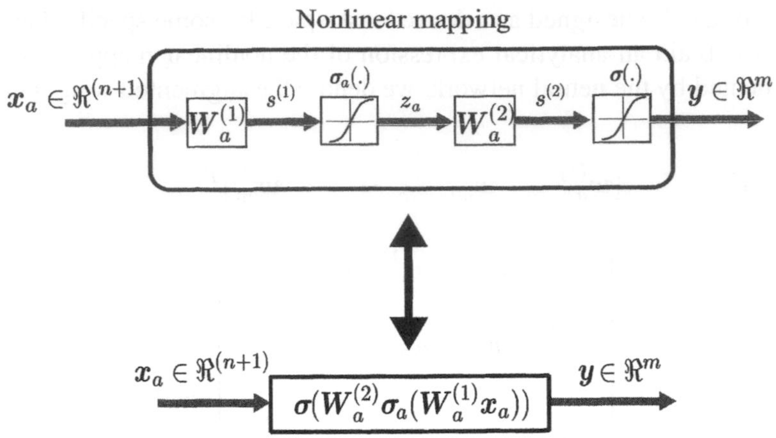

Figure 4.3 Two-layered neural network: nonlinear mapping for input ($\boldsymbol{x}_a \in \Re^{(n+1)}$) to output ($\boldsymbol{y} \in \Re^m$).

where the augmented vector-valued sigmoid function $\boldsymbol{\sigma}_a(.) : \Re^n \longrightarrow [-1, 1]^{(n+1)}$ is defined as

$$\boldsymbol{\sigma}_a(.) = \begin{bmatrix} 1 \\ \sigma(.) \end{bmatrix} \in \Re^{(n+1)}$$

and

$$\text{Output layer:} \qquad \left\{ \begin{array}{lcl} \boldsymbol{s}^{(2)} & = & \boldsymbol{W}_a^{(2)} \boldsymbol{z}_a \\ \boldsymbol{y} & = & \boldsymbol{\sigma}(\boldsymbol{s}^{(2)}) \end{array} \right. \tag{4.15}$$

Or simply

$$\boldsymbol{y} = \boldsymbol{\sigma}\left(\boldsymbol{W}_a^{(2)} \boldsymbol{\sigma}_a(\boldsymbol{W}_a^{(1)} \boldsymbol{x}_a) \right) \in \Re^m \tag{4.16}$$

Thus, the neural output vector $\boldsymbol{y} \in \Re^m$ is a vector-valued nonlinear function of the input signal vector $\boldsymbol{x} \in \Re^n$. In other words, the neural network deals with the operation on the input signals through a nonlinear mapping processing as shown in Fig. 4.3.

4.1.2 Generalized Delta Rule

A feedforward neural network is capable of processing continuous-time or discrete-time information through a nonlinear mapping function. However, in the following discussions of this chapter, we will consider the discrete-time version of the neural networks where both the inputs and outputs of the network are considered in a discrete-time domain.

Given a desired output response vector $\boldsymbol{d}(k) = [d_1(k) \quad d_2(k) \quad \cdots \quad d_m(k)]^T$, the adaptive weight learning rule characterized by the generalized delta rule was proposed by Rumelhart and McClelland (1986). This rule performs an optimization process such that each output error, defined as the error between the desired output $\boldsymbol{d}(k)$ and the output of the neural network $\boldsymbol{y}(k)$, is minimized.

To address this problem mathematically, an instantaneous error function for the network is given as a sum of the squares of the output errors for all the output units

$$\begin{aligned} E &= \tfrac{1}{2}\sum_{j=1}^{m}[d_j(k) - y_j(k)]^2 \\ &= \tfrac{1}{2}\sum_{j=1}^{m} e_j^2(k) \end{aligned} \tag{4.17}$$

where the output error e_j describes the error between the jth desired response and the jth network output at the output $neuron(2, j)$, and is defined as

$$e_j = (d_j - y_j)$$

The factor $\frac{1}{2}$ in Eqn. (4.17) is introduced for convenience in calculating the derivatives. The instantaneous sum of the output error squares E is a function of all the synaptic weights and thresholds involved in the network.

For a given desired response $\{k, \boldsymbol{d}(k)\}$, E represents the *cost function* as the measure of the learning performance of the network. In a manner similar to the gradient descent technique used in Chapter 3 for minimizing the error function, the correction in the weight vectors are made in the direction of decreasing error function and are, therefore, proportional to the negative gradients of the error function with respect to the weight vectors; that is

$$\Delta \boldsymbol{w}_{ai}^{(1)} = -\eta \nabla_{\boldsymbol{w}_{ai}^{(1)}}(E) = -\eta \frac{\partial E}{\partial \boldsymbol{w}_{ai}^{(1)}}, \qquad i = 1, 2, \ldots, p \tag{4.18}$$

and

$$\Delta \boldsymbol{w}_{aj}^{(2)} = -\eta \nabla_{\boldsymbol{w}_{aj}^{(2)}}(E) = -\eta \frac{\partial E}{\partial \boldsymbol{w}_{aj}^{(2)}}, \qquad j = 1, 2, \ldots, m \tag{4.19}$$

where $\eta > 0$ is a learning rate constant whose choice will affect the convergence speed of the updating process, and the gradient of E determines both the magnitude and the directions in which to change the weight vectors.

Like the derivative procedure used in Chapter 3 for the weight learning, the definition of the partial derivatives δs plays an important role in the final learning formulations. For such a two-layered structure, these intermediate variables are defined as

$$\delta_i^{(1)} \triangleq -\frac{\partial E}{\partial s_i^{(1)}}, \quad i = 1, 2, \ldots, p \tag{4.20}$$

$$\delta_j^{(2)} \triangleq -\frac{\partial E}{\partial s_j^{(2)}}, \quad j = 1, 2, \ldots, m \tag{4.21}$$

where $\delta_i^{(1)}$ is the partial derivative for the $neuron(1, i)$, and $\delta_j^{(2)}$ is the partial derivative for the $neuron(2, j)$.

4.1.2.1 Adaptation for the Output Neurons

To obtain the detailed expressions of these delta variables, one starts the derivation from the output layer, that is, with Eqn. (4.21). Expanding the error function on the right-hand side of Eqn. (4.21) by Eqns. (4.7) and (4.17) yields

$$\begin{aligned}
\delta_j^{(2)} &= -\frac{1}{2}\frac{\partial \sum_{\ell=1}^{m}(d_\ell - y_\ell)^2}{\partial s_j^{(2)}} \\
&= -\frac{1}{2}\frac{\partial \sum_{\ell=1}^{m}(d_\ell - \sigma(s_\ell^{(2)}))^2}{\partial s_j^{(2)}} \\
&= -\frac{1}{2}\sum_{\ell=1}^{m}\frac{\partial(d_\ell - \sigma(s_\ell^{(2)}))^2}{\partial s_j^{(2)}}
\end{aligned} \tag{4.22}$$

Since d_ℓ, $s_j^{(2)}$, and $s_\ell^{(2)}$ $(\ell \neq j)$ are independent, we obtain

$$\begin{aligned}
\delta_j^{(2)} &= (d_j - \sigma(s_j^{(2)}))\frac{\partial \sigma(s_j^{(2)})}{\partial s_j^{(2)}} \\
&= e_j \sigma'(s_j^{(2)}) \; \left(\equiv e_j^{(2)} \sigma'(s_j^{(2)})\right)
\end{aligned} \tag{4.23}$$

Thus, a δ corresponding to the neuron in the output layer, $\delta_j^{(2)}$ is the product of the output error e_j and the differential signal of the nonlinear activation function $\sigma'(s_j^{(2)})$.

In order to obtain the weight updating formulation, we will now evaluate the gradient of the error index E with respect to the weight vector $\boldsymbol{w}_{aj}^{(2)}$ using the notations of the derivatives δs. First, we have

$$\begin{aligned} \nabla_{\boldsymbol{w}_{aj}^{(2)}}(E) &= \frac{\partial E}{\partial \boldsymbol{w}_{aj}^{(2)}} \\ &= \sum_{\ell=1}^{m} \frac{\partial E}{\partial s_{\ell}^{(2)}} \frac{\partial s_{\ell}^{(2)}}{\partial \boldsymbol{w}_{aj}^{(2)}} \end{aligned} \tag{4.24}$$

Since $s_{\ell}^{(2)}$ $(\ell \neq j)$ is independent of $\boldsymbol{w}_{aj}^{(2)}$, we have

$$\nabla_{\boldsymbol{w}_{aj}^{(2)}}(E) = \frac{\partial E}{\partial s_{j}^{(2)}} \frac{\partial s_{j}^{(2)}}{\partial \boldsymbol{w}_{aj}^{(2)}}$$

Hence

$$s_j^{(2)} = (\boldsymbol{w}_{aj}^{(2)})^T \boldsymbol{z}_a$$

yields

$$\frac{\partial s_j^{(2)}}{\partial \boldsymbol{w}_{aj}^{(2)}} = \boldsymbol{z}_a$$

Thus

$$\begin{aligned} \nabla_{\boldsymbol{w}_{aj}^{(2)}}(E) &= -\delta_j^{(2)} \boldsymbol{z}_a \\ &= -e_j \sigma'(s_j^{(2)}) \boldsymbol{z}_a \end{aligned} \tag{4.25}$$

Finally, the weight updating formulations for the output layer are as follows:

$$\begin{aligned} \boldsymbol{w}_{aj}^{(2)}(k+1) &= \boldsymbol{w}_{aj}^{(2)}(k) - \eta \nabla_{\boldsymbol{w}_{aj}^{(2)}} \Big(E(k) \Big) \\ &= \boldsymbol{w}_{aj}^{(2)}(k) + \eta \delta_j^{(2)}(k) \boldsymbol{z}_a(k) \\ &= \boldsymbol{w}_{aj}^{(2)}(k) + \eta e_j(k) \sigma'(s_j^{(2)}(k)) \boldsymbol{z}_a(k) \end{aligned} \tag{4.26}$$

4.1.2.2 Adaptation for the Input Neurons

To obtain the weight adapting formulations for the input neurons, the δs associated with the neurons in the input layer are calculated first by using the chain rule

$$\begin{aligned} \delta_i^{(1)} &= -\sum_{\ell=1}^{m} \frac{\partial E}{\partial s_{\ell}^{(2)}} \frac{\partial s_{\ell}^{(2)}}{\partial s_i^{(1)}} \\ &= \sum_{\ell=1}^{m} \delta_{\ell}^{(2)} \frac{\partial s_{\ell}^{(2)}}{\partial s_i^{(1)}} \end{aligned}$$

From the input–output equations, Eqns. (4.6) and (4.7), one obtains

$$\begin{aligned}\frac{\partial s_\ell^{(2)}}{\partial s_i^{(1)}} &= \frac{\partial \sum_{q=0}^{p}(w_{\ell q}^{(2)} z_q)}{\partial s_i^{(1)}} \\ &= \sum_{q=0}^{p} \frac{\partial(w_{\ell q}^{(2)}\sigma(s_q^{(1)}))}{\partial s_i^{(1)}} \\ &= w_{\ell i}^{(2)}\sigma'(s_i^{(1)}) \end{aligned} \tag{4.27}$$

Thus

$$\delta_i^{(1)} = \sum_{\ell=1}^{m} \delta_\ell^{(2)} w_{\ell i}^{(2)} \sigma'(s_i^{(1)}) \tag{4.28}$$

Now, we introduce the definition for the propagation error $e_i^{(1)}$ as

$$e_i^{(1)} \triangleq \sum_{\ell=1}^{m} \delta_\ell^{(2)} w_{\ell i}^{(2)} \tag{4.29}$$

This propagation error represents the error in the input layer due to all the output errors. Substituting Eqn. (4.29) into Eqn. (4.28) gives

$$\delta_i^{(1)} = e_i^{(1)} \sigma'(s_i^{(1)}) \tag{4.30}$$

It can thus be seen that each output error produced in the output layer makes its own contribution to the derivatives δs associated with the neurons in the input layer. This error backpropagation process is similar to the one that transmits the forward input signals where each input signal is transmitted forward to every neuron in the input layer, and each output of the input neurons is further transmitted to the output neurons.

On the other hand, the gradient with respect to the input neural weight vector may be conducted using the chain rule as follows:

$$\begin{aligned}\nabla_{\boldsymbol{w}_{ai}^{(1)}}(E) &= \frac{\partial E}{\partial \boldsymbol{w}_{ai}^{(1)}} \\ &= \sum_{j=1}^{m}\sum_{q=1}^{p} \frac{\partial E}{\partial s_j^{(2)}} \frac{\partial s_j^{(2)}}{\partial s_q^{(1)}} \frac{\partial s_q^{(1)}}{\partial \boldsymbol{w}_{ai}^{(1)}}\end{aligned}$$

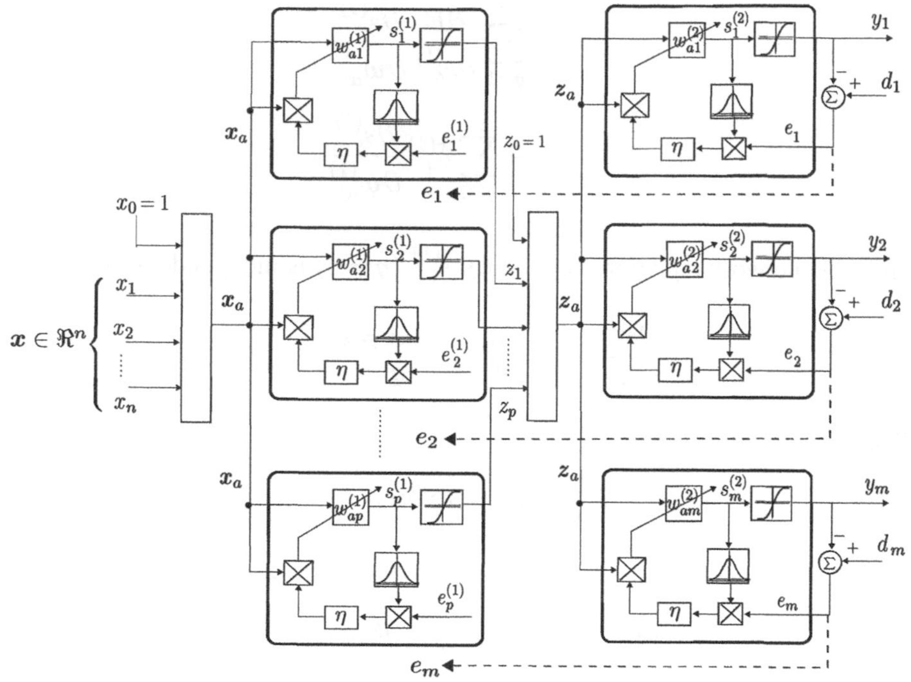

Figure 4.4 Backpropagation learning (generalized delta rule) for a two-layered feedforward neural network: neural inputs, $x \in \Re^n$; neural outputs, $y \in \Re^m$ and the desired outputs $d \in \Re^m$.

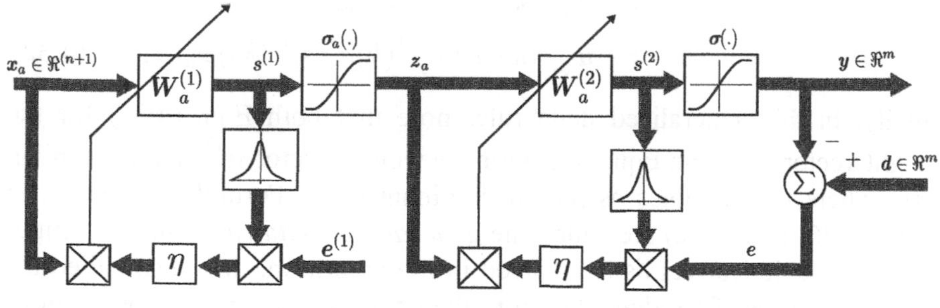

Figure 4.5 Matrix representation of backpropagation learning (generalized delta rule) for a two-layered feedforward neural network.

$$= \sum_{q=1}^{p} \frac{\partial E}{\partial s_q^{(1)}} \frac{\partial s_q^{(1)}}{\partial \boldsymbol{w}_{ai}^{(1)}}$$

$$= -\sum_{q=1}^{p} \delta_q^{(1)} \frac{\partial s_q^{(1)}}{\partial \boldsymbol{w}_{ai}^{(1)}}$$

From the network equation, Eqn. (4.6), $s_q^{(1)}$ $(q \neq i)$ is independent of $\boldsymbol{w}_{ai}^{(1)}$:

$$\frac{\partial s_q^{(1)}}{\partial \boldsymbol{w}_{ai}^{(1)}} = \begin{cases} 0, & q \neq i \\ \boldsymbol{x}_a, & q = i \end{cases}$$

Thus

$$\nabla_{\boldsymbol{w}_{ai}^{(1)}}(E) = \delta_i^{(1)} \boldsymbol{x}_a$$

Substituting the value of $\delta_i^{(1)}$ from Eqn. (4.30) into this equation yields

$$\nabla_{\boldsymbol{w}_{ai}^{(1)}}(E) = e_i^{(1)} \sigma'(s_i^{(1)}) \boldsymbol{x}_a \tag{4.31}$$

Therefore, the weight updating formulations for the hidden layer are as follows:

$$\begin{aligned} \boldsymbol{w}_{ai}^{(1)}(k+1) &= \boldsymbol{w}_{ai}^{(1)}(k) - \eta \nabla_{\boldsymbol{w}_{ai}^{(1)}} \Big(E(k) \Big) \\ &= \boldsymbol{w}_{ai}^{(1)}(k) + \eta \delta_i^{(1)}(k) \boldsymbol{x}_a(k) \\ &= \boldsymbol{w}_{ai}^{(1)}(k) + \eta e_i^{(1)}(k) \sigma'(s_i^{(1)}(k)) \boldsymbol{x}_a(k) \end{aligned} \tag{4.32}$$

Finally, in this generalized delta rule, note that both Eqn. (4.32) for the weight vector $\boldsymbol{w}_j^{(2)}$ and Eqn. (4.26) for the weight vector $\boldsymbol{w}_i^{(1)}$ have a similar form where the variables δs play a dominant role. Formulations given in Eqns. (4.26) and (4.32) are called the *generalized delta rule* since a computation of the derivatives δs is involved in the algorithm. It is also called the *backpropagation* (BP) *algorithm* from the error signal transmission point of view. This backpropagation algorithm is illustrated in Figs. 4.4 and 4.5.

4.1.3 Network with Linear Output Units

As discussed in the previous sections, the outputs of the feedforward neural network are constrained by the nonlinear function. In this case it is the sigmoidal function that yields the outputs $y_j \in [-1, 1]$, $j = 1, 2, \ldots, p$. To modify this type of feedforward neural network so that the neural outputs may be any real value, the sigmoidal activation function used for the output neurons is replaced with a simple linear function; that is, $\sigma(x) = x$. The output neurons then become linear combiners whose functions are only the sum of the weighted inputs. In this case, for a linear function in the output layer the input–output relationship of the network is described by

$$\begin{aligned} y_j &= \sum_{q=1}^{p} w_{jq}^{(2)} z_q \\ &= \sum_{q=1}^{p} w_{jq}^{(2)} \sigma(s_q^{(1)}) \\ &= \sum_{q=1}^{p} w_{jq}^{(2)} \sigma\left(\sum_{k=0}^{n} w_{qk}^{(1)} x_k\right) \\ & j = 1, 2, \ldots, p \end{aligned} \tag{4.33}$$

or simply in a vectorform

$$\boldsymbol{y} = \boldsymbol{W}^{(2)} \boldsymbol{\sigma}(\boldsymbol{W}_a^{(1)} \boldsymbol{x}_a) \tag{4.34}$$

Block diagram representations of the preceding vector operation equation are given in Figs. 4.6–4.8.

The weight updating formulation derived in the previous section may thus be changed for the output layer. The derivatives δs associated with the output neurons given by Eqn. (4.23) become

$$\delta_j^{(2)} = e_j \tag{4.35}$$

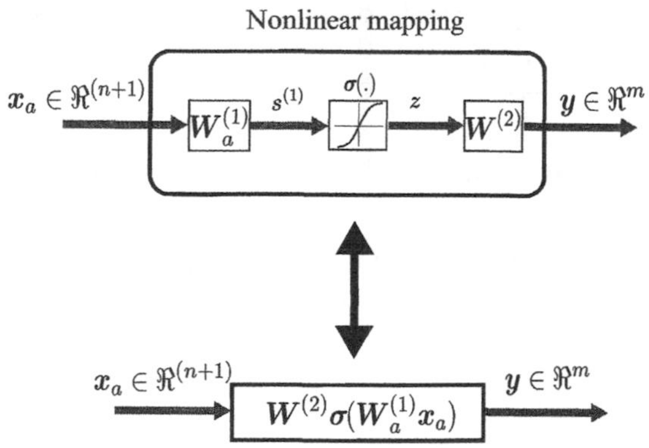

Figure 4.6 Nonlinear mapping implemented by the two-layered network with *linear output neurons.*

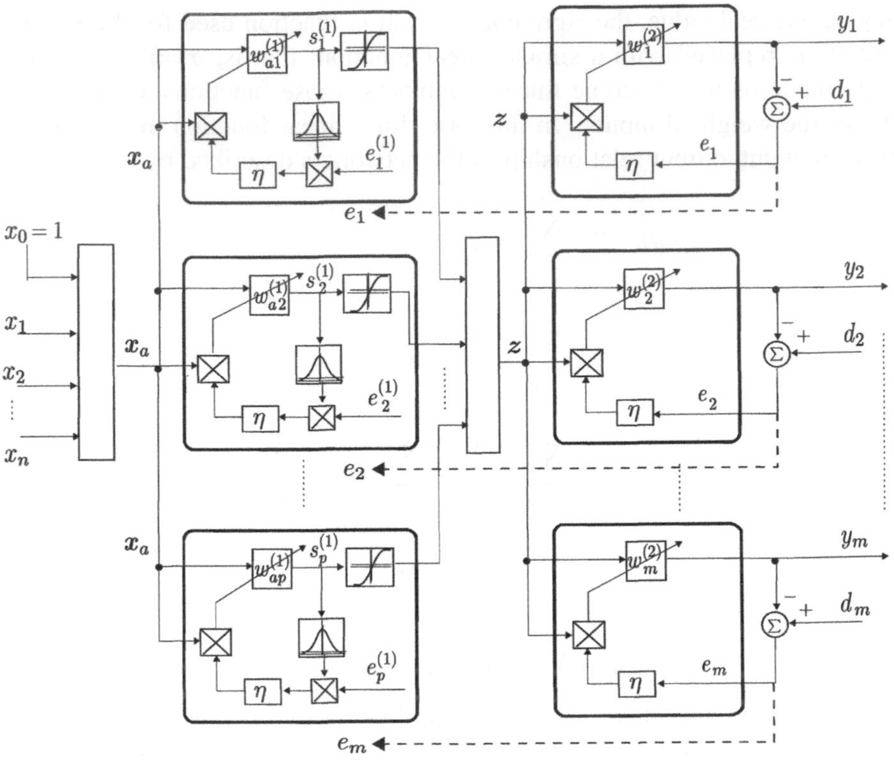

Figure 4.7 Backpropagation learning for a two-layered feedforward neural network with *linear output neurons*.

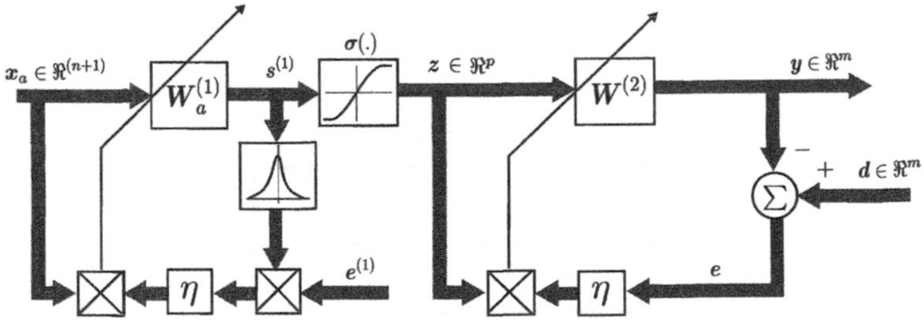

Figure 4.8 The matrix representation of backpropagation learning for a two-layered feedforward neural network with *linear output neurons*.

The updating equation for the output weight vector is simplified as follows:

$$\boldsymbol{w}_j^{(2)}(k+1) = \boldsymbol{w}_j^{(2)}(k) + \eta e_j(k)\boldsymbol{z}(k) \tag{4.36}$$

This result also shows that the output neurons may be considered as m linear combiners of the weighted input vector $\boldsymbol{z}$. Thus, Eqn. (4.36) may also be implied directly by applying the learning algorithm for the individual linear combiner discussed in Chapter 3.

4.2 EXAMPLE 4.1: XOR NEURAL NETWORK

4.2.1 Network Model

It was shown in Chapter 3 that a two-variable exclusive or (XOR) function $f(x_1, x_2) = x_1 \oplus x_2$ can be implemented by using a neural network with three neurons and preselected connecting weights. This is of great historical significance because it is one of the simplest logic functions that cannot be realized by a single neuron; that is, it requires at least two layers of neurons. This problem is now discussed using a network with three neurons as shown in Fig. 4.9 incorporating the BP weight learning processing.

In this case, the augmented weight vectors associated with $neuron(1,1)$, $neuron(1,2)$, and $neuron(2,1)$ may be denoted as

$$\begin{aligned}
\boldsymbol{w}_{a1}^{(1)} &= [w_{10}^{(1)} \quad w_{11}^{(1)} \quad w_{12}^{(1)}]^T \\
\boldsymbol{w}_{a2}^{(1)} &= [w_{20}^{(1)} \quad w_{21}^{(1)} \quad w_{22}^{(1)}]^T \\
\boldsymbol{w}_{a1}^{(2)} &= [w_{10}^{(2)} \quad w_{11}^{(2)} \quad w_{12}^{(2)}]^T
\end{aligned}$$

and the input vectors for layers 1 and 2 are respectively

$$\begin{aligned}
\boldsymbol{x}_a &= [x_0 \quad x_1 \quad x_2]^T, \quad x_0 = 1 \\
\boldsymbol{z}_a &= [z_0 \quad z_1 \quad z_2]^T, \quad z_0 = 1
\end{aligned}$$

where $x_0 = 1$ and $z_0 = 1$ are the bias terms. Then, the input–output equations of the neurons may be given as

$$neuron(1,1): \begin{cases} s_1^{(1)} = (\boldsymbol{w}_{a1}^{(1)})^T \boldsymbol{x}_a \\ z_1 = \sigma(s_1^{(1)}) \end{cases}$$

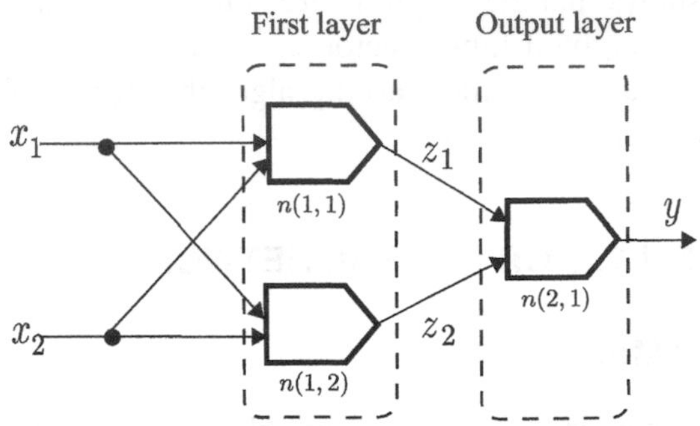

(a) Topological structure representation

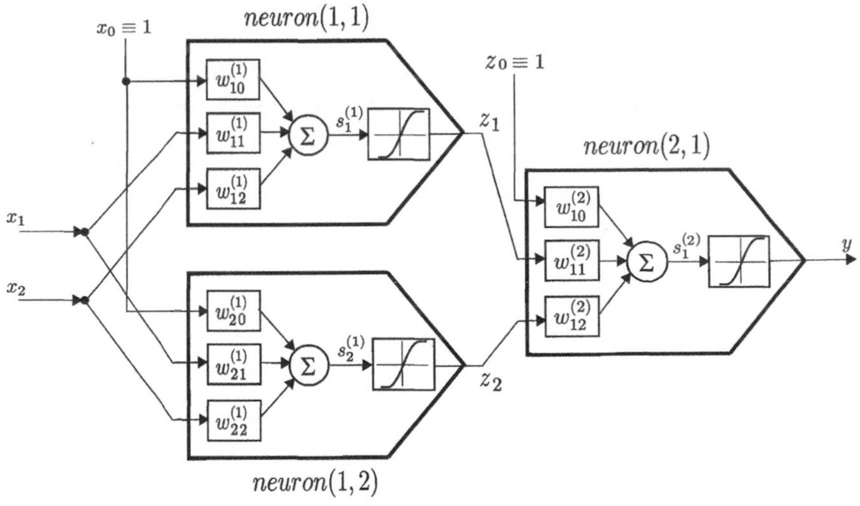

(b) Block diagram

Figure 4.9 Example 4.1: a two-layered neural network with three neurons for the implementation of XOR neural network.

$$neuron(1,2): \begin{cases} s_2^{(1)} & = & (\boldsymbol{w}_{a2}^{(1)})^T \boldsymbol{x}_a \\ z_2 & = & \sigma(s_2^{(1)}) \end{cases}$$

$$neuron(2,1): \begin{cases} s_1^{(2)} & = & (\boldsymbol{w}_{a1}^{(2)})^T \boldsymbol{z}_a \\ y & = & \sigma(s_1^{(2)}) \end{cases}$$

For the nonlinearity $\sigma(.)$, using the sigmoidal function

$$\sigma(s) = \tanh(s)$$

and its derivative

$$\begin{aligned} \sigma'(s) &= \operatorname{sech}^2(s) = 1 - \tanh^2(s) \\ &= [1 - \sigma^2(s)] \end{aligned}$$

the incremental equations for the weight vectors may be derived. Thus, for $neuron(2,1)$ in the output layer, the change in the weight vector is

$$\begin{aligned} \Delta \boldsymbol{w}_1^{(2)} &= \eta \delta_1^{(2)} \boldsymbol{z}_a \\ &= \eta(1 - \sigma^2(s_1^{(2)}))e\boldsymbol{z}_a \end{aligned}$$

where the output error $e \triangleq d - y$. Similarly, changes in the weight vectors for the neurons in the first layer are given by

$$\begin{aligned} \Delta \boldsymbol{w}_1^{(1)} &= \eta \delta_1^{(1)} \boldsymbol{x}_a \\ &= \eta(1 - \sigma^2(s_1^{(1)}))e_1^{(1)} \boldsymbol{x}_a \\ &= \eta(1 - \sigma^{(2)}(s_1^{(2)})w_{11}^{(2)} \delta_1^{(2)} \boldsymbol{x}_a \end{aligned}$$

and

$$\begin{aligned} \Delta \boldsymbol{w}_2^{(1)} &= \eta \delta_2^{(1)} \boldsymbol{x}_a \\ &= \eta(1 - \sigma^2(s_2^{(1)}))e_2^{(1)} \boldsymbol{x}_a \\ &= \eta(1 - \sigma^2(s_2^{(1)}))w_{12}^{(2)} \delta_1^{(2)} \boldsymbol{x}_a \end{aligned}$$

4.2.2 Simulation Results

To implement the XOR function using the network shown in Fig. 4.9, the four learning patterns corresponding to the four combinations of the two bipolar inputs $(x_1, x_2) = \{(-1,-1), (-1,1), (1,-1), (1,1)\}$ given in Table 4.1 were

Table 4.1 **Truth table of XOR function $f(x_1, x_2) = x_1 \oplus x_2$**

Pattern	Input x_1	Input x_2	Output d
A	-1	-1	-1
B	-1	1	1
C	1	-1	1
D	1	1	-1

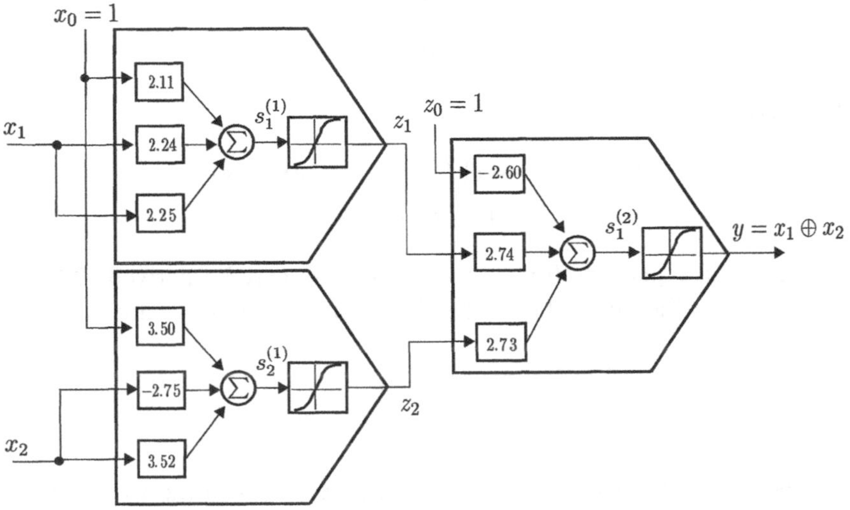

Figure 4.10 Example 4.1: a XOR neural network obtained by the BP algorithm with the learning rate $\eta = 0.8$ and the following initial weight conditions:

$$\begin{aligned} \boldsymbol{w}_1^{(1)}(0) &= [-1.3280 \quad 0.3345 \quad 1.5873]^T \\ \boldsymbol{w}_2^{(1)}(0) &= [2.0472 \quad -2.1382 \quad -2.3985]^T \\ \boldsymbol{w}_1^{(2)}(0) &= [-3.1753 \quad -1.2566 \quad 1.2546]^T \end{aligned}$$

used repeatedly in the learning process until a set of converged values of the weight vectors are obtained. For this purpose, the learning rate chosen was $\eta = 0.8$, and the randomly chosen initial weight values were as follows:

$$\begin{aligned} \boldsymbol{w}_1^{(1)}(0) &= [-1.3280 \quad 0.3345 \quad 1.5873]^T \\ \boldsymbol{w}_2^{(1)}(0) &= [2.0472 \quad -2.1382 \quad -2.3985]^T \\ \boldsymbol{w}_1^{(2)}(0) &= [-3.1753 \quad -1.2566 \quad 1.2546]^T \end{aligned}$$

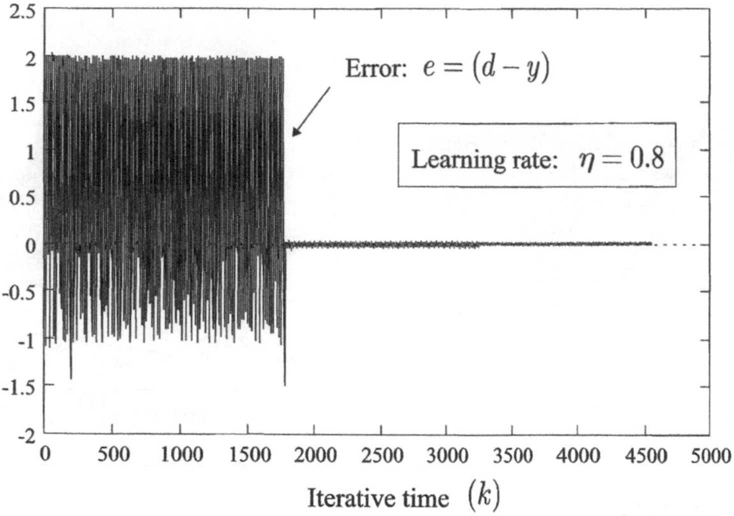

Figure 4.11 Example 4.1: the learning error $e = d - y$ for a XOR neural network with the learning rate $\eta = 0.8$.

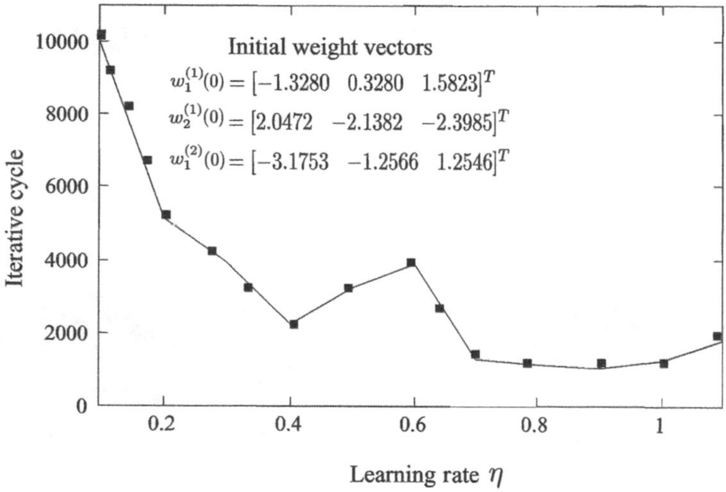

Figure 4.12 Example 4.1: the relationship between the learning rate and iteration cycle for the XOR.

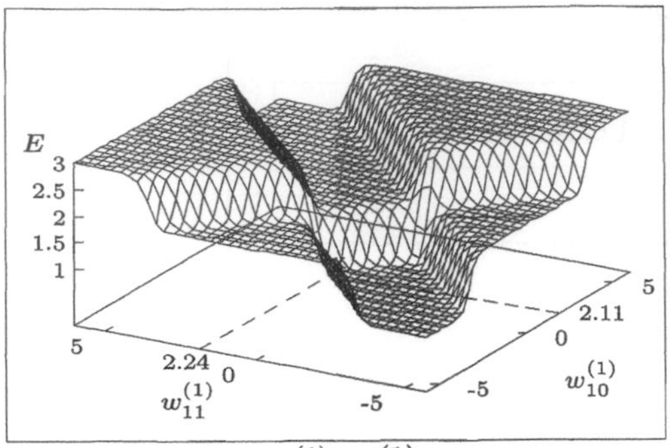

(a) $E(w_{10}^{(1)}, w_{11}^{(1)})$

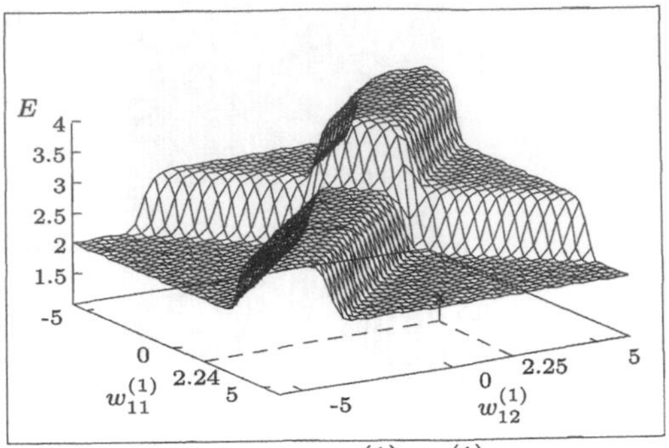

(b) $E(w_{11}^{(1)}, w_{12}^{(1)})$

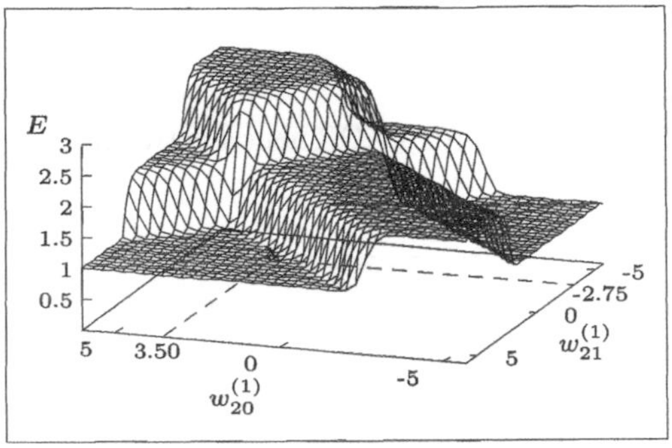

(c) $E(w_{20}^{(1)}, w_{21}^{(1)})$

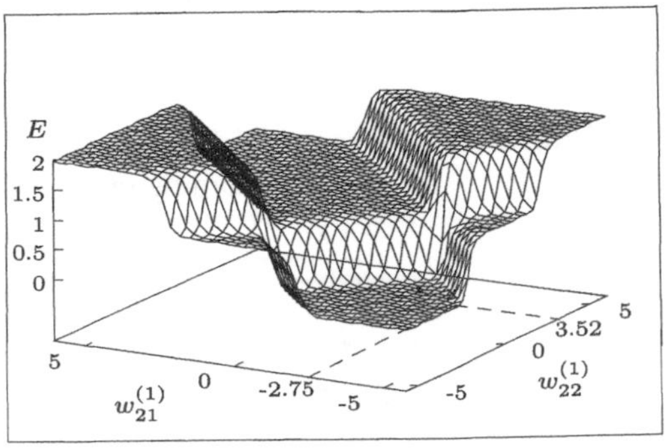

(d) $E(w_{21}^{(1)}, w_{22}^{(1)})$

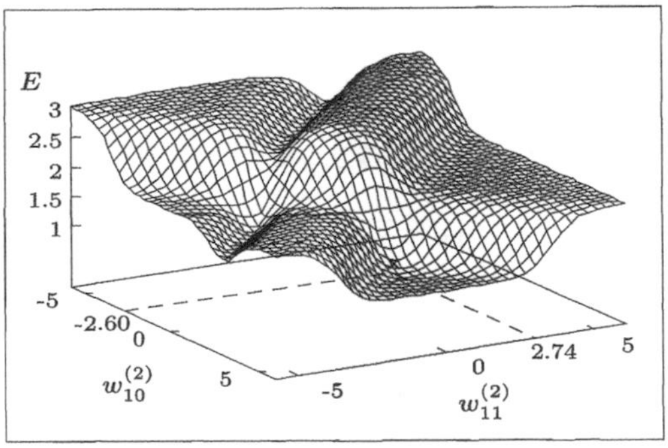

(e) $E(w_{10}^{(2)}, w_{11}^{(2)})$

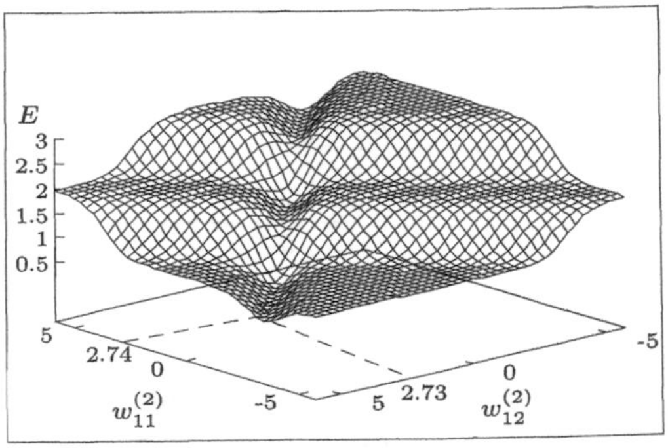

(f) $E(w_{11}^{(2)}, w_{12}^{(2)})$

Figure 4.13 Error surfaces of the XOR neural network.

The learning process stopped when any one of the absolute values of the output errors e overall the four patterns was less than the tolerance parameter $\epsilon = 0.0001$, that is

$$|e(i)| \leq 0.0001, \quad \text{for} \quad i = 1, 2, 3, 4$$

where $i = 1, 2, 3, 4$ corresponds to the patterns A, B, C, and D, respectively.

After 1173 learning cycles, or equivalently $1173 \times 4 = 4692$ iterations through the four learning patterns, the resulting weight vectors were obtained (Fig. 4.10)

$$\begin{aligned} \boldsymbol{w}_1^{(1)} &= [2.1081 \quad 2.2440 \quad 2.2533]^T \\ \boldsymbol{w}_2^{(1)} &= [3.4963 \quad -2.7463 \quad 3.5200]^T \\ \boldsymbol{w}_1^{(2)} &= [-2.5983 \quad 2.7354 \quad 2.7255]^T \end{aligned}$$

The learning error is shown in Fig. 4.11.

Simulation studies for different learning rates from $\eta = 0.1$ to $\eta = 1.1$ were also conducted. When the learning rate overtook this range the convergence of the learning phase could not be ensured. The learning cycle required for the learning processing with the same initial weights choice given in Fig. 4.10 is shown in Fig. 4.12 for different values of the learning rate. The results indicate that the best choice of the learning rate η should be around $\eta = 0.9$. However, this relationship between the learning cycle required for a successful learning process and the learning rate could change for another choice of the initial weight values. The convergence speed of a learning process depends not only on the choice of the learning rate but also on the choice of the initial weight values. It should be noted that for a suitable choice of the learning rate η, a considerable improvement in the convergence speed can be achieved. In other words, the BP algorithm can take varying amounts of time to solve this problem depending on the values of the initial weights and the learning rate η. The error surfaces of the error function with respect to two of the varying weights of the neural network are illustrated in Fig. 4.13.

4.2.3 Geometric Explanation

Since the XOR neural network solves a pattern classification problem, the nonlinear mapping from an input binary pattern space to an output binary pattern space implemented by the neural network may be analyzed using a geometric explanation as shown in Fig. 4.14. It can be seen from Fig. 4.14a that $neuron(1, 1)$ and $neuron(1, 2)$ in layer 1 yield two discriminant lines in the input pattern plane $x_1 - x_2$

$$L_{11}: \quad 2.1081 + 2.244x_1 + 2.2533x_2 = 0$$

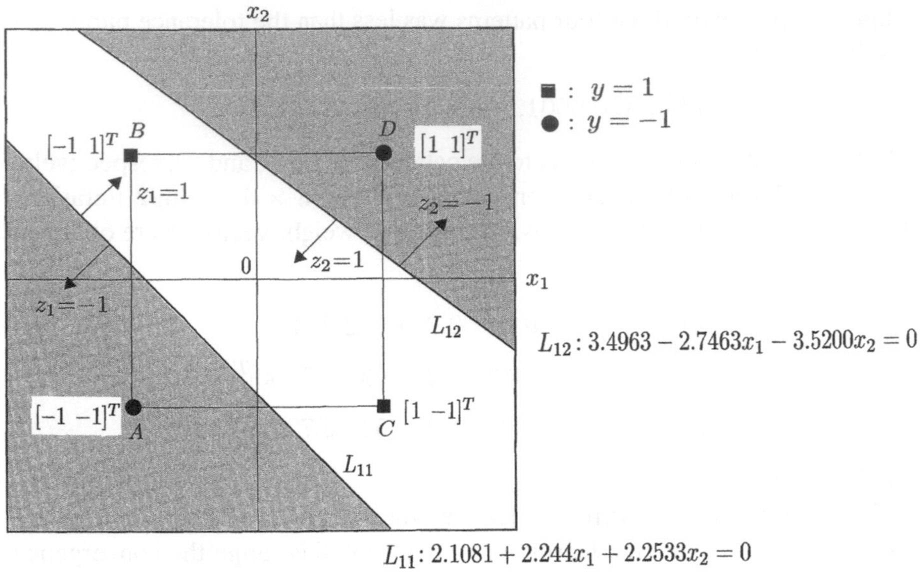

(a) Neural layer 1: discriminant lines L_{11} and L_{12} in $x_1 - x_2$ plane

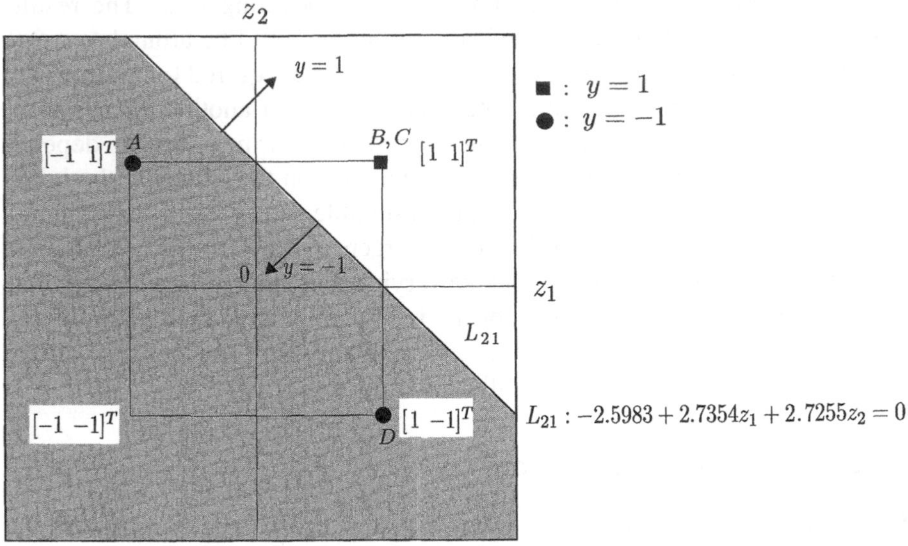

(b) Neural layer 2: mapping of points A, B, C, and D in $z_1 - z_2$ plane and the discriminant line L_{21}

Figure 4.14 Example 4.1: a geometric explanation for the XOR neural network.

$$L_{12}: \quad 3.4963 - 2.746x_1 - 3.52x_2 = 0$$

which classify the patterns A, B, C, and D into two parts. This fact can be found in Fig. 4.14a. The patterns $A(x_1 = -1,\ x_2 = -1)$ and $D(x_1 = 1,\ x_2 = 1)$ are located outside the two lines in the plane and correspond to the output z_1 of $neuron(1,1)$ and the output z_2 of $neuron(1,2)$ given below

$$D(1,1): \begin{cases} z_1 &= 1 \\ z_2 &= -1 \end{cases}$$

and

$$A(-1,-1): \begin{cases} z_1 &= -1 \\ z_2 &= 1 \end{cases}$$

Patterns $B(x_1 = -1,\ x_2 = 1)$ and $C(x_1 = 1,\ x_2 = -1)$ are positioned between the two lines L_{11} and L_{12} and produce

$$B(-1,1) \text{ and } C(1,-1): \begin{cases} z_1 = 1 \\ z_2 = 1 \end{cases}$$

Furthermore, $neuron(2,1)$ in layer 2 provides, as shown in Fig. 4.14b, a discriminant line

$$L_{21}: -2.5983 + 2.7354z_1 + 2.7255z_2 = 0$$

on a new pattern plane $z_1 - z_2$ such that the network output $y = 1$ occurs in the upper part of this line, and $y = -1$ corresponds to the points in the lower part of this line. The patterns A, B, C, and D in the input pattern plane $x_1 - x_2$ are mapped into the plane $z_1 - z_2$ whose coordinates are the outputs of the neurons in layer 1. The patterns A and D with $y = -1$ are located in the lower part of the line, whereas the patterns B and C, which correspond to $y = 1$, are mapped to the upper part of the line. It should be noted that there are many possible solutions to this problem, and that in this simulation example the network has correctly learned one of these. ■

4.3 BACKPROPAGATION (BP) ALGORITHMS FOR MFNN

We now discuss the topic of backpropagation (BP) algorithms in more detail. This arises from the realization that several hidden layers in a neural network may be used to create a general neural computing structure.

A two-layered feedforward neural network is a simple structure of the general multilayered feedforward network where multiple hidden layers are employed. Since it has the potential of approximating a general class of nonlinear functions with a desirable degree of accuracy, it has been widely employed in many applications such as system identification, control, and pattern recognition problems. As a natural extension of this simple type of feedforward neural network, a few results regarding a general model and the BP learning algorithm of the multilayered feedforward neural network (MFNN) with multiple hidden neural layers are now presented. The ideas and methods used in the previous section provoke and inspire the development in the following descriptions.

4.3.1 General Neural Structure for MFNNs

In a MFNN the neurons are organized into layers with no feedback or cross connections. The lowest layer of the MFNN is the input layer in which the processing elements have received all the weighted neural inputs, and provide their outputs to the processing elements of the first hidden layer. The highest layer of the MFNN is the output layer. The outputs from a given layer are transmitted only to the higher layers. A basic structure of the M-multilayered feedforward neural networks (MFNNs) with feedforward connections is shown in Fig. 4.15.

Let the neural layers be numbered from the first layer and M be the total number of layers of the MFNN including the input, hidden, and output layers.

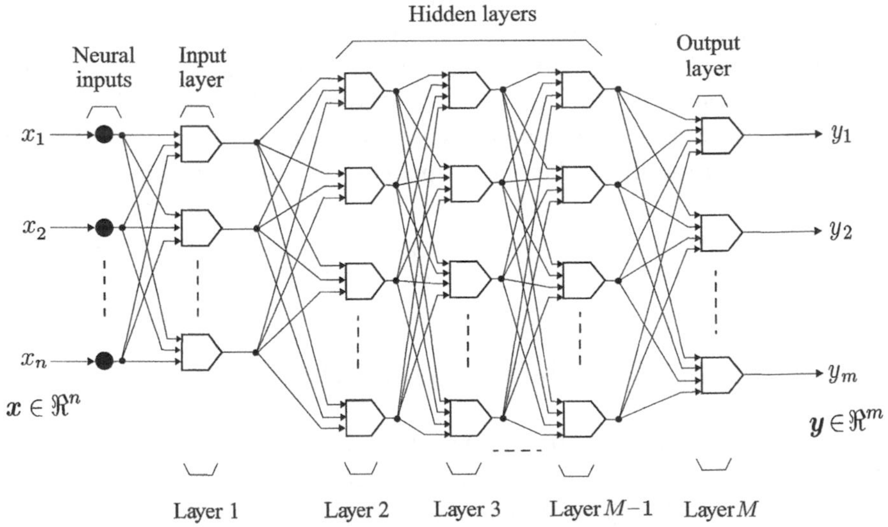

Figure 4.15 A multilayered feedforward neural network with input layer, output layer and $(M-2)$ hidden layers.

Let the ith neuron in the sth layer be denoted by $neuron(s,i)$, and n_s be the total number of neurons in the sth layer. The input to the first layer (input layer) is $\boldsymbol{x} \in \Re^n$. The outputs of the first layer is a nonlinear function of the sum of the weighted inputs, and these outputs are transmitted to all the neural units of the second layer. This process is repeated for the following neural layers. The basic notations with the corresponding meaning used in the MFNN are listed in Table 4.2.

The signal processing involved in each single neuron is summarized in Fig. 4.16.

Table 4.2 **Basic notations used in MFNN**

Notation	Meaning
$neuron(i,j)$	jth neuron in layer i
$s_j^{(i)}$	Output of linear combiner in $neuron(i,j)$
$x_j^{(i)}$	Output of $neuron(i,j)$
$w_{j\ell}^{(i)}$	Weight between $neuron(i,j)$ and $neuron(i-1,\ell)$
x_j	jth external input to the network
y_i	ith output of the network
n_i	Number of neurons in layer i
M	Number of layers in the network

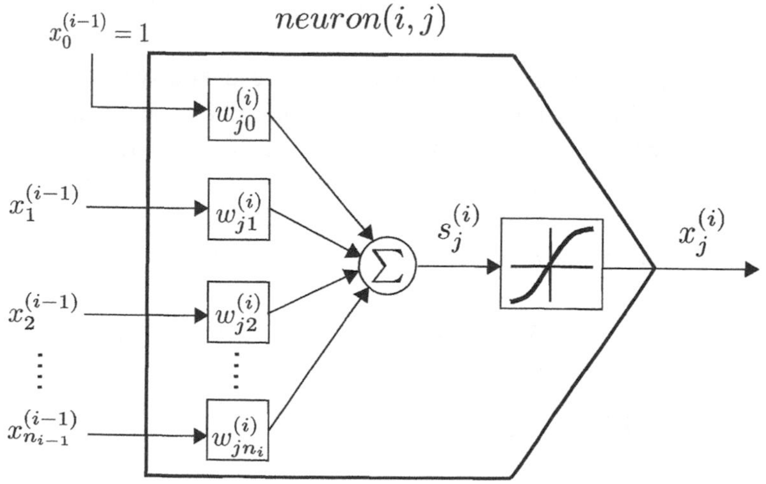

Figure 4.16 Block diagram representation for $neuron(i,j)$ in the ith layer.

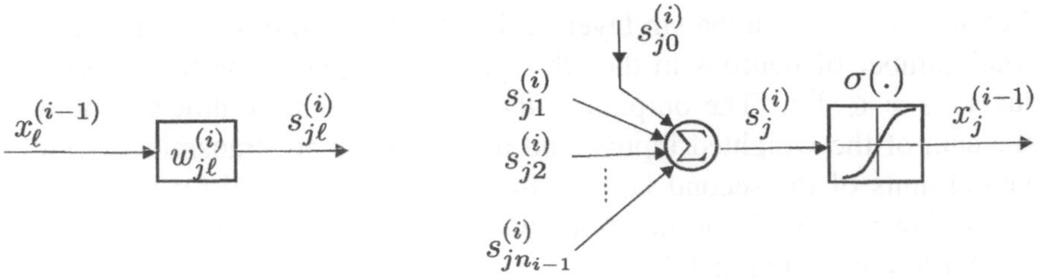

(a) synaptic operation (b) somatic operation

Figure 4.17 Synaptic and somatic operations in the $neuron(i, j)$.

A biological interpretation of the operation is demonstrated in Fig. 4.17, which defines that the neuronal operation in a single neuron consists of both synaptic and somatic operations. Mathematically, the operations of $neuron(i, j)$ are defined as

$$\text{(a)} \quad \text{Synaptic operation :} \quad s_{j\ell}^{(i)} = w_{j\ell}^{(i)} x_\ell^{(i-1)}, \quad \ell = 0, 1, \ldots, n_{i-1},\ n_0^{(i-1)} = 1 \tag{4.37}$$

$$\text{(b)} \quad \text{Somatic operation :} \quad \begin{cases} s_j^{(i)} = \sum_{\ell=0}^{n_{i-1}} s_{j\ell}^{(i)} \\ x_j^{(i)} = \sigma(s_j^{(i)}) \end{cases} \tag{4.38}$$

$$i = 1, 2, \ldots, M; j = 1, 2, \ldots, n_i$$

As a biological equivalence, the first equation represents a synaptic operation in which the signal through the synapse is multiplied by the synaptic weight (the past experience, memory), and the second and third equations implement a somatic operation that consists of the summation of all the synaptic outputs and the threshold. The nonlinear operation on this summation is shown in Fig. 4.17b. Equations (4.37) and (4.38) may be rewritten as

$$\begin{cases} s_j^{(i)} = \sum_{\ell=0}^{n_{i-1}} w_{j\ell}^{(i)} x_\ell^{(i-1)}, & x_0^{(i-1)} = 1 \\ x_j^{(i)} = \sigma(s_j^{(i)}) \end{cases} \tag{4.39}$$

$$i = 1, 2, \ldots, M; j = 1, 2, \ldots, n_i$$

where $s_j^{(i)}$ is the output of the linear combiner corresponding to *neuron* (i, j), $w_{j\ell}^{(i)}$ is the connection weight between the output of $neuron(i-1, \ell)$ and $neuron(i, j)$, $x_\ell^{(i-1)}$ is the output of $neuron(i-1, \ell)$, and $\sigma(.)$ is the nonlinear activation function. Indeed, for convenience, let $x_\ell^{(0)} \triangleq x_\ell$, $(\ell = 1, 2, \ldots, n_0 \equiv n)$ be the ℓth input of the network and $x_\ell^{(M)}$, $(\ell = 1, 2, \ldots, n_M \equiv m)$ the ℓth output of the network. A multidimensional output vector from layer $(i-1)$ is then used directly as an input vector to layer i.

The augmented forms of the neural inputs and neural weights, as introduced in Chapter 3, may be written as

$$\begin{aligned} \boldsymbol{x}_a^{(i-1)} &= \left[x_0^{(i-1)} \; x_1^{(i-1)} \; x_2^{(i-1)} \; \cdots \; x_{n_{i-1}}^{(i-1)}\right]^T, \quad x_0^{(i-1)} \equiv 1 \\ \boldsymbol{w}_{aj}^{(i)} &= \left[w_{j0}^{(i)} \; w_{j1}^{(i)} \; w_{j2}^{(i)} \; \cdots \; w_{jn_{i-1}}^{(i)}\right]^T \end{aligned}$$

The introduction of the augmented output vectors and the weight matrices is due to the existence of the thresholds in the nonlinear neural activation function. With these notations, the operation equation or transfer function of the network can be written, therefore, as

$$\begin{cases} s_j^{(i)} = (\boldsymbol{w}_{aj}^{(i)})^T \boldsymbol{x}_a^{(i-1)} \\ x_j^{(i)} = \sigma(s_j^{(i)}) \end{cases} \tag{4.40}$$

$$i = 1, 2, \ldots, M; j = 1, 2, \ldots, n_i$$

The total number of the weights n_T in such a MFNN is, thus, given by

$$n_T = \sum_{s=1}^{M} n_{s-1} n_s + \sum_{s=1}^{M} n_s \quad , \quad n_0 \equiv n$$

where the first term is the number of all the synaptic connection weights and the second term represents the number of all the thresholds.

An explicit representation of the input–output relationship of the network with n-dimensional input vector $\boldsymbol{x} \in \Re^n$ and m-dimensional output vector $\boldsymbol{y} \in [-1, 1]^m$ may be given as follows

$$\begin{aligned} \boldsymbol{y} &= \boldsymbol{\sigma}(\boldsymbol{s}^{(M)}) \\ &= \boldsymbol{\sigma}(\boldsymbol{W}_a^{(M)} \boldsymbol{\sigma}_a(\boldsymbol{s}^{(M-1)})) \\ &\vdots \end{aligned}$$

$$= \sigma(\boldsymbol{W}_a^{(M)}\boldsymbol{\sigma}_a(\boldsymbol{W}_a^{(M-1)}\boldsymbol{\sigma}_a(\cdots\boldsymbol{\sigma}_a(\boldsymbol{W}_a^{(1)}\boldsymbol{x}_a))))$$

$$\triangleq \boldsymbol{f}(\boldsymbol{W}^{(M)}, \boldsymbol{W}^{(M-1)}, \ldots, \boldsymbol{W}^{(1)}, \boldsymbol{x}) \in \Re^m \tag{4.41}$$

where

$$\boldsymbol{s}^{(i)} = [s_1^{(i)} \quad s_2^{(i)} \quad \cdots \quad s_{n_i}^{(i)}]^T$$

and

$$\begin{aligned} \boldsymbol{W}_a^{(i)} &= [\boldsymbol{w}_{a1}^{(i)} \quad \boldsymbol{w}_{a2}^{(i)} \quad \cdots \quad \boldsymbol{w}_{an_i}^{(i)}]^T \\ &= \begin{bmatrix} w_{10}^{(i)} & w_{11}^{(i)} & w_{12}^{(i)} & \cdots & w_{1n_{i-1}}^{(i)} \\ w_{20}^{(i)} & w_{21}^{(i)} & w_{22}^{(i)} & \cdots & w_{2n_{i-1}}^{(i)} \\ \vdots & \vdots & \vdots & \ddots & \vdots \\ w_{n_i0}^{(i)} & w_{n_11}^{(i)} & w_{n_i2}^{(i)} & \cdots & w_{n_in_{i-1}}^{(1)} \end{bmatrix} \end{aligned}$$

A diagram representation of this nonlinear mapping is given in Fig. 4.18. Since the nonlinear activation function $\sigma(.)$ is continuous and differentiable, the mapping function $f(.)$ in Eqn. (4.41) is a continuous and differentiable nonlinear function from the input space to the output space. Therefore, the nonlinear mapping function $f(.)$ in Eqn. (4.41), which contains many synaptic weights, may be considered as a nonlinear neural mapping function from the input pattern space to the output pattern space, where this mapping

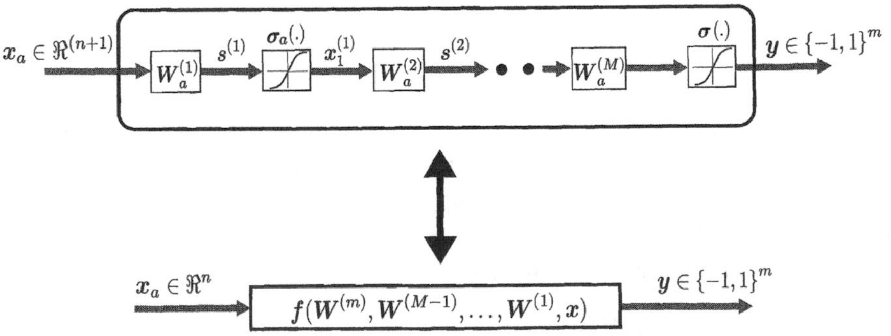

Figure 4.18 Nonlinear mapping implemented by an M-layered feedforward neural network.

function is formulated through the process of learning as opposed to being preprogramming as done in the conventional methods. In other words, in the MFNN architecture, the input information is fed forward recursively to the higher hidden layers, and finally to the output layer. It is for this reason that the networks are also called *propagation networks* (Hecht-Nielsen 1989). Since the input–output relationship of a MFNN is described by static algebraic manipulations, the neural outputs are computed in a straightforward fashion. Note that the MFNNs are static neural networks and do not have any dynamics. However, an extension of MFNN to dynamic neural networks will be introduced in Part III of this book.

4.3.2 Extension of the Generalized Delta Rule to General MFNN Structures

As seen in the previous section, the δs-based backpropagation paradigm provides a weight learning procedure for a static MFNN and is one of the most important approaches to the training of such neural networks. The interest in this backpropagation paradigm and its algorithm structure is due to the function of the progress that makes it possible to propagate the output error of the network from the output layer to the hidden layers and, thereby, to adapt the synaptic weights.

4.3.2.1 Formulation of the BP Algorithm

Assuming that the discrete-time desired output vector $\boldsymbol{d}(k)$ is given, it can be concluded that, as will be seen in a later discussion, based on the BP algorithm developed for a two-layered feedforward neural network by Rumelhart et al. (1986), an extension version of the BP algorithm to the M-layered MFNN, which minimizes the error function E defined in Eqn. (4.17) as the summation of squares of the differences between the desired output $\boldsymbol{d}(k)$ and actual neural network outputs $\boldsymbol{y}(k)$, may be given as

$$\begin{aligned} \Delta \boldsymbol{w}_{aj}^{(i)} &= -\eta \frac{\partial E}{\partial \boldsymbol{w}_{aj}^{(i)}} \\ &= \eta \delta_j^{(i)} \boldsymbol{x}_a^{(i-1)} \\ &= \eta e_j^{(i)} \sigma'(s_j^{(i)}) \boldsymbol{x}_a^{(i-1)} \end{aligned} \tag{4.42}$$

$$i = 1, 2, \ldots, M; j = 1, 2, \ldots, n_i$$

where

$$\delta_j^{(i)} \triangleq -\frac{\partial E}{\partial s_j^{(i)}} = e_j^{(i)} \sigma'(s_j^{(i)}) \tag{4.43}$$

$$e_j^{(i)} = \sum_{l=1}^{n_{i+1}} \delta_l^{(i+1)} w_{lj}^{(i+1)} \tag{4.44}$$

The starting condition for the recursive calculation is given from the output layer as follows

$$\delta_j^{(M)} = e_j^{(M)} \sigma'(s_j^{(M)}) \tag{4.45}$$

with

$$e_j^{(M)} \triangleq e_j = d_j - y_j \tag{4.46}$$

For an individual neuron the above weight learning algorithm is schematically shown in Fig. 4.19, and the feedforward and backward signal processing in Fig. 4.20. Here, the feedforward path is used to propagate the input function signal while the backward channels are designed for transmitting the output error signals.

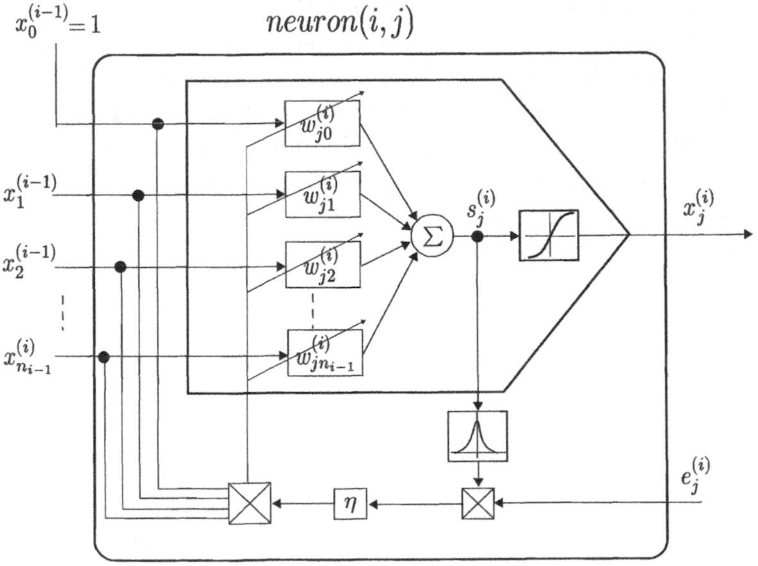

Figure 4.19 Backpropagation (BP) algorithm for the adaptation of the weights $w_j^{(i)}$ of the $neuron(i,j)$.

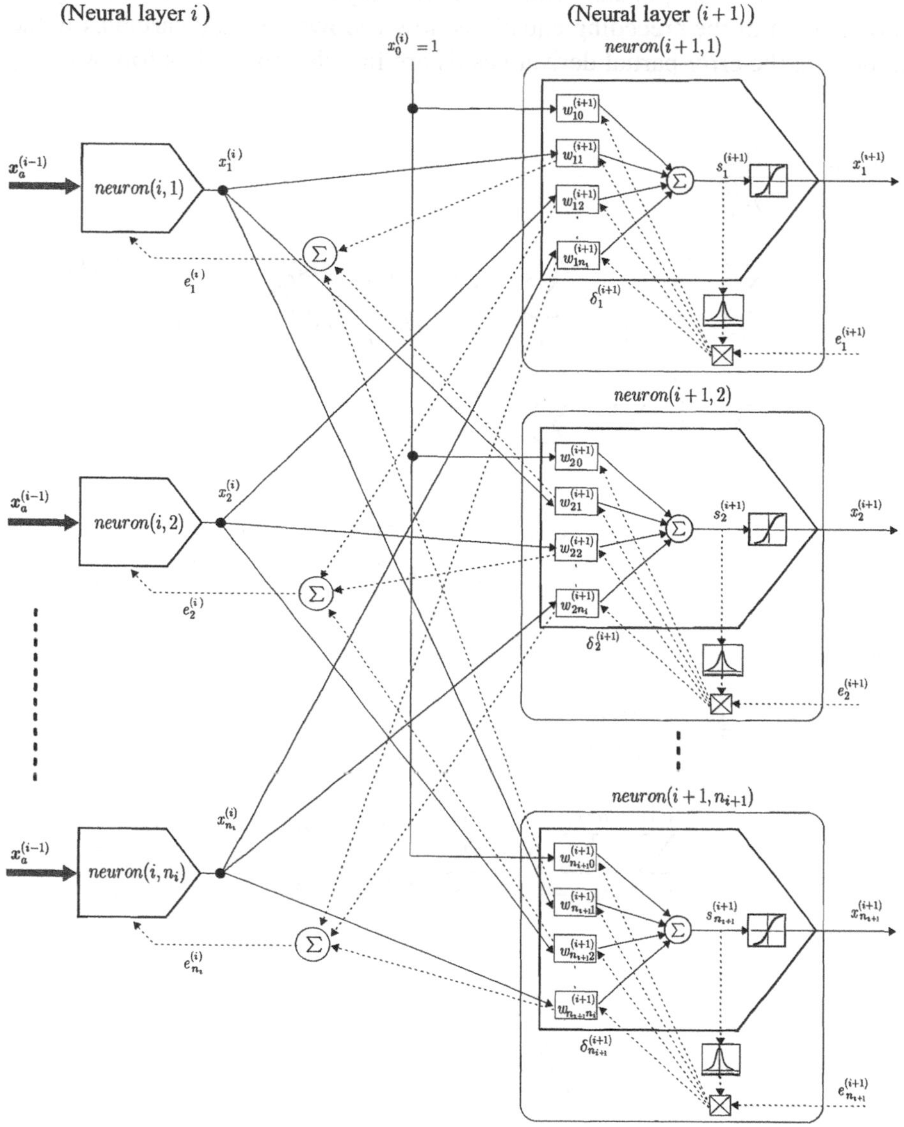

Figure 4.20 Schematic representation of the forward propagation process of the function signal (—) and backpropagation of the error signal $(\cdots\cdot)$ between the layer i and the layer $(i+1)$.

4.3.2.2 Recursive Computation of δs

The updating formulations given in Eqns. (4.42)–(4.46) involve a recursive calculation of the δs gradually from the output layer to the lower hidden layers. A derivation of the preceding equations now follows. As key variables in the algorithm, the error partial derivatives δs are first determined as follows:

$$
\begin{aligned}
\delta_j^{(i)} &\triangleq -\frac{\partial E}{\partial s_j^{(i)}} \\
&= -\sum_{\ell_M=1}^{n_M}\sum_{\ell_{M-1}=1}^{n_{M-1}}\cdots\sum_{\ell_{i+2}=1}^{n_{i+2}}\sum_{\ell_{i+1}=1}^{n_{i+1}}\frac{\partial E}{\partial s_{\ell_m}^{(m)}}\frac{\partial s_{\ell_m}^{(m)}}{\partial s_{\ell_{m-1}}^{(m-1)}}\cdots\frac{\partial s_{\ell_{i+2}}^{(i+2)}}{\partial s_{\ell_{i+1}}^{(i+1)}}\frac{\partial s_{\ell_{i+1}}^{(i+1)}}{\partial s_{\ell_i}^{(i)}} \\
&= -\sum_{\ell_{i+1}=1}^{n_{i+1}}\left(\sum_{\ell_M=1}^{n_M}\sum_{\ell_{M-1}=1}^{n_{M-1}}\cdots\right. \\
&\qquad\left.\sum_{\ell_{i+2}=1}^{n_{i+2}}\frac{\partial E}{\partial s_{\ell_m}^{(m)}}\frac{\partial s_{\ell_m}^{(m)}}{\partial s_{\ell_{m-1}}^{(m-1)}}\cdots\frac{\partial s_{\ell_{i+2}}^{(i+2)}}{\partial s_{\ell_{i+1}}^{(i+1)}}\right)\frac{\partial s_{\ell_{i+1}}^{(i+1)}}{\partial s_{\ell_i}^{(i)}}
\end{aligned}
$$

where

$$
\begin{aligned}
\delta_{\ell_{i+1}}^{(i+1)} &\triangleq -\frac{\partial E}{\partial s_{\ell_{i+1}}^{(i+1)}} \\
&= \sum_{\ell_M=1}^{n_M}\sum_{\ell_{M-1}=1}^{n_{M-1}}\cdots\sum_{\ell_{i+2}=1}^{n_{i+2}}\frac{\partial E}{\partial s_{\ell_m}^{(m)}}\frac{\partial s_{\ell_m}^{(m)}}{\partial s_{\ell_{m-1}}^{(m-1)}}\cdots\frac{\partial s_{\ell_{i+2}}^{(i+2)}}{\partial s_{\ell_{i+1}}^{(i+1)}}
\end{aligned}
$$

Thus

$$
\delta_j^{(i)} = \sum_{\ell_{i+1}=1}^{n_{i+1}}\delta_{\ell_{i+1}}^{(i+1)}\frac{\partial s_{\ell_{i+1}}^{(i+1)}}{\partial s_{\ell_i}^{(i)}}
$$

For convenience, the subscript ℓ_{i+1} is replaced with ℓ. The relationship between $s_\ell^{(i+1)}$ and $s_j^{(i)}$ implied by the following network equation

$$
s_\ell^{(i+1)} = \sum_{p=1}^{n_i} w_{\ell p}^{(i+1)}\sigma(s_p^{(i)}) + \theta_\ell^{(i+1)}
$$

yields

$$\frac{\partial s_\ell^{(i+1)}}{\partial s_j^{(i)}} = w_{\ell j}^{(i+1)} \sigma'(s_j^{(i)})$$

Therefore

$$\begin{aligned} \delta_j^{(i)} &= \sum_{\ell=1}^{n_{i+1}} \delta_\ell^{(i+1)} w_{\ell j}^{(i+1)} \sigma'(s_j^{(i)}) \\ &= e_j^{(i)} \sigma'(s_j^{(i)}) \end{aligned} \tag{4.47}$$

with

$$e_j^{(i)} = \sum_{\ell=1}^{n_{i+1}} \delta_\ell^{(i+1)} w_{\ell j}^{(i+1)} \tag{4.48}$$

The gradient of E with respect to the weight vectors is

$$\frac{\partial E}{\partial \boldsymbol{w}_{aj}^{(i)}} = \sum_{\ell=1}^{n_i} \frac{\partial E}{\partial s_\ell^{(i)}} \frac{\partial s_\ell^{(i)}}{\partial \boldsymbol{w}_{aj}^{(i)}}$$

where the second term on the right-hand side depends only on the neuron characteristics, and is not related to the error measure index E. Moreover, since

$$\frac{\partial s_\ell^{(i)}}{\partial \boldsymbol{w}_{aj}^{(i)}} = \begin{cases} \boldsymbol{x}_a^{(i)}, & \text{if } \ell = j \\ 0, & \text{otherwise} \end{cases}$$

one obtains

$$\begin{aligned} \frac{\partial E}{\partial \boldsymbol{w}_{aj}^{(i)}} &= \frac{\partial E}{\partial s_j^{(i)}} \frac{\partial s_j^{(i)}}{\partial \boldsymbol{w}_{aj}^{(i)}} \\ &= -\delta_j^{(i)} \boldsymbol{x}_a^{(i)} \end{aligned} \tag{4.49}$$

Hence, this shows the derivation of the backpropagation algorithm described by Eqns. (4.42)–(4.46). During such a BP learning phase, each pattern presentation in the output components differs, in general, from the corresponding desired (target) components. After a batch of presentations, corrections are made to the parameters of the neural network described by the weights and thresholds that minimize the mean squared error E.

So far the term *backpropagation* has been used to represent an entire supervised learning algorithm, complete with a particular choice of the neural transfer function and the weight updating rule. On the other hand, it is often convenient to use it in a more restrictive sense to represent the single component of this algorithm that determines the relevant partial derivatives by means of the backward pass. In this sense, it is simply a computational implementation of the chain rule. Thus, the *backpropagation learning algorithm* is a supervised learning algorithm that uses backpropagation to compute partial derivatives.

4.4 DERIVING BP ALGORITHM USING VARIATIONAL PRINCIPLE

The BP learning algorithm has recently emerged as one of the most efficient learning procedures for MFNNs. One reason for the success of this algorithm is its simplicity. In fact, the BP algorithm is little more than an extremely judicious application of the chain rule and the gradient descent method (LeCun 1988).

There are a number of approaches for deriving the BP algorithm. The simplest derivation is the one presented in the previous section. Alternatively, the variational principle may be used to obtain the BP algorithm formulations as proposed by Fogelman-Soulie et al. (1987) and LeCun (1988). This approach is inspired directly from the optimal control theory, which uses Lagrange multipliers to find the optimal values of a set of control variables. Variational calculus may help us find a function that minimizes an objective function subject to constraints. A procedure for obtaining the BP algorithm in terms of the variational principle is now reviewed.

4.4.1 Optimality Conditions

For a MFNN with M neural layers, the network or transfer equations of the neurons in the different layers are

$$\begin{cases} s_j^{(i)} &= (\boldsymbol{w}_{aj}^{(i)})^T \boldsymbol{x}_a^{(i-1)} \\ x_j^{(i)} &= \sigma(s_j^{(i)}) \end{cases}$$

$$i = 1, 2, \ldots, M; \quad j = 1, 2, \ldots, n_i$$

The parameter optimization problem for a specific desired task may be described as follows

$$\min_{\boldsymbol{w}} E = \tfrac{1}{2} \min_{\boldsymbol{w}} \sum_{j=1}^{n_M} (d_j - x_j^{(m)})^2 \tag{4.50}$$

To solve the problem described above, introduce the Lagrangian

$$L = \tfrac{1}{2} \sum_{j=1}^{n_M} (d_j - x_j^{(M)})^2 + \sum_{i=1}^{M} \sum_{j=1}^{n_i} \lambda_j^{(i)} \left(x_j^{(i)} - \sigma(s_j^{(i)}) \right) \tag{4.51}$$

where $\lambda_j^{(i)} \in \Re$ are Lagrange multipliers. As stated above, the Lagrangian L consists of two terms. The first term is the squared output error while the second term is due to the network equations that provide constraints on the MFNN parameters. The first variation yields

$$\delta L = \sum_{i=1}^{M} \sum_{j=1}^{n_M} \left(\frac{\partial L}{\partial \lambda_j^{(i)}} \delta \lambda_j^{(i)} + \frac{\partial L}{\partial x_j^{(i)}} \delta x_j^{(i)} + \left(\frac{\partial L}{\partial \boldsymbol{w}_{aj}^{(i)}} \right)^T \delta \boldsymbol{w}_{aj}^{(i)} \right) \tag{4.52}$$

It is easy to show that (Bryson and Ho 1969)

$$\delta L = 0 \tag{4.53}$$

is a necessary condition that defines a local minimum of the error function E with respect to the network constraint equations. This single condition, which totally describes the behavior of the network, implies the following optimality conditions

$$\frac{\partial L}{\partial \lambda_j^{(i)}} = 0 \tag{4.54}$$

$$\frac{\partial L}{\partial x_j^{(i)}} = 0 \tag{4.55}$$

$$\frac{\partial L}{\partial \boldsymbol{w}_{aj}^{(i)}} = 0 \tag{4.56}$$

$$i = 1, 2, \ldots, M; \quad j = 1, 2, \ldots, n_i$$

Each of these equations represents one of the three elements of the back-propagation network. The first equation defines the feedforward pass of the network represented by the network equations and the second, the backward propagation pass in terms of the gradient. The third equation does not imply a direct way to update the weight vectors, but it does give the optimality condition that must be fulfilled.

It is easy to show that Eqn. (4.54) implies the network equations. From Eqn. (4.55) we have

$$\begin{aligned} \lambda_j^{(i)} &= \sum_{\ell=1}^{n_i} \lambda_\ell^{(i+1)} \frac{\partial \sigma(s_\ell^{(i+1)})}{\partial x_j^{(i)}} \\ &= \sum_{\ell=1}^{n_i} \lambda_\ell^{(i+1)} w_{\ell j}^{(i+1)} \sigma'(s_\ell(i+1)) \end{aligned} \tag{4.57}$$

$$i = 1, 2, \ldots, M-1; \;\; j = 1, 2, \ldots, n_i$$

and

$$\lambda_j^{(M)} = (d_j - x_j^{(M)}), \qquad j = 1, 2, \ldots, n_M \tag{4.58}$$

The third optimality equation; that is, Eqn. (4.56) implies

$$\frac{\partial L}{\partial \boldsymbol{w}_{aj}^{(i)}} = -\lambda_j^{(i)} \frac{\partial \sigma(s_j^{(i)})}{\partial \boldsymbol{w}_{aj}^{(i)}} = 0 \tag{4.59}$$

that is

$$\lambda_j^{(i)} \sigma'(s_j^{(i)}) \boldsymbol{x}_a^{(i-1)} = 0 \tag{4.60}$$

This condition states that the weight vectors $\boldsymbol{w}_{aj}^{(i)}$ correspond to a stationary point of L, that is, a local minimum or a saddle point.

4.4.2 Weight Updating

Finding a minimum of the error function with respect to the weight vectors is equivalent to finding a minimum of L while satisfying the network equations and Eqn. (4.53). The network equations, Eqn. (4.57), and Eqn. (4.60) form a complete system for the problem represented by a two-point boundary-value problem (TPBVP). There is even no magical solution. Fortunately, the gradient descent method provides the following weight iterative algorithm

$$\boldsymbol{w}_{aj}^{(i)}(k+1) = \boldsymbol{w}_{aj}^{(i)}(k) - \eta \frac{\partial L}{\partial \boldsymbol{w}_{aj}^{(i)}(k)} \tag{4.61}$$

$$i = 1, 2, \ldots, M; \;\; j = 1, 2, \ldots, n_i$$

Substituting the results described by Eqns. (4.59) and (4.60) into the above equation yields

$$\boldsymbol{w}_{aj}^{(i)}(k+1) = \boldsymbol{w}_{aj}^{(i)}(k) + \eta \lambda_j^{(i)}(k) \sigma'(s_j^{(i)}(k)) \boldsymbol{x}_a^{(i-1)}(k) \tag{4.62}$$

$$i = 1, 2, \ldots, M; \;\; j = 1, 2, \ldots, n_i$$

which is equivalent to the BP updating formulations given in the previous section with the following relations

$$\lambda_j^{(i)} \equiv e_j^{(i)}$$

$$\lambda_j^{(i)} \sigma'(s_j^{(i)}) \equiv \delta_j^{(i)}$$

It is clear that this derivation procedure is simpler than the derivation procedure used in the last section with the gradient descent method and the chain rule. The physical meaning of the equations are not difficult to show.

4.4.3 Transforming the Parameter Space

The gradient descent method based BP learning algorithm is often considered as an iterative search for a minimum of the error function in weight space. In some cases, however, it is interesting to consider the weights not as independent variables or elementary variables, but as functions of some elementary parameters in a parameter space. The functions of utilizing these elementary parameters may be considered from two perspectives: (1) this allows the designer to insert a priori knowledge about the task into the network (e.g., some equality constraints between some weights can be enforced to make the network response invariant under certain types of input signals) and (2) when the weight space is ill-conditioned or too complicated to search, appropriate transformations can be applied to improve its geometric properties and accelerate the learning.

For this purpose, one may assume that the weights are functions of a n_p-dimensional parameter vector $\boldsymbol{p} \in \Re^{n_p}$:

$$\boldsymbol{w}_{aj}^{(i)} = \boldsymbol{w}_{aj}^{(i)}(\boldsymbol{p})$$

Then, the optimality condition given in Eqn. (4.53) becomes

$$\frac{\partial L}{\partial \boldsymbol{p}} = 0 \tag{4.63}$$

or equivalently

$$\frac{\partial L}{\partial \boldsymbol{p}} = \sum_{i=1}^{M} \sum_{j=1}^{n_i} \frac{\partial \boldsymbol{w}_{aj}^{(i)}}{\partial \boldsymbol{p}} \frac{\partial L}{\partial \boldsymbol{w}_{aj}^{(i)}} = 0 \tag{4.64}$$

Thus, an iterative algorithm for the parameter vector may be obtained as follows

$$\boldsymbol{p}(k+1) = \boldsymbol{p}(k) - \eta \frac{\partial L}{\partial \boldsymbol{p}(k)} \tag{4.65}$$

that is

$$\boldsymbol{p}(k+1) = \boldsymbol{p}(k) + \eta \sum_{i=1}^{M} \sum_{j=1}^{n_i} \lambda_j^{(i)}(k) \sigma'(s_j^{(i)}(k)) \left(\frac{\partial \boldsymbol{w}_{aj}^{(i)}}{\partial \boldsymbol{p}(k)} \right) \boldsymbol{x}_a^{(i-1)}(k) \quad (4.66)$$

It may also be assumed that several weights share a single parameter p. This then provides a method of implementing equality constraints between the weights with very little overhead.

4.5 MOMENTUM BP ALGORITHM

One of the most common variants of the standard BP algorithm is the *momentum* algorithm. In order to avoid oscillations due to a large η for rapid learning and the acceleration of the learning speed, a modified version of the backpropagation learning algorithm may be derived using the concept of momentum term suggested by Rumelhart et al. (1986).

4.5.1 Modified Increment Formulation

Let a new output error index at the current time k be based on the overall measure of the error among all the past and current patterns as

$$E_m(k) = \sum_{p=1}^{k} E(p) \quad (4.67)$$

where

$$E(p) \triangleq \frac{1}{2} \sum_{j=1}^{m} e_j^2(p)$$

is the quadratic error function and m is the number of neural outputs. Then, the gradient of the error function E_m with respect to the weight vectors is as follows:

$$\begin{aligned} \frac{\partial E_m}{\partial w_{aj}^{(i)}} &= \sum_{p=1}^{k} \frac{\partial E(p)}{\partial w_{aj}^{(i)}} \\ &= \sum_{p=1}^{k} \sum_{\ell=1}^{n_i} \frac{\partial E(p)}{\partial s_\ell^{(i)}} \frac{\partial s_\ell^{(i)}}{\partial w_{aj}^{(i)}} \end{aligned}$$

$$= -\sum_{p=1}^{k} \delta_j^{(i)}(p)\boldsymbol{x}_a^{(i-1)}(p)$$

$$= -\delta_j^{(i)}(k)x_a^{(i-1)}(k) - \sum_{p=1}^{k-1} \delta_j^{(i)}(p)x_a^{(i-1)}(p) \tag{4.68}$$

Hence, using the gradient descent method, the incremental change for the weight updating may be expressed as

$$\Delta \boldsymbol{w}_{aj}^{(i)}(k) = -\frac{\partial E_m(k)}{\partial \boldsymbol{w}_{aj}^{(i)}}$$

$$= \eta\delta_j^{(i)}(k)\boldsymbol{x}_a^{(i-1)}(k) + \eta\sum_{p=1}^{k-1} \delta_j^{(i)}(p)\boldsymbol{x}_a^{(i-1)}(p)$$

Note that the previous incremental term at time $k-1$ is defined as

$$\Delta \boldsymbol{w}_{aj}^{(i)}(k-1) = -\frac{\partial E_m(k-1)}{\partial \boldsymbol{w}_{aj}^{(i)}}$$

$$= \eta\sum_{p=1}^{k-1} \delta_j^{(i-1)}(p)\boldsymbol{x}_a^{(i-1)}(p)$$

Thus, the weight vector updating process given in the standard generalized delta rule may be modified as

$$\boldsymbol{w}_{aj}^{(i)}(k+1) = \boldsymbol{w}_{aj}^{(i)}(k) + \Delta\boldsymbol{w}_{aj}^{(i)}(k)$$

with

$$\Delta\boldsymbol{w}_{aj}^{(i)}(k) = \eta\delta_j^{(i)}(k)\boldsymbol{x}_a^{(i-1)}(k) + \Delta\boldsymbol{w}_{aj}^{(i)}(k-1) \tag{4.69}$$

Let us introduce a parameter α, $0 \leq \alpha < 1$, called the *momentum constant*, in the second term on the right side of Eqn. (4.69).

$$\Delta\boldsymbol{w}_{aj}^{(i)}(k) = \eta\delta_j^{(i)}(k)\boldsymbol{x}_a^{(i-1)}(k) + \alpha\Delta\boldsymbol{w}_{aj}^{(i)}(k-1) \tag{4.70}$$

$$i = 1, 2, \ldots, M; \quad j = 1, 2, \ldots, n_i$$

In practice α is usually set between 0.8 and 0.9. The second term on the right-hand side of Eqn. (4.70) is a momentum term that determines the influence of the past weight changes on the current direction of movement in the weight space. In this algorithm, an inertia function is built in, and the momentum in the rate of change is conserved to some degree. In fact, evaluation of the system output error over a large number of steps in the updating process to a solution will generally show that a finite α tends to dampen the oscillations but can also serve to slow the speed of the learning convergence. It will be shown analytically below that adding the momentum term is beneficial when the values η and α are well chosen.

4.5.2 Effect of Momentum Term

To further explore the function of the momentum term in the modified formulation given in Eqn. (4.70) for the weight updating process, consider a scalar form of the incremental formulation for each individual weight given by

$$\Delta w_{j\ell}^{(i)}(k) = \eta \delta_j^{(i)}(k) x_\ell^{(i-1)}(k) + \alpha \Delta w_{j\ell}^{(i)}(k-1) \tag{4.71}$$

$$i = 1, 2, \ldots, M; \quad j = 1, 2, \ldots, n_i; \quad \ell = 0, 1, 2, \ldots, n_{i-1}$$

For convenience, omit the superscripts and subscripts in this equation and define

$$g(k) = \delta_j^{(i)}(k) x_\ell^{(i-1)}(k)$$

where $g(k)$ is the error gradient. Then, the momentum equation, Eqn. (4.71), can be reexpressed as

$$\Delta w(k+1) = \alpha \Delta w(k) + \eta g(k) \tag{4.72}$$

Note that a first-order linear difference equation of a general form

$$x(k+1) = a(k)x(k) + b(k)$$

has as its solution

$$x(k+1) = \prod_{i=1}^{k} a(i)x(1) + \sum_{j=1}^{k} \prod_{\ell=j+1}^{k} a(\ell)b(j)$$

The momentum equation, Eqn. (4.72), can then be rewritten as

$$\Delta w(k+1) = \alpha^k \Delta w(1) + \eta \sum_{j=1}^{k} \alpha^{k-j} g(j) \tag{4.73}$$

since $a(k) = \alpha$ and $b(k) = \eta g(k)$.

On the other hand, since

$$\begin{cases} \Delta w(k+1) = w(k+1) - w(k) \\ \Delta w(1) = w(1) - w(0) = \eta g(0) \end{cases}$$

Equation (4.73) becomes

$$w(k+1) = w(k) + \eta \sum_{j=0}^{k} \alpha^{k-j} g(j)$$

This, in turn, is a first-order difference equation in w, which can be solved in the same way

$$\begin{cases} a(k) & = & 1 \\ b(k) & = & \eta \sum_{j=0}^{k} \alpha^{k-j} g(j) \end{cases}$$

Thus

$$w(k+1) = w(0) + \eta \sum_{\ell=0}^{k} \alpha^{\ell} \sum_{j=0}^{k-\ell} g(j)$$

Now assume that the error gradient $g(k)$ is approximately constant in a certain region of the weight space:

$$g(k) \approx g(k-1) = g$$

Hence,

$$w(k+1) = w(0) + \eta g \sum_{\ell=0}^{k} (k - \ell + 1) \alpha^{\ell}$$

Expressing the finite sum as a difference of infinite sums, and simplifying gives

$$w(k+1) = w(0) + \eta g \left[(k+1) \sum_{\ell=0}^{\infty} \alpha^{\ell} - (1 - \alpha^{k+1}) \sum_{\ell=0}^{\infty} \ell \alpha^{\ell} \right]$$

Using the binomial series expansion, this can be rewritten as

$$w(k+1) = w(0) + \eta g \left[\frac{k+1}{1-\alpha} \right] \left[1 - \frac{(1-\alpha^{k+1})}{k+1} \frac{\alpha}{1-\alpha} \right] \tag{4.74}$$

for $|\alpha| < 1$.

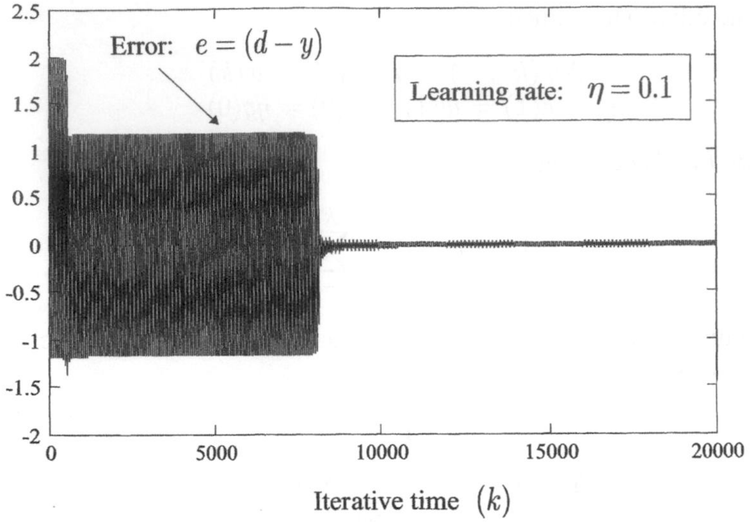

(a) The standard BP algorithm with the learning rate $\eta = 0.1$

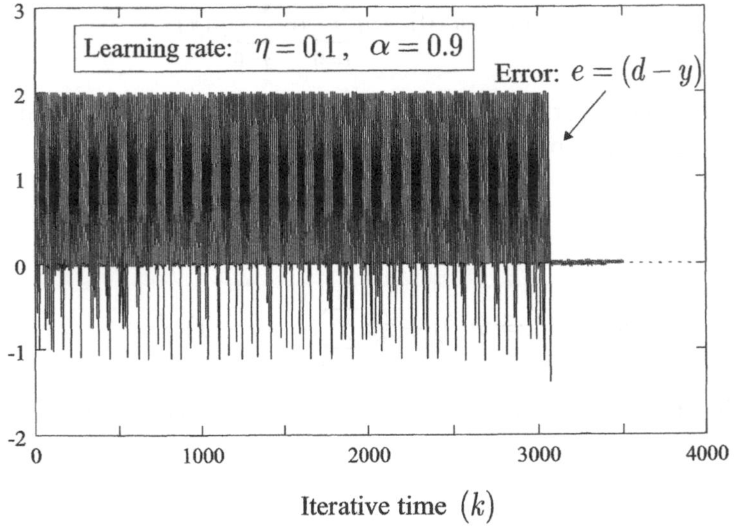

(b) The momentum version of BP algorithm with the learning rates $\eta = 0.1$ and $\alpha = 0.9$

Figure 4.21 Example 4.2: simulation results for a XOR network comparing the speed of convergence without and with the momentum term.

This equation indicates clearly the effect of the acceleration term α on the weight update formula. If the gradient is relatively small, as in a plateau, the weight increment is small, and the number of iterations to cross the plateau can be quite large. As k becomes larger, $(1-\alpha^{k+1})/(k+1)$ becomes smaller, and the effective acceleration factor approaches $1/(1-\alpha)$. The effect of the momentum term for the narrow steep regions of the weight learning space is to focus the movement in a downhill direction by averaging out the components of the gradient which alternate in sign.

Example 4.2 In this example, we will reconsider the solution for the XOR problem given in Example 4.1 in Section 4.2. For the initial weight values given in Example 4.1, and as illustrated in Figs. 4.12 and 4.21a, the standard BP algorithm with a learning rate $\eta = 0.1$ takes as many as 10,070 learning cycles, or equivalently 10,070×4 =40,280 iterations, to train the three-neuron network for implementing a two-variable XOR function. But the momentum version of the BP algorithm with the learning parameters $\eta = 0.1$ and $\alpha = 0.9$ performs the learning task, as illustrated in Fig. 4.21b, in only 877 cycles, or equivalently $877 \times 4 = 3,508$ iterations. Obviously, the convergence speed of the learning process may be improved through a suitable selection of the parameters η and α. ■

4.6 A SUMMARY OF BP LEARNING ALGORITHM

4.6.1 Updating Procedure

The key distinguishing characteristic of a MFNN with the backpropagation learning algorithm is that it forms a nonlinear mapping from a set of input stimuli to a set of outputs using features extracted from the input patterns. The neural network can be designed and trained to accomplish a wide variety of nonlinear mappings, some of which are very complex. This is because the neural units in the neural network learn to respond to features found in the input. By applying the set of formulations of the BP algorithm obtained in the previous subsection, a calculation procedure of such a learning process is summarized in Table 4.3.

In the procedure listed in Table 4.3, several learning factors such as the initial weights, the learning rate, and the number of the hidden neural layers and the number of neurons in each layer, may be reselected if the iterative learning process does not converge quickly to the desired point. This issue is dealt with in Section 4.7.

Table 4.3 **The summary of the BP learning algorithm for MFNN**

Given a finite length input patterns $x_1(k)$, $x_2(k)$, ..., $x_n(k) \in \Re$, $(1 \leq k \leq K)$ and the desired patterns $d_1(k)$, $d_2(k)$, ...,$d_m(k) \in \Re$,

Step 1: Select the total number of layers M, the number n_i $(i = 1, 2, \ldots, M-1)$ of the neurons in each hidden layer, and an error tolerance parameter $\epsilon > 0$.

Step 2: Randomly select the initial values of the weight vectors $\boldsymbol{w}_{aj}^{(i)}$ for $i = 1, 2, \ldots, M$ and $j = 1, 2, \ldots, n_i$.

Step 3: Initialization:

$$\boldsymbol{w}_{aj}^{(i)} \longleftarrow \boldsymbol{w}_{aj}^{(i)}(0), \qquad E \longleftarrow 0, \qquad k \longleftarrow 1$$

Step 4: Calculate the neural outputs

$$\begin{cases} s_j^{(i)} &= (\boldsymbol{w}_{aj}^{(i)})^T \boldsymbol{x}_a^{(i-1)} \\ x_j^{(i)} &= \sigma(s_j^{(i)}) \end{cases}$$

for $i = 1, 2, \ldots, M$ and $j = 1, 2, \ldots, n_i$.

Step 5: Calculate the output error $e_j = d_j - x_j^{(M)}$ for $j = 1, 2, \ldots, m$.

Step 6: Calculate the output delta's $\delta_j^{(M)} = e_j \sigma'(s_j^{(M)})$.

Step 7: Recursively calculate the propagation errors of the hidden neurons

$$e_j^{(i)} = \sum_{\ell=1}^{n_{i+1}} \delta_\ell^{(i+1)} w_{\ell j}^{(i+1)}$$

from the layer $M-1$, $M-2$, ..., to layer 1.

Step 8: Recursively calculate the hidden neuronal delta values:

$$\delta_j^{(i)} = e_j^{(i)} \sigma'(s_j^{(i)})$$

Step 9: Update weight vectors

$$\boldsymbol{w}_{aj}^{(i)} = \boldsymbol{w}_{aj}^{(i)} + \eta \delta_j^{(i)} \boldsymbol{x}_a^{(i-1)}$$

Step 10: Calculate the error function

$$E = E + \frac{1}{k} \sum_{j=1}^{m} e_j^2$$

Step 11: If $k = K$ then go to Step 12; otherwise, $k \longleftarrow k + 1$ and go to Step 4.

Step 12: If $E \leq \epsilon$ then go to Step 13; otherwise go to Step 3.

Step 13: Learning is completed. Output the weights.

4.6.2 Signal Propagation in MFNN Architecture

In a MFNN, with the backpropagation learning algorithm presented in the previous sections, the information propagation is performed in two directions on the synaptic connections. The input signals are propagated *forward* from the lower neural layers to the higher layers, and meanwhile the output error signals are propagated *backward* from the neurons in the output layer as shown in Fig. 4.22.

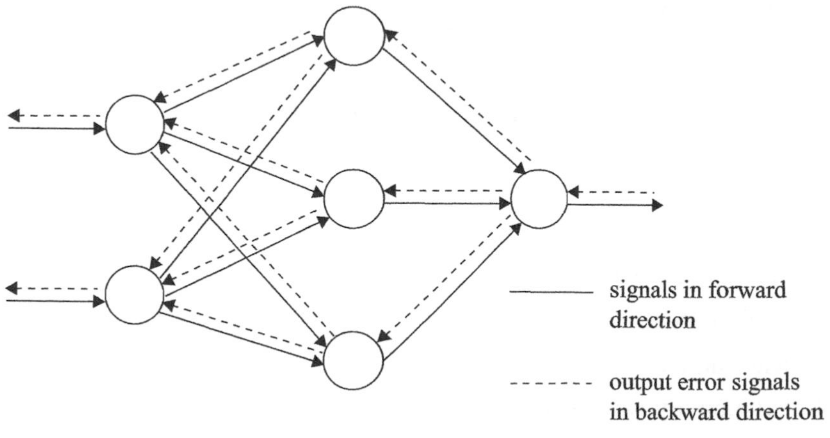

Figure 4.22 An example of a backpropagation network.

In addition to the feedforward information processing path mentioned previously, each unit of each layer receives an error feedback connection from each of the units above it. In fact, after the network output $\boldsymbol{y}(k)$ is emitted through a feedforward path at time k, each of the output units is supplied with

Table 4.4 **Neural processing in feedforward and feedback paths**

<u>*Forward Path*</u>

Synaptic Processing

Neural inputs used:	$x_p^{(i-1)}$ (where $x_0^{(i-1)} \equiv 1$)
Weight value used:	$w_{jp}^{(i)}$
Local memory value used:	None
Output:	$w_{jp}^{(i)} x_p^{(i-1)}$
Weight and local memory value update:	None

Somatic Processing (Input and Hidden Layers)
$(1 \leq i \leq M-1)$

Input used:	$w_{j0}^{(i)} x_0^{(i-1)}, w_{j1}^{(i)} x_1^{(i-1)}, \ldots, w_{jn_{i-1}}^{(i)} x_{n_{i-1}}^{(i-1)}$
Local memory value used:	None
Output:	$x_j^{(i)} = \sigma(\sum_p w_{jp}^{(i)} x_p^{(i-1)})$
Local memory value stored:	$s_j^{(i)} = \sum_p w_{jp}^{(i)} x_p^{(i-1)}$

Somatic Processing (Output Layer)

Input used:	$w_{j0}^{(M)} x_0^{(M-1)}, w_{j1}^{(M)} x_1^{(M-1)}, \ldots, w_{jn_{M-1}}^{(M)} x_{n_{M-1}}^{(M-1)}$
Local memory value used:	None
Sigmoid output:	$y_j = \sigma(\sum_p w_{jp}^{(M)} x_p^{(M-1)})$
Linear output:	$y_j = \sum_p w_{jp}^{(M)} x_p^{(M-1)}$
Local memory value stored:	$s_j^{(M)} = \sum_p w_{jp}^{(M)} x_p^{(M-1)}$

Backward Path

Synaptic Processing

Input used:	$\delta_j^{(i+1)}$
Weight value used:	$w_{j\ell}^{(i+1)}$
Local memory value used:	$x_j^{(i)}$
Output:	$w_{j\ell}^{(i+1)}\delta_j^{(i+1)}$
Weight and local memory value update:	$w_{j\ell}^{(i+1)}(k+1) = w_{j\ell}^{(i+1)}(k) + \eta\delta_j^{(i+1)}(k)x_\ell^{(i)}(k)$

Somatic Processing (Input and Hidden Layers)
$(1 \le i \le M-1)$

Input used:	$w_{1j}^{(i+1)}\delta_1^{(i+1)}, w_{2j}^{(i+1)}\delta_2^{(i+1)}, \ldots, w_{n_{i+1}j}^{(i+1)}\delta_{n_{i+1}}^{(i+1)}$
Local memory value used:	$s_j^{(i)}$
Output:	$\delta_j^{(i)} = \sigma'(s_j^{(i)})\sum_\ell w_{\ell j}^{(i+1)}\delta_\ell^{(i+1)}$
Local memory value stored:	None

Somatic Processing (Output Layer)

Input used:	d_j
Local memory value used:	$s_j^{(M)}, y_j$
Sigmoid output:	$\delta_j^{(M)} = \sigma'(s_j^{(M)})(d_j - y_j)$
Linear output:	$\delta_j^{(M)} = d_j - y_j$
Local memory value stored:	None

its component of the desired output vector $\boldsymbol{d}(k)$, starting the second backward sweep through the network (the backward path as shown in Fig. 4.23). For the neurons in the output layer, the somatic operations give $\delta_j^{(M-1)}$ and transmit these to their synaptic operations. The synaptic operations then update their weights and transmit the values $w_{\ell j}^{M}\delta_\ell^{(M-1)}$ to the neurons in the lower layer.

This process continues until the neurons of layer 1 have been updated. The cycle can then be repeated. In short, each cycle consists of the inputs to the network "bubbling forward" from the input node to the output node of the network and then the errors "percolating back" from the output node to the input node of the network. Furthermore, these information processing procedures in the forward and backward paths are summarized respectively in Table 4.4.

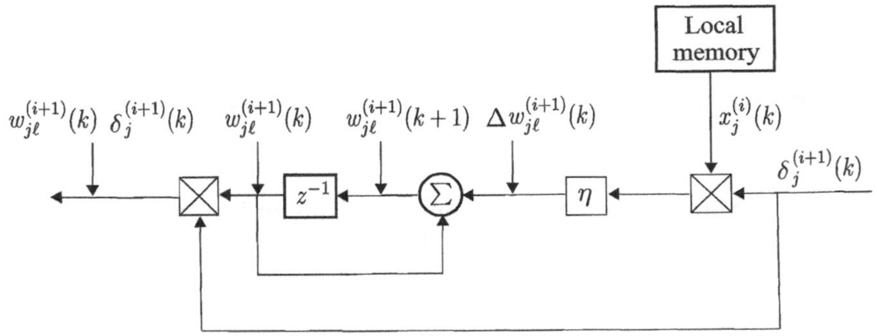

(a) The synaptic operation

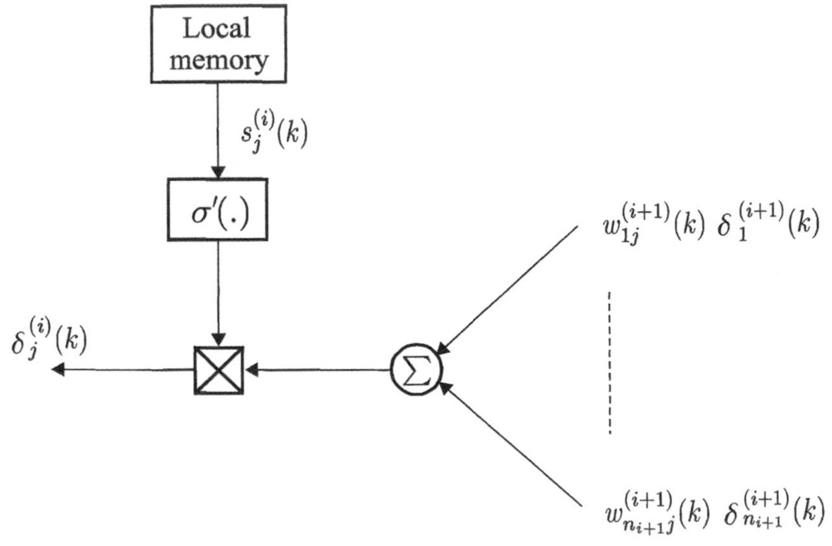

(b) The somatic operation

Figure 4.23 The backward information processing of $neuron(s,i)$.

4.7 SOME ISSUES IN BP LEARNING ALGORITHM

Although, the BP learning algorithm provides a method for training MFNNs to accomplish a specified task in terms of the internal nonlinear mapping representations, it is not free from problems. Many factors affect the learning performance and must be dealt with in order to have a successful learning process. Mainly, these factors include the initial parameters, learning rate, network size, and learning database. A good choice of these items may greatly speed up the learning process to reach the target, and we will discuss some of these issues in the following sections, although there is no universal answer for these issues.

4.7.1 Initial Values of Weights and Learning Rate

4.7.1.1 Random Selection for Initial Weights

The values of the weights selected initially in the weight space for the BP learning algorithm are one of the most important aspects that affect the learning procedure. The learning convergence, however, is theoretically independent of this initial point. It is difficult to choose the initial value of the weights so that it is as close as possible to one of the global minima in the weight space. Since a priori knowledge about the global minima is limited, the initial weights must be estimated. It is common practice to initialize randomly the weights with small values, for example, between -0.5 and 0.5. A simple methodology for selecting a better starting point is one that first chooses a few sets of the weights, and calculates the error function for these different sets. Finally, a set of the weights that correspond to the minimum value of the error function among these selections is made. It is obvious that the learning procedure does not function well if the initial values of the weights are set at the same value. The convergence of the learning procedure will not be ensued if the initial point is too far from any minimum point. In such cases, the network learning should be restarted with a new choice of the random initial weights.

4.7.1.2 Learning Rate Adaptation

The learning rate η, which determines the scale of the increments of the weight at every updating step, definitely affects the learning performance. Roughly speaking, an excessively large learning rate value may cause chattering or unstable oscillations while a very small learning rate η may slow down the learning procedure. In the conventional BP algorithm, described in the previous sections, the learning rate is assumed to be fixed and to be uniform for all the weights. Further, the learning rate is usually kept small to prevent oscillations and thus to ensure convergence.

Analytically, at the beginning of the learning, a larger learning rate η is required to move the weights rapidly toward the minimum point since a larger distance usually exists between the current point of the weights and the minimum point in the weight space during the initial stages of learning. A smaller learning rate is suitable for the final stage of the learning to avoid overshooting the solution. On the other hand, with a different surface of the error function in the weight space, which is associated with both the network structure and the task especially when the error surface has a broad minima with small gradient values, a larger value of the learning rate will result a more rapid descent. However, for cases with steep and narrow minima, a small value η should be chosen to guarantee the learning stability. This leads to the conclusion that the learning rate η should be properly chosen so that it reduces the learning time and thus obtains a faster convergence.

To select adaptively the learning rate η, many attempts have been recently carried out by researchers. Some of the results will be presented in the following discussions. The *search-then-converge* strategy was proposed by Darken and Moody (1991) and is a task-independent approach. This approach provides an adaptive formulation for η that is only a function of the learning time. In the first phase of learning, which is also called the *search phase*, the learning rate is set to a large value and then it is decreased exponentially. In the second phase, or the "convergent phase," the learning rate is set to a small value and then is decreased gradually to zero. The two possible formulations for η proposed by Darken and Moody (1991, 1992) are

$$\eta(k) = \eta_0 \frac{1}{1 + \frac{k}{k_0}} \tag{4.75}$$

and

$$\eta(k) = \eta_0 \frac{1 + \frac{c}{\eta_0}\frac{k}{k_0}}{1 + \frac{c}{\eta_0}\frac{k}{k_0} + k_0\left(\frac{k}{k_0}\right)^2} \tag{4.76}$$

where the parameters $\eta_0 > 0$, $c > 0$, and $k \gg 1$ are appropriately chosen. Since $\eta(k)$ is not very sensitive to the choice of the constant k_0, the range over which it may be chosen is large. It has been indicated that the adoption of these algorithms with the proper choice of parameters may have the potential for improving the convergence of the speed.

It is evident that the disadvantage of the preceding algorithm is linked with that of the characteristics of the network. In fact, the value of adaptive learning rate value should be kept as large as possible at each iterative step while retaining a stable learning process. To implement this goal, one of the simplest heuristic strategies for adapting η is to increase it if the total error function E is decreased and to decrease it rapidly if the new error exceeds the old error by more than a prespecified ratio. Mathematically, this process is described as (Vogl et al. 1988)

$$\eta(k) = \begin{cases} a\eta(k-1), & E(k) < E(k-1) \\ b\eta(k-1), & E(k) \geq c_1 E(k-1) \\ \eta(k-1), & \text{otherwise} \end{cases} \tag{4.77}$$

where typical values of the parameters are $a = 1.05$, $b = 0.7$, and $c_1 = 1.04$.

Except for the preceding adaptive algorithms for the learning rate that has a uniform parameter for all the weights, some local algorithms that consider the adaptation process for each learning rate parameter $\eta_{j\ell}^{(i)}$ corresponding to the individual weight parameter $w_{j\ell}^{(i)}$ are useful. In other words, each weight parameter $w_{j\ell}^{(i)}$ involved in the network is updated by the BP algorithm equation

$$\begin{aligned} \Delta w_{j\ell}^{(i)} &= -\eta_{j\ell}^{(i)} \frac{\partial E}{\partial w_{j\ell}^{(i)}} \\ &= \eta_{j\ell}^{(i)} e_j^{(i)} \sigma'(s_j^{(i)}) x_\ell^{(i-1)} \end{aligned} \tag{4.78}$$

where $\eta_{j\ell}^{(i)}$ is a learning rate parameter.

To solve this problem, the following heuristics were introduced by Jacobs (1988):

(i) When the gradient component $\partial E / \partial w_{j\ell}^{(i)}$ has the same sign for several iterations, the corresponding learning rate $\eta_{j\ell}^{(i)}$ is increased;

(ii) When the gradient component changes sign for several consecutive time steps, the corresponding learning rate $\eta_{j\ell}^{(i)}$ is reduced exponentially to allow rapid decay.

On the basis of these heuristics, a *delta–bar–delta* algorithm for adapting the learning rate $\eta_{j\ell}^{(i)}$ at each iteration time was developed by Jacobs (1988) as

$$\eta_{j\ell}^{(i)} = \begin{cases} \eta_{j\ell}^{(i)} + a, & \text{if } \bar{\delta}_{j\ell}^{(i)}(k-1)\hat{\delta}_{j\ell}^{(i)}(k) > 0 \\ b\eta_{j\ell}^{(i)}, & \text{if } \bar{\delta}_{j\ell}^{(i)}(k-1)\hat{\delta}_{j\ell}^{(i)}(k) < 0 \\ 0, & \text{otherwise} \end{cases}$$

with

$$\begin{aligned}\bar{\delta}_{j\ell}^{(i)}(k) &= \frac{\partial E(k)}{\partial w_{j\ell}^{(i)}}\\ \bar{\delta}_{j\ell}^{(i)}(k-1) &= (1-\theta)\bar{\delta}_{j\ell}^{(i)}(k)\theta\bar{\delta}_{j\ell}^{(i)}(k-1)\end{aligned}$$

where a is a parameter for an additive increase and b is a parameter for an exponential decrease in the learning rate $\eta_{j\ell}^{(i)}$, and θ is a momentum parameter. The typical ranges proposed for these parameters are

$$\begin{aligned}10^{-4} \le a \le 0.1\\ 0.5 \le b \le 0.9\\ 0.1 \le \theta \le 0.7\end{aligned}$$

On the other hand, if the momentum version of the BP algorithm is applied to train the MFNN, an adaptive process for both the learning rate η and the momentum parameter α may speed up the learning procedure. One of the simplest and most efficient algorithms with the locally adaptive algorithm for the problem was proposed by Silva and Almeida (1990). This algorithm is given by the following batch formulations

$$\Delta w_{j\ell}^{(i)}(k) = -\eta_{j\ell}^{(i)}\left[\frac{\partial E(k)}{\partial w_{j\ell}^{(i)}} + \beta\Delta_{j\ell}^{(i)}(k-1)\right]$$

where the learning rate is computed at each instant by

$$\eta_{j\ell}^{(i)} = \begin{cases} a\eta_{j\ell}^{(i)}, & \text{if } \frac{\partial E(k)}{\partial w_{j\ell}^{(i)}}\frac{\partial E(k-1)}{\partial w_{j\ell}^{(i)}} \ge 0\\ b\eta_{j\ell}^{(i)}, & \text{otherwise}\end{cases}$$

The recommended values of the parameters were obtained as

$$\begin{aligned}&1.1 \le a \le 1.3, \quad 0.75 \le b \le 0.9 \quad a \approx b^{-1}\\ &\eta_{j\ell}^{(i)} = 10^{-3}, \quad \beta = 0.1\end{aligned}$$

4.7.2 Number of Hidden Layers and Neurons

It is known that the BP learning algorithm may be used to train a layered neural network because of its efficiency. In addition to the issues of selecting the initial weights and the learning rate, the optimal numbers of the input and hidden neurons as well as the hidden layers are not known in advance. Usually, they have to be determined by trial and error. A structural capability of a MFNN for implementing a nonlinear mapping is the basic requirement for ensuring a successful learning for a desired task. Naturally, this capability may be guaranteed by the neural network structure being assigned a sufficient number of hidden neural layers and hidden neurons. From the computational point of view, one always demands as few as possible hidden layers and input and hidden neurons. Thus, the term *optimal structure* is defined here as the network that has the fewest hidden layers, and input and hidden neurons, and that is capable of performing the given task.

A simple example is given in Fig. 4.24 to explain this fact. To implement a two-variable XOR logic function, the optimal structure is a two-layered network with three neurons given in Fig. 4.24b. In fact, if the input neurons are reduced from two to one as shown in Fig. 4.24a, the network is incapable of realizing the function. On the other hand, as shown in Fig. 4.24c, even if the network with three input neurons is employed to implement the problem,

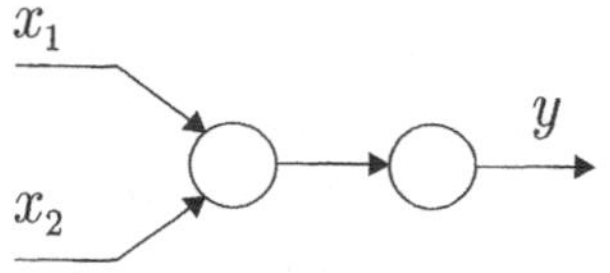

(a) The network with only single input neuron fails to implement the XOR logic function

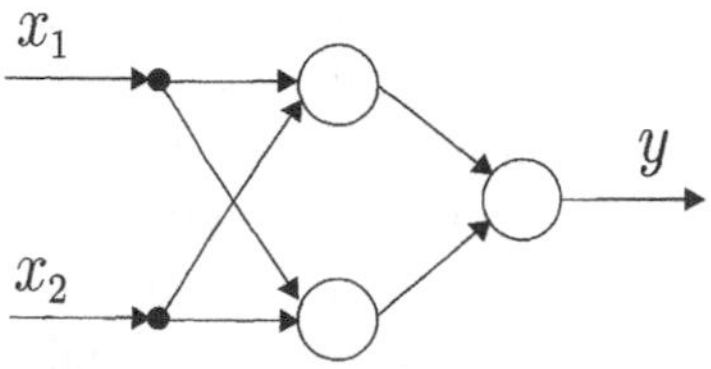

(b) The network of two input neurons is an optimal structure

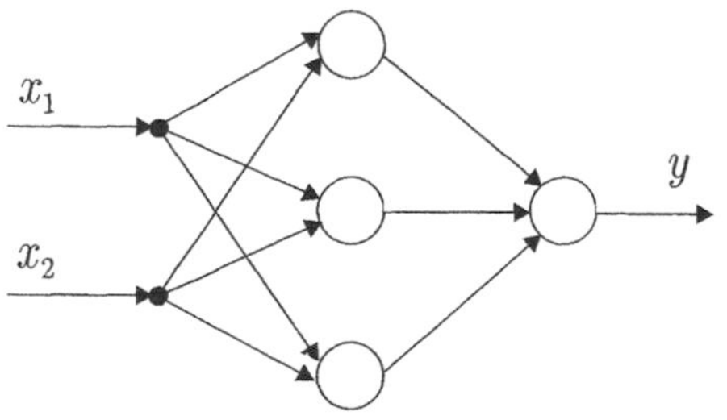

(c) The network with three input neurons increases the complexity

Figure 4.24 Two-layered network implementing the XOR logic function $y = f(x_1, x_2) = x_1 \oplus x_2$.

the unnecessary complexities of the network structure and computations are increased.

Although the number of the output neurons may easily be decided for a specific task, there is no universal criterion to determine an appropriate number of inputs and hidden units. However, a strict mathematical proof, as will be seen in a later chapter, has verified that networks with only an input layer; that is, without hidden layers, are always capable of approximating the arbitrary nonlinear mapping function. It seems sometimes that a network with two hidden layers solves the problem easier than does a network with a single hidden layer. In this case, the word *easier* indicates that the learning procedure converges faster. It has been suggested that networks with more hidden layers and fewer units in each layer may generate a better performance than "shallow" networks with many units in a single layer. However, narrow networks with many hidden layers are harder to train than the broad networks with one or two hidden layers.

Selecting the appropriate number of the neural units involved in the input and hidden layers is rarely as straightforward as determining the number of the input and output neurons. To solve this problem, two approaches of dynamically changing the number of input and hidden units may be used to optimize the structure during the learning process. The first approach (Hirose et al. 1991) initially uses a reasonable small number of input and hidden units for the learning. When a learning procedure is trapped in a local minimum, new input and hidden units are added. The learning process then proceeds because the shape of the weight space is changed. A simple example is given in Fig. 4.25, where a two-variable XOR function problem is considered. In the second approach proposed by Sietsma and Dow (1991) a network, having a larger number of the hidden units than actually required, is constructed. Redundant units are then gradually removed during the learning process. An example given in Fig. 4.26 is used to explain the procedure described above.

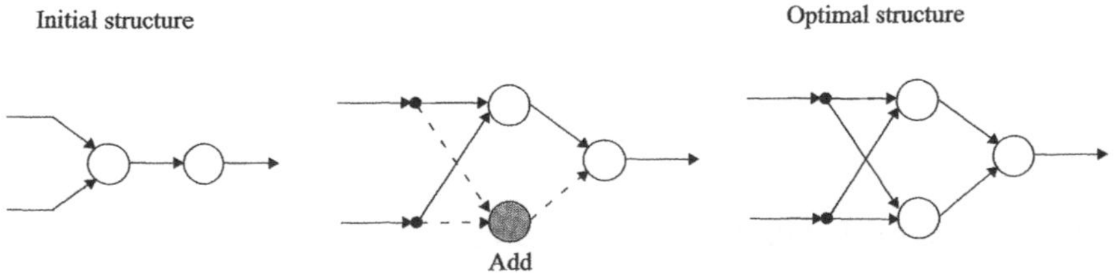

(a) Initial network (b) Adding a new unit (c) Optimal network structure

Figure 4.25 Optimizing network size by dynamical adding hidden units.

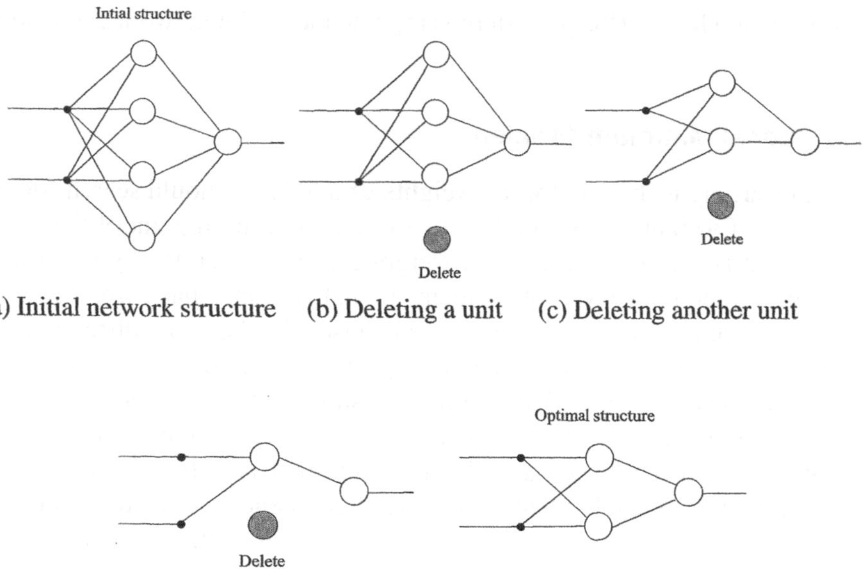

(a) Initial network structure (b) Deleting a unit (c) Deleting another unit

(d) The network is incapable of learning if one more unit is deleted (e) Optimal network structure

Figure 4.26 Optimizing network size by dynamical deleting hidden units.

It seems that the former has a more practical potential for finding a proper network size. There are two advantages of the approach in which we add dynamically new units:

(i) The computation complexity will increase slowly when a new unit is added to the input or hidden layer;

(ii) The optimal size of the network may always be obtained through such an adjustment.

An important step involved in such an iterative procedure is the approach for monitoring and examining the occurrence of the local minimum during learning. To decide when and how the input and hidden units should be added, Hirose et al. (1991) used an algorithm to conduct this task. In case the error function does not decrease or decreases very slowly, for example, less than 1% every 100 iterations for the weights, then the network is probably trapped in a local minimum or the number of input or hidden units is insufficient to ensure convergence, and a new input or hidden unit is added. The network is trained again, and if the error function E fails to decrease by more than 1% within the next 100 iterations of the learning, another unit is added to the input or hidden layer. This procedure is repeated until the network eventually converges.

4.7.3 Local Minimum Problem

An ideal learning technique for the weights of a MFNN should search for an optimal set of weights corresponding to a global minimum point of the error function that is a hypersurface in the weight space. In fact, the hypersurface of the error function may contain many global minima that correspond to different sets of the weight permutations because a MFNN with different sets of the weights may have the same output properties. However, the gradient descent method based on the BP algorithm ensures that the converged point is only a local minimum or even a saddle point. Generally speaking, the gradient descent algorithm may reach a stationary point that is either a point of the local minimum or a saddle point. Thus, the phenomenon of the local minima as shown in Fig. 4.27 may occur in the BP learning procedure. Usually, these local minima correspond to a very high level of the error surface.

Let $E(\boldsymbol{w})$ be an error function with $\boldsymbol{w} \in \Re^n$. Usually, a local minimum occurs when the partial derivative $\partial E/\partial \boldsymbol{w}$ is zero or very small but $E(\boldsymbol{w})$ is still at a very high error level. Theoretically, in a gradient descent method the searching algorithm with

$$\Delta \boldsymbol{w} = -\eta \frac{\partial E}{\partial \boldsymbol{w}} = 0$$

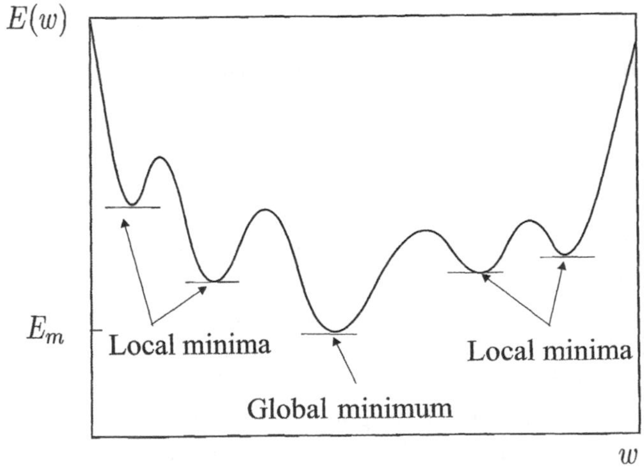

Figure 4.27 Global minimum and local minima of the error function: a one-dimensional example.

or

$$\frac{dw}{dt} = -\eta \frac{\partial E}{\partial w} = 0$$

would be stopped. Even though $E(w)$ is at a higher level in the weight space, the output errors of MFNN described with the weights learned are unacceptable. Naturally, the gradient descent searching is not capable of dropping the iterative learning from the local minimum and continuing the learning toward the global minima. At this point, an automatic judgment process for both the magnitudes of the error function and the measure of the gradient vector must be incorporated into the learning process to avoid nonstop iterations occurring at a local minimum point. If the updating procedure indicates that there are zero gradient vectors and an unacceptable error function, the procedure must be restarted by a new permutation of the initial weights, a new learning rate parameter, or a new network size, so that an acceptable value of the error function is finally obtained. Of course, if the surface of the error function is a monotonic function of the weights and does not have a local minimum, the gradient learning procedure will always converge to the global minimum. However, the descent speed becomes very low near the global minimum point, and a smaller learning rate is more effective during this period of learning for avoiding the chattering.

4.8 CONCLUDING REMARKS

Multilayered feedforward neural networks (MFNNs), as we have studied in this chapter, are capable of solving complex problems as proved in many engineering and science applications. In this chapter, we introduced the basic notion of MFNNs with the network models and adaptive learning equations as an extension of the delta rule discussed in Chapter 3.

The process of learning and adaptation associated with a MFNN was demonstrated as key features of neural networks, and was explored in detail by using the backpropagation (BP) learning algorithm. The mathematical proofs, derivations, and equations of the BP learning algorithm presented in this chapter provide a basis for further applications of MFNNs that are described mathematically by a static nonlinear mapping for many science and engineering applications. Several examples were used to help us to understand the theoretical foundations. In summary, the following important results were obtained in this chapter: (i) general mathematical model of MFNNs and (ii) adaptation or learning equations for MFNNs by using the BP learning algorithm. There are several factors that may affect the performance of a BP learning algorithm as discussed in Chapter 5.

Problems

4.1 Derive a continuous-time version of the BP learning algorithm for the MFNN.

4.2 Consider the two-layered network with three input neurons and two output neurons shown in Fig. 4.28. If an input pattern is given as

$$\begin{bmatrix} x_1 \\ x_2 \end{bmatrix} = \begin{bmatrix} -3.0 \\ 1.5 \end{bmatrix}$$

(a) Calculate $s_1^{(1)}$, $s_2^{(1)}$, $s_3^{(1)}$, $s_1^{(2)}$, $s_2^{(2)}$, y_1, and y_2;

(b) Given a desired output pattern

$$\mathbf{d} = \begin{bmatrix} d_1 \\ d_2 \end{bmatrix} = \begin{bmatrix} -1.0 \\ -2.5 \end{bmatrix}$$

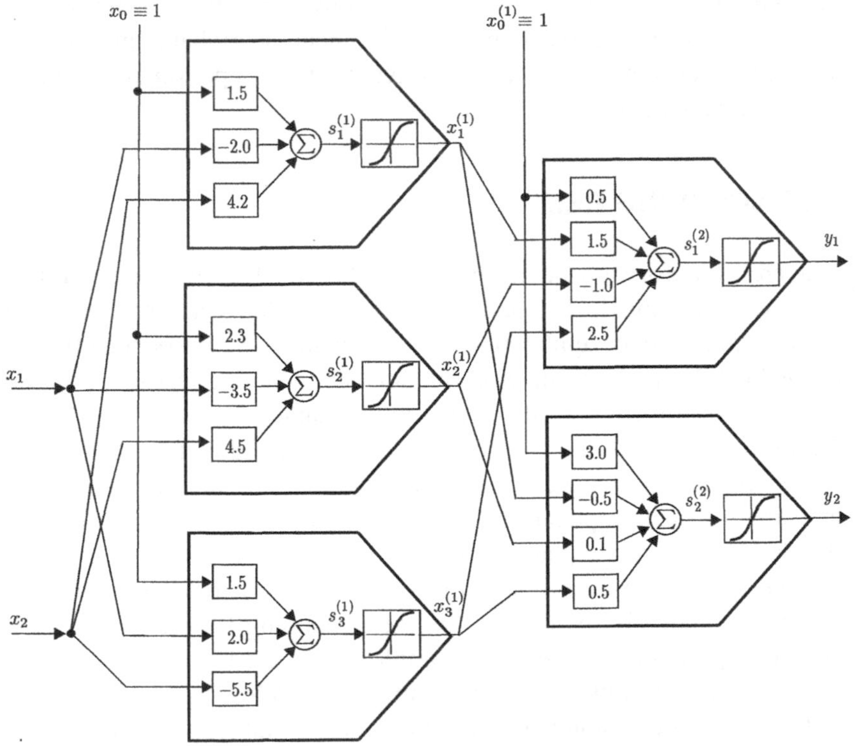

Figure 4.28 Problem 4.2: a two-layered feedforward neural network with input layer (three neurons) and output layer (two neurons).

calculate the error partial derivatives $\delta_1^{(1)}$, $\delta_2^{(1)}$, $\delta_3^{(1)}$, $\delta_1^{(2)}$, and $\delta_2^{(2)}$.

4.3 In a MFNN with $(M-2)$ hidden layers, let $\boldsymbol{W}_a^{(i)}$ represent the weight matrix of the layer i. Derive the matrix version of the BP learning algorithm for the MFNN.

4.4 A two-layered network with two input neurons and a linear output neuron is given in Fig. 4.29:

(a) Using the BP algorithm, train the three-neuron network with a linear output neuron as illustrated in Fig. 4.29 to realize a two-variable XOR function $f(x_1, x_2) = x_1 \oplus x_2$;

(b) Give a geometrical explanation for the realization of the XOR logic in the pattern plane.

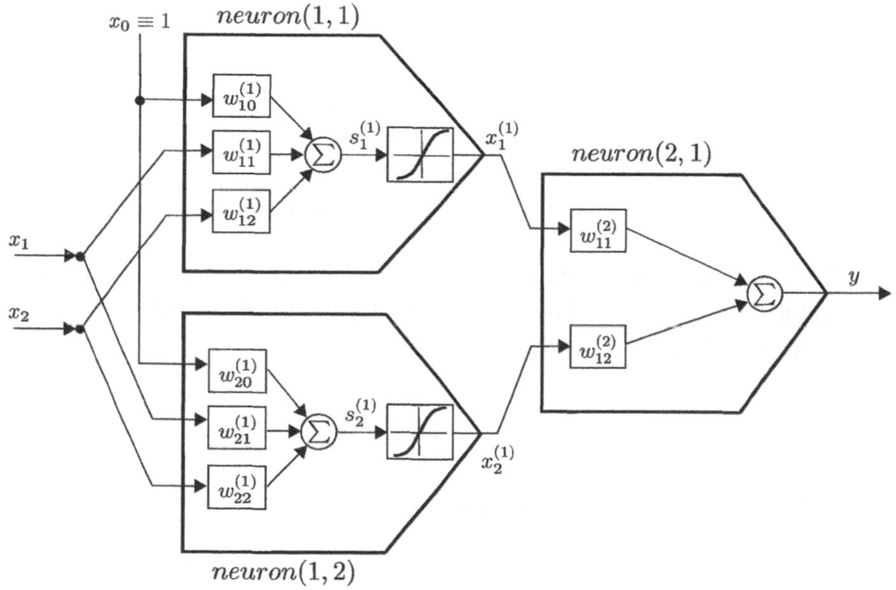

Figure 4.29 Problem 4.4: three-neuron network with a linear output unit for implementing a XOR function $f(x_1, x_2) = x_1 \oplus x_2$.

4.5 Using the BP algorithm, train a two-layered neural network with two input neurons and one output neuron to implement the logic function

$$f(x_1, x_2, x_3) = x_2(\bar{x}_1 + \bar{x}_3)$$

4.6 Given the following linearly nonseparable patterns

$$\text{Class I:} \quad x_1 = \begin{bmatrix} 1 \\ 0 \end{bmatrix}, \quad x_2 = \begin{bmatrix} 2 \\ 1 \end{bmatrix}, \quad x_3 = \begin{bmatrix} 4 \\ 1 \end{bmatrix}, \quad x_4 = \begin{bmatrix} -5 \\ 1 \end{bmatrix}$$

$$\text{Class II:} \quad x_5 = \begin{bmatrix} 1 \\ 2 \end{bmatrix}, \quad x_6 = \begin{bmatrix} -2 \\ 2 \end{bmatrix}, \quad x_7 = \begin{bmatrix} 3 \\ 4 \end{bmatrix}, \quad x_8 = \begin{bmatrix} 1 \\ -1 \end{bmatrix}$$

(a) Design a two-layered network to classify these two class patterns;

(b) Give a geometric interpretation of the nonlinear mapping implemented by the network in the pattern plane.

4.7 A three-variable XOR function is defined as

$$\begin{aligned} y &= f(x_1, x_2, x_3) \\ &= (x_1 \oplus x_2) \oplus x_3 = x_1 \oplus (x_2 \oplus x_3) = x_1 \oplus x_2 \oplus x_3 \end{aligned}$$

The eight learning patterns are given in Table 4.5. Using the BP algorithm, train a two-layered network for the implementation of this three-variable XOR function.

Table 4.5 **Truth table of XOR function** $f(x_1, x_2, x_3) = x_1 \oplus x_2 \oplus x_3$

Pattern	Input x_1	Input x_2	Input x_3	Output y
A	-1	-1	-1	-1
B	-1	-1	1	1
C	-1	1	-1	1
D	-1	1	1	-1
E	1	-1	-1	1
F	1	-1	1	-1
G	1	1	-1	-1
H	1	1	1	1

4.8 Give a geometric explanation for the three-variable XOR network obtained in Problem 4.7 in the three-dimensional pattern space shown in Fig. 4.30.

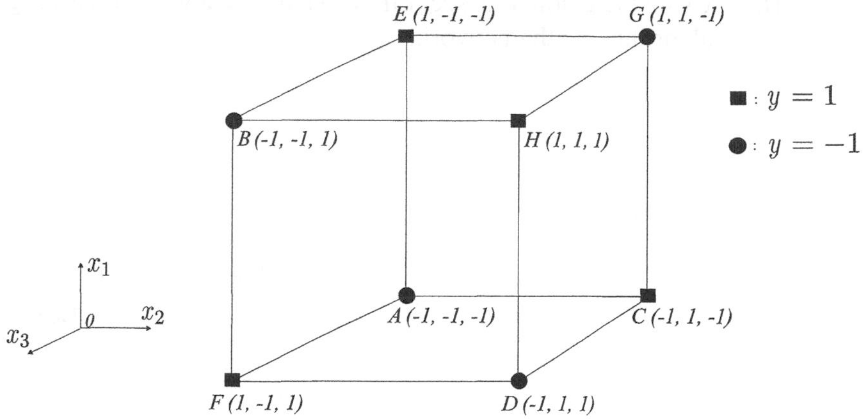

Figure 4.30 Problem 4.8: three-dimensional pattern space for the XOR function $y = f(x_1, x_2, x_3) = x_1 \oplus x_2 \oplus x_3$.

4.9 Find the optimal network size of a two-layered network that is capable of implementing the three-variable XOR logic function given in Problem 4.7.

4.10 A two-element threshold network is illustrated in Fig. 4.31:

(a) Write the input–output equation $y = y(x_1, x_2)$;

(b) Find a solution of the weights such that a two-variable XOR function $f(x_1, x_2) = x_1 \oplus x_2$ is implemented by the network;

(c) Give the separating plane provided by the network.

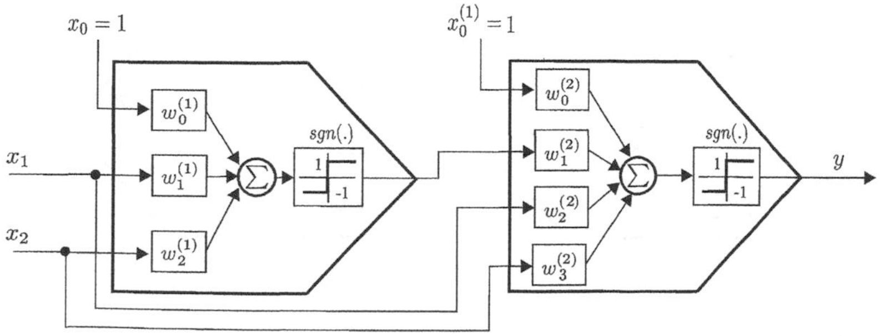

Figure 4.31 Problem 4.10: two-element threshold network with two inputs.

4.11 A two-layered feedforward network with fully feedforward interlayer connections is given in Fig. 4.32:

(a) Give input–output equations for the network;

(b) Using the gradient descent method, derive a weight learning algorithm for the network.

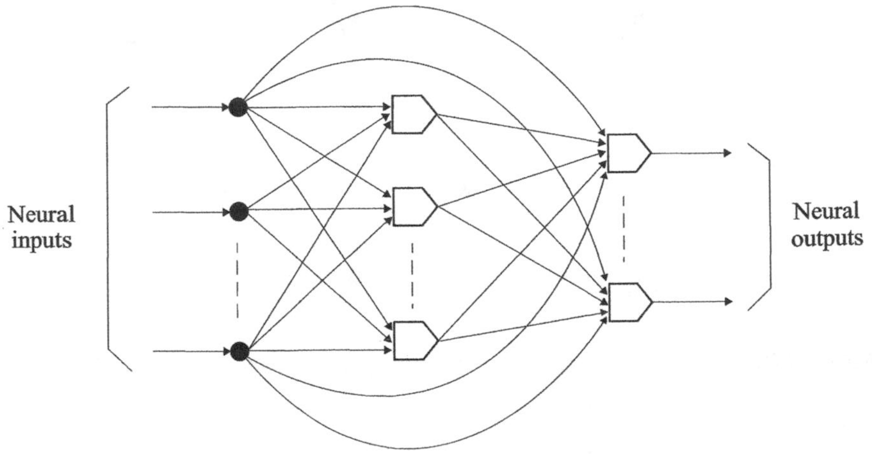

Figure 4.32 Problem 4.11: two-layered feedforward neural network with fully feedforward interlayer connections.

4.12 Using the learning algorithm obtained in Problem 4.11, train the two-input, two-neuron network shown in Fig. 4.33 such that a two-variable XOR function is implemented by the network.

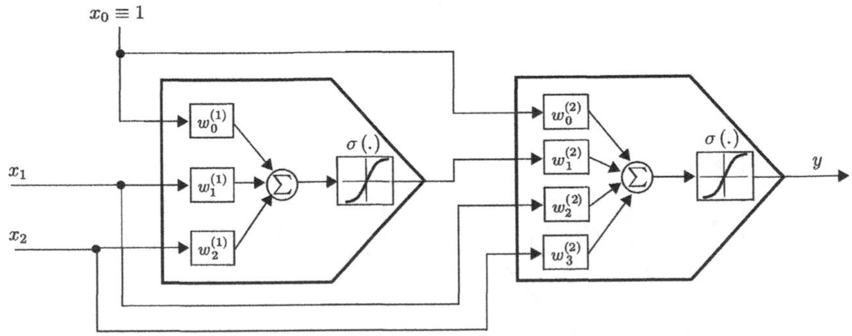

Figure 4.33 Problem 4.12: two-layered feedforward neural network for implementing a two-variable XOR function.

4.13 Using the BP algorithm, design a two-layered feedforward network to approximate the following nonlinear functions:

(a) $y_1 = f_1(x_1, x_2) = \sin(x_1 + x_1 x_2 + x_2);$

(b) $y_2 = f_2(x_1, x_2) = \dfrac{x_1 + x_1 x_2}{1 + x_1^2 + x_2^2}.$

4.14 Show mathematically why the BP algorithm will not converge if all the initial weights are selected as the same value.

4.15 Consider a sigmoid activation function $\sigma(x) = \tanh(\lambda x)$ where λ is the gain. If every neuron in a MFNN has a gain parameter $\lambda_j^{(i)}$, derive the updating formulation in terms of the gradient descent method:

$$\Delta \lambda_j^{(i)} = -\eta \frac{\partial E}{\partial \lambda_j^{(i)}}$$

4.16 Using the network equations of the MFNN, variational equation for optimality and Eqn. (4.55), derive Eqn. (4.57).

4.17 Explain why the MFNN network equation [Eqn. (4.57)] and Eqn. (4.60) form a so-called a two-point boundary-value problem (TPBVP). Give an alterative solution for this problem.

4.18 Verify the following partial derivative formulations of the outputs of a MFNN with respect to the weight vectors

$$\frac{\partial x_j^{(M)}}{\partial \boldsymbol{w}_{aj}^{(i)}} = \bar{\delta}_{j\ell}^{(i)} \boldsymbol{x}_a^{(i-1)}$$

where

$$\bar{\delta}_{j\ell}^{(i)} = \frac{\partial x_j^{(M)}}{\partial s_\ell^i} = \sum_{p=1}^{n_{i+1}} \bar{\delta}_{jp}^{(i+1)} w_{p\ell}^{(i+1)} \sigma'(s_\ell^{(i)})$$

with the initial condition

$$\bar{\delta}_{j\ell}^{(M)} = \begin{cases} 1, & \text{if } j = \ell \\ 0 \end{cases}$$

4.19 When the weight updating is moving through a plateau region of the error function surface, the gradient component $\partial E/\partial w_{j\ell}^{(i)}$ will be approximated by a constant at each timestep. Show that in this case the momentum BP learning algorithm may be approximately represented as

$$\begin{aligned}\Delta w_{j\ell}^{(i)}(k) &= -\eta \frac{\partial E}{\partial w_{j\ell}^{(i)}(k)} + \alpha \Delta w_{j\ell}^{(i)}(k-1) \\ &\approx -\frac{\eta}{1-\alpha} \frac{\partial E}{\partial w_{j\ell}^{(i)}(k)}\end{aligned}$$

where $0 \leq \alpha < 1$. This result means that the effective learning rate increases to the new value $\eta/(1-\alpha)$.

5

Advanced Methods for Learning and Adaptation in MFNNs

5.1 Different Error Measure Criteria

5.2 Complexities in Regularization

5.3 Network Pruning through Sensitivity Calculations

5.4 Evaluation of the Hessian Matrix

5.5 Second-Order Optimization Learning Algorithms

5.6 Linearized Recursive Estimation Learning Algorithms

5.7 Tapped Delay Line Neural Networks (TDLNNs)

5.8 Applications of TDLNNs for Adaptive Control Systems

5.9 Concluding Remarks

Problems

The basic topics of multilayered feedforward neural networks (MFNNs), such as the network structures, mathematical descriptions, and backpropagation (BP) learning algorithms were discussed extensively in the previous chapters. Beyond these aspects, significant progress has been made on many related issues. In fact, numerous extensions to the basic MFNNs with the BP algorithm have emerged. Most of these were developed to overcome some of the inherent limitations of the basic BP learning algorithms.

In order to provide a more comprehensive viewpoint of the neural network structures and learning algorithms for MFNNs, some further problems associated with MFNNs are presented in this chapter. First, the alternative error measure criteria for the standard BP learning algorithm, where a least squares error index is employed, are addressed in Section 5.1. Complex regularization techniques are then discussed in Section 5.2 for both improving the generalization capability of MFNNs and pruning the networks. Sensitivity-calculation-based network pruning techniques for the purpose of optimizing the network structure and accelerating the learning phase are then studied in Section 5.3. In Section 5.4, a procedure for dealing with the second derivatives of MFNNs is discussed. To improve the convergence speed of the BP algorithm, some commonly used second-order optimization methods are presented in Section 5.5. An important class of supervised learning algorithms for static feedforward neural networks, the linearized recursive estimation methods, are discussed in Section 5.6. MFNNs with tapped delay inputs and outputs signals are introduced for applications such as system identification, control systems, and channel equalization in Section 5.7. An application of such neural networks for nonlinear adaptive control is studied in Section 5.8.

5.1 DIFFERENT ERROR MEASURE CRITERIA

As shown in Fig. 5.1, the BP algorithm, or the generalized delta rule, for the weight learning involved in a MFNN can be interpreted as an optimization process where one of the most important choices is the selection of an optimality index or error function that gives a suitable global measure of the distribution of the errors. The choice of an appropriate error measure norm can be crucial for obtaining a reasonable solution of the problem at hand. Several criteria exist to define an optimality index. Among them, those based on an L_p norm ($1 \leq p \leq \infty$) have the advantage of allowing an easy mathematical formulation. In particular, the least squares (LS) criterion (L_2 norm criterion) is widely used because of its simplicity. In this section, we focus on MFNNs with a BP algorithm. A general framework is proposed within which it is possible to justify the selection of a particular L_p norm for carrying out the BP learning procedure. On the other hand, if some stochastic factors are

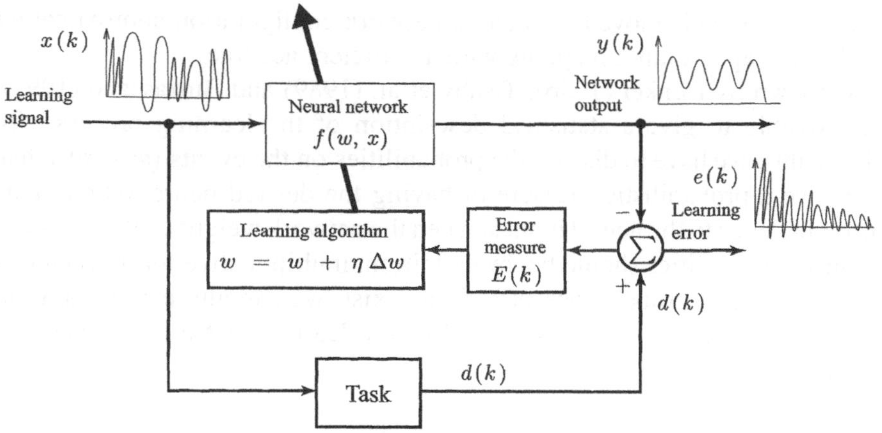

Figure 5.1 The weight learning process for neural networks.

considered for MFNNs, the choice of a particular L_p norm must be linked to the particular distribution of the output errors because the particular L_p norm is an overall measure of the output error components. Consequently, the effort is to define a correspondence between the error distributions and the L_p norms.

5.1.1 Error Distributions and L_p Norms

The BP algorithm discussed in Chapter 4 relies on a quadratic error measure, regardless of the output error distributions. The focal point of the following discussion was developed by Burrascano (1991). It is to define a possible link between the error distribution at the output of a MFNN and the L_p norms. Given a set of n-dimensional neural input vector $\boldsymbol{x} \in \Re^n$ and an m-dimensional desired neural output vector $\boldsymbol{d} \in \Re^m$, what is generally used for the learning phase of a MFNN is an additive error function

$$E(\boldsymbol{w}, \boldsymbol{x}) = \sum_{i=1}^{m} e_i(d_i, \boldsymbol{x}) = \sum_{i=1}^{m} D\left(d_i - y_i(\boldsymbol{x})\right) \tag{5.1}$$

where $D(.)$ denotes a distance measure between the ith desired output d_i and the ith current network output $y_i(\boldsymbol{x})$ for a given input $\boldsymbol{x}$. If we consider the n_t-dimensional Euclidean space $\Re^{n_t}$, where n_t is the number of parameters consisting of all the weights and thresholds involved in the network, the learning algorithm provides a strategy to minimize the error function. The point $\boldsymbol{w}$ defining all the weights and thresholds in the network configuration space ($\boldsymbol{w} \in \Re^{n_t}$) is moved to obtain a network configuration approximating the desired input–output mapping with a sufficient accuracy.

As shown by Denker (1986), Tishby et al. (1989) and Burrascano (1991), it is possible to give a statistical description of the learning process. To achieve this, we have to discuss the probabilities on the events $(\boldsymbol{x}, d_i|\boldsymbol{w})$, that is, to give a probabilistic measure of having the desired neural output d_i in correspondence to the neural input $\boldsymbol{x}$ when the network weight configuration is $\boldsymbol{w}$. Such probabilities should be, by definition, multiplicative for independent samples. If such probabilities $p(\boldsymbol{x}, d_i|\boldsymbol{w})$ exist, we can alternately train the network by maximizing the likelihood of the learning set over the network parameters:

$$\max_{\boldsymbol{w} \in \Re^{n_t}} P(\boldsymbol{x}, \boldsymbol{d}|\boldsymbol{w}) \triangleq \max_{\boldsymbol{w} \in \Re^{n_t}} \prod_{i=1}^{m} p(\boldsymbol{x}, d_i|\boldsymbol{w}) \tag{5.2}$$

A fundamental requirement is that this maximization of the likelihood must be equivalent to the minimization of the additive error given in Eqn. (5.1) for every set of independent learning points. The only way that these two optimization criteria can be simultaneously fulfilled is if the error functions are directly related through an arbitrary monotonic and smooth function ϕ:

$$\prod_{i=1}^{m} p(\boldsymbol{x}, d_i|\boldsymbol{w}) = \phi\left(\sum_{i=1}^{m} e(\boldsymbol{x}, d_i|\boldsymbol{w})\right) \tag{5.3}$$

This equation puts a strong constraint on the possible form of $p(\boldsymbol{x}, d_i|\boldsymbol{w})$. It can be shown that the only solution to the functional equation [Eqn. (5.3)] for the smooth positive error function $e(\boldsymbol{x}, d_i|\boldsymbol{w})$ is given by

$$\begin{aligned} p(\boldsymbol{x}, d_i|\boldsymbol{w}) &= \frac{1}{z(\beta)} \exp\Big(-\beta e(\boldsymbol{x}, d_i|\boldsymbol{w})\Big) \\ z(\beta) &= \int_{X,D} \exp\Big(-\beta e(\boldsymbol{x}, \zeta|\boldsymbol{w})\Big)\, d\boldsymbol{x}\, d\zeta \end{aligned} \tag{5.4}$$

where $X \in \Re^{n}$ and $D \in \Re^{n_t}$ are the admissible sets of the input signal vector $\boldsymbol{x}$ and the weight vector $\boldsymbol{w}$, respectively, and β is a positive constant that determines the sensitivity of the probability $p(\boldsymbol{x}, d_i|\boldsymbol{w})$ to the error values.

Moreover, let the error function be defined in the L_p norm

$$e(\boldsymbol{x}, d_i|\boldsymbol{w}) = |d_i - y_i(\boldsymbol{x})|^{p} \tag{5.5}$$

for $\boldsymbol{x} \in X$. If we can model the data distribution in the domain T with a uniform distribution

$$p_I(\boldsymbol{x}|\boldsymbol{w}) = \int_T p(\boldsymbol{x}, \zeta|\boldsymbol{w}) d\zeta = \frac{1}{k} \tag{5.6}$$

then

$$p(d_i|\boldsymbol{x}, \boldsymbol{w}) = \frac{p(\boldsymbol{x}, d_i|\boldsymbol{w})}{p_I(\boldsymbol{x}|\boldsymbol{w})} = kp(\boldsymbol{x}, d_i|\boldsymbol{w}) \tag{5.7}$$

and, therefore, Eqn. (5.7) gives us the desired result: when the output error function is defined in the L_p norm, the consistent $p(d_i|\boldsymbol{x}, \boldsymbol{w})$ is the generalized Gaussian of the order of p

$$p(d_i|\boldsymbol{x}, \boldsymbol{w}) = \frac{k}{z(\beta)} \exp\left(-\beta|d_i - y_i(\boldsymbol{x})|^p\right) \tag{5.8}$$

In particular, for $p = 2$ (the quadratic error function in the range T), one has

$$p(d_i|\boldsymbol{x}, w) = \sqrt{2\pi\sigma^2} \exp\left(-\frac{[d_i - y_i(\boldsymbol{x})]^2}{2\sigma^2}\right) \tag{5.9}$$

with

$$\beta = \frac{1}{2\sigma^2}, \qquad z(\beta) = k\sqrt{\frac{\pi}{\beta}} \tag{5.10}$$

5.1.2 The Case of Generic L_p Norm

In the backpropagation paradigm, as presented in the previous chapters, the learning procedure is based on the minimization of a quadratic error measure that is actually an error function defined by the square of the L_2 norm of the output error vector. Now, let us investigate how the generalized delta rule must be changed in order to perform a minimization in the pth power of the generic L_p norm. We may reflect that the characteristic that renders the backpropagation rule particularly interesting is the fact that the gradient of the error function with respect to the weight vectors can be evaluated in a simple way in terms of the definition of the derivative δs since

$$\begin{aligned}\frac{\partial E}{\partial \boldsymbol{w}_{aj}^{(i)}} &= \sum_{l=1}^{n_i} \frac{\partial E}{\partial s_l^{(i)}} \frac{\partial s_l^{(i)}}{\partial \boldsymbol{w}_{aj}^{(i)}} \\ &= -\delta_j^{(i)} \frac{\partial s_j^{(i)}}{\partial \boldsymbol{w}_{aj}^{(i)}}\end{aligned}$$

where

$$\delta_j^{(i)} = -\frac{\partial E}{\partial s_j^{(i)}}$$

and the second term on the right-hand side depends on only the neural characteristics, and is not related to the error measure index E. Furthermore, note that the recursive algorithm for the δs of the hidden layers given by

$$\delta_j^{(i)} = \sum_{l=1}^{n_{i+1}} \delta_l^{(i+1)} w_{lj}^{(i+1)}$$

must start from the initial condition given in the output layer:

$$\begin{aligned}\delta_j^{(M)} &= -\frac{\partial E}{\partial s_j^{(M)}} \\ &= \frac{\partial E}{\partial y_j} \sigma'(s_j^{(M)}) \qquad (5.11)\end{aligned}$$

Thus, for a different definition of the error function E, only the formulations for the derivative δs of the output layer have to be modified. In fact, when the error function is defined in terms of the generic L_p $(1 \leq p < \infty)$ norm as follows

$$E = \frac{1}{p} \sum_{j=1}^{m} |d_j - y_j(\boldsymbol{x})|^p \qquad (5.12)$$

one may easily obtain

$$\begin{aligned}\frac{\partial E}{\partial y_j} &= -sgn\Big(d_j - y_j(\boldsymbol{x})\Big) |d_j - y_j(\boldsymbol{x})|^{p-1} \\ &= -sgn(e_j)|e_j|^{p-1} \qquad (5.13)\end{aligned}$$

The formulations for the δs of the output layer are then given by

$$\delta_j^{(M)} = -sgn(e_j)|e_j|^{p-1}\sigma'(s_j^{(M)}) \qquad (5.14)$$

On the other hand, it can be seen that a modified version of the delta formulations for the output layer in the particular case of the L_∞ norm may be of some special interest. The problem of defining an L_∞ version error function of the generalized delta rule must be approached by showing how the overall error measure E^∞ is employed starting from the output error components, and how the derivative $\partial E^{\infty}/\partial s_l^{(i)}$ can be evaluated. Let us define the error function in the Chebyshev case as

$$E^{\infty} = \max\Big[\, |d_j - y_j(\boldsymbol{x})| : j = 1, 2, \ldots, m\Big] \tag{5.15}$$

where max[.] denotes a function selecting the largest component in the error vector defined by $[\boldsymbol{d} - \boldsymbol{y}(\boldsymbol{x})]$. The preceding definition implies that the overall error measure E^{∞} equals the largest component of the error vector, while all the other error components are neglected. Let us denote the index of this output error component with j^*:

$$|d_{j^*} - y_{j^*}(\boldsymbol{x})| = \max\Big[\, |d_j - y_j(\boldsymbol{x})| : j = 1, 2, \ldots, m\Big]$$

As far as the output layer is concerned, one has

$$\begin{aligned}
\delta_j^{(M)} &= -\frac{\partial E^{\infty}}{\partial s_j^M} \\
&= \begin{cases} 0, & \text{if } j \neq j^* \\ -sgn\left(d_{j^*} - y_{j^*}(\boldsymbol{x})\right) \sigma'(s_{j^*}^{(M)}), & \text{if } j = j^* \end{cases} \\
&= \begin{cases} 0, & \text{if } j \neq j^* \\ -sgn(e_{j^*}^{(M)})\sigma'(s_{j^*}^{(M)}), & \text{if } j = j^* \end{cases}
\end{aligned}$$

Thus, the maximum output error in the output layer is propagated back to the lower layers during the learning phase. In a practical updating process, this unit with the maximum error must be determined at each instant.

5.2 COMPLEXITIES IN REGULARIZATION

The concept of generalization for a neural network is used to measure how well the network performs on the actual problem once learning is complete. It is usually tested by evaluating the performance of the network on the new data set outside the learning set. As shown in Fig. 5.2, generalization is mainly influenced by three factors: the number and performance of the learning data samples, which represent how well the problem at hand is characterized, the complexity of the learning algorithm employed, and the network size. Generally speaking, a larger number of learning data samples can provide a better representation for the underlying problem, and if a suitable learning algorithm and network size are used, a better solution to the problem should be obtained. The third factor, the network size of the generalization for the neural networks, is discussed in the following text.

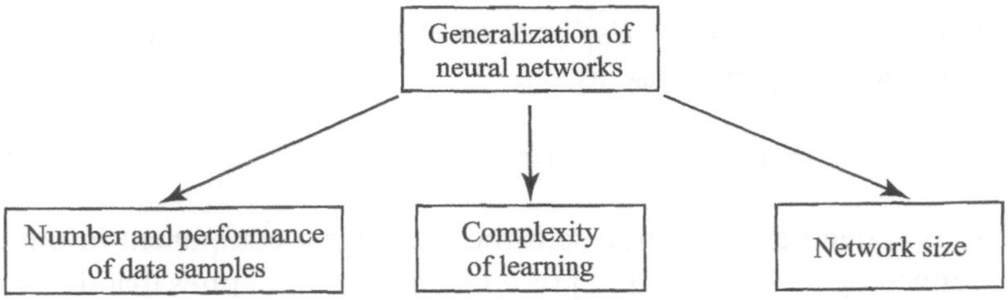

Figure 5.2 Factors influencing the generalization for neural networks.

It is generally admitted that the generalization of performance of the back-propagation architecture will depend on the relative size of the training data and the trained network. However, it is observed that the BP networks are sometimes very slow in learning. This is because the synaptic connection weights, especially the hidden connection weights (connections among hidden neurons), are significantly smaller for a large network. This means that the networks cannot utilize hidden connections efficiently. Thus, hidden neurons cannot be appropriately used in speeding up the learning. This situation is illustrated in Fig. 5.3. The network in Fig. 5.3a is a BP network in which the hidden connections among the hidden neurons are inactive, while the input and output connections are active. If the hidden connections are weak; that is, the absolute values of the hidden weights are small, it is certain that the hidden neurons are not appropriately used in speeding up the learning. As shown in Fig. 5.3b, some hidden connections of the network are active. In this case,

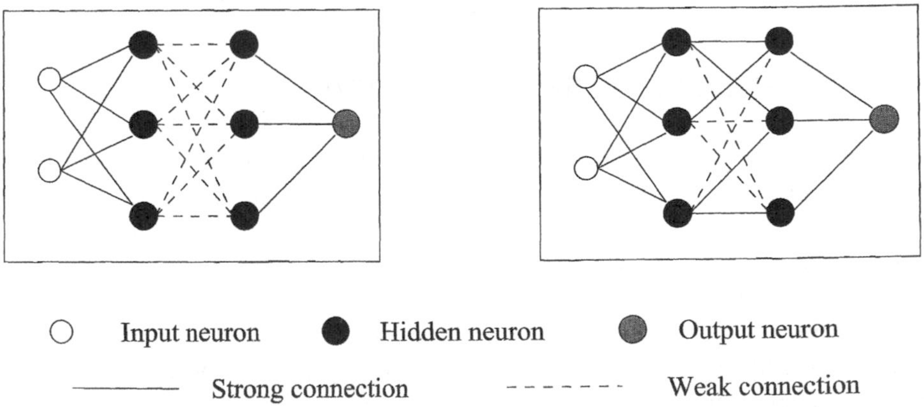

(a) All hidden connections are inactive

(b) Some hidden connections are active

Figure 5.3 The status of hidden neural connections.

the hidden neurons are expected to be used in improving the generalization as well as speeding up the learning.

In order to adapt the size of the BP network and activate hidden connections, an approach of complexity regularization may be applied. In this approach, a term is added to the error measure function that discourages the learning algorithm from seeking solutions that are too complex. This term represents, in fact, a measure of the network's complexity; that is, both the quantities and number of weights. The resulting criterion or cost function is of the form

$$Cost = network\ error\ measure + model\ complexity\ measure$$

where the first term on the right-hand side measures the network error between the network outputs and the task or desired outputs, while the second term is determined only by the complexity of the network structure.

This type of criterion is sometimes referred to as the *minimum description length* (MDL) criterion because it has the same form as the information-theoretic measure of description length. Simply speaking, the description length of a set of data is defined as the total number of bits required to represent the data. But for a neural network that is designed to represent a set of data, the total description length should be defined as the sum of the number of bits required to encode the errors. The cost function introduced above may be considered as one such form if the term of the network error measure is related to the number of bits required to encode the errors, and the term of complexity measure corresponds to the number of bits required to describe the network model. The learning process that minimizes this cost function then, to a certain degree, provides a minimal description of the data.

In the context of BP learning, or any other supervised learning procedure, such a cost function may be represented as

$$E_t(\boldsymbol{w}) = E(\boldsymbol{w}) + \lambda E_c(\boldsymbol{w}) \tag{5.16}$$

where the first term on the right-hand side is the error function used in the standard BP learning, $E_c(\boldsymbol{w})$ is the complexity measure, and the parameter λ is a small positive constant that is used to control the influence of the term of the complexity measure $E_c(\boldsymbol{w})$ in relation to the conventional error measure $E(\boldsymbol{w})$. Consequently, the learning algorithm derived using such a criterion is a simple extension of the BP algorithm. Later, we will see that for different choices of the complexity measure, the *weight decay* approach, the *weight elimination* approach, and many similar approaches may be obtained.

5.2.1 Weight Decay Approach

The *weight decay approach* is a method of reducing the effective number of weights in the network by encouraging the learning algorithm to seek solutions that use as many zero weights as possible. This is accomplished by adding a term that is the sum of all the squared weights to the criterion function that penalizes the network for using the nonzero weights. Then, the new criterion function is formulated as

$$\begin{aligned} E_t(\boldsymbol{w}) &= E(\boldsymbol{w}) + \frac{\lambda}{2}||\boldsymbol{w}|| \\ &= E(\boldsymbol{w}) + \frac{\lambda}{2}\sum_i w_i^2 \end{aligned} \tag{5.17}$$

where the sum in the second term on the right-hand side performed over all the weights represents the complexity measure E_c of the network. It is to be seen that in this modification of the standard BP learning algorithm, an extra term of the form $\lambda \boldsymbol{w}$ is added for updating the weight vector. Therefore, one has the following new updating formulation:

$$\begin{aligned} \boldsymbol{w}(k+1) &= \boldsymbol{w}(k) - \eta\left(\frac{\partial E}{\partial \boldsymbol{w}(k)} + \lambda \boldsymbol{w}(k)\right) \\ &= (1-\eta\lambda)\boldsymbol{w}(k) - \eta\frac{\partial E}{\partial \boldsymbol{w}(k)} \end{aligned} \tag{5.18}$$

It is evident that the effect of λ is to "decay" the weight vector by a factor of $(1 - \eta\lambda)$. The weight decay approach does not actually delete weights from the network, nor does it typically produce weights that are exactly zero. Weights that are not essential to the solution decay to zero and can be removed. When some weights are forced to take on values near zero, some other weights remain relatively large. The result is that the average weight size is smaller.

Another simple weight decay method is to define the cost function as

$$E_t(\boldsymbol{w}) = E(\boldsymbol{w}) + \lambda\sum_i |w_i| \tag{5.19}$$

In this case, an additional term $-\lambda sgn(\boldsymbol{w})$ is used in the weight vector updating rule, Eqn. (5.18). If $w_i > 0$, the weight is decremented by λ; otherwise, if $w_i < 0$, then it is incremented by λ.

5.2.2 Weight Elimination Approach

Similar to the weight decay approach, an alternative technique is called the *weight elimination approach* was proposed first by Rumelhart and McClelland (1986). In this weight elimination approach the complexity regularization term is of the form

$$E_c(\boldsymbol{w}) = \sum_i \frac{(w_i/w_0)^2}{1+(w_i/w_0)^2} \tag{5.20}$$

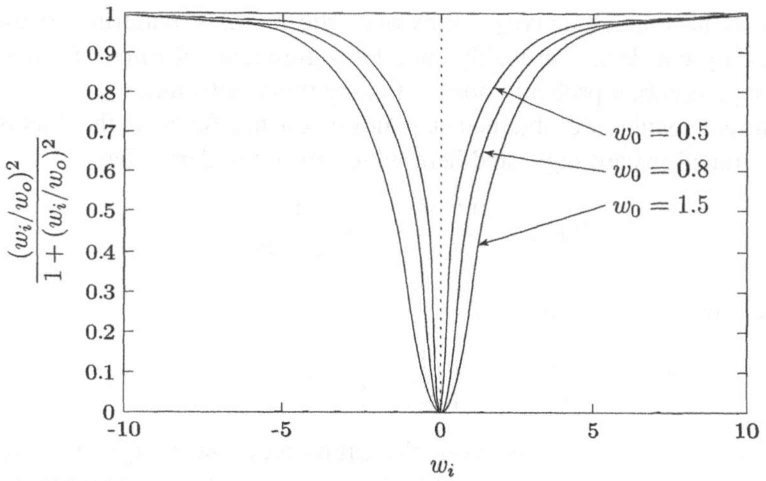

Figure 5.4 The curve for function $(w_i/w_0)^2/[1 + (w_i/w_0)^2]$ with various values of w_0, $w_0 = 0.5, 0.8$, and 1.5.

where w_0 is a fixed weight normalization factor. As shown in Fig. 5.4, when $(w_i/w_0) \gg 1$, the terms inside the sum are close to unity, and thus this criterion essentially counts the number of weights. The purpose of introducing a complexity term into the error function is to push the negative values of the weights toward larger absolute values, while the positive values are pushed toward zero. Thus, it can be expected that some hidden connections will be large enough to speed up the learning that is due to the complexity term $E_c(\boldsymbol{w})$. In fact, when $(w_i/w_0) \ll 1$, the term inside the sum is proportional to w_i^2, and this approach acts like the weight decay approach. Through the appropriate choice of w_0, we can encourage the network to have a few large weights with a small w_0, or many small weights with a large w_0.

5.2.3 Chauvin's Penalty Approach

To effectively prune the network by driving the weights to zero during learning, Chauvin (1989) introduced the following complexity measure

$$E_c(\boldsymbol{w}) = \sum_{j,p} \zeta(x_j^2(p)) \tag{5.21}$$

where $\zeta(.)$ is a positive monotonic function. The sums are over the set of the output units, the set of the hidden neurons, and the set of the input patterns. Chauvin indicated that this term measures the average "energy" expanded by the hidden units. It is important to note that the "energy" expanded by a unit represents how much activity varies over the learning patterns. If the unit changes a great deal, it probably encodes significant information. If it does not change much, it probably does not carry much information.

Different results are obtained depending on the form of the function ζ. Various functions are suggested here which have the derivative

$$\zeta'(x^2) = \frac{\partial \zeta(x^2)}{\partial x^2} = \frac{1}{(1+x^2)^n} \tag{5.22}$$

or, by defining $z = x^2$, we write

$$\zeta'(z) = \frac{\partial \zeta(z)}{\partial z} = \frac{1}{(1+z)^n}, \qquad n = 0, 1, 2, \ldots$$

For $n = 0$, ζ is linear, and both the high- and low-energy units receive equal penalties. As shown in Table 5.1, for $n = 1$, ζ is logarithmic and the low-energy units are penalized more heavily than the high-energy units. For $n = 2$, the penalty approaches an asymptote as the energy increases, which means that the high-energy units are not penalized much more than the medium-energy units.

Chauvin also proposed the following two types of cost functions for constrained BP algorithms:

$$E_t(\boldsymbol{w}) = E(\boldsymbol{w}) + \lambda_1 \sum_{j,p} \zeta(x_j^2(p)) + \lambda_2 \sum_i w_i^2 \tag{5.23}$$

and

$$E_t(\boldsymbol{w}) = E(\boldsymbol{w}) + \lambda_1 \sum_{j,p} \frac{x_j^2}{1+x_j^2} + \lambda_2 \sum_i \frac{w_i^2}{1+w_i^2} \tag{5.24}$$

The numerical analysis results show that under these choices of the cost functions, the network may be reduced to an optimal number of hidden units independently of the starting size.

Table 5.1 **Energy functions ζ for various values of n, Eqns. (5.21) and (5.22)**

n	$\zeta(x^2)$	$\zeta'(x) = \frac{\partial \zeta(x^2)}{\partial x^2} = \frac{1}{(1+x^2)^n}$
0	x^2	1
1	$\log(1+x^2)$	$\frac{1}{(1+x^2)}$
2	$\frac{x^2}{1+x^2}$	$\frac{1}{(1+x^2)^2}$

5.3 NETWORK PRUNING THROUGH SENSITIVITY CALCULATIONS

It is generally true that there is a large amount of redundant information contained in the weights of a fully connected MFNN. In terms of information content or complexity, some studies, like the concept of *minimum description length* (MDL) (Rissanen 1989), have shown that a "simple" network whose description needs a small number of bits is more likely to generalize correctly than a more complex network. Presumably, this is because it has extracted the essence of the data and removed the redundancy from them. Thus, it seems plausible that we could remove explicitly some *insignificant* weights from the network, and at the same time retain the functional capability needed to solve the specified problem. This process is known as *pruning* the network. Generally speaking, there are two advantages to pruning: (i) with a fixed number of learning samples, the reduction in the amount of weights can lead to a marked improvement in the generalization properties of the network; and (ii) by isolating the relevant parameters, learning is easier.

The simplest approach to pruning is to delete the smallest weights in the network. This, however, is not always the best approach since the network output can be quite sensitive to these weights. A much better approach is to eliminate the weights that contribute the least to the solution. According to this theory, some network pruning methods have been developed through sensitivity calculations for the units or the weights (Hassibi and Stork 1993, Karnin 1990, LeCun et al. 1990, Reed 1993, Segee and Carter 1991). Because of the evaluation procedures of the sensitivities, which may involve the first-order or second-order error partial derivatives, these pruning methods are categorized as *first- and second-order pruning procedures*. We will now discuss these pruning methods.

5.3.1 First-Order Pruning Procedures

5.3.1.1 Relevance for Deleting Hidden Units

It is of interest to note that a simple network pruning algorithm for deleting hidden neural units, rather than weights, was proposed by Mozer and Smolensky (1989), who defined an important measure (*measure of the relevance*) for every neuron and deleted the neurons with the least importance in the network.

The *measure of the relevance* ρ of a neuron is the error between the cost function without the neuron and the cost function with the neuron. To avoid a direct calculation for each neuron, ρ is approximated by introducing a gating term α for each unit, as shown for a two-layered network in Fig. 5.5, such that

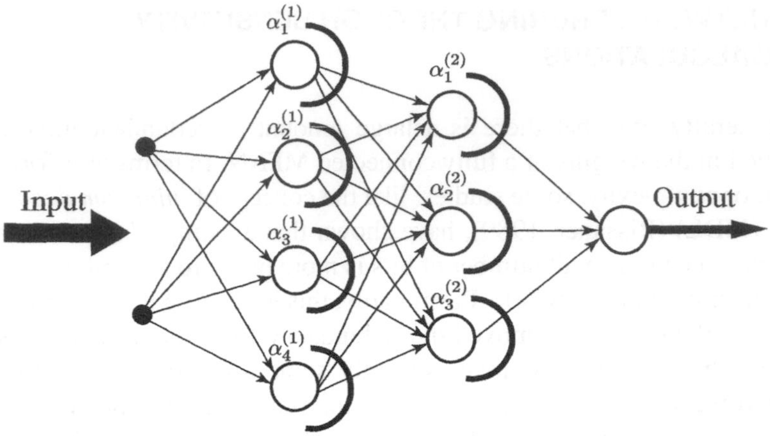

Figure 5.5 A three-layered network with attentional coefficients on the hidden units.

$$x_j = \sigma\left(\sum_i w_{ij}\alpha_i x_i\right) \tag{5.25}$$

where x_j is the output of unit j, w_{ij} is the weight from unit i to unit j, and $\sigma(.)$ is the sigmoidal function. If $\alpha = 0$, the unit has no influence on the network; if $\alpha = 1$, the unit behaves normally. The importance of a unit is then approximated by the derivative

$$\hat{\rho}_i = -\left.\frac{\partial E^l}{\partial \alpha_i}\right|_{\alpha_i=1} \tag{5.26}$$

which can be calculated using the same approach as that of the BP algorithm. Since the gating parameter α is unity in the calculation, it is only the notation for the relevance evaluation rather than a parameter that must be implemented in the network equations. When $\hat{\rho}_i$ falls below a certain threshold, the unit can be deleted.

Even though the squared error is usually used for the BP learning, it is wise to use the absolute value error for measuring the relevance:

$$E^l = \sum_p |d_j(p) - y_j(p)| \tag{5.27}$$

Because this provides a better estimate of relevance when the error is small. In addition, an exponentially decaying average is proposed to suppress fluctuations (Mozer and Smolensky 1989)

$$\hat{\rho}_i(k+1) = 0.8\hat{\rho}_i(k) + 0.2\frac{\partial E^l}{\partial \alpha_i} \tag{5.28}$$

This pruning method was used by Segee and Carter (1991) to determine its effect on the fault tolerance of MFNNs. They pointed out that the pruned network is not significantly more sensitive to a damage even though it has fewer parameters. When the increase in error is considered as a function of the magnitude of a weight that is deleted by a fault, the curves for the pruned and unpruned networks are almost the same.

5.3.1.2 Karnin's Pruning Method

In the network pruning method proposed by Karnin (1990), the procedure is to estimate the first-order sensitivity of the error function for the exclusion of each synaptic weight, and then to prune the weights with the low sensitivity parameters. The sensitivity associated with a weight w is defined as

$$S = E(w = 0) - E(w = w^f) = -\frac{E(w^f) - E(0)}{w^f - 0} w^f \tag{5.29}$$

where w^f is the final value of the weight w on the completion of the learning phase, $w = 0$ represents its value on removal, and $E(0)$ is the error when it is removed.

Since $E(0)$ is unknown, we consider a point w^i between 0 and w^f. Then, the slope of $E(w)$ may be approximated by the average slope measured between w^i and w^f:

$$S \approx -\frac{E(w^f) - E(w^i)}{w^f - w^i} w^f \tag{5.30}$$

Finally, the following approximation is used for the evaluation of the sensitivity to the removal of the connection weight w_i

$$\hat{S}_i = -\sum_{n=1}^{N} \frac{\partial E}{\partial w_i}(n) \Delta w_i(n) \frac{w_i^f}{w_i^f - w_i^i} \tag{5.31}$$

where N is the number of learning patterns. All terms involved in the calculation above are available during the learning phase so that the evaluation is easily performed and a separate sensitivity calculation is avoided. Moreover, if a standard BP algorithm is employed, Eqn. (5.31) can be rewritten as

$$\hat{S}_i = -\sum_{n=1}^{N} (\Delta w_i(n))^2 \frac{w_i^f}{w_i^f - w_i^i} \tag{5.32}$$

On the basis of the preceding algorithm, each weight has an estimated sensitivity parameter and the weights with lower sensitivity are deleted. It is readily seen that if all the output connection weights associated with a unit are

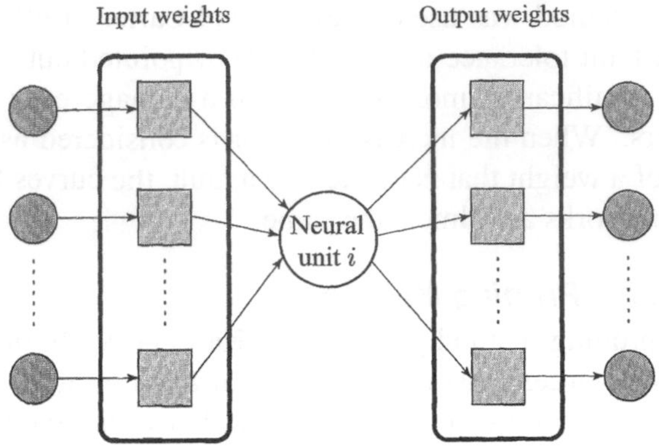

Figure 5.6 The input and output weights of the neural unit i.

removed, the unit itself should be deleted. If all the input connection weights, as shown in Fig. 5.6, are deleted, the network will have a constant output and it can be deleted by adjusting the thresholds of the following units that receive the output from the unit deleted.

5.3.2 Second-Order Pruning Procedures

Another effective pruning method, which is based on the second-order Taylor series expansion of the error function, is the *optimal brain damage* (OBD) (LeCun et al. 1990). It is used for reducing the size of a learning network by selectively deleting the weights. Further development of this method is the *optimal brain surgeon* (OBS) proposed by Hassibi and Stork (1993). The key step in both strategies is that how to define the term *saliency* corresponding to every weight parameter that measures the importance of the weight parameter in terms of the network output. A reasonable deleting process is the one which operates on the weights that have small saliency values. We will now start our discussion of the second-order Taylor series expansion of the error function around a local or global minimum point.

5.3.2.1 Taylor Expansion of Error Functions

Let $E(\boldsymbol{w}) : \Re^n \longrightarrow \Re$ be an error function of an n-dimensional weight parameter vector $\boldsymbol{w} = [w_1 \; w_2 \; \dots \; w_n]^T$. Fortunately, it is possible to construct a local model to analytically predict the effect of perturbing the parameter vector around a point $\boldsymbol{w}^*$, called the *nominal point*, where the error function has a local minimum. Expanding the objective function $E(\boldsymbol{w})$ at this point by using the Taylor series yields

$$\begin{aligned} E(\boldsymbol{w}) &= E(\boldsymbol{w}^*) + \boldsymbol{g}^T \Delta \boldsymbol{w} + \frac{1}{2} (\Delta \boldsymbol{w})^T \boldsymbol{H} \Delta \boldsymbol{w} + 0(\|\Delta \boldsymbol{w}\|^3) \\ &= E(\boldsymbol{w}^*) + \sum_{i=1}^{n} g_i \Delta w_i + \frac{1}{2} \sum_{i=1}^{n} \sum_{j=1}^{n} h_{ij} \Delta w_i \Delta w_j + 0(\|\Delta \boldsymbol{w}\|^3) \end{aligned} \tag{5.33}$$

with

$$\Delta \boldsymbol{w} = \boldsymbol{w} - \boldsymbol{w}^*, \quad \boldsymbol{g} = \left.\frac{\partial E}{\partial \boldsymbol{w}}\right|_{\boldsymbol{w}=\boldsymbol{w}^*} \quad \boldsymbol{H} = \left.\frac{\partial^2 E}{\partial \boldsymbol{w} \partial \boldsymbol{w}}\right|_{\boldsymbol{w}=\boldsymbol{w}^*}$$

or

$$\Delta w_i = w_i - w_i^*, \quad g_i = \left.\frac{\partial E}{\partial w_i}\right|_{\boldsymbol{w}=\boldsymbol{w}^*}, \quad h_{ij} = \left.\frac{\partial E^2}{\partial w_i \partial w_j}\right|_{\boldsymbol{w}=\boldsymbol{w}^*}$$

where Δw_i is the difference between the current value and the nominal value, g_i is the first-order partial derivative of the error function with respect to the parameter w_i, h_{ij} is the second-order partial derivative of the error function with respect to the parameters w_i and w_j, and the last term contains all the terms that are higher than second order.

First, one assumes that the error function E has a minimum value at the point $\boldsymbol{w} = \boldsymbol{w}^*$. Then at the minimum error value, we have

$$g_i = 0, \quad \text{for all} \quad i = 1, 2, \ldots, n$$

and

$$h_{ij} \geq 0, \quad \text{for all} \quad i, j = 1, 2, \ldots, n$$

Second, one assumes that the error function around a local minimum or global minimum is nearly *quadratic*. Thus, neglecting the higher-order terms in Eqn. (5.33) yields

$$\begin{aligned} \Delta E &\triangleq E(\boldsymbol{w}) - E(\boldsymbol{w}^*) \\ &= \tfrac{1}{2} (\Delta \boldsymbol{w})^T \boldsymbol{H} \Delta \boldsymbol{w} \\ &= \tfrac{1}{2} \sum_{i=1}^{n} \sum_{j=1}^{n} h_{ij} \Delta w_i \Delta w_j \end{aligned} \tag{5.34}$$

where ΔE represents the error due to the changes of the weights around the nominal weight vector $\boldsymbol{w}^*$.

5.3.2.2 Optimal Brain Damage (OBD)

The objective here is to find a set of parameters using the second-order Taylor series expansion whose deletion will cause the least change of E. This problem is practically insolvable in the general case. One reason is that the number of the second-order partial derivatives is so enormous (6.76×10^6 terms for a 2600-parameter network) that they are very difficult to compute. Therefore, we must introduce some simplifications to the algorithm. An effective method (LeCun et al. 1990) is a "diagonal" approximation which considers only ΔE caused by deleting several parameters individually where the cross terms are neglected. Thus, in Eqn. (5.34), deleting the terms of the second derivative h_{ij} for $i \neq j$; that is

$$h_{ij} = \frac{\partial E^2}{\partial w_i \partial w_j} = 0, \quad \text{for} \quad i \neq j$$

gives

$$\Delta E = \tfrac{1}{2} \sum_{i=1}^{n} h_{ii} (\Delta w_i)^2 \tag{5.35}$$

Furthermore, if the ith parameter w_i is deleted; that is, $w_i = 0$ or $\Delta w_i = w_i^*$, this deletion causes an error

$$\Delta E_{w_i} = \tfrac{1}{2} h_{ii} (w_i^*)^2$$

Thus, the saliency for parameter w_i may be defined as

$$S_i = \tfrac{1}{2} h_{ii} (w_i^*)^2 \tag{5.36}$$

where the second-order partial derivatives may be recursively calculated using the formulations obtained in Section 5.3.2.1.

In summary, the OBD (optimal brain damage) procedure for a MFNN is as follows (LeCun et al. 1990):

(i) Select a reasonable network architecture;

(ii) Train the network until a desired solution is obtained;

(iii) Compute the second-order derivatives $h_{ii} \triangleq \partial^2 E / \partial w_i^2$;

(iv) Compute the saliencies for weights: $S_i = h_{ii} (w_i^*)^2 / 2$;

(v) Delete some weights that have small saliencies;

(vi) Return to step (ii).

It may be noted that deleting a parameter is carried out by setting it to zero. As an interactive tool for network design and analysis, LeCun et al. (1989) conducted a network pruning task for a backpropagation network applied to the problem of handwritten digit recognition. The initial network was trained on a database of segmented handwritten zip-code digits and printed digits containing approximately 9300 training examples and parameters, 33,210 test examples, and 10^{17} connections controlled by 21,778 weight parameters. To reduce the number of parameters in this network, the simulation studies carried out by LeCun et al. (1989) indicated that up to approximately 800 parameters (approximately 30% of the parameters) could be deleted with small changes in the error function.

An extension of the OBD method that uses the full second-order derivatives instead of just the diagonal elements, called the *optimal brain surgeon* (OBS), is described in the following discussion.

5.3.2.3 Optimal Brain Surgeon (OBS)

An important simplification used in the OBD is where only the diagonal terms of the second-order Taylor series expansion are considered in defining the saliency of the parameters. In other words, the nondiagonal elements of the Hessian matrix are ignored. Sometimes this assumption may cause large errors during the network pruning process. To overcome this drawback, the more complex method, called the *optimal brain surgeon* (OBS), was proposed by Hassibi and Stork (1993). The main difference between the OBD and OBS methods is that the latter deals with a full consideration of the second-order Taylor series expansion of the error function around a local or global minimum point while the former neglects the nondiagonal elements of the Hessian matrix.

Like the deleting procedure used in the OBD, the key task of the OBS is to define the saliency of the weights, which is the incremental of the error function E due to the elimination of the weight parameter w_i. Let $\boldsymbol{w}^*$ be the weight vector where the error function $E(\boldsymbol{w}^*)$ has a local or global minimum value. If the ith weight w_i is deleted, the elimination of this weight is equivalent to the condition

$$\Delta w_i = -w_i^*$$

or

$$\mathbf{1}_i^T \Delta \boldsymbol{w} + w_i^* = 0 \tag{5.37}$$

where $\mathbf{1}_i$ is the unit vector whose ith element is one and all other elements are zero:

$$\mathbf{1}_i = [0 \ \cdots \ 0 \qquad \underset{\leftarrow\, i\text{th} \,\rightarrow}{1} \qquad 0 \ \cdots \ 0]^T$$

Subject to the constraint condition given in Eqn. (5.37), a useful suggestion proposed by Hassibi and Stork (1993) is one that defines the saliency parameter of w_i in the OBS as a minimum value of $\Delta E(\boldsymbol{w})$ with respect to the incremental change $\delta \boldsymbol{w}$ of the whole weight vector. Mathematically, this problem can be described as

$$\min_{\Delta \boldsymbol{w}} \Delta E(\Delta \boldsymbol{w}) = \tfrac{1}{2} (\Delta \boldsymbol{w})^T \boldsymbol{H} \Delta \boldsymbol{w} \tag{5.38}$$

with the constraint condition given in Eqn. (5.37). To find an analytic solution of this constrained optimization problem, the Lagrangian is given as

$$L_i = \tfrac{1}{2} (\Delta \boldsymbol{w})^T \boldsymbol{H} \Delta \boldsymbol{w} + \lambda_i (\boldsymbol{1}_i^T \Delta \boldsymbol{w} + w_i^*) \tag{5.39}$$

where $\lambda_i \in \Re$ is the Lagrangian multiplier with respect to the constraint condition given in Eqn. (5.37). The optimality conditions may be obtained by taking partial derivatives of the Lagrangian L_i respectively with respect to $\Delta \boldsymbol{w}$ and λ_i as follows:

$$\frac{\partial L_i}{\partial (\Delta \boldsymbol{w})} = \boldsymbol{H} \Delta \boldsymbol{w} + \lambda_i \boldsymbol{1}_i = 0 \tag{5.40}$$

$$\frac{\partial L_i}{\partial \lambda_i} = \boldsymbol{1}_i^T \Delta \boldsymbol{w} + w_i^* = 0 \tag{5.41}$$

In addition to the fact that the second equation implies constraint condition given in Eqn. (5.37), Eqn. (5.40) yields

$$\Delta \boldsymbol{w} = -\boldsymbol{H}^{-1} \lambda_i \boldsymbol{1}_i \tag{5.42}$$

To solve the Lagrangian multiplier λ_i, one may use the ith equation of the vector equation above:

$$\Delta w_i = -\lambda_i [\boldsymbol{H}^{-1}]_{ii} \tag{5.43}$$

By using the constraint condition given in Eqn. (5.37), we easily obtain

$$\lambda_i = \frac{w_i^*}{[\boldsymbol{H}^{-1}]_{ii}} \tag{5.44}$$

Hence, the optimal increment of the weight vector due to the elimination of the weight w_i is

$$\Delta \boldsymbol{w} = -\frac{w_i^*}{[\boldsymbol{H}^{-1}]_{ii}} \boldsymbol{H}^{-1} \boldsymbol{1}_i \tag{5.45}$$

and the minimum value of the Lagrangian with respect to the weight vector increment, which is also defined as the saliency of w_i, is finally obtained as

$$L_i = \frac{1}{2} \frac{(w_i^*)^2}{[\boldsymbol{H}^{-1}]_{ii}} \tag{5.46}$$

where $\boldsymbol{H}^{-1}$ is the inverse of the Hessian matrix $\boldsymbol{H}$, and $[\boldsymbol{H}^{-1}]_{ii}$ is the ith diagonal element of $\boldsymbol{H}^{-1}$. The preceding optimization procedure finds the minimum value of the quadratic error function by using the results of deleting the weight w_i and of the weight vector change $\Delta\boldsymbol{w}$.

However, the OBS procedure gives a more accurate definition of the saliency of the parameters than that in the OBD approach discussed in Section 5.3.2.2. The main difficulty of the OBS is associated with calculating the inverse of the Hessian matrix. Of course, the algorithm requires the nonsingularity of the Hessian matrix to ensure the existence of its inverse. In general, the Hessian matrix, which is calculated at a local or global minimum point, is nonsingular if the network is learned by the BP learning algorithm. A study presented by Saarinen et al. (1991, 1992) shows that the neural network learning problems may be ill-conditioned, resulting in computational difficulties of the inverse of the Hessian matrix.

5.4 EVALUATION OF THE HESSIAN MATRIX

The BP learning algorithm, which originally employed only the first-order partial derivatives, has emerged as the most popular learning method for the MFNNs. However, several of the more recent developments of the BP algorithm require the second-order partial derivatives in addition to the first-order derivatives. These second-order derivatives are typically partial derivatives of either the network output or the error function with respect to the weights and thresholds. Such a matrix of second-order derivatives is usually called a *Hessian*.

As pointed out by Buntine and Weigend (1994), second-order derivatives are important in the following different contexts:

(i) Direct second-order learning methods:

The standard BP algorithm is a first-order gradient descent method. The convergence speed of the learning phase can be significantly improved if the information pertaining to the second-order derivatives is available. As we will see later, a typical example is the *Newton–Raphson*-type framework. Since the second-order derivatives have to be computed at each instant, the computation speed is crucial here.

(ii) Indirect second-order learning methods:

There is another class of second-order optimization algorithms that do not require the direct calculation of the Hessian because they operate in an iterative manner. The conjugate gradient and related algorithms are generally considered the most powerful all-purpose minimization algorithms. Here, the second-order derivatives are used during line searches so that the full Hessian is not required; only the product of the Hessian and a given vector is needed.

(iii) Network pruning:

Second-order derivatives are also used in some postlearning phases such as parameter evaluation and network pruning. Since these postlearning methods do not require second-order derivatives in each learning iteration, the efficiency of their computation is less crucial here than in the previous two cases.

Second-order derivatives can be calculated exactly, or calculated using approximations and ignoring certain terms, or calculated using numerical differentiation. Derivations of these calculation procedures are discussed in detail in the following text.

5.4.1 Diagonal Second-Order Derivatives

As seen in the last section, an efficient method of computing the diagonal second-order derivatives of the error function with respect to the weights plays an important role in a weight-deleting process. A derivative procedure that is very similar to the BP algorithm used for computing the first-order derivatives was presented by LeCun (1987). The basic idea and formulations are outlined in the following description.

We still assume that the error function is expressed as a mean-squared error function; generalization to other additive error measures is straightforward. For convenience, the basic network transfer equations for an M-layered network may be re-listed as follows:

$$\left.\begin{array}{rcl} s_j^{(i)} & = & \sum_{p=0}^{n_{i-1}} w_{jp}^{(i)} x_p^{(i-1)} \\ x_j^{(i)} & = & \sigma(s_j^{(i)}) \end{array}\right\} \quad i = 1, 2, \ldots, M; j = 1, 2, \ldots, n_i \tag{5.47}$$

An instantaneous error function is also defined as

$$E = \frac{1}{2} \sum_{j=1}^{n_M} \left(d_j - x_j^{(M)}\right)^2 \tag{5.48}$$

Before discussing the second-order partial derivatives, one has to review some basic results of the first-order partial derivatives. From the network transfer equations one may directly obtain the following results:

$$\frac{\partial x_j^{(i)}}{\partial s_j^{(i)}} = \sigma'(s_j^{(i)})$$

$$\frac{\partial s_j^{(i)}}{\partial w_{jp}^{(i)}} = x_p^{(i-1)}$$

$$\frac{\partial s_j^{(i)}}{\partial x_p^{(i-1)}} = w_{jp}^{(i)}$$

These basic first-order partial derivatives, which are derived from only the network equations, are repeatedly used in the following derivations for dealing with the second-order partial derivatives. Let us consider the first-order partial derivative of the error function with respect to the weights, which is given by the chain rule as

$$\frac{\partial E}{\partial w_{jp}^{(i)}} = \frac{\partial E}{\partial s_j^{(i)}} \frac{\partial s_j^{(i)}}{\partial w_{jp}^{(i)}} = \frac{\partial E}{\partial s_j^{(i)}} x_p^{(i-1)} \tag{5.49}$$

As shown previously, the first-order partial derivative $\partial E / \partial s_j^{(i)}$ may be recursively calculated from the output layer. In fact

$$\frac{\partial E}{\partial s_j^{(i)}} = \sum_{l=1}^{n_{i+1}} \frac{\partial E}{\partial s_l^{(i+1)}} \frac{\partial s_l^{(i+1)}}{\partial x_j^{(i)}} \frac{\partial x_j^{(i)}}{\partial s_j^{(i)}} = \sum_{l=1}^{n_{i+1}} \frac{\partial E}{\partial s_l^{(i+1)}} w_{lj}^{(i+1)} \sigma'(s_j^{(i)}) \tag{5.50}$$

and the initial conditions given in the output layer are

$$\frac{\partial E}{\partial s_l^{(M)}} = -\left(d_l - x_l^{(M)}\right) \sigma'(s_l^{(M)}) \tag{5.51}$$

Using these results, the second-order partial derivatives may be evaluated as

$$\frac{\partial^2 E}{\partial (w_{jp}^{(i)})^2} = \frac{\partial}{\partial w_{jp}^{(i)}} \frac{\partial E}{\partial w_{jp}^{(i)}} = \frac{\partial}{\partial w_{jp}^{(i)}} \left(\frac{\partial E}{\partial s_j^{(i)}} x_p^{(i-1)} \right)$$

Since $x_p^{(i-1)}$, the output of the $neuron(i-1, p)$ in the layer $(i-1)$, is independent of the weights $w_{jp}^{(i)}$ for the neurons in the layer i, it yields

$$\frac{\partial^2 E}{\partial (w_{jp}^{(i)})^2} = \frac{\partial}{\partial w_{jp}^{(i)}} \left(\frac{\partial E}{\partial s_j^{(i)}} \right) x_p^{(i-1)} = \frac{\partial^2 E}{\partial (s_j^{(i)})^2} (x_p^{(i-1)})^2$$

The next task is to obtain a recursive computing formulation for the second-order partial derivative $\partial^2 E / \partial (s_j^{(i)})^2$. The partial derivative of the two sides of Eqn. (5.50) with respect to the parameter $s_j^{(i)}$ yields

$$\frac{\partial^2 E}{\partial (s_j^{(i)})^2} = \sum_{l=1}^{n_{i+1}} \frac{\partial^2 E}{\partial (s_l^{(i+1)})^2} \frac{\partial s_l^{(i+1)}}{\partial s_j^{(i)}} w_{lj}^{(i+1)} \sigma'(s_j^{(i)}) + \left(\sum_{l=1}^{n_{i+1}} \frac{\partial E}{\partial s_l^{(i+1)}} w_{lj}^{(i+1)} \right) \sigma''(s_j^{(i)})$$

Note that

$$\frac{\partial s_l^{(i+1)}}{\partial s_j^{(i)}} = \frac{\partial s_l^{(i+1)}}{\partial x_j^{(i)}} \frac{\partial x_j^{(i)}}{\partial s_j^{(i)}} = w_{lj}^{(i+1)} \sigma'(s_j^{(i)})$$

Finally, for the hidden layers $(1 \leq i \leq M-1)$, we have

$$\frac{\partial^2 E}{\partial (s_j^{(i)})^2} = (\sigma'(s_j^{(i)}))^2 \sum_{l=1}^{n_{i+1}} (w_{lj}^{(i+1)})^2 \frac{\partial^2 E}{\partial (s_l^{(i+1)})^2} + \left(\sum_{l=1}^{n_{i+1}} \frac{\partial E}{\partial s_l^{(i+1)}} w_{lj}^{(i+1)} \right) \sigma''(s_j^{(i)}) \tag{5.52}$$

and for the output layer

$$\frac{\partial^2 E}{\partial (s_j^{(M)})^2} = (\sigma'(s_j^{(M)}))^2 - (d_j - y_j)\sigma''(s_j^{(M)}) \tag{5.53}$$

Also, using the propagation errors associated with the hidden neurons and the delta's notations, which were discussed extensively in Chapter 4, one may simplify Eqn. (5.52) to

$$\frac{\partial^2 E}{\partial (s_j^{(i)})^2} = (\sigma'(s_j^{(i)}))^2 \sum_{l=1}^{n_{i+1}} (w_{lj}^{(i+1)})^2 \frac{\partial^2 E}{\partial (s_l^{(i+1)})^2} - e_j^{(i)} \sigma''(s_j^{(i)}) \tag{5.54}$$

where

$$e_j^{(i)} \triangleq \sum_{l=1}^{n_{i+1}} \delta_l^{(i+1)} w_{lj}^{(i+1)}$$

$$\delta_l^{(i+1)} \triangleq -\frac{\partial E}{\partial s_l^{(i+1)}}$$

Here, the second-order derivative of the sigmoidal function $\sigma(.)$ is shown in Fig. 5.7.

Using the same procedure as for the backpropagation, the computation will start recursively from the output layer to the hidden layers. The calculation procedure for the diagonal second-order partial derivatives is summarized in Table 5.2. As can be seen, computing the second-order derivatives is of the same order of complexity as computing the gradient.

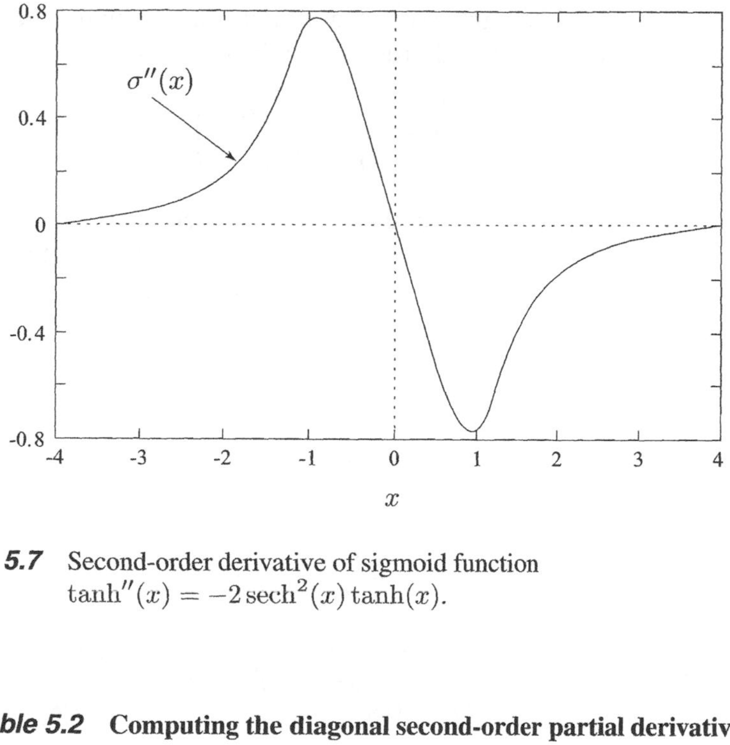

Figure 5.7 Second-order derivative of sigmoid function $\tanh''(x) = -2\,\mathrm{sech}^2(x)\tanh(x)$.

Table 5.2 **Computing the diagonal second-order partial derivatives**

Step 1:	Calculate initial conditions $\partial E/\partial s_j^{(M)}, j = 1, 2, \ldots, n_M$ using Eqn. (5.51) and $\partial^2 E/\partial (s_j^{(M)})^2, j = 1, 2, \ldots, n_M$ using Eqn. (5.53);
Step 2:	Let $i \longleftarrow M - 1$, then calculate $\partial^2 E/\partial (s_j^{(i)})^2$, $j = 1, 2, \ldots, n_i$ using Eqn. (5.54);
Step 3:	If $i \leq 1$, then go to Step 4, otherwise, if $i \longleftarrow i - 1$, go to Step 2;
Step 4:	Calculation is completed. Output $\partial^2 E/\partial (s_j^{(i)})^2$, $i = 1, 2, \ldots, M$.

5.4.2 General Second-Order Derivative Formulations

The number of elements of the Hessian matrix is the square of the number of the parameters including all the weights and thresholds involved in the network. For example, if the number of the parameters is n then the number of the elements of the Hessian matrix is n^2. To evaluate the off-diagonal elements of the Hessian matrix, one has to consider the second-order derivative of the error index E with respect to the weights $w_{jp}^{(i)}$ associated with the neuron in the layer i, and $w_{qr}^{(l)}$, the weight associated with the neuron in the the layer l. From the symmetry of the second-order derivatives, that is

$$\frac{\partial}{\partial w_{qr}^{(l)}}\left(\frac{\partial E}{\partial w_{jp}^{(i)}}\right) = \frac{\partial}{\partial w_{jp}^{(i)}}\left(\frac{\partial E}{\partial w_{qr}^{(l)}}\right) \tag{5.55}$$

it may thus be assumed that $l \leq i$ in the following discussions.

From Eqn. (5.49), which gives the results of the first-order partial derivatives of the error index with respect to the weights, one obtains

$$\begin{aligned}
\frac{\partial}{\partial w_{qr}^{(l)}}\left(\frac{\partial E}{\partial w_{jp}^{(i)}}\right) &= \frac{\partial}{\partial w_{qr}^{(l)}}\left(\frac{\partial E}{\partial s_j^{(i)}} x_p^{(i-1)}\right) \\
&= \frac{\partial s_q^{(l)}}{\partial w_{qr}^{(l)}} \frac{\partial}{\partial s_q^{(l)}}\left(\frac{\partial E}{\partial s_j^{(i)}} x_p^{(i-1)}\right) \\
&= x_r^{(l-1)} \frac{\partial}{\partial s_q^{(l)}}\left(\frac{\partial E}{\partial s_j^{(i)}} x_p^{(i-1)}\right) \\
&= x_r^{(l-1)} \frac{\partial E}{\partial s_j^{(i)}} \frac{\partial x_p^{(i-1)}}{\partial s_q^{(l)}} + x_r^{(l-1)} x_p^{(i-1)} \frac{\partial^2 E}{\partial s_q^{(l)} \partial s_j^{(i)}} \\
&= x_r^{(l-1)} \frac{\partial E}{\partial s_j^{(i)}} \frac{\partial x_p^{(i-1)}}{\partial s_p^{(i-1)}} \frac{\partial s_p^{(i-1)}}{\partial s_q^{(l)}} + x_r^{(l-1)} x_p^{(i-1)} \frac{\partial^2 E}{\partial s_q^{(l)} \partial s_j^{(i)}} \\
&= x_r^{(l-1)} \sigma'(s_p^{(i-1)}) \frac{\partial E}{\partial s_j^{(i)}} \frac{\partial s_p^{(i-1)}}{\partial s_q^{(l)}} \\
&\quad + x_r^{(l-1)} x_p^{(i-1)} \frac{\partial^2 E}{\partial s_q^{(l)} \partial s_j^{(i)}}
\end{aligned} \tag{5.56}$$

The partial derivative $\partial E/\partial s_j^{(i)}$ can be calculated using Eqn. (5.50) with the initial conditions given in Eqn. (5.51). Next, one has to derive the recursive formulations for the partial derivatives $\partial s_p^{(i-1)}/\partial s_q^{(l)}$ and $\partial^2 E/\partial s_q^{(l)} \partial s_j^{(i)}$.

First, one has

$$\frac{\partial s_j^{(i-1)}}{\partial s_q^{(l)}} = \sum_{r=1}^{n_{l+1}} \frac{\partial s_j^{(i)}}{\partial s_r^{(l+1)}} \frac{\partial s_r^{(l+1)}}{\partial x_q^{(l)}} \frac{\partial x_q^{(l)}}{\partial s_q^{(l)}} = \sum_{r=1}^{n_{l+1}} \frac{\partial s_j^{(i-1)}}{\partial s_r^{(l+1)}} w_{rq}^{(l+1)} \sigma'(s_q^{(l)}) \tag{5.57}$$

with the initial condition

$$\frac{\partial s_j^{(i-1)}}{\partial s_q^{(i-1)}} = \begin{cases} 0, & q \neq j \\ 1, & q = j \end{cases}$$

From Eqn. (5.50) one obtains

$$\begin{aligned} \frac{\partial^2 E}{\partial s_q^{(l)} \partial s_j^{(i)}} &= \frac{\partial}{\partial s_q^{(l)}} \left(\sum_{r=1}^{n_{i+1}} \frac{\partial E}{\partial s_r^{(i+1)}} w_{rj}^{(i+1)} \sigma'(s_j^{(i)}) \right) \\ &= \sum_{r=1}^{n_{i+1}} \left[\frac{\partial^2 E}{\partial s_r^{(i+1)} \partial s_q^{(l)}} w_{rj}^{(i+1)} \sigma'(s_j^{(i)}) \right. \\ &\qquad \left. + \frac{\partial E}{\partial s_r^{(i+1)}} w_{rj}^{(i+1)} \sigma''(s_j^{(i)}) \frac{\partial s_j^{(i)}}{\partial s_q^{(l)}} \right] \end{aligned} \tag{5.58}$$

The initial conditions for the second-order partial derivative $\partial^2 E/\partial s_q^{(l)} \partial s_j^{(i)}$ may be obtained from Eqn. (5.51) as follows:

$$\frac{\partial^2 E}{\partial s_q^{(l)} \partial s_j^{(M)}} = \sigma'(s_j^{(M)}) \frac{\partial x_j^{(M)}}{\partial s_j^{(M)}} \frac{\partial s_j^{(M)}}{\partial s_q^{(l)}} - \left(d_j - x_j^{(M)} \right) \sigma''(s_j^{(M)}) \frac{\partial s_j^{(M)}}{\partial s_q^{(l)}}$$

Using the basic first-order partial derivatives, one finally obtains

$$\frac{\partial^2 E}{\partial s_q^{(l)} \partial s_j^{(M)}} = \left[(\sigma'(s_j^{(M)}))^2 - \left(d_j - x_j^{(M)} \right) \sigma''(s_j^{(M)}) \right] \frac{\partial s_j^{(M)}}{\partial s_q^{(l)}} \tag{5.59}$$

The computing procedure of the second-order partial derivatives, which begins from the output layer in the manner of the backpropagation, is summarized in Table 5.3.

Table 5.3 **Computing the second-order partial derivatives of the error index with respect to the weight parameters**

Step 1:	Calculate initial conditions for the first-order partial derivatives $\partial E/\partial s_j^{(M)}, j = 1, 2, \ldots, n_M$ using Eqn. (5.51);
Step 2:	Let $i \longleftarrow M$ and $l \longleftarrow (M-1)$ calculate $\partial s_j^{(i)}/\partial s_q^{(l)}$, $(j = 1, 2, \ldots, n_M; q = 1, 2, \ldots, n_l)$;
Step 3:	Calculate the second-order partial derivatives $\partial^2 E/[\partial s_q^{(l)} \partial s_j^{(i)}]$, $(j = 1, 2, \ldots, n_i; q = 1, 2, \ldots, n_l)$ using Eqn. (5.58);
Step 4:	Calculate the second-order partial derivatives $\partial^2 E/[\partial w_{qr}^{(l)} \partial w_{jp}^{(i)}]$, $(q = 1, 2, \ldots, n_l, r = 1, 2, \ldots, n_{l-1}; j = 1, 2, \ldots, n_i, p = 1, 2, \ldots, n_{i-1})$ using Eqn. (5.56);
Step 5:	If $l \leq 1$ go to Step 6; otherwise let $l \longleftarrow (l-1)$ then go to Step 2;
Step 6:	If $i \leq 1$ go to Step 7, otherwise let $i \longleftarrow (i-1)$ and $l \longleftarrow i-1$ then go to Step 2;
Step 7:	Calculation is completed. Output $\partial^2 E/[\partial w_{qr}^{(l)} \partial w_{jp}^{(i)}]$, $(q = 1, 2, \ldots, n_l, r = 1, 2, \ldots, n_{l-1};$ $j = 1, 2, \ldots, n_i, p = 1, 2, \ldots, n_{i-1})$.

5.5 SECOND-ORDER OPTIMIZATION LEARNING ALGORITHMS

As discussed in the previous section, the backpropagation (BP) learning algorithm and its modified versions which employ only the first-order partial derivatives of the error function have proved their usefulness in dealing with a large number of classification and function approximation problems. In many cases, the large number of learning iterations needed to optimally adjust the weights of the networks is prohibitive for online applications to problems such as vision systems and adaptive control. An alterative way for speeding up the learning phase is by using higher-order optimization methods that utilize the second-order partial derivatives. In fact, numerical analysis has always focused on methods using not only the local gradient of the function but also the second derivatives. In the former case the function is approximated by only the linear terms that include the first-order derivatives in a Taylor series expansion. In the second case the second-order nonlinear terms that include the second-order derivatives are also used in the Taylor series expansion, resulting in a more precise approximation.

In Section 5.4 we discussed the second-order pruning procedure. In the following discussion, we will study the use of the second-order partial derivatives in the development of some learning algorithms.

Given a vector $\boldsymbol{w}_0$ in the weight space, a second-order Taylor series approximation of the error function around this vector is expressed as

$$E(\boldsymbol{w}) = E(\boldsymbol{w}_0) + \boldsymbol{g}^T \Delta\boldsymbol{w} + \tfrac{1}{2}(\Delta\boldsymbol{w})^T \boldsymbol{H} \Delta\boldsymbol{w} \tag{5.60}$$

where

$$\boldsymbol{g} = \left.\frac{\partial E}{\partial \boldsymbol{w}}\right|_{\boldsymbol{w}=\boldsymbol{w}_0} \quad \text{and} \quad \boldsymbol{H} = \left.\frac{\partial^2 E}{\partial \boldsymbol{w}^2}\right|_{\boldsymbol{w}=\boldsymbol{w}_0}$$

are the gradient vector and the Hessian matrix, respectively. The minima of the function E are located where the gradient of E expressed by Eqn. (5.60) is zero:

$$\frac{\partial E}{\partial \boldsymbol{w}} = \boldsymbol{g} + \boldsymbol{H}\Delta\boldsymbol{w} = 0 \tag{5.61}$$

Therefore, the optimal value of $\boldsymbol{w}$ is given by

$$\boldsymbol{w} = \boldsymbol{w}_0 - \boldsymbol{H}^{-1}\boldsymbol{g} \tag{5.62}$$

Equation (5.62) is a basic formulation for the second-order optimization methods. The key issue related to the second-order methods is in computing the inversion of the Hessian matrix $\boldsymbol{H}$. The numerical approximation for such a complex calculation may help us overcome the difficulties associated with the exact calculation.

5.5.1 Quasi-Newton Methods

The objective of the quasi-Newton methods, such as the Broyden–Fletcher–Goldfarb–Shannon (BFGS) and Davidson–Fletcher–Powell (DFP) methods, is to iteratively compute matrices $\boldsymbol{Q}(k)$ such that

$$\lim_{k \longrightarrow \infty} \boldsymbol{Q}(k) = \boldsymbol{H}^{-1} \tag{5.63}$$

The term *quasi-Newton* is applied since

$$\boldsymbol{Q}(k+1)\Big[\boldsymbol{g}(k+1) - \boldsymbol{g}(k)\Big] = \boldsymbol{w}(k+1) - \boldsymbol{w}(k) \tag{5.64}$$

is satisfied. Thus, the resulting $\boldsymbol{Q}(k)$ can then be used in the following updating equation

$$\boldsymbol{w}(k+1) = \boldsymbol{w}(k) - \boldsymbol{Q}(k)\boldsymbol{g}(k) \tag{5.65}$$

until a minimum is reached. It is relatively easy to verify that the DFP updating formulation for $\boldsymbol{Q}(k)$, which is

$$\begin{aligned} \boldsymbol{Q}(k+1) &= \boldsymbol{Q}(k) + \frac{\Delta\boldsymbol{w}(k+1)(\Delta\boldsymbol{w}(k+1))^T}{(\Delta\boldsymbol{w}(k+1))^T\Delta\boldsymbol{g}(k+1)} \\ &\quad - \frac{(\boldsymbol{Q}(k)\Delta\boldsymbol{g}(k+1))(\boldsymbol{Q}(k)\Delta\boldsymbol{g}(k+1))^T}{(\Delta\boldsymbol{g}(k+1))^T\boldsymbol{Q}(k)\Delta\boldsymbol{g}(k+1)} \end{aligned} \tag{5.66}$$

with

$$\begin{cases} \Delta\boldsymbol{w}(k+1) = \boldsymbol{w}(k+1) - \boldsymbol{w}(k) \\ \Delta\boldsymbol{g}(k+1) = \boldsymbol{g}(k+1) - \boldsymbol{g}(k) \end{cases}$$

satisfies Eqn. (5.64). It can be shown that $\boldsymbol{Q}(k)$ converges to $\boldsymbol{H}^{-1}$. A slightly different version for updating $\boldsymbol{Q}(k)$ is the BFGS algorithm. Battiti and Masulli (1990) pointed out that the BFGS algorithm, as an alternative learning algorithm for the feedforward neural networks, yields an acceleration in computation of about one order of magnitude compared to the BP learning algorithm when tested on the parity problem. As with any second-order optimization methods, the disadvantage of these methods is that the storage of the matrix $\boldsymbol{Q}$ is quadratic in the number of weights of the network.

5.5.2 Conjugate Gradient (CG) Methods for Learning

Another second-order optimization method which has been used in supervised neural learning is the *conjugate gradient* (CG) *method*. Several conjugate gradient algorithms have been proposed as learning algorithms in neural networks (Battiti 1992, Johansson et al. 1990, Moller 1993). Johansson et al. (1990) described the theory of general conjugate gradient methods and how to apply the methods in feedforward neural networks. They also concluded that the standard conjugate gradient method with line search (CGL) is an order of magnitude faster than the standard BP learning algorithm when tested on the parity problem (Johansson et al. 1990). A novel conjugate gradient algorithm, called the *scaled conjugate gradient* (SCG) *method*, was developed by Moller (1993) to avoid the line search per learning iteration. The basic algorithm of conjugate gradient and the related topics for neural learning are now reviewed.

The form of the basic updating equation of the CG algorithm is the same as the general gradient algorithm and is given by

$$\boldsymbol{w}(k+1) = \boldsymbol{w}(k) + \eta(k)\Delta\boldsymbol{w}(k) \tag{5.67}$$

where $\eta(k)$ is a time-varying learning parameter that may be updated using the following line search method:

$$\eta(k) = \min_{\eta}\{E(\boldsymbol{w}(k) + \eta\Delta\boldsymbol{w}(k)) : \eta \geq 0\} \tag{5.68}$$

The conjugate condition for the incremental weight vector $\Delta\boldsymbol{w}$ is designed as (Smagt 1994)

$$(\Delta\boldsymbol{w}(k))^T\boldsymbol{H}(k)\Delta\boldsymbol{w}(k+1) = 0 \tag{5.69}$$

where the Hessian matrix $\boldsymbol{H}(k)$ is calculated at the point $\boldsymbol{w}(k)$. The updating for $\Delta\boldsymbol{w}$, in this case, is chosen as (Smagt 1994)

$$\Delta\boldsymbol{w}(k) = -\boldsymbol{g}(k) + \alpha(k-1)\Delta\boldsymbol{w}(k-1) \tag{5.70}$$

To satisfy the conjugate condition between the vectors $\Delta\boldsymbol{w}(k)$ and $\Delta\boldsymbol{w}(k+1)$, the expressions for the updating parameter $\alpha(k)$ are given as

(i) The Fletcher–Reeves formulation:

$$\alpha(k) = \frac{(\boldsymbol{g}(k+1))^T\boldsymbol{g}(k+1)}{(\boldsymbol{g}(k))^T\boldsymbol{g}(k)} \tag{5.71}$$

(ii) The Polak–Ribiere formulation:

$$\alpha(k) = \frac{(\boldsymbol{g}(k+1))^T(\boldsymbol{g}(k+1) - \boldsymbol{g}(k))}{(\boldsymbol{g}(k))^T\boldsymbol{g}(k)} \tag{5.72}$$

(iii) The Hestenes–Stiefel formulation:

$$\alpha(k) = \frac{[\boldsymbol{g}(k) - \boldsymbol{g}(k-1)]^T\boldsymbol{g}(k)}{(\Delta\boldsymbol{w}(k-1))^T[\boldsymbol{g}(k) - \boldsymbol{g}(k-1)]} \tag{5.73}$$

However, the best formula for updating α is highly problem-dependent. Many studies indicate that the Polak–Ribiere and the Hestenes–Stiefel methods provide a better performance. It can be immediately concluded that Eqns. (5.67)–(5.70) implement the momentum version BP learning algorithm with the learning rate $\eta(k)$ and the momentum parameter α, which is determined subject to the conjugate condition given in Eqn. (5.69). Therefore, the CG learning algorithm is a special type of BP learning algorithms, where the information of the second-order partial derivatives is used to update the learning rate and the momentum parameter. In fact, the preceding conjugate gradient algorithm utilizes information about the direction search for $\Delta\boldsymbol{w}$ from the previous iteration in order to accelerate the convergence. Each search direction is conjugate if the objective function is quadratic.

5.6 LINEARIZED RECURSIVE ESTIMATION LEARNING ALGORITHMS

If the structure of a MFNN is considered as a mapping from the neural input to the neural output, which is at the heart of many problems in system identification, control, equalization, and pattern recognition, the weight learning problem of MFNNs can be considered as the parameter identification problem of a nonlinear system with a known structure. More recently, Singhal and Wu (1989), using an *extended Kalman filter* (EKF) algorithm, and Douglas and Meng (1991) using a least squares (LS) estimation algorithm, improved the BP learning strategies for MFNNs. Although these two algorithms were derived independently using different approaches, they are equivalent. In these approaches, the convergence speed of the BP algorithms is significantly improved, but they are computationally more complex and require more storage. The weight updating requires a centralized computing facility, and this means that the parallel computation structure of the learning is not exploited. The practical applications of the EKF and LS algorithms are thus limited because of their computational and storage complexities. Considering the real-time capability of the learning algorithm, the important research topics in the field of recursive estimation learning algorithm for MFNNs are the problems of reducing the computational and storage requirements. To overcome the difficulties associated with some of these complexities, some decoupled versions of the recursive estimation learning algorithms have been developed.

5.6.1 Linearized Least Squares Learning (LLSL)

Linearized least squares learning (LLSL) can simply represent the input and output transfer function of a MFNN as follows

$$\boldsymbol{y}(k) = \boldsymbol{f}(\boldsymbol{w}, \boldsymbol{x}(k)) \tag{5.74}$$

where $\boldsymbol{x} \in \Re^l$ and $\boldsymbol{y} \in \Re^m$ are, respectively, the neural input vector and the output vector of the network, and $\boldsymbol{w} \in \Re^n$ is the weight parameter vector used to describe the internal network structure. The purpose of weight learning for MFNNs is to estimate the weight vectors $\boldsymbol{w}$ such that the output $\boldsymbol{y}(k)$ of a MFNN tracks the desired output $\boldsymbol{d}(k)$ with an error that converges to zero as $k \longrightarrow \infty$. Hence, if the weights of a MFNN are taken into account as the unknown parameters of a nonlinear input–output system, the weight learning problem of a MFNN can be phrased as the parameter identification process of a nonlinear system.

In other words, if the network structure represented by the number of layers, and the number of hidden neural units is predetermined, the implementation of a known task, which is either a function or input–output pattern pairs, becomes the parameter estimation problem of finding the weight vector $\boldsymbol{w}$ that "solves" the particular input–output mapping problem. However, if $\boldsymbol{f}(.)$ is parameterized by the weight vector $\boldsymbol{w}$, the equation is not linear in the parameter vector $\boldsymbol{w}$ and thus it would seem that the well-known recursive techniques for estimating parameters for stationary linear systems are unable to be applied to the problem. The idea is to linearize the function $\boldsymbol{f}(\boldsymbol{w}, \boldsymbol{x})$ about the current estimate of the parameter vector $\boldsymbol{w}(k)$ to obtain a linearized problem that we can approach with the standard techniques.

Assume that the known pattern pairs $\{\boldsymbol{x}(k), \boldsymbol{d}(k)\}$ may be modeled using the network given in Eqn. (5.74) as

$$\boldsymbol{d}(k) = \boldsymbol{f}(\boldsymbol{w}, \boldsymbol{x}(k)) + \boldsymbol{v}(k) \tag{5.75}$$

where $\boldsymbol{v}(k)$ is a zero-mean stationary white noise disturbance. Let an estimate of $\boldsymbol{w}$ at time k be $\boldsymbol{w}(k)$. A simple linearization of $\boldsymbol{f}(.)$ about $\boldsymbol{w}(k)$ yields

$$\boldsymbol{f}(\boldsymbol{w}, \boldsymbol{x}(k)) \approx \boldsymbol{f}(\boldsymbol{w}(k), \boldsymbol{x}(k)) + (\boldsymbol{G}(k))^T (\boldsymbol{w} - \boldsymbol{w}(k)) \tag{5.76}$$

where

$$\boldsymbol{G}(k) = \left.\frac{\partial \boldsymbol{f}(\boldsymbol{w}, \boldsymbol{x}(k))}{\partial \boldsymbol{w}}\right|_{\boldsymbol{w}=\boldsymbol{w}(k)}$$

is a Jacobian matrix dependent on the current estimate of the weight vector $\boldsymbol{w}(k)$.

Define

$$\hat{\boldsymbol{d}}(k) \triangleq \boldsymbol{d}(k) - \boldsymbol{f}(\boldsymbol{w}(k), \boldsymbol{x}(k)) + (\boldsymbol{G}(k))^T \boldsymbol{w}(k) = (\boldsymbol{G}(k))^T \boldsymbol{w} + \boldsymbol{v}(k) \tag{5.77}$$

Then, $\hat{\boldsymbol{d}}(k)$, which is a linear in the unknown parameter vector $\boldsymbol{w}$, can be calculated at time k using the given weight vector estimate $\boldsymbol{w}(k)$. Thus, we can apply a least squares minimization to $\boldsymbol{w}$ using the new "observed" data $\hat{\boldsymbol{d}}(k)$.

For this linearized problem, a cost function is expressed as

$$E(\boldsymbol{w}(k)) = \frac{1}{k} \sum_{l=1}^{k} \alpha_k \left[\hat{\boldsymbol{d}}(l) - (\boldsymbol{G}(l))^T \boldsymbol{w}\right]^2 \tag{5.78}$$

where α_l are the appropriate weighting factors. Minimization of $E(\boldsymbol{w}(k))$ with respect to $\boldsymbol{w}$ yields the solution

$$\boldsymbol{w}(k+1) = \left[\sum_{l=1}^{k} \alpha_l \boldsymbol{G}(l)(\boldsymbol{G}(l))^T\right]^{-1} \sum_{l=1}^{k} \alpha_l \boldsymbol{G}(l)\hat{\boldsymbol{d}}(l) \tag{5.79}$$

Let us introduce the conditional covariance matrix defined as

$$\boldsymbol{R}(k) = \sum_{l=1}^{k} \alpha_l \boldsymbol{G}(l)(\boldsymbol{G}(l))^T = \boldsymbol{R}(k-1) + \alpha_k \boldsymbol{G}(k)(\boldsymbol{G}(k))^T \tag{5.80}$$

Then, one finally obtains (Douglas and Meng 1991)

$$\boldsymbol{w}(k+1) = \boldsymbol{w}(k) + \alpha_k \boldsymbol{R}^{-1}(k)\boldsymbol{G}(k)\boldsymbol{e}(k) \tag{5.81}$$

$$\boldsymbol{R}(k) = \boldsymbol{R}(k-1) + \alpha_k \boldsymbol{G}(k)(\boldsymbol{G}(k))^T \tag{5.82}$$

$$\boldsymbol{e}(k) = \boldsymbol{d}(k) - \boldsymbol{f}(\boldsymbol{w}(k), \boldsymbol{x}(k)) \tag{5.83}$$

The computational difficulty that existed in the algorithm above is the inversion of the matrix $\boldsymbol{R}(k)$. Since the number of the weights is very large, this calculation is almost prohibitive. However, the matrix inversion lemma may help to simplify the computation of the LLSL algorithm described by Eqns. (5.81)–(5.83) by reducing the order of the matrix involved in the inverse computation. Defining the matrix $\boldsymbol{P}(k) = \boldsymbol{R}^{-1}(k)$ and the gain sequence $\alpha_l = \lambda^{k-1}, 0 < \lambda \leq 1$, we may derive the following algorithm for the weight vector updating (Singhal and Wu 1989, Douglas and Meng 1991)

$$\boldsymbol{A}(k) = \left[\lambda \boldsymbol{I} + (\boldsymbol{G}(k))^T \boldsymbol{P}(k-1)\boldsymbol{G}(k)\right]^{-1} \tag{5.84}$$

$$\boldsymbol{K}(k) = \boldsymbol{P}(k-1)\boldsymbol{G}(k)\boldsymbol{A}(k) \tag{5.85}$$

$$\boldsymbol{P}(k) = \frac{1}{\lambda}\left[\boldsymbol{P}(k-1) - \boldsymbol{K}(k)(\boldsymbol{G}(k))^T \boldsymbol{P}(k-1)\right] \tag{5.86}$$

$$\boldsymbol{w}(k+1) = \boldsymbol{w}(k) + \boldsymbol{K}(k)\boldsymbol{e}(k) \tag{5.87}$$

where $\boldsymbol{A}(k)$ is an $(m \times m)$ matrix, and $\boldsymbol{K}(k)$ is an $(n \times m)$ matrix of the filtering gains. Equations (5.84)–(5.87) are called an *extended Kalman filter* (EKF), which reduces the computation of an $(n \times n)$ matrix inversion to that of an $(m \times m)$ matrix inversion. When $m \ll n$, that is, the number of the neural outputs is much smaller than the number of the weight parameters, the algorithm provides a significant improvement over the direct inversion of $\boldsymbol{R}(k)$. Note that Eqn. (5.87) is similar to the weight updating equation in the BP algorithm with the error term $\boldsymbol{e}(k)$ measured at the output layer of the network. However, unlike the BP algorithm, this error is propagated to the weights through the filtering gain matrix $\boldsymbol{K}(k)$, which updates each weight through the entire gradient matrix $\boldsymbol{G}(k)$ and the conditional covariance matrix $\boldsymbol{P}(k)$.

5.6.2 Decomposed Extended Kalman Filter (DEKF) Learning

Since the dimension of the weight vector that consists of all the weights of a MFNN is usually very high, an efficient approach for reducing the computational and storage requirements of the extended Kalman filter (EKF)-based weight learning algorithm derived above is to decompose the weight vector into several subvectors as shown in Fig. 5.8. The decomposed extended Kalman filter (DEKF) algorithm will be used in this section to perform the weight learning algorithm of MFNNs.

Let the network contain N_n neurons. Naturally, it is easy to group the input weights of a neuron as a sub-vector. Then, the weight vector $\boldsymbol{w}$ in Eqns. (5.84)–(5.87) may be divided into several groups

$$\boldsymbol{w} = \begin{bmatrix} \boldsymbol{w}_1 \\ \boldsymbol{w}_2 \\ \vdots \\ \boldsymbol{w}_{N_n} \end{bmatrix} \in \Re^n, \qquad \boldsymbol{w}_i = \begin{bmatrix} w_{i1} \\ w_{i2} \\ \vdots \\ w_{in_i} \end{bmatrix} \in \Re^{n_i} \tag{5.88}$$

where

$$n = \sum_{j=1}^{N_n} n_j$$

is the total number of the weights involved in the network. Then, the decomposed extended Kalman filtering (DEKF) equations may be obtained from the

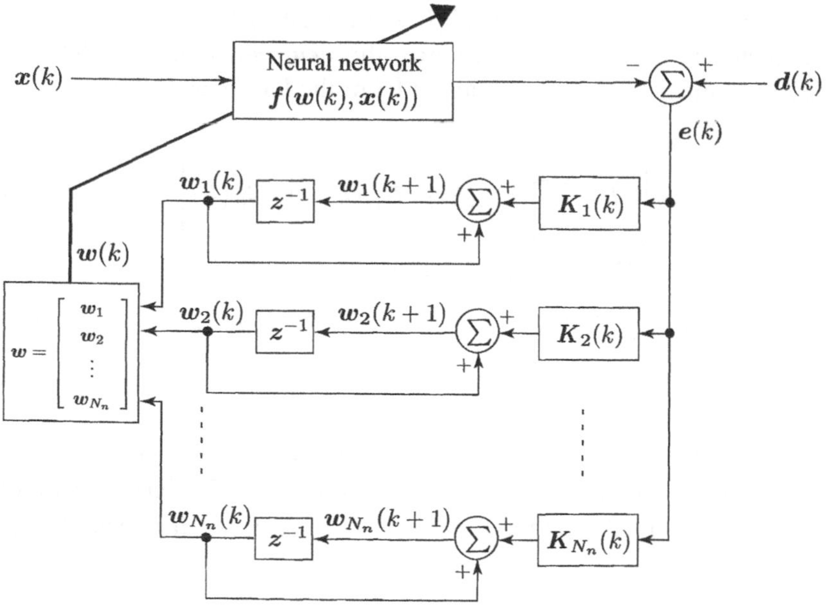

Figure 5.8 Weight learning by the decomposed extended Kalman filter (DEKF), Eqns. (5.89)–(5.92).

standard EKF formulations given in Eqns. (5.84)–(5.87) as follows

$$\boldsymbol{A}(k) = \left[\lambda \boldsymbol{I} + \sum_{\alpha,\beta=1}^{N_n} (\boldsymbol{G}_\alpha(k))^T \boldsymbol{P}_{\alpha\beta}(k-1)\boldsymbol{G}_\beta(k)\right]^{-1} \tag{5.89}$$

$$\boldsymbol{K}_i(k) = \sum_{\alpha=1}^{M} \boldsymbol{P}_{i\alpha}(k-1)\boldsymbol{G}_\alpha(k)\boldsymbol{A}(k) \tag{5.90}$$

$$\boldsymbol{P}_{ij}(k) = \frac{1}{\lambda}\left[\boldsymbol{P}_{ij}(k-1) - \sum_{\alpha=1}^{N_n} \boldsymbol{K}_i(k)(\boldsymbol{G}_\alpha(k))^T \boldsymbol{P}_{i\alpha}(k-1)\right] \tag{5.91}$$

$$\boldsymbol{w}_i(k+1) = \boldsymbol{w}_i(k) + \boldsymbol{K}_i(k)\boldsymbol{e}(k) \tag{5.92}$$

where $\boldsymbol{G}_i(k)$ are $(n_i \times m)$, $(1 \le i \le N_n)$ matrices of the filtering gains and $\boldsymbol{P}_{ij}(k) = (\boldsymbol{P}_{ji}(k))^T$ are $(n_i \times n_j)$ matrices of the error covariance between the estimations $\boldsymbol{w}_i(k)$ and $\boldsymbol{w}_j(k)$. A comparison of the EKF and DEKF shows that even if the storage requirements for the error covariance matrices $\boldsymbol{P}_{ij}(k)$ are the same, each step of the learning algorithm requires $O(n(n+1)/2)$ storage for the $\boldsymbol{P}_{ij}$ matrices, whereas the DEKF algorithm avoids the multiplications of the matrices with very high dimensions at every iteration.

If the error covariance matrices $\boldsymbol{P}_{ij}(k)$ of the estimations $\boldsymbol{w}_i(k)$ and $\boldsymbol{w}_j(k)$ are neglected in the iterative procedure, the *neuron-decoupled* EKF, or the NDEKF formulations, may be obtained from the DEKF as follows

$$\boldsymbol{A}(k) = \left[\lambda I + \sum_{\alpha=1}^{N_n} (\boldsymbol{G}_\alpha(k))^T \boldsymbol{P}_\alpha(k-1)\boldsymbol{G}_\alpha(k)\right]^{-1} \tag{5.93}$$

$$\boldsymbol{K}_i(k) = \boldsymbol{P}_i(k-1)\boldsymbol{G}_i(k)\boldsymbol{A}(k) \tag{5.94}$$

$$\boldsymbol{P}_i(k) = \frac{1}{\lambda}\left[\boldsymbol{P}_i(k-1) - \boldsymbol{K}_i(k)(\boldsymbol{G}_i(k))^T \boldsymbol{P}_i(k-1)\right] \tag{5.95}$$

$$\boldsymbol{w}_i(k+1) = \boldsymbol{w}_i(k) + \boldsymbol{K}_i(k)\boldsymbol{e}(k) \tag{5.96}$$

where $\boldsymbol{P}_i(k) = \boldsymbol{P}_{ii}(k)$ are the $(n_i \times n_i)$ matrices of the error variance of the estimations $\boldsymbol{w}_i(k)$. It is obvious that the NDEKF algorithm requires $O(\sum_{i=1}^{N_n} n_i(n_i+1)/2)$ storage for the $\boldsymbol{P}_i(k)$ matrices. It is easy to verify that

$$\sum_{i=1}^{N_n}\sum_{j=1}^{N_n} n_i n_j \gg \sum_{i=1}^{N_n} n_i^2$$

for $N_n \gg 1$. Thus

$$\frac{n(n+1)}{2} \gg \sum_{i=1}^{N_n} \frac{n_i(n_i+1)}{2}$$

Hence, the computational and storage requirements of the NDEKF are significantly less than those of the DEKF, but the cost associated with this reduction is a decrease in the accuracy of the recursive learning algorithm.

It is known that the NDEKF learning algorithm is a type of partial decoupled algorithm in which the interactions between the neurons of each layer are still considered in the updating process. Furthermore, in order to achieve fully decoupled learning for each weight of the MFNN, a simple and natural extension based on the parallel feature of the BP algorithm is assumed where the error covariance $p_{ij}(k)$ of the weights $w_i(k)$ and $w_j(k)$ is neglected in the NDEKF algorithm. Another approximate *weight-decoupled* EKF (WDEKF) may be derived from the NDEKF formulations given in Eqns. (5.93)–(5.96) as follows

$$w_i(k+1) = w_i(k) + \sum_{v=1}^{M} \mu_{iv}(k) h_{vi}(k) e_v(k) \tag{5.97}$$

$$\mu_{iv}(k) = p_i(k-1) a_v(k) \tag{5.98}$$

$$p_i(k) = \frac{1}{\lambda}\left(1 - \sum_{v=1}^{m} \mu_{iv}(k) h_{vi}^2(k)\right) p_i(k-1) \tag{5.99}$$

$$a_v(k) = \frac{1}{\lambda + \sum_{s=1}^{n} h_{vs}^2(k) p_s(k-1)} \tag{5.100}$$

$$e_v(k) = d_v(k) - f_v(\boldsymbol{w}(k-1), \boldsymbol{x}(k)) \tag{5.101}$$

$$h_{vi}(k) = \frac{\partial e_v(k)}{\partial w_i(k-1)} \tag{5.102}$$

where $\mu_{iv}(k)$ is the learning rate of the weight w_i at time k with respect to the vth output error, $a_v(k)$ are the central adjustment parameters, $p_i(k)$ are the variances of the weights $w_i(k)$, and all iterative variables are scalars. In addition to the advantages associated with the computation and storage, the other attractive feature of the WDEKF is that it can be integrated into the parallel structure of the network similar to the conventional backpropagation algorithm. The WDEKF algorithm is, of course, computationally more complex than the gradient-search-based backpropagation algorithm. However, the convergence rate of the former is much faster than that of the latter. This characteristic of the WDEKF algorithm is very useful in real-time applications of neural networks such as neural identification and control problems.

Equation (5.97) is similar to the weight updating equation of the conventional BP learning algorithm, which is a learning algorithm with a constant learning rate. In the course of numerical simulations with the conventional BP algorithm, it becomes clear that the learning rate μ is critical. If μ is too large, the algorithm will not converge, while if μ is too small, the convergence will be too slow to be practical. The WDEKF learning algorithm overcomes this difficulty by using a varying learning rate that is adjusted adaptively to reach the optimal value at each instant. In other words, the WDEKF may be treated as a type of the BP algorithm with an optimal learning rate.

5.7 TAPPED DELAY LINE NEURAL NETWORKS (TDLNNs)

The so-called tapped delay line neural networks (TDLNNs) consist of MFNNs and some time delay operators as shown in Fig. 5.9. Let $y(k) \in \Re$ be an internal state variable at the time instant k. The delayed states $y(k), y(k-1), \ldots, y(k-n)$ are used as inputs of a TDLNN. The various type of TDLNNs can be further defined on the basis of specified applications.

For time series analysis, the one-step and q-step prediction equations of the TDLNNs, as shown in Fig. 5.9, can be given as follows:

(i) One-step prediction:

$$y(k+1) = F(\boldsymbol{w}, y(k), \ldots, y(k-n), u(k)) \tag{5.103}$$

(2) q-step prediction:

$$y(k+q) = F(\boldsymbol{w}, y(k), \ldots, y(k-n), u(k)) \tag{5.104}$$

In these equations $F(.)$ is a continuous and differentiable function that may be obtained from the operation equation of the MFNN given in Section 5.6. The input components of the neural networks are the time-delayed versions of the outputs of the networks. In this case, Eqns. (5.103) and (5.104) represent, respectively, a one-step-ahead nonlinear predictor and a q-steps-ahead nonlinear predictor. For identification and control applications, the input–output equations of TDLNNs with relative degree one and q steps as illustrated in Fig. 5.10 are

$$y(k+1) = F(\boldsymbol{w}, y(k), \ldots, y(k-n), u(k), \ldots, u(k-m)) \tag{5.105}$$

and

$$y(k+q) = F(\boldsymbol{w}, y(k), \ldots, y(k-n), u(k), \ldots, u(k-m)) \tag{5.106}$$

respectively, where the inputs to the networks are the time-delayed terms of the neural outputs and the current neural inputs. These neural network

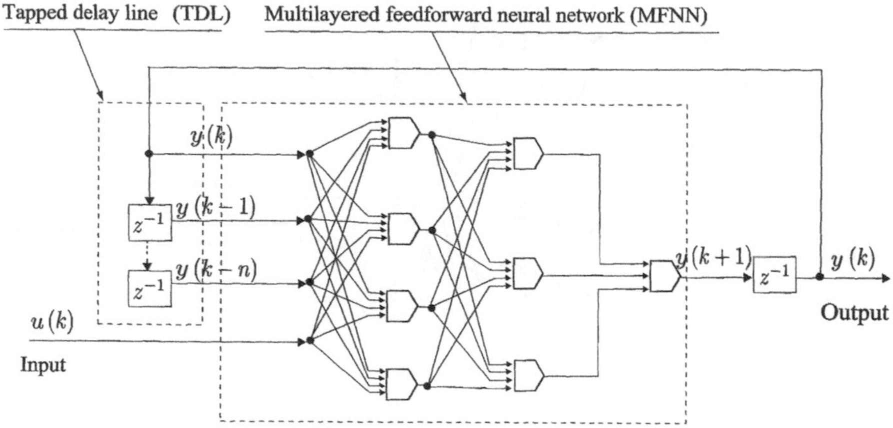

(a) TDLNN with one-step prediction, Eqn. (5.103)

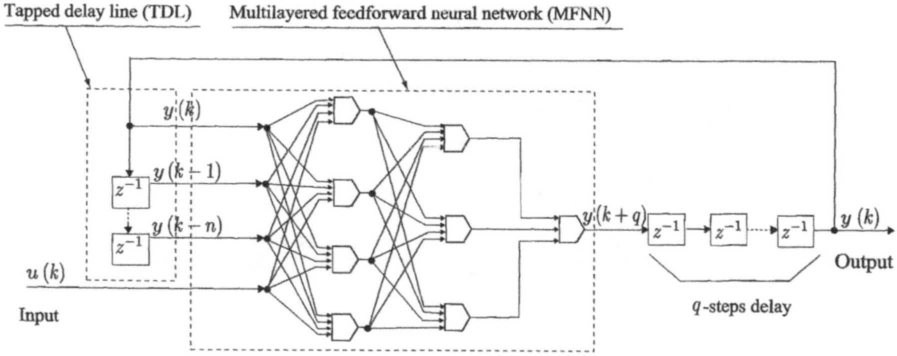

(b) TDLNN with q-steps prediction, Eqn. (5.104)

Figure 5.9 Tapped delay line neural networks (TDLNNs) for time series analysis.

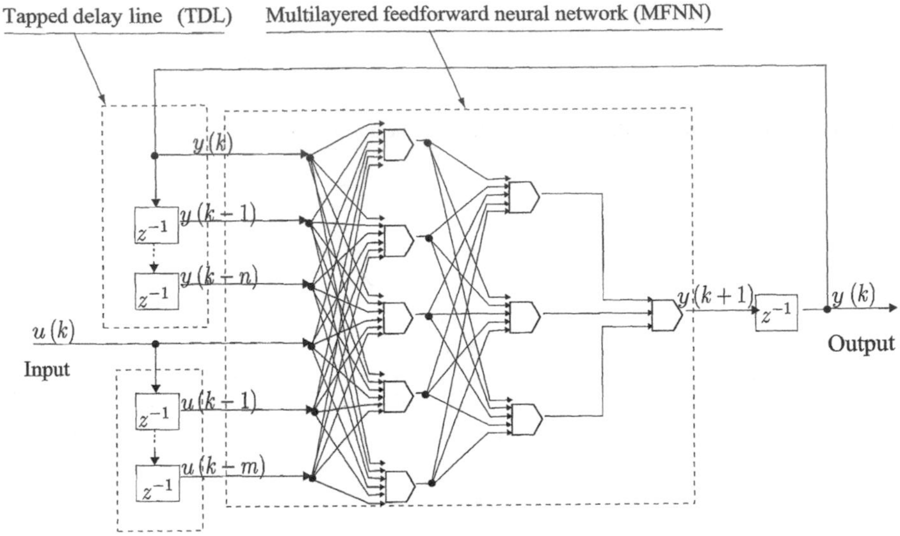

(a) TDLNN with relative degree one, Eqn. (5.105)

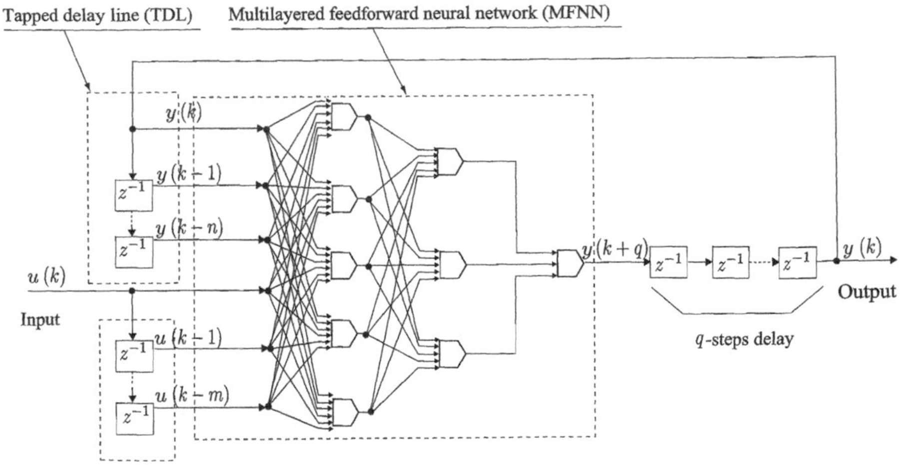

(b) TDLNN with relative degrees q, Eqn. (5.106)

Figure 5.10 Tapped delay line neural networks (TDLNNs) for identification and control.

structures have the potential to represent a class of nonlinear input–output mappings of unknown nonlinear systems or communication channels without internal dynamics, and have been successfully applied to the design of adaptive control systems (Narendra and Parthasarathy 1990). Because there are no state feedback connections in the network, the static backpropagation (BP) learning algorithm may be used to train the TDLNN so that the processes of system modeling or function approximation are carried out.

5.8 APPLICATIONS OF TDLNNs FOR ADAPTIVE CONTROL SYSTEMS

Consider a single-input/single-output (SISO) unknown nonlinear system that has the following input–output equation expressed in a canonical form

$$\begin{aligned} y_p(k+1) &= f(y_p(k), \ldots, y_p(k-n), u(k), \ldots, u(k-m)) \\ &= f(\boldsymbol{x}(k), u(k)) \end{aligned} \tag{5.107}$$

where $\boldsymbol{x}(k) = [y_p(k) \ \cdots \ y_p(k-n) \ u(k-1) \ \cdots \ u(k-m)]^T$ is a state vector, and $f(.)$ is an unknown nonlinear function that satisfies $\partial f(x,u)/\partial u \neq 0$. The *canonical form* of Eqn. (5.107) represents a general class of input–output nonlinear systems without the *internal dynamics*. For a desired output $y_d(k)$, some control schemes for the purpose of adaptive output tracking using TDLNNs are now discussed.

In direct inverse control (DIC), as shown in Fig. 5.11, the input–output equation of the TDLNN that produces the control signal to the system is

$$u(k) = F(\boldsymbol{w}, \boldsymbol{x}(k), r(k+1)) \tag{5.108}$$

where $r(k+1)$ is a reference input defined by

$$r(k+1) = y_d(k+1) + \sum_{i=1}^{\gamma} \beta_i \left[y_d(k-i+1) - y_p(k-i+1) \right], \quad \gamma \leq k \tag{5.109}$$

Let the nonlinear mapping $F(.)$ be trained to approximate the inverse system of the unknown nonlinear system, that is

$$F(\boldsymbol{w}, \boldsymbol{x}, r) \longrightarrow f_u^{-1}(\boldsymbol{x}, r)$$

where $f_u^{-1}(\boldsymbol{x}, r)$ satisfies

$$\begin{aligned} y_p(k+1) &= f(\boldsymbol{x}(k), u(k)) \\ &= f(\boldsymbol{x}(k), f_u^{-1}(\boldsymbol{x}(k), r(k+1)) \\ &= r(k+1) \end{aligned} \tag{5.110}$$

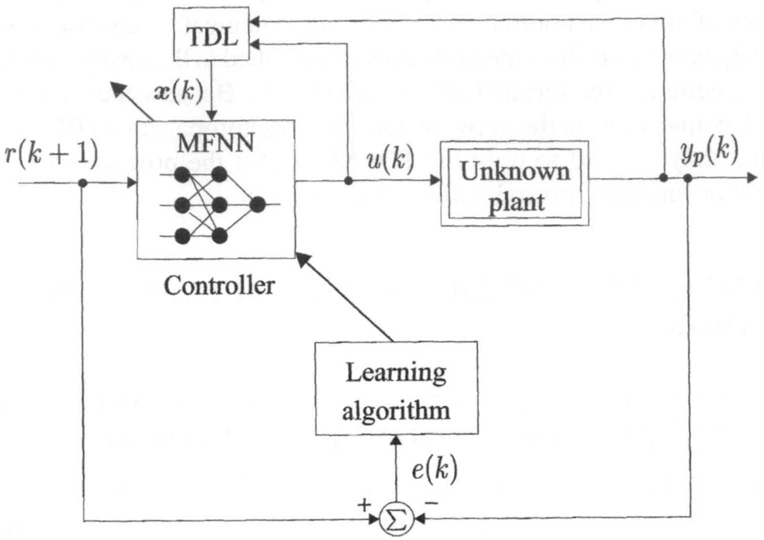

Figure 5.11 Direct inverse control (DIC) using tapped delay line neural network (TDLNN).

Then

$$\begin{aligned} y_p(k+1) &= f(x(k), u(k)) \\ &= f(x(k), F(w, x(k), r(k+1)) \longrightarrow r(k+1) \end{aligned}$$

The output tracking control can be accomplished as long as the parameters $\beta_i, i = 1, \ldots, \gamma$ are chosen so that the roots of the characteristic equation

$$z^\gamma + \beta_\gamma z^{\gamma-1} + \cdots + \beta_1 = 0$$

lie inside the unit circle. If one chooses all $\beta_i = 0$, $i = 1, 2, \ldots, \gamma$, then Eqn. (5.109) becomes

$$y_p(k+1) \longrightarrow y_d(k+1)$$

which describes an output deadbeat response. In terms of robustness, the deadbeat response is not a good choice although the closed-loop response of such a system is the fastest achievable closed-loop response in terms of tracking the desired output $y_d(k)$ (Isermann 1989).

Furthermore, the error index used to train the TDLNN is defined as

$$E(k) = \tfrac{1}{2}(r(k) - y_p(k))^2 = \tfrac{1}{2}e^2(k) \tag{5.111}$$

The partial derivative of $E(k)$ with respect to the weight vector is

$$\frac{\partial E}{\partial \boldsymbol{w}} = -e\frac{\partial y_p}{\partial u}\frac{\partial F}{\partial \boldsymbol{w}} \tag{5.112}$$

If the sign of the $\partial y_p/\partial u$ is known, the BP learning algorithm may be applied to train the TDLNN so that the output tracking control is accomplished. Although TDLNN's simpler structure and a need for less computation are significant advantages for the direct inverse control (DIC) scheme, this method needs more a priori knowledge about the unknown plant.

An indirect inverse control (IIC) scheme is shown in Fig. 5.12. The input–output equation of the TDLNN is

$$y_n(k+1) = F(\boldsymbol{x}(k), u(k)) \tag{5.113}$$

Let the TDLNN be used to approximate the unknown plant through a weight learning process:

$$F(\boldsymbol{w}, \boldsymbol{x}, u) \longrightarrow f(\boldsymbol{x}, u)$$

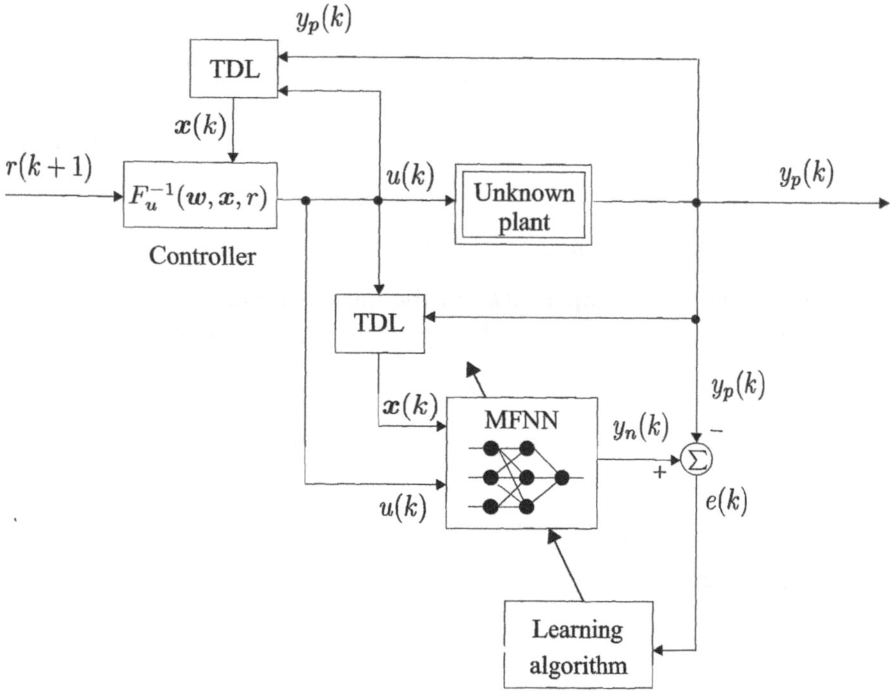

Figure 5.12 Indirect inverse control (IIC) using TDLNN.

The controller may then be obtained by inverting the TDLNN equation as follows

$$u(k) = F_u^{-1}(\boldsymbol{w}, \boldsymbol{x}(k), r(k+1)) \tag{5.114}$$

which, implicitly, is the inverse of the input–output equation of the TDLNN with respect to the current control $u(k)$. Let the reference input $r(k+1)$ be designed as

$$r(k+1) = y_d(k+1) + \sum_{i=1}^{\gamma} \beta_i \left[y_d(k-i+1) - y_n(k-i+1) \right], \quad \gamma \leq k \tag{5.115}$$

where the parameters β_i, $i = 1, \ldots, \gamma$ are chosen so that the roots of the characteristic equation

$$z^\gamma + \beta_\gamma z^{\gamma-1} + \cdots + \beta_1 = 0$$

lie inside the unit circle. Substituting Eqn. (5.115) in Eqn. (5.113) yields

$$\begin{aligned} y_n(k+1) &= F(\boldsymbol{w}, \boldsymbol{x}(k), u(k)) \\ &= F(\ \boldsymbol{w}, \boldsymbol{x}(k), F_u^{-1}(\boldsymbol{w}, \boldsymbol{x}(k), r(k+1))\ ) \\ &= r(k+1) \\ &= y_d(k+1) + \sum_{i=1}^{\gamma} \beta_i \left[y_d(k-i+1) - y_n(k-i+1) \right] \end{aligned} \tag{5.116}$$

that is

$$\lim (y_d(k) - y_n(k)) = 0$$

On the other hand, if the output $y_p(k)$ of the unknown plant is approximated by the output $y_n(k)$ of the TDLNN through a learning process

$$\lim (y_p(k) - y_n(k)) = 0$$

then the output tracking error of the unknown plant with respect to the desired output satisfies

$$|y_d(k) - y_p(k)| \leq |y_d(k) - y_n(k)| + |y_p(k) - y_n(k)| \longrightarrow 0 \tag{5.117}$$

In this case, the error index is represented as

$$\begin{aligned} E(k) &= \tfrac{1}{2}(r(k) - y_p(k))^2 \\ &= \tfrac{1}{2}(y_n(k) - y_p(k))^2 \\ &= \tfrac{1}{2}(F(\boldsymbol{w}, \boldsymbol{x}(k-1), u(k-1)) - y_p(k))^2 \end{aligned} \tag{5.118}$$

5.9 CONCLUDING REMARKS

In this chapter we have provided a more comprehensive view of neural network structures and learning algorithms. Generally speaking, neural network architectures can be used to solve a variety of problems. However, each class of problems that needs to be solved requires a different architecture and learning approach. The exposition in this chapter has focused on some new learning algorithms as extensions and additions to the commonly used BP learning algorithm. Different error measure criteria, neural network pruning through sensitivity calculations, second-order optimization learning algorithms, and tapped delay line neural network structures are some of the important topics that were discussed in this chapter. Some of these discussions may lead to a better design of learning algorithms for situations such as incremental learning, signal and image processing, and adaptive control systems (Brown and Card 2001, Card 2001, Fernandez et al. 2001, Fu 2001, Fujimori 2001b, Homma and Gupta 2002a, Hoya and Chambers 2001, Hyvarinen 2001, Hyvarinen et al. 2001, Hyvarinen and Oja 1997, Iyer and Wunsch 2001, Jin et al. 1993a, Kalman and Bertram 1960, Kim et al. 2000, Ko et al. 2000a, 2000b, Li et al. 2001, McLachlan and Peel 2000, Mozer et al. 2000, Pham and Cardoso 2000, Wang 2000).

Problems

5.1 For the XOR network discussed in Section 4.2, define an error function in the L_1 norm as

$$E = |d - y|$$

Conduct a simulation process for the initial weight values used in Section 4.2 and compare the results obtained with those presented in Section 4.2.

5.2 Consider a two-layered neural network with a single output:

$$y = \sum_{i=1}^{n_2} w_i^{(2)} \sigma \left(\sum_{j=1}^{n_1} w_{ij}^{(1)} x_j + \theta_i \right)$$

Derive the BP learning rule for the error function, called the *loglikelihood* loss or *cross-entropy cost function*, defined as

$$E(\boldsymbol{w}) = -d \ln(y) - (1 - d) \ln(1 - y)$$

5.3 For an m-layered MFNN, an exponential error function for the weight learning is defined as

$$E_e = e^{kE}$$

where

$$E = \frac{1}{2}\sum_{j=1}^{m}(d_j - y_j)^2$$

(a) Derive the gradient formulations

$$\nabla_{w_{jl}^{(i)}} E_e = \frac{\partial E_e}{\partial w_{jl}^{(i)}}$$

(b) Prove that

$$\nabla_{w_{jl}^{(i)}} E_e = K \nabla_{w_{jl}^{(i)}} E$$

where

$$K \triangleq kE_e = ke^{kE}$$

5.4 To minimize a function of the "energy" spent by the hidden neurons throughout the MFNN, an error function may be defined as (Chauvin 1989)

$$E = \frac{\mu_1}{2}\sum_{j=1}^{m}(d - y_j)^2 + \frac{\mu_2}{2}\sum_{i=1}^{M-1}\sum_{j=1}^{n_i}(x_j^{(i)})^2$$

where μ_1 and μ_2 are weight coefficients. Using the gradient descent algorithm, derive a weight learning algorithm and analyze the possible advantages of the second term in the error function.

5.5 Consider a single-input/single-output (SISO) feedforward neural network with the following transfer function

$$y(x, \boldsymbol{w}) = \sum_{i=1}^{n_1} w_i^{(2)} \sigma(w_i^{(1)} x + \theta_i)$$

where $w_i^{(2)}$ and $w_i^{(1)}$ are, respectively, the input and output weights of the hidden unit i, θ_i is the threshold, and $\sigma(.)$ is the sigmoidal function. The cost function, which includes the term of the complexity measure, is defined as

$$E_t(\boldsymbol{w}) = \frac{1}{2N}\sum_{p=1}^{N}(y_d(p) - y(x(p), \boldsymbol{w}))^2 + \lambda \sum_{i=1}^{n_1}\sum_{j=1}^{i-1} S_i S_j$$

where

$$S_i \triangleq \frac{(w_i^{(1)})^2}{1 + (w_i^{(1)})^2} \frac{(w_i^{(2)})^2}{1 + (w_i^{(2)})^2}$$

Using the gradient descent algorithm, derive the weight updating algorithm.

5.6 Verify the following approximate recursive form of the second-order derivative formulation

$$\frac{\partial^2 E}{\partial (s_j^{(i)})^2} \approx (\sigma'(s_j^{(i)}))^2 \sum_{l=1}^{n_{i+1}} (w_{lj}^{(i+1)})^2 \frac{\partial^2 E}{\partial (s_l^{(i+1)})^2}$$

where the second-order derivative of the sigmoidal function is neglected.

5.7 Consider a MFNN with only linear output neurons. Derive the diagonal second-order partial derivative formulations of the error function with respect to the output weights, that is, $\partial^2 E/\partial (w_{ij}^{(M)})^2$.

5.8 Consider a two-layered network given in Fig. 5.13. Let the neural inputs and the desired neural output pairs be

$$\boldsymbol{x}_A = \begin{bmatrix} 1 \\ -1 \end{bmatrix}, \qquad d_A = 0.58$$

$$\boldsymbol{x}_B = \begin{bmatrix} 0.5 \\ 1.5 \end{bmatrix}, \qquad d_B = 0.95$$

$$\boldsymbol{x}_C = \begin{bmatrix} 1.5 \\ -2.0 \end{bmatrix}, \qquad d_C = 0.52$$

$$\boldsymbol{x}_D = \begin{bmatrix} -3 \\ 2 \end{bmatrix}, \qquad d_D = 0.99$$

(a) For given neural inputs $\boldsymbol{x}_A, \boldsymbol{x}_B, \boldsymbol{x}_C$, and $\boldsymbol{x}_D$, calculate the corresponding outputs;

(b) Calculate the saliency for all the weights;

(c) Remove the weight that has the smallest saliency and give the new network structure diagram;

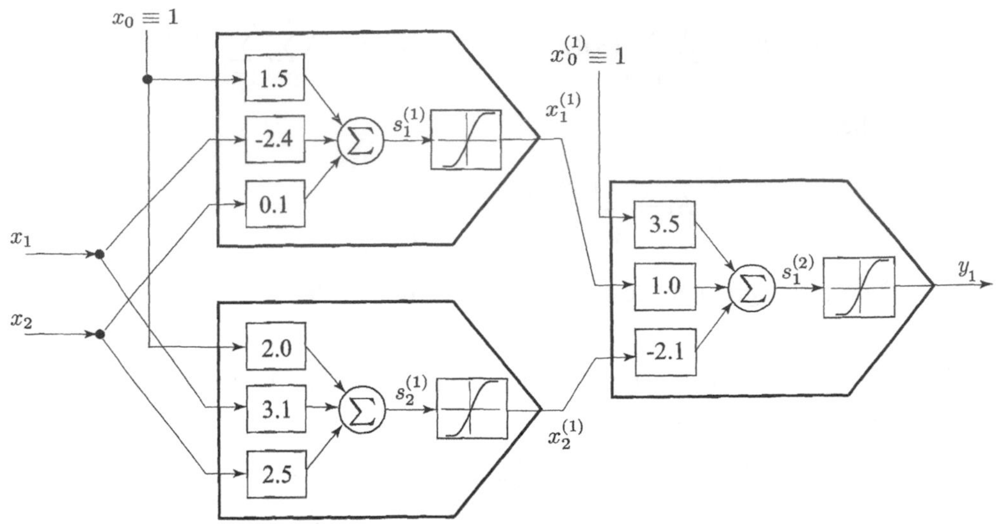

Figure 5.13 Problem 5.8: a two-layered network with the neural inputs $\boldsymbol{x} = [x_1\ x_2]^T$ and the neural output $y = y_1$.

(d) For given inputs $\boldsymbol{x}_A$, $\boldsymbol{x}_B$, $\boldsymbol{x}_C$, and $\boldsymbol{x}_D$ and the new neural network structure derived in **(c)** calculate the corresponding outputs.

5.9 Show that the optimal brain damage (OBD) method for the network pruning may be obtained from the optimal brain surgeon (OBS) method by neglecting the off-diagonal elements of the Hessian matrix.

5.10 Except for the quasi-Newton and conjugate gradient algorithms, give another type of higher-order optimization methods for the weight learning problem.

5.11 Show that in the Fletcher–Reeves conjugate gradient, if one takes

$$\eta(k) = \frac{(\boldsymbol{g}(k))^T \boldsymbol{g}(k)}{(\Delta \boldsymbol{w}(k))^T \boldsymbol{H} \Delta \boldsymbol{w}(k)}$$

and

$$\boldsymbol{g}(k+1) = \boldsymbol{g}(k) - \eta(k) \boldsymbol{H}(k) \Delta \boldsymbol{w}(k)$$

then, $\Delta \boldsymbol{w}(k)$ and $\Delta \boldsymbol{w}(i)$ $(i \neq k)$ are conjugate, that is,

$$\Delta \boldsymbol{w}^T(k) \boldsymbol{H}(k) \Delta \boldsymbol{w}(i) = 0, \quad i \neq k$$

and, $\boldsymbol{g}(k)$ and $\boldsymbol{g}(i)$ $(i \neq k)$ are orthogonal:

$$(\boldsymbol{g}(k))^T \boldsymbol{g}(i) = 0$$

5.12 Consider the weight updating algorithm given by

$$\begin{aligned} \Delta\boldsymbol{w}(k+1) &= \boldsymbol{w}(k) + \eta(k)\Delta\boldsymbol{w}(k) \\ \Delta\boldsymbol{w}(k) &= -\boldsymbol{g}(k) + \alpha_1(k-1)\Delta\boldsymbol{w}(k-1) \\ &\quad + \alpha_2(k-1)\Delta\boldsymbol{w}(i) \end{aligned}$$

where $i < (k-1)$. Give an algorithm for both the parameters α_1 and α_2 such that $\Delta\boldsymbol{w}(k+1)$ is not only conjugate to $\Delta\boldsymbol{w}(k)$ but also to $\Delta\boldsymbol{w}(i)$ (Smagt 1994).

5.13 Consider a multiinput/multioutput (MIMO) linear network described by

$$\boldsymbol{y} = \boldsymbol{W}\boldsymbol{x} + \boldsymbol{v}$$

where $\boldsymbol{y} \in \Re^m$ is the output vector, $\boldsymbol{x} \in \Re^n$ is the input vector, $\boldsymbol{W} \in \Re^{m\times n}$ is the weight matrix, and $\boldsymbol{v}$ is the zero-mean stationary white noise. Let $\{\boldsymbol{x}(k), \boldsymbol{d}(k)\}$ be a desired task pair.

(a) Derive the recursive least squares algorithm for estimating the matrix $\boldsymbol{W}$;

(b) Derive the Kalman filter equation.

5.14 To simplify the linearized least squares learning (LLSL) algorithm given in Eqns. (5.81)-(5.83), one assumes that the off-diagonal elements of the conditional variance matrix $\boldsymbol{R}(k)$ are negligible:

$$\boldsymbol{R}(k) \approx diag[r_1(k), r_2(k), \ldots, r_n(k)]$$

Give the learning formulation for each weight w_i and compare the algorithm obtained with the WDEKF algorithm given in Eqns. (5.97)–(5.102).

5.15 An unknown nonlinear plant to be controlled is assumed to be governed by the difference equation

$$y(k+1) = \frac{[2 + \cos\left(\,7\pi\{y^2(k-1) + y^2(k-2)\}\,\right)] + e^{-u(k)}}{[1 + u^2(k-1) + u^2(k-2)]}$$

Design a TDLNN to adaptive control such a nonlinear system. Show simulation results for the system designed.

5.16 Consider a system identification problem for the nonlinear system of the form

$$\begin{aligned} y(k+1) &= f(y(k), y(k-1), \cdots, y(k-n)) \\ &\quad + g(y(k), y(k-1), \cdots, y(k-m))u(k) \end{aligned}$$

where $f(.)$ and $g(.)$ are two continuous functions. Give a system structure consisting of two TDLNNs for this system identification problem.

5.17 Let the nonlinear function in the above problem be given by

$$f(.) = \frac{y(k)y(k-1)}{1 + y^2(k) + y^2(k-1)}$$

and

$$g(.) = \frac{1}{1 + y^2(k) + y^2(k-1) + y^2(k-2)}$$

Give the simulation results for this nonlinear system identification problem.

5.18 An adaptive echo cancellation mechanism for a telephone system is shown in Fig. 5.14. Let $x(k)$ be a received signal from the channel, and $s(k)$ be a transmitted signal from the speaker. As the impedance mismatch at the hybrid circuit of the system, the received signal $x(k)$ will be returned or reflected as an echo. The objective of the adaptive echo cancellation is to remove the echo signal by using the output of the echo canceller, that is

$$e(k) = r(k) + s(k) - \hat{r}(k) \quad \longrightarrow \quad s(k)$$

(a) Design a linear combiner for such a linear echo canceller. Derive the training algorithm for online adaptation of the echo canceller.

(b) Design a tapped delay line neural network (TDLNN) based echo canceller for dealing with the nonlinear echo dynamics.

(c) Discuss the advantages of using such a neural network based nonlinear version echo cancellation mechanism for a telephone system.

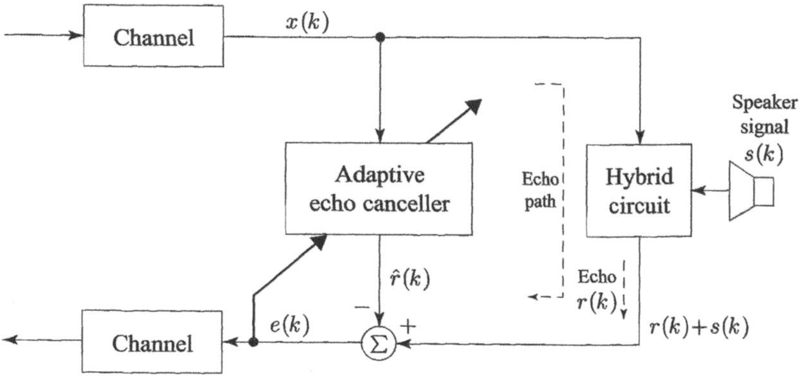

Figure 5.14 Problem 5.18: adaptive echo cancellation.

5.19 In Problem 5.18, let the nonlinear dynamics of the hybrid circuit for generating echo is characterized by a discrete-time nonlinear model

$$r(k+1) = \frac{r(k)}{1+r^2(k)} + x^3(k)$$

where $x(k)$ is the input of the echo path and $r(k)$ is the output of the echo path or simply echo. Design a neural network based echo canceller for cancelling such a nonlinear echo signal.

6

Radial Basis Function Neural Networks

6.1 Radial Basis Function Networks (RBFNs)

6.2 Gaussian Radial Basis Function Neural Networks

6.3 Learning Algorithms for Gaussian RBF Neural Networks

6.4 Concluding Remarks

Problems

Radial basis function (RBF) neural networks have recently been studied intensively. In addition to many applications and improvements, several theoretical results have also been obtained. The RBF neural network has the universal approximation ability, therefore, the RBF neural network can be used for the interpolation problem. A Gaussian radial basis function, an unnormalized form of the Gaussian density function, is highly nonlinear, and it provides some good characteristics for incremental learning, and has many well-defined mathematical features. Gaussian neural networks, which have been found to be powerful scheme for learning complex input–output mapping, have been used in learning, identification, equalization, and control of nonlinear dynamic systems. In this chapter we introduce the concepts of RBF and give some of its applications.

6.1 RADIAL BASIS FUNCTION NETWORKS (RBFNs)

6.1.1 Basic Radial Basis Function Network Models

The *radial basis function network* (RBFN), or the *potential function network*, as an alternative to the multilayered feedforward neural networks (MFNNs), has been studied intensively. A RBFN is a multidimensional nonlinear function mapping that depends on the distance between the input vector and the center vector. A RBFN with an n-dimensional input $\boldsymbol{x} \in \Re^n$ and a single output $y \in \Re$ can be represented, as shown in Fig. 6.1, by the weighted summation of a finite number of radial basis functions as follows

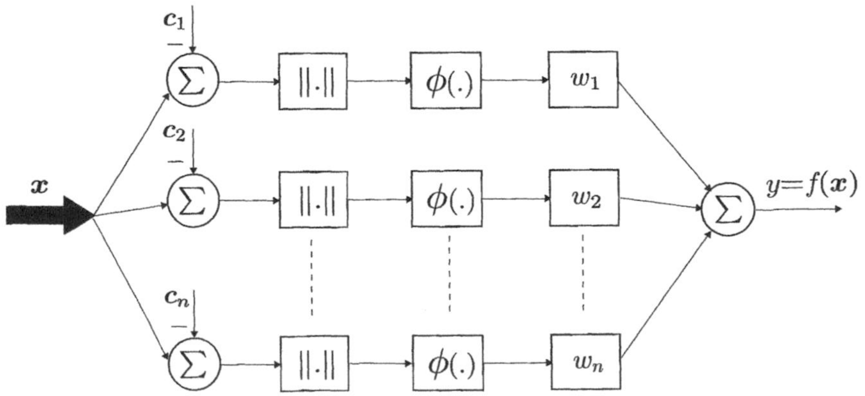

Figure 6.1 Block diagram representation of the radial basis function network (RBFN) with input $\boldsymbol{x} \in \Re^n$ and output $y \in \Re$.

$$y \triangleq f(\boldsymbol{x}) = \sum_{i=1}^{n} w_i \phi_i(||\boldsymbol{x} - \boldsymbol{c}_i||) \tag{6.1}$$

where $\phi_i(||\boldsymbol{x} - \boldsymbol{c}_i||)$ is the *radial basis function* of $\boldsymbol{x}$, obtained by shifting $\phi_i(||\boldsymbol{x}||)$ by $\boldsymbol{c}_i$. For simplicity, it can always chosen the same type of radial basis function ϕ for all weighted summation given in the above, therefore, Eqn. (6.1) can be rewritten as

$$y \triangleq f(\boldsymbol{x}) = \sum_{i=1}^{n} w_i \phi(||\boldsymbol{x} - \boldsymbol{c}_i||) \tag{6.2}$$

In this equation $\phi(.)$ is an arbitrary nonlinear function, $||.||$ denotes a norm that is usually assumed to be Euclidean, the known vectors $\boldsymbol{c}_i \in \Re^n$ are viewed as the centers of the radial basis functions, and w_i is a weight parameter. For instance, the radial basis function $\phi(||\boldsymbol{x} - \boldsymbol{c}_i||)$, which has been used in classical physics, has the maximum value at $\boldsymbol{x} = \boldsymbol{c}_i$ and decreases monotonically to zero as $||\boldsymbol{x} - \boldsymbol{c}_i||$ approaches infinity. The term *radial basis function* derives from the fact that these functions are radially symmetric; that is, each node produces an identical output for inputs that lie at a fixed radial distance from the center. In other words, a radial basis function $\phi(||\boldsymbol{x} - \boldsymbol{c}_i||)$ has the same value for all neural inputs $\boldsymbol{x}$ that lie on a hypersphere with the center $\boldsymbol{c}_i$. A two-dimensional example is shown in Fig. 6.2a.

If the individual elements of the input vector $\boldsymbol{x}$ belong to different classes, it is more appropriate to introduce a weighted norm (Poggio and Girosi 1990) in the radial basis function such that the RBFN may be represented as

$$y = f(\boldsymbol{x}) = \sum_{i=1}^{n} w_i \phi(||\boldsymbol{x} - \boldsymbol{c}_i||_{\boldsymbol{K}_i}) \tag{6.3}$$

where $\boldsymbol{K}_i \in \Re^{n \times n}$ is a weight matrix and the weighted Euclidean norm is given by

$$\begin{aligned} ||\boldsymbol{x} - \boldsymbol{c}_i||^2_{\boldsymbol{K}_i} &= ||\boldsymbol{K}_i(\boldsymbol{x} - \boldsymbol{c}_i)||^2 \\ &= (\boldsymbol{x} - \boldsymbol{c}_i)^T \boldsymbol{K}_i^T \boldsymbol{K}_i (\boldsymbol{x} - \boldsymbol{c}_i) \end{aligned} \tag{6.4}$$

In a simple case, $\boldsymbol{K}_i$ is a diagonal matrix, $\boldsymbol{K}_i = diag[k_{i1}, k_{i2}, \ldots, k_{in}]$ and the diagonal elements k_{ij} are assigned a specific weight to each input coordinate, and the standard Euclidean norm is obtained when $\boldsymbol{K}_i$ is set to the identity matrix. However, the radially symmetric property is no longer true for the weighted norms. The radial basis function (RBF) produces the same value for all inputs $\boldsymbol{x}$ that lie on a hyperellipsoid with the center $\boldsymbol{c}_i$ and the axes are determined by the weight matrix $\boldsymbol{K}_i$ as shown in Fig. 6.2b for a

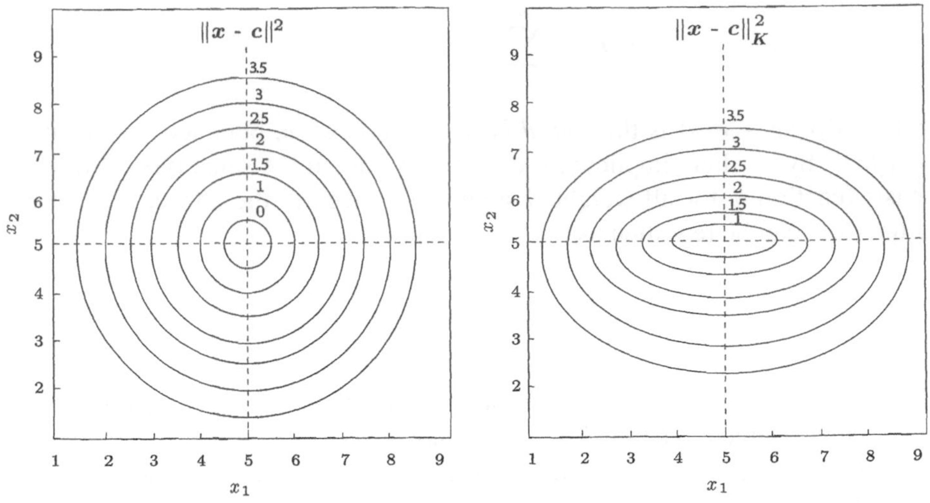

(a) $\| \boldsymbol{x} - \boldsymbol{c} \|^2$ with $\boldsymbol{c} = [5, 5]^T$

(b) $\| \boldsymbol{x} - \boldsymbol{c} \|^2_{\boldsymbol{K}}$ with $\boldsymbol{c} = [5, 5]^T$ and $\boldsymbol{K} = diag[4, 3]$

Figure 6.2 A two-dimensional example for $\| \boldsymbol{x} - \boldsymbol{c} \|^2$ and $\| \boldsymbol{x} - \boldsymbol{c} \|^2_{\boldsymbol{K}}$.

two-dimensional example. The introduction of the concept of the weighted norm plays a critical role whenever different types of inputs are presented.

Like the MFNNs, the RBFNs can be used for both classification and functional approximation. A simple classification example is given in Fig. 6.3, where three classes of patterns can be effectively classified using a single linear radial basis function neural unit

$$\phi(||\boldsymbol{x} - \boldsymbol{c}||) = ||\boldsymbol{x} - \boldsymbol{c}|| \tag{6.5}$$

and the decision functions are easily obtained as

$$\begin{array}{ll} \phi(||\boldsymbol{x} - \boldsymbol{c}||) < r_1 : & \text{class 1} \\ r_1 < \phi(||\boldsymbol{x} - \boldsymbol{c}||) < r_2 : & \text{class 2} \\ \phi(||\boldsymbol{x} - \boldsymbol{c}||) > r_2 : & \text{class 3} \end{array}$$

where $\boldsymbol{c}$ is selected as the center of the patterns, and decision radii r_1 and r_2 are appropriately valued to produce the circular decision boundaries as shown in Fig. 6.3. However, a conventional single neuron with a sigmoidal activation function will not be able to carry out such a classification task.

For the case of multiple-output, the RBFN given by Eqn. (6.2) can be extended as

$$y_j \triangleq f_j(\boldsymbol{x}) = \sum_{i=1}^{n} w_{ij}\phi(||\boldsymbol{x} - \boldsymbol{c}_i||); \quad j = 1, 2, \ldots, m$$

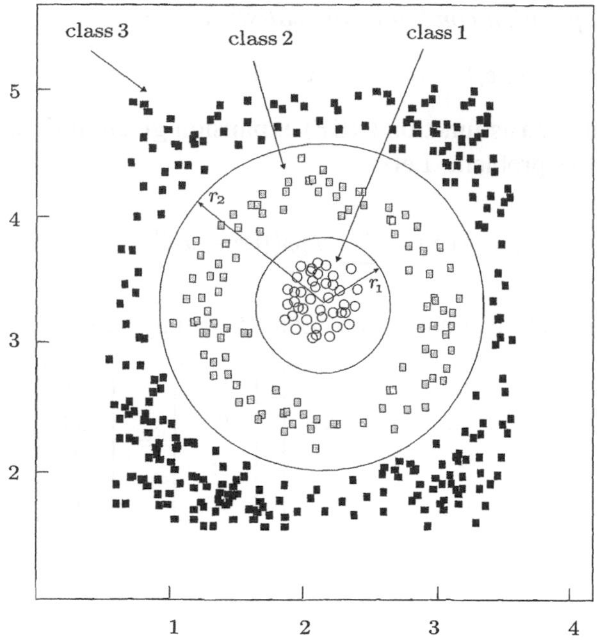

Figure 6.3 An example of a two-dimensional classification example problem using RBF neural units.

or a vector form

$$\boldsymbol{y} \triangleq \boldsymbol{f}(\boldsymbol{x}) = \boldsymbol{W}\boldsymbol{\phi} \tag{6.6}$$

where

$$\boldsymbol{W} = \begin{bmatrix} w_{11} & w_{12} & \cdots & w_{1n} \\ w_{21} & w_{22} & \cdots & w_{2n} \\ \vdots & \vdots & \ddots & \vdots \\ w_{n1} & w_{n2} & \cdots & w_{nn} \end{bmatrix} \quad \text{and} \quad \boldsymbol{\phi} = \begin{bmatrix} \phi(\|\boldsymbol{x} - \mathbf{c}_1\|) \\ \phi(\|\boldsymbol{x} - \mathbf{c}_2\|) \\ \vdots \\ \phi(\|\boldsymbol{x} - \mathbf{c}_n\|) \end{bmatrix}$$

6.1.2 RBFNs and Interpolation Problem

The radial basis function (RBFN) can naturally be derived from the classic interpolation problem. The RBFN is one of the possible solutions to the *real multivariable interpolation problem* for data that are nonuniformly sampled. Mathematically, this problem can be stated as follows:

Given n different points $\{\boldsymbol{x}_i \in \Re^p,\ i = 1, 2, \ldots, n\}$ and n real numbers $\{y_i \in \Re,\ i = 1, 2, \ldots, n\}$, find a function $f : \Re^n \longrightarrow \Re$ such that the *following interpolation conditions are satisfied:*

$$f(\boldsymbol{x}_i) = y_i, \qquad i = 1, 2, \ldots, n \tag{6.7}$$

In fact, the radial basis function (RBF) expansion given in Eqn. (6.2) may be used to solve this problem. Let

$$y = f(\boldsymbol{x}) = \sum_{i=1}^{n} w_i \phi(||\boldsymbol{x} - \boldsymbol{x}_i||) \tag{6.8}$$

Then, the interpolation conditions of Eqn. (6.7) may be interpreted as

$$\begin{bmatrix} \phi_{11} & \phi_{12} & \cdots & \phi_{1n} \\ \phi_{21} & \phi_{22} & \cdots & \phi_{2n} \\ \vdots & \vdots & \ddots & \vdots \\ \phi_{n1} & \phi_{n2} & \cdots & \phi_{nn} \end{bmatrix} \begin{bmatrix} w_1 \\ w_2 \\ \vdots \\ w_n \end{bmatrix} = \begin{bmatrix} y_1 \\ y_2 \\ \vdots \\ y_n \end{bmatrix} \tag{6.9}$$

where

$$\phi_{ij} \triangleq \phi(||\boldsymbol{x}_j - \boldsymbol{x}_i||); \quad i, j = 1, 2, \ldots, n$$

Also, let

$$\boldsymbol{y} = \begin{bmatrix} y_1 \\ y_2 \\ \vdots \\ y_n \end{bmatrix} \in \Re^n, \qquad \boldsymbol{w} = \begin{bmatrix} w_1 \\ w_2 \\ \vdots \\ w_n \end{bmatrix} \in \Re^n$$

and

$$\boldsymbol{\Phi} = \begin{bmatrix} \phi_{11} & \phi_{12} & \cdots & \phi_{1n} \\ \phi_{21} & \phi_{22} & \cdots & \phi_{2n} \\ \vdots & \vdots & \ddots & \vdots \\ \phi_{n1} & \phi_{n2} & \cdots & \phi_{nn} \end{bmatrix} \in \Re^{n \times n}$$

be the desired value vector, the weight vector, and the interpolation matrix, respectively. Then, Eqn. (6.7) in a compact form is expressed as

$$\boldsymbol{\Phi w} = \boldsymbol{y} \tag{6.10}$$

A necessary and sufficient condition to solve the interpolation problem is the invertibility of the matrix $\boldsymbol{\Phi}$. Hence, if we can suitably select the radial basis function $\phi(.)$ such that $\boldsymbol{\Phi}$ is nonsingular, then the solution of the weight vector $\boldsymbol{w}$ is obtained as

$$\boldsymbol{w} = \boldsymbol{\Phi}^{-1} \boldsymbol{y} \tag{6.11}$$

Fortunately, the previous results due to Micchelli (1986) have shown that for n distinct points $\boldsymbol{x}_1, \boldsymbol{x}_2, \ldots, \boldsymbol{x}_n \in \Re^p$, the following classes of radial basis functions, as shown in Fig. 6.4, may guarantee the nonsingularity of $\boldsymbol{\Phi}$:
(i) Gaussian radial basis function:

$$\phi(r) = e^{-(r/c)^2} \tag{6.12}$$

(ii) Multiquadratic radial basis function:

$$\phi(r) = (c^2 + r^2)^\beta, \qquad (0 < \beta < 1) \tag{6.13}$$

(iii) Inverse multiquadratic radial basis function:

$$\phi(r) = \frac{1}{(c^2 + r^2)^\alpha}, \qquad (\alpha > 0) \tag{6.14}$$

(iv) Thin plate splines radial basis function:

$$\phi(r) = r^2 \log(r) \tag{6.15}$$

(v) Cubic splines radial basis function:

$$\phi(r) = r^3 \tag{6.16}$$

(vi) Linear splines radial basis function:

$$\phi(r) = r \tag{6.17}$$

Functions given in Eqns. (6.12)–(6.17) can be used in practice for data interpolation by means of the RBF given in Eqn. (6.8). In particular, in a one-dimensional linear case, the Eqn. (6.17) RBF corresponds to piecewise linear interpolation; that is, the simplest case of spline interpolation. The function given in Eqn. (6.13) is multiquadric for $\beta = \frac{1}{2}$, while the function given in Eqn. (6.14) is inverse multiquadric for $\alpha = \frac{1}{2}$. More recently, Light (1992) proved that for the Gaussian radial basis function given in Eqn. (6.12) and the inverse multiquadric function

$$\phi(r) = \frac{1}{(c^2 + r^2)^{1/2}} \qquad \text{for some} \quad c > 0, \quad \text{and} \quad r \geq 0 \tag{6.18}$$

the interpolation matrix is not only nonsingular but is also a positive definite function. However, there exists a problem of selecting the parameters in these radial basis functions.

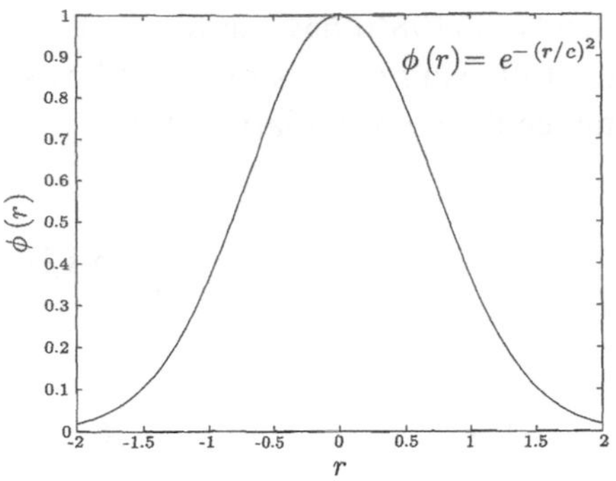

(a) Gaussian radial basis function, $\phi(r) = e^{-(r/c)^2}$ with $c = 1$, Eqn. (6.12)

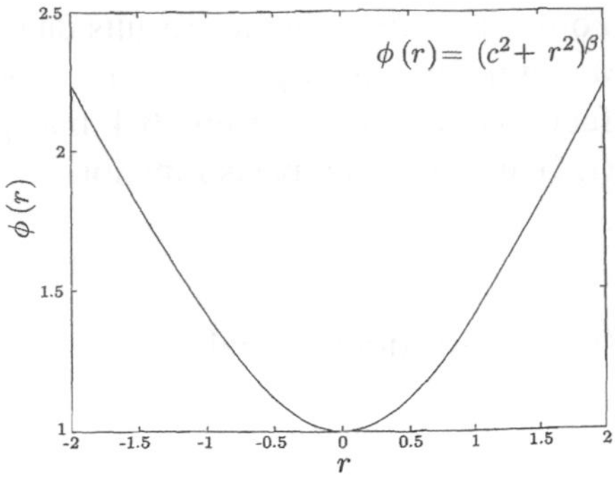

(b) Multiquadratic radial basis function, $\phi(r) = (c^2+r^2)^\beta$ with $c = 1$ and $\beta = 0.5$, Eqn. (6.13)

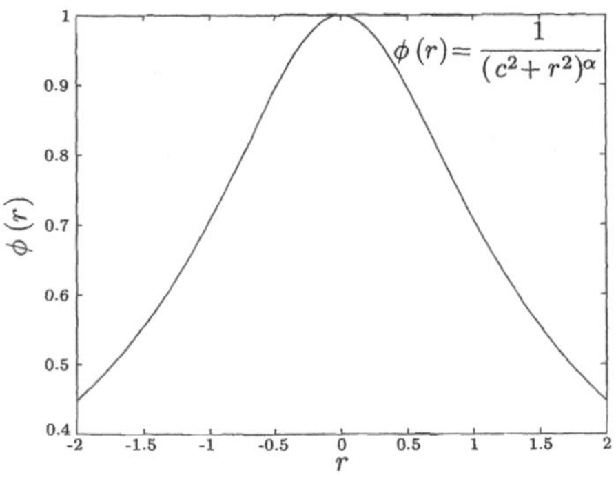

(c) Inverse multiquadratic radial basis function, $\phi(r) = 1/(c^2 + r^2)^\alpha$ with $c = 1$ and $\alpha = 0.5$, Eqn. (6.14)

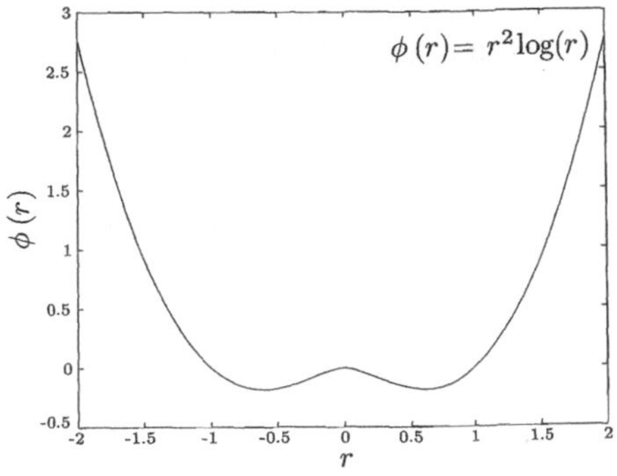

(d) Thin plate splines radial basis function, $\phi(r) = r^2 \log(r)$, Eqn. (6.15)

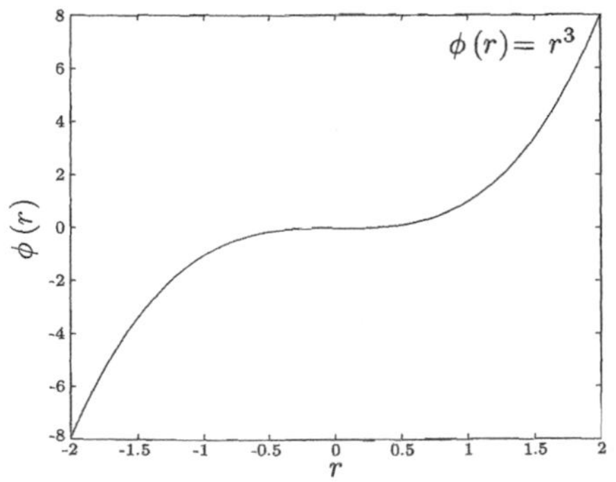

(e) Cubic splines radial basis function, $\phi(r) = r^3$, Eqn. (6.16)

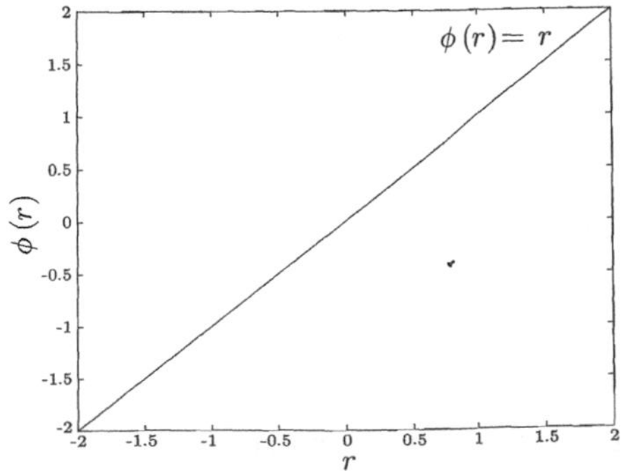

(f) Linear splines radial basis function, $\phi(r) = r$, Eqn. (6.17)

Figure 6.4 Radial basis functions that guarantee the nonsingularity of $\mathbf{\Phi}$ in Eqn. (6.11).

Example 6.1 In this example we consider a two-variable XOR problem using the RBFN with the linear radial basis function (RBF) $\phi(r) = r$.

The RBF network with four linear radial basis functions, as shown in Fig. 6.5, is assumed to be of the following form:

$$y = \sum_{i=1}^{4} w_i ||\boldsymbol{x} - \boldsymbol{c}_i||$$

The four binary input vectors and the associated output vector are

$$\boldsymbol{x}_1 = \begin{bmatrix} -1 \\ -1 \end{bmatrix}, \quad \boldsymbol{x}_2 = \begin{bmatrix} 1 \\ -1 \end{bmatrix}, \quad \boldsymbol{x}_3 = \begin{bmatrix} -1 \\ 1 \end{bmatrix}, \quad \boldsymbol{x}_4 = \begin{bmatrix} 1 \\ 1 \end{bmatrix}$$

and

$$\boldsymbol{y} = \begin{bmatrix} -1 \\ 1 \\ 1 \\ -1 \end{bmatrix}$$

respectively. Correspondingly, the center parameter vectors in the linear radial basis functions are selected as

$$\begin{cases} \boldsymbol{c}_1 = \boldsymbol{x}_1 \\ \boldsymbol{c}_2 = \boldsymbol{x}_2 \\ \boldsymbol{c}_3 = \boldsymbol{x}_3 \\ \boldsymbol{c}_4 = \boldsymbol{x}_4 \end{cases}$$

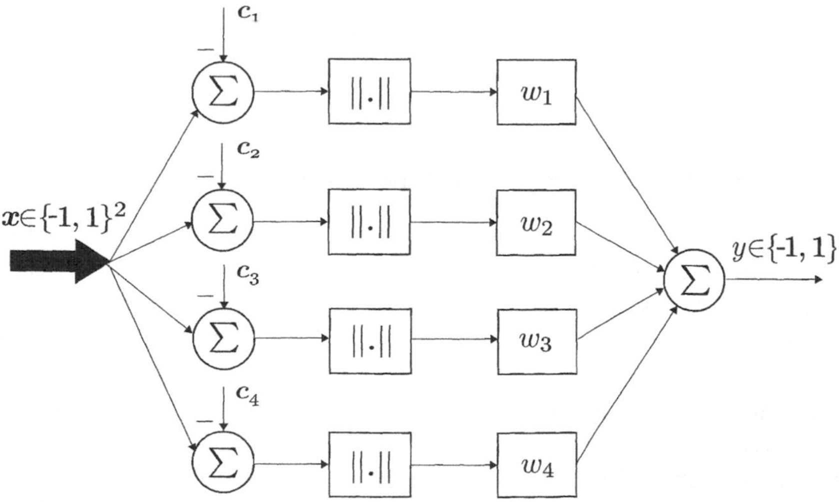

Figure 6.5 Example 6.1: a radial basis function network (RBFN) for the two-variable XOR problem.

In this case, the interpolation matrix $\mathbf{\Phi}$ may be calculated as

$$\begin{aligned}\mathbf{\Phi} &= \begin{bmatrix} \|\boldsymbol{x}_1 - \mathbf{c}_1\| & \|\boldsymbol{x}_1 - \mathbf{c}_2\| & \|\boldsymbol{x}_1 - \mathbf{c}_3\| & \|\boldsymbol{x}_1 - \mathbf{c}_4\| \\ \|\boldsymbol{x}_2 - \mathbf{c}_1\| & \|\boldsymbol{x}_2 - \mathbf{c}_2\| & \|\boldsymbol{x}_2 - \mathbf{c}_3\| & \|\boldsymbol{x}_2 - \mathbf{c}_4\| \\ \|\boldsymbol{x}_3 - \mathbf{c}_1\| & \|\boldsymbol{x}_3 - \mathbf{c}_2\| & \|\boldsymbol{x}_3 - \mathbf{c}_3\| & \|\boldsymbol{x}_3 - \mathbf{c}_4\| \\ \|\boldsymbol{x}_4 - \mathbf{c}_1\| & \|\boldsymbol{x}_4 - \mathbf{c}_2\| & \|\boldsymbol{x}_4 - \mathbf{c}_3\| & \|\boldsymbol{x}_4 - \mathbf{c}_4\| \end{bmatrix} \\ &= \begin{bmatrix} 0 & 2 & 2 & 2\sqrt{2} \\ 2 & 0 & 2\sqrt{2} & 2 \\ 2 & 2\sqrt{2} & 0 & 2 \\ 2\sqrt{2} & 2 & 2 & 0 \end{bmatrix}\end{aligned}$$

It is easy to verify that the 4×4 matrix $\mathbf{\Phi}$ is nonsingular. Thus, the weight vector $\boldsymbol{w} = [w_1\ w_2\ w_3\ w_4]^T$ may be solved by the matrix equation

$$\mathbf{\Phi}\boldsymbol{w} = \boldsymbol{y}$$

that is

$$\begin{bmatrix} 0 & 2 & 2 & 2\sqrt{2} \\ 2 & 0 & 2\sqrt{2} & 2 \\ 2 & 2\sqrt{2} & 0 & 2 \\ 2\sqrt{2} & 2 & 2 & 0 \end{bmatrix} \begin{bmatrix} w_1 \\ w_2 \\ w_3 \\ w_4 \end{bmatrix} = \begin{bmatrix} -1 \\ 1 \\ 1 \\ -1 \end{bmatrix}$$

which yields

$$\begin{cases} w_1 = w_4 = \dfrac{2+\sqrt{2}}{4} \\ w_2 = w_3 = -\dfrac{2+\sqrt{2}}{4} \end{cases}$$

■

6.1.3 Solving Overdetermined Equations

Determining the proper number of hidden nodes and their specific locations is of fundamental importance since they provide the basis to the interpolation problem. As discussed in Example 6.1, the obvious choice for a RBF is to place the center vectors of the radial basis functions on every known point such that $\mathbf{\Phi}$ is a nonsingular square matrix. Thus, an *exact* problem with the weight parameters whose number is the same as that of the equations can be easily solved.

It can be seen easily that, if the number n of the sample points is very large, the above method is somewhat unrealistic (Lee and Kil 1991). In this case, this scheme will encounter some limitations due to the speed and memory problems in computer simulations, also due to hardware restrictions in VLSI implementations. Hence, it is of interest to study the problem for using as small as possible the number of radial basis functions for solving the interpolation problem. In this case, let

$$y = f(\boldsymbol{x}) = \sum_{i=1}^{m} w_i \phi(||\boldsymbol{x} - \boldsymbol{c}_i||) \tag{6.19}$$

and

$$\boldsymbol{w} = \begin{bmatrix} w_1 \\ w_2 \\ \vdots \\ w_m \end{bmatrix}, \quad \text{and} \quad \boldsymbol{\Phi} = \begin{bmatrix} \phi_{11} & \phi_{12} & \cdots & \phi_{1m} \\ \phi_{21} & \phi_{22} & \cdots & \phi_{2m} \\ \vdots & \vdots & \cdots & \vdots \\ \phi_{n1} & \phi_{n2} & \cdots & \phi_{nm} \end{bmatrix} \tag{6.20}$$

where

$$\phi_{ij} \triangleq \phi(||\boldsymbol{x}_j - \boldsymbol{c}_i||), \quad i = 1, 2, \ldots, m; \; j = 1, 2, \ldots, n \tag{6.21}$$

For a set of known $\boldsymbol{c}_i \in \Re^p$, $(i = 1, 2, \ldots, m)$, the interpolation problem may be redescribed as a solution of the following equation:

$$\boldsymbol{\Phi w} = \boldsymbol{y} \tag{6.22}$$

The question is whether and how, for a given $\boldsymbol{y}$, we can adjust $\boldsymbol{\Phi}$ to find an exact solution for $\boldsymbol{w}$ satisfying Eqn. (6.22) or an optimal solution minimizing the error

$$E \triangleq ||\boldsymbol{y} - \boldsymbol{\Phi w}||^2 \tag{6.23}$$

In the case when $m \geq n$, there always exists one or more exact solutions for $\boldsymbol{w}$ that satisfies Eqn. (6.22); this is because of the properties of the radial basis function $\phi(.)$. However, the condition $m \geq n$ is unrealistic since n is usually selected very large for the minimization of the interpolation errors. For $m < n$, Eqn. (6.22) represents an over-determined set of equations in the sense that there are more data points than the weighted parameters to be determined. The existence condition of the exact solution that depends on both the matrix $\boldsymbol{\Phi}$ and the vector $\boldsymbol{y}$ may be given as

$$rank[\boldsymbol{\Phi} \;\vdots\; \boldsymbol{y}] = m \tag{6.24}$$

Whether $\boldsymbol{\Phi}$ can be chosen to satisfy this condition, by adjusting the parameter vectors $\boldsymbol{c}_i$, is a problem that needs to be further studied.

In fact, the condition in Eqn. (6.24) is equivalent to the condition that $\boldsymbol{y}$ is embedded in the subspace S_ϕ defined by

$$S_\phi \triangleq span\{\phi_1, \phi_2, \ldots, \phi_m\} \tag{6.25}$$

where $\boldsymbol{\phi}_i = [\phi_{i1}\, \phi_{i2} \cdots \phi_{in}]^T \in \Re^n$. In other words, the solvability condition requires that $\boldsymbol{y}$ lies in the linear subspace spanned by the column vectors ϕ_i, $i = 1, 2, \ldots, m$. However, there exists the possibility that an adjustment of the center parameter vectors $\boldsymbol{c}_i$ in the radial basis functions may provide the setting of ϕ_i, $i = 1, 2, \ldots, m$ such that $\boldsymbol{y}$ is embedded in S_ϕ. In this case, the solutions of the weight vector $\boldsymbol{w}$ may be given by the following recursive formulations (Barmann and Biegler-Konig 1992)

$$w_j = \frac{< \boldsymbol{\phi}_j, \boldsymbol{s}_j >}{||\boldsymbol{\phi}_j||^2}, \quad j = 1, 2, \ldots, m \tag{6.26}$$

where $< \cdot, \cdot >$ represents the inner product of the two vectors, and

$$\begin{cases} \boldsymbol{s}_1 & \triangleq & \boldsymbol{y} \\ \boldsymbol{s}_j & \triangleq & \boldsymbol{y} - \sum_{k=1}^{j-1} w_k \boldsymbol{\phi}_j, \quad j = 2, 3, \ldots, m \end{cases} \tag{6.27}$$

This algorithm is called the *projection method*. The computational procedure has to be started recursively from the first component of the weight vector $\boldsymbol{w}$. Alternatively, an iterative version of this algorithm may be given as follows

$$w_j(k+1) = \frac{< \boldsymbol{\phi}_j, \boldsymbol{s}_j(k+1) >}{||\boldsymbol{\phi}_j||^2} \tag{6.28}$$

$$\boldsymbol{s}_j(k+1) = \boldsymbol{y} - \sum_{k=1, k\neq j}^{n} w_k(k) \boldsymbol{\phi}_k, \quad j = 1, 2, \ldots, m \tag{6.29}$$

with the initial condition $w_j(0) = 0$ for all $j = 1, 2, \ldots, m$. It is easy to see that this algorithm will converge at least linearly to the projection solution given above.

Note that with fixed $\boldsymbol{\phi}_i$, $i = 1, 2, \ldots, m$, $\boldsymbol{y} \in S_\phi$ implies that no exact solution for $\boldsymbol{w}$ exists. Alternatively, the optimal solution $\boldsymbol{w}^*$ that minimizes the error given in Eqn. (6.23) can be obtained by projecting $\boldsymbol{y}$ onto S_ϕ such that

$$\boldsymbol{w}^* = \boldsymbol{\Phi}^+ \boldsymbol{y} \tag{6.30}$$

and

$$E_{min} = ||(\boldsymbol{I} - \boldsymbol{P})\boldsymbol{y}||^2 \tag{6.31}$$

where $\boldsymbol{\Phi}^+$ represents the generalized inverse of $\boldsymbol{\Phi}$ given by

$$\boldsymbol{\Phi}^+ \triangleq [\boldsymbol{\Phi}^T \boldsymbol{\Phi}]^{-1} \boldsymbol{\Phi}^T \tag{6.32}$$

and $\boldsymbol{P}$ is the projection matrix described by

$$\boldsymbol{P} \triangleq \boldsymbol{\Phi}\boldsymbol{\Phi}^T \tag{6.33}$$

To avoid a direct computation for the matrix inversion that is involved in the generalized inverse $\boldsymbol{\Phi}^+$ given above, an effective and straightforward algorithm is the singular-value decomposition. The detailed procedure of this algorithm may be found in the text books on matrix analysis (Horn and Johnson 1985) and signal processing (Haykin 1991).

6.2 GAUSSIAN RADIAL BASIS FUNCTION NEURAL NETWORKS

6.2.1 Gaussian RBF Network Model

A *Gaussian* radial basis function neural network, or simply the Gaussian neural network, which consists of an unnormalized form of Gaussian density function given by

$$\phi(r) = \exp\left(-\left(\frac{r}{c}\right)^2 \right) \tag{6.34}$$

is the most important class network of the RBFNs. As shown in Fig. 6.6, a Gaussian function which is bounded, strictly positive and continuous on $\Re^n$, has a peak at the center $r = 0$, and decreases monotonically as the distance from the center increases. Note also that the Gaussian radial basis function

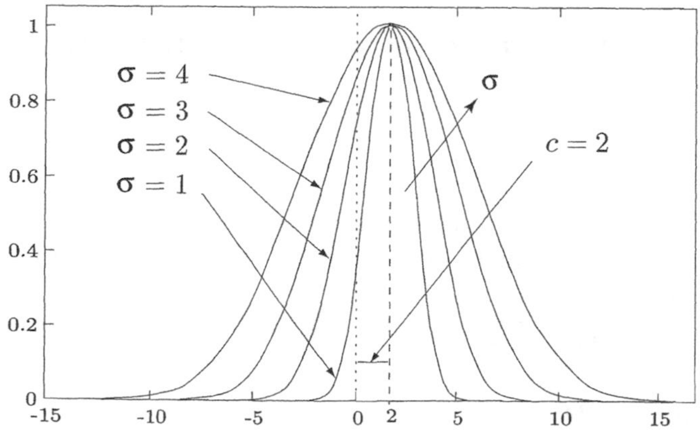

Figure 6.6 Gaussian radial basis function $f(x) = \exp(-\frac{1}{2}[(x-c)/\sigma]^2)$ with $c = 2$ and various values of σ, $(\sigma = 1, 2, 3, 4)$.

has a separable nonlinearity, that is

$$\begin{aligned}\phi(||\boldsymbol{x}-\mathbf{c}||) &= \phi(x_1-c_1)\phi(x_2-c_2)\ldots\phi(x_n-c_n) \\ &= \prod_{i=1}^{n}\phi(x_i-c_i)\end{aligned} \tag{6.35}$$

or any intermediate combination of such terms, so that instead of computing a single nonlinear transform of the entire input vector, individual subspaces of $\Re^n$ may be transformed separately, and then multiplied to obtain the final expression. The Gaussian networks are highly nonlinear and provide good locality for incremental learning. It has been proved that Gaussian networks have many well-defined mathematical features and can be used in the learning and control of nonlinear dynamic systems, and as some powerful schemes for modeling complex input–output mappings. Moreover, these properties make the Gaussian networks particularly amenable for their implementation in parallel analog hardware.

A typical Gaussian network is a three-stage network with an input stage, an intermediate stage of Gaussian units and an output stage of conventional summation units as shown in Fig. 6.7. A block diagram showing the input–output of the Gaussian RBF is shown in Fig. 6.8.

Let $\boldsymbol{x} = [x_1\ x_2\ \ldots\ x_n]^T$ and $\boldsymbol{y} = [y_1\ y_2\ \ldots\ y_m]^T$ be the input and output of the network, respectively, and $\boldsymbol{u} = [u_1\ u_2\ \ldots\ u_\ell]^T$ be the ℓ outputs of the ℓ Gaussian units. A Gaussian radial basis function ϕ_i with a weighted norm is defined by

$$\phi(||\boldsymbol{x}-\boldsymbol{c}_i||_{\boldsymbol{K}_i}) = e^{-d(\boldsymbol{x},\boldsymbol{c}_i,\boldsymbol{H}_i)/2} \tag{6.36}$$

where

$$d(\boldsymbol{x},\boldsymbol{c}_i,\boldsymbol{H}_i) \triangleq ||\boldsymbol{x}-\boldsymbol{c}_i||_{\boldsymbol{K}_i} = (\boldsymbol{x}-\boldsymbol{c}_i)^T\boldsymbol{H}_i(\boldsymbol{x}-\boldsymbol{c}_i) \tag{6.37}$$

with

$$\boldsymbol{H}_i = \boldsymbol{K}_i^T\boldsymbol{K}_i \tag{6.38}$$

and $\boldsymbol{c}_i \in \Re^n$ and $\boldsymbol{H}_i \in \Re^{n\times n}$ represent, respectively, the mean vector and the shape matrix defined by the inverse of the covariance matrix of the ith radial basis function.

Furthermore, $d(\boldsymbol{x},\boldsymbol{c}_i,\boldsymbol{H}_i)$ can be rewritten in an expanded form

$$d(\boldsymbol{x},\boldsymbol{c}_i,\boldsymbol{H}_i) = \sum_{j=1}^{n}\sum_{k=1}^{n} h_{ijk}(x_j-c_{ij})(x_k-c_{ik}) \tag{6.39}$$

where c_{ij} is the jth element of $\boldsymbol{c}_i$, and h_{ijk} is the (j,k)th element of $\boldsymbol{H}_i$.

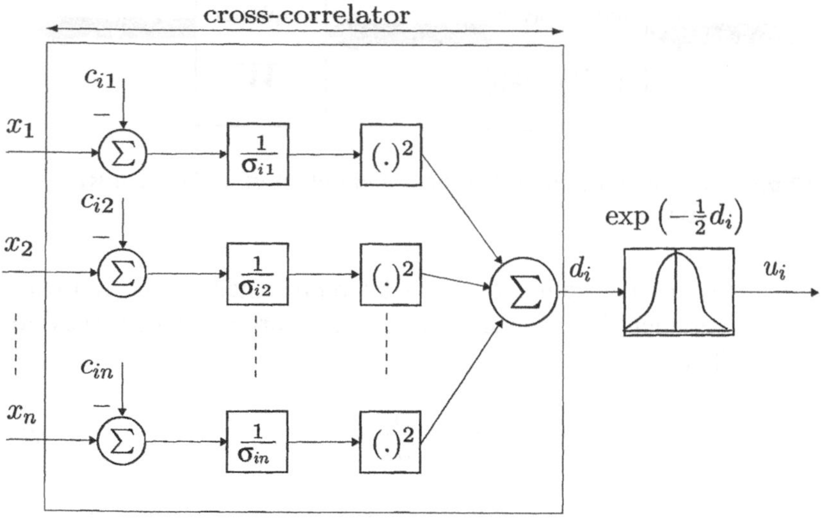

(a) The cross-correlator: connections between the inputs $x_1, x_2, \ldots, x_n$ and the ith Gaussian unit, $d_i = \sum_{k=1}^{\ell}[(x_i - c_{ik})/\sigma_{ik}]^2$, and $u_i = \exp\left(-\frac{1}{2}d_i\right)$

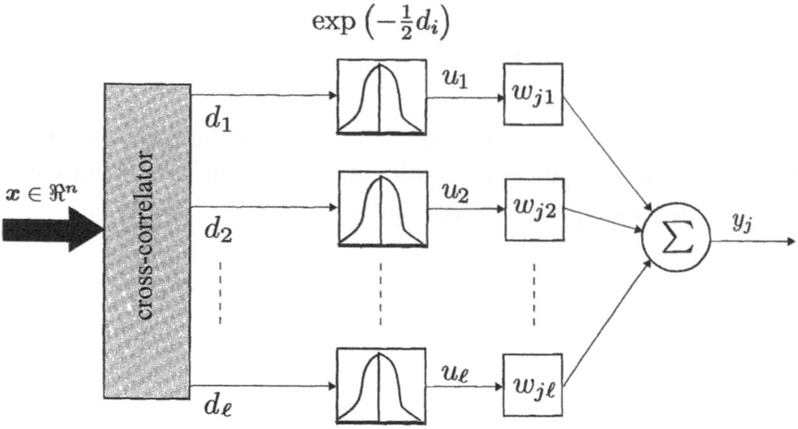

(b) Connections between the nodes in the hidden layer and the output y_j

Figure 6.7 The schematic diagram of a Gaussian radial basis function neural network (GRBF-NN).

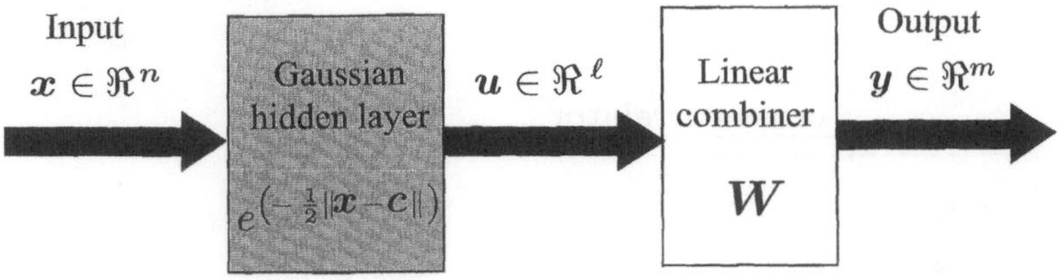

Figure 6.8 A block diagram of the input and output of a Gaussian RBF neural network.

Without loss of generality, h_{ijk} can be represented as the ratio of the correlation coefficient k_{ijk} and the product of the marginal standard deviations σ_{ij} and σ_{ik}. Thus

$$h_{ijk} = \frac{k_{ijk}}{\sigma_{ij}\sigma_{ik}} \tag{6.40}$$

where σ_{ij} is positive real number, and $k_{ijk} = 1$ for $j = k$, and $|k_{ijk}| \leq 1$, $j \neq k$.

Instead of using the general form of h_{ijk} given by Eqn. (6.40), we may simply assume that the shaping matrix $\boldsymbol{H}_i$ is positive diagonal; that is

$$h_{ijk} = \begin{cases} \dfrac{1}{\sigma_{ij}^2}, & \text{if} \quad j = k \\ 0, & \text{otherwise} \end{cases} \tag{6.41}$$

where σ_{ij}^2 is the variance for controlling the width of the Gaussian function. Therefore, the input–output relationship of a Gaussian neural network that might have multiple outputs is described by

$$u_i = \exp\left(-\frac{1}{2}\sum_{k=1}^{n}\left[\frac{x_k - c_{ik}}{\sigma_{ik}}\right]^2\right), \quad 1 \leq i \leq \ell \tag{6.42}$$

and

$$\begin{aligned} y_j &= \sum_{i=1}^{\ell} w_{ji} u_i \\ &= \sum_{i=1}^{\ell} w_{ij} \exp\left(-\frac{1}{2}\sum_{k=1}^{n}\left[\frac{x_k - c_{ik}}{\sigma_{ik}}\right]^2\right), \quad 1 \leq j \leq m \end{aligned} \tag{6.43}$$

where u_i is the output of the ith hidden Gaussian neuron described by a Gaussian function that forms a hyperellipsoid in the n-dimensional space $\Re^n$

rather than a hyperplane; c_{ik} and σ_{ik}^2 are respectively, the center and variance parameters, of the ith Gaussian function, which determine the geometric shape and position of the hyperellipsoid in $\Re^n$; and ℓ is the number of the Gaussian neurons. As seen above, the intermediate stage in a Gaussian network consists of an array of nodes c_i that contain some parameter vectors called *centers*. These intermediate nodes calculate the weighted Euclidean distance between the center and the network input vector and the result is passed through a Gaussian function. The output stage of the neuron is just a set of linear combiners.

Using the notation of the variance matrices defined as

$$\Sigma_i \triangleq diag[\sigma_{i1}^2, \sigma_{i2}^2, \ldots, \sigma_{in}^2] \tag{6.44}$$

Eqns. (6.42) and (6.43) may be rewritten as

$$u_i = \exp\left(-\tfrac{1}{2}(\boldsymbol{x} - \boldsymbol{c}_i)^T \Sigma_i^{-1} (\boldsymbol{x} - \boldsymbol{c}_i)\right), \quad 1 \le i \le \ell \tag{6.45}$$

and

$$\begin{aligned} y_j &= \sum_{i=1}^{\ell} w_{ji} u_i \\ &= \sum_{i=1}^{\ell} w_{ij} \exp\left(-\tfrac{1}{2}(\boldsymbol{x}_i - \boldsymbol{c}_i)^T \Sigma_i^{-1} (\boldsymbol{x} - \boldsymbol{c}_i)\right) \\ & \qquad 1 \le j \le m \end{aligned} \tag{6.46}$$

6.2.2 Gaussian RBF Networks as Universal Approximator

The approximation capability of such a Gaussian RBF network has been addressed using the multipoint interpolation approximation technique in the previous section. However, this issue is discussed extensively in Chapter 7 using the well-known Stone–Weierstrass theorem, which is a basis theorem of functional analysis and approximation theory. A practical statement of the theorem is given in Theorem 6.1.

Theorem 6.1 [Stone-Weierstrass Theorem II (Ray 1988)] *Let S be a compact set with n dimensions, and $\Omega \supset C[S]$ be a set of continuous real-valued functions on S satisfying the conditions:*

(i) *Identity function: The constant function $f(x) = 1$ is in Ω;*

(ii) *Separability: For any two points $\boldsymbol{x}_1, \boldsymbol{x}_2 \in S$ and $\boldsymbol{x}_1 \neq \boldsymbol{x}_2$, there exists a $f \in \Omega$ such that $f(\boldsymbol{x}_1) \neq f(\boldsymbol{x}_2)$;*

(iii) Algebraic closure: For any $f, g \in \Omega$ and $\alpha, \beta \in \Re$, the functions fg and $(\alpha f + \beta g)$ are in Ω.

Then, Ω is dense in $C[S]$. In other words, for any $\varepsilon > 0$ and any function $g \in C[S]$, there is a function $f \in \Omega$ such that

$$|g(\boldsymbol{x}) - f(\boldsymbol{x})| < \varepsilon$$

for all $\boldsymbol{x} \in S$. ■

To ensure the function approximation capability of the Gaussian RBF networks using the Stone–Weierstrass theorem, one has to verify that the networks satisfy conditions (i)–(iii).

Note that the fact that exponential function can process the multiplication into addition as follows:

$$\exp(x)\exp(y) = \exp(x + y)$$

Hence, it can be verified that the Gaussian RBF network satisfies the Stone–Weierstrass theorem.

Theorem 6.2 *Let Ω be the set of all functions that can be computed by Gaussian RBF neural network on a compact set $S \supset R^n$:*

$$\Omega_N = \left\{ f(\boldsymbol{x}) = \sum_{i=1}^{N} w_i \exp\left(-\frac{1}{2} \sum_{k=1}^{n} \left[\frac{x_k - c_{ik}}{\sigma_{ik}} \right]^2 \right) : \quad w_i, c_{ik}, \sigma_{ik} \in \Re, \boldsymbol{x} \in S \right\}$$

$$\Omega = \bigcup_{N=1}^{\infty} \Omega_N$$

Then Ω is dense in $C[S]$.

Proof: The function $f(\boldsymbol{x}) = 1$ belongs to Ω since it can be considered as a Gaussian function with infinite variance σ, and for any distinct points $\boldsymbol{x}$ and $\boldsymbol{y} \in S$, we can obviously verify that $f(\boldsymbol{x}) \neq f(\boldsymbol{y})$ since the exponential function is strictly monotonic. Furthermore, we can show that the product of two of the elements of Ω yields another element of Ω. Let f and g be two functions in Ω and be represented by the Gaussian functions as

$$f(x_1, \ldots, x_n) = \sum_{i=1}^{N_f} w_i^f \exp\left(-\frac{1}{2} \sum_{k=1}^{n} \left[\frac{x_k - c_{ik}^f}{\sigma_{ik}^f} \right]^2 \right)$$

and

$$g(x_1, \ldots, x_n) = \sum_{j=1}^{N_g} w_j^g \exp\left(-\frac{1}{2}\sum_{k=1}^{n}\left[\frac{x_k - c_{jk}^g}{\sigma_{jk}^g}\right]^2\right)$$

Since

$$\begin{aligned}
fg &= \sum_{i=1}^{N_f}\sum_{j=1}^{N_g} w_i^f w_j^g \exp\left(-\frac{1}{2}\sum_{k=1}^{n}\left[\frac{x_k - c_{ik}^f}{\sigma_{ik}^f}\right]^2\right) \\
&\quad \times \exp\left(-\frac{1}{2}\sum_{k=1}^{n}\left[\frac{x_k - c_{jk}^g}{\sigma_{jk}^g}\right]^2\right) \\
&= \sum_{i=1}^{N_f}\sum_{j=1}^{N_g} w_i^f w_j^g \exp\left(-\frac{1}{2}\left\{\sum_{k=1}^{n}\left[\frac{x_k - c_{ik}^f}{\sigma_{ik}^f}\right]^2\right.\right. \\
&\quad \left.\left. + \sum_{k=1}^{n}\left[\frac{x_k - c_{jk}^g}{\sigma_{jk}^g}\right]^2\right\}\right) \\
&= \sum_{i=1}^{N_f}\sum_{j=1}^{N_g} w_{ij} \exp\left(-\frac{1}{2}\sum_{k=1}^{n}\left[\frac{x_k - c_{ijk}^f}{\sigma_{ijk}^f}\right]^2\right)
\end{aligned}$$

where

$$\begin{aligned}
w_{ij} &= w_i^f w_j^g \exp\left(-\frac{1}{2}\sum_{k=1}^{n}\left[\frac{a_{ijk} - c_{ijk}^2}{\sigma_{ijk}^2}\right]\right) \\
c_{ijk} &= \frac{(\sigma_{ik}^f)^2[c_{ik}^f + c_{jk}^g]}{(\sigma_{ik}^f)^2 + (\sigma_{jk}^g)^2} \\
\sigma_{ijk} &= \frac{\sigma_{ik}^f \sigma_{jk}^g}{[(\sigma_{ik}^f)^2 + (\sigma_{jk}^g)^2]^{1/2}} \\
a_{ijk} &= \frac{(c_{ik}^f)^2(\sigma_{jk}^g)^2 + (c_{ik}^f)^2(\sigma_{jk}^g)^2}{(\sigma_{ik}^f)^2 + (\sigma_{ik}^g)^2}
\end{aligned}$$

Hence, the product fg is in Ω so that the Gaussian RBF neural network satisfies the Stone–Weierstrass theorem. It follows that Ω is dense in $C[S]$. ■

For the other choices of the radial basis functions given in the preceding section, it can be shown that the resulting RBFNs do not satisfy the algebraic closure condition required by the Stone–Weierstrass theorem. Thus, the approximation capability of this class of the RBFNs cannot be ensured using the theorem. However, we have demonstrated their ability for solving interpolation problems in the last section.

6.3 LEARNING ALGORITHMS FOR GAUSSIAN RBF NEURAL NETWORKS

It has been shown that the Gaussian RBF neural networks are capable of uniformly approximating arbitrary continuous functions defined on a compact set to satisfy a given approximation error. This approximation process is usually carried out by a learning phase where the number of hidden nodes and the network parameters are appropriately adjusted so that the approximation error is minimized. There are a variety of approaches for using the Gaussian networks. Most of them start by breaking the problem into two stages: *learning in the intermediate stage*, that is, adjusting the center and variance parameters, followed by learning or adjusting the weight parameters of the *linear combiners* in the output stage. Learning in the intermediate stage is typically performed using the clustering algorithm, while learning in the output stage is a supervised learning. Once an initial solution is found using this approach, a supervised learning algorithm is sometimes applied to both stages simultaneously to update the parameters of the network.

6.3.1 K-Means Clustering-Based Learning Procedures in Gaussian RBF Neural Network

Numerous clustering algorithms can be used in the intermediate stage for determining the center parameter vectors c_i. The simplest way is to choose these vectors randomly from the set of the learning data. However, this must be done in such a way that the number of the hidden Gaussian units must be relatively large to cover the input pattern domain. One of the most popular choices is K-means clustering, which has been widely accepted because of its simplicity and ability to produce good results. The basic idea of this algorithm is to group the learning data into some subsets or clusters and further select the centers according to the natural measure of the attracting centers in the sense of the Euclidean distance. Each cluster center is associated with one of the hidden Gaussian units. Next, let us examine not only the original

Table 6.1 **K-means clustering algorithm for Gaussian RBF**

Step 1: Select the number $\ell < m$ of the clusters;

Step 2: Take the first ℓ learning data $\boldsymbol{x}_1, \boldsymbol{x}_2, \ldots, \boldsymbol{x}_\ell$ as the center vectors:

$$\boldsymbol{c}_j = \boldsymbol{x}_j, \quad j = 1, 2, \ldots, \ell;$$

Step 3: Assign $\boldsymbol{x}_i$ $(i = \ell+1, \ell+2, \ldots, m)$ to one of the clusters with the least distance criterion; that is, $\boldsymbol{x}_i$ belongs to the j^*th cluster if

$$||\boldsymbol{x}_i - \boldsymbol{c}_j^*|| = \min_{j^*} ||\boldsymbol{x}_i - \boldsymbol{c}_j||, \quad 1 \leq j \leq \ell;$$

Step 4: Recompute the center vectors using the new mean, that is

$$\boldsymbol{c}_j = \frac{1}{m_j} \sum_{i \in C_j} \boldsymbol{x}_j; \quad 1 \leq j \leq \ell$$

where m_j is the number of the learning data belonging to the jth cluster C_j.

K-means clustering algorithm but also some modified versions proposed relatively recently.

Given m data $\boldsymbol{x}_1, \boldsymbol{x}_2, \ldots, \boldsymbol{x}_m \in \Re^n$, the standard K-means clustering for the Gaussian networks is as given in Table 6.1.

The initial selection of the centers of the clusters dealt with in Step 2 may also be carried out by randomly choosing ℓ data from the data domain. As soon as the clustering algorithm is complete, the variance or width parameters may be taken into account. These parameters control the amount of overlap of the radial basis functions as well as the network generalizations. A small value yields a rapidly decreasing function, whereas a large value results in a more gently varying function. Although they can be determined in a variety of ways, the most common one is to make them equal to the average distance between the cluster centers and the data; that is

$$\sigma_{ij} = \frac{1}{m_j} \sum_{k \in C_j} (x_{kj} - c_{ij})^2, \quad 1 \leq i \leq \ell; \; 1 \leq j \leq n \tag{6.47}$$

where x_{kj} is the jth component of $\boldsymbol{x}_k$. They represent a measure of the spread of the data associated with each node.

It is to be noted that the problem existing in the K-meaning clustering described above is that the data points that belong to the old clusters may not be in the corresponding new clusters since the centers of the clusters are updated. A simple two-dimension example is shown in Fig. 6.9 where the datum d_1 is initially in the cluster 1, but after updating the centers it switches to the cluster 2 since it is closest to the new center 2. The so-called convergent K-means clustering algorithm described by Anderberg (1973) and Spath (1980) may be used to achieve the goal that the data points are finally in the current clusters in the sense of the nearest distance. This task is easily carried out by adding an additional iterative process to the K-means clustering and as is shown in Table 6.2.

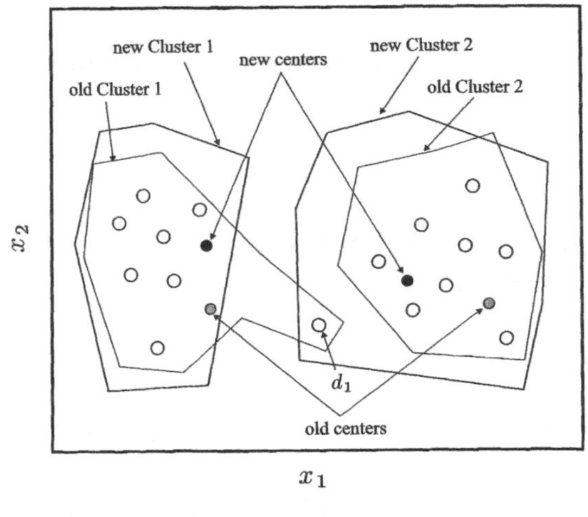

Figure 6.9 An example of the K-means clustering algorithm where the datum d_1 switches from the cluster 1 to cluster 2 after the centers are updated.

Table 6.2 **Convergent K-means clustering algorithm**

Steps 1–4:	These are the same as those in the K-means clustering algorithm given in Table 6.1;
Step 5:	Assign $\boldsymbol{x}_i$ $(i = 1, 2, \ldots, n)$ to one of the clusters with the nearest distance criterion;
Step 6:	If at least one data point switches to another cluster, then recompute the centers using the new mean and go to Step 5; otherwise, stop the procedure.

It is worth indicating that the K-means clustering is a task-independent procedure where no error feedback or supervised function are reflected in such an algorithm. The number of clusters in the K-means clustering is preselected; however, the algorithm is so fast that it can be repeated using different values of ℓ. Some self-organizing approaches for dynamically determining ℓ have also been conducted by Weymaere and Martens (1991), Lee and Kil (1991), and Musavi et al. (1992). In fact, large number of clusters may increase the accuracy of the learning phase, but at the cost of additional computational requirements.

6.3.2 Supervised (Gradient Descent) Parameter Learning in Gaussian Networks

With the center and variance parameters that are initialized to nearly optimum values using K-means clustering at hand, we may use either the well-known least mean square (LMS) or the generalized inverse methods for updating the unknown weights that are linear in the Gaussian network as discussed in the previous section. The learning problem in such linear combiners that finally produce the outputs of the network has been studied extensively in the previous sections. Furthermore, like the BP algorithm for the MFNNs, if all of the free parameters, such as the weights, centers, and variance parameters, in the Gaussian network are considered as the unknown parameters, we may use the gradient descent method to form the updating equations for the parameters.

Assume that the learning task is described by the input–output data pairs $\{\boldsymbol{x}(k), \boldsymbol{d}(k)\}$. The number of such sets of data might be either finite or infinite. As seen in the previous sections, the first step for developing such a gradient-descent-technique-based supervised learning procedure is to define the instantaneous value of the cost function as follows

$$E = \frac{1}{2}\sum_{j=1}^{m}(d_j - y_j)^2 = \frac{1}{2}\sum_{j=1}^{m} e_j^2 \tag{6.48}$$

where

$$\begin{aligned} e_j &\triangleq d_j - y_j \\ &= d_j - \sum_{i=1}^{\ell} w_{ij} \exp\left(-\frac{1}{2}\sum_{p=1}^{n}\left[\frac{x_k - c_{ip}}{\sigma_{ip}}\right]^2\right) \end{aligned} \tag{6.49}$$

Using both the above definition and the network equations, Eqns. (6.42)–(6.43), the following set of the updating equations for the parameters may be obtained

$$w_{ij}^{new} = w_{ij}^{old} + \eta_1 u_i e_j \tag{6.50}$$

$$c_{ip}^{new} = c_{ip}^{old} + \eta_2 \frac{(x_p - c_{ip})}{\sigma_{ip}^2} \sum_{j=1}^{m} u_j e_j \tag{6.51}$$

$$\sigma_{ip}^{new} = \sigma_{ip}^{old} + \eta_3 \frac{(x_p - c_{ip})^2}{\sigma_{ip}^3} \sum_{j=1}^{m} u_j e_j \tag{6.52}$$

$$1 \leq i \leq \ell; \quad 1 \leq j \leq m; \quad 1 \leq p \leq n$$

where η_1, η_2, and η_3 are the learning rates associated with the weights, centers, and variance parameters, respectively. The verification of the above formulations may easily be obtained, and is left as an exercise for the reader. The iterative process goes repeatedly around the given learning data until the convergence values of the parameters are obtained.

An obvious drawback of this supervised algorithm for all the free parameters is its computational complexity compared with the clustering method just discussed. If the parameters c_{ip} and σ_{ip} are predetermined using K-means clustering, only Eqn. (6.50) is required to update the weights w_{ij}. This might reduce the learning time and avoid problems of getting trapped into the local minima. Furthermore, the supervised learning issues and approaches discussed in the previous chapters for feedforward neural networks are also applicable to the learning for RBF networks, as it can also be considered as a class of feedforward neural networks in terms of their input–output relationship.

6.4 CONCLUDING REMARKS

In this chapter, we have introduced the *radial basis function* (RBF), another form of feedforward neural networks, which has been proved useful for solving many engineering problems such as adaptive communication channels, adaptive modeling, classification, and clustering problems. In particular, we introduced the Gaussian radial basis function neural networks (GRBF-NNs) which have, unlike the conventional multilayered feedforward neural networks introduced in previous chapters, some impressive neural network characteristics for effectively resolving many approximation, adaptive, nonlinear issues existing in many engineering applications.

Problems

6.1 Let a Gaussian network with an n-dimensional input $\boldsymbol{x} \in \Re^n$ and a single output $y \in \Re$ be described by the following equation:

$$y = \sum_{i=1}^{\ell} w_i \exp\left(-\frac{1}{2} \sum_{j=1}^{n} \left[\frac{x_j - c_{ij}}{\sigma_{ij}} \right]^2 \right)$$

Given an input–output data pair $\{\boldsymbol{x}(k), y(k)\}$ $(k = 1, 2, \ldots, n)$, design a learning algorithm for adjusting the center parameters c_{ij}, the variances σ_{ij}, and the weight parameters w_i using the gradient descent algorithm.

6.2 Verify the supervised learning algorithm given in Section 6.3.2 for the Gaussian networks.

6.3 Use mathematical language to show that, in the classical interpolation problem, the radial basis function f is determined such that $f(x_k) = f_k$ where f_k are some data values. Also show that, in this case, there is exactly one linear constraint per radial basis function, and the corresponding linear system of equations is invertible.

6.4 Show that the Gaussian radial basis function with the weighted norm has the following separable nonlinearity

$$\phi(||\boldsymbol{x} - \mathbf{c}||_{\boldsymbol{K}}) = \prod_{i,j=1}^{n} \phi\Big((x_i - c_i)(x_j - c_j) h_{ij} \Big)$$

where $\boldsymbol{x}, \boldsymbol{c} \in \Re^n$, $\boldsymbol{K} \in \Re^{n \times n}$, and

$$\boldsymbol{H} = [h_{ij}]_{n \times n} \triangleq \boldsymbol{K}^T \boldsymbol{K}$$

6.5 Given six data as follows

$$\boldsymbol{x}_1 = \begin{bmatrix} 1 \\ -1 \\ 1 \\ -1 \\ -1 \end{bmatrix}, \quad \boldsymbol{x}_2 = \begin{bmatrix} 1 \\ -1 \\ 1 \\ 1 \\ -1 \end{bmatrix}, \quad \boldsymbol{x}_3 = \begin{bmatrix} -1 \\ 1 \\ -1 \\ 1 \\ 1 \end{bmatrix},$$

$$\boldsymbol{x}_4 = \begin{bmatrix} -1 \\ 1 \\ -1 \\ -1 \\ -1 \end{bmatrix}, \quad \boldsymbol{x}_5 = \begin{bmatrix} -1 \\ -1 \\ -1 \\ 1 \\ -1 \end{bmatrix}, \quad \boldsymbol{x}_6 = \begin{bmatrix} -1 \\ -1 \\ 1 \\ 1 \\ -1 \end{bmatrix}.$$

Let the cluster number be chosen as $\ell = 2$. Use the convergent K-means clustering algorithm to group these data.

6.6 Consider a conventional two-layered feedforward neural network and a Gaussian network that have the same number of inputs, outputs, and intermediate units. Show that the Gaussian network represents more degree of freedom than the conventional one in terms of the free parameters.

6.7 Show that a RBF network with a *multiquadratic radial basis function*

$$\phi(r) = (c^2 + r^2)^{\beta} \qquad (0 < \beta < 1)$$

does not satisfy algebraic closure condition required by the Stone–Weierstrass theorem.

6.8 A generalized Gaussian radial basis function network is described by the equation

$$\begin{aligned} y = f(\boldsymbol{x}) &= \sum_{i=1}^{m} w_i \phi(\| \boldsymbol{x} - \boldsymbol{c}_i \|_{\boldsymbol{K}_i}) \\ &= \sum_{i=1}^{m} w_i e^{-d(\boldsymbol{x}, \boldsymbol{c}_i, \boldsymbol{H}_i)/2} \end{aligned}$$

where

$$\begin{aligned} d(\boldsymbol{x}, \boldsymbol{c}_i, \boldsymbol{H}_i) &= (\boldsymbol{x} - \boldsymbol{c}_i)^T \boldsymbol{H}_i (\boldsymbol{x} - \boldsymbol{c}_i) \\ \boldsymbol{H}_i &= \boldsymbol{K}_i^T \boldsymbol{K}_i \end{aligned}$$

Derive the learning algorithm for the network parameters $w_i \in \Re$, $\boldsymbol{c}_i \in \Re^n$, and $\boldsymbol{H}_i \in \Re^{n \times n}$ by minimizing an error function.

6.9 Given a time series of $y(n), y(n-1), \ldots, y(n-m+1)$. Find an input–output mapping $f(.)$ of the prediction model for the following optimization problem

$$\hat{f} = \arg\min_{\hat{f}} \left\{ \sum_{n=m}^{N-1} [y(n+1) - \hat{y}(n+1)]^2 + \lambda \| \mathrm{P}\hat{f} \|^2 \right\}$$

where

$$\hat{y}(n+1) = \hat{f}(y(n), y(n-1), \ldots, y(n-m+1))$$

The P is a differentiable operator. Show that with an appropriate choice of the differential operator P, we obtain the solution

$$\begin{aligned}
\hat{f}(y) &= \boldsymbol{w}^T \boldsymbol{g}(\boldsymbol{y}) \\
\boldsymbol{y}(n) &= [y(n) \quad y(n-1) \quad \cdots \quad y(n-m+1)]^T \\
\boldsymbol{g}(\boldsymbol{y}) &= [g_1(\boldsymbol{y}) \quad g_2(\boldsymbol{y}) \quad \cdots \quad g_{N-1}(\boldsymbol{y})]^T \\
g_j(\boldsymbol{y}) &= \exp\left(-\tfrac{1}{2} \parallel \boldsymbol{y} - \boldsymbol{c}_j \parallel_{\boldsymbol{K}}\right), \quad j = 1, 2, \ldots, N-1
\end{aligned}$$

where $\boldsymbol{w} \in \Re^{N-1}$, $\boldsymbol{c}_j \in \Re^m$, and $\boldsymbol{K} \in \Re^{m \times m}$.

6.10 Using the extended Kalman filtering algorithm discussed in Chapter 5, derive a learning algorithm for a Gaussian network.

6.11 For a sinusoidal radial basis function network (RBFN) of the form

$$\begin{aligned}
f(\boldsymbol{x}) &= \sum_{i=1}^{n} w_i \phi_i(\boldsymbol{x}) \\
\phi_i(\boldsymbol{x}) &= \frac{\sin(\parallel \boldsymbol{x} - \boldsymbol{c}_i \parallel)}{\parallel \boldsymbol{x} - \boldsymbol{c}_i \parallel}, \quad \boldsymbol{x},\ \boldsymbol{c}_i \in \Re^m
\end{aligned}$$

(a) Discuss the universal approximation capability of the above RBFN by using Stone–Weierstrass theorem;

(b) Derive a learning algorithm for updating the parameters of the RBFN.

6.12 In most communication systems, channel equalizers are employed to deal with channel characteristics that are unknown a priori and, in many cases, time-variant and nonlinear. In such a case, the equalizers are designed to be adjustable to the channel response and, for time-variant and nonlinear channels, to be adaptive to the time variations and nonlinear characteristics in the channel response. As shown in Fig. 6.10, a neural network based adaptive equalizer is used to process on the received signal $y(k)$ such that the output of the equalizer satisfies

$$\hat{x}(k) \longrightarrow x(k) \quad \text{or} \quad e(k) = \hat{x}(k) - x(k) \longrightarrow 0$$

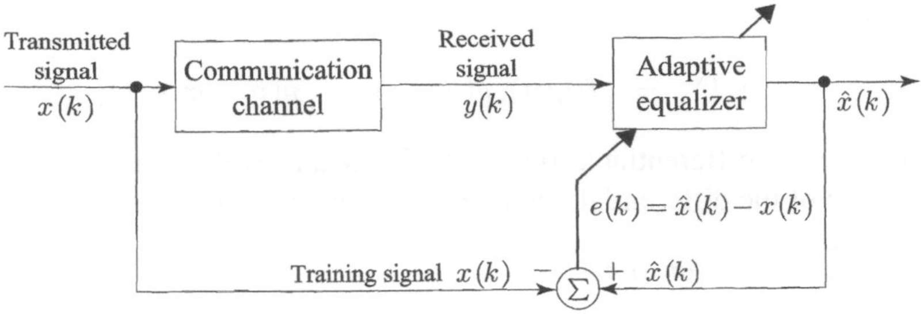

Figure 6.10 Problem 6.12: adaptive channel equalizer.

(a) Design a linear combiner based linear tapped delay line neural network as an adaptive equalizer and give a training equation for online adjusting the parameters;

(b) Design a Gaussian radial basis function based tapped delay line neural network as an adaptive equalizer and give a training equation for online adjusting the parameters;

(c) Discuss the advantages of using such a Gaussian radial basis function based equalizer for a communication system.

6.13 Let the channel model in Problem 6.12 be a nonlinear system

$$\begin{aligned} y(k+1) &= f\Big(y(k), y(k-1), y(k-2), x(k)\Big) + n(k) \\ &= \frac{y(k)y(k-1)y(k-2)[y(k-2)-1] + x(k)}{1 + y^2(k-1) + y^2(k-2)} + n(k) \end{aligned}$$

where $n(k)$ is a white noise with zero mean value. Train the Gaussian radial basis function network based equalizer designed in Problem 6.12 for the equalization of such a nonlinear channel.

6.14 Many digital communication channels can usually be characterized by a finite impulse response (FIR) filter and an additive noise source as shown in Fig. 6.11. Let $x(k)$ be the digital data sequence passing

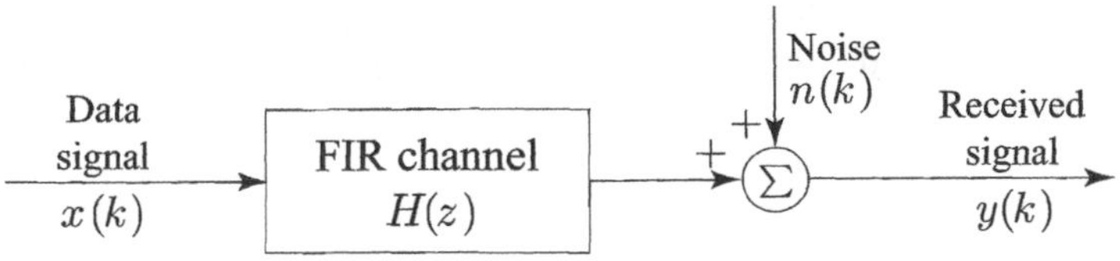

Figure 6.11 Problem 6.14: Digital communication channel.

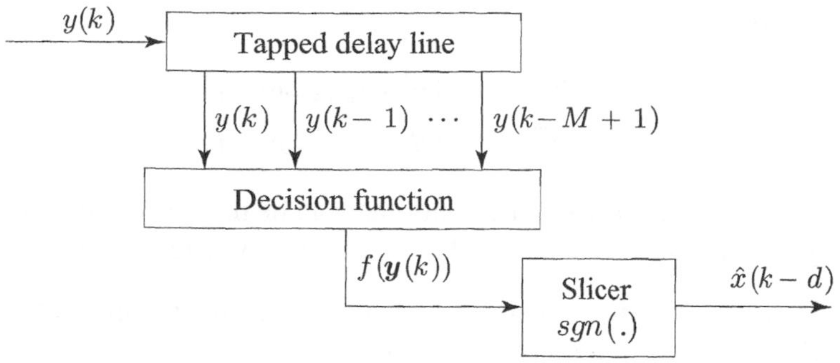

Figure 6.12 Problem 6.14: Feedforward channel equalizer.

through the channel of FIR, and $y(k)$ be the received digital data sequence, which is formed by adding Gaussian random noise $n(k)$ to the output of the FIR. The input and output equation of such a system is given by

$$y(k) = \sum_{i=1}^{N-1} h_i x(k-i) + n(k)$$

$$H(z) = \sum_{i=0}^{N-1} h_i z^{-i}$$

where N is the length of the impulse response.

The channel equalization problem is that of using the information present in the observed channel output $\boldsymbol{y}(k) = [y(k)\ y(k-1)\ \cdots\ y(k-M+1)]^T$ to generate an estimate $\hat{x}(k-d)$, as shown in Fig. 6.12, of the channel input $x(k-d)$. Therefore, the objective of designing such a channel equalizer is to find the decision function $f(\boldsymbol{y}(k))$. One may use a Bayesian approach to select an optimal decision boundary that is the locus of all values of $\boldsymbol{y}(k)$ for which the probability $x(k-d) = +1$ is equal to the probability that $x(k-d) = -1$, given the same values of $\boldsymbol{y}(k)$. Show that such a Bayesian decision function can be described by a Gaussian radial basis function network of the form

$$f(\boldsymbol{y}(k)) = \sum_{\boldsymbol{y}'_i \in S^+} \frac{\exp\left(-\frac{\|\boldsymbol{y}(k)-\boldsymbol{y}'_i\|}{2\sigma_n^2}\right)}{(2\pi\sigma_n^2)^{N_r/2} N_r} - \sum_{\boldsymbol{y}'_j \in S^-} \frac{\exp\left(-\frac{\|\boldsymbol{y}(k)-\boldsymbol{y}'_j\|}{2\sigma_n^2}\right)}{(2\pi\sigma_n^2)^{N_r/2} N_r}$$

where

$$
\begin{aligned}
S^{+} &= \{\boldsymbol{y}'(k)|_{x(k-d)=+1}\} \\
S^{-} &= \{\boldsymbol{y}'(k)|_{x(k-d)=-1}\}
\end{aligned}
$$

$(2\pi\sigma_n^2)^{N_r/2}N_r$ is a scaling factor that can be normalized to unity, and $\boldsymbol{y}'_i$ are the parameters needed to be adaptively determined.

6.15 Derive a training algorithm for updating the parameters of the Bayesian decision function obtained in Problem 6.14.

7

Function Approximation Using Feedforward Neural Networks

7.1 Stone–Weierstrass Theorem and its Feedforward Networks

7.2 Trigonometric Function Neural Networks

7.3 MFNNs as Universal Approximators

7.4 Kolmogorov's Theorem and Feedforward Networks

7.5 Higher-Order Neural Networks (HONNs)

7.6 Modified Polynomial Neural Networks

7.7 Concluding Remarks

Problems

The functional approximation capability of a feedforward neural network architecture is one of the most exciting properties of the neural structures and has potentials for applications to problems such as system identification, communication channel equalization, signal processing, control, and pattern recognition. Since the 1990's the rigorous investigation of the approximation capabilities of various types of multilayered feedforward architectures has received much research interest. A feedforward network structure may be treated as a rule for computing the output values of the neurons in the ℓth layer using the output values of the $(\ell - 1)$th layer, hence implementing a class of mapping from the input space $\Re^n$ to the output space $\Re^m$. Of interest in this study is what type and how well the mappings from $\Re^n$ to $\Re^m$ can be approximated by the network, and how many neural layers and neurons in such layers are sufficient for this approximating process. This issue has been investigated by many authors, including Carroll and Dickinson (1989), Cybenko (1989), Funahashi (1989), Gallant and White (1988), Hecht-Nielsen (1989), Hornik et al. (1989, 1990), and Hornik (1991).

For function approximation, both the series expansion approach and the Stone–Weierstrass theorem are effective analytic tools. Hecht-Nielsen (1987, 1989) first found the relationship between Kolmogorov's theorem and the approximation principle of the feedforward networks. On the other hand, functional analytic methods have been used successfully to show that feedforward neural structures with at least one hidden layer are capable of simultaneously approximating continuous functions in several variables and their derivatives if the neural activation functions of the hidden neural units are differentiable.

In this chapter, the universal approximation capabilities of feedforward neural networks are studied mainly using the well-known Stone–Weierstrass theorem. After an introduction of this theorem in Section 7.1, the function approximation capabilities of the trigonometric function network structures are discussed in Section 7.2. The functional approximation capabilities of multilayered feedforward neural networks (MFNNs) are addressed in Section 7.3. In Section 7.4, the relationships between Kolmogorov's theorem and feedforward neural networks are presented. As alternative structures of feedforward neural networks, some structures of higher-order neural networks are proposed in Section 7.5 for the purpose of universal approximation. In Section 7.6, for the purpose of the functional approximation, a modified version of MFNNs is also presented.

7.1 STONE–WEIERSTRASS THEOREM AND ITS FEEDFORWARD NETWORKS

There have been attempts to find a mathematical justification for employing MFNNs for function approximation. Typical studies have dealt with the possibility of approximating any continuous function using MFNNs. In mathematical terms this means that approximation can be achieved by a dense network in the space of continuous functions defined on some subset of $\Re^n$. We show next that the Stone–Weierstrass theorem plays an important role in exploring the function approximation capabilities of feedforward neural networks.

7.1.1 Basic Definitions

As seen in the following discussion, to study the approximation capabilities of the neural networks, we have to know some basic concepts and definitions of functional analysis. We will now review some of the definitions that will be used in this chapter. First, every set will be assumed to have the structure of metric space, unless specified otherwise, and the concepts of limit point, infimum and supremum are assumed to be known. All these definitions and theorems can be found in any standard text on functional analysis and in many books on approximation theory. An important concept is that of *closure.*

Definition 7.1 *If Ω is a set of elements, then by the closure $[\Omega]$ of Ω, we mean the set of all points in Ω together with the set of all limit points of Ω.* ■

A definition of closed sets is as follows.

Definition 7.2 *A set Ω is closed if it is coincident with its closure $[\Omega]$.* ■

Thus, a closed set contains all its limit points. Another important definition related to the concept of closure is that of *dense sets.*

Definition 7.3 *Let V be a subset of the set Ω. V is dense in Ω if $[V] = \Omega$.* ■

From the approximation theory point of view, if V is dense in Ω, then each element of Ω can be approximated arbitrary well by elements of V. This denseness will play a key role in our later discussions on the approximation capabilities of neural networks. In order to extend some properties of the real-valued functions defined on an interval to real-valued functions defined on a more complex metric space, it is of interest to give the following concepts.

Definition 7.4 *A set is said to be compact if every infinite subset of the set contains at least one limit point.* ■

It can be shown that, in finite-dimensional metric space, there exists a simple characterization of compact sets. In fact, the following theorem holds.

Theorem 7.1 *Every closed, bounded, finite-dimensional set in a metric linear space is compact.* ■

Furthermore, a continuous function defined on a compact set has the following property.

Theorem 7.2 *A continuous real valued function defined on a compact set in a metric space achieves its infimum and supremum on the set.* ■

7.1.2 Stone–Weierstrass Theorem and Approximation

The Stone–Weierstrass theorem, as a basis theorem of functional analysis and approximation theory, has been very useful for applications to neural networks (Cotter 1990, Hornik 1991). Two equivalent descriptions of this theorem are as follows (Ray 1988).

Theorem 7.3 [Stone–Weierstrass Theorem I (Ray 1988)] *Let S be a compact set with n dimensions, and $\Omega \supset C(S)$ be a set of continuous real-valued functions on S satisfying the following conditions:*

(i) Identity function: The constant function $f(x) = 1$ is in Ω;

(ii) Separability: For any two points $\boldsymbol{x}_1, \boldsymbol{x}_2 \in S$, and $\boldsymbol{x}_1 \neq \boldsymbol{x}_2$, there exists a $f(.) \in \Omega$ such that $f(\boldsymbol{x}_1) \neq f(\boldsymbol{x}_2)$;

(iii) Linear subspace: For any $f, g \in \Omega$ and $\alpha \in \Re$, the functions (αf) and $(f + g)$ are in Ω;

(iv) Lattice property: For any $f, g \in \Omega$, the functions $(f \vee g) = \max(f, g)$, and $(f \wedge g) = \min(f, g)$, are in Ω.

Then, Ω is dense in $C[S]$. In other words, for any $\varepsilon > 0$ and any function $g \in C[S]$, there is a function $f \in \Omega$ such that

$$|g(\boldsymbol{x}) - f(\boldsymbol{x})| < \varepsilon$$

for all $\boldsymbol{x} \in S$. ■

The lattice property is somewhat difficult to verify. Consequently, a slightly different statement of this theorem with respect to the properties of algebraic closure is sometimes more useful in applications.

Theorem 7.4 [Stone–Weierstrass Theorem II (Ray 1988)] *Let S be a compact set with n dimensions, and $\Omega \supset C[S]$ be a set of continuous real-valued functions on S satisfying the following conditions:*

(i) Identity function: The constant function $f(x) = 1$ *is in* Ω;

(ii) Separability: For any two points $\boldsymbol{x}_1, \boldsymbol{x}_2 \in S$ *and* $\boldsymbol{x}_1 \neq \boldsymbol{x}_2$, *there exists a* $f \in \Omega$ *such that* $f(\boldsymbol{x}_1) \neq f(\boldsymbol{x}_2)$;

(iii) Algebraic closure: For any $f, g \in \Omega$ *and* $\alpha, \beta \in \Re$, *the functions* fg *and* $(\alpha f + \beta g)$ *are in* Ω.

Then, Ω *is dense in* $C[S]$. ■

Although the Stone–Weierstrass theorem has a potential application for continuous function approximation, many interesting functions, including step functions, are discontinuous. These functions are members of the set of bounded measurable functions that are continuous and bounded functions and have a finite number of discontinuities. Fortunately, the Stone–Weierstrass theorem can be extended to bounded measurable functions by applying the following theorem.

Theorem 7.5 *If* g *is a measurable real-valued function that is bounded almost everywhere on a compact set* $S \supset \Re^n$, *then, given* $\delta > 0$, *there is a continuous real-valued function* f *on* S *such that the measure of the set where* f *is not equal to* g *is less than* δ

$$m\{\boldsymbol{x} : f(\boldsymbol{x}) \neq g(\boldsymbol{x}), \boldsymbol{x} \in S\} < \delta$$

In other words, the minimum total volume of open spheres required to cover the set where $f \neq g$ *is less than* δ. ■

Theorem 7.5 shows that the continuous functions are dense in the space of the bounded measurable functions on a compact set S. Generally, for a compact set $S \supset \Re^n$, the space $L^p[S], 1 \leq p < \infty$, which consists of all the real measurable Lebesgue-integrable functions with finite L_p norm, is

$$L^p[S] = \{f(\boldsymbol{x}) : \| f(\boldsymbol{x}) \|_p < \infty, \quad \boldsymbol{x} \in S\}$$

where $L_p, 1 \leq p < \infty$, norm is defined as

$$\| f \|_p \equiv \left\{ \int_S |f|_p d\boldsymbol{x} \right\}^{1/p}$$

Therefore, the continuous function space $C[S]$ in the Stone–Weierstrass theorem may be replaced by $L^p[S]$ so that we can consider not only the continuous function approximation problem but also discontinuous cases.

For the applications of neural networks we have to assume that S is an arbitrary compact set in $\Re^n$. An important concept of the uniformly denseness is defined as follows.

Definition 7.5 *Let $S \in \Re^n$ be a compact set, and $\Omega \supset C[S]$ be a set of continuous real-valued functions on S. If Ω for arbitrary S is dense in $C[S]$ then Ω is uniformly dense in $C[S]$.* ■

An important consequence of the Stone–Weierstrass theorem is that the polynomial functions are dense in $C[a,b]$. Since for two arbitrary sets of real numbers $a_i \in \Re$, $(i = 1, 2, \ldots, n)$ and $b_j \in \Re$, $(j = 1, 2, \ldots, m)$, one has

$$\left(\sum_{i=1}^{n} a_i x^i\right)\left(\sum_{j=1}^{m} b_j x^j\right) = \sum_{k=1}^{n+m} c_k x^k$$

where c_k is uniquely determined by a_i and b_j, the product is still a polynomial function in $C[a,b]$. Thus, the set

$$\left\{\sum_{i=1}^{n} a_i x^i : x \in [a,b], \quad a_i \in \Re\right\}\Bigg|_{|n|=0}^{\infty}$$

is dense in $C[a,b]$. Indeed, let $P[0,2\pi]$ be a set of all the continuous functions $f \in C[0,2\pi]$ satisfying $f(0) = f(2\pi)$, since

$$\begin{aligned}
&[\cos(nx) + \sin(nx)][\cos(mx) + \sin(mx)] \\
&\qquad = \cos(-nx)\cos(mx) - \sin(-nx)\sin(mx) \\
&\qquad\qquad + \cos(nx)\sin(mx) + \sin(nx)\cos(mx) \\
&\qquad = \cos((m-n)x) + \sin((n+m)x)
\end{aligned}$$

It is easy to show that the span of $\{\cos(nx) + \sin(nx)\}|_{|n|=0}^{\infty}$ is dense in $P[0,2\pi]$. This property of trigonometric functions provides a foundation for the Fourier series. Obviously, the Stone–Weierstrass theorem states the principle for the infinitely close approximation; however, a finite number of the terms of the sequence may be used to approximate a function over a compact set as accurately as we desire.

7.1.3 Implications for Neural Networks

To establish the function approximation capabilities of nonlinear neural networks that are described by nonlinear mapping from input space to output space directly using the Stone–Weierstrass theorem, one has to verify that the networks satisfy the following three conditions:

(i) The ability of the approximating network to generate $f(x) = 1$. This is always satisfied in many feedforward neural networks due to the existence of the threshold parameters.

(ii) The second condition that requires the separability of the function is satisfied since the activation functions of the neural networks are strictly monotonic. In fact, the neural networks generate different outputs for different inputs.

(iii) The algebraic closure condition requires that the nonlinear mappings of the neural networks are able to generate sums and products of functions.

If a network spans a function space that satisfies the conditions of the Stone–Weierstrass theorem, then the network not only is able to approximate arbitrary continuous real-valued functions on a compact set but can also approximate the weighted sum $(f + g)$ and the product (fg) of arbitrary two continuous functions, f,g, using two networks with smaller sizes. For example, a polynomial expression may be separated into smaller terms that can be approximated by neural networks. A simple recombination of these networks may provide an exact approximation of the original polynomial. Thus, the identity function condition and separability are satisfied for all the feedforward neural structures discussed in this chapter. In fact, only the multiplicative condition of the algebraic closure is needed to be verified for these networks.

Since a feedforward neural structure satisfies these conditions, it can be simply concluded that this network structure has the capability, on a compact set, to approximate arbitrary continuous real-valued functions to any desired degree of accuracy. However, the Stone–Weierstrass theorem gives only a set of sufficient conditions for the universal approximation capabilities. In some cases, even if the network transfer functions do not satisfy the conditions given in the Stone–Weierstrass theorem, one may prove the approximation capabilities of the networks using indirect approaches. A typical example of this group of networks is the well-known multilayered feedforward neural networks (MFNNs), where the function space formed by the network transfer functions with sigmoidal functions such as the popular logistic function $\sigma(x) = 1/(1 + e^{-x})$, or the hyperbolic tangent function $\sigma(x) = \tanh(x)$, does not match the conditions of the theorem because the multiplication condition is not satisfied; that is, the spanned function space is not algebraic. However, as will be seen in the later discussion, the universal approximation capabilities of this network structure may also be ensured.

Feedforward neural networks as described by nonlinear mappings from the input pattern space to the output pattern space are said to be universal approximators in that they are capable of approximating arbitrary nonlinear functions on compact sets to any degree of error. However, implementing such an approximation process fully depends on an effective weight learning procedure. According to the principle offered by the Stone–Weierstrass theorem, as another objective of the next several sections, we will design some feedforward neural network structures that are different from conventional MFNNs with sigmoidal activation functions and that satisfy the Stone–Weierstrass theorem so that they are also universal approximators.

7.2 TRIGONOMETRIC FUNCTION NEURAL NETWORKS

Trigonometric functions have been used extensively in Fourier series analysis for representing functions in the form of trigonometric series consisting of sines and cosines. In this section we will show that as a choice of the nonlinear activation functions in the feedforward neural networks, trigonometric functions, in particular sines and cosines, may be employed in the hidden neural units so that the resulting networks satisfy the conditions of the Stone–Weierstrass theorem. Also, in this section studies on trigonometric function networks will prepare us for exploring the universal approximation of MFNNs, which are addressed in the next section. Without loss of generality, the case of a single output is discussed. However, extension of the results to networks with multiple outputs is straightforward.

By the basic trigonometric system, we mean the system of functions

$$1, \cos(x), \sin(x), \cos(2x), \sin(2x), \ldots, \cos(nx), \sin(nx)$$

All these functions have the common period 2π.

A two-layered trigonometric network with a single hidden layer, as shown in Fig. 7.1, is described by the following input–output transfer function

$$y = \sum_{i=1}^{N} u_i \phi_i \left(\sum_{j=1}^{n} w_{ij} x_j + \theta_i \right) \tag{7.1}$$

which is obtained by replacing the sigmoid function with a trigonometric function $\phi(x)$ in the conventional two-layered neural network. The trigonometric activation function ϕ_i may be chosen as

(i) All $\phi_i(x) = \cos(x)$ (cosine network);
(ii) All $\phi_i(x) = \sin(x)$ (sine network);
(iii) $\phi_i(x) = \cos(x)$ or $\sin(x)$ (trigonometric network).

Trigonometric functions can process signals by transforming multiplication into addition with the following familiar trigonometric formulas

$$\begin{aligned}
2\cos(x)\cos(y) &= \cos(x+y) + \cos(x-y) \\
2\sin(x)\sin(y) &= \sin\left(\frac{\pi}{2} - x + y\right) - \sin\left(\frac{\pi}{2} - x - y\right) \\
2\sin(x)\cos(y) &= \sin(x+y) + \sin(x-y)
\end{aligned}$$

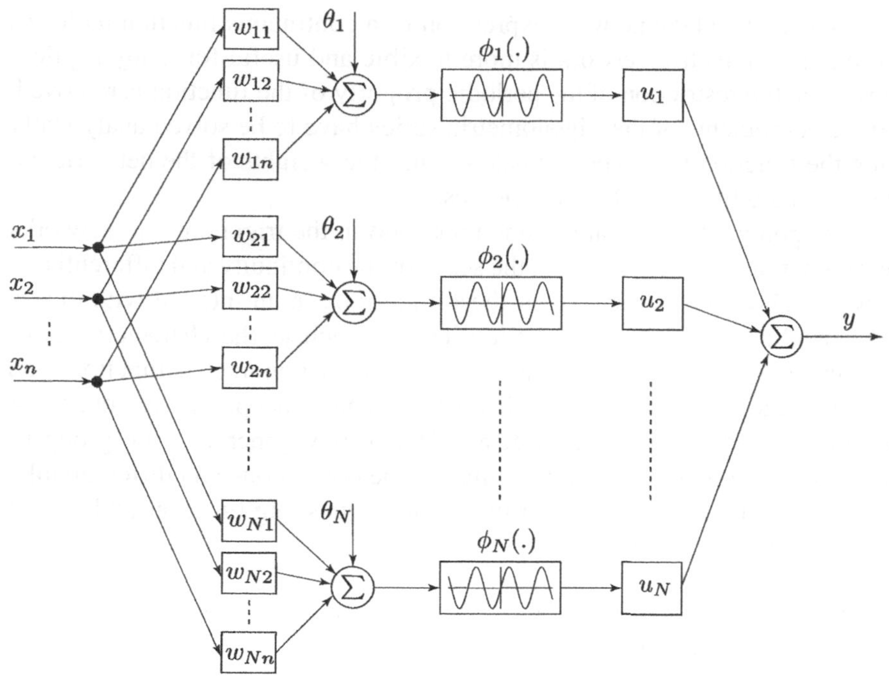

Figure 7.1 Block diagram of the trigonometric neural network, Eqn. (7.1).

Hence, the following theorem of the trigonometric network given in Eqn. (7.1) ensures the universal approximation capability.

Theorem 7.6 *Let Ω be the set of all the functions that can be represented by the trigonometric networks on a compact set $S \supset \Re^n$:*

$$\Omega_N = \left\{ f(\boldsymbol{x}) = \sum_{i=1}^{N} u_i \phi \left(\sum_{j=1}^{n} w_{ij} x_j + \theta_i \right) : \right.$$
$$\left. u_i, w_{ij}, \theta_i \in \Re, \boldsymbol{x} \in S \right\} \qquad (7.2)$$

$$\Omega = \bigcup_{N=1}^{\infty} \Omega_N$$

Then, Ω is dense in $C[S]$. ■

The proof of Theorem 7.6 is easy and is left as an exercise for the readers.

Trigonometric networks are a typical class of feedforward neural networks with nonsigmoidal functions. A comparison of the classical trigonometric series expansion and the network expression of a continuous function indicates that the trigonometric network is more flexible and useful for many applications since the restriction of the periodic property of the function is removed, and the coefficients of the trigonometric series have to be solved analytically using the function to be approximated while the weights of the network can be determined through a learning process.

The trigonometric activation functions used in the trigonometric networks are well defined on the real axis in the sense of the continuity and differentiable property. Having a closer look at these functions in an interval with only a half period reveals that some similarities exit such as the characteristics of nondecreasing and the boundedness between the trigonometric functions and the sigmoidal functions used in MFNNs. The concept of the squashing functions introduced by Hornik et al. (1989) may generalize the group of the sigmoidal functions that are assumed to be continuous and differentiable. For convenience, we will consider the bipolar squashing functions, which are formally defined as follows.

Definition 7.6 *A function* $\psi : \Re \longrightarrow [-1, 1]$ *is a squashing function if it is nondecreasing and satisfies*

$$\lim_{x \to +\infty} \psi(x) = 1, \quad \textit{and} \quad \lim_{x \to -\infty} \psi(x) = -1 \qquad \blacksquare$$

Squashing functions have at the most countable discontinuities that are measurable. In addition to the sigmoidal functions, which are obviously squashing functions, some other examples of squashing functions are the signum function $sgn(x)$ defined by

$$sgn(x) = \begin{cases} -1 & \text{if} \quad x < -1 \\ 1 & \text{if} \quad x \geq 1 \end{cases} \tag{7.3}$$

and the saturating function $Sat(x)$ defined by

$$Sat(x) = \begin{cases} -1 & \text{if} \quad x < -1 \\ x & \text{if} \quad -1 \leq x \leq 1 \\ 1 & \text{if} \quad x > 1 \end{cases} \tag{7.4}$$

Trigonometric functions defined on the whole real axis do not belong to the group of squashing functions. However, because of their periodic property, they may be used to form a new class of squashing functions as seen in the following discussion.

The Fourier network is a direct extension of the cosine network. It is another two-layered network with a nonsigmoidal function and was proposed by Gallant and White (1988) who implemented the Fourier series in the network structure. The activation function in the original Fourier networks was obtained by chopping the sinusoids into halfcycle sections and adding flat trails. The resulting function is called a *bipolar sigmoidal cosine activation function*. Fourier neural networks with a bipolar activation function may be represented, therefore, by

$$y = \sum_{i=1}^{N} w_i \psi \left(\sum_{j=1}^{n} w_{ij} x_j + \theta_i \right) \tag{7.5}$$

where $\psi(.)$ is a sigmoidal cosine squashing function, as shown in Fig. 7.2, with the form

$$\psi(x) = \begin{cases} -1 & \text{if} \quad x < -\frac{\pi}{2} \\ \cos\left(x + \frac{3}{2}\pi\right) & \text{if} \quad -\frac{\pi}{2} \leq x \leq \frac{\pi}{2} \\ 1 & \text{if} \quad x > \frac{\pi}{2} \end{cases} \tag{7.6}$$

A slightly modified version of the sigmoidal cosine squashing function $\psi(x)$ is a cosine squashing function, called a *cosig function* (Cotter 1990)

$$cosig(x) = \begin{cases} -1 & \text{if} \quad x < -12 \\ \cos(2\pi x) & \text{if} \quad -\frac{1}{2} \leq x \leq 0 \\ 1 & \text{if} \quad x > 0 \end{cases} \tag{7.7}$$

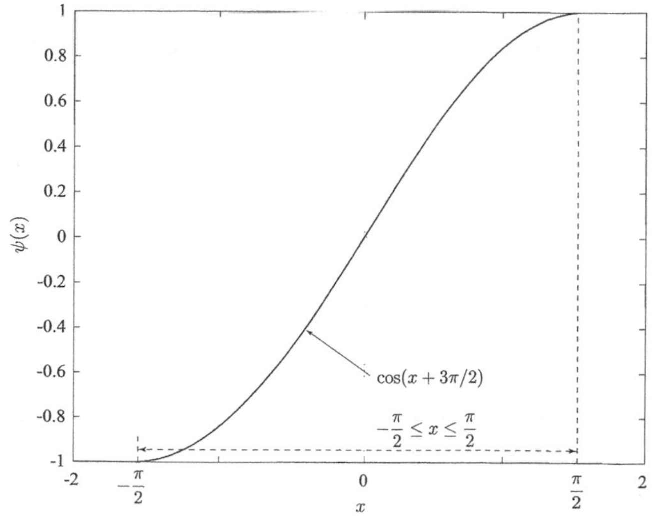

Figure 7.2 Sigmoidal cosine squashing function $\psi(x)$, Eqn. (7.6).

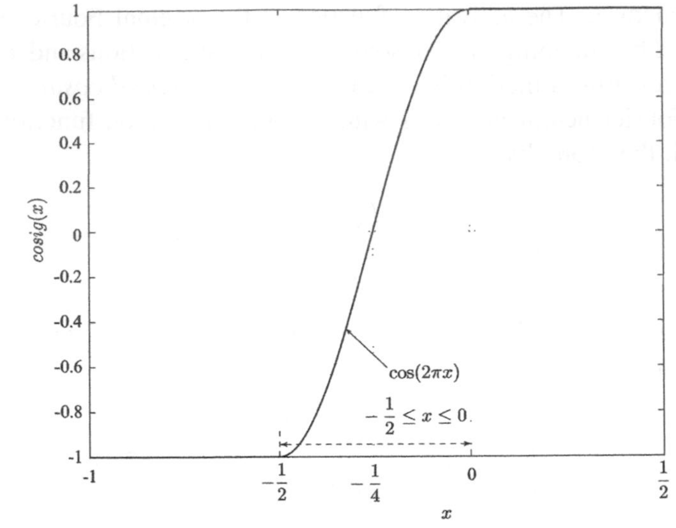

Figure 7.3 Cosine squashing function $cosig(x)$, Eqn. (7.7).

which is shown in Fig. 7.3.

Corresponding to the cosig activation function, a two-layered cosig network is given by

$$y = \sum_{i=1}^{N} w_i \, cosig\left(\sum_{j=1}^{n} w_{ij}x_j + \theta_i\right) \tag{7.8}$$

which deals with only the left-half set of functions computed by the Fourier neural networks given in Eqn. (7.5).

Theorem 7.7 *Let Ω be the set of all the functions that can be represented by either the Fourier neural network or the cosig network on a compact set $S \supset \Re^n$, then Ω is uniformly dense in $C[S]$.*

Proof: We only prove the denseness of the Fourier neural network here. In this case, the set Ω_N is defined as

$$\Omega_N = \left\{ f(\boldsymbol{x}) = \sum_{i=1}^{N} u_i \phi\left(\sum_{j=1}^{n} w_{ij}x_j + \theta_i\right) : \quad u_i, w_{ij}, \theta_i \in \Re, \boldsymbol{x} \in S \right\} \tag{7.9}$$

where the function ψ is given by Eqn. (7.6). Obviously, $f(\boldsymbol{x}) = 1$ is an element of the set Ω_N.

Now consider two arbitrary functions in Ω_N

$$f(\boldsymbol{x}) = \sum_{i_1=1}^{N_1} u_{i_1}^f \psi\left(\sum_{j_1=1}^{n} w_{i_1 j_1}^f x_{j_1} + \theta_{i_1}^f\right) \tag{7.10}$$

$$g(\boldsymbol{x}) = \sum_{i_2=1}^{N_2} u_{i_2}^g \psi\left(\sum_{j_2=1}^{n} w_{i_2 j_2}^g x_{j_2} + \theta_{i_2}^g\right) \tag{7.11}$$

Then, for the arbitrary constants α and $\beta \in \Re$, $\alpha f + \beta g \in \Omega$. Furthermore, noting the definition of the function $\psi(x)$, the product of $\psi(x)$ and $\psi(y)$, $\psi(x)\psi(y)$, can be expressed as

$$\psi(x)\psi(y) = \begin{cases} \psi(x), & \text{if } x, y > \frac{\pi}{2}, \quad \text{or } x < -\frac{\pi}{2},\ y > \frac{\pi}{2} \\ & \quad \text{or } -\frac{\pi}{2} \le x \le \frac{\pi}{2},\ y > \frac{\pi}{2} \\ \psi(y), & \text{if } x > \frac{\pi}{2},\ y < -\frac{\pi}{2} \\ & \quad \text{or } x > \frac{\pi}{2},\ -\frac{\pi}{2} \le y \le \frac{\pi}{2} \\ -\psi(x), & \text{if } -\frac{\pi}{2} \le x \le \frac{\pi}{2},\ y < -\frac{\pi}{2} \\ -\psi(y), & \text{if } x < -\frac{\pi}{2},\ -\frac{\pi}{2} \le y \le \frac{\pi}{2} \end{cases}$$

and, for $-(\pi/2) \le x, y \le (\pi/2)$,

$$\psi(x)\psi(y) = \begin{cases} \psi\left(z_1 - \frac{\pi}{2}\right) + \psi\left(z_2 + \frac{\pi}{2}\right) \\ \quad \text{if } 0 \le z_1 \le \pi,\ -\pi \le z_2 \le 0 \\ -\psi\left(z_1 + \frac{\pi}{2}\right) + \psi\left(z_2 + \frac{\pi}{2}\right) \\ \quad \text{if } -\pi \le z_1 \le 0,\ -\pi \le z_2 \le 0 \\ \psi\left(z_1 - \frac{\pi}{2}\right) - \psi\left(z_2 - \frac{\pi}{2}\right) \\ \quad \text{if } 0 \le z_1 \le \pi,\ 0 \le z_2 \le \pi \\ -\psi\left(z_1 + \frac{\pi}{2}\right) - \psi\left(z_2 + \frac{\pi}{2}\right) \\ \quad \text{if } -\pi \le z_1 \le 0,\ 0 \le z_2 \le \pi \end{cases}$$

where $z_1 \triangleq x + y$ and $z_2 \triangleq x - y$. Therefore

$$f(\boldsymbol{x})g(\boldsymbol{x}) = \sum_{i=1}^{N} u_i \psi \left(\sum_{j=1}^{n} w_{ij} x_j + \theta_i \right) \tag{7.12}$$

where the parameters u_i, w_{ij}, θ_i and N are uniquely determined by the networks of $f(\boldsymbol{x})$ and $g(\boldsymbol{x})$. Therefore, from the Stone–Weierstrass theorem, the set $\Omega = \bigcup \Omega_N$ is uniformly dense in $C[S]$. ■

The critical step in the proof of Theorem 7.7 is to verify the multiplicative condition. A similar approach may be employed to prove the denseness of the cosig networks. It seems that the approach used in this proof provides a basic procedure for showing that a neural network that satisfies the Stone–Weierstrass theorem has the universal approximation capability. Both the cosine squashing functions $\psi(x)$ and $cosig(x)$ are nondecreasing and satisfy

$$\lim_{x \to +\infty} \psi(x) = \lim_{x \to +\infty} cosig(x) = 1$$

and

$$\lim_{x \to -\infty} \psi(x) = \lim_{x \to -\infty} cosig(x) = -1$$

The performance of such networks is very similar to that of three-layered neural networks with sigmoidal functions. This important observation will help us to establish the function approximation capabilities of the MFNNs in the next section.

7.3 MFNNs AS UNIVERSAL APPROXIMATORS

The commonly used two-layered feedforward neural network with a continuous sigmoidal function does not satisfy the Stone–Weierstrass theorem because the multiplicative condition fails. Hence, the denseness of such a feedforward neural network cannot be immediately implied using the Stone–Weierstrass theorem. Using the functional analysis methods, the capabilities of MFNNs may be addressed in a constructive way. These analysis procedures, however, require more mathematical explanation. The scope of all these proofs is too ambitious, even if some significant proofs are worth reviewing. In particular, the Hornik et al. proof (1989) used the trigonometric networks as an intermediate tool to study the problem. However, trigonometric networks are not the unique choice for the basis functions as pointed by Blum and Li (1991). Chebyshev polynomials may replace the trigonometric functions as the basis functions. Blum and Li (1991) addressed the approximation of real functions by feedforward neural networks based on the fundamental principle of approximation by piecewise-constant function. Other approaches to the approximation problem by feedforward neural networks may be found in Cybenko (1989), Lapedes and Farber (1987), and Funahashi (1989). All of these studies used semilinear units and, for the most part, monotonic threshold functions. The proofs are nonconstructive in a simple way, since they depend on the Fourier transformation, Radon transforms, the Hahn–Banach theorem, and so on.

7.3.1 Sketch Proof for Two-Layered Networks

In this section the approximation capabilities of MFNNs will be presented using the denseness of the cosig network presented above. Hornik et al. (1989) proposed an elegant approach to indirectly prove the denseness of the space spanned by two-layered networks with sigmoidal functions in continuous function space. The first step shows that a single-variable cosine squasher function can be uniformly approximated by a single-input, two-layered network with a sigmoidal function. In the second step, one proves that the arbitrary cosig network discussed above can be uniformly approximated by a two-layered network with a sigmoidal function. Finally, the denseness of the space spanned by the cosig network, as was shown above, implies the denseness of the space of the two-layered networks with sigmoidal functions. We will now outline a proof that is based mainly on the work of Hornik et al. (1989), starting from the following lemma with a more readable description.

Lemma 7.1 *Let* $\sigma : \Re \longrightarrow [-1, 1]$ *be a sigmoidal function and* $cosig : \Re \longrightarrow [-1, 1]$ *be a cosine squashing function defined in Eqn. (7.7). For every* $\varepsilon > 0$ *there exists a two-layered network*

$$f(x) = \sum_{i=1}^{N} u_i \sigma(w_i x + \theta_i), \quad x,\ u_i,\ w_i,\ \theta_i \in \Re \tag{7.13}$$

such that

$$\sup_{x \in \Re} |f(x) - cosig(x)| < \varepsilon \tag{7.14}$$

Proof: For an arbitrary $\varepsilon > 0$, without the loss of generality, assume $\varepsilon < 1$. We will now find a finite collection of constants u_i, w_i, and θ_i such that

$$\sup_{x \in \Re} \left| \sum_{i=1}^{N} u_i \sigma(wix + \theta_i) - cosig(x) \right| < \varepsilon \tag{7.15}$$

Select N such that $1/(N+1) < \varepsilon/2$. For $i \in \{1, 2, \ldots, N\}$, set

$$u_i = \frac{1}{N+1} \tag{7.16}$$

Choose $M > 0$ such that $\sigma(-M) < \varepsilon/2(N+1)$ and $\sigma(M) > [1 - \varepsilon/2(N+1)]$. Because $\sigma(.)$ is a sigmoidal function such an M can be found as shown in Fig. 7.4. Furthermore, for the $i \in \{1, 2, \ldots, N\}$ set

$$r_i = \sup\left\{\lambda : \; cosig(\lambda) = \frac{i}{N+1}\right\} \tag{7.17}$$

and

$$r_{N+1} = \sup\left\{\lambda : \; cosig(\lambda) = 1 - \frac{1}{2(N+1)}\right\} \tag{7.18}$$

Since $cosig(.)$, as shown in Fig. 7.4, is a continuous squashing function, such r_j values exist.

Next, a choice of the constants w_i and θ_i is given. Let

$$w_i r_i + \theta_i = M$$

and

$$w_i r_{i+1} + \theta_i = -M$$

Then, a unique set of w_i and θ_i may be determined using these two equations as follows:

$$w_i = \frac{2M}{r_i - r_{i+1}} \tag{7.19}$$

$$\theta_i = -\frac{M(r_i + r_{i+1})}{r_i - r_{i+1}} \tag{7.20}$$

It is easy to verify that for u_i, w_i and θ_i given in Eqns. (7.19) and (7.20)

$$\left| \sum_{i=1}^{N} u_i \sigma(w_i x + \theta_i) - cosig(x) \right| < \varepsilon$$

on each of the intervals $(-\infty, r_1], (r_1, r_2], \ldots, (r_N, r_{N+1}], (r_{N+1}, +\infty)$. ■

Lemma 7.1 not only shows the capability of the two-layered networks for approximating a cosig function that is a special class of the squashing functions but also gives an analytic formulation for selecting the number of the hidden units for a desired degree of approximation. Next, using the results obtained in Lemma 7.1, we will show that an arbitrary cosig network may be uniformly approximated by a two-layered network with a sigmoidal function.

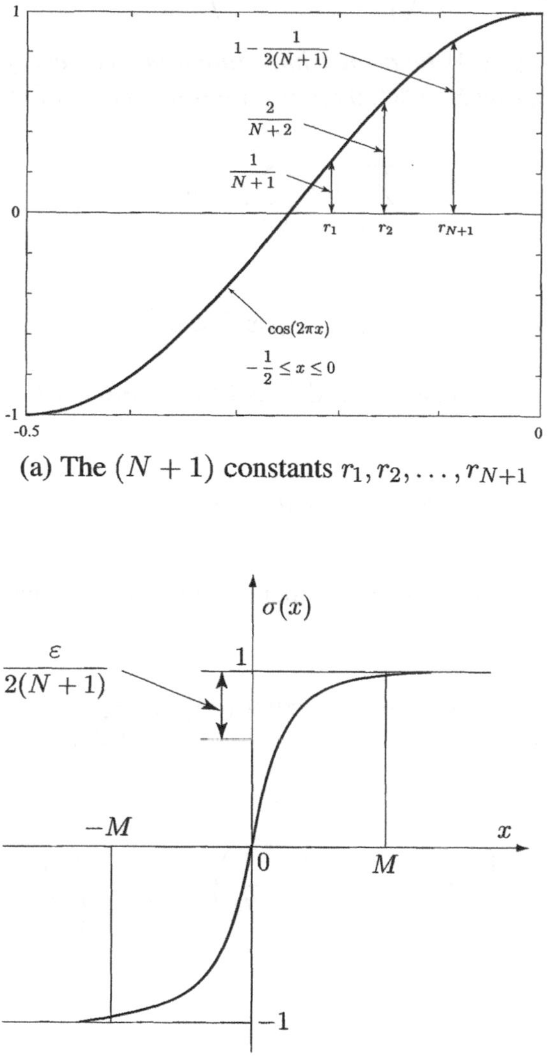

(a) The $(N+1)$ constants $r_1, r_2, \ldots, r_{N+1}$

(b) The constant M

Figure 7.4 Choice of the constant used in the proof of Lemma 7.1.

Lemma 7.2 *Let $x \in \Re^n$, be an arbitrary two-layered cosig network*

$$g(\boldsymbol{x}) = \sum_{i=1}^{N} u_i \, cosig\left(\sum_{j=1}^{n} w_{ij}x_j + \theta_i\right), \qquad u_i,\ w_{ij},\ \theta_i \in \Re \tag{7.21}$$

and $\sigma : \Re \longrightarrow [-1, 1]$ be a squashing function. For every $\varepsilon > 0$ and an arbitrary compact set $S \supset \Re^n$, there is a two-layered feedforward network

$$f(\boldsymbol{x}) = \sum_{\ell=1}^{N} \alpha_i \sigma \left(\sum_{p=1}^{n} \beta_{\ell p} x_p + \gamma_\ell\right) \tag{7.22}$$

such that

$$\sup_{\boldsymbol{x} \in S} |f(\boldsymbol{x}) - g(\boldsymbol{x})| < \varepsilon$$

Proof: Since S is a compact set and N is finite, there is $M > 0$ such that for $i \in \{1, 2, \ldots, N\}$

$$-M \leq \sum_{j=1}^{n} w_{ij}x_j + \theta_i \leq M, \quad \boldsymbol{x} \in S$$

From Lemma 7.1, for every $\varepsilon > 0$, there is a set of constants $\overline{u}_\ell, \overline{w}_\ell$, and $\overline{\theta}_\ell$ such that

$$\sup_{\lambda \in \Re} \left| \sum_{\ell=1}^{Q} \overline{u}_\ell \sigma(\overline{w}_\ell \lambda + \overline{\theta}_\ell) - cosig(\lambda) \right| < \frac{\varepsilon}{N \sum_{i=1}^{N} |u_i|}$$

Hence

$$\sup_{\boldsymbol{x} \in S} \left| \sum_{\ell=1}^{Q} \overline{u}_\ell \sigma \left(\overline{w}_\ell \left[\sum_{j=1}^{n} w_{ij}x_j + \theta_i \right] + \overline{\theta}_\ell \right) - cosig\left(\sum_{j=1}^{n} w_{ij}x_j + \theta_i \right) \right| < \frac{\varepsilon}{N \sum_{i=1}^{N} |u_i|}$$

that is

$$\sup_{\boldsymbol{x} \in S} \left| \sum_{i=1}^{N} u_i \sum_{\ell=1}^{Q} \overline{u}_\ell \sigma \left(\overline{w}_\ell \left[\sum_{j=1}^{n} w_{ij}x_j + \theta_i \right] + \overline{\theta}_\ell \right) - \sum_{i=1}^{N} u_i \, cosig\left(\sum_{j=1}^{n} w_{ij}x_j + \theta_i \right) \right| < \varepsilon$$

Let

$$f(\boldsymbol{x}) = \sum_{i=1}^{N} \sum_{\ell=1}^{Q} u_i \overline{u}_\ell \sigma \left(\overline{w}_\ell \left[\sum_{j=1}^{n} w_{ij} x_j + \theta_i \right] + \overline{\theta}_\ell \right)$$

Then

$$\sup_{\boldsymbol{x} \in S} |f(\boldsymbol{x}) - g(\boldsymbol{x})| < \varepsilon \qquad \blacksquare$$

Lemma 7.2 indicates that the function space spanned by the two-layered networks with sigmoidal functions is uniformly dense in the cosig network function space if both the networks are defined on a compact set. These preliminary results allow the following main theorem to be derived.

Theorem 7.8 *Let $\sigma : \Re \longrightarrow [-1, 1]$ be a sigmoidal function and Ω be the set of all functions that can be represented by a two-layered network on an arbitrary compact set $S \supset \Re^n$:*

$$\begin{aligned} \Omega_N &= \left\{ f(\boldsymbol{x}) = \sum_{i=1}^{N} u_i \phi \left(\sum_{j=1}^{n} w_{ij} x_j + \theta_i \right) \; : \; u_i, w_{ij}, \theta_i \in \Re, \boldsymbol{x} \in S \right\} \\ \Omega &= \bigcup_{N=1}^{\infty} \Omega_N \end{aligned}$$

Then Ω is uniformly dense in $C[\Re^n]$.

Proof: Since the function space spanned by the cosig network is uniformly dense in $C[S]$, and Ω is uniformly dense in the cosig network space by Lemma 7.2, the proof of the theorem is implied. $\blacksquare$

7.3.2 Approximation Using General MFNNs

The approximation capabilities of two-layered neural networks with sigmoidal functions is ensured by Theorem 7.8. However, no information is given on the number of the hidden units needed to achieve a satisfactory approximation even for the continuous function that is to be approximated. On the other hand, one may note that the continuity of the sigmoidal functions is not necessary in the proof of Theorem 7.8. This leads to a natural extension that the sigmoidal functions often used in conventional neural networks may be replaced with a more general class of squashing functions for achieving the universal approximation.

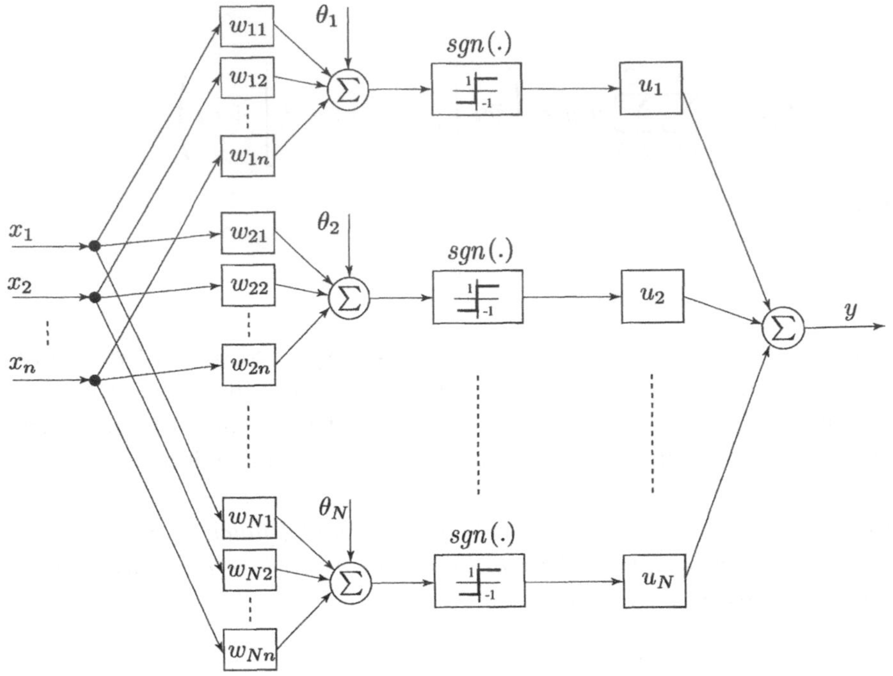

Figure 7.5 Two-layered network with the Mc-P hidden units, Eqn. (7.23).

An interesting consequence is that the approximation using a two-layered network (Fig. 7.5) with the hidden units of McCulloch–Pitts, called the "Mc-P units," is easily implied. This type of feedforward neural network, called a *neural logic network* may be obtained by replacing the sigmoidal function $\sigma(x)$ with the signum function as follows

$$y = f(\boldsymbol{x}) = \sum_{i=1}^{N} u_i \, sgn \left(\sum_{j=1}^{n} w_{ij} x_j + \theta_i \right) \tag{7.23}$$

where the signum function $sgn(.)$ is defined by

$$sgn(x) \quad = \quad \begin{cases} 1 & \text{if} \quad x \geq 0 \\ -1 & \text{if} \quad x < 0 \end{cases}$$

The network in Eqn. (7.23) consists of the hidden units of the threshold elements that deal with a threshold logic on the real inputs $x_1, x_2, \ldots, x_n$. When the input $\boldsymbol{x}$ is restricted on a compact set in $\Re^n$ the network is capable of approximating any continuous function to a desired degree of accuracy. This conclusion is summarized in the following corollary.

Corollary 7.1 *Let $S \supset \Re^n$ be a compact set and $g \in C[S]$ be a continuous function. For any $\varepsilon > 0$, there is a two-layered network consisting of Mc-P units in the hidden layer with the form*

$$f(\boldsymbol{x}) = \sum_{i=1}^{N} u_i \, sgn\left(\sum_{j=1}^{n} w_{ij}x_j + \theta_i\right) \tag{7.24}$$

such that

$$|f(\boldsymbol{x}) - g(\boldsymbol{x})| < \varepsilon, \quad \boldsymbol{x} \in S$$ ■

Although two-layered networks with Mc-P hidden neurons are capable of approximating arbitrary continuous functions, Blum and Li (1991) proved that there is a class of piecewise constant functions which cannot be implemented by a two-layered Mc-P network. Therefore, in the direct approach to function approximation three-layered Mc-P networks with two hidden layers are generally required. Using the results on the three-layered networks, the approximation capabilities of the multilayered feedforward neural networks (MFNNs) may be easily explored.

Corollary 7.2 *Let $S \supset \Re^n$ be a compact set and $g \in C[S]$ be a continuous function. For any $\varepsilon > 0$, there is a MFNN with arbitrary hidden layers and the sigmoidal function that approximates g uniformly on S with error $< \varepsilon$.*

Proof: We need only to prove that the three-layered network

$$f(\boldsymbol{x}) = \sum_{i=1}^{N_1} u_i \, \sigma\left(\sum_{j=1}^{N_2} v_{ij}\sigma\left(\sum_{k=1}^{n} w_{ijk}x_k + \theta_j\right) + \ell_i\right)$$

can approximate g on S with error $< \varepsilon$.

For every $\varepsilon > 0$, using Theorem 7.8, there is a three-layered network

$$\overline{f}(\boldsymbol{x}) = \sum_{i=1}^{N} u_i \, \sigma\left(\sum_{j=1}^{n} w_{ij}x_j + \ell_i\right)$$

such that

$$\left|\overline{f}(\boldsymbol{x}) - g(\boldsymbol{x})\right| < \frac{\varepsilon}{2}$$

for all $\boldsymbol{x} \in S$. On the other hand, the sigmoidal function $\sigma(x)$ is uniformly continuous on the compact set S. Then for a given set of constants

$$\varepsilon_i' = \frac{\varepsilon}{N_1|u_i|}, \quad i = 1, 2, \ldots, N_1$$

there are constants δ_i, and thus we may find a set of the three-layered networks

$$\sum_{j=1}^{N_2} v_{ij}\,\sigma\left(\sum_{k=1}^{n} w_{ijk}x_k + \theta_j\right)$$

such that

$$\left|\sum_{j=1}^{N_2} v_{ij}\,\sigma\left(\sum_{k=1}^{n} w_{ijk}x_k + \theta_j\right) - \sum_{j=1}^{n} w_{ij}x_j\right| < \delta_i$$

and

$$\left|\sigma\left(\sum_{j=1}^{N_2} v_{ij}\,\sigma\left(\sum_{k=1}^{n} w_{ijk}x_k + \theta_j\right) + \ell_i\right) - \sigma\left(\sum_{j=1}^{n} w_{ij}x_j + \ell_i\right)\right| < \varepsilon_i'$$

Hence

$$\left|f(\boldsymbol{x}) - \overline{f}(\boldsymbol{x})\right| < \sum_{i=1}^{N_1} \frac{\varepsilon_i'}{|u_i|} = \varepsilon$$

Finally

$$|f(\boldsymbol{x}) - g(\boldsymbol{x})| \le \left|f(\boldsymbol{x}) - \overline{f}(\boldsymbol{x})\right| + \left|\overline{f}(\boldsymbol{x}) - g(\boldsymbol{x})\right| < \varepsilon \qquad \blacksquare$$

Corollary 7.2 gives the results of the approximation capabilities of general MFNNs with sigmoidal functions. In fact, the neural activation functions in MFNNs may be relaxed to any continuous, bounded and nonconstant function (Hornik 1991).

7.4 KOLMOGOROV'S THEOREM AND FEEDFORWARD NETWORKS

Applications of Kolmogorov's superposition theorem, which is considered as the representation of continuous functions defined on an n-dimensional cube by sums and superpositions to feedforward neural networks, were first studied by Hecht-Nielsen (1987, 1990). This study gives an existence of an exact implementation of every continuous function in a structure of the three-layered networks. As one of the pioneers in the field of neural networks, Hecht-Nielsen gave some interpretations of the approximation principle of Kolmogorov's theorem in terms of feedforward neural networks before some more practical achievements of the universal approximation capabilities of feedforward networks were developed independently by Cybenko (1989), Funahashi (1989), and Hornik et al. (1989). More recently, Sprecher (1993) presented some new results that may be viewed as a stronger version of the results obtained by Hecht-Nielsen. However, Poggio and Girosi (1989) pointed out that the one-variable functions constructed by Kolmogorov (1957), and its later improvements by Lorentz (1966, 1986) and Sprecher (1965), are far from being any of the type of functions used in feedforward neural networks.

Let $I = [0, 1]$ denote the closed unit interval and $I^n = [0, 1]^n$, $(n \geq 2)$ be the Cartesian product of I. The superposition theorem of Kolmogorov (1957) established that for each integer $n \geq 2$ there are $n \times (2n + 1)$ continuous monotonically increasing function h_{pq}, and $(2n+1)$ continuous functions g_q which can be used to represent exactly every real-valued continuous function $f : I^n = [0, 1]^n \longrightarrow \Re$. The original statement of Kolmogorov is as follows.

Theorem 7.9 (Kolmogorov's Superposition Theorem) *There exist a set of increasing continuous functions $h_{pq} : I = [0, 1] \longrightarrow \Re$ such that each continuous function f on I^n can be written in the form*

$$f(\boldsymbol{x}) = \sum_{q=1}^{2n+1} g_q \left(\sum_{p=1}^{n} h_{pq}(x_p) \right) \tag{7.25}$$

where g_q are the properly chosen continuous functions of one variable. ■

Kolmogorov's theorem shows that any continuous function of several variables can be represented exactly by means of the superposition of continuous functions of a single variable and the operation of addition. Moreover, the functions h_{pq} are universal for the given dimension n; they are independent of the given function f. Only the function g_q is specific for the given function f. Using the language of neural networks, we may explain Kolmogorov's theorem as follows:

Any continuous function defined on an n-dimensional cube can be implemented exactly by a two-layered feedforward network, as shown in Fig. 7.6, which has $n(2n + 1)$ units with the increasing continuous functions $h_{pq} : I \longrightarrow \Re$ in the first hidden layer and $(2n + 1)$ units with the continuous functions g_q in the second hidden layer.

The main improvements to the Kolmogorov's original theorem concentrate on the possibility of replacing the function g_q by a single function g (Lorentz 1962), and of transforming h_{pq} into $\ell_p h_q$ (Sprecher 1965) as shown in Fig. 7.7. Let H be the space with the uniform norm consisting of all nondecreasing continuous functions on the closed interval $I = [0, 1]$ and $H^k = H \times \cdots \times H$

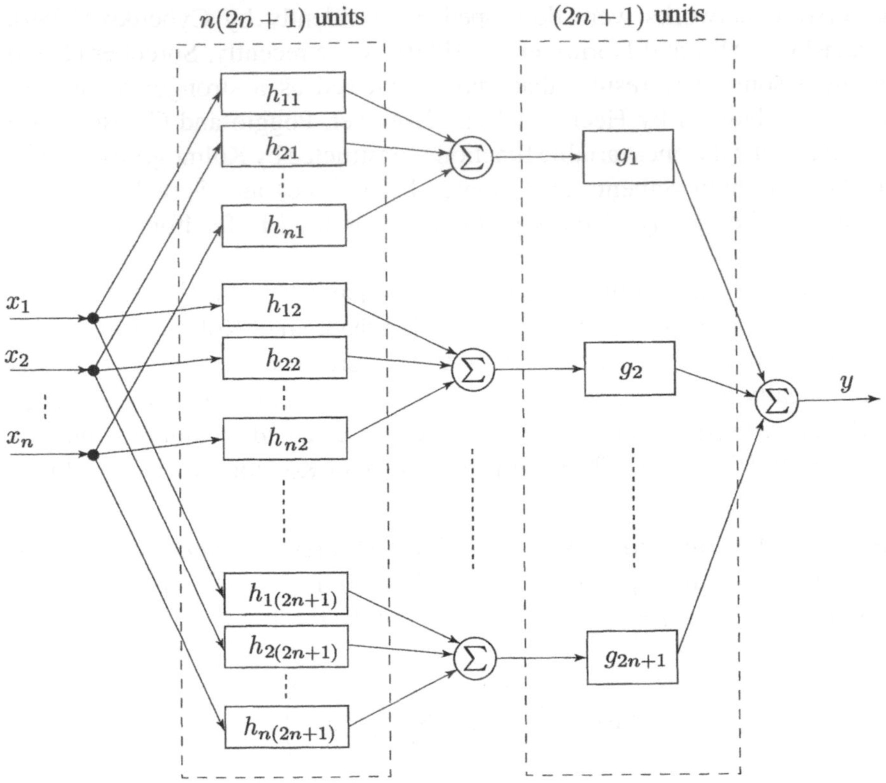

Figure 7.6 Systematic representation of the Kolmogorov superposition theorem using a two-layered network structure, Eqn. (7.25).

be the kth power of space. Kahane (1975) modified Kolmogorov's theorem using the following results.

Theorem 7.10 *Let ℓ_p $(p = 1, \ldots, n)$ be a collection of rationally independent constants. Then for quasicollection $\{h_1, \ldots, h_{2n+1}\} \in H^{2n+1}$, and any function $f \in C(I^n)$, it can be represented on I^n in the form*

$$y = f(x_1, \ldots, x_n) = \sum_{q=1}^{2n+1} g\left(\sum_{p=1}^{n} \ell_p h_q(x_p)\right) \tag{7.26}$$

where g is a continuous function. ■

In order to give a geometric interpretation of Theorem 7.10, consider the mapping of I^n into a $(2n + 1)$-dimensional space defined by

$$y_q = \ell_1 h_q(x_1) + \cdots + \ell_n h_q(x_n), \quad q = 1, \ldots, (2n + 1) \tag{7.27}$$

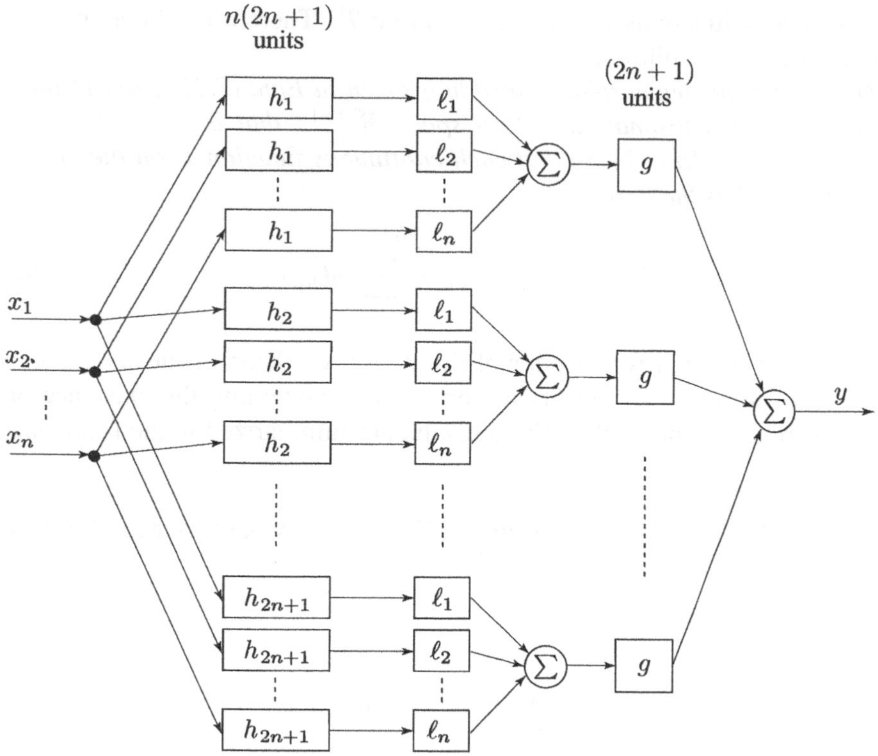

Figure 7.7 The modified Kolmogorov network, where the connection weights between the input and the hidden layers are equal to 1 and the weights between the hidden and output layers are $\{\ell_1, \ldots, \ell_n, \ldots, \ell_1, \ldots, \ell_n\}$, Eqn. (7.26).

This is a continuous and one-to-one mapping. Otherwise, two points would exist of I^n which are not distinguished by the family of functions $y_q(x_1, \ldots, x_n)$, $q = 1, \ldots, (2n+1)$. All functions would then be represented by Eqn. (7.27) and would coincide at these two points. Equation (7.27) would then be impossible for some functions $f \in C[I^n]$. Indeed, since I^n is compact, its image under mapping is

$$T \triangleq \left\{ y = (y_1, \ldots, y_{2n+1}) : \ y_q = \sum_{p=1}^{n} \ell_p h_q(x_p), \quad \boldsymbol{x} \in I^n \right\} \tag{7.28}$$

which is also compact, and the mapping given in Eqn. (7.27) is a homeomorphism between I^n and T. This implies that there exists a one-to-one relationship between all the continuous functions $f(x_1, \ldots, x_n)$ on I^n and all the continuous functions $F(y_1, \ldots, y_{2n+1})$ on T. Therefore, Theorem 7.10 can be rewritten as follows:

There exists homeomorphic embedding given in Eqn. (7.27) from I^n into the $(2n+1)$-dimensional Euclidean space $\Re^{2n+1}$; that is, $y_q : I^n \longrightarrow \Re$, $q = 1, \ldots, (2n+1)$, so that each continuous function F on the image space T of I^n has the form

$$F(y_1, \ldots, y_{2n+1}) = \sum_{p=1}^{2n+1} g(y_p) \tag{7.29}$$

More recently, an improved version of Kolmogorov's theorem due to Sprecher (1965) was presented by Hecht-Nielsen (1987) concerning the existence of feedforward neural networks. These results are summarized in the following theorem.

Theorem 7.11 [Kolmogorov's Mapping Neural Network Existence Theorem (Hecht-Nielsen 1987)] *Given any continuous function $f : I^n \longrightarrow \Re^m$ with $n \geq 2$, $\boldsymbol{f}(\boldsymbol{x}) = \boldsymbol{y}$. Then $\boldsymbol{f}$ can be implemented exactly by the following network*

$$z_k = \sum_{j=1}^{n} \lambda^k h(x_j + k\varepsilon) + k \tag{7.30}$$

$$y_i = f_i(\boldsymbol{x}) = \sum_{k=1}^{2n+1} g_i(z_k) \tag{7.31}$$

where the real constant λ and the continuous real monotonically increasing function h are independent of f although they do depend on n. The real and continuous g_i are dependent on the function f_i and the constant ε, where ε is a rational number $0 \leq \varepsilon \leq \delta$, and δ is an arbitrary chosen positive constant. ■

The proof of this theorem may be completed directly by applying the results of Sprecher (1965) to each of the m coordinates of $\boldsymbol{y}$ separately. As shown in Fig. 7.8, the implementation given in Theorem 7.11 is a two-layered neural network having n processing units in the input layer, $(2n+1)$ processing units in the hidden layer that receive the input $\boldsymbol{x}$ and create the outputs $z_1, z_2, \ldots, z_{2n+1}$, and m processing units in the output layer which give the outputs $y_1, y_2, \ldots, y_m$.

Kolmogorov's theorem provides only a structure for a three-layered feedforward network that can represent exactly an arbitrary continuous function. No further results concerning the network functions g and h_q have been obtained yet. The proof of the theorem is not constructive, as it does not show us

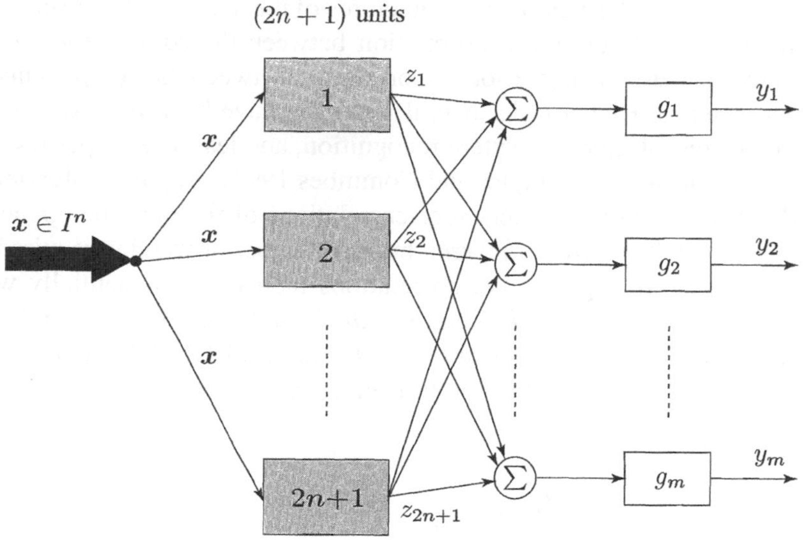

Figure 7.8 A schematic representation of the Kolmogorov mapping neural network existence theorem presented by Hecht-Nielsen (1987).

how to select these quantities. It is strictly an existence theorem, and this is the main limitation for the application of Kolmogorov's theorem. As suggested by Hecht-Nielsen (1987), a potentially high-payoff challenge is to discover an adaptive mechanism where the g_i values could self-organize themselves in response to incoming x/y vector pairs. However, exact network expressions of the arbitrary continuous functions are very attractive for function approximation issues. In addition, some progress on the applications of Kolmogorov's theorem for constructing multilayered neural networks has been made (Kurkova 1992, Sprecher 1993). In particular, work on the estimation of the number of the hidden units of a three-layered network using Kolmogorov's theorem presented by Kurkova (1992) is one of the more interesting examples of these applications.

7.5 HIGHER-ORDER NEURAL NETWORKS (HONNs)

As seen previously, a conventional neuron in a MFNN has only a linear correlation between the input vector and the synaptic weight vector. This correlation was described as a type of synaptic operation. To capture the higher-order nonlinear properties of the input pattern space, extensive attempts have been made by Rumelhart et al. (1986), Giles and Maxwell (1987), Softky and Kammen (1991), Xu et al. (1992), Taylor and Commbes (1993), and Homma and

Gupta (2002b) toward developing architectures of the neurons that are capable of capturing not only the linear correlation between the components of the input pattern but also the higher-order correlation between the components of the input patterns. Higher-order neural networks have been proved to have good computational, storage, pattern recognition, and learning properties and are realizable in hardware (Taylor and Commbes 1993). Regular polynomial networks that contain the higher-order correlations of the input components satisfy the *Stone–Weierstrass theorem*, but the number of weights required to accommodate all the higher-order correlations increases exponentially with the number of the inputs. *Higher-order neural units* (HONUs) are the *basic building block* for such a *higher-order neural network* (HONN). For such a HONN as shown in Fig. 7.9, the output is given by

$$y = \phi(z) \tag{7.32}$$

$$\begin{aligned} z &= w_0 + \sum_{i_1}^{n} w_{i_1} x_{i_1} + \sum_{i_1, i_2}^{n} w_{i_1 i_2} x_{i_1} x_{i_2} + \cdots \\ &\quad + \sum_{i_1, \cdots, i_N}^{n} w_{i_1 \cdots i_N} x_{i_1} \cdots x_{i_N} \end{aligned} \tag{7.33}$$

where $\boldsymbol{x} = [x_1\ x_2\ \cdots\ x_n]^T$ is the vector of neural inputs, y is an output, and $\phi(.)$ is a strictly monotonic activation function such as a sigmoidal function whose inverse, $\phi^{-1}(.)$, exists. The summation for the kth-order correlation is taken on a set $C(i_1 \cdots i_j)$, $(1 \le j \le N)$ which is a set of the combinations of j indices $1 \le i_1 \cdots i_j \le n$ defined by

$$C(i_1 \cdots i_j) \triangleq \{< i_1 \cdots i_j >: 1 \le i_1 \cdots i_j \le n, i_1 \le i_2 \le \cdots \le i_j\} \quad 1 \le j \le N$$

Also, the number of the Nth order correlation terms is given by

$$\binom{n+j-1}{j} = \frac{(n+j-1)!}{j!(n-1)!}, \quad 1 \le j \le N$$

The introduction of the set $C(i_1 \cdots i_j)$ is to absorb the redundant terms due to the symmetry of the induced combinations. In fact, Eqn. (7.33) is a truncated Taylor series with some adjustable coefficients. The Nth-order neural unit needs a total of

$$\sum_{j=0}^{N} \binom{n+j-1}{j} = \sum_{j=0}^{N} \frac{(n+j-1)!}{j!(n-1)!}$$

weights including the basis of all of the product up to N components.

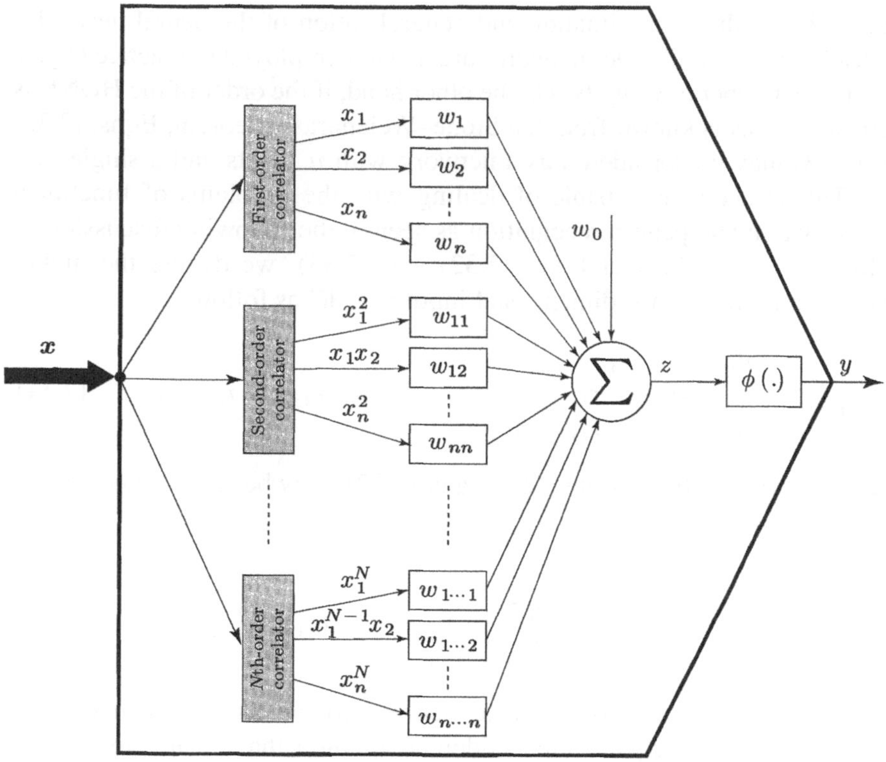

Figure 7.9 Block diagram of the higher-order neural unit (HONU), Eqns. (7.32) and (7.33).

Example 7.1 In this example we consider a case of the third-order ($N = 3$) neural network with two neural inputs ($n = 2$). Here

$$\begin{aligned} C(i) &= \{0, 1, 2\} \\ C(i_1 i_2) &= \{11, 12, 22\} \\ C(i_1 i_2 i_3) &= \{111, 112, 122, 222\} \end{aligned}$$

and the network equation is

$$\begin{aligned} y &= \phi\Big(w_0 + w_1 x_1 + w_2 x_2 + w_{11} x_1^2 + w_{12} x_1 x_2 + w_{22} x_2^2 \\ &\quad + w_{111} x_1^3 + w_{112} x_1^2 x_2 + w_{122} x_1 x_2^2 + w_{222} x_2^3 \Big) \end{aligned}$$

■

The higher-order neural units (HONUs) may be used in conventional feedforward neural network structures as the hidden units to form HONNs. In this case, however, consideration of the higher correlation may improve the capabilities of the approximation and generalization of the neural networks. Typically only second-order networks are usually employed in practice to give a tolerable number of weights. On the other hand, if the order of the HONU is high enough, as is known from the Stone–Weierstrass theorem, Eqns. (7.32) and (7.33) may be considered as a network with n inputs and a single output. This structure is capable of dealing with the problems of functional approximation and pattern recognition as seen in the following discussion.

To get a closer look at Eqns. (7.32) and (7.33), we denote the higher correlation terms of an n-dimensional input $\boldsymbol{x} \in \Re^n$ as follows:

$$\begin{cases} u_{i_1} &= x_{i_1} \\ u_{i_1 i_2} &= x_{i_1} x_{i_2} \\ u_{i_1 i_2 \cdots i_N} &= x_{i_1} x_{i_2} \cdots x_{i_N} \end{cases}, \quad 1 \leq i_1, i_2, \ldots, i_N \leq n \tag{7.34}$$

Then network equations, Eqns. (7.32) and (7.33), may be represented as

$$y = \phi(z) \tag{7.35}$$

$$z = w_0 + \sum_{j=1}^{N} \left(\sum_{i_1 \cdots i_j} w_{i_1 \cdots i_j} u_{i_1 \cdots i_j} \right) \tag{7.36}$$

and may be treated as a two-layered neural network as shown in Fig.7.9. Here, $u_{i_1 \cdots i_j}$ are the outputs of the hidden neural units that are able to produce the higher-order correlations between the components for each vector input pattern $\boldsymbol{x}$. The output neuron is a simple linear combiner with an activation function $\phi(.)$.

To accomplish an approximation task for given input–output data $\{\boldsymbol{x}(k), y(k)\}$, the learning algorithm for the higher-order neural network can easily be developed on the basis of the gradient descent method. Let us assume that the error function is formulated as

$$E(k) = \tfrac{1}{2}\left[d(k) - y(k)\right]^2 = \tfrac{1}{2}e^2(k)$$

where $e(k) = d(k) - y(k)$, $d(k)$ is the desired output and $y(k)$ is the output of the neural networks. Minimization of the error function by a standard steepest-descent technique yields the following set of learning equations

$$w_0^{new} = w_0^{old} + \eta(d - y)\phi'(z) \tag{7.37}$$

$$w_{ij}^{new} = w_{ij}^{old} + \eta(d - y)\phi'(z)u_{i_1 \cdots i_j} \tag{7.38}$$

where $\phi'(z) = d\phi/dz$. Like the BP algorithm for a MFNN, a momentum version of the above is easily obtained.

Alternatively, since all the weights of the higher-order networks appear linearly in Eqn. (7.36), one may use the method for solving linear algebraic equations to carry out the preceding learning task if the number of patterns is finite. To do so, one has to introduce the following two augmented vectors

$$\boldsymbol{w} \triangleq \begin{bmatrix} w_0 \\ w_1 \\ \vdots \\ w_n \\ w_{11} \\ w_{12} \\ \vdots \\ w_{nn} \\ \vdots \\ w_{1\cdots 1} \\ w_{1\cdots 2} \\ \vdots \\ w_{n\cdots n} \end{bmatrix} \quad \text{and} \quad \boldsymbol{u}(\boldsymbol{x}) \triangleq \begin{bmatrix} x_0 \\ x_1 \\ x_2 \\ \vdots \\ x_n \\ x_1^2 \\ x_1 x_2 \\ \vdots \\ x_n^2 \\ \vdots \\ x_1^N \\ x_1^{N-1} x_2 \\ \cdots \\ x_n^N \end{bmatrix}$$

where $x_0 \triangleq 1$, so that the network equations, Eqns. (7.35) and (7.36), may be rewritten into the following compact form:

$$y = \phi\left(\boldsymbol{w}^T \boldsymbol{u}(\boldsymbol{x})\right) \tag{7.39}$$

For the given p pattern pairs $\{\boldsymbol{x}(k), d(k)\}$, $(1 \leq k \leq p)$, define the following vectors and matrix

$$\boldsymbol{U} = \begin{bmatrix} \boldsymbol{u}^T(1) \\ \boldsymbol{u}^T(2) \\ \vdots \\ \boldsymbol{u}^T(p) \end{bmatrix}, \qquad \boldsymbol{d} = \begin{bmatrix} \phi^{-1}(d(1)) \\ \phi^{-1}(d(2)) \\ \vdots \\ \phi^{-1}(d(p)) \end{bmatrix}$$

where $\boldsymbol{u}(k) = \boldsymbol{u}(\boldsymbol{x}(k))$, $1 \leq k \leq p$. Then, the learning problem becomes one of finding a solution of the following linear algebraic equation

$$\boldsymbol{U}\boldsymbol{w} = \boldsymbol{d} \tag{7.40}$$

If the number of the weights is equal to the number of the data and the matrix $\boldsymbol{U}$ is nonsingular, then Eqn. (7.40) has a unique solution

$$\boldsymbol{w} = \boldsymbol{U}^{-1}\boldsymbol{d}$$

A more interesting case is that when the dimension of the weight vector $\boldsymbol{w}$ is less than the number of data p. Thus, the existence of the exact solution for the above linear equation is given by

$$rank\left[\, \boldsymbol{U} \vdots \boldsymbol{d} \,\right] = rank[\boldsymbol{U}] \tag{7.41}$$

In case this condition is not satisfied, the pseudoinverse solution is usually an option and gives the best fit.

Examples 7.2 and 7.3 show how to use the higher-order neural network presented in this section to deal with pattern recognition problems. It is of interest to show that solving these problems is equivalent to finding the decision surfaces in the pattern space such that the given data patterns are located on the surfaces.

Example 7.2 Consider a two-variable *XOR* functions defined as

$$f(x_1, x_2) = (x1 \oplus x2) = \begin{cases} 1 & \text{if} \quad x_1 = 1 \quad \text{and} \quad x_2 = -1 \\ 1 & \text{if} \quad x_1 = -1 \quad \text{and} \quad x_2 = 1 \\ -1 & \text{if} \quad x_1 = 1 \quad \text{and} \quad x_2 = 1 \\ -1 & \text{if} \quad x_1 = -1 \quad \text{and} \quad x_2 = -1 \end{cases}$$

where $x_1, x_2 \in \{-1, 1\}$ are the bipolar binary inputs. A second-order neural network used to realize this logic function is assumed to be

$$y = w_0 + w_1 x_1 + w_2 x_2 + w_{12} x_1 x_2$$

whose weights may be determined by the following set of linear algebraic equations:

$$\begin{cases} w_0 + w_1 - w_2 - w_{12} &= 1 \\ w_0 - w_1 + w_2 - w_{12} &= 1 \\ w_0 + w_1 + w_2 + w_{12} &= -1 \\ w_0 - w_1 - w_2 + w_{12} &= -1 \end{cases}$$

It is easily observed that the coefficient matrix of these equations is nonsingular and the equations have a unique solution

$$w_0 = 0, \quad w_1 = 0, \quad w_2 = 0, \quad w_{12} = -1$$

Hence, the logic function is implemented by a simple second-order polynomial

$$y = -x_1 x_2$$

■

Example 7.3 Consider a three-variable *XOR* function defined as

$$y = f(x_1, x_2, x_3) = (x_1 \oplus x_2) \oplus x_3 = x_1 \oplus (x_2 \oplus x_3) = x_1 \oplus x_2 \oplus x_3$$

Table 7.1 Truth table of *XOR* function $x_1 \oplus x_2 \oplus x_3$

Pattern	Input x_1	Input x_2	Input x_3	Output y
A	1	1	1	1
B	−1	1	1	−1
C	−1	−1	1	1
D	−1	−1	−1	−1
E	1	−1	−1	1
F	1	1	−1	−1
G	1	−1	1	−1
H	−1	1	−1	1

The eight input pattern pairs and corresponding outputs are given in Table 7.1. This is a typical nonlinear pattern classification problem. A single linear neuron with a nonlinear activation function is unable to form a decision surface such that the patterns are separated in the pattern space. Our objective here is to find all the possible solutions using the third-order network to realize the logic function.

A third-order neural network is designed as

$$\begin{aligned} y &= w_0 + w_1x_1 + w_2x_2 + w_3x_3 + w_{12}x_1x_2 + w_{13}x_1x_3 \\ &\quad + w_{23}x_2x_3 + w_{123}x_1x_2x_3 \end{aligned}$$

where $x_1, x_2, x_3 \in \{-1, 1\}$ are the binary inputs, and the network contains eight weights. To implement the above mentioned logic (*XOR*) function, one may consider the solution of the following set of linear algebraic equations:

$$\left\{ \begin{array}{rcr} w_0 + w_1 + w_2 + w_3 + w_{12} + w_{13} + w_{23} + w_{123} &=& 1 \\ w_0 - w_1 + w_2 + w_3 - w_{12} - w_{13} + w_{23} - w_{123} &=& -1 \\ w_0 - w_1 - w_2 + w_3 + w_{12} - w_{13} - w_{23} + w_{123} &=& 1 \\ w_0 - w_1 - w_2 - w_3 + w_{12} + w_{13} + w_{23} - w_{123} &=& -1 \\ w_0 + w_1 - w_2 - w_3 - w_{12} - w_{13} + w_{23} + w_{123} &=& 1 \\ w_0 + w_1 + w_2 - w_3 + w_{12} - w_{13} - w_{23} - w_{123} &=& -1 \\ w_0 + w_1 - w_2 + w_3 - w_{12} + w_{13} - w_{23} - w_{123} &=& -1 \\ w_0 - w_1 + w_2 - w_3 - w_{12} + w_{13} - w_{23} + w_{123} &=& 1 \end{array} \right.$$

The coefficient matrix U is given by

$$
\boldsymbol{U} = \begin{bmatrix}
1 & 1 & 1 & 1 & 1 & 1 & 1 & 1 \\
1 & -1 & 1 & 1 & -1 & -1 & 1 & -1 \\
1 & -1 & -1 & 1 & 1 & -1 & -1 & 1 \\
1 & -1 & -1 & -1 & 1 & 1 & 1 & -1 \\
1 & 1 & -1 & -1 & -1 & -1 & 1 & 1 \\
1 & 1 & 1 & -1 & 1 & -1 & -1 & -1 \\
1 & 1 & -1 & 1 & -1 & 1 & -1 & -1 \\
1 & -1 & 1 & -1 & -1 & 1 & -1 & 1
\end{bmatrix}
$$

which is nonsingular. The equations have a unique set of solutions:

$$w_0 = w_1 = w_2 = w_3 = w_{12} = w_{13} = w_{23} = 0, \qquad w_{123} = 1$$

Therefore, the logic function is realized by the third-order polynomial $y = x_1 x_2 x_3$. This solution is unique in terms of the third-order polynomial. It is of interest to mention that when a unipolar binary system is used for the *XOR* problem, a numerical solution was introduced by Pao (1989). A comparison of the convergence speed of the HONN described by

$$
\begin{aligned}
y &= \phi(w_1 x_1 + w_2 x_2 + w_3 x_3 + w_{12} x_1 x_2 + w_{23} x_2 x_3 \\
&\quad + w_{13} x_1 x_3 + w_{123} x_1 x_2 x_3)
\end{aligned}
$$

with a sigmoidal function

$$\phi(.) = \frac{1}{1 + e^{-(.)}}$$

and a two-layered feedforward neural network with three hidden neurons was given in this book. These results indicate that as far as the gradient descent technique learning algorithms are considered, the HONN has a faster convergence property than the MFNN. ■

These examples show that the higher-order networks are capable of dealing with pattern classification problems. Xu et al. (1992), Taylor and Commbes (1993) also demonstrated that they may be effectively applied to problems using a model of a curve, surface, or hypersurface to fit a given data set. This problem, called *nonlinear surface fitting*, is often encountered in many engineering applications. Some learning algorithms for solving such problems may be found in their papers. Moreover, if one assumes $\phi(x) = x$ in the HONU, the weight exhibits linearity in the networks and the learning algorithms for the HONNs may be characterized as a linear LS procedure. Then the well-known local minimum problems existing in many nonlinear neural learning schemes may be avoided.

7.6 MODIFIED POLYNOMIAL NEURAL NETWORKS

7.6.1 Sigma–Pi Neural Networks (S-PNNs)

Note that a higher-order neural unit (HONU) contains all the linear and nonlinear correlation terms of the input components to the order n. A slightly generalized structure of the HONU is a polynomial network that includes weighted sums of products of selected input components with an appropriate power. Mathematically, the input–output transfer function of this network structure is given by

$$u_i = \prod_{j=1}^{n} x_j^{w_{ij}} \tag{7.42}$$

$$y = \phi\left(\sum_{i=1}^{N} w_i u_i\right) \tag{7.43}$$

where $w_i, w_{ij} \in \Re$, is the order of the network, and u_i is the output of the ith hidden unit. This type of feedforward networks is called a *sigma–pi network* (Rumelhart et al. 1986). It is easy to show that this network satisfies the Stone–Weierstrass theorem if $\phi(x) = x$ is a linear function. From the network structure point of view, the *sigma–pi network* shown in Fig. 7.10 may be considered as a two-layered network with a hidden layer and an output layer, where the units in the hidden layer create the products of selected input components computed with a power operation, while, like the conventional weighted combiners, the output unit makes a weighted summation of all the outputs of the hidden units. Moreover, a modified version of the sigma–pi networks, as proposed by Hornik et al. (1989) and Cotter (1990), is

$$u_i = \prod_{j=1}^{n} \Big(p(x_j)\Big)^{w_{ij}} \tag{7.44}$$

$$y = \phi\left(\sum_{i=1}^{N} w_i u_i\right) \tag{7.45}$$

where $w_i, w_{ij} \in \Re$ and $p(x_j)$ is a polynomial of x_j. It is easy to verify that this network satisfies the Stone–Weierstrass theorem, and thus, it can be an approximator for problems of functional approximations. The sigma–pi networks defined in Eqns. (7.42) and (7.43) is a special case of the above network while $p(x_j)$ is assumed to be a linear function of x_j. In fact, the weights w_{ij} in both the networks given in Eqns. (7.44) and (7.45) may be restricted to integer or nonnegative integer values.

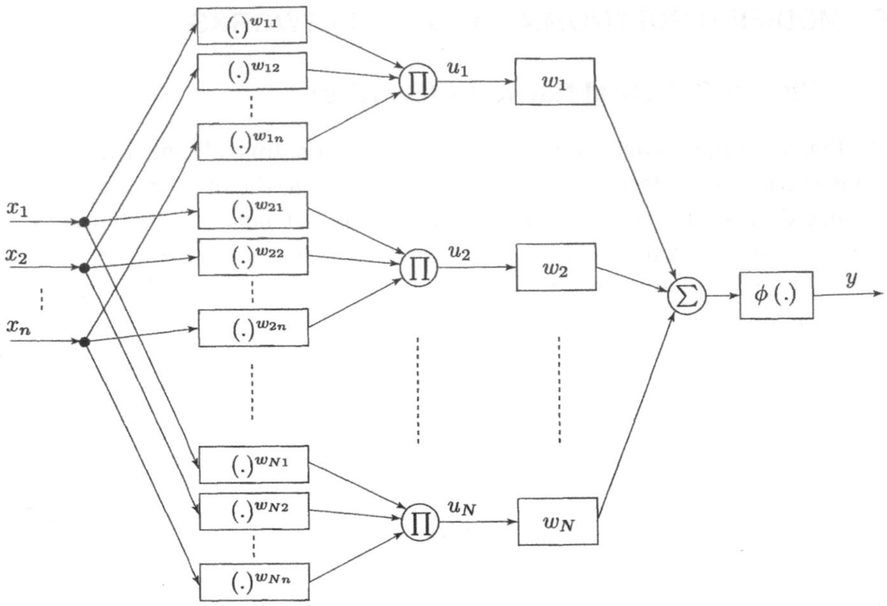

Figure 7.10 Block diagram of the sigma–pi network, Eqns. (7.42) and (7.43).

7.6.2 Ridge Polynomial Neural Networks (RPNNs)

To obtain fast learning and powerful mapping capabilities, and to avoid the combinatorial increase in the number of weights of the higher-order networks, some modified polynomial network structures were introduced recently. One of these is the *pi–sigma network* (PSN) (Shin and Ghosh 1991), which is a regular higher-order structure and involves a much smaller number of weights than the higher-order neural networks (HONNs). The mapping equation of a *pi–sigma network*, as depicted in Fig. 7.11, can be represented as

$$\begin{aligned} u_i &= \sum_{j=1}^{n} w_{ij} x_j + \theta_i \\ y &= \phi\left(\prod_{i=1}^{N} u_i\right) \\ &= \phi\left(\prod_{i=1}^{N}\left[\sum_{j=1}^{n} w_{ij} x_j + \theta_i\right]\right) \end{aligned} \tag{7.46}$$

The total number of weights for an Nth-order pi–sigma network with n inputs is only $(n+1)N$. Compared with the sigma–pi structure, the number

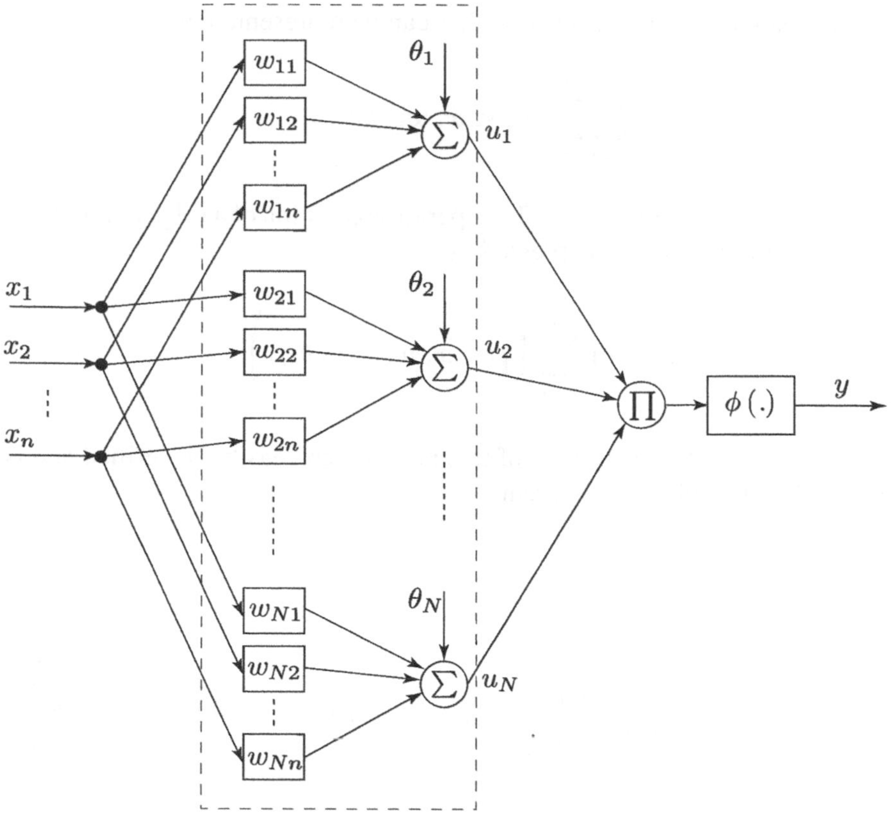

Figure 7.11 Block diagram of the pi–sigma network, Eqn. (7.46).

of weights involved in this network is significantly reduced. Unfortunately, when $\phi(x) = x$, the pi–sigma network does not match the conditions provided by the Stone–Weierstrass theorem because the linear subspace condition is not satisfied. However, some studies have shown that it is a good network model for smooth functions (Shin and Ghosh 1991).

To modify the structure of the above mentioned pi–sigma networks such that they satisfy the Stone–Weierstrass theorem, Shin and Ghosh (1991) suggested considering the *ridge polynomial neural network* (RPNN). For the vectors $\boldsymbol{w}_{ij} = [w_{ij1} \ \cdots \ w_{ijn}]^T$, and $\boldsymbol{x} = [x_1 \ \cdots \ x_n]^T$, let

$$< \boldsymbol{x}, \boldsymbol{w}_{ij} >= \sum_{k=1}^{n} w_{ijk} x_k$$

which represents an inner product between the two vectors. A one-variable continuous function f of the form $< \boldsymbol{x}, \boldsymbol{w}_{ij} >$ is called a *ridge function.* A *ridge polynomial* is a ridge function that can be represented as

$$\sum_{i=0}^{N}\sum_{j=0}^{M} a_{ij} < \boldsymbol{x}, \boldsymbol{w}_{ij} >^{i}$$

for some $a_{ij} \in \Re$ and $\boldsymbol{w}_{ij} \in \Re^n$. The operation equation of a ridge polynomial neural network (RPNN) is expressed as

$$y = \phi\left(\sum_{j=1}^{N}\prod_{i=1}^{n}(< \boldsymbol{x}, \boldsymbol{w}_{ij} > +\theta_{ji})\right) \tag{7.47}$$

where $\phi(x) = x$. The denseness of this network can easily be verified and is described in the following theorem.

Theorem 7.12 *Let Ω be the set of all the functions that can be represented by the ridge polynomial network on a compact set $S \supset \Re^n$:*

$$\begin{aligned}\Omega_N &= \left\{ f(\boldsymbol{x}) = \sum_{j=1}^{N}\prod_{i=1}^{j}\left(\sum_{k=1}^{n} w_{ijk}x_k + \theta_{ji}\right) : w_{jik}, \theta_{ji} \in \Re, \boldsymbol{x} \in S \right\} \\ \Omega &= \bigcup_{N=1}^{\infty} \Omega_N\end{aligned}$$

Then, Ω is uniformly dense in $C[\Re^n]$. ■

As shown in Fig. 7.12, Theorem 7.12 shows that an arbitrary continuous function $f : [a, b]^n \longrightarrow \Re$ may be uniformly approximated by

$$\begin{aligned} f(\boldsymbol{x}) \approx\ & (< \boldsymbol{x}, \boldsymbol{w}_{11} > +\theta_{11}) + (< \boldsymbol{x}, \boldsymbol{w}_{21} > +\theta_{21})(< \boldsymbol{x}, \boldsymbol{w}_{22} > +\theta_{22}) \\ & + \cdots + (< \boldsymbol{x}, \boldsymbol{w}_{N1} > +\theta_{N1}) \cdots (< \boldsymbol{x}, \boldsymbol{w}_{NN} > +\theta_{NN}) \end{aligned} \tag{7.48}$$

However, the results do not show how many neural units are needed to attain a given degree of approximation.

The total number of weights involved in this structure is $N(N+1)(n+1)/2$. A comparison of the number of weights of the three types of polynomial network structures is given in Table 7.2. The results show that when the networks have the same higher-order terms, the weights of a RPNN are significantly less than those of a HONN. In particular, this is a very attractive improvement offered by RPNNs.

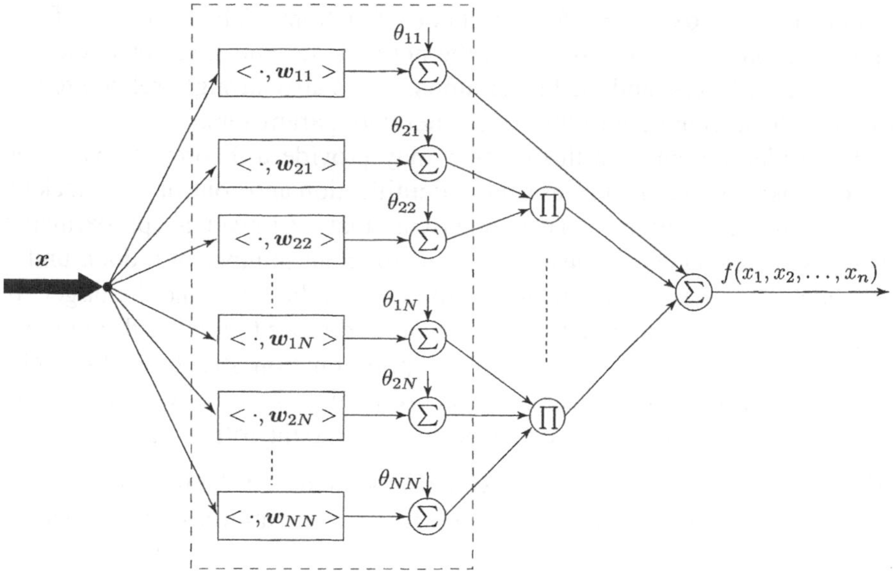

Figure 7.12 Ridge polynomial neural network (RPNN), Eqn. (7.47).

Table 7.2 **The number of weights in the polynomial networks**

Order of Network	Number of Weights					
	Pi–sigma		RPNN		HONN	
N	$n = 5$	$n = 10$	$n = 5$	$n = 10$	$n = 5$	$n = 10$
2	12	22	18	33	21	66
3	18	33	36	66	56	286
4	24	44	60	110	126	90

7.7 CONCLUDING REMARKS

The approximation capabilities of feedforward neural networks were discussed in this chapter. Feedforward neural networks, as intelligent computing tools, contain many types of neural network structures that have various different mathematical expressions and have different similarities to biological neural models. These studies focused only on a few commonly used static neural network structures such as multilayered feedforward networks, trigonometric networks, and higher-order neural networks. On the other hand, the Gaussian radial basis function networks are also universal approximators as shown in Chapter 6. One may then conclude that feedforward neural networks are universal approximators for continuous functions. The accuracy of the approximations not only depends on the network structures selected such as the number of layers, and the hidden units, but is also strongly related to the design of the learning algorithms of the network parameters.

The results presented in this chapter may provide a theoretical basis for applications to problems such as neural identification and control. Any lack of success in the applications of a neural network that is a universal approximator must arise from inadequate learning, an insufficient number of hidden units, or the lack of a deterministic relationship between the input and the target. It is a fact that different neural networks result in different learning difficulties. Therefore, the choice of an appropriate approximation structure ultimately determines the success of an application. From this point of view, a successful neural approximation procedure may be divided into the following three steps:

(i) Determine the universal approximation structure of the neural network; that is, ensure the inherent approximation capabilities of the neural networks by adjusting the numbers of the hidden units and layers.

(ii) Choose an adequate learning algorithm.

(iii) Use learning signals that contain sufficient information.

Problems

7.1 Prove the results given in Theorem 7.6.

7.2 Give five squashing functions that are continuous and differentiable.

7.3 The input–output transfer function of a *decaying exponential* network defined on a compact set is given by (Cotter 1990)

$$y = \sum_{i=1}^{\ell} w_i^{(2)} \exp\left(-\sum_{j=1}^{n} w_{ij}^{(1)} x_j\right)$$

Prove that the network is dense in $C[S]$.

7.4 The modified logistic neural network (MLNN) (Cotter 1990) is defined as

$$f(x) = \sum_{i=1}^{N_1} \frac{u_i}{1 + \sum_{j=1}^{N_2} \exp\left(-\sum_{k=1}^{n} w_{ijk} x_k + \theta_{ij}\right)}, \qquad x \in [a, b]^n$$

Prove that the network is dense in $C[S]$.

7.5 Let $S \supset \Re^n$ be a compact set and $g \in C[S]$ be a continuous function. Prove that for any $\varepsilon > 0$, there is a MFNN with Mc-P hidden units that approximates g uniformly on S with error $< \varepsilon$.

7.6 For a single variable function $\sigma(x)$ (Kurkova 1992), let

$$\Omega_N(\sigma) = \left\{ f(x) = \sum_{i=1}^{N} w_i \sigma(u_i x + v_i) \; : \; w_i, u_i, v_i \in \Re \right\}$$

$$\Omega = \bigcup_{N=1}^{\infty} \Omega_N$$

and $f \in C[I^n]$ be a continuous function. Prove that for any $\varepsilon > 0$, there exist the functions, $\phi_i, \psi_{pi} \in \Omega(\sigma)$ such that

$$\left| f(x_1, \cdots, x_n) - \sum_{q=1}^{2n+1} \phi_q \left(\sum_{p=1}^{n} \psi_{pq}(x_p) \right) \right| < \varepsilon$$

7.7 For any $\varepsilon > 0$, prove that the two-variable trigonometric network (Blum and Li 1991)

$$y(x_1, x_2) = \sum_{n,m=1}^{N} a_{nm} \cos(nx_1) \cos(mx_2)$$

may be used to approximate an arbitrary two-dimensional continuous function $f(x_1, x_2)$ defined on a compact set S with error $< \varepsilon$.

7.8 Using trigonometric functions, design a two-layered neural network

$$y = \sum_{i=1}^{N} u_i \psi \left(\sum_{j=1}^{n} w_{ij} x_j + \theta_i \right)$$

such that

(a) $\psi(x) = 1$ if $x \geq 1$, and $\psi(x) = -1$, if $x \leq -1$;

(b) The network satisfies the conditions of the Stone–Weierstrass theorem.

7.9 Prove that there exists a single-input two-layered network with a sigmoidal function that can uniformly approximate the function $\psi(x)$ defined in Problem 7.5 to any degree of error on $\Re$.

7.10 Find a single-variable continuous function $f: S \supset \Re \longrightarrow \Re$ defined on a compact set S that cannot exactly be implemented by an arbitrary two-layered neural network

$$y = \sum_{i=1}^{N} u_i \sigma(w_i x + \theta_i)$$

7.11 A function $g: S \supset \Re^n \longrightarrow \Re$ is simple with a finite range if S is the union of a finite family of a pairwise disjoint sets, D_i, such that g is constant on each D_i. Let $f: [a, b] \longrightarrow \Re$ be a simple function on a subinterval partition. Prove that f can be exactly implemented by a two-layered network with Mc-P hidden units described by

$$y = \sum_{i=1}^{N} u_i \, sgn(w_i x + \theta_i)$$

7.12 Let Ω be the set of functions that can be represented by the cosig networks on a compact set $S \supset \Re^n$. Prove that Ω is uniformly dense in $C[S]$.

7.13 Given a two-variable nonlinear function

$$f(x_1, x_2) = \frac{x_1 x_2 + x_1 + x_2}{x_1^2 + x_2^2}, \qquad x_1, x_2 \in [-1, 1]$$

obtain the network representation of the function $f(x_1, x_2)$ using the two-layered cosine function network, Fourier network, cosig network, and the conventional feedforward neural network with sigmoidal function.

7.14 Using the gradient descent technique, design the weight learning algorithms for both the pi–sigma and ridge polynomial networks neural presented in Section 7.6.

Part III

DYNAMIC NEURAL NETWORKS

Chapter 8. Dynamic Neural Units (DNUs): Nonlinear Models and Dynamics

Chapter 9. Continuous-Time Dynamic Neural Networks

Chapter 10. Learning and Adaptation in Dynamic Neural Networks

Chapter 11. Stability of Continuous-Time Dynamic Neural Networks

Chapter 12. Discrete-Time Dynamic Neural Networks and Their Stability

8

Dynamic Neural Units (DNUs): Nonlinear Models and Dynamics

8.1 Models of Dynamic Neural Units (DNUs)

8.2 Models and Circuits of Isolated DNUs

8.3 Neuron with Excitatory and Inhibitory Dynamics

8.4 Neuron with Multiple Nonlinear Feedback

8.5 Dynamic Temporal Behavior of DNN

8.6 Nonlinear Analysis for DNUs

8.7 Concluding Remarks

Problems

Neural units with learning and adaptive capabilities discussed so far had only static input–output functional relationships. This implies, therefore, that for a given input pattern to such a static neural unit, an instantaneous output is obtained through a linear or nonlinear mapping procedure. The history of these neural models is strongly related to the McCulloch–Pitts neuron model and the threshold logic as seen in previous chapters. In fact, a biological neuron not only contains a nonlinear mapping operation on the weighted sum of the input signals but also has some dynamic processes such as the state signal feedback, time delays, hysteresis, and limit cycles. To emulate such a complex behavior, a number of dynamic or feedback neural units have been proposed relatively recently. As the basic building blocks of the dynamic feedback neural networks, these dynamic neural units may be used to construct a complex dynamic neural network structure through internal synaptic connections.

As a demonstration of a simple dynamic neural architecture, some structures and electronic implementations of dynamic neural units (DNUs), that is, a single dynamic neuron that is the basic computing element of the dynamic neural networks, are first discussed in this chapter. Some important aspects of the nonlinear dynamic phenomena of such nonlinear elements are then explored. Since a dynamic recurrent neural network is a population, or a so-called large-scale system, which consists of individual neurons with some complex synaptic connections, each neuron involved in the network makes its own contribution to the dynamic properties of the whole system. From the aspect of dynamic systems, a dynamic neural unit forms a nonlinear dynamic subsystem that is described by a single-variable nonlinear dynamic equation. The analysis of a dynamic neural unit provides an understanding of the dynamic properties of the network system in which the DNU is a basic unit fully or partially connected to other neural units.

In this chapter we explore various configurations of dynamic neural units and study some of their dynamic properties that will be useful in forming neural architectures.

8.1 MODELS OF DYNAMIC NEURAL UNITS (DNUs)

8.1.1 A Generalized DNU Model

Dynamic feedback plays an essential role in the study of neural systems, where we say that an organism or machine has feedback if its activity is controlled to some extent by the comparison of its actual performance with some tested performance. Dynamic neural units (DNUs), as the basic elements of dynamic neural networks, receive not only external inputs but also state feedback sig-

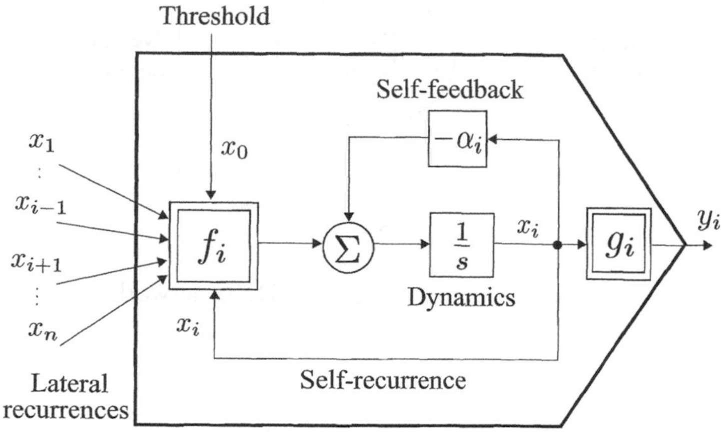

(a) Schematic representation of the ith DNU

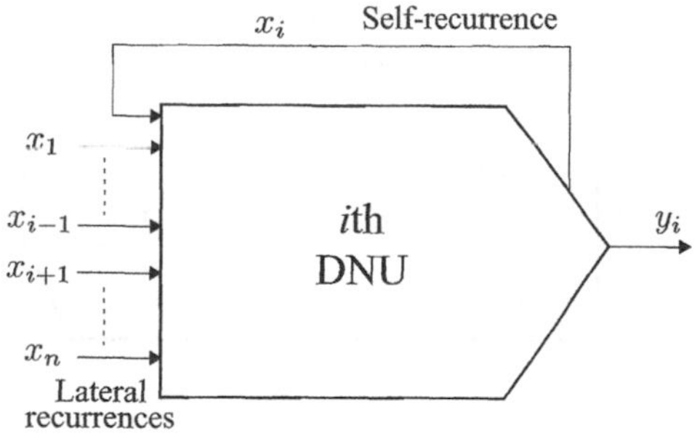

(b) Symbolic representation of the ith DNU

Figure 8.1 Schematic and symbolic representations of a dynamic neural unit (DNU), Eqns. (8.1) and (8.2).

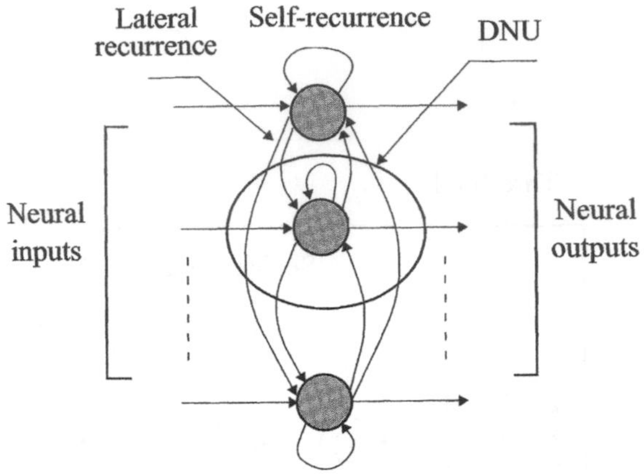

(a) Topological structure of a DNU network

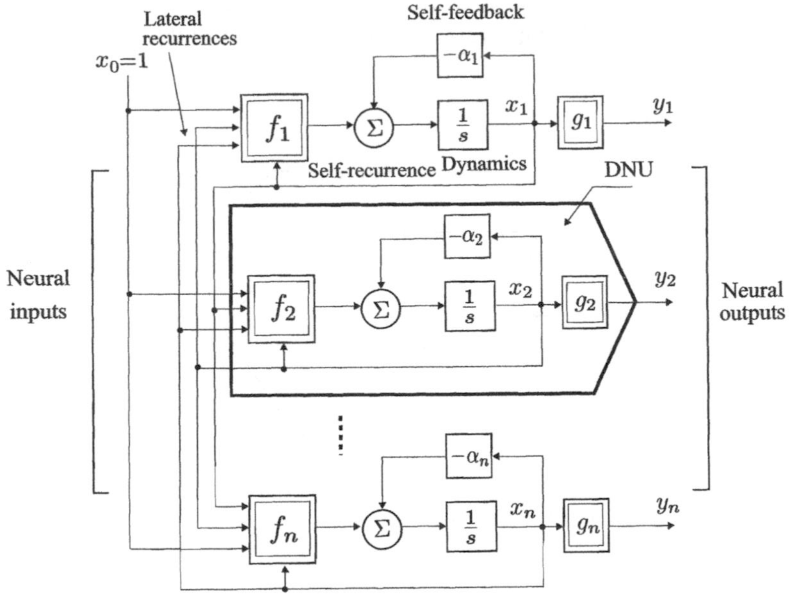

(b) Schematic representation of a DNU network

Figure 8.2 A topological structure and schematic representation of a DNU network.

nals from themselves and other neurons. The synaptic connections in a DNU contain a self-recurrent connection that represents a weighted feedback signal of its state and lateral inhibition connections, which are the state feedback signals from other DNUs in the network. In terms of information processing, the feedback signals involved in a DNU deal with some processing of the past knowledge and store current information for future usage. Each DNU has its own internal potential or internal state that is used to describe the dynamic characteristics of the network.

A general mathematical model of the ith DNU that is connected to other $(n-1)$ DNUs in an n-neuron dynamic network structure may be described as

$$\frac{dx_i(t)}{dt} = -\alpha_i x_i(t) + f_i(\boldsymbol{w}_{ai}, \boldsymbol{x}_a) \tag{8.1}$$

$$y_i(t) = g_i(x_i(t)) \tag{8.2}$$

where $\boldsymbol{x}_a = [x_0\ x_1\ x_2\ \cdots\ x_n]^T \in \Re^{n+1}$ = augmented vector of n-neural states (internal state of DNU neurons) including bias

$x_0 = 1$ = threshold (bias) of neuron

$\boldsymbol{w}_{ai} = [w_{i0}\ w_{i1}\ \cdots\ w_{in}]^T \in \Re^{n+1}$ = augmented vector of synaptic weights vector associated with ith DNU

$w_{ij} (1 \le i, j \le n)$ = synaptic connection between ith DNU and state of jth DNU associated with network

$y_i(t)$ = output of ith DNU

$f_i(.)$ = nonlinear activation function that is usually assumed to be continuous and differentiable

$g_i(.)$ = neural output function

Figure 8.1 illustrates schematic and symbolic representations of the individual dynamic neural unit (DNU) described in Eqns. (8.1) and (8.2). An ensemble of dynamic neural unit can be used to form a DNU network. A topological structure and schematic representation of such a DNU network is shown in Fig. 8.2.

8.1.2 Some Typical DNU Structures

Due to the different choices of the nonlinear function f_i in the general DNU model given in Eqns. (8.1) and (8.2), and the different types of synaptic connection that possibly exists among the DNUs, one may have different dynamic neural models as seen in the following discussion. In other words, the general model of a dynamic neural unit (DNU), Eqns. (8.1) and (8.2), may be further expanded into various mathematical representations based on the selections of the nonlinear function f_i. Some of these configurations are discussed in this subsection, and their important nonlinear dynamics properties are examined in the next section.

8.1.2.1 DNU-1

This dynamic neural unit, DNU-1, is the extension of the generalized DNU described in Eqns. (8.1) and (8.2), and is based on the early work of Hopfield (1982). The mathematical description of DNU-1 is given by

$$\begin{aligned}\frac{dx_i(t)}{dt} &= -\alpha_i x_i(t) + \boldsymbol{w}_{ai}^T \boldsymbol{f}(\boldsymbol{x}_a(t)) \\ &= -\alpha_i x_i(t) + w_{ii} f_i(x_i(t)) + \sum_{j=0, j\neq i}^{n} w_{ij} f_j(x_j(t)), \quad x_0 = 1\end{aligned} \tag{8.3}$$

$$y_i(t) = g_i(x_i(t)), \quad i = 1, 2, \ldots, n \tag{8.4}$$

where $\boldsymbol{f} = [f_0\ f_1\ f_2\ \cdots\ f_n]^T \in \Re^{n+1}$ = vector-valued nonlinear functions

$\boldsymbol{x}_a = [x_0\ x_1\ x_2\ \cdots\ x_n]^T \in \Re^{n+1},\ x_0 = 1$ = augmented state vector of n neural units

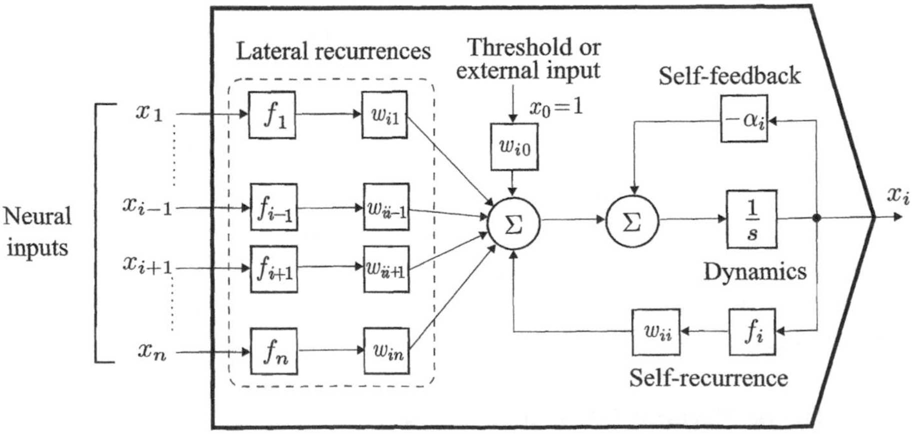

Figure 8.3 DNU-1: the state feedback structure associated with Eqns. (8.3) and (8.4).

In the neural state equation, Eqn. (8.3), the first term $-\alpha_i x_i$ is called the *self-feedback* term representing the passive exponential decay in the absence of both the state recurrent signals and the direct external input. Also, $w_{ii} f_i(x_i)$ is the self-recurrence term, and $\sum_{j=0,j\neq i}^{n} w_{ij} f_j(x_j)$ is the lateral recurrence contributions from other neurons. The neural output y_i is defined by the output equation, Eqn. (8.4). The state structure of the DNU-1 is shown in Fig. 8.3.

8.1.2.2 DNU-2

It may be noted that the terms on the right-hand side of Eqn. (8.3) associated with the recurrence synaptic connections may be directly represented using the output feedback structure. Thus, the DNU-1, Eqns. (8.3)-(8.4), may be rewritten as follows with the output feedback

$$
\begin{aligned}
\frac{dx_i(t)}{dt} &= -\alpha_i x_i(t) + \boldsymbol{w}_{ai}^T \boldsymbol{y}_a(t) \\
&= -\alpha_i x_i(t) + w_{ii} y_i(t) + \sum_{j=0, j\neq i}^{n} w_{ij} y_j(t), \quad x_0 = 1 \qquad (8.5) \\
y_i(t) &= f_i(x_i(t)), \quad i = 1, 2, \ldots, n \qquad (8.6)
\end{aligned}
$$

where

$$\boldsymbol{y}_a = [y_0 \; y_1 \; y_2 \; \cdots \; y_n]^T \in \Re^{n+1}, \quad y_0 = 1$$

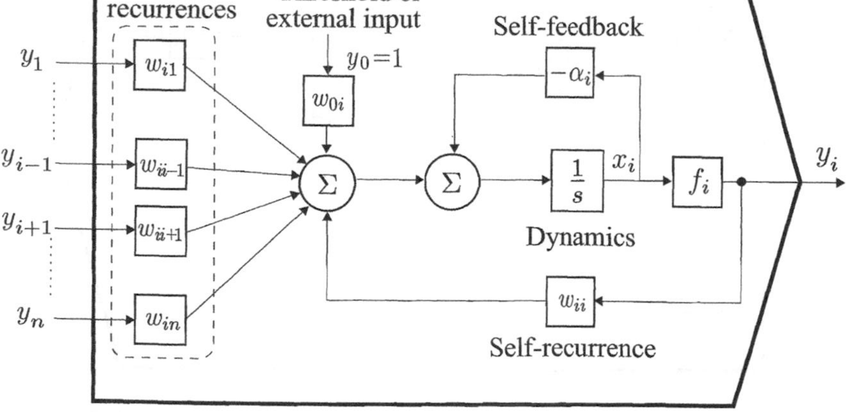

Figure 8.4 Block diagram of the ith DNU-2: the output feedback structure associated with Eqns. (8.5) and (8.6).

is the output vector of the network. The block diagram of the above mentioned DNU-2 is shown in Fig. 8.4.

8.1.2.3 DNU-3

The mathematical description of the DNU-3 (Pineda 1988) is given by

$$
\begin{aligned}
\frac{dx_i(t)}{dt} &= -\alpha_i x_i(t) + f_i\left(\boldsymbol{w}_{ai}^T \boldsymbol{x}_a(t)\right) \\
&= -\alpha_i x_i(t) + f_i\left(w_{ii} x_i(t) + \sum_{j=0, j\neq i}^{n} w_{ij} x_j(t)\right), \quad x_0 = 1
\end{aligned}
\tag{8.7}
$$

$$
y_i(t) = x_i(t), \quad i = 1, 2, \ldots, n \tag{8.8}
$$

In terms of neural structure, unlike the neural models DNU-1 and DNU-2, DNU-3, described by Eqns. (8.7) and (8.8) and shown in Fig. 8.5, provides first a weighted summation that is associated directly with the state feedback signals and the synaptic weights, and then a nonlinear operation is applied to this summation. On the other hand, the output of DNU-3 is the same as the internal state of DNU-3.

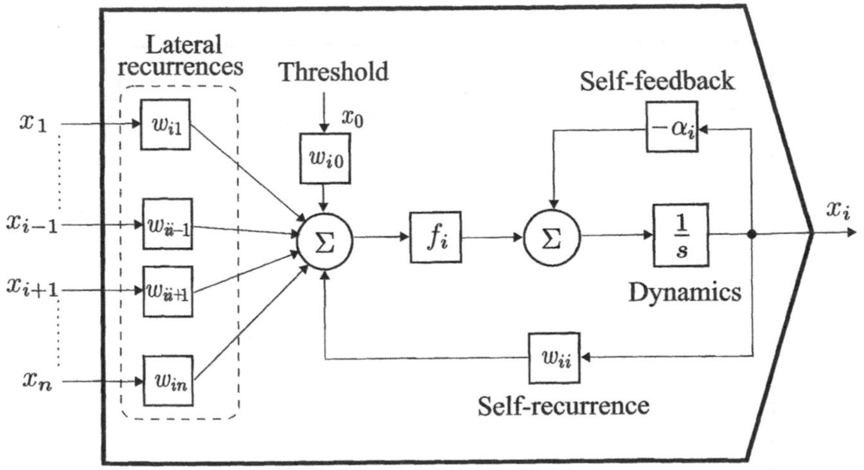

Figure 8.5 Block diagram of the ith DNU-3 structure associated with Eqns. (8.7) and (8.8) in which the external input is summed before a nonlinear operation f_i.

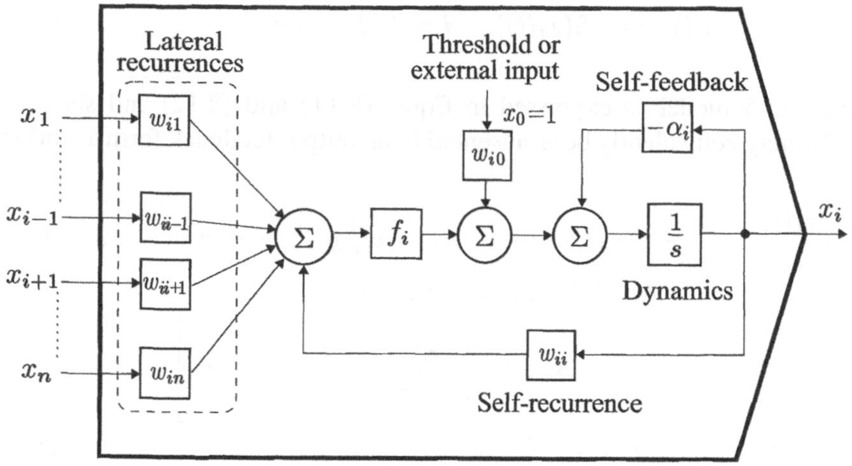

Figure 8.6 Block diagram of the ith DNU-4 associated with Eqns. (8.9) and (8.10) in which the external inputs are summed after a nonlinear operation f_i.

8.1.2.4 DNU-4

A slightly different version of the DNU structure (Pineda 1987), may be obtained by moving the threshold input out of the nonlinear activation function f_i in Eqn. (8.7). Thus, DNU-4 is described as

$$\begin{aligned} \frac{dx_i(t)}{dt} &= -\alpha_i x_i(t) + f_i\left(\boldsymbol{w}_i^T \boldsymbol{x}(t)\right) + x_0 w_{0i}, \qquad x_0 = 1 \\ &= -\alpha_i x_i(t) + f_i\left(w_{ii} x_i(t) + \sum_{j=1, j\neq i}^{n} w_{ij} x_j(t)\right) + x_0 w_{0i} \quad (8.9) \\ y_i(t) &= x_i(t), \quad i = 1, 2, \ldots, n \quad (8.10) \end{aligned}$$

The block diagram of the DNU-4 described by Eqns. (8.9) and (8.10) is illustrated in Fig. 8.6.

8.1.2.5 DNU-5

DNU-5 can be used to form the so-called *additive and shunting* networks and has the following mathematical form (Grossberg 1990):

$$\begin{aligned} \frac{dx_i(t)}{dt} &= -\alpha_i x_i(t) + (\gamma_i - \beta_i x_i)\left[\boldsymbol{w}_{ai}^T \boldsymbol{f}(\boldsymbol{x}_a(t))\right] \\ &= -\alpha_i x_i(t) + (\gamma_i - \beta_i x_i) w_{ii} f_i(x_i(t)) \\ &\quad + (\gamma_i - \beta_i x_i)\left[\sum_{j=0, j\neq i}^{n} w_{ij} f_j(x_j(t))\right] \quad (8.11) \end{aligned}$$

$$y_i(t) = f_i(x_i(t)), \quad i = 1, 2, \ldots, n \tag{8.12}$$

The DNU-5 model as expressed in Eqns. (8.11) and (8.12) and shown in Fig. 8.7 may equivalently be represented in an output feedback form as follows

$$\begin{aligned} \frac{dx_i(t)}{dt} &= -\alpha_i x_i(t) + (\gamma_i - \beta_i x_i)\left[\boldsymbol{w}_i^T \boldsymbol{y}(t) + w_{i0}x_0\right], \quad x_0 = 1 \\ &= -\alpha_i x_i(t) + (\gamma_i - \beta_i x_i(t)) w_{ii} y_i(t) \\ &\quad + (\gamma_i - \beta_i x_i(t)) \left[\sum_{j=1, j\neq i}^{n} w_{ij} y_j(t) + w_{i0}\right] \end{aligned} \tag{8.13}$$

$$y_i(t) = f_i(x_i(t)), \quad i = 1, 2, \ldots, n \tag{8.14}$$

where the term $(\gamma_i - \beta_i x_i)$ represents the refractory process of the ith DNU and the parameters γ_i and β_i perform, respectively, an automatic gain control and total normalization for the internal state of the ith DNU. Block diagrams of the models given in Eqns. (8.11), (8.12) and Eqns. (8.13), (8.14) are shown in Figs. 8.7 and 8.8, respectively.

A more general model of DNU-5 for additive and shunting networks may be obtained by separating the contributions corresponding to the synaptic connections and the external inputs into excitatory and inhibitory parts. Some aspects of this model will be further addressed in the next section.

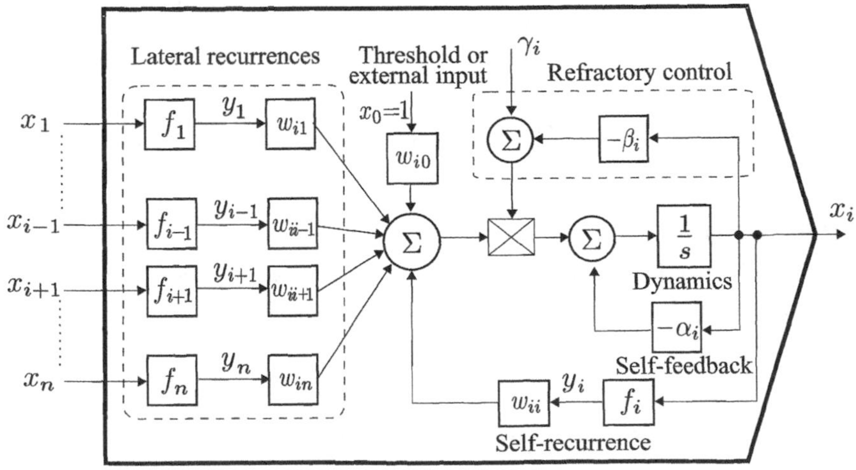

Figure 8.7 Block diagram of the ith DNU-5 with state feedback associated with Eqns. (8.11) and (8.12).

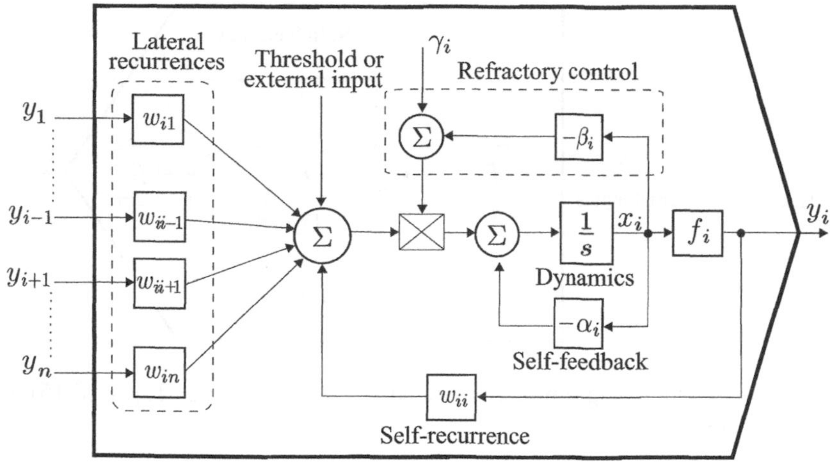

Figure 8.8 Block diagram of the equivalent ith DNU-5 with output feedback associated with Eqns. (8.13) and (8.14).

8.2 MODELS AND CIRCUITS OF ISOLATED DNUs

8.2.1 An Isolated DNU

As described in Section 8.1, the dynamic neural response generated by a population of dynamic neural units, such as DNU-1 through DNU-5, shows highly coupled nonlinear activities and, as such, is extremely difficult to analyze because of the immense numbers of inherent nonlinearities and complex feedback interactions involved. Therefore, in this section, an investigation of such a nonlinear neural system will begin by examining a spatially isolated DNU that has no lateral synaptic connections with other DNUs in the network as shown in Fig. 8.9. In other words, the terms corresponding to the lateral recurrent connections may be viewed as some external inputs on the right-hand side of Eqn. (8.1), and these terms, without loss of generality, may be absorbed into u. Consequently, the dynamic property of an isolated DNU may be given by a single-variable nonlinear differential equation

$$\frac{dx(t)}{dt} = -\alpha x(t) + f(w, x(t), u) \tag{8.15}$$

$$y(t) = g(x(t)) \tag{8.16}$$

where x and y are, respectively, the state and output of the DNU, and α, w, and u are the neural parameters. For simplicity, the subscript that represents the position of the DNU in the network is dropped from all the variables used in describing the dynamics of an isolated DNU. The results developed for

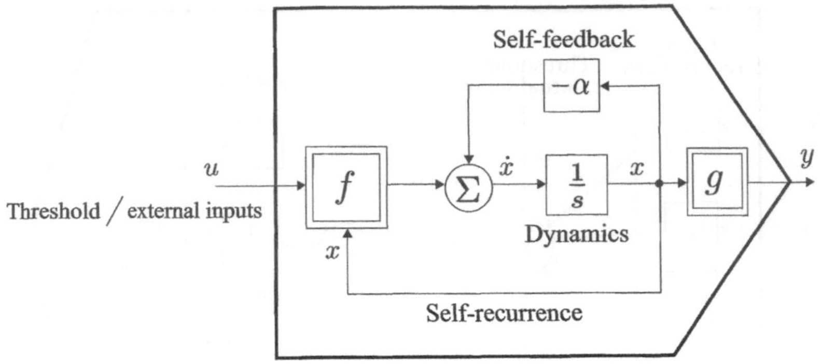

Figure 8.9 A block diagram of an isolated DNU described by Eqns. (8.15) and (8.16).

this isolated case provide a basis for studying the complex dynamic neural networks in later chapters.

8.2.2 DNU Models: Some Extensions and Their Properties

The neural network structure DNU-1 or DNU-2 initially proposed by Hopfield (1982, 1984) is one of the most successful neural models developed since the 1980s. It has a strong biological motivation and can easily be implemented by an electric circuit. The basic neural unit, or single neuron, in the Hopfield neural network may be implemented by the circuit shown in Fig. 8.10a, which consists of a capacitor C, resistors R and ρ, and a nonlinear operational amplifier with a sigmoidal transfer function $\sigma(x)$. To ensure that all resistors

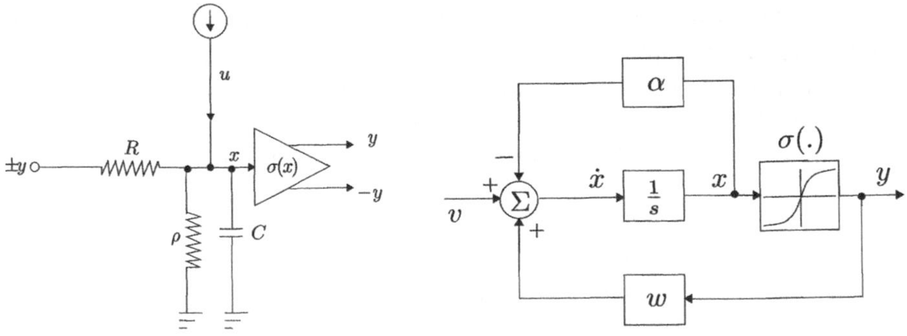

(a) Circuit structure

(b) Block diagram of a single-dynamic neural unit

Figure 8.10 DNU-1 single neuron.

simulating the synaptic weights have positive values, the amplifier is assumed to provide dual voltage outputs, $+y$ and $-y$, such that a positive synaptic weight is realized by connecting the resistor R to $+y$ and a negative weight by connecting R to $-y$. The current u represents a bias or an external input signal.

Let x represent a voltage at the input port of the amplifier. Using Ohm's and Kirchhoff's laws, the dynamic equation of such a circuit may be expressed as

$$C\frac{dx(t)}{dt} = -\frac{x(t)}{R_p} + \frac{y(t)}{R} + u \tag{8.17}$$

$$y(t) = \sigma(x(t)) \tag{8.18}$$

where

$$R_p = \left(\frac{1}{\rho} + \frac{1}{R}\right)^{-1} = \frac{\rho R}{\rho + R} \tag{8.19}$$

By means of biological interpretations, x may be viewed as the mean soma potential of a neuron from the total effect of its excitatory and inhibitory inputs, and y as the short term average of the firing rate of the cell.

The preceding dynamic equation for DNU-1 may also be rewritten as

$$\frac{dx(t)}{dt} = -\alpha x(t) + wy(t) + v \tag{8.20}$$

$$y(t) = \sigma(x(t)) \tag{8.21}$$

where $x \in \Re$ is an internal neural state, or neural potential, $y \in \Re$ is an output voltage or output potential, $\alpha = 1/(R_pC)$ is the inverse time-constant or decay, $w = 1/(RC)$ is the synaptic weight, and $v = u/C$ is the bias or external input signal. The block diagram of the system is given in Fig. 8.10b.

Since the sigmoidal function $\sigma(x)$ is monotonic, as shown in Fig. 8.11, there exists a unique inverse function of $\sigma(x)$

$$x = \sigma^{-1}(y)$$

Thus, Eqn. (8.20) may be represented in terms of the neural output y as a state variable. Therefore

$$\frac{dy(t)}{dt} = \frac{d\sigma(x(t))}{dx(t)}\frac{dx(t)}{dt} = h(y(t))\left[-\alpha x(t) + wy(t) + v\right] \tag{8.22}$$

where

$$h(y(t)) = \left.\frac{d\sigma(x(t))}{dx(t)}\right|_{x=\sigma^{-1}(y)} \tag{8.23}$$

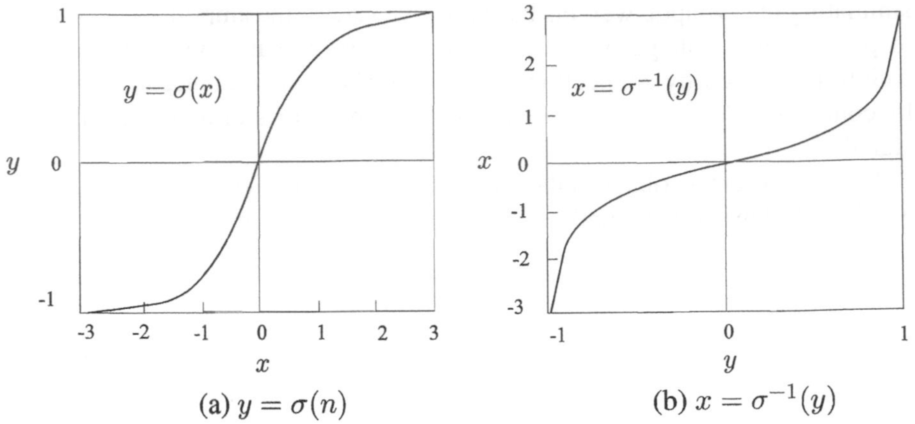

Figure 8.11 Sigmoid function $y = \sigma(x)$ and its inverse function $x = \sigma^{-1}(y)$.

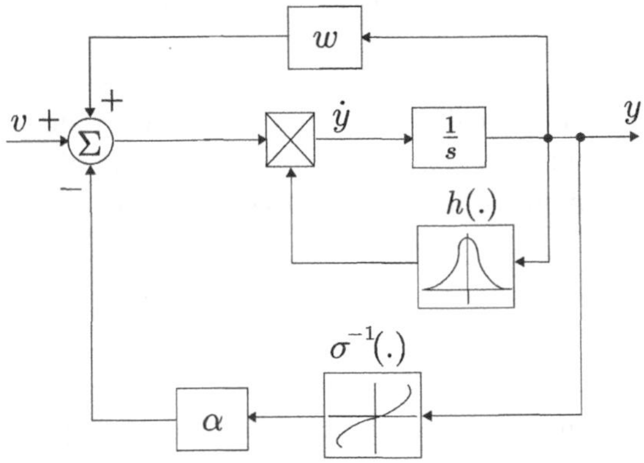

Figure 8.12 An equivalent representation of DNU-1, Eqn. (8.24).

Equation (8.22) may be rewritten as follows using the output y as a state variable

$$\frac{dy(t)}{dt} = h(y(t))\left[-\alpha\sigma^{-1}(y(t)) + wy(t) + v\right] \tag{8.24}$$

A block diagram of the above system is depicted in Fig. 8.12.

8.2.2.1 Convergence Properties of DNU-1

To study the state convergence of DNU-1, Eqn. (8.20), a Lyapunov function for the DNU-1 may be expressed as

$$E(y) = -\frac{1}{2}wy^2 + \alpha\int_0^y \sigma^{-1}(\eta)d\eta - vy \tag{8.25}$$

where $\alpha > 0$.

In order to apply LaSalle's invariant set principle (Khalil 1992), the derivative of the function E with respect to time t needs to be evaluated as follows:

$$\begin{aligned}\frac{dE}{dt} &= -wy\frac{dy}{dt} + \alpha\sigma^{-1}(y)\frac{dy}{dt} - v\frac{dy}{dt} \\ &= -\frac{dy}{dt}\left[-\alpha\sigma^{-1}(y) + wy + v\right] \\ &= -\frac{dy}{dt}\frac{dx}{dt}\end{aligned} \tag{8.26}$$

Note that

$$\frac{dy}{dt} = \sigma'(x)\frac{dx}{dt}$$

with the derivative $\sigma'(x) > 0$. Therefore, one has

$$\frac{dE}{dt} = -\sigma'(x)\left[\frac{dx}{dt}\right]^2 < 0 \tag{8.27}$$

and

$$\frac{dE}{dt} = 0, \quad \text{only if} \quad \frac{dx}{dt} = 0 \tag{8.28}$$

This analysis shows that the state trajectory of DNU-1 given in Eqn. (8.20) will always converge to one of the equilibrium points that satisfies

$$\frac{dx}{dt} = -\alpha x + w\sigma(x) + v = 0 \tag{8.29}$$

regardless of the initial value of the neural state x. At these equilibrium points, the Lyapunov function E has the local minimum value.

8.2.2.2 DNU-6

The neural system described by Eqns. (8.24) and (8.25) has sets of equilibrium points and asymptotically stable equilibrium points identical to those in the following neural system shown in Fig. 8.13:

$$\frac{dy(t)}{dt} = -\alpha\sigma^{-1}(y(t)) + wy(t) + v \tag{8.30}$$

Verification of the preceding statement is straightforward and is left for the readers as an exercise.

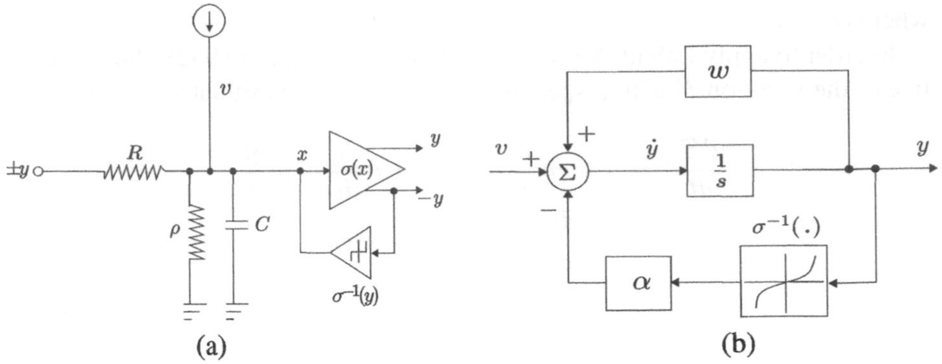

Figure 8.13 Circuit implementation and block diagram of DNU-6, Eqn. (8.30).

8.2.2.3 DNU-7: Dynamic Neuron with Saturation

This DNU-7 is a modification of DNU-1 obtained by replacing the sigmoidal function by a saturating function $Sat(x)$ shown in Fig. 8.14 and defined as

$$Sat(x) = \begin{cases} 1, & \text{if} \quad x > 1 \\ x, & \text{if} \quad -1 \leq x \leq 1 \\ -1, & \text{if} \quad x < -1 \end{cases} \tag{8.31}$$

In this case, the equations of the DNU may easily be obtained directly from Eqns. (8.20) and (8.21) as follows:

$$\frac{dx(t)}{dt} = -\alpha x(t) + wy(t) + v \tag{8.32}$$

$$y(t) = Sat(x(t)) \tag{8.33}$$

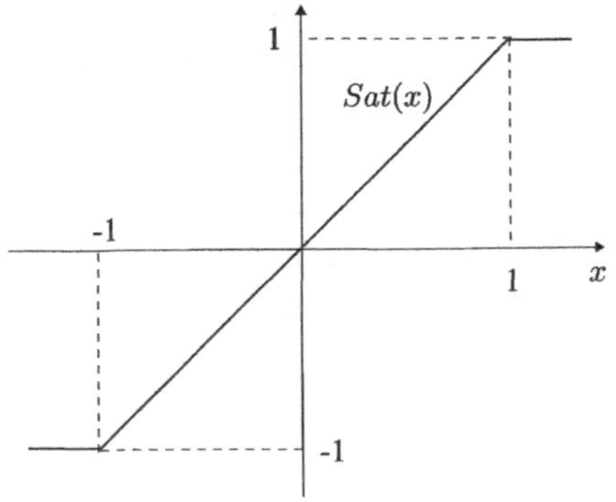

Figure 8.14 The saturating function $Sat(x)$ defined by Eqn. (8.31).

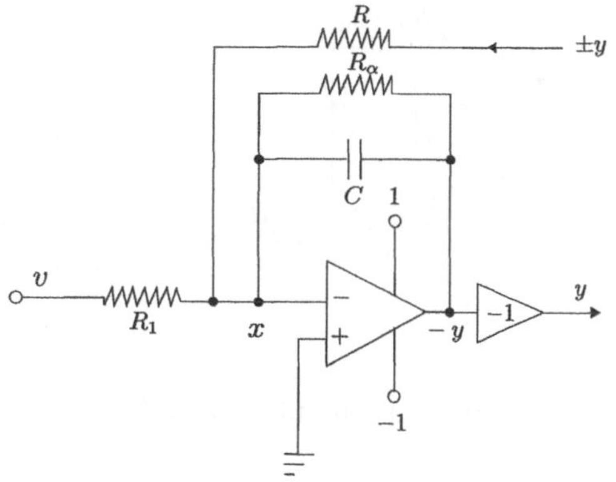

(a) Circuit structure of DNU-7 with saturation

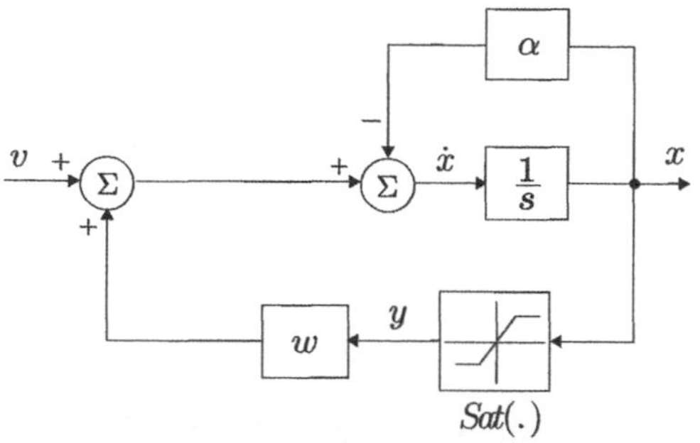

(b) Block diagram of DNU-7 with saturation

Figure 8.15 DNU-7: neuron with the saturating function, Eqns. (8.32) and (8.33).

These two equations represent a linear system operating on a closed cube. A circuit implementation that contains an ideal operational amplifier with a saturation and a block diagram of this type of DNUs is given in Fig. 8.15.

8.2.2.4 DNU-8

DNU-8, an extended version of DNU-7 with the saturating neural activation function and a double integrator, was proposed by Yanai and Sawada (1990). The dynamic equations of DNU-8 are described by

$$\frac{dx(t)}{dt} = -\alpha x(t) + w\, Sat(y(t)) + v \tag{8.34}$$

$$\frac{dy(t)}{dt} = x(t) \tag{8.35}$$

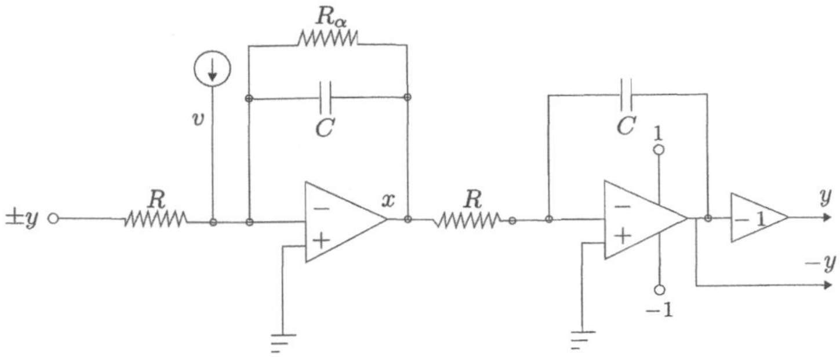

(a) Circuit implementation of DNU-8

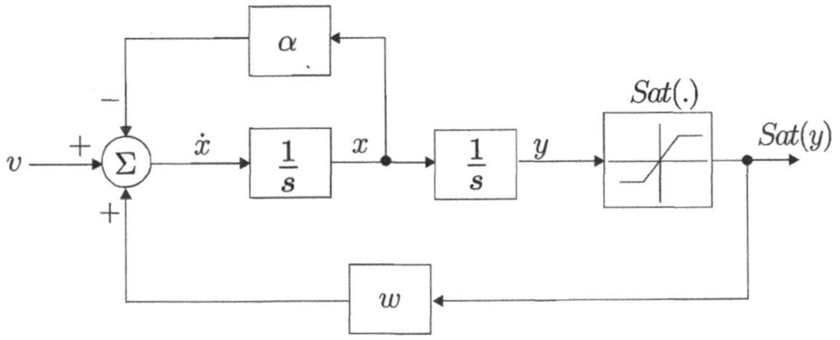

(b) Block diagram of DNU-8

Figure 8.16 Circuit structure and block diagram of the double-integrator neuron DNU-8, Eqns. (8.34) and (8.35).

The circuit implementation of the neural structure of DNU-8 is shown in Fig. 8.16a. It shows that DNU-8 consists of the two integrators: an integrator with losses and a lossless integrator with saturation. A block diagram of this neural structure is given in Fig. 8.16b. As pointed out by Yanai and Sawada (1990), if the autocorrelation type associative memory is considered, then, from a hardware implementation perspective, the integrators are more useful in a wider range of parameters than are the amplifiers. However, amplifiers as the output part of a neuron may have a sufficiently rapid response to the internal neural state.

8.2.2.5 DNU-9

Another type of DNU structure, shown in Fig. 8.17, based on the network proposed in DNU-3 and DNU-4 is described by the following nonlinear

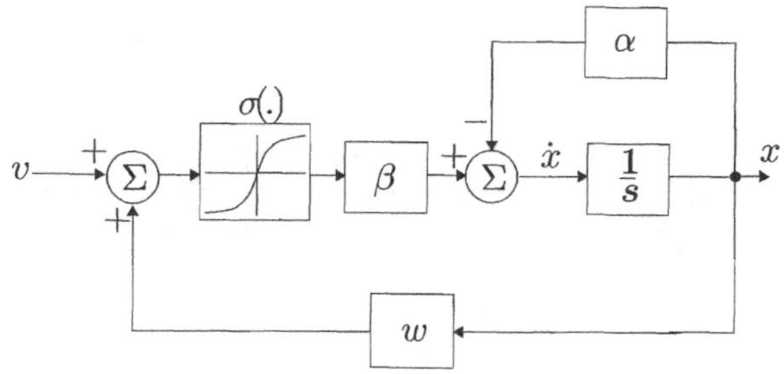

Figure 8.17 A block diagram of DNU-9, Eqn. (8.36).

differential equation

$$\frac{dx(t)}{dt} = -\alpha x(t) + \beta\sigma[wx(t) + v] \tag{8.36}$$

$$y(t) = x(t) \tag{8.37}$$

where $\beta \neq 0$ is a neural gain. The nonlinear neural activation function in this model acts on the summation of two terms: the product of the synaptic weight w and the neural state x, and the bias v. If an affine coordinate transformation is introduced

$$z(t) = wx(t) + v \tag{8.38}$$

the system presented above may be equivalently represented as

$$\begin{aligned}\frac{dz(t)}{dt} &= w\frac{dx(t)}{dt} = w[-\alpha x(t) + \beta\sigma(z(t))] \\ &= -\alpha z(t) + \bar{w}\sigma(z(t)) + \bar{v}\end{aligned} \tag{8.39}$$

where $\bar{w} = w\beta$ and $\bar{v} = \alpha v$. Since $w \neq 0$, the coordinate transformation expressed by Eqn. (8.38) is invertible. Hence, the single-neuron models represented in Eqns. (8.20) and (8.36) are equivalent. If $\alpha = \beta = 1$, they are identical.

8.2.2.6 DNU-10

As shown in Fig. 8.18, after changing the position of the function $\sigma(.)$ in the single neuron such that the neural activation function maps only the product of the synaptic weight and the neural state, another type of dynamic neuron, DNU-10, which was used by Pineda (1987), is described by

$$\frac{dx(t)}{dt} = -\alpha x(t) + \beta\sigma(wx(t)) + v \tag{8.40}$$

$$y(t) = x(t) \tag{8.41}$$

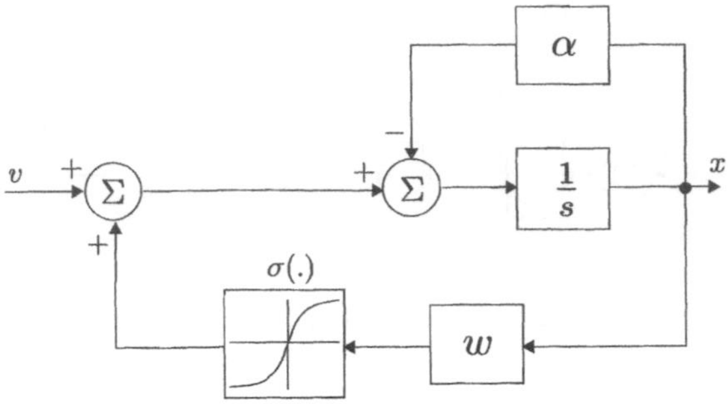

Figure 8.18 A block diagram of the DNU-10, Eqn. (8.40).

where $\beta \neq 0$. Using a simple coordinate transformation

$$z(t) = wx(t) \tag{8.42}$$

it is found that

$$\begin{aligned} \frac{dz(t)}{dt} &= w\frac{dx(t)}{dt} = -\alpha wx(t) + \beta w\sigma[z(t)] + wv \\ &= -\alpha z(t) + \bar{w}\sigma(z(t)) + \bar{v} \end{aligned} \tag{8.43}$$

where $\bar{w} = \beta w$ and $\bar{v} = wv$. A comparison of the three neural models, DNU-8, DNU-9, and DNU-10 reveals that in single neural structures, the different structures which are due to the different positions of the nonlinear neural activation function in the single neuron may be described by a unified mathematical model. However, this convenient property may not be retained in the dynamic neural network structures consisting of many such DNUs because of the complexity of the nonlinear dynamic characteristics.

8.2.2.7 DNU-11

This type of dynamic neural structure is obtained from the more general formulations of the dynamic neural network DNU-5 as was proposed by Grossberg (1990). It is based on population biology, neurobiology, and evolutionary theory. This single neuron structure is shown in Fig. 8.19 and can be described mathematically by the following equations

$$\frac{dx(t)}{dt} = -\alpha x(t) + (\gamma - \beta x(t))[wy(t) + v] \tag{8.44}$$

$$y(t) = \sigma(x(t)) \tag{8.45}$$

where x is the internal neural activity, y is the neural output, which is related to the internal neural activity x by the output equation, Eqn. (8.45); α is a constant

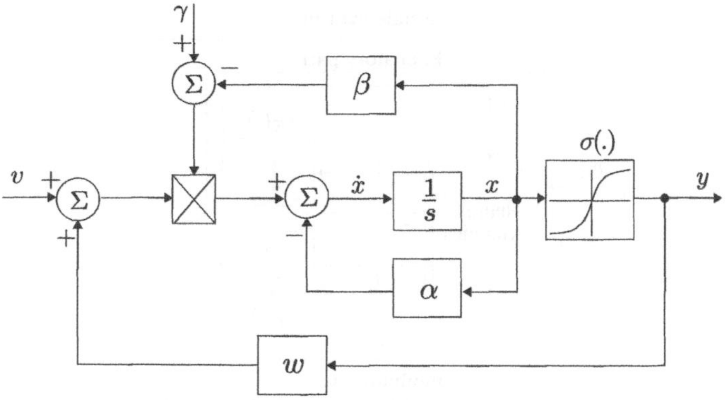

Figure 8.19 A block diagram of DNU-11, Eqns. (8.44) and (8.45).

responsible for the state decay; β is the gain of the somatic operation; γ is the total activity normalization coefficient; and w is the synaptic weight. The difference between the Hopfield's and Grossberg's neural models is the term $(\gamma - \beta x)$ on the right-hand side of Eqn. (8.44), which represents a *refractory period* of the neuron. In fact, the DNU-1 model given in Eqns. (8.20) and (8.21) of the single neuron is one of the special cases of the DNU-10 model in Eqns. (8.44) and (8.45) for $\gamma = 1$ and $\beta = 0$.

8.3 NEURON WITH EXCITATORY AND INHIBITORY DYNAMICS

8.3.1 A General Model

As discussed in Chapter 2, in biological systems the electrochemical potential of each neuron is determined by the integrated effects of all the excitatory (positive) and inhibitory (negative) postsynaptic potentials transmitted to the nerve cell for an integrating period of several milliseconds. If an intrinsic threshold of the potential is reached, then the neuron will fire an action potential. A biological neural cell contains two groups of operations—the excitatory and the inhibitory operations—and these two types of neural operations have the same internal states and dynamics as shown in Fig. 8.20a.

The dynamic neural model as proposed in Eqn. (8.44) and shown in Fig. 8.19 can be generalized to form a pair of excitatory–inhibitory neural models. Thus

$$\begin{aligned}\frac{dx(t)}{dt} &= -\alpha x(t) + (\gamma_E - \beta_E x(t))[w_E \sigma_E(x(t)) + v_E] \\ &\quad - (\gamma_I - \beta_I x(t))[w_I \sigma_I(x(t)) + v_I] \qquad (8.46)\end{aligned}$$

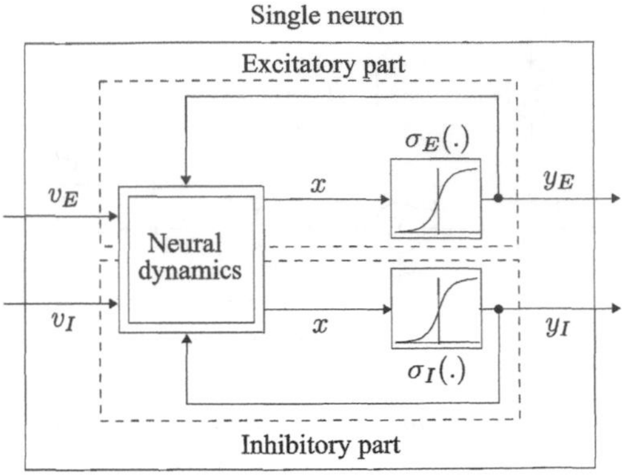

(a) Excitatory and inhibitory neuron

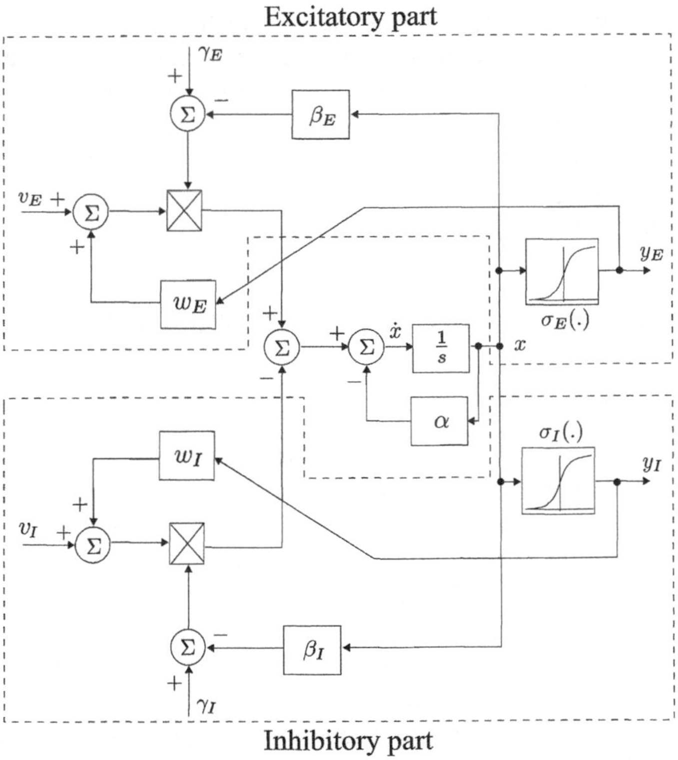

(b) Details of the excitatory and inhibitory neuron, Eqn. (8.46)

Figure 8.20 Block diagrams of the single neuron that contains both the excitatory and inhibitory parts.

where γ_E, β_E and γ_I, β_I are, respectively, the excitatory and inhibitory parameters; w_E and w_I are, respectively, the excitatory and inhibitory weights, which are always positive; and v_E and v_I are, respectively, the excitatory and inhibitory neural inputs. This particular model of the excitatory and inhibitory neuron is shown in Fig. 8.20.

In this case, the sigmoidal activation functions $\sigma_E(x)$ and $\sigma_I(x)$ are assumed to be always positive, that is

$$\begin{cases} \sigma_E(x) > 0 \\ \sigma_I(x) > 0 \end{cases}$$

for all $x \in \Re$. Some commonly used choices of such a neural activation function are

$$\sigma_E(x) = \sigma_I(x) = \tfrac{1}{2}[1 + \tanh(x)] \tag{8.47}$$

$$\sigma_E(x) = \sigma_I(x) = \frac{1}{(1 + e^{-x})} \tag{8.48}$$

Figure 8.21 shows the sigmoidal function $\sigma(x)$ as defined in Eqn. (8.47) and its derivative $\sigma'(x)$. Additionally, the terms $(\gamma_E - \beta_E x)$ and $(\gamma_I - \beta_I x)$ represent, respectively, the refractory periods of the excitatory and inhibitory processes in the single neuron. It is worth mentioning that the neural model in Fig. 8.20 has two outputs that can be computed by

$$y_E(t) = \sigma_E(x(t)) \tag{8.49}$$

$$y_I(t) = \sigma_I(x(t)) \tag{8.50}$$

where y_E and y_I are, respectively, the excitatory and inhibitory outputs that are the functions of the same internal state x. Many known models of the

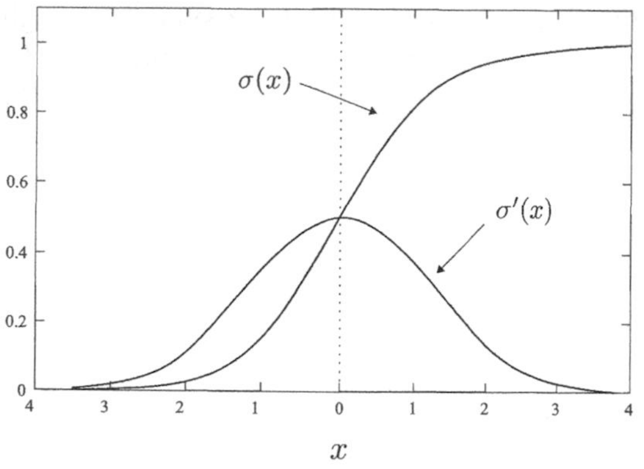

Figure 8.21 The unipolar sigmoidal function $\sigma(x) = \frac{1}{2}[1 + \tanh(x)]$ and its derivative $\sigma'(x) = \frac{1}{2}[\text{sech}^2(x)]$, Eqn. (8.47).

dynamic neural units (DNUs) may be considered as special cases of this general model.

8.3.2 Positive–Negative (PN) Neural Structure

The two parts in the excitatory–inhibitory neural structure described above and shown in Fig. 8.20 have a similar dynamic structure but different feedback parameters from each other. A different type of neural structure has been developed (Gupta and Knopf 1992) which introduces the notion of the positive neuron (corresponding to the excitatory portion of the neuron) and the negative neuron (corresponding to the inhibitory portion of the neuron). This neural model has been referred to as a *positive–negative* (PN) *neuron*, and is expressed by the following coupled nonlinear differential equations

$$\begin{cases} \dfrac{dx_E(t)}{dt} = -\alpha_E x_E(t) + (\gamma_E - \beta_E x_E(t))(w_{EE} y_E(t) - w_{EI} y_I(t) + v_E) \\ \dfrac{dx_I(t)}{dt} = -\alpha_I x_I(t) + (\gamma_I - \beta_I x_I(t))(w_{IE} y_E(t) - w_{II} y_I(t) + v_I) \end{cases} \tag{8.51}$$

and

$$\begin{cases} y_E(t) = \sigma_E(x_E(t)) \\ y_I(t) = \sigma_I(x_I(t)) \end{cases}$$

where x_E and x_I are respectively the excitatory (positive) and inhibitory (negative) states; y_E and y_I are respectively the output from the excitatory and inhibitory parts; v_E and v_I are respectively the inputs to the excitatory and inhibitory parts of the single neuron; and all the synaptic weights w_{EE}, w_{EI}, w_{IE}, and w_{II} are positive. The terms $(\gamma_E - \beta_E x_E)$ and $(\gamma_I - \beta_I x_I)$ represent, respectively, the excitatory and inhibitory refractory periods. Equations (8.51) and (8.52) represent a two-state nonlinear dynamic system. We introduce the following notations:

$$\boldsymbol{x}(t) = \begin{bmatrix} x_E(t) \\ x_I(t) \end{bmatrix}, \qquad \boldsymbol{v} = \begin{bmatrix} v_E \\ v_I \end{bmatrix}, \qquad \boldsymbol{y}(t) = \begin{bmatrix} y_E(t) \\ y_I(t) \end{bmatrix}$$

$$\boldsymbol{A} = \begin{bmatrix} \alpha_E & 0 \\ 0 & \alpha_I \end{bmatrix}, \qquad \boldsymbol{B} = \begin{bmatrix} \beta_E & 0 \\ 0 & \beta_I \end{bmatrix}$$

$$\boldsymbol{C} = \begin{bmatrix} \gamma_E & 0 \\ 0 & \gamma_I \end{bmatrix}, \qquad \boldsymbol{W} = \begin{bmatrix} w_{EE} & -w_{EI} \\ w_{IE} & -w_{II} \end{bmatrix}$$

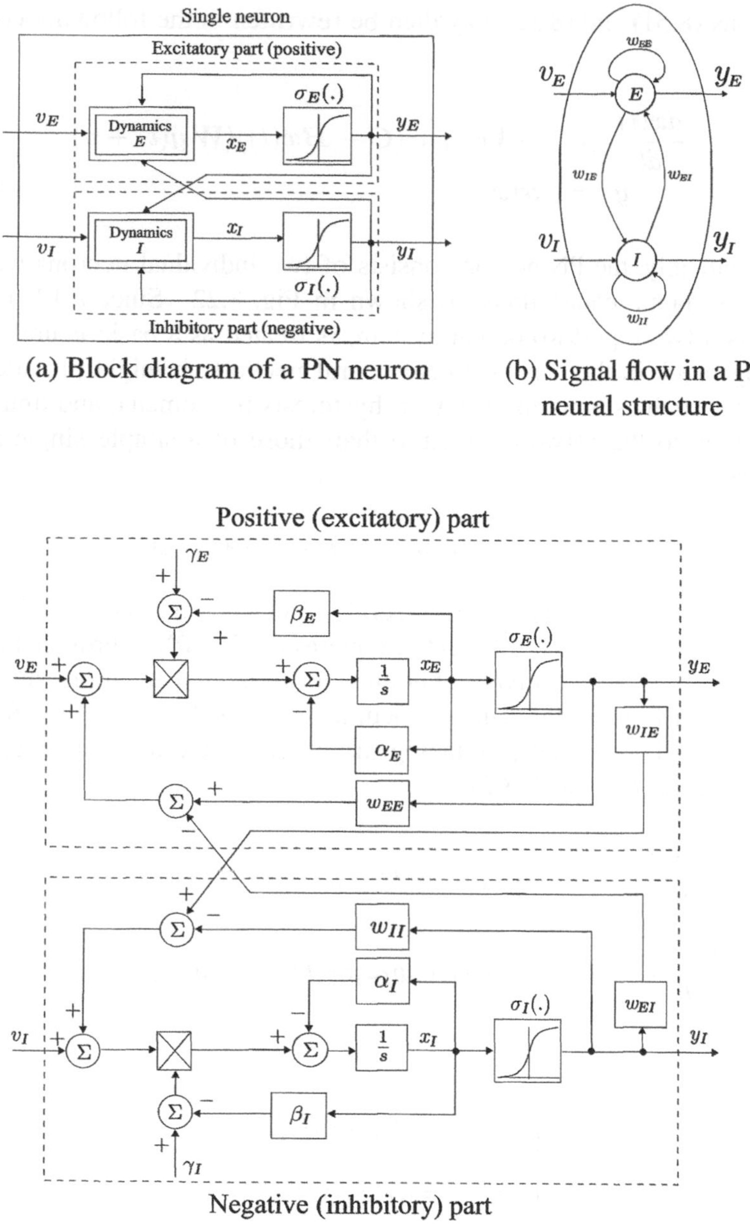

(a) Block diagram of a PN neuron

(b) Signal flow in a PN neural structure

(c) Details of the PN dynamic neuron

Figure 8.22 Schematic representations of a PN neural structure containing both positive (excitatory) and negative (inhibitory) dynamics, Eqns. (8.51)–(8.53).

Equations (8.51) and (8.52) may then be rewritten in the following compact form

$$\begin{aligned} \frac{d\boldsymbol{x}(t)}{dt} &= -\boldsymbol{A}\boldsymbol{x}(t) + (\boldsymbol{C} - \boldsymbol{B}\boldsymbol{x}(t))(\boldsymbol{W}\boldsymbol{y}(t) + \boldsymbol{v}) && (8.52) \\ \boldsymbol{y} &= \boldsymbol{\sigma}(\boldsymbol{x}) && (8.53) \end{aligned}$$

Mathematically, the PN neuron consists of two individual neurons with full internal synaptic connections, as shown in Fig. 8.22. Since a PN neuron, which is a two-input/two-output system, is treated as a basic neural unit or building block in the computational neural network, it might provide more properties such as transient behavior, hysteresis phenomena, and limit-cycle oscillations to the network structure than those of a simple single-neuron structure.

8.3.3 Further Extension to the PN Neural Model

As shown in Eqn. (8.51), the PN neural structure is formed by using a set of two coupled nonlinear differential equations. The PN neuron can also be formed by using different types of nonlinear differential equations such as we have used in forming the dynamic neural units (DNUs) earlier, in Sections 8.1 and 8.2. For example, by taking the model of the dynamic neural unit DNU-1, Eqns. (8.20) and (8.21):

$$\left\{ \begin{aligned} \frac{dx_E(t)}{dt} &= -\alpha_E x_E(t) + w_{EE} y_E(t) - w_{EI} y_I(t) + v_E \\ \frac{dx_I(t)}{dt} &= -\alpha_I x_I(t) + w_{IE} y_E(t) - w_{II} y_I(t) + v_I \end{aligned} \right. \qquad (8.54)$$

and

$$\left\{ \begin{aligned} y_E(t) &= \sigma_E(x_E(t)) \\ y_I(t) &= \sigma_I(x_I(t)) \end{aligned} \right.$$

A circuit implementation that contains two nonlinear operational amplifiers and a block diagram of the above PN neuron are given in Fig. 8.23. The oscillatory and excitable behaviors of the simplified PN neuron model presented above when $\alpha_E = \alpha_I = 1$ were studied by Sakaguchi (1988). Some applications in the neurocontrol and neurovision fields have also been reported by Gupta and Rao (1994a) and Gupta and Knopf (1994).

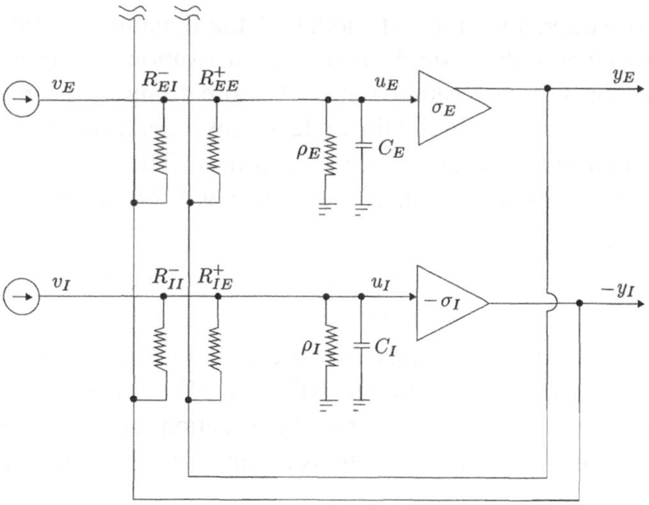

(a) Circuit implementation of a PN neuron

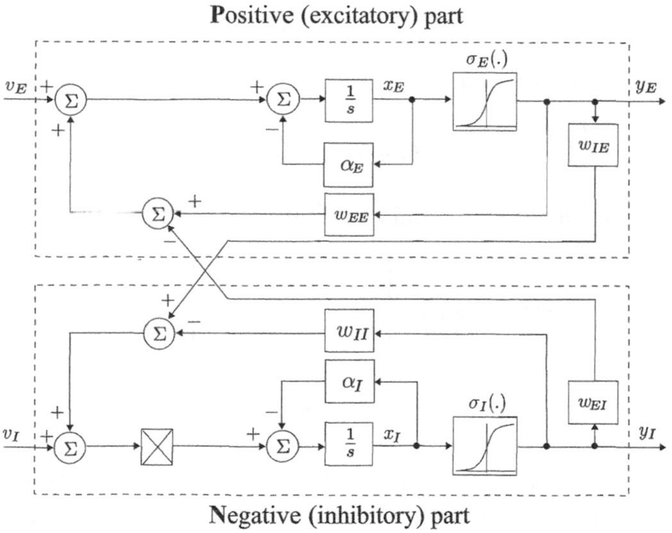

(b) Block diagram of a PN neuron

Figure 8.23 The simplified PN single neuron which contains both the excitatory and inhibitory parts with different dynamics, Eqns. (8.54) and (8.55).

8.4 NEURON WITH MULTIPLE NONLINEAR FEEDBACK

As discussed earlier, the simplest model of the dynamic neural structures, the DNU, involves only a single nonlinear activation function that has a nonlinear feedback of the neural state. A more complicated model of the DNU that contains multiple nonlinear feedback operations is achieved by neural activation functions and is introduced now. The mathematical model of such a dynamic single neuron, as shown in Fig. 8.24, is represented as

$$\frac{dx(t)}{dt} = -\alpha x(t) + \sum_{i=1}^{n} a_i \sigma(b_i x(t) + c_i) + v \tag{8.55}$$

where a_i, b_i, and c_i are the parameters associated with the ith nonlinear feedback function. The neural model given in Eqn. (8.55) increases the capabilities of the dynamic single neuron for storing information, and for approximating an arbitrary nonlinear dynamic system as a universal approximator.

After introducing the notations

$$\begin{aligned} \boldsymbol{a} &= [a_1\ a_2\ \cdots\ a_n]^T \\ \boldsymbol{b} &= [b_1\ b_2\ \cdots\ b_n]^T \\ \boldsymbol{c} &= [c_1\ c_2\ \cdots\ c_n]^T \end{aligned}$$

Eqn. (8.55) may be rewritten as

$$\frac{dx(t)}{dt} = -\alpha x(t) + \boldsymbol{a}^T \boldsymbol{\sigma}(\boldsymbol{b}x + \boldsymbol{c}) + v \tag{8.56}$$

where the vector-valued sigmoidal function is defined as

$$\boldsymbol{\sigma}(\boldsymbol{b}x + \boldsymbol{c}) = \begin{bmatrix} \sigma(b_1 x + c_1) \\ \vdots \\ \sigma(b_n x + c_n) \end{bmatrix}$$

The following description shows that the dynamic properties of the neural model given in Eqn. (8.56) may be described by n dynamic single neurons that are fully connected to each other. In other words, the neural model given in Eqn. (8.56) can be represented by a dynamic neural network that contains n neurons. At this point, a new vector is introduced

$$\boldsymbol{y} = \boldsymbol{b}x + \boldsymbol{c}$$

which yields

$$\frac{dy_i(t)}{dt} = b_i \frac{dx(t)}{dt} = -\alpha y_i(t) + \sum_{j=1}^{n} w_{ij} \sigma(y_j) + \bar{v}_i \tag{8.57}$$

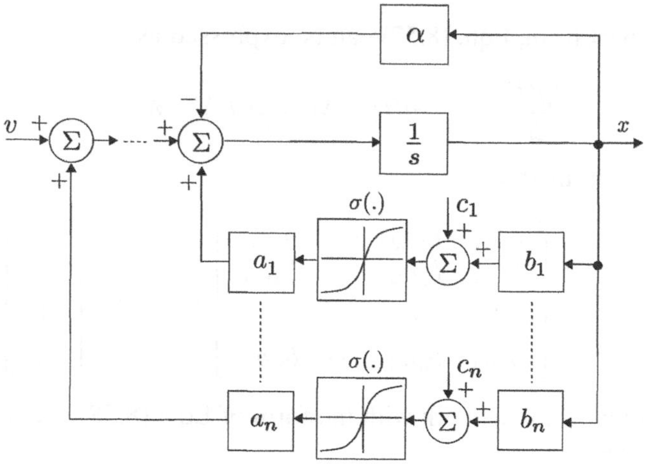

(a) Block diagram of DNU with multiple nonlinear feedback

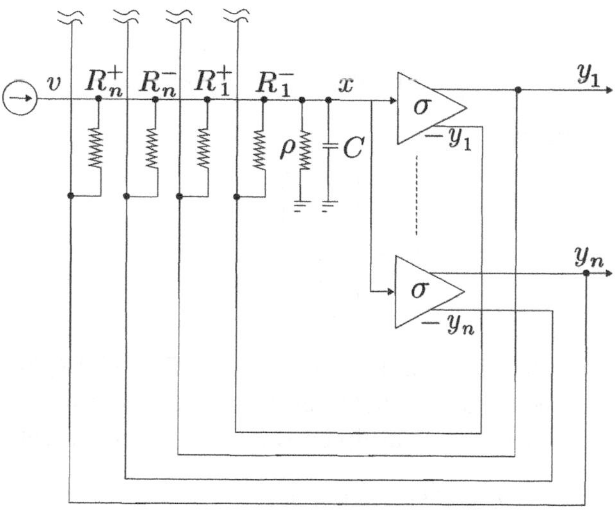

(b) Circuit implementation of DNU with multiple nonlinear feedback

Figure 8.24 Block diagram and circuit implementation of the dynamic neural unit (DNU) with multiple nonlinear feedback, Eqns. (8.55) and (8.56).

where

$$w_{ij} \triangleq b_i a_j, \qquad \bar{v}_i \triangleq b_i v + c_i \alpha$$

Or, in a compact form, Eqn. (8.57) can be expressed as

$$\frac{d\boldsymbol{y}(t)}{dt} = -\alpha \boldsymbol{y}(t) + \boldsymbol{W}\sigma(\boldsymbol{y}(t)) + \bar{\boldsymbol{v}} \tag{8.58}$$

where the weight matrix

$$\boldsymbol{W} = \boldsymbol{b}\boldsymbol{a}^T = \begin{bmatrix} b_1 a_1 & b_1 a_2 & \cdots & b_1 a_n \\ b_2 a_1 & b_2 a_2 & \cdots & b_2 a_n \\ \vdots & \vdots & \ddots & \vdots \\ b_n a_1 & b_n a_2 & \cdots & b_n a_n \end{bmatrix}, \qquad \bar{\boldsymbol{v}} = \begin{bmatrix} \bar{v}_1 \\ \bar{v}_2 \\ \vdots \\ \bar{v}_n \end{bmatrix}$$

If a dynamic neural network with the form of Eqn. (8.58) is defined with a synaptic matrix

$$\boldsymbol{W} = \begin{bmatrix} w_{11} & w_{12} & \cdots & w_{1n} \\ w_{21} & w_{22} & \cdots & w_{2n} \\ \vdots & \vdots & \ddots & \vdots \\ w_{n1} & w_{n2} & \cdots & w_{nn} \end{bmatrix}$$

and a threshold vector

$$\bar{\boldsymbol{v}} = \begin{bmatrix} \bar{v}_1 \\ \bar{v}_2 \\ \vdots \\ \bar{v}_n \end{bmatrix}$$

it is not necessary that the neural model given in Eqn. (8.58) be transformed equivalently into the dynamic single-neuron model given in Eqn. (8.56), except when the following relationship between the weights is satisfied

$$\frac{w_{ij}}{w_{lj}} = \frac{w_{ik}}{w_{lk}}, \qquad 1 \le i, l, j, k \le n$$

and

$$\bar{v}_i = \bar{\bar{v}}_i + c_i \alpha$$

with

$$\frac{\bar{\bar{v}}_i}{\bar{\bar{v}}_l} = \frac{w_{ij}}{w_{lj}}, \qquad 1 \le i, l, j \le n$$

where c_i are constants. In this case, let

$$\begin{aligned} b_1 &\triangleq 1 \\ b_l &= \frac{w_{lj}}{w_{1j}}, \quad 2 \le l \le n, \quad 1 \le j \le n \end{aligned}$$

and

$$\begin{aligned} v &= \overline{\overline{v}}_1 \\ a_i &= w_{1i}, \quad 1 \le i \le n \end{aligned}$$

Then, the dynamic model of the dynamic neural network (DNN) given in Eqn. (8.58) is equivalent to the model of the dynamic neural unit (DNU) given in Eqn. (8.56).

8.5 DYNAMIC TEMPORAL BEHAVIOR OF DNN

As pointed out in Chapter 2 on biological neurons, stimulus information is encoded by a single neuron as spike trains that typically have a constant spiking amplitude or potential and the information contents of the stimulus are encoded in the form of frequency modulation. The temporal phenomena generated by an isolated DNU with multiple steady states exhibit not only the dynamic characteristics of the state trajectory of the DNU before it reaches an equilibrium state but also an encoding capability for the external signal. For a slowly time-varying external input signal, the temporal dynamics are primarily the switching action between the stable equilibrium points as shown in Fig. 8.25. For a rapidly varying external input signal, the DNU produces a specific state trajectory that is the result of encoding the time-varying input signal as shown in Fig. 8.26. These temporal responses generated by a DNU are very useful for control systems, vision systems, and, in general, for information processing. Some mathematical processes of such temporal dynamics are as follows.

Consider a general model of an isolated DNU described by

$$\tau \frac{dx(t)}{dt} = -\alpha x(t) + f(w, x(t), v) \tag{8.59}$$

where $\alpha > 0$. Let the external input v be a time-dependent stimulus $v = v(t)$. Then, for the arbitrary initial state value $x(0)$ the solution of Eqn. (8.59) is given by

$$x(t) = x(0)e^{-\frac{\alpha}{\tau}t} + \frac{1}{\tau}\int_0^t e^{-\frac{\alpha}{\tau}(t-\zeta)} f(w, x(\zeta), v(\zeta))d\zeta \tag{8.60}$$

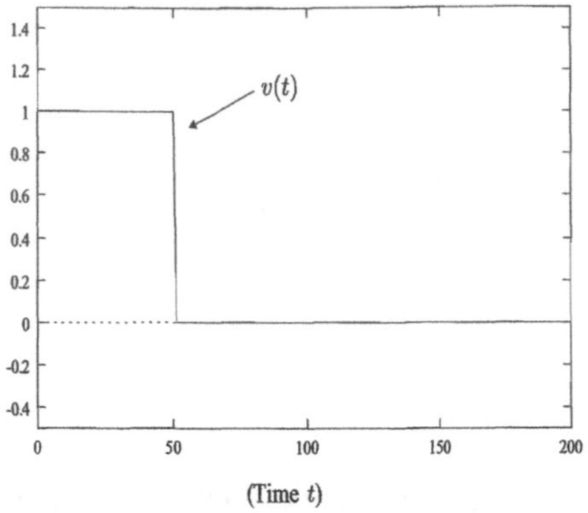

(a) Input signal $v(t)$

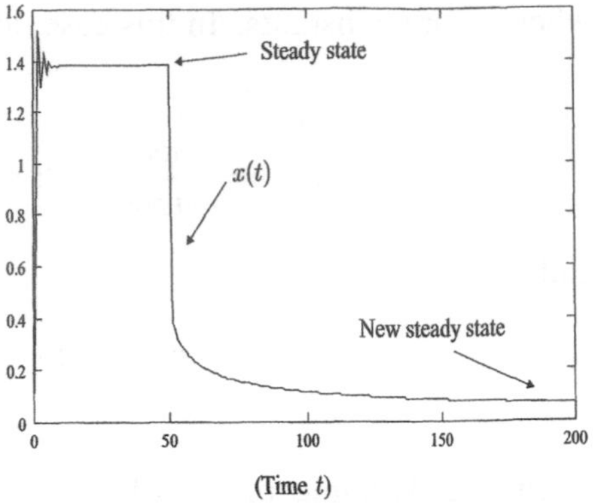

(b) Neural state response $x(t)$

Figure 8.25 The temporal response of an isolated DNU-1 with the parameters $\alpha = 1$ and $w = 1.5$ for a narrow pulse stimulus input $v(t)$.

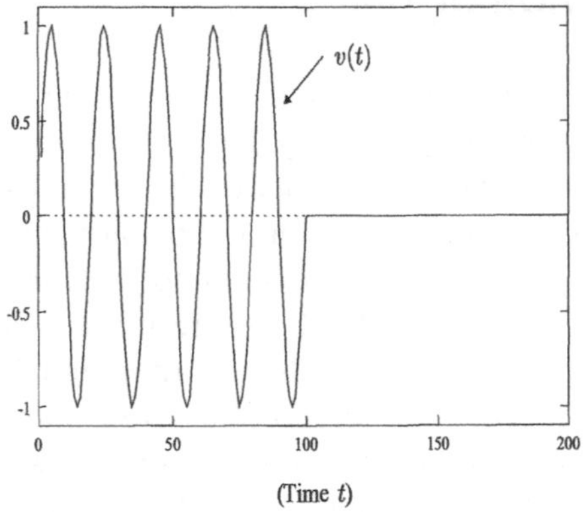

(a) Input signal

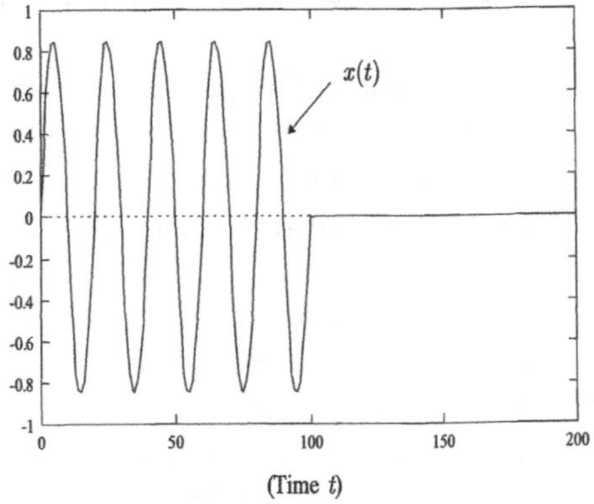

(b) Neural state signal

Figure 8.26 The encoding capability of an isolated DNU-1 with the parameters $\alpha = 1$ and $w = 1.5$ for a rapidly varying stimulus input $v(t)$.

For a sufficiently long time $t = t^*$, if

$$\lim_{t \longrightarrow t^*} e^{-\frac{\alpha}{\tau}t} = e^{-\frac{\alpha}{\tau}t^*} \approx 0$$

one may deal with the limitation for both sides of the equality in Eqn. (8.60), yielding

$$\begin{aligned}\lim_{t \longrightarrow t^*} x(t) &= \lim_{t \longrightarrow t^*} x(0)e^{-\frac{\alpha}{\tau}t} + \lim_{t \longrightarrow t^*} \frac{1}{\tau}\int_0^t e^{-\frac{\alpha}{\tau}(t-\zeta)} f(w, x(\zeta), v(\zeta))d\zeta \\ &= \lim_{t \longrightarrow t^*} \frac{1}{\tau}\int_0^t e^{-\frac{\alpha}{\tau}(t-\zeta)} f(w, x(\zeta), v(\zeta))d\zeta\end{aligned}$$

On the other hand, without loss of generality, let the activation function f be a continuous function for both the variables x and v. Then

$$\lim_{t \longrightarrow t^*} \frac{1}{\tau} \int_0^t e^{-\frac{\alpha}{\tau}(t-\zeta)} f(w, x(\zeta), v(\zeta)) d\zeta = \lim_{t \longrightarrow t^*} \frac{\int_0^t e^{\frac{\alpha}{\tau}\zeta} f(w, x(\zeta), v(\zeta)) d\zeta}{\tau e^{\frac{\alpha}{\tau}t}}$$

$$= \lim_{t \longrightarrow t^*} \frac{1}{\alpha} f(w, x(t), v(t))$$

$$= \frac{1}{\alpha} f(w, x(t^*), v(t^*))$$

where

$$x(t^*) \triangleq \lim_{t \longrightarrow t^*} x(t)$$

$$v(t^*) \triangleq \lim_{t \longrightarrow t^*} v(t)$$

Hence

$$x(t^*) = \frac{1}{\alpha} f(w, x(t^*), v(t^*)) \tag{8.61}$$

or simply denote

$$x(t^*) = x(t^*, v(t^*)) \tag{8.62}$$

This relationship shows that for a time-varying input signal $v(t)$ the neural state's response eventually converges to a solution of a static algebraic equation at each time t. This algebraic equation is the equilibrium equation of the DNU for the stimulus input at time t, and its solution is independent of the initial state value. If $v(t)$ is a slowly varying signal within an interval $t \in [t^*, t^* + \Delta t]$, then

$$v(t) \approx v^* = constant$$

and Eqn. (8.61) can be rewritten as

$$-\alpha x^* + f(w, x^*, v^*) = 0 \tag{8.63}$$

where

$$x^* \triangleq \lim_{t \longrightarrow t^*} x(t)$$

In this case, within a time interval where the stimulus remains approximately constant, the state trajectory reaches a steady state x^* that satisfies the equilibrium given in Eqn. (8.61). This process is shown in Fig. 8.25, where an isolated DNU-1 is considered.

If $v(t)$ is a rapidly varying signal compared with the function f, the solution x given in Eqn. (8.62) is an encoded representation of the input signal. In this case, $v(t)$ appears linearly on the right-hand side of the DNU model:

$$f(w, x, v) = f(w, x) + v$$

The neural state response at time $t > t^*$ may be determined by the following equation:

$$-\alpha x(t) + f(w, x(t)) + v(t) = 0 \tag{8.64}$$

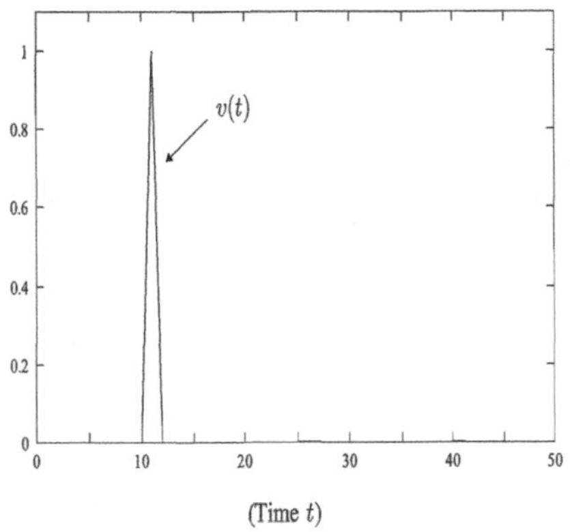

(a) Input signal $v(t)$

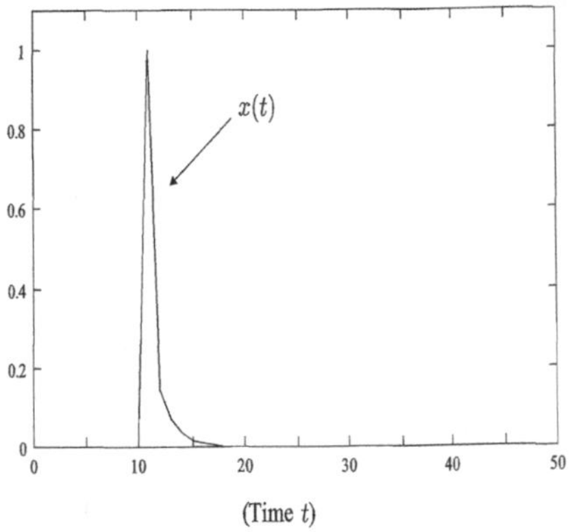

(b) Neural state $x(t)$

Figure 8.27 The temporal response of an isolated DNU-1 with the parameters $\alpha = 1$ and $w = 1.5$ to an impulse stimulus $v(t)$.

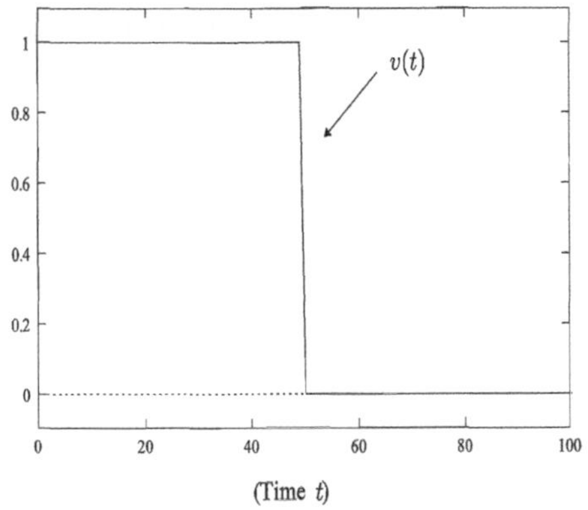

(a) Input signal $v(t)$

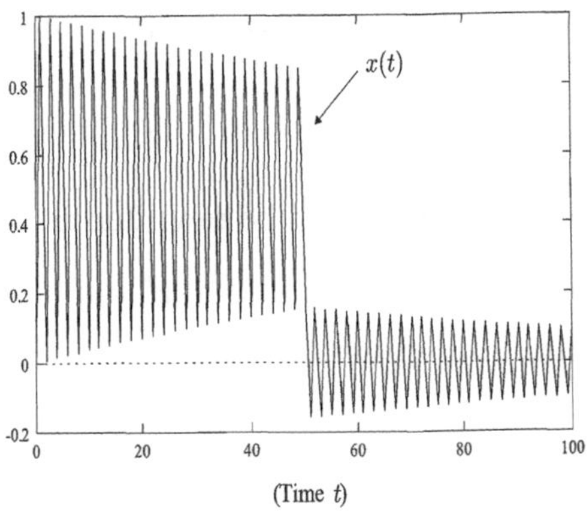

(b) Neural state $x(t)$

Figure 8.28 The damped oscillatory temporal response of an isolated DNU-1 with the parameters $\alpha = 1$ and $w = 0.05$.

In this case, the solution of x in the above equation is almost a linear function of v, and the shape and frequency of the stimulus input signal, which contains the most information, can be perfectly retained by the neural activity.

From this analysis it is observed that this important class of temporal behavior is the transient activity that is generated around a single stable attractor. A variety of neurons in the nervous system generate transient activity in response to an impulse or narrow pulse stimulus. On the initial application of a stimulus, the activity exhibited by a neural element corresponds to a rapid rise, leading to a steady state value. After the stimulus is removed, the neural activity returns to its original rest state. An example of the neural state response to an impulse stimulus input is shown in Fig. 8.27. The characteristics of the transient activity generated by a DNU are a function of the parameters employed. In certain circumstances, the damped oscillatory phenomenon is induced by small synaptic weight parameters as depicted in Fig. 8.28.

8.6 NONLINEAR ANALYSIS FOR DNUs

8.6.1 Equilibrium Points of a DNU

Let us consider a DNU having the form described by the nonlinear differential equation

$$\frac{dx}{dt} = -\alpha x + w\sigma(x) + v \equiv f(x) \tag{8.65}$$

where $x \in \Re$, $\alpha \neq 0$, $w \neq 0$, and v are the scalars. The special properties of the sigmoidal function $\sigma(x)$ provide the possibility that we may analytically exploit the equilibrium points of the DNU. The equilibrium points x^* of the DNU, Eqn. (8.65), are given by the roots of the equation $dx/dt = 0$, that is

$$x^* = \frac{w}{\alpha}\sigma(x^*) + \frac{v}{\alpha} = g(x^*) \tag{8.66}$$

where

$$g(x) = (w/\alpha)\sigma(x) + (v/\alpha)$$

Obviously, the equilibrium points x^* may be determined by considering directly the roots of the nonlinear function $f(x)$, or indirectly by the intersection of the curve $y = (w/\alpha)\sigma(x) + (v/\alpha)$ and the line $y = x$ in the x–y plane. The former approach will now be used for determining the number and locations of the equilibrium points.

Note that for all $x \in \Re$, the function $g(x)$ satisfies

$$\left[\frac{v}{\alpha} - \left|\frac{w}{\alpha}\right|\right] \leq g(x) \leq \left[\frac{v}{\alpha} + \left|\frac{w}{\alpha}\right|\right]$$

that is

$$g(x) : \left[\frac{v}{\alpha} - \left|\frac{w}{\alpha}\right|, \frac{v}{\alpha} + \left|\frac{w}{\alpha}\right|\right] \longrightarrow \left[\frac{v}{\alpha} - \left|\frac{w}{\alpha}\right|, \frac{v}{\alpha} + \left|\frac{w}{\alpha}\right|\right] \tag{8.67}$$

Hence, $g(x)$ is a continuous nonlinear function that maps a closed interval $[(v/\alpha) - |(w/\alpha)|, (v/\alpha) + |(w/\alpha)|]$ onto itself. Using Brouwer's fixed-point theorem, there is at least one equilibrium point x^* of the system in the interval $[(v/\alpha) - |(w/\alpha)|, (v/\alpha) + |(w/\alpha)|]$:

$$x^* \in \left[\frac{v}{\alpha} - \left|\frac{w}{\alpha}\right|, \frac{v}{\alpha} + \left|\frac{w}{\alpha}\right|\right]$$

Thus, x^* is located in an interval with the center (v/α) and the radius $|(w/\alpha)|$ as shown in Fig. 8.29. The equilibrium point x^* may be placed anywhere in the range $(-\infty, +\infty)$ by adjusting the parameters α, w, and v. The function $f(x)$ is a continuous and differentiable function, and satisfies $f(x) \rightarrow \infty$ as $x \rightarrow \infty$. If $v = 0$, the fact that $f(-x) = -f(x)$ shows that the curve of $f(x)$ is the skew–symmetric with respect to the axis $x = 0$ in the x–$f(x)$ plane. In this case, the system has a unique equilibrium point, or an even number of equilibrium points. According to the sign and values of the parameters α, w, and v, we may discuss the number and location of the roots of the nonlinear function $f(x) = -\alpha x + w\sigma(x) + v$, which are the equilibrium points of the system given in Eqn. (8.65). It can be further shown that a DNU with a sigmoidal activation function has at the most three, and at the least one equilibrium point in the interval $|x^* - (v/\alpha)| < |(w/\alpha)|$.

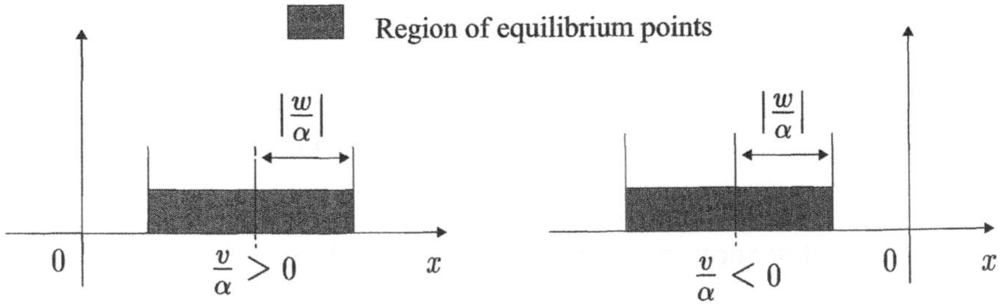

Figure 8.29 Region of the equilibrium point for DNU, Eqn. (8.65).

8.6.2 Stability of the DNU

An asymptotically stable equilibrium point, also called a *state attractor*, can be used for storing information in the associative memories. Following the results obtained in the last section, two questions immediately arise:

(i) Which of these equilibrium points are stable (or unstable) in the sense of Lyapunov?

(ii) How is the stability (or instability) affected as the parameters are varied?

To answer these questions, the asymptotic stability of these equilibrium points under the choice of the parameters of the single dynamic neural unit is now briefly addressed.

For convenience, assume that the maximum slope of the sigmoidal function $\sigma'(x)$ is 1. Then, the nonlinear sigmoid function $\sigma(x)$ satisfies

$$-1 \leq \sigma(x) \leq 1, \quad \text{and} \quad 0 \leq \sigma'(x) \leq 1, \quad \forall x \in \Re$$

Next, one may test the exponential stability of x^* using the Lyapunov function method. Let $z = x - x^*$ be a new variable of the system. Then

$$\frac{dz(t)}{dt} = -\alpha z(t) + wf(z(t)) \tag{8.68}$$

has a unique equilibrium point at $z = 0$ and the function $f(z) \equiv \sigma(z + x^*) - \sigma(x^*)$ satisfies

$$0 \leq f'(z) \leq 1$$
$$f(z)z \geq 0$$

To investigate the Lyapunov stability of the equilibrium point, let us choose the function

$$V(z) = \tfrac{1}{2}z^2$$

Then, for $\alpha > 0$ and $w < 0$

$$\begin{aligned} \frac{dV(z)}{dt} &= z\frac{dz}{dt} \\ &= z(-\alpha z + wf(z)) \\ &= -\alpha z^2 + wzf(z) \\ &\leq -\alpha z^2 \\ &= -2\alpha V(z) \end{aligned} \tag{8.69}$$

Therefore, if $\alpha > 0$ and $w < 0$, since $V(z) > 0$ and $dV(z)/dt < 0$, then $z = 0$ or equivalently $x = x^*$ is a globally exponentially stable equilibrium point. On the other hand, if $\alpha > 0,\ w > 0$ with $(w/\alpha) < 1$, then

$$\begin{aligned}\frac{dV(z)}{dt} &= -\alpha z^2 + wzf(z) \\ &\leq -\alpha z^2 + wz^2 \\ &= -2(\alpha - w)V(z)\end{aligned} \tag{8.70}$$

Hence, $z = 0$, or equivalently, $x = x^*$ is a globally exponentially stable equilibrium point.

In case of $\alpha < 0$, $w > 0$, we have

$$\frac{dV(z)}{dt} = z\frac{dz}{dt} = -\alpha z^2 + wzf(z) > 0 \tag{8.71}$$

Therefore, the equilibrium point x^* is *unstable*. Also, if $\alpha < 0,\ w < 0$ with $w > \alpha$, then

$$\frac{dV(z)}{dt} = -\alpha z^2 + wzf(z) \leq -\alpha z^2 + wz^2 > 0 \tag{8.72}$$

Thus, $z = 0$; that is, $x = x^*$ will be an *unstable* equilibrium point. For other combinations of the parameters α and w of the DNU, the equilibrium stability of the DNU can also be studied using the same analysis procedure.

8.6.3 Pitchfork Bifurcation in the DNU

The phenomenon of the appearance and disappearance of equilibrium points, accompanied by changes of the stability properties when some parameters in the differential equation are varied, is known as *bifurcation*. In other words, bifurcation describes the process of quantitative changes of the parameters leading to qualitative changes of the system properties such as the number of equilibrium points and their stability. We now discuss the bifurcation phenomenon in a single DNU whose properties of the equilibrium points were addressed in the previous sections. Several kinds of equilibrium point bifurcations have been discussed in the literature. Kelly et al. (1993) reported that a *pitchfork bifurcation* exists in the dynamic neural unit (DNU) of Eqn. (8.65). To study bifurcation in a single dynamic neuron, some preliminaries of bifurcation theory are discussed first.

Consider a single-variable first-order differential equation

$$\frac{dx}{dt} = f(x, \mu), \qquad x \in \Re, \qquad \mu \in \Re \tag{8.73}$$

where μ is a constant parameter. We assume that the right-side function in this equation satisfies

$$f(0,0) = 0 \tag{8.74}$$

$$\frac{\partial f}{\partial x}(0,0) = 0 \tag{8.75}$$

Equation (8.74) is simply an equilibrium condition. Thus, Eqn. (8.74) implies that for $\mu = 0$, $x = 0$ is an equilibrium point. Equation (8.75) provides the nonhyperbolic equilibrium condition, which is one of the necessary conditions that $(x, \mu) = (0, 0)$ is a bifurcation point and μ is a bifurcation value.

Without loss of generality, let the nonlinear function for a DNU be a sigmoidal function, $\sigma(x) = \tanh(x)$, and $\alpha \in \Re$ be a fixed constant in the following discussion. Let the DNU be described by the following differential equation

$$\frac{dx}{dt} = -\alpha x + w \tanh(x) + v \tag{8.76}$$

By defining $w = (\mu + \alpha)$, this equation can be rewritten as

$$\begin{aligned} \frac{dx}{dt} &= -\alpha x + (\mu + \alpha) \tanh(x) + v \\ &\equiv f(x, \mu, v) \end{aligned} \tag{8.77}$$

The state $x(t)$ of the DNU as described in Eqn. (8.76) is dependent on the two variable parameters w and v. Alternatively, by defining $w = (\mu + \alpha)$, the state $x(t)$ of the DNU of Eqn. (8.76) is expressed in Eqn. (8.77) with another set of two variable parameters $\mu = (w - \alpha)$ and bias v. It can be shown that the preceding differential equation of the DNU has pitchfork bifurcation when the bias $v = 0$ and the bifurcation is broken when $v \neq 0$.

8.6.3.1 Case (A) with zero bias, $v = 0$

In the case of a zero bias, that is, for $v = 0$, Eqn. (8.76) has a pitchfork bifurcation at the origin in the x–μ plane, that is, at $(x, \mu) = (0, 0)$, or equivalently at $x = 0$ and $w = \alpha$ in the x–w plane, that is, at $(x, w) = (0, \alpha)$. Hence, $(x, w) = (0, \alpha)$ is a bifurcation point through which more than one curve of the equilibrium point passes through this point in the w–x plane. The stability of the locus of the equilibrium point $x = 0$ also changes when passing through the point $(0, \alpha)$ as discussed in the last subsection. As well, there are three equilibrium points, two of which are stable and one unstable for $w > \alpha > 0$, and two unstable and one stable for $w < \alpha < 0$. The bifurcation diagram for the DNU is shown in Fig. 8.30, where the dashed

—— (continuous lines): locus of *stable* equilibrium points
– – – (dashed lines): locus of *unstable* equilibrium points

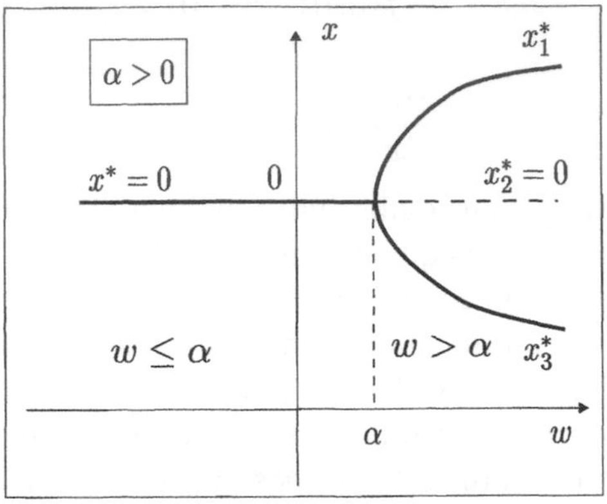

(a) Dynamic neural unit: $\dot{x} = -\alpha x + w\tanh(x)$, $\alpha > 0$

(i) For $w \le \alpha$, the DNU has a locus of a unique *stable* equilibrium point at $x^* = 0$.

(ii) For $w > \alpha$, the DNU has loci of *two stable* (x_1^* and x_3^*) and *one unstable* (x_2^*) equilibrium points.

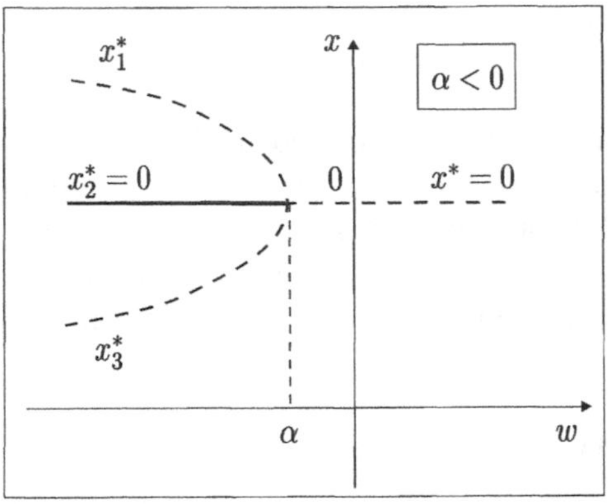

(b) Dynamic neural unit: $\dot{x} = -\alpha x + w\tanh(x)$, $\alpha < 0$

(i) For $w \ge \alpha$, the DNU has a locus of a unique *unstable* equilibrium point at $x^* = 0$.

(ii) For $w < \alpha$, the DNU has loci of *two unstable* (x_1^* and x_3^*) and *one stable* (x_2^*) equilibrium points.

Figure 8.30 Case (A), with zero bias, $v = 0$, pitchfork bifurcation in the DNU with $v = 0$, Eqn. (8.76).

—— (continuous lines): locus of *stable* equilibrium points
– – – (dashed lines): locus of *unstable* equilibrium points

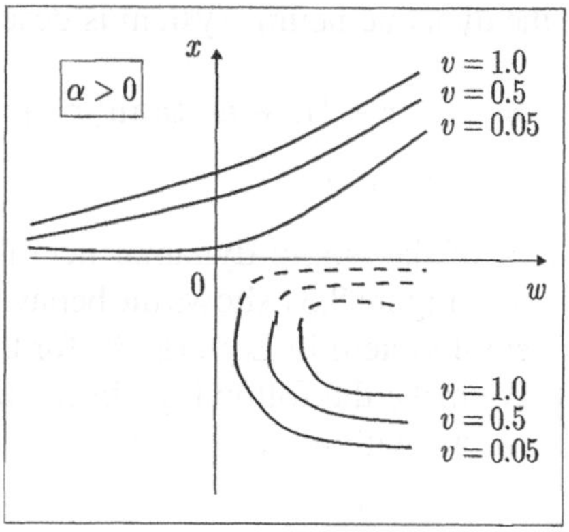

(a) For $\alpha > 0$ with increasing w, sudden appearance of two equilibrium points

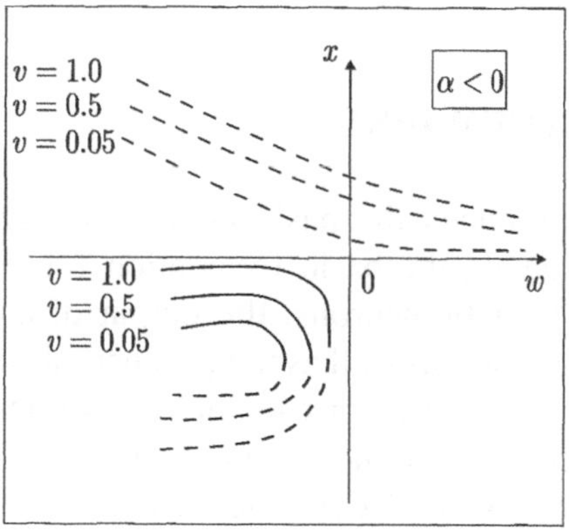

(b) For $\alpha < 0$ with increasing w, sudden disappearance of two equilibrium points

Figure 8.31 Case (B), DNU with bias v, the equilibrium curves of the single DNU, Eqn. (8.78). When $v \neq 0$, the pitchfork bifurcation disappears.

lines represent the locus of the unstable equilibrium points and the continuous lines represent the locus of the stable equilibrium points. Obviously, when $w > \alpha$, the equilibrium point $x^* = 0$ loses its stability for all values of α as shown in Fig. 8.30a for $\alpha > 0$, and in Fig. 8.30b for $\alpha < 0$.

8.6.3.2 Case (B) with bias $v, v \neq 0$

For the case of $v \neq 0$, the dynamic neural system is described as

$$\begin{aligned} \frac{dx}{dt} &= -\alpha x + (\mu + w)\tanh(x) + v \\ &\equiv f(x, \mu, v) \end{aligned} \tag{8.78}$$

The pitchfork bifurcation of the single dynamic neural unit at $(x, \mu, v) = (0, 0, 0)$ is broken for $v \neq 0$. Figure 8.31 shows the behavior of the equilibrium points of the dynamic neural system in Eqn. (8.78) for the DNU with bias v, and $\alpha > 0$ and $\alpha < 0$. We make the following observations on the dynamic behavior of equilibrium points with increasing w.

(i) In Fig. 8.31a, for $\alpha > 0$ and $w > 0$, when the parameter w is increased, two equilibrium points suddenly appear; one is stable and the other one is unstable.

(ii) In Fig. 8.31b, for $\alpha < 0$, when w is increased two equilibrium points suddenly disappear.

8.7 CONCLUDING REMARKS

In this chapter we introduced the basic concept of *feedback* phenomenon in neural units, thus laying the basic foundation for *dynamic neural units* (DNUs). In contrast to static neurons, the output of a dynamic neural unit depends on the present inputs as well as the past neural states. This concept of a *dynamic neural unit* (DNU) gives rise to some very important characteristics such as *equilibrium memory* and the *dynamic temporal behavior* of a DNU.

The input–output behavior of dynamic neural units as described in this chapter is characterized by nonlinear differential or difference equations. After introducing the basic equations of the dynamic neural units, we studied various types of dynamic neural units, including neurons with *excitatory* and *inhibitory* dynamics. The phenomena of multiple equilibrium points and their stability characteristics are discussed. The concept of pitchfork bifurcation, which can be found in certain parameter conditions in dynamic neural units (DNUs), was also explored. The dynamic neural units studied in this chapter provide a basic understanding for a further study of dynamic neural networks (DNNs) in the following chapters.

Problems

8.1 Given a nonlinear dynamic system of the form

$$\frac{d\boldsymbol{x}(t)}{dt} = \boldsymbol{f}(\boldsymbol{x}(t), \boldsymbol{u}(t)), \qquad \boldsymbol{x}(0) = \boldsymbol{x}_0$$

where $\boldsymbol{x} \in \Re^n$ is the state vector, $\boldsymbol{u}(t) \in \Re^n$ is the external input vector, and $\boldsymbol{f} : \Re^n \times \Re^n \longrightarrow \Re^n$ is a nonlinear function.

(a) Can dynamic responses of such a nonlinear dynamic system with respect to a specific external input $\boldsymbol{u}(t)$ be used to emulate the phenomenon of short-term memory?

(b) Can steady states of such a dynamic system with respect to an specific external input $\boldsymbol{u}(t)$ be used to emulate the phenomenon of long-term memory?

(c) Compare biological memory systems with that of the memory associated with this type of nonlinear dynamic system.

8.2 Show that the DNU model

$$\frac{dy}{dt} = h(y)\left[-\alpha\sigma^{-1}(y) + wy + v\right]$$

has the identical set of equilibrium points and the identical set of asymptotically stable equilibrium points as that of the following system

$$\frac{dy}{dt} = -\alpha\sigma^{-1}(y) + wy + v$$

where

$$h(y) = \left.\frac{d\sigma(x)}{dx}\right|_{x=\sigma^{-1}(y)}$$

8.3 Let all the parameters in the models of the Hopfield (DNU-1) and Grossberg (DNU-5) be 1 and the initial values of the state $x(0) = 0$. Give the numerical solutions of the states of both neurons.

8.4 Consider a two-neuron dynamic network described by

$$\begin{aligned} \frac{dx_1}{dt} &= -\alpha x_1 + \beta_1 w_1 \sigma(x_1) + \beta_1 w_2 \sigma(x_2) + \beta_1 v \\ \frac{dx_2}{dt} &= -\alpha x_2 + \beta_2 w_1 \sigma(x_1) + \beta_2 w_2 \sigma(x_2) + \beta_2 v \end{aligned}$$

Prove that this system is equivalent to the following single-neuron structure with the two nonlinear activation operations

$$\frac{dy}{dt} = -\alpha y + w_1\sigma(\beta_1 y) + w_2\sigma(\beta_2 y) + v$$

where $y = x_1/\beta_1 = x_2/\beta_2$.

8.5 Consider a nonlinear system described by the following differential equation:

$$\begin{aligned} \frac{dx(t)}{dt} &= -\alpha x(t) + \sigma(w_1 x(t) + w_2 x^2(t) + v) \\ y(t) &= \sigma(x(t)) \end{aligned}$$

Give a block diagram of this system and compare the difference between the model described above and the Hopfield neuron (DNU-1).

8.6 Let the external input $v(t)$ be a square-wave function with the amplitude -1 and 1, and period 0.1 second. Using computer simulation, design an isolated DNU such that the error between the input $v(t)$ and the temporal neural state response $x(t)$ is less than 0.2 at any time t.

8.7 Consider a dynamic neural unit (DNU) with the following form:

$$\frac{dx(t)}{dt} = -0.6x(t) + 1.5\tanh(2x(t)) + 1.7$$

(a) Determine all the equilibrium points of the above system;
(b) Discuss the stability of the equilibrium points.

8.8 Determine the parameters α, w, c, d, and v such that the following neural equation

$$\frac{dx(t)}{dt} = -\alpha x(t) + w\left[\tanh(c(x+d)) + \tanh(c(x-d))\right] + v$$

has three asymptotically stable equilibrium points.

8.9 For the continuous-time dynamic neural unit (CT-DNU)

$$\frac{dx(t)}{dt} = -\alpha x(t) + w\sigma(x(t)) + v$$

use the first-difference approximation expression of dx/dt as

$$\left.\frac{dx(t)}{dt}\right|_{t=kT} = \frac{x((k+1)T) - x(kT)}{T} = \frac{x(k+1) - x(k)}{T}$$

where T is the timestep.

(a) Obtain the discrete version of the CT-DNU model;

(b) Draw the block diagram of the discrete-time DNU model;

(c) Determine the stable regions of the equilibrium points;

(d) Discuss the effect on the stability of the equilibrium points for a different sampling period T.

8.10 Consider an isolated CT-DNU model of the form

$$\frac{dx}{dt} = -\alpha x + (\gamma - \beta x)(w\sigma(x) + v)$$

(a) Show that the equilibrium points are given by

$$x = \frac{\gamma w\sigma(x) + \gamma v}{\alpha + \beta w\sigma(x) + \beta v}$$

(b) Discuss the number and location of these equilibrium points;

(c) Discuss the stability of these equilibrium points.

8.11 Consider an isolated CT-DNU model of the form

$$\frac{dx}{dt} = -\alpha x + w\tanh(x) + v$$

Discuss the number and location of the equilibrium points of the DNU for the following choices of parameters:

(a) $\alpha > 0, w > 0$

(b) $\alpha < 0, w < 0, (w/\alpha) \leq 1$

(c) $\alpha < 0, w < 0, (w/\alpha) > 1$

8.12 Discuss the stability of the equilibrium points of the CT-DNU given in Problem 8.11 and having the parameters given in (a), (b), and (c), respectively.

8.13 Consider a linear differential equation

$$\frac{dx}{dt} = -\alpha x + wx + v$$

(a) Determine the solution of the above system;

(b) Discuss the asymptotic stability condition of the equilibrium point in terms of the parameters α, w, and v;

(c) Let $\alpha = 1$, $w = 0.5$, and

$$v = \begin{cases} 1, & \text{for } 0 \leq t \leq 10 \\ 0, & \text{otherwise} \end{cases}$$

Obtain the response of the system for the zero initial condition, $x(0) = 0$.

8.14 Consider an isolated DNU of the form

$$\frac{dx}{dt} = -\alpha x + w \tanh(x) + v$$

where $-2 \leq v \leq 2$.

(a) Select the parameters α and w such that the system has a unique stable equilibrium point $x^*(\alpha, w, v)$;

(b) Let

$$v = \begin{cases} 0.5, & \text{for } 0 \leq t \leq 10 \\ 1.5, & \text{otherwise} \end{cases}$$

Obtain the response of the system for zero initial condition.

8.15 Give a definition of the equilibrium bifurcation for a one-parameter family of a one-dimensional differential equation.

8.16 Give two types of equilibrium bifurcations that exist in nonlinear dynamic systems that are different with the pitchfork bifurcation.

8.17 Find a two-dimension nonlinear system

$$\begin{aligned} \frac{dx_1}{dt} &= f_1(x_1, x_2) \\ \frac{dx_2}{dt} &= f_2(x_1, x_2) \end{aligned}$$

such that the system has at least one nonhyperbolic equilibrium point; that is, at least one of the eigenvalues of the Jacobian

$$v = \begin{bmatrix} \frac{\partial f_1}{\partial x_1} & \frac{\partial f_2}{\partial x_1} \\ \frac{\partial f_1}{\partial x_2} & \frac{\partial f_2}{\partial x_2} \end{bmatrix}$$

has a zero real part at the equilibrium point.

8.18 Consider a differential equation

$$\frac{dx}{dt} = \mu x - x^2$$

where $x \in \Re$ is the state and $\mu \in \Re$ is the parameter.

(a) Determine the equilibrium points of the system;

(b) Show that $x = 0$ is a nonhyperbolic equilibrium point;

(c) Analyze the change of the stability of the equilibrium for $\mu = 0$.

8.19 Consider a differential equation

$$\frac{dx}{dt} = \mu - x^2$$

where $x \in \Re$ is the state and $\mu \in \Re$ is the parameter.

(a) Determine the equilibrium points of the system;

(b) Show that $x = 0$ is a nonhyperbolic equilibrium point;

(c) Analyze the change of the stability of the equilibrium at $\mu = 0$.

9

Continuous-Time Dynamic Neural Networks

9.1 Dynamic Neural Network Structures: An Introduction

9.2 Hopfield Dynamic Neural Network (DNN) and Its Implementation

9.3 Hopfield Dynamic Neural Networks (DNNs) as Gradient-like Systems

9.4 Modifications of Hopfield Dynamic Neural Networks

9.5 Other DNN Models

9.6 Conditions for Equilibrium Points in DNN

9.7 Concluding Remarks

Problems

As seen in the previous chapters, a neural network consists of many interconnected simple processing units, called *neurons*, which form the layered configurations. An individual neuron aggregates its weighed inputs and yields an output through a nonlinear activation function with a threshold. In artificial neural networks there are three types of connections: intralayer, interlayer, and recurrent connections. The *intralayer* connections, which are also called *lateral* connections or *cross-layer* connections, are links between neurons in the same layer of the network. The *interlayer* connections are links between neurons in different layers. The *recurrent* connections provide self-feedback links to the neurons. In interlayer connections, the signals are transformed in one of the two ways: either feedforward or feedback.

From the computational point of view, a dynamic neural structure that contains the state feedback may provide more computational advantages than a static neural structure, which contains only a feedforward neural structure. In general, a small feedback system is equivalent to a large and possibly infinite feedforward system (Hush and Horne 1993). A well-known example is that an infinite number of feedforward logic gates are required to emulate an arbitrary finite-state machine. Also an infinite order *finite impulse response* (FIR) filter is required to emulate a single-pole *infinite impulse response* (IIR). A nonlinear dynamic recurrent neural network structure is particularly appropriate for system identification, control and filtering applications because of its distributed information processing ability as in biological neural systems. In fact, a class of dynamic neural mechanisms has been exploited for learning, information storing, and using knowledge that might be found widely in the brain. In these new neural machines the physics of the machines and algorithms of the computation are intimately related.

The introduction of feedback in neural networks produces a dynamic neural system with several stable equilibrium points. A universally agreed-on definition of neural network models does not exist, but for purposes of theoretical analysis and applications it is useful to define the most general features of the dynamic neural systems that are to be considered in this book. The entire discussion in this chapter, unless otherwise specified, will be limited to systems that have continuous valued states and equations of motion that can be expressed as differential equations.

9.1 DYNAMIC NEURAL NETWORK STRUCTURES: AN INTRODUCTION

Consider a continuous-time dynamic neural network structure defined as

$$\text{State equation:} \quad \frac{dx(t)}{dt} = f(x(t), u(t), w) \tag{9.1}$$

$$\text{Output equation:} \quad y(t) = h(x(t), w) \tag{9.2}$$

where $x \in \Re^n$ represents the state vector, $u \in \Re^m$ is the external input vector, and $w \in \Re^\ell$ is the neural parameters vector, which contains the synaptic connection weights and somatic operational parameters; $f(.)$ is a function that represents the structure of the neural network, and $h(.)$ is a function that represents the relationship between the state vector $x(t)$ and the output vector $y(t) \in \Re^p$.

Equivalently, a discrete-time dynamic neural structure can be defined as

$$\text{State equation:} \quad x(k+1) = f(x(k), u(k), w) \tag{9.3}$$

$$\text{Output equation:} \quad y(k) = h(x(k), w) \tag{9.4}$$

These dynamic neural structures possess three general characteristics as pointed out by Pineda (1988):

(i) First, they generally have many degrees of freedom. The human brain, as a basis of these dynamic models, is believed to have between 10^{11} and 10^{13} biological neurons. The state of each of these neurons can be modeled by different dynamic equations. It is generally believed that the computational power and fault tolerance capabilities of the neural systems result from the collective dynamics of the neural networks. Collective effects account for the properties of many physical systems including magnetism, superconductivity, and fluid dynamics. These static neural networks are trivial in some respects. They can all be characterized by only one or two coupling constants. Dynamic neural systems, on the other hand, are characterized by many synaptic connecting weights.

(ii) The second general characteristic is that the dynamic neural structures are nonlinear. Linear dynamic systems are characterized by the fact that any two solutions of the system may be added together to produce a third solution. Accordingly, linear dynamic systems can perform linear mappings only and, therefore, are limited in their computational ability. In fact, nonlinearity is a required property in associative memories if they are to distinguish between two stored patterns.

(iii) The third characteristic of dynamic neural systems is that they are dissipative. A dissipative system is characterized by the convergence of the flow onto a manifold of lower dimensionality as the system evolves. General dissipative systems, as shown in Fig. 9.1, can exhibit complicated behavior. For example, they may converge onto manifolds with

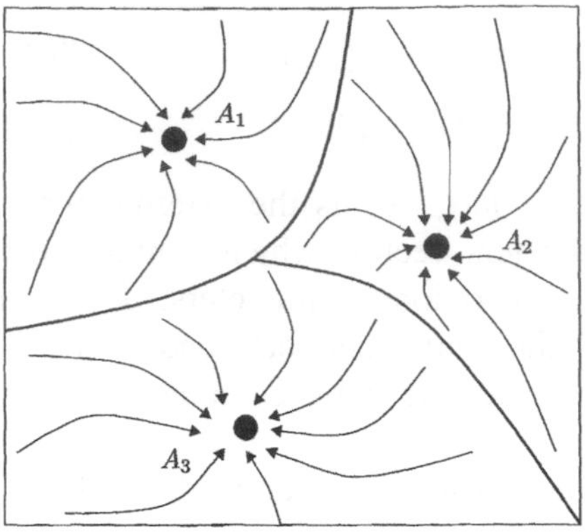

(a) Attractors A_1, A_2, and A_3

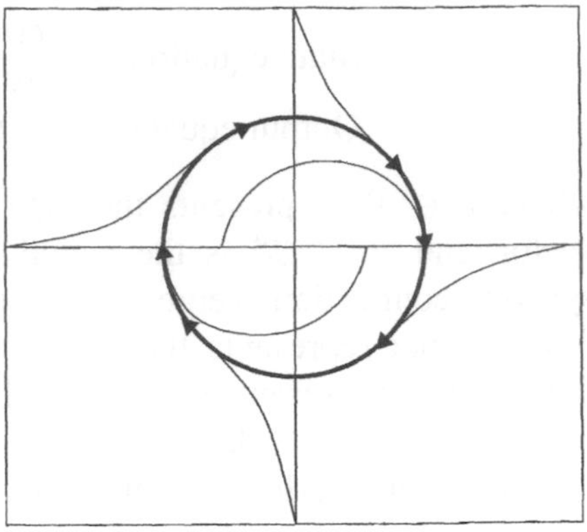

(b) Biological neural network

Figure 9.1 A two-dimensional (2-D) illustration for the orbit of a dissipative system.

fractional dimensions (attractors) or onto a one-dimensional manifold with periodic orbits.

Parallel to the development of static feedforward neural networks, dynamic recurrent neural networks were first proposed in the context of *associative* or *content-addressable memory* (CAM) problems (Hopfield 1982, 1984; Kohonen 1988) for pattern recognition. The uncorrupted pattern is used as a stable equilibrium point and its noisy versions as its basin of attraction. In this way, a dynamic neural system associated with a set of patterns is created. If the whole working space is correctly partitioned by such a content-addressable memory (CAM), then a system should have a steady-state solution corresponding to the uncorrupted pattern for any initial condition which represents a sample pattern. The neural network dynamics of such a classifier serve as a filter.

A well-known model of dynamic recurrent neural networks with some useful collective computational properties is due to Hopfield (1982, 1984). This dynamic neural structure consists of a large number of the dynamic neurons that were introduced in Chapter 8. A continuous-time model of an analog neural network can be described by the following system of nonlinear differential equations

$$\text{State equation:} \quad \frac{dx_i(t)}{dt} = -\alpha_i x_i(t) + \sum_{j=1}^{n} w_{ij} y_j(t) + s_i \qquad i = 1, 2, \ldots, n \tag{9.5}$$

$$\text{Output equation:} \quad y_i(t) = \sigma_i(x_i(t)), \quad i = 1, 2, \ldots, n \tag{9.6}$$

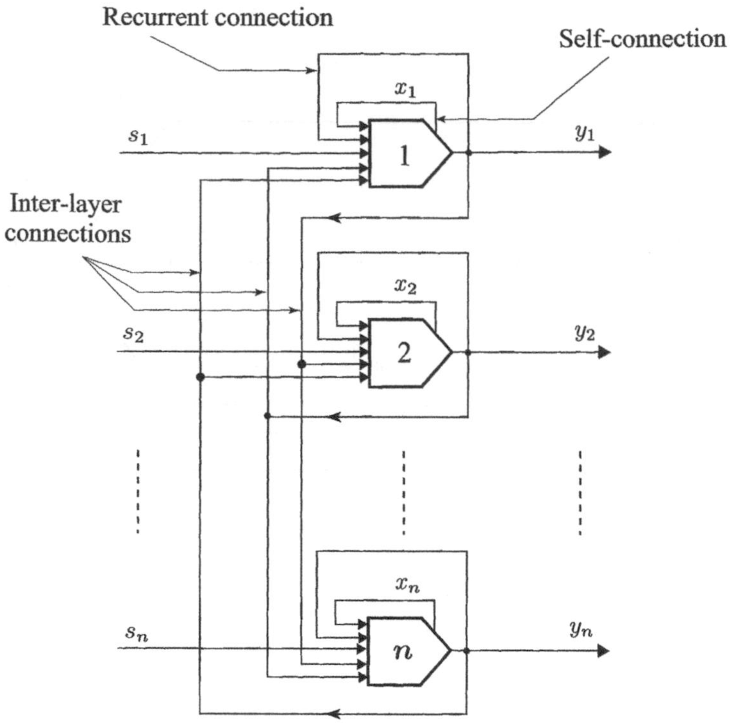

Figure 9.2 A basic dynamic neural network structure, Eqns. (9.5) and (9.6).

where x_i represents the state of the ith neuron, y_i is the output of the ith neuron, w_{ij} is the synaptic connection weight from the ith neuron to the jth neuron, s_i is a constant external input, the constant α_i is a positive constant, and $\sigma_i(.)$ is assumed to be a monotonic sigmoidal function as discussed in the previous chapters.

Figure 9.2 shows a single-layer dynamic neural structure as described by Eqns. (9.5) and (9.6). Each dynamic neuron receives three types of input:

$s_i(t)$: an external input signal for its dynamic processing

$x_i(t)$: self-connection: a state feedback signal

$y_i(t)$: inter-layer connections: an output signal from each neuron including the ith neuron

The accomplishment of both recurrent and interlayer connections involves synaptic operations. From the system's perspective, the model of this dynamic neural network is a continuous deterministic nonlinear dynamic system and is illustrated by the block diagram in Fig. 9.3. More detailed studies about this type of DNN will follow in the later sections of this chapter.

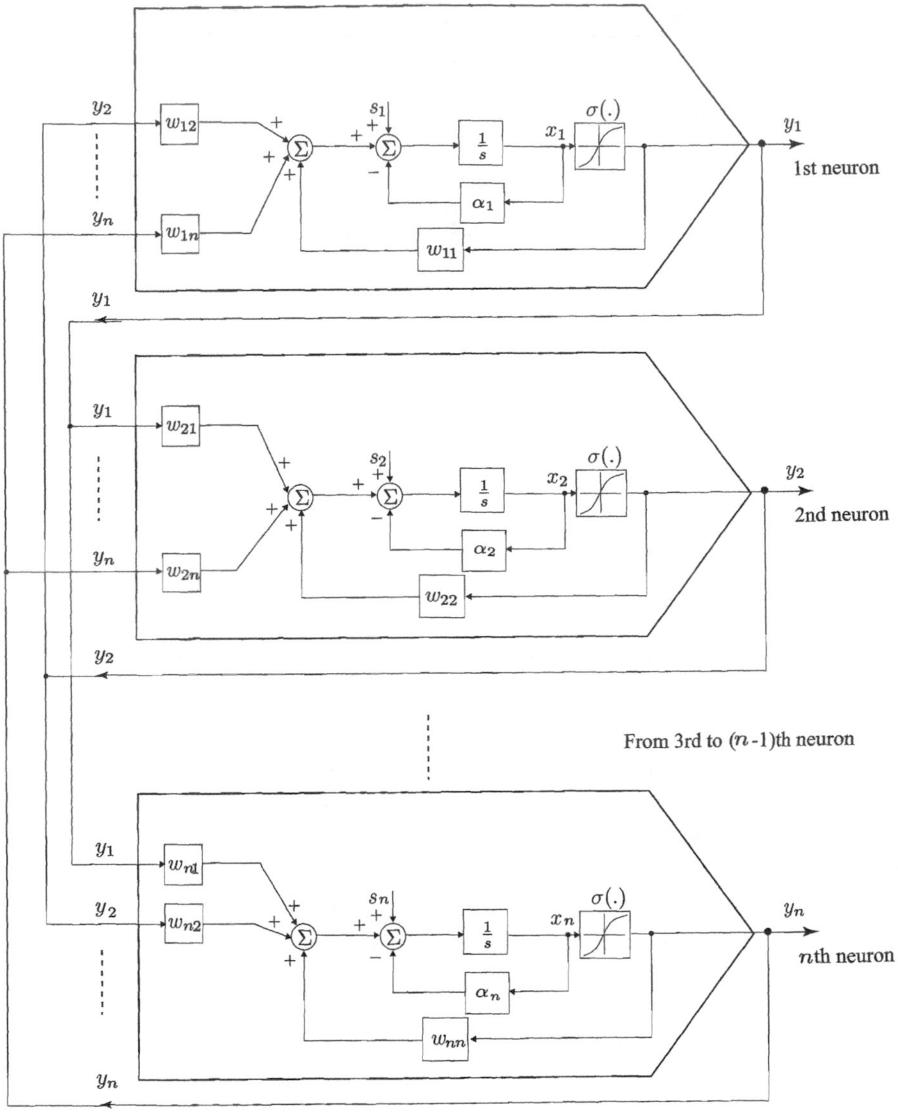

Figure 9.3 Block diagram of a continuous-time dynamic neural structure, Eqns. (9.5) and (9.6).

9.2 HOPFIELD DYNAMIC NEURAL NETWORK (DNN) AND ITS IMPLEMENTATION

This dynamic neural network (DNN), as introduced in Eqns. (9.5) and (9.6), has evolved from the original work of Hopfield (1984), who used an electronic circuit implementation of such a network.

In this section, we describe the Hopfield neural network and its electronic circuit implementation. Some of its important properties, such as the stability and equilibrium points, will be discussed. An extensive study of some of the other dynamic characteristics that are useful in the design and applications of these DNUs is addressed in the following sections.

9.2.1 State Space Model of the Hopfield DNN

A continuous-time dynamic neural network containing n dynamic neural units (DNUs), introduced by Hopfield (1984), is described by the following nonlinear differential equations

$$\text{State equation:} \quad C_i \frac{dx_i(t)}{dt} = -\frac{x_i(t)}{R_i} + \sum_{j=1}^{n} w_{ij} y_j(t) + s_i(t) \qquad i = 1, 2, \ldots, n \tag{9.7}$$

$$\text{Output equation:} \quad y_i(t) = \sigma_i(x_i(t)) \tag{9.8}$$

This nonlinear system can be implemented by an analog RC (resistance–capacitance) network circuit. As shown in Fig. 9.4, such a circuit contains a RC network at the input of each amplifier. The capacitance $C_i > 0$ and the resistance $\rho_i > 0$ represent the total shunt capacitance and shunt resistance at the input of the ith amplifier. Since the intrinsic delay exhibited by any physical amplifier is modeled by an input resistance ρ_i and C_i, which are drawn as external components in Fig. 9.4, an actual operational amplifier can, therefore, be assumed as an ideal amplifier without delay. Furthermore, let R_{ij} be the resistor connecting the output of the jth amplifier to the input of the ith amplifier, and s_i the fixed external input current.

Let

$u_i \triangleq x_i$: input voltage of the ith amplifier

$V_i = \sigma_i(u_i)$: output of the ith amplifier, where each operational amplifier has two output terminals each providing V_i and $-V_i$

One may write the current equation at the input node of the ith amplifier using Kirchhoff's current law as follows

$$
\begin{aligned}
C_i \frac{du_i}{dt} + \frac{u_i}{\rho_i} &= \frac{(\pm V_1 - u_i)}{R_{i1}} + \ldots + \frac{(\pm V_j - u_i)}{R_{in}} + s_i \\
&= -u_i \sum_{j=1}^{n} \frac{1}{R_{ij}} + \sum_{j=1}^{n} \frac{(\pm V_j)}{R_{ij}} + s_i
\end{aligned}
$$

or

$$
C_i \frac{du_i}{dt} + u_i \left(\frac{1}{\rho_i} + \sum_{j=1}^{n} \frac{1}{R_{ij}} \right) = \sum_{j=1}^{n} \frac{(\pm V_j)}{R_{ij}} + s_i \tag{9.9}
$$

and

$$
V_i = \sigma_i(u_i) \tag{9.10}
$$

By introducing a new parameter R_i defined as

$$
\frac{1}{R_i} = \frac{1}{\rho_i} + \sum_{j=1}^{n} \frac{1}{R_{ij}}
$$

the dynamic neural network given in Eqns. (9.9) and (9.10) may be rewritten in a compact form as

$$
\begin{aligned}
C_i \frac{du_i}{dt} + \frac{u_i}{R_i} &= \sum_{j=1}^{n} \frac{(\pm V_j)}{R_{ij}} + s_i \\
&= \sum_{j=1}^{n} G_{ij}(\pm V_j) + s_i
\end{aligned} \tag{9.11}
$$

where, $G_{ij} = 1/R_{ij}$.

Moreover, by defining the neural weighting function w_{ij} as

$$
w_{ij} = \begin{cases} +\dfrac{1}{R_{ij}}, & \text{if } R_{ij} \text{ is connected to the } V_j \\ -\dfrac{1}{R_{ij}}, & \text{if } R_{ij} \text{ is connected to the } -V_j \end{cases}
$$

the DNN in Eqn. (9.11) may be rewritten as

$$
C_i \frac{du_i}{dt} = -\frac{1}{R_i} u_i + \sum_{j=1}^{n} w_{ij} y_j(t) + s_i(t) \tag{9.12}
$$

where

$$
y_i = \sigma_i(u_i) \tag{9.13}
$$

These equations are the same as those given in Eqns. (9.7) and (9.8).

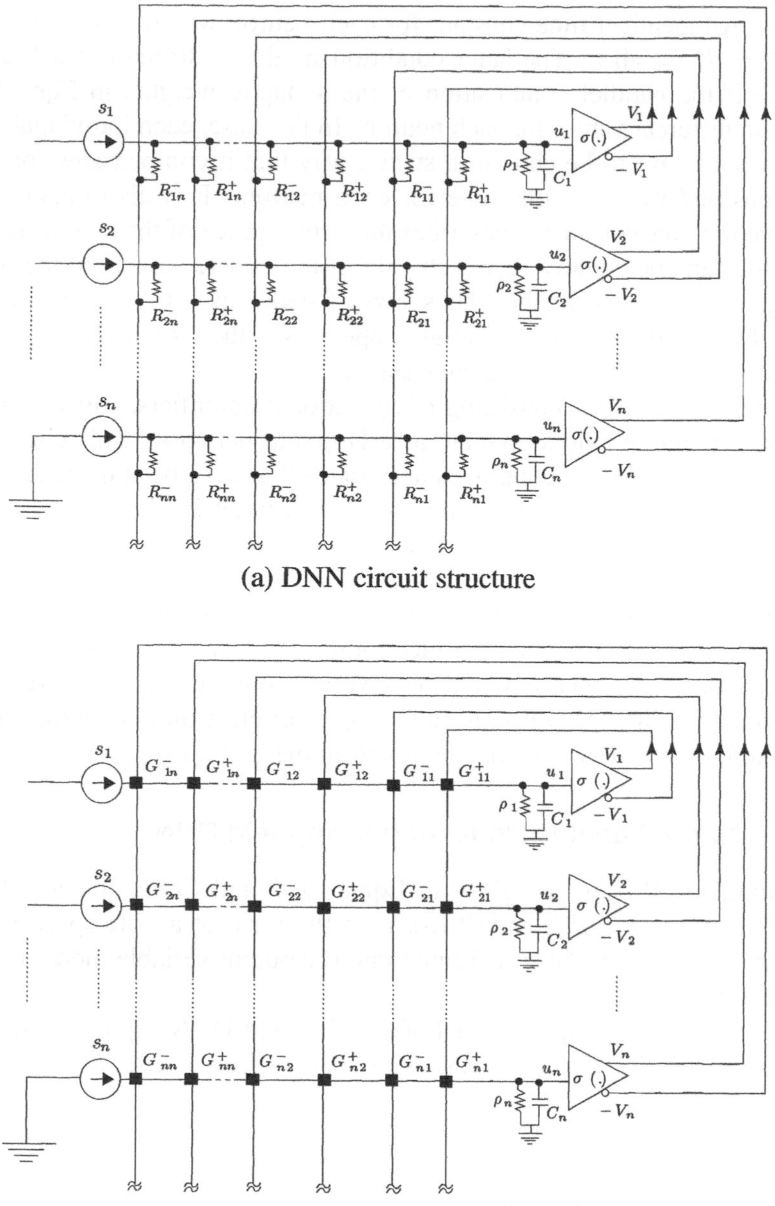

(a) DNN circuit structure

(b) A simplified DNN circuit structure, $G_{ij} = 1/R_{ij}$

Figure 9.4 Circuit representation of continuous-time dynamic neural network (DNN) structure; Eqns. (9.12) and (9.13).

The product $R_iC_i = \tau_i$ is often referred to as the time constant of the ith neuron. An identical time constant for each neuron would require $C_i = C$ and $R_i = R$ for all i. The latter condition might be difficult to achieve in practice if the parallel combination of the synaptic weights in Eqn. (9.11) results in different values for each neuron. In this case, each individual value for ρ_i would have to be chosen in such a way that it compensates for these variations and keeps R_i the same for each neuron. It is also important to note that the time constant τ_i describes the convergence of the neural state u_i. Because of the potentially very high gain of the transfer function, the output V_i might saturate very quickly. Thus, even if state u_i is still far from reaching its equilibrium point, output V_i might appear as if the circuit had converged in merely a fraction of the time constant τ_i.

An electronic circuit consisting of operational amplifiers, capacitors, and resistors should be able to operate as a Hopfield network. This circuit can be designed by reconstructing the stable states that have been designed using the proper value of w_{ij}, and as long as w_{ij} is symmetric; that is, $w_{ij} = w_{ji}$, and the amplifiers are quick compared with the characteristic of the neural time constant R_iC_i. In this case, the neural system converges to stable states and will not oscillate or display chaotic behavior. The novel concepts and implementations of a single-chip electronic neural network along the lines just discussed have been reported by several groups using *very large-scale integration* (VLSI). Many details on the topics of electronic implementations of dynamic neural networks may be found in the literature.

9.2.2 Output Variable Model of the Hopfield DNN

The Hopfield DNN model given in Eqns. (9.7) and (9.8), or equivalently expressed in Eqns. (9.12) and (9.13), is in the form of a state space model. These models can also be transformed into the output variable model form as described below.

To rewrite the state space model of the Hopfield DNN expressed in Eqns. (9.7) and (9.8) using the output variable $y_i = \sigma_i(x_i)$, $i = 1, 2, \dots, n$, we have

$$\begin{aligned}\frac{dy_i}{dt} &= \frac{d\sigma_i}{dx_i} \cdot \frac{dx_i}{dt} \\ &= \frac{d\sigma_i}{dx_i} \cdot \frac{1}{C_i}\left[-\frac{x_i(t)}{R_i} + \sum_{j=1}^{n} w_{ij} y_j(t) + s_i(t)\right] \qquad (9.14)\end{aligned}$$

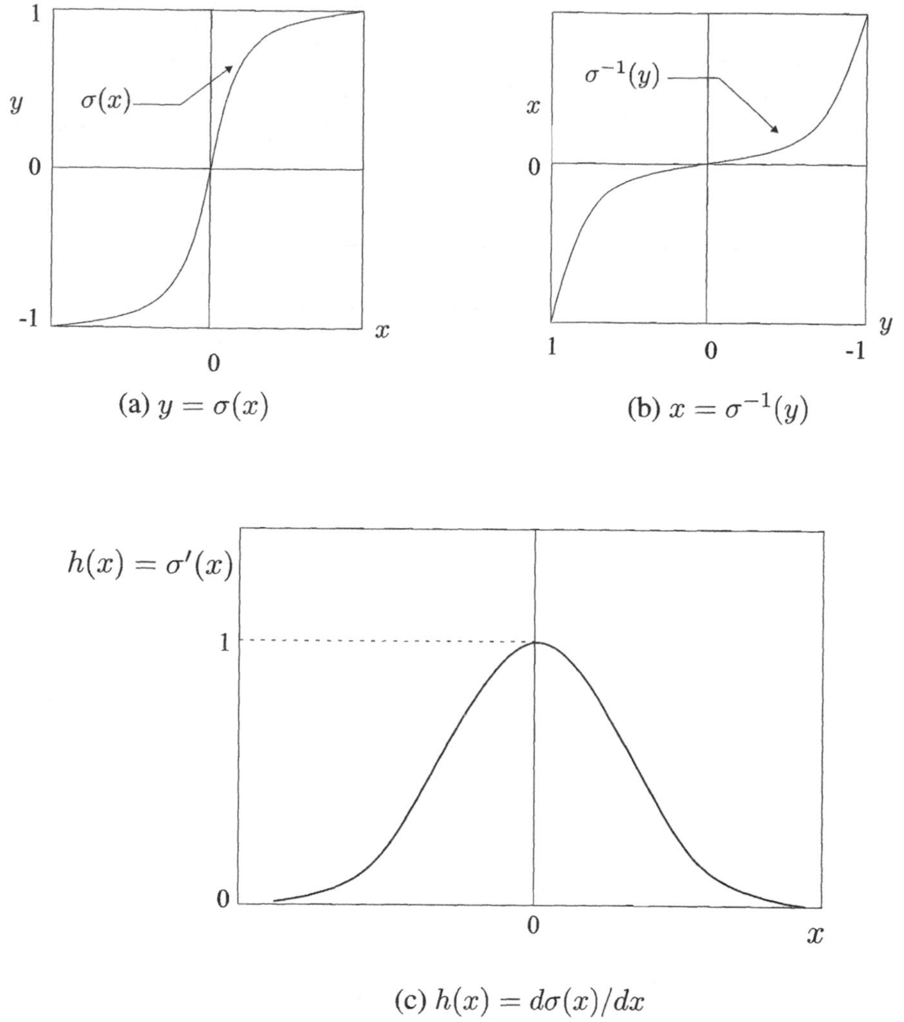

Figure 9.5 Sigmoidal function $y = \sigma(x)$, its inverse $x = \sigma^{-1}(y)$, and its derivative $\sigma'(x) = h(x) = d\sigma(x)/dx$.

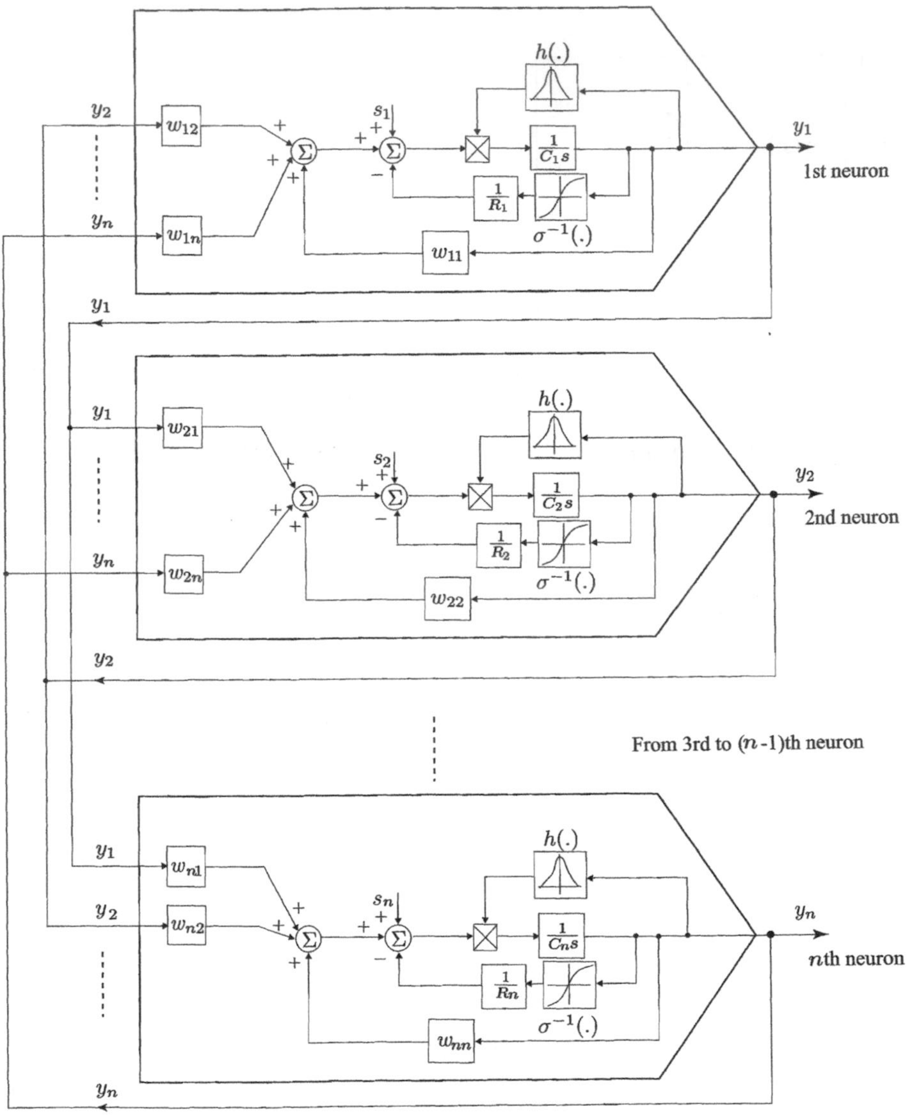

Figure 9.6 Block diagram of the output variable model of the Hopfield dynamic neural network, Eqn. (9.18).

Define

$$h_i(y_i) = \left.\frac{d\sigma_i}{dx_i}\right|_{x_i=\sigma_i^{-1}(y_i)} \tag{9.15}$$

Then Eqn. (9.14) can be rewritten as

$$\frac{dy_i}{dt} = \frac{1}{C_i} h_i(y_i(t)) \left[-\frac{1}{R_i}\sigma_i^{-1}(y_i(t)) + \sum_j^n w_{ij} y_j(t) + s_i(t) \right] \tag{9.16}$$

for $i = 1, 2, \ldots, n$. Note that, as shown in Fig. 9.5, due to the sigmoid characteristic of $\sigma_i(y_i)$, the function $h_i(y_i) = d\sigma_i/dx_i$ satisfies

$$h_i(y_i) > 0, \qquad y_i \in (-1, 1) \tag{9.17}$$

Hence, the Hopfield dynamic neural networks can be written using the output variable $y_i(t)$ as

$$C_i \frac{dy_i(t)}{dt} = h_i(y_i(t)) \left[-\frac{1}{R_i}\sigma^{-1}(y_i(t)) + \sum_{j=1}^n w_{ij} y_j(t) + s_i(t) \right] \tag{9.18}$$

This output variable model of the Hopfield DNN shown in Fig. 9.6 has the same equilibrium points as the original state space model of the Hopfield DNN defined in Eqns. (9.12) and (9.13).

9.2.3 State Stability of Hopfield DNN

The Hopfield dynamic neural network (DNN) is a nonlinear dynamic system that has the potential for exhibiting a wide range of complex behaviors. Depending on how the network parameters are chosen, the systems behavior may be stable, oscillatory, or even chaotic. In fact, most applications of the Hopfield DNN require that the network be a stable system with multiple asymptotically stable equilibrium points. In this section, we will study the stability behavior of its equilibrium points.

Consider an energy function E defined as

$$E = -\frac{1}{2}\sum_{i=1}^n \sum_{j=1}^n w_{ij} y_i y_j + \sum_{i=1}^n \frac{1}{R_i} \int_0^{y_i} h_i(y)\sigma^{-1}(y)dy - \sum_{i=1}^n s_i y_i \tag{9.19}$$

which is also referred to as the *computational energy* function of the system by Hopfield (1984), and describes the macroscopic characteristic of the network behavior. It is easy to verify that for a symmetric weight matrix $\boldsymbol{W}$

$$\begin{aligned}\frac{\partial E}{\partial y_i} &= -\sum_{j=1}^{n} w_{ij}y_j + h_i(y_i)\sigma_i^{-1}(y_i) - s_i \\ &= -C_i\frac{dx_i}{dt}\end{aligned} \tag{9.20}$$

Hence, the time derivative of the computational energy function E is

$$\begin{aligned}\frac{dE}{dt} &= \sum_{i=1}^{n} \frac{\partial E}{\partial y_i}\frac{dy_i}{dt} \\ &= -\sum_{i=1}^{n} C_i\left(\frac{dx_i}{dt}\right)\left(\frac{dy_i}{dt}\right) \\ &= -\sum_{i=1}^{n} C_i\sigma'(x_i)\left(\frac{dx_i}{dt}\right)^2\end{aligned} \tag{9.21}$$

Since $y_i = \sigma(x_i)$, a substitution for (dx_i/dt) in Eqn. (9.21) yields

$$\frac{dE}{dt} = -\sum_{i=1}^{n} C_i(\sigma_i^{-1}(y_i))'\left(\frac{dy_i}{dt}\right)^2 \tag{9.22}$$

Since $\sigma_i(y_i)$ is a monotonically increasing function, its derivative is positive-definite and so is C_i. Hence, each term on the right-hand side of Eqns. (9.21) and (9.22) is nonnegative. Therefore

$$\frac{dE}{dt} \leq 0 \tag{9.23}$$

and

$$\frac{dE}{dt} = 0 \longrightarrow \frac{dy_i}{dt} = 0, \text{ and } \frac{dx_i}{dt} = 0 \text{ for all } i \tag{9.24}$$

This means that the dynamic neural system moves from any initial point in the state space in the direction that decreases its energy E and comes to a stop at one of the many local minima of the energy function. Hence, E is a Lyapunov function for the system. Because of the existence of the multiple equilibrium points in the system, the energy function E converges to the nearest stable equilibrium point from the initial starting position, as will be seen in the later discussions.

Equations (9.20) and (9.22) indicate that the convergence of the neural state of the continuous deterministic Hopfield model to its stable equilibrium points is based on the existence of an energy function that directs the flows in state space. Such a function can be constructed as a continuous deterministic model when the weight matrix $\boldsymbol{W}$ is symmetric. The importance of this simple symmetric system lies not only in its state convergence but also in its potential as a computing device for applications to systems such as *content-addressable memory* (CAM).

Example 9.1 Consider the Hopfield DNN described by Eqns. (9.7) and (9.10) with the following set of parameters:

$$n = 2, \; C_1 = C_2 = 1, \; R_1 = R_2 = 1$$
$$w_{11} = w_{22} = 1, \; w_{12} = w_{21} = 1.5, \; \text{and } s_1 = s_2 = 0$$

The DNN equations are, therefore, described as

$$\begin{cases} \dfrac{dx_1}{dt} & = & -x_1 + \sigma(x_1) + 1.5\sigma(x_2) \\ \\ \dfrac{dx_2}{dt} & = & -x_2 + 1.5\sigma(x_1) + \sigma(x_2) \end{cases} \tag{9.25}$$

The equilibrium points are defined as the solution of Eqn. (9.25) for $dx_1/dt = dx_2/dt = 0$:

$$\begin{cases} x_1 & = & \sigma(x_1) + 1.5\sigma(x_2) \\ \\ x_2 & = & 1.5\sigma(x_1) + \sigma(x_2) \end{cases} \tag{9.26}$$

The solution of these equations yields two stable equilibrium points

$$\begin{aligned} \boldsymbol{x}^{*1} &= [x_1^* \; x_2^*]^T = [2.4641 \;\; 2.4641]^T \\ \boldsymbol{x}^{*2} &= [x_1^* \; x_2^*]^T = [-2.4641 \;\; -2.4641]^T \end{aligned}$$

which correspond to the two minima of the energy function $E(x_1, \; x_2)$ as described in Eqn. (9.19).

There is also another solution of Eqn. (9.25) and this solution lies at the *unstable equilibrium* point

$$\boldsymbol{x}^{*3} = [0 \;\; 0]^T$$

Figure 9.7 shows the surface of the computational energy function E with two stable and one unstable equilibrium points.

Figure 9.8 demonstrates an energy contour for this two neural system showing both the stable $(\boldsymbol{x}^{*1}, \boldsymbol{x}^{*2})$ and unstable $(\boldsymbol{x}^{*3})$ equilibrium points. ■

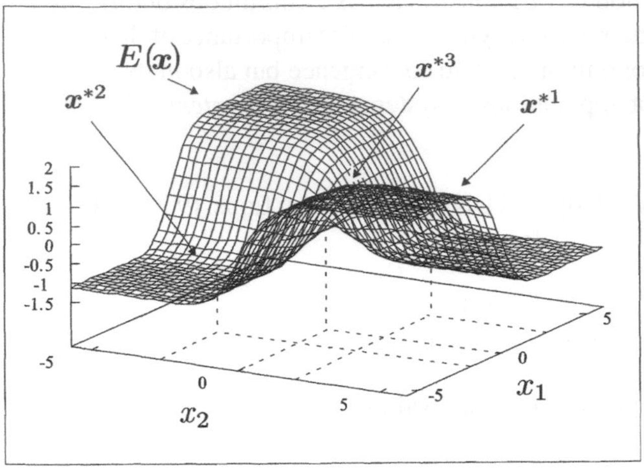

Stable equilibrium points:

$$\boldsymbol{x}^{*1} = [2.4641 \quad 2.4641]^T$$

$$\boldsymbol{x}^{*2} = [-2.4641 \quad -2.4641]^T$$

Unstable equilibrium point:

$$\boldsymbol{x}^{*3} = [0 \quad 0]^T$$

(a) Front view

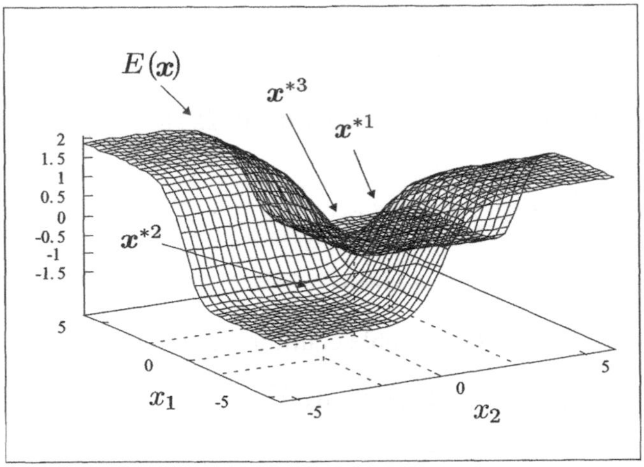

(b) Side view

Figure 9.7 Example 9.1: the surface of the computational energy function E. A two-neuron system with the parameters $C_1 = C_2 = 1$, $R_1 = R_2 = 1$, $w_{11} = w_{22} = 1.0$, $w_{12} = w_{21} = 1.5$, and $s_1 = s_2 = 0$. The system's two stable equilibrium points are at $\boldsymbol{x}^{*1} = [2.4641 \quad 2.4641]^T$ and $\boldsymbol{x}^{*2} = [-2.4641 \quad -2.4641]^T$, which correspond to the two minima of the energy function $E(x_1, x_2)$. Also, the unstable equilibrium point is at $\boldsymbol{x}^{*3} = [0 \quad 0]^T$.

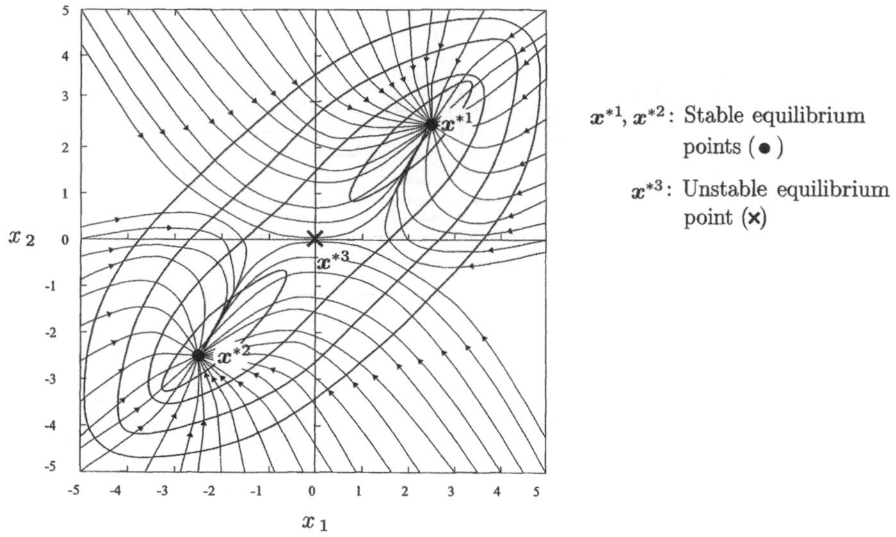

Figure 9.8 Example 9.1: an energy contour map for the two-neural system.

9.2.4 A General Form of Hopfield DNN

A general form of the Hopfield dynamic neural network can be expressed as

$$\frac{dx_i(t)}{dt} = -\alpha_i x_i(t) + \sum_{j=1}^{n} w_{ij}\sigma_j(x_j(t)) + s_i \tag{9.27}$$

or

$$\frac{dy_i(t)}{dt} = h_i(y_i(t)) \left[-\alpha_i \sigma_i^{-1}(y_i(t)) + \sum_{j=1}^{n} w_{ij} y_j(t) + s_i \right] \tag{9.28}$$

where

$$h_i(y_i) = \left. \frac{d\sigma_i}{dx_i} \right|_{x_i=\sigma_i^{-1}(y_i)}, \qquad y_i = \sigma_i(x_i)$$

and $\alpha_i > 0$ is the inverse of the time constant governing the rate of change of the ith neuron. Moreover, a vector form of the system given in Eqn. (9.27) can be expressed as

$$\frac{d\boldsymbol{x}(t)}{dt} = -\boldsymbol{A}\boldsymbol{x}(t) + \boldsymbol{W}\boldsymbol{\sigma}(\boldsymbol{x}(t)) + \boldsymbol{s} \tag{9.29}$$

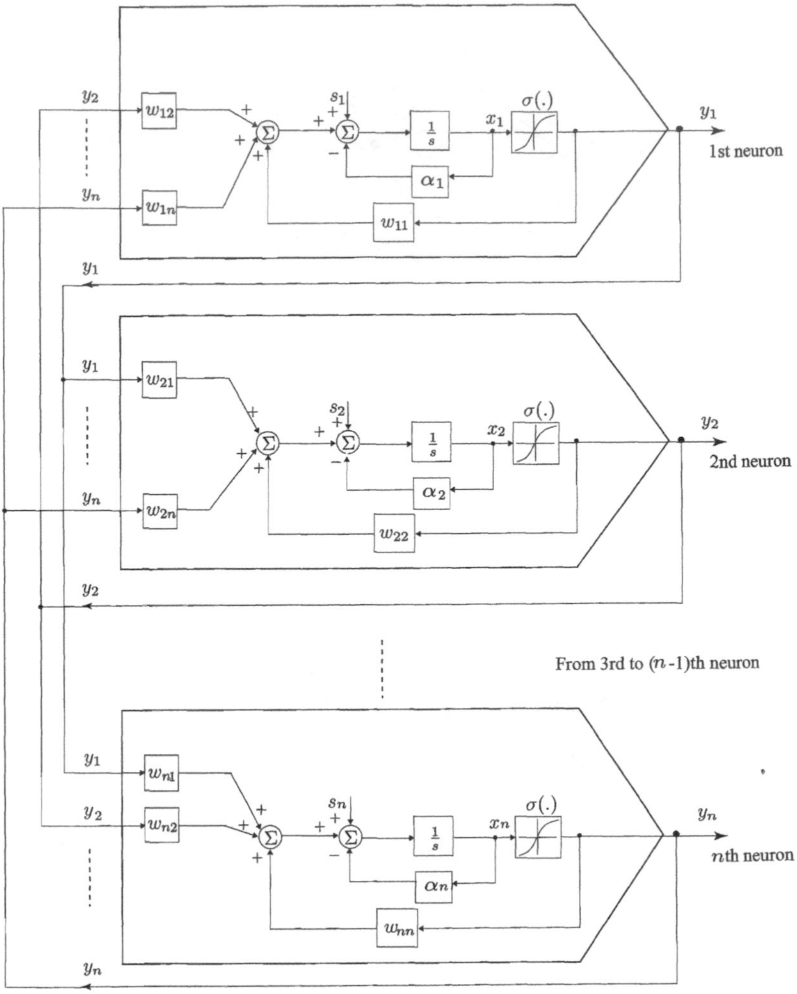

(a) A general form of the Hopfield DNN, Eqn. (9.27)

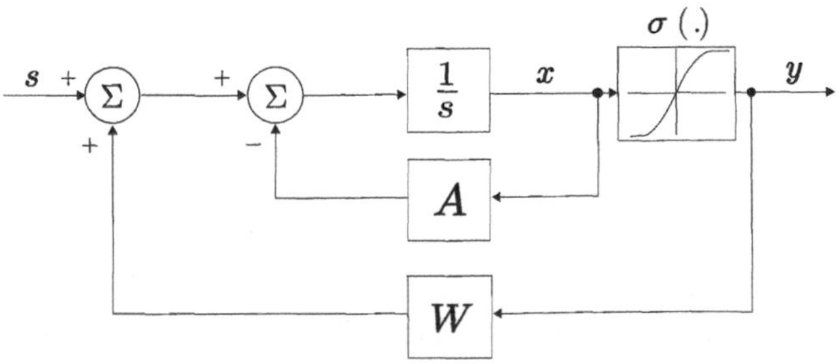

(b) Block diagram of the Hopfield DNN, Eqn. (9.29)

Figure 9.9 A general form of the Hopfield DNN.

where, $\boldsymbol{x} = [x_1 \ \cdots \ x_n]^T$ is the state vector of the network, $\boldsymbol{s} = [s_1 \ \cdots \ s_n]^T$ is the input vector, $\boldsymbol{y} = \boldsymbol{\sigma}(\boldsymbol{x}) = [\sigma_1(x_1) \ \cdots \ \sigma_n(x_n)]^T$, is the output vector, $\boldsymbol{A} = diag[\alpha_1 \ \cdots \ \alpha_n]^T$, and

$$\boldsymbol{W} = \begin{bmatrix} w_{11} & \cdots & w_{1n} \\ \vdots & \ddots & \vdots \\ w_{n1} & \cdots & w_{nn} \end{bmatrix}$$

is the synaptic weight matrix. The block diagrams of the individual neuron given in Eqn. (9.27) and the neural system given in Eqn. (9.29) are shown in Fig. 9.9.

If $\boldsymbol{W}$ is symmetric, the energy function of the system expressed in Eqn. (9.28) is defined as

$$\begin{aligned} E &= -\tfrac{1}{2}\sum_{i=1}^{n}\sum_{j=1}^{n} w_{ij}y_iy_j + \sum_{i=1}^{n}\alpha_i\int_0^{y_i}\sigma_i^{-1}(y)dy - \sum_{i=1}^{n}s_iy_i \\ &= -\tfrac{1}{2}\boldsymbol{y}^TW\boldsymbol{y} - \boldsymbol{y}^T\boldsymbol{s} + \sum_{i=1}^{n}\alpha_i\int_0^{\boldsymbol{y}}\sigma_i^{-1}(\boldsymbol{y})d\boldsymbol{y} \end{aligned} \quad (9.30)$$

9.3 HOPFIELD DYNAMIC NEURAL NETWORKS (DNNs) AS GRADIENT-LIKE SYSTEMS

The state stability of the Hopfield DNN may also be referred to as the convergence to its equilibrium points. This topic is explored in more detail by using the energy function method in this section.

The continuous-time Hopfield dynamic neural network discussed in Section 9.2 was represented by

$$\left.\begin{aligned} C_i\frac{dx_i(t)}{dt} &= -\frac{x_i(t)}{R_i} + \sum_{j=1}^{n} w_{ij}y_i(t) + s_i, \\ y_i &= \sigma_i(x_i(t)) \end{aligned}\right\} \quad (9.31)$$

where s_i are the constant inputs, $R_i > 0$ and $C_i > 0$, and $w_{ij} = w_{ji}$ satisfies the symmetric condition. In matrix form, this system can be rewritten as

$$\boldsymbol{C}\frac{d\boldsymbol{x}(t)}{dt} = -\boldsymbol{R}^{-1}\boldsymbol{x}(t) + \boldsymbol{W}\boldsymbol{y}(t) + \boldsymbol{s} \quad (9.32)$$

$$\boldsymbol{y}(t) = \boldsymbol{\sigma}(\boldsymbol{x}(t)) \quad (9.33)$$

where $\boldsymbol{C} = diag[C_1, \ \ldots, \ C_n]$, and $\boldsymbol{R}^{-1} = diag[1/R_1, \ \ldots, \ 1/R_n]$. Also, as in Eqn. (9.16) using the output y_i as the state variables, Eqn. (9.31) can be rewritten as

$$\frac{dy_i(t)}{dt} = \frac{1}{C_i}h_i(y_i(t))\left[-\frac{1}{R_i}\sigma_i^{-1}(y_i(t)) + \sum_{j=1}^{n} w_{ij}y_j(t) + s_i\right] \tag{9.34}$$

or in matrix form as

$$\frac{d\boldsymbol{y}(t)}{dt} = \boldsymbol{C}^{-1}\boldsymbol{h}(\boldsymbol{y}(t))\left[-\boldsymbol{R}^{-1}\boldsymbol{\sigma}^{-1}(\boldsymbol{y}(t)) + \boldsymbol{W}\boldsymbol{y}(t) + \boldsymbol{s}\right] \tag{9.35}$$

where the function $\sigma_i^{-1}(y_i)$ is the inverse of the sigmoid function and

$$h_i(x_i) = \left.\frac{d\sigma_i}{dx_i}\right|_{x_i=\sigma_i^{-1}(y_i)} > 0, \qquad \forall y_i \in (-1, 1) \tag{9.36}$$

It is seen that the range of the state $\boldsymbol{y}$ in Eqn. (9.35) is an n-dimensional hypercube

$$H = \{\boldsymbol{y} \in \Re^n : -1 < y_I < 1\} = (-1, 1)^n$$

The computational energy function $E(\boldsymbol{y})$ for this neural network may be written as

$$E(\boldsymbol{y}) = -\frac{1}{2}\sum_{i=1}^{n}\sum_{j=1}^{n} w_{ij}y_iy_j + \sum_{i=1}^{n}\frac{1}{R_i}\int_0^{y_i}\sigma_i^{-1}(s)ds - \sum_{i=1}^{n} s_iy_i \tag{9.37}$$

or in vector form as

$$E(\boldsymbol{y}) = -\tfrac{1}{2}\boldsymbol{y}^T\boldsymbol{W}\boldsymbol{y} - \boldsymbol{s}^T\boldsymbol{y} + \hat{\boldsymbol{R}}^T\hat{\boldsymbol{\sigma}}(\boldsymbol{y}) \tag{9.38}$$

where $\hat{\boldsymbol{R}} = [R_1^{-1} \cdots R_n^{-1}]^T$ and $\hat{\boldsymbol{\sigma}}(\boldsymbol{y}) = [\int_0^{y_1}\sigma_1^{-1}(s)ds \cdots \int_0^{y_n}\sigma_n^{-1}(s)ds]^T$. This function is continuously differentiable, but not positive-definite. From the symmetric property, it is easy to verify that

$$\frac{\partial E(\boldsymbol{y})}{\partial \boldsymbol{y}} \equiv \nabla E(\boldsymbol{y}) = -\boldsymbol{R}^{-1}\boldsymbol{\sigma}^{-1}(\boldsymbol{y}) + \boldsymbol{W}\boldsymbol{y} + \boldsymbol{s} \tag{9.39}$$

Hence, the dynamic equation of the Hopfield neural network can also be expressed in the form of the energy function as

$$\boldsymbol{C}\frac{d\boldsymbol{x}(t)}{dt} = -\nabla E(\boldsymbol{y}(t)) \tag{9.40}$$

$$\boldsymbol{y}(t) = \boldsymbol{\sigma}(\boldsymbol{x}(t)) \tag{9.41}$$

or

$$C\frac{d\boldsymbol{y}(t)}{dt} = \hat{\boldsymbol{h}}(\boldsymbol{y}(t))\nabla E(\boldsymbol{y}(t)) \tag{9.42}$$

where, $\hat{\boldsymbol{h}}(\boldsymbol{y}) = diag[h_1(y_1), \ldots, h_n(y_n)]$ is a positive-definite and invertible matrix. Equation (9.42) describes a *gradient-like system* (Hirsch and Smale 1974). Some basic properties of the system in Eqn. (9.42) are now discussed.

Theorem 9.1 *$dE(\boldsymbol{y})/dt \leq 0$ for any $\boldsymbol{y} \in H^n$, and $dE(\boldsymbol{y})/dt = 0$ if and only if $\boldsymbol{y}$ is an equilibrium point of Eqn. (9.40). Thus, the set of critical points of $E(\boldsymbol{y})$ is identical to the set of equilibrium points of the system in Eqn. (9.31).*

Proof: The derivative of $E(\boldsymbol{y})$ along the trajectories of the system is given by

$$\begin{aligned} \frac{dE(\boldsymbol{y})}{dt} &= \frac{\partial E(\boldsymbol{y})}{\partial \boldsymbol{y}}\frac{d\boldsymbol{y}}{dt} \\ &= < \nabla E(\boldsymbol{y}), -C^{-1}\hat{\boldsymbol{h}}(\boldsymbol{y})\nabla E(\boldsymbol{y}) > \\ &= -(\nabla E(\boldsymbol{y}))^T[C^{-1}\hat{\boldsymbol{h}}(\boldsymbol{y})]\nabla E(\boldsymbol{y}) \\ &= -\sum_{i=1}^{n}\frac{1}{C_i}h_i(y_i)\left(\frac{\partial E(\boldsymbol{y})}{\partial y_i}\right)^2 \leq 0 \end{aligned} \tag{9.43}$$

where $C^{-1}\hat{\boldsymbol{h}}(\boldsymbol{y}) > 0$ by assumption. Furthermore,

$$\frac{dE(\boldsymbol{y})}{dt} = 0 \Longleftrightarrow \nabla E(y) = 0 \Longleftrightarrow \frac{dy}{dt} = 0$$

Hence, $dE(\boldsymbol{y})/dt = 0$ only at the equilibrium points. ■

Theorem 9.2 *Let $\boldsymbol{y}^*$ be an isolated local minimum of $E(\boldsymbol{y})$. Then $\boldsymbol{y}^*$ is a locally asymptotically stable equilibrium point of the system in Eqn. (9.32).*

Proof: For the isolated local minimum $\boldsymbol{y}^*$, one may define a function

$$V(\boldsymbol{y}) = E(\boldsymbol{y}) - E(\boldsymbol{y}^*)$$

for $\forall \boldsymbol{y} \in \Omega \equiv \{\boldsymbol{y} : ||\boldsymbol{y} - \boldsymbol{y}^*|| < \delta, \text{ for } 0 < \delta \leq 1\}$. Then, the expansion about the equilibrium point $\boldsymbol{y}^*$ yields

$$\begin{aligned} V(\boldsymbol{y}) &= V(\boldsymbol{y}^*) + \left\langle \frac{\partial V(\boldsymbol{y}^*)}{\partial \boldsymbol{y}}, (\boldsymbol{y} - \boldsymbol{y}^*) \right\rangle \\ &= (\boldsymbol{y} - \boldsymbol{y}^*)^T \frac{\partial^2 V(\boldsymbol{y})}{\partial \boldsymbol{y}^2}(\boldsymbol{y} - \boldsymbol{y}^*) + O(||\boldsymbol{y} - \boldsymbol{y}^*||^3) \end{aligned}$$

Since for the isolated local minimum $\boldsymbol{y}^*$

$$\frac{\partial V(\boldsymbol{y}^*)}{\partial \boldsymbol{y}} = \frac{\partial E(\boldsymbol{y}^*)}{\partial \boldsymbol{y}} = 0$$

and

$$\frac{\partial^2 V(\boldsymbol{y}^*)}{\partial \boldsymbol{y}^2} = \frac{\partial^2 E(\boldsymbol{y}^*)}{\partial \boldsymbol{y}^2} > 0$$

Hence

$$V(\boldsymbol{y}) > 0, \quad \text{for} \quad \boldsymbol{y} \in \Omega \quad \text{and} \quad \boldsymbol{y} \neq \boldsymbol{y}^*$$

Therefore, $V(\boldsymbol{y})$ is a Lyapunov function of the system in Eqn. (9.32), and this proves the theorem. ∎

Theorem 9.3 *The eigenvalues of the Jacobian of the system in Eqn. (9.32) are real.*

Proof: Note that

$$-\nabla^2 E(\boldsymbol{y}) \equiv -\left[\frac{\partial^2 E(\boldsymbol{y})}{\partial y_i \partial y_j}\right]$$

is symmetric. ∎

Theorem 9.4 *All trajectories of the Hopfield dynamic neural network in Eqn. (9.32) converge to one of the equilibrium points.*

Proof: Consider a globally positive-definite function

$$V(\boldsymbol{x}) = \tfrac{1}{2}\boldsymbol{x}^T \boldsymbol{R}\boldsymbol{C}\boldsymbol{x} \tag{9.44}$$

where $\boldsymbol{RC} = diag[R_1C_1, \ldots, R_nC_n]$ is a diagonal positive definite matrix. Then, along the trajectories we have

$$\begin{aligned}
\frac{dV(\boldsymbol{x})}{dt} &= \boldsymbol{x}^T \boldsymbol{RC}\dot{\boldsymbol{x}} \\
&= \boldsymbol{x}^T \boldsymbol{R}(-\boldsymbol{R}^{-1}\boldsymbol{x} + \boldsymbol{W}\boldsymbol{y} + \boldsymbol{s}) \\
&= -\boldsymbol{x}^T\boldsymbol{x} + \boldsymbol{x}^T\boldsymbol{R}(\boldsymbol{W}\boldsymbol{y} + \boldsymbol{s}) \\
&\leq -\boldsymbol{x}^T\boldsymbol{x} + |\boldsymbol{x}^T\boldsymbol{R}(\boldsymbol{W}\boldsymbol{y} + \boldsymbol{s})| \\
&\leq -||\boldsymbol{x}||_2^2 + ||\boldsymbol{x}||_2||\boldsymbol{R}||_2(||\boldsymbol{W}||_2||\boldsymbol{y}||_2 + ||\boldsymbol{s}||_2) \\
&= -||\boldsymbol{x}||_2\left[||\boldsymbol{x}||_2 - ||\boldsymbol{R}||_2\left(||\boldsymbol{W}||_2||\boldsymbol{y}||_2 + ||\boldsymbol{s}||_2\right)\right] \\
&< 0
\end{aligned} \tag{9.45}$$

for all $\boldsymbol{x} \in \bar{\Omega} = \{\boldsymbol{x} : ||\boldsymbol{x}||_2 \leq ||\boldsymbol{R}||_2(||\boldsymbol{W}||_2||\boldsymbol{y}||_2 + ||\boldsymbol{s}||_2)\}$. Consequently, all solutions must converge to the closed set $\bar{\Omega}$. Additionally, using the results given in Theorem 9.1, all the equilibrium points of the Hopfield dynamic neural network in Eqn. (9.53) must be inside the set $\bar{\Omega}$. Since $\bar{\Omega}$ consists of isolated equilibrium points, it can be shown that a trajectory approaching $\bar{\Omega}$ must approach one of these equilibrium points. Thus, for all the possible initial conditions, the trajectory of the system will always converge to one of the equilibrium points. This ensures that the system will not oscillate. ■

It is to be noted that the proof of Theorem 9.4 is independent of the symmetry of the synaptic weight matrix $\boldsymbol{W}$; it can be applied for any weight matrix $\boldsymbol{W}$. Thus, the conclusions drawn from Theorem 9.4 are beyond the results derived by Khalil (1992) using LaSalle's well-known theorem.

In the following example, we will show that even if the trajectories of a Hopfield dynamic neural network always converge to the equilibrium points for all the possible initial conditions, the system may still contain isolated local unstable equilibrium points. In other words, the trajectories will converge only to the asymptotically stable equilibrium points.

Example 9.2 Consider a DNN with two-neurons without the self-feedback connections described by

$$\begin{cases} \dfrac{dx_1(t)}{dt} = -x_1(t) + w_{12}\tanh(x_2(t)) + s_1 \\ \\ \dfrac{dx_2(t)}{dt} = -x_2(t) + w_{21}\tanh(x_1(t)) + s_2 \end{cases} \tag{9.46}$$

The Jacobian of the system in Eqn. (9.46) is given by

$$J(\boldsymbol{x}) = \begin{bmatrix} -1 & w_{12}\text{sech}^2(x_2) \\ \\ w_{21}\text{sech}^2(x_1) & -1 \end{bmatrix}$$

The eigenvalues of $J(\boldsymbol{x})$ are

$$\lambda_{1,2}(\boldsymbol{x}) = \begin{cases} -1 + \text{sech}(x_1)\text{sech}(x_2)\sqrt{w_{12}w_{21}} \\ \\ -1 - \text{sech}(x_1)\text{sech}(x_2)\sqrt{w_{12}w_{21}} \end{cases}$$

Obviously, if the weight w_{12} has the opposite sign to that of the weight w_{21}, the system eigenvalues are complex conjugate with negative real parts, and the system in Eqn. (9.46) has a unique global asymptotically stable equilibrium point. Otherwise, the system may have unstable equilibrium points.

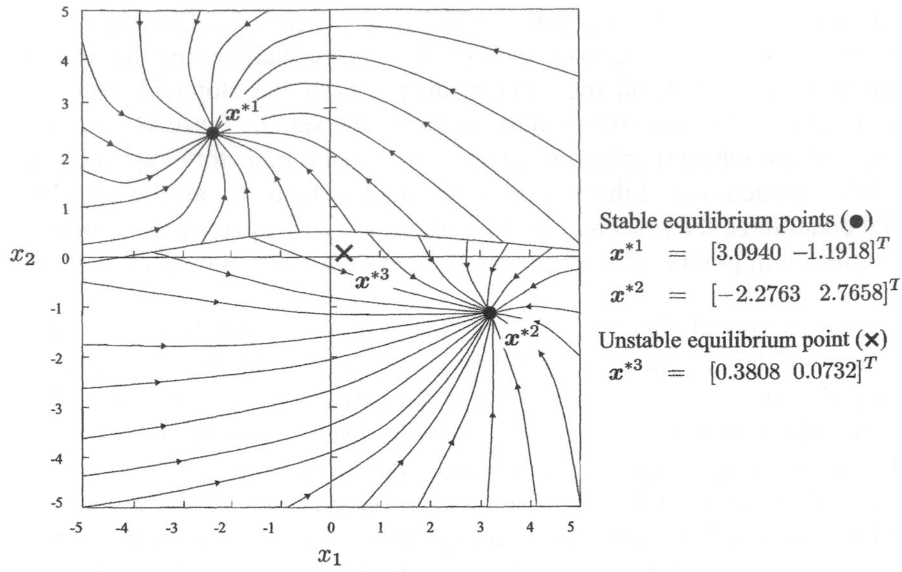

Figure 9.10 Example 9.2: phase plane diagram of the neural system in Eqn. (9.46). $w_{12} = -3$, $w_{21} = -2$, and $s_1 = 0.6$, $s_2 = 0.8$, where the equilibrium points $\boldsymbol{x}^{*1} = [3.0940 \quad -1.1918]^T$ and $\boldsymbol{x}^{*2} = [-2.2763 \quad 2.7658]^T$ are locally stable, and the equilibrium point $\boldsymbol{x}^{*3} = [0.3808 \quad 0.0732]^T$ is unstable.

For example, if $w_{12} = -3.0$, $w_{21} = -2.0$, and $s_1 = 0.6$, $s_2 = 0.8$, the system in Eqn. (9.46) has three equilibrium points $\boldsymbol{x}^{*1} = [3.0940 \quad -1.19179]^T$, $\boldsymbol{x}^{*2} = [-2.3763 \quad 2.7658]^T$, and $\boldsymbol{x}^{*3} = [0.3808 \; 0.0732]^T$. Then the eigenvalues of the Jacobian $J(\boldsymbol{x})$ at the equilibrium points $\boldsymbol{x}^{*1}$, $\boldsymbol{x}^{*2}$ and $\boldsymbol{x}^{*3}$ are respectively,

$$\lambda_{1,2}(\boldsymbol{x}^{*1}) = \begin{cases} -0.8769 \\ -1.1232 \end{cases}$$

$$\lambda_{1,2}(\boldsymbol{x}^{*2}) = \begin{cases} -1.0566 \\ -0.9434 \end{cases}$$

$$\lambda_{1,2}(\boldsymbol{x}^{*3}) = \begin{cases} 1.2759 \\ -3.2759 \end{cases}$$

Hence, using the Lyapunov's first method (Khalil 1992), we find that the equilibrium points $\boldsymbol{x}^{*1}$ and $\boldsymbol{x}^{*2}$ are only locally stable, not globally stable, and $\boldsymbol{x}^{*3}$ is unstable. This fact is shown in the phase plane diagram of the system in Eqn. (9.46), given in Fig. 9.10. ■

9.4 MODIFICATIONS OF HOPFIELD DYNAMIC NEURAL NETWORKS

9.4.1 Hopfield Dynamic Neural Networks with Triangular Weighting Matrix

The symmetric connection weighting matrix assumption in the Hopfield dynamic neural network is useful from a design viewpoint, especially for problems that can be described in terms of the minimization of a quadratic function. Nevertheless, the existence of many equilibrium points for the energy function E implies that, in general, a global asymptotically stable equilibrium point that corresponds to a global minimum of the energy function E is not guaranteed; that is, the network will compute the local stable equilibrium states that are associated with the local minima of the energy function E. It follows, then, that the Hopfield dynamic neural network has many equilibrium points and, thus, it has the potential capability for implementing neural associative memories. Some applications demand that the network computing have a globally optimal solution. For example, in the neuron-based analog-to-digital (A/D) converter proposed by Hopfield and Tank (1986), the existence of many equilibrium points for E requires in a practical implementation the use of separate electronics to impose zero initial conditions before each conversion. Essentially, this is due to the fact that for nonzero initial conditions, the network may stop in a *spurious state*; that is, at an equilibrium point that corresponds to a locally optimal solution and does not correspond to the correct digital representation of the analog input signal.

To guarantee the uniqueness of the equilibrium point in the Hopfield dynamic neural network, the simplest structure is described by a strict lower (upper) triangular weighting matrix, as will be seen in the following discussion.

Consider a trivial network structure where the weighting matrix is strictly a lower triangular matrix with $w_{ij} = 0$, for all $j \geq i$:

$$\boldsymbol{W} = \begin{bmatrix} 0 & 0 & 0 & \cdots & 0 & 0 \\ w_{21} & 0 & 0 & \cdots & 0 & 0 \\ w_{31} & w_{32} & 0 & \cdots & 0 & 0 \\ \vdots & \vdots & \vdots & \ddots & \vdots & \vdots \\ w_{n1} & w_{n2} & w_{n3} & \cdots & w_{n,n-1} & 0 \end{bmatrix} \tag{9.47}$$

In this case, the neural network contains interlayer connections as shown in Figs. 9.11 and 9.12.

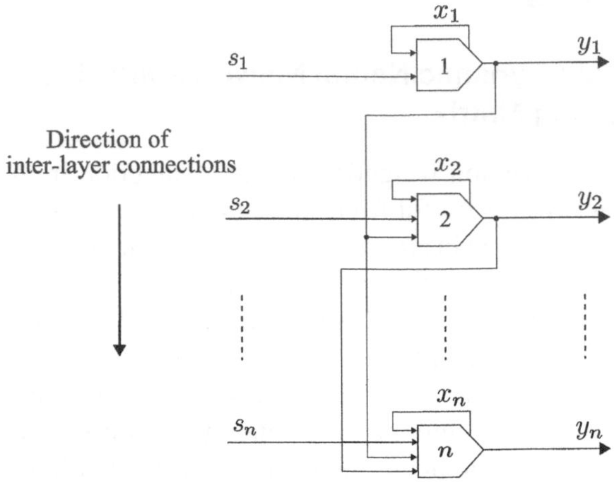

Figure 9.11 Hopfield dynamic neural network with a lower triangular weighting matrix, Eqn. (9.47).

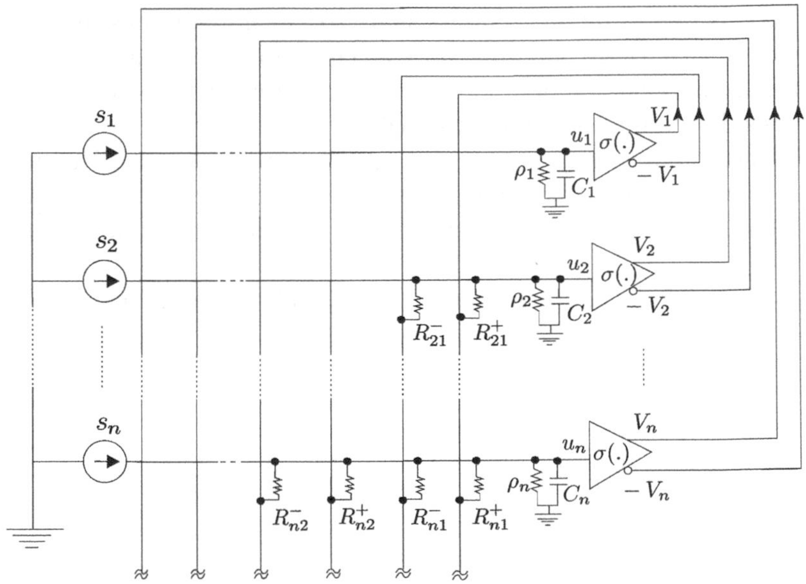

Figure 9.12 Circuit representation of the continuous-time Hopfield dynamic neural network with a lower triangular connection weighting matrix.

Using the lower triangular weighting matrix, the dynamic neural networks equations can be expressed as

$$\left.\begin{aligned}\frac{dx_1(t)}{dt} &= -\alpha_1 x_1(t) + s_1\\ \frac{dx_2(t)}{dt} &= -\alpha_2 x_2(t) + w_{21}\sigma_1(x_1(t)) + s_2\\ &\vdots\\ \frac{dx_n(t)}{dt} &= -\alpha_n x_n(t) + w_{n1}\sigma_1(x_1(t)) + w_{n,n-1}\sigma_{n-1}(x_{n-1}(t)) + s_n\end{aligned}\right\} \tag{9.48}$$

or

$$\left.\begin{aligned}\frac{dx_1(t)}{dt} &= -\alpha_1 x_1(t) + s_1\\ \frac{dx_i(t)}{dt} &= -\alpha_i x_i(t) + \sum_{j=1}^{i-1} w_{ij}\sigma_j(x_j(t)) + s_i, \quad i = 2, \ldots, n\end{aligned}\right\} \tag{9.49}$$

The equilibrium equations of the dynamic neural network are defined by

$$\frac{dx_i}{dt} = 0, \qquad i = 2, \ldots, n$$

that is

$$\left.\begin{aligned}&-\alpha_1 x_1^* + s_1 = 0\\ \text{and}\quad &-\alpha_i x_i^* + \sum_{j=1}^{i-1} w_{ij}\sigma_j(x_j^*) + s_i = 0, \quad i = 2, \ldots, n\end{aligned}\right\} \tag{9.50}$$

The analytic solution of the steady state of this system is given by

$$\left.\begin{aligned}x_1^* &= \frac{s_1}{\alpha_1}\\ x_i^* &= \frac{1}{\alpha_i}\left[\sum_{j=1}^{i-1} w_{ij}\sigma_j(x_j^*) + s_i\right], \quad i = 2, \ldots, n\end{aligned}\right\} \tag{9.51}$$

Furthermore, the general solution of the DNN system in Eqn. (9.49) for an arbitrary initial condition $x_i(0)$ is derived as

$$\begin{aligned}x_1(t) &= x_1(0)e^{-\alpha_1 t} + \int_0^t e^{-\alpha_1(t-\tau)} s_1 d\tau\\ &= \left(x_1(0) - \frac{s_1}{\alpha_1}\right) e^{-\alpha_1 t} + \frac{s_1}{\alpha_1}\end{aligned}$$

and

$$\begin{aligned} x_i(t) &= x_i(0)e^{-\alpha_i t} + \int_0^t e^{-\alpha_i(t-\tau)}\left(\sum_{j=1}^{i-1} w_{ij}\sigma_j(x_j(\tau)) + s_j\right)d\tau \\ &= \left(x_i(0) - \frac{s_i}{\alpha_i}\right)e^{-\alpha_i t} + \frac{s_i}{\alpha_i} + e^{-\alpha_i \tau}\int_0^t e^{\alpha_i \tau}\sum_{j=1}^{i-1} w_{ij}\sigma_j(x_j(\tau))d\tau \\ & \quad i = 2, \ldots, n \end{aligned} \tag{9.52}$$

It is easy to verify that

$$\begin{aligned} \lim_{t\to\infty} e^{-\alpha_i \tau}\int_0^t e^{\alpha_i \tau}\sum_{j=1}^{i-1} w_{ij}\sigma_j(x_j(\tau))d\tau &= \lim_{t\to\infty}\frac{1}{\alpha_i}\sum_{j=1}^{i-1} w_{ij}\sigma_j(x_j(t)) \\ &= \frac{1}{\alpha_i}\sum_{j=1}^{i-1} w_{ij}\sigma_j(x_{ej}) \end{aligned} \tag{9.53}$$

Therefore

$$\lim_{t\to\infty} x_i(t) = x_{ei}, \qquad i = 1, 2, \ldots, n$$

This implies that this type of Hopfield dynamic neural network has a unique asymptotic stable equilibrium state $\boldsymbol{x}_e$ for any arbitrary inputs $\boldsymbol{s}$. The same result can be obtained for the Hopfield DNN with a strict upper triangular weighting matrix.

9.4.2 Hopfield Dynamic Neural Network with Infinite Gain (Hard Threshold Switch)

The Hopfield dynamic neural network represented by the system of equations

$$\boldsymbol{C}\frac{d\boldsymbol{x}(t)}{dt} = -\boldsymbol{R}^{-1}\boldsymbol{x}(t) + \boldsymbol{W}\boldsymbol{\sigma}(\boldsymbol{x}(t)) + \boldsymbol{s} \tag{9.54}$$

can be realized by electronic circuits in which each nonlinear activation $\sigma(.)$ is implemented by a nonlinear operational amplifier with an input voltage x_i, output voltage $y_i = \sigma(x_i)$, and gain λ. In practice, λ is a very large positive number. It is of interest to know what happens when λ becomes arbitrarily large. In this case, the nonlinear amplifiers may be viewed as hard threshold switches. For instance, let $\sigma(x_i) = \tanh(\lambda x_i)$. Then

$$\sigma(x_i) = \lim_{\lambda\to\infty}\tanh(\lambda x_i) = \begin{cases} 1, & \text{if } x_i > 0 \\ -1, & \text{if } x_i < 0 \end{cases} \tag{9.55}$$

and

$$\begin{cases} \lim_{x_i \to 0+} \lim_{\lambda \to \infty} \tanh(\lambda x_i) &= 1 \\ \\ \lim_{x_i \to 0-} \lim_{\lambda \to \infty} \tanh(\lambda x_i) &= -1 \end{cases} \tag{9.56}$$

Hence, for a sufficiently large enough gain λ, the sigmoidal function $\sigma(.)$ becomes discontinuous and can be replaced using the $sgn(.)$ function defined by

$$sgn(x_i) = \begin{cases} 1, & \text{if } x_i > 0 \\ -1, & \text{if } x_i < 0 \\ \text{undefined}, & \text{if } x_i = 0 \end{cases} \tag{9.57}$$

To understand the dynamic behavior of the neural network with this type of activation function, we need to study an ideal mathematical model described by the equation

$$\boldsymbol{C}\frac{d\boldsymbol{x}(t)}{dt} = -\boldsymbol{R}^{-1}\boldsymbol{x}(t) + \boldsymbol{W}\,\boldsymbol{sgn}(\boldsymbol{x}(t)) + \boldsymbol{s} \tag{9.58}$$

where $\boldsymbol{sgn}(\boldsymbol{x}) = [sgn(x_1) \ \cdots \ sgn(x_n)]^T$.

9.4.3 Some Restrictions on the Internal Neural States of the Hopfield DNN

The Hopfield dynamic neural network discussed in the previous section is a continuous-time analog information processor in which the internal states may lie in a large range as a function of the variable parameters. However, the external behavior described by the neural outputs are bounded because of the characteristics of the sigmoidal activation function. The advantage of this model lies in its capabilities for dealing with temporal information processing and steady-state memory problems even if there are some difficulties associated with the analysis and electronic implementation, as will be seen in the following discussion.

(i) In the electronic implementation of Eqn. (9.58), since the internal state variable $\boldsymbol{x} = [x_1 \ x_2 \ \cdots \ x_n]^T$ of the network varies in $\Re^n$, x_i $(1 \leq i \leq n)$ may assume very large values, and scaling may pose problems in implementation. Furthermore, whenever the value of R_{ij} is altered to adjust the corresponding value of w_{ij} in Eqn. (9.54), the value of R_i also changes;

(ii) Because of the complicated nonlinearity of the sigmoidal function, the analysis and determination of the equilibrium points from the equilibrium equations

$$-\frac{x_i}{R_i} + \sum_{j=1}^{n} w_{ij}\sigma_i(x_j) + s_i = 0, \quad i = 1, \ldots, n$$

are difficult and, hence, it is difficult to check the performance of the system;

(iii) The integrator term involved in the energy function

$$E = -\frac{1}{2} \sum_{i=1,j=1}^{n} w_{ij} y_i y_j + \sum_{i=1}^{n} \frac{1}{R_i} \int_{0}^{y_i} \sigma_i^{-1}(y) dy - \sum_{i=1}^{n} s_i y_i$$

may cause some difficulties in the synthesis procedure of the system.

To overcome such drawbacks, some modified versions of the Hopfield dynamic neural network have been proposed. We now present two modified versions.

9.4.4 Dynamic Neural Network with Saturation (DNN-S)

A simple modification for the Hopfield dynamic neural network, as introduced by Li et al. (1989), is to restrict the internal state of the network in a closed hypercube. This modified version of DNN is given by

$$C_i \frac{dx_i(t)}{dt} = -\frac{x_i(t)}{R_i} + \sum_{j=1}^{n} w_{ij} x_j(t) + s_i, \quad i = 1, 2, \ldots, n$$

with the constraints

$$-1 \leq x_i \leq 1, \quad i = 1, 2, \ldots, n \tag{9.59}$$

This dynamic neural network, given in Eqn. (9.59), will be named as a dynamic neural network with saturation (DNN-S). As discussed by Li et al. (1989), the main difference between the DNN-S and the usual linear system is that the former is defined on the closed subset of $\Re^n$, while the latter is defined on the open subsets of $\Re^n$. The dynamic neural system in Eqn. (9.59) may also be expressed in the following vector form

$$\boldsymbol{C} \frac{d\boldsymbol{x}(t)}{dt} = \boldsymbol{R}^{-1}\boldsymbol{x}(t) + \boldsymbol{W}\boldsymbol{x}(t) + \boldsymbol{s} \tag{9.60}$$

where $\boldsymbol{x} = [x_1 \cdots x_n]^T \in [-1, 1]^n$, $\boldsymbol{C} = diag[c_1, \ldots, c_n]$, $\boldsymbol{R} = diag[r_1, \ldots, r_n]$, $\boldsymbol{W} = [w_{ij}]_{n \times n}$, and $\boldsymbol{s} = [s_1 \cdots s_n]^T$. An energy function for the above system may be defined as

$$
\begin{aligned}
E &= -\tfrac{1}{2} \sum_{j=1,i=1}^{n} w_{ij} x_i x_j + \tfrac{1}{2} \sum_{i=1}^{n} \frac{1}{R_i} x_i^2 - \sum_{j=1}^{n} s_i x_i \\
&= -\tfrac{1}{2} \boldsymbol{x}^T \boldsymbol{W} \boldsymbol{x} + \tfrac{1}{2} \boldsymbol{x}^T \boldsymbol{R}^{-1} \boldsymbol{x} - \boldsymbol{s}^T \boldsymbol{x}
\end{aligned} \tag{9.61}
$$

For a symmetric weight matrix $\boldsymbol{W}$, it is easy to verify that

$$
-\frac{\partial E}{\partial \boldsymbol{x}} = \boldsymbol{C} \frac{d\boldsymbol{x}(t)}{dt} = -\boldsymbol{R}^{-1} \boldsymbol{x}(t) + \boldsymbol{W} \boldsymbol{x}(t) + \boldsymbol{s} \tag{9.62}
$$

Hence, the convergence of the dynamic neural system given in Eqn. (9.60) is ensured.

Figure 9.13 shows the block diagram of the DNN-S expressed by Eqn. (9.60). The dynamic neural system in Eqn. (9.60) can be easily implemented using the electronic circuit given in Fig. 9.14. There are n identical operational amplifiers in this circuit. Let u_i and V_i be the input and output voltages of the ith amplifier, respectively, and let $\pm V_{cc}$ denote the power supply voltage. The input–output relation of the ith operational amplifier is, therefore, given by

$$
u_i = \begin{cases} V_{cc}, & \text{if} \quad u_i > \dfrac{V_{cc}}{\lambda} \\[2ex] \lambda u_i, & \text{if} \quad -\dfrac{V_{cc}}{\lambda} \le u_i \le \dfrac{V_{cc}}{\lambda} \\[2ex] -V_{cc}, & \text{if} \quad u_i < -\dfrac{V_{cc}}{\lambda} \end{cases} \tag{9.63}
$$

where λ is the gain of the operational amplifiers. By employing a feedback capacitor C_i, the ith operational amplifier becomes an integrator. If we assign

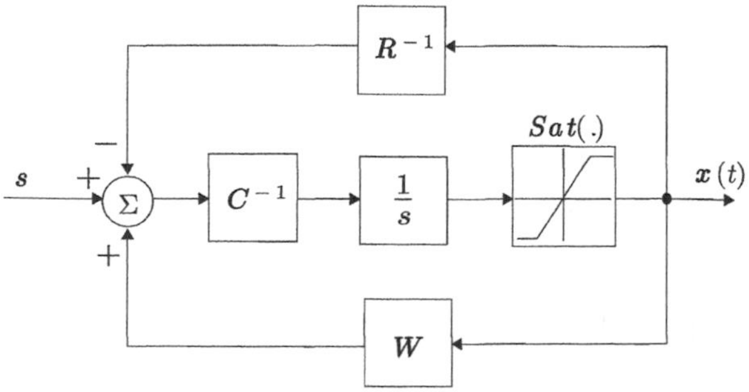

Figure 9.13 Block diagram of the dynamic neural network with saturation (DNN-S), Eqn. (9.60).

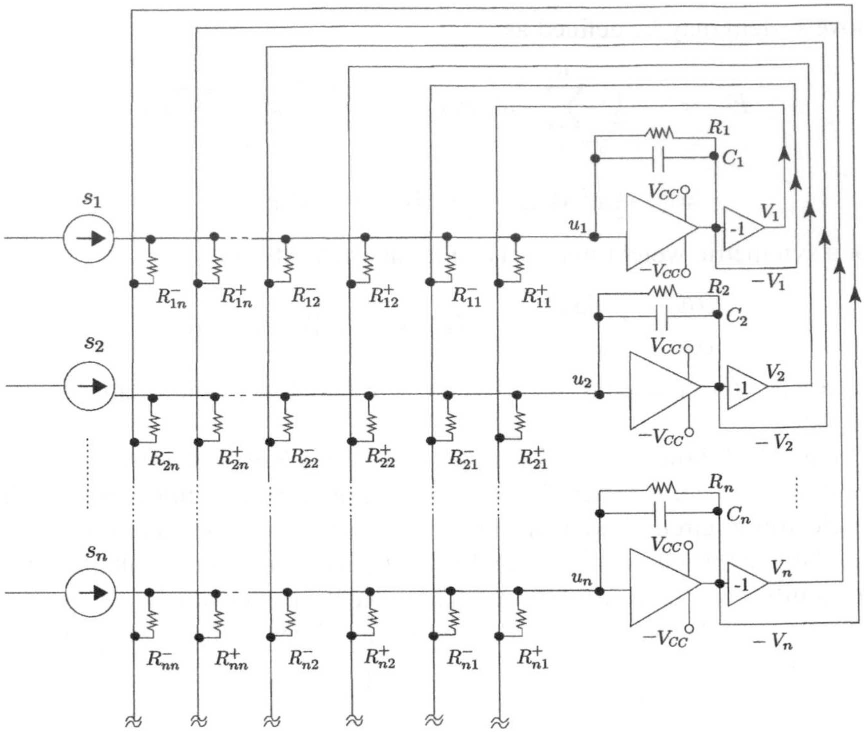

Figure 9.14 The circuit implementation of the dynamic neural network with saturation (DNN-S), Eqn. (9.60).

the values of unity to the gain λ and voltage V_{cc}, then each component V_i can vary from -1 to 1. In this case, the circuit can be described by a set of linear differential equations as

$$C_i \frac{dV_i(t)}{dt} + \frac{V_i(t)}{R_i} = \sum_{j=1}^{n} \frac{1}{R_{ij}} (\pm V_j(t)) + s_i, \quad i = 1, 2, \ldots, n \tag{9.64}$$

with the constraints

$$-1 \le V_i \le 1, \quad i = 1, 2, \ldots, n$$

Furthermore, let $\boldsymbol{x} = [V_1 \ \ldots \ V_n]^T$, $\boldsymbol{s} = [s_1 \ \ldots \ s_n]^T$, and

$$w_{ij} = \begin{cases} +\dfrac{1}{R_{ij}}, & \text{if } R_{ij} \text{ is connected to the } V_j \\ \\ -\dfrac{1}{R_{ij}}, & \text{if } R_{ij} \text{ is connected to the } -V_j \end{cases}$$

Then, Eqn. (9.64) may be transformed into the form of Eqn. (9.62). Without loss of generality, if the first term $\boldsymbol{B}^{-1}\boldsymbol{x}(t)$ in Eqn. (9.60) is absorbed in the second term $\boldsymbol{W}\boldsymbol{x}(t)$, the modified version of the DNN-S is

$$\frac{d\boldsymbol{x}(t)}{dt} = \boldsymbol{W}\boldsymbol{x}(t) + \boldsymbol{s}, \quad \boldsymbol{x} \in [-1, 1]^n \tag{9.65}$$

The system in Eqn. (9.65) may be implemented by the block diagram shown in Fig. 9.15.

An electronic implementation of the circuit may also be expressed by the equations

$$\frac{dV_i(t)}{dt} = \frac{1}{C_i}\left\{\sum_{j=1}^{n}\frac{1}{R_{ij}}(\pm V_j(t)) + s_i\right\}, \quad i = 1, 2, \ldots, n \tag{9.66}$$

with the constraints

$$-1 \leq V_i \leq 1, \quad i = 1, 2, \ldots, n$$

If, we let $C_i = 1$, $(1 \leq i \leq n)$, $\boldsymbol{x} = [V_1 \ \ldots \ V_n]^T$, $\boldsymbol{s} = [s_1 \ \ldots \ s_n]^T$, and $\boldsymbol{W} = [w_{ij}]_{n\times n}$, where $w_{ij} = 1/R_{ij}$, then Eqn. (9.66) may be written in the same form as the DNN-S in Eqn. (9.65). Also, for the DNN-S in Eqn. (9.65), the stability of the equilibrium points may be investigated by considering the energy function defined as

$$\begin{aligned} E &= -\tfrac{1}{2}\sum_{j=1,i=1}^{n} w_{ij}x_i x_j - \sum_{j=1}^{n} s_i x_i \\ &= -\tfrac{1}{2}\boldsymbol{x}^T\boldsymbol{W}\boldsymbol{x} - \boldsymbol{s}^T\boldsymbol{x}, \quad \boldsymbol{x} \in [-1, 1]^n \end{aligned} \tag{9.67}$$

Further analysis for the stability of equilibrium points can be conducted as was done before.

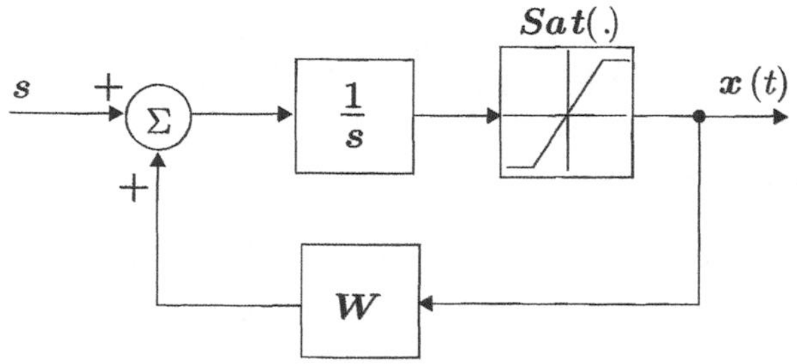

Figure 9.15 Block diagram of the modified DNN-S, Eqn. (9.65).

9.4.5 Dynamic Neural Network with Integrators

If at the output stages the nonlinear amplifiers in the Hopfield dynamic neural network are replaced using integrators with saturation, then the dynamic neural network is described by

$$\begin{aligned} C_i \frac{dx_i(t)}{dt} &= -\frac{x_i(t)}{R_i} + \sum_{j=1}^{n} w_{ij} y_j(t) + s_i \\ \frac{dy_i(t)}{dt} &= x_i(t), \quad -1 \le x_i \le 1, \quad i = 1, 2, \ldots, n \end{aligned} \tag{9.68}$$

or equivalently

$$\begin{aligned} \boldsymbol{C} \frac{d\boldsymbol{x}(t)}{dt} &= -\boldsymbol{R}^{-1}\boldsymbol{x}(t) + \boldsymbol{W}\boldsymbol{y}(t) + \boldsymbol{s} \\ \frac{d\boldsymbol{y}(t)}{dt} &= \boldsymbol{x}(t), \quad \boldsymbol{x} \in [-1, 1]^n \end{aligned} \tag{9.69}$$

Obviously, this is an integrator with decay to x_i. An additional integrator may seem meaningless, but in an analog neural network of this type the decaying term in the dynamics provides a mechanism for avoiding unnecessary local minima of the energy function of the Hopfield dynamic neural network.

For the DNN described in Eqn. (9.70), and depicted in Figs. 9.16 and 9.17, we may define the following energy function

$$\begin{aligned} E &= -\frac{1}{2} \sum_{i,j=1}^{n} w_{ij} y_i y_j + \frac{1}{2} \sum_{j=1}^{n} \frac{1}{R_j} x_j^2 + \sum_{j=1} s_j y_j \\ &= -\frac{1}{2} \sum_{i,j=1}^{n} w_{ij} y_i y_j + \frac{1}{2} \sum_{j=1}^{n} \frac{1}{R_j} \left(\frac{dy_j}{dt} \right)^2 + \sum_{j=1} s_j y_j \\ &= -\frac{1}{2} \boldsymbol{y}^T \boldsymbol{W} \boldsymbol{y} + \frac{1}{2} \left(\frac{d\boldsymbol{y}}{dt} \right)^T \boldsymbol{R}^{-1} \left(\frac{d\boldsymbol{y}}{dt} \right) + \boldsymbol{s}^T \boldsymbol{y} \end{aligned} \tag{9.70}$$

The time derivative of E is

$$\begin{aligned} \frac{dE}{dt} &= \left[\frac{\partial E}{\partial \boldsymbol{x}} \right]^T \frac{d\boldsymbol{x}}{dt} + \left[\frac{\partial E}{\partial \boldsymbol{y}} \right]^T \frac{d\boldsymbol{y}}{dt} \\ &= -\left[\frac{d\boldsymbol{y}}{dt} \right]^T \frac{d\boldsymbol{y}}{dt} \le 0 \end{aligned} \tag{9.71}$$

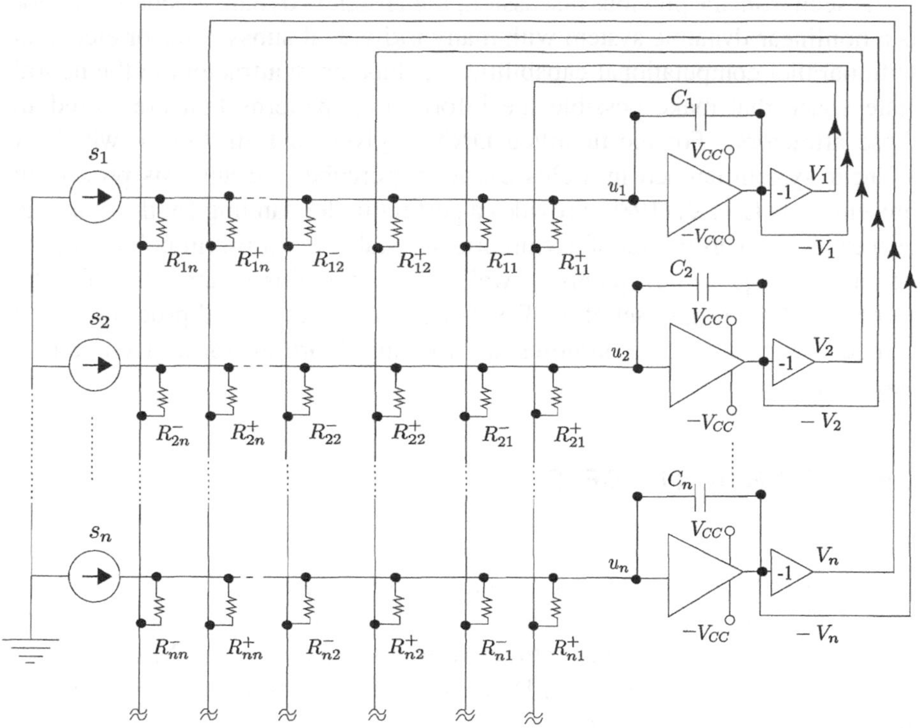

Figure 9.16 The circuit implementation of the dynamic neural network, Eqn. (9.70).

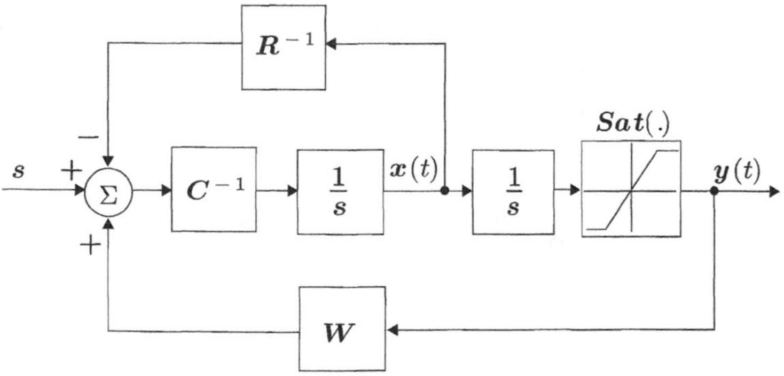

Figure 9.17 Block diagram of the dynamic neural network, Eqn. (9.70).

which guarantees the stability of the equilibrium points.

As seen from the previous discussion, the Hopfield dynamic neural network is a nonlinear dynamic system with many individual subsystems or elements with parallel computational capabilities. It has many attractors in the neural state space that make possible the information patterns that are stored in these attractors. For the modified DNN-S given in Eqn. (9.63), which is a linear system defined in a closed-unit hypercube, the analysis procedure presented by Li et al. (1989) provides a perfect understanding for the dynamic properties, such as the set of asymptotically stable equilibrium points, the set of unstable equilibrium points as well as the domains of attraction for the elements of the former set of the DNN-S as a dynamic neural processor. The synthesis procedure also proposes an efficient algorithm for a given pattern vector storage.

9.5 OTHER DNN MODELS

As discussed in the beginning of this chapter, a dynamic neural network can be described by either a set of continuous-time differential equations or a set of discrete-time difference equations. The Hopfield DNN is a widely studied model of DNNs, as it has very attractive nonlinear dynamics. Moreover, we will present some other types of DNNs that may also show some interesting and useful nonlinear behaviors.

9.5.1 The Pineda Model of Dynamic Neural Networks

The next model that we now discuss is very similar to the Hopfield network. This model, called the *continuous-time recurrent neural network*, was first studied by Pineda (1988). Like the Hopfield dynamic neural network, this network consists of a single layer of neurons that are fully interconnected and contains recurrent connections and intra-layer connections as shown in Fig. 9.18. The dynamics of the network are described by the differential equation

$$\frac{dx_i(t)}{dt} = -\alpha_i x_i(t) + \beta_i g_i \left(\sum_{j=1}^{n} w_{ij} y_j(t) + s_i \right), \quad i = 1, \ldots, n \tag{9.72}$$

or

$$\frac{d\boldsymbol{x}(t)}{dt} = -\boldsymbol{A}\boldsymbol{x}(t) + \boldsymbol{B}\boldsymbol{g}(\boldsymbol{W}\boldsymbol{x}(t) + \boldsymbol{s}) \tag{9.73}$$

where, all $\alpha_i \neq 0$, $i = 1, \ldots, n$.

The topological structure and the block diagram of this dynamic neural network are shown in Figs. 9.18 and 9.19, respectively.

Let all $\alpha_i = 1$ and $\beta_i = 1$, and $\boldsymbol{s}$ be a constant input; that is, matrices $\boldsymbol{A}$ and $\boldsymbol{B}$ are unity matrices. It is easy to see that if the weighting matrix $\boldsymbol{W}$ is invertible, then the preceding model is an equivalent form of the Hopfield dynamic neural network expressed in Eqn. (9.5). In this case, let $\boldsymbol{u} = \boldsymbol{W}\boldsymbol{x}+\boldsymbol{s}$. Then

$$\begin{aligned}\frac{d\boldsymbol{u}(t)}{dt} &= \boldsymbol{W}\frac{d\boldsymbol{x}(t)}{dt} \\ &= -\boldsymbol{W}\boldsymbol{x}(t) + \boldsymbol{W}\boldsymbol{g}(\boldsymbol{W}\boldsymbol{x} + \boldsymbol{s}) \\ &= -\boldsymbol{u}(t) + \boldsymbol{W}\boldsymbol{g}(\boldsymbol{u}) + \boldsymbol{s} \qquad (9.74)\end{aligned}$$

From the nonlinear system dynamics point of view, if the number of inputs for the recurrent neural system is smaller than that of the neural states, then we can introduce an input weight matrix such that the equation of the recurrent

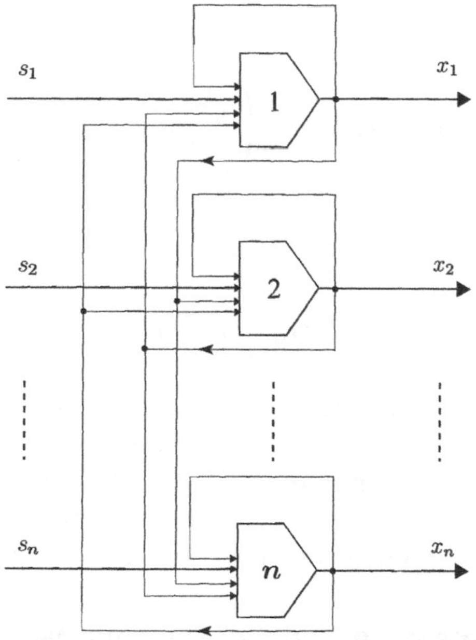

Figure 9.18 Topological structure of the continuous-time recurrent neural network, Eqn. (9.72).

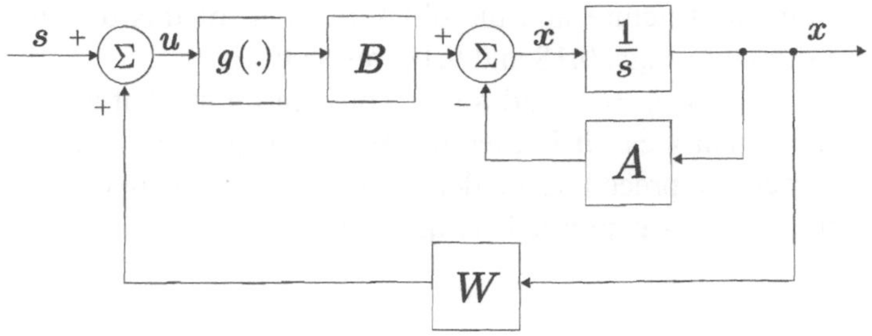

Figure 9.19 Block diagram of the continuous-time recurrent neural network.

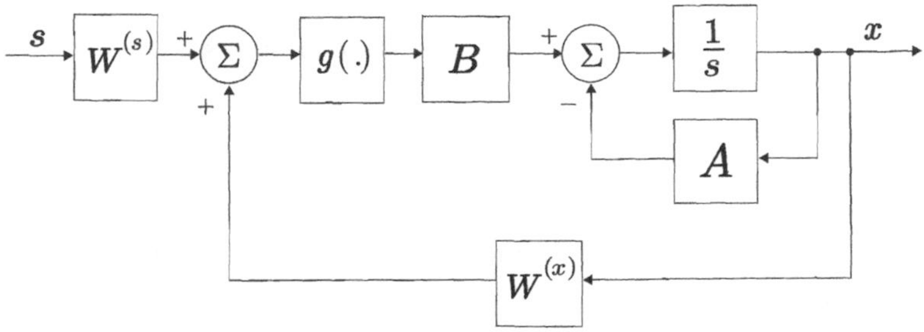

Figure 9.20 Continuous-time recurrent neural network, Eqn. (9.76).

neural network becomes

$$\frac{dx_i(t)}{dt} = -\alpha_i x_i(t) + \beta_i g_i \left(\sum_{j=1}^{n} w_{ij}^{(x)} x_j(t) + \sum_{p=1}^{l} w_{ip}^{(s)} s_p \right)$$
$$i = 1, \ldots, n \tag{9.75}$$

or

$$\frac{d\boldsymbol{x}(t)}{dt} = -\boldsymbol{A}\boldsymbol{x}(t) + \boldsymbol{B}\boldsymbol{g}\left(\boldsymbol{W}^{(x)}\boldsymbol{x}(t) + \boldsymbol{W}^{(s)}\boldsymbol{s}\right) \tag{9.76}$$

where $\boldsymbol{W}^{(x)}$ is a weight matrix associated with the neural state vector $\boldsymbol{x}$ and $\boldsymbol{W}^{(s)}$ is a weight matrix associated with the external input vector $\boldsymbol{s}$. The block diagram of this network is given in Fig. 9.20. The dynamic neural model in Eqn. (9.76) has some advantages for control applications because most of the control systems involve different numbers of inputs, outputs, and states.

9.5.2 Cohen–Grossberg Model of Dynamic Neural Network

From the absolute stability point of view, Cohen and Grossberg (1983) attempted to represent a class of dynamic neural systems using a competitive dynamic system described as

$$\frac{dx_i}{dt} = a_i(x_i)\left[b_i(x_i) - \sum_{j=1}^{n} w_{ij} d_j(x_j)\right], \quad i = 1, \ldots, n \tag{9.77}$$

The following hypotheses were made for the above neural model in Eqn. (9.77):

(i) *Symmetry*: $w_{ij} \geq 0$ and $w_{ij} = w_{ji}$;

(ii) *Continuity*: $a_i(\xi)$ is continuous for $\xi \geq 0$; function $b_i(\xi)$ is continuous for $\xi > 0$;

(iii) *Positivity*: function $a_i(\xi) > 0$ for $\xi > 0$; function $d_i(\xi) \geq 0$ for $\xi \in (-\infty, \infty)$;

(iv) *Smoothness* and *monotonicity*: function $d_i(\xi)$ is differentiable and monotonically nondecreasing for $\xi \geq 0$.

Obviously, condition (i), in which $w_{ij} \geq 0$, is a strong condition. Furthermore, Cohen and Grossberg assumed that

(v) $\lim\limits_{\xi}[b_i(\xi) - w_{ij} g_j(\xi)] < 0$, for all $i = 1, 2, \ldots, n$;

(vi) And either
$\lim_{\xi \to 0^+} b_i(\xi) = \infty$, or
$\lim_{\xi \to 0^+} b_i(\xi) < 0$, and
$\int_0^{\xi} d\xi / a_i(\xi) = \infty$ for some $\xi > 0$.

Let us define a Lyapunov function for the neural system in Eqn. (9.77) as

$$V(\boldsymbol{x}) = -\sum_{i=1}^{n} \int_0^{x_i} b_i(x_i) d_i'(x_i) d(x_i) + \tfrac{1}{2} \sum_{j,k=1}^{n} w_{jk} d_j(x_j) d_k(x_k) \tag{9.78}$$

and its time derivative satisfies

$$\begin{aligned} \frac{dV(t)}{dt} &= -\sum_{i=1}^{n} a_i(x_i) d_i'(x_i) [b_i(x_i) - \sum_{j=1}^{n} w_{ij} d_j(x_j)]^2 \\ &\leq 0 \end{aligned} \tag{9.79}$$

This Lyapunov function guarantees the stability of the equilibrium points.

9.6 CONDITIONS FOR EQUILIBRIUM POINTS IN DNN

As stated earlier, equilibrium points are an important notion in dynamic neural networks, which are essentially the steady-state points of a nonlinear dynamic system. In this section we will study some existence conditions of the equilibrium points for two different dynamic neural networks: DNN-1 and DNN-2.

9.6.1 Conditions for Equilibrium Points of DNN-1

First, let us consider the dynamic neural network, DNN-1, described earlier by Eqn. (9.29):

$$\frac{d\boldsymbol{x}(t)}{dt} = -\boldsymbol{A}\boldsymbol{x}(t) + \boldsymbol{W}\boldsymbol{\sigma}(\boldsymbol{x}) + \boldsymbol{s} \tag{9.80}$$

Given a set of nonzero vectors $\{\boldsymbol{x}^1, \ldots, \boldsymbol{x}^m\} \equiv \{\boldsymbol{x}^i\}$ that represent some specific information, we will now study the conditions for which the vectors $\{\boldsymbol{x}^i\}$ are the equilibrium points of the dynamic neural network in Eqn. (9.80). For convenience, assume that the input or bias $\boldsymbol{s} = 0$ and $\{\boldsymbol{x}^i\}$ are the equilibrium points of the system in Eqn. (9.80). Then, for each vector $\boldsymbol{x}^i$ at the equilibrium points, $d\boldsymbol{x}^i/dt = 0$, and, the following equality is thus satisfied

$$0 = -\boldsymbol{A}\boldsymbol{x}^i + \boldsymbol{W}\boldsymbol{\sigma}(\boldsymbol{x}^i) \tag{9.81}$$

That is

$$\boldsymbol{A}[\boldsymbol{x}^1 \ \cdots \ \boldsymbol{x}^m] = \boldsymbol{W}[\boldsymbol{\sigma}(\boldsymbol{x}^1) \ \cdots \ \boldsymbol{\sigma}(\boldsymbol{x}^m)] \tag{9.82}$$

or

$$\boldsymbol{A}\boldsymbol{X} = \boldsymbol{W}\boldsymbol{\Sigma} \tag{9.83}$$

where $\boldsymbol{X} = [\boldsymbol{x}^1 \ \cdots \ \boldsymbol{x}^m]$ and $\boldsymbol{\Sigma} = [\boldsymbol{\sigma}(\boldsymbol{x}^1) \ \cdots \ \boldsymbol{\sigma}(\boldsymbol{x}^m)]$. Furthermore, assume that $m \geq n$, and $rank[\boldsymbol{\sigma}(\boldsymbol{x}^1), \ldots, \boldsymbol{\sigma}(\boldsymbol{x}^m)] = n$, where n is the number of neurons. Then Eqn. (9.83) leads to

$$\boldsymbol{W} = \boldsymbol{A}\boldsymbol{X}\boldsymbol{\Sigma}^T(\boldsymbol{\Sigma}\boldsymbol{\Sigma}^T)^{-1} \tag{9.84}$$

Since $\boldsymbol{W}$ is a symmetric matrix, the right-hand side of this equation is equal to the transposition of itself, that is

$$\begin{aligned} \boldsymbol{A}\boldsymbol{X}\boldsymbol{\Sigma}^T(\boldsymbol{\Sigma}\boldsymbol{\Sigma}^T)^{-1} &= \left(\boldsymbol{A}\boldsymbol{X}\boldsymbol{\Sigma}^T(\boldsymbol{\Sigma}\boldsymbol{\Sigma}^T)^{-1}\right)^T \\ &= (\boldsymbol{\Sigma}\boldsymbol{\Sigma}^T)^{-1}\boldsymbol{\Sigma}\boldsymbol{X}^T\boldsymbol{A} \end{aligned}$$

which is equivalent to

$$\Sigma\Sigma^T A X \Sigma^T = \Sigma X^T A \Sigma\Sigma^T \tag{9.85}$$

The preceding equation is satisfied if

$$\Sigma^T A X = X^T A \Sigma \tag{9.86}$$

that is

$$[\sigma(x^1) \ \cdots \ \sigma(x^m)]^T A [x^1 \ \cdots \ x^m] = [x^1 \ \cdots \ x^m]^T A [\sigma(x^1) \ \cdots \ \sigma(x^m)]$$

or

$$\sigma^T(x^j) A x^i = \sigma^T(x^i) A x^j, \quad i, j = 1, 2, \ldots, m \tag{9.87}$$

Consequently, Eqn. (9.87) is a *sufficient* condition that the set of nonzero vectors $\{x^1, \ldots, x^m\}$ are the equilibrium points of the system of Eqn. (9.80) for the nonlinear vector function $\sigma(.)$.

In fact, the sufficient condition in Eqn. (9.87) is also *necessary* for all m. To verify this, using Eqns. (9.82) and (9.87), we obtain

$$\sigma^T(x^j) A x^i = \sigma^T(x^j) W \sigma(x^i) \tag{9.88}$$

Using the same procedure, we obtain

$$\sigma^T(x^i) A x^j = \sigma^T(x^i) W \sigma(x^j) \tag{9.89}$$

Then, the symmetry of the matrix W gives

$$\sigma^T(x^j) W \sigma(x^i) = \sigma^T(x^i) W \sigma(x^j) \tag{9.90}$$

Therefore

$$\sigma^T(x^i) A x^j = \sigma^T(x^j) A x^i, \quad i, j = 1, 2, \ldots, m \tag{9.91}$$

These calculations are summarized into the following theorem.

Theorem 9.5 *Let $s = 0$ in the system described in Eqn. (9.80) and $x^1, \ldots, x^m$ be a set of nonzero constant vectors in H^n. Then*

(i) The condition given in Eqn. (9.82) is necessary for $x^1, \ldots, x^m$ to be the equilibrium points of the system in Eqn. (9.80),

(ii) If $m \geq n$ and $rank[\sigma(x^1), \ldots, \sigma(x^m)] = n$, the condition in Eqn. (9.82) is also sufficient for $x^1, \ldots, x^m$ to be the equilibrium points of the system in Eqn. (9.80).

Proof: We only need to prove the sufficient part; that is, if $m \geq n$ and $rank[\sigma(\boldsymbol{x}^1), \ldots, \sigma(\boldsymbol{x}^m)] = n$, then there is a symmetric matrix $\boldsymbol{W}$ such that $\boldsymbol{x}^1, \ldots, \boldsymbol{x}^m$ are the equilibrium points of the system in Eqn. (9.80). In this case, we construct

$$\begin{aligned} \boldsymbol{W} &= \{[\sigma(\boldsymbol{x}^1) \ \cdots \ \sigma(\boldsymbol{x}^m)][\sigma(\boldsymbol{x}^1) \cdots \ \sigma(\boldsymbol{x}^m)]^T\}^{-1} \\ &\qquad [\sigma(\boldsymbol{x}^1) \ \cdots \ \sigma(\boldsymbol{x}^m)][\boldsymbol{x}^1 \ \cdots \ \boldsymbol{x}^m]^T \boldsymbol{A} \\ &= (\boldsymbol{\Sigma}\boldsymbol{\Sigma}^T)^{-1}\boldsymbol{\Sigma}\boldsymbol{X}^T\boldsymbol{A} \end{aligned} \tag{9.92}$$

Then, using the condition in Eqn. (9.84), it is easy to verify that $\boldsymbol{W}$ is a symmetric matrix. Multiplying both sides of the equality above by $\boldsymbol{\Sigma} = [\sigma(\boldsymbol{x}^1) \ \cdots \ \sigma(\boldsymbol{x}^m)]$ yields the equilibrium equations

$$\begin{aligned} \boldsymbol{W}\boldsymbol{\Sigma} &= (\boldsymbol{\Sigma}\boldsymbol{\Sigma}^T)^{-1}\boldsymbol{\Sigma}\boldsymbol{X}^T\boldsymbol{A}\boldsymbol{\Sigma} \\ &= (\boldsymbol{\Sigma}\boldsymbol{\Sigma}^T)^{-1}\boldsymbol{\Sigma}\boldsymbol{\Sigma}^T\boldsymbol{A}\boldsymbol{X} \\ &= \boldsymbol{A}\boldsymbol{X} \end{aligned}$$

that is

$$\boldsymbol{W}[\sigma(\boldsymbol{x}^1) \ \cdots \ \sigma(\boldsymbol{x}^m)] = \boldsymbol{A}[\boldsymbol{x}^1 \ \cdots \ \boldsymbol{x}^m] \tag{9.93}$$

Hence, $\boldsymbol{x}^1, \ldots, \boldsymbol{x}^m$ are the equilibrium points of the system in Eqn. (9.80). ■

9.6.2 Conditions for Equilibrium Points of DNN-2

Next, we consider the conditions that $\{\boldsymbol{x}^i\}$ are the equilibrium points of the following DNN-2 neural system

$$\frac{d\boldsymbol{x}(t)}{dt} = -\boldsymbol{A}\boldsymbol{x}(t) + \boldsymbol{B}\sigma(\boldsymbol{W}\boldsymbol{x}(t)) \tag{9.94}$$

where $\boldsymbol{B} > 0$ and $\boldsymbol{W}$ is symmetric. Let $\{\boldsymbol{x}^i\}$ be the equilibrium points of the system in Eqn. (9.94). Then each vector $\boldsymbol{x}^i$ satisfies

$$0 = -\boldsymbol{A}\boldsymbol{x}^i + \boldsymbol{B}\sigma(\boldsymbol{W}\boldsymbol{x}^i) \tag{9.95}$$

By denoting $\sigma^{-1}(.)$ as the inverse of $\sigma(.)$, we have

$$0 = -\sigma^{-1}(\boldsymbol{B}^{-1}\boldsymbol{A}\boldsymbol{x}) + \boldsymbol{W}\boldsymbol{x} \tag{9.96}$$

that is

$$[\sigma^{-1}(\boldsymbol{B}^{-1}\boldsymbol{A}\boldsymbol{x}^1) \ \cdots \ \sigma^{-1}(\boldsymbol{B}^{-1}\boldsymbol{A}\boldsymbol{x}^m)] = \boldsymbol{W}[\boldsymbol{x}^1 \ \cdots \ \boldsymbol{x}^m] \tag{9.97}$$

Furthermore, if $m \geq n$ and $rank[\boldsymbol{x}^1, \ldots, \boldsymbol{x}^m] = n$, using the same derivation procedure as for DNN-1, we obtain the following condition:

$$(\boldsymbol{x}^i)^T \boldsymbol{\sigma}^{-1}(\boldsymbol{B}^{-1}\boldsymbol{A}\boldsymbol{x}^j) = (\boldsymbol{x}^j)^T \boldsymbol{\sigma}^{-1}(\boldsymbol{B}^{-1}\boldsymbol{A}\boldsymbol{x}^i), \quad i, j = 1, 2, \ldots, m \tag{9.98}$$

These results may be summarized in the following theorem.

Theorem 9.6 *Let $\boldsymbol{x}^1, \ldots, \boldsymbol{x}^m$ be a set of nonzero constant vectors in H^n. Then*

(i) The condition in Eqn. (9.98) is necessary for $\boldsymbol{x}^1, \ldots, \boldsymbol{x}^m$ to be the equilibrium points of the system in Eqn. (9.94),

(ii) If $m \geq n$ and $rank[\boldsymbol{x}^1, \ldots, \boldsymbol{x}^m] = n$, the condition in Eqn. (9.98) is also sufficient for $\boldsymbol{x}^1, \ldots, \boldsymbol{x}^m$ to be the equilibrium points of the system in Eqn. (9.94). ■

If $m \geq n$ and $rank[\boldsymbol{x}^1, \ldots, \boldsymbol{x}^m] = n$, and the condition in Eqn. (9.98) is satisfied, the weight matrix is calculated as follows:

$$\begin{aligned} \boldsymbol{W} = & \{[\boldsymbol{x}^1 \cdots \boldsymbol{x}^m][\boldsymbol{x}^1 \cdots \boldsymbol{x}^m]^T\}^{-1}[\boldsymbol{x}^1 \cdots \boldsymbol{x}^m] \\ & [\boldsymbol{\sigma}^{-1}(\boldsymbol{B}^{-1}\boldsymbol{A}\boldsymbol{x}^1) \cdots \boldsymbol{\sigma}^{-1}(\boldsymbol{B}^{-1}\boldsymbol{A}\boldsymbol{x}^m)]^T \boldsymbol{A} \end{aligned} \tag{9.99}$$

9.7 CONCLUDING REMARKS

Dynamic neural networks, for both continuous and discrete time, are a very important topic. Since these dynamic neural networks form complex nonlinear dynamic equations, the study of their properties such as the equilibrium points and their stability, are important notions. These notions lead to the design of frameworks for the dynamic neural networks for specific tasks. In this chapter we introduced basic mathematical models of continuous-time dynamic neural networks and their analog circuit implementations. In particular, we discussed at length the model of the Hopfield DNN and its variations. We also studied the state stability and the convergence properties of the equilibrium points for some important classes of dynamic neural networks.

Problems

9.1 Consider a system with the form

$$\dot{\boldsymbol{x}} = \boldsymbol{A}\boldsymbol{x} + \boldsymbol{g}(\boldsymbol{x}) \tag{9.100}$$

where $\boldsymbol{A} = [a_{ij}]$ is an $n \times n$ constant matrix with $a_{ij} = 0$ for $i < j$,

$\boldsymbol{x} \in \Re^n$ is a n-dimensional state vector, and $\boldsymbol{g}\colon \Re^n \longrightarrow \Re^n$ is a continuous vector function $\boldsymbol{g} = [g_1\ g_2\ \cdots\ g_n]^T$ such that

$$g_1(\boldsymbol{x}) = k \quad \text{(constant)}$$
$$g_i(\boldsymbol{x}) = g_i(x_1, \ldots, x_{i-1}), \quad i = 2, \ldots, n$$

Prove that if the matrix $\boldsymbol{A}$ is stable, then the system in Eqn. (9.100) has only one equilibrium point that is globally asymptotically stable.

9.2 Consider a nonlinear system of the form

$$\dot{\boldsymbol{x}} = \boldsymbol{f}(\boldsymbol{x}), \quad \boldsymbol{f}\colon \Re^n \longrightarrow \Re^n$$

Let $\boldsymbol{y} = \boldsymbol{T}(\boldsymbol{x})$ with $\boldsymbol{T}(0) = 0$ be a *diffeomorphism* in the neighborhood of the origin, that is, the inverse map $\boldsymbol{T}^{-1}(.)$ exists, and both $\boldsymbol{T}(.)$ and $\boldsymbol{T}^{-1}(.)$ are differentiable. The transformed system is

$$\dot{\boldsymbol{y}} = \hat{\boldsymbol{f}}(\boldsymbol{y}) \quad \text{with} \quad \hat{\boldsymbol{f}}(\boldsymbol{y}) = \frac{\partial \boldsymbol{T}}{\partial \boldsymbol{x}} \boldsymbol{f}(\boldsymbol{x})\bigg|_{\boldsymbol{x}=\boldsymbol{T}^{-1}(\boldsymbol{y})}$$

(a) Show that $\boldsymbol{x} = 0$ is an equilibrium point of $\dot{\boldsymbol{x}} = \boldsymbol{f}(\boldsymbol{x})$ if and only if $\boldsymbol{y} = 0$ is an equilibrium point of $\dot{\boldsymbol{y}} = \hat{\boldsymbol{f}}(\boldsymbol{y})$;

(b) Show that $\boldsymbol{x} = 0$ is stable (asymptotically stable, unstable) if and only if $\boldsymbol{y} = 0$ is stable (asymptotically stable, unstable).

9.3 Let the nonlinear sigmoidal function in the continuous-time Hopfield dynamic neural network be chosen as $y_i = \sigma_i(\lambda x_i)$, where $\lambda > 0$ is an activation gain and the neural output y is used as the state variable in a continuous-time system. Analyze the changes of the minima of the continuous-time energy function due to the changes of the gain λ. [*Hints*: $y_i = \sigma_i(\lambda x_i)$ implies $x_i = (1/\lambda)\sigma_i^{-1}(y_i)$.]

9.4 Show that output variable model of the Hopfield DNN has the same equilibrium points as that of the original state space model of the Hopfield DNN.

9.5 Let the Hopfield DNN have a strict upper triangular weighting matrix of the form

$$\boldsymbol{W} = \begin{bmatrix} 0 & w_{12} & w_{13} & \cdots & w_{1,n-1} & w_{1,n} \\ 0 & 0 & w_{23} & \cdots & w_{2,n-1} & w_{2,n} \\ 0 & 0 & 0 & \cdots & w_{3,n-1} & w_{3,n} \\ \vdots & \vdots & \vdots & \ddots & \vdots & \vdots \\ 0 & 0 & 0 & \cdots & 0 & 0 \end{bmatrix}$$

Show that this type of Hopfield DNN has a unique asymptotic stable equilibrium state for an arbitrary input.

9.6 Consider a general class of neural networks with the following form

$$\frac{dx_i(t)}{dt} = -x_i(t) + \sum_{j=1}^{n} w_{ij}\sigma_j(x_j(t)) + v_i, \quad i = 1, 2, \ldots, n$$

or

$$\frac{d\boldsymbol{x}(t)}{dt} = -\boldsymbol{A}\boldsymbol{x}(t) + \boldsymbol{W}\boldsymbol{\sigma}(\boldsymbol{x}(t)) + \boldsymbol{v}$$

where $\boldsymbol{W} \in \Re^{n \times n}$. Show that for any given connection weight matrix $\boldsymbol{W}$ and input $\boldsymbol{v}$, there exists at least one equilibrium point $\boldsymbol{x}^* \in H^n \equiv \{\boldsymbol{x} : ||\boldsymbol{x} - \boldsymbol{v}||_\infty \leq ||\boldsymbol{W}||_\infty, \boldsymbol{x} \in \Re^n\}$ such that

$$\boldsymbol{x}^* = \boldsymbol{W}\boldsymbol{\sigma}(\boldsymbol{x}^*) + \boldsymbol{v}$$

9.7 Consider a general class of neural networks with the following form

$$\frac{dx_i(t)}{dt} = -\alpha_i x_i(t) + \sum_{j=1}^{n} w_{ij}\sigma_j(x_j(t)) + v_i, \quad i = 1, 2, \ldots, n \tag{9.101}$$

or

$$\frac{d\boldsymbol{x}(t)}{dt} = -\boldsymbol{A}\boldsymbol{x}(t) + \boldsymbol{W}\boldsymbol{\sigma}(\boldsymbol{x}(t)) + \boldsymbol{v} \tag{9.102}$$

where $\boldsymbol{A} = diag[\alpha_1, \ldots, \alpha_n]$ and $\boldsymbol{W} \in \Re^{n \times n}$. Let all $\alpha_i \neq 0$, $i = 1, 2, \ldots, n$ in Eqn. (9.101) and $\alpha = \max\{|1/\alpha_i| : i = 1, 2, \ldots, n\}$. Show that for any given input $\boldsymbol{v}$ and the connection weight matrices $\boldsymbol{W}$, there exists at least one equilibrium point $\boldsymbol{x}^* \in H^n \equiv \{\boldsymbol{x} : ||\boldsymbol{x} - \boldsymbol{v}||_\infty \leq \alpha||\boldsymbol{W}||_\infty, \boldsymbol{x} \in \Re^n\}$ of the dynamic system in Eqn. (9.102); that is, $\boldsymbol{A}\boldsymbol{x}^* = \boldsymbol{W}\sigma(\boldsymbol{x}^*) + \boldsymbol{v}$.

9.8 Show that for any given connection weight matrix $\boldsymbol{W}$ and input $\boldsymbol{v}$, there exists at least one equilibrium point $\boldsymbol{x}^* \in [-1, 1]^n$ of the dynamic neural system

$$\frac{d\boldsymbol{x}(t)}{dt} = -\boldsymbol{x}(t) + \boldsymbol{\sigma}(\boldsymbol{W}\boldsymbol{x} + \boldsymbol{v})$$

that is, $\boldsymbol{x}^* = \boldsymbol{\sigma}(\boldsymbol{W}\boldsymbol{x}^* + \boldsymbol{v})$.

9.9 Consider a general class of recurrent neural network of the form

$$\frac{dx_i(t)}{dt} = -\alpha_i x_i(t) + \beta_i \sigma_i \left(\sum_{j=1}^{n} w_{ij} x_j(t) + v_i \right), \quad i = 1, 2, \ldots, n \tag{9.103}$$

or, equivalently, in vector form

$$\frac{d\boldsymbol{x}(t)}{dt} = -\boldsymbol{A}\boldsymbol{x}(t) + \boldsymbol{B}\boldsymbol{\sigma}(\boldsymbol{W}\boldsymbol{x}(t) + \boldsymbol{v}) \tag{9.104}$$

where $\boldsymbol{B} = diag[\beta_1, \beta_2, \ldots, \beta_n]$. Let all $\alpha_i \neq 0$, $i = 1, 2, \ldots, n$ in Eqn. (9.103) and $\beta = \max\{|\beta_i/\alpha_i| : i = 1, 2, \ldots, n\}$. Show that for any given input $\boldsymbol{v}$ and the connection weight matrix $\boldsymbol{W}$, there exists at least one equilibrium point $\boldsymbol{x}^* \in [-\beta, \beta]^n$ of the dynamic system in Eqn. (9.103); that is, $\boldsymbol{A}\boldsymbol{x}^* = \boldsymbol{B}\boldsymbol{\sigma}(\boldsymbol{W}\boldsymbol{x}^* + \boldsymbol{v})$ will have at least one solution $\boldsymbol{x}^* \in [-\beta, \beta]^n$.

9.10 Consider a general class of recurrent neural network of the form

$$\frac{dx_i(t)}{dt} = \beta_i \sigma_i \left(\sum_{j=1}^{n} w_{ij} x_j(t) + v_i \right), \quad i = 1, 2, \ldots, n$$

or, equivalently, in vector form

$$\frac{d\boldsymbol{x}(t)}{dt} = \boldsymbol{B}\boldsymbol{\sigma}(\boldsymbol{W}\boldsymbol{x}(t) + \boldsymbol{v})$$

where $\boldsymbol{B} = diag[\beta_1, \beta_2, \ldots, \beta_n]$. Show that the dynamical neural system has at least one equilibrium point $\boldsymbol{x}^* \in \Re^n$ if and only if the given input $\boldsymbol{v}$ and the connection weight matrix satisfy

$$rank[\boldsymbol{W} \vdots \ -\boldsymbol{v}] = n$$

Furthermore, show that the system has a unique equilibrium point if and only if the weight matrix $\boldsymbol{W}$ is invertible, and this equilibrium point is $\boldsymbol{x}^* = -\boldsymbol{W}^{-1}\boldsymbol{v}$.

9.11 For the dynamic neural network (DNN)

$$\frac{d\boldsymbol{x}(t)}{dt} = -\boldsymbol{A}\boldsymbol{x}(t) + \boldsymbol{W}\boldsymbol{\sigma}(\boldsymbol{x}(t))$$

if

$$\alpha \equiv ||\boldsymbol{A}|| + ||\boldsymbol{W}|| < 1$$

then $f(x) = -Ax + W\sigma(x)$ is a contraction. Show that

(a) The system has a unique equilibrium point x^* that is globally asymptotically stable;

(b) For any $x^0 \in \Re^n$, the sequence $\{x^n\}$ defined by $x^{n+1} = f(x^n)$ satisfies

$$||x^n - x^*|| \le \frac{\alpha^n}{1-\alpha}||x^1 - x^0||$$

that is, the sequence $\{x^n\}$ converges to x^* at an exponential rate.

9.12 For the neural system given in Problem 9.11, we may consider the possibility of using the equilibrium point $\bar{x}^*$ of a linear network

$$\frac{d\bar{x}(t)}{dt} = -A\bar{x} + W\bar{x}$$

as an estimation of the equilibrium point x^* of the nonlinear neural network. Let

$$\sigma_j(0) = 0, \quad \sigma_j'(0) = 1, \quad |\sigma_j''(x_j)| \le \gamma$$

Show that

$$||x^* - \bar{x}^*|| \le \frac{\gamma||W||}{2(1-\alpha)}$$

The simple observation is that if the equilibrium of the linear network is within a region in which $\sigma(x)$ is well approximated by x. In other words, if $\bar{x}^*$ is in a small neighborhood of the origin, then the equilibrium point of the nonlinear network will be in that neighborhood.

9.13 (Multimodal Sigmoidal Function) A symmetric multimodal sigmoidal function is given by

$$\sigma_m(x) = \frac{1}{2m}\sum_{i=1}^{m}[\sigma(c_i(x-d_i)) + \sigma(c_i(x+d_i))]$$

where the constants c_i and d_i determine, respectively, the slope and the positions of the inflation points of $\sigma_m(x)$. Show that a dynamic neural network (DNN) with such a multimodal sigmoidal function may have more equilibrium points than that with nonmodal sigmoidal function $\sigma(x)$.

9.14 Consider a two-neuron system with the external inputs described by

$$\begin{aligned}\frac{dx_1}{dt} &= -x_1 + 3\tanh(x_1) + 0.5\tanh(x_2) + 0.7\\ \frac{dx_2}{dt} &= -x_2 + 0.5\tanh(x_1) + 2\tanh(x_2) + 0.5\end{aligned}$$

(a) Show that the system has only four equilibrium points;

(b) Give solutions of those four equilibrium pints;

(c) Show that three of those four equilibria are asymptotical stable while another one is unstable.

9.15 Consider again a two-neuron system with the following form:

$$\begin{aligned}\frac{dx_1}{dt} &= -\alpha_1 x_1 + w_1\tanh(x_2)\\ \frac{dx_2}{dt} &= -\alpha_2 x_2 + w_2\tanh(x_1)\end{aligned}$$

Show that the number of equilibrium points and their stability of this dynamic neural system.

9.16 Consider again a two-neuron system with the following form

$$\begin{aligned}\frac{dx_1}{dt} &= -x_1 + 2\tanh(x_2)\\ \frac{dx_2}{dt} &= -x_2 + \tanh(x_1)\end{aligned}$$

(a) Show that the system has only three equilibrium points;

(b) Give solutions of those three equilibrium points;

(c) Show that two of those three equilibria are asymptotical stable while another one is unstable.

10

Learning and Adaptation in Dynamic Neural Networks

10.1 Some Observation on Dynamic Neural Filter Behaviors

10.2 Temporal Learning Process I: Dynamic Backpropagation (DBP)

10.3 Temporal Learning Process II: Dynamic Forward Propagation (DFP)

10.4 Dynamic Backpropagation (DBP) for Continuous-Time Dynamic Neural Networks (CT-DNNs)

10.5 Concluding Remarks

Problems

As a demonstration of a simple dynamic neural architecture, some structures and essential dynamics of a single dynamic neuron which is a basic computing unit of dynamic neural networks (DNNs) were discussed in Chapter 8, and other earlier chapters. Generally speaking, a single dynamic neuron is designed as a nonlinear and dissipative system, where the nonlinearities ensure that the multiple equilibrium points occur in the steady state of the neuron, and the dissipative property provides the convergence of the state flow and exhibit some behaviors such as stable equilibrium points, periodic orbits, and state attractors. Usually, discussion of dynamic neural systems is confined to systems whose only behavior is to converge onto state attractors for given ranges of neural parameters and initial conditions. As we discussed earlier, the notion of state attractors is an important dynamic property in dynamic neural computing because the corresponding state values can be used to represent specified patterns such as memories, data structures, or rules.

Apart from the complicated inherent architecture of the single dynamic neuron, another important characteristic is the capability of learning from the external environment. From the biological perspective, the phenomenon of the general dynamic neural unit described in earlier chapters can be exploited to construct *filters*. Here the term "filter" refers to an architectural component that performs a nonlinear mapping operation from the input (receiving port) to the output. The architecture of a processor, the design of a program, or the organization of the brain can be described as a hierarchy of filters. A single dynamic neuron, which is an intelligent processor when learning algorithms are introduced, changes its nonlinear mapping operation. From the systems point of view, if suitable learning algorithms are adapted, a single dynamic neuron is capable of dealing with the processing of either time-independent analog patterns or time-dependent continuous-time trajectories, where the former is represented by steady states and the latter correspond to temporal or state trajectories. Therefore, we conclude that dynamic neural networks possessing the same structure but distinct learning algorithms can exhibit different dynamic behaviors. In other words, the neural system is a composition of two dynamic systems: the signal transmission and the parameter adjusting systems. The overall input–output behavior thus is a result of the interaction of both.

Roughly speaking, there are two general concepts of dynamic neural learning. *Equilibrium point learning* is designed for the purpose of implementing neural associative memories and is aimed at making the system reach the prescribed equilibrium points or perform steady state matching. The requirements of this dynamic learning are the stability of the equilibrium points with decaying transients. *Dynamic temporal learning* performs an adjusting process for the parameters of a neural system such that the state or output of the system follows the desired trajectory in time. In particular, when the time becomes long enough, it will also reach the prescribed steady state, so the latter algorithm can be considered as a generalization of the equilibrium point learning algorithm.

In this chapter we introduce temporal learning methods for dynamic neural units (DNUs) and dynamic neural networks (DNNs). These methods may be expanded further; but, we will limit ourselves to some new notions and new concepts of learning.

The temporal learning process, which represents the capability of dynamic neural units for continuous and discrete-time processes, is discussed in Sections 10.2 and 10.3. Finally, in Section 10.4, we present dynamic backpropagation (DBP) for dynamic neural networks. Hopefully, an exposition to some of these advanced topics presented in this chapter will lead the readers to some new directions in the field of neural network, memory, and processing of signals and images.

10.1 SOME OBSERVATION ON DYNAMIC NEURAL FILTER BEHAVIORS

As seen in the previous chapters, a universally agreed-on definition of dynamic neural networks does not exist, but for purposes of analysis and applications of DNNs, it is useful to define their most general features that are capable of emulating biological neural behavior and, thus, providing some useful tools for practical applications. With respect to the dynamic property, Pineda (1988) pointed out that, in general, a successful model of dynamic neural networks should involve the following important features:

(i) *Collective or population effects due to many degrees of freedom*: It is generally believed that the computational capabilities of neural systems result from the collective dynamics of the system. The number of neurons in the human brain, for example, is believed to range between 10^{11} and 10^{13}. The state of each of these neurons can be modeled by one or more dynamic variables.

(ii) *Nonlinear characteristics of dynamic neural dynamics*: Nonlinearity is a basic property in associative memories since it is required to store multiple patterns and is thus capable of distinguishing between two stored patterns. The conventional linear mechanisms fail to accomplish such complicated tasks.

(iii) *Dissipative dynamic property*: A dissipative nonlinear dynamic system is characterized by the convergence of the state flow onto a manifold of lower dimensions as the system evolves. Point attractors are important in dynamic neural computing systems because the corresponding state vector values can be used to represent specified computational tasks such as associative memories and knowledge representations. Also, from the biological cognitive perspective, chaotic attractors can be used for knowledge representations (Skarda and Freeman 1987, Honma et al. 1999b).

A general model of the continuous-time dynamic neural networks (CT-DNNs) may be presented by the following set of nonlinear differential equations

$$\frac{d\boldsymbol{x}(t)}{dt} = \boldsymbol{F}(\boldsymbol{x}(t), \boldsymbol{W}, \boldsymbol{s}), \quad \boldsymbol{x}(0) = \boldsymbol{x}^0 \tag{10.1}$$

where $\boldsymbol{x}$ is an n-dimensional internal state vector, $\boldsymbol{W}$ is an $n \times n$ synaptic weighting parameters matrix, and $\boldsymbol{s}$ represents the set of the external control vector or external bias. It is assumed that trajectories of this system converge onto point attractors for some values of $\boldsymbol{W}$ and $\boldsymbol{s}$, and an initial state vector value $\boldsymbol{x}^0$ in some *operating region*. The concept of an operating region of the system means the set of $\boldsymbol{x}$, $\boldsymbol{W}$, and $\boldsymbol{s}$ that are permitted by the dynamics of the external environment.

Quantities evaluated at equilibrium points will be denoted by a superscript f. In particular, the point attractors will be denoted by $\boldsymbol{x}^f$, which are solutions of a set of nonlinear algebraic equations:

$$\frac{d\boldsymbol{x}}{dt} = 0 \quad \longrightarrow \quad \boldsymbol{F}(\boldsymbol{x}^f, \boldsymbol{W}, \boldsymbol{s}) = 0 \tag{10.2}$$

For a given $\boldsymbol{W}$, $\boldsymbol{s}$ and the set of initial state vectors $\boldsymbol{x}(0) = \boldsymbol{x}^0$, the basin of attraction $B(\boldsymbol{x}^0)$ that evolves into a particular equilibrium point $\boldsymbol{x}^f$ is defined as

$$B(\boldsymbol{x}^0) \equiv \left\{ \boldsymbol{x}^0 : \lim_{t \longrightarrow \infty} \boldsymbol{x}(\boldsymbol{x}^0, t) = \boldsymbol{x}^f \right\} \tag{10.3}$$

where $\boldsymbol{x}(\boldsymbol{x}^0, t)$ represents a state trajectory of the system in Eqn. (10.1) with an initial state $\boldsymbol{x}(0) = \boldsymbol{x}^0$. Obviously, the locations of the equilibrium point and the basin boundaries are inexplicit functions of $\boldsymbol{W}$ and $\boldsymbol{s}$. Figure 10.1 shows a typical diagram for the points of attractors $\boldsymbol{x}^f$ and the attraction basin $B(\boldsymbol{x}^0)$ with initial condition $\boldsymbol{x}^0$.

Information processing in the basin of attractors of the dynamic neural system described by Eqn. (10.3) may be exploited to construct *neural filters*. The term *filter* in this context refers to an architectural component that performs a mapping operation from some input to some output. The architecture of a conventional computer that processes the input information through the

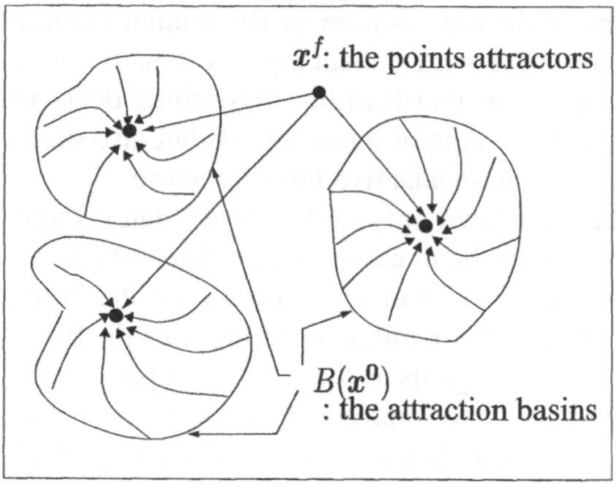

Figure 10.1 Attraction basin $B(x^0)$ of the attractor x^f: From a set of initial state vector x^0, the solution of the system in Eqn. (10.1) with initial condition x^0 converges to the attractor x^f.

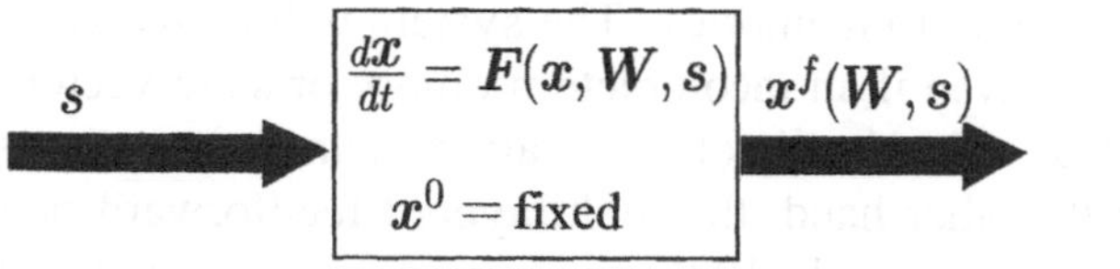

(a) *Continuous-time mapper*: In this type of filter the input of the filter is the external environmental signal s, and the output $x(W, s)$ is an implicit continuous function of s.

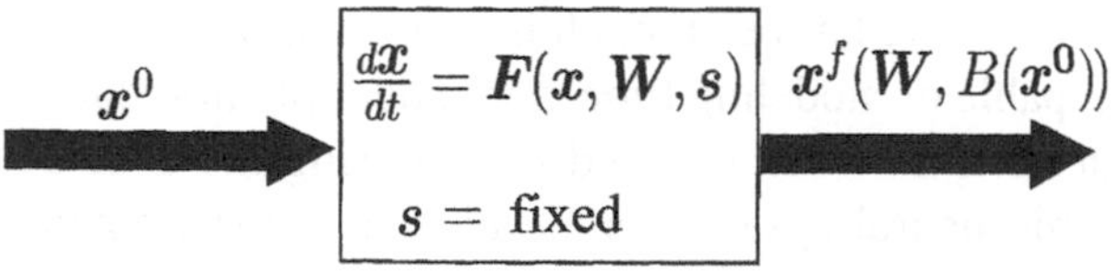

(b) *Autoassociative memory*: For this second type of filter, the input to the filter is the initial state x^0, and the output $x^f(W, B(x^0))$ depends on the basin of attraction which contains the input state, x^0.

Figure 10.2 Structures of two possible types of dynamic neural filters.

designed program, or the organization of the human brain, can be described as a designed filter under such a meaning. A dynamic neural network that involves some adaptive weight learning algorithms deals with the mapping operation not only on the current input signals but also on the past history of the inputs. Thus, it forms an adaptive filter structure.

If the filters are considered only in the steady states, there are two general approaches of exploiting the dynamic neural filter structures for the system. In both cases the steady states of the network are the outputs of the filters. As shown in Fig. 10.2a, the first filter structure uses the bias s that represents the external environment signals as the external input of the filter. The initial states of the system are set to some constant vector x^0 for all external inputs. In the second case, which is shown schematically in Fig. 10.2b, the initial state x^0 of the dynamic neural system represents the external input to the filter, and the bias s is set to some constant vector for all initial condition vector x^0 as external inputs. The first filter is also called the *continuous-time mapper*, while the second type of the filter is termed an *autoassociative memory*.

In fact, there are two well-known examples of these two types of filter structures. As explored in the previous chapters, the continuous-time Hopfield neural network is an example of the second filter, the *autoassociative memory*. In a Hopfield network, information patterns are stored by attractors in the state space that correspond to memories. The system will converge to a complete memory attractor even if an incomplete memory or state vector is presented as an initial state. The details of associative memory are discussed in later chapters. On the other hand, the multilayered feedforward neural network proposed by Rumelhart et al. (1986) is a limiting case of the first filter. In this case, the bias s represents an input to the network.

10.2 TEMPORAL LEARNING PROCESS I: DYNAMIC BACKPROPAGATION (DBP)

Since the late 1980s, there has been much interest in developing learning algorithms that are capable of modeling time-dependent phenomena. In particular, considerable attention has been devoted to capturing the time-dependent dynamics of dynamic neural systems embedded in some known or observed temporal sequences. Note that this temporal learning can be applied for providing time-independent equilibrium neural outputs for time-independent inputs. The problem of temporal learning can typically be formulated as a minimization of an appropriate error index function over an arbitrary but finite time interval. The gradients of the index with respect to the parameters of the neural system are essential elements of the minimization process. We discuss the basic framework of temporal learning in a dynamic neural unit (DNU) in Sections 10.2.1 and 10.2.2.

10.2.1 Dynamic Backpropagation for CT-DNU

Consider a continuous-time dynamic neural unit (CT-DNU) with multiple nonlinear operations described by the nonlinear differential equation

$$\begin{aligned}\frac{dx}{dt} &= -\alpha x + \sum_{i=1}^{n} a_i \sigma(b_i x(t) + c_i) + s(t) \\ &= -\alpha x(t) + \boldsymbol{a}^T \sigma(\boldsymbol{b} x(t) + \mathbf{c}) + s(t) \qquad (10.4)\end{aligned}$$

where $\boldsymbol{a} = [a_1\ a_2\ \cdots\ a_n]^T$, $\boldsymbol{b} = [b_1\ b_2\ \cdots\ b_n]^T$, and $\mathbf{c} = [c_1\ c_2\ \cdots\ c_n]^T$. The theoretical studies provided in a later discussion will show that for any trajectory of a given nonlinear system defined on a compact set D with the form

$$\frac{dy(t)}{dt} = f(y(t))$$

where the function on the right-hand side is *Lipschitz*; that is, with an initial value $x(0) \in D$ and an arbitrary small number $\epsilon > 0$, there exist an integer n and an appropriate initial state of the CT-DNU given in Eqn. (10.4) such that

$$|x(t) - y(t)| < \epsilon$$

These results show that the CT-DNU described by Eqn. (10.4) is capable of approximating an arbitrary nonlinear system or a nonlinear continuous function with a desired accuracy.

To simplify the description, Eqn. (10.4) is represented in the following compact form

$$\frac{dx(t)}{dt} = -\alpha x(t) + f(x(t), \boldsymbol{w}) + s(t) \qquad (10.5)$$

where $\boldsymbol{w}$ is a $3n$-dimensional parameter vector defined by

$$\begin{aligned}\boldsymbol{w} &= [w_1\ \cdots\ w_n\ w_{n+1}\ \cdots\ w_{2n}\ w_{2n+1}\ \cdots\ w_{3n}]^T \\ &= [a_1\ \cdots a_n\ b_1\ \cdots\ b_n\ c_1\ \cdots\ c_n]^T \\ &= [\boldsymbol{a}^T\ \boldsymbol{b}^T\ \mathbf{c}^T]^T\end{aligned}$$

and

$$f(x, \boldsymbol{w}) = \sum_{i=1}^{n} a_i \sigma(b_i x + c_i) = \boldsymbol{a}^T \boldsymbol{\sigma}(\boldsymbol{b} x + \mathbf{c})$$

Let $x_d(t)$ be a known time trajectory in the interval $[t_0, t_f]$. Usually, the time-dependent external input $s(t)$ is used to encode the target temporal pattern via the expression $s(t) = x_d(t)$. To proceed formally with the development of a temporal learning algorithm, we will consider an approach based on the minimization of an error function, E, defined over the fixed time interval $[t_0, t_f]$ by the following expression

$$
\begin{aligned}
E &= \tfrac{1}{2}(x_d(t_f) - x(t_f))^2 + \tfrac{1}{2}\int_{t_0}^{t_f} (x_d(t) - x(t))^2 dt \\
&= \tfrac{1}{2}e^2(t_f) + \tfrac{1}{2}\int_{t_0}^{t_f} e^2(t)dt \qquad (10.6)
\end{aligned}
$$

where $e(t) = x_d(t) - x(t)$ represents the difference between the desired and actual value of the neural state.

We may use the *variational principle* to study this fixed time optimization problem in dynamic systems. Introducing the Lagrangian L as

$$
\begin{aligned}
L = \tfrac{1}{2}e^2(t_f) + \int_{t_0}^{t_f} \Big\{ & \tfrac{1}{2}(x_d(t) - x(t))^2 \\
& - z(t)[\dot{x}(t) + \alpha x(t) - f(x(t), \boldsymbol{w}) - s(t)] \Big\} dt \\
= \tfrac{1}{2}e^2(t_f) + \int_{t_0}^{t_f} \Big\{ & \tfrac{1}{2}e^2(t) - z(t)[\dot{x}(t) + \alpha x(t) - f(x(t), \boldsymbol{w}) - s(t)] \Big\} dt \qquad (10.7)
\end{aligned}
$$

where $z \in \Re$ is the Lagrange multiplier. Now, the first variation in L yields

$$
\begin{aligned}
\delta L &= e(t_f)\delta x(t_f) + \int_{t_0}^{t_f} \Big\{ e(t)\delta x(t) - z(t)[\delta\dot{x}(t) + \alpha\delta x(t) + x(t)\delta\alpha \\
&\quad - (\boldsymbol{f}_w(x(t), \boldsymbol{w}))^T \delta\boldsymbol{w} - f_x(x(t), \boldsymbol{w})\delta x(t)] \Big\} dt \\
&= e(t_f)\delta x(t_f) + \int_{t_0}^{t_f} \Big\{ [e(t) - z(t)\alpha + z(t) f_x(x(t), \boldsymbol{w})]\delta x(t) \\
&\quad - z\delta\dot{x}(t) + z(t)x(t)\delta\alpha + z(t)(\boldsymbol{f}_w(x(t), \boldsymbol{w}))^T \delta\boldsymbol{w} \Big\} dt \qquad (10.8)
\end{aligned}
$$

where $\delta x \in \Re$, $\delta \dot{x} \in \Re$, $\delta \alpha \in \Re$, and $\delta \boldsymbol{w} \in \Re^{3n}$ are the first variations of x, $\dot{x}$, α, and $\boldsymbol{w}$, respectively; $f_x(x, \boldsymbol{w}) = \partial f / \partial x$ is a scalar; and $\boldsymbol{f}_w(x, \boldsymbol{w}) = \partial f / \partial \boldsymbol{w}$ is a $3n$-dimensional vector.

Defining the adjoint equation

$$\frac{dz(t)}{dt} = [\alpha - f_x(x(t), \boldsymbol{w})]z(t) - e(t) \tag{10.9}$$

it follows that

$$\begin{aligned} \delta L &= e(t_f)\delta x(t_f) + \int_{t_0}^{t_f} \{[-\dot{z}(t)\delta x(t) - z\delta\dot{x}(t)] \\ &\quad - z(t)x(t)\delta\alpha + z(t)(\boldsymbol{f}_w(x(t), \boldsymbol{w}))^T \delta\boldsymbol{w}\} dt \\ &= z(t_0)\delta x(t_0) - (z(t_f) - e(t_f))\delta x(t_f) \\ &\quad + \int_{t_0}^{t_f} \{-z(t)x(t)\delta\alpha + z(t)(\boldsymbol{f}_w(x(t), \boldsymbol{w}))^T \delta\boldsymbol{w}\} dt \end{aligned} \tag{10.10}$$

Since the initial condition $x(t_0)$ does not depend on the parameters adapted, $\delta x(t_0) = 0$. If, additionally, one chooses the boundary value

$$z(t_f) = e(t_f) \tag{10.11}$$

then

$$\begin{aligned} \delta L &= \int_{t_0}^{t_f} \{-z(t)x(t)\delta\alpha + z(t)(\boldsymbol{f}_w(x(t), \boldsymbol{w}))^T \delta\boldsymbol{w}\} dt \\ &= \left[\int_{t_0}^{t_f} -z(t)x(t)dt\right]\delta\alpha + \left[\int_{t_0}^{t_f} z(t)(\boldsymbol{f}_w(x(t), \boldsymbol{w}))^T dt\right]\delta\boldsymbol{w} \end{aligned} \tag{10.12}$$

Therefore

$$\frac{\partial E}{\partial \alpha} = -\int_{t_0}^{t_f} z(t)x(t)dt \tag{10.13}$$

$$\frac{\partial E}{\partial \boldsymbol{w}} = \int_{t_0}^{t_f} z(t)\boldsymbol{f}_w(x(t), \boldsymbol{w})dt \tag{10.14}$$

Finally, the parameter updating equations are

$$\frac{d\alpha}{dt} = -\eta_\alpha \frac{\partial E}{\partial \alpha} \tag{10.15}$$

$$\frac{d\boldsymbol{w}}{dt} = -\eta_w \frac{\partial E}{\partial \boldsymbol{w}} \tag{10.16}$$

where $\eta_\alpha > 0$ and $\eta_w > 0$ are the learning rates associated with the parameters α and $\boldsymbol{w}$, respectively. Note that the partial derivatives involved on the right-hand side of Eqns. (10.15) and (10.16) are constants. Hence, the algorithms for the parameter adaptations for α and w are

$$\alpha_{new} = \alpha_{old} - \eta_\alpha(t_{new} - t_{old})\frac{\partial E}{\partial \alpha} \tag{10.17}$$

$$\boldsymbol{w}_{new} = \boldsymbol{w}_{old} - \eta_w(t_{new} - t_{old})\frac{\partial E}{\partial \boldsymbol{w}} \tag{10.18}$$

When the state equation, given in Eqn. (10.4), has an initial condition $x(t_0) = x_0$, the adjoint equation involves a final condition $z(t_f) = 0$. This means that the state and adjoint equations must be integrated forward and backward, respectively. Hence, the resulting formulations form a classical nonlinear *two-point boundary-value problem* (TPBVP) (Bryson and Ho 1969). Although much attention has been paid to this interesting computational problem, these iterative calculations should be performed off line, even though, there exists the theoretical possibility of an online algorithm (Williams and Zipser 1990), but the calculations would have to be performed at every step, requiring unlimited memory and computational power.

The difference between the TPBVPs arising from optimal control processes and the parameter optimization problems is that the forward state equations contain backward adjoint variables that are used to represent the optimal control variables in the former TPBVP and the forward state equations involve only the parameters in the latter. Hence, in the procedure of iterative learning computing, first the forward state equation, given in Eqn. (10.12), may be integrated from the initial time t_0 to the final time t_f to obtain the final state value $x(t_f)$ for a set of given values of the parameters. Afterward, the forward and backward equations may be integrated together from the final time t_f to the initial time t_0 because the adjoint equation contains both the state and adjoint variables. Meanwhile, to update the parameters, the partial derivatives $\partial E/\partial \alpha$ and $\partial E/\partial \boldsymbol{w}$ in Eqns. (10.13) and (10.14) need to be computed in the backward process:

$$\frac{\partial E}{\partial \alpha} = \int_{t_f - t_0}^{0} z(t_f - \tau) x(t_f - \tau) d\tau \tag{10.19}$$

$$\frac{\partial E}{\partial \boldsymbol{w}} = -\int_{t_f - t_0}^{0} z(t_f - \tau) \boldsymbol{f}_w(x(t_f - \tau), \boldsymbol{w}) d\tau \tag{10.20}$$

Of course, the history of $x(t)$ ($t_0 \leq t \leq t_f$) may be memorized during the forward integration for the utilization in the backward integration. The updating could be finished, when the difference between the old and new values of the performance index becomes as small as desired. This learning algorithm is referred to as *dynamic backpropagation* by Williams and Zipser (1990).

10.2.2 Dynamic Backpropagation for DT-DNU

Using Euler's method, the first-order derivative is approximated as

$$\left. \frac{dx}{dt} \right|_{t=kT} = \frac{x((k+1)T) - x(kT)}{T} \tag{10.21}$$

where T is the sampling period and k is the sampling instant. If $T = 1$, this derivative can be approximated to

$$\frac{dx}{dt} = x(k+1) - x(k)$$

Thus, for a continuous-time dynamic neural unit (CT-DNU)

$$\begin{aligned} \frac{dx}{dt} &= -\alpha x(k) + w y(t) + s \\ y(t) &= \sigma(x(t)) \end{aligned}$$

the equivalent model of the DNU in discrete time (DT-DNU) is given by

$$\begin{aligned} x(k+1) &= -(\alpha - 1) x(k) + w y(k) + s \\ y(k) &= \sigma(x(k)) \end{aligned} \tag{10.22}$$

The block diagram of the above discrete-time model is given in Fig. 10.3. Usually, the discrete-time representations of dynamic neural systems may provide some computational advantages on digital computers.

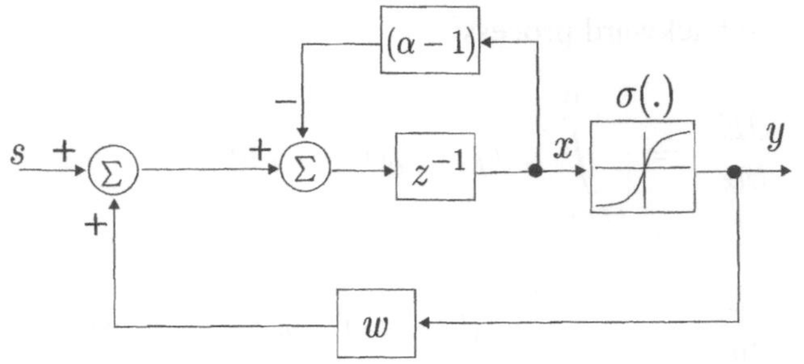

Figure 10.3 Block diagram of a discrete-time dynamic neural unit DT-DNU, Eqn. (10.22).

Given a finite length discrete-time sequence $x_d(k)$, $k = 1, 2, \ldots, N$, we wish to design a discrete-time temporal learning algorithm such that the state of the following discrete-time dynamic neural unit (DT-DNU)

$$\begin{aligned} x(k+1) &= -(\alpha-1)x(k) + \sum_{i=1}^{n} a_i\sigma(b_i x(k) + c_i) + s(k) \\ &= -(\alpha-1)x(k) + \boldsymbol{a}^T\boldsymbol{\sigma}(\boldsymbol{b}x(k) + \boldsymbol{c}) + s(k) \\ &= -(\alpha-1)x(k) + f(x(k), \boldsymbol{w}) + s(k) \end{aligned} \tag{10.23}$$

will asymptotically track the sequence $x_d(k)$. Here

$$f(x, \boldsymbol{w}) = \sum_{i=1}^{n} a_i\sigma(b_i x + c_i) = \boldsymbol{a}^T\boldsymbol{\sigma}(\boldsymbol{b}x + \boldsymbol{c})$$

In this case, an error index with quadratic form is defined by

$$\begin{aligned} E(k) &= \tfrac{1}{2}(x_d(N) - x(N))^2 + \tfrac{1}{2}\sum_{k=0}^{N-1}[x_d(k) - x(k)]^2 \\ &= \tfrac{1}{2}e^2(N) + \tfrac{1}{2}\sum_{k=0}^{N-1} e^2(k) \end{aligned} \tag{10.24}$$

where $e(k) = x_d(k) - x(k)$ and $e(N) = x_d(N) - x(N)$. Using the discrete-time variational principle, a discrete-time Lagrangian is defined by

$$\begin{aligned} \Phi &= \tfrac{1}{2}(x_d(N) - x(N))^2 + \sum_{k=0}^{N-1}\{\tfrac{1}{2}(x_d(k) - x(k))^2 \\ &\quad - z(k+1)[x(k+1) + (\alpha-1)x(k) - f(x(k), \boldsymbol{w}) - s(k)]\} \end{aligned}$$

$$
\begin{aligned}
&= \tfrac{1}{2}e^2(N) + \sum_{k=0}^{N-1}\{\tfrac{1}{2}e^2(N) - z(k+1)[x(k+1) \\
&\quad + (\alpha - 1)x(k) - f(x(k), \boldsymbol{w}) - s(k)]\}
\end{aligned}
\tag{10.25}
$$

The reason that the discrete time $(k+1)$ is associated with the Lagrange multiplier is due to the simplicity of the final condition, as will be apparent in the following discussion.

Like the method used for the continuous-time case, the first variation of Φ may be represented as

$$
\begin{aligned}
\delta\Phi &= e(N)\delta x(N) + \sum_{k=0}^{N-1}\{e(k)\delta x(k) \\
&\quad - z(k+1)[\delta x(k+1) + (\alpha - 1)\delta x(k) + x(k)\delta\alpha \\
&\quad - f_x(x(k), \boldsymbol{w})\delta x(k) - \boldsymbol{f}_w(x(k), \boldsymbol{w})^T\delta\boldsymbol{w}]\} \\
&= e(N)\delta x(N) + \sum_{k=0}^{N-1}\{[e(k) - (\alpha - 1)z(k+1) \\
&\quad + f_x(x(k), \boldsymbol{w})z(k+1)]\delta x(k) - z(k+1)\delta x(k+1) \\
&\quad - z(k+1)x(k)\delta\alpha + z(k+1)(\boldsymbol{f}_w(x(k), \boldsymbol{w}))^T\delta\boldsymbol{w}\}
\end{aligned}
\tag{10.26}
$$

Let the Lagrange multiplier $z(k)$ satisfy

$$
z(k) = e(k) + [f_x(x(k), \boldsymbol{w}) - (\alpha - 1)]z(k+1) \tag{10.27}
$$

or

$$
z(k+1) = \frac{z(k) - e(k)}{f_x(x(k), \boldsymbol{w}) - (\alpha - 1)} \tag{10.28}
$$

Then

$$
\begin{aligned}
\delta\Phi &= e(N)\delta x(N) + \sum_{k=0}^{N-1}[z(k)\delta x(k) - z(k+1)\delta x(k+1) \\
&\quad - z(k+1)x(k)\delta\alpha + z(k+1)(\boldsymbol{f}_w(x(k), \boldsymbol{w}))^T\delta\boldsymbol{w}]
\end{aligned}
$$

$$= z(0)\delta x(0) - [z(N) - e(N)]\delta x(N)$$

$$+ \sum_{k=0}^{N-1}[-z(k+1)x(k)\delta\alpha + z(k+1)(\boldsymbol{f}_w(x(k),\boldsymbol{w}))^T\delta\boldsymbol{w}] \quad (10.29)$$

Since the initial value $x(0)$ does not depend on the parameters, $\delta x(0) = 0$. If we choose additionally the final condition of the Lagrange multiplier

$$z(N) = e(N) \quad (10.30)$$

then

$$\delta\Phi = \sum_{k=0}^{N-1}[-z(k+1)x(k)\delta\alpha + z(k+1)(\boldsymbol{f}_w(x(k),\boldsymbol{w}))^T\delta\boldsymbol{w}]$$

$$= \left(\sum_{k=0}^{N-1} -z(k+1)x(k)\right)\delta\alpha + \left(\sum_{k=0}^{N-1} z(k+1)(\boldsymbol{f}_w(x(k),\boldsymbol{w}))^T\right)\delta\boldsymbol{w}$$

Therefore, the partial derivatives of the error index with respect to the parameters are given by

$$\frac{\partial E}{\partial \alpha} = -\sum_{k=0}^{N-1} z(k+1)x(k) \quad (10.31)$$

$$\frac{\partial E}{\partial \boldsymbol{w}} = \sum_{k=0}^{N-1} z(k+1)\boldsymbol{f}_w(x(k),\boldsymbol{w}) \quad (10.32)$$

and the incremental terms of the parameters are

$$\Delta\alpha(k) = -\eta_\alpha\frac{\partial E}{\partial \alpha} = \eta_\alpha\sum_{k=0}^{N-1} z(k+1)x(k) \quad (10.33)$$

$$\Delta\boldsymbol{w}(k) = -\eta_w\frac{\partial E}{\partial \boldsymbol{w}} = -\eta_w\sum_{k=0}^{N-1} z(k+1)\boldsymbol{f}_w(x(k),\boldsymbol{w}) \quad (10.34)$$

that is, the updating equations are obtained as

$$\alpha(k+1) = \alpha(k) + \eta_\alpha\sum_{k=0}^{N-1} z(k+1)x(k) \quad (10.35)$$

$$\boldsymbol{w}(k+1) = \boldsymbol{w}(k) - \eta_w\sum_{k=0}^{N-1} z(k+1)\boldsymbol{f}_w(x(k),\boldsymbol{w}) \quad (10.36)$$

The learning algorithm given above for such a fixed time sequence learning problem involves a discrete-time two-point boundary-value problem (TPBVP) that can be solved, in general, by reiterative technique. Here, the initial condition $x(0)$ of the state is known, and the final condition $z(N)$ of the Lagrange multiplier is a linear function of the unknown final condition $x(N)$ of the state.

10.2.3 Comparison between Continuous and Discrete-Time Dynamic Backpropagation Approaches

Having discussed both the continuous and discrete-time dynamic backpropagation (DBP) learning algorithms for the models of the dynamic neural units (DNUs), we will now compare the two approaches. It is only natural to expect that both the continuous and discrete-time backpropagation algorithms will yield either very similar solutions, or the same solution to a given problem. Obviously, there are two discrete-time backpropagation approaches. One may be obtained directly from the results of the continuous-time backpropagation algorithm discussed in the previous section using the first-difference discretization. The other was given in the last subsection using the discrete-time variational principle for a DNU with the first-difference approximation. We will show in this subsection that the two approaches that we have proposed earlier are somewhat different. For some sample periods, however, the computational solutions for the two approaches will be essentially the same.

Consider the continuous-time backpropagation using the first variational calculus. We wish to minimize

$$\begin{aligned} E &= \tfrac{1}{2}(x_d(t_f) - x(t_f))^2 + \tfrac{1}{2}\int_{t_0}^{t_f} (x_d(t) - x(t))^2 dt \\ &= \tfrac{1}{2}e^2(t_f) + \tfrac{1}{2}\int_{t_0}^{t_f} e^2(t)dt \end{aligned} \tag{10.37}$$

subject to the equality constant

$$\frac{dx(t)}{dt} = -\alpha x(t) + f(x(t), \boldsymbol{w}) + s(k), \qquad x(t_0) = x_0 \tag{10.38}$$

where $e(t) = x_d(t) - x(t)$ and $e(t_f) = x_d(t_f) - x(t_f)$. The continuous-time dynamic backpropagation learning algorithm, which involves the two-point boundary-value problem (TPBVP), is obtained from the variational principle as follows. The adjoint equation and associated boundary conditions are

$$\frac{dz(t)}{dt} = [\alpha - f_x(x(t), \boldsymbol{w})]z(t) - e(t), \qquad z(t_f) = e(t_f) \tag{10.39}$$

The parameter updating equations are determined by

$$\frac{d\alpha}{dt} = \eta_\alpha \int_{t_0}^{t_f} z(t)x(t)dt \tag{10.40}$$

$$\frac{d\boldsymbol{w}}{dt} = -\eta_w \int_{t_0}^{t_f} z(t)\boldsymbol{f}_w(x(t), \boldsymbol{w})dt \tag{10.41}$$

Hence the continuous-time DBP problem to be solved is given by Eqns. (10.37)–(10.41), where the neural state equation given in Eqn. (10.38) has an initial condition and the adjoint equation given in Eqn. (10.39) has a final condition. Using the first-difference approximations

$$\left.\frac{dx}{dt}\right|_{t=kT} = \frac{x((k+1)T) - x(kT)}{T} \equiv \frac{x(k+1) - x(k)}{T} \tag{10.42}$$

$$\left.\frac{dz}{dt}\right|_{t=kT} = \frac{z((k+1)T) - z(kT)}{T} \equiv \frac{z(k+1) - z(k)}{T} \tag{10.43}$$

and discretizing the integral in the parameter updating equations using an infinite summation, the resulting discrete-time DBP becomes

$$\begin{cases} x(k+1) = -(\alpha T - 1)x(k) + Tf(x(k), \boldsymbol{w}) + Ts(k) \\ x(0) = x_0 \end{cases} \tag{10.44}$$

$$\begin{cases} z(k+1) = [(\alpha T + 1) - Tf_x(x(k), \boldsymbol{w})]z(k) - Te(k) \\ z(N) = e(N) \end{cases} \tag{10.45}$$

$$\Delta\alpha(k) = T\eta_\alpha \sum_{k=0}^{N-1} z(k)x(k) \tag{10.46}$$

$$\Delta\boldsymbol{w} = -T\eta_w \sum_{k=0}^{N-1} z(k)\boldsymbol{f}_w(x(k), \boldsymbol{w}) \tag{10.47}$$

The alternate approach, using the discrete-time variational principle as seen in the last subsection is now given. The first-difference approximation to the equality constraint yields

$$\begin{aligned} x(k+1) &= -(\alpha T - 1)x(k) + Tf(x(k), \boldsymbol{w}) + Ts(k) \qquad (10.48) \\ x(0) &= x_0 \end{aligned}$$

A direct discretization of the continuous-time integral error index yields

$$\begin{aligned} E &= \tfrac{1}{2}(x_d(N) - x(N))^2 + T\tfrac{1}{2}\sum_{k=0}^{N-1}(x_d(k) - x(k))^2 \\ &= \tfrac{1}{2}e^2(N) + T\sum_{k=1}^{N-1} e^2(k) \qquad (10.49) \end{aligned}$$

where $e(k) = x_d(k) - x(k)$ and $e(N) = x_d(N) - x(N)$. Thus, the adjoint equation with a final condition is given by

$$\begin{aligned} z(k) &= Te(k) + [Tf_x(x(k), \boldsymbol{w}) - (T\alpha - 1)]z(k+1) \qquad (10.50) \\ z(N) &= e(N) \end{aligned}$$

or

$$\begin{aligned} z(k+1) &= \frac{z(k) - Te(k)}{Tf_x(x(k), \boldsymbol{w}) - (T\alpha - 1)} \qquad (10.51) \\ z(N) &= e(N) \end{aligned}$$

The parameter updating equations are easily obtained as

$$\Delta\alpha(k) = T\eta_\alpha \sum_{k=0}^{N-1} z(k+1)x(k) \qquad (10.52)$$

$$\Delta\boldsymbol{w}(k) = -T\eta_w \sum_{k=0}^{N-1} z(k+1)\boldsymbol{f}_w(x(k), \boldsymbol{w}) \qquad (10.53)$$

Equations (10.48)–(10.53) constitute the discrete-time two-point boundary-value (TPBV) nonlinear difference equations to be solved. The state and adjoint equations with the boundary conditions are Eqns. (10.48) and (10.51) together with updating equations, Eqns. (10.52) and (10.53). It is immediately apparent that these equations are not the same as those obtained when we discretized the continuous nonlinear TPBVP consisting of Eqns. (10.38)–(10.41). The discrete-time state equations given in Eqns. (10.38) and (10.48) of the DNUs and their initial conditions, are the same as the final conditions of the adjoint equations. However, the parameters updating equations and the adjoint equations are different, although similar. If the $z(k+1)$ term in Eqns. (10.52) and (10.53) is replaced by $z(k)$, the two sets of parameters updating equations are the same. For a sufficiently small sampling period, this is not an unreasonable approximation since the change in $z(k)$ from instant k to instant $(k+1)$ will be small.

Moreover, for a sufficiently small sampling period T, a Taylor series expansion yields

$$\begin{aligned}\frac{1}{Tf_x(x,w)-(T\alpha-1)} &= \frac{1}{1+(f_x(x,w)-\alpha)T} \\ &= 1-(f_x(x,w)-\alpha)T+O(T^2) \\ &= (\alpha T+1)-Tf_x(x,w)+O(T^2) \qquad (10.54)\end{aligned}$$

where $O(T^2)$ includes the terms of T higher than the first. Hence, if $O(T^2)$ terms are neglected, we obtain

$$z(k+1) = [(T\alpha+1)-Tf_x(x(k),w)]z(k)-Te(k)$$

This is identical to Eqn. (10.45), the discretized adjoint equation for the continuous-time dynamic backpropagation algorithm. Therefore, as previously stated, the computational results for the two approaches will be essentially the same for small sampling periods. However, the sensitivity effects of the sampling periods are considerably important for discretization of continuous-time dynamic neural systems.

The essential difference between the two approaches lies in the manner in which the discrete approximation is made. The discrete-time DBP algorithm yields a TPBVP in the form of a set of nonlinear difference equations whose solution is precisely the solution that optimizes the stated discrete temporal learning problem. The continuous-time DBP algorithm yields a TPBVP in the form of a set of nonlinear differential equations whose solution is precisely the solution that minimizes the stated continuous-time temporal learning problem. The solution of a discrete version of this continuous-time DBP yields a temporal state trajectory that does not optimize either the continuous-time problem or a discrete-time version of the continuous-time problem. For most situations, this creates no difficulties.

10.3 TEMPORAL LEARNING PROCESS II: DYNAMIC FORWARD PROPAGATION (DFP)

10.3.1 Continuous-Time Dynamic Forward Propagation (CT-DFP)

The dynamic backpropagation through time discussed in the last section is inherently an off line technique due to introducing an error index on the fixed time interval. The following algorithm, which is a slight modification of the algorithms proposed by Robinson and Fallside (1987) and Williams and Zipser (1989), overcomes the difficulty associated with the two-point boundary-value problem (TPBVP).

Let us consider a dynamic neural unit (DNU) of the form

$$\frac{dx(t)}{dt} = -\alpha x(t) + f(x(t), \boldsymbol{w}) + s(k) \tag{10.55}$$

where α and $\boldsymbol{w}$ are adjustable parameters. Define a time-varying error function E over the time-varying interval $[t_0, t]$ by the following expression:

$$E(t) = \frac{1}{2}\int_{t_0}^{t}(x_d(\tau) - x(\tau))^2 d\tau = \frac{1}{2}\int_{t_0}^{t} e^2(\tau) d\tau \tag{10.56}$$

In this case, the error index is a function of time. Usually, learning algorithms are constructed by invoking Lyapunov stability arguments; that is, by requiring that the error index be monotonically decreasing during the learning time τ. This requirement may be translated into

$$\frac{dE}{d\tau} = \frac{\partial E}{\partial \alpha}\frac{d\alpha}{d\tau} + \left(\frac{\partial E}{\partial \boldsymbol{w}}\right)^T \frac{d\boldsymbol{w}}{d\tau} \tag{10.57}$$

One can always choose

$$\frac{d\alpha}{d\tau} = -\eta_\alpha \frac{\partial E}{\partial \alpha} \tag{10.58}$$

$$\frac{d\boldsymbol{w}}{d\tau} = -\eta_w \frac{\partial E}{\partial \boldsymbol{w}} \tag{10.59}$$

Equations (10.58) and (10.59) implement the learning algorithms for the adjustments of the parameters α and $\boldsymbol{w}$ in terms of an inherently local minimization procedure. Attention should be paid to the fact that the state equation and the learning equations may operate on different timescales with parameter adaptation occurring at a slower rate. Integrating the parameter adaptive equations given in Eqns. (10.58) and (10.59) over the time interval $[\tau, \tau+\Delta\tau]$, one obtains

$$\alpha(\tau+\Delta\tau) = \alpha(\tau) - \eta_\alpha \int_{\tau}^{\tau+\Delta\tau} \frac{\partial E}{\partial \alpha} d\tau \tag{10.60}$$

$$\boldsymbol{w}(\tau+\Delta\tau) = \boldsymbol{w}(\tau) - \eta_w \int_{\tau}^{\tau+\Delta\tau} \frac{\partial E}{\partial \boldsymbol{w}} d\tau \tag{10.61}$$

These equations imply that, in order to evaluate the system parameters, one must calculate the "*sensitivity*" or the gradient of E with respect to the parameters adapted. Using the error index equation, one can obtain

$$\frac{\partial E}{\partial \alpha} = -\int_{t_0}^{t} (x_d(\tau) - x(\tau)) \frac{\partial x(\tau)}{\partial \alpha} d\tau = -\int_{t_0}^{t} e(\tau) \frac{\partial x(\tau)}{\partial \alpha} d\tau \tag{10.62}$$

$$\frac{\partial E}{\partial \boldsymbol{w}} = -\int_{t_0}^{t} (x_d(\tau) - x(\tau)) \frac{\partial x(\tau)}{\partial \boldsymbol{w}} d\tau = -\int_{t_0}^{t} e(\tau) \frac{\partial x(\tau)}{\partial \boldsymbol{w}} d\tau \tag{10.63}$$

The derivatives on the right-hand side of these equations may be evaluated from the original state system as follows:

$$\frac{\partial}{\partial \alpha}\left(\frac{dx}{dt}\right) = -\alpha \frac{\partial x}{\partial \alpha} - x + f_x(x, \boldsymbol{w}) \frac{\partial x}{\partial \alpha} \tag{10.64}$$

$$\frac{\partial}{\partial \boldsymbol{w}}\left(\frac{dx}{dt}\right) = -\alpha \frac{\partial x}{\partial \boldsymbol{w}} + \boldsymbol{f}_w(x, \boldsymbol{w}) + f_x(x, \boldsymbol{w}) \frac{\partial x}{\partial \boldsymbol{w}} \tag{10.65}$$

Note that the derivative with respect to the time and the partial derivatives with respect to the parameters on the left-hand side of these equations are commutable:

$$\frac{\partial}{\partial \alpha}\left(\frac{dx}{dt}\right) = \frac{d}{dt}\left(\frac{\partial x}{\partial \alpha}\right)$$

$$\frac{\partial}{\partial w}\left(\frac{dx}{dt}\right) = \frac{d}{dt}\left(\frac{\partial x}{\partial \boldsymbol{w}}\right)$$

Hence, let

$$z_\alpha \triangleq \frac{\partial x}{\partial \alpha} \in \Re$$

$$\boldsymbol{z}_w \triangleq \frac{\partial x}{\partial \boldsymbol{w}} \in \Re^{3n}$$

Then the partial derivatives of x with respect to the parameters may be generated by the following new dynamic system:

$$\frac{dz_\alpha}{dt} = -x + [f_x(x, \boldsymbol{w}) - \alpha] z_\alpha \tag{10.66}$$

$$\frac{d\boldsymbol{z}_w}{dt} = \boldsymbol{f}_w(x, \boldsymbol{w}) + [f_x(x, \boldsymbol{w}) - \alpha] \boldsymbol{z}_w \tag{10.67}$$

Since the initial condition $x(0)$ does not depend on the parameters α and $\boldsymbol{w}$, the initial conditions of Eqns. (10.66) and (10.67) are set to

$$z_\alpha(0) = 0, \qquad \boldsymbol{z}_w(0) = 0$$

Equations (10.66) and (10.67) are referred to as equations of *sensitivity systems* associated respectively with the parameters α and $\boldsymbol{w}$ (see Fig. 10.4). The

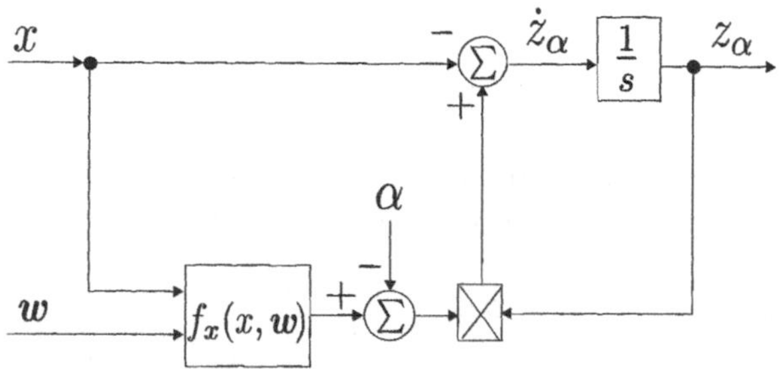

(a) Partial derivative $z_\alpha = \partial x / \partial \alpha$, Eqn. (10.66)

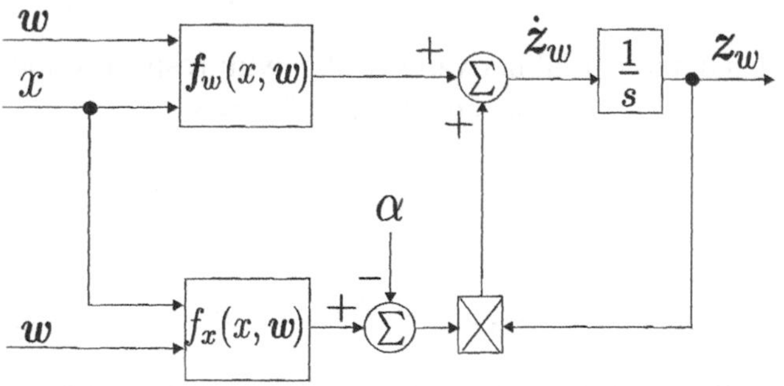

(b) Partial derivative $\boldsymbol{z}_w = \partial x / \partial \boldsymbol{w}$, Eqn. (10.67)

Figure 10.4 Block diagrams for the sensitivity functions for the partial derivatives $z_\alpha = \partial x / \partial \alpha$ and $\boldsymbol{z}_w = \partial x / \partial \boldsymbol{w}$.

replacement of the final condition of the adjoint equation in the dynamic backpropagation (DBP) algorithm discussed in the previous section with the initial conditions of the above mentioned sensitivity systems allows online calculations in the updating process.

10.3.2 Discrete-Time Dynamic Forward Propagation (DT-DFP)

For a given discrete-time sequence $x_d(i)$, $i = 1, 2, \ldots$, we are given the discrete-time model of the DNU

$$x(k+1) = -(\alpha - 1)x(k) + f(x(k), \boldsymbol{w}) + s(k) \tag{10.68}$$

Define a time-varying error index over the interval $[0, k]$ as

$$\begin{aligned} E(k) &= \tfrac{1}{2}\sum_{i=0}^{k}[x_d(i) - x(i)]^2 \\ &= \tfrac{1}{2}\sum_{i=0}^{k} e^2(i) \end{aligned} \tag{10.69}$$

where $e(i) = x_d(i) - x(i)$. Using the gradient descent method, the incremental terms of the parameters α and w are obtained as

$$\Delta\alpha(k) = -\eta_\alpha \frac{\partial E}{\partial \alpha} = -\eta_\alpha \sum_{i=1}^{k}\left(e(i)\frac{\partial x(i)}{\partial \alpha}\right) \tag{10.70}$$

$$\Delta\boldsymbol{w}(k) = -\eta_w \frac{\partial E}{\partial \boldsymbol{w}} = -\eta_w \sum_{i=1}^{k}\left(e(i)\frac{\partial x(i)}{\partial \boldsymbol{w}}\right) \tag{10.71}$$

On the other hand, the partial derivatives of x with respect to the parameters may be dealt with using the state equation as follows:

$$\begin{aligned} \frac{\partial}{\partial \alpha}x(k+1) &= -x(k) + [f_x(x(k), \boldsymbol{w}) - (\alpha - 1)]\frac{\partial}{\partial \alpha}x(k) \\ \frac{\partial}{\partial \boldsymbol{w}}x(k+1) &= \boldsymbol{f}_w(x(k), \boldsymbol{w}) + [f_x(x(k), \boldsymbol{w}) - (\alpha - 1)]\frac{\partial}{\partial \boldsymbol{w}}x(k) \end{aligned}$$

By introducing the sensitivity parameters z_α and $\boldsymbol{z}_w$ defined as

$$z_\alpha \triangleq \frac{\partial x}{\partial \alpha} \tag{10.72}$$

$$\boldsymbol{z}_w \triangleq \frac{\partial x}{\partial \boldsymbol{w}} \tag{10.73}$$

the parameter sensitivity equations may then be rewritten as in the following form:

$$\begin{aligned} z_\alpha(k+1) &= -x(k) + [f_x(x(k), \boldsymbol{w}) - (\alpha - 1)]z_\alpha(k) \\ z_\alpha(0) &= 0 \end{aligned} \tag{10.74}$$

$$\begin{aligned} \boldsymbol{z}_w(k+1) &= \boldsymbol{f}_w(x(k), \boldsymbol{w}) + [f_x(x(k), \boldsymbol{w}) - (\alpha - 1)]\boldsymbol{z}_w(k) \\ \boldsymbol{z}_w(0) &= 0 \end{aligned} \tag{10.75}$$

Hence, the updating equations for the parameters may be written as

$$\alpha(k+1) = \alpha(k) - \eta_\alpha \sum_{i=0}^{k} e(i) z_\alpha(i) \tag{10.76}$$

$$\boldsymbol{w}(k+1) = \boldsymbol{w}(k) - \eta_w \sum_{i=0}^{k} e(i) \boldsymbol{z}_w(i) \tag{10.77}$$

Example 10.1 Let the desired discrete-time signal $x_d(k)$ be a square wave with a period of 10 iterations and an amplitude of -1 and 1. Using the discrete-time sequence learning algorithm presented above, we adapt the discrete-time DNU model such that the sequence $x(k)$ of the state of the DT-DNU with a simple form

$$\frac{dx(t)}{dt} = -\alpha x(t) + w \tanh(x) + s(t) \tag{10.78}$$

will approach the given sequence $x_d(k)$.

Using the parameter sensitivity equations, Eqns. (10.74) and (10.75), the parameter adaptation equations for the DT-DNU described in Eqn. (10.78) are given by (see also Fig. 10.5)

$$\begin{aligned} z_\alpha(k+1) &= -x(k) + [w \operatorname{sech}^2(x(k)) - (\alpha - 1)]z_\alpha(k) \\ z_\alpha(0) &= 0 \end{aligned} \tag{10.79}$$

$$\begin{aligned} z_w(k+1) &= \tanh(x(k)) + [w \operatorname{sech}^2(x(k)) - (\alpha - 1)]z_w(k) \\ z_w(0) &= 0 \end{aligned} \tag{10.80}$$

The updating equations of the parameters are

$$\alpha(k+1) = \alpha(k) - \eta_\alpha \sum_{i=0}^{k} e(i) z_\alpha(i) \tag{10.81}$$

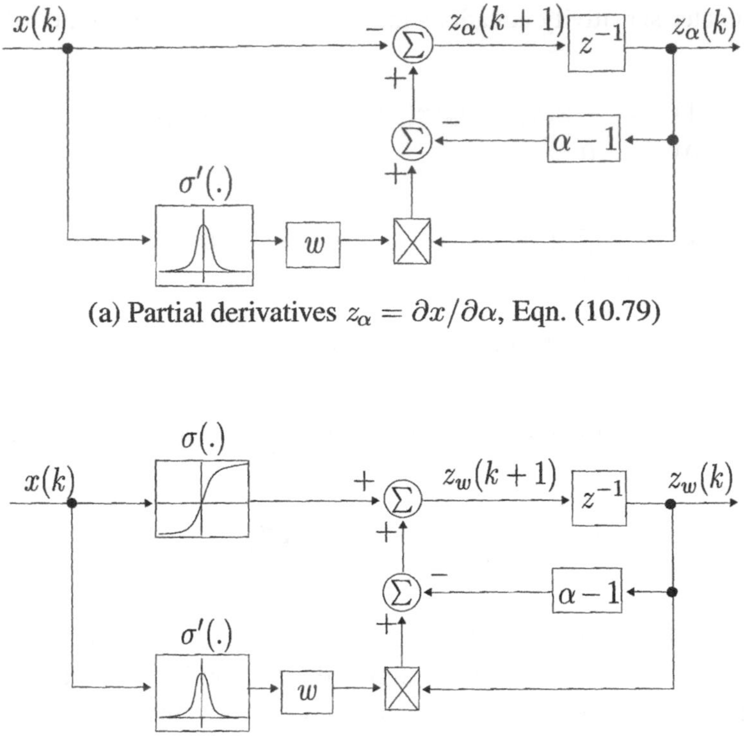

(a) Partial derivatives $z_\alpha = \partial x/\partial \alpha$, Eqn. (10.79)

(b) Partial derivatives $z_w = \partial x/\partial w$, Eqn. (10.80)

Figure 10.5 Example 10.1: block diagrams for the sensitivity functions for the partial derivatives $z_\alpha = \partial x/\partial \alpha$ and $z_w = \partial x/\partial w$.

$$w(k+1) = w(k) - \eta_w \sum_{i=0}^{k} e(i) z_w(i) \tag{10.82}$$

The initial values of the parameters α and w were chosen randomly in the interval $[-1, 1]$. Assume that the external input of the DT-DNU is $s(k) = x_d(k)$. Using such a learning process, the parameters were adapted as $\alpha = -0.22837$, and $w = -0.29986$. The simulation results of the state $x(k)$ of the DT-DNU, the desired $x_d(k)$, and the error $e(k)$ between $x_d(k)$ and $x(k)$ are shown in Fig. 10.6 for two different learning rates: (i) $\eta_w = \eta_\alpha = 0.008$, and (ii) $\eta_w = \eta_\alpha = 0.04$. The convergence process of the parameters was very fast for the higher learning rate of 0.04, and the smaller learning rate of 0.008 causes the convergence speed to decrease. ■

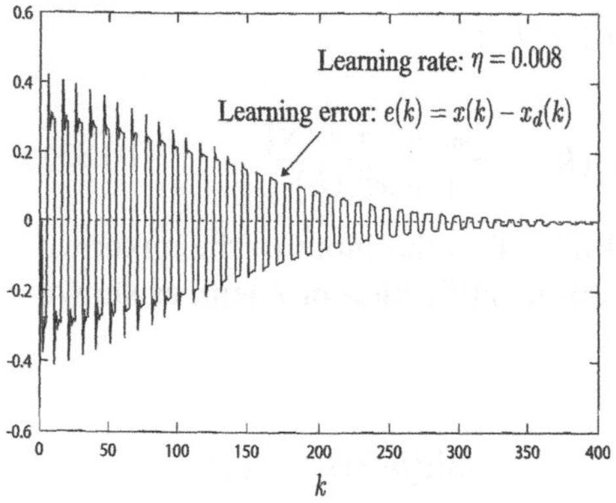

(a) Learning error during the learning process with a smaller learning rate $\eta_\alpha = \eta_w = 0.008$

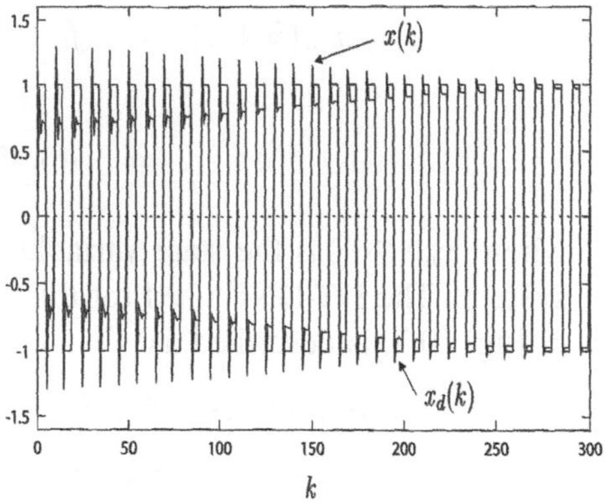

(b) State of the DT-DNU and the desired state $x_d(k)$ during the learning process with a smaller learning rate $\eta_\alpha = \eta_w = 0.008$

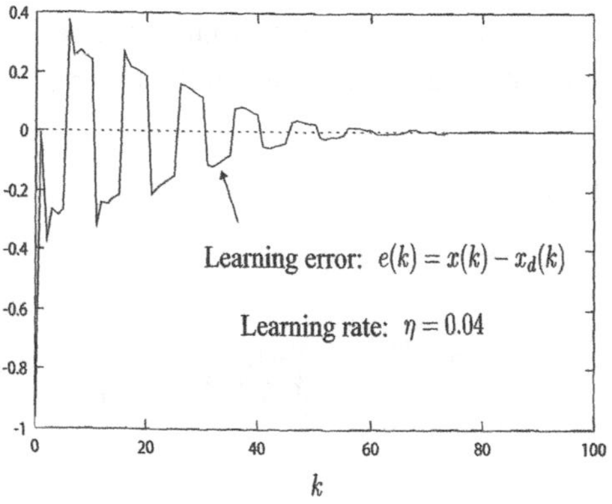

(c) Learning error during the learning process with a larger learning rate $\eta_\alpha = \eta_w = 0.04$

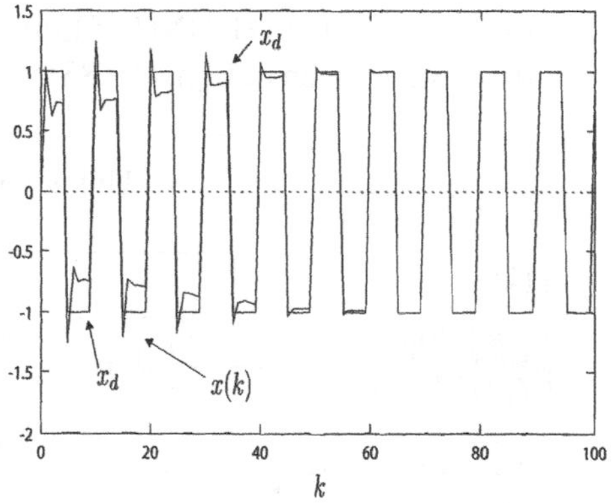

(d) State $x(k)$ of the DT-DNU and the desired state $x_d(k)$ during the learning process with a larger learning rate $\eta_\alpha = \eta_w = 0.04$

Figure 10.6 Example 10.1: simulation results with two different learning rates.

Example 10.2 In this example we consider the problem of identification of an unknown nonlinear discrete-time system described by

$$\begin{aligned} x_m(k+1) &= f_m(x_m(k), s(k)) \\ &= -0.25x_m(k) + \frac{x_m(k)+u(k)}{1+x_m^2(k)} \end{aligned} \tag{10.83}$$

where $x_m \in \Re$ is the state variable and $u \in \Re$ is the input to the unknown system. The DT-DNU used for this system identification problem, as shown in Fig. 10.7, is described as

$$\begin{aligned} x(k+1) &= f(x(k), u(k)) \\ &= -(\alpha-1)x(k) + a_1 \tanh(b_1 x(k) + c_1) \\ &\quad + a_2 \tanh(b_2 x(k) + c_2) + u(k) \end{aligned} \tag{10.84}$$

Using the identification procedure, parameters α and $\boldsymbol{w}$ were updated so that

$$\lim_{k\to\infty} (x_m(k) - x(k)) = 0 \tag{10.85}$$

In other words, the DT-DNU of Eqn. (10.84) becomes an approximate model of the system given in Eqn. (10.83) with an acceptable error between the states

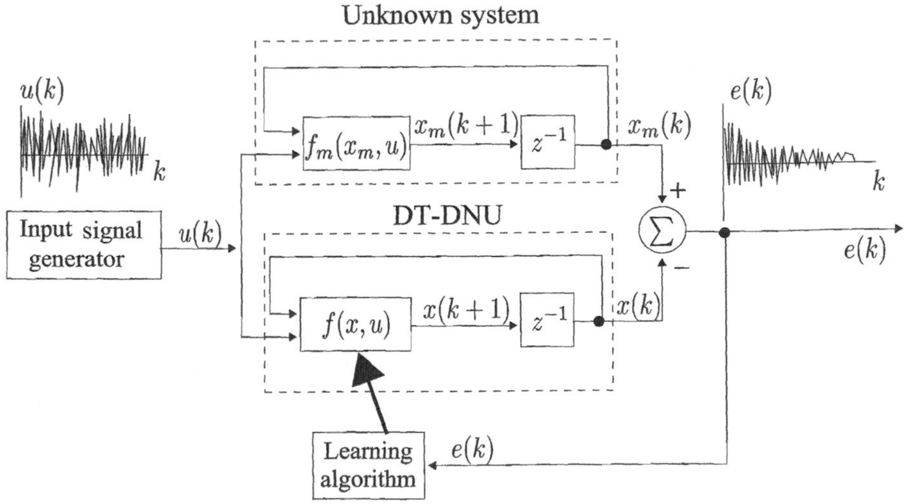

Figure 10.7 Example 10.2: system identification of an unknown discrete-time nonlinear system using a discrete-time dynamic neural unit (DT-DNU).

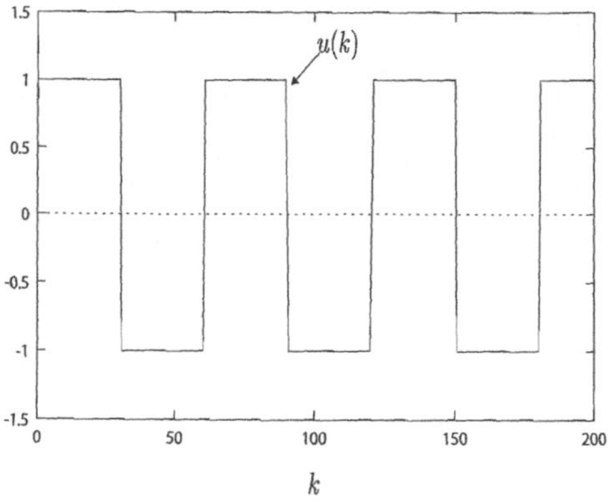

(a) Square-wave input signal with a period of 60 iterations and amplitude ±1

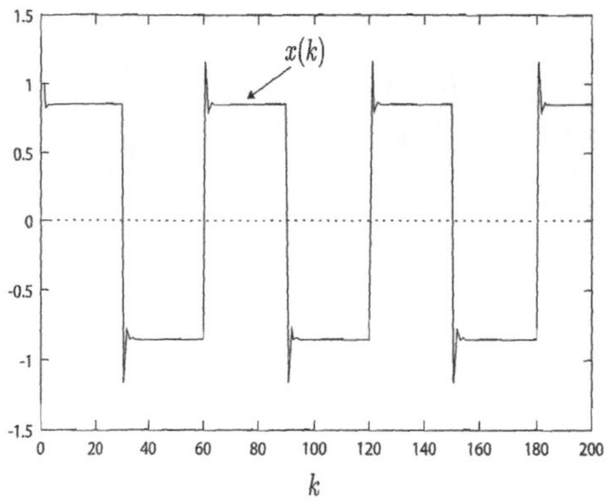

(b) State response of the adapted DT-DNU for square-wave inputs

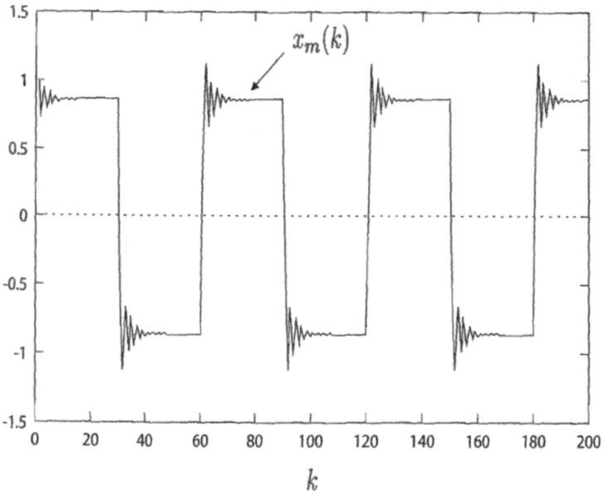

(c) State response of the unknown system with a square-wave input

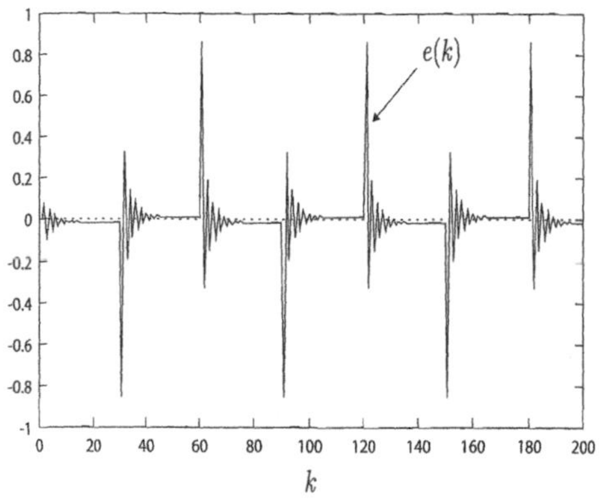

(d) Error response between the states of the unknown system and the adapted DT-DNU

Figure 10.8 Example 10.2: simulation results for identifying an unknown nonlinear dynamic system given in Eqn. (10.83) with a DT-DNU model, Eqn. (10.84). After 50,000 iterations for system identification, simulation results were obtained for a square-wave input signal.

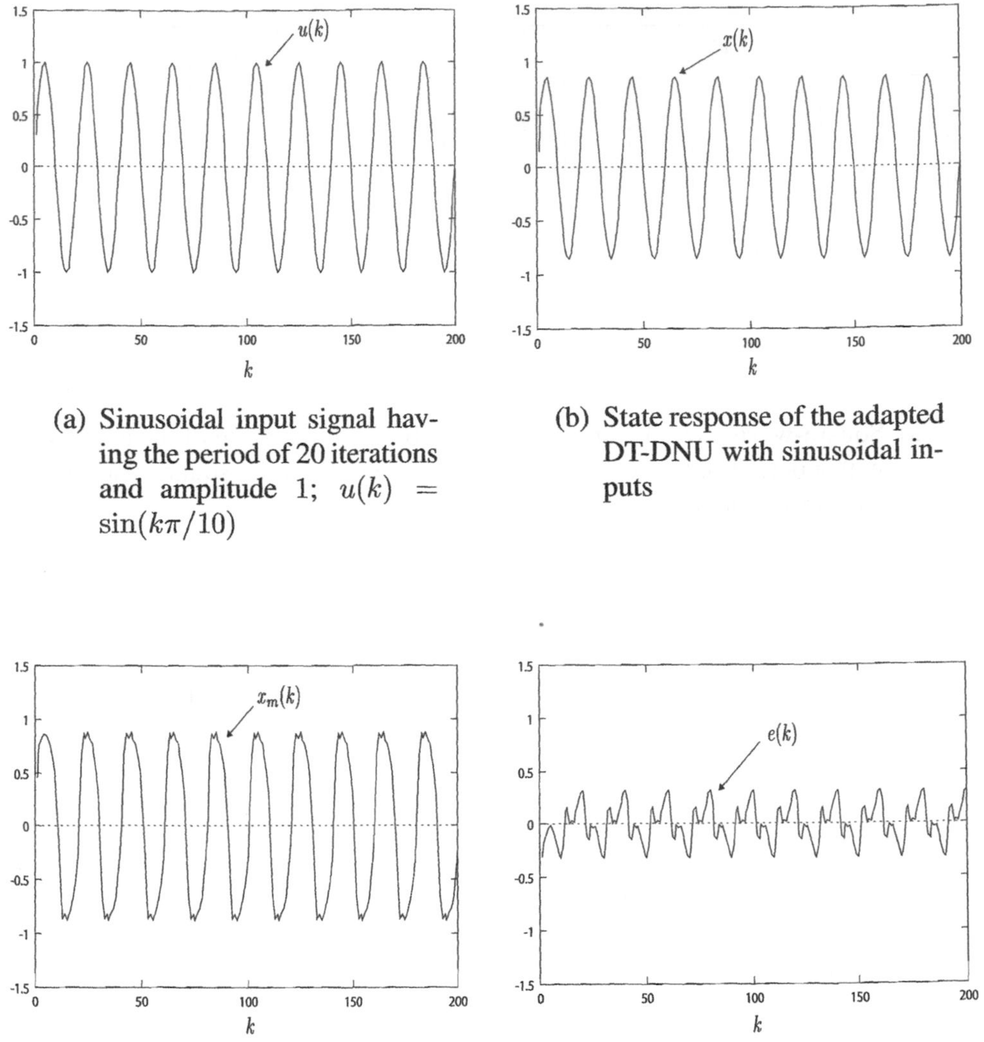

(a) Sinusoidal input signal having the period of 20 iterations and amplitude 1; $u(k) = \sin(k\pi/10)$

(b) State response of the adapted DT-DNU with sinusoidal inputs

(c) State response of the unknown system with sinusoidal inputs

(d) Error response between the state of the unknown system and the adapted DT-DNU

Figure 10.9 Example 10.2: simulation results with sinusoidal inputs. After 50,000 iterations were carried out for identifying a unknown nonlinear system, Eqn. (10.83), using a DT-DNU, a sine-wave input signal $u(k) = \sin(k\pi/10)$ was applied to both the unknown system and the DT-DNU.

of the unknown system and the DT-DNU adapted for an arbitrary input signal $u(k)$.

During the learning phase, the input signal $u(k)$ was designed to be random in the closed interval $[-1, 1]$, the initial values of the parameters α and $\boldsymbol{w}$ were chosen randomly in the closed interval $[-1, 1]$, and the initial values of both the unknown system and DT-DNU were set at zero. After 50,000 learning iterations, the parameters converged to the following values

$$\alpha = 1.15433, \qquad \begin{cases} a_1 = -0.39846 \\ a_2 = 0.34944, \end{cases}$$

$$\begin{cases} b_1 = 0.01169 \\ b_2 = 0.00838, \end{cases} \qquad \begin{cases} c_1 = 0.28653 \\ c_2 = 0.18433 \end{cases}$$

At this point, the learning phase was stopped and a binary square-wave with an amplitude of $[-1, 1]$ and a period of 60 iterations was applied simultaneously as the inputs to the unknown plant and the DNU model. Simulation results are shown in Fig. 10.8. It is to be noted that the error during the transient period is high; otherwise the DNU model is able to adapt the nonlinear plant fairly well.

Figure 10.9 shows the simulation results for this system with a sinusoidal signal of amplitude $(-1, 1)$ and a period of 50 iterations applied as inputs to both the unknown plants and the DT-DNU model. These simulation studies show that the DT-DNU model was able to identify fairly well the unknown plant.

Such DT-DNU models with higher-order dynamics may be used for better approximations of complex nonlinear and time-varying plants. Such analytic tools provided by the neural processes may be useful for both the analysis and design of the complex feedback control systems. ■

10.4 DYNAMIC BACKPROPAGATION (DBP) FOR CONTINUOUS-TIME DYNAMIC NEURAL NETWORKS (CT-DNNs)

10.4.1 General Representation of Network Models

Consider a general form of a continuous-time dynamic neural network (CT-DNN) shown in Fig. 10.10 and described by a continuous-time nonlinear system of the following form

$$\frac{d\boldsymbol{x}(t)}{dt} = -\boldsymbol{A}\boldsymbol{x}(k) + \boldsymbol{f}(\boldsymbol{x}(t), \boldsymbol{W}, \boldsymbol{\theta}) \in \Re^n$$

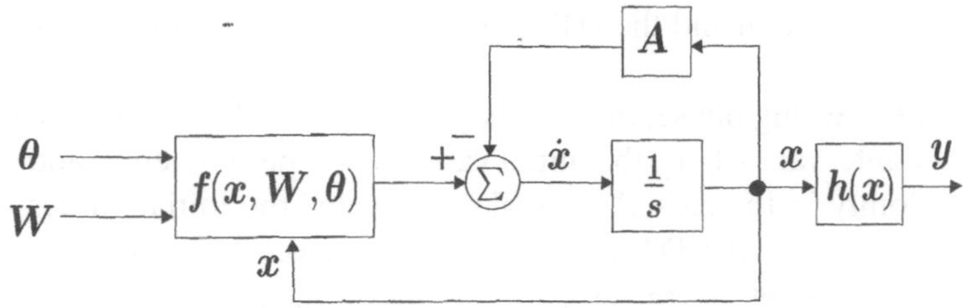

Figure 10.10 Block diagram of the continuous-time dynamic neural network (CT-DNN), Eqn. (10.86).

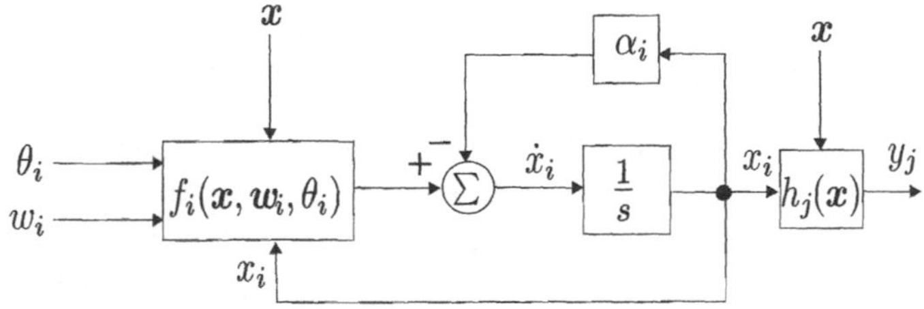

Figure 10.11 Block diagram of the ith neuron of the model given in Eqn. (10.87).

$$y(t) = h(x(t)) \in \Re^m \tag{10.86}$$

where $\boldsymbol{x} = [x_1 \;\cdots\; x_n]^T \in \Re^n$ is the state vector of the dynamic neural network, x_i represents the internal state of the ith neuron, $\boldsymbol{A} = diag[\alpha_1, \ldots, \alpha_n]$ with all $\alpha_i > 0$, $\boldsymbol{W} = [w_{ij}]_{n\times n}$ is the real-valued matrix of the synaptic weight matrix, $\boldsymbol{\theta} = [\theta_1 \;\cdots\; \theta_n]^T$ is a threshold vector (somatic vector), $\boldsymbol{y} = [y_1 \;\cdots\; y_m]^T$ is an observation vector or output vector, $\boldsymbol{f}$: $\Re^n \times \Re^{n\times n} \times \Re^n \longrightarrow \Re^n$ is a continuous and differentiable vector-valued function, $f_i(.)$ and $\partial f_i/\partial \boldsymbol{x}$ are respectively bounded and uniformly bounded, and $\boldsymbol{h}(\boldsymbol{x})$: $\Re^n \longrightarrow \Re^m$ is a known continuous and differentiable vector-valued function.

The dynamic neural network consists of both the feedforward and feedback connections between the layers; thus, these neurons form a complex nonlinear dynamic system. In fact, the weight w_{ij} represents a synaptic connection parameter between the ith and jth neurons, and θ_i is a threshold at the ith neuron. An arbitrary neuron in the network may have synaptic connections with itself and all the other neurons. Also, the output of a neuron is not only a function of its own state but also a combination of states of the other neurons in the networks. Hence, as shown in Fig. 10.11, the nonlinear vector-valued function on the right side of the system given in Eqn. (10.86) may be represented as

Table 10.1 **Three continuous-time dynamic neural models**

Neural Model No.	Dynamic Neural Models	
	Network Equations	Region of Equilibrium
I	$\frac{dx_i(t)}{dt} = -\alpha_i x_i(t) + \beta_i \sigma_i \left(\sum_{j=1}^{n} w_{ij} x_j(t) + \theta_i \right)$ $y_j(t) = x_j(t)$	$[-\|\beta_i\|, \|\beta_i\|]^n$
II	$\frac{dx_i(t)}{dt} = -\alpha_i x_i(t) + \sigma_i \left(\sum_{j=1}^{n} w_{ij} x_j(t) \right) + \theta_i$ $y_j(t) = x_j(t)$	$[\|\theta_i\| - 1, \|\theta_i\| + 1]^n$
III	$\frac{dx_i(t)}{dt} = -\alpha_i x_i(t) + \sum_{j=1}^{n} w_{ij} y_j(t) + \theta_i$ $y_j(t) = \sigma_j(x_j(t))$	$[\|\theta_i\| - W_i, \|\theta_i\| + W_i]^n$ where $W_i = \sum_{j=1}^{n} \|w_{ij}\|$

$$\begin{aligned} \frac{dx_i(t)}{dt} &= -\alpha_i x_i(t) + f_i(\boldsymbol{x}(t), \boldsymbol{w}_i, \theta_i), \qquad i = 1, \ldots, n \\ y_j(t) &= h_j(\boldsymbol{x}(t)), \quad j = 1, \ldots, m \end{aligned} \tag{10.87}$$

where

$$\boldsymbol{W} = \begin{bmatrix} w_{11} & \cdots & w_{1n} \\ \vdots & \ddots & \vdots \\ w_{n1} & \cdots & w_{nn} \end{bmatrix} = \begin{bmatrix} \boldsymbol{w}_1^T \\ \vdots \\ \boldsymbol{w}_n^T \end{bmatrix} \tag{10.88}$$

and

$$\boldsymbol{w}_i = \begin{bmatrix} w_{i1} \\ \vdots \\ w_{in} \end{bmatrix}, \qquad i = 1, \ldots, n \tag{10.89}$$

Equation (10.87) indicates that the dynamics of the ith neuron in the network are associated with all the states of the network, the synaptic weights $w_{i1}, \ldots, w_{in}$, and the somatic threshold parameter θ_i.

The three main types of continuous-time dynamic neural models are given in Table 10.1. These neural model describe the different dynamic properties due to the different neural state equations. Models I and II are defined by nonlinear differential equations. Model III, however, is defined by the seminonlinear equations, which contain the linear terms on the right side of the model and nonlinear terms in the output equation. In these neural models, $\boldsymbol{W} = [w_{ij}]_{n\times n}$ is the synaptic connection weight matrix, β_i is the neural gain of the ith neuron, $0 < \alpha_i < 1$ is the self-state feedback gain of the ith neuron, and θ_i is a threshold at the ith neuron. The neural activation function $\sigma(.)$ may be chosen as the continuous and differentiable nonlinear sigmoidal function as used in the previous sections.

10.4.2 DBP Learning Algorithms

The dynamic backpropagation (DBP) algorithm for a class of continuous-time recurrent neural networks was first proposed by Pineda (1988). A DBP learning algorithm for a general class of dynamic neural systems with nonlinear output equations will be developed in this section for the purpose of analog target pattern storage. Let $\boldsymbol{t} = [t_1 \ \cdots \ t_m]^T$ be an analog target pattern that is to be implemented by a steady state output vector that is a nonlinear vector function of an equilibrium point $\boldsymbol{x}^f$ of the neural system given in Eqn. (10.86); that is, $\boldsymbol{t} = \boldsymbol{h}(\boldsymbol{x}^f)$. The purpose of the learning procedure is to adjust the synaptic weights w_{ij} and the somatic threshold parameter θ_i

such t_i can be realized by the nonlinear function $h_i(\boldsymbol{x}^f)$. Note that, however, we can derive the learning procedure for two-point boundary-value problems (TPBVPs) instead of steady state pattern.

Define an error function as

$$\begin{aligned} E &= \tfrac{1}{2}\sum_{\ell=1}^{m}[t_\ell - h_\ell(\boldsymbol{x}^f)]^2 = \tfrac{1}{2}\sum_{\ell=1}^{m}(J_\ell^f(\boldsymbol{x}^f))^2 \\ &= \tfrac{1}{2}\left(\boldsymbol{J}^f(\boldsymbol{x}^f)\right)^T \boldsymbol{J}^f(\boldsymbol{x}^f) \end{aligned} \tag{10.90}$$

where

$$\boldsymbol{J}^f(\boldsymbol{x}^f) = [J_1^f(\boldsymbol{x}^f) \ \cdots \ J_m^f(\boldsymbol{x}^f)]^T \in \Re^m$$

whose components are defined by

$$\boldsymbol{J}_\ell^f(\boldsymbol{x}^f) = t_\ell - h_\ell(\boldsymbol{x}^f), \quad \ell = 1, \ldots, m$$

and $\boldsymbol{x}^f$ is an equilibrium state vector of the system, which satisfies the following equilibrium equation

$$\frac{d\boldsymbol{x}^f}{dt} = 0 \quad \longrightarrow \quad -\boldsymbol{A}\boldsymbol{x}^f + \boldsymbol{f}(\boldsymbol{x}^f, \boldsymbol{W}, \boldsymbol{\theta}) = 0$$

that is

$$\boldsymbol{A}\boldsymbol{x}^f = \boldsymbol{f}(\boldsymbol{x}^f, \boldsymbol{W}, \boldsymbol{\theta}) \tag{10.91}$$

Next, we discuss the learning formulations of the synaptic weights and somatic parameters. After performing a gradient descent in E, the incremental change of the weight $w_{i,j}$ is given by

$$\begin{aligned} \frac{dw_{ij}}{dt} &= -\eta_w \frac{\partial E}{\partial w_{ij}} \\ &= -\eta_w \left(\frac{\partial E}{\partial \boldsymbol{x}^f}\right)^T \frac{\partial \boldsymbol{x}^f}{\partial w_{ij}} \\ &= -\eta_w \sum_{p=1}^{n} \frac{\partial E}{\partial x_p{}^f} \frac{\partial x_p^f}{\partial w_{ij}} \end{aligned} \tag{10.92}$$

where η_w is a learning rate associated with the synaptic weights. On the other hand, for the somatic parameter θ_i, the incremental formulation is

$$\frac{d\theta_i}{dt} = -\eta_\theta \frac{\partial E}{\partial \theta_i}$$

$$
\begin{aligned}
&= -\eta_\theta \left(\frac{\partial E}{\partial \boldsymbol{x}^f}\right)^T \frac{\partial \boldsymbol{x}^f}{\partial w_{ij}} \\
&= -\eta_\theta \sum_{p=1}^{n} \frac{\partial E}{\partial {x_p}^f} \frac{\partial x_p^f}{\partial w_{ij}} \qquad (10.93)
\end{aligned}
$$

where η_θ is the learning rate associated with the somatic parameters.

Using Eqn. (10.90), one may easily obtain

$$
\begin{aligned}
\frac{\partial E}{\partial x_p^f} &= \sum_{\ell=1}^{m} J_\ell^f \frac{\partial J_\ell^f}{\partial x_p^f} \\
&= -\sum_{\ell=1}^{m} [t_\ell - h_\ell(\boldsymbol{x}^f)] \frac{\partial h_\ell(\boldsymbol{x}^f)}{\partial x_p^f} \qquad (10.94)
\end{aligned}
$$

Substituting this expression in Eqns. (10.92) and (10.93), respectively, yields

$$
\begin{aligned}
\frac{dw_{ij}}{dt} &= -\eta_w \frac{\partial E}{\partial w_{ij}} \\
&= \eta_w \sum_{p=1}^{n} \sum_{\ell=1}^{m} [t_\ell - h_\ell(\boldsymbol{x}^f)] \frac{\partial h_\ell(\boldsymbol{x}^f)}{\partial x_p^f} \frac{\partial x_p^f}{\partial w_{ij}} \\
&= \eta_w \sum_{p=1}^{n} \sum_{\ell=1}^{m} J_\ell^f \frac{\partial h_\ell(\boldsymbol{x}^f)}{\partial x_p^f} \frac{\partial x_p^f}{\partial w_{ij}} \qquad (10.95)
\end{aligned}
$$

and

$$
\begin{aligned}
\frac{d\theta_i}{dt} &= -\eta_\theta \frac{\partial E}{\partial \theta_i} \\
&= \eta_\theta \sum_{p=1}^{n} \sum_{\ell=1}^{m} [t_\ell - h_\ell(\boldsymbol{x}^f)] \frac{\partial h_\ell(\boldsymbol{x}^f)}{\partial x_p^f} \frac{\partial x_p^f}{\partial \theta_i} \\
&= \eta_\theta \sum_{p=1}^{n} \sum_{\ell=1}^{m} J_\ell^f \frac{\partial h_\ell(\boldsymbol{x}^f)}{\partial x_p^f} \frac{\partial x_p^f}{\partial \theta_i} \qquad (10.96)
\end{aligned}
$$

On the basis of the equilibrium point equation given in Eqn. (10.91), the partial derivative of x_i^f with respect to w_{ij}, results in the following expression

$$
\alpha_p \frac{\partial x_p^f}{\partial w_{ij}} = \delta_{i,p} \frac{\partial f_p}{\partial w_{ij}} + \sum_{\ell=1}^{n} \frac{\partial f_p}{\partial x_\ell^f} \frac{\partial x_\ell^f}{\partial w_{ij}} \qquad (10.97)
$$

where $\delta_{i,j}$ is the *Krönecker* delta function:

$$\delta_{i,j} = \begin{cases} 0, & i \neq j \\ 1, & i = j \end{cases}$$

Moreover, let us denote

$$\frac{\partial x_p^f}{\partial w_{ij}} = \sum_{\ell=1}^{n} \delta_{p,\ell} \frac{\partial x_\ell^f}{\partial w_{ij}} \tag{10.98}$$

Then, Eqn. (10.97) can be represented as

$$\sum_{\ell=1}^{n} \left[\alpha_p \delta_{p,\ell} - \frac{\partial f_p}{\partial x_\ell^f} \right] \frac{\partial x_\ell^f}{\partial w_{ij}} = \delta_{i,p} \frac{\partial f_p}{\partial w_{ij}} \tag{10.99}$$

For convenience, let the matrix $\boldsymbol{M}$ be introduced whose elements are defined by

$$m_{p\ell} = \alpha_p \delta_{p,\ell} - \frac{\partial f_p}{\partial x_\ell^f} \tag{10.100}$$

Then, Eqn. (10.99) can be rewritten as

$$\sum_{\ell=1}^{n} m_{p\ell} \frac{\partial x_\ell^f}{\partial w_{ij}} = \delta_{i,p} \frac{\partial f_p}{\partial w_{ij}} \tag{10.101}$$

Let $\boldsymbol{M}^{-1} = [\overline{m}_{\ell i}]_{n \times n}$ be the inverse of the matrix $\boldsymbol{M}$. Then $\partial x_\ell^f / \partial w_{ij}$ may be solved as

$$\frac{\partial x_\ell^f}{\partial w_{ij}} = \overline{m}_{\ell i} \frac{\partial f_i}{\partial w_{ij}} \tag{10.102}$$

Hence, the updating equations for the weight w_{ij} and threshold θ_i are expressed as

$$\frac{dw_{ij}}{dt} = \eta_w \sum_{p=1}^{n} \sum_{\ell=1}^{m} \left[J_\ell^f \frac{\partial h_\ell(\boldsymbol{x}^f)}{\partial x_p^f} \overline{m}_{pi} \right] \frac{\partial f_i}{\partial w_{ij}} \tag{10.103}$$

Using the same procedure, one obtains

$$\frac{\partial x_\ell^f}{\partial \theta_i} = \overline{m}_{\ell i} \frac{\partial f_i}{\partial \theta_i} \tag{10.104}$$

Hence

$$\frac{d\theta_i}{dt} = \eta_\theta \sum_{p=1}^{n} \sum_{\ell=1}^{m} \left[J_\ell^f \frac{\partial h_\ell(\boldsymbol{x}^f)}{\partial x_p^f} \overline{m}_{pi} \right] \frac{\partial f_i}{\partial \theta_i} \tag{10.105}$$

Furthermore, let us introduce a new n-dimensional vector

$$\boldsymbol{z}^f = [z_1^f \; \cdots \; z_n^f]^T$$

whose components are defined as

$$z_i^f = \sum_{p=1}^{n} \sum_{\ell=1}^{m} J_\ell^f \frac{\partial h_\ell(\boldsymbol{x}^f)}{\partial x_p^f} \overline{m}_{pi}, \qquad i = 1, \ldots, n \tag{10.106}$$

It can be shown that

$$\sum_{p=1}^{n} \left[\alpha_p \delta_{p,i} - \frac{\partial f_p}{\partial x_i^f} \right] z_p^f = \sum_{\ell=1}^{m} J_\ell^f \frac{\partial h_\ell(\boldsymbol{x}^f)}{\partial x_i^f} \tag{10.107}$$

that is

$$\alpha_i z_i^f = \sum_{p=1}^{n} \frac{\partial f_p}{\partial x_i^f} z_p^f + \sum_{\ell=1}^{m} J_\ell^f \frac{\partial h_\ell(\boldsymbol{x}^f)}{\partial x_i^f} \tag{10.108}$$

Hence, Eqns. (10.103) and (10.105) can be represented, respectively by

$$\frac{dw_{ij}}{dt} = \eta_w z_i^f \frac{\partial f_i}{\partial w_{i,j}} \tag{10.109}$$

and

$$\frac{d\theta_i}{dt} = \eta_\theta z_i^f \frac{\partial f_i}{\partial \theta_i} \tag{10.110}$$

Equation (10.108) is said to be the steady adjoint equation associated with the equilibrium point equation given in Eqn. (10.91) of the dynamic neural system given in Eqn. (10.87). It is easy to define the adjoint equation for the adjoint vector $\boldsymbol{z}(t)$ as follows

$$\begin{aligned} \frac{dz_i(t)}{dt} &= -\alpha_i z_i(t) + \sum_{p=1}^{n} \frac{\partial f_p(\boldsymbol{x}(t), \boldsymbol{w}_p, \theta_p)}{\partial x_i} z_p(t) \\ &\quad + \sum_{\ell=1}^{m} J_\ell(\boldsymbol{x}(t)) \frac{\partial h_\ell(\boldsymbol{x}(t))}{\partial x_i} \end{aligned} \tag{10.111}$$

or, in a more compact form

$$\frac{dz(t)}{dt} = -\boldsymbol{A}z(t) + \left[\frac{\partial \boldsymbol{f}(\boldsymbol{x}, \boldsymbol{W}, \boldsymbol{\theta})}{\partial \boldsymbol{x}}\right]^T z(t) + \left[\frac{\partial \boldsymbol{h}(\boldsymbol{x}(t))}{\partial \boldsymbol{x}}\right]^T \boldsymbol{J}(\boldsymbol{x}) \quad (10.112)$$

where $J_i(\boldsymbol{x}(t)) = t_i - h_i(\boldsymbol{x}(t))$. Equation (10.111) is said to be the adjoint equation associated with the dynamic neural systems given in Eqn. (10.86).

The updating rules given in Eqns. (10.109) and (10.110) are not able to guarantee the stability of both of the systems given in Eqn. (10.86) and its adjoint, Eqn. (10.112), and a checking procedure for the stability of both equations is needed in such a dynamic learning process. The first approach is to verify that the stability condition of the equilibrium may be carried out after the dynamic learning process has been completed. In this case, if the network is unstable, the learning phase must be repeated, and the steady states $\boldsymbol{x}^f$ and $\boldsymbol{z}^f$ must be solved using the nonlinear algebraic equations, Eqns. (10.91)

Table 10.2 **Four discrete-time dynamic neural models**

Model No.	Dynamic Neural Models: State Equations	Dynamic Neural Models: Region of Equilibrium
I	$x_i(k+1) = \beta_i \sigma_i \left(\sum_{j=1}^{n} w_{ij} x_j(t) + \theta_i \right)$	$[-\lvert\beta_i\rvert, \lvert\beta_i\rvert]^n$
II	$x_i(k+1) = \sigma_i \left(\sum_{j=1}^{n} w_{ij} x_j(t) \right) + \theta_i$	$[\lvert\theta_i\rvert - 1, \lvert\theta_i\rvert + 1]^n$
III	$x_i(k+1) = \alpha_i x_i(t) + (1-\alpha_i) \times \sigma_i \left(\sum_{j=1}^{n} w_{ij} x_j(t) + \theta_i \right)$ $0 < \alpha_i < 1$	$[-1, 1]^n$
IV	$x_i(k+1) = \alpha_i x_i(t) + \beta_i \sigma_i \left(\sum_{j=1}^{n} w_{ij} x_j(t) + \theta_i \right)$ $0 < \alpha_i < 1$	$\left[1 - \left\lvert\frac{\beta_i}{1-\alpha_i}\right\rvert, 1 + \left\lvert\frac{\beta_i}{1-\alpha_i}\right\rvert\right]^n$

and (10.108), at each iterative instant. The second approach is to verify the known stability of the network at each iterative instant. When the network is unstable, [i.e., when Eqns. (10.91) and (10.108) do not converge to the stable equilibrium points $\boldsymbol{x}^f$ and $\boldsymbol{z}^f$], the iterative process must be repeated by adjusting the learning rates η_w and η_θ, until the solutions of Eqns. (10.91) and (10.108) converge to some stable equilibrium points as time k becomes large. Both of these methods for studying the stability are very time-consuming.

For the discrete-time dynamic neural models given in Table 10.2, the DBP learning algorithms for the synaptic weight w_{ij}, and the threshold θ_i are respectively summarized in Table 10.3. The steady state adjoint equations corresponding to these neural models are also summarized in Table 10.3.

Table 10.3 **DBP learning algorithms for the models given in Table 10.2**

Model No.	DBP Learning Algorithms: Updating Laws	DBP Learning Algorithms: Steady Adjoint Equations
I	$\Delta w_{i,j} = \eta z_i^f \beta_i \sigma'(u_i^f) x_j^f$ $\Delta \theta_i = \eta_\theta z_i^f \sigma'(u_i^f)$	$z_i^f = \sum_{p=1}^{n} \beta_p \sigma'(u_p^f) w_{p,i} z_p^f + \sum_{l=1}^{m} J_l^f \frac{\partial h_l(x^f)}{\partial x_i}$
II	$\Delta w_{i,j} = \eta z_i^f \sigma' \left(\sum_{j=1}^{n} w_{i,j} x_j^f \right) x_j^f$ $\Delta \theta_i = \eta_\theta z_i^f$	$z_i^f = \sum_{p=1}^{n} \sigma' \left(\sum_{j=1}^{n} w_{p,j} x_j^f \right) w_{p,i} z_p^f + \sum_{l=1}^{m} J_l^f \frac{\partial h_l(x^f)}{\partial x_i}$
III	$\Delta w_{i,j} = \eta (1 - \alpha_i) z_i^f \sigma'(u_i^f) x_j^f$ $\Delta \theta_i = \eta_\theta z_i^f (1 - \alpha_i) \sigma'(u_i^f)$	$z_i^f = \sum_{p=1}^{n} \Big[\alpha_p \delta_{p,i} + (1 - \alpha_p) \sigma'(u_p^f) w_{p,i} \Big] z_p^f + \sum_{l=1}^{m} J_l^f \frac{\partial h_l(x^f)}{\partial x_i}$
IV	$\Delta w_{i,j} = \eta z_i^f \beta_i \sigma'(u_i^f) x_j^f$ $\Delta \theta_i = \eta_\theta z_i^f \beta_i \sigma'(u_i^f)$	$z_i^f = \sum_{p=1}^{n} \Big[\alpha_p \delta_{p,i} + \beta_p \sigma'(u_p^f) w_{p,i} \Big] z_p^f + \sum_{l=1}^{m} J_l^f \frac{\partial h_l(x^f)}{\partial x_i}$
where $u_i^f = \sum_{j=1}^{n} w_{i,j} x_j^f + \theta_i$		

The preceding iterative process for updating the parameters toward a target set is the *adaptive learning process* of the parameters. During this learning phase, the parameters are adjusted according to the error between the equilibrium point of the current system at each learning instant and the target point. In other words, the error is propagated into the neural system as a function of supervision for updating the parameters. This is why this approach is called *error backpropagation*. From the systems point of view, a system which consists of the forward state equation and backward learning equations forms a closed loop feedback system in which the error is a basic feedback signal. From the biological point of view, the forward state equation of the neural system describes a process of *information receiving and transmission*, and the backward learning equations emulate a *thinking* process. It is evident that this two-way information propagation exists in many human cognitive processes.

It is important to stress that this system evolves both in the space of activations (state space) and in the space of weights (weight space or parameter space). The evolution in the state space is determined by Eqn. (10.86) whereas the evolution in the parameter space is determined by Eqns. (10.109) and (10.110). The iterative learning algorithm can be implemented online by computing a set of differential equations. This will bring potential benefits for applications to problems such as neurovision systems, real-time control systems, and identification.

10.5 CONCLUDING REMARKS

Learning and *adaptation* are the two keywords associated with the notion of neural networks. We have studied in detail dynamic backpropagation methods for the temporal learning process for both continuous-time and discrete-time dynamic neural networks. These learning algorithms provide a special attribute for the design and operation of the dynamic neural network for a given task such as in the processing of signals and images and their storage, and in the design of controllers for complex dynamic systems.

This discussion will expose the readers to certain innovations in the field of neural network learning and adaptation. Indeed, some of the advanced learning methods can make the neural network perform chaotic state trajectories (Principe and Kuo 1995, Deco and Schürmann 1997, Honma et al. 1999a). Also, some of the new learning methods such as the decomposed extended Kalman filter (DEKF) and recursive least squares (RLS) approaches may lead to a better design of learning algorithms for many practical applications (Haykin 1991, Xu et al. 2002).

Problems

10.1 Using the dynamic backpropagation (DBP) learning method developed in Section 10.2, train a dynamic neural unit with the following form

$$\frac{dx(t)}{dt} = -x + w\tanh(x(t)) + s$$

to store an analog pattern, $\nu = 6.0$.

10.2 Derive a dynamic backpropagation learning algorithm for continuous-time dynamic neural networks (CT-DNNs) to solve two-point boundary-value problems (TPBVPs).

10.3 Consider the following CT-DNN with six dynamic neural units and two neural outputs of the network given as

$$\begin{aligned}\frac{dx_i(t)}{dt} &= -x_i(t) + \tanh\left(\sum_{j=1}^{6} w_{ij}x_j(t)\right), \quad i = 1, 2, \ldots, 6 \\ y_k(t) &= x_k(t), \quad k = 1, 2\end{aligned}$$

Train the CT-DNN to follow a *circular trajectory* by using the dynamic backpropagation learning method developed in Problem 10.2.

10.4 Determine the region of equilibrium points for discrete-time dynamic neural models given in Table 10.2.

10.5 Prove the DBP learning algorithms given in Table 10.3 for the neural models given in Table 10.2.

10.6 Design a discrete-time dynamic neural network for the time series prediction of the Logistic or Feigenbaum map

$$x(k+1) = 4x(k)(1 - x(k)), \quad k = 0, 1, \ldots$$

10.7 Design a continuous-time dynamic neural network to model the Mackey–Glass system (Mackey and Glass, 1977) described by the following delay-differential equation

$$\frac{dy(t)}{dt} = \frac{0.2y(t - T_d)}{1 + y^{10}(t - T_d)} - 0.1y(t)$$

with $T_d = 30$, sampled at $1/6$ Hz.

10.8 Design a continuous-time dynamic neural network to model the Lorenz attractor whose dynamics are described by a coupled system of three nonlinear differential equations (Haykin and Principe, 1998)

$$\begin{aligned}\frac{dx(t)}{dt} &= -\sigma x(t) + \sigma y(t)\\ \frac{dy(t)}{dt} &= -x(t)z(t) + \gamma x(t) - y(t)\\ \frac{dz(t)}{dt} &= x(t)y(t) - bz(t)\end{aligned}$$

where σ, γ, and b are dimensionless parameters. Typical values for these parameters are $\sigma = 10$, $\gamma = 28$, and $b = 8/3$.

10.9 Consider a dynamic neural network with the following differential equation

$$\dot{\boldsymbol{x}}(t) = -\boldsymbol{x}(t) + \boldsymbol{\sigma}(\boldsymbol{W}\boldsymbol{x}(t)) + \boldsymbol{I}$$

where $\boldsymbol{x} \in \Re^n$, $\boldsymbol{W} \in \Re^{n\times n}$, $\boldsymbol{I} \in \Re^n$, and $\boldsymbol{\sigma}: \Re^n \longrightarrow \Re^n$. Let $\boldsymbol{d}(t) = [d_1(t)\ d_2(t)\ \cdots\ d_n(t)]^T$ be a differentiable trajectories. Define an error function of the form

$$E(t) = \tfrac{1}{2} \parallel \boldsymbol{x}(t) - \boldsymbol{d}(t) \parallel^2$$

Derive the learning equation for the weight matrix $\boldsymbol{W}$ by minimizing

$$\begin{aligned}J(\boldsymbol{W}) &= \int_0^T E(t)dt\\ &= \tfrac{1}{2}\int_0^T \parallel \boldsymbol{x}(t) - \boldsymbol{d}(t) \parallel^2 dt\end{aligned}$$

10.10 (Universal Approximation of Nonlinear Systems) Consider a discrete-time dynamic neural network of the form

$$\begin{aligned}\boldsymbol{x}(k+1) &= -\alpha\boldsymbol{x}(k) + \boldsymbol{A}\boldsymbol{\sigma}(\boldsymbol{x}(k) + \boldsymbol{B}\boldsymbol{u}(k))\\ \boldsymbol{y}(k) &= \boldsymbol{C}\boldsymbol{x}(k)\end{aligned}$$

where $\boldsymbol{x} \in \Re^N$, $\boldsymbol{u} \in \Re^m$, and $\boldsymbol{y} \in \Re^n$ are the neural state, input, and output vectors, respectively. $\boldsymbol{A} \in \Re^{N\times N}$, $\boldsymbol{B} \in \Re^{N\times n}$, and $\boldsymbol{C} \in \Re^{n\times n}$ are the connecting weight matrices associated with the neural state, input, and output vectors, respectively. α is a fixed constant for controlling state decaying and is chosen as $-1 \leq \alpha \leq 1$.

$\boldsymbol{\sigma}(\boldsymbol{x})$ is a vector neural activation function.

Let $S \subset \Re^n$ and $U \subset \Re^m$ be open sets, $D_s \subset S$ and $D_u \subset U$ be compact sets, $Z \subset D_s$ be an open set, and $\boldsymbol{f}\colon\ S \times U \longrightarrow \Re^n$ be a continuous vector-valued function. For a discrete-time nonlinear system of the form

$$\boldsymbol{z}(k+1) \;=\; \boldsymbol{f}(\boldsymbol{z}(k), \boldsymbol{u}(k)), \quad \boldsymbol{z} \in \Re^n,\ \boldsymbol{u} \in \Re^m$$

with an initial state $\boldsymbol{z}(0) \in Z$, whose solution $\boldsymbol{z}(k) \in D_s$, show that for an arbitrary $\varepsilon > 0$ and an integer $0 < I < +\infty$, there exist an integer N and an appropriate initial state $\boldsymbol{x}(0)$ such that for any bounded input $\boldsymbol{u}\colon\ \Re^+ = [0+, \infty) \longrightarrow D_u$

$$\max_{0 \le k \le I} \| \boldsymbol{z}(k) - \boldsymbol{y}(k) \| < \varepsilon$$

10.11 (Universal Approximation of Nonlinear Functions) Consider a simplified version of the discrete-time dynamic neural network in Problem 10.10 of the form

$$\begin{aligned} \boldsymbol{x}(k+1) &= -\alpha \boldsymbol{x}(k) + \boldsymbol{A}\boldsymbol{\sigma}(\boldsymbol{x}(k)) \\ \boldsymbol{y}(k) &= \boldsymbol{C}\boldsymbol{x}(k) \end{aligned}$$

Let $\boldsymbol{f}\colon\ \Re \longrightarrow \Re^n$ be a continuous function, and $\boldsymbol{f}(k),\ 0 \le k \le I < +\infty$, be a discrete-time trajectories. Show that for an arbitrary number $\varepsilon > 0$, there exist an integer N and an appropriate initial state $\boldsymbol{x}(0)$ such that

$$\max_{0 \le k \le I} \| \boldsymbol{f}(k) - \boldsymbol{y}(k) \| < \varepsilon$$

10.12 Define a class of continuous-time dynamic neural network that can universally approximate a class of nonlinear systems as discussed in Problem 10.10.

11

Stability of Continuous-Time Dynamic Neural Networks

11.1 Local Asymptotic Stability

11.2 Global Asymptotic Stability of Dynamic Neural Network

11.3 Local Exponential Stability of DNNs

11.4 Global Exponential Stability of DNNs

11.5 Concluding Remarks

Problems

Complex nonlinear structures of dynamic neural networks (DNNs) used in computing tasks such as information processing, or in associative memory for storing patterns, present a challenge in stability investigations. In this chapter, some stability analysis approaches and stability results for a general class of continuous-time dynamic neural networks (CT-DNNs) are presented.

The notion of the stability of an equilibrium point of a dynamic system is of fundamental importance in dynamic neural networks. An equilibrium point is stable if the state trajectory stays in the neighborhood of the point. It is asymptotically stable if all nearby solutions not only stay in the neighborhood but also approach the equilibrium point. The *stability* of the equilibrium points of a dynamic neural network is one of the most basic and important properties for many engineering applications. It is important to note that we refer to stability in the sense of Lyapunov (Khalil 1992).

The dynamic behavior and the notions of stability of CT-DNNs described by a set of nonlinear differential equations have been widely studied since the early 1990s. A series of local and global stable conditions were derived using different nonlinear analysis approaches by Cohen and Grossberg (1983), Guez et al. (1988), Kelly (1990), and Matsuoka (1992) for a general class of continuous-time dynamic neural networks, which may be considered as generalized versions of the well-known Hopfield dynamic neural networks.

After discussing some basic results of Lyapunov stability theories, the local asymptotic stability of the equilibrium points of continuous-time DNNs is studied in Section 11.1. Using the position estimation of the eigenvalues of the matrix, some local asymptotic stability criteria that contain the parameters of the neural network and have simple algebraic expressions are also presented in this section. On the basis of Lyapunov's second method, the global asymptotic stability of neural systems is investigated in Section 11.2 using the Lyapunov diagonal function approach, and the corresponding conditions are derived. Also, the exponential stability of dynamic neural networks is studied in Section 11.3, and some explicit estimations formulations of the attraction domains are given in these studies.

11.1 LOCAL ASYMPTOTIC STABILITY

The trajectories of a dynamic neural network (DNN) for an arbitrary set of initial conditions are usually required to converge to the equilibrium points that are asymptotically stable. In addition to the convergence properties of the solutions, the local asymptotic stability, in the sense of Lyapunov, of the isolated equilibrium points should be addressed such that the dynamic orbits around the equilibrium points become clear. In fact, the attraction behaviors of the asymptotically stable equilibrium points provide a basis for neural associative memories and for other applications of the dynamic neural networks.

11.1.1 Lyapunov's First Method

Consider a general form of the continuous-time dynamic neural networks given by

$$\frac{d\boldsymbol{x}(t)}{dt} = \boldsymbol{f}(\boldsymbol{x}(t), \boldsymbol{W}, \boldsymbol{s}) \tag{11.1}$$

where $\boldsymbol{f} : \Re^n \times \Re^{n \times n} \times \Re^n \longrightarrow \Re^n$ is a continuously differentiable vector-valued function. Although the convergence of dynamic neural networks ensures that the trajectory of the system from a given initial condition will converge to one of the equilibrium points, we are often interested in determining which equilibrium points are the target points or the convergent points of the trajectories of the system for all possible initial conditions. In other words, we need to discuss the stability of the equilibrium points. We study the stability issue for the equilibrium points that are isolated; that is, if $\boldsymbol{x}^*$ is an equilibrium point of the system given in Eqn. (11.1), we may find a neighborhood $B = \{\boldsymbol{x} : ||\boldsymbol{x} - \boldsymbol{x}^*|| < r, r > 0\}$ such that there is no other equilibrium point in B of the system given in Eqn. (11.1).

Definition 11.1 *The equilibrium point $\boldsymbol{x}^*$ of the system in Eqn. (11.1) is*

(i) Stable, if for each $\epsilon > 0$, there is $\delta = \delta(\epsilon) > 0$ such that

$$||\boldsymbol{x}(0) - \boldsymbol{x}^*|| < \delta \Longrightarrow ||\boldsymbol{x}(t) - \boldsymbol{x}^*|| < \epsilon, \quad \forall t \geq 0$$

(ii) Locally asymptotically stable, if it is stable and δ can be chosen such that

$$||\boldsymbol{x}(0) - \boldsymbol{x}^*|| < \delta \Longrightarrow \lim_{t \to \infty} ||\boldsymbol{x}(t) - \boldsymbol{x}^*|| = 0 \qquad \blacksquare$$

We now discuss the local asymptotic stability of an equilibrium point $\boldsymbol{x}^*$ of the system in Eqn. (11.1). If $\boldsymbol{x}^*$ is locally asymptotically stable, we may find a constant δ such that any trajectories that start in a δ neighborhood of the equilibrium $\boldsymbol{x}^*$ will eventually tend to $\boldsymbol{x}^*$. The region of attraction, or region of asymptotic stability, of an equilibrium point is defined as the set of all points $\boldsymbol{x}_0$ such that the solution of the system in Eqn. (11.1) satisfies

$$\lim_{t \to \infty} ||\boldsymbol{x}(t, \boldsymbol{x}_0) - \boldsymbol{x}^*|| = 0$$

However, determining analytically the exact region of attraction might be difficult or even impossible for a nonlinear dynamic system (Khalil 1992).

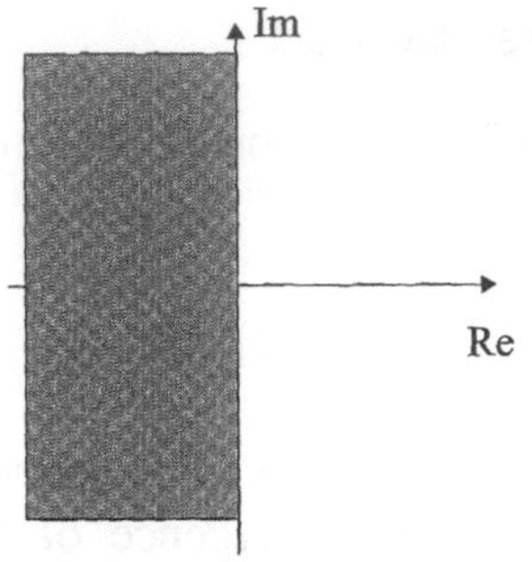

(a) x^* is an asymptotically stable point (a *sink*)

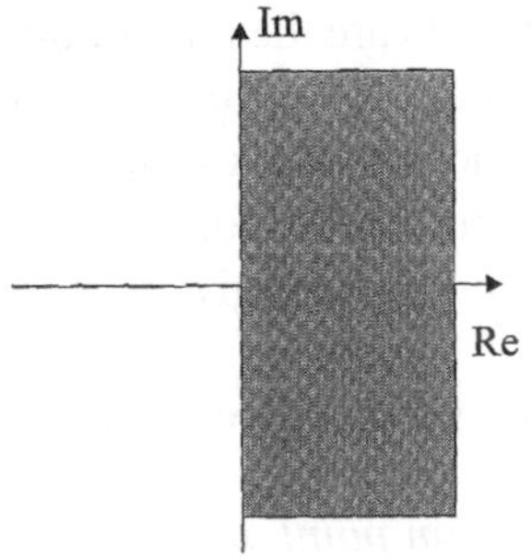

(b) x^* is an unstable equilibrium point (a *source*)

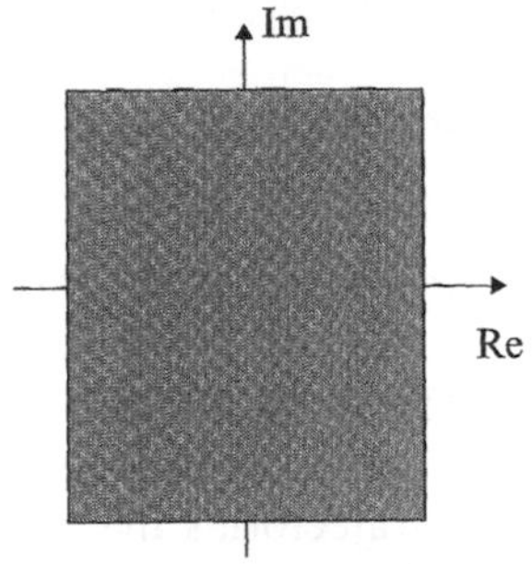

(c) x^* is a saddle point

Figure 11.1 The domains of the eigenvalues of the Jacobian $J(x^*)$.

Let $\boldsymbol{x}^*$ be an equilibrium point of the nonlinear system in Eqn. (11.1). The Jacobian at this equilibrium point is given by

$$J(\boldsymbol{x}^*) = \left.\frac{\partial \boldsymbol{f}(\boldsymbol{x}, \boldsymbol{W}, \boldsymbol{s})}{\partial \boldsymbol{x}}\right|_{\boldsymbol{x}=\boldsymbol{x}^*}$$

Lyapunov's first method, or Lyapunov's indirect method, which uses the real part of the eigenvalues $\lambda(J(\boldsymbol{x}^*))$ of the Jacobin $J(\boldsymbol{x}^*)$, states that

(i) $\boldsymbol{x}^*$ is asymptotically stable if $Re[\lambda(J(\boldsymbol{x}^*))] < 0$ for all eigenvalues of $J(\boldsymbol{x}^*)$.

(ii) $\boldsymbol{x}^*$ is unstable if $Re[\lambda(J(\boldsymbol{x}^*))] > 0$ for one or more of the eigenvalues of $J(\boldsymbol{x}^*)$.

In other words, for the local asymptotic stability of the equilibrium point $\boldsymbol{x}^*$, the eigenvalues of the Jacobian at the equilibrium point $\boldsymbol{x}^*$ need to be examined as shown in Fig. 11.1. If all the eigenvalues of the Jacobian at $\boldsymbol{x}^*$ are in the left-half complex plane, then $\boldsymbol{x}^*$ is a locally asymptotically stable equilibrium point of the system in Eqn. (11.1), and this equilibrium point is a *sink* (stable). If all the eigenvalues of the Jacobian at $\boldsymbol{x}^*$ are in the right-half complex plane, it is a *source* (unstable). If some eigenvalues are in the left-half complex plane and some are in the right-half complex plane, the equilibrium point is a *saddle* or unstable equilibrium point. Lyapunov's first method has been used widely in the fields of engineering and sciences. However, when some of the eigenvalues are located on the imaginary axis in the complex plane, this approach fails to determine the stability of the equilibrium point.

Example 11.1 Consider a two-neuron system described by

$$\begin{aligned} \frac{dx_1}{dt} &= -\alpha_1 x_1 + w \tanh(x_2), \quad \alpha_1 > 0 \\ \frac{dx_2}{dt} &= -\alpha_2 x_2 + w \tanh(x_1), \quad \alpha_2 > 0 \end{aligned} \tag{11.2}$$

We will consider the location of the equilibrium points for this two-neuron interactive system. The Jacobian of this system is easily obtained as

$$J(x_1, x_2) = \begin{bmatrix} -\alpha_1 & w \operatorname{sech}^2(x_2) \\ w \operatorname{sech}^2(x_1) & -\alpha_2 \end{bmatrix} \tag{11.3}$$

The two eigenvalues λ_1 and λ_2 of $J(x_1, x_2)$ are the solutions of the following equation

$$det \begin{bmatrix} \lambda + \alpha_1 & w \operatorname{sech}^2(x_2) \\ w \operatorname{sech}^2(x_1) & \lambda + \alpha_2 \end{bmatrix} = 0 \tag{11.4}$$

that is

$$\lambda^2 + (\alpha_1 + \alpha_2)\lambda + \alpha_1\alpha_2 - w^2\text{sech}^2(x_1)\text{sech}^2(x_2) = 0 \tag{11.5}$$

Hence

$$\lambda_{1,2}(J(x_1, x_2)) = \frac{-(\alpha_1 + \alpha_2) \pm \sqrt{(\alpha_1 - \alpha_2)^2 + 4w^2\text{sech}^2(x_1)\text{sech}^2(x_2)}}{2}$$

Obviously, if $\boldsymbol{x}^* = [x_1^* \quad x_2^*]^T = [0 \quad 0]^T$ is an equilibrium point of the neural system in Eqn. (11.2), then $\text{sech}(0) = 1$ is the maximum value of $\text{sech}(\boldsymbol{x})$ for all $\boldsymbol{x} \in \Re$. One may observe that

$$(\alpha_1 - \alpha_2)^2 + 4w^2 \;\; > \;\; (\alpha_1 - \alpha_2)^2 + 4w^2\text{sech}^2(x_1)\text{sech}^2(x_2)$$

for $x_1, x_2 \neq 0$, which implies

$$Re(\lambda_{1,2}(J(0,0))) \leq 0 \quad \Longrightarrow \quad Re(\lambda_{1,2}(J(x_1, x_2))) < 0$$

for $x_1, x_2 \neq 0$, where $Re(.)$ represents the real part of a complex number. Therefore, if $\boldsymbol{x}^* = [x_1^* \quad x_2^*]^T = [0 \quad 0]^T$ is an asymptotically stable equilibrium point, the eigenvalues of the Jacobian always have negative real parts for all $x_1, x_2 \neq 0$. In this case, the system in Eqn. (11.2) is a contractive system that has a unique stable equilibrium point $\boldsymbol{x}^* = 0$.

On the other hand, $Re(\lambda_{1,2}(J(0,0))) < 0$ if and only if

$$(\alpha_1 - \alpha_2)^2 + 4w^2 < (\alpha_1 + \alpha_2)^2$$

that is

$$|w| < \sqrt{\alpha_1\alpha_2} \tag{11.6}$$

Thus, the condition for the stability of the equilibrium states of the neural system in Eqn. (11.2) is given by Eqn. (11.6). ■

11.1.2 Determination of Eigenvalue Position

A dynamic neural system is usually a large-scale nonlinear dynamic system, and the direct computation of the eigenvalues of the Jacobian is usually complicated. The development of some indirect test approaches for the eigenvalues of the dynamic neural network is usually useful. To discuss the positions of the eigenvalues of a matrix $\boldsymbol{W} = [w_{ij}]_{n\times n}$ in the complex plane, some mathematical preliminaries are required, which are given in the following discussion.

Let $W = [w_{ij}]_{n\times n}$ be a complex matrix. We can always write $W = U + V$, where $U = diag[w_{11}, \ldots, w_{nn}]$ is the main diagonal part of W and V represents the rest of the matrix with a zero main diagonal. If we set $W_\epsilon \equiv U + \epsilon V$ for any $\epsilon \in C$, then $W_0 = U$ and $W_1 = W$. The eigenvalues of $W_0 = U$ are easy to locate, for they are just the points of the diagonal elements $w_{11}, \ldots, w_{nn}$ in the complex plane. We suspect, however, that if ϵ is small enough, then the eigenvalues of W_ϵ will be located in some small neighborhoods of the points $w_{11}, \ldots, w_{nn}$. There are indeed some easily computed disks centered at the points w_{ii} that are guaranteed to contain the eigenvalues. The following theorem makes this observation.

Lemma 11.1 [Gerschgorin's (1931) Theorem] *Let $W = [w_{ij}]_{n\times n}$ be a complex matrix and*

$$R_i = \sum_{j=1, j\neq i}^{n} |w_{ij}|, \quad i = 1, 2, \ldots, n \tag{11.7}$$

denote the deleted row absolute value sums of W. Then, all the eigenvalues of W are located in the union of n closed disks in the complex plane with the center w_{ii} and radius R_i, $i = 1, 2, \ldots, n$. Furthermore, if a union of k of these n disks forms a connected region that is disjointed from the remaining $n - k$ disks, then there are precisely k eigenvalues of W in this region. ■

Since W and W^T have the same eigenvalues, one can obtain Gerschgorin's theorem for the columns by applying that theorem to W^T and obtain a region that contains the eigenvalues of W which are specified in terms of the deleted column absolute value sums.

Corollary 11.1 *Let $W = [w_{ij}]_{n\times n}$ be a complex matrix and*

$$C_j = \sum_{i=1, i\neq j}^{n} |w_{ij}|, \quad j = 1, 2, \ldots, n \tag{11.8}$$

denote the deleted column absolute value sums of W. Then all the eigenvalues of W are located in the union of n closed disks in the complex plane with the center w_{ii} and radius C_i, $i = 1, 2, \ldots, n$. Furthermore, if a union of k of these n disks forms a connected region that is disjointed from all the remaining $n - k$ disks, then there are precisely k eigenvalues of W in this region. ■

Let

$$G(W) = \bigcup_{i=1}^{n} \{z \in C : |z - w_{ii}| \leq R_i\} \tag{11.9}$$

and

$$G(\boldsymbol{W}^T) = \bigcup_{j=1}^{n} \{z \in C : |z - w_{jj}| \le C_j\} \tag{11.10}$$

Then, all the eigenvalues of $\boldsymbol{W}$ lie in the intersection of the regions in Eqns. (11.9) and (11.10); that is, in $G(\boldsymbol{W}) \bigcap G(\boldsymbol{W}^T)$.

For the stability analysis of continuous-time systems, we will determine whether the eigenvalues of the Jacobian are located in the left-half complex plane. The following corollary provides the sufficient conditions.

Corollary 11.2 *Let* $\boldsymbol{W} = [w_{ij}]_{n \times n}$ *be a complex matrix, and* R_i *and* C_i *be defined by Eqns. (11.7) and (11.8), respectively. If*

$$w_{ii} + R_i < 0, \quad i = 1, 2, \ldots, n \tag{11.11}$$

or

$$w_{jj} + C_j < 0, \quad j = 1, 2, \cdots, n \tag{11.12}$$

all the eigenvalues of $\boldsymbol{W}$ *are then located in the left-half complex plane.* ■

The proof of Corollary 11.2 is easily obtained from Gerschgorin's theorem. The geometric meaning of Corollary 11.2 is given in Fig. 11.2. It is easy to see that all $w_{ii} < 0$ are sufficient conditions of the conclusions obtained in this corollary.

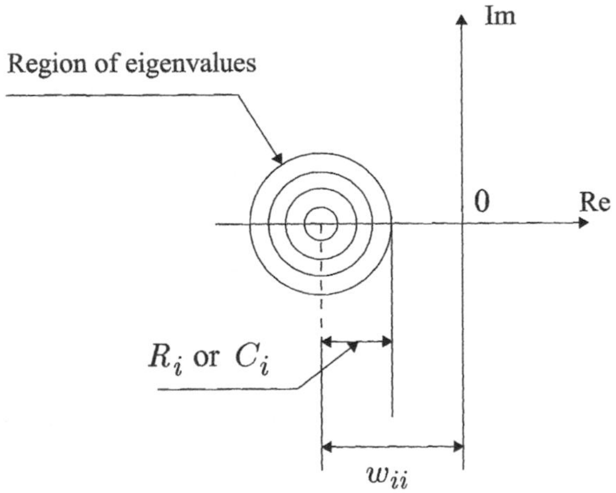

Figure 11.2 The positions of all the eigenvalues of a matrix $\boldsymbol{W}$, where R_i and C_i satisfy respectively the inequalities given in Eqns. (11.11) and (11.12).

11.1.3 Local Asymptotic Stability Conditions

Consider a general class of dynamic neural networks with the following form

$$\frac{dx_i(t)}{dt} = -\alpha_i x_i(t) + \sum_{j=1}^{n} w_{ij}\sigma_j(x_j) + s_i, \quad i = 1, 2, \ldots, n \qquad (11.13)$$

or

$$\frac{d\boldsymbol{x}(t)}{dt} = -\boldsymbol{A}\boldsymbol{x}(t) + \boldsymbol{W}\boldsymbol{\sigma}(\boldsymbol{x}(t)) + \boldsymbol{s} \qquad (11.14)$$

where $\alpha_i \neq 0$, $\boldsymbol{A} = diag[\alpha_1, \ldots, \alpha_n]$, and the weight matrix $\boldsymbol{W}$ may not be symmetric.

For the local asymptotic stability of the equilibrium point $\boldsymbol{x}^*$ of the system in Eqn. (11.14), the eigenvalues of the Jacobian at the equilibrium point $\boldsymbol{x}^*$ must be examined. The Jacobian of the function $\boldsymbol{f}(\boldsymbol{x}) = -\boldsymbol{A}\boldsymbol{x}+\boldsymbol{W}\boldsymbol{\sigma}(\boldsymbol{x})+\boldsymbol{s}$ is given by

$$J(x) = \frac{\partial \boldsymbol{f}}{\partial \boldsymbol{x}} = \boldsymbol{f}'(\boldsymbol{x}) = -\boldsymbol{A} + \boldsymbol{W}\boldsymbol{\sigma}'(\boldsymbol{x}) = -\boldsymbol{A} + \boldsymbol{W}\boldsymbol{\Sigma}(\boldsymbol{x}) \qquad (11.15)$$

where $\boldsymbol{\Sigma}(\boldsymbol{x}) = diag[\Sigma_{11}(\boldsymbol{x}), \ldots, \Sigma_{nn}(\boldsymbol{x})]$ with $\Sigma_{ii}(\boldsymbol{x}) = \sigma_i'(x_i)$. The following theorem gives some local stability conditions that can be used to verify whether an equilibrium point $\boldsymbol{x}^*$ is stable.

Theorem 11.1 *Let $\boldsymbol{x}^*$ be an equilibrium state of the system in Eqn. (11.13). If*

$$-\alpha_i + w_{ii}\frac{\partial \sigma_i(x_i^*)}{\partial x_i} + \sum_{j=1, j\neq i}^{n} \left| w_{ij}\frac{\partial \sigma_j(x_j^*)}{\partial x_j} \right| < 0 \qquad (11.16)$$

$$i = 1, 2, \ldots, n$$

or

$$-\alpha_j + w_{jj}\frac{\partial \sigma_j(x_j^*)}{\partial x_j} + \sum_{i=1, i\neq j}^{n} \left| w_{ij}\frac{\partial \sigma_j(x_j^*)}{\partial x_j} \right| < 0 \qquad (11.17)$$

$$j = 1, 2, \ldots, n$$

then $\boldsymbol{x}^*$ is a locally asymptotically stable equilibrium state of the neural system in Eqn. (11.13).

Proof: This theorem may be proved using Corollary 11.2 to the Jacobian $[\partial \boldsymbol{f}/\partial \boldsymbol{x}]$. ■

The stability conditions in Theorem 11.1 involve only some algebraic manipulations about the network parameters such as the time constants, the synaptic weights, and the elements of the Jacobian at an equilibrium point. These results provide us with simple procedures for determining the local asymptotic stability of an equilibrium point. The locally asymptotically stable conditions given in Theorem 11.1 are derived using Lyapunov's first method. It may be more conservative than directly verifying the position of the eigenvalues of the Jacobian; but, it is easier to use. Therefore, these conditions are the indirect conditions for verifying the local asymptotic stability of an equilibrium point.

11.2 GLOBAL ASYMPTOTIC STABILITY OF DYNAMIC NEURAL NETWORK

11.2.1 Lyapunov Function Method

When $\boldsymbol{x}^*$ is asymptotically stable and the trajectory $\boldsymbol{x}(t, \boldsymbol{x}_0)$ approaches $\boldsymbol{x}^*$ as $t \to \infty$, regardless of how large $||\boldsymbol{x}_0 - \boldsymbol{x}^*||$ is, in other words, for an arbitrary initial state $\boldsymbol{x}(0)$, the state of the system in Eqn. (11.13) converges to $\boldsymbol{x}^*$ for a given weight matrix $\boldsymbol{W}$ and input $\boldsymbol{s}$. In this case $\boldsymbol{x}^*$ is said to be a globally asymptotically stable equilibrium point, and the system is referred to as a *globally asymptotically stable* system. If $\boldsymbol{x}^*$ is a globally asymptotically stable equilibrium point of a neural system, it must be the unique equilibrium point of the system. If there is another equilibrium point $\bar{\boldsymbol{x}}^*$, the trajectory starting at $\bar{\boldsymbol{x}}^*$ would remain at $\bar{\boldsymbol{x}}^*$ for all $t \geq 0$. Hence, it would not approach $\boldsymbol{x}^*$, which contradicts the evidence that $\boldsymbol{x}^*$ is a globally asymptotically stable equilibrium point. Therefore, the use of global asymptotic stability is not applicable to a dynamic neural network having multiple equilibrium points. The *Lyapunov's second method* or *Lyapunov function method* given below has been widely used to build some globally asymptotically stable conditions.

Theorem 11.2 (Lyapunov Function Method) *Let $\boldsymbol{x}^*$ be an equilibrium point for the system in Eqn. (11.1). Let $V : \Re^n \to \Re$ be a continuously differentiable function such that*

(i) $V(\boldsymbol{x}^*) = 0$ *and* $V(\boldsymbol{x}) > 0, \forall \boldsymbol{x} \neq \boldsymbol{x}^*$

(ii) $V(\boldsymbol{x}) \to \infty$ *when* $||\boldsymbol{x}|| \to \infty$

(iii) $\dfrac{dV(\boldsymbol{x})}{dt} < 0, \forall \boldsymbol{x} \neq \boldsymbol{x}^*$

Then, $\boldsymbol{x} = \boldsymbol{x}^*$ *is globally asymptotically stable.* ■

11.2.2 Diagonal Lyapunov Function for DNNs

The *diagonal Lyapunov function method*, first proposed by Persidskii (1969) for studying the absolute stability, is based on the existence of a diagonal solution of the Lyapunov equation. Kaszkurewicz and Bhaya (1993) used this approach to discuss the robust stability of a class of continuous-time and discrete-time nonlinear systems. Matsuoka (1992) derived a diagonal Lyapunov function for a Hopfield neural network with an asymmetric weight matrix, and established some absolute stability conditions.

We will now explore the global stability conditions of the system in Eqn. (11.14) using a global diagonal Lyapunov function method in this section. Let $\boldsymbol{x}^* = [x_1^* \ \cdots \ x_n^*]^T$ be an equilibrium state of this system. We introduce a new variable $\boldsymbol{z}$ as

$$\boldsymbol{z} = [z_1 \ \cdots \ z_n]^T = \boldsymbol{x} - \boldsymbol{x}^*$$

Then, the system in Eqn. (11.14) can be rewritten in terms of $\boldsymbol{z}$ as

$$\frac{d\boldsymbol{z}}{dt} = -\boldsymbol{A}\boldsymbol{z} + \boldsymbol{W}\boldsymbol{f}(\boldsymbol{z}) \tag{11.18}$$

where

$$\boldsymbol{f}(\boldsymbol{z}) = \begin{bmatrix} f_1(z_1) \\ \vdots \\ f_n(z_n) \end{bmatrix} \equiv \begin{bmatrix} \sigma_1(z_1 + x_1^*) - \sigma_1(x_1^*) \\ \vdots \\ \sigma_n(z_n + x_n^*) - \sigma_n(x_n^*) \end{bmatrix} \tag{11.19}$$

Since

$$0 < \sigma_i'(z_i + x_i^*) = f_i'(z_i) \leq 1, \quad i = 1, 2, \ldots, n$$

we have

$$z_i \leq f_i(z_i) < 0 \quad \text{for} \quad z_i < 0 \tag{11.20}$$
$$0 < f_i(z_i) \leq z_i \quad \text{for} \quad z_i > 0 \tag{11.21}$$

that is

$$|f_i(z_i)| \leq |z_i| \tag{11.22}$$

Theorem 11.3 *Let all $\alpha_i \geq 0$ in Eqn. (11.13). The system in Eqn. (11.18) is globally asymptotically stable if, for a positive diagonal matrix $\boldsymbol{P} = diag[p_1, \ldots, p_n]$ with $p_i > 0$, there exists a positive matrix $\boldsymbol{Q} > 0$ such that*

$$\boldsymbol{P}\boldsymbol{W} + \boldsymbol{W}^T\boldsymbol{P} = -\boldsymbol{Q} + 2\boldsymbol{P}\boldsymbol{A} \tag{11.23}$$

Proof: We will find a global Lyapunov function for the system in Eqn. (11.18). Consider the following positive definite function of $\boldsymbol{z}$

$$V(\boldsymbol{z}) = \sum_{i=1}^{n} \int_{0}^{z_i} p_i f_i(\zeta) d\zeta \tag{11.24}$$

where

$$V(\boldsymbol{z}) = 0 \quad \text{only at} \quad \boldsymbol{z} = 0$$

Differentiating $V(\boldsymbol{z})$ with respect to time, we obtain

$$\begin{aligned} \frac{dV(\boldsymbol{z})}{dt} &= \boldsymbol{f}^T(\boldsymbol{z})\boldsymbol{P}\left(\frac{d\boldsymbol{z}}{dt}\right) \\ &= \boldsymbol{f}^T(\boldsymbol{z})\boldsymbol{P}\{-\boldsymbol{A}\boldsymbol{z} + \boldsymbol{W}\boldsymbol{f}(\boldsymbol{z})\} \end{aligned} \tag{11.25}$$

where $dV(\boldsymbol{z})/dt = 0$ for $\boldsymbol{z} = 0$. Note, since the inequality in Eqn. (11.22) implies

$$|f_i(z_i)| \leq |z_i|$$

$$f_i(z_i)z_i \geq f_i(z_i)f_i(z_i)$$

that the first term in Eqn. (11.25) satisfies

$$\begin{aligned} -\boldsymbol{f}^T(\boldsymbol{z})\boldsymbol{P}\boldsymbol{A}\boldsymbol{z} &= -\sum_{i=1}^{n} f_i(z_i)z_i p_i \alpha_i \\ &\leq -\sum_{i=1}^{n} f_i(z_i)f_i(z_i)p_i \alpha_i \\ &= -\boldsymbol{f}^T(\boldsymbol{z})\boldsymbol{P}\boldsymbol{A}\boldsymbol{f}(\boldsymbol{z}) \end{aligned} \tag{11.26}$$

Hence, the differential of $V(\boldsymbol{z})$ with respect to time can be modified as

$$\begin{aligned} \frac{dV(\boldsymbol{z})}{dt} &= -\boldsymbol{f}^T(\boldsymbol{z})\boldsymbol{P}\boldsymbol{A}\boldsymbol{z} + \boldsymbol{f}^T(\boldsymbol{z})\boldsymbol{P}\boldsymbol{W}\boldsymbol{f}(\boldsymbol{z}) \\ &\leq \boldsymbol{f}^T(\boldsymbol{z})\{-\boldsymbol{P}\boldsymbol{A} + \boldsymbol{P}\boldsymbol{W}\}\boldsymbol{f}(\boldsymbol{z}) \\ &= \boldsymbol{f}^T(\boldsymbol{z})\{-\boldsymbol{P}\boldsymbol{A} + (\boldsymbol{P}\boldsymbol{W} + \boldsymbol{W}^T\boldsymbol{P})/2\}\boldsymbol{f}(\boldsymbol{z}) \end{aligned} \tag{11.27}$$

Therefore, if

$$-2\boldsymbol{P}\boldsymbol{A} + (\boldsymbol{P}\boldsymbol{W} + \boldsymbol{W}^T\boldsymbol{P}) < 0 \tag{11.28}$$

then

$$\frac{dV(\boldsymbol{z})}{dt} < 0, \qquad \boldsymbol{z} \neq 0$$

This implies that $V(\boldsymbol{z})$ is a Lyapunov function for the system in Eqn. (11.18) and the origin $\boldsymbol{z} = 0$ is the only globally asymptotically stable equilibrium of the system. ■

Remark 11.1 A limitation of the nonlinear-dependent Lyapunov function in Eqn. (11.24) is that it is valid only for the diagonal state-dependent nonlinear function $\sigma_j(x_j)$.

Remark 11.2 When all $\alpha_i = 1$ in Eqn. (11.13), the result in Theorem 11.2 is also valid for the dynamic neural model given by

$$\frac{d\boldsymbol{x}(t)}{dt} = -\boldsymbol{x}(t) + \boldsymbol{\sigma}(\boldsymbol{W}\boldsymbol{x}(t) + \boldsymbol{s}) \tag{11.29}$$

Using the coordinate transformation defined as

$$\boldsymbol{y}(t) = \boldsymbol{W}\boldsymbol{x}(t) + \boldsymbol{s} \tag{11.30}$$

Eqn. (11.29) can be rewritten as

$$\frac{d\boldsymbol{y}(t)}{dt} = -\boldsymbol{y}(t) + \boldsymbol{W}\boldsymbol{\sigma}(\boldsymbol{y}(t)) + \boldsymbol{s} \tag{11.31}$$

Hence, the global asymptotic stability of the system in Eqn. (11.29) implies the system described by Eqn. (11.31). The inverse implication needs the inversion of the weight matrix $\boldsymbol{W}$.

Furthermore, if all $\alpha_i > 0$ in Eqn. (11.13), then $\boldsymbol{A} = diag[\alpha_1, \ldots, \alpha_n] > 0$. One may set the positive diagonal matrix $\boldsymbol{P} = \boldsymbol{A}^{-1}$ in Eqn. (11.28) such that

$$-\boldsymbol{U} + \frac{\boldsymbol{A}^{-1}\boldsymbol{W} + \boldsymbol{W}^T\boldsymbol{A}^{-1}}{2} < 0 \tag{11.32}$$

which is equivalent to

$$-1 + \lambda_{max}\left(\frac{\boldsymbol{A}^{-1}\boldsymbol{W} + \boldsymbol{W}^T\boldsymbol{A}^{-1}}{2}\right) < 0$$

or

$$\lambda_{max}\left(\boldsymbol{A}^{-1}\boldsymbol{W} + \boldsymbol{W}^T\boldsymbol{A}^{-1}\right) < 2 \tag{11.33}$$

We summarize these results in the following theorem and its corollaries.

Theorem 11.4 *If*

$$\lambda_{max}\left(\boldsymbol{A}^{-1}\boldsymbol{W} + \boldsymbol{W}^T\boldsymbol{A}^{-1}\right) < 2 \tag{11.34}$$

then the system in Eqn. (11.13) is globally asymptotically stable. ■

Corollary 11.3 *If*

$$||\boldsymbol{A}^{-1}\boldsymbol{W} + \boldsymbol{W}^T\boldsymbol{A}^{-1}||_2 = \left[\sum_{i,j}\left(\frac{w_{ij}}{\alpha_i} + \frac{w_{ji}}{\alpha_j}\right)^2\right]^{1/2} < 2 \tag{11.35}$$

then the system in Eqn. (11.13) is globally asymptotically stable. ■

Corollary 11.4 *If*

$$\frac{2w_{ii}}{\alpha_i} + \sum_{j=1,j\neq i}^{n}\left|\frac{w_{ij}}{\alpha_i} + \frac{w_{ji}}{\alpha_j}\right| < 2 \tag{11.36}$$

then the system in Eqn. (11.13) is globally asymptotically stable. ■

11.2.3 DNNs with Synapse-Dependent Functions

We now consider a more general class of dynamic neural models that is described by the equations

$$\frac{dx_i(t)}{dt} = -\alpha_i x_i(t) + \sum_{j=1}^{n} w_{ij}\sigma_{ij}(x_j(t)) + s_i, \quad i = 1, \ldots, n \tag{11.37}$$

where $\alpha_i \geq 0$ and $\sigma_{ij}(x_j)$ are sigmoidal functions. Equation (11.37) represents a dynamic neural network (DNN) model with synapse-dependent nonlinear activation functions. In other words, each neural unit in such a network structure may have a set of its own nonlinear activation functions.

Since $0 \leq \sigma'_{ij}(x) \leq 1$, using the mean-value theorem, it is easy to verify that

$$|\sigma_{ij}(x_j) - \sigma_{ij}(y_j)| \leq |x_j - y_j| \tag{11.38}$$

where $\boldsymbol{x} = [x_1 \ \cdots \ x_n]^T$ and $\boldsymbol{y} = [y_1 \ \cdots \ y_n]^T$ are two arbitrary n-dimensional vectors. Let $\boldsymbol{x}^* = [x_1^* \cdots x_n^*]^T$ be an equilibrium state of the system in Eqn. (11.37). We will now use the new state variables, $\boldsymbol{z} = [z_1 \cdots z_n]^T$

and $z = x - x^*$, such that

$$\frac{dz_i(t)}{dt} = -\alpha_i z_i(t) + \sum_{j=1}^{n} w_{ij} f_{ij}(z_j(t)) \tag{11.39}$$

where

$$f_{ij}(z_j) = \sigma_{ij}(z_j + x_j^*) - \sigma_{ij}(x_j^*) \tag{11.40}$$

satisfies

$$|f_{ij}(z_j)| \leq |z_j| \tag{11.41}$$

It is easy to show that $z = 0$ is a unique equilibrium point of the system in Eqn. (11.39). Define a Metzler matrix $\overline{W}$ as

$$\overline{W} = [\bar{w}_{ij}]_{n \times n}$$

$$\bar{w}_{ij} = \begin{cases} w_{ij}, & i = j \\ |w_{ij}|, & i \neq j \end{cases}$$

We then have the following theorem.

Theorem 11.5 *The system in Eqn. (11.37) is globally and asymptotically stable if for a positive diagonal matrix $P = diag[p_1, \ldots, p_n]$ with $p_i > 0$, there exists a positive matrix $Q > 0$ such that*

$$P\overline{W} + \overline{W}^T P = -Q + 2PA \tag{11.42}$$

Proof: Define the diagonal Lyapunov function

$$V(z) = \tfrac{1}{2} \sum_{j=1}^{n} p_i z_i^2 = \tfrac{1}{2} z^T p z \tag{11.43}$$

Computing $dV(z)/dt$ along the trajectories of Eqn. (11.37) gives

$$\frac{dV(z)}{dt} = \sum_{i=1}^{n} \Big(-p_i \alpha_i z_i^2 + \sum_{j=1}^{n} p_i w_{ij} z_i f_{ij}(z_j) \Big) \tag{11.44}$$

Using the condition of Eqn. (11.41) gives

$$\frac{dV(z)}{dt} \leq \sum_{i=1}^{n} \Big(-p_i \alpha_i |z_i|^2 + \sum_{j=1}^{n} p_i \bar{w}_{ij} |z_i||z_j| \Big) \tag{11.45}$$

Let $z = [z_1 \ \cdots \ z_n]^T$, and let the vectorial norm $\langle|.|\rangle$ be defined as

$$\langle|z|\rangle = \begin{bmatrix} |z_1| \\ |z_2| \\ \vdots \\ |z_n| \end{bmatrix}$$

Then, the inequality of Eqn. (11.45) can be rewritten in the form

$$\frac{dV(z)}{dt} \leq \langle|z|\rangle^T(-PA + P\overline{W} + \overline{W}^T P)\langle|z|\rangle \tag{11.46}$$

where

$$-PA + P\overline{W} + \overline{W}^T P < 0 \tag{11.47}$$

that is

$$\frac{dV(z)}{dt} < 0, \quad \text{for} \quad \text{all} \quad z \neq 0$$

Hence, the global asymptotic stability of the system in Eqn. (11.37) is guaranteed. ■

11.2.4 Some Examples

Example 11.2 (DNN with Lotka–Volterra Equations) Consider the nonadditive network or the generalized Lotka–Volterra equations (Guez et al. 1988) given by

$$\frac{dx_i(t)}{dt} = -\alpha_i x_i(t) + \sum_{j=1}^{n} w_{ij} x_i(t) x_j(t), \qquad i = 1, \ldots, n \tag{11.48}$$

By assuming $x_i(t) \neq 0$, $i = 1, \ldots, n$, these equations can be rewritten as

$$\frac{\dot{x}_i(t)}{x_i(t)} = -\alpha_i + \sum_{j=1}^{n} w_{ij} x_j(t), \qquad i = 1, \ldots, n \tag{11.49}$$

which is equivalent to

$$\frac{d(\ln x_i(t))}{dt} = -\alpha_i + \sum_{j=1}^{n} w_{ij} \exp(\ln x_j(t)), \qquad i = 1, \ldots, n \tag{11.50}$$

Defining $y_i(t) = \ln x_i(t)$, we have

$$\frac{dy_i(t)}{dt} = -\alpha_i + \sum_{j=1}^{n} w_{ij} f(y_j(t)) \tag{11.51}$$

where $f(.) = \exp(.)$. Let $\boldsymbol{y}^* = [y_1^* \ \cdots \ y_n^*]^T$ be an equilibrium state of the system in Eqn. (11.51) that satisfies

$$-\alpha_i + \sum_{j=1}^{n} w_{ij} f(y_j^*) = 0 \tag{11.52}$$

Introducing the new variables $z_i(t) = y_i(t) - y_i^*$ yields

$$\frac{dz_i(t)}{dt} = \sum_{j=1}^{n} w_{ij} g(z_j(t)) \tag{11.53}$$

where $g(z_i(t)) \equiv \exp(z_i(t) + y_i^*) - \exp(y_i^*)$. Therefore, $g(0) = 0$, and $g(z_i)z_i > 0$ for $z_i \neq 0$. Using Theorem 11.2, the global asymptotically stability conditions for the Lotka–Volterra network in Eqn. (11.48) is one of the following:

(i) For a positive diagonal matrix $\boldsymbol{P} = diag[p_1, \ldots, p_n]$ with $p_i > 0$ there exists a positive matrix $\boldsymbol{Q} > 0$ such that

$$\boldsymbol{PW} + \boldsymbol{W}^T\boldsymbol{P} = -\boldsymbol{Q} \tag{11.54}$$

(ii) The matrix $(\boldsymbol{W} + \boldsymbol{W}^T)$ is negative:

$$\boldsymbol{W} + \boldsymbol{W}^T < 0 \tag{11.55}$$

(iii) The maximum eigenvalue of the matrix $(\boldsymbol{W} + \boldsymbol{W}^T)$ is negative:

$$\lambda_{max}(\boldsymbol{W} + \boldsymbol{W}^T) < 0 \tag{11.56}$$

■

Example 11.3 Let us consider a continuous-time dynamic neural network (CT-DNN) in which the first n_1 neural units have *linear activation functions* and the other n_2 neural units have *nonlinear sigmoidal functions*. Let $\boldsymbol{u} \in \Re^{n_1}$ and $\boldsymbol{v} \in \Re^{n_2}$ represent the state vectors of the first n_1 neurons and the remaining n_2 neurons, respectively. The dynamic equations of this neural model are given by

$$\begin{aligned}
\frac{d\boldsymbol{u}}{dt} &= -\boldsymbol{A}^u\boldsymbol{u} + \boldsymbol{W}^{uu}\boldsymbol{u} + \boldsymbol{W}^{uv}\boldsymbol{\sigma}(\boldsymbol{v}) + \boldsymbol{s}^u \\
\frac{d\boldsymbol{v}}{dt} &= -\boldsymbol{A}^v\boldsymbol{v} + \boldsymbol{W}^{vu}\boldsymbol{u} + \boldsymbol{W}^{vv}\boldsymbol{\sigma}(\boldsymbol{v}) + \boldsymbol{s}^v
\end{aligned}$$

where $\boldsymbol{A}^u = diag[\alpha_1^u, \ldots, \alpha_{n1}^u]$, $\boldsymbol{A}^v = diag[\alpha_1^v, \ldots, \alpha_{n2}^v]$, $\boldsymbol{W}^{uu} \in \Re^{n_1 \times n_1}$, $\boldsymbol{W}^{uv} \in \Re^{n_1 \times n_2}$, $\boldsymbol{W}^{vu} \in \Re^{n_2 \times n_1}$, and $\boldsymbol{W}^{vv} \in \Re^{n_2 \times n_2}$, and $\boldsymbol{s}^u \in \Re^{n_1}$ and $\boldsymbol{s}^v \in \Re^{n_2}$ are the input or bias constant vectors.

Without loss of generality, let $\boldsymbol{s}^u = 0$ and $\boldsymbol{s}^v = 0$ in these system. Define a diagonal Lyapunov function of the system as

$$V(\boldsymbol{u}, \boldsymbol{v}) = \tfrac{1}{2}\sum_{i=1}^{n_1} p_i^u u_i^2 + \sum_{j=1}^{n_2} \int_0^{v_j} p_j^v \sigma(\zeta) d\zeta$$

where, $p_i^u > 0$ for all $i \in [1, n_i]$, and $p_j^v > 0$ for all $j \in [1, n_i]$. Furthermore, denote

$$\boldsymbol{A} = \begin{bmatrix} \boldsymbol{A}^u & 0 \\ 0 & \boldsymbol{A}^v \end{bmatrix}, \qquad \boldsymbol{W} = \begin{bmatrix} \boldsymbol{W}^{uu} & \boldsymbol{W}^{uv} \\ \boldsymbol{W}^{vu} & \boldsymbol{W}^{vv} \end{bmatrix}$$

Using the same derivation procedure used to prove Theorem 11.3, it can be shown that one of the sufficient conditions for the global asymptotic stability of the system is satisfying the Lyapunov equation given in Theorem 11.3. ■

11.3 LOCAL EXPONENTIAL STABILITY OF DNNs

The exponential stability of an equilibrium point $\boldsymbol{x}^*$ guarantees that the state trajectories of the neural system converge to the equilibrium point with a specified degree of exponential convergence speed. Sudharsanan and Sundareshan (1991a) studied the exponential stability and instability properties of the equilibrium points for a class of dynamic neural networks, and provided an explicit estimation method for the degree of exponential stability and the regions of attraction of the stable equilibrium points. Moreover, the stability results were used in the synthesis procedure for associative memories. However, most results on the exponential stability introduced by Sudharsanan and Sundareshan (1991a) are local. Obviously, the concept of the exponential stability is stronger than the asymptotic stability; that is, if an equilibrium point $\boldsymbol{x}^*$ of the system is exponentially stable, it must be asymptotically stable.

11.3.1 Lyapunov Function Method for Exponential Stability

Let a constant $r > 0$ and $B = \{\boldsymbol{x} : ||\boldsymbol{x}|| < r\} \subset \Re^n$ be an r neighborhood of the origin $\boldsymbol{x}^* = 0$.

Consider the dynamic system

$$\frac{d\boldsymbol{x}(t)}{dt} = \boldsymbol{f}(\boldsymbol{x}(t)), \qquad \boldsymbol{f}(0) = 0 \tag{11.57}$$

where $\boldsymbol{x} \in \Re^n$, and $\boldsymbol{f} : \Re^n \longrightarrow \Re^n$. Assume that $\boldsymbol{x}^* = 0$ is an isolated equilibrium point of the above system in B. We have the following definition.

Definition 11.2 *The isolated equilibrium point $\boldsymbol{x}^* = 0$ of the system in Eqn. (11.57) is exponentially stable in B with degree η if every trajectory of the system in Eqn. (11.57) starting at any initial condition $\boldsymbol{x}(t_0) = \boldsymbol{x}_0 \in B$ satisfies the condition*

$$||\boldsymbol{x}(t)|| \leq \pi ||\boldsymbol{x}_0|| \exp(-\eta(t - t_0)), \quad \forall t \geq t_0, \quad \forall x \in B \tag{11.58}$$

■

It should be noted that there is no loss of generality in the discussion of the equilibrium point at the origin. If $\boldsymbol{x}^* \neq 0$, a coordinate transformation $\boldsymbol{y} = \boldsymbol{x} - \boldsymbol{x}^*$ will transfer this equilibrium point to the origin, which will be an equilibrium point of the new system. A basic result for the exponential stability can be given as follows and will be used in studying the exponential stability condition for the equilibrium points of dynamic neural networks.

Lemma 11.2 *The equilibrium point $\boldsymbol{x}^* = 0$ of the system in Eqn. (11.57) is exponentially stable in B with degree η if there exists a Lyapunov function $V : \Re^n \longrightarrow \Re$ satisfying the following conditions:*

(i) $V(\boldsymbol{x})$ has a continuous partial derivative with respect to each element of $\boldsymbol{x} \in \Re^n$;

(ii) $V(\boldsymbol{x})$ is positive-definite in B; that is, $V(\boldsymbol{x}) > 0$, and $V(0) = 0$;

(iii) The time derivative of $V(\boldsymbol{x})$ along the trajectories of the system in Eqn. (11.57) satisfies

$$\frac{dV(\boldsymbol{x})}{dt} \leq -2\eta V(\boldsymbol{x}), \quad \forall \boldsymbol{x} \in \boldsymbol{B}, \quad \forall t \geq t_0 \tag{11.59}$$

■

11.3.2 Local Exponential Stability Conditions for DNNs

Consider a dynamic neural network (DNN) of the following form:

$$\frac{d\boldsymbol{x}(t)}{dt} = -\boldsymbol{A}\boldsymbol{x}(t) + \boldsymbol{W}\boldsymbol{\sigma}(\boldsymbol{x}(t)) + \boldsymbol{s} \tag{11.60}$$

Let $\boldsymbol{x}^* = [x_1^* \cdots x_n^*]^T$ be an equilibrium state of the system in Eqn. (11.60), for transforming the equilibrium point to the origin. If a new variable $\boldsymbol{z}$ is introduced as

$$\boldsymbol{z} = [z_1 \cdots z_n]^T = \boldsymbol{x} - \boldsymbol{x}^*$$

Then, the system in Eqn. (11.60) can be rewritten in terms of z as

$$\frac{dz}{dt} = -Az + Wf(z) \tag{11.61}$$

where

$$f(z) = \begin{bmatrix} f_1(z_1) \\ \vdots \\ f_n(z_n) \end{bmatrix} \equiv \begin{bmatrix} \sigma_1(z_1 + x_1^*) - \sigma_1(x_1^*) \\ \vdots \\ \sigma_n(z_n + x_n^*) - \sigma_n(x_n^*) \end{bmatrix} \tag{11.62}$$

Theorem 11.6 *For the equilibrium point x^* of the system in Eqn. (11.60), let $(W\Sigma(x^*) - A)$ be a stable matrix. There then exists a constant $r > 0$ such that*

$$||f(z) - \Sigma(x^*)z|| \leq k||z||_2 \tag{11.63}$$

for all $z \in B = \{z : ||z|| < r\}$. Then, the equilibrium point x^* is locally exponentially stable if

$$||W||_2 < \frac{\lambda_{min}(Q)}{2k\lambda_{max}(P)} \tag{11.64}$$

where $Q = Q^T > 0$ is an arbitrary positive symmetric matrix and $P = P^T > 0$ is a unique positive symmetric solution of the Lyapunov function

$$P(W\Sigma(x^*) - A) + (W\Sigma(x^*) - A)^T P = -Q \tag{11.65}$$

Proof: Since $W\Sigma(x^*) - A$ is a Hurwitz, for a given $Q = Q^T > 0$, the Lyapunov equation

$$P(W\Sigma(x^*) - A) + (W\Sigma(x^*) - A)^T P = -Q \tag{11.66}$$

has a unique positive symmetric solution $P = P^T > 0$. A quadratic Lyapunov function may be defined as

$$V(z) = z^T P z \tag{11.67}$$

which satisfies

$$\lambda_{min}(P)||z||_2^2 \leq V(z) \leq \lambda_{max}(P)||z||_2^2 \tag{11.68}$$

$$\frac{\partial V}{\partial z}(W\Sigma(x^*) - A)z = -z^T Q z \leq -\lambda_{min}(Q)||z||_2^2 \tag{11.69}$$

$$\left|\left|\frac{\partial V}{\partial z}\right|\right|_2 = ||2z^T P||_2 \leq 2||P||_2||z||_2 = 2\lambda_{max}(P)||z||_2 \tag{11.70}$$

The time derivative of $V(z)$ along the trajectories of the system in Eqn. (11.61) is

$$\begin{aligned}\frac{dV(z)}{dt} &= z^T P\frac{dz}{dt} + \left(\frac{dz}{dt}\right)^T Pz \\ &= z^T[P(W\Sigma(x^*) - A) + (W\Sigma(x^*) - A)^T P]z \\ &\quad - 2z^T PW\Sigma(x^*)z + 2z^T PWf(z) \\ &= -z^T Qz - 2z^T PW\Sigma(x^*)z + 2z^T PWf(z) \\ &= -z^T Qz + 2z^T PW[f(z) - \Sigma(x^*)z] \end{aligned} \tag{11.71}$$

Using the inequality of Eqn. (11.64), one obtains

$$\frac{dV(z)}{dt} \leq -\lambda_{min}(Q)||x||_2^2 + 2k\lambda_{max}(P)||W||_2||x||_2^2 \tag{11.72}$$

if

$$||W||_2 < \frac{\lambda_{min}(Q)}{2k\lambda_{max}(P)} \tag{11.73}$$

Define

$$\eta = \frac{\lambda_{min}(Q) - 2k\lambda_{max}(P)||W||_2}{2\lambda_{max}(P)} \tag{11.74}$$

Then Eqn. (11.72) becomes

$$\begin{aligned}\frac{dV(z)}{dt} &\leq -2\eta\lambda_{max}(P)||z||_2^2 \\ &\leq -2\eta V(z)\end{aligned} \tag{11.75}$$

Hence, the origin is locally exponentially stable in $B(r)$. ■

Remark 11.3 The inequality assumption of Eqn. (11.64) is trivial for nonlinear functions $f(z)$ whose elements satisfy the conditions stated in Eqn. (11.63). Since a Taylor series expansion around $z = 0$ is

$$\begin{aligned}f(z) &= f(0) + \left[\frac{\partial f(0)}{\partial z}\right] z + 0(||z||^2) \\ &= f(0) + \Sigma(x^*)z + 0(||z||^2) \\ &= \Sigma(x^*)z + 0(||z||^2)\end{aligned} \tag{11.76}$$

where $0(||z||^2)$ contains the higher-order terms; that is

$$\lim_{z \to 0} \frac{0(||z||^2)}{||z||} = 0$$

then, for any given k it is possible to find a constant $r = r(k) > 0$ such that $0(||\boldsymbol{z}||^2) = \boldsymbol{f}(\boldsymbol{z}) - \boldsymbol{\Sigma}(\boldsymbol{x}^*)\boldsymbol{z}$ is bounded by the linear term $k||\boldsymbol{x}||_2$ in the r neighborhood $B = \{\boldsymbol{z} : ||\boldsymbol{z}|| < r\}$ of $\boldsymbol{z} = 0$.

Furthermore, for $\boldsymbol{z} \neq 0$, we may rewrite the function $\boldsymbol{f}(\boldsymbol{z})$ as

$$\boldsymbol{f}(\boldsymbol{z}) = \begin{bmatrix} f_1(z_1) \\ \vdots \\ f_n(z_n) \end{bmatrix} = \begin{bmatrix} \frac{f_1(z_1)}{z_1} & \cdots & 0 \\ \vdots & \ddots & \vdots \\ 0 & \cdots & \frac{f_n(z_n)}{z_n} \end{bmatrix} \begin{bmatrix} z_1 \\ \vdots \\ z_n \end{bmatrix} \tag{11.77}$$

$$\equiv \boldsymbol{F}(\boldsymbol{z})\boldsymbol{z} \tag{11.78}$$

where

$$\boldsymbol{F}(\boldsymbol{z}) = \begin{bmatrix} f_1(z_1)/z_1 & \cdots & 0 \\ \vdots & \ddots & \vdots \\ 0 & \cdots & f_n(z_n)/z_n \end{bmatrix} \tag{11.79}$$

Theorem 11.7 *Let all $\alpha_i > 0$ in the system given in Eqn. (11.60). For a constant $r > 0$, the equilibrium point $\boldsymbol{x}^*$ of this system is locally exponentially stable in $\boldsymbol{B} = \{\boldsymbol{z} : ||\boldsymbol{z}|| < r|\}$ if there exists a constant $\eta > 0$ such that for all $\boldsymbol{z} \in \boldsymbol{B}$ and $\boldsymbol{z} \neq 0$*

$$(2\eta\boldsymbol{P} - \boldsymbol{Q}) - \boldsymbol{PWF}(\boldsymbol{z}) - \boldsymbol{F}(\boldsymbol{z})\boldsymbol{W}^T\boldsymbol{P} \geq 0 \tag{11.80}$$

where $\boldsymbol{Q} = \boldsymbol{Q}^T > 0$ is an arbitrary positive symmetric matrix and $\boldsymbol{P} = \boldsymbol{P}^T > 0$ is a unique positive symmetric solution of the Lyapunov function

$$\boldsymbol{PA} + \boldsymbol{AP} = \boldsymbol{Q} \tag{11.81}$$

Proof: Note that if the matrix $\boldsymbol{A} = diag[\alpha_1, \ldots, \alpha_n] > 0$, then $-\boldsymbol{A}$ is a stable matrix. Hence, for a given $\boldsymbol{Q} = \boldsymbol{Q}^T > 0$, the Lyapunov equation

$$\boldsymbol{PA} + \boldsymbol{AP} = \boldsymbol{Q} \tag{11.82}$$

has a unique positive symmetric solution $\boldsymbol{P} = \boldsymbol{P}^T > 0$. A quadratic Lyapunov function may be defined as

$$V(\boldsymbol{z}) = \boldsymbol{z}^T\boldsymbol{P}\boldsymbol{z} \tag{11.83}$$

For $z \neq 0$ and $\eta > 0$, the time derivative of $V(z)$ along the trajectories of the system is

$$\begin{aligned}\frac{dV(z)}{dt} &= z^T(-PA - AP)z + 2z^T PWf(z) \\ &= -z^T Qz + 2z^T PWF(z)z \\ &= -2\eta z^T Pz - z^T(Q - 2\eta P)z - 2z^T PWF(z)z \\ &= -2\eta V(z) - z^T[(Q - 2\eta P) - 2PWF(z)]z \\ &= -2\eta V(z) - z^T\Big[(Q - 2\eta P) \\ &\quad - PWF(z) - F(z)W^T P \Big] z \end{aligned} \tag{11.84}$$

Hence, if

$$z^T[(Q - 2\eta P) - PWF(z) - F(z)W^T P]z \geq 0 \tag{11.85}$$

that is

$$(Q - 2\eta P) - PWF(z) - F(z)W^T P \geq 0 \tag{11.86}$$

then

$$\frac{dV(z)}{dt} \leq -2\eta V(z) \tag{11.87}$$

This proves the theorem. ■

Lemma 11.3 *Let x^* be an equilibrium point of the system in Eqn. (11.60) and*

$$E(z) = F(z) - \Sigma(x^*) \tag{11.88}$$

where $E(z) = diag[e_1(z_1), \ldots, e_n(z_n)]$. Then for an arbitrary $\epsilon > 0$, there exists a $r > 0$ such that for all $z \in B = \{z : ||z|| < r\}$ and $z \neq 0$

$$||E(z)||_2 < \epsilon \tag{11.89}$$

Proof: The Taylor series expansion of the functions $f_i(z_i)$ around $z_i = 0$ is

$$\begin{aligned} f_i(z_i) &= \left.\frac{\partial f_i(z_i)}{\partial z_i}\right|_{z_i=0} z_i + 0(||z_i||^2) \\ &= \frac{\partial f_i(0)}{\partial z_i} z_i + 0(||z_i||^2) \end{aligned} \tag{11.90}$$

Hence, for $z_i \neq 0$, one has

$$\frac{f_i(z_i)}{z_i} - \frac{\partial f_i(z_i)}{\partial z_i} = \frac{0(||z||^2)}{z_i}$$

that is

$$e_i(z_i) = \frac{0(||z||^2)}{z_i}$$

Since

$$\lim_{z_i \to 0} \frac{0(||z||^2)}{z_i} = 0$$

for an arbitrary $\epsilon > 0$ there exists an $r_i > 0$ such that for all $|z_i| < r_i$ and $z_i \neq 0$

$$|e_i(z_i)| < \epsilon \tag{11.91}$$

Setting $r = \min\{r_i : i = 1, 2, \ldots, n\}$, it is easy to show that

$$||\boldsymbol{E}(\boldsymbol{z})||_2 < \epsilon \tag{11.92}$$

for all $\boldsymbol{z} \in B = \{\boldsymbol{z} : ||\boldsymbol{z}|| < r\}$ and $\boldsymbol{z} \neq 0$. ■

Corollary 11.5 *Let $\alpha_i > 0$ in the system described in Eqn. (11.60) and $\boldsymbol{x}^*$ be an equilibrium point of the system. If the matrix*

$$\boldsymbol{M} \equiv \boldsymbol{s} - \tfrac{1}{2}(\boldsymbol{A}^{-1}\boldsymbol{W}\boldsymbol{\Sigma}(\boldsymbol{x}^*) + \boldsymbol{\Sigma}(\boldsymbol{x}^*)\boldsymbol{W}^T\boldsymbol{A}^{-1}) > 0 \tag{11.93}$$

then $\boldsymbol{x}^*$ is locally exponentially stable in the neighborhood of $\boldsymbol{x}^*$.

Proof: Denote

$$\boldsymbol{F}(\boldsymbol{z}) = \boldsymbol{\Sigma}(\boldsymbol{x}^*) + \boldsymbol{E}(\boldsymbol{z})$$

Then, from Lemma 11.3, for a given $\epsilon > 0$ there exists a constant $r > 0$ such that for all $\boldsymbol{z} \in \boldsymbol{B} = \{\boldsymbol{z} : ||\boldsymbol{z}||_2 < r\}$ and $\boldsymbol{z} \neq 0$

$$||\boldsymbol{E}(\boldsymbol{z})||_2 < \epsilon \tag{11.94}$$

On the other hand, since all $\alpha_i > 0$, $\boldsymbol{A} = diag[\alpha_1, \ldots, \alpha_n] > 0$, we may choose $\boldsymbol{Q} = \boldsymbol{s}$, then the solution of the Lyapunov equation, Eqn. (11.83), is $\boldsymbol{P} = \boldsymbol{A}^{-1}/2$. Hence, the purpose of the following proof is to verify that

$$\begin{aligned}&\boldsymbol{s} - 2\eta\boldsymbol{P} - \boldsymbol{P}\boldsymbol{W}\boldsymbol{F}(\boldsymbol{z}) - \boldsymbol{F}(\boldsymbol{z})\boldsymbol{W}^T\boldsymbol{P}\\ &\quad = \boldsymbol{s} - \eta\boldsymbol{A}^{-1} - \tfrac{1}{2}[\boldsymbol{A}^{-1}\boldsymbol{W}\boldsymbol{F}(\boldsymbol{z}) + \boldsymbol{F}(\boldsymbol{z})\boldsymbol{W}^T\boldsymbol{A}^{-1}] \geq 0\end{aligned} \tag{11.95}$$

for all $z \in B$ and $z \neq 0$.

Note that

$$\begin{aligned} & s - \eta A^{-1} - \tfrac{1}{2}[A^{-1}WF(z) + F(z)W^T A^{-1}] \\ = \; & s - \eta A^{-1} - \tfrac{1}{2}[A^{-1}W(\Sigma(x^*) + E(z)) + (\Sigma(x^*) + E(z))WA^{-1}] \\ = \; & Y + Y^T - \tfrac{1}{2}[A^{-1}WE(z) + E(z)WA^{-1}] \end{aligned} \tag{11.96}$$

where

$$Y = \tfrac{1}{2}(s - \eta A^{-1}) - \tfrac{1}{2}A^{-1}W\Sigma(x^*) \tag{11.97}$$

Furthermore

$$\begin{aligned} Y + Y^T &= s - \tfrac{1}{2}(A^{-1}W\Sigma(x^*) + \Sigma(x^*)W^T A^{-1}) - \eta A^{-1} \\ &= M - \eta A^{-1} \end{aligned} \tag{11.98}$$

According to the assumption of the theorem, M is a positive-definite matrix; that is, $\lambda_{max}(M) > 0$. Hence, if

$$\lambda_{min}(M) > \eta \lambda_{max}(A^{-1}) = \frac{\eta}{\alpha_{min}} \tag{11.99}$$

where $\alpha_{min} = \min\{\alpha_i : i = 1, 2, \ldots, n\}$, then

$$Y + Y^T > 0 \tag{11.100}$$

In this case, it can be shown that Eqn. (11.100) is satisfied if

$$\tfrac{1}{2}||A^{-1}WE(z) + E(z)W^T A^{\;1}|| \leq \lambda_{min}(Y + Y^T) \tag{11.101}$$

or

$$\frac{\epsilon}{\alpha_{min}}||W||_2 \leq \lambda_{min}(Y + Y^T) \tag{11.102}$$

which may be ensured by the choice of an appropriate ϵ given in Eqn. (11.92). Thus, the corollary is proved. ■

Theorem 11.8 *The equilibrium point x^* of Eqn. (11.60) is locally exponentially stable if $(W\Sigma(x^*) - A)$ is a stable matrix and*

$$||W||_2 < \frac{\lambda_{min}(Q)}{4\lambda_{max}(P)} \tag{11.103}$$

where $Q = Q^T > 0$ is an arbitrary positive symmetric matrix and $P = P^T > 0$ is a unique positive symmetric solution of the Lyapunov equation

$$P(W\Sigma(x^*) - A) + (W\Sigma(x^*) - A)^T P = -Q \tag{11.104}$$

Proof: Note that in the transformed system in Eqn. (11.61) we have

$$x_i \leq f_i(z_i) < 0 \quad \text{if} \quad z_i < 0$$

$$0 < f_i(z_i) \leq z_i \quad \text{if} \quad z_i > 0$$

It is easy to verify that

$$||\boldsymbol{f}(\boldsymbol{z})||_2 \leq ||\boldsymbol{z}||_2 \tag{11.105}$$

and

$$\begin{aligned} ||\boldsymbol{W}\boldsymbol{f}(\boldsymbol{z})||_2 &\leq ||\boldsymbol{W}||_2||\boldsymbol{f}(\boldsymbol{z})||_2 \\ &\leq ||\boldsymbol{W}||_2||\boldsymbol{z}||_2 \end{aligned} \tag{11.106}$$

for all $t \geq 0$ and $\boldsymbol{x} \in \Re^n$. Since $\boldsymbol{W\Sigma}(\boldsymbol{x}^*) - \boldsymbol{A}$ is a Hurwitz, for a given $\boldsymbol{Q} = \boldsymbol{Q}^T > 0$, the Lyapunov equation

$$\boldsymbol{P}(\boldsymbol{W\Sigma}(\boldsymbol{x}^*) - \boldsymbol{A}) + (\boldsymbol{W\Sigma}(\boldsymbol{x}^*) - \boldsymbol{A})^T\boldsymbol{P} = -\boldsymbol{Q} \tag{11.107}$$

has a unique positive symmetric solution $\boldsymbol{P} = \boldsymbol{P}^T > 0$. A quadratic Lyapunov function may be defined as

$$V(\boldsymbol{z}) = \boldsymbol{z}^T\boldsymbol{P}\boldsymbol{z} \tag{11.108}$$

which satisfies

$$\lambda_{min}(\boldsymbol{P})||\boldsymbol{z}||_2^2 \leq V(\boldsymbol{z}) \leq \lambda_{max}(\boldsymbol{P})||\boldsymbol{z}||_2^2$$

$$\begin{aligned} \frac{\partial V}{\partial \boldsymbol{z}}(\boldsymbol{W\Sigma}(\boldsymbol{x}^*) - \boldsymbol{A})\boldsymbol{z} &= -\boldsymbol{z}^T\boldsymbol{Q}\boldsymbol{z} \leq -\lambda_{min}(\boldsymbol{Q})||\boldsymbol{z}||_2^2 \\ \left\|\frac{\partial V}{\partial \boldsymbol{z}}\right\|_2 &= ||2\boldsymbol{z}^T\boldsymbol{P}||_2 \leq 2||\boldsymbol{P}||_2||\boldsymbol{z}||_2 = 2\lambda_{max}(\boldsymbol{P})||\boldsymbol{z}||_2 \end{aligned}$$

The time derivative of $V(\boldsymbol{z})$ along the trajectories of the system in Eqn. (11.61) is

$$\begin{aligned} \frac{dV(\boldsymbol{z})}{dt} &= \boldsymbol{z}^T\boldsymbol{P}\frac{d\boldsymbol{z}}{dt} + \left(\frac{d\boldsymbol{z}}{dt}\right)^T\boldsymbol{P}\boldsymbol{z} \\ &= \boldsymbol{z}^T[\boldsymbol{P}(\boldsymbol{W\Sigma}(\boldsymbol{x}^*) - \boldsymbol{A}) + (\boldsymbol{W\Sigma}(\boldsymbol{x}^*) - \boldsymbol{A})^T\boldsymbol{P}]\boldsymbol{z} \\ &\quad - 2\boldsymbol{z}^T\boldsymbol{P}\boldsymbol{W\Sigma}(x^*)\boldsymbol{z} + 2\boldsymbol{z}^T\boldsymbol{P}\boldsymbol{W}\boldsymbol{f}(\boldsymbol{z}) \\ &= -\boldsymbol{z}^T\boldsymbol{Q}\boldsymbol{z} - 2\boldsymbol{z}^T\boldsymbol{P}\boldsymbol{W\Sigma}(\boldsymbol{x}^*)\boldsymbol{z} + 2\boldsymbol{z}^T\boldsymbol{P}\boldsymbol{W}\boldsymbol{f}(\boldsymbol{z}) \end{aligned} \tag{11.109}$$

Note that

$$\Sigma(x^*) = diag\left[\frac{\partial\sigma_1(x_1^*)}{\partial x_1}, \ldots, \frac{\partial\sigma_n(x_n^*)}{\partial x_n}\right]$$

with all

$$0 < \frac{\partial\sigma_i(x_i^*)}{\partial x_i} < 1 \tag{11.110}$$

one obtains

$$||\Sigma(x^*)||_2 \leq 1$$

Hence

$$\begin{aligned}\frac{dV(z)}{dt} &\leq -\lambda_{min}(Q)||x||_2^2 + 2\lambda_{max}(P)||W||_2||z||_2^2 \\ &\quad + 2\lambda_{max}(P)||W||_2||z||_2||f(z)||_2 \\ &\leq -\lambda_{min}(Q)||z||_2^2 + 4\lambda_{max}(P)||W||_2||z||_2^2\end{aligned} \tag{11.111}$$

if

$$||W||_2 < \frac{\lambda_{min}(Q)}{4\lambda_{max}(P)} \tag{11.112}$$

and

$$\eta = \frac{\lambda_{min}(Q) - 4\lambda_{max}(P)||W||_2}{2\lambda_{max}(P)} \tag{11.113}$$

then

$$\begin{aligned}\frac{dV(z)}{dt} &\leq -2\eta\lambda_{max}(P)||z||_2^2 \\ &\leq -2\eta V(z)\end{aligned} \tag{11.114}$$

Hence, the origin is locally exponentially stable. ■

11.4 GLOBAL EXPONENTIAL STABILITY OF DNNs

If the r neighborhood of the equilibrium point is replaced by the whole state space $\Re^n$ in Definition 11.2 and Theorem 11.6, the exponential stability is then global. In this case, for an arbitrary initial condition $x(t_0) = x_0 \in \Re^n$, the trajectory of the system will tend to the unique equilibrium point with an exponential convergence rate η.

Theorem 11.9 *The system given in Eqn. (11.60) is globally exponentially stable if* $(\boldsymbol{W} - \boldsymbol{A})$ *is a stable matrix and*

$$||\boldsymbol{W}||_2 < \frac{\lambda_{min}(\boldsymbol{Q})}{4\lambda_{max}(\boldsymbol{P})} \tag{11.115}$$

where $\boldsymbol{Q} = \boldsymbol{Q}^T > 0$ *is an arbitrary positive symmetric matrix and* $\boldsymbol{P} = \boldsymbol{P}^T > 0$ *is a unique positive symmetric solution of the Lyapunov function*

$$\boldsymbol{P}(\boldsymbol{W} - \boldsymbol{A}) + (\boldsymbol{W} - \boldsymbol{A})^T\boldsymbol{P} = -\boldsymbol{Q} \tag{11.116}$$

Proof: The proof procedure is the same as that used in Theorem 11.8. ■

The results given in Theorem 11.9 do not have any restrictions on the sign of the constants α_i in Eqn. (11.79).

Corollary 11.6 *Let all* $\alpha_i > 0$ *in Eqn. (11.60). The system in Eqn. (11.60) is globally exponentially stable if*

$$||\boldsymbol{W}||_2 < \frac{\alpha_{min}}{2} \tag{11.117}$$

where $\alpha_{min} = \min\{\alpha_i : i = 1, \ldots, n\}$. *In this case, the exponential convergence degree is*

$$\eta = \frac{\alpha_{min}}{2} - ||\boldsymbol{W}||_2 \tag{11.118}$$

Proof: Note that matrix $\boldsymbol{A} = diag[\alpha_1, \ldots, \alpha_n] > 0$ and $-\boldsymbol{A}$ is a stable matrix. Hence, for a given $\boldsymbol{Q} = \boldsymbol{Q}^T > 0$ the Lyapunov equation

$$\boldsymbol{P}\boldsymbol{A} + \boldsymbol{A}\boldsymbol{P} = \boldsymbol{Q} \tag{11.119}$$

has a unique positive symmetric solution $\boldsymbol{P} = \boldsymbol{P}^T > 0$. A quadratic Lyapunov function may be defined as

$$V(\boldsymbol{z}) = \boldsymbol{z}^T\boldsymbol{P}\boldsymbol{z} \tag{11.120}$$

which satisfies

$$\lambda_{min}(\boldsymbol{P})||\boldsymbol{z}||_2^2 \leq V(\boldsymbol{z}) \leq \lambda_{max}(\boldsymbol{P})||\boldsymbol{z}||_2^2$$

$$\begin{aligned}
\frac{\partial V}{\partial \boldsymbol{z}}(-\boldsymbol{A})\boldsymbol{z} &= -\boldsymbol{z}^T\boldsymbol{Q}\boldsymbol{z} \leq -\lambda_{min}(\boldsymbol{Q})||\boldsymbol{z}||_2^2 \\
\left\|\frac{\partial V}{\partial \boldsymbol{z}}\right\|_2 &= ||2\boldsymbol{z}^T\boldsymbol{P}||_2 \leq 2||\boldsymbol{P}||_2||\boldsymbol{z}||_2 = 2\lambda_{max}(\boldsymbol{P})||\boldsymbol{z}||_2
\end{aligned}$$

The time derivative of $V(\boldsymbol{z})$ along the trajectories of the system in Eqn. (11.61) is

$$\begin{aligned}\frac{dV(\boldsymbol{z})}{dt} &= \boldsymbol{z}^T(-\boldsymbol{PA} - \boldsymbol{AP})\boldsymbol{z} + 2\boldsymbol{z}^T\boldsymbol{PW}f(\boldsymbol{z}) \\ &= -\boldsymbol{z}^T\boldsymbol{Q}\boldsymbol{z} + 2\boldsymbol{z}^T\boldsymbol{PW}f(\boldsymbol{z}) \\ &\leq -\lambda_{min}(\boldsymbol{Q})||\boldsymbol{z}||_2^2 + 2\lambda_{max}(\boldsymbol{P})||\boldsymbol{W}||_2||\boldsymbol{z}||_2^2 \qquad (11.121)\end{aligned}$$

If

$$||\boldsymbol{W}||_2 < \frac{\lambda_{min}(\boldsymbol{Q})}{2\lambda_{max}(\boldsymbol{P})} \qquad (11.122)$$

and

$$\eta = \frac{\lambda_{min}(\boldsymbol{Q}) - 2\lambda_{max}(\boldsymbol{P})||\boldsymbol{W}||_2}{2\lambda_{max}(\boldsymbol{P})} \qquad (11.123)$$

then

$$\begin{aligned}\frac{dV(\boldsymbol{z})}{dt} &\leq -2\eta\lambda_{max}(\boldsymbol{P})||\boldsymbol{x}||_2^2 \\ &\leq -2\eta V(\boldsymbol{z}) \qquad (11.124)\end{aligned}$$

Hence, the origin $\boldsymbol{z} = 0$, that is, $\boldsymbol{x} = \boldsymbol{x}^*$ is globally exponentially stable. Since this condition depends on the choice of $\boldsymbol{Q}$, one may choose $\boldsymbol{Q}$ such that the ratio $\lambda_{min}(\boldsymbol{Q})/\lambda_{max}(\boldsymbol{P})$ reaches the maximum. In this case the optimal solution is $\boldsymbol{Q} = \boldsymbol{s}$, and $\boldsymbol{P}$ may be solved from Eqn. (11.119) as

$$\boldsymbol{P} = \tfrac{1}{2}\boldsymbol{A}^{-1} \qquad (11.125)$$

Hence

$$\lambda_{min}(\boldsymbol{Q}) = 1$$

$$\lambda_{max}(\boldsymbol{P}) = \frac{1}{\alpha_{min}}$$

where $\alpha_{min} = \min\{\alpha_i : i = 1, \ldots, n\}$. Then, the global exponential stability condition of Eqn. (11.124) may be simplified to

$$||\boldsymbol{W}||_2 < \frac{\alpha_{min}}{2} \qquad (11.126)$$

and the exponential convergence rate is

$$\eta = \frac{\alpha_{min}}{2} - ||\boldsymbol{W}||_2 \qquad (11.127)$$

■

11.5 CONCLUDING REMARKS

The notion of stability is of fundamental importance in dynamic systems. Dynamic neural networks (DNNs) form a class of highly nonlinear dynamic systems, and this chapter was devoted to study of the stability of continuous-time dynamic neural networks (CT-DNNs) that are described by a set of differential equations. In the study of the stability of continuous-time dynamic neural networks, we discussed the basic notions of local asymptotic stability, global asymptotic stability, and exponential asymptotic stability. The local stability conditions for a general class of DNNs are presented by using Lyapunov's first method, while the global asymptotic stability are studied by the well-known Lyapunov function method. The results presented in this chapter form a basis for further investigating stability conditions of any type of continuous-time DNNs with complex nonlinear dynamics.

Problems

11.1 Using Gerschgorin's theorem (Lemma 11.1), prove Corollary 11.2.

11.2 Using Corollary 11.2 to the Jacobian of the neural network given in Eqn. (11.13), prove Theorem 11.1.

11.3 Discuss the stability of the following two-neuron network system using Theorem 11.1:

$$\begin{aligned} \frac{dx_1}{dt} &= -x_1 - 3\tanh(x_2) + 0.6 \\ \frac{dx_2}{dt} &= -x_2 - 2\tanh(x_1) + 0.8 \end{aligned}$$

11.4 Discuss the stability of the two-neuron network system in Problem 11.3 using the following stability condition, which can be derived using Krasovskii's theorem (Krasovskii 1963): For an equilibrium point $\boldsymbol{x}^*$ of the system given in Eqn. (11.13), if

$$2w_{ii}\frac{\partial\sigma_i(x_i^*)}{\partial x_i} + \sum_{j=1,j\neq i}^{n}\left|w_{ij}\frac{\partial\sigma_j(x_j^*)}{\partial x_j} + w_{ji}\frac{\partial\sigma_i(x_i^*)}{\partial x_i}\right| < 2\alpha_i$$

$$i = 1, 2, \cdots, n$$

then $\boldsymbol{x}^*$ is a locally asymptotic stable equilibrium point.

11.5 Let all $\alpha_i = \alpha > 0$ in the system given in Eqn. (11.13). Show that the system given in Eqn. (11.13) is globally asymptotic stable if the weight matrix $\boldsymbol{W}$ is skew–symmetric; that is, $\boldsymbol{W} = -\boldsymbol{W}^T$.

11.6 Consider a general class of neural networks having the form

$$\frac{dx_i(t)}{dt} = -\alpha_i x_i(t) + \sum_{j=1}^{n} w_{ij}\sigma_j(x_j(t)) + v_i, \quad i = 1, 2, \ldots, n \tag{11.128}$$

or

$$\frac{d\boldsymbol{x}(t)}{dt} = -\boldsymbol{A}\boldsymbol{x}(t) + \boldsymbol{W}\boldsymbol{\sigma}(\boldsymbol{x}(t)) + \boldsymbol{v} \tag{11.129}$$

where $\boldsymbol{A} = diag[\alpha_1, \ldots, \alpha_n]$ and $\boldsymbol{W} \in \Re^{n \times n}$. Let $\boldsymbol{W}$ be a symmetric matrix and $\boldsymbol{\sigma}(\boldsymbol{x})$ be a monotonical sigmoidal function. Show that if $\boldsymbol{x}^*$ is an asymptotically stable equilibrium point of the system in Eqn. (11.129), there is then no other asymptotically stable equilibrium point $\boldsymbol{y}^*$ that satisfies

$$|y_i^*| \geq |x_i^*|, \quad sgn(y_i^*) = sgn(x_i^*), \quad \text{for all } i \text{ such that} \quad x_i^* \neq 0$$

or

$$|y_i^*| \leq |x_i^*|, \quad sgn(y_i^*) = sgn(x_i^*), \quad \text{for all } i$$

11.7 For the dynamic neural network given in Problem 11.6, show that

(a) $\boldsymbol{x} = 0$ is an equilibrium point of the system if and only if the threshold $\boldsymbol{v} = 0$;

(b) If the origin is an asymptotically stable point of the neural system, then there are no other asymptotically stable points of the system.

11.8 As pointed out by Kelly (1990), even though simplicity and the theoretical tractability of a linear system is obvious, and the general conclusion is that nonlinearity is an essential feature of biological neural processes. The linear case can still be used to explain the first-approximation model of the neural processing of input by the primary sensory cortex. Give a stability analysis of a linear neural network shown in Fig. 11.3 with the following form

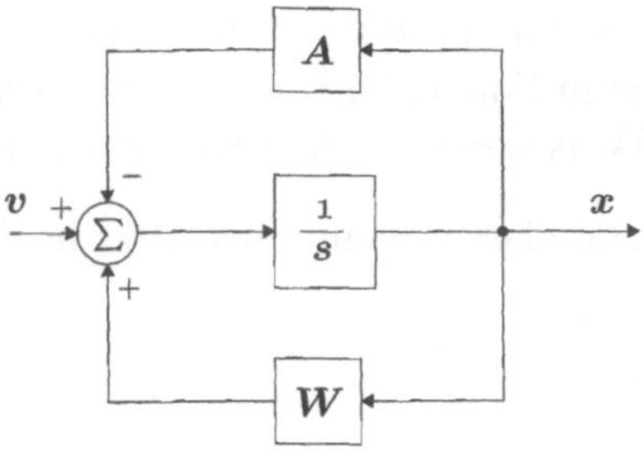

Figure 11.3 Problem 11.8: block diagram of the linear neural network.

$$\frac{d\boldsymbol{x}}{dt} = -\boldsymbol{A}\boldsymbol{x} + \boldsymbol{W}\boldsymbol{x} + \boldsymbol{v}$$

where $\boldsymbol{A} = diag[\alpha_1, \ldots, \alpha_n]$.

11.9 Show that the linear neural system given in Problem 11.8 has a unique global asymptotically stable equilibrium point $\boldsymbol{x}^*$ if and only if for any given positive-definite symmetric matrix $\boldsymbol{Q}$ there exists a positive-definite symmetric matrix $\boldsymbol{P}$ that satisfies the Lyapunov equation

$$-2\boldsymbol{P}\boldsymbol{A} + \boldsymbol{P}\boldsymbol{W} + \boldsymbol{W}^T\boldsymbol{P} = -\boldsymbol{Q}$$

Moreover, if $(\boldsymbol{A} - \boldsymbol{W})$ is a stable matrix, then $\boldsymbol{P}$ is the unique solution of the Lyapunov equation.

11.10 Let all $\alpha_i > 0$ or all $\alpha_i < 0$ in the linear neural system. Show that the system is globally asymptotically stable if

$$\lambda_{max}(\boldsymbol{A}^{-1}\boldsymbol{W} + \boldsymbol{W}^T\boldsymbol{A}^{-1}) < 2, \quad \text{for } \alpha_i > 0, \quad i = 1, \ldots, n$$

or

$$\lambda_{min}(\boldsymbol{A}^{-1}\boldsymbol{W} + \boldsymbol{W}^T\boldsymbol{A}^{-1}) > 2, \quad \text{for } \alpha_i < 0, \quad i = 1, \ldots, n$$

11.11 Let all $\alpha_i = \alpha > 0$ or all $\alpha_i = \alpha < 0$ in the linear neural system. Show that the system is globally asymptotically stable if

$$\lambda_{max}(\boldsymbol{W} + \boldsymbol{W}^T) < 2\alpha$$

11.12 Let $\alpha_i = \alpha$ and the weight matrix of the linear neural system be given as a strict lower triangular matrix as follows:

$$W = \begin{bmatrix} 0 & 0 & 0 & \cdots & \cdots & 0 \\ w_{21} & 0 & 0 & \cdots & \cdots & 0 \\ w_{31} & w_{32} & 0 & \cdots & \cdots & 0 \\ \vdots & \vdots & \vdots & \vdots & \vdots & \vdots \\ w_{n1} & w_{n2} & w_{n3} & \cdots & w_{n,n-1} & 0 \end{bmatrix}$$

In this case, the linear neural system is called as a *linear dynamic feedforward neural network.* Show that this linear neural system is globally asymptotic stable regardless of the magnitudes of the synaptic weights.

11.13 Show that the weight matrix in Problem 11.12 can also be a strict upper triangular matrix.

11.14 (Skew–Symmetric Linear Neural Network) Consider a dynamic linear neural network with n interconnected neural units. Let the synaptic strengths from unit j to unit k, and from the inverse propagation direction have the same magnitude but a different sign; that is, $w_{ij} = -w_{ji}$, and all self-connection strengths are set to zero. The network is then said to be a skew–symmetric linear neural network and is defined as

$$\dot{x}(t) = Wx(t)$$

Show that

(a) The system is globally asymptotic stable regardless of the magnitudes of the synaptic weights;

(b) Give the weight matrix of the skew–symmetric linear network with four neural, and draw a diagram to show the internal connections of those four neurons.

11.15 (Spatially Homogeneous Neural Network) Let a linear neural network have a *circulant* weight matrix of the form

$$W = \begin{bmatrix} w_0 & w_1 & \cdots & w_{n-1} \\ w_{n-1} & w_0 & \cdots & w_{n-2} \\ \vdots & \vdots & \ddots & \vdots \\ w_1 & w_2 & \cdots & w_0 \end{bmatrix}$$

Show that a set of analytic solutions of the eigenvalues and eigenvectors associated with the former may be obtained as

$$\lambda_j = \sum_{s=1}^{n-1} w_s e^{i(2\pi j s/n)}$$

and

$$x^j = \begin{bmatrix} 1 \\ e^{i(2\pi j/n)} \\ \vdots \\ e^{i(2\pi j(n-1)/n)} \end{bmatrix} = \begin{bmatrix} 1 \\ \cos\frac{2\pi j}{n} \\ \vdots \\ \cos\frac{2\pi j(n-1)}{n} \end{bmatrix} + i \begin{bmatrix} 1 \\ \sin(\frac{2\pi j}{n}) \\ \vdots \\ \sin\frac{2\pi j(n-1)}{n} \end{bmatrix}$$

where i is the imaginary unit, $i^2 = -1$. An interesting fact is that the eigenvectors of $\boldsymbol{W}$ are expressed in a complex spatial sinusoidal form that, due to the properties of the circulant matrix, does not depend on the values of the weights w_{ij}.

11.16 Show that the spatially homogeneous neural network given in Problem 11.15 is globally asymptotically stable if and only if $Re(\lambda_j) < \alpha$ for all j.

11.17 Show that for the spatially homogeneous neural network given in Problem 11.16, the equilibrium state components $x_0^*, x_1^*, \ldots, x_{n-1}^*$ can be obtained as

$$x_k^* = \sum_{j=0}^{n-1} \frac{\pi_j}{\alpha - \lambda_j} e^{i(2\pi jk/n)}, \quad k = 0, 1, \ldots, (n-1)$$

where

$$\pi_j = \frac{1}{n} \sum_{k=0}^{n-1} v_k e^{-i(2\pi jk/n)}$$

12

Discrete-Time Dynamic Neural Networks and Their Stability

12.1 General Class of Discrete-Time Dynamic Neural Networks (DT-DNNs)

12.2 Lyapunov Stability of Discrete-Time Nonlinear Systems

12.3 Stability Conditions for Discrete-Time DNNs

12.4 More General Results on Globally Asymptotic Stability

12.5 Concluding Remarks

Problems

The nonlinear dynamic behavior and stability of continuous-time dynamic neural networks (CT-DNNs) described by a set of nonlinear differential equations were studied extensively in Chapter 11. It was shown that Lyapunov's first and second methods can be used to study the equilibrium stability for a general class of continuous-time dynamic neural networks. In this chapter, the Lyapunov methods are extended to a general class of discrete-time dynamic neural networks (DT-DNNs). In Section 12.1, the general model of discrete-time DNNs is represented by a set of nonlinear difference equations. This model presents a number of discrete-time models derived from the notions of population biology, neurobiology, and evolutionary theory. The Lyapunov stability of the neural model is verified in Section 12.2. The stability conditions of the neural model are studied in Section 12.3. More general results on globally asymptotical stability are discussed in Section 12.4. For a given discrete-time DNN model, these conditions are determined only by the synaptic weight matrix of the network. It is shown that these results need fewer constraints on the synaptic weight matrix than the models described in the previous studies.

12.1 GENERAL CLASS OF DISCRETE-TIME DYNAMIC NEURAL NETWORKS (DT-DNNs)

Consider a general class of discrete-time dynamic neural networks (DT-DNNs) with continuous states as shown in Fig. 12.1 and described by the following set of difference equations

$$x_i(k+1) = -\alpha_i x_i(k) + \sum_{j=1}^{n} w_{ij}\sigma_j(\mu_j x_j(k)) + s_i, \quad i = 1, 2, \ldots, n \tag{12.1}$$

or equivalently in a vector form, the discrete-time dynamic neural network is described as

$$\boldsymbol{x}(k+1) = -\boldsymbol{A}\boldsymbol{x}(k) + \boldsymbol{W}\boldsymbol{\sigma}(\boldsymbol{\Psi}\boldsymbol{x}(k)) + \boldsymbol{s} \tag{12.2}$$

where $\boldsymbol{x} = [x_1, x_2, \ldots, x_n]^T$ is the neural state vector, $\boldsymbol{W} = [w_{ij}]_{n\times n}$ is the synaptic weight matrix, $\boldsymbol{s} = [s_1, s_2, \ldots, s_n]^T$ is the constant threshold vector, $\boldsymbol{A} = diag[\alpha_1, \alpha_2, \ldots, \alpha_n]$ with $|\alpha_i| < 1$ is the self-feedback coefficient matrix, $\boldsymbol{\Psi} = diag[\mu_1, \mu_2, \ldots, \mu_n]$ is the matrix of activation gains for controlling the state decay, and $\boldsymbol{\sigma}(\boldsymbol{\Psi x}) = [\sigma(\mu_1 x_1), \sigma(\mu_2 x_2), \ldots, \sigma(\mu_n x_n)]^T$ is the vector-valued activation function with the gain matrix $\boldsymbol{\Psi}$. The first term in Eqn. (12.2) is called the *self-feedback linear term* of the network.

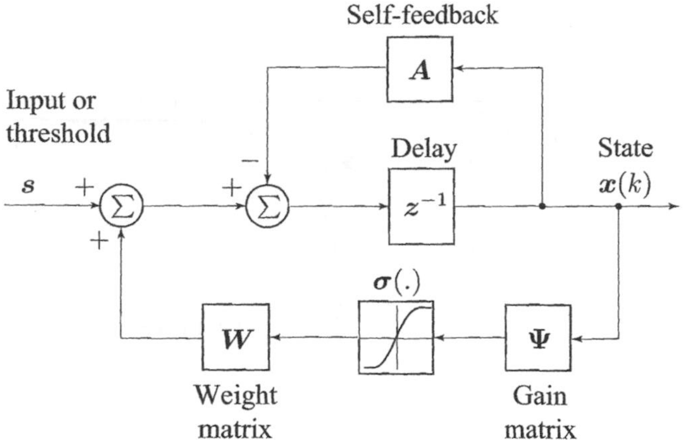

Figure 12.1 Block diagram of the discrete-time dynamic neural network (DT-DNN) defined in Eqn. (12.2).

As in continuous-time DNNs, the nonlinear neural activation function $\sigma(.)$ may be chosen as a continuous and differentiable nonlinear sigmoidal function satisfying the following conditions:

(i) $\sigma(x) \longrightarrow \pm 1$ as $x \longrightarrow \pm\infty$;

(ii) $\sigma(x)$ is bounded with the upper bound 1 and the lower bound -1;

(iii) $\sigma(x) = 0$ at a unique point $x = 0$;

(iv) $\sigma'(x) > 0$ and $\sigma'(x) \longrightarrow 0$ as $x \longrightarrow \pm\infty$;

(v) $\sigma'(x)$ has a global maximal value of 1.

In this section, $\sigma(.)$ is chosen as the *hyperbolic tangent sigmoidal function* $\sigma(x) = \tanh(x)$ shown in Fig. 12.2. The activation gain $\mu > 0$ is a constant that determines the slope of $\sigma(\mu x)$. The activation function $\sigma(\mu_i x_i) = \tanh(\mu_i x_i)$ associated with the ith neuron in Eqn. (12.2) is assumed to have its own gain $\mu_i > 0$. It is easy to verify the following inequalities:

(i) $|\sigma(\mu_i x_i)| \leq \mu_i |x_i|$;

(ii) $|\boldsymbol{\sigma}(\boldsymbol{\Psi x})| \leq \mu |\boldsymbol{x}|$;

(iii) $|\boldsymbol{\sigma}(\boldsymbol{\Psi x})| \leq \sqrt{n}$.

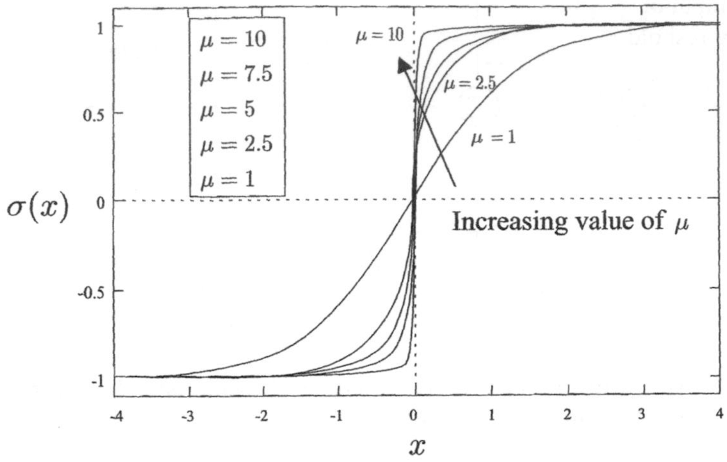

(a) $\sigma(x) = \tanh(\mu x)$

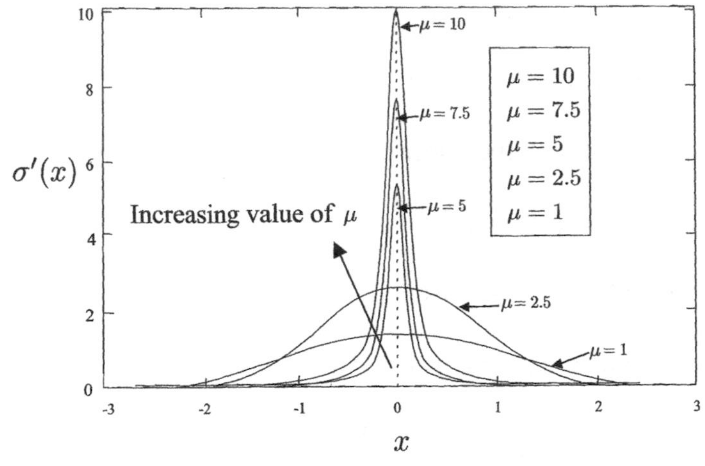

(b) $\sigma'(x) = \mu \operatorname{sech}^2(\mu x)$

Figure 12.2 The nonlinear neural activation function $\sigma(x) = \tanh(\mu x)$ and its derivative $\sigma'(x) = \mu \operatorname{sech}^2(\mu x)$, where $\mu = 1$, $\mu = 2.5$, $\mu = 5$, $\mu = 7.5$, and $\mu = 10$, respectively.

Given an initial condition $\boldsymbol{x}(0)$ of the neural network given in Eqn. (12.2), the state solution of the network at the instant k can be represented as

$$\begin{aligned}\boldsymbol{x}(k) &= (-\boldsymbol{A})^k\boldsymbol{x}(0) + \sum_{i=1}^{k-1}(-\boldsymbol{A})^{k-(i+1)}\boldsymbol{W}\boldsymbol{\sigma}(\boldsymbol{\Psi}\boldsymbol{x}(i)) + \boldsymbol{s} \\ &\triangleq \boldsymbol{\phi}(k, \boldsymbol{x}(0), \boldsymbol{s})\end{aligned}$$

One important characteristic of Eqn. (12.2) is its equilibrium points defined by the condition $\boldsymbol{x}(k+1) = \boldsymbol{x}(k)$. The equilibrium state equation of the system may also be represented as

$$\boldsymbol{x} = (\boldsymbol{I} + \boldsymbol{A})^{-1}[\boldsymbol{W}\boldsymbol{\sigma}(\boldsymbol{\Psi}\boldsymbol{x}) + \boldsymbol{s}] \triangleq \boldsymbol{g}(\boldsymbol{x}) \tag{12.3}$$

The equilibrium points of the neural system given in Eqn. (12.2) are the fixed points of the mapping $\boldsymbol{g}(\boldsymbol{x})$ defined by Eqn. (12.3). For an arbitrary given constant input $\boldsymbol{s} \in \Re^n$, let Ω be a hypercube defined by

$$\Omega = \left\{\boldsymbol{x} : |\boldsymbol{x} - (\boldsymbol{I} + \boldsymbol{A})^{-1}\boldsymbol{s}| \leq \frac{\sqrt{n}}{1+\alpha}||\boldsymbol{W}||_2\right\}$$

where $\alpha = \min\{\alpha_i\}$ and $\mu = \max\{\mu_i\}$, $|.|$ is the Euclidean norm and $||.||$ represents the induced matrix norm throughout this section. Then for an arbitrary $\boldsymbol{x} \in \Omega$

$$\begin{aligned}|\boldsymbol{g}(\boldsymbol{x}) - (\boldsymbol{I} + \boldsymbol{A})^{-1}\boldsymbol{s}| &= |(\boldsymbol{I} + \boldsymbol{A})^{-1}\boldsymbol{W}\boldsymbol{\sigma}(\boldsymbol{\Psi}\boldsymbol{x})| \\ &\leq ||(\boldsymbol{I} + \boldsymbol{A})^{-1}||_2||\boldsymbol{W}||_2|\boldsymbol{\sigma}(\boldsymbol{\Psi}\boldsymbol{x})| \\ &\leq \frac{\sqrt{n}}{1+\alpha}||\boldsymbol{W}||_2\end{aligned}$$

holds. Hence, $\boldsymbol{g}(\boldsymbol{x})$ is a continuous mapping from a bounded, convex and closed set Ω onto itself; that is, $\boldsymbol{g}(\boldsymbol{x}) : \Omega \longrightarrow \Omega$. According to Brouwer's fixed-point theorem, $\boldsymbol{g}$ has at least one fixed point in Ω for any choice of the weight matrix $\boldsymbol{W}$.

As in conventional nonlinear systems, the neural network given in Eqn. (12.2) is said to be *globally asymptotically stable*, or *asymptotically stable in large*, if it has a unique equilibrium point that is globally asymptotically stable in the sense of Lyapunov. In this case, for the arbitrary initial state $\boldsymbol{x}(0) \in \Re^n$ the state solution $\boldsymbol{\phi}(k, \boldsymbol{x}(0), \boldsymbol{s})$ will converge to the unique equilibrium point $\boldsymbol{x}^*$ satisfying Eqn. (12.3):

$$\boldsymbol{x}^* = \lim_{k \longrightarrow +\infty} \boldsymbol{\phi}(k, \boldsymbol{x}(0), \boldsymbol{s})$$

Moreover, if for an arbitrary initial state $\boldsymbol{x}(0) \in \Re^n$ the state solution $\boldsymbol{\phi}(k, \boldsymbol{x}(0), \boldsymbol{s})$ approaches this unique equilibrium point $\boldsymbol{x}^*$ exponentially in terms of the norm, that is, if there exist two positive constants $c_1, c_2 > 0$ such that

$$|\boldsymbol{x}(k)| \leq c_1 |\boldsymbol{x}^*| \exp(-c_2 k) \qquad \text{for } k \geq 0$$

then the network given in Eqn. (12.2) is *globally exponentially stable*.

12.2 LYAPUNOV STABILITY OF DISCRETE-TIME NONLINEAR SYSTEMS

12.2.1 Lyapunov's Second Method of Stability

Let a discrete-time nonlinear system be described by

$$\boldsymbol{x}(k+1) = \boldsymbol{f}(\boldsymbol{x}(k)) \tag{12.4}$$

where $\boldsymbol{x} \in \Re^n$ is the state vector, and $\boldsymbol{f}(\boldsymbol{x}(k))$ is an $n \times 1$ vector-valued function. Let $\boldsymbol{x}^*$ be an equilibrium point of the system; that is, $\boldsymbol{x}^* = \boldsymbol{f}(\boldsymbol{x}^*)$. Introducing an equivalent coordinate transformation $\boldsymbol{z} = \boldsymbol{x} - \boldsymbol{x}^*$, the neural system described by Eqn. (12.4) can be written in terms of $\boldsymbol{z}$ as

$$\begin{aligned} \boldsymbol{z}(k+1) &= \boldsymbol{f}(\boldsymbol{z}(k) + \boldsymbol{x}^*) - \boldsymbol{f}(\boldsymbol{x}^*) \\ &= \tilde{\boldsymbol{f}}(\boldsymbol{z}(k)) \end{aligned} \tag{12.5}$$

where $\tilde{\boldsymbol{f}}(\boldsymbol{z}) = \boldsymbol{f}(\boldsymbol{z} + \boldsymbol{x}^*) - \boldsymbol{f}(\boldsymbol{x}^*)$ and the origin $\boldsymbol{z}^* = 0$ is an equilibrium point of the new system corresponding to the equilibrium point $\boldsymbol{x}^*$ in the original neural system defined in Eqn. (12.4). Therefore, in the following discussion about the stability of the equilibrium point, we will study the stability or instability of the origin $\boldsymbol{x}^* = 0$ for the discrete-time nonlinear neural system given in Eqn. (12.4).

Lemma 12.1 [Local Stability Theorem of Lyapunov (Khalil 1992)] *Let $\boldsymbol{x} = 0$ be an equilibrium point of the system in Eqn. (12.4) and $V : D \longrightarrow \Re$ be a continuously differentiable function in a neighborhood D of $\boldsymbol{x} = 0$ such that*

(i) $V(\boldsymbol{x}(k) = 0) = V(0) = 0$

(ii) $V(\boldsymbol{x}(k)) = V(\boldsymbol{x}) > 0 \quad for \quad \boldsymbol{x} \neq 0 \quad and \quad \boldsymbol{x} \in D$

(iii) $\Delta V(\boldsymbol{x}) = V(\boldsymbol{x}(k+1)) - V(\boldsymbol{x}(k)) < 0 \quad for \quad \boldsymbol{x} \neq 0 \quad and \quad \boldsymbol{x} \in D$

Then the equilibrium point $\boldsymbol{x} = 0$ is asymptotically stable and $V(\boldsymbol{x})$ is a local Lyapunov function. ■

Lemma 12.2 [Global Stability Theorem of Lyapunov (Khalil 1992)] *Let* $\boldsymbol{x} = 0$ *be an equilibrium point of the system in Eqn. (12.4) and* $V : \Re^n \longrightarrow \Re$ *be a continuously differentiable function such that*

(i) $V(\boldsymbol{x}(k) = 0) = V(0) = 0$

(ii) $V(\boldsymbol{x}(k)) = V(\boldsymbol{x}) > 0 \quad for \quad \boldsymbol{x} \neq 0$

(iii) $V(\boldsymbol{x}) \longrightarrow \infty, \quad as \quad ||\boldsymbol{x}|| \longrightarrow \infty$

(iv) $\Delta V(\boldsymbol{x}) \leq 0 \quad for \quad \boldsymbol{x} \neq 0$

Then the equilibrium point $\boldsymbol{x} = 0$ *is asymptotically stable and* $V(\boldsymbol{x})$ *is a global Lyapunov function.* ■

The stability and instability theorems of Lyapunov are valid for both linear and nonlinear systems. In fact, a successful execution of the Lyapunov test depends on the selection of $V(\boldsymbol{x})$ or $\Delta V(\boldsymbol{x})$, which is always a difficult task.

LaSalle's invariance principle can be extended to discrete-time systems for deriving stability conditions based on the so-called energy function, which is not a Lyapunov function in the strict mathematical sense. The discrete-time version LaSalle's invariance principle can be stated as follows.

Lemma 12.3 (Energy Function Method) *Let* Ω *be a compact set with the property that every solution of the neural system in Eqn. (12.4) that starts in* Ω *remains for all future time instants* k *in* Ω. *Let* $E : \Omega \longrightarrow \Re$ *be a function such that*

(i) $\Delta E(\boldsymbol{x}) = E(\boldsymbol{x}(k+1)) - E(\boldsymbol{x}(k)) < 0 \quad for \quad \boldsymbol{x} \in \Omega$

(ii) $\Delta E(\boldsymbol{x}) = E(\boldsymbol{x}(k+1)) - E(\boldsymbol{x}(k)) = 0$, *only* $\Delta \boldsymbol{x}(k) = \boldsymbol{x}(k+1) - \boldsymbol{x}(k) = 0$

Then, for any $\boldsymbol{x}(0) \in \Omega$, *the solution of the neural system given in Eqn. (12.4) will approach one equilibrium of the system as* $k \longrightarrow \infty$. ■

Unlike the Lyapunov function method, the energy function approach does not require the function $E(\boldsymbol{x})$ to be positive define. The system satisfying the conditions in Lemma 12.3 has a global state convergence that ensures that the state of such a nonlinear system will converge to an equilibrium.

12.2.2 Lyapunov's First Method

In general, finding a suitable Lyapunov function for a given nonlinear dynamic system is a difficult task. Special stability properties of the nonlinear neural activation function $\sigma(\boldsymbol{x})$ were discussed earlier. An equivalent analysis process using the Lyapunov function approach is to test the positions of all the eigenvalues of the Jacobian of the neural system. This approach is known as *Lyapunov's indirect method* or *Lyapunov's first method.*

The Jacobian of the function $\boldsymbol{f}(\boldsymbol{x})$ is defined as

$$J = \frac{d\boldsymbol{f}}{d\boldsymbol{x}} = \boldsymbol{f}'(\boldsymbol{x}) \tag{12.6}$$

which can also be used to analyze the stability of the equilibrium points.

For the local asymptotical stability of the equilibrium point $\boldsymbol{x}^*$, the eigenvalues of the Jacobian at the equilibrium point $\boldsymbol{x}^*$ should be examined. Let us go back to the nonlinear system

$$\boldsymbol{x}(k+1) = \boldsymbol{f}(\boldsymbol{x}(k))$$

where $\boldsymbol{f} : D \longrightarrow \Re^n$ is a continuously differentiable map from a domain $D \in \Re^n$ into $\Re^n$. The following lemma gives the local stability and instability conditions.

Lemma 12.4 (Lyapunov's First Method) *Let $\boldsymbol{x}^* = 0$ be an equilibrium point of system*

$$\boldsymbol{x}(k+1) = \boldsymbol{f}(\boldsymbol{x}(k)) \tag{12.7}$$

where $\boldsymbol{f} : D \longrightarrow \Re^n$ is continuously differentiable and D is a neighborhood of the origin. Define the Jacobian of Eqn. (12.7) in the neighborhood of the equilibrium point $\boldsymbol{x}^* = 0$ as

$$J = \frac{\partial \boldsymbol{f}}{\partial \boldsymbol{x}}(0) \equiv \boldsymbol{A} \tag{12.8}$$

Then

(i) The origin is locally asymptotically stable if all the eigenvalues of $\boldsymbol{J}$ are inside the unit circle in the complex plane;

(ii) The origin is unstable if one or more of the eigenvalues of $\boldsymbol{J}$ are outside the unit circle in the complex plane. ■

Lemma 12.4 shows that, as illustrated in Fig. 12.3, if all the eigenvalues of the Jacobian $\boldsymbol{A}$ at $\boldsymbol{x}^*$ are within the unit circle, then $\boldsymbol{x}^*$ is a local asymptotical stable equilibrium point of the neural system given in Eqn. (12.7), and this equilibrium point is called a *sink.* If all the eigenvalues of the Jacobian at $\boldsymbol{x}^*$ are outside the unit circle, then $\boldsymbol{x}^*$ is unstable and it is called a *source.* If some eigenvalues are inside and some are outside the unit circle, the equilibrium point is a *saddle* equilibrium point. For a local asymptotical stable equilibrium point, it is important to find the region of attraction of the point. Khalil (1992) indicates that whenever the Jacobian matrix $\boldsymbol{A}$ at the equilibrium point x^* is a stable matrix, that is, when all the eigenvalues are located inside the unit circle, we can estimate the region of attraction for that equilibrium point.

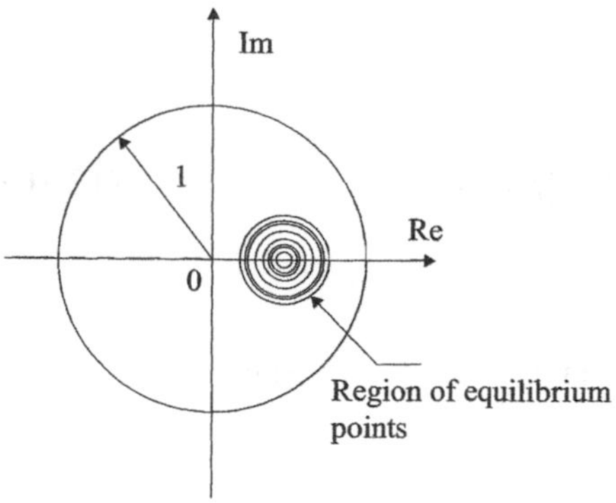

(a) Region of stable (sink) equilibrium points

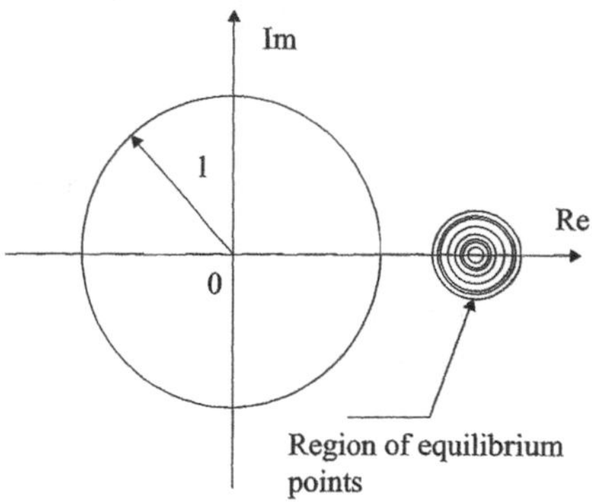

(b) Region of unstable (source) equilibrium points

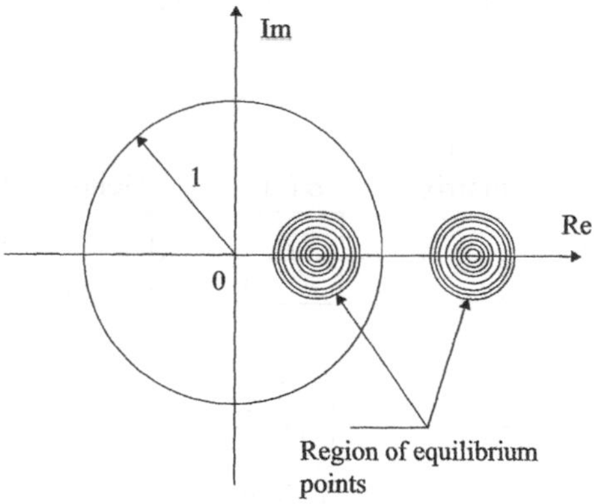

(c) Saddle equilibrium points

Figure 12.3 Positions and classification of the equilibrium points.

12.3 STABILITY CONDITIONS FOR DISCRETE-TIME DNNs

If the self-feedback or linear term in Eqn. (12.2) is neglected; that is, $\boldsymbol{A} \equiv 0$ in Eqn. (12.2), a simplified model of discrete-time dynamic neural networks (DT-DNNs) is shown in Fig. 12.4a and given by

$$x_i(k+1) = \sum_{j=1}^{n} w_{ij}\sigma_j(\mu_j x_j(k)) + s_i, \quad i = 1, 2, \ldots, n \tag{12.9}$$

or

$$\boldsymbol{x}(k+1) = \boldsymbol{W}\boldsymbol{\sigma}(\boldsymbol{\Psi}\boldsymbol{x}(k)) + \boldsymbol{s} \tag{12.10}$$

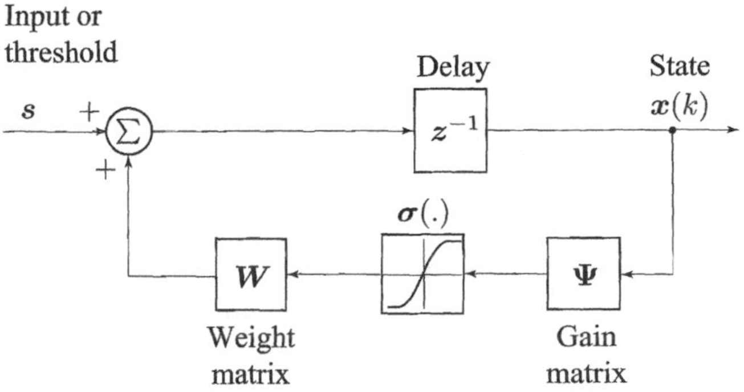

(a) The network described by Eqn. (12.10)

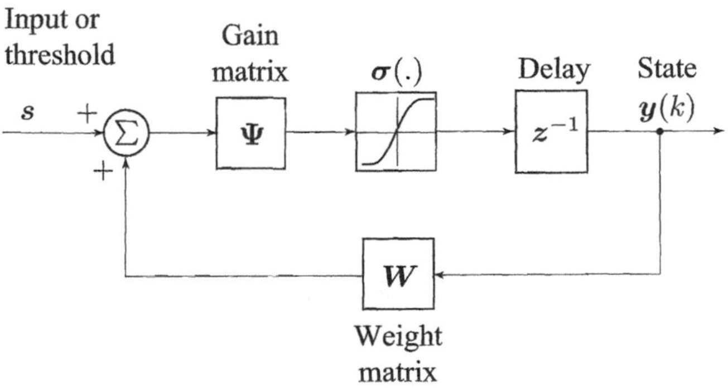

(b) The network described by Eqn. (12.11)

Figure 12.4 Block diagrams of the dynamic neural networks without the linear term.

Using a linear coordinate transformation $\boldsymbol{x} = \boldsymbol{W}\boldsymbol{y} + \boldsymbol{s}$, Eqn. (12.10) may be written equivalently in terms of the new state vector $\boldsymbol{y} \in \Re^n$ as follows:

$$\boldsymbol{y}(k+1) = \boldsymbol{\sigma}(\boldsymbol{\Psi}\boldsymbol{W}\boldsymbol{y}(k) + \boldsymbol{\Psi}\boldsymbol{s}) \tag{12.11}$$

This network is shown in Fig. 12.4b. Therefore, the two neural networks illustrated in Fig. 12.4 have the same stability property. As seen in the previous section, to apply the Lyapunov function method, Eqn. (12.10) can be transferred into the following equivalently form

$$\boldsymbol{z}(k+1) = \boldsymbol{W}\boldsymbol{f}(\boldsymbol{z}(k)) \tag{12.12}$$

where the vector-valued function $\boldsymbol{f}: \Re^n \longrightarrow \Re^n$ is given by

$$\boldsymbol{f}(\boldsymbol{z}) = \begin{bmatrix} f_1(z_1) \\ f_2(z_2) \\ \vdots \\ f_n(z_n) \end{bmatrix} \triangleq \begin{bmatrix} \sigma(\mu_1(z_1 + x_1^*)) - \sigma(\mu_1 x_1^*) \\ \sigma(\mu_2(z_2 + x_2^*)) - \sigma(\mu_2 x_2^*) \\ \vdots \\ \sigma(\mu_n(z_n + x_n^*)) - \sigma(\mu_n x_n^*) \end{bmatrix} \tag{12.13}$$

and satisfies $\boldsymbol{f}(0) = 0$. Thus, $\boldsymbol{z} = 0$ is a unique equilibrium point of the new system expressed in Eqn. (12.12).

12.3.1 Global State Convergence for Symmetric Weight Matrix

Like continuous-time Hopfield neural networks, one can also explore the global state convergence of the discrete-time DNN with a symmetric weight matrix. For instances, when the synaptic weight matrix $\boldsymbol{W}$ is symmetric, that is, when $\boldsymbol{W} = \boldsymbol{W}^T$, Marcus and Westervelt (1989) proposed an energy function for the neural system given in Eqn. (12.11), which is of the form

$$\begin{aligned} E(k) &= -\tfrac{1}{2}\sum_{i=1}^{n}\sum_{j=1}^{n} \mu_i w_{ij} y_i(k) y_j(k) - \sum_{i=1}^{n} y_i(k)\mu_i s_i \\ &\quad + \sum_{i=1}^{n} \int_0^{y_i(k)} \sigma_i^{-1}(\tau)d\tau \\ &= -\tfrac{1}{2}\boldsymbol{y}^T(k)\boldsymbol{\Psi}\boldsymbol{W}\boldsymbol{y}(k) - \boldsymbol{y}^T(k)\boldsymbol{\Psi}\boldsymbol{s} + \sum_{i=1}^{n} G_i(y_i(k)) \end{aligned} \tag{12.14}$$

where

$$G_i(y_i) = \int_0^{y_i} \sigma_i^{-1}(\tau)d\tau \tag{12.15}$$

Using symmetry, $w_{ij} = w_{ji}$, the change in $E(k)$ between the time k and $k+1$, defined as $\Delta E(k) \triangleq E(k+1) - E(k)$, can be given as

$$\begin{aligned}\Delta E(k) &= -\tfrac{1}{2}\Delta \boldsymbol{y}^T(k)\boldsymbol{\Psi W}\Delta \boldsymbol{y}(k) - \Delta \boldsymbol{y}^T(k)\boldsymbol{\Psi W y}(k) \\ &\quad - \Delta \boldsymbol{y}^T(k)\boldsymbol{\Psi s} + \sum_{i=1}^{n}\Big[G_i(y_i(k+1)) - G_i(y_i(k))\Big] \\ &= -\tfrac{1}{2}\Delta \boldsymbol{y}^T(k)\boldsymbol{\Psi W}\Delta \boldsymbol{y}(k) - \Delta \boldsymbol{y}^T(k)\boldsymbol{\sigma}^{-1}(\boldsymbol{y}(k+1)) \\ &\quad + \sum_{i=1}^{n}\Delta G_i(k) \end{aligned} \tag{12.16}$$

where $\Delta \boldsymbol{y}(k) \triangleq \boldsymbol{y}(k+1) - \boldsymbol{y}(k)$ and

$$\Delta G_i(k) \;=\; G_i(y_i(k+1)) - G_i(y_i(k))$$

Considering up to the second derivatives, one obtains the following inequality (Marcus and Westervelt 1989)

$$\Delta G_i(k) \le G_i'(y_i(k+1))\Delta y_i(k) - \tfrac{1}{2}\min_{y_i}\left(\frac{d^2G_i(y_i)}{dy_i^2}\right)\Big[\Delta y_i(k)\Big]^2 \tag{12.17}$$

where $G_i'(y_i(k+1))$ is the derivative of $G_i(y_i)$ at the point $y_i = y_i(k+1)$. Since the minimum curvature of G_i is given by the inverse number of the maximum slope of the function $\sigma(.)$; that is 1, the minimum second derivative can be expressed as

$$\min_{y_i}\left(\frac{d^2G_i(y_i)}{dy_i^2}\right) = 1^{-1} = 1 \tag{12.18}$$

Equations (12.16)–(12.18) and equality $G_i'(y_i) = \sigma_i^{-1}(y_i)$ from Eqn. (12.15) yield

$$\begin{aligned}\Delta E(k) &\le -\tfrac{1}{2}\Delta \boldsymbol{y}^T(k)\boldsymbol{\Psi W}\Delta \boldsymbol{y}(k) - \tfrac{1}{2}\Delta \boldsymbol{y}^T(k)\Delta \boldsymbol{y}(k) \\ &= -\tfrac{1}{2}\Delta \boldsymbol{y}^T(k)\left[\boldsymbol{\Psi W} + \boldsymbol{I}\right]\Delta \boldsymbol{y}(k)\end{aligned} \tag{12.19}$$

If the matrix $\boldsymbol{\Psi W} + \boldsymbol{I}$ is positive-definite; that is

$$\boldsymbol{W} + \boldsymbol{\Psi}^{-1} > 0 \tag{12.20}$$

then

$$\Delta E(k) \le 0; \quad \Delta E(k) = 0 \Longrightarrow \Delta \boldsymbol{y} = 0 \tag{12.21}$$

Therefore, all the attractors of the dynamic neural system described in Eqn. (12.11) are fixed points, and the condition in Eqn. (12.20) is a global convergence condition. A sufficient condition for $\boldsymbol{W} + \boldsymbol{\Psi}^{-1}$ to be positive-definite is

$$|\lambda_{min}(\boldsymbol{W})| < \frac{1}{\mu} \tag{12.22}$$

where $\lambda_{min}(\boldsymbol{W})$ represents the minimum eigenvalue of the matrix $\boldsymbol{W}$. If this condition is satisfied, the states of the system in Eqn. (12.10) or Eqn. (12.11) will always converge to one of their asymptotically stable equilibrium points regardless of the initial values of the states.

12.3.2 Norm Stability Conditions

We will now obtain a sufficient condition that guarantees the origin $\zeta = 0$ to be a globally asymptotical stable equilibrium point. The contraction of the nonlinear neural function can be used to develop a stability condition. It is easy to verify that the nonlinear neural function satisfies

$$||\boldsymbol{f}(\boldsymbol{z})|| \le ||\boldsymbol{\Psi}\boldsymbol{z}|| \le ||\boldsymbol{\Psi}||||\boldsymbol{z}||$$

Therefore, we can choose another Lyapunov function for the equivalent neural system in Eqn. (12.12) as

$$V(\boldsymbol{z}) = ||\boldsymbol{z}||$$

Furthermore, we have

$$\begin{aligned} \Delta V(\boldsymbol{z}) &= ||\boldsymbol{W}\boldsymbol{f}(\boldsymbol{z})|| - ||\boldsymbol{z}|| \\ &\le ||\boldsymbol{W}||||\boldsymbol{f}(\boldsymbol{z})|| - ||\boldsymbol{z}|| \\ &\le (||\boldsymbol{W}||||\boldsymbol{\Psi}|| - 1)||\boldsymbol{z}|| \end{aligned}$$

Hence, if

$$||\boldsymbol{W}|| < \frac{1}{||\boldsymbol{\Psi}||} \tag{12.23}$$

then ΔV is negative-definite, and the neural system in Eqn. (12.10) is globally asymptotically stable. Equation (12.23) is the so-called norm stability condition.

12.3.3 Diagonal Lyapunov Function Method

In the discrete-time domain, the well-known Lyapunov equation for a test matrix $\boldsymbol{M}$ is given by

$$\boldsymbol{M}^T\boldsymbol{P}\boldsymbol{M} - \boldsymbol{P} = -\boldsymbol{Q}$$

If there exists a positive-definite matrix $\boldsymbol{Q} > 0$ such that this Lyapunov equation has a positive diagonal solution $\boldsymbol{P}$, then the matrix $\boldsymbol{M}$ is said to be diagonally stable. The diagonal stability implies the Schur stability of the matrix. Moreover, if the tested matrix is a nonnegative or M matrix, the diagonal stability is equivalent to the Schur stability (Kaszkurewicz and Bhaya 1993, Michel and Miller 1977), or simply speaking, in this case, the diagonal stability is equivalent to all the eigenvalues of the matrix being located inside the unit circle.

Theorem 12.1 *The neural system in Eqn. (12.12) is globally asymptotically stable if for an $n \times n$ positive diagonal matrix $\boldsymbol{P} = diag[p_1, p_2, \ldots, p_n]$ with $p_i > 0$ for all $1 \leq i \leq n$, there exists a positive-definite matrix $\boldsymbol{Q} > 0$ such that*

$$\boldsymbol{W}^T \boldsymbol{P} \boldsymbol{W} - \boldsymbol{\Psi}^{-2} \boldsymbol{P} = -\boldsymbol{Q} \tag{12.24}$$

where $\boldsymbol{\Psi}^{-2} = \boldsymbol{\Psi}^{-1}\boldsymbol{\Psi}^{-1} = diag[1/p_1^2, 1/p_2^2, \ldots, 1/p_n^2]$.

Proof: Let a function be defined as

$$V(\boldsymbol{z}(k)) = \sum_{i=1,j=1}^{n} p_{ij} z_i(k) z_j(k) = \boldsymbol{z}^T \boldsymbol{P} \boldsymbol{z} \tag{12.25}$$

where $\boldsymbol{P} = diag[p_1, p_2, \ldots, p_n] > 0$. This function satisfies

$$V(\boldsymbol{z}) = 0, \qquad \text{if and only if } \boldsymbol{z} = 0$$

and

$$V(\boldsymbol{z}) > 0, \qquad \text{for } \boldsymbol{z} \neq 0$$

Noting that

$$\boldsymbol{z}^T \boldsymbol{P} \boldsymbol{z} \geq \boldsymbol{f}^T(\boldsymbol{z}) \boldsymbol{\Psi}^{-2} \boldsymbol{P} \boldsymbol{f}(\boldsymbol{z})$$

one obtains

$$\begin{aligned}
\Delta V(\boldsymbol{z}(k)) &= \boldsymbol{z}^T(k+1)\boldsymbol{P}\boldsymbol{z}(k+1) - \boldsymbol{z}^T(k)\boldsymbol{P}\boldsymbol{z}(k) \\
&= \boldsymbol{f}^T(\boldsymbol{z}(k))\boldsymbol{W}^T\boldsymbol{P}\boldsymbol{W}\boldsymbol{f}(\boldsymbol{z}(k)) - \boldsymbol{z}^T(k)\boldsymbol{P}\boldsymbol{z}(k) \\
&\leq \boldsymbol{f}^T(\boldsymbol{z}(k))\boldsymbol{W}^T\boldsymbol{P}\boldsymbol{W}\boldsymbol{f}(\boldsymbol{z}(k)) - \boldsymbol{f}^T(\boldsymbol{z}(k))\boldsymbol{\Psi}^{-2}\boldsymbol{P}\boldsymbol{f}(\boldsymbol{z}(k)) \\
&= \boldsymbol{f}^T(\boldsymbol{z}(k))[\boldsymbol{W}^T\boldsymbol{P}\boldsymbol{W} - \boldsymbol{\Psi}^{-2}\boldsymbol{P}]\boldsymbol{f}(\boldsymbol{z}(k))
\end{aligned}$$

Therefore, the theorem is proved. ■

The Lyapunov function defined by Eqn. (12.25) is a *diagonal Lyapunov function* (Kaszkurewicz and Bhaya 1993), and Eqn. (12.24) is consequentially a *diagonal Lyapunov equation.* Theorem 12.1 indicates that if there exists a positive-definite matrix $\boldsymbol{Q}$ such that the solution $\boldsymbol{P}$ of Eqn. (12.24) is a positive diagonal matrix, then the neural system in Eqn. (12.12) is globally asymptotically stable. In other words, if the product of the synaptic weight matrix $\boldsymbol{W}$ and the gain matrix $\boldsymbol{\Psi}$, that is, $\boldsymbol{W\Psi}$, is diagonally stable, the neural system in Eqn. (12.12) is then globally asymptotically stable. As a consequence of Theorem 12.1, the following corollaries can be stated:

Corollary 12.1 *The neural system in Eqn. (12.12) is globally asymptotically stable if one of the following conditions is satisfied*

$$(i) \quad \lambda_{max}(\boldsymbol{\Psi W}^T\boldsymbol{W\Psi}) < 1; \tag{12.26}$$

$$(ii) \quad \sum_{j,k=1}^{n} \mu_i\mu_j|w_{ik}w_{jk}| < 1, \quad i = 1, 2, \ldots, n; \tag{12.27}$$

$$(iii) \quad \sum_{i,k=1}^{n} \mu_i\mu_j|w_{ik}w_{jk}| < 1, \quad j = 1, 2, \ldots, n. \tag{12.28}$$

Proof: The stability condition given in Eqn. (12.24) can be represented equivalently as

$$\boldsymbol{\Psi W}^T\boldsymbol{P W\Psi} - \boldsymbol{P} < 0$$

Let $\boldsymbol{P} = \boldsymbol{I}$ in the matrix inequality above. One then obtains

$$\boldsymbol{\Psi W}^T\boldsymbol{W\Psi} - \boldsymbol{I} < 0$$

Thus, a sufficient condition is

$$\lambda_{max}(\boldsymbol{\Psi W}^T\boldsymbol{W\Psi} - \boldsymbol{I}) = \lambda_{max}(\boldsymbol{\Psi W}^T\boldsymbol{W\Psi}) - 1 < 0$$

which proves condition (i).

Moreover, applying Gerschgorin's theorem (Horn and Johnson 1985) to the matrix

$$\boldsymbol{\Psi W}^T\boldsymbol{W\Psi} = \begin{bmatrix} \sum_{k=1}^{n} \mu_1^2 w_{ik}^2 & \sum_{k=1}^{n} \mu_1 w_{1k} w_{2k} \mu_2 & \cdots & \sum_{k=1}^{n} \mu_1 w_{1k} w_{nk} \mu_n \\ \sum_{k=1}^{n} \mu_2 w_{2k} w_{1k} \mu_1 & \sum_{k=1}^{n} \mu_2^2 w_{2k}^2 & \cdots & \sum_{k=1}^{n} \mu_2 w_{2k} w_{nk} \mu_n \\ \vdots & \vdots & \ddots & \vdots \\ \sum_{k=1}^{n} \mu_n w_{nk} w_{1k} \mu_1 & \sum_{k=1}^{n} \mu_n w_{nk} w_{2k} \mu_2 & \cdots & \sum_{k=1}^{n} \mu_n^2 w_{nk}^2 \end{bmatrix}$$

This proves conditions (ii) and (iii). ■

When the absolute values of the elements of the weight matrix are considered, the following results can be obtained.

Corollary 12.2 *The neural system in Eqn. (12.12) is globally asymptotically stable if there exist a positive-diagonal matrix* $\boldsymbol{P} = diag[p_1, p_2, \ldots, p_n]$ *and a positive definite matrix* $\boldsymbol{Q} > 0$ *such that*

$$\boldsymbol{\Psi}|\boldsymbol{W}|^T\boldsymbol{P}|\boldsymbol{W}|\boldsymbol{\Psi} - \boldsymbol{P} = -\boldsymbol{Q} \tag{12.29}$$

Proof: Since for a positive diagonal matrix $\boldsymbol{P} > 0$

$$|\boldsymbol{W}|^T\boldsymbol{P}|\boldsymbol{W}| \geq \boldsymbol{W}^T\boldsymbol{P}\boldsymbol{W}$$

Thus

$$\boldsymbol{\Psi}|\boldsymbol{W}|^T\boldsymbol{P}|\boldsymbol{W}|\boldsymbol{\Psi} - \boldsymbol{P} \geq \boldsymbol{\Psi}\boldsymbol{W}^T\boldsymbol{P}\boldsymbol{W}\boldsymbol{\Psi} - \boldsymbol{P}$$

This means that if Eqn. (12.29) is valid, then Eqn. (12.24) is satisfied. The result is proved. ■

Corollary 12.2 shows that if the nonnegative matrix $|\boldsymbol{W}|\boldsymbol{\Psi}$ is diagonally stable, the neural system in Eqn. (12.12) is globally asymptotically stable.

Noting that the equivalence between the diagonal stability and the Schur stability when the matrix is nonnegative (Kaszkurewicz and Bhaya 1993), Michel and Miller 1977), one obtains the conditions for asymptotically stability as given in the following corollary.

Corollary 12.3 *The neural system in Eqn. (12.12) is globally asymptotically stable if one of the following conditions is satisfied:*

(i) There exist positive matrices $\boldsymbol{P} > 0$ *and* $\boldsymbol{Q} > 0$ *such that*

$$\boldsymbol{\Psi}|\boldsymbol{W}|^T\boldsymbol{P}|\boldsymbol{W}|\boldsymbol{\Psi} - \boldsymbol{P} = -\boldsymbol{Q} \tag{12.30}$$

(ii) All eigenvalues of the matrix $|\boldsymbol{W}|\boldsymbol{\Psi}$ *are located inside the unit circle.*

Proof: For the nonnegative matrix $|\boldsymbol{W}|\boldsymbol{\Psi}$, the diagonal stability is equivalent to the Schur stability. Thus, conditions (i) and (ii) are true. ■

Moreover, a real square matrix is said to be an M matrix (Kaszkurewicz and Bhaya 1993, Michel and Miller 1977) if all the off-diagonal elements of the matrix are nonpositive and all the principal minor determinants of the matrix are positive. The following results may then be stated.

Corollary 12.4 *The neural system in Eqn. (12.12) is globally asymptotically stable if*

(i) The matrix $\boldsymbol{D} \triangleq \boldsymbol{I} - |\boldsymbol{W}|\boldsymbol{\Psi}$ *is an* M *matrix;*

(ii) There exist n *constants* $c_1, c_2, \ldots, c_n > 0$ *such that*

$$\sum_{j=1}^{n} c_j(\delta_{ij} - |w_{ij}|\mu_j) > 0, \quad i = 1, 2, \ldots, n \tag{12.31}$$

(iii) There exist n *constants* $\eta_1, \eta_2, \ldots, \eta_n > 0$ *such that*

$$\sum_{i=1}^{n} \eta_i(\delta_{ij} - |w_{ij}|\mu_j) > 0, \quad j = 1, 2, \ldots, n \tag{12.32}$$

where δ_{ij} *is a delta function defined by* $\delta_{ij} = 1$ *for* $i = j$ *and by* $\delta_{ij} = 0$ *for* $i \neq j$.

Proof: Equation (12.24) has a positive diagonal solution $\boldsymbol{P} > 0$ if and only if matrix $(\boldsymbol{I} - |\boldsymbol{W}|\boldsymbol{\Psi})$ is an M matrix (Michel and Miller 1977). Thus, condition (i) is proved. Moreover, matrix $(\boldsymbol{I} - |\boldsymbol{W}|\boldsymbol{\Psi})$ being an M matrix is equivalent to conditions (ii) and (iii) (Michel and Miller 1977). ■

Remark 12.1 The global stability conditions presented above are independent of the threshold vector $\boldsymbol{s}$ of the network.

Remark 12.2 The global stability conditions presented above for the neural system in Eqn. (12.12) are also the sufficient conditions of the global stability for the neural network described by Eqn. (12.11).

Note that the discrete-time diagonal Lyapunov equation given in Eqn. (12.24) may be relaxed as

$$\boldsymbol{W}^T\boldsymbol{P}\boldsymbol{W} - \frac{1}{\mu^2}\boldsymbol{P} = -\boldsymbol{Q} \tag{12.33}$$

If the positive diagonal matrix $\boldsymbol{P}$ is chosen as an identity matrix $\boldsymbol{I}$, the fact that $(\boldsymbol{W}^T\boldsymbol{W} - \boldsymbol{I}/\mu^2)$ is negative-definite is equivalent to

$$\lambda_{max}(\boldsymbol{W}^T\boldsymbol{W} - \frac{\boldsymbol{I}}{\mu^2}) = \lambda_{max}(\boldsymbol{W}^T\boldsymbol{W}) - \frac{1}{\mu^2} < 0$$

In this case, a globally asymptotical stability condition is given by

$$||\boldsymbol{W}||_2 = \left(\lambda_{max}(\boldsymbol{W}^T\boldsymbol{W})\right)^{1/2} < \frac{1}{\mu}$$

which is equivalent to Li's norm stability condition (Li 1992), where the Euclidean norm is applied, given as

$$||\boldsymbol{W}|| < \frac{1}{\mu} \tag{12.34}$$

Thus, the norm stability condition is, in fact, a special case of the result given in Theorem 12.1 in terms of the Euclidean norm.

Furthermore, if $\boldsymbol{W}$ is a symmetric matrix; that is, $\boldsymbol{W} = \boldsymbol{W}^T$, then

$$||\boldsymbol{W}||_2 = \left(\lambda_{max}(\boldsymbol{W}^T\boldsymbol{W}) \right)^{1/2} = \max_i \{|\lambda_i(\boldsymbol{W})|\} < \frac{1}{\mu}$$

is a sufficient condition for the global stability. When this condition is true, the global convergence condition in Eqn. (12.22) is always satisfied.

12.3.4 Examples

Example 12.1 In this example it will be shown that if a suitable positive diagonal matrix $\boldsymbol{P}$ is chosen, the global stability condition presented in Theorem 12.1 is more relaxed than the norm conditions of Eqn. (12.34). Consider a simple two-neuron system without external inputs and with the following form

$$\begin{cases} x_1(k+1) &= \left(\frac{1}{2}\right)\tanh(x_1(k)) + \left(\frac{3}{4}\right)\tanh(x_2(k)) \\ x_2(k+1) &= \left(\frac{1}{3}\right)\tanh(x_1(k)) + \left(\frac{4}{9}\right)\tanh(x_2(k)) \end{cases} \tag{12.35}$$

where the 2×2 weight matrix is

$$\boldsymbol{W} = \begin{bmatrix} w_{11} & w_{12} \\ w_{21} & w_{22} \end{bmatrix} = \begin{bmatrix} \frac{1}{2} & \frac{3}{4} \\ \frac{1}{3} & \frac{4}{9} \end{bmatrix}$$

The stability of this neural system can now be tested using the norm stability condition of Eqn. (12.34) as follows:

$$\begin{aligned} ||\boldsymbol{W}||_1 &= \max_j \sum_{i=1}^{2} |w_{ij}| = \tfrac{5}{4} > 1 \\ ||\boldsymbol{W}||_\infty &= \max_i \sum_{j=1}^{2} |w_{ij}| = \tfrac{43}{36} > 1 \\ ||\boldsymbol{W}||_2 &= \{\lambda_{max}(\boldsymbol{W}^T\boldsymbol{W})\}^{1/2} = 1.065 \end{aligned}$$

Unfortunately, according to the choices of the matrix norms indicated above, the norm stability conditions cannot ensure the stability of the neural system defined in Eqn. (12.35). The global stability condition given in Theorem 12.1 will now be used to test the stability of the system. Let $P = diag[p_1, p_2]$ with $p_1 > 0$ and $p_2 > 0$; then

$$W^T P W - P = \begin{pmatrix} \frac{1}{9}p_2 - \frac{3}{4}p_1 & \frac{3}{8}p_1 + \frac{4}{27}p_1 \\ \frac{3}{8}p_1 + \frac{4}{27}p_2 & \frac{9}{16}p_1 - \frac{65}{81}p_2 \end{pmatrix}$$

If we let $p_1 = 1$ and $p_2 = 2$, then

$$W^T P W - P = -\begin{pmatrix} \frac{19}{36} & -\frac{145}{216} \\ -\frac{145}{216} & \frac{1351}{1296} \end{pmatrix} = -Q$$

where

$$Q = \begin{pmatrix} \frac{19}{36} & -\frac{145}{216} \\ -\frac{145}{216} & \frac{1351}{1296} \end{pmatrix}$$

is positive-definite. Therefore, the neural system of Eqn. (12.35) is globally asymptotically stable. ■

Example 12.2 Consider a discrete-time dynamic neural network (DT-DNN) with three neurons described by

$$\begin{bmatrix} x_1(k+1) \\ x_2(k+1) \\ x_3(k+1) \end{bmatrix} = \begin{bmatrix} 0 & -\alpha & 0 \\ 0 & 0 & \beta \\ \gamma & 0 & 0 \end{bmatrix} \begin{bmatrix} \tanh(\mu_1 x_1(k)) \\ \tanh(\mu_2 x_2(k)) \\ \tanh(\mu_3 x_3(k)) \end{bmatrix} + \begin{bmatrix} s_1 \\ s_2 \\ s_3 \end{bmatrix} \tag{12.36}$$

where

$$W = \begin{bmatrix} 0 & -\alpha & 0 \\ 0 & 0 & \beta \\ \gamma & 0 & 0 \end{bmatrix}$$

Using the norm stability condition of Eqn. (12.34), one obtains the following global stability condition

$$\begin{cases} \mu|\alpha| < 1 \\ \mu|\beta| < 1 \\ \mu|\gamma| < 1 \end{cases} \tag{12.37}$$

where $\mu = \max\{\mu_i\}$.

On the other hand, since

$$\Psi W^T W \Psi = \begin{bmatrix} \alpha^2\mu_1^2 & 0 & 0 \\ 0 & \beta^2\mu_2^2 & 0 \\ 0 & 0 & \gamma^2\mu_3^2 \end{bmatrix}$$

the global stability condition may be represented as

$$\begin{cases} \mu_1|\alpha| < 1 \\ \mu_2|\beta| < 1 \\ \mu_3|\gamma| < 1 \end{cases} \tag{12.38}$$

Obviously, in some cases, the condition in Eqn. (12.38) is more relaxed than that in Eqn. (12.37). For example, if

$$\begin{cases} \alpha = \frac{1}{2}, & \mu_1 = 1 \\ \beta = 1, & \mu_2 = \frac{2}{3} \\ \gamma = 2, & \mu_3 = \frac{1}{3} \end{cases}$$

then the condition in Eqn. (12.37) fails to establish the stability of this neural network. However, the condition given in Eqn. (12.38) ensures the global stability of this neural network. ■

12.4 MORE GENERAL RESULTS ON GLOBALLY ASYMPTOTIC STABILITY

To apply the Lyapunov function method for studying the global stability of the neural system of Eqn. (12.2), one has to transfer this neural system into a new system where the origin is an equilibrium point. Let $\boldsymbol{x}^* = [x_1^*, x_2^*, \ldots, x_n^*]^T$ be an equilibrium state of the original neural system and $\boldsymbol{z} = [z_1, z_2, \ldots, z_n]^T = \boldsymbol{x} - \boldsymbol{x}^*$ be a new state vector. Then, Eqn. (12.2) can be represented in terms of $\boldsymbol{z}$ as

$$\boldsymbol{z}(k+1) = -\boldsymbol{A}\boldsymbol{z}(k) + \boldsymbol{W}\boldsymbol{f}(\boldsymbol{z}(k)) \tag{12.39}$$

where the vector-valued function $\boldsymbol{f} : \Re^n \longrightarrow \Re^n$ is defined by Eqn. (12.13). Thus, $\boldsymbol{z} = 0$ is a unique equilibrium point of the new neural system given by Eqn. (12.39). Since

$$0 < \sigma'(\mu_i(z_i + x_i^*)) = f_i'(z_i) \leq \mu_i, \quad i = 1, 2, ..., n$$

one obtains

$$\begin{cases} \mu_i z_i & \leq & f_i(z_i) & < & 0, & \text{for} & z_i < 0 \\ 0 & < & f_i(z_i) & \leq & \mu_i z_i, & \text{for} & z_i > 0 \end{cases}$$

The contraction property of a nonlinear mapping may be used to determine the global stability of the nonlinear neural systems (Kelly 1990, Li 1992). For two arbitrary vectors $\boldsymbol{x}_1$ and $\boldsymbol{x}_2 \in \Re^n$, using the *mean-value theorem*, one obtains

$$|\boldsymbol{\sigma}(\boldsymbol{\Psi}\boldsymbol{x}_1) - \boldsymbol{\sigma}(\boldsymbol{\Psi}\boldsymbol{x}_2)| \leq \mu|\boldsymbol{x}_1 - \boldsymbol{x}_2|$$

This implies that for two arbitrary vectors $\boldsymbol{z}_1$ and $\boldsymbol{z}_2 \in \Re^n$, one obtains

$$\begin{aligned} |\boldsymbol{f}(\boldsymbol{z}_1) - \boldsymbol{f}(\boldsymbol{z}_2)| &= |\boldsymbol{\sigma}(\boldsymbol{\Psi}(\boldsymbol{z}_1 + \boldsymbol{x}^*)) - \boldsymbol{\sigma}(\boldsymbol{\Psi}(\boldsymbol{z}_2 + \boldsymbol{x}^*))| \\ &\leq \mu|\boldsymbol{z}_1 - \boldsymbol{z}_2| \end{aligned}$$

Thus

$$\begin{aligned} &| - \boldsymbol{A}\boldsymbol{z}_1 + \boldsymbol{W}\boldsymbol{f}(\boldsymbol{z}_1) + \boldsymbol{A}\boldsymbol{z}_2 - \boldsymbol{W}\boldsymbol{f}(\boldsymbol{z}_2)| \\ &\qquad \leq ||\boldsymbol{A}||_2|\boldsymbol{z}_1 - \boldsymbol{z}_2| + ||\boldsymbol{W}||_2|\boldsymbol{f}(\boldsymbol{z}_1) - \boldsymbol{f}(\boldsymbol{z}_2)| \\ &\qquad \leq (||\boldsymbol{A}||_2 + \mu||\boldsymbol{W}||_2)|\boldsymbol{z}_1 - \boldsymbol{z}_2| \end{aligned}$$

From the *contraction mapping theorem* (Hirsch 1989), if

$$||\boldsymbol{A}||_2 + \mu||\boldsymbol{W}||_2 < 1 \tag{12.40}$$

then the neural network of Eqn. (12.39) is a contractive system and has a unique equilibrium point $\boldsymbol{z} = 0$ that is globally asymptotically stable, so that the inequality of Eqn. (12.40) is a sufficient condition for the global stability. Furthermore, as far as the matrix norms $||.||_1$, $||.||_2$, and $||.||_\infty$ are concerned, one has the following three sufficient conditions for the global stability of the neural system given in Eqn. (12.39):

$$\text{(i)} \quad \max_j \sum_{i=1}^{n} |w_{ij}| < \frac{1}{\mu}(1 - \max_j(|\alpha_j|)) \tag{12.41}$$

$$\text{(ii)} \quad \Big(\lambda_{max}(\boldsymbol{W}^T\boldsymbol{W})\Big)^{1/2} < \frac{1}{\mu}(1 - \max_i(|\alpha_i|)) \tag{12.42}$$

$$\text{(iii)} \quad \max_i \sum_{j=1}^{n} |w_{ij}| < \frac{1}{\mu}(1 - \max_i(|\alpha_i|)) \tag{12.43}$$

where $\lambda_{max}(.)$ represents the maximum eigenvalue of the matrix. Equations (12.41)–(12.43) are referred to as the norm condition for the global stability in this section. In this case, the equilibrium point of the network may be iteratively computed (Kelly 1990) since the state of the network starting from an arbitrary initial position will converge to the unique equilibrium point.

Moreover, note that the state solution of the neural system defined in Eqn. (12.39) at the instant k

$$\boldsymbol{z}(k) = (-\boldsymbol{A})^k\boldsymbol{z}(0) + \sum_{i=0}^{k-1}(-\boldsymbol{A})^{k-(i+1)}\boldsymbol{W}\boldsymbol{f}(\boldsymbol{z}(i))$$

yields

$$\begin{aligned} |\boldsymbol{z}(k)| &\leq ||\boldsymbol{A}^k||_2|\boldsymbol{z}(0)| + \sum_{i=0}^{k-1} ||\boldsymbol{A}^{k-(i+1)}||_2||\boldsymbol{W}||_2|\boldsymbol{f}(\boldsymbol{z}(i))| \\ &\leq ||\boldsymbol{A}||_2^k|\boldsymbol{z}(0)| + \sum_{i=0}^{k-1} ||\boldsymbol{A}||_2^{k-(i+1)}\mu||\boldsymbol{W}||_2|\boldsymbol{z}(i)| \end{aligned}$$

that is

$$|\boldsymbol{z}(k)|||\boldsymbol{A}||_2^{-k} \leq |\boldsymbol{z}(0)| + \mu||\boldsymbol{W}||_2 \sum_{i=0}^{k-1} ||\boldsymbol{A}||_2^{-(i+1)}|\boldsymbol{z}(i)|$$

Applying Gronwall's inequality (Hirsch and Smale 1974) yields

$$|\boldsymbol{z}(\boldsymbol{k})|||\boldsymbol{A}||_2^{-k} \leq |\boldsymbol{z}(0)| \exp(\mu||\boldsymbol{W}||_2 k)$$

or equivalently

$$|\boldsymbol{z}(k)| \leq |\boldsymbol{z}(0)| \exp(k(\ln ||\boldsymbol{A}||_2 + \mu||\boldsymbol{W}||_2))$$

Thus, a sufficient condition for the globally exponential stability is obtained as

$$\ln ||\boldsymbol{A}||_2 + \mu||\boldsymbol{W}||_2 < 0 \tag{12.44}$$

12.4.1 Main Stability Results

Even if there is no universal way to find a global Lyapunov function for such a nonlinear system, because of the structures of the dynamic neural networks and the properties of the sigmoid function, one may attempt a diagonal Lyapunov function for the network as seen in the following discussion which starts with Theorem 12.2.

Theorem 12.2 *The neural system given in Eqn. (12.39) is globally asymptotically stable if there exist a $\gamma > 0$, a positive diagonal matrix $\boldsymbol{P} = diag[p_1, p_2, \ldots, p_n] > 0$, and a positive definite matrix $\boldsymbol{Q} > 0$ such that*

$$(i) \quad |\alpha_i| \leq \frac{1}{\sqrt{1+\gamma}}, \qquad \text{for all} \quad 1 \leq i \leq n; \tag{12.45}$$

$$(ii) \quad [(1+\gamma)\boldsymbol{APA} - \boldsymbol{P}]\Psi^{-2} + (1+\gamma^{-1})\boldsymbol{W}^T\boldsymbol{PW} = -\boldsymbol{Q} \tag{12.46}$$

Proof: Consider the following diagonal Lyapunov function

$$V(\boldsymbol{z}) = \sum_{i=1}^{n} p_i z_i^2 = \boldsymbol{z}^T \boldsymbol{P} \boldsymbol{z}$$

where $\boldsymbol{P} = diag[p_1, p_2, \ldots, p_n] > 0$. Then

$$\begin{aligned}\Delta V(\boldsymbol{z}(k)) &= V(\boldsymbol{z}(k+1)) - V(\boldsymbol{z}(k)) \\ &= \boldsymbol{z}^T(\boldsymbol{APA} - \boldsymbol{P})\boldsymbol{z} - 2\boldsymbol{z}^T \boldsymbol{APWf}(\boldsymbol{z}) \\ &\quad + \boldsymbol{f}^T(\boldsymbol{z})\boldsymbol{W}^T \boldsymbol{PWf}(\boldsymbol{z})\end{aligned} \tag{12.47}$$

For $\gamma > 0$

$$(\gamma^{1/2}\boldsymbol{Az} + \gamma^{-1/2}\boldsymbol{Wf}(\boldsymbol{z}))^T \boldsymbol{P}(\gamma^{1/2}\boldsymbol{Az} + \gamma^{-1/2}\boldsymbol{Wf}(\boldsymbol{z})) \geq 0$$

that is

$$\gamma \boldsymbol{z}^T \boldsymbol{APAz} + \gamma^{-1}\boldsymbol{f}^T(\boldsymbol{z})\boldsymbol{W}^T \boldsymbol{PWf}(\boldsymbol{z}) \geq -2\boldsymbol{z}^T \boldsymbol{APWf}(\boldsymbol{z})(\boldsymbol{z})$$

Substituting this inequality into the right-hand side of Eqn. (12.47) yields

$$\begin{aligned}\Delta V(\boldsymbol{z}(k)) &\leq \boldsymbol{z}^T[(1+\gamma)\boldsymbol{APA} - \boldsymbol{P}]\boldsymbol{z} \\ &\quad + (1+\gamma^{-1})\boldsymbol{f}^T(\boldsymbol{z})\boldsymbol{W}^T \boldsymbol{PWf}(\boldsymbol{z})\end{aligned}$$

Since

$$|\alpha_i| \leq \frac{1}{\sqrt{1+\gamma}}$$

implies that

$$(1+\gamma)\alpha_i^2 - 1 \leq 0, \quad \text{for all} \quad 1 \leq i \leq n$$

Therefore

$$(1+\gamma)\boldsymbol{APA} - \boldsymbol{P} \leq 0$$

and

$$\boldsymbol{z}^T[(1+\gamma)\boldsymbol{APA} - \boldsymbol{P}]\boldsymbol{z} \leq \boldsymbol{f}^T(\boldsymbol{z})[(1+\gamma)\boldsymbol{APA} - \boldsymbol{P}]\boldsymbol{\Psi}^{-2}\boldsymbol{f}(\boldsymbol{z})$$

Therefore

$$\Delta V(\boldsymbol{z}) \leq \boldsymbol{f}^T(\boldsymbol{z})\{[(1+\gamma)\boldsymbol{APA} - \boldsymbol{P}]\boldsymbol{\Psi}^{-2} + (1+\gamma^{-1})\boldsymbol{W}^T \boldsymbol{PW}\}\boldsymbol{f}(\boldsymbol{z}) \tag{12.48}$$

If there exists a positive definite matrix $\boldsymbol{Q} > 0$ such that

$$[(1+\gamma)\boldsymbol{APA} - \boldsymbol{P}]\boldsymbol{\Psi}^{-2} + (1+\gamma^{-1})\boldsymbol{W}^T\boldsymbol{PW} = -\boldsymbol{Q} \tag{12.49}$$

then $\Delta V(\boldsymbol{z}) \leq 0$, and $\boldsymbol{z} = 0$ is a globally stable equilibrium point of the network. ■

The matrix equation given in Eqn. (12.46) is a modified diagonal Lyapunov equation and involves an adjustable parameter $\gamma > 0$. This matrix equation can equivalently be written as

$$\left(\gamma\boldsymbol{APA} - \frac{\gamma}{1+\gamma}\boldsymbol{P}\right)\boldsymbol{\Psi}^{-2} + \boldsymbol{W}^T\boldsymbol{PW} = -\boldsymbol{Q} \tag{12.50}$$

or

$$\left(\gamma\boldsymbol{APA} - \frac{\gamma}{1+\gamma}\boldsymbol{P}\right) + \boldsymbol{\Psi W}^T\boldsymbol{PW\Psi} = -\boldsymbol{Q} \tag{12.51}$$

When $\boldsymbol{A} \equiv 0$, letting $\gamma \longrightarrow +\infty$ in Eqn. (12.50) one obtains

$$\boldsymbol{W}^T\boldsymbol{PW} - \boldsymbol{\Psi}^{-2}\boldsymbol{P} = -\boldsymbol{Q}$$

which was derived in Theorem 12.1. In this sense, the result obtained in Theorem 12.1 can be treated as a special case of that presented in Theorem 12.2. It follows, therefore, that the choice of the parameter $\gamma > 0$ in Eqn. (12.46) plays an important role in determination of the global stability of the network. Some corollaries of Theorem 12.2 are now presented.

Theorem 12.3 *The neural system in Eqn. (12.39) is globally asymptotically stable if there exist a positive diagonal matrix $\boldsymbol{P} = diag[p_1, p_2, \ldots, p_n] > 0$ and a positive-definite matrix $\boldsymbol{Q} > 0$ such that*

$$\left[\left(\frac{1-\alpha_m}{\alpha_m}\right)\boldsymbol{APA} - (1-\alpha_m)\boldsymbol{P}\right]\boldsymbol{\Psi}^{-2} + \boldsymbol{W}^T\boldsymbol{PW} = -\boldsymbol{Q} \tag{12.52}$$

where $\alpha_m = \max\{|\alpha_i|\}$.

Proof: In the proof of Theorem 12.2, an optimal selection of the parameter γ is such that

$$\lambda_{min}\left(\gamma\boldsymbol{A}^2 - \frac{\gamma}{1+\gamma}\boldsymbol{I}\right) = min$$

Then γ can be chosen as

$$\gamma = \frac{1-\alpha_m}{\alpha_m} \tag{12.53}$$

In this case, for all $|\alpha_i| < 1$, we obtain

$$\frac{1}{\sqrt{1+\gamma_m}} = \sqrt{\alpha_m} \geq |\alpha_i|, \quad i = 1, 2, \ldots, n$$

that is, condition (i) in Theorem 12.2 is satisfied. Substitution of Eqn. (12.53) in Eqn. (12.46) yields Eqn. (12.52). ■

If all the neural units of the network have the same self-feedback coefficient $\alpha_i = \alpha$ with $\alpha < 1$, that is, $\boldsymbol{A} = \alpha \boldsymbol{I}$, then Eqn. (12.52) can be simplified to

$$-(1 - |\alpha|)^2 \boldsymbol{P}\boldsymbol{\Psi}^{-2} + \boldsymbol{W}^T \boldsymbol{P}\boldsymbol{W} = -\boldsymbol{Q} \tag{12.54}$$

In the derivations above, only the contribution of the maximum absolute value of the self-feedback coefficients was considered in the selection of the parameter $\gamma > 0$. To replace the scalar parameter γ in the proof of Theorem 12.2 with a positive diagonal matrix associated with all self-feedback coefficients $|\alpha_i| < 1$, a theorem can be stated as follows.

Theorem 12.4 *The neural system in Eqn. (12.39) is globally asymptotically stable if there exist a positive diagonal matrix $\boldsymbol{P} = diag[p_1, p_2, \ldots, p_n] > 0$ and a positive-definite matrix $\boldsymbol{Q} > 0$ such that*

$$-(\boldsymbol{I} - |\boldsymbol{A}|)\boldsymbol{P}(\boldsymbol{I} - |\boldsymbol{A}|) + \boldsymbol{\Psi}\boldsymbol{W}^T \boldsymbol{P}\boldsymbol{W}\boldsymbol{\Psi} = -\boldsymbol{Q} \tag{12.55}$$

Proof: First, let all $\alpha_i \neq 0$, $i = 1, 2, \ldots, n$, and let there be a positive diagonal matrix $\boldsymbol{F} = diag[\gamma_1, \gamma_2, \ldots, \gamma_n]$ whose elements satisfy

$$\gamma_i > 0 \tag{12.56}$$

$$|\alpha_i| \leq \frac{1}{\sqrt{1+\gamma_i}}, \quad i = 1, 2, \ldots, n \tag{12.57}$$

Indeed, for a positive diagonal matrix $\boldsymbol{P}$

$$(\boldsymbol{F}^{1/2}\boldsymbol{A}\boldsymbol{z} + \boldsymbol{F}^{-1/2}\boldsymbol{W}\boldsymbol{f}(\boldsymbol{z}))^T \boldsymbol{P}(\boldsymbol{F}^{1/2}\boldsymbol{A}\boldsymbol{z} + \boldsymbol{F}^{-1/2}\boldsymbol{W}\boldsymbol{f}(\boldsymbol{z})) \geq 0$$

that is

$$\boldsymbol{F}\boldsymbol{z}^T \boldsymbol{A}\boldsymbol{P}\boldsymbol{A}\boldsymbol{z} + \boldsymbol{F}^{-1}\boldsymbol{f}^T(\boldsymbol{z})\boldsymbol{W}^T \boldsymbol{P}\boldsymbol{W}\boldsymbol{f}(\boldsymbol{z}) \geq -2\boldsymbol{z}^T \boldsymbol{A}\boldsymbol{P}\boldsymbol{W}\boldsymbol{f}(\boldsymbol{z})$$

Thus, Eqn. (12.47) in the proof of Theorem 12.2 can be rewritten as

$$\Delta V(\boldsymbol{z}) \leq \boldsymbol{z}^T[(\boldsymbol{I} + \boldsymbol{F})\boldsymbol{A}\boldsymbol{P}\boldsymbol{A} - \boldsymbol{P}]\boldsymbol{z} + (\boldsymbol{I} + \boldsymbol{F}^{-1})\boldsymbol{f}^{-1}(\boldsymbol{z})\boldsymbol{W}^T \boldsymbol{P}\boldsymbol{W}\boldsymbol{f}(\boldsymbol{z}) \tag{12.58}$$

Noting that

$$(\boldsymbol{I} + \boldsymbol{F})\boldsymbol{A}\boldsymbol{P}\boldsymbol{A} - \boldsymbol{P} \leq 0$$

one obtains

$$\begin{aligned}\Delta V(\boldsymbol{z}) &\le \boldsymbol{f}^T(\boldsymbol{z})\Big\{ [(\boldsymbol{I}+\boldsymbol{F})\boldsymbol{APA}-\boldsymbol{P}]\boldsymbol{\Psi}^{-2} \\ &\quad + (\boldsymbol{I}+\boldsymbol{F}^{-1})\boldsymbol{W}^T\boldsymbol{PW} \Big\}\boldsymbol{f}(\boldsymbol{z}) \\ &\le \boldsymbol{f}^T(\boldsymbol{z})(\boldsymbol{I}+\boldsymbol{F}^{-1})\boldsymbol{\Psi}^{-1}\Big\{ [\boldsymbol{FAPA}-\boldsymbol{F}(\boldsymbol{I}+\boldsymbol{F})^{-1}\boldsymbol{P}] \\ &\quad + \boldsymbol{\Psi}\boldsymbol{W}^T\boldsymbol{PW}\boldsymbol{\Psi} \Big\}\boldsymbol{\Psi}^{-1}\boldsymbol{f}(\boldsymbol{z})\end{aligned}$$

Thus, if there exists a positive definite $\boldsymbol{Q} > 0$ such that

$$[\boldsymbol{FAPA}-\boldsymbol{F}(\boldsymbol{I}+\boldsymbol{F})^{-1}\boldsymbol{P}] + \boldsymbol{\Psi}\boldsymbol{W}^T\boldsymbol{PW}\boldsymbol{\Psi} = -\boldsymbol{Q} \tag{12.59}$$

then $\Delta V(\boldsymbol{z}) \le 0$ and $\boldsymbol{z} = 0$ is a globally stable equilibrium point of the network. Moreover, if one selects γ_i such that Eqns. (12.56) and (12.57) are satisfied and

$$\gamma_i \alpha_i^2 - \frac{\gamma_i}{1+\gamma_i} = min$$

then

$$\gamma_i = \frac{1-|\alpha_i|}{|\alpha_i|}$$

It can be verified that for $|\alpha_i| < 1$, the choice of γ_i satisfies

$$\frac{1}{\sqrt{1+\gamma_i}} = \sqrt{|\alpha_i|} \ge |\alpha_i|$$

The matrix $\boldsymbol{F}$ is then given by

$$\boldsymbol{F} = (\boldsymbol{I} - |\boldsymbol{A}|)|\boldsymbol{A}|^{-1}$$

Thus

$$\begin{aligned}[\boldsymbol{FAPA}-\boldsymbol{F}(\boldsymbol{I}+\boldsymbol{F})^{-1}\boldsymbol{P}] &= [\boldsymbol{F}|\boldsymbol{A}|\boldsymbol{P}|\boldsymbol{A}| - \boldsymbol{F}(\boldsymbol{I}+\boldsymbol{F})^{-1}\boldsymbol{P}] \\ &= \boldsymbol{P}|\boldsymbol{A}| - |\boldsymbol{A}|\boldsymbol{P}|\boldsymbol{A}| - \boldsymbol{P} + |\boldsymbol{A}|\boldsymbol{P} \\ &= -(\boldsymbol{I}-|\boldsymbol{A}|)\boldsymbol{P}(\boldsymbol{I}-|\boldsymbol{A}|) \qquad (12.60)\end{aligned}$$

Substituting this result in Eqn. (12.59) proves Eqn. (12.55). When there are an i^* such that $\alpha_{i^*} = 0$ and $\alpha_i \ne 0$, $(1 \le i \le n, i \ne i^*)$, and the elements of the matrix $\boldsymbol{F} = diag[\gamma_1, \gamma_2, \ldots, \gamma_n]$ are chosen as

$$\begin{aligned}\gamma_i &> 0 \\ |\alpha_i| &\le \frac{1}{\sqrt{1+\gamma_i}}, \qquad i = 1, 2, \ldots, i^*-1, i^*+1, \ldots, n\end{aligned}$$

and

$$-1 < \gamma_{i^*} < 0$$

then Eqn. (12.59) is still valid. Furthermore, let the elements of a nonsingularly diagonal matrix $\boldsymbol{B} = diag[b_1, b_2, \ldots, b_n]$ be defined as

$$\begin{cases} b_i = |\alpha_i|, \quad i = 1, 2, \ldots, i^* - 1, i^*, i^* + 1, \ldots, n \\ -1 < b_{i^*} < 0 \end{cases}$$

and the matrix $\boldsymbol{F}$ be given by

$$\boldsymbol{F} = (\boldsymbol{I} - \boldsymbol{B})\boldsymbol{B}^{-1}$$

It can be seen that for a positive diagonal matrix $\boldsymbol{P} > 0$

$$\begin{aligned} [\boldsymbol{FAPA} - \boldsymbol{F}(\boldsymbol{I} + \boldsymbol{F})^{-1}\boldsymbol{P}] &= \boldsymbol{P}|\boldsymbol{A}| - |\boldsymbol{A}|\boldsymbol{P}|\boldsymbol{A}| - \boldsymbol{P} + \boldsymbol{BP} \\ &< \boldsymbol{P}|\boldsymbol{A}| - |\boldsymbol{A}|\boldsymbol{P}|\boldsymbol{A}| - \boldsymbol{P} + |\boldsymbol{A}|\boldsymbol{P} \\ &= -(\boldsymbol{I} + |\boldsymbol{A}|)\boldsymbol{P}(\boldsymbol{I} + |\boldsymbol{A}|) \end{aligned}$$

Thus, Eqn. (12.55) is valid. Using the same procedure, one may also prove that the theorem is valid when there exist more than one $\alpha_i = 0$. ■

Theorem 12.5 *The neural system in Eqn. (12.39) is globally asymptotically stable if there exist a positive-diagonal matrix $\boldsymbol{P} = diag[p_1, p_2, \ldots, p_n]$ and a positive definite matrix $\boldsymbol{Q} > 0$ such that*

$$(|\boldsymbol{A}| + |\boldsymbol{W}|\boldsymbol{\Psi})^T \boldsymbol{P}(|\boldsymbol{A}| + |\boldsymbol{W}|\boldsymbol{\Psi}) - \boldsymbol{P} = -\boldsymbol{Q} \tag{12.61}$$

Proof: Since for a positive diagonal matrix $\boldsymbol{P} > 0$

$$\begin{aligned} &-(\boldsymbol{I} - |\boldsymbol{A}|)\boldsymbol{P}(\boldsymbol{I} - |\boldsymbol{A}|) + \boldsymbol{\Psi W}^T\boldsymbol{PW\Psi} \\ &\quad = -\boldsymbol{P} + |\boldsymbol{A}|\boldsymbol{P}|\boldsymbol{A}| + |\boldsymbol{A}|\boldsymbol{P} + \boldsymbol{P}|\boldsymbol{A}| + \boldsymbol{\Psi W}^T\boldsymbol{PW\Psi} \\ &\quad \le -\boldsymbol{P} + |\boldsymbol{A}|\boldsymbol{P}|\boldsymbol{A}| + |\boldsymbol{A}|\boldsymbol{P} + \boldsymbol{\Psi}|\boldsymbol{W}|^T\boldsymbol{P}|\boldsymbol{A}| \\ &\quad\quad + |\boldsymbol{A}|\boldsymbol{P}|\boldsymbol{W}\boldsymbol{\Psi} + \boldsymbol{P}|\boldsymbol{A}| + \boldsymbol{\Psi W}^T\boldsymbol{PW\Psi} \\ &\quad \le (|\boldsymbol{A}| + |\boldsymbol{W}|\boldsymbol{\Psi})^T\boldsymbol{P}(|\boldsymbol{A}| + |\boldsymbol{W}|\boldsymbol{\Psi}) - \boldsymbol{P} \end{aligned}$$

Thus, if the condition given in Eqn. (12.61) holds, then the condition of Eqn. (12.55) is satisfied. This proves the theorem. ■

A sufficient condition of Eqn. (12.61) for the global stability is also reported by (Jin and Gupta 1996b) who applied a different technique. The matrix equation, Eqn. (12.61), is a diagonal Lyapunov equation in terms of the nonnegative matrix $|\boldsymbol{A}| + |\boldsymbol{W}|\boldsymbol{\Psi}$. Theorem 12.5 shows that if the nonnegative matrix $|\boldsymbol{A}| + |\boldsymbol{W}|\boldsymbol{\Psi}$ is diagonally stable, then it implies that the neural system given in Eqn. (12.39) is globally asymptotically stable.

Remark 12.3 Unlike continuous-time dynamic neural networks (CT-DNNs) where the negative self-feedback coefficients increase the stability degree of the network (Matsuoka 1992), the self-feedback coefficients $|\alpha_i| < 1$ that are either positive or negative in Eqn. (12.39) reduce the degree of stability for the network in terms of the global stability conditions obtained from Theorems 12.4 and 12.5.

To determine the global stability of a given network using the preceding results, the positive diagonal matrix $\boldsymbol{P}$ and the positive-definite matrix $\boldsymbol{Q}$ must be found. Usually, for a given $\boldsymbol{Q} > 0$, it is difficult to verify that these matrix equations have such a positive diagonal solution. Corollaries of these theorems, which give simplified expressions of the theorems, have been presented by Jin and Gupta (1996b). It is noted that these corollaries involve only network parameters such as the self-feedback coefficients, connection weights, and the gains. In the following, one of the corollaries will be presented, and it will be used in the next examples.

Corollary 12.5 *The neural system in Eqn. (12.39) is globally asymptotically stable if one of the following conditions is satisfied:*

(i) There exist positive matrices $\boldsymbol{P} > 0$ and $\boldsymbol{Q} > 0$ such that

$$((|\boldsymbol{A} + |\boldsymbol{W}|\boldsymbol{\Psi})^T \boldsymbol{P})(|\boldsymbol{A}| + |\boldsymbol{W}|\boldsymbol{\Psi}) - \boldsymbol{P} = -\boldsymbol{Q} \tag{12.62}$$

(ii) All eigenvalues of the matrix $(|\boldsymbol{A}| + |\boldsymbol{W}|\boldsymbol{\Psi})$ are located inside the unit circle.

Proof: For the nonnegative matrix $(|\boldsymbol{A}| + |\boldsymbol{W}|\boldsymbol{\Psi})$, the diagonal stability is equivalent to the Schur stability. This proves the corollary. ■

12.4.2 Examples

Example 12.3 Consider a trivial discrete-time dynamic neural network (DT-DNN) structure, as shown in Fig. 12.5, where some feedback connections in the network have been eliminated so that the network has become a dynamic feedforward network. In this case, the weight matrix is a lower triangular

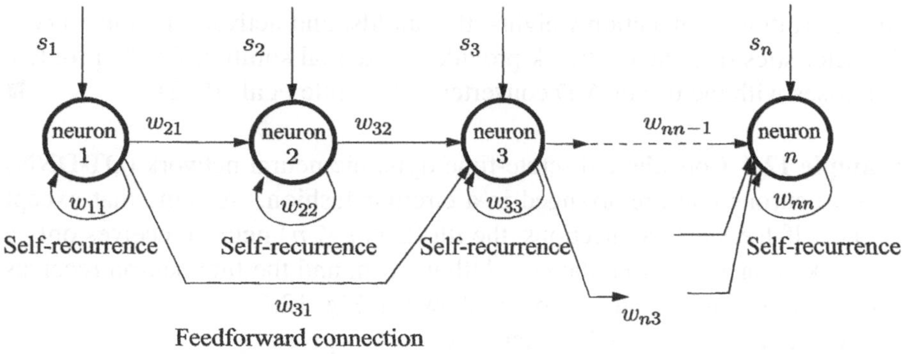

Figure 12.5 Block diagram of a dynamic feedforward neural network discussed in Example 12.3.

matrix (possibly after a renaming of all the neurons) of the form

$$\boldsymbol{W} = \begin{bmatrix} w_{11} & 0 & 0 & \cdots & 0 \\ w_{21} & w_{22} & 0 & \cdots & 0 \\ w_{31} & w_{32} & w_{33} & \cdots & 0 \\ \vdots & \vdots & \vdots & \ddots & \vdots \\ w_{n1} & w_{n2} & w_{n3} & \cdots & w_{nn} \end{bmatrix}$$

In this case

$$|\boldsymbol{A}| + |\boldsymbol{W}|\boldsymbol{\Psi} = \begin{bmatrix} |\alpha_1| + |w_{11}|\mu_1 & 0 & \cdots & 0 \\ |w_{21}|\mu_1 & |\alpha_2| + |w_{22}|\mu_2 & \cdots & 0 \\ \vdots & \vdots & \ddots & 0 \\ |w_{n1}|\mu_1 & |w_{n2}|\mu_2 & \cdots & |\alpha_n| + |w_{nn}|\mu_n \end{bmatrix}$$

and the eigenvalues of the above matrix are obtained as

$$\lambda_i = |\alpha_i| + |w_{ii}|\mu_i, \quad i = 1, 2, \ldots, n$$

It is seen that the global stability condition given by condition (ii) of Corollary 12.5 becomes

$$|\alpha|_i + |w_{ii}|\mu_i < 1, \quad i = 1, 2, \ldots, n$$

Thus, the global stability of the network is determined by only the self-recurrence connections described by the weights w_{ii}. Moreover, even if all the self-recurrence connections w_{ii} are removed, the network is always satisfied for the arbitrary connection weights. Hence, the network without the recurrent connections ($w_{ij} = 0$, for $j \geq i$) is inherently globally stable for the arbitrary connection weights, thresholds, and activation gains. These characteristics of such a network provide a potential solution for the problem that arises with the use of A/D converters (Avitabile et al. 1992). ■

Example 12.4 Consider a discrete-time dynamic neural network (DT-DNN) with n neurons that are arranged in a circular fashion. Assume that except for the self-feedback connections, the ith $(2 \le i \le n)$ neuron receives only a feedback connection from the $(i-1)$th neuron, and the first neuron receives a connection from the nth neuron as shown in Fig. 12.6.

The mathematical model of such a network is given by

$$\begin{bmatrix} x_1(k+1) \\ x_2(k+1) \\ \vdots \\ x_n(k+1) \end{bmatrix} = -\alpha \begin{bmatrix} x_1(k) \\ x_2(k) \\ \vdots \\ x_n(k) \end{bmatrix} + \begin{bmatrix} 0 & 0 & \cdots & 0 & w_{1n} \\ w_{21} & 0 & \cdots & 0 & 0 \\ \vdots & \vdots & \ddots & \vdots & \vdots \\ 0 & 0 & \cdots & w_{nn-1} & 0 \end{bmatrix} \times \begin{bmatrix} \tanh(\mu_1 x_1(k)) \\ \tanh(\mu_2 x_2(k)) \\ \vdots \\ \tanh(\mu_n x_n(k)) \end{bmatrix} + \begin{bmatrix} s_1 \\ s_2 \\ \vdots \\ s_n \end{bmatrix}$$

where $0 < \alpha < 1$ and all the weight parameters are positive.

Using the norm stability condition of Eqn. (12.40), one obtains the following global stability condition

$$\begin{cases} \alpha + \mu w_{1n} & < \; 1 \\ \alpha + \mu w_{ii-1} & < \; 1, \quad i = 2, 3, \ldots, n \end{cases} \tag{12.63}$$

where $\mu = \max\{\mu_i\}$.

On the other hand, using the new condition given by condition (ii) of Corollary 12.5, one tests the eigenvalues of the following matrix:

$$|\boldsymbol{A}| + |\boldsymbol{W}|\boldsymbol{\Psi} = \begin{bmatrix} \alpha & 0 & \cdots & 0 & w_{1n}\mu_n \\ w_{21}\mu_1 & \alpha & \cdots & 0 & 0 \\ \vdots & \vdots & \cdots & \vdots & \vdots \\ 0 & 0 & \cdots & w_{nn-1}\mu_{n-1} & \alpha \end{bmatrix}$$

If n is odd, then

$$\lambda_{1,2,\ldots,n} = \sqrt[n]{\left(\prod_{i=1}^{n} \mu_i\right)\left(w_{1n} \prod_{i=2}^{n} w_{ii-1}\right)} + \alpha$$

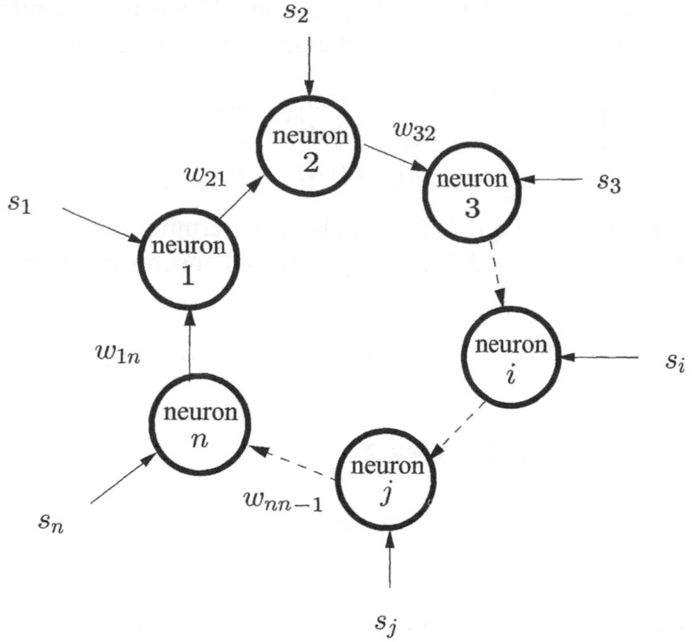

Figure 12.6 Block diagram of a circle dynamic neural network discussed in Example 12.4.

If n is even, then

$$\lambda_{1,2,\ldots,n/2} = -\sqrt[n]{(\prod_{i=1}^{n} \mu_i)(w_{1n} \prod_{i=2}^{n} w_{ii-1})} + \alpha$$

and

$$\lambda_{n/2,n/2+1,\ldots,n} = \sqrt[n]{(\prod_{i=1}^{n} \mu_i)(w_{1n} \prod_{i=2}^{n} w_{ii-1})} + \alpha$$

Thus, the global stability condition may be represented as

$$\sqrt[n]{\left(\prod_{i=1}^{n} \mu_i\right) \left(w_{1n} \prod_{i=2}^{n} w_{ii-1}\right)} < 1 - \alpha \tag{12.64}$$

Obviously, in some cases the condition of Eqn. (12.64) is more relaxed than that of Eqn. (12.63). For example, for the three-neuron structure if

$$\begin{cases} \alpha = 0.5, & w_{13} = 0.6, & \mu_1 = 1 \\ & w_{21} = 0.4, & \mu_2 = \frac{1}{2} \\ & w_{32} = 0.4, & \mu_3 = \frac{1}{2} \end{cases}$$

then, the condition in Eqn. (12.63) fails to determine the stability of the network. However, the condition in Eqn. (12.64) ensures the global stability of the network because of

$$\sqrt[3]{\mu_1\mu_2\mu_3 w_{13} w_{21} w_{32}} = 0.2885 < 1 - \alpha = 0.5$$ ■

12.5 CONCLUDING REMARKS

In this chapter, we have studied the stability problems for a general class of discrete-time dynamic neural network (DT-DNN) using Lyapunov's first and second methods. On the basis of the special nonlinear structures of the neural networks and properties of the neural activation function, some stability conditions were derived. For a given dynamic neural network with bounded derivatives of the nonlinear activation functions, these stability conditions, which are determined only by the synaptic connection weight matrix $\boldsymbol{W}$ of the network, are easy to check by using simple algebraic manipulations on the connecting weights. The analytic approaches and results that were presented in this chapter can be generalized to other models of discrete-time neural networks and to more complicated discrete-time neural networks.

Problems

12.1 Consider a discrete-time linear system described by

$$\boldsymbol{x}(k+1) = \boldsymbol{A}\boldsymbol{x}(k)$$

(a) Show that $\boldsymbol{x}(k) \to 0$ as $k \to \infty$ if and only if all eigenvalues of $\boldsymbol{A}$ satisfy $|\lambda_i| < 1$;

(b) Can we conclude that the mapping $\boldsymbol{A}\boldsymbol{x}$ is a contraction mapping if all eigenvalues of $\boldsymbol{A}$ satisfy $|\lambda_i| < 1$?

12.2 Consider a discrete-time nonlinear system

$$\boldsymbol{x}(k+1) = \boldsymbol{f}(\boldsymbol{x}(k)); \quad \boldsymbol{f}(0) = 0$$

Let

$$A = \left.\frac{\partial f}{\partial x}\right|_{x=0}$$

be the linearization of the above system. Show that the origin is asymptotically stable if all the eigenvalues of A have magnitudes less than one.

12.3 Consider a discrete-time linear system described by

$$x(k+1) = Ax(k)$$

where x is an n-dimensional vector and A is an $n \times n$ matrix. Letting P be a positive-definite real symmetric matrix, show that

$$V(x) = x^T P x$$

is a Lyapunov function for the system, and the equilibrium state $x^* = 0$ is asymptotically stable if and only if for a given positive-definite real symmetric matrix Q, there exists a positive-definite real symmetric matrix P such that

$$A^T P A - P = -Q$$

12.4 A vector function $f(x)$ is said to be a "contraction" if

$$||f|| < ||x||$$

where $||.||$ is the norm of the vector (.). For the neural system in Eqn. (12.4), if f is a contraction for all x, show that the neural system in Eqn. (12.4) is globally asymptotical stable, and one of its Lyapunov functions is

$$V(x) = ||x||$$

12.5 Consider a discrete-time DNN described by

$$x(k+1) = f(Wx(k) + s)$$

where $x \in \Re^n$, $W = W^T \in \Re^{n \times n}$, $s \in \Re^n$, and f is a sigmoidal function, $f = [f_1 \; f_2 \; \cdots \; f_n]^T$ with $f_i = \tanh(.)$. Show that the attractors of the neural system are either fixed points or period 2 limit cycles by constructing an energy function $E(k)$ as

$$
\begin{aligned}
E(k) &= -\sum_{i=1}^{n}\sum_{j=1}^{n} w_{ij} y_i(k) y_j(k-1) \\
&\quad - \sum_{i=1}^{n} s_I[x_i(k) + x_i(k-1)] \\
&\quad + \sum_{i=1}^{n} [g_i(x_i(k)) + g_i(x_i(k-1))]
\end{aligned}
$$

where

$$
g_i(y_i) = \int_0^{x_i} f_i^{-1}(\tau) d\tau
$$

12.6 Discuss the stability of the following two discrete-time neural network system using Lyapunov's first method:

$$
\begin{cases}
x_1(k+1) = \tanh\left(\frac{1}{4}x_1(k) - \frac{1}{5}x_2(k)\right) \\
x_2(k+1) = \tanh\left(\frac{1}{2}x_2(k) + \frac{3}{4}x_2(k)\right)
\end{cases}
$$

12.7 Discuss the stability of the following two discrete-time neural network system:

$$
\begin{cases}
x_1(k+1) = -\frac{1}{2}x_1(k) + \tanh\left(\frac{1}{3}x_1(k) - \frac{1}{8}x_2(k)\right) \\
x_2(k+1) = \frac{1}{2}x_2(k) + \tanh\left(\frac{1}{5}x_2(k) - \frac{1}{3}x_2(k)\right)
\end{cases}
$$

12.8 Rederive the results obtained in Section 12.3.1 for the global state convergence for a symmetric weight matrix and give a two-neuron system that satisfies the global state convergence condition.

12.9 In Example 12.4, let the weight matrix have a form of

$$
\boldsymbol{W} = \begin{bmatrix}
0 & w_{12} & 0 & \cdots & 0 \\
0 & 0 & w_{23} & \cdots & 0 \\
\vdots & \vdots & \vdots & \ddots & \vdots \\
0 & 0 & 0 & \cdots & w_{n-1,n} \\
w_{n1} & 0 & 0 & \cdots & 0
\end{bmatrix}
$$

Analyze the global stability conditions of the network by using both the norm stability condition of Eqn. (12.40) and Corollary 12.5.

12.10 Consider a two-neuron discrete-time system

$$\begin{bmatrix} x_1(k+1) \\ x_2(k+1) \end{bmatrix} = \begin{bmatrix} \alpha & \beta \\ \beta & \gamma \end{bmatrix} \begin{bmatrix} \tanh(x_1(k)) \\ \tanh(x_2(k)) \end{bmatrix}$$

Discuss both local and global stability conditions of the system.

12.11 Consider a discrete-time dynamic neural network of the form

$$\boldsymbol{x}(k+1) = \boldsymbol{W}\sigma(\boldsymbol{x}(k)), \qquad \boldsymbol{x} \in \Re^n, \ \boldsymbol{W} \in \Re^{n\times n}$$

Show that $V(\boldsymbol{x}) = \boldsymbol{x}^T\boldsymbol{x}$ is a Lyapunov function if $(\boldsymbol{W}^T\boldsymbol{W} - \boldsymbol{I})$ is a negative definite matrix. Discuss the global stability condition derived by this Lyapunov function.

12.12 Consider a single-input/single-output (SISO) nonlinear system

$$y(k+1) = f(\, y(k), \ldots, y(k-n_y), u(k), \ldots, u(k-n_u)\,)$$

(a) Give a state equation expression of the above system;

(b) If the external input $u(k)$ is designed as a state feedback

$$u(k) = g(\, y(k), \ldots, y(k-n_y), u(k-1), \ldots, u(k-n_u)\,)$$

Derive the Jacobian of the system and discuss the local stability of the equilibrium point of the system based on the Jacobian obtained.

12.13 Consider a nonlinear discrete-time dynamic neural network of the form

$$\boldsymbol{x}(k+1) = -\boldsymbol{A}\boldsymbol{x}(k) + \boldsymbol{B}\sigma(\boldsymbol{W}\boldsymbol{x}(k) + \boldsymbol{s}) \qquad (12.65)$$

where $\boldsymbol{x} \in \Re^n$, $\boldsymbol{A} \in \Re^{n\times n}$, $\boldsymbol{B} \in \Re^{n\times n}$, $\boldsymbol{W} \in \Re^{n\times n}$, and $s \in \Re^n$.

(a) Let $\boldsymbol{P} \in \Re^{n\times n}$ be a nonsingular matrix. Show that $\boldsymbol{P}^{-1}\boldsymbol{W}\boldsymbol{P}$ has the same eigenvalues as $\boldsymbol{W}$;

(b) Let $\boldsymbol{P} = diag[p_1, p_2, \ldots, p_n]$ for all $p_i > 0, \ i = 1, 2, \ldots, n$. Show that the neural system

$$\boldsymbol{z}(k+1) = -\boldsymbol{P}^{-1}\boldsymbol{A}\boldsymbol{P}\boldsymbol{z}(k) + \boldsymbol{P}^{-1}\boldsymbol{B}\sigma(\boldsymbol{W}\boldsymbol{P}\boldsymbol{z}(k) + \boldsymbol{s})$$

has the same local stability of the system given in Eqn. (12.65).

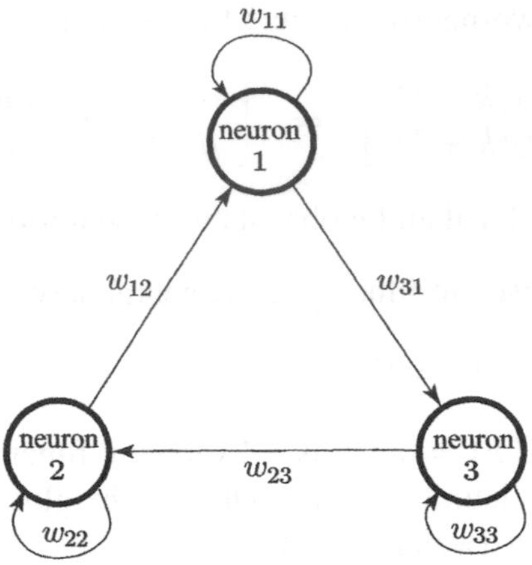

Figure 12.7 Problem 12.14: the three-neuron system.

12.14 As shown in Fig. 12.7, consider a three-neuron network with the following equation

$$\begin{aligned} x_1(k+1) &= w_{11}\tanh(x_1(k)) + w_{12}\tanh(x_2(k)) \\ x_2(k+1) &= w_{22}\tanh(x_2(k)) + w_{23}\tanh(x_3(k)) \\ x_3(k+1) &= w_{31}\tanh(x_1(k)) + w_{33}\tanh(x_3(k)) \end{aligned}$$

(a) Analyze the equilibrium points of the above system;

(b) Study global stability condition of the system;

(c) Let

$$w_{11} = \frac{1}{2}, \quad w_{12} = \frac{1}{3}, \quad w_{22} = \frac{1}{2}$$

$$w_{23} = \frac{1}{4}, \quad w_{31} = \frac{2}{5}, \quad w_{33} = \frac{1}{2}$$

Calculate all equilibrium point of the system and study the stability of those equilibrium points.

12.15 Consider the global stability condition of an n-neuron system with a circle connection as shown in Fig. 12.8, which is a generalized version of the three-neuron system discussed in Problem 12.14

$$\boldsymbol{x}(k+1) = \boldsymbol{W}\,\mathbf{tanh}(\boldsymbol{x}(k)), \qquad \boldsymbol{x} \in \Re^n, \ \boldsymbol{W} \in \Re^{n\times n}$$

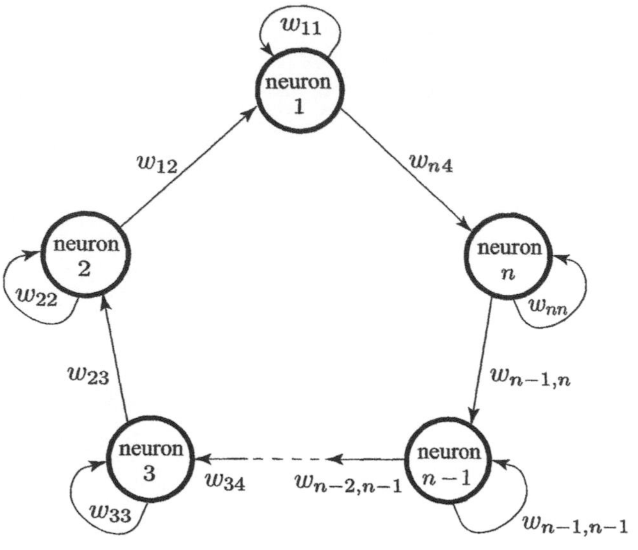

Figure 12.8 Problem 12.15: the n-neuron system with a circle connection.

where

$$\boldsymbol{W} = \begin{bmatrix} w_{11} & w_{12} & 0 & \cdots & 0 & 0 \\ 0 & w_{22} & w_{23} & \cdots & 0 & 0 \\ \vdots & \vdots & \vdots & \ddots & \vdots & \vdots \\ 0 & 0 & 0 & \cdots & w_{n-1,n-1} & w_{n-1,n} \\ w_{n1} & 0 & 0 & \cdots & 0 & w_{nn} \end{bmatrix}$$

(a) Analyze the equilibrium points of the above system;

(b) Study global stability condition of the system.

Part IV

SOME ADVANCED TOPICS IN NEURAL NETWORKS

Chapter 13. Binary Neural Networks

Chapter 14. Feedback Binary Associative Memories

Chapter 15. Fuzzy Sets and Fuzzy Neural Networks

13

Binary Neural Networks

13.1 Discrete-Time Two-State Systems

13.2 Asynchronous Operating Hopfield Neural Network

13.3 An Alternative Version of the Asynchronous Binary Neural Network

13.4 Neural Network in Synchronous Mode of Operation

13.5 Block Sequential Operation of the Hopfield Neural Network

13.6 Concluding Remarks

Problems

Most models of the neural networks discussed in the previous chapters were described mathematically by a set of either continuous-time differential equations or discrete-time difference equations with continuous state values. Those neural networks can be implemented by analog integrated circuits or by computer emulations. The binary neural networks to be studied in this chapter are a class of neural networks with only two states in a discrete-time domain. This type of neural networks can be considered as an extension of finite-state machines and can be implemented by integrated digital logic circuits for various engineering applications.

In this chapter, we will first present models of binary neural networks by using the dynamic system language. As the most famous and typical binary neural network, the binary Hopfield neural networks are then studied extensively in terms of their operation mode and convergence. A Lyapunov function or energy-function-based method for analyzing the stability of such nonlinear and discrete-time dynamic systems is introduced. Moreover, the convergence of various types of binary neural networks is also studied in this chapter. The results form a basis for the further study of neural associative memories in Chapter 14.

13.1 DISCRETE-TIME TWO-STATE SYSTEMS

13.1.1 Basic Definitions

13.1.1.1 Binary States of Neural Systems

From a dynamic system point of view, discrete-time binary neural networks shown in Fig. 13.1 may be considered as a special class of discrete-time dynamic systems, where the state space is a unipolar or bipolar two-state hypercube. Let $S = \{-1, 1\}^n$ be a bipolar two-state hypercube. A general state space equation of a discrete-time binary neural network containing n neurons is given by

$$\begin{aligned} x_1(k+1) &= f_1\left(\sum_{j=1}^{n} w_{1j}x_j(k) + \theta_1\right) \\ x_2(k+1) &= f_2\left(\sum_{j=1}^{n} w_{2j}x_j(k) + \theta_2\right) \\ &\vdots \\ x_n(k+1) &= f_n\left(\sum_{j=1}^{n} w_{nj}x_j(k) + \theta_n\right) \end{aligned} \tag{13.1}$$

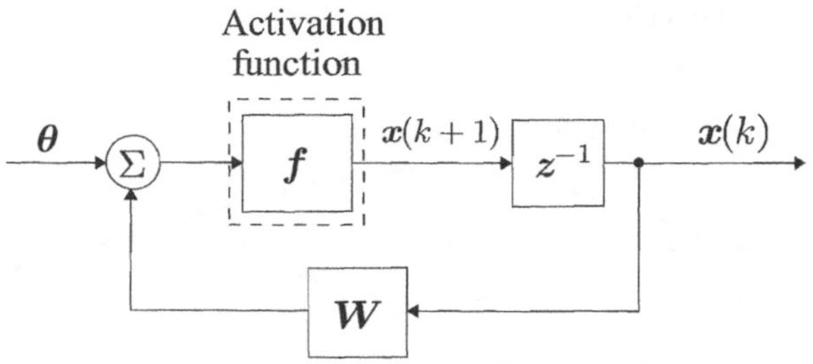

Figure 13.1 Block diagram of the discrete-time binary neural network.

where x_i is the state of neuron i that is either 1 or -1, w_{ij} is the synaptic weight from neuron j to neuron i, θ_i is the threshold of neuron i, and the nonlinear activation function $f_i : \{-1, 1\}^n \longrightarrow \{-1, 1\}$ is a Boolean function whose value is either 1 or -1. Let the neural state values 1 and -1 represent the active (firing) and nonactive (rest) states of the neurons, respectively. The ith neuron has n two-valued inputs, $x_1(k)$, $x_2(k)$, ..., $x_n(k)$, and a single two-valued output $x_i(k+1)$. Its internal parameters are weights w_{i1}, w_{i2}, ..., w_{in} and its threshold is θ_i, where each weight w_{ij} is associated with a particular input variable x_j. The values of the weights w_{ij} and the threshold θ_i may be any real, finite, positive, or negative values.

Equation (13.1) may be rewritten in the following vector form

$$\boldsymbol{x}(k+1) = \boldsymbol{f}(\boldsymbol{W}\boldsymbol{x}(k) + \boldsymbol{\theta}) \tag{13.2}$$

where

$$\boldsymbol{x} \triangleq \begin{bmatrix} x_1 \\ x_2 \\ \vdots \\ x_n \end{bmatrix} \in \{-1, 1\}^n$$

and

$$\boldsymbol{f} \triangleq \begin{bmatrix} f_1 \\ f_2 \\ \vdots \\ f_n \end{bmatrix} : \{-1, 1\}^n \longrightarrow \{-1, 1\}^n$$

$$\boldsymbol{\theta} \triangleq \begin{bmatrix} \theta_1 \\ \theta_2 \\ \vdots \\ \theta_n \end{bmatrix} \in \Re^n$$

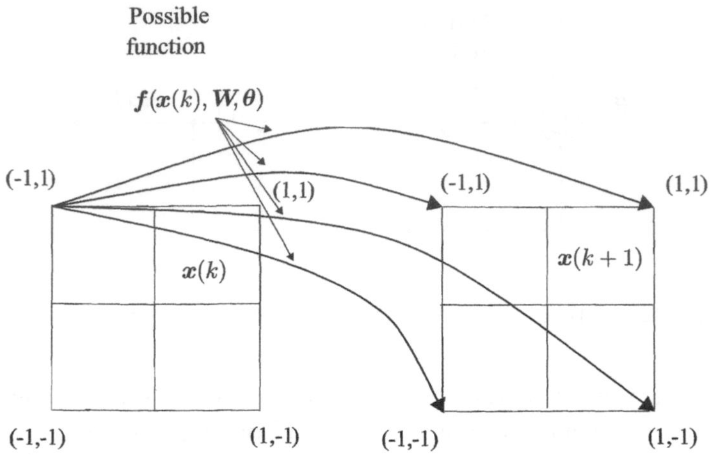

Figure 13.2 A two-neuron discrete-time binary neural network, where the state space is $\{[-1 \quad -1]^T, [-1 \quad 1]^T, [1 \quad -1]^T, [1 \quad 1]^T\}$.

$$\boldsymbol{W} = \begin{bmatrix} w_{11} & \cdots & w_{1n} \\ w_{21} & \cdots & w_{2n} \\ \vdots & \ddots & \vdots \\ w_{n1} & \cdots & w_{nn} \end{bmatrix} \in \Re^{n \times n}$$

Generally speaking, the state space in a continuous-time dynamic system is taken to be a topological space or smooth manifold, and the function f is assumed to be continuous or smooth. For a discrete-time binary neural network, the state space will be a finite set and the conditions of continuity or smoothness will not be applied. A two-neuron system is shown in Fig. 13.2.

Definition 13.1 *The state trajectory* $\boldsymbol{x} \in \{-1, 1\}^n$ *under* $\boldsymbol{f}$ *is the set*

$$\{\boldsymbol{x}, \boldsymbol{f}(\boldsymbol{x}, \boldsymbol{W}, \boldsymbol{\theta}), \ldots, \boldsymbol{f}^n(\boldsymbol{x}, \boldsymbol{W}, \boldsymbol{\theta}), \ldots\}, \text{ with } \boldsymbol{f}^n(\boldsymbol{x}) \triangleq \boldsymbol{f}(\boldsymbol{f}(\cdots \boldsymbol{f}(\boldsymbol{x})))$$

which is a subset of the state space $\{-1, 1\}^n$. ■

The points of the state space $\{-1, 1\}^n$ whose trajectory exhibits persistent steady state behavior are the basis for the analysis of the neural system given in Eqn. (13.2).

Definition 13.2 $\boldsymbol{x} \in \{-1, 1\}^n$ *is an equilibrium point of the system described by Eqn. (13.2) if* $\boldsymbol{x}(k) = \boldsymbol{x}(k-1)$ *for time* k*; that is,* $\boldsymbol{f}(\boldsymbol{x}, \boldsymbol{W}, \boldsymbol{\theta}) = \boldsymbol{x}$. $\boldsymbol{x} \in \{-1, 1\}^n$ *is a periodic point of the system if there exists a positive integer*

p such that $x(k+p) = x(k)$ for time k; that is, $f(f \cdots (f(f(x)))) = f^p(x) = x$. The minimum number of such an integer p is called the "period" of the system. ■

13.1.1.2 Modes of Neural State Updating

Note from Eqns. (13.1) and (13.2) that every unit in the neural network is a linear threshold element with inputs $x_i(k)$, $i = 1, \ldots, n$ and threshold θ_i. For a given neural weight $\boldsymbol{w}$ and threshold $\boldsymbol{\theta}$, the next state $\boldsymbol{x}(k+1)$ of the neural network is computed from the current state $\boldsymbol{x}(k)$. Depending on the number of the states $x_i(k)$, $i = 1, 2, \ldots, N$, where N is a subset integer of n employed in Eqn. (13.2), the network operation may be divided into three different modes of operation. To define these modes, let us denote a subset N of the integer set n (where n is the number of neural units), and assume that there are N neural units $Nu(N)$ in operation during each interval of time. Then, these three modes of operation of the neural networks are defined as follows:

(i) *Asynchronous or serial mode of operation:* For this case, only one unit is in operation during any time interval:

$$Nu(N) = 1$$

(ii) *Synchronous or (fully) parallel mode of operation:* For this case, the computation is performed in the synchronous mode. All the neural units are in operation during each time interval:

$$Nu(N) = n$$

(iii) *Block Sequential or partial parallel mode of operation:* For this case, only a specified block of neural units are in operation during any time interval:

$$1 < Nu(N) < n$$

In all these modes of operation the integer set $N \in n$ can be chosen randomly or by using some deterministic rule.

An n-dimensional state vector $\boldsymbol{x} \in \{-1, 1\}^n$ is called a *stable* state if and only if

$$\boldsymbol{x} = \boldsymbol{f}(\boldsymbol{W}\boldsymbol{x} + \boldsymbol{\theta}) \tag{13.3}$$

that is, if there is no change in the state of the network no matter what the mode of operation is.

13.1.1.3 Cycle Length and Transient Time

A state vector $\boldsymbol{x}$ is said to be stable if and only if there is no further change in the state of the network. Obviously, the equilibrium points may be considered as special cases of the periodic points. Clearly, since the state space of the system, which is an n-dimensional two-state hypercube $\{-1, 1\}^n$, is a finite set, all the state trajectories $\{\boldsymbol{x}(k)\}_{k\geq 0}$ of any updating mode are ultimately periodic. Hence, the length of such a periodic sequence and the maximum time that the state vector enters the periodic iteration plays an important role in analyzing the dynamic characteristics of the network. They are also referred to as the *cycle lengths* and the *transient time* of the system. The exact mathematical definitions of those two key parameters, the cycle length and the transient time, for a given binary neural network system are now studied.

Definition 13.3 *For every $\boldsymbol{x} \in \{-1, 1\}^n$ let two functions $p(\boldsymbol{x})$ and $t(\boldsymbol{x})$ of $\boldsymbol{x}$ satisfy*

$$\boldsymbol{x}(k + p(\boldsymbol{x})) = \boldsymbol{x}(k), \quad \textit{for all} \quad k \geq t(\boldsymbol{x})$$

$$\boldsymbol{x}(k + q) \neq \boldsymbol{x}(k), \quad \textit{for any} \quad k \leq t(\boldsymbol{x}), \quad q \leq p(\boldsymbol{x})$$

Then, for the neural system defined in Eqn. (13.2) two constants are defined:

$$\text{Cycle length:} \qquad P(\boldsymbol{W}, \boldsymbol{\theta}) = \max_{\boldsymbol{x}\in\{-1,1\}^n} \Big\{ p(\boldsymbol{x}) \Big\} \tag{13.4}$$

$$\text{Transient time:} \qquad T(\boldsymbol{W}, \boldsymbol{\theta}) = \max_{\boldsymbol{x}\in\{-1,1\}^n} \Big\{ t(\boldsymbol{x}) \Big\} \tag{13.5}$$

■

The transient time $T(\boldsymbol{W}, \boldsymbol{\theta})$ describes the dynamic temporal process, while the cycle length $P(\boldsymbol{W}, \boldsymbol{\theta})$ shows the internal structure of the steady states that are either stable equilibrium points or periodic points with a certain period. The above definition can be used to describe the dynamic properties of the binary Hopfield neural network with an asynchronous operating mode as well as other operating modes such as synchronous and block sequential operating modes as discussed later. Also, from Definition 13.3, it is worth noting that if

$$P(\boldsymbol{W}, \boldsymbol{\theta}) = 1$$

that is, the length of the periodic state sequence is one, then the system has only stable equilibrium points, called the *attractors*. The exact positions of the equilibrium states, which represent the ultimate position of the states, depend on the initial points. As discussed later, the application of associative

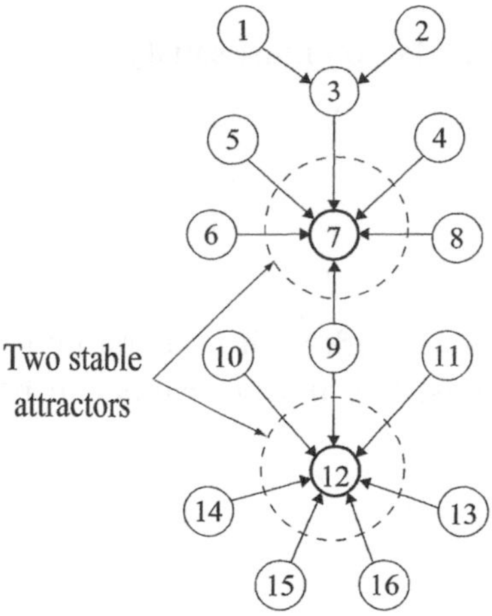

(a) Steady states contain two stable equilibrium points (attractors)

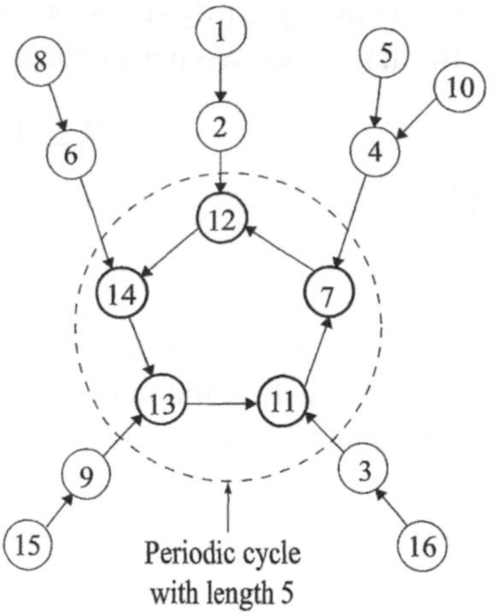

(b) Steady states are a periodic cycle with length 5

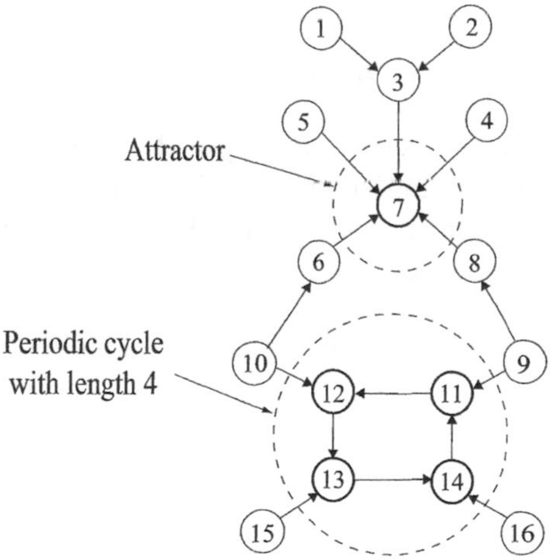

(c) Steady states are both an attractor and a periodic cycle with length 4

Figure 13.3 The steady states of a four-neuron binary neural network, where each circle represents a state of the system, and the heavy circle represents the steady state of the normal system.

memories utilizes the *attraction* function of an equilibrium to ensure the recall or retrieval capability of associative memories.

In fact, these two parameters $T(\boldsymbol{W},\boldsymbol{\theta})$ and $P(\boldsymbol{W},\boldsymbol{\theta})$ must satisfy

$$0 \le T(\boldsymbol{W},\boldsymbol{\theta}) \le 2^n$$

and

$$1 \le P(\boldsymbol{W},\boldsymbol{\theta}) \le 2^n$$

where 2^n is the total number of the states for a network with n neural units. In case these two inequalities become equalities, two trivial results can be obtained as follows. If

$$T(\boldsymbol{W},\boldsymbol{\theta}) = 0$$

or

$$P(\boldsymbol{W},\boldsymbol{\theta}) = 1$$

the network has only equilibrium states; that is, all 2^n possible states are isolated stable equilibrium states, but they are not attractors. Indeed

$$T(\boldsymbol{W},\boldsymbol{\theta}) = 0$$

and

$$P(\boldsymbol{W},\boldsymbol{\theta}) = 2^n$$

imply that the network has a cycle with length 2^n. Figure 13.3 illustrates an example of a system exhibiting stable equilibrium points (attractors) and a periodic cycle. We now present two examples to illustrate the dynamic behaviors of such neural networks.

Example 13.1 Consider an n-neuron network with a weight matrix

$$\boldsymbol{W} = \boldsymbol{I}$$

where $\boldsymbol{I}$ is an identity matrix. The vector-valued nonlinear activation function is selected as

$$\boldsymbol{f}(\boldsymbol{W}\boldsymbol{x}) = \boldsymbol{sgn}(\boldsymbol{W}\boldsymbol{x}) = \begin{bmatrix} sgn((\boldsymbol{W}\boldsymbol{x})_1) \\ sgn((\boldsymbol{W}\boldsymbol{x})_2) \\ \vdots \\ sgn((\boldsymbol{W}\boldsymbol{x})_n) \end{bmatrix}$$

where the signum function, or the so-called hard-limiting quantizer $sgn(.)$, is defined as

$$sgn(x) = \begin{cases} 1, & \text{if} \quad x \geq 0 \\ \\ -1, & \text{if} \quad x < 0 \end{cases}$$

Then, all the possible 2^n binary states are the equilibrium points of the following binary network

$$\boldsymbol{x}(k+1) = \boldsymbol{sgn}(\boldsymbol{x}(k))$$

For a binary network, the equilibrium states satisfy

$$\boldsymbol{x}(k+1) = \boldsymbol{x}(k)$$

Hence, for such a binary network, one has

$$\text{Transient time:} \qquad T(\boldsymbol{W}, \boldsymbol{\theta}) = 0$$

$$\text{Cycle length:} \qquad P(\boldsymbol{W}, \boldsymbol{\theta}) = 1$$

■

Example 13.2 Consider a two-neuron binary network, as shown in Fig. 13.4a, described by

$$\begin{aligned} x_1(k+1) &= sgn(x_2(k)) \\ x_2(k+1) &= sgn(-x_1(k)) \end{aligned}$$

The corresponding weight matrix

$$\boldsymbol{W} = \begin{bmatrix} 0 & 1 \\ -1 & 0 \end{bmatrix}$$

is skew–symmetric, and the system has four possible states

$$\begin{bmatrix} 1 \\ 1 \end{bmatrix}, \quad \begin{bmatrix} -1 \\ 1 \end{bmatrix}, \quad \begin{bmatrix} 1 \\ -1 \end{bmatrix}, \quad \begin{bmatrix} -1 \\ -1 \end{bmatrix}$$

As depicted in Fig. 13.4b, the system starting from any one of the four states will go back to the original starting point after four steps of updating. Thus

$$\text{Transient time:} \qquad T(\boldsymbol{W}, \boldsymbol{\theta}) = 0$$

$$\text{Cycle length:} \qquad P(\boldsymbol{W}, \boldsymbol{\theta}) = 4$$

■

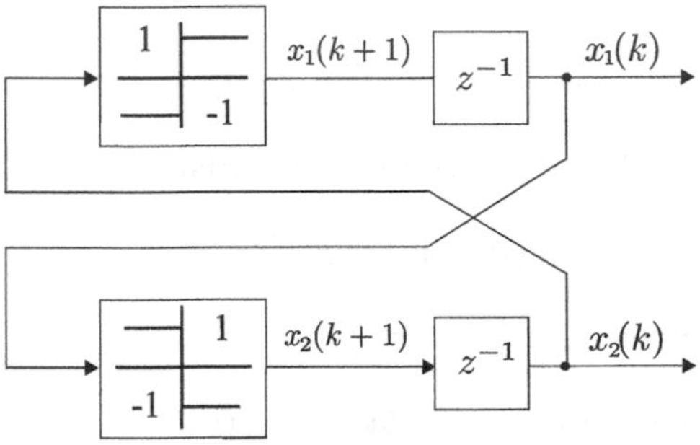

(a) Block diagram of the network

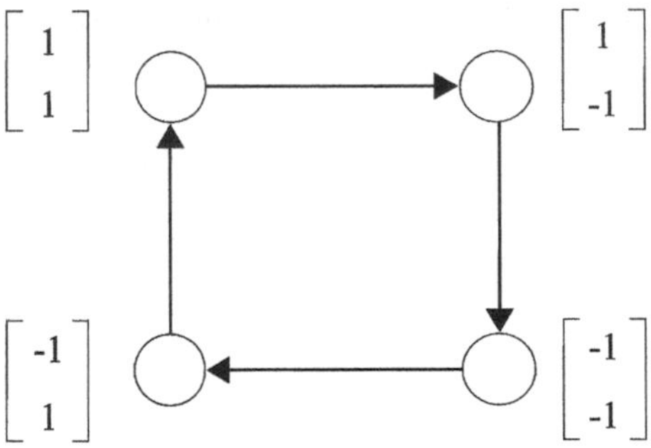

(b) The state transfer diagram of the network: cycle length 4

Figure 13.4 Example 13.2: cyclic phenomenon in a two-neuron binary network.

13.1.2 Lyapunov Function Method

It is well known that the nature of the stability of deterministic dynamic systems can be determined if Lyapunov functions with certain specified properties are constructed. The Lyapunov stability analysis method has been widely used in studying the state convergence and the stability of discrete-time neural networks as well. Let $E(\boldsymbol{x}) : \{-1, 1\}^n \longrightarrow \Re$ be a Lyapunov function, or the so-called energy function, which is defined on the state space $\{-1, 1\}^n$ and is nonincreasing along all the state trajectories

$$E(\boldsymbol{x}(k)) \geq E(\boldsymbol{x}(k+1)), \quad \text{for all} \quad \boldsymbol{x}(k+1) \neq \boldsymbol{x}(k)$$

and there exists a constant E^- such that

$$E(\boldsymbol{x}) \leq E^-, \quad \forall \boldsymbol{x} \in \{-1, 1\}^n \tag{13.6}$$

In this case, the steady state of the system may be one of the following three possible types:

(i) *Stable equilibrium points:* If

$$\Delta E(k) \triangleq E(\boldsymbol{x}(k+1)) - E(\boldsymbol{x}(k)) = 0 \tag{13.7}$$

then

$$\boldsymbol{x}(k) = \boldsymbol{x}(k+1) \tag{13.8}$$

and the neural system has only stable equilibrium points;

(ii) *Limit-cycle oscillations:* If there is a positive integer p such that

$$\begin{aligned} \Delta E(k) &= 0 \\ \text{iff} \quad \boldsymbol{x}(k) &= \boldsymbol{x}(k+p) \end{aligned} \tag{13.9}$$

the neural system then has limit-cycle oscillations with a period p;

(iii) *Stable equilibrium points and limit-cycle oscillations:* If there is a positive integer p such that

$$\begin{aligned} \Delta E(k) &= 0 \\ \text{iff} \quad \boldsymbol{x}(k) &= \boldsymbol{x}(k+1) \quad \text{or} \quad \boldsymbol{x}(k) = \boldsymbol{x}(k+p) \end{aligned} \tag{13.10}$$

the system may have then either stable equilibrium points or a limit-cycle oscillation with a period p.

Furthermore, assume that an upper bound E^+ of the energy function $E(\boldsymbol{x})$ is given by

$$E^+ \geq E(\boldsymbol{x}), \quad \forall \boldsymbol{x} \in \{-1, 1\}^n \tag{13.11}$$

and before the system reaches the steady state the minimum absolute value of the difference of the energy function $E(\boldsymbol{x})$ from time k to $(k+1)$ is

$$\epsilon(\boldsymbol{W}, \boldsymbol{\theta}) \triangleq \min\{|E(\boldsymbol{x}(k+1)) - E(\boldsymbol{x}(k))|\} \tag{13.12}$$

Since the time that the energy function E reaches the minimum value from its maximum value must not be less than the transient time of the system, one obtains

$$T(\boldsymbol{W}, \boldsymbol{\theta})\epsilon(\boldsymbol{W}, \boldsymbol{\theta}) \leq (E^+ - E^-) \tag{13.13}$$

Hence

$$T(\boldsymbol{W}, \boldsymbol{\theta}) \leq \frac{1}{\epsilon(\boldsymbol{W}, \boldsymbol{\theta})}(E^+ - E^-) \tag{13.14}$$

Figure 13.5 shows the relationship between the transient length $T(\boldsymbol{W}, \boldsymbol{\theta})$ and the energy function $E(\boldsymbol{x})$.

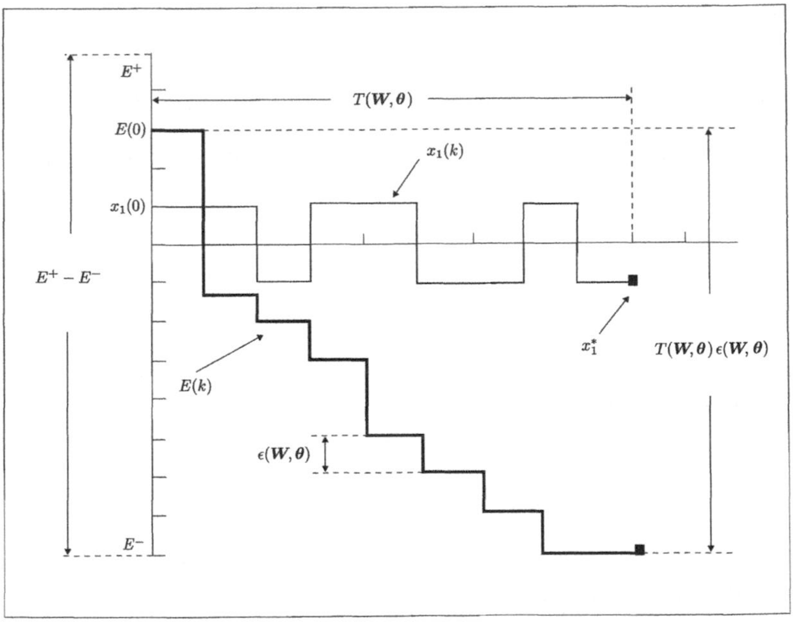

Figure 13.5 The relationship between the transient length $T(\boldsymbol{W}, \boldsymbol{\theta})$ and the energy function $E(\boldsymbol{x})$, where $x_1(0)$ is the first component of the initial state $\boldsymbol{x}(0)$, and x_1^* is the first component of the stable state $\boldsymbol{x}^*$.

13.2 ASYNCHRONOUS OPERATING HOPFIELD NEURAL NETWORK

13.2.1 State Operating Equations

The original discrete-time Hopfield neural network defined by Hopfield (1982) is a binary pattern processor consisting of n two-state neurons, and it was designed only for the unipolar step function shown in Fig. 13.6a and defined as

$$\mathbf{1}(y_i(k)) = \begin{cases} 1 & \text{if} \quad y_i(k) > 0 \\ 0 & \text{if} \quad y_i(k) < 0 \end{cases} \tag{13.15}$$

where

$$y_i(k) = \sum_{j=1}^{n} w_{ij} x_j(k) + \theta_i \tag{13.16}$$

is the internal potential of the ith neuron. As an intermediate variable, the expression of the internal potential plays an important role in dealing with binary neural computing.

The bipolar choice, as shown in Fig. 13.6b, is often mathematically preferable and is used in the following discussion, is described by the hard-limiting nonlinearity

$$sgn(y_i(k)) = \begin{cases} 1, & \text{if} \quad y_i(k) \geq 0 \\ -1, & \text{if} \quad y_i(k) < 0 \end{cases} \tag{13.17}$$

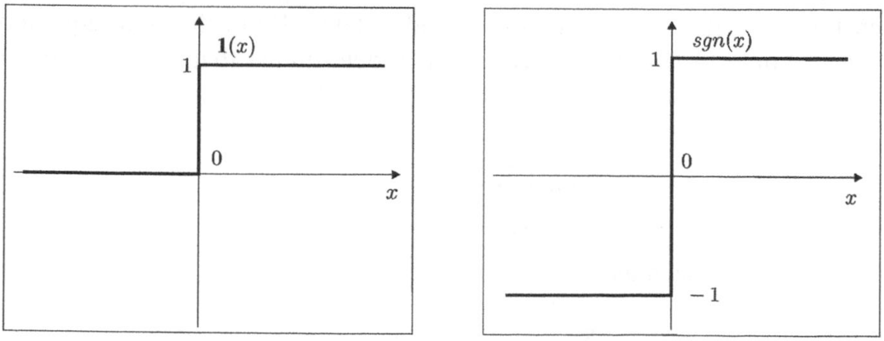

(a) Step-like unipolar function, $\mathbf{1}(x)$ (b) Bipolar signum function, $sgn(x)$

Figure 13.6 Nonlinear activation functions for binary neural network.

where x_i is the state of neuron i, which is either 1 or -1; y_i is the internal field; w_{ij} is the synaptic weight from neuron j to neuron i; and θ_i is a threshold of neuron i. Let the neural state values 1 and -1 represent the states of the active and rest of the neurons, respectively. In the asynchronous operating mode, only one neuron is assumed to be in the state of firing (active), and all the others neurons are in the state of rest at each operating time. In other words, only the state of one neuron is updated, and the states of all other neurons are unchanged at each time. Moreover, as shown in Fig. 13.7, the number p of the unique active neuron is chosen randomly from the integer set $N_n = \{1, 2, \ldots, n\}$; that is, the firing probability of every neuron is $1/n$.

In this case, the information processing of the neurons in the neural system is accomplished in the asynchronous mode or the serial mode. The state equation of the neural system is given as follows

$$\begin{aligned} x_i(k+1) &= f_i(\boldsymbol{x}(k)) \\ &= f_i(x_1(k), \ldots, x_n(k)), \quad i = 1, 2, \ldots, n \end{aligned} \tag{13.18}$$

where the right-hand function is defined as

$$f_i(\boldsymbol{x}(k)) = \begin{cases} sgn(y_i(k)), & \text{if} \quad i = p, \; y_p(k) \neq 0 \\ x_i(k), & \text{otherwise} \end{cases} \tag{13.19}$$

and the state space is $\{-1, 1\}^n$. Hence, the discrete-time Hopfield neural network may be viewed as a special class of discrete-time dynamic systems. The steady states are reached if

$$x_i(k+1) = x_i(k), \quad \text{for} \quad \text{all} \quad i = 1, 2, \ldots, n$$

that is, if none of the states x_1, x_2, ..., x_n change during an operation, then the network is said to be in a steady state. From the state equation given in Eqn. (13.18) of the network, it is determined that a binary vector $\boldsymbol{x} \in \{-1, 1\}^T$ is a steady state of the network if it obeys

$$x_i = sgn\left(\sum_{j=1}^{n} w_{ij} x_j + \theta_i\right)$$

for all $1 \leq i \leq n$ such that

$$\sum_{j=1}^{n} w_{ij} x_j + \theta_i \neq 0$$

In this serial mode of operation, the final steady state depends not only on the initial state but also on the updating sequence of the neurons.

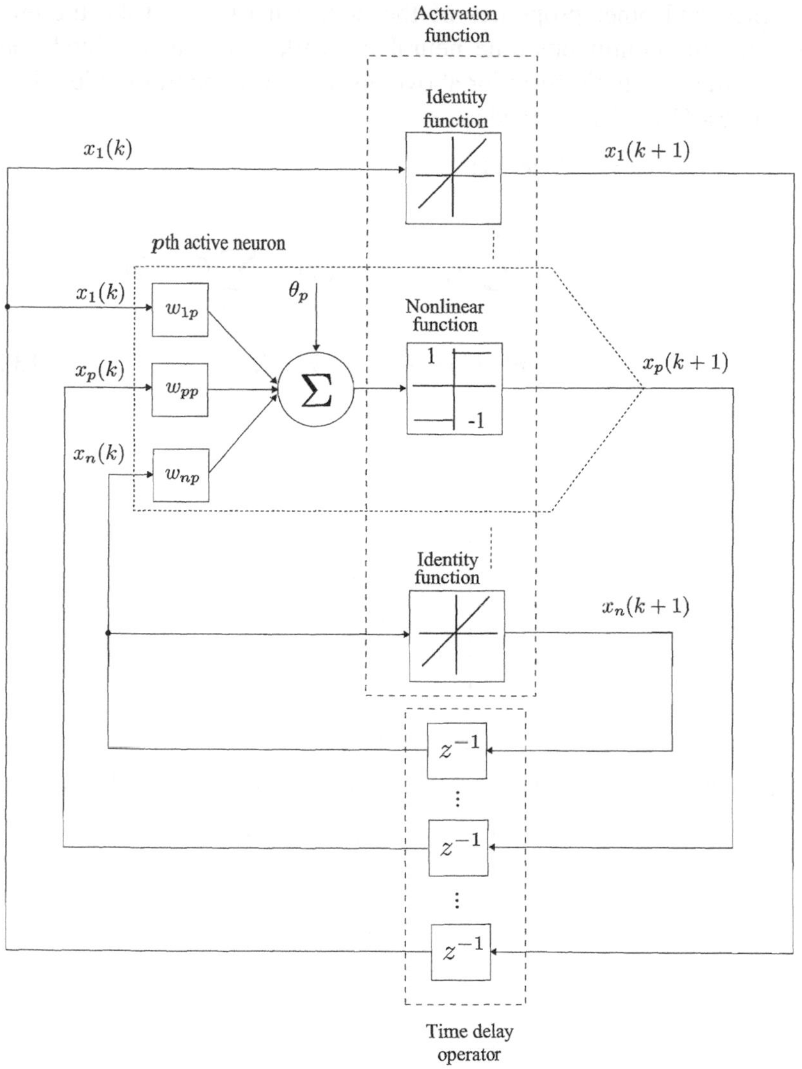

Figure 13.7 Block diagram of a binary Hopfield dynamic neural network with an asynchronous operating mode, where only the pth neuron is in active state.

13.2.2 State Convergence of Hopfield Neural Network with Zero-Diagonal Elements

An energy function was introduced by Hopfield to facilitate the study of convergence and other properties of the neural network. Like the energy function for the continuous-time neural network, the scalar-valued energy function with a quadratic form for above discrete-time neural model given in Eqns. (13.16)–(13.19) is defined as

$$\begin{aligned} E(k) &\triangleq E(\boldsymbol{x}(k)) \\ &= -\tfrac{1}{2}\sum_{i,j=1}^{n} w_{ij}x_i(k)x_j(k) - \sum_{i=1}^{n}\theta_i x_i(k) \\ &= -\tfrac{1}{2}\boldsymbol{x}^T(k)\boldsymbol{W}\boldsymbol{x}(k) - \boldsymbol{\theta}^T\boldsymbol{x}(k) \end{aligned} \tag{13.20}$$

Assume that a given state vector at time k is

$$\boldsymbol{x}(k) = \begin{bmatrix} x_1(k) \\ x_2(k) \\ \vdots \\ x_{p-1}(k) \\ x_p(k) \\ x_{p+1}(k) \\ \vdots \\ x_n(k) \end{bmatrix}$$

then any changes to $x_p(k)$ change the state vector at time $(k+1)$ as

$$\boldsymbol{x}(k+1) = \begin{bmatrix} x_1(k) \\ \vdots \\ x_{p-1}(k) \\ x_p(k) + \Delta x_p(k) \\ x_{p+1}(k) \\ \vdots \\ x_n(k) \end{bmatrix}$$

as a result of operation in the pth neuron, where

$$\Delta x_p(k) = x_p(k+1) - x_p(k) \tag{13.21}$$

Let the connecting weight matrix $\boldsymbol{W}$ be symmetric with zero-diagonal elements:

$$w_{ij} = w_{ji} \qquad \text{and} \qquad w_{ii} = 0$$

The assumption of the zero-diagonal element means that no units have self-connections. To show that the energy function does not change when the time increases

$$\Delta E(k) = E(k+1) - E(k) \leq 0 \tag{13.22}$$

we may express the changes in the energy function as

$$\begin{aligned}\Delta E(k) &= -\tfrac{1}{2}\Delta x_p(k)\left[\sum_{j=1,j\neq p}^{n} w_{pj}x_j(k) + \sum_{i=1,i\neq p}^{n} w_{ip}x_i(k)\right] \\ &\quad - \Delta x_p(k)\theta_p \\ &= -\Delta x_p(k)\left[\sum_{j=1,j\neq p}^{n} w_{pj}x_j(k) + \theta_p\right] \end{aligned} \tag{13.23}$$

In view of the operation equation, we may note that if

$$\Delta x_p(k) = x_p(k+1) - x_p(k) > 0$$

implies that

$$\longrightarrow x_p(k+1) = 1$$

and

$$\longrightarrow y_p(k) = \left[\sum_{j=1,j\neq p}^{n} w_{pj}x_j(k) + \theta_p\right] > 0 \tag{13.24}$$

and if

$$\Delta x_p(k) = x_p(k+1) - x_p(k) < 0$$

implies that

$$\longrightarrow x_p(k+1) = -1$$

$$\longrightarrow y_p(k) = \left[\sum_{j=1,j\neq p}^{n} w_{pj}x_j(k) + \theta_p\right] < 0 \tag{13.25}$$

Thus, one obtains

$$\Delta E(k) < 0 \tag{13.26}$$

that is, when $\boldsymbol{x}(k) \neq \boldsymbol{x}(k+1)$, the energy function E decreases strictly with each updating. Furthermore, either of the following results are obtained:

$$\Delta E(k) = 0 \longleftarrow \Delta x_p(k) = 0 \longleftrightarrow x_p(k+1) = x_p(k) \tag{13.27}$$

$$\Delta E(k) = 0 \longleftarrow \left[\sum_{j=1}^{n} w_{pj} x_j(k) + \theta_p\right] = 0$$
$$\longrightarrow x_p(k+1) = x_p(k) \tag{13.28}$$

Hence, using such an asynchronous mode of operation, the discrete-time neural network presented above will finally converge to a stable steady state. In fact, the energy function E cannot decrease infinitely because it is bounded from below

$$E(k) \geq -\frac{1}{2} \sum_{i,j=1}^{n} |w_{ij}| - \sum_{i=1}^{n} |\theta_i| \tag{13.29}$$

that is, once the minimum energy state is reached, no further transitions are possible and the network is said to have reached a steady state as an attractor. It is evident that the main reason for showing the convergence properties of the state is to define a so-called energy function and to prove that this energy function is nonincreasing when the state of the network changes as a result of computation. Since the energy function is bounded from below, it may be concluded that the network will converge to some steady state as an attractor.

Example 13.3 (Serial Operation) A general structure of a two-neuron network with serial operation is shown in Fig. 13.8. Consider the neural network with the weight matrix

$$\boldsymbol{W} = \begin{bmatrix} 0 & 1 \\ 1 & 0 \end{bmatrix}$$

and the threshold $\boldsymbol{\theta}$ is a 0 vector. It can be verified that when the neural network is operating in a serial mode, the state of the system with an arbitrary initial condition will converge to one of the following stable equilibrium points

$$\left\{ \begin{bmatrix} 1 \\ 1 \end{bmatrix}, \begin{bmatrix} -1 \\ -1 \end{bmatrix} \right\}$$

and the energy function E at every state is given as

$$E([1 \quad 1]^T) = -1$$
$$E([-1 \quad -1]^T) = -1$$
$$E([-1 \quad 1]^T) = 1$$
$$E([1 \quad -1]^T) = 1$$

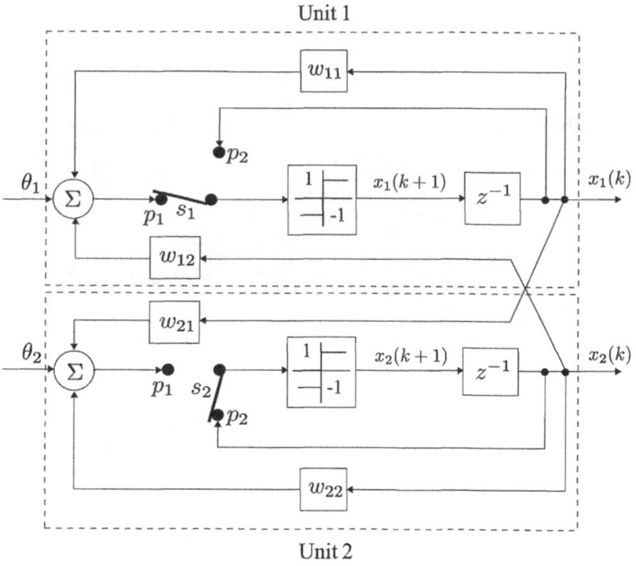

(a) General structure of the two-neuron system

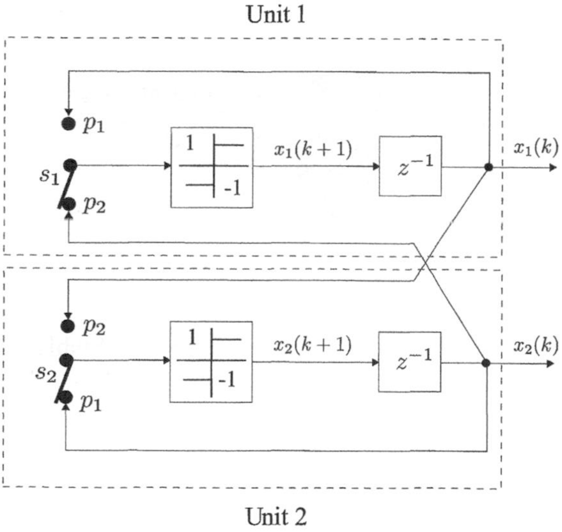

(b) Two-neuron system with parameters $w_{11} = w_{22} = 0$, $w_{12} = w_{21} = 1.0$, and $\theta_1 = \theta_2 = 0$

Figure 13.8 Example 13.3: block diagram of a two-neuron system with an asynchronous operating mode. Switches s_1 and s_2 always have different positions. For example, when the switch s_1 is in the position p_1, switch s_2 is in the position p_2.

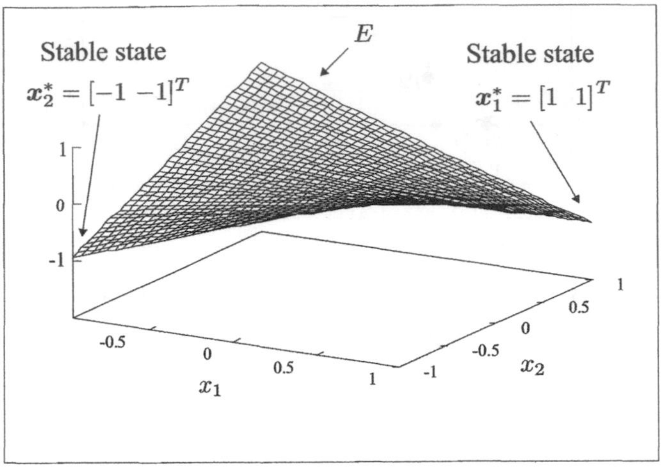

(a) Front view of energy function E

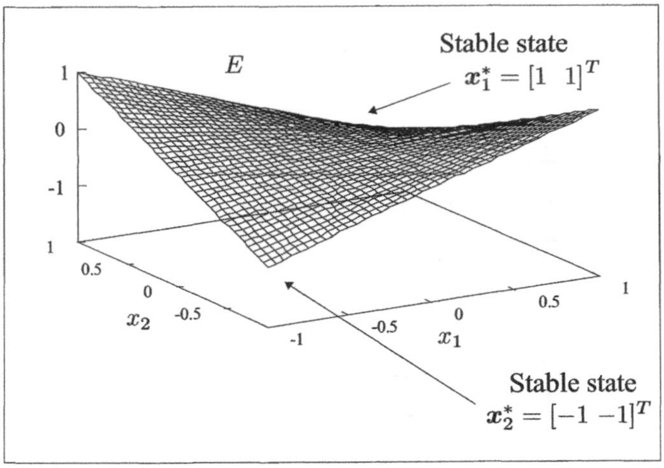

(b) Rear view of energy function E

Figure 13.9 Example 13.3: the surface of energy function E for a two-neuron system with parameters $w_{11} = w_{22} = 0$, $w_{12} = w_{21} = 1.0$, and $\theta_1 = \theta_2 = 0$. The system has two stable equilibrium points $x_1^* = [1\ \ 1]^T$ and $x_2^* = [-1\ -1]^T$, which correspond to the two minima of the energy function $E(x_1, x_2)$.

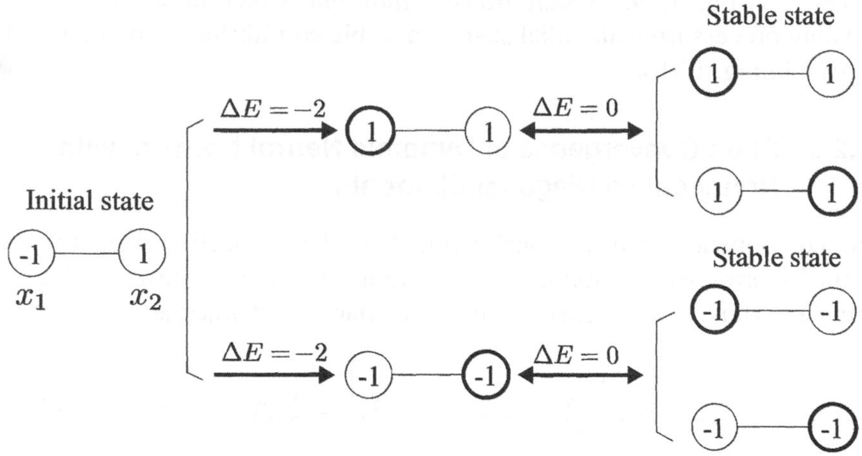

(a) Neural system operation with initial state $[-1\ \ 1]^T$

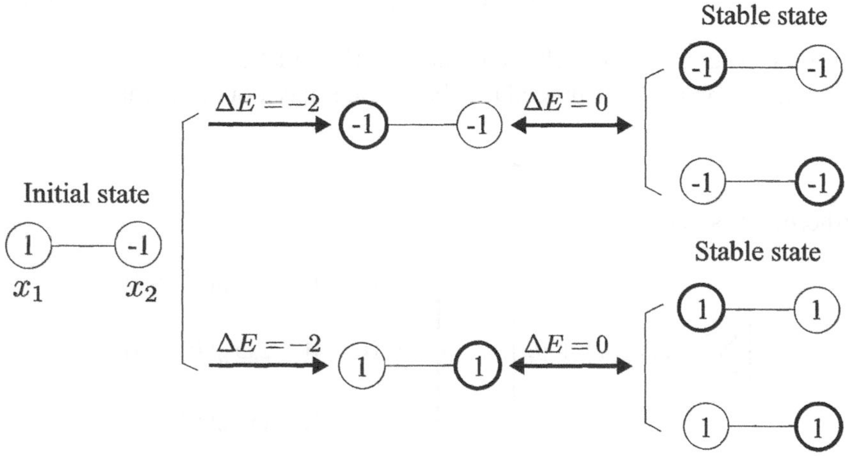

(b) Neural system operation with initial state $[1\ \ -1]^T$

Figure 13.10 State transfer diagram of a sequence operating processing of a two-neuron system using a serial (asynchronous) mode. The parameters of the network are: $w_{11} = w_{22} = 0$, $w_{12} = w_{21} = 1.0$, and $\theta_1 = \theta_2 = 0$. The possibly final stable states are either $[1\ \ 1]^T$ or $[-1\ \ -1]^T$. The heavy cycle represents the neuron tha is in operation.

Hence, the energy function E has the minimum value in the equilibrium states, as shown in Fig. 13.9. A *state transfer diagram*, which describes the state updating process from an initial state to a stable equilibrium point or a cycle, is given in Fig. 13.10. ■

13.2.3 State Convergence of Dynamic Neural Network with Nonnegative Diagonal Elements

The requirement of zero-diagonal elements in the connection weight matrix originally proposed by Hopfield may be relaxed as that of positive diagonal elements. Thus, in the energy function the change is defined as

$$\Delta E(k) = -\Delta x_p(k)\left[\sum_{j=1}^{n} w_{pj}x_j(k) + \theta_p\right] - \tfrac{1}{2}(\Delta x_p(k))^2 w_{pp} \tag{13.30}$$

Note that in the results given by Eqns. (13.28) and (13.29) if

$$w_{pp} \geq 0, \quad \text{for} \quad 1 \leq p \leq n \tag{13.31}$$

then the last term on the right-hand side of Eqn. (13.30) is always negative. Hence, from the analysis procedure above, one may conclude that

$$\Delta E(k) < 0$$

Furthermore, since

$$\left[\sum_{j=1}^{n} w_{pj}x_j(k) + \theta_p\right] \quad \begin{cases} = 0, & \text{if} \quad \Delta x_p(k) = 0 \\ < 0, & \text{if} \quad \Delta x_p(k) > 0 \\ > 0, & \text{if} \quad \Delta x_p(k) < 0 \end{cases}$$

therefore, for $\Delta x_p(k) \neq 0$

$$\left[\sum_{j=1}^{n} w_{pj}x_j(k) + \theta_p\right] \neq -\tfrac{1}{2}(\Delta x_p(k))^2 w_{pp} \tag{13.32}$$

which implies

$$\Delta E(k) = 0 \longleftrightarrow \Delta x_p(k) = 0 \longleftrightarrow x_p(k+1) = x_p(k) \tag{13.33}$$

Therefore, one may summarize the above results in the following theorem.

Theorem 13.1 (Convergence Theorem for Serial Operating Mode) *Let the weight matrix* $\mathbf{W}$ *be symmetric with nonnegative diagonal elements. Then, the Hopfield neural network with an asynchronous operation is such that*

(i) $\forall k,\ \boldsymbol{x}(k+1) \neq \boldsymbol{x}(k) \longrightarrow E(\boldsymbol{x}(k+1)) < E(\boldsymbol{x}(k))$*;*

(ii) The system has only stable equilibrium points

$$P(\mathbf{W}, \boldsymbol{\theta}) = 1 \tag{13.34}$$

(iii) The transient length satisfies

$$T(\mathbf{W}, \boldsymbol{\theta}) \leq \frac{1}{\epsilon(\mathbf{W}, \boldsymbol{\theta})} \left[||\mathbf{W}|| + 2||\boldsymbol{\theta}|| - \sum_{i=1}^{n} w_{ii} \right] \tag{13.35}$$

where

$$\begin{aligned}
\epsilon(\mathbf{W}, \boldsymbol{\theta}) &= \min\{|E(k+1) - E(k)| : \boldsymbol{x}(k) \neq \boldsymbol{x}(k+1)\} \\
||\mathbf{W}|| &= \sum_{i=1}^{n} \sum_{j=1}^{n} |w_{ij}| \\
||\boldsymbol{\theta}|| &= \sum_{i=1}^{n} |\theta_i|
\end{aligned}$$

Proof: Conditions (i) and (ii) follow from the discussion above, and only condition (iii) needs to be proved. It is easy to see that, for any $\boldsymbol{x}(k) \in \{-1, 1\}^n$, the energy function

$$\begin{aligned}
E(k) &= -\tfrac{1}{2} \sum_{i=1}^{n} \sum_{j=1}^{n} w_{ij} x_i(k) x_j(k) - \sum_{i=1}^{n} \theta_i x_i(k) \\
&= -\tfrac{1}{2} \sum_{i=1}^{n} \sum_{j=1, j \neq i}^{n} w_{ij} x_i(k) x_j(k) - \tfrac{1}{2} \sum_{i=1}^{n} w_{ii} - \sum_{i=1}^{n} \theta_i x_i(k)
\end{aligned}$$

satisfies

$$E(k) \geq -\tfrac{1}{2} \sum_{i=1}^{n} \sum_{j=1, j \neq i}^{n} |w_{ij}| - \tfrac{1}{2} \sum_{i=1}^{n} w_{ii} - \sum_{i=1}^{n} |\theta_i|$$

and

$$E(k) \leq \tfrac{1}{2} \sum_{i=1}^{n} \sum_{j=1, j \neq i}^{n} |w_{ij}| + \tfrac{1}{2} \sum_{i=1}^{n} w_{ii} + \sum_{i=1}^{n} |\theta_i|$$

On the other hand, for $k < t(\boldsymbol{x})$, $\boldsymbol{x}(k+1) \neq \boldsymbol{x}(k)$, which implies

$$|\Delta E(k)| \geq \epsilon(\boldsymbol{W}, \boldsymbol{\theta}) > 0$$

and, from condition (i)

$$\begin{aligned} T(\boldsymbol{W}, \boldsymbol{\theta})\epsilon(\boldsymbol{W}, \boldsymbol{\theta}) \quad \leq & \left[\frac{1}{2} \sum_{i=1}^{n} \sum_{j=1, j \neq i}^{n} |w_{ij}| + \frac{1}{2} \sum_{i=1}^{n} w_{ii} + \sum_{i=1}^{n} |\theta_i| \right] \\ & - \left[-\frac{1}{2} \sum_{i=1}^{n} \sum_{j=1, j \neq i}^{n} |w_{ij}| - \frac{1}{2} \sum_{i=1}^{n} w_{ii} - \sum_{i=1}^{n} |\theta_i| \right] \end{aligned}$$

which proves condition (iii). ■

In a serial mode of operation, each neuron in the network may be fired several times until the states of all the network neurons converge to an asymptotically stable steady state that depends not only on the initial state but also on the operating sequence of neurons as shown in Example 13.3. The major advantage of the asynchronous update mode is that since the units are independently updated, and if we look at a short time interval, we see that only one unit is being updated at a time. Among other things, as discussed above, this system can help the stability of the network by preventing oscillations that are more readily entered into with such a serial mode of updating.

Example 13.4 Consider a binary neural network with $10 \times 10 = 100$ neural units. Let the (100×100)-dimensional symmetric weight matrix with zero-diagonal elements be determined by

$$\begin{aligned} w_{ij} &= x_i \times x_j, \qquad (i \neq j) \\ w_{ii} &= 0, \quad i = 1, 2, \ldots, 100 \end{aligned}$$

where the 100-dimensional binary pattern vector $\boldsymbol{x}_d$ represents digit 5 and has the bitmap pattern as depicted in Fig. 13.11j, where the state -1 or 1 of the network represents, respectively, a white and a black image block. In fact, the preceding algorithm for the weights is Hebb's rule, which will be studied in Chapter 14. The asynchronous operating process for such a binary network with 100 units is illustrated in Fig. 13.11. The desired stable state of the network, which represents a desired or stored binary pattern, is designed to represent the pattern of digit 5. If the input pattern, which is viewed as a corrupted or noisy version of the desired pattern and is given in Fig. 13.11a, is used as an initial state of the network. The states of the network converge to

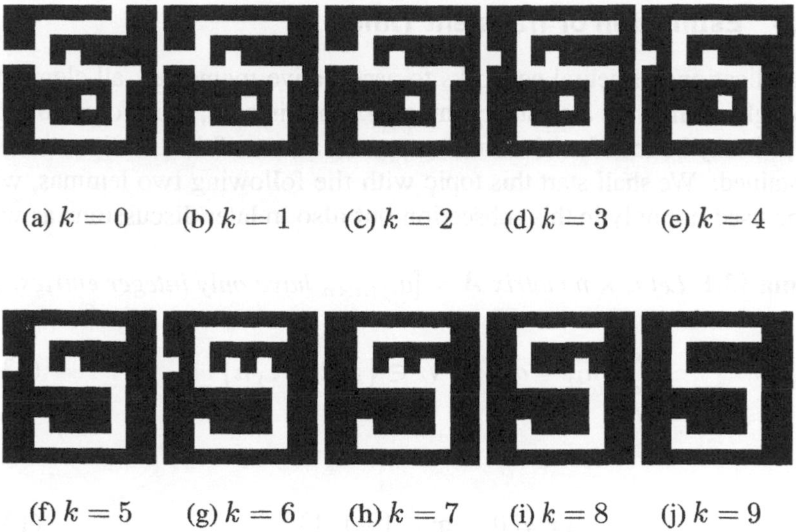

Figure 13.11 Example 13.4: the asynchronous updating process of a 10×10 bitmap of digit 5.

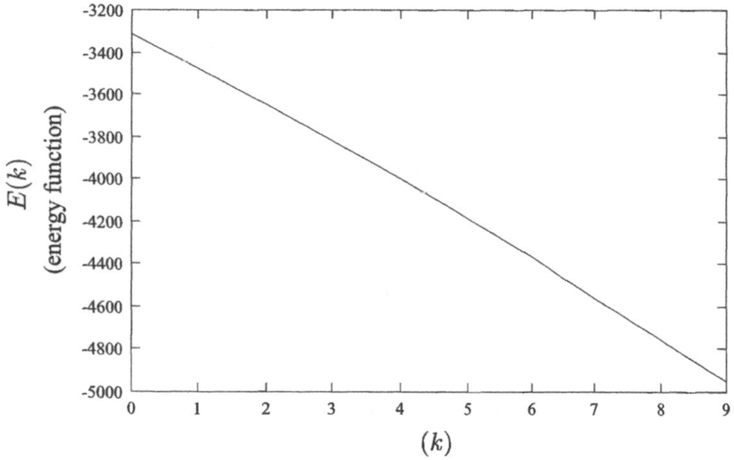

Figure 13.12 Example 13.4: the energy of the network during the state updating process.

the stable states, as shown in Fig. 13.11j, after 10 states updating. During such an updating process, since the asynchronous operating mode was employed, only one of the states was fired at each updating instant. The decreasing phase of the energy function during the state updating is shown in Fig. 13.12. ■

13.2.4 Estimation of Transient Time

For applications of neural networks to associative memories, all elements of the weight matrix $\boldsymbol{W}$ are usually integers. In this case, a uniform bound for $\epsilon(\boldsymbol{W}, \boldsymbol{\theta})$ may be found so that the exact estimations of the transient time may be obtained. We shall start this topic with the following two lemmas, which will be used not only in this subsection but also in later discussions as well.

Lemma 13.1 *Let $n \times n$ matrix $\boldsymbol{A} = [a_{ij}]_{n\times n}$ have only integer entries. If*

$$\sum_{j=1}^{n} a_{ij} = odd, \quad \forall i \in \{1, 2, \ldots, n\} \tag{13.36}$$

then

$$\boldsymbol{A}\boldsymbol{x} \neq 0, \quad \boldsymbol{x} \in \{-1, 1\}^n \tag{13.37}$$

Proof: If all components of the state vector $\boldsymbol{x}$ have the same sign, that is, all components of $\boldsymbol{x}$ are 1 or -1, the result is obvious. Let $\boldsymbol{x} \in \{-1, 1\}^n$ and

$$\boldsymbol{x} = \begin{bmatrix} x_1 \\ \vdots \\ x_{i^*} \\ \vdots \\ x_n \end{bmatrix}$$

with

$$x_{i^*} = -1$$

and

$$x_i = 1, \quad i = 1, ..., i^* - 1, i^* + 1, \ldots, n$$

If

$$\sum_{j=1}^{n} a_{ij}x_j = 0, \quad \forall i \in \{1, 2, \ldots, n\}$$

one has

$$\sum_{j=1, j\neq i^*}^{n} a_{ij}x_j = a_{ii^*}$$

Substituting a_{ii^*} into the left-hand side of Eqn. (13.36) yields

$$\sum_{j=1, j \neq i^*}^{n} a_{ij}(1 + x_j) = \text{odd}$$

Since all a_{ij} are integers, the left side satisfies

$$\sum_{j=1, j \neq i^*}^{n} a_{ij}(1 + x_j) = 2 \sum_{j=1, j \neq i^*}^{n} a_{ij} \neq \text{odd}$$

Therefore, the contradiction is due to the assumption in Eqn. (13.36). The result is proved. ■

Lemma 13.2 *Let $n \times n$ matrix $\boldsymbol{A} = [a_{ij}]_{n \times n}$ have only integer entries. If*

$$\sum_{j=1}^{n} a_{ij} = \textit{even}, \quad \forall i \in \{1, 2, \ldots, n\} \tag{13.38}$$

then

$$(\boldsymbol{Ax})_i = \textit{even}, \quad \forall i \in \{1, 2, \ldots, n\} \quad \textit{and} \quad \boldsymbol{x} \in \{-1, 1\}^n \tag{13.39}$$

■

The proof of this lemma is left to the readers as an exercise. One may use the same approach that was used in the proof of Lemma 13.1.

Corollary 13.1 *Let the integer weight matrix **W** with nonnegative diagonal elements and the threshold vector $\boldsymbol{\theta}$ have integer entries. Then*

$$T(\boldsymbol{W}, \boldsymbol{\theta}) \leq \frac{\frac{1}{2}\left[||\boldsymbol{W}|| + 2||\boldsymbol{\theta}|| - \sum_{i=1}^{n} w_{ii}\right]}{1 + \min_{p} w_{pp}} \tag{13.40}$$

Proof: Since for any $\boldsymbol{x}(k)$, and $\boldsymbol{x}(k+1) \in \{-1, 1\}^n$ and $\boldsymbol{x}(k+1) \neq \boldsymbol{x}(k)$, one has

$$\Delta x_p(k) = 2, \quad \text{and} \quad \left[\sum_{i=1}^{n} w_{pj} x_j(k) + \theta_p\right] > 0, \quad \text{for} \quad 1 \leq p \leq n$$

$$\Delta x_p(k) = -2, \quad \text{and} \quad \left[\sum_{i=1}^{n} w_{pj} x_j(k) + \theta_p\right] < 0, \quad \text{for} \quad 1 \leq p \leq n$$

which are equivalent to

$$\Delta x_p(k) = 2, \quad \text{and} \quad \left[\sum_{i=1}^{n} w_{pj}x_j(k) + \theta_p\right] \geq 1, \quad \text{for} \quad 1 \leq p \leq n$$

$$\Delta x_p(k) = -2, \quad \text{and} \quad \left[\sum_{i=1}^{n} w_{pj}x_j(k) + \theta_p\right] \leq -1, \quad \text{for} \quad 1 \leq p \leq n$$

respectively. Thus, for $\Delta x_p(k) \neq 0$, one obtains

$$\left|\left[\sum_{j=1}^{n} w_{pj}x_j(k) + \theta_p\right]\right| \geq 1$$

Furthermore, one has

$$\begin{aligned} \Delta E(k) &= -\Delta x_p(k)\left[\sum_{j=1}^{n} w_{pj}x_j(k) + \theta_p\right] - \tfrac{1}{2}(\Delta x_p(k))^2 w_{pp} \\ &\leq -2 - 2w_{pp} \end{aligned} \tag{13.41}$$

Therefore

$$\epsilon(\boldsymbol{W}, \boldsymbol{\theta}) = 2 + 2\min_p w_{pp} \tag{13.42}$$

Substituting this result in Eqn. (13.35) in Theorem 13.1 leads to the proof of the corollary. ■

Corollary 13.2 *Let the integer weight matrix* $\boldsymbol{W}$ *with nonnegative diagonal elements and the threshold vector* $\boldsymbol{\theta}$ *have integer entries. If*

$$\sum_{j=1}^{n} w_{ij} + \theta_i = \textit{even}, \quad \textit{for all} \quad i \in \{1, 2, \ldots, n\} \tag{13.43}$$

then

$$T(\boldsymbol{W}, \boldsymbol{\theta}) \leq \frac{\frac{1}{2}\left[||\boldsymbol{W}|| + 2||\boldsymbol{\theta}|| - \sum_{i=1}^{n} w_{ii}\right]}{2 + \min_p w_{pp}} \tag{13.44}$$

Proof: Using the result of Lemma 13.2, one obtains

$$\Delta x_p(k) = 2, \quad \text{and} \quad \left[\sum_{i=1}^{n} w_{pj}x_j(k) + \theta_p\right] \geq 2, \quad \text{for} \quad 1 \leq p \leq n$$

$$\Delta x_p(k) = -2, \quad \text{and} \quad \left[\sum_{i=1}^{n} w_{pj}x_j(k) + \theta_p\right] \leq -2, \quad \text{for} \quad 1 \leq p \leq n$$

that is

$$\left| \left[\sum_{j=1}^{n} w_{pj} x_j(k) + \theta_p \right] \right| \geq 2$$

Thus, in this case

$$\epsilon(\boldsymbol{W}, \boldsymbol{\theta}) = 4 + 2 \min_p w_{pp} \tag{13.45}$$

The result is obvious. ■

Example 13.5 Consider a binary neural network with $30 \times 30 = 900$ neural units with an asynchronous updating mode. Given a 30×30 $\boldsymbol{x}_d \in \{-1, 1\}^{900}$ binary pattern that corresponds to the bitmap depicted in Fig. 13.13i, to store this known binary pattern as one of the stable equilibrium points, the elements of a symmetric and zero-diagonal weight matrix $\boldsymbol{W}$ are computed using the Hebb's rule as follows:

$$\begin{aligned} w_{ij} &= x_i \times x_j, \quad (i \neq j) \\ w_{ii} &= 0, \quad i = 1, 2, \ldots, 900 \end{aligned}$$

Since all components of the weight matrix $\boldsymbol{W}$ are integers, the bound of the transient time of this network may be estimated according to the formulation given in Corollary 13.1. In this case, it is easy to obtain

$$||\boldsymbol{W}|| = 809{,}100$$

and

$$T(\boldsymbol{W}) \leq \tfrac{1}{2} ||\boldsymbol{W}|| = 404{,}550$$

If the initial binary state values of the network are chosen randomly, the convergence time from an initial point to a stable equilibrium, which is a known and is a desired binary pattern vector, consists of 899 steps. The state updating process is shown in Fig. 13.13, where the bitmaps are used to express the state vectors at a different time k. For such an asynchronous network with a large number of neural units, and since only one unit is updated at each time, the system takes a long time to reach an equilibrium state. However, the convergence is ensured in the asynchronous updating mode of operation. The energy function during such a state updating is given in Fig. 13.14. ■

(a) $k = 0$ (b) $k = 200$ (c) $k = 300$

(d) $k = 400$ (e) $k = 500$ (f) $k = 600$

(g) $k = 700$ (h) $k = 800$ (i) $k = 898$

Figure 13.13 Example 13.5: state bitmaps of an asynchronous network with $30 \times 30 = 900$ units. The elements of the symmetric weight matrix with zero-diagonal elements are determined using Hebb's rule. All the initial state values are selected as 1. The convergence time of the network from the initial state (a) at $k = 0$ to the stable equilibrium state shown in (i) is $k = 898$.

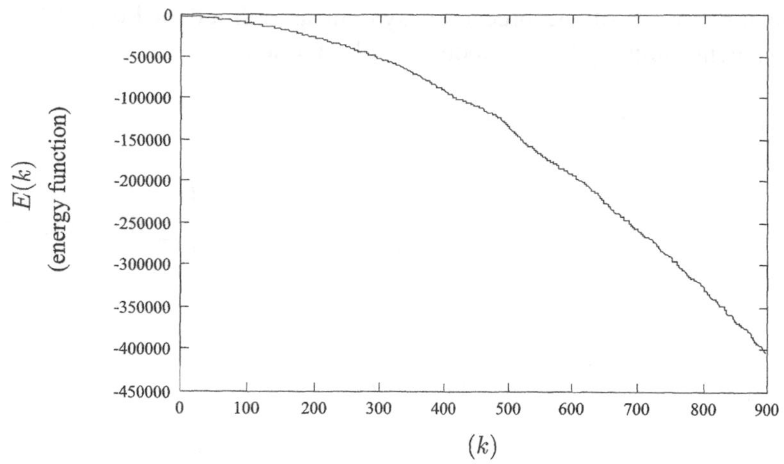

Figure 13.14 Example 13.5: the energy curve of the network during the state updating.

13.3 AN ALTERNATIVE VERSION OF THE ASYNCHRONOUS BINARY NEURAL NETWORK

13.3.1 Binary State Updating

A slight modification of the original Hopfield binary neural network may be made for the definition of the state values when the corresponding internal potentials are zero. For an asynchronous updating mode, a state equation that appears very often in the literature is

$$x_i(k+1) = \begin{cases} sgn(y_i(k)), & \text{if} \quad i = p \\ x_i(k), & \text{otherwise} \end{cases} \tag{13.46}$$

It can be seen that the difference between the above model and Hopfield's original network, discussed extensively in Section 13.2 is the definition of $x_p(k+1)$ when $y_p(k) = 0$. The value of $x_p(k+1)$ is always set to 1 for $y_p(k) = 0$ in Eqn. 13.46, while $x_p(k+1)$ remains unchanged for $y_p(k) = 0$ in the Hopfield's original neural model. The preceding model is also called the *Hopfield neural network* in much of the literature. A binary vector $\boldsymbol{x} \in \{-1, 1\}^n$ is a stable state of the network described in Eqn. (13.46) if it obeys

$$\boldsymbol{x} = \boldsymbol{sgn}(\boldsymbol{W}\boldsymbol{x} + \boldsymbol{\theta}) \tag{13.47}$$

In the following discussion, the state convergence property of this model is first considered by using the energy function method. The dynamics of the model is then addressed in detail.

For the function E of the preceding system as defined in Eqn. (13.20), when an asynchronous updating mode is applied, one has

$$\Delta x_p(k) > 0 \longrightarrow x_p(k+1) = 1$$
$$\longrightarrow y_p(k) = \left[\sum_{j=1}^{n} w_{pj} x_j(k) + \theta_p \right] \geq 0 \qquad (13.48)$$

and

$$\Delta x_p(k) < 0 \longrightarrow x_p(k+1) = -1$$
$$\longrightarrow y_p(k) = \left[\sum_{j=1}^{n} w_{pj} x_j(k) + \theta_p \right] < 0 \qquad (13.49)$$

Thus, when $\boldsymbol{x}(k) \neq \boldsymbol{x}(k+1)$, the energy function satisfies

$$\Delta E(k) \leq 0 \qquad (13.50)$$

that is, the energy function E either decreases or remains constant. Furthermore

$$\Delta E(k) = 0 \longleftarrow \Delta x_p(k) = 0 \longleftrightarrow x_p(k+1) = x_p(k) \qquad (13.51)$$

or

$$\Delta E(k) = 0 \longleftarrow y_p(k) = 0$$
$$\longrightarrow \begin{cases} \text{if} \quad x_p(k) = 1, & \text{then} \quad x_p(k+1) = x_p(k) = 1 \\ \text{if} \quad x_p(k) = -1, & \text{then} \quad x_p(k+1) = 1 \text{ and } y_k(k+1) > 0 \end{cases}$$
$$\longrightarrow \boldsymbol{x}(k+1) \text{ is a stable equilibrium state} \qquad (13.52)$$

Hence, one may conclude that this analysis results in the following theorem.

Theorem 13.2 *Let the weight matrix* $\mathbf{W}$ *be symmetric with nonnegative diagonal elements. Then, the Hopfield neural network in Eqn. (13.46) with an asynchronous operation is such that*

(i) $\forall k,\ \boldsymbol{x}(k+1) \neq \boldsymbol{x}(k) \longrightarrow E(\boldsymbol{x}(k+1)) \leq E(\boldsymbol{x}(k))$

(ii) The system has only stable equilibrium points:

$$P(\boldsymbol{W}, \boldsymbol{\theta}) = 1 \tag{13.53}$$

(iii) The transient length satisfies

$$T(\boldsymbol{W}, \boldsymbol{\theta}) \leq \frac{1}{\epsilon(\boldsymbol{W}, \boldsymbol{\theta})} \left[||\boldsymbol{W}|| + 2||\boldsymbol{\theta}|| - \sum_{i=1}^{n} w_{ii} \right] \tag{13.54}$$

where

$$\begin{aligned}
\epsilon(\boldsymbol{W}, \boldsymbol{\theta}) &= \min\{|E(k+1) - E(k)| : \boldsymbol{x}(k) \neq \boldsymbol{x}(k+1)\} \\
||\boldsymbol{W}|| &= \sum_{i=1}^{n} \sum_{j=1}^{n} |w_{ij}| \\
||\boldsymbol{\theta}|| &= \sum_{i=1}^{n} |\theta_i|
\end{aligned}$$

■

It is important to note the following facts:

(i) The energy function E is not always decreasing even before the state reaches one of the stable equilibrium states. However, the energy function has a local minimum value at the arbitrary stable equilibrium point;

(ii) If $\boldsymbol{x}^*$ is the state where the energy function has the minimum value, then $\boldsymbol{x}^*$ is a stable equilibrium state only if

$$(\boldsymbol{W}\boldsymbol{x}^* + \boldsymbol{\theta})_i \neq 0, \quad \text{for all} \quad i = 1, 2 \ldots, n \tag{13.55}$$

(iii) Let $\boldsymbol{\theta} = 0$ in the network and $\boldsymbol{x}^*$ be a stable state that must satisfy

$$\boldsymbol{x}^* = \boldsymbol{sgn}(\boldsymbol{W}\boldsymbol{x}^*) \tag{13.56}$$

Then $-\boldsymbol{x}^*$ is also a stable equilibrium state only if

$$(\boldsymbol{W}\boldsymbol{x}^*)_i \neq 0, \quad \text{for all} \quad i = 1, 2, \ldots, n \tag{13.57}$$

It is to be noted that points (ii) and (iii) show that the two networks may have different stable states, and that the stable equilibrium states of the modified model must be the stable equilibrium states of the original Hopfield neural network, but the inverse implication is not always true.

Example 13.6 Consider a three-neuron network with a zero threshold vector and a weight matrix

$$\boldsymbol{W} = \begin{bmatrix} 0 & 1 & 2 \\ 1 & 0 & -1 \\ 2 & -1 & 0 \end{bmatrix}$$

The energy function as defined in Eqn. (13.20) is obtained as

$$E(x_1, x_2, x_3) = -x_1x_2 - 2x_1x_3 + x_2x_3$$

The minimum value of E is

$$\min_{\boldsymbol{x}} E(x_1, x_2, x_3) = -2$$

It is easy to verify that there are four binary vectors such that E has a minimum value. These vectors are

$$\boldsymbol{x}^{(1)} = \begin{bmatrix} 1 \\ 1 \\ 1 \end{bmatrix}, \quad \boldsymbol{x}^{(2)} = \begin{bmatrix} -1 \\ 1 \\ -1 \end{bmatrix}$$

and

$$\boldsymbol{x}^{(3)} = -\boldsymbol{x}^{(1)} = \begin{bmatrix} -1 \\ -1 \\ -1 \end{bmatrix}, \quad \boldsymbol{x}^{(4)} = -\boldsymbol{x}^{(2)} = \begin{bmatrix} 1 \\ -1 \\ 1 \end{bmatrix}$$

Since

$$\begin{aligned} \boldsymbol{sgn}(\boldsymbol{W}\boldsymbol{x}^{(1)}) &= \boldsymbol{sgn} \begin{bmatrix} 3 \\ 0 \\ 1 \end{bmatrix} = \begin{bmatrix} 1 \\ 1 \\ 1 \end{bmatrix} = \boldsymbol{x}^{(1)} \\ \boldsymbol{sgn}(\boldsymbol{W}\boldsymbol{x}^{(2)}) &= \boldsymbol{sgn} \begin{bmatrix} -1 \\ 0 \\ -3 \end{bmatrix} = \begin{bmatrix} -1 \\ 1 \\ -1 \end{bmatrix} = \boldsymbol{x}^{(2)} \end{aligned}$$

Thus, $\boldsymbol{x}^{(1)}$ and $\boldsymbol{x}^{(2)}$ are two stable equilibrium points of the network. On the other hand, since

$$\begin{aligned} \boldsymbol{sgn}(\boldsymbol{W}\boldsymbol{x}^{(3)}) &= \boldsymbol{sgn}(-\boldsymbol{W}\boldsymbol{x}^{(1)}) = \boldsymbol{sgn} \begin{bmatrix} -3 \\ 0 \\ -1 \end{bmatrix} = \begin{bmatrix} -1 \\ 1 \\ -1 \end{bmatrix} \neq \boldsymbol{x}^{(3)} \\ \boldsymbol{sgn}(\boldsymbol{W}\boldsymbol{x}^{(4)}) &= \boldsymbol{sgn}(-\boldsymbol{W}\boldsymbol{x}^{(2)}) = \boldsymbol{sgn} \begin{bmatrix} 1 \\ 0 \\ 3 \end{bmatrix} = \begin{bmatrix} 1 \\ 1 \\ 1 \end{bmatrix} \neq \boldsymbol{x}^{(4)} \end{aligned}$$

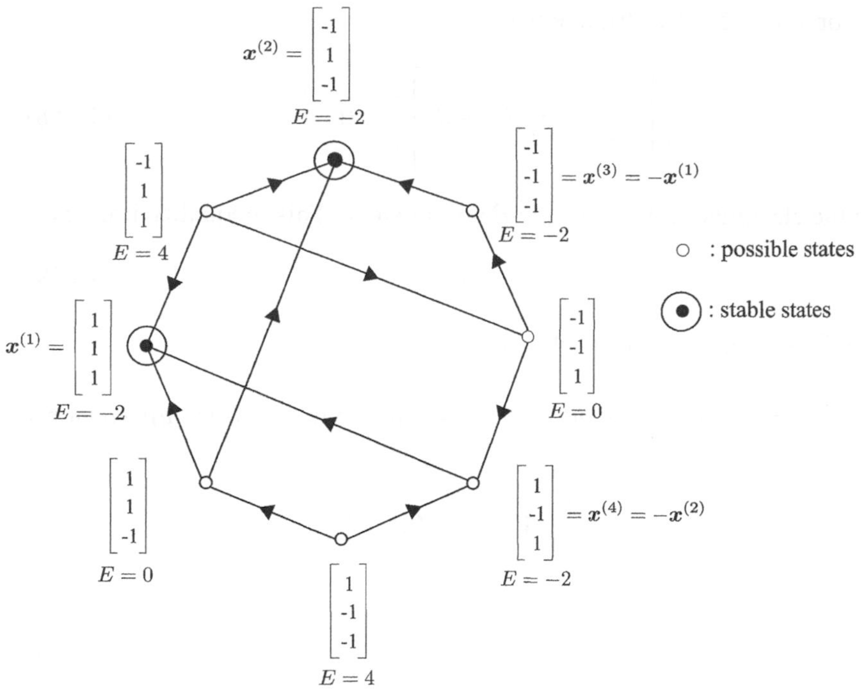

Figure 13.15 Example 13.6: state transfer map of the network.

the complements $\boldsymbol{x}^{(3)} = -\boldsymbol{x}^{(1)}$ and $\boldsymbol{x}^{(4)} = -\boldsymbol{x}^{(2)}$ are not stable states. The instability for $\boldsymbol{x}^{(3)}$ and $\boldsymbol{x}^{(4)}$ as inputs arises mainly because of the definition of the $sgn(.)$ function at $x = 0$; that is, $sgn(0) = 1$. The state transfer map of the network with such a weight matrix is shown in Fig. 13.15. ■

13.3.2 Formulations for Transient Time in Asynchronous Mode

13.3.2.1 The Case with Positive Diagonal Elements of W

To obtain an estimation of the transient time of the network, one needs first to derive the bound of the ΔE when $\boldsymbol{x}(k) = \boldsymbol{x}(k+1)$. Note that if

$$\Delta x_p(k) = 2 \longrightarrow \left[\sum_{j=1}^{n} w_{pj} x_j(k) + \theta_p\right] \geq 0, \quad \text{for} \quad 1 \leq p \leq n$$

and, if

$$\Delta x_p(k) = -2 \longrightarrow \left[\sum_{j=1}^{n} w_{pj} x_j(k) + \theta_p\right] \leq 0, \quad \text{for} \quad 1 \leq p \leq n$$

Thus, for $\boldsymbol{x}(k+1) \neq \boldsymbol{x}(k)$, one has

$$\left\| \left[\sum_{j=1}^{n} w_{pj} x_j(k) + \theta_p \right] \right\| \geq 0 \qquad (13.58)$$

where the elements of both $\boldsymbol{W}$ and $\boldsymbol{\theta}$ are integers. This inequality implies

$$\Delta E \leq -2w_{pp} \qquad (13.59)$$

and the following corollary is obvious.

Corollary 13.3 *Let the weight matrix* $\boldsymbol{W}$ *have positive diagonal elements. Then*

$$T(\boldsymbol{W}, \boldsymbol{\theta}) \leq \frac{\frac{1}{2}\left[||\boldsymbol{W}|| + 2||\boldsymbol{\theta}|| - \sum_{i=1}^{n} w_{ii} \right]}{\min_p w_{pp}} \qquad (13.60)$$

■

13.3.2.2 Improved Results of Transient Time

When the weight matrix $\boldsymbol{W}$ has at least one zero-diagonal component, the formulation given in Corollary 13.3 fails to provide an estimation of the transient time. It is of interest to develop a new algorithm for the transient time. It is important to note that the definition of the energy function used previously plays a key role in the analysis of the state convergence as well as the transient time for a binary neural network with an asynchronous updating rule. However, since the state convergence of the network is invariant, there is the need to find again a monotonic energy function that is associated with the network under consideration so that a better estimation of the transient time may be found. Floréen (1991) modified the original energy function defined by Hopfield for the network when $\boldsymbol{W}$ and $\boldsymbol{\theta}$ have only integer components. On the basis of this novel energy function, a formulation of transient time is now presented.

Let the weight matrix $\boldsymbol{W}$ be a symmetric integer matrix with nonnegative diagonal elements and $\boldsymbol{\theta}$ be an integer vector. Choose the energy function as

$$\begin{aligned} E(\boldsymbol{x}) &= -\tfrac{1}{2} \sum_{i=1}^{n} \sum_{j=1}^{n} w_{ij} x_i x_j - \sum_{i=1}^{n} (\theta_i + e_i) x_i \\ &= -\tfrac{1}{2} \boldsymbol{x}^T \boldsymbol{W} \boldsymbol{x} - (\boldsymbol{\theta} + \boldsymbol{e})^T \boldsymbol{x} \end{aligned} \qquad (13.61)$$

where

$$\boldsymbol{e} = \begin{bmatrix} e_1 \\ e_2 \\ \vdots \\ e_n \end{bmatrix}$$

and the coefficients e_i are defined as

$$e_i = \begin{cases} 1, & \text{if } \sum_{j=1}^{n} w_{ij} + \theta_i \text{ is even} \\ 0, & \text{otherwise} \end{cases}$$

The last term on the right-hand side of E creates a difference between this novel energy function and the one defined previously. Now, let us study the change of the energy function from time k to time $k+1$ when, in the asynchronous mode, only the pth state is updated at time k and the other states remain unchanged. The difference in the energy function E is given by

$$\begin{aligned} \Delta E(k) &= E(k+1) - E(k) \\ &= -\Delta x_p(k) \left\{ \left[\sum_{j=1}^{n} w_{pj} x_j(k) + \theta_p \right] + e_p \right\} - \tfrac{1}{2}(\Delta x_p(k))^2 w_{pp} \\ &= -\Delta x_p(k) \left[y_p(k) + e_p \right] - \tfrac{1}{2}(\Delta x_p(k))^2 w_{pp} \end{aligned} \tag{13.62}$$

The energy function E is then bounded as follows:

$$E \geq E^{+} \triangleq -\tfrac{1}{2} \sum_{i=1}^{n} \sum_{j=1}^{n} |w_{ij}| - \tfrac{1}{2} \sum_{i=1}^{n} w_{ii} - \sum_{i=1}^{n} (|\theta_i| + |e_i|) \tag{13.63}$$

$$E \leq E^{-} \triangleq \tfrac{1}{2} \sum_{i=1}^{n} \sum_{j=1}^{n} |w_{ij}| - \tfrac{1}{2} \sum_{i=1}^{n} w_{ii} + \sum_{i=1}^{n} (|\theta_i| + |e_i|) \tag{13.64}$$

In view of the operating equation, we know that for $\boldsymbol{x}(k+1) = \boldsymbol{x}(k)$ there are only two choices for Δx_p, namely

$$x_p(k+1) = 1 \quad \text{and} \quad x_p(k) = -1 \Longleftrightarrow \Delta x_p(k) = 2 \tag{13.65}$$

or

$$x_p(k+1) = -1 \quad \text{and} \quad x_p(k) = 1 \Longleftrightarrow \Delta x_p(k) = -2 \tag{13.66}$$

On the other hand, noting the definition of e_i and using Lemma 13.1, one has

$$e_p = 0 \quad \text{and} \quad |y_p(k)| \geq 0 \tag{13.67}$$

which is equivalent to

$$e_p = 0 \quad \text{and} \quad |y_p(k)| \geq 1 \tag{13.68}$$

and using Lemma 13.2, one has

$$e_p = 1 \quad \text{and} \quad y_p(k) < 0 \tag{13.69}$$

which is equivalent to

$$e_p = 1 \quad \text{and} \quad y_p(k) < -2 \tag{13.70}$$

We will examine the following cases to determine a minimum bound of $|\Delta E|$:

(i) If $\Delta x_p(k) = 2$ and $e_p = 1$, we have

$$y_p(k) \geq 0 \tag{13.71}$$

Thus

$$\Delta E \leq -2 - 2w_{pp} \tag{13.72}$$

Note that without the e_p values, this bound would be

$$\Delta E \leq -2w_{pp} \tag{13.73}$$

as used previously.

(ii) If $\Delta x_p(k) = 2$ and $e_p = 0$, we have

$$y_p(k) \geq 1 \tag{13.74}$$

Thus

$$\Delta E \leq -2 - 2w_{pp} \tag{13.75}$$

(iii) If $\Delta x_p = -2$ and $e_p = 1$, we have

$$y_p(k) < -2 \tag{13.76}$$

Thus

$$\Delta E \leq -2 - 2w_{pp} \tag{13.77}$$

(iv) If $\Delta x_p(k) = -2$ and $e_p = 0$, we have

$$y_p(k) \leq -1 \tag{13.78}$$

Thus

$$\Delta E \leq -2 - 2w_{pp} \tag{13.79}$$

Consequently, whenever the state value of the pth neuron changes, the absolute value of the energy decreases at least by an amount of

$$2 + \min_p w_{pp} \tag{13.80}$$

that is

$$\epsilon(\boldsymbol{W}, \boldsymbol{\theta}) \leq 2 + \min_p w_{pp} \tag{13.81}$$

Hence, an estimation of the transient time of the network may then be given by

$$\begin{aligned} T(\boldsymbol{W}, \boldsymbol{\theta}) &\leq \frac{1}{\epsilon(\boldsymbol{W}, \boldsymbol{\theta})}(E^+ - E^-) \\ &\leq \frac{\frac{1}{2}\sum_{i=1}^{n}\sum_{j=1}^{n}|w_{ij}| + \sum_{i=1}^{n}(|\theta_i| + e_i)}{1 + \min_p w_{pp}} \end{aligned} \tag{13.82}$$

Hence, the preceding results can be summarized in the following corollary.

Corollary 13.4 (Floréen 1991) *Let $\boldsymbol{W}$ be a symmetric integer matrix with nonnegative diagonal elements, and $\boldsymbol{\theta}$ be an integer vector. Then, the transient time of the network satisfies*

$$T(\boldsymbol{W}, \boldsymbol{\theta}) \leq \frac{\frac{1}{2}\sum_{i=1}^{n}\sum_{j=1}^{n}|w_{ij}| + \sum_{i=1}^{n}(|\theta_i| + e_i)}{1 + \min_p w_{pp}} \tag{13.83}$$

■

13.4 NEURAL NETWORK IN SYNCHRONOUS MODE OF OPERATION

13.4.1 Neural Network with Symmetric Weight Matrix

13.4.1.1 State Operating Equation

The state of a Hopfield neural network consisting of a symmetric connecting weight matrix $\boldsymbol{W}$ with nonnegative diagonal elements and operating in an asynchronous operating mode always converges to one of the stable equilibrium points. In some neural models there is a central timing pulse, and after each timing pulse a new value of the state is determined simultaneously for all the neural units. This is a *synchronous state* mode of operation. If the operations of the neurons in the Hopfield neural network are synchronously coordinated at each instant with the hard limit nonlinearity (sign function) given in Eqn. (13.17), then the operational equations of the neuron states, as illustrated in Fig. 13.16, may be represented as

$$\begin{aligned} x_i(k+1) &= f\left(\sum_{j=1}^{n} w_{ij}x_j(k) + \theta_i\right) \\ &= f(y_i(k)), \quad i = 1, 2, \ldots, n \end{aligned} \tag{13.84}$$

where

$$y_i = \sum_{j=1}^{n} w_{ij}x_j + \theta_i$$

and

$$f_i(y_i) = \begin{cases} sgn(y_i), & \text{if} \quad y_i \neq 0 \\ x_i, & \text{if} \quad y_i = 0 \end{cases} \tag{13.85}$$

that is

$$f_i(y_i) = \begin{cases} 1, & \text{if} \quad y_i > 0 \\ x_i, & \text{if} \quad y_i = 0 \\ -1, & \text{if} \quad y_i < 0 \end{cases} \tag{13.86}$$

Equation (13.84) may also be rewritten into the following compact form

$$\boldsymbol{x}(k+1) = \boldsymbol{f}(\boldsymbol{W}\boldsymbol{x}(k) + \boldsymbol{\theta}) \tag{13.87}$$

where

$$\boldsymbol{f} \triangleq \begin{bmatrix} f_1 \\ f_2 \\ \vdots \\ f_n \end{bmatrix}$$

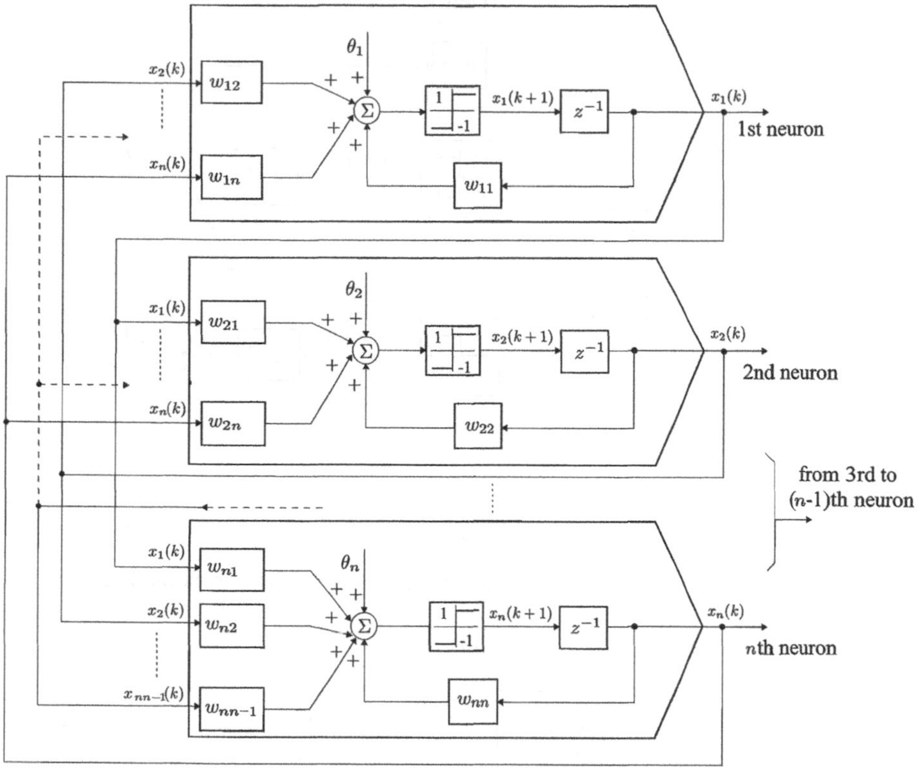

(a) Synchronous operating structure with n neurons

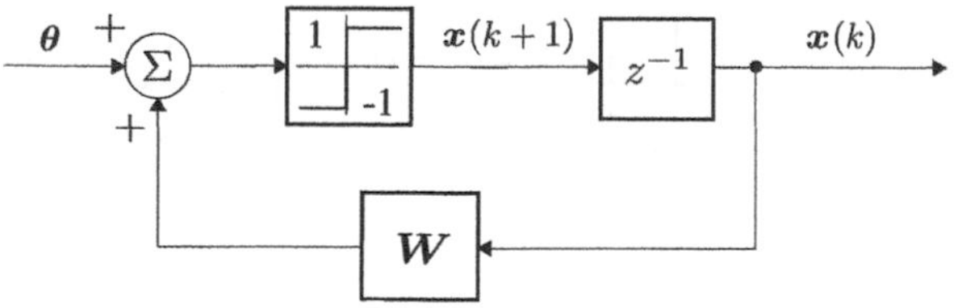

(b) Block diagram of synchronous operating structure of NN

Figure 13.16 Discrete-time Hopfield neural network with synchronous operating structure.

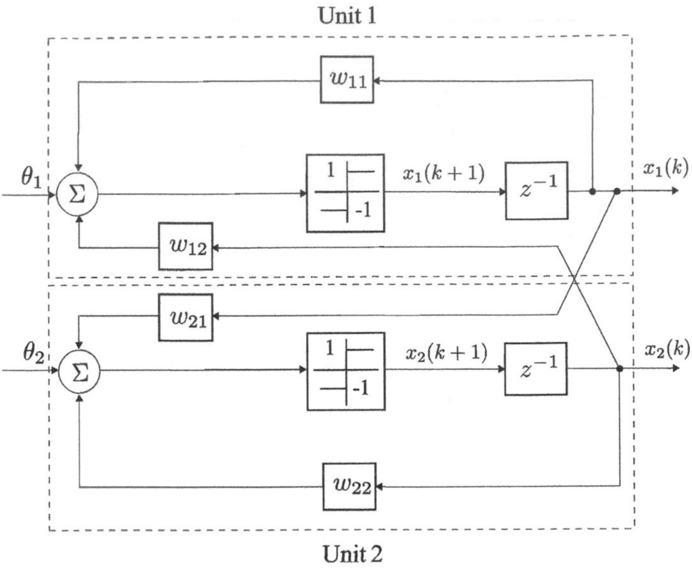

(a) General structure of a two-neuron system in the synchronous mode

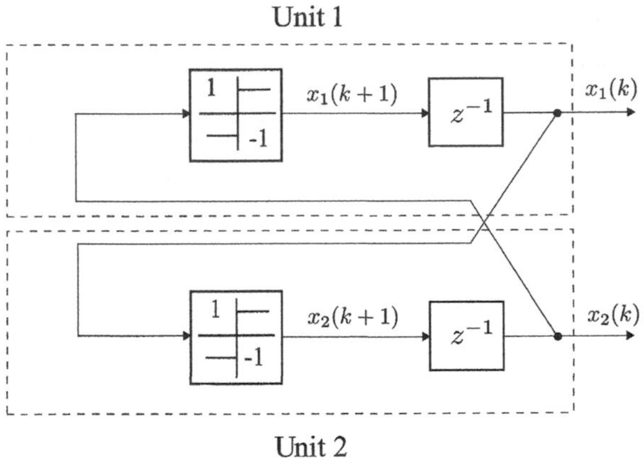

(b) A two-neuron system in the synchronous mode with parameters: $w_{11} = w_{22} = 0, w_{12} = w_{21} = 1, \theta_1 = \theta_2 = 0$

Figure 13.17 Example 13.7: block diagram of a two-neuron system with a synchronous operating mode.

represents the vector-valued activation function of the network, $\boldsymbol{\theta}$ is the threshold vector, and $\boldsymbol{W} = [w_{ij}]_{n\times n}$ is the connecting weight matrix. Equation (13.87) describes a fully parallel operating mode. However, the function E defined earlier is no longer an energy function for the synchronous neural network model in Eqn. (13.87).

The following example shows that the states of the Hopfield neural network with the fully parallel operating mode do not always converge to a set of stable equilibrium states even if the connection weight matrix $\boldsymbol{W}$ is chosen as a symmetric matrix with nonnegative diagonal elements.

Example 13.7 (Synchronous Operation with Symmetric Matrix) A two-neuron system with a synchronous (fully parallel) operation is given in Fig. 13.17. Let the weight matrix be the same one as discussed in Example 13.3:

$$\boldsymbol{W} = \begin{bmatrix} 0 & 1 \\ 1 & 0 \end{bmatrix}$$

When the network is operating in a fully parallel mode, as shown in Figs. 13.17 and 13.18, the state of the system may converge to one of the stable equilibrium states

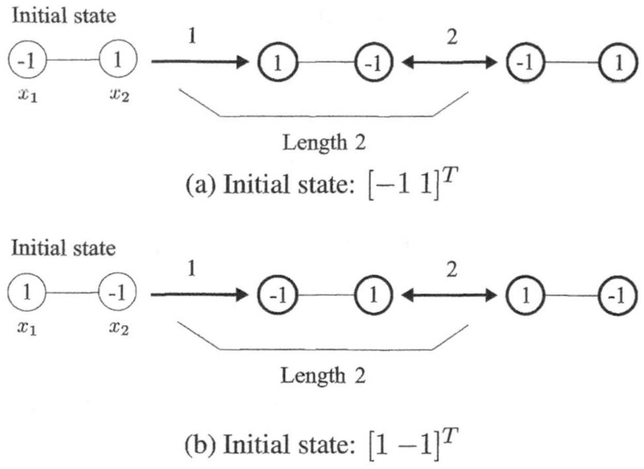

Figure 13.18 Example 13.7: state transfer diagram of a sequence processing of a two-neuron system in a synchronous operation (fully parallel). Here, the network parameters are the same as those given in Fig. 13.17, and the states of the network converge to a periodic sequence of length 2.

$$\text{Stable states:} \quad \left\{ \begin{bmatrix} 1 \\ 1 \end{bmatrix}, \text{ and } \begin{bmatrix} -1 \\ 1 \end{bmatrix} \right\}$$

or one of the periodic cycles

$$\text{Periodic:} \quad \left\{ \begin{bmatrix} -1 \\ 1 \end{bmatrix}, \begin{bmatrix} 1 \\ -1 \end{bmatrix} \right\}$$

and

$$\text{Periodic:} \quad \left\{ \begin{bmatrix} 1 \\ -1 \end{bmatrix}, \begin{bmatrix} -1 \\ 1 \end{bmatrix} \right\}$$

The energy function E is a constant in the cycles. ■

13.4.1.2 Energy Function for Convergence

For instances in which the synaptic weight matrix $\boldsymbol{W}$ is symmetric, an energy function for the neural system in Eqn. (13.84) was presented by Goles et al. (1985) of the following form:

$$\begin{aligned} E(k) &= -\tfrac{1}{2}\sum_{i=1}^{n}\sum_{j=1}^{n} w_{ij}x_i(k)x_j(k-1) - \tfrac{1}{2}\sum_{i=1}^{n}\theta_i[x_i(k) + x_i(k-1)] \\ &= -\tfrac{1}{2}\boldsymbol{x}^T(k)\boldsymbol{W}\boldsymbol{x}(k-1) - \tfrac{1}{2}\boldsymbol{\theta}^T(\boldsymbol{x}(k) + \boldsymbol{x}(k-1)) \end{aligned} \tag{13.88}$$

For the evaluation of the function E, one may have

$$\begin{aligned} \Delta E(k) &= E(k+1) - E(k) \\ &= \left[-\tfrac{1}{2}\boldsymbol{x}^T(k+1)\boldsymbol{W}\boldsymbol{x}(k) - \tfrac{1}{2}\boldsymbol{\theta}^T(\boldsymbol{x}(k+1) + \boldsymbol{x}(k))\right] \\ &\quad + \left[\tfrac{1}{2}\boldsymbol{x}^T(k)\boldsymbol{W}\boldsymbol{x}(k-1) + \tfrac{1}{2}\boldsymbol{\theta}^T(\boldsymbol{x}(k) + \boldsymbol{x}(k-1))\right] \\ &= -\tfrac{1}{2}[\boldsymbol{x}(k+1) - \boldsymbol{x}(k-1)]^T[\boldsymbol{W}\boldsymbol{x}(k) + \boldsymbol{\theta}] \end{aligned} \tag{13.89}$$

Using the synchronous operational equation, the following relationships may be derived:

$$[\boldsymbol{x}(k+1) - \boldsymbol{x}(k-1)] > 0 \longrightarrow \boldsymbol{x}(k+1) > 0 \longrightarrow [\boldsymbol{W}\boldsymbol{x}(k) + \boldsymbol{\theta}] > 0 \tag{13.90}$$

$$[\boldsymbol{x}(k+1) - \boldsymbol{x}(k-1)] < 0 \longrightarrow \boldsymbol{x}(k+1) < 0 \longrightarrow [\boldsymbol{W}\boldsymbol{x}(k) + \boldsymbol{\theta}] < 0 \tag{13.91}$$

Hence

$$\boldsymbol{x}(k+1) \neq \boldsymbol{x}(k-1) \longrightarrow \Delta E(k) < 0$$

Furthermore

$$\Delta E(k) = 0 \longrightarrow \boldsymbol{x}(k+1) = \boldsymbol{x}(k-1) \tag{13.92}$$

or

$$\begin{aligned}\Delta E(k) = 0 \quad &\longrightarrow \quad [\boldsymbol{W}\boldsymbol{x} + \boldsymbol{\theta}] = 0 \\ &\longrightarrow \quad \boldsymbol{x}(k+1) = \boldsymbol{x}(k)\end{aligned} \tag{13.93}$$

Thus, $\Delta E(k) \leq 0$, and the state of the system with the synchronous (fully parallel) operating mode always converges to either a stable equilibrium state or a periodic sequence of length 2. It is also seen that

$$-\tfrac{1}{2}\sum_{i=1}^{n}\sum_{j=1}^{n}|w_{ij}| - \sum_{i=1}^{n}|\theta_i| \leq E(k) \leq \tfrac{1}{2}\sum_{i=1}^{n}\sum_{j=1}^{n}|w_{ij}| + \sum_{i=1}^{n}|\theta_i|$$

These results may be summarized in the following theorem.

Theorem 13.3 (Convergence Theorem for Synchronous Operating Neural Network) *Let the weight matrix* $\mathbf{W}$ *be symmetric. The Hopfield neural network with a synchronous operating mode is such that*

(i) $\forall k,\ \boldsymbol{x}(k+1) \neq \boldsymbol{x}(k-1) \longrightarrow E(k+1) < E(k)$

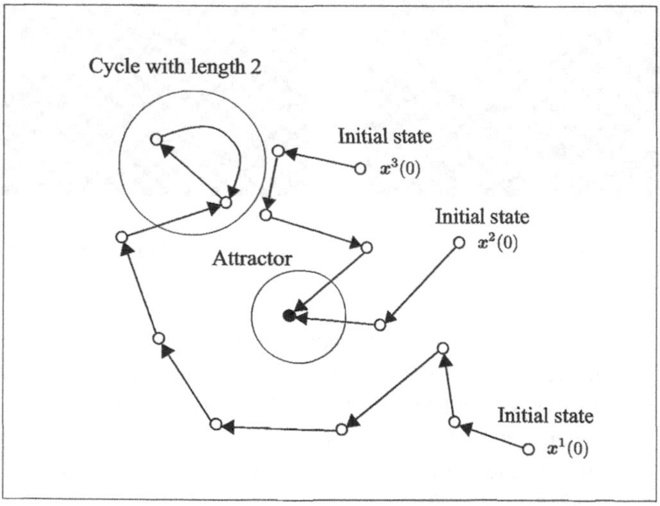

Figure 13.19 Schematic representation of a state transient process of a neural network in a synchronous operating mode. Trajectory with initial state $\boldsymbol{x}^1(0)$ results in a periodic cycle with length 2, and trajectories with initial states $\boldsymbol{x}^2(0)$ and $\boldsymbol{x}^3(0)$ converge to a stable attractor.

(a) $k = 0$

(b) $k = 86$

(c) $k = 87$

(d) $k = 88$

Figure 13.20 Example 13.8: state bitmaps of a synchronous network with 40×40 neural units. Elements of a symmetric and zero-diagonal weight matrix $\boldsymbol{W}$ and initial state values are chosen randomly from the binary set $\{-1, 1\}$. The convergence time of the network from the initial state in (a) at $k = 0$ to a cycle of length 2 as illustrated in (c) and (d) is $k = 86$.

(ii) The system has either a stable equilibrium state or a periodic sequences of length 2:

$$P(\boldsymbol{W}, \boldsymbol{\theta}) \leq 2$$

(iii) The transient length satisfies

$$T(\boldsymbol{W}, \boldsymbol{\theta}) \leq \frac{1}{\epsilon(\boldsymbol{W}, \boldsymbol{\theta})}[||\boldsymbol{W}|| + 2||\boldsymbol{\theta}||] \tag{13.94}$$

where

$$\epsilon(\boldsymbol{W}, \boldsymbol{\theta}) = \min\left\{|E(k+1) - E(k)| : \begin{array}{l} \boldsymbol{x}(k+1) \neq \boldsymbol{x}(k) \\ \boldsymbol{x}(k+1) \neq \boldsymbol{x}(k-1) \end{array}\right\}$$

■

The results of this theorem are illustrated in Fig. 13.19. Note that the trajectory with the initial state $\boldsymbol{x}^1(0)$ results in a periodic cycle of length 2, while the trajectories with the initial states $\boldsymbol{x}^2(0)$ and $\boldsymbol{x}^3(0)$ converge to a stable attractor.

Example 13.8 (Synchronous Network with 40×40 Neural Units) Consider a synchronous network with $40 \times 40 = 1600$ neural units. Let a (1600×1600)-dimensional weight matrix be symmetric and have a zero-diagonal component. The elements of the weight matrix are selected randomly from the binary set $\{-1, 1\}$. As shown in Fig. 13.20, from an initial 1600-dimensional binary

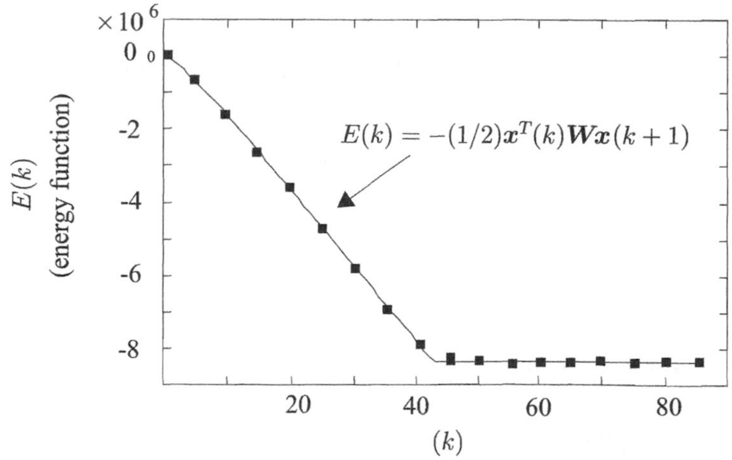

Figure 13.21 Example 13.8: the energy curve of the network described in Fig. 13.20 during the synchronous state updating.

state vector selected randomly, the network state converges to a periodic cycle of length 2 after 86 fully parallel iterations according to the network equation defined by Eqn. (13.86). The energy function $E(k)$ in Eqn. (13.88), illustrated in Fig. 13.21 decreases during such an iterative procedure and finally reaches its minimum value. ■

13.4.2 Neural Network with Skew–Symmetric Weight Matrix

An interesting case considered by Goles (1986) is a synaptic weight matrix in the neural system given in Eqn. (13.84), having a skew–symmetric form with zero-diagonal elements

$$\boldsymbol{W} = -\boldsymbol{W}^T \tag{13.95}$$

and a zero threshold vector. In this case, the neural system equation, Eqn. (13.84), can be simplified to

$$\boldsymbol{x}(k+1) = \boldsymbol{f}(\boldsymbol{W}\boldsymbol{x}(k)) = -\boldsymbol{f}(\boldsymbol{W}^T\boldsymbol{x}(k)) \tag{13.96}$$

where the vector-valued function $\boldsymbol{f}$ is defined by Eqn. (13.85). Furthermore, we shall assume that the weight matrix $\boldsymbol{W}$ satisfies

$$\sum_{j=1}^{n} w_{ij}x_j \neq 0, \quad \forall i \in \{1, \ldots, n\}, \quad \forall \boldsymbol{x} \in \{-1, 1\}^n$$

that is

$$\boldsymbol{W}\boldsymbol{x} \neq 0, \quad \forall \boldsymbol{x} \in \{-1, 1\}^n$$

Because of the skew–symmetry of $\boldsymbol{W}$, this condition is equivalent to

$$\sum_{i=1}^{n} w_{ij}x_i \neq 0, \quad \forall j \in \{1, \ldots, n\}, \quad \forall \boldsymbol{x} \in \{-1, 1\}^n$$

That is

$$\boldsymbol{W}^T\boldsymbol{x} \neq 0, \quad \forall \boldsymbol{x} \in \{-1, 1\}^n$$

In this case, the energy function is defined as

$$\begin{aligned} E(k) &= -\tfrac{1}{2}\sum_{j=1}^{n}\sum_{i=1}^{n} w_{ij}x_j(k)x_i(k-1) \\ &= -\tfrac{1}{2}\boldsymbol{x}^T(k)\boldsymbol{W}\boldsymbol{x}(k-1) \end{aligned} \tag{13.97}$$

Since $\boldsymbol{W}$ is skew–symmetric, we have

$$\begin{aligned}\Delta E(k) &= E(k+1) - E(k) \\ &= -\tfrac{1}{2}\boldsymbol{x}^T(k+1)\boldsymbol{W}\boldsymbol{x}(k) + \tfrac{1}{2}\boldsymbol{x}^T(k)\boldsymbol{W}\boldsymbol{x}(k-1)\end{aligned}$$

Since $\boldsymbol{W}^T = -\boldsymbol{W}$, we have

$$\begin{aligned}\Delta E(k) &= -\tfrac{1}{2}\boldsymbol{x}^T(k+1)\boldsymbol{W}\boldsymbol{x}(k) - \tfrac{1}{2}\boldsymbol{x}^T(k-1)\boldsymbol{W}\boldsymbol{x}(k) \\ &= -\tfrac{1}{2}[\boldsymbol{x}(k+1) + \boldsymbol{x}(k-1)]^T\boldsymbol{W}\boldsymbol{x}(k) \qquad (13.98)\end{aligned}$$

Hence

$$\text{If} \quad \boldsymbol{x}(k+1)+\boldsymbol{x}(k-1) > 0 \longrightarrow \boldsymbol{x}(k+1) > 0 \longrightarrow \boldsymbol{W}\boldsymbol{x}(k) > 0 \qquad (13.99)$$

$$\text{If} \quad \boldsymbol{x}(k+1)+\boldsymbol{x}(k-1) < 0 \longrightarrow \boldsymbol{x}(k+1) < 0 \longrightarrow \boldsymbol{W}\boldsymbol{x}(k) < 0 \qquad (13.100)$$

That is

$$\Delta E(k) < 0, \quad \text{iff} \quad \boldsymbol{x}(k+1) \neq -\boldsymbol{x}(k-1) \qquad (13.101)$$

and

$$\Delta E(k) = 0, \quad \text{iff} \quad \boldsymbol{x}(k+1) = -\boldsymbol{x}(k-1) \qquad (13.102)$$

Hence, it is concluded that in the steady state the energy is constant and the only possible period is 4; that is

$$\boldsymbol{x}(k+4) = \boldsymbol{x}(k), \quad \text{for any} \quad k \geq q$$

where q is a transient length. The state of the network will converge to a cycle of length 4 for such a choice of the network parameters.

Example 13.9 (Synchronous Mode Operation with Skew–Symmetric Weight Matrix) Consider a two-neuron system with the skew–symmetric weight matrix

$$\boldsymbol{W} = \begin{bmatrix} 0 & -1 \\ 1 & 0 \end{bmatrix}$$

where the threshold $\boldsymbol{\theta}$ is the zero vector. The block diagram of the network is depicted in Fig. 13.22. It can be verified that when the network is operating in a synchronous (fully parallel) mode, there are no stable states and the set of the states

$$\left\{ \begin{bmatrix} -1 \\ 1 \end{bmatrix}, \begin{bmatrix} -1 \\ -1 \end{bmatrix}, \begin{bmatrix} 1 \\ -1 \end{bmatrix}, \begin{bmatrix} 1 \\ 1 \end{bmatrix} \right\}$$

results in a cyclic process with the period 4 as illustrated in Fig. 13.23. ■

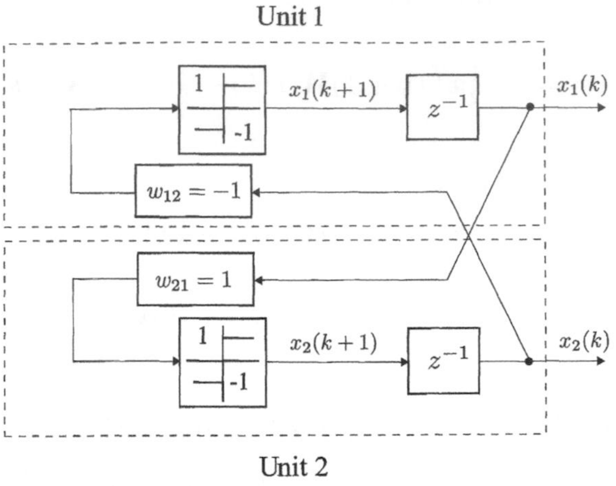

Figure 13.22 Example 13.9: block diagram of a two-neuron system operating in a synchronous mode with a skew–symmetric weight matrix. The neural network parameters of the network are $w_{11} = w_{22} = 0$, $w_{12} = -1$, $w_{21} = 1$, and $\theta_1 = \theta_2 = 0$.

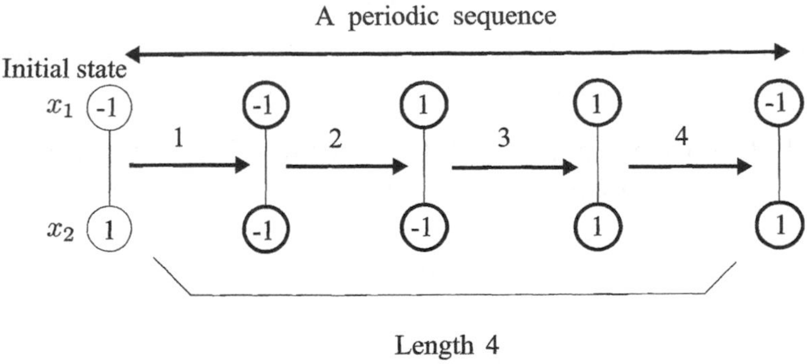

Figure 13.23 Example 13.9: state transfer diagram of a sequence operating processing of a two-neuron system with a skew–symmetric weight matrix operating in a synchronous mode. The network parameters are $w_{11} = w_{22} = 0$, $w_{12} = -1$, $w_{21} = 1$, $\theta_1 = \theta_2 = 0$. The states of the network converge to a periodic sequence with length 4.

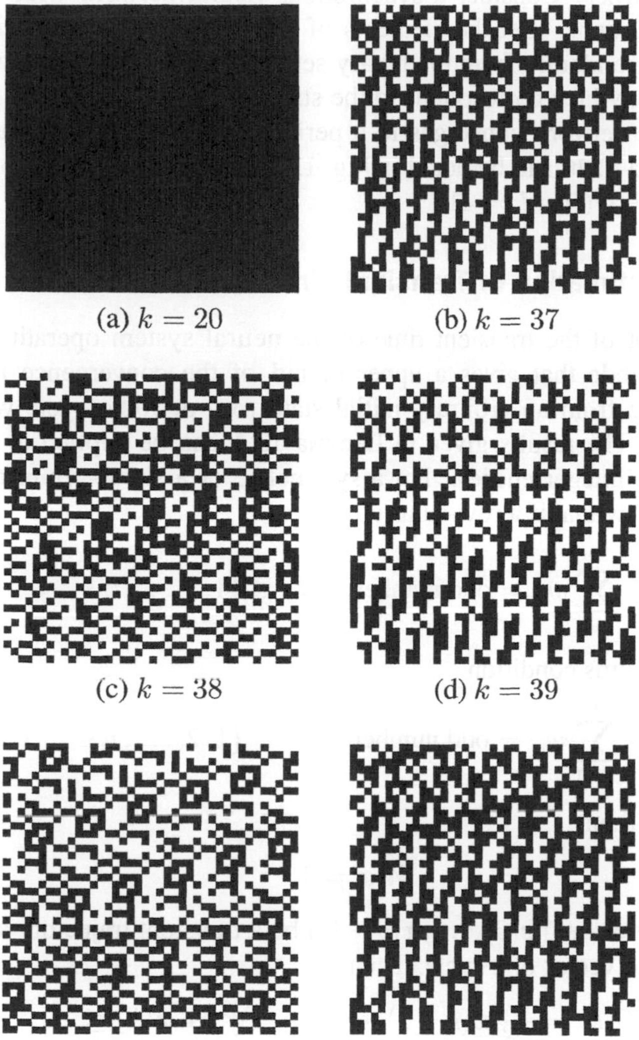

(a) $k = 20$ (b) $k = 37$

(c) $k = 38$ (d) $k = 39$

(e) $k = 40$ (f) $k = 41$

Figure 13.24 Example 13.10: state bitmaps of a synchronous network with $40 \times 40 = 1600$ neural units. The elements of the skew–symmetric weight matrix are chosen randomly from $\{-1, 1\}$. All the selected initial state values are 1. The convergence times of the network from the initial state described in (a) to the final state as shown in (b) is $k = 37$. This state is a periodic cycle of length 4 as shown in panels (b)–(f).

Example 13.10 (Synchronous Mode Operation with 40×40 Skew–Symmetric Weight Matrix) Consider a synchronous neural network with $40 \times 40 = 1600$ neural units. Let the elements of the skew–symmetric weight matrix be selected randomly from the binary set $\{-1, 1\}$. If all the initial states are chosen as 1, which corresponds to the state bit map given in Fig. 13.24a, the state of the network converges to a periodic cycle of length 4 as shown in Figs. 13.24b–f. It is to be noted in Fig. 13.24 that the pattern in (b) at $k = 37$ repeats pattern (f) at $k = 41$. ■

13.4.3 Estimation of Transient Time

The concept of the transient time of the neural system operating in a synchronous mode that gives a upper bound of the convergence time of the system state from an arbitrary initial state to a periodic cycle will now be addressed. The results given in Lemma 13.1 can be applied to any $n \times n$ matrix with integer entries. For a symmetric or a skew–symmetric matrix, one may show that if a row-sums condition

$$\sum_{i=1}^{n} w_{ij} = \text{odd number}, \quad \forall j \in \{1, 2, \ldots, n\} \tag{13.103}$$

or column-sums condition

$$\sum_{j=1}^{n} w_{ij} = \text{odd number}, \quad \forall i \in \{1, 2, \ldots, n\} \tag{13.104}$$

is satisfied, then

$$\boldsymbol{W}\boldsymbol{x} \neq 0$$

is always true. Let $(\boldsymbol{x}(0), \ldots, \boldsymbol{x}(q-1))$ be a transient trajectory and $\boldsymbol{x}(q)$ be the first state vector of a cycle. Then

$$\Delta E(k) = -\tfrac{1}{2}[\boldsymbol{x}(k+1) + \boldsymbol{x}(k-1)]^T \boldsymbol{W}\boldsymbol{x}(k) \leq -1$$

and

$$-\tfrac{1}{2}||\boldsymbol{W}|| \leq E(k) \leq 0, \quad \text{for any} \quad k \in (1, 2, \ldots, q-1)$$

Hence

$$-\tfrac{1}{2}||\boldsymbol{W}|| \leq E(k) \leq -(k-1), \quad \text{for any} \quad k \in (1, 2, \ldots, q-1)$$

Furthermore, since $\boldsymbol{x}(q)$ is the first state vector belonging to a periodic cycle, one obtains

$$-\tfrac{1}{2}||\boldsymbol{W}|| + 2 \leq E(q-1) \leq -(q-2)$$

Hence

$$q \leq \tfrac{1}{2}||\boldsymbol{W}||$$

We summarize these results in the following theorem.

Theorem 13.4 (Goles 1986) *Let $\boldsymbol{W}$ be a skew–symmetric matrix with integer entries and all row sums or all column sums are odd. Then the transient length $T(\boldsymbol{W})$ of the system in Eqn. (13.96) is bounded by*

$$T(\boldsymbol{W}) \leq \tfrac{1}{2}||\boldsymbol{W}||, \quad \textit{where} \quad ||\boldsymbol{W}|| = \sum_{i=1}^{n}\sum_{j=1}^{n} |w_{ij}| \qquad \blacksquare$$

13.5 BLOCK SEQUENTIAL OPERATION OF THE HOPFIELD NEURAL NETWORK

As seen in the previous sections, the convergence properties of the two-state discrete-time Hopfield neural network are dependent on the structure of the weight matrix $\boldsymbol{W}$ and the method by which the states of the units are updated. When an asynchronous (serial) operating mode is employed, the state of the Hopfield neural network that has a symmetric weight matrix with nonnegative diagonal elements will always converge to one of its stable equilibrium states regardless of the position of the initial states. However, the stable equilibrium points of the target must have an attracting region in which the initial state is located. When a synchronous (parallel) operating mode is used, the Hopfield neural network with a symmetric weight matrix converges to either one stable equilibrium state or a periodic sequence of length (period) 2, and the state of the Hopfield neural network with a skew–symmetric converges to a periodic sequence with length 4.

The operating mode considered in this section is a *block sequential* (BS) operating mode for the Hopfield neural network. It is a state updating process by which some of the units are fired simultaneously and the others are in the rest state at each operating time. The block sequential operating mode may be considered as a generalization of both the asynchronous and synchronous operating modes discussed in the previous sections.

13.5.1 State Updating with Ordered Partition

A partition $(N_\ell)_{\ell=1,\ldots,p}$ of the integer set $\{1,\ldots,n\}$ must satisfy

$$\{1,\ldots,n\} = N_1 \bigcup \cdots \bigcup N_p$$

where the elements of N_ℓ ($\ell = 1, \ldots, p$) are the integers between 1 and n. For example, a partition of the integer set $\{1, 2, \ldots, 10\}$ may be given as

$$N_1 = \{1, 2, 3\}, \quad N_2 = \{4, 3, 6, 5\}, \quad N_3 = \{7, 9, 8, 10\}$$

An *ordered partition* of the integer set $\{1, \ldots, n\}$ is a partition $(N_\ell)_{\ell=1,\ldots,p}$ such that

$$\forall m_1 \in N_{i_1} \quad \text{and} \quad \forall m_2 \in N_{i_2}$$

implies

$$i_1 < i_2 \longrightarrow m_1 < m_2$$

For example, an ordered partition of the integer set $\{1, 2, \ldots, 10\}$ is

$$N_1 = \{1, 2, 3\}, \quad N_2 = \{4, 5, 6\}, \quad N_3 = \{7, 8, 9, 10\}$$

Let a known *ordered partition* of the integer set $\{1, \ldots, n\}$ be $(N_\ell)_{\ell=1,\ldots,p}$. The block sequential (BS) operation of the Hopfield neural network associated with the ordered partition $(N_\ell)_{\ell=1,\ldots,p}$ assumes that only the units belonging to the set N_ℓ are fired at time k. Hence, the state updating equations for the BS operation may be expressed as

$$x_i(k+1) = \begin{cases} sgn\left(\sum_{j=1}^{n} w_{ij} x_j(k) + \theta_i\right), & \text{if} \quad i \in N_\ell \\ \\ x_i(k), & \text{otherwise} \end{cases}$$

Furthermore, let

$$n_\ell = \text{element number of } N_\ell$$

which satisfies

$$n = \sum_{s=1}^{p} n_s$$

and the ordered partition expressions for the state vector $\boldsymbol{x}$, weight matrix $\boldsymbol{W}$, and threshold vector $\boldsymbol{\theta}$ may be expressed as

$$\boldsymbol{x}^T = \begin{bmatrix} \boldsymbol{x}_1^T \\ \boldsymbol{x}_2^T \\ \vdots \\ \boldsymbol{x}_\ell^T \\ \vdots \\ \boldsymbol{x}_p \end{bmatrix}, \quad \text{with } \boldsymbol{x}_\ell \in \Re^{N_\ell}$$

$$\boldsymbol{\theta}^T = \begin{bmatrix} \boldsymbol{\theta}_1^T \\ \boldsymbol{\theta}_2^T \\ \vdots \\ \boldsymbol{\theta}_\ell^T \\ \vdots \\ \boldsymbol{\theta}_p^T \end{bmatrix}, \quad \text{with } \boldsymbol{\theta}_\ell \in \Re^{N_\ell}$$

$$\boldsymbol{W} = \begin{bmatrix} \boldsymbol{W}_{11} & \cdots & \boldsymbol{W}_{1p} \\ \boldsymbol{W}_{21} & \cdots & \boldsymbol{W}_{2p} \\ \vdots & \ddots & \vdots \\ \boldsymbol{W}_{p1} & \cdots & \boldsymbol{W}_{pp} \end{bmatrix}, \quad \text{with } \boldsymbol{W}_{rs} \in \Re^{N_r \times N_s}$$

Then, the operating equation can be rewritten in the following vector form

$$\boldsymbol{x}_r(k+1) = \begin{cases} \boldsymbol{sgn}\left(\sum_{s=1}^{p} \boldsymbol{W}_{rs}\boldsymbol{x}_s(k) + \boldsymbol{\theta}_r\right), & \text{if} \quad r = \ell \\ \boldsymbol{x}_r(k), & \text{if} \quad r \neq \ell \end{cases} \tag{13.105}$$

where ℓ represents the units belonging to the ordered partition N_ℓ that are fired at the time k, and vector-valued function $\boldsymbol{sgn}(.)$ is defined by

$$\boldsymbol{sgn}(.) = \begin{bmatrix} sgn(.) \\ sgn(.) \\ \vdots \\ sgn(.) \end{bmatrix}$$

Particular cases of the block sequential operation discussed above that correspond to particular choices of the partition may be expressed as follows:

(i) When the partition is

$$N_\ell = \ell, \quad \text{and} \quad \ell = 1, 2 \ldots, n$$

that is, $(\{\ell\})_{\ell=1,\ldots,n}$, the BS operation mode becomes as an asynchronous operation mode for the Hopfield neural network. This case was discussed in Section 13.2;

(ii) When the partition is trivially reduced to

$$N_\ell = \{1, 2, \ldots, n\}, \quad \text{and} \quad \ell = 1$$

that is, the unique integer set $\{1, 2, \ldots, n\}$, the BS operation becomes the synchronous operation mode of the Hopfield neural network, which was studied extensively in Section 13.4.

As pointed out previously, since $\{-1,1\}^n$ is a finite set, the possible states of the system are 2^n, and all the trajectories $(\boldsymbol{x}(k))_{k\geq 0}$ of any block sequential (BS) operating mode are ultimately periodic. It is obvious that, for a given weight matrix $\boldsymbol{W}$ and threshold $\boldsymbol{\theta}$, the different block sequential operation, or different ordered partitions of the integer set $\{1,2,\ldots,n\}$, have the same stable equilibrium points, but they may have different periodic sequences.

13.5.2 Guaranteed Convergence Results for Block Sequential Operation

The energy function approach is still used to deal with the state convergence properties of the block sequential operating neural network. In this case, an energy function at time k is defined as

$$E(k) = -\tfrac{1}{2}\sum_{i=1}^{n}\sum_{j=1}^{n} w_{ij}x_i(k)x_j(k) - \sum_{i=1}^{n}\theta_i x_i(k)$$

which, for the block sequential form, can be written as

$$E(k) = -\tfrac{1}{2}\sum_{s=1}^{p}\sum_{r=1}^{p} \boldsymbol{x}_s^T(k)\boldsymbol{W}_{sr}\boldsymbol{x}_r(k) - \sum_{s=1}^{p}\boldsymbol{\theta}_s^T\boldsymbol{x}_s(k) \qquad (13.106)$$

Let the units belonging to the partition N_ℓ be fired at time k, and the state vector at time k

$$\boldsymbol{x}(k) = \begin{bmatrix} \boldsymbol{x}_1(k) \\ \boldsymbol{x}_2(k) \\ \vdots \\ \boldsymbol{x}_\ell(k) \\ \vdots \\ \boldsymbol{x}_p(k) \end{bmatrix}$$

changes to a new state vector at time $(k+1)$

$$\boldsymbol{x}(k+1) = \begin{bmatrix} \boldsymbol{x}_1(k) \\ \boldsymbol{x}_2(k) \\ \vdots \\ \boldsymbol{x}_{\ell-1}(k) \\ \boldsymbol{x}_\ell(k) + \Delta\boldsymbol{x}_\ell(k) \\ \boldsymbol{x}_{\ell+1}(k) \\ \vdots \\ \boldsymbol{x}_p(k) \end{bmatrix}$$

where

$$\Delta \boldsymbol{x}_\ell(k) = \boldsymbol{x}_\ell(k+1) - \boldsymbol{x}_\ell(k) \tag{13.107}$$

Let the weight matrix $\boldsymbol{W}$ be symmetric, that is

$$\boldsymbol{W}_{sr} = \boldsymbol{W}_{rs}^T, \quad \text{for all} \quad 1 \leq s, r \leq p$$

and all matrices $\boldsymbol{W}_{\ell\ell}$ ($\ell = 1, \ldots, p$) be nonnegative definite. Then, the increment of the energy function $E(k)$ at time k can be evaluated as follows:

$$\begin{aligned}
\Delta E(k) &= E(k+1) - E(k) \\
&= -\tfrac{1}{2} \sum_{s=1}^{p} \boldsymbol{x}_s^T(k) \boldsymbol{W}_{s\ell} \Delta \boldsymbol{x}_\ell(k) \\
&\quad - \tfrac{1}{2} \sum_{s=1}^{p} \Delta \boldsymbol{x}_\ell^T(k) \boldsymbol{W}_{s\ell} \boldsymbol{x}_s(k) - \boldsymbol{\theta}_\ell^T \Delta \boldsymbol{x}_\ell(k) \\
&= -\Delta \boldsymbol{x}_\ell^T(k) \left[\sum_{s=1}^{p} \boldsymbol{W}_{\ell s} \boldsymbol{x}_s(k) + \boldsymbol{\theta}_\ell \right] - \Delta \boldsymbol{x}_\ell^T(k) \boldsymbol{W}_{\ell\ell} \Delta \boldsymbol{x}_\ell(k)
\end{aligned} \tag{13.108}$$

Since the matrix $\boldsymbol{W}_{\ell\ell}$ is nonnegative definite, this implies that

$$\Delta \boldsymbol{x}_\ell^T(k) \boldsymbol{W}_{\ell\ell} \Delta \boldsymbol{x}_\ell(k) \geq 0$$

Applying the same analysis procedure as used in Section 13.1, one may conclude that

$$\Delta \boldsymbol{x}_\ell \neq 0, \quad \text{or} \quad \boldsymbol{x}_\ell(k+1) \neq \boldsymbol{x}_\ell(k) \quad \longrightarrow \quad \Delta E(k) < 0$$

and

$$\Delta E(k) = 0, \quad \longleftrightarrow \quad \Delta \boldsymbol{x}_\ell(k) = 0$$

The results of this analysis can be summarized in the following theorem.

Theorem 13.5 *Let the weight matrix* $\boldsymbol{W}$ *be symmetric and for any ordered partition* $(N_\ell)_{\ell=1,\ldots,n}$ *of the integer set* $\{1, 2, \ldots, n\}$ *the matrices* $\boldsymbol{W}_{\ell\ell}$ *be nonnegative-definite. Then, the Hopfield neural network with a block sequential operating mode associated with the partition* $(N_\ell)_{\ell=1,\ldots,n}$ *is such that* *(i)* $\forall k,\ \boldsymbol{x}(k+1) \neq \boldsymbol{x}(k) \longrightarrow E(\boldsymbol{x}(k+1)) < E(\boldsymbol{x}(k))$

(ii) The system has only stable equilibrium states:

$$P(\boldsymbol{W}, \boldsymbol{\theta}) = 1$$

(iii) The transient length satisfies

$$T(\boldsymbol{W}, \boldsymbol{\theta}) \leq \frac{1}{\epsilon(\boldsymbol{W}, \boldsymbol{\theta})} \left[||\boldsymbol{W}|| + 2||\boldsymbol{\theta}|| - \sum_{i=1}^{n} w_{ii} \right] \tag{13.109}$$

where

$$\epsilon(\boldsymbol{W}, \boldsymbol{\theta}) = \min\{|E(k+1) - E(k)| : \boldsymbol{x}(k) \neq \boldsymbol{x}(k+1)\} \qquad \blacksquare$$

Example 13.11 (Block Sequential Operating Mode with Three Neurons) Consider a three-neuron system with the following weight matrix and threshold vector:

$$\boldsymbol{W} = \begin{bmatrix} 0 & -1 & 1 \\ -1 & 0 & 1 \\ 1 & 1 & 0 \end{bmatrix}, \quad \text{and} \quad \boldsymbol{\theta} = \begin{bmatrix} 1 \\ -1 \\ 2 \end{bmatrix}$$

Let $\{N_1, N_2\}$ be a partition of the integer set $\{1, 2, 3\}$ and the neurons belonging to N_ℓ $(1 \leq \ell \leq 2)$ be fired at time k. Then, the updating equation may be represented as

$$x_i(k+1) = \begin{cases} sgn(y_i), & \text{if} \quad i \in N_\ell \\ x_i(k), & \text{otherwise} \end{cases}$$

where

$$\begin{cases} y_1(k) & = & sgn(-x_2(k) + x_3(k) + 1) \\ y_2(k) & = & sgn(-x_1(k) + x_3(k) - 1) \\ y_3(k) & = & sgn(x_1(k) + x_2(k) + 2) \end{cases}$$

The energy function E given in Eqn. (13.106) is obtained as

$$E(x) = x_1x_2 - x_1x_3 - x_2x_3 - x_1 + x_2 - 2x_3$$

This neural system has $2^3 = 8$ states, and the values of the energy function E at these possible states are as follows:

$$\begin{array}{lcr} E([-1 \;\; -1 \;\; -1]^T) & = & 1 \\ E([-1 \;\; -1 \;\; 1]^T) & = & 1 \\ E([-1 \;\; 1 \;\; -1]^T) & = & 3 \\ E([-1 \;\; 1 \;\; 1]^T) & = & -1 \\ E([1 \;\; -1 \;\; -1]^T) & = & -1 \\ E([1 \;\; -1 \;\; 1]^T) & = & -5 \\ E([1 \;\; 1 \;\; -1]^T) & = & 5 \\ E([1 \;\; 1 \;\; 1]^T) & = & -3 \end{array}$$

Thus, the neural system has the least energy function $E([1 \;\; -1 \;\; 1]^T) = -5$, and it has a unique stable equilibrium state

$$\boldsymbol{x}^* = \begin{bmatrix} 1 \\ -1 \\ 1 \end{bmatrix}$$

Two sets of ordered partitions of the integer set $\{1, 2, 3\}$ are selected as

$$P_1 : N_1 = \{1, 2\}, \quad \text{and} \quad N_2 = \{3\} \tag{13.110}$$

$$P_2 : N_1 = \{1\}, \quad \text{and} \quad N_2 = \{2, 3\} \tag{13.111}$$

For the following eight possible initial states

$$\begin{bmatrix} -1 \\ -1 \\ -1 \end{bmatrix}, \begin{bmatrix} -1 \\ -1 \\ 1 \end{bmatrix}, \begin{bmatrix} -1 \\ 1 \\ -1 \end{bmatrix}, \begin{bmatrix} -1 \\ 1 \\ 1 \end{bmatrix}$$

$$\begin{bmatrix} 1 \\ -1 \\ -1 \end{bmatrix}, \begin{bmatrix} 1 \\ -1 \\ 1 \end{bmatrix}, \begin{bmatrix} 1 \\ 1 \\ -1 \end{bmatrix}, \begin{bmatrix} 1 \\ 1 \\ 1 \end{bmatrix}$$

the transient processes of the Hopfield network with the BS operating mode that are, respectively, associated with the ordered partition P_1 in Eqn. (13.110) and the ordered partition P_2 in Eqn. (13.111) are shown in Fig. 13.25. It is evident that because of the different choices of the partition, even if the transient processes of the neural system state from the initial point to the stable equilibrium point are different, each state still converges to the same stable equilibrium point $[1 \;\; -1 \;\; 1]^T$. ■

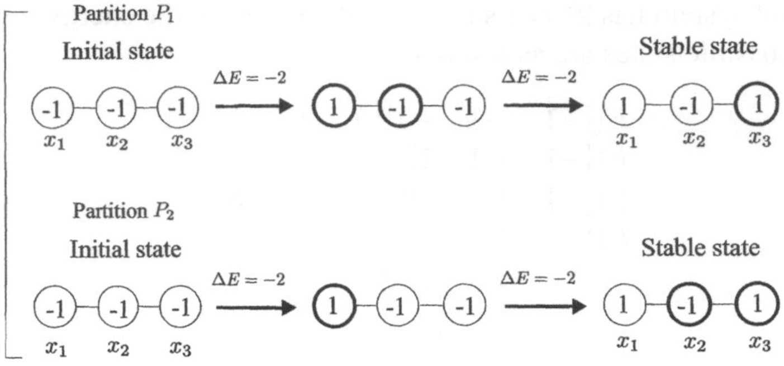

(a)

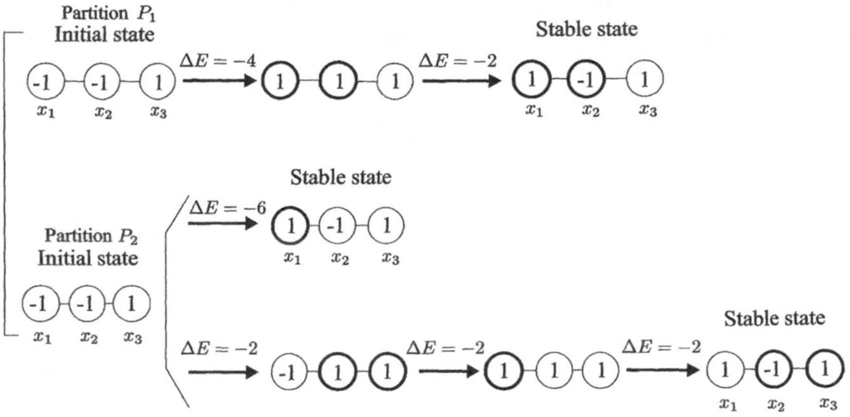

(b)

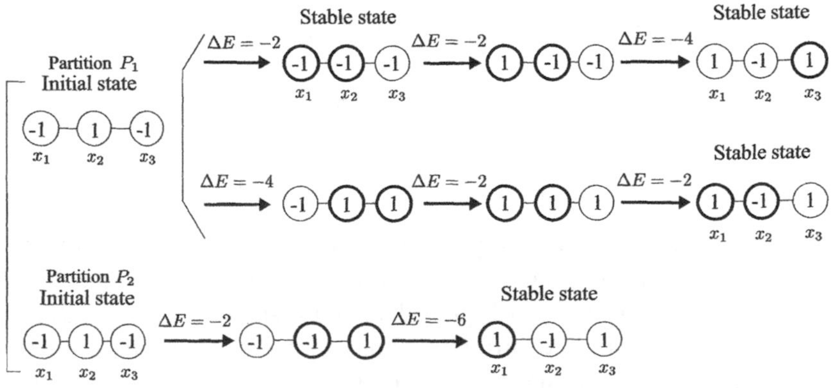

(c)

Figure 13.25 (Continued)

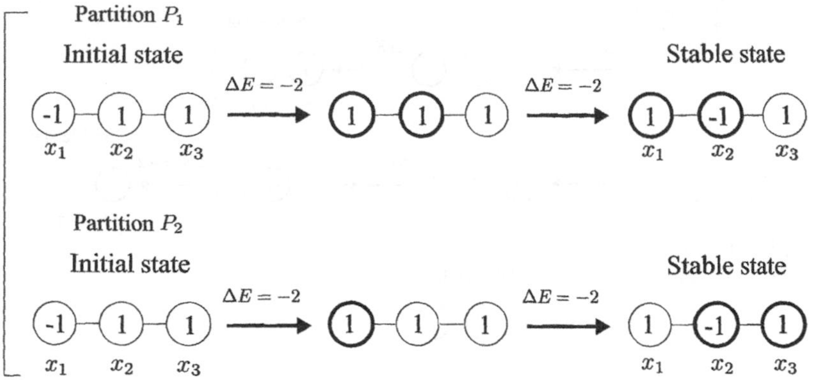

(d)

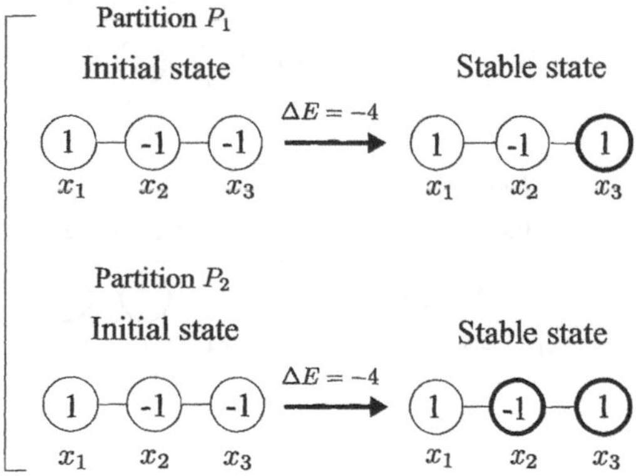

(e)

Figure 13.25 (Continued)

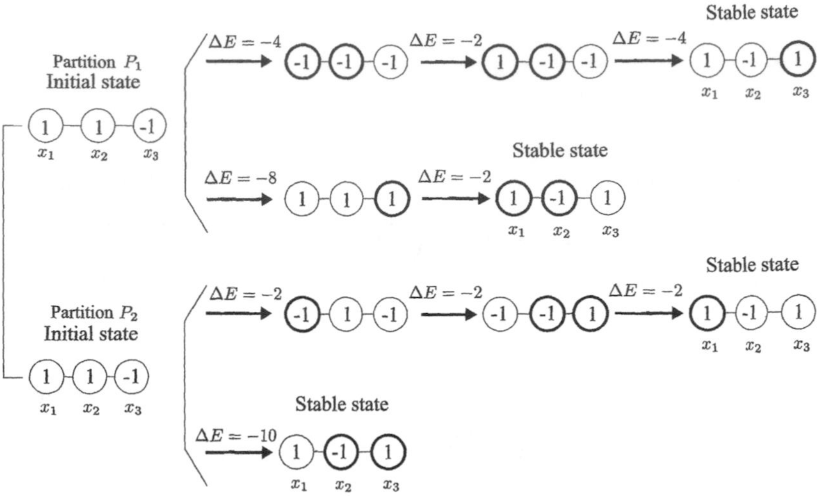

(f)

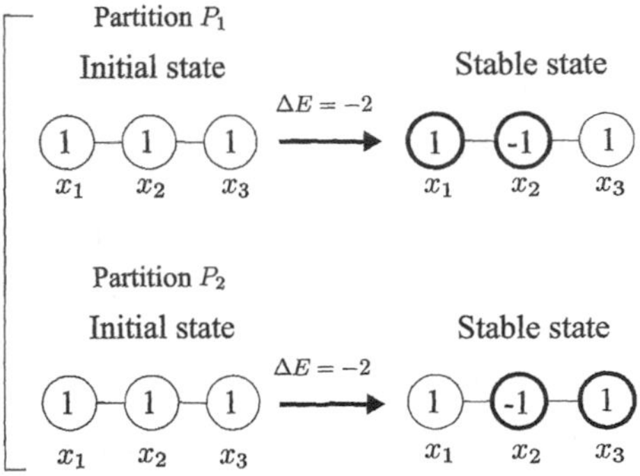

(g)

Figure 13.25 Example 13.11: state transfer diagram of a block sequential operating processing of a three-neuron system. The parameters of the network are chosen as $w_{11} = w_{22} = w_{33} = 0$, $w_{12} = w_{21} = -1$, $w_{13} = w_{31} = 1$, $w_{23} = w_{32} = 1$, and $\theta_1 = 1$, $\theta_2 = -1$, $\theta_3 = 2$. The 2-ordered partitions of the integer set $\{1, 2, 3\}$ considered are as follows:

$$P_1: \quad N_1 = \{1, 2\}, N_2 = \{3\}$$
$$P_2: \quad N_1 = \{1\}, N_2 = \{2, 3\}$$

13.6 CONCLUDING REMARKS

Binary neural networks can be described by a set of discrete-time and discrete-state nonlinear difference equations. One of the most interesting properties of the binary neural network model is the fact that, since the state space of the neural network is finite, it will converge to stable states or enter into a periodic cycle in the binary state space $\{-1, 1\}^n$. However, the convergence properties of a binary network are dependent on the structure of the weight matrix $\boldsymbol{W}$ and the method by which the states of the neurons are updated. The Lyapunov function or energy function method can be employed to analyze the stability of the networks in terms of their equilibrium points. As the most famous and important class of binary neural networks, the binary Hopfield neural networks demonstrate the stability of their equilibrium points. More details on the convergence analysis for various types of binary neural networks can be found in the next chapter.

The main idea in deriving the convergence properties of a binary network is to define an energy function and to show that it is nonincreasing when the state of the network changes as a result of computation. Since the energy function is a bounded function from below, it follows that the states will converge to some value. Meanwhile, as an alternative method, it is interesting to note that the undirected graph theory may be applied to address the issue of the state convergence (Bruck 1990b) where the concept of an energy function may not be involved.

The convergence properties of some important network architectures discussed in this chapter may be summarized as follows:

(i) Convergence to a stable state when the neural network is operating in a serial (asynchronous) mode with a symmetric nonnegative diagonal weight matrix $\boldsymbol{W}$.

(ii) Convergence to a cycle of length at the most 2 when the neural network is operating in a fully parallel (synchronous) mode with symmetric weight matrix $\boldsymbol{W}$.

(iii) Convergence to a periodic process of length 4 when the neural network is operating in a fully parallel (synchronous) mode with a skew–symmetric $\boldsymbol{W}$.

(iv) Convergence to a stable state when the neural network is operating in a block sequential mode with a symmetric weight $\boldsymbol{W}$ and all nonnegative-definite main diagonal submatrices.

Problems

13.1 Compare the similarities and differences of the Lyapunov function approach for both continuous and discrete-time systems.

13.2 Consider a *unipolar* Hopfield binary neural network with an asynchronous operating equation

$$x_i(k+1) = \begin{cases} \mathbf{1}(y_i(k)), & \text{if} \quad i = p \quad \text{and} \quad y_i(k) \neq 0 \\ x_i(k), & \text{otherwise} \end{cases}$$

where

$$y_i = \sum_{j=1}^{n} w_{ij} x_j + \theta_i$$

and

$$\mathbf{1}(y_i) = \begin{cases} 1, & y_i \geq 0 \\ 0, & y_i < 0 \end{cases}$$

(a) Find an energy function for this binary neural network and analyze the state convergence of the network.

(b) Give a formula for the transient time of the network.

13.3 Consider a three-neuron binary neural network with a zero-threshold vector and the weight matrix

$$\boldsymbol{W} = \begin{bmatrix} 0 & 1 & 0 \\ 0 & 0 & 1 \\ 1 & 0 & 0 \end{bmatrix}$$

(a) Give all the possible binary states of the binary neural network.

(b) Analyze the characteristics of the equilibrium points of the network.

(c) Calculate the transient time and cycle length of the network.

13.4 Consider a two-neuron binary Hopfield neural network with the weight matrix

$$W = \begin{bmatrix} -2 & 1 \\ 1 & -2 \end{bmatrix}$$

Show that given any initial state, the network will not converge to a stable state in any sequential mode.

13.5 Prove the results given in Lemma 13.2.

13.6 Show that the binary Hopfield neural network with a zero-threshold vector converges for any hybrid mode of operation if the weight matrix W is symmetric, and positive-semidefinite (i.e., $x^T W x \geq 0$ for all $x \in \Re^n$).

13.7 For the binary Hopfield neural network with an asynchronous operation mode, if an energy function is defined as

$$\begin{aligned} E &= -\tfrac{1}{2}\sum_{i=1}^{n}\sum_{j=1}^{n} w_{ij}x_i(k)x_j(k-1) - \tfrac{1}{2}\sum_{i=1}^{n} v_i(x_i(k) + x_i(k-1)) \\ &= -\tfrac{1}{2}x^T(k)Wx(k-1) - \tfrac{1}{2}v^T(x(k) + x(k-1)) \end{aligned}$$

show that the energy function E is bounded from below as

$$E \geq -\sum_{i,j=1}^{n} |w_{ij}| - \sum_{i=1}^{n} |v_i|$$

13.8 Consider a Hopfield binary neural network with the weight matrix

$$W = \begin{bmatrix} 1 & -1 & 2 \\ -1 & 2 & 1 \\ 2 & 1 & 0 \end{bmatrix}$$

and an asynchronous updating equation

$$x_i(k+1) = \begin{cases} sgn((Wx)_i), & \text{if } \ i = p \ \text{ and } \ (Wx)_i \neq 0 \\ x_i(k), & \text{otherwise} \end{cases}$$

where $p \in \{1, 2, \ldots, n\}$ is selected randomly at every discrete-time k.

(a) Calculate all the stable states of the network.
(b) Draw the state transfer map of the network.
(c) Give an estimate of the transient time of the network.

13.9 Redefine the asynchronous updating equation in Problem 13.8 as follows:

$$x_i(k+1) = \begin{cases} sgn((\boldsymbol{W}\boldsymbol{x})_i), & \text{if} \quad i = p \\ x_i(k), & \text{otherwise} \end{cases}$$

Repeat (a), (b), and (c) of Problem 13.8.

13.10 Show that for the original Hopfield binary neural network, if there exists a nonnegative-definite diagonal matrix

$$\boldsymbol{C} = diag[c_1 \; c_2 \; \cdots \; c_n] \quad \text{with} \quad c_i \geq 0$$

such that

$$\boldsymbol{W}\boldsymbol{x} + \boldsymbol{\theta} = \boldsymbol{C}\boldsymbol{x}$$

then $\boldsymbol{x} \in \{-1, 1\}^n$ is a stable state of the network.

13.11 Consider a Hopfield binary neural network defined by

$$\boldsymbol{x}(k+1) = \boldsymbol{sgn}(\boldsymbol{W}\boldsymbol{x}(k) + \boldsymbol{\theta})$$

Prove that if

$$\boldsymbol{W}\boldsymbol{x} + \boldsymbol{\theta} = \boldsymbol{C}\boldsymbol{x}$$

where $\boldsymbol{C}$ is a nonnegative-definite diagonal matrix, $\boldsymbol{C} = diag[c_1, c_2, \ldots, c_n]$ with $c_i \geq 0$, $i = 1, 2, \ldots, n$, and when

$$(\boldsymbol{W}\boldsymbol{x} + \boldsymbol{\theta})_{i^*} = 0, \qquad 1 \leq i^* \leq n$$

corresponds only to the state

$$x_{i^*} = 1$$

then $\boldsymbol{x} \in \{-1, 1\}^n$ is a stable state of the network.

13.12 Consider a Hopfield binary neural network with the weight matrix

$$\boldsymbol{W} = \begin{bmatrix} 1 & -1 & 2 \\ -1 & 2 & 1 \\ 2 & 1 & 0 \end{bmatrix}$$

and an asynchronous updating equation

$$x_i(k+1) = \begin{cases} sgn((\boldsymbol{W}\boldsymbol{x})_i), & \text{if} \quad i = p \quad \text{and} \quad (\boldsymbol{W}\boldsymbol{x})_i \neq 0 \\ x_i(k), & \text{otherwise} \end{cases}$$

where $p \in \{1, 2, \ldots, n\}$ is selected randomly at every discrete-time k.

(a) Calculate all the stable states of the network.
(b) Draw the state transfer map of the network.
(c) Give an estimate of the transient time of the network.

13.13 Let the elements of the threshold vector $\boldsymbol{\theta}$ satisfy

$$N_i \leq \theta_i < N_i + 1, \quad \text{for} \quad \text{integer} \quad N_i$$

Show that there exists an integer weight matrix $\boldsymbol{W}$ with nonnegative diagonal elements such that the transient time of the Hopfield neural network with an asynchronous operating mode is

$$T(\boldsymbol{W}, \boldsymbol{\theta}) \leq \frac{1}{2\zeta}\left[||\boldsymbol{W}|| + 2||\boldsymbol{\theta}|| - \sum_{i=1}^{n} w_{ii}\right]$$

where

$$\zeta = \begin{cases} 1, & \text{if} \quad \text{all} \quad \theta_i = N_i \\ \min_i\{|N_i - \theta_i|, |N_i + 1 - \theta_i|\}, & \text{otherwise} \end{cases}$$

13.14 Let N_0 and N_1 be a partition of an integer set $\{1, 2, \ldots, n\}$. A binary network with a symmetric weight matrix and nonnegative diagonal elements has the following asynchronous operating equation

$$x_i(k+1) = \begin{cases} sgn(y_i(k)), & \text{if} \quad i = p, \quad y_p(k) \neq 0 \\ x_i(k), & \text{if} \quad i \in N_0, \quad i = p, \quad y_p(k) = 0 \\ -x_i(k), & \text{if} \quad i \in N_1, \quad i = p, \quad y_p(k) = 0 \\ x_i(k), & \text{if} \quad i \neq p \end{cases}$$

where the integer p represents the pth unit that is fired at time k, and

$$y_p(k) = \sum_{j=1}^{n} w_{pj} x_j(k) + \theta_p$$

Let the energy function of this system be defined by

$$E(k) = -\tfrac{1}{2}\boldsymbol{x}^T(k)\boldsymbol{W}\boldsymbol{x}(k) - \boldsymbol{\theta}^T\boldsymbol{x}(k)$$

Prove that

(a) $\forall k, \boldsymbol{x}(k+1) \neq \boldsymbol{x}(k) \longrightarrow \Delta E(k) \leq 0$;

(b) In any limit-cycle oscillations, the states of all the units i with $i \in N_0$ are stable, and the states of all the units i with $i \in N_1$ are changed only when $y_i = 0$.

13.15 Let $(N_l)_{l=1,2,\ldots,p}$ ($p > 1$) be the partition of the integer set $\{1, 2, \ldots, n\}$ and the weight matrix $\boldsymbol{W}$ be symmetric with all nonnegative definite partition matrices, that is, $\boldsymbol{W}_{ll} \leq 0$. Prove that if the weight matrix $\boldsymbol{W}$ and the threshold vector $\boldsymbol{\theta}$ have integer entries, the Hopfield network with the block sequential operation associated with the partition $(N_l)_{l=1,2,\ldots,p}$ has

$$|\Delta E(k)| \geq 2, \quad \text{for} \quad \boldsymbol{x}(k+1) \neq \boldsymbol{x}(k), \quad \boldsymbol{x} \in \{-1, 1\}^n$$

where $E(k)$ is the energy function defined by Eqn. (13.106).

13.16 A multivalued Hopfield neural network is defined as

$$x_i(k+1) = f_i\left(\sum_{j=1}^{n} w_{ij} x_j(k) + \theta_i\right), \quad i = 1, 2, \ldots, n$$

where f_i is a multivalued function defined by

$$f_i(y_i) = \begin{cases} N, & \text{if} \quad y_i \geq N \\ v, & \text{if} \quad v \leq y_i < v+1 \\ 0, & \text{if} \quad y_i < 0 \end{cases}$$

where $y_i = \sum_{j=1}^{n}(w_{ij}x_j(k) + \theta_i)$, and $N > 1$ is a integer. Define the energy function

$$E = -\frac{1}{2}\sum_{i=1}^{n}\sum_{j=1, j\neq i}^{n} w_{ij} x_i x_j - \sum_{j=1}^{n} \theta_j x_j$$

Show that

(a) If $\boldsymbol{W}$ is symmetric, then the neural network with an asynchronous operating mode will converge to the stable equilibrium point states;

(b) If $\boldsymbol{W}$ is a positive-definite and symmetric matrix, then the network with a synchronous operating mode will converge to the stable equilibrium state;

(c) Discuss the upper bound on the transient time.

13.17 Consider a four-neuron Hopfield binary neural network with the following weight matrix:

$$\boldsymbol{W} = \begin{bmatrix} 0 & 1 & 2 & -1 \\ 1 & 0 & -1 & 2 \\ 2 & -1 & 0 & 1 \\ -1 & 2 & 1 & 0 \end{bmatrix}$$

Two sets of ordered partitions of the integer set $\{1, 2, 3, 4\}$ are selected as

$$P_1: \quad N_1 = \{1, 2\}, \quad N_2 = \{3, 4\}$$

and

$$P_2: \quad N_1 = \{1\}, \quad N_2 = \{2, 3, 4\}$$

Obtain the transfer maps for the partitions P_1 and P_2.

13.18 [Traveling Salesman Problem (TSP)] Given n cites C_i, $i = 1, 2, \ldots, n$, and the distances w_{ij} between cities C_i and C_j. A salesman wants to make a closed tour that visits each city once and then return to its starting point. TSP is to find a closed tour of the minimum length among all possible choices. Show that a selection of weight w_{ij} and threshold θ_i in a way such that the global minimum of

$$E = \sum_{j=1}^{n} \theta_j x_j - \frac{1}{2} \sum_{i,j}^{n} w_{ij} x_i x_j$$

would correspond to a minimum length valid tour.

14

Feedback Binary Associative Memories

14.1 Hebb's Neural Learning Mechanisms

14.2 Information Retrieval Process

14.3 Nonorthogonal Fundamental Memories

14.4 Other Learning Algorithms for Associative Memory

14.5 Information Capacity of Binary Hopfield Neural Network

14.6 Concluding Remarks

Problems

In the preceding chapters we studied the equilibrium analysis and memory capacity of dynamic neural networks (DNNs). In those studies we showed that the dynamic behavior of such neural networks exhibits stable equilibrium points during the system's evolution in time. In this chapter we study feedback binary associative memories.

An associative memory can store a large number of patterns. Those stored patterns can be recalled through the association of the key pattern and the information stored.

Donald Hebb (Hebb 1949) was the first to propose a neural learning scheme for updating the synaptic weights for associative memories, now known as the *Hebbian learning rule*. He stated that the information can be stored in synaptic weights, and postulated the learning techniques that have had a profound impact on some of the developments in the field of neural learning and associative memories. Indeed, Hebb's learning rule has made some profound contributions to the theory of neural networks and associative memories.

In this chapter we first discuss Hebb's learning mechanisms and study the convergence consideration of such mechanisms. Then, in Section 14.2, we study the information retrieval process and self-recall of stored patterns. In Section 14.3, we discuss the convergence property and pattern storage for *nonorthogonal fundamental memories*. Other learning algorithms for associative memory such as the *projection learning rule* and the *generalized learning rule* are discussed in Section 14.4. In Section 14.5 we discuss an interesting topic that is the information capacity of the binary Hopfield network.

14.1 HEBB'S NEURAL LEARNING MECHANISMS

14.1.1 Basis of Hebb's Learning Rule

A neural network of the type discussed in Chapter 13 exhibits the so-called associative (or content-addressable) memory property. A system is said to possess the property of associative memory if it is capable of storing several types of patterns in its memory, and when presented with a corrupted version of one of these patterns, it retrieves the corresponding prototype pattern. Given a binary n string with 1 and -1 as the initial state of a system, the mathematical recognition amounts to a sequence of state transitions to one of several attractors referred to as *associative memories*. An associative memory acts, therefore, as a classifier of input patterns by assigning each of them to one of the stored prototypes. As we know, a Hopfield neural network can be used as an associative memory since it can be constructed so that it has many stable states, each corresponding to a prototype pattern.

The Hebbian learning rule is one of the most popular approaches for adjusting the weights of a binary neural network for an associative memory. The concept of Hebb's learning rule comes from experimental data on biological neural systems, whereby the synaptic weight between two neurons is enhanced if both neurons are active at the same time. The original statement given by Hebb (1949) in his classical book *Organization of Behavior* is quoted as

> When an axon of cell A is near enough to excite a cell B, and repeatedly or persistently takes part in firing it, some growth process or metabolic change takes place in one or both cells such that A's efficiency as one of the cells firing B is increased.

In mathematical language, if the neural activities of the source neuron i and the destination neuron j at time k are denoted, respectively, by the state variables $x_i(k)$ and $x_j(k)$, the basic interpretation of Hebb's learning mechanism then can be expressed as

$$\Delta w_{ij}(k) = x_i(k)x_j(k) \tag{14.1}$$

that is, the increment of the weight w_{ij} between the two neurons is the product of the states of the neurons i and j. Hebb's learning rule described by Eqn. (14.1) indicates two basic facts:

(i) The connection weight between the two neurons should be increased when the two neural states have the same sign such that a position correlation between the two neural states takes placc.

(ii) The increment of the weight from neuron i to neuron j is equal to that from neuron j to neuron i.

Some further modifications of Eqn. (14.1) can be also given as follows

$$\Delta w_{ij}(k) = h_1(x_i(k))h_2(x_j(k)) \tag{14.2}$$

or

$$\Delta w_{ij}(k) = h_3(x_i(k), x_j(k)) \tag{14.3}$$

where $h_1(.)$, $h_2(.)$, and $h_3(.)$ are some suitable functions of the states x_i and x_j.

Since Hebb's learning rule was proposed, many extended versions of it have been developed for designing weight learning processes for neural networks. The most direct extension of Eqn. (14.3) for the individual neuron is the vector correlation technique, which can be employed to deal with the weight learning process for the neural network structure.

14.1.2 Hebb's Learning Formulations

Given m $(m \leq n)$ n-dimensional *bipolar* binary pattern vectors $\boldsymbol{y}^{(k)} \in \{-1, 1\}^n$, $k = 1, 2, \ldots, m$:

$$\boldsymbol{y}^{(k)} = \begin{bmatrix} y_1^{(k)} \\ y_2^{(k)} \\ \vdots \\ y_n^{(k)} \end{bmatrix}, \quad k = 1, 2, \ldots, m \tag{14.4}$$

Hopfield proposed that Hebb's learning rule may be used to encode m binary patterns, $\boldsymbol{y}^{(k)}$, $k = 1, \ldots, m$, as stable equilibrium points of the binary neural network with the synaptic weight matrix $\boldsymbol{W}$ by choosing

$$w_{ij} = \sum_{k=1}^{m} y_i^{(k)} y_j^{(k)} - m\delta_{ij} \tag{14.5}$$

and the threshold weight $w_{00} = 0$.

The second term δ_{ij} on the right-hand side is the Dirac's delta function and is used to ensure that the diagonal elements are zero. This Dirac's delta function δ_{ij} is defined as

$$\delta_{ij} = \begin{cases} 1, & i = j \\ 0, & i \neq j \end{cases}$$

Equation (14.5) shows that if two neurons have correlated states, the weights between them increase. It is easy to see that this process gives the same value for w_{ij} as for w_{ji} leading to the symmetric network with the nonnegative diagonal elements. The formulation of Eqn. (14.5) may be rewritten in the following matrix form

$$\boldsymbol{W}_k \triangleq (\boldsymbol{y}^{(k)})(\boldsymbol{y}^{(k)})^T - \boldsymbol{I} \tag{14.6}$$

and

$$\boldsymbol{W} = \sum_{k=1}^{m} \boldsymbol{W}_k = \sum_{k=1}^{m} (\boldsymbol{y}^{(k)})(\boldsymbol{y}^{(k)})^T - m\boldsymbol{I} \tag{14.7}$$

where $\boldsymbol{W}_k$ is a $(n \times n)$-dimensional matrix that represents the contribution associated with the pattern $\boldsymbol{y}^{(k)}$. Equations (14.6) and (14.7) lead to the following rule, which is called the *outer-product rule*.

The pattern storage algorithm given in Eqns. (14.5) and (14.7), as originally proposed by Hopfield for the *unipolar* binary vector $\boldsymbol{y}^{(1)}$, $\boldsymbol{y}^{(2)}$, ..., $\boldsymbol{y}^{(m)} \in$

$\{0, 1\}^n$, can also be modified for *bipolar* binary vectors through a simple mapping process with the entries $(2y_i^{(k)} - 1)$ and $(2y_j^{(k)} - 1)$ in Eqn. (14.5). This leads to the following formulation for bipolar binary vectors

$$w_{ij} = \sum_{k=1}^{m} (2y_i^{(k)} - 1)(2y_j^{(k)} - 1) - m\delta_{ij}$$

or in a compact matrix form

$$\boldsymbol{W}_k \triangleq (2\boldsymbol{y}^{(k)} - \mathbf{1})(2\boldsymbol{y}^{(k)} - \mathbf{1})^T - \boldsymbol{I} \tag{14.8}$$

and

$$\begin{aligned} \boldsymbol{W} &= \sum_{k=1}^{m} \boldsymbol{W}_k \\ &= \sum_{k=1}^{m} (2\boldsymbol{y}^{(k)} - \mathbf{1})(2\boldsymbol{y}^{(k)} - \mathbf{1})^T - m\boldsymbol{I} \end{aligned} \tag{14.9}$$

where $\mathbf{1}$ is an n-dimensional unity vector $\mathbf{1} \triangleq [1 \quad 1 \quad \cdots \quad 1]^T$.

Recall the binary neural networks with a zero-threshold vector discussed in Chapter 13 of the form

$$\boldsymbol{x}(k+1) = \boldsymbol{sgn}(\boldsymbol{W}\boldsymbol{x}(k))$$

With the choicc of $\boldsymbol{W}$ given by Eqn. (14.7), the energy function E for this binary neural network may be evaluated as follows:

$$\begin{aligned} E(\boldsymbol{x}) &= -\tfrac{1}{2}\boldsymbol{x}^T \boldsymbol{W} \boldsymbol{x} \\ &= -\tfrac{1}{2}\boldsymbol{x}^T \sum_{k=1}^{m} (\boldsymbol{y}^{(k)})(\boldsymbol{y}^{(k)})^T \boldsymbol{x} - \tfrac{1}{2} m \boldsymbol{x}^T \boldsymbol{x} \\ &= -\tfrac{1}{2}\boldsymbol{x}^T \sum_{k=1}^{m} (\boldsymbol{y}^{(k)})(\boldsymbol{y}^{(k)})^T \boldsymbol{x} - \tfrac{1}{2} mn \end{aligned} \tag{14.10}$$

It can be noted from Eqn. (14.7) that $\boldsymbol{W}$ is a symmetric real matrix with zero-diagonal elements, and that the binary patterns $\boldsymbol{y}^{(k)}$ are all orthogonal, specifically

$$\frac{1}{n} \sum_{j=1}^{n} y_j^{(i)} y_j^{(\ell)} = \delta_{i\ell} \tag{14.11}$$

or

$$\frac{1}{n} < \boldsymbol{y}^{(i)}, \boldsymbol{y}^{(\ell)} >= \frac{1}{n}(\boldsymbol{y}^{(i)})^T(\boldsymbol{y}^{(\ell)}) = \delta_{i\ell} \tag{14.12}$$

As a consequence, all the eigenvalues of $\boldsymbol{W}$ are real and their sum is zero. This implies that if $\boldsymbol{W}$ is not a zero matrix, it must involve both the positive and negative eigenvalues. One may prove that the energy function E will have the same minimum at each $\boldsymbol{y}^{(\ell)}$:

$$\begin{aligned} E(\boldsymbol{y}^{(\ell)}) &= -\tfrac{1}{2}(\boldsymbol{y}^{(\ell)})^T \sum_{k=1}^{m}(\boldsymbol{y}^{(k)})(\boldsymbol{y}^{(k)})^T(\boldsymbol{y}^{(\ell)}) - \tfrac{1}{2}mn \\ &= -n\tfrac{1}{2}(\boldsymbol{y}^{(\ell)})^T(\boldsymbol{y}^{(\ell)}) - \tfrac{1}{2}nm \\ &= -n\tfrac{1}{2}\sum_{i=1}^{n}(y_i^{(\ell)})^2 - \tfrac{1}{2}nm \\ &= -\tfrac{1}{2}n(n+m), \qquad \ell = 1, 2, \ldots, m \end{aligned} \tag{14.13}$$

Thus, all the given pattern vectors have the same energy, which is the lowest possible energy. Hopefully, the dynamics of the system will have a region of attraction about each pattern $\boldsymbol{y}^{(k)}$ that associates the initial state values of the neural input vector $\boldsymbol{x}$. To ensure this property, we should first give the Hebbian rule encoding process, by which the binary pattern $\boldsymbol{y}^{(k)}$ is supposed to be stored or encoded as the equilibrium points of the binary neural network with the weight matrix $\boldsymbol{W}$.

14.1.3 Convergence Considerations

Using the analysis method described below, we may verify that the given binary pattern vectors $\boldsymbol{y}^{(1)}$, $\boldsymbol{y}^{(2)}$, ..., $\boldsymbol{y}^{(m)}$, which are orthogonal, are stored as stable equilibrium states of the network with the choice of $\boldsymbol{W}$ given by the formulation in Eqn. (14.7):

$$\boldsymbol{y}^{(\ell)} = \boldsymbol{sgn}(\boldsymbol{W}\boldsymbol{y}^{(\ell)}), \quad \text{for all} \quad 1 \leq \ell \leq m \tag{14.14}$$

To prove this, we consider the internal field of the neural network defined by

$$
\boldsymbol{y} = \begin{bmatrix} y_1 \\ y_2 \\ \vdots \\ y_n \end{bmatrix} = \begin{bmatrix} \sum_{j=1}^{n} w_{1j}x_j \\ \sum_{j=1}^{n} w_{2j}x_j \\ \vdots \\ \sum_{j=1}^{n} w_{nj}x_j \end{bmatrix}
$$

It is easy to understand that when the "direction" of y_i $(1 \leq i \leq n)$ coincides with the "direction" of x_i $(1 \leq i \leq n)$, or simply speaking, when all the y_i are zero or have the same sign as the corresponding component x_i, the system attains a stable equilibrium state. In this case, the following relationship must be satisfied:

$$
x_i y_i \geq 0, \quad \text{for all} \quad 1 \leq i \leq m \tag{14.15}
$$

Let us test this for the given patterns $\boldsymbol{y}^{(1)}, \ldots, \boldsymbol{y}^{(m)}$ by calculating $x_i y_i$ for the case when the weight matrix $\boldsymbol{W}$ is designed by Hebb's learning rule, namely, Eqn. (14.7). For the pattern $\boldsymbol{y}^{(\ell)}$ $(1 \leq \ell \leq m)$ and an arbitrary $1 \leq i \leq n$, let

$$
x_i = y_i^{(\ell)}
$$

and

$$
y_i = \sum_{j=1}^{n} w_{ij} x_j
$$

Then

$$
\begin{aligned}
x_i y_i &= \sum_{j=1}^{n} w_{ij} x_i x_j \\
&= \sum_{j=1}^{n} \left[\sum_{k=1}^{m} y_i^{(k)} y_j^{(k)} - m\delta_{ij} \right] y_i^{(\ell)} y_j^{(\ell)} \\
&= \sum_{j=1}^{n} \sum_{k=1}^{m} y_i^{(k)} y_j^{(k)} y_i^{(\ell)} y_j^{(\ell)} - \sum_{j=1}^{n} m\delta_{ij} y_i^{(\ell)} y_j^{(\ell)}
\end{aligned} \tag{14.16}
$$

Invoking the orthogonality relation, one obtains

$$
\sum_{j=1}^{n} \sum_{k=1}^{m} y_i^{(k)} y_j^{(k)} y_i^{(\ell)} y_j^{(\ell)} = \sum_{j=1}^{n} \sum_{k=1}^{m} \left[y_i^{(k)} y_i^{(\ell)} \right] \left[y_j^{(k)} y_j^{(\ell)} \right]
$$

$$\begin{aligned} &= \left[y_i^{(\ell)} y_i^{(\ell)}\right] \sum_{j=1}^{n} \left[y_j^{(\ell)} y_j^{(\ell)}\right] \\ &= n \end{aligned} \tag{14.17}$$

and

$$\sum_{j=1}^{n} m\delta_{ij} y_i^{(\ell)} y_j^{(\ell)} = m y_i^{(\ell)} y_j^{(\ell)} = m \tag{14.18}$$

Hence, Eqn. (14.15) reduces to

$$x_i y_i = n - m \geq 0 \tag{14.19}$$

Thus, the stored pattern $\boldsymbol{y}^{(\ell)}$ is indeed a stable equilibrium state. The discussion above is summarized in the following theorem.

Theorem 14.1 (Convergence for Orthogonal Pattern) *Given m $(m \leq n)$ binary pattern vectors, $\boldsymbol{y}^{(1)}$, $\boldsymbol{y}^{(2)}$, ..., $\boldsymbol{y}^{(m)}$ that are orthogonal, then all the m patterns are the stable states of the neural network with a zero threshold vector and a weight matrix*

$$\boldsymbol{W} = \sum_{k=1}^{m} (\boldsymbol{y}^{(k)})(\boldsymbol{y}^{(k)})^T - m\boldsymbol{I} \tag{14.20}$$

■

This conclusion may be confirmed using the results of the eigenvalues of the weighting matrix $\boldsymbol{W}$. Thus, using Eqns. (14.5) and (14.18), we have

$$\begin{aligned} \sum_{j=1}^{n} w_{ij} y_j^{(\ell)} &= \sum_{j=1}^{n} \left[\sum_{k=1}^{m} y_i^{(k)} y_j^{(k)} y_j^{(\ell)} - m\delta_{ij} y_j^{(\ell)} \right] \\ &= \sum_{j=1}^{n} \left[y_i^{(\ell)} y_j^{(\ell)} y_j^{(\ell)} - m\delta_{ij} y_j^{(\ell)} \right] \\ &= y_i^{(\ell)} \sum_{j=1}^{n} y_j^{(\ell)} y_j^{(\ell)} - m \sum_{j=1}^{n} \delta_{ij} y_j^{(\ell)} \\ &= (n-m) y_i^{(\ell)} \end{aligned} \tag{14.21}$$

that is

$$\boldsymbol{W}\boldsymbol{y}^{(\ell)} = (n-m)\boldsymbol{y}^{(\ell)} \tag{14.22}$$

Hence, the stored patterns, $\boldsymbol{y}^{(\ell)}$, $(1 \le \ell \le m)$, are the eigenvectors of the matrix $\boldsymbol{W}$ with the eigenvalue $(n-m)$. Also, since $n \ge m$

$$\begin{aligned} \boldsymbol{sgn}(\boldsymbol{W}\boldsymbol{y}^{(\ell)}) &= \boldsymbol{sgn}\left((n-m)\boldsymbol{y}^{(\ell)}\right) \\ &= \boldsymbol{sgn}(\boldsymbol{y}^{(\ell)}) \end{aligned} \tag{14.23}$$

which implies that $\boldsymbol{y}^{(\ell)}$ is a stable vector.

However, in the discussion above, we selected the threshold vector as a zero vector. We may find from the previous derivation that the threshold vector $\boldsymbol{\theta}$ is not necessary to be selected as a zero vector. Let the components of the threshold vector $\boldsymbol{\theta}$ satisfy

$$-(n-m) \le \theta_i \le (n-m) \tag{14.24}$$

Then

$$\begin{aligned} y_i^{(\ell)}\left(\sum_{j=1}^{n} w_{ij} y_j^{(\ell)} + \theta_i\right) &= (n-m) + \theta_i y_i^{(\ell)} \\ &\ge n - m - (n-m) = 0 \end{aligned} \tag{14.25}$$

or

$$\begin{aligned} \boldsymbol{sgn}(\boldsymbol{W}\boldsymbol{y}^{(\ell)} + \boldsymbol{\theta}) &= \boldsymbol{sgn}\left((n-m)\boldsymbol{y}^{(\ell)} + \boldsymbol{\theta}\right) \\ &= \boldsymbol{sgn}\left((n-m)\boldsymbol{y}^{(\ell)}\right) \\ &= \boldsymbol{sgn}(\boldsymbol{y}^{(\ell)}) \end{aligned} \tag{14.26}$$

Therefore, we have the following corollary.

Corollary 14.1 (Convergence for Nonzero Threshold) *Given m, $(m \le n)$, orthogonal binary pattern vectors $\boldsymbol{y}^{(1)}$, $\boldsymbol{y}^{(2)}$, ..., $\boldsymbol{y}^{(m)}$, then all the m patterns are the stable states of the neural network with the weight matrix*

$$\boldsymbol{W} = \sum_{k=1}^{m} (\boldsymbol{y}^{(k)})(\boldsymbol{y}^{(k)})^T - m\boldsymbol{I}$$

and with the threshold vector $\boldsymbol{\theta}$ whose components satisfy

$$-(n-m) \le \theta_i \le (n-m) \tag{14.27}$$

■

Table 14.1 Orthogonal patterns storage using Hebb's learning rule

Given m bipolar pattern vectors

$$y^{(1)}, y^{(2)}, \ldots, y^{(m)} \in \{-1, 1\}^n$$

that satisfy

$$\frac{1}{n}(y^{(i)})^T(y^{(\ell)}) = \delta_{i\ell}, \quad 1 \le i,\ \ell \le n$$

Step 1: The $(n \times n)$-dimensional weight matrix W is

$$W \longleftarrow 0,\ k \longleftarrow 1$$

Step 2: Storing the pattern vector $y^{(k)}$ results in

$$W \longleftarrow (y^{(k)})(y^{(k)})^T - I$$

Step 3: If $k < m$ then $k \leftarrow k + 1$ and go to Step 2. Otherwise, go to Step 4.

Step 4: The n-dimensional threshold vector is

$$\theta \longleftarrow 0$$

Step 5: Storing is completed. Output the weight matrix W.

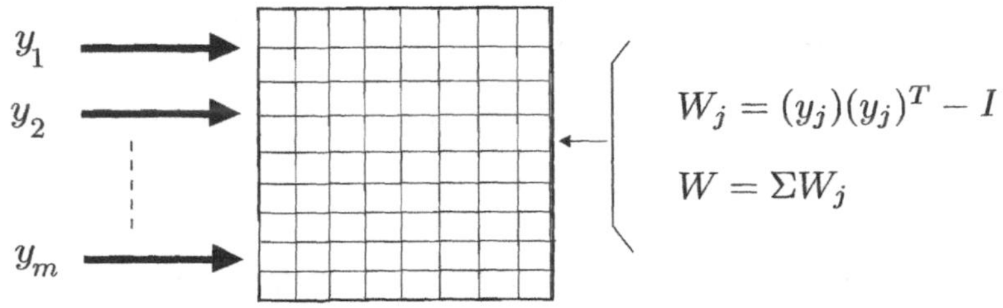

Figure 14.1 Schematic representation of the pattern storage process.

If all prototype patterns $y^{(k)}$ are orthogonal, as originally assumed, then every such pattern can be represented as a vector in an n-dimensional Euclidean space. Since the total number of orthogonal vectors in this space cannot exceed the dimensionality of the space, we immediately see that the network of n neurons can store as many as n orthogonal patterns. Given m orthogonal binary pattern vectors, the weight construction process, as shown in Fig. 14.1, is summarized in Table 14.1.

Example 14.1 Given three binary pattern vectors

$$y^{(1)} = \begin{bmatrix} -1 \\ 1 \\ -1 \\ 1 \end{bmatrix}, \quad y^{(2)} = \begin{bmatrix} 1 \\ -1 \\ 1 \\ -1 \end{bmatrix}, \quad y^{(3)} = \begin{bmatrix} -1 \\ -1 \\ -1 \\ -1 \end{bmatrix}$$

where, $n = 4$ and $m = 3$.

It is easy to verify that the three patterns are orthogonal since

$$(\boldsymbol{y}^{(1)})^T(\boldsymbol{y}^{(2)}) = 0$$
$$(\boldsymbol{y}^{(1)})^T(\boldsymbol{y}^{(3)}) = 0$$
$$(\boldsymbol{y}^{(2)})^T(\boldsymbol{y}^{(3)}) = 0$$

Using Hebb's learning rule, we have

$$\boldsymbol{W}_1 = (\boldsymbol{y}^{(1)})(\boldsymbol{y}^{(1)})^T - \boldsymbol{I} = \begin{bmatrix} 0 & -1 & 1 & -1 \\ -1 & 0 & -1 & 1 \\ 1 & -1 & 0 & -1 \\ -1 & 1 & -1 & 0 \end{bmatrix}$$

$$\boldsymbol{W}_2 = (\boldsymbol{y}^{(2)})(\boldsymbol{y}^{(2)})^T - \boldsymbol{I} = \begin{bmatrix} 0 & -1 & 1 & -1 \\ -1 & 0 & -1 & 1 \\ 1 & -1 & 0 & -1 \\ -1 & 1 & -1 & 0 \end{bmatrix}$$

$$\boldsymbol{W}_3 = (\boldsymbol{y}^{(3)})(\boldsymbol{y}^{(3)})^T - \boldsymbol{I} = \begin{bmatrix} 0 & 1 & 1 & 1 \\ 1 & 0 & 1 & 1 \\ 1 & 1 & 0 & 1 \\ 1 & 1 & 1 & 0 \end{bmatrix}$$

Finally, the weight matrix is obtained as

$$\boldsymbol{W} = \boldsymbol{W}_1 + \boldsymbol{W}_2 + \boldsymbol{W}_3 = \begin{bmatrix} 0 & -1 & 3 & -1 \\ -1 & 0 & -1 & 3 \\ 3 & -1 & 0 & -1 \\ -1 & 3 & -1 & 0 \end{bmatrix}$$

Moreover, we have

$$\boldsymbol{W}\boldsymbol{y}^{(1)} = \begin{bmatrix} -5 \\ 5 \\ -5 \\ 5 \end{bmatrix}, \quad \boldsymbol{W}\boldsymbol{y}^{(2)} = \begin{bmatrix} 5 \\ -5 \\ 5 \\ -5 \end{bmatrix}, \quad \boldsymbol{W}\boldsymbol{y}^{(3)} = \begin{bmatrix} -1 \\ -1 \\ -1 \\ -1 \end{bmatrix}$$

This implies that the ith component of $\boldsymbol{W}\boldsymbol{y}^{(\ell)}$ $(\ell = 1, 2, 3)$ has the same sign as the ith component of the pattern $\boldsymbol{y}^{(\ell)}$. Hence, all three patterns are at the stable equilibrium points of the neural network with the weight matrix $\boldsymbol{W}$ and a zero-threshold vector $\boldsymbol{\theta}$. Figure 14.2 shows the state transfer map of the neural network containing four neurons. ■

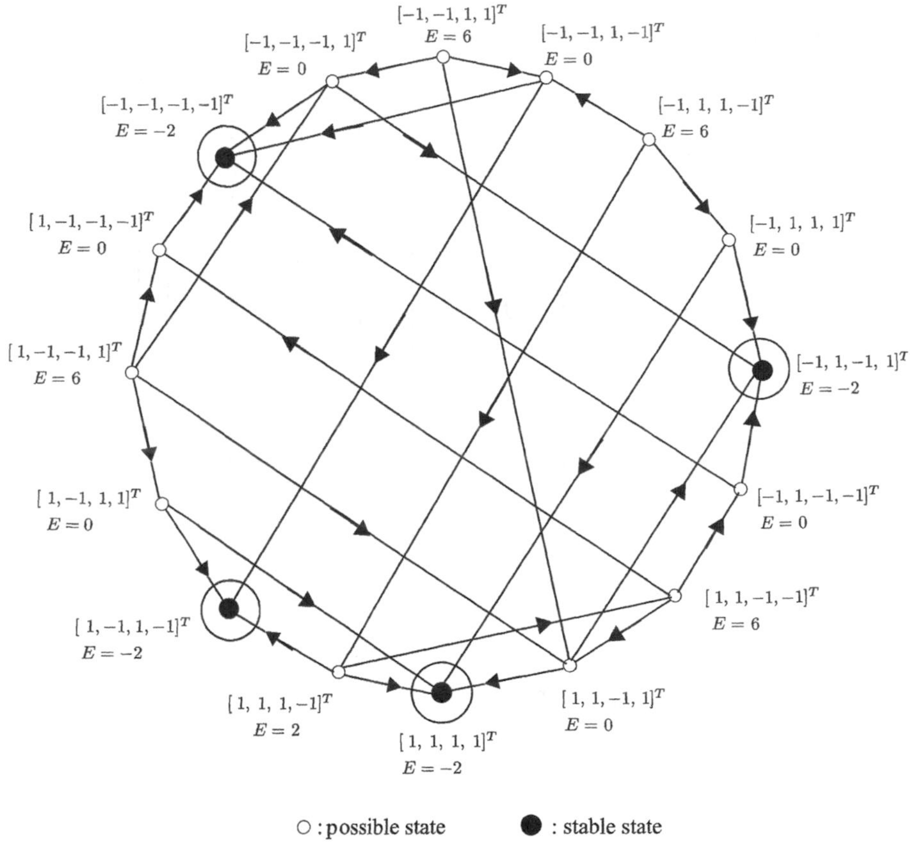

Figure 14.2 Example 14.1: state transfer map of the four-neuron network where the network has the four stable states $[-1, 1, -1, 1]^T$, $[1, -1, 1, -1]^T$, $[-1, -1, -1, -1]^T$, and $[1, 1, 1, 1]^T$.

14.2 INFORMATION RETRIEVAL PROCESS

14.2.1 The Hamming Distance (HD)

The concept of the Hamming distance (HD) between two binary patterns has been widely used to evaluate the performance of the associative memory. For two n-dimensional bipolar binary vectors $\boldsymbol{x}$ and $\boldsymbol{y}$, the similarity between two binary patterns may be shown by counting the number of the same position components that have the same sign. When the two patterns have more numbers of the same components, the similarity is higher. The Hamming distance between the two binary patterns $\boldsymbol{x} \in \Re^n$ and $\boldsymbol{y} \in \Re^n$, $x_i, y_i \in -1, 1$ is defined as

$$HD(\boldsymbol{x}, \boldsymbol{y}) \triangleq \frac{1}{2} \sum_{i=1}^{n} |x_i - y_i|$$

which gives a measurement for dissimilarity between the two patterns. In other words, the Hamming distance is the number of elements in which the two vectors differ from one another. When the two patterns have more numbers of the same components, the similarity is smaller. Obviously, the Hamming distance function satisfies

$$HD(\boldsymbol{x}, \boldsymbol{y}) = HD(\boldsymbol{y}, \boldsymbol{x})$$

and the maximum value of the Hamming distance between $\boldsymbol{x}$ and $\boldsymbol{y}$ is n; that is, if $\boldsymbol{x} \neq \boldsymbol{y}$, then

$$HD(\boldsymbol{x}, \boldsymbol{y}) = n, \quad \text{iff} \quad x_i \neq y_i, \quad \text{for all} \quad 1 \leq i \leq n \tag{14.28}$$

Also, for $\boldsymbol{x} = \boldsymbol{y}$, then

$$HD(\boldsymbol{x}, \boldsymbol{y}) = 0, \quad \text{iff} \quad \boldsymbol{x} = \boldsymbol{y} \tag{14.29}$$

If a network is designed using the Hebbian learning rule and a pattern $\boldsymbol{y}^{(i)}$, which is a stable state vector, the complement $-\boldsymbol{y}^{(i)}$ is also a stable state vector. It is useful to evaluate the Hamming distance between a pattern $\boldsymbol{y}^{(j)}$ and $\boldsymbol{y}^{(i)}$ and the distance between $\boldsymbol{y}^{(j)}$ and $-\boldsymbol{y}^{(i)}$. To simplify this comparison Dasgupta et al. (1989) introduced the following concept of the *effective Hamming distance* (EHD) between two binary vectors.

Given two binary patterns $\boldsymbol{x}$ and $\boldsymbol{y}$, the EHD between the two binary vectors $\boldsymbol{x}$ and $\boldsymbol{y}$ is defined as

$$EHD(\boldsymbol{x}, \boldsymbol{y}) \triangleq \min\{HD(\boldsymbol{x}, \boldsymbol{y}), HD(\boldsymbol{x}, -\boldsymbol{y})\} \tag{14.30}$$

Since

$$HD(\boldsymbol{x}, \boldsymbol{y}) = HD(\boldsymbol{y}, \boldsymbol{x}) \tag{14.31}$$

and

$$HD(\boldsymbol{x}, -\boldsymbol{y}) = HD(\boldsymbol{y}, -\boldsymbol{x}) \tag{14.32}$$

Thus

$$EHD(\boldsymbol{x}, \boldsymbol{y}) = EHD(\boldsymbol{y}, \boldsymbol{x}) \tag{14.33}$$

On the other hand, the EHD between the pattern vector and itself, or between a vector and its complement, is zero. Similarly, the EHD between $\boldsymbol{x}$ and $\boldsymbol{y}$ equals that between $-\boldsymbol{x}$ and $-\boldsymbol{y}$. To facilitate further analysis, we state the following simple lemma. The proof may be obtained by the reader as an exercise.

Lemma 14.1 *Given two n-dimensional binary patterns $\boldsymbol{x}$ and $\boldsymbol{y}$, $\boldsymbol{x}, \boldsymbol{y} \in -1, 1^n$, then*

$$\begin{aligned} (i) \quad HD(\boldsymbol{x}, \boldsymbol{y}) &= \tfrac{1}{2}(n - <\boldsymbol{x}, \boldsymbol{y}>) = \tfrac{1}{2}(n - \boldsymbol{x}^T\boldsymbol{y}) \\ &= \tfrac{1}{2}(n - \sum_{j=1}^{n} x_j y_j); \end{aligned} \tag{14.34}$$

$$\begin{aligned} (ii) \quad EHD(\boldsymbol{x}, \boldsymbol{y}) &= \tfrac{1}{2}(n - | <\boldsymbol{x}, \boldsymbol{y}> |) = \tfrac{1}{2}(n - |\boldsymbol{x}^T\boldsymbol{y}|) \\ &= \tfrac{1}{2}(n - |\sum_{j=1}^{n} x_j y_j|) \end{aligned} \tag{14.35}$$

■

Using this relationship, it is seen that if the patterns $\boldsymbol{x}$ and $\boldsymbol{y}$ are orthogonal, that is

$$<\boldsymbol{x}, \boldsymbol{y}> = \boldsymbol{x}^T\boldsymbol{y} = 0$$

then

$$HD(\boldsymbol{x}, \boldsymbol{y}) = EHD(\boldsymbol{x}, \boldsymbol{y}) = \frac{n}{2}$$

14.2.2 Self-Recall of Stored Patterns

Given m, $(m \leq n)$, the binary pattern vectors that are to be stored as stable states (memories) of a binary neural network, the weight matrix $\boldsymbol{W}$ and the threshold vector $\boldsymbol{\theta}$ may be constructed using the method discussed in Section 14.2.1. The weight matrix $\boldsymbol{W}$ obtained is also referred to as a *memory matrix*. The network designed by Hebb's learning rule may have not only the

m pattern vectors but also other pattern vectors as the stable states that are, however, usually undesirable. Here, the m given pattern vectors are referred to as the *fundamental memories*, while the other stable states are the *spurious memories*. In fact, if $\boldsymbol{y}^{(1)}, \boldsymbol{y}^{(2)}, \ldots, \boldsymbol{y}^{(m)}$ are the fundamental memories, then the complements of the original patterns, $-\boldsymbol{y}^{(1)}, -\boldsymbol{y}^{(2)}, \ldots, -\boldsymbol{y}^{(m)}$ are the spurious memories since

$$\boldsymbol{sgn}\left(\boldsymbol{W}(-\boldsymbol{y}^{(j)})\right) = -\boldsymbol{sgn}\left(\boldsymbol{W}(\boldsymbol{y}^{(j)})\right)$$

Note that the weight matrix $\boldsymbol{W}$ for the pattern $\boldsymbol{y}^{(k)}$ and its complement $-\boldsymbol{y}^{(k)}$ are the same since

$$\begin{aligned} \boldsymbol{W} &= \sum_{k=1}^{m}(\boldsymbol{y}^{(k)})(\boldsymbol{y}^{(k)})^T - m\boldsymbol{I} \\ &= \sum_{k=1}^{m}(-\boldsymbol{y}^{(k)})(-\boldsymbol{y}^{(k)})^T - m\boldsymbol{I} \end{aligned} \tag{14.36}$$

Fundamental and spurious memories are shown in Fig. 14.3.

For a network with the weight matrix $\boldsymbol{W}$ and the threshold vector $\boldsymbol{\theta}$, the information retrieval or recall, as shown in Fig. 14.4, works as follows. Let an n-dimensional binary pattern vector $\boldsymbol{x} = [x_1\ x_2\ \cdots\ x_n]^T$ be given as a so-called key pattern vector or probe vector. Then, using the network structure and the updating procedure discussed earlier, we wish to find the "correct memory" $\boldsymbol{x}^*$, which is the stored memory closest to $\boldsymbol{x}$ in the sense of Hamming distance. In fact, for a network with a weight matrix $\boldsymbol{W}$ obtained

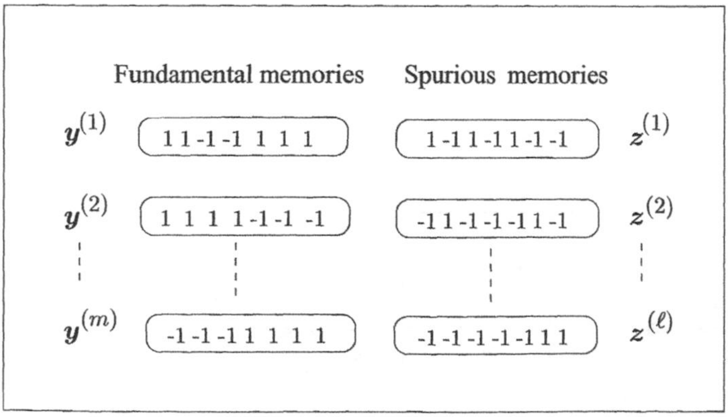

Figure 14.3 Fundamental ($\boldsymbol{y}^{(j)}$) and spurious ($\boldsymbol{z}^{(j)}$) memories stored in a seven-neuron network.

by Hebb's learning rule, the state that starts from any key pattern vector x will always reach a stable equilibrium point when an asynchronous updating mode is employed. Although all the fundamental memories themselves may be stored as stable equilibrium points, the resulting memory that is one of stable equilibrium points may not be one of the fundamental memories, or even if it is, it may not be the "correct (nearest) memory." An undesirable convergence to a fundamental memory that is not the closest to the pattern vector will be illustrated in the next example, Example 14.2. The process of self-recall is summarized in Table 14.2, with a schematic representation in Fig. 14.5.

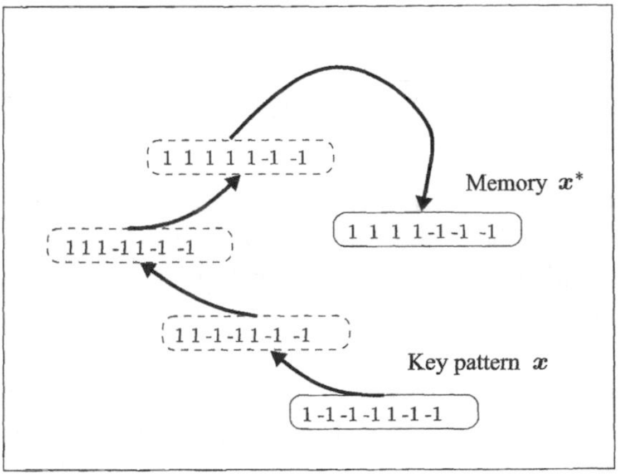

Figure 14.4 Schematic representation of a memory recall process.

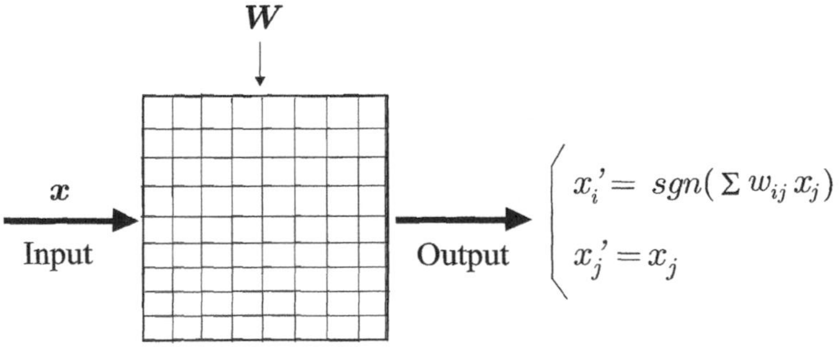

Figure 14.5 Schematic representation of self-recall process.

Table 14.2 **Information recall process using an asynchronous updating**

Given an $(n \times n)$-dimensional weight matrix $\boldsymbol{W}$ with nonnegative diagonal elements, an n-dimensional threshold vector $\boldsymbol{\theta}$, and an n-dimensional key pattern vector $\boldsymbol{x}(0)$. **Step 1:** Initialize $\boldsymbol{x} \longleftarrow \boldsymbol{x}(0), \quad k \longleftarrow 1, \quad \ell \longleftarrow 1$ **Step 2:** Choose randomly an integer i from the integer set $\{1, 2, \ldots, n\}$; **Step 3:** Compute the internal potential y_i: $y_i = \sum_{j=1}^{n} w_{ij} x_j + \theta_i$ **Step 4:** Update the state of the neuron i: $x_i = \begin{cases} sgn(y_i), & \text{if } \; y_i \neq 0 \\ x_i, & \text{if } \; y_i = 0 \end{cases}$ **Step 5:** If $\ell \neq i$ and $x_i y_i \geq 0$, then go to Step 6. Otherwise, $k \longleftarrow k+1, \ell \longleftarrow i$ and go to Step 2; **Step 6:** Recall is completed. Output the recalled pattern $\boldsymbol{x}(k)$ and k.

Example 14.2 (McEliece et al. 1987) Given the following three pattern vectors

$$\boldsymbol{y}^{(1)} = \begin{bmatrix} 1 \\ 1 \\ 1 \\ 1 \\ 1 \end{bmatrix}, \quad \boldsymbol{y}^{(2)} = \begin{bmatrix} 1 \\ -1 \\ -1 \\ 1 \\ -1 \end{bmatrix}, \quad \boldsymbol{y}^{(3)} = \begin{bmatrix} -1 \\ 1 \\ -1 \\ -1 \\ -1 \end{bmatrix}$$

then, we have

$$\boldsymbol{W}_1 = (\boldsymbol{y}^{(1)})(\boldsymbol{y}^{(1)})^T - \boldsymbol{I} = \begin{bmatrix} 0 & 1 & 1 & 1 & 1 \\ 1 & 0 & 1 & 1 & 1 \\ 1 & 1 & 0 & 1 & 1 \\ 1 & 1 & 1 & 0 & 1 \\ 1 & 1 & 1 & 1 & 0 \end{bmatrix}$$

$$\boldsymbol{W}_2 = (\boldsymbol{y}^{(2)})(\boldsymbol{y}^{(2)})^T - \boldsymbol{I} = \begin{bmatrix} 0 & -1 & -1 & 1 & -1 \\ -1 & 0 & 1 & -1 & 1 \\ -1 & 1 & 0 & -1 & 1 \\ 1 & -1 & -1 & 0 & -1 \\ -1 & 1 & 1 & -1 & 0 \end{bmatrix}$$

$$\boldsymbol{W}_3 = (\boldsymbol{y}^{(3)})(\boldsymbol{y}^{(3)})^T - \boldsymbol{I} = \begin{bmatrix} 0 & -1 & 1 & 1 & 1 \\ -1 & 0 & -1 & -1 & -1 \\ 1 & -1 & 0 & 1 & 1 \\ 1 & -1 & 1 & 0 & 1 \\ 1 & -1 & 1 & 1 & 0 \end{bmatrix}$$

Hence

$$\boldsymbol{W} = \boldsymbol{W}_1 + \boldsymbol{W}_2 + \boldsymbol{W}_3 = \begin{bmatrix} 0 & -1 & 1 & 3 & 1 \\ -1 & 0 & 1 & -1 & 1 \\ 1 & 1 & 0 & 1 & 3 \\ 3 & -1 & 1 & 0 & 1 \\ 1 & 1 & 3 & 1 & 0 \end{bmatrix}$$

and the threshold is chosen as a zero vector.

Also, since

$$\boldsymbol{W}\boldsymbol{y}^{(1)} = \begin{bmatrix} 4 \\ 0 \\ 6 \\ 4 \\ 6 \end{bmatrix}, \quad \boldsymbol{W}\boldsymbol{y}^{(2)} = \begin{bmatrix} 2 \\ -2 \\ -2 \\ 2 \\ -2 \end{bmatrix}, \quad \boldsymbol{W}\boldsymbol{y}^{(3)} = \begin{bmatrix} -4 \\ 0 \\ -4 \\ -6 \\ -4 \end{bmatrix}$$

the three patterns $\boldsymbol{y}^{(1)}$, $\boldsymbol{y}^{(2)}$, and $\boldsymbol{y}^{(3)}$ are memorized as the stable equilibrium points of the network with the weight matrix $\boldsymbol{W}$.

Now suppose that a key pattern $\boldsymbol{x}$ is given as

$$\boldsymbol{x} = [1 \quad -1 \quad -1 \quad 1 \quad 1]^T$$

The Hamming distances between the key pattern $\boldsymbol{x}$ and the memories $\boldsymbol{y}^{(1)}$, $\boldsymbol{y}^{(2)}$, and $\boldsymbol{y}^{(3)}$ are easily obtained as

$$\begin{aligned} HD(\boldsymbol{x}, \boldsymbol{y}^{(1)}) &= 2 \\ HD(\boldsymbol{x}, \boldsymbol{y}^{(2)}) &= 1 \\ HD(\boldsymbol{x}, \boldsymbol{y}^{(3)}) &= 4 \end{aligned}$$

Hence, we assume that the key pattern should converge to the correct target memory $\boldsymbol{y}^{(2)}$ that has the least $HD(\boldsymbol{x}, \boldsymbol{y}^{(2)}) = 1$. In fact

$$\boldsymbol{W}\boldsymbol{x} = \begin{bmatrix} 4 \\ -3 \\ 4 \\ 4 \\ -2 \end{bmatrix}$$

where the signs of the third and fifth components are different from that of $\boldsymbol{x}$. Hence, only the third and fifth components of $\boldsymbol{x}$ will change when an asynchronous operating mode is applied. If we had decided to update the fifth component of $\boldsymbol{x}$ first, the new state vector would be

$$\boldsymbol{x}' = [1 \quad -1 \quad -1 \quad 1 \quad -1]^T$$

Hence, the state has converged to the "correct memory" $\boldsymbol{y}^{(2)}$, which is closest to the initial key pattern $\boldsymbol{x}$.

On the other hand, as noted earlier, the convergence to the correct memory is not guaranteed by the Hopfield neural network. Indeed, if we select the third component to be updated first, the new state will be

$$\boldsymbol{x}' = [1 \ -1 \ 1 \ 1 \ 1]^T$$

Furthermore, we compute

$$\boldsymbol{W}\boldsymbol{x}' = [6 \ 0 \ 4 \ 6 \ 4]^T$$

It is easy to see that we will ultimately have to update the second component of the state $\boldsymbol{x}'$ to 1, reaching the fundamental memory $\boldsymbol{y}^{(1)}$. However, $\boldsymbol{y}^{(1)}$ is at a distance 2 from $\boldsymbol{x}$, whereas $\boldsymbol{y}^{(2)}$, the "correct memory" is only at a distance 1 from $\boldsymbol{x}$. In this case, the system has converged to an incorrect memory. ■

14.2.3 Attractivity in Synchronous Mode

Synchronous information retrieval from the synaptic matrix $\boldsymbol{W}$ proceeds as follows (Dasgupta et al. 1989).

Given a binary probe vector $\boldsymbol{x}(0)$, the object is to find the stored fundamental memory $\boldsymbol{y}^{(\ell)}$ that is, in a sense, closest to $\boldsymbol{x}(0)$. A sequence of binary vectors $\boldsymbol{x}(k)$, $k \geq 1$, are generated using a synchronous operating mode such that

$$\boldsymbol{x}(k+1) = \boldsymbol{f}(\boldsymbol{W}\boldsymbol{x}(k)) \tag{14.37}$$

where

$$\boldsymbol{f}(\boldsymbol{W}\boldsymbol{x}) = \begin{bmatrix} f_1((\boldsymbol{W}\boldsymbol{x})_1) \\ f_2((\boldsymbol{W}\boldsymbol{x})_2) \\ \vdots \\ f_n((\boldsymbol{W}\boldsymbol{x})_n) \end{bmatrix}$$

with the following definition:

$$f_i((\boldsymbol{W}\boldsymbol{x})_i) = \begin{cases} sgn((\boldsymbol{W}\boldsymbol{x})_i), & \text{if} \quad (\boldsymbol{W}\boldsymbol{x})_i \neq 0 \\ x_i, & \text{if} \quad (\boldsymbol{W}\boldsymbol{x})_i = 0 \end{cases} \tag{14.38}$$

The process of information recall using the synchronous updating mode is summarized in Table 14.3.

A key function of a content-addressable memory relates to its error-correcting ability. Given a key pattern vector that is not identical to any fundamental memories, then such a content-addressable memory is able to identify the key pattern with the memory contents closest to it. Indeed, the updating equation given in Eqn. (14.37) may be viewed as an algorithm for performing this task with $\boldsymbol{x}(0)$ as an incorrect word. The role of Eqn. (14.37) is to generate a sequence $\boldsymbol{x}(k)$ whose limit point is the memory content $\boldsymbol{y}^{(\ell)}$ or $-\boldsymbol{y}^{(\ell)}$, closest in the effective Hamming distance (EHD) to $\boldsymbol{x}(0)$. As pointed out in the previous section, the state vector of such a network with the weight matrix $\boldsymbol{W}$ may converge either to a stable state that represents a memory, or to a cycle with length 2. Next, we present the conditions that the probe vector $\boldsymbol{x}(0)$ converges to a cycle and to a fundamental memory vector using the description of the Hamming distance between the probe and the fundamental memories.

Table 14.3 **Information recall process using a synchronous updating**

Given an $(n \times n)$-dimensional weight matrix $\boldsymbol{W}$ with nonnegative diagonal elements, an n-dimensional threshold vector $\boldsymbol{\theta}$, and an n-dimensional key pattern vector $\boldsymbol{x}(0)$.

Step 1: Initialize

$$\boldsymbol{x} \longleftarrow \boldsymbol{x}(0), \quad \boldsymbol{z} \longleftarrow \boldsymbol{z}(0), \quad k \longleftarrow 1, \quad \ell \longleftarrow 1$$

Step 2: Compute the internal potential vector

$$\boldsymbol{y} = \boldsymbol{W}\boldsymbol{x} + \boldsymbol{\theta}$$

Step 3: Update the neural states for $i = 1, 2, \ldots, n$

$$x_i = \begin{cases} sgn(y_i), & \text{if} \quad y_i \neq 0 \\ x_i, & \text{if} \quad y_i = 0 \end{cases}$$

Step 4: If $x_i y_i \geq 0$ for all $i = 1, 2, \ldots, n$ or $z_i x_i \geq 0$ for all $i = 1, 2, \ldots, n$
then go to Step 6. Otherwise, $k \longleftarrow k+1$, $\ell \longleftarrow \ell+1$ and go to Step 5.

Step 5: If $\ell = 2$, update vector $\boldsymbol{z}$ by

$$z_i = x_i, \quad i = 1, 2, \ldots, n$$

and $\ell \longleftarrow 0$, then go to Step 2. Otherwise, go to Step 6.

Step 6: Recall is completed. If $x_i y_i \geq 0$ for all $i = 1, 2, \ldots, n$, then output $\boldsymbol{x}$ and k. Otherwise, output $\boldsymbol{x}$, $\boldsymbol{z}$, and k.

Let $\boldsymbol{x}(0)$ be a binary probe vector. After p iterations using a synchronous operating mode, one obtains

$$\begin{aligned} \boldsymbol{x} \triangleq \boldsymbol{x}(p) &= \boldsymbol{f}^p(\boldsymbol{W}\boldsymbol{x}(0)) \\ &= \boldsymbol{f}(\boldsymbol{W}\boldsymbol{f}(\boldsymbol{W}\ldots\boldsymbol{f}(\boldsymbol{W}\boldsymbol{x}(0))\ldots)) \end{aligned} \tag{14.39}$$

It is seen that the ith component of the vector $(\boldsymbol{W}\boldsymbol{x})$ is

$$(\boldsymbol{W}\boldsymbol{x})_i = \sum_{j=1}^{n} w_{ij}x_j$$

Since $w_{ij} = \sum_{k=1}^{m} y_i^{(k)} y_j^{(k)}(1 - m\delta_{ij})$, we have

$$\begin{aligned} (\boldsymbol{W}\boldsymbol{x})_i &= \sum_{j=1}^{n}\sum_{k=1}^{m} y_i^{(k)} y_j^{(k)}(1 - m\delta_{ij})x_j \\ &= \sum_{k=1}^{m} y_i^{(k)}(\boldsymbol{x}^T\boldsymbol{y}^{(k)}) - mx_i \end{aligned} \tag{14.40}$$

Hence

$$\begin{aligned} (\boldsymbol{W}\boldsymbol{x})_i &\le \left| \sum_{k=1}^{m} y_i^{(k)}(\boldsymbol{x}^T\boldsymbol{y}^{(k)}) \right| - mx_i \\ &\le \sum_{k=1}^{m} |\boldsymbol{x}^T\boldsymbol{y}^{(k)}| - mx_i \end{aligned} \tag{14.41}$$

and

$$(\boldsymbol{W}\boldsymbol{x})_i \ge -\sum_{k=1}^{m} |\boldsymbol{x}^T\boldsymbol{y}^{(k)}| - mx_i \tag{14.42}$$

Hence, if one chooses

$$\sum_{k=1}^{m} |\boldsymbol{x}^T\boldsymbol{y}^{(k)}| < m \tag{14.43}$$

or, equivalently

$$\sum_{k=1}^{m} \mathit{EHD}(\boldsymbol{x}, \boldsymbol{y}^{(k)}) > \frac{(n-1)m}{2} \tag{14.44}$$

then

$$-m(1+x_i) < (\boldsymbol{W}\boldsymbol{x})_i \le m(1-x_i) \tag{14.45}$$

which implies

$$\begin{aligned} x_i = 1 &\longrightarrow -2m < (\boldsymbol{W}\boldsymbol{x})_i < 0 \longrightarrow x_i' = -1 \\ x_i = -1 &\longrightarrow 0 < (\boldsymbol{W}\boldsymbol{x})_i < 2m \longrightarrow x_i' = 1 \end{aligned}$$

that is

$$\boldsymbol{x}' \triangleq \boldsymbol{sgn}(\boldsymbol{W}\boldsymbol{x}) = -\boldsymbol{x} \tag{14.46}$$

This result may be summarized in the following theorem.

Theorem 14.2 (Dasgupta et al. 1989) *Given a key pattern $\boldsymbol{x}$, if there exists an integer p such that $\boldsymbol{x} \triangleq \boldsymbol{x}(p)$ that satisfies*

$$\sum_{k=1}^{n} EHD(\boldsymbol{x}, \boldsymbol{y}^{(k)}) > \frac{(n-1)m}{2} \tag{14.47}$$

then the state converges to only a cycle of length 2. ■

This theorem shows that if a probe vector $\boldsymbol{x}$ satisfies the condition of the theorem, it is inadequate for reaching a fundamental memory vector in the sense that the synchronous operating algorithm fails to register any impact on it. The successive $\boldsymbol{x}(k)$ simply oscillates between $\boldsymbol{x}'$ and $-\boldsymbol{x}'$.

Next, we study the condition where a probe $\boldsymbol{x}$ can be identified with a fundamental memory $\boldsymbol{y}^{(\ell)}$ that is closest to it in the Hamming distance. If a given probe $\boldsymbol{x}(0)$ is close enough to a particular $\boldsymbol{y}^{(\ell)}$ and far enough from all other fundamental memories, the probe $\boldsymbol{x}(0)$ may be updated to reach $\boldsymbol{y}^{(\ell)}$ using a synchronous operating mode.

Theorem 14.3 *Given a probe vector $\boldsymbol{x}(0)$, if there exist integers p and $\ell \in \{1, 2, \ldots, n\}$ such that $\boldsymbol{x} \triangleq \boldsymbol{x}(p)$ satisfies*

$$HD(\boldsymbol{x}, \boldsymbol{y}^{(\ell)}) \le \sum_{k=1, k\neq\ell}^{m} EHD(\boldsymbol{x}, \boldsymbol{y}^{(\ell)}) + n - \frac{m(n+1)}{2}$$

then the state converges to the fundamental memory $\boldsymbol{y}^{(\ell)}$.

Proof: Using the expressions of the Hamming distance (HD) and the effective Hamming distance (EHD) given in Lemma 14.1, one has

$$y_i^{(\ell)}(\boldsymbol{W}\boldsymbol{x})_i \quad = \quad y_i^{(\ell)} \left[\sum_{k=1}^{m} y_i^{(k)}(\boldsymbol{x}^T \boldsymbol{y}^{(k)}) - m x_i \right]$$

$$
\begin{aligned}
&= \sum_{k=1,k\neq\ell}^{m} y_i^{(k)} y_i^{(\ell)} (\boldsymbol{x}^T \boldsymbol{y}^{(k)}) + (\boldsymbol{x}^T \boldsymbol{y}^{(k)})(y_i^{(k)})^2 - m x_i y_i^{(\ell)} \\
&\geq - \sum_{k=1,k\neq\ell}^{m} |\boldsymbol{x}^T \boldsymbol{y}^{(k)}| + (\boldsymbol{x}^T \boldsymbol{y}^{(k)}) - m \\
&= 2 \sum_{k=1,k\neq\ell}^{m} EHD(\boldsymbol{x}, \boldsymbol{y}^{(k)}) - (m-1)n \\
&\quad + n - 2HD(\boldsymbol{x}, \boldsymbol{y}^{(\ell)}) - m
\end{aligned}
\tag{14.48}
$$

Hence, if

$$
HD(\boldsymbol{x}, \boldsymbol{y}^{(\ell)}) \leq \sum_{k=1,k\neq\ell}^{m} EHD(\boldsymbol{x}, \boldsymbol{y}^{(k)}) + n - \frac{m(n+1)}{2} \tag{14.49}
$$

then

$$
y_i^{(\ell)} (\boldsymbol{W}\boldsymbol{x})_i \geq 0 \tag{14.50}
$$

that is

$$
\boldsymbol{y}^{(\ell)} = \boldsymbol{sgn}(\boldsymbol{W}\boldsymbol{x}) \tag{14.51}
$$

■

Because of the existence of the spurious memory $-\boldsymbol{y}^{(\ell)}$, one further conclusion proposed by Dasgupta et al. (1989) is as follows:

If the condition in Theorem 14.3 is modified as

$$
EHD(\boldsymbol{x}, \boldsymbol{y}^{(\ell)}) \leq \sum_{k=1,k\neq\ell}^{m} EHD(\boldsymbol{x}, \boldsymbol{y}^{(\ell)}) + n - \frac{m(n+1)}{2} \tag{14.52}
$$

then

$$
\boldsymbol{sgn}(\boldsymbol{W}\boldsymbol{x}) = \boldsymbol{y}^{(\ell)} \quad \text{if} \quad HD(\boldsymbol{x}, \boldsymbol{y}^{(\ell)}) < HD(\boldsymbol{x}, -\boldsymbol{y}^{(\ell)}) \tag{14.53}
$$

$$
\boldsymbol{sgn}(\boldsymbol{W}\boldsymbol{x}) = -\boldsymbol{y}^{(\ell)} \quad \text{if} \quad HD(\boldsymbol{x}, \boldsymbol{y}^{(\ell)}) > HD(\boldsymbol{x}, -\boldsymbol{y}^{(\ell)}) \tag{14.54}
$$

That is, in this case, if the Hamming distance (HD) between $\boldsymbol{x}$ and $\boldsymbol{y}^{(\ell)}$ is smaller than that between $\boldsymbol{x}$ and $-\boldsymbol{y}^{(\ell)}$, then the state converges to $\boldsymbol{y}^{(\ell)}$. Otherwise, the state converges to the spurious memory $-\boldsymbol{y}^{(\ell)}$.

This analysis shows that the convergence of an initial probe vector varies with respect to one of the fundamental memories. It can be applied to the case of either orthogonal or nonorthogonal fundamental memories. Given an initial probe vector, the possibility of updating that probe vector to one of the fundamental memories may be verified using Theorem 14.3. The explicit estimation of the attractive region in the sense of the Hamming distance of a fundamental memory is somewhat difficult to obtain.

Next, we present a method for analyzing the attractive regions of the fundamental memories (see Fig. 14.6). This method was first proposed by Personnaz et al. (1986) for orthogonal patterns, and then was extended to the nonorthogonal patterns.

Let $\boldsymbol{x}$ be a probe vector that differs from the fundamental memories. We investigate the evolution of the system when started with state $\boldsymbol{x}$. Using the result given in Lemma 14.1, one has

$$\begin{aligned} \boldsymbol{W}\boldsymbol{x} &= \sum_{k=1}^{m} (\boldsymbol{y}^{(k)})(\boldsymbol{y}^{(k)})^T \boldsymbol{x} - m\boldsymbol{x} \\ &= \sum_{k=1}^{m} (n - 2\ HD(\boldsymbol{x}, \boldsymbol{y}^{(k)}))\boldsymbol{y}^{(k)} - m\boldsymbol{x} \qquad (14.55) \end{aligned}$$

To study the attractivity of the pattern vector $\boldsymbol{y}^{(\ell)}$, we try to find a sufficient condition for the system to evolve from the state $\boldsymbol{x}$ to the state $\boldsymbol{y}^{(\ell)}$ in one iteration. It may be concluded that if each component of $\boldsymbol{W}\boldsymbol{x}$ has the same

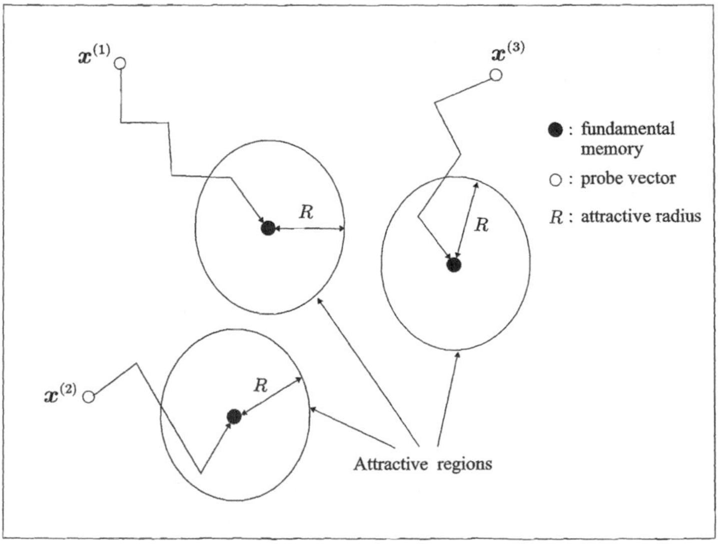

Figure 14.6 Attractive regions of fundamental memory.

sign as the corresponding component of $y^{(\ell)}$, the network evolves from the state $\boldsymbol{x}$ to the state $\boldsymbol{y}^{(\ell)}$ in one iteration.

This condition can be expressed as

$$\begin{aligned}(\boldsymbol{W}\boldsymbol{x})_i y_i^{(\ell)} &= (n - 2\,HD(\boldsymbol{x}, \boldsymbol{y}^{(\ell)}) \\ &\quad + \sum_{k=1,k\neq\ell}^{m} \left(n - 2\,HD(\boldsymbol{x}, \boldsymbol{y}^{(k)})\right) y_i^{(k)} y_i^{(\ell)} - m x_i y_i^{(\ell)} \\ &\geq 0, \quad \text{for all} \quad i \end{aligned} \tag{14.56}$$

Also

$$n - 2\,HD(\boldsymbol{x}, \boldsymbol{y}^{(\ell)}) + \sum_{k=1,k\neq\ell}^{m} (n - 2\,HD(\boldsymbol{x}, \boldsymbol{y}^{(k)})) y_i^{(k)} y_i^{(\ell)} - m \geq 0, \quad \text{for all} \quad i \tag{14.57}$$

This condition is satisfied if

$$n - 2\,HD(\boldsymbol{x}, \boldsymbol{y}^{(\ell)}) > |\sum_{k=1,k\neq\ell}^{m} (n - 2\,HD(\boldsymbol{x}, \boldsymbol{y}^{(k)})) y_i^{(k)} y_i^{(\ell)}| - m \tag{14.58}$$

Using the notation of the correlation coefficient $r_{k\ell}$, one has

$$HD(\boldsymbol{y}^{(\ell)}, \boldsymbol{y}^{(k)}) = \frac{n}{2} - \frac{r_{k\ell}}{2}$$

Using the triangular inequality, one has

$$\begin{aligned} HD(\boldsymbol{x}, \boldsymbol{y}^{(k)}) &\leq HD(\boldsymbol{x}, \boldsymbol{y}^{(\ell)}) + HD(\boldsymbol{y}^{(\ell)}, \boldsymbol{y}^{(k)}) \\ &= HD(\boldsymbol{x}, \boldsymbol{y}^{(\ell)}) + \frac{n}{2} - \frac{r_{k\ell}}{2} \end{aligned}$$

and

$$\begin{aligned} HD(\boldsymbol{y}^{(\ell)}, \boldsymbol{y}^{(k)}) &= \frac{n}{2} - \frac{r_{k\ell}}{2} \\ &\leq HD(\boldsymbol{y}^{(k)}, \boldsymbol{x}) + HD(\boldsymbol{y}^{(\ell)}, \boldsymbol{x}) - \frac{r_{k\ell}}{2} \end{aligned}$$

which implies

$$|n - 2\,HD(\boldsymbol{x}, \boldsymbol{y}^{(k)})| \leq 2\,HD(\boldsymbol{x}, \boldsymbol{y}^{(\ell)})) + |r_{k\ell}| \tag{14.59}$$

Therefore

$$\begin{aligned}
&\left| \sum_{k=1,k\neq\ell}^{m} \left(n - 2\,HD(\boldsymbol{x}, \boldsymbol{y}^{(k)})\right) y_i^{(k)} y_i^{(\ell)} \right| \\
&\leq \; 2\,HD(\boldsymbol{x}, \boldsymbol{y}^{(\ell)})(m-1) + \sum_{k=1,k\neq\ell}^{m} |r_{k\ell}| \\
&= \; 2\,HD(\boldsymbol{x}, \boldsymbol{y}^{(\ell)})(m-1) + \mu_\ell \qquad (14.60)
\end{aligned}$$

Consequently, if the condition

$$2\,HD(\boldsymbol{x}, \boldsymbol{y}^{(\ell)})(m-1) + \mu_\ell \leq n - 2\,HD(\boldsymbol{x}, \boldsymbol{y}^{(\ell)}) - m \qquad (14.61)$$

or equivalently

$$HD(\boldsymbol{x}, \boldsymbol{y}^{(\ell)}) \leq \frac{n - m - \mu_\ell}{2m} \qquad (14.62)$$

then the inequality given in Eqn. (14.56) is verified. Thus, the network will certainly reach the fundamental memory $y^{(\ell)}$. It can be checked from the inequality given in Eqn. (14.62) that if a probe state lies within a distance of $(n - m - \mu_\ell)/2m$ from a fundamental memory, its distance from any other fundamental memory is greater than $(n - m - \mu_\ell)/2m$

$$n - [2\,HD(\boldsymbol{x}, \boldsymbol{y}^{(k)})] \leq 2\,HD(\boldsymbol{x}, \boldsymbol{y}^{(\ell)}) \leq \frac{n - m - \mu_\ell}{m} \qquad (14.63)$$

Hence

$$HD(\boldsymbol{x}, \boldsymbol{y}^{(k)}) \geq \frac{n - m - \mu_\ell}{2m} \qquad (14.64)$$

Theorem 14.4 *Given a probe vector $\boldsymbol{x}(0)$, if there exist integers p and $\ell \in \{1, 2, \ldots, n\}$ such that $\boldsymbol{x} \triangleq \boldsymbol{x}(p)$ satisfies*

$$HD(\boldsymbol{x}, \boldsymbol{y}^{(\ell)}) \leq \frac{n - m - \mu_\ell}{2m} \qquad (14.65)$$

then the state converges to the fundamental memory $y^{(\ell)}$. ■

If the fundamental memories are orthogonal, then

$$\mu_\ell = 0, \quad \text{for all} \quad 1 \leq \ell \leq m \qquad (14.66)$$

In this case, however, these fundamental memories are guaranteed to be stable states.

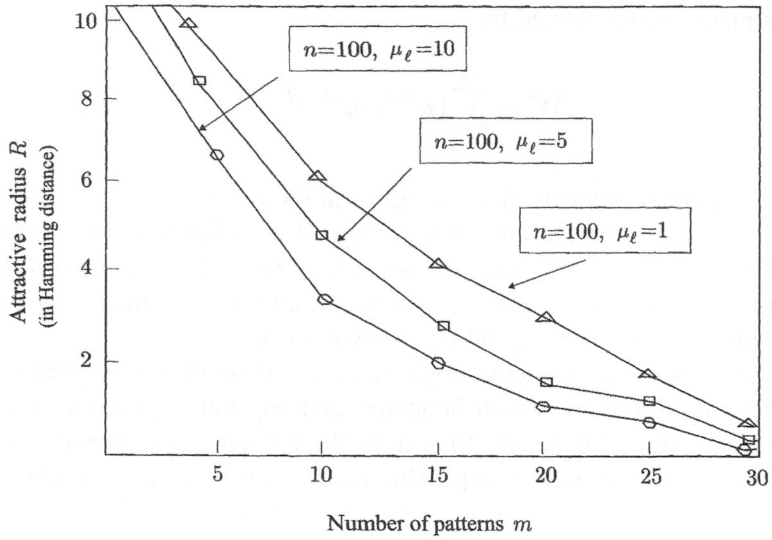

Figure 14.7 The attractive radius R of *nonorthogonal* fundamental memories as a function of the number of patterns m and various values of μ_ℓ.

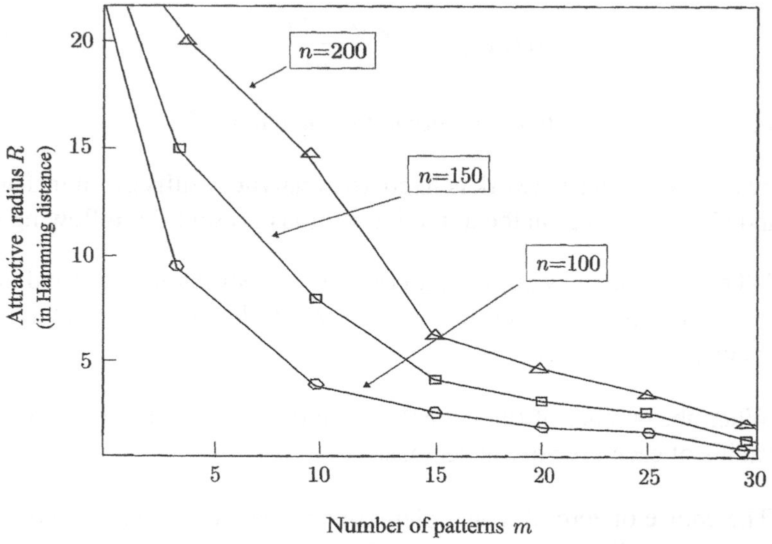

Figure 14.8 The attractive radius R of *orthogonal* fundamental memories as a function of the number of patterns m and various values of n.

Now we need to explore the attractivity of these memory vectors. If the weight matrix is determined by

$$\boldsymbol{W} = \sum_{k=1}^{m} (\boldsymbol{y}^{(k)})(\boldsymbol{y}^{(k)})^T$$

then the diagonal elements of the weight matrix are m.

Figure 14.7 shows the attractive radius R as a function of the number of patterns m, $n = 100$, and various values of μ_ℓ for the *nonorthogonal* fundamental memories. Figure 14.8 shows the attractive radius R as a function of the number of patterns m and various values of n.

An analysis of the attractive regions of the memories was presented by Personnaz et al. (1986), which indicates that any initial probe vector lying within a Hamming distance $(n/2m)$ from the fundamental memory will converge to this memory in one step. This result may be easily extended to the weight matrix with zero-diagonal elements using the procedure given in the following corollary.

Corollary 14.2 *Let all the fundamental memories be orthogonal. Given a probe vector $\boldsymbol{x}(0)$, if there exist integers p and $\ell \in \{1, 2, \ldots, n\}$ such that $\boldsymbol{x} \triangleq \boldsymbol{x}(p)$ satisfies*

$$HD(\boldsymbol{x}, \boldsymbol{y}^{(\ell)}) \leq \frac{n - m}{2m} \tag{14.67}$$

then the state converges to the fundamental memory $\boldsymbol{y}^{(\ell)}$. ■

If the dimension of a network is fixed, the analytic results given in Theorem 14.4 and Corollary 14.2 on the attractive regions present the following facts:

(i) When the absolute values of the correlation coefficients of a fundamental memory with rest memories are increased, the attractive radius of this memory is decreased;

(ii) When the number of fundamental memories is increased, the attractive radius of each memory is decreased;

(iii) The choice of zero-diagonal elements of the weight matrix reduces the attractive radii of the fundamental memories. However, this structure of the weight matrix, as discussed in a later section, may eliminate the undesirable spurious memories.

Example 14.3 Consider the memory storage case when $n = 24$, $m = 4$, and there are four patterns to be stored

$$\boldsymbol{y}^{(1)} = \begin{bmatrix} e \\ e \\ e \\ e \end{bmatrix}, \quad \boldsymbol{y}^{(2)} = \begin{bmatrix} e \\ e \\ -e \\ -e \end{bmatrix}, \quad \boldsymbol{y}^{(3)} = \begin{bmatrix} e \\ -e \\ e \\ -e \end{bmatrix}, \quad \boldsymbol{y}^{(4)} = \begin{bmatrix} e \\ -e \\ -e \\ e \end{bmatrix}$$

where

$$e = [1\ 1\ 1\ 1\ 1\ 1]^T$$

is a vector of six 1s. Clearly these four vectors are mutually orthogonal. Hence, the neural network with the weight matrix $\boldsymbol{W}$ designed by the Hebb learning rule is able to recognize each of the four patterns. In this case

$$\frac{n-m}{2m} = \frac{5}{2}$$

Hence, if

$$HD(\boldsymbol{x}, \boldsymbol{y}^{(\ell)}) \leq 2$$

the network transforms $\boldsymbol{x}$ to $\boldsymbol{y}^{(\ell)}$ in a single timestep. This means that the network is able to recognize even a corrupted version of the pattern $\boldsymbol{y}^{(\ell)}$, provided the number of errors is no more than 2.

Now, if $y_4^{(4)}$ is changed to $-e$, the first three patterns continue to be mutually orthogonal, but the fourth pattern is no longer orthogonal to the others. The correlation coefficients $r_{\ell k}$ can be readily computed as follows:

$$\begin{bmatrix} - & r_{12} & r_{13} & r_{14} \\ r_{21} & - & r_{13} & r_{14} \\ r_{31} & r_{32} & - & r_{34} \\ r_{41} & r_{42} & r_{43} & - \end{bmatrix} = \begin{bmatrix} - & 0 & 0 & -2 \\ 0 & - & 0 & 2 \\ 0 & 0 & - & 2 \\ -2 & 2 & 2 & - \end{bmatrix}$$

Hence

$$\mu_1 = \mu_2 = \mu_3 = 2, \qquad \mu_4 = 6$$

Since

$$\mu_\ell < (n-m) = 20, \qquad \ell = 1, 2, 3, 4$$

these four patterns stored in the neural network are stable. Furthermore

$$\frac{n-m-\mu_\ell}{2m} = \begin{cases} 2.25, & \text{for } \ell = 1, 2, 3 \\ 1.75, & \text{for } \ell = 4 \end{cases}$$

Hence, if the weight matrix is chosen by Hebb's learning rule, the network continues to recognize each of the four patterns. However, the attractive region of the fourth pattern, which is not orthogonal with the other patterns, is reduced. ■

14.3 NONORTHOGONAL FUNDAMENTAL MEMORIES

14.3.1 Convergence for Nonorthogonal Patterns

As an associative memory mechanism, a memory pattern is valid only if it is stable or retrievable. The memory pattern is valid when all the given patterns belong to a set of orthogonal vectors. However, nonorthogonal pattern vectors may not be the stable states if Hebb's learning rule with a zero-threshold vector is applied as shown in Example 14.4. This means that these pattern vectors may not be retrievable regardless of the state updating modes used. Since

$$\boldsymbol{sgn}(\boldsymbol{W}\boldsymbol{y}^{(\ell)}) = \boldsymbol{sgn}(\lambda^{(\ell)}\boldsymbol{y}^{(\ell)}) = \boldsymbol{y}^{(\ell)} \tag{14.68}$$

a necessary condition that the fundamental memory $\boldsymbol{y}^{(\ell)}$ is a stable state is that $\boldsymbol{y}^{(\ell)}$ is an eigenvector of $\boldsymbol{W}$ with a positive eigenvalue $\lambda^{(\ell)} > 0$. This condition is always satisfied for m orthogonal fundamental memory vectors. However, it may not be true when the given m fundamental memories are nonorthogonal because $\boldsymbol{y}^{(\ell)}$ may not be an eigenvector of $\boldsymbol{W}$.

Example 14.4 In this example we shall show that the Hebb learning rule given by Eqns. (14.6) and (14.7) fails to store two pattern vectors that are nonorthogonal if these two pattern vectors differ in only one component. Assume that there exist two stable vectors $\boldsymbol{y}^{(1)}$ and $\boldsymbol{y}^{(2)}$ of the weight matrix with zero diagonal elements so that

$$y_j^{(1)} = y_j^{(2)}, \quad \text{for all} \quad 1 \le j \le n \quad \text{and} \quad j \ne i$$

and

$$y_i^{(1)} = -y_i^{(2)}$$

Since both $\boldsymbol{y}^{(1)}$ and $\boldsymbol{y}^{(2)}$ are stable vectors of the network, we have

$$\begin{aligned} y_i^{(1)} &= sgn\left(\sum_{j=1}^{n} w_{ij} y_j^{(1)}\right) \\ &= sgn\left(\sum_{j=1, j\ne i}^{n} w_{ij} y_j^{(1)}\right) \\ &= sgn\left(\sum_{j=1, j\ne i}^{n} w_{ij} y_j^{(2)}\right) \end{aligned}$$

$$
\begin{aligned}
&= sgn\left(\sum_{j=1}^{n} w_{ij} y_j^{(2)}\right) \\
&= y_i^{(2)}
\end{aligned}
$$

Since we started with the assumption that $\boldsymbol{y}^{(1)}$ and $\boldsymbol{y}^{(2)}$ are different, the result in this equation represents a contradiction. In fact

$$
\begin{aligned}
(\boldsymbol{y}^{(1)})^T(\boldsymbol{y}^{(2)}) &= \sum_{j=1, j\neq i}^{n} (y_j^{(1)})^2 + y_i^{(1)} y_i^{(2)} \\
&= n - 2
\end{aligned}
$$

that is, $\boldsymbol{y}^{(1)}$ and $\boldsymbol{y}^{(2)}$ are two nonorthogonal vectors. ■

Example 14.5 Given two n-dimensional patterns $\boldsymbol{y}^{(1)}$ and $\boldsymbol{y}^{(2)}$ defined by

$$
y_i^{(1)} = -1, \quad \text{for all} \quad i = 1, 2, \ldots, n
$$

and

$$
\begin{aligned}
y_1^{(2)} &= -1 \\
y_i^{(2)} &= 1, \qquad \text{for all} \quad i = 2, 3, \ldots, n
\end{aligned}
$$

it is easy to verify that

$$
\left|(\boldsymbol{y}^{(1)})^T(\boldsymbol{y}^{(2)})\right| = (n-2)
$$

which means that the two pattern vectors are nonorthogonal. Using Hebb's learning rule, we have

$$
\begin{aligned}
\boldsymbol{W}_1 &= (\boldsymbol{y}^{(1)})(\boldsymbol{y}^{(1)})^T - \boldsymbol{I} = \begin{bmatrix} 0 & 1 & \cdots & 1 \\ 1 & 0 & \cdots & 1 \\ \vdots & \vdots & \ddots & \vdots \\ 1 & 1 & \cdots & 0 \end{bmatrix} \\
\boldsymbol{W}_2 &= (\boldsymbol{y}^{(2)})(\boldsymbol{y}^{(2)})^T - \boldsymbol{I} = \begin{bmatrix} 0 & -1 & \cdots & -1 \\ -1 & 0 & \cdots & 1 \\ \vdots & \vdots & \ddots & \vdots \\ -1 & 1 & \cdots & 0 \end{bmatrix}
\end{aligned}
$$

Thus

$$\boldsymbol{W} = \boldsymbol{W}_1 + \boldsymbol{W}_2 = \begin{bmatrix} 0 & 0 & 0 & \cdots & 0 \\ 0 & 0 & 2 & \cdots & 2 \\ \vdots & \vdots & \vdots & \ddots & \vdots \\ 0 & 2 & 2 & \cdots & 0 \end{bmatrix}$$

Since

$$\begin{aligned} sgn(\boldsymbol{W}\boldsymbol{y}^{(1)}) &= [1 \quad -1 \quad \cdots \quad -1]^T \neq \boldsymbol{y}^{(1)} \\ sgn(\boldsymbol{W}\boldsymbol{y}^{(2)}) &= [1 \quad 1 \quad \cdots \quad 1]^T \neq \boldsymbol{y}^{(2)} \end{aligned}$$

neither $\boldsymbol{y}^{(1)}$ nor $\boldsymbol{y}^{(2)}$ is stable. ■

An inspection of the patterns in Example 14.5 gives the effective Hamming distance between patterns $\boldsymbol{y}^{(1)}$ and $\boldsymbol{y}^{(2)}$ as

$$EHD(\boldsymbol{y}^{(1)}, \boldsymbol{y}^{(2)}) = 1$$

which is "too small." This fact may be considered as the reason that the patterns could not be stored as stable states. This leads us to finding the sufficient conditions that the nonorthogonal patterns can be stored as the stable states using the measurement of the Hamming distance between the patterns. We will review the results obtained by Dasgupta et al. (1989).

Given m binary pattern vectors $\boldsymbol{y}^{(1)}$, $\boldsymbol{y}^{(2)}$, ..., $\boldsymbol{y}^{(m)}$, which may be nonorthogonal, for $\forall k, \ell \in \{1, 2, \ldots, n\}$, define the correlation coefficient as

$$r_{k\ell} \triangleq \langle \boldsymbol{y}^{(k)}, \boldsymbol{y}^{(\ell)} \rangle = (\boldsymbol{y}^{(k)})^T (\boldsymbol{y}^{(\ell)}) = \sum_{j=1}^{n} y_j^{(k)} y_j^{(\ell)} \tag{14.69}$$

Since

$$HD(\boldsymbol{y}^{(k)}, \boldsymbol{y}^{(\ell)}) = \tfrac{1}{2} \left[n - (\boldsymbol{y}^{(k)})^T (\boldsymbol{y}^{(\ell)}) \right] \tag{14.70}$$

one has

$$r_{k\ell} = n - 2\, HD(\boldsymbol{y}^{(k)}, \boldsymbol{y}^{(\ell)}) \tag{14.71}$$

Hence, $r_{\ell k}$ is a measure of the nonorthogonality of the patterns $\boldsymbol{y}^{(\ell)}$ and $\boldsymbol{y}^{(k)}$ and is called the *correlation coefficient* between the two patterns.

Let us define an integer μ_ℓ as a measure of how $\boldsymbol{y}^{(\ell)}$ is correlated with the remaining $(m-1)$ patterns as

$$\mu_\ell = \sum_{k=1, k \neq \ell}^{m} |r_{k\ell}| \tag{14.72}$$

Note that μ_ℓ can be large in a number of ways:

(i) $\boldsymbol{y}^{(\ell)}$ is *strongly* correlated with some other patterns $\boldsymbol{y}^{(k)}$;

(ii) $\boldsymbol{y}^{(\ell)}$ is *somewhat* correlated with *several* other patterns;

(iii) A combination of conditions (i) and (ii): $\boldsymbol{y}^{(\ell)}$ is *strongly* correlated with some patterns and *somewhat* correlated with several others.

Lemma 14.2 *Given m binary vectors, $\boldsymbol{y}^{(1)}, \boldsymbol{y}^{(2)}, \ldots, \boldsymbol{y}^{(m)}$, if*

$$\mu_\ell \leq (n - m) \tag{14.73}$$

then the pattern $\boldsymbol{y}^{(\ell)}$ is in the stable state of the neural network designed by Hebb's learning rule, Eqn. (14.7).

Proof: As discussed previously, a sufficient and necessary condition for ensuring the stability of these patterns is

$$\left(\sum_{j=1}^{n} w_{ij} y_j^{(\ell)}\right) y_i^{(\ell)} \leq 0$$

where

$$w_{ij} = \sum_{k=1}^{n} y_i^{(k)} y_j^{(k)} - m\delta_{ij} \tag{14.74}$$

and

$$\begin{aligned}
\sum_{j=1}^{n} w_{ij} y_j^{(\ell)} &= \sum_{j=1}^{n}\sum_{k=1}^{m} y_i^{(k)} y_j^{(k)} (1 - m\delta_{ij}) y_j^{(\ell)} \\
&= \sum_{j=1}^{n}\left(y_i^{(\ell)} y_j^{(\ell)} y_j^{(\ell)} + \sum_{k=1, k\neq\ell}^{m} y_i^{(k)} y_j^{(k)} y_j^{(\ell)} - m\delta_{ij} y_j^{(\ell)} \right) \\
&= (n - m) y_i^{(\ell)} + \sum_{j=1}^{n} \sum_{k=1, k\neq\ell}^{m} y_i^{(k)} y_j^{(k)} y_j^{(\ell)} \qquad (14.75)
\end{aligned}$$

Thus

$$\left(\sum_{j=1}^{n} w_{ij} y_j^{(\ell)}\right) y_i^{(\ell)} = (n - m)(y_i^{(\ell)} y_i^{(\ell)}) + \sum_{j=1}^{n} \sum_{k=1, k\neq\ell}^{m} y_i^{(k)} y_j^{(k)} y_j^{(\ell)} y_i^{(\ell)}$$

$$
\begin{aligned}
&= n - m + \sum_{k=1,k\neq\ell}^{m} y_i^{(k)} y_i^{(\ell)} ((\boldsymbol{y}^{(k)})^T \boldsymbol{y}^{(\ell)}) \\
&\geq n - m - \sum_{k=1,k\neq\ell}^{m} |(\boldsymbol{y}^{(k)})^T \boldsymbol{y}^{(\ell)}| \\
&\geq 0 \qquad (14.76)
\end{aligned}
$$

This implies that

$$
(n-m) \geq \sum_{k=1,k\neq\ell}^{m} |r_{k\ell}| = \mu_\ell \qquad (14.77)
$$

Then, the inequality given in Eqn. (14.73) is satisfied and the pattern $y^{(\ell)}$ is in the stable state of the network designed using Hebb's learning rule. ■

Furthermore, from Lemma 14.1 one has

$$
2\,EHD(\boldsymbol{y}^{(\ell)}, \boldsymbol{y}^{(k)}) + |(\boldsymbol{y}^{(\ell)})^T (\boldsymbol{y}^{(k)})| = n
$$

that is

$$
\sum_{k=1,k\neq\ell}^{m} \left(2\,EHD(\boldsymbol{y}^{(\ell)}, \boldsymbol{y}^{(k)}) + |(\boldsymbol{y}^{(\ell)})^T (\boldsymbol{y}^{(k)})| \right) = (m-1)n \qquad (14.78)
$$

If

$$
\sum_{k=1,k\neq\ell}^{m} EHD(\boldsymbol{y}^{(\ell)}, \boldsymbol{y}^{(K)}) > \frac{m(n+1)}{2} - n \qquad (14.79)
$$

or

$$
EHD(\boldsymbol{y}^{(\ell)}, \boldsymbol{y}^{(k)}) \geq \frac{m(n+1) - 2n}{2(m-1)} \qquad (14.80)
$$

then

$$
m(n+1) - 2n + \sum_{k=1,k\neq\ell}^{n} |\boldsymbol{y}^{(k)} \boldsymbol{y}^{(\ell)}| \leq n(m-1) \qquad (14.81)
$$

that is, the inequality given in Eqn. (14.73) is satisfied. A summary of the above derivation is given in the following theorem.

Theorem 14.5 (Dasgupta et al. 1989) *Given m binary pattern vectors $\boldsymbol{y}^{(1)}$, $\boldsymbol{y}^{(2)}$, ..., $\boldsymbol{y}^{(m)}$, if one of the following conditions is satisfied*

(i) for $\ell \in \{1, 2, \ldots, m\}$

$$\sum_{k=1, k\neq\ell}^{m} EHD(\boldsymbol{y}^{(\ell)}, \boldsymbol{y}^{(K)}) > \frac{m(n+1)}{2} - n \tag{14.82}$$

or

(ii) for $\ell, k \in \{1, 2, \ldots, m\}$ and $k \neq \ell$

$$EHD(\boldsymbol{y}^{(\ell)}, \boldsymbol{y}^{(k)}) \geq \frac{m(n+1) - 2n}{2(m-1)} \tag{14.83}$$

then the pattern $\boldsymbol{y}^{(\ell)}$ is in the stable state of the network if it is designed using Hebb's learning rule given in Eqn. (14.7). ■

14.3.2 Storage of Nonorthogonal Patterns

Hebb's learning rule is suitable for designing an associative memory that guarantees perfect retrieval of the stored information if the given binary pattern vectors are orthogonal. If the given pattern vectors are not orthogonal, the stable condition given in Eqn. (14.1) is no longer true. The requirement of strict orthogonality imposes severe restrictions on the possible prototypes or memory vector to be stored. On the other hand, it is known that if n is large, any two randomly selected patterns will almost be orthogonal, and this is usually sufficient in many practical applications. However, in many practical problems one has to deal with finite systems having a small n. In this case, the information to be stored is neither random nor orthogonal, and the prototype patterns will, in general, be correlated, causing a low storage capacity. Therefore, it is important to develop a weight learning method exhibiting the same stability property for any set of pattern vectors, as we are going to explore in this section.

Given m binary pattern vectors that are nonorthogonal, the stability conditions of the states associated with the given patterns may be expressed as

$$\left(\sum_{j=1}^{n} w_{ij} y_j^{(\ell)} + \theta_i\right) y_i^{(\ell)} \geq 0 \tag{14.84}$$

$$1 \leq i \leq n, \quad 1 \leq \ell \leq m$$

Here, the unknown variables are the n components θ_i of $\boldsymbol{\theta}$. Hence, a proper choice of the threshold $\boldsymbol{\theta}$ may ensure the stability of the stored pattern vectors. Moreover, the determination of such a vector requires solving a system of $n \times m$ inequalities. These inequalities cannot be solved easily and do not always have a solution.

Next, a simplified approach is introduced to find the solutions of the set of inequalities given in Eqn. (14.84). In fact, small deviations from orthogonality lead to random variations in the internal field y_i, and an estimate of this variation can be obtained by calculating the actual value of y when it coincides with one of the stored patterns; that is, when $x_i = y_i^{(\ell)}$. Then

$$\begin{aligned} y_i &= \sum_{j=1}^{n} w_{ij} x_j + \theta_i \\ &= \sum_{j=1}^{n} \sum_{k=1}^{m} y_i^{(k)} y_j^{(k)} (1 - m\delta_{ij}) y_j^{(\ell)} + \theta_i \\ &= \sum_{j=1}^{n} \left(y_i^{(\ell)} y_j^{(\ell)} y_j^{(\ell)} + \sum_{k=1, k \neq \ell}^{m} y_i^{(k)} y_j^{(k)} y_j^{(\ell)} - m\delta_{ij} y_j^{(\ell)} \right) + \theta_i \end{aligned} \tag{14.85}$$

Using $r_{k\ell}$ as the correlation coefficients between the patterns $\boldsymbol{y}^{(k)}$ and $\boldsymbol{y}^{(\ell)}$ yields

$$y_i = (n - m) y_i^{(\ell)} + \sum_{k=1, k \neq \ell}^{m} r_{k\ell} y_i^{(k)} + \theta_i \tag{14.86}$$

The second term of this equation shows a contribution from all the other stored patterns due to their nonorthogonality. In order to ensure the stability of the pattern $\boldsymbol{y}^{(\ell)}$ that is an equilibrium state, one may assume $x_i y_i \geq 0$, that is

$$\begin{aligned} &\left[(n - m) y_i^{(\ell)} + \sum_{k=1, k \neq \ell}^{m} r_{k\ell} y_i^{(k)} + \theta_i \right] y_i^{(\ell)} \\ &= (n - m) + \left[\sum_{k=1, k \neq \ell}^{m} r_{k\ell} y_i^{(k)} + \theta_i \right] y_i^{(\ell)} \\ &\geq 0 \end{aligned} \tag{14.87}$$

Table 14.4 **Nonorthogonal patterns storage using Hebb's learning rule, Eqn. (14.7)**

Given m bipolar pattern vectors:

$$\boldsymbol{y}^{(1)}, \boldsymbol{y}^{(2)}, \ldots, \boldsymbol{y}^{(m)} \in \{-1, 1\}^n$$

Steps 1–3: These are the same as that in Table 14.3;

Step 4: The correlation coefficients are: $r_{k\ell} \longleftarrow 0,\ k \longleftarrow 1,\ \ell \longleftarrow 1$

Step 5: $r_{k\ell} \longleftarrow (\boldsymbol{y}^{(k)})(\boldsymbol{y}^{(\ell)})$

Step 6: If $k < m$, then $k \longleftarrow k+1$ and go to Step 5; otherwise go to Step 7;

Step 7: If $\ell < m$, then $\ell \longleftarrow \ell+1$, $k \longleftarrow 1$, and go to Step 8;

Step 8: Initialization: $r_{i\ell} \longleftarrow 0,\ i \longleftarrow 1,\ \ell \longleftarrow 1,\ k \longleftarrow 1$

Step 9: If $k \neq \ell$, then $r_{i\ell} \longleftarrow r_{k\ell} y_i^{(k)}$ and go to Step 8; otherwise, go to Step 10;

Step 10: If $k \leq m$, then $k \longleftarrow k+1$, and go to Step 9; otherwise go to Step 11;

Step 11: If $i \leq n$, then $i \longleftarrow i+1$, $k \longleftarrow 1$, and go to Step 9; otherwise go to Step 12;

Step 12: If $\ell \leq m$, then $\ell \longleftarrow \ell+1$, and go to Step 9; otherwise go to Step 13;

Step 13: Initialization: $\gamma_i^- \longleftarrow \gamma_{i\ell},\quad \gamma_i^+ \longleftarrow \gamma_{i\ell},\quad \ell \longleftarrow 1,\quad k \longleftarrow 1$

Step 14: If $\ell \leq m$ then $\ell \longleftarrow \ell+1$, and go to Step 15; otherwise, go to Step 16;

Step 15: If $\gamma_i^- \leq \gamma_{i\ell}$ then go to Step 14; otherwise, $\gamma_i^- = \gamma_{i\ell}$ and go to Step 14;

Step 16: If $k \leq m$ then $k \longleftarrow k+1$, and go to Step 17; otherwise, go to Step 18;

Step 17: If $\gamma_i^+ \geq \gamma_{i\ell}$ then go to Step 16; otherwise, $\gamma_i^+ = \gamma_{i\ell}$ and go to Step 16;

Step 18: The threshold vector $\boldsymbol{\theta}$ is

$$-(n-m) - \gamma_i^- \leq \theta_i \leq (n-m) - \gamma_i^+, \quad i = 1, 2, \ldots, n$$

Step 19: Storing is completed. Output $\boldsymbol{W}$ and $\boldsymbol{\theta}$.

Hence the component θ_i of the threshold vector that satisfies the inequality may be chosen such that

$$-(n-m) \leq \sum_{k=1, k\neq \ell}^{m} r_{k\ell} y_i^{(k)} + \theta_i \leq (n-m) \tag{14.88}$$

Define the coefficients

$$\gamma_{i\ell} \triangleq \sum_{k=1, k\neq \ell}^{m} r_{k\ell} y_i^{(k)}, \quad i = 1, 2, \ldots, n, \quad \ell = 1, 2 \ldots, m \tag{14.89}$$

Then, a further relationship may be given by

$$-(n-m) - \gamma_i^- \leq \theta_i \leq (n-m) - \gamma_i^+ \tag{14.90}$$

where

$$\gamma_i^- \triangleq \min_{\ell}\{\gamma_{i\ell}\}$$

and

$$\gamma_i^+ \triangleq \max_{\ell}\{\gamma_{i\ell}\}$$

A storage process for m binary pattern vectors that may be nonorthogonal is summarized in Table 14.4.

Example 14.6 Given three binary pattern vectors

$$\boldsymbol{y}^{(1)} = \begin{bmatrix} -1 \\ 1 \\ -1 \\ 1 \end{bmatrix}, \quad \boldsymbol{y}^{(2)} = \begin{bmatrix} -1 \\ -1 \\ -1 \\ 1 \end{bmatrix}, \quad \boldsymbol{y}^{(3)} = \begin{bmatrix} -1 \\ -1 \\ -1 \\ -1 \end{bmatrix}$$

It is to be noted that the two patterns are nonorthogonal since the correlation coefficient between the two patterns is

$$r_{12} = r_{21} = (\boldsymbol{y}^{(1)})(\boldsymbol{y}^{(2)}) = 2$$
$$r_{13} = r_{31} = (\boldsymbol{y}^{(1)})(\boldsymbol{y}^{(3)}) = 0$$
$$r_{23} = r_{32} = (\boldsymbol{y}^{(2)})(\boldsymbol{y}^{(3)}) = 2$$

Using Hebb's learning rule, the weight matrix is obtained as

$$\boldsymbol{W}_1 = (\boldsymbol{y}^{(1)})(\boldsymbol{y}^{(1)})^T - \boldsymbol{I} \quad = \begin{bmatrix} 0 & -1 & 1 & -1 \\ -1 & 0 & -1 & 1 \\ 1 & -1 & 0 & -1 \\ -1 & 1 & -1 & 0 \end{bmatrix}$$

$$W_2 = (y^{(2)})(y^{(2)})^T - I = \begin{bmatrix} 0 & 1 & 1 & -1 \\ 1 & 0 & 1 & -1 \\ 1 & 1 & 0 & -1 \\ -1 & -1 & -1 & 0 \end{bmatrix}$$

$$W_3 = (y^{(3)})(y^{(3)})^T - I = \begin{bmatrix} 0 & 1 & 1 & 1 \\ 1 & 0 & 1 & 1 \\ 1 & 1 & 0 & 1 \\ 1 & 1 & 1 & 0 \end{bmatrix}$$

Therefore, the weight matrix is given by

$$W = W_1 + W_2 + W_3 = \begin{bmatrix} 0 & 1 & 3 & -1 \\ 1 & 0 & 1 & 1 \\ 3 & 1 & 0 & -1 \\ -1 & 1 & -1 & 0 \end{bmatrix} \tag{14.91}$$

Since

$$Wy^{(1)} = \begin{bmatrix} -3 \\ -1 \\ -3 \\ 3 \end{bmatrix}, \quad Wy^{(2)} = \begin{bmatrix} -5 \\ -1 \\ -5 \\ 1 \end{bmatrix}, \quad Wy^{(3)} = \begin{bmatrix} -3 \\ -3 \\ -3 \\ 1 \end{bmatrix}$$

it follows that if the threshold vector θ is chosen as zero, the patterns $y^{(1)}$ and $y^{(2)}$ are not the stable equilibrium points of the designed network. One has to reselect the threshold vector using the procedure given in Table 14.4. By using Eqn. (14.89), we have

$$\begin{aligned} \gamma_{i1} &= r_{21}y_i^{(2)} + r_{31}y_i^{(3)} = 2y_i^{(2)} \\ \gamma_{i2} &= r_{12}y_i^{(1)} + r_{32}y_i^{(3)} = 2y_i^{(1)} + 2y_i^{(3)} \\ \gamma_{i3} &= r_{13}y_i^{(1)} + r_{23}y_i^{(2)} = 2y_i^{(2)} \end{aligned}$$

Hence

$$\begin{cases} \gamma_{11} = -2 \\ \gamma_{12} = -4 \\ \gamma_{13} = -2 \end{cases}, \quad \begin{cases} \gamma_{21} = -2 \\ \gamma_{22} = 0 \\ \gamma_{23} = -2 \end{cases}, \quad \begin{cases} \gamma_{31} = -2 \\ \gamma_{32} = -4 \\ \gamma_{33} = -2 \end{cases}, \quad \begin{cases} \gamma_{41} = 2 \\ \gamma_{42} = 0 \\ \gamma_{43} = 2 \end{cases}$$

and

$$\begin{cases} \gamma_1^- = -4 \\ \gamma_1^+ = -2 \end{cases}, \quad \begin{cases} \gamma_2^- = -2 \\ \gamma_2^+ = 0 \end{cases}, \quad \begin{cases} \gamma_3^- = -4 \\ \gamma_3^+ = -2 \end{cases}, \quad \begin{cases} \gamma_4^- = 0 \\ \gamma_4^+ = 2 \end{cases}$$

Therefore, the four components of the threshold vector θ may be chosen as

$$\theta_1 = 3, \quad \theta_2 = 1, \quad \theta_3 = 3, \quad \theta_3 = -1$$

or

$$\boldsymbol{\theta} = [3 \quad 1 \quad 3 \quad -1]^T \tag{14.92}$$

In this case

$$\boldsymbol{W}\boldsymbol{y}^{(1)} + \boldsymbol{\theta} = \begin{bmatrix} 0 \\ 0 \\ 0 \\ 2 \end{bmatrix} \tag{14.93}$$

$$\boldsymbol{W}\boldsymbol{y}^{(2)} + \boldsymbol{\theta} = \begin{bmatrix} -2 \\ 0 \\ -2 \\ 0 \end{bmatrix} \tag{14.94}$$

$$\boldsymbol{W}\boldsymbol{y}^{(3)} + \boldsymbol{\theta} = \begin{bmatrix} 0 \\ -2 \\ 0 \\ 0 \end{bmatrix} \tag{14.95}$$

Hence, with the weight matrix $\boldsymbol{W}$ and the threshold vector $\boldsymbol{\theta}$ as given in Eqns. (14.91) and (14.92), respectively, all three patterns are in the stable equilibrium states of the neural network. ■

14.4 OTHER LEARNING ALGORITHMS FOR ASSOCIATIVE MEMORY

In this section we will show that there exists a choice of the coupling weight matrix $\boldsymbol{W}$ which guarantees the stability for a set of given binary pattern vectors, which are either orthogonal or nonorthogonal. We will also analyze to what extent the neural structures designed with such a weight matrix can be useful as associative memories.

14.4.1 The Projection Learning Rule

For the known m binary pattern vectors $\boldsymbol{y}^{(1)}, \ldots, \boldsymbol{y}^{(m)}$, it is easy to show that one of the sufficient conditions that the following equilibrium equation exists

$$\begin{aligned} \boldsymbol{signa}(\boldsymbol{W}\boldsymbol{y}^{(\ell)} + \boldsymbol{I}) &= \boldsymbol{signa}(\boldsymbol{z}) \\ &= \boldsymbol{y}^{(\ell)}, \quad \ell = 1, 2, \ldots, m \end{aligned} \tag{14.96}$$

where $\boldsymbol{z} = [z_1 \ \cdots \ z_n]^T$, $z_i = \sum_{j=1}^{n} w_{ij} y_j^{(\ell)} + I_i$, $(i = 1, 2, \ldots, n)$ and

$$signa(z_i) = \begin{cases} 1, & \text{if} \quad z_i > 0 \\ y_j^{(\ell)}, \text{(unchanged)} & \text{if} \quad z_i = 0 \\ -1, & \text{if} \quad z_i < 0 \end{cases} \tag{14.97}$$

with

$$-1 \leq I_i \leq 1, \quad i = 1, 2, \ldots, n \tag{14.98}$$

is

$$\boldsymbol{W}\boldsymbol{y}^{(\ell)} = \boldsymbol{y}^{(\ell)}, \quad \ell = 1, 2, \ldots, m \tag{14.99}$$

This sufficient condition for equilibrium can be rewritten equivalently as

$$\boldsymbol{W}\boldsymbol{Y} = \boldsymbol{Y} \tag{14.100}$$

where $\boldsymbol{Y}$ is an $(n \times m)$ pattern matrix defined by

$$\boldsymbol{Y} = [\boldsymbol{y}^{(1)} \ \cdots \ \boldsymbol{y}^{(m)}] \tag{14.101}$$

Equation (14.96) represents an *orthogonal projection* in the subspace spanned by the pattern vectors family $\{\boldsymbol{y}^{(\ell)}\}$, and $\boldsymbol{W}$ is the *orthogonal projection matrix*, which can be solved from Eqn. (14.100) as

$$\boldsymbol{W} = \boldsymbol{Y}\boldsymbol{Y}^I \tag{14.102}$$

where $\boldsymbol{Y}^I$ is the Moore–Penrose pseudoinverse of $\boldsymbol{Y}$. Equation (14.102) is termed as the *projection rule* or the *pseudoinverse rule*. The weight matrix $\boldsymbol{W}$, being an orthogonal projection matrix, is symmetric.

It should be noted that this projection rule does not place any limit on the storage capacity of a network. Nevertheless, this property does not mean that the network will always achieve the desired associative memory function. In fact, the memory capacity can be expressed directly in terms of the rank r of the family of the m pattern vectors. If $r = n$, $(n \leq m)$, the projection matrix is the identity matrix and the 2^n states of the network are stable. If $r < n$, the associative memory function is possible; the retrieval efficiency of a pattern will fall sharply as (r/n) becomes of the order of 0.5. Therefore, it is possible to memorize more than n patterns without complete memory degeneracy; the only condition is $r < n$. Among the m patterns, therefore, the linear combinations of r are linearly independent pattern vectors. The detailed analysis about those conclusions is left as an exercise for the readers.

In a general case, the coupling matrix $\boldsymbol{W}$ can be computed conveniently without matrix inversion using an iterative algorithm. It yields the exact solution of the system given in Eqn. (14.102) after a finite number of iterations, which is equal to the number of pattern vectors. This kind of computation is typical of a learning process. Once the synaptic matrix has been computed from a given set of pattern vectors, the addition of one extra item of knowledge does not require that the whole computation be performed again; one just has to run one iteration, starting from the previous matrix. Therefore, memorization through the projection rule retains the same iterative nature as the classical Hebb rule. In fact, the following points should be noted:

(i) In a particular case where the pattern vectors $y^{(\ell)}$, $\ell = 1, 2, \ldots, m$ are linearly independent, the synaptic matrix $\boldsymbol{W}$ takes the form

$$\boldsymbol{W} = \boldsymbol{Y}(\boldsymbol{Y}^T\boldsymbol{Y})^{-1}\boldsymbol{Y}^T \tag{14.103}$$

Since for orthogonal vectors

$$(\boldsymbol{Y}^T\boldsymbol{Y})^{-1} = \boldsymbol{U}$$

where $\boldsymbol{U}$ is the identity matrix, the projection rule reduces exactly to Hebb's rule:

$$\boldsymbol{W} = \boldsymbol{Y}\boldsymbol{Y}^T \tag{14.104}$$

(ii) A zero-diagonal matrix has been used by several authors. Since the diagonal coefficients of the projection matrix are smaller than or equal to one, the stability of the pattern vectors after canceling the diagonal terms is preserved, but their attractivity is altered.

(iii) Finally, one can ensure the stability of the pattern vectors with the projection rule without any restriction on the thresholds. The thresholds v_i are directly related to the scaling of the matrix. If one has $-\lambda \leq v_i \leq \lambda$ for all i, one can just chose $\boldsymbol{W} = \lambda \boldsymbol{Y}\boldsymbol{Y}^I$.

14.4.2 A Generalized Learning Rule

The learning rules discussed above provide some effective approaches for storing given binary pattern vectors as stable equilibrium states with an associative memory function. We now present a generalized learning rule for the association that was first introduced by Personnaz et al. (1986). This generalized learning rule not only implies the mere stability of the pattern vectors but also provides a possible method to design binary Hopfield neural networks that satisfy a given set of constraints. For instance, one may wish to design a neural network that exhibits a given set of stable states, and a given set of transitions as well as a given set of cycles.

There are two sets of given pattern vectors $\{\boldsymbol{y}^{(\ell)}\}$ and $\{\boldsymbol{z}^{(\ell)}\}$, $\ell = 1, 2, \ldots,$ n. Suppose that we want to determine the synaptic weight matrix $\boldsymbol{W}$ such that the network has the following transitions in state space

$$\boldsymbol{x}(k) = \boldsymbol{y}^{(\ell)} \tag{14.105}$$

$$\boldsymbol{x}(k+1) = \boldsymbol{z}^{(\ell)}, \quad 1 \leq \ell \leq m \tag{14.106}$$

that is, using the function $signa(.)$ given as Eqn. (14.97), we obtain

$$\boldsymbol{z}^{(\ell)} = \boldsymbol{signa}(\boldsymbol{W}\boldsymbol{y}^{(\ell)} + \boldsymbol{\theta}), \quad 1 \leq \ell \leq m \tag{14.107}$$

Note that if $\boldsymbol{z}^{(\ell)} = \boldsymbol{y}^{(\ell)}$ for all $1 \leq \ell \leq m$, the problem reduces to imposing the stability condition on the pattern vectors. The problem described by Eqn. (14.107) can be expressed as a system consisting of $n \times m$ inequalities

$$(\boldsymbol{W}\boldsymbol{y}^{(\ell)} + \boldsymbol{\theta})\boldsymbol{z}^{(\ell)} > 0, \quad 1 \leq \ell \leq m \tag{14.108}$$

from which the elements of the matrix $\boldsymbol{W}$ should be solved. As pointed out by Personnaz et al. (1986), in analogy to magnetic systems, these inequalities express simply the fact that the spin vector $\boldsymbol{y}^{(\ell)}$ will flip into the direction of its local field with the bias vector $\boldsymbol{\theta}$ as

$$(\boldsymbol{W}\boldsymbol{y}^{(\ell)} + \boldsymbol{\theta}) \tag{14.109}$$

to give the spin vector $\boldsymbol{z}^{(\ell)}$. Instead of trying to solve the inequality system given in Eqn. (14.108), one may transform it to a linear problem

$$(\boldsymbol{W}\boldsymbol{y}^{(\ell)} + \boldsymbol{\theta}) = \boldsymbol{A}^{(\ell)}\boldsymbol{z}^{(\ell)}, \quad 1 \leq \ell \leq m \tag{14.110}$$

where $\boldsymbol{A}^{(\ell)}$ is an arbitrary diagonal matrix with all the positive diagonal elements. Equation (14.110) may further be reduced into a single matrix equation

$$\boldsymbol{W}\boldsymbol{Y} = \boldsymbol{F} \tag{14.111}$$

where

$$\boldsymbol{Y} = [\boldsymbol{y}^{(1)} \quad \boldsymbol{y}^{(2)} \quad \cdots \quad \boldsymbol{y}^{(m)}]$$

$$\boldsymbol{F} = [\boldsymbol{f}^{(1)} \quad \boldsymbol{f}^{(2)} \quad \cdots \quad \boldsymbol{f}^{(m)}]$$

with

$$\boldsymbol{f}^{(\ell)} = \boldsymbol{A}^{(\ell)}\boldsymbol{z}^{(\ell)} + \boldsymbol{\theta}$$

Equation (14.111) does not always have an exact solution, as indicated in the following discussion.

14.4.2.1 Case A: Exact Solution

If

$$\boldsymbol{F}\boldsymbol{Y}^I\boldsymbol{Y} = \boldsymbol{F}$$

Equation (14.111) has an exact solution, the general form of which is

$$\boldsymbol{W} = \boldsymbol{F}\boldsymbol{Y}^I + \boldsymbol{B}(\boldsymbol{\theta} - \boldsymbol{Y}\boldsymbol{Y}^I) \tag{14.112}$$

where $\boldsymbol{Y}^I$ is the Moore-Penrose pseudo-inverse, and $\boldsymbol{B}$ is an arbitrary $(n \times n)$ matrix. Without loss of generality, assume $\boldsymbol{B} = 0$ so that Eqn. (14.112) is simplified to

$$\boldsymbol{W} = \boldsymbol{F}\boldsymbol{Y}^I \tag{14.113}$$

However, in some cases, $\boldsymbol{B}$ provides a degree of freedom that has already been proved fruitful for the modeling of biological processes. Since $\boldsymbol{Y}^I\boldsymbol{Y}$ is the orthogonal projection matrix into the subspace spanned by the rows of $\boldsymbol{Y}$, the condition $\boldsymbol{F}\boldsymbol{Y}^I\boldsymbol{Y} = \boldsymbol{F}$, which can be rewritten equivalently as $\boldsymbol{Y}^I\boldsymbol{Y}\boldsymbol{F} = \boldsymbol{F}^I$, means that the rows of $\boldsymbol{F}$ are linear combinations of the rows of $\boldsymbol{W}$.

In the particular case where the vectors $\boldsymbol{y}^{(\ell)}$ are linearly independent, as mentioned earlier, the pseudoinverse has the form

$$\mathbf{Y}^I = (\mathbf{Y}^T\mathbf{Y})^{-1}\mathbf{Y}^T, \quad \mathbf{Y}^I\mathbf{Y} = \boldsymbol{I} \tag{14.114}$$

14.4.2.2 Case B: Inexact Solution

If

$$\boldsymbol{F}\mathbf{Y}^I\mathbf{Y} \neq \boldsymbol{F} \tag{14.115}$$

where

$$\begin{aligned} \boldsymbol{Y} &= [\boldsymbol{y}^{(1)} \quad \boldsymbol{y}^{(2)} \quad \cdots \quad \boldsymbol{y}^{(m)}] \\ \boldsymbol{F} &= [\boldsymbol{f}^{(1)} \quad \boldsymbol{f}^{(2)} \quad \cdots \quad \boldsymbol{f}^{(m)}] \end{aligned}$$

with

$$\boldsymbol{f}^{(\ell)} = \boldsymbol{A}^{(\ell)}\boldsymbol{z}^{(\ell)} + \boldsymbol{\theta}$$

there is no exact solution but $\boldsymbol{W} = \boldsymbol{F}\boldsymbol{Y}^I$ is the matrix that minimizes the Euclidean norm of the error matrix $(\boldsymbol{W}\boldsymbol{Y} - \boldsymbol{F})$.

14.4.2.3 Discussion

In Case A, when an exact solution exists, there are still an infinite number of possible matrices $\boldsymbol{W}$ satisfying the required set of constraints given in Eqn. (14.115) depending on $\boldsymbol{F}$.

The computation of the coupling matrix $\boldsymbol{W}$ may be further simplified by the following argument. For a given $\boldsymbol{\theta}$, it is possible to find λ such that

$$-\lambda < v_i < \lambda, \quad 1 \leq i \leq n \tag{14.116}$$

It can be easily shown that a set of positive diagonal matrices $\boldsymbol{A}^{(\ell)}$ exists if we choose

$$\boldsymbol{F} = \lambda \boldsymbol{Z}, \quad \boldsymbol{Z} = [\boldsymbol{z}^{(1)}\ \boldsymbol{z}^{(2)}\ \cdots\ \boldsymbol{z}^{(m)}] \tag{14.117}$$

so that matrix $\boldsymbol{W}$ reduces to

$$\boldsymbol{W} = \lambda \boldsymbol{Z}\boldsymbol{Y}^I \tag{14.118}$$

This rule is called the *associating learning rule* because it allows us to impose the condition that the network performs the associations $\boldsymbol{y}^{(\ell)} \longrightarrow \boldsymbol{z}^{(\ell)}$ for $\ell = 1, 2, \ldots, m$. If $\boldsymbol{Z} = \boldsymbol{Y}$, disregarding the scaling factor λ, the learning rule in Eqn. (14.118) reduces to the projection rule.

Example 14.7 Consider a two-neuron system with the given two sets of binary pattern vectors

$$\boldsymbol{y}^{(1)} = \begin{bmatrix} -1 \\ 1 \end{bmatrix}, \quad \boldsymbol{y}^{(2)} = \begin{bmatrix} 1 \\ 1 \end{bmatrix}$$

$$\boldsymbol{z}^{(1)} = \begin{bmatrix} -1 \\ -1 \end{bmatrix}, \quad \boldsymbol{z}^{(2)} = \begin{bmatrix} -1 \\ 1 \end{bmatrix}$$

We determine a synaptic weight matrix $\boldsymbol{W}$ such that every pattern $\boldsymbol{y}^{(\ell)}$ $(1 \leq \ell \leq 2)$ will be followed by the pattern $\boldsymbol{z}^{(\ell)}$ $(1 \leq \ell \leq 2)$. In this case, the weight matrix $\boldsymbol{W}$ may be solved by the matrix equation

$$\boldsymbol{W}\boldsymbol{Y} = \boldsymbol{Z}$$

that is

$$\boldsymbol{W} = \boldsymbol{Z}\boldsymbol{Y}^{-1}$$

where

$$\boldsymbol{Y} = [\boldsymbol{y}^{(1)}\boldsymbol{y}^{(2)}] = \begin{bmatrix} -1 & 1 \\ 1 & 1 \end{bmatrix}$$

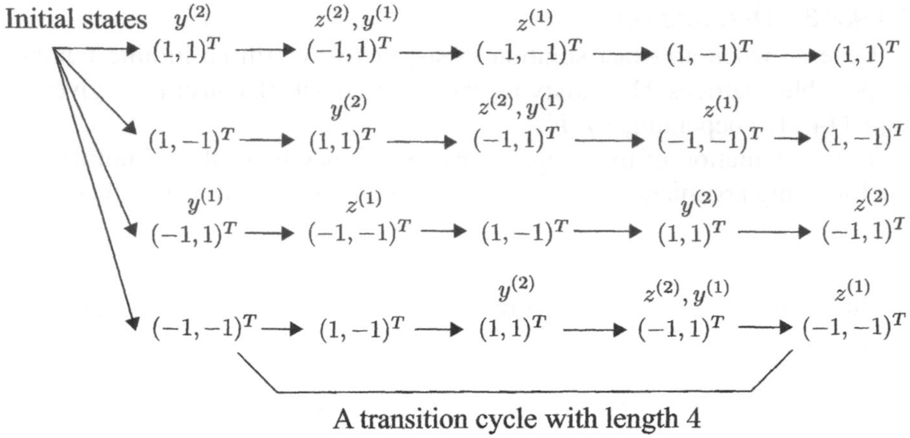

Figure 14.9 Example 14.7: the transition process of the network for different initial conditions. Here, the given pattern vectors $\boldsymbol{y}^{(\ell)}$ $(1 \leq \ell \leq 2)$ and $\boldsymbol{z}^{(\ell)}$ $(1 \leq \ell \leq 2)$ are associatively implemented.

$$\boldsymbol{Z} = [\boldsymbol{z}^{(1)} \boldsymbol{z}^{(2)}] = \begin{bmatrix} -1 & -1 \\ -1 & 1 \end{bmatrix}$$

Then

$$\boldsymbol{Y}^{-1} = -\frac{1}{2} \begin{bmatrix} 1 & -1 \\ -1 & -1 \end{bmatrix}$$

and

$$\boldsymbol{W} = \begin{bmatrix} 0 & -1 \\ 1 & 0 \end{bmatrix}$$

This transition process of the designed network, with a cycle length of 4 with all the different possible initial conditions, is shown in Fig. 14.9. ■

14.5 INFORMATION CAPACITY OF BINARY HOPFIELD NEURAL NETWORK

From the information theory point of view, a discrete-time binary Hopfield dynamic neural network is a *dynamic memory* that can store information in the form of a collection of specified binary pattern vectors. A binary pattern with n dimensions and components either 1 or -1 is called an *n-bit pattern*. We may now ask how many n-bit patterns can be stored in a Hopfield dynamic neural network with n neurons or what is the information storage capacity of a

Hopfield dynamic neural network. In order to study the information capacity C of a Hopfield dynamic neural network, let us first look at the following example given by Abu-Mostafa and Jacques (1985).

As shown in Fig. 14.10, a random access memory (RAM) with M address lines and one data line [i.e., an $(M \times 1)$ RAM] contains 2^M memory locations. Each location contains 1 bit of stored data and is accessed by an M-bit address line. It is easy to see that in a RAM with an M-bit address line, 2^M bits of information can be stored. This is because, given an arbitrary string of 2^M bits, we can load the $(M \times 1)$ RAM with a string and then later retrieve the string from the memory. On the other hand, since there are 2^{2^M} strings of 2^M bits, the memory can distinguish between the 2^{2^M} cases. Consequently, *the information capacity C of a memory may be defined as the logarithm of the number of cases that it can distinguish*:

$$C = \log 2^{2^M} = 2^M \text{ bit} \tag{14.119}$$

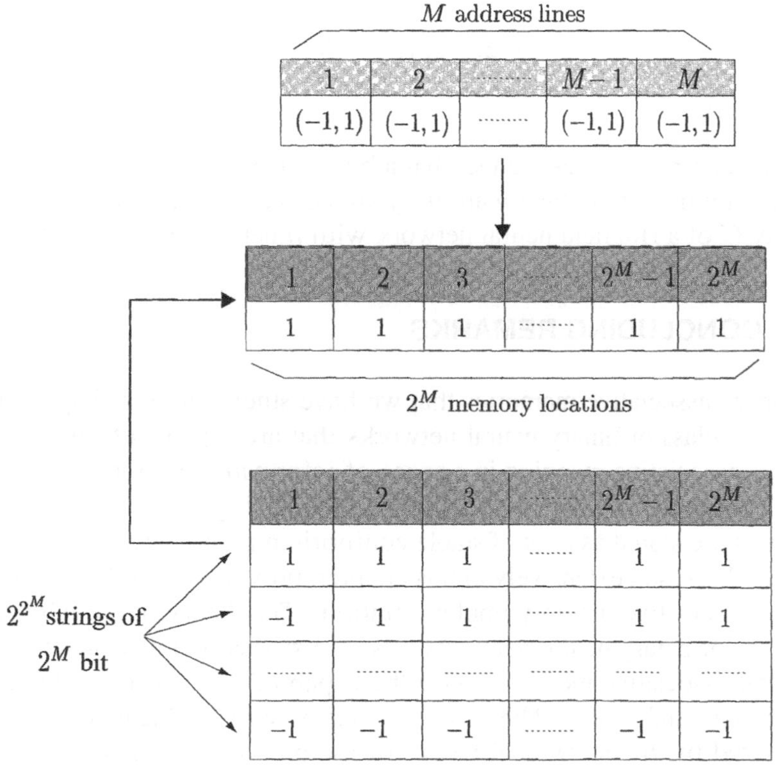

Figure 14.10 A random access memory (RAM) with M address lines and $C = 2^M$ bits information capacity.

Information in the Hopfield dynamic neural network is stored as stable states. As seen from the previous subsections, each state of the neuron in a Hopfield dynamic neural network is randomly and repeatedly fired through the threshold function operation on the weighted sum of all previous states that are the inputs to the current neural operation. It is of interest to determine n neurons. In other words, how many n-bit binary patterns can be stored and retrieved in a Hopfield dynamic neural network as stable states? Abu-Mostafa and Jacques proposed a result that shows the number of stable states K can be at the most n, no matter how the synaptic weight matrix $\boldsymbol{W}$ is designed.

Theorem 14.6 (Abu-Mostafa and Jacques 1985) *Let $\boldsymbol{W}$ denote a real-valued zero diagonal $n \times n$ matrix, and let $\boldsymbol{v}$ denote a real-valued n vector. For any K n-bit binary patterns $\boldsymbol{y}^{(1)}, \ldots, \boldsymbol{y}^{(K)}$, there is a matrix $\boldsymbol{W}$ and a vector $\boldsymbol{v}$ such that*

$$sgn\left(\sum_{j=1}^{n} w_{ij} y_j^{(\ell)} + v_i\right) = y_i^{(\ell)}$$

$$\ell = 1, 2, \ldots, K; \quad i = 1, 2, \ldots, n$$

then $K \leq n$. ■

This theorem indicates the fact that a binary Hopfield dynamic neural network cannot have more than n arbitrary stable states. Hence, the information capacity C of a Hopfield neural network with n neurons is at most 2^n.

14.6 CONCLUDING REMARKS

The binary associative memories that we have studied in this chapter are essentially a class of binary neural networks that are capable of implementing complex associative mapping in a space of information vectors. The domain of such mapping is a set of memory vectors having binary values. Those memories are stored as a set of stable equilibrium points. Hebb's learning algorithm, discussed extensively in this chapter, provides a simple approach for such an associative memory implementation. The theory of the information capability of binary neural networks was also studied in this chapter.

Neural associative memories have the capabilities of storing patterns, images, signals, and speech. The characteristics of retrievalable memories stored are ensured by the operational modes of the binary neural networks. There are many other avenues of dynamic neural networks, which are to be explored in the context of design and applications of feedback binary associative memories.

Problems

14.1 For the discrete-time Hopfield neural network

$$\boldsymbol{x}(k+1) = \boldsymbol{A}\boldsymbol{x}(k) + \boldsymbol{W}\boldsymbol{\sigma}(\boldsymbol{x}) + \boldsymbol{\theta}$$

with the threshold vector $\boldsymbol{\theta} = 0$, let m, $(m \leq n)$, binary pattern vectors $\boldsymbol{y}^{(1)}, \ldots, \boldsymbol{y}^{(m)} \in \Re^n$ be an orthogonal set of vectors, and let the weight matrix $\boldsymbol{W}$ determined by Hebb's learning rule be defined as

$$\boldsymbol{W} = \sum_{\ell=1}^{m} (\boldsymbol{y}^{(\ell)})(\boldsymbol{y}^{(\ell)})^T = \boldsymbol{Y}\boldsymbol{Y}^T$$

(a) Calculate all the eigenvectors and the corresponding eigenvalues of $\boldsymbol{W}$;

(b) If the energy function is defined as

$$E = -\tfrac{1}{2}\boldsymbol{x}^T\boldsymbol{W}\boldsymbol{x}$$

then for an arbitrary $\boldsymbol{x} \in \Re^n$ and $\boldsymbol{y}^{(\ell)} \in \Re^m$, $\boldsymbol{x} \neq \boldsymbol{y}^{(\ell)}$, $1 \leq \ell \leq m$, show that

$$E(\boldsymbol{x}) \geq E(\boldsymbol{y}^{(\ell)}), \quad 1 \leq \ell \leq m$$

14.2 Show that Hebb's learning rule may be modified to

$$\boldsymbol{W} = \boldsymbol{sgn}\left(\boldsymbol{Y}\boldsymbol{Y}^T\right)$$

where $\boldsymbol{Y} = [\boldsymbol{y}^{(1)} \; \cdots \; \boldsymbol{y}^{(m)}]$.

14.3 A model of the *full* 2-order discrete-time binary neural network is given by Psaltis et al. (1988) as follows

$$\begin{aligned} x_i(k+1) \quad &= \quad signa\left(\sum_{j=1}^{n} w_{ij}^{(1)} x_j(k)\right. \\ &\left. + \sum_{j=1,p=1}^{n} w_{ijp}^{(1)} x_j(k) x_p(k) + \theta_i\right), \quad i = 1, 2, \ldots, n \end{aligned}$$

(a) Design a Hebb learning rule for the above network;

(b) Give a model of the arbitrary *full* r-order discrete-time binary neural network and design a Hebb learning rule for this model.

14.4 A model of the *single* 2-order discrete-time binary neural network is given by Psaltis et al. (1988):

$$x_i(k+1) = signa\left(\sum_{j=1,p=1}^{n} w_{ijp}^{(1)} x_j(k) x_p(k) + \theta_i\right)$$
$$i = 1, 2, \ldots, n$$

(a) Use Hebb's learning rule for designing the network above;

(b) Find a possible energy function for the system;

(c) Give a model of the arbitrary *single* r-order discrete-time binary neural network and design a Hebb learning rule for the model.

14.5 Given three binary vectors $\boldsymbol{x}$, $\boldsymbol{y}$, and $\boldsymbol{z} \in -1, 1^n$. Prove that the following inequalities for both Hamming distance (HD) and effective Hamming distance (EHD):

(a) $HD(\boldsymbol{x}, \boldsymbol{z}) \leq HD(\boldsymbol{x}, \boldsymbol{y}) + HD(\boldsymbol{y}, \boldsymbol{z})$

(b) $EHD(\boldsymbol{x}, \boldsymbol{z}) \leq EHD(\boldsymbol{x}, \boldsymbol{y}) + EHD(\boldsymbol{y}, \boldsymbol{z})$

14.6 Given two binary vectors $\boldsymbol{x}$ and $\boldsymbol{y} \in -1, 1^n$, prove that the effective Hamming distance (EHD) satisfies

(a) $EHD(\boldsymbol{x}, \boldsymbol{x}) = 0$

(b) $EHD(\boldsymbol{x}, -\boldsymbol{x}) = 0$

(c) $EHD(\boldsymbol{x}, \boldsymbol{y}) = EHD(-\boldsymbol{x}, -\boldsymbol{y})$

(d) $2\, EHD(\boldsymbol{x}, \boldsymbol{y}) + |\boldsymbol{x}^T \boldsymbol{y}| = n$

14.7 Let $\boldsymbol{W}$ be an $n \times n$ symmetric real matrix with zero-diagonal elements.

(a) Prove that all eigenvalues of $\boldsymbol{W}$ are real and their sum is zero.

(b) Give a formulation for calculating all eigenvalues of $\boldsymbol{W}$.

14.8 For a set of m, $(m \leq n)$, binary pattern vectors $\boldsymbol{y}^{(1)}, \boldsymbol{y}^{(2)}, \ldots, \boldsymbol{y}^{(m)}$, a Hebb learning rule for the weight matrix $\boldsymbol{W}$ and the threshold vector $\boldsymbol{\theta}$ of an n-dimensional binary Hopfield neural network is given by

$$w_{ij} = \sum_{k=1}^{m} y_i^{(k)} y_j^{(k)}, \quad -m \le \theta_i \le m$$

that is

$$\boldsymbol{W} = \sum_{k=1}^{m} (\boldsymbol{y}^{(k)})(\boldsymbol{y}^{(k)})^T, \quad -m \le \theta_i \le m$$

Prove that all the given pattern vectors are stored as stable equilibrium states of the neural network.

14.9 (Gram–Schmidt Orthogonalization) Given m binary pattern vectors $\boldsymbol{y}^{(1)}, \boldsymbol{y}^{(2)}, \ldots, \boldsymbol{y}^{(m)}$ that may be mutually correlated. Construct m new pattern vectors as

$$\boldsymbol{z}^{(1)} = \boldsymbol{y}^{(1)}$$

$$\boldsymbol{z}^{(\ell)} = \boldsymbol{y}^{(\ell)} - \sum_{k=1}^{\ell-1} \frac{< \boldsymbol{z}^{(k)}, \boldsymbol{y}^{(\ell)} >}{< \boldsymbol{z}^{(k)}, \boldsymbol{z}^{(k)} >} \boldsymbol{z}^{(k)}, \quad 2 \le \ell \le m$$

Show that the new pattern vectors $\boldsymbol{z}^{(1)}, \boldsymbol{z}^{(2)}, \ldots, \boldsymbol{z}^{(m)}$ are orthogonal.

14.10 Consider ten $5 \times 5 = 25$-dimensional pattern vectors which are used to represent 10 digits $0, \ldots, 9$ as shown in Fig. 14.11, where the black square corresponds to 1 and the white square represents -1. The binary patterns are represented as below.

$$\boldsymbol{y}^{(0)} = [-----\vdots--++-\vdots-+--+\vdots-+--+\vdots--++-]^T$$

$$\boldsymbol{y}^{(1)} = [--+--\vdots+++--\vdots-++--\vdots-++--\vdots-++--]^T$$

$$\boldsymbol{y}^{(2)} = [+++++\vdots----+\vdots--+--\vdots+----\vdots+++++]^T$$

$$\boldsymbol{y}^{(3)} = [-+++-\vdots----+\vdots--++-\vdots----+\vdots-+++-]^T$$

$$\boldsymbol{y}^{(4)} = [--++-\vdots-+-+-\vdots+++++\vdots---+-\vdots---+-]^T$$

$$\boldsymbol{y}^{(5)} = [++++-\vdots+----\vdots++++-\vdots----+\vdots++++-]^T$$

$$y^{(6)} = [- - - + - \vdots - - + - - \vdots - + + + - \vdots + - - - + \vdots - + + + -]^T$$

$$y^{(7)} = [+ + + + + \vdots - - - + - \vdots - - + - - \vdots - + - - - \vdots + - - - -]^T$$

$$y^{(8)} = [- - + + - \vdots - + - - + \vdots - - + + - \vdots - + - - + \vdots - - + + -]^T$$

$$y^{(9)} = [- - + + - \vdots - + - - + \vdots - - + + + \vdots - - - - + \vdots - - - - +]^T$$

(a) Determine whether these 10 pattern vectors are orthogonal;

(b) Calculate the weighting matrix W such that these pattern vectors are stored as memories of a binary neural network;

(c) Discuss whether these memories stored are retrievable.

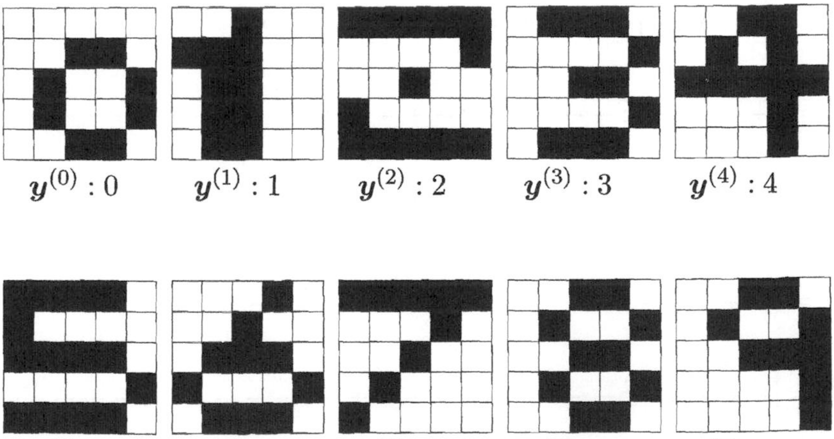

$y^{(0)}$: 0 $y^{(1)}$: 1 $y^{(2)}$: 2 $y^{(3)}$: 3 $y^{(4)}$: 4

$y^{(5)}$: 5 $y^{(6)}$: 6 $y^{(7)}$: 7 $y^{(8)}$: 8 $y^{(9)}$: 9

Figure 14.11 Problem 14.10: bitmaps of 10 sample digit patterns, $0, 1, \ldots, 9$. $\square \Rightarrow -1$, $\blacksquare \Rightarrow +1$.

14.11 Given three binary patterns

$$y^{(1)} = \begin{bmatrix} 1 \\ -1 \\ 1 \\ 1 \end{bmatrix}, \quad y^{(2)} = \begin{bmatrix} 1 \\ 1 \\ 1 \\ 1 \end{bmatrix}, \quad y^{(3)} = \begin{bmatrix} -1 \\ -1 \\ -1 \\ 1 \end{bmatrix}$$

(a) Design a four-neuron binary network using Hebb's learning rule such that the patterns $y^{(1)}$, $y^{(2)}$, and $y^{(3)}$ are the stable equilibrium states of the network;

(b) Given a key pattern $x = [1 \quad 1 \quad -1 \quad -1]^T$, compute the Hamming distance (HD) between the key pattern x and the memories $y^{(1)}$, $y^{(2)}$, and $y^{(3)}$;

(c) Let an asynchronous operating mode be applied. Draw the state transfer diagram for the given key pattern.

14.12 Prove the results given in Lemma 14.1.

14.13 Consider the case where $n = 16$, $m = 4$, and four pattern vectors to be stored are

$$y^{(1)} = \begin{bmatrix} e^* \\ e \\ e \\ e \end{bmatrix}, y^{(2)} = \begin{bmatrix} e \\ e \\ -e \\ -e \end{bmatrix}, y^{(3)} = \begin{bmatrix} e \\ -e \\ e \\ -e \end{bmatrix}, y^{(4)} = \begin{bmatrix} e \\ -e \\ -e \\ e \end{bmatrix}$$

where $e^* = [-1 \quad 1 \quad 1 \quad 1]^T$ is a vector of one -1 and three 1s and $e = [1 \quad 1 \quad 1 \quad 1]^T$ is a vector of four 1s.

(a) Calculate the weight matrix W using Hebb's learning rule;

(b) Verify the stability of the given four patterns;

(c) Estimate the attractive regions of the memories patterns.

14.14 Let an $(n \times n)$ memory matrix W be determined by Hebb's rule with a unique n-dimensional pattern vector y as follows:

$$W = yy^T - \theta$$

For a probe vector x given by

$$x_i = \begin{cases} -y_i, & i = 1, 2, \ldots, n_1 \\ y_i, & i = n_1 + 1, \ldots, n_1 \end{cases}$$

Prove that if $n_1 \leq ((n/2) + 1)$, then $\boldsymbol{x}$ can be updated to the memory vector $\boldsymbol{y}$ in a single step.

14.15 For the binary patterns given in Problem 14.11, use the projection rule discussed in this chapter to calculate the projection matrix $\boldsymbol{W}$. Also, discuss the stability of these stored memory patterns.

14.16 Given m binary patter vectors $\boldsymbol{y}^{(1)}, \boldsymbol{y}^{(2)}, \ldots, \boldsymbol{y}^{(m)} \in \{-1, 1\}^n$. Let $\boldsymbol{Y}$ be an $(n \times m)$ pattern matrix defined by

$$\boldsymbol{Y} = [\boldsymbol{y}^{(1)} \boldsymbol{y}^{(2)} \cdots \boldsymbol{y}^{(m)}]$$

and r be the rank of the matrix $\boldsymbol{Y}$.

(a) Prove that if $r = n$, the projection matrix

$$\boldsymbol{W} = \boldsymbol{Y}\boldsymbol{Y}^I$$

is an identity matrix;

(b) Prove that 2^n states of the binary neural network are stable;

(c) Show that if $r \leq n$, the retrieval efficiency of a pattern vector stored will fall sharply as (r/n) becomes of the order of 0.5.

15

Fuzzy Sets and Fuzzy Neural Networks

15.1 Fuzzy Sets and Systems: An Overview

15.2 Building Fuzzy Neurons (FNs) Using Fuzzy Arithmetic and Fuzzy Logic Operations

15.3 Learning and Adaptation for Fuzzy Neurons (FNs)

15.4 Regular Fuzzy Neural Networks (RFNNs)

15.5 Hybrid Fuzzy Neural Networks (HFNNs)

15.6 Fuzzy Basis Function Networks (FBFNs)

15.7 Concluding Remarks

Problems

Fuzzy logic, which was introduced by Lotfi A. Zadeh in 1965 (Zadeh 1965), is a powerful tool for modeling human thinking and cognition. Instead of bivalent propositions, fuzzy logic systems deal with reasoning with multivalued sets, stored rules, and estimated sampled functions from linguistic input to linguistic output. The effectiveness of the human brain not only is due to the numerical data but also depends on fuzzy concepts, fuzzy judgment, fuzzy reasoning, and cognition. The most successful domain of fuzzy logic has been in the field of feedback control of various physical and chemical processes such as temperature, electric current, flow of liquid/gas, and the motion of machines (Gupta 1994; Gupta and Rao 1994b; Jang and Sun 1993; Kaufmann and Gupta 1988; Kiszka et al. 1985; Langari and Berenji 1992; Lee 1990a, 1990b). Fuzzy logic principles can also be applied to other areas as well. For example, these fuzzy principles have been used in the area such as fuzzy knowledge–based systems that use fuzzy IF–THEN rules, *fuzzy software engineering*, which may incorporate fuzziness in data and programs, and fuzzy database systems in the field of medicine, economics, and management problems. It is exciting to note that some consumer electronic and automotive industry products in the current market have used technology based on fuzzy logic, and the performance of these products has significantly improved (Al-Holou et al. 2002; Eichfeld et al. 1996).

Conventional forms of fuzzy systems have low capabilities for learning and adaptation. Fuzzy mathematics provides an inference mechanism for approximate reasoning under cognitive uncertainty, while neural networks offer exciting advantages such as learning and adaptation, generalization, approximation and fault tolerance. These networks are also capable of dealing with computational complexity, nonlinearity, and uncertainty. The integration of these two fields, *fuzzy logic and neural networks*, has given birth to an innovative technological field called *fuzzy neural networks* (FNNs) (Gupta and Qi 1991, 1992a, 1992b; Gupta and Rao 1994b; Jin et al. 1995a). Extensive studies have indicated that FNNs, with the unique capabilities of dealing with numerical data, and linguistic knowledge and information, have the potential of capturing the attributes of these two fascinating fields—fuzzy logic and neural networks—into a single capsule, *fuzzy neural networks*. In view of the robust capabilities of FNNs, it is believed that they posses a great potential as emulation machines for a variety of behaviors associated with human cognition and intelligence (Sinha and Gupta 1999).

Although much progress has been made in the field of fuzzy neural networks (FNNs), there are no universally accepted models of FNNs so far. Two main classes of FNNs have been studied extensively, and have been proved to have robust capabilities for processing fuzzy information for specified tasks. The first category of FNNs has fuzzy triangular inputs and outputs, and it implements a mapping from a fuzzy input set to a fuzzy output set, and has the potential for realizing fuzzy logic functions on a compact fuzzy set. The other class of FNNs deals with crisp input and output signals. However, the internal structure of this type of FNN contains many fuzzy operations and approximate reasoning using the rule-based knowledge framework. It can be expected that this type of FNNs could implement fuzzy systems for real-world applications. Studies on the first class of FNNs can be traced back to 1974 (Lee and Lee 1974), when the concepts of fuzzy sets into neural networks were introduced for the generalization of the McCulloch–Pitts (Mc-P) model by using intermediate values between zero and one. Various types of fuzzy neurons were developed using the notions of standard fuzzy arithmetic and fuzzy logic such as t-norm, t-conorm, and fuzzy implications (Buckley and Hayashi, 1993a, 1993b, 1993c, 1994a, 1994b; Pedrycz 1991b, 1993). Some applications of this class of FNNs have been reported (Jang and Sun 1993; Kosko 1992; Wang 1993). Important contributions have also been made on the universal approximation capabilities of fuzzy systems that can be expressed in the form of FNNs, and genetic algorithms have also been used in the learning schemes of FNNs (Buckley and Hayashi 1994b; Jang and Sun 1990; Jang 1992; Kosko 1994; Pedrycz 1995; Wang and Mendel 1992b, 1993; Wang 1993).

The objective of this chapter is to provide an overview of the basic principles, mathematical descriptions, and the state-of-the-art developments of FNNs. It contains seven sections. In Section 15.1 the foundations of fuzzy sets and systems are briefly reviewed in order to provide the necessary mathematical background. The basic definitions of fuzzy neurons with fuzzy input signals and weights are introduced in Section 15.2. Following this introduction, some basic methods of fuzzy neural learning and adaptation are introduced in Section 15.3. Fuzzy neural networks (FNNs) formed by a number of interconnected fuzzy neurons are addressed in Section 15.4. Fuzzy backpropagation (FBP) is also introduced in this section. Both the structures and learning mechanisms of hybrid fuzzy neural networks (HFNNs) are studied in Section 15.5. A fuzzy basis function network (FBFN), which is used to express a fuzzy system that has a singleton fuzzifier, product inference, and centroid defuzzifier, is discussed in Section 15.6. These results indicate that if a Gaussian membership function is applied, the fuzzy system is functionally equivalent to a modified Gaussian network. Thus, well-known results for the Gaussian network such as online and offline learning algorithms, and universal approximation capabilities might be employed directly in the design and analysis of fuzzy systems. The material presented in this chapter not only provides an overview of the existing results but also presents some state-of-the-art new achievements and open problems in the field of fuzzy neural computing.

15.1 FUZZY SETS AND SYSTEMS: AN OVERVIEW

Fuzzy set theory is a generalization of conventional set theory and was introduced by Zadeh in 1965 (Zadeh 1965, 1972a, 1973). It provides a mathematical tool for dealing with linguistic variables associated with natural languages. Some introductory definitions of fuzzy sets, fuzzy logic, and fuzzy systems are reviewed in this section. Systematic descriptions of these topics can be found in several texts (Bellman and Zadeh 1977; Dubois and Prade 1980; Kaufmann and Gupta 1985, 1988). A central notion of fuzzy set theory, as described in the following sections, is that it is permissible for elements to be only partial elements of a set rather than full membership.

15.1.1 Some Preliminaries

A "fuzzy" set is defined as a set whose boundary is not sharp. Let $\boldsymbol{X} = \{x\}$ be a conventional set with generic elements x. A fuzzy set A is characterized by a membership function $\mu_A(x)$ defined on $\boldsymbol{X}$, a set of ordered pairs $A = \{x, \mu_A(x)\}, x \in \boldsymbol{X}$, where $\mu_A(x)$ is the grade of membership of x in A, and is defined as

$$\mu_A : \boldsymbol{X} \to [0,1] \tag{15.1}$$

Thus, a fuzzy set A in $\boldsymbol{X}$ can also be represented as

$$A = \{(x, \mu_A(x)) : x \in \boldsymbol{X}\} \tag{15.2}$$

The set $\boldsymbol{X}$ may be either a discrete set with discrete elements or a continuous set with continuous elements. For instance, $\boldsymbol{X} = \{1, 2, 3, \ldots, 35\}$ is a discrete set, and $\boldsymbol{X} = \Re^+ = [0, +\infty)$ is a continuous set. In this case, an alternative way of expressing a fuzzy set A of $\boldsymbol{X}$ is

$$A = \begin{cases} \displaystyle\sum_{x \in \boldsymbol{X}} \mu_A(x_i)/x_i, & \text{if } \boldsymbol{X} \text{ is a discrete set} \\ \displaystyle\int_{\boldsymbol{X}} \mu_A(x)/x, & \text{if } \boldsymbol{X} \text{ is a continuous set} \end{cases}$$

where the signs $\sum$ and $\int$ do not mean conventional summation and integration, and "/" is only a marker between the membership $\mu_A(x_i)$ and its element x_i and does not represent division.

A fuzzy set is said to be a *normal fuzzy set* if and only if

$$\max_{x \in \boldsymbol{X}} \mu_A(x) = 1$$

Assume that A and B are two fuzzy sets defined on $\boldsymbol{X}$ with membership functions $\mu_A(x)$ and $\mu_B(x)$. The set-theoretic definitions and operations such as inclusion ($\subset$), intersection ($\cap$), union ($\cup$), and the complement of the two fuzzy sets are defined as follows:

(i) The *intersection* of fuzzy sets A and B corresponds to the connective "*AND*." Thus, $A \cap B = A\ AND\ B$.

Table 15.1 **Fuzzy set–theoretic definitions and operations**

Inclusion:	$A \subset B$ implies that $\mu_A(x) \leq \mu_B(x), \quad \forall x \in \boldsymbol{X}$;
Intersection:	$A \cap B$, an intersection of A and B, implies that $\mu_{A \cap B}(x) = \min[\mu_A(x), \mu_B(x)] = \mu_A(x) \wedge \mu_B(x) = A\ AND\ B, \quad \forall x \in \boldsymbol{X}$
Union:	$A \cup B$, a union of A and B, implies that $\mu_{A \cup B}(x) = \max[\mu_A(x), \mu_B(x)] = \mu_A(x) \vee \mu_B(x) = A\ OR\ B, \quad \forall x \in \boldsymbol{X}$
Complement:	$\overline{A}$, a complement of A, implies that $\mu_{\overline{A}} = 1 - \mu_A(x) = NOT\ A, \quad \forall x \in \boldsymbol{X}$;

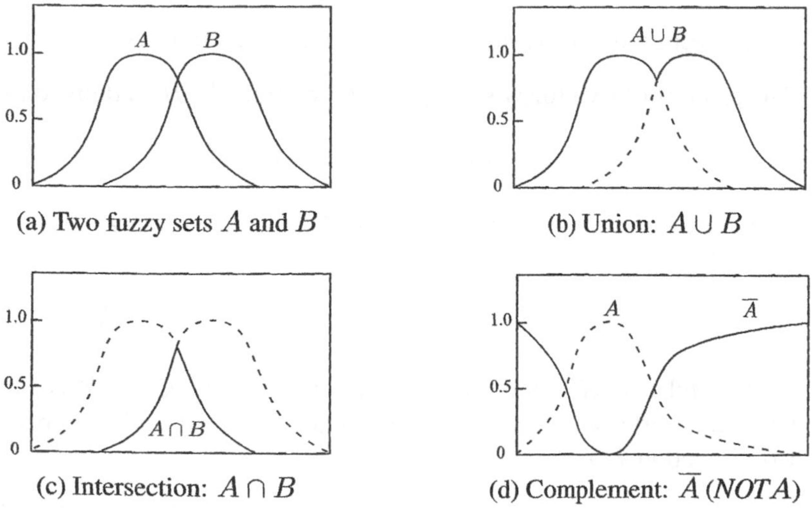

Figure 15.1 Some logic operations on fuzzy sets.

(ii) The *union* of fuzzy sets A and B corresponds to the connective "*OR*." Thus, $A \cup B = A \ OR \ B$.

(iii) The operation of *complementation* corresponds to the negation *NOT*. Thus, $\overline{A} = NOT \ A$.

Fuzzy set operations are summarized in Table 15.1.

Given two sets A and B as shown in Fig. 15.1a, the logic operations listed above are shown in Figs. 15.1b–15.1d. An example is also given below.

Example 15.1 Assume $\boldsymbol{X} = \{a, b, c, d, e\}$. Let

$$A = \{0.5/a,\ 0.9/b,\ 0.7/c,\ 0.6/d,\ 1/e\}$$

and

$$B = \{0.7/a,\ 1/b,\ 0.8/c,\ 0.5/d,\ 0/e\}$$

Then

$$A \cap B = \{0.5/a,\ 0.9/b,\ 0.7/c,\ 0.5/d,\ 0/e\}$$

and

$$A \cup B = \{0.7/a,\ 1/b,\ 0.8/c,\ 0.6/d,\ 1/e\}$$

and

$$\overline{A} = \{0.5/a,\ 0.1/b,\ 0.3/c,\ 0.4/d,\ 0/e\}$$ ■

Some other operations of two-fuzzy sets are defined as follows:

(i) The product of two fuzzy sets A and B, written $A \cdot B$, is defined as

$$\mu_{A \cdot B} = \mu_A(x) \cdot \mu_B(x), \quad \forall x \in \boldsymbol{X} \tag{15.3}$$

(ii) The algebraic sum of two fuzzy sets A and B, written as $A \oplus B$, is defined as

$$\mu_{A \oplus B} = \mu_A(x) + \mu_B(x) - \mu_A(x) \cdot \mu_B(x), \ \forall x \in \boldsymbol{X} \tag{15.4}$$

(iii) A fuzzy relation $\boldsymbol{R}$ between the two (nonfuzzy) sets $\boldsymbol{X}$ and $\boldsymbol{Y}$ is a fuzzy set in the Cartesian product $\boldsymbol{X} \times \boldsymbol{Y}$; that is, $\boldsymbol{R} \subset \boldsymbol{X} \times \boldsymbol{Y}$. Hence, the fuzzy relation $\boldsymbol{R}$ is defined as

$$\boldsymbol{R} = \{\mu_{\boldsymbol{R}}(x, y), (x, y)\} = \{\mu_{\boldsymbol{R}}(x, y)/(x, y)\}, \ \forall (x, y) \in \boldsymbol{X} \times \boldsymbol{Y} \tag{15.5}$$

(iv) The max–min composition of two fuzzy relations $\boldsymbol{R} \subset \boldsymbol{X} \times \boldsymbol{Y}$ and $\boldsymbol{S} \subset \boldsymbol{Y} \times \boldsymbol{Z}$, written $\boldsymbol{R} \circ \boldsymbol{S}$, is defined as a fuzzy relation $\boldsymbol{R} \circ \boldsymbol{S} \subset \boldsymbol{X} \times \boldsymbol{Z}$ such that

$$\mu_{\boldsymbol{R} \circ \boldsymbol{S}}(x, z) = \max_{y \in \boldsymbol{Y}} (\mu_{\boldsymbol{R}}(x, y) \wedge \mu_{\boldsymbol{S}}(y, z)) \tag{15.6}$$

for each $x \in \boldsymbol{X}, z \in \boldsymbol{Z}$, where $\wedge = \min$.

(v) The Cartesian product of two fuzzy sets $A \subset \boldsymbol{X}$ and $B \subset \boldsymbol{Y}$, written as $A \times B$, is defined as a fuzzy set in $\boldsymbol{X} \times \boldsymbol{Y}$, such that

$$\mu_{A \times B}(x, y) = \mu_A(x) \wedge \mu_B(y) \tag{15.7}$$

for each $x \in \boldsymbol{X}$ and $y \in \boldsymbol{Y}$.

15.1.2 Fuzzy Membership Functions (FMFs)

The definitions of *fuzzy membership functions* (FMFs) of fuzzy sets play an important role in fuzzy set theory and its applications. The following are several types of fuzzy membership functions, as illustrated in Fig. 15.2, which are either continuous, or discontinuous in terms of a finite number of switching points:

(i) Triangular function:

$$\mu(x, a, b, c) = \max\left(\min\left(\frac{x-a}{b-a}, \frac{c-x}{c-b}\right), 0\right), \quad a \neq b \text{ and } c \neq b \tag{15.8}$$

(ii) Trapezoidal function:

$$\mu(x, a, b, c, d) = \max\left(\min\left(\frac{x-a}{b-a}, 1, \frac{d-x}{d-c}\right), 0\right) \qquad a \neq b \text{ and } c \neq d \tag{15.9}$$

(iii) Sinusoidal function:

$$\mu(x, a, b) = \begin{cases} \sin(ax - b), & \text{if } \dfrac{b}{a} \leq x \leq \dfrac{\pi + b}{a}, \ a \neq 0 \\ 0, & \text{otherwise} \end{cases} \tag{15.10}$$

(iv) Gaussian function:

$$\mu(x, \sigma, c) = e^{-[(x-c)/\sigma]^2} \tag{15.11}$$

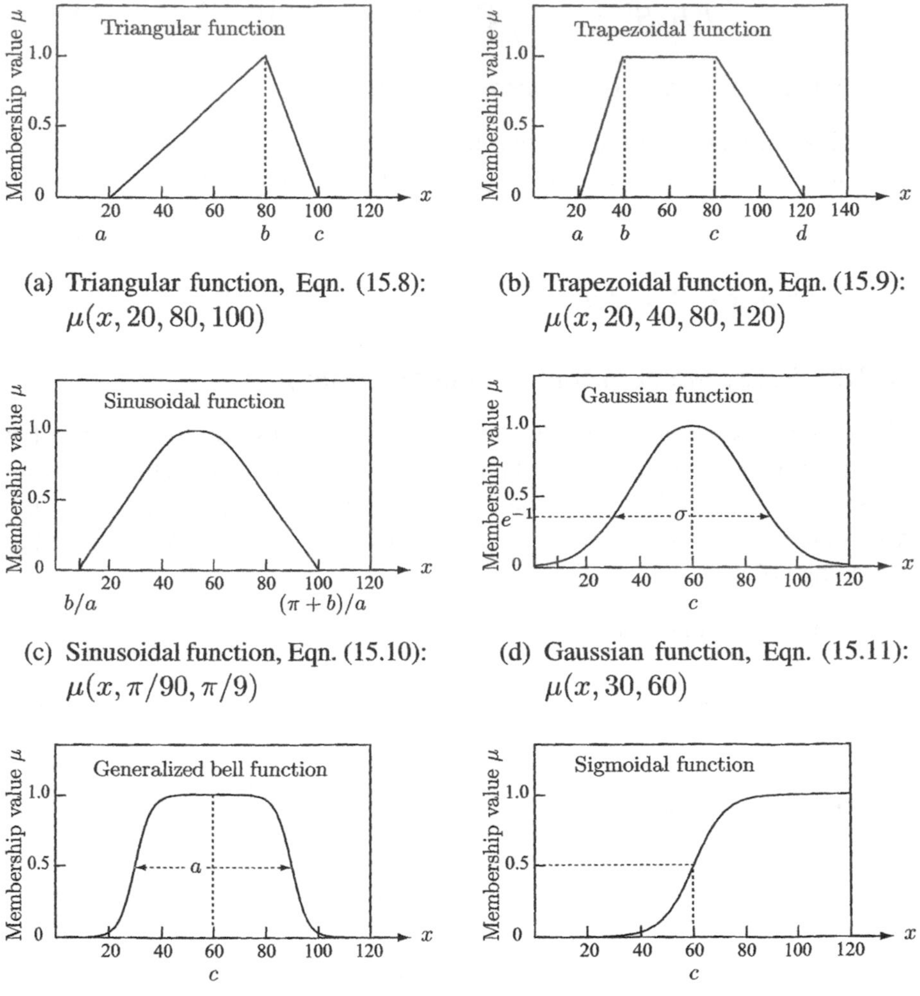

(a) Triangular function, Eqn. (15.8): $\mu(x, 20, 80, 100)$

(b) Trapezoidal function, Eqn. (15.9): $\mu(x, 20, 40, 80, 120)$

(c) Sinusoidal function, Eqn. (15.10): $\mu(x, \pi/90, \pi/9)$

(d) Gaussian function, Eqn. (15.11): $\mu(x, 30, 60)$

(e) Generalized bell function, Eqn. (15.12): $\mu(x, 5, 35, 85, 115)$

(f) Sigmoidal function, Eqn. (15.13): $\mu(x, 1, 60)$

Figure 15.2 Examples of some membership functions (FMFs), Eqns. (15.8)–(15.13).

where c is a center parameter for controlling the center position of $\mu(x, \sigma, c)$ and σ is a parameter for defining the width of $\mu(x, \sigma, c)$.

(v) Generalized bell function:

$$\mu(x, a, b, c) = \frac{1}{1 + \left|\frac{x-c}{a}\right|^{2b}}, \quad \text{with} \quad b > 0 \tag{15.12}$$

(vi) Sigmoidal function:

$$\mu(x, a, c) = \frac{1}{1 + \exp(\,-a(x - c)\,)} \tag{15.13}$$

where the parameter c determines the position of $\mu(x, a, c)|_{x=c} = 0.5$.

It should be noted that a FMF contains a set of parameters that define the shape of the membership function. Usually, these parameters can be predetermined by human experience, knowledge, or known data. However, in fuzzy-neural systems they can be adapted online according to the specified environment in order to achieve the optimal performance.

Since the early 1970s, because of the simplicity in their formulations and computational efficiency, both triangular and trapezoid functions have been used extensively as FMFs in fuzzy logical systems (Kaufmann and Gupta 1985, 1988). However, these two types of FMFs consist of straight line segments, and are not smooth at the switching points, which are determined by the preselected parameters. This raises some difficulties for fuzzy neural computing. Some studies have indicated that continuous and differentiable FMFs such as Gaussian functions, sigmoidal functions, and sinusoidal functions are good candidates for fuzzy neural computing (Jang and Sun 1993; Jin et al. 1994a, 1995a).

15.1.3 Fuzzy Systems

A fuzzy system with a basic configuration as depicted in Fig. 15.3 has four principal elements: *fuzzifier*, *fuzzy rule base*, *fuzzy inference engine*, and *defuzzifier*. Without the loss of generality, we will consider here multiinput single-output fuzzy systems: $S \subset \Re^n \to \Re$, where S is a compact set.

In such a fuzzy system, the *fuzzifier* deals with a mapping from the input space $S \in \Re^n$ to the fuzzy sets defined in S, which are characterized by a membership function $\mu_F : S \to [0,1]$, and is labeled by a linguistic variable F such as "small," "medium," "large," or "very large." The most commonly used fuzzifier is a singleton fuzzifier, which is defined as follows:

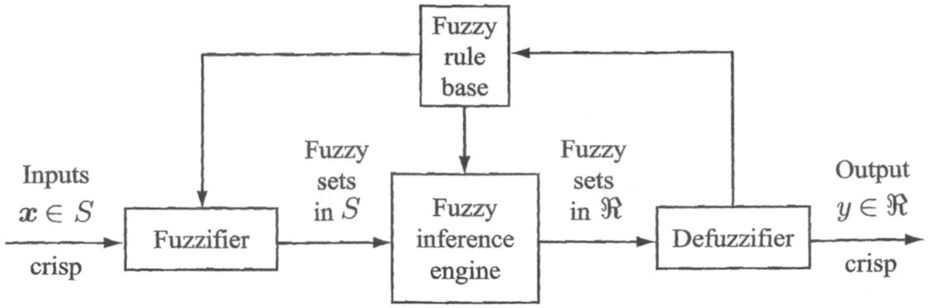

Figure 15.3 A schematic representation of a fuzzy system.

$$\boxed{\begin{array}{l} \boldsymbol{x} \in S \rightarrow \text{fuzzy set } A_x \subset S \text{ with } \mu_{A_{\boldsymbol{x}}}(\boldsymbol{x}) = 1, \text{ and} \\ \mu_{A_{\boldsymbol{x}}}(\boldsymbol{x}') = 0 \text{ for } \boldsymbol{x}' \in S \text{ and } \boldsymbol{x}' \neq \boldsymbol{x} \end{array}} \tag{15.14}$$

Thus, the fuzzifier changes the range of crisp values of input variables into a corresponding universe of discourse, and converts nonfuzzy (crisp) input data into suitable linguistic values.

The *fuzzy rule base* consists of a set of linguistic rules of the following form: "IF a set of conditions are satisfied, THEN a set of consequences are inferred."

In other words, a fuzzy rule base is a collection of IF–THEN values. Moreover, we consider in this text a fuzzy rule base having M rules of the following forms

$$\boxed{\begin{array}{l} \boldsymbol{R}_j(j = 1, 2, \ldots, M)\text{: IF } x_1 \text{ is } A_1^j, \textit{ AND } x_2 \text{ is } A_2^j, \\ \textit{AND}, \ldots, \textit{AND } x_n \text{ is } A_n^j, \text{ THEN } y \text{ is } B^j. \end{array}} \tag{15.15}$$

where $x_i(i = 1, 2, \ldots, n)$ are the input variables to the fuzzy system, y is the output variable of the fuzzy system, and A_i^j and B^j are the linguistic variables characterized by the fuzzy membership functions $\mu_{A_i^j}$ and μ_{B^j}, respectively. In practical applications, the rules can be extracted from either numerical data or human knowledge for the problem of concern. A simple example is given in Fig. 15.4.

Each rule R_j can be viewed as a fuzzy implication

$$A_1^j \times \cdots \times A_n^j \rightarrow B^j$$

which is a fuzzy set in $S \times \Re$ with

$$\mu_{A_1^j \times \cdots \times A_n^j \rightarrow B^j}(x_1, \ldots, x_n, y) = \mu_{A_1^j}(x_1) \otimes \cdots \otimes \mu_{B^j}(y) \tag{15.16}$$

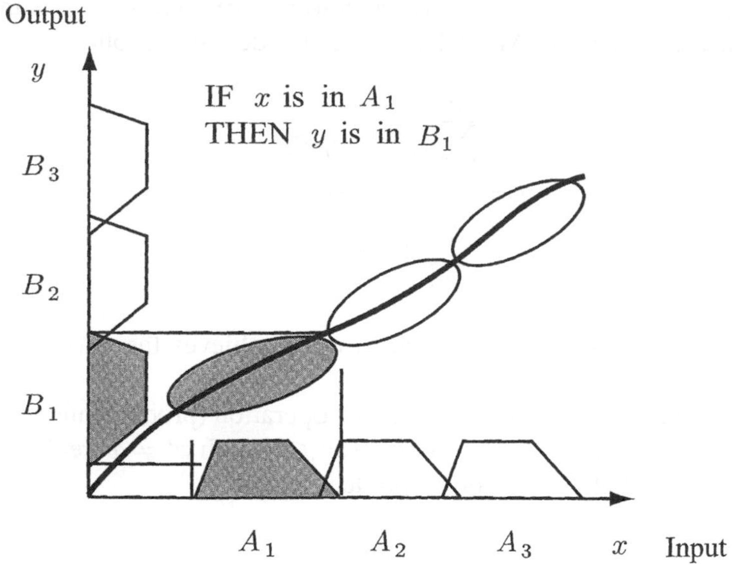

Figure 15.4 An example of the fuzzy IF–THEN rule.

for $\boldsymbol{x} \in S$ and $y \in \Re$. The most commonly used operations for $\otimes$ are product and min operations defined as

$$\text{Product operation: } \mu_{A_1^j}(x_1) \otimes \mu_{A_2^j}(x_2) = \left[\mu_{A_1^j}(x_1) \cdot \mu_{A_2^j}(x_2)\right] \quad (15.17)$$

$$\text{Min operation: } \mu_{A_1^j}(x_1) \otimes \mu_{A_2^j}(x_2) = \min\left[\mu_{A_1^j}(x_1), \mu_{A_2^j}(x_2)\right] \quad (15.18)$$

The *fuzzy inference engine* is a decisionmaking logic that uses the fuzzy rules provided by the fuzzy rule base to implement a mapping from the fuzzy sets in the input space S to the fuzzy sets in the output space $\Re$. The efficiency of a fuzzy inference engine greatly depends on the knowledge base of the system considered. Let A_x be an arbitrary fuzzy set in S. Then each R_j of the fuzzy rule base creates a fuzzy $A_x \circ R_j$ in $\Re$ based on the sup–star composition:

$$\begin{aligned} \mu_{A_x \circ R_j} &= \sup_{\boldsymbol{x}' \in S}\left[\mu_{A_x}(\boldsymbol{x}') \otimes \mu_{A_1^j \times \cdots \times A_n^j \to B^j}(x_1, \ldots, x_n, z)\right] \\ &= \sup_{\boldsymbol{x}' \in S}\left[\mu_{A_x}(\boldsymbol{x}') \otimes \mu_{A_1^j}(x_1') \otimes \cdots \otimes \mu_{A_n^j}(x_n') \otimes \mu_{B^j}(z)\right] \end{aligned} \quad (15.19)$$

The *defuzzifier* provides a mapping from the fuzzy sets in $\Re$ to crisp points in $\Re$. The following centroid defuzzifier, which performs a mapping from the fuzzy set $A_x \circ R_j (j = 1, 2, \ldots, M)$ in $\Re$ to a crisp point $y \in \Re$, is the most commonly used method (Mendel 1995), and is defined as follows:

$$y = \frac{\displaystyle\sum_{j=1}^{M} c_j \mu_{A_x \circ R_j}(c_j)}{\displaystyle\sum_{j=1}^{M} \mu_{A_x \circ R_j}(c_j)} \tag{15.20}$$

where c_j is the point in $\Re$ at which $\mu_{B^j}(c_j)$ achieves the maximum value $\mu_{B^j}(c_j) = 1$.

Next, if one assumes that $\otimes$ is a product operation (product inference), then for $\mu_{A_x}(\boldsymbol{x}) = 1$ and $\mu_{A_x}(\boldsymbol{x}') = 0$ for all $\boldsymbol{x}' \in S$ with $\boldsymbol{x}' \neq \boldsymbol{x}$, replacing $\otimes$ in Eqn. (15.19) with the conventional product yields

$$\begin{aligned} \mu_{A_x \circ R_j}(c_j) &= \sup_{\boldsymbol{x}' \in S} \left[\mu_{A_x}(\boldsymbol{x}') \, \mu_{A_1^j}(x_1') \cdots \mu_{A_n^j}(x_n') \, \mu_{B^j}(c_j) \right] \\ &= \prod_{i=1}^{n} \mu_{A_i^j}(x_i) \end{aligned} \tag{15.21}$$

Thus, the analytical relationship between the crisp input $\boldsymbol{x}$ and the crisp output y is

$$y = \frac{\displaystyle\sum_{j=1}^{M} c_j \left(\prod_{i=1}^{n} \mu_{A_i^j}(x_i) \right)}{\displaystyle\sum_{j=1}^{M} \left(\prod_{i=1}^{n} \mu_{A_i^j}(x_i) \right)} \tag{15.22}$$

Other types of defuzzifiers, such as a maximum defuzzifier, mean of maxima defuzzifier, and height defuzzifier, can also be applied to form the mapping from the crisp input $\boldsymbol{x}$ to the crisp output $y \in \Re$.

15.2 BUILDING FUZZY NEURONS (FNs) USING FUZZY ARITHMETIC AND FUZZY LOGIC OPERATIONS

Following the basic mathematics of fuzzy logic and the basic structure of the neurons discussed in the previous sections, some models of fuzzy neurons (FNs) are introduced in this section.

15.2.1 Definition of Fuzzy Neurons

When we consider fuzzy uncertainties within neural units, the inputs and/or the weights of a neuron can be expressed in terms of their membership functions, and several types of *fuzzy neurons* (FNs) based on fuzzy logic operations can be defined. According to the nature of neural inputs and weights (fuzzy or nonfuzzy), we define the following three types of fuzzy neurons:

(i) FN_1 has nonfuzzy neural inputs but fuzzy synaptic weights;

(ii) FN_2 has fuzzy neural inputs and nonfuzzy synaptic weights;

(iii) FN_3 has fuzzy neural inputs and fuzzy synaptic weights.

Restricting the synaptic weights to fuzzy quantities may avoid deformation of fuzzy input signals in fuzzy neural computation. Since FN_1 and FN_2 may be considered as special cases of FN_3, emphasis will be devoted only to FN_3, which will be simply referred to as a FN in the following discussion.

It has been seen that the mathematical operations involved in a conventional neuron discussed in the previous chapters are

(i) The weighting of the neural inputs with synaptic weights;

(ii) The aggregation of these weighted neural inputs;

(iii) The nonlinear operation on this aggregation.

The mathematical operations in fuzzy neural networks can be carried out using either fuzzy arithmetic operations or fuzzy logic operations. In this section, we briefly describe fuzzy neurons first using fuzzy arithmetic operations and then using fuzzy logic operations.

15.2.1.1 Fuzzy Arithmetic–Based Fuzzy Neurons

The weighting of fuzzy neural inputs using the synaptic weights can be expressed by fuzzy multiplication, and the aggregation operation of weighted neural inputs by fuzzy addition, and these modifications lead to a fuzzy neural architecture. On the basis of fuzzy arithmetic operations, the mathematical expression of such a FN is given by the following equation

$$y = \sigma\left((+)_{i=0}^{n} w_i (\cdot) x_i \right), \quad x_0 = 1 \tag{15.23}$$

where $(+)$ and $(\cdot)$ respectively are the fuzzy addition and fuzzy multiplication operators, and w_0 is the threshold.

Fuzzy neural inputs and fuzzy synaptic weights are defined on an n-dimensional hypercube in terms of their membership functions x_i and w_i,

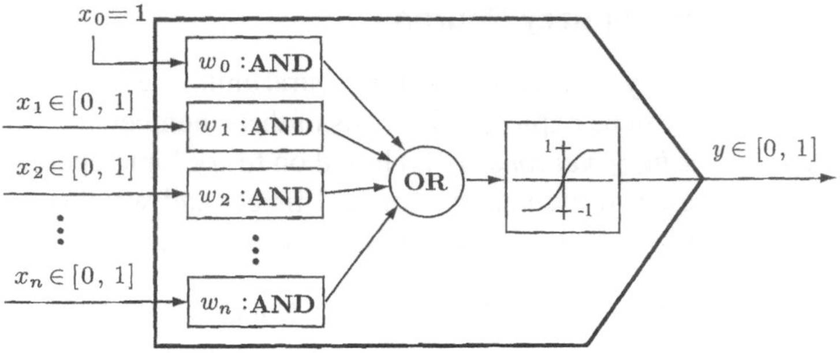

Figure 15.5 *OR–AND*-type fuzzy neuron.

and are as follows:

$$\left.\begin{array}{rcl} \boldsymbol{x} & = & [x_0\, x_1\, x_2\, \cdots\, x_n]^T \in [0,1]^{(n+1)}, \quad x_0 = 1 \\ \boldsymbol{w} & = & [w_0\, w_1\, w_2\, \cdots\, w_n]^T \in [0,1]^{(n+1)} \end{array}\right\} \tag{15.24}$$

15.2.1.2 Fuzzy Logic–Based Fuzzy Neurons

Alternatively, fuzzy logic operations, using *OR*, *AND*, and *NOT*, or their generalized versions, can be employed to perform fuzzy neural operations. In this case, fuzzy logic operations can be expressed by the following two neural models

(i) OR–AND-type fuzzy neuron (Fig. 15.5):

This type of fuzzy neuron is shown in Fig. 15.5, and is described by

$$\begin{aligned} y &= \sigma(\ OR_{i=0}^{n}(w_i\ AND\ x_i)\ ) \\ &= \sigma(\ OR(w_0\ AND\ x_0,\ w_1\ AND\ x_1,\ \ldots, w_n\ AND\ x_n)\ ) \end{aligned} \tag{15.25}$$

A schematic representation of this neuron is shown in Fig. 15.5. This *OR–AND* fuzzy operations–based neuron is similar to that of the conventional type of neurons described in the earlier chapters.

(ii) AND–OR-type fuzzy neuron (Fig. 15.6):

This type of fuzzy neuron is shown in Fig. 15.6, and is described by

$$\begin{aligned} y &= \sigma(\ AND_{i=0}^{n}(w_i\ OR\ x_i)\ ) \\ &= \sigma(\ AND(w_0\ OR\ x_0,\ w_1\ OR\ x_1,\ \ldots, w_n\ OR\ x_n)\ ) \end{aligned} \tag{15.26}$$

This *AND–OR*-type of fuzzy neuron is similar to that of the radial basis function (RBF) neurons, and is useful for pattern recognition and other decisionmaking problems. However, only the *OR–AND*-type of fuzzy neurons are explored in the following discussions.

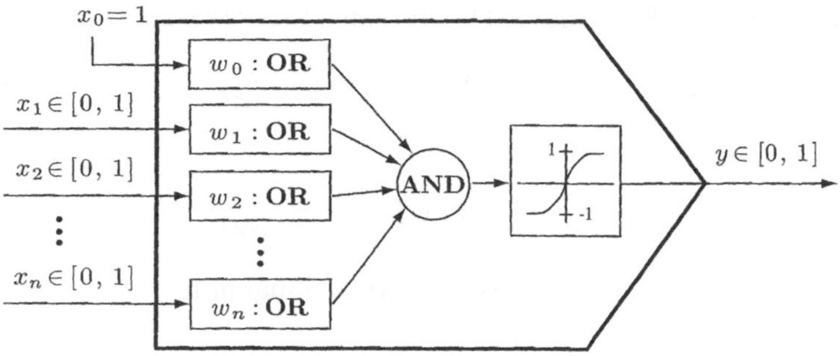

Figure 15.6 *AND–OR*-type fuzzy neuron.

15.2.2 Utilization of T and S Operators

15.2.2.1 Definition and Properties

The **T** operator (t-norm) and **S** operator (t-conorm), which are generalized *AND* and *OR* operations, respectively, can be employed effectively to deal with the fuzzy operations given in Eqns. (15.25) and (15.26). Let $x_1, x_2 \in [0,1]$ be two triangular fuzzy numbers. The **T** operator $\mathbf{T} : [0,1] \times [0,1] \rightarrow [0,1]$ represents the generalized *AND* operation, and is defined as

$$(x_1 \; AND \; x_2) \triangleq (x_1 \; \mathbf{T} \; x_2) = \mathbf{T}(x_1, x_2) \tag{15.27}$$

Similarly, the **S** operator $\mathbf{S} : [0,1] \times [0,1] \rightarrow [0,1]$ represents the generalized *OR* operation, and is defined as

$$(x_1 \; OR \; x_2) \triangleq (x_1 \; \mathbf{S} \; x_2) = \mathbf{S}(x_1, x_2) \tag{15.28}$$

In fact, a **T** operator (t-norm) is a nonlinear mapping from $[0,1] \times [0,1]$ onto $[0,1]$. For three fuzzy numbers x, y, and $z \in [0,1]$ the **T** operator satisfies the following properties

(i) $\mathbf{T}(x, y) = \mathbf{T}(y, x)$ (commutativity)
(ii) $\mathbf{T}(\mathbf{T}(x, y), z) = \mathbf{T}(x, \mathbf{T}(y, z))$ (associativity)
(iii) $\mathbf{T}(x_1, y_1) \geq \mathbf{T}(x_2, y_2)$ if $x_1 \geq x_2$ and $y_1 \geq y_2$ (monotonicity)
(iv) $\mathbf{T}(x, 1) = x$ (boundary condition)

A **S** operator (t-conorm) is also a nonlinear mapping from $[0,1] \times [0,1]$ onto $[0,1]$ that differs from a **T** operator only in the property (iv), the boundary condition. For the **S** operator, the boundary conditions are

$$\mathbf{S}(x, 0) = x \tag{15.29}$$

Some additional properties of the **T** and **S** operators are

$$\left.\begin{array}{ll} \mathbf{T}(0,0) = 0, & \mathbf{T}(1,1) = 1 \\ \mathbf{S}(0,0) = 0, & \mathbf{S}(1,1) = 1 \end{array}\right\} \tag{15.30}$$

Also, using the **T** and **S** operators, De Morgan's theorems are stated as follows

$$\mathbf{T}(x_1, x_2) = 1 - \mathbf{S}(1 - x_1, 1 - x_2) \tag{15.31}$$

and

$$\mathbf{S}(x_1, x_2) = 1 - \mathbf{T}(1 - x_1, 1 - x_2) \tag{15.32}$$

Indeed, negation **N** on $x_1 \in [0,1]$ is defined as a mapping

$$\mathbf{N}(x_1) = 1 - x_1 \tag{15.33}$$

which implies $\mathbf{N}(0) = 1, \mathbf{N}(1) = 0$, and $\mathbf{N}(\mathbf{N}(x)) = x$.

15.2.2.2 Fuzzy Logic Neuronal Equations

By means of the **T** and **S** operators just discussed, the input–output function $y = f(x_1, x_2, \ldots, x_n)$ of the *OR–AND* fuzzy neuron defined in Eqn. (15.25) can be represented further as

$$\begin{aligned} u &= \mathbf{S}_{i=0}^{n}\left[(w_i \ \mathbf{T} \ x_i)\right] \\ &= \mathbf{S}_{i=0}^{n}\left[\mathbf{T}(w_i, x_i)\right] \\ &= \mathbf{S}\left[\mathbf{T}(w_0, x_0), \ \mathbf{T}(w_1, x_1), \ \ldots, \mathbf{T}(w_n, x_n)\right] \in [0,1], \quad x_0 = 1 \end{aligned} \tag{15.34}$$

and

$$y = \sigma(u) \in [0,1], \quad \text{for} \quad u \geq 0 \tag{15.35}$$

where $u \in [0,1]$ is an intermediate variable that is introduced to simplify the mathematical expression of such a fuzzy neural operation. It can be noted that even if a bipolar activation function $\sigma(\cdot)$ is employed in Eqn. (15.35), the output y, which is also a fuzzy quantity in terms of the membership grade, is always located in the unit interval [0,1] because $u \geq 0$.

There are many alternative ways to define the expressions for the **T** and **S** operators. However, for simplicity, only the three types of **T** and **S** operators proposed previously are summarized in Table 15.2. Since in fuzzy neural computing, the operations of the **T** and **S** operators defined in Table 15.2 are often on more than two fuzzy variables, the generalized versions of **T** and **S** operators given in Table 15.2 are provided in Table 15.3 for dealing with n fuzzy variables $x_1, x_2, \ldots, x_n \in [0,1]$.

According to the three definitions of the **T** and **S** operators given in Tables 15.2 and 15.3, we now give the mathematical expressions for three different types of *OR–AND* fuzzy neurons.

Table 15.2 T and S operators on fuzzy variables x and $y \in [0,1]$

No.	$\mathbf{T}(x, y)$: *AND* operation	$\mathbf{S}(x, y)$: *OR* operation	$\mathbf{N}(x)$
1	$\min(x, y)$	$\max(x, y)$	$1 - x$
2	xy	$x + y - xy$	$1 - x$
3	$\max(x + y - 1, 0)$	$\min(x + y, 1)$	$1 - x$

Table 15.3 T and S operators for n fuzzy variables $x_1, x_2, \ldots, x_n \in [0,1]$

No.	$\mathbf{T}(x_1, x_2, \ldots, x_n)$ (*AND* operation)	$\mathbf{S}(x_1, x_2, \ldots, x_n)$ (*OR* operation)
1	$\min(x_1, x_2, \ldots, x_n)$	$\max(x_1, x_2, \ldots, x_n)$
2	$\prod_{i=1}^{n} x_i$	$\sum_{i=1}^{n} x_i - \sum_{j=1}^{n} \sum_{1 \le i_1 < \cdots < i_j \le n} x_{i_1} \cdots x_{i_j}$ or equivalently $\begin{cases} v_1 = x_1 \\ v_i = v_{i-1} + x_i - x_i v_{i-1}, \\ \qquad i = 2, 3, \ldots, n \\ x_n + v_{n-1} - x_n v_{n-1} \end{cases}$
3	$\begin{cases} v_1 = x_1 \\ v_i = \max(v_{i-1} + x_i - 1, 0), \\ \qquad i = 2, 3, \ldots, n \\ \max(v_{n-1} + x_n - 1, 0) \end{cases}$	$\min(x_1 + x_2 + \cdots + x_n,\ 1)$

(i) Type I (min–max fuzzy neuron):

The operational equation for this type of min–max FN is obtained using the first type of **T** and **S** operators given in Table 15.3 as follows

$$\begin{aligned} u &= \max_{0 \le i \le n} (\min(w_i, x_i)) \\ &= \max(\min(w_0, x_0), \min(w_1, x_1), \ldots, \min(w_n, x_n)) \end{aligned} \tag{15.36}$$

and

$$y = \sigma(u)$$

Type II (product–sum fuzzy neuron):

The product–sum fuzzy neuron is of the second type and is expressed by the following recursive formulations

$$\left.\begin{aligned} v_0 &= w_0 x_0 \\ v_i &= w_i x_i + v_{i-1} - w_i x_i v_{i-1}, \quad i = 1, 2, 3, \ldots, n \\ u &= v_n \end{aligned}\right\} \tag{15.37}$$

and

$$y = \sigma(u) = \sigma(v_n) \tag{15.38}$$

or equivalently

$$\left.\begin{aligned} v_i &= w_i x_i, \quad i = 0, 1, 2, \ldots, n \\ u &= \sum_{i=0}^{n} v_i - \sum_{j=1}^{n} \sum_{0 \le i_1 < i_2 < \cdots < i_j \le n} v_{i_1} v_{i_2} \cdots v_{i_j} \end{aligned}\right\} \tag{15.39}$$

and

$$y = \sigma(u)$$

For instance, when $n = 2$, Eqn. (15.37) becomes

$$\left.\begin{aligned} v_0 &= w_0 x_0, x_0 = 1 \\ v_1 &= w_1 x_1 + w_0 x_0 - w_1 x_1 w_0 x_0 \\ v_2 &= w_2 x_2 + w_1 x_1 + w_0 x_0 - w_1 x_1 w_0 x_0 \\ &\quad - w_2 x_2 w_1 x_1 - w_2 x_2 w_0 x_0 - w_2 x_2 w_1 x_1 w_0 x_0 \\ u &= v_2 \end{aligned}\right\}$$

and

$$y = \sigma(u) \tag{15.40}$$

Type III (max–min fuzzy neuron):

The third type of fuzzy neuron is the max–min fuzzy neuron, which is obtained by using the third type of **T** and **S** operators given in Table 15.3.

$$\begin{aligned} u &= \min\Big(\max(w_0 + x_0 - 1, 0) + \max(w_1 + x_1 - 1, 0) + \cdots \\ &\qquad + \max(w_n + x_n - 1, 0), 1\Big) \\ &= \min\left(\sum_{i=0}^{n} \max(w_i + x_i - 1, 0), 1\right) \end{aligned} \tag{15.41}$$

Noting that since for x_1 and $x_2 \in [0,1]$

$$\max(x_1 + x_2 - 1, 0) = \max(x_1 + x_2, 1) - 1$$

Eqn. (15.41) can equivalently be expressed as follows:

$$\begin{aligned} u &= \min\Big(\max(w_0 + x_0, 1) - 1 + \max(w_1 + x_1, 1) - 1 + \cdots \\ &\quad + \max(w_n + x_n, 1) - 1, 1\Big) \\ &= \min\left(\sum_{i=0}^{n} \max(w_i + x_i, 1) - n, 1\right) \end{aligned} \tag{15.42}$$

and

$$y = \sigma(u) \tag{15.43}$$

Example 15.2 Consider a fuzzy neuron with four inputs x_1, x_2, x_3, and x_4 as shown in Fig. 15.7. Let the nonlinear activation function be a sigmoidal

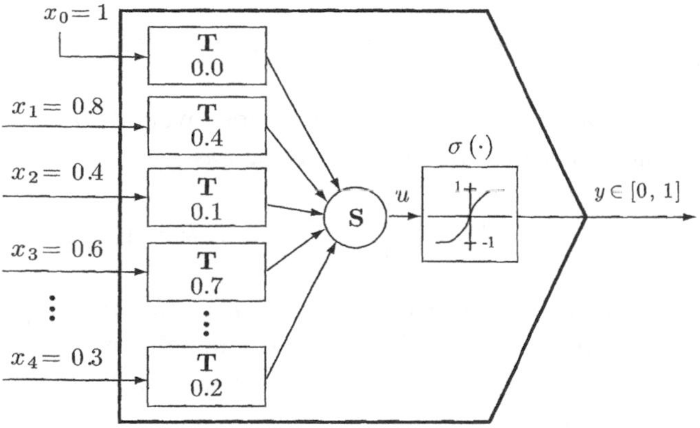

Figure 15.7 Example 15.2: the fuzzy neuron.

Table 15.4 **Example 15.2: output of the fuzzy neurons**

Type	u	Output $y = \tanh(u)$
I: min–max	0.6	0.8090
II: product–sum	0.6441	0.8478
III: max–min	0.5	0.7071

function $\sigma(u) = \tanh(u)$. Using the three types of fuzzy neural operations just discussed above, the output of the function neuron can be obtained as given in Table 15.4. ■

15.3 LEARNING AND ADAPTATION FOR FUZZY NEURONS (FNs)

In order to update the connection weights involved in the fuzzy neurons (FNs), some learning and adaptation mechanisms for the FN models that were proposed in the last section are presented in this section. Like the least square error functions used in the conventional BP algorithm for multilayered feedforward neural networks (MFNNs), the generic performance index used here is also expressed as a squared error between the output of the fuzzy neuron and a desired value.

15.3.1 Updating Formulation

For the batch of learning data $x(i), i = 1, \ldots, N$, described as the following input–output pairs

$$\Big(\boldsymbol{x}(1), y^d(1)), (\boldsymbol{x}(2), y^d(2)), \ldots, (\boldsymbol{x}(N), y^d(N)\Big) \tag{15.44}$$

let the adjustable parameters for a FN be the synaptic weights $\boldsymbol{w}_a = [w_0\, w_1 \cdots w_n]^T$. An instantaneous error function is defined as

$$E(k) = \tfrac{1}{2}\left[y^d(k) - y(\boldsymbol{x}_a(k), \boldsymbol{w}_a)\right]^2 = \tfrac{1}{2}e^2(k), \quad k = 1, 2, \ldots, N \tag{15.45}$$

where $(e(k) = (y^d(k) - y(\boldsymbol{x}_a(k), \boldsymbol{w}_a))$, and $y(\boldsymbol{x}_a(k), \boldsymbol{w}_a)$ represents the output of the FN for the neural input $\boldsymbol{x}_a(k)$ and the neural weight $\boldsymbol{w}_a$. The updating algorithms for the parameters of such a FN can be derived using the standard gradient decent technique. For the unipolar weights $w_0, w_1, \ldots, w_n \in [0,1]$, the updating formulations for the weights are

$$w_i(k+1) = sat\,(\, w_i(k) + \Delta w_i(k)\,)\,, \quad i = 0, 1, \ldots, n \tag{15.46}$$

where $sat(\cdot)$ is a unipolar saturating function as shown in Fig. 15.8 and which is mathematically defined as

$$sat(x) = \begin{cases} 1, & \text{if} \quad x > 1 \\ x, & \text{if} \quad 0 \le x \le 1 \\ 0, & \text{if} \quad x < 0 \end{cases} \tag{15.47}$$

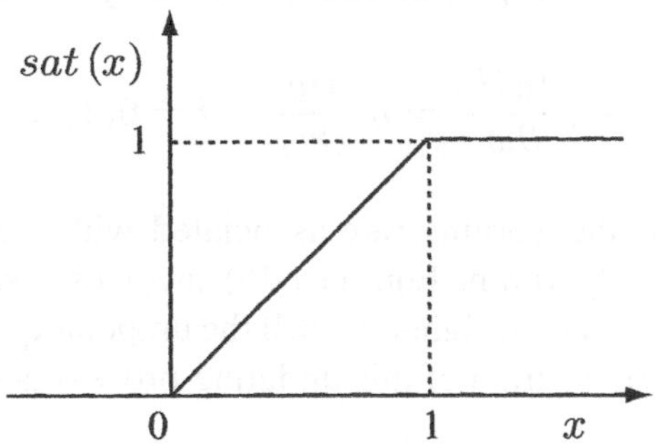

Figure 15.8 Unipolar saturating function $sat(x)$.

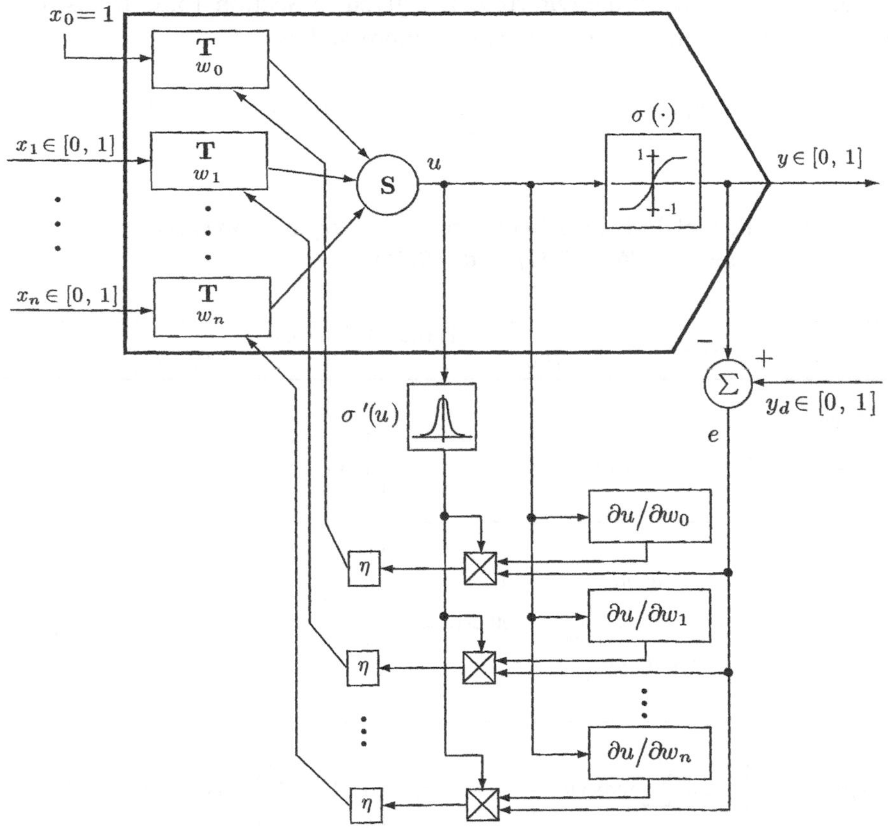

Figure 15.9 Schematic representation of the weight updating process of a fuzzy neuron.

The incremental term $\Delta w_i(k)$ in Eqn. (15.46) is given as

$$\Delta w_i(k) = -\eta \frac{\partial E(k)}{\partial w_i} = \eta e \frac{\partial y}{\partial w_i}, \quad i = 0, 1, \ldots, n \tag{15.48}$$

where $0 < \eta < 1$ is the learning rate associated with the weights. Unlike the conventional BP algorithm, Eqn. (15.46) involves a saturating function $sat(\cdot)$ by which the updated weights are still the unipolar quantities on the unit interval [0,1]. A block diagram of this updating process is given in Fig. 15.9.

15.3.2 Calculations of Partial Derivatives

To evaluate further the updating formulations presented above, the partial derivatives on the right-hand side of Eqn. (15.48) must be computed using the operations equations of the *OR–AND* FN given in Section 15.3. It has been known that the operation of a FN can be expressed as

$$y = \sigma(u(\boldsymbol{x}, \boldsymbol{w})), \quad \text{with} \quad u = \mathbf{S}_{i=0}^{n}(w_i \; \mathbf{T} \; x_i), \quad x_0 = 1$$

Table 15.5 **Partial derivative formulation for fuzzy neuron (FN), Eqns. (15.36), (15.37), and (15.41)**

Type of Neuron	Partial Derivatives: $\partial u / \partial x_i$	Partial Derivatives: $\partial u / \partial w_i$
Type I, Eqn. (15.36)	$\begin{cases} 1, & \text{if} \quad u = x_i \\ 0. & \text{otherwise} \end{cases}$	$\begin{cases} 1, & \text{if} \quad u = w_i \\ 0. & \text{otherwise} \end{cases}$
Type II, Eqn. (15.37)	$\begin{cases} w_n - w_n u_{n-1}, & \text{if} \quad i = n \\ (1 - w_n x_n)\dfrac{\partial u_{n-1}}{\partial x_i}, & \text{otherwise} \end{cases}$ where $u = u_n$	$\begin{cases} x_n - x_n u_{n-1}, & \text{if} \quad i = n \\ (1 - w_n x_n)\dfrac{\partial u_{n-1}}{\partial x_i}, & \text{otherwise} \end{cases}$
Type III, Eqn. (15.41)	$\begin{cases} 1, \text{if} \sum_{j=1}^{n} \max(w_j + x_j - 1) < 1 \\ \quad \text{and } (w_i + x_i - 1) > 0 \\ 0, \text{otherwise} \end{cases}$	$\begin{cases} 1, \text{if} \sum_{j=1}^{n} \max(w_j + x_j - 1) < 1 \\ \quad \text{and } (w_i + x_i - 1) > 0 \\ 0, \text{otherwise} \end{cases}$

Thus, the partial derivatives of the output with respect to the weights can be expressed using the chain law as follows:

$$\frac{\partial y}{\partial w_i} = \frac{\partial y}{\partial u}\frac{\partial u}{\partial w_i} = \sigma'(u)\frac{\partial u}{\partial w_i} = \sigma'(u)\frac{\partial\left(\mathbf{S}_{i=1}^{n}(w_i\ \mathbf{T}\ x_i)\right)}{\partial w_i} \tag{15.49}$$

On the basis of the different definitions of the **T** and **S** operators and the corresponding operation equations of the FNs, the detailed expressions of the partial derivatives $\partial u/\partial w_i$ and $\partial u/\partial x_i$ corresponding to the three types of **T** and **S** operators as illustrated in Fig. 15.9 and defined in Table 15.2 can be obtained as shown in Table 15.5. Even if the various versions of the partial derivatives are conceptually quite different, their final numerical effects of learning should be similar.

15.4 REGULAR FUZZY NEURAL NETWORKS (RFNNs)

The three types of fuzzy neural units discussed in the previous section can be used to form a class of fuzzy neural networks (FNNs). These FNNs can be used for approximating mappings from the input hypercube $[0,1]^n$ to the output hypercube $[0,1]^m$ in a fuzzy logic–based format. Since these FN

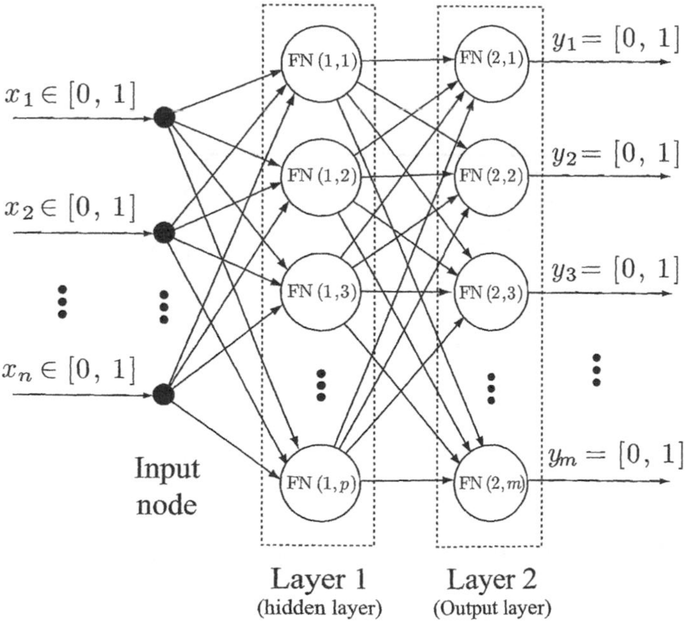

Figure 15.10 A two-layered regular fuzzy neural network (RFNN).

models are built by using the standard fuzzy logic, the networks formed by these FNs are termed *regular fuzzy neural networks* (RFNNs).

15.4.1 Regular Fuzzy Neural Network (RFNN) Structures

The RFNN shown in Fig. 15.10 with one hidden layer is considered in this section. In such a RFNN, the neurons are organized into layers with no feedback or cross-layer connections. A basic structure of such a RFNN is shown in Fig. 15.11.

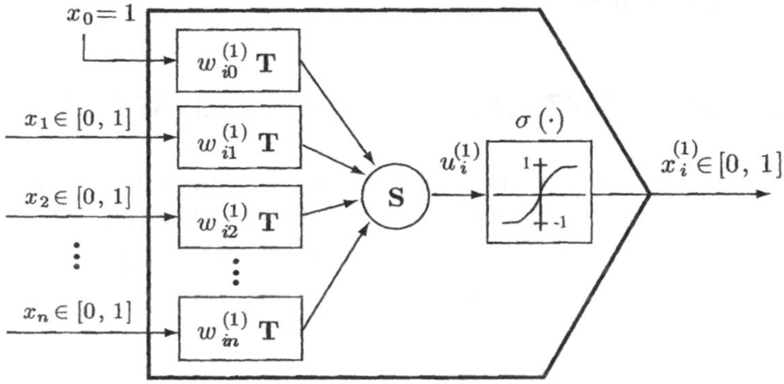

(a) FN $(1, i)$, $i = 0, 1, 2, \ldots, p$, in the first layer, Eqn. (15.50)

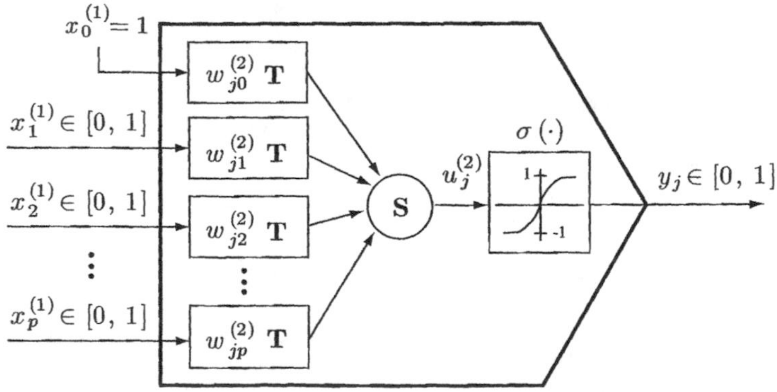

(b) FN $(2, j)$, $j = 0, 1, 2, \ldots, m$, in the second layer, Eqn. (15.51)

Figure 15.11 First and second neural layers in regular fuzzy neural networks (RFNNs).

Assume that the neurons in the first layer are denoted by FN$(1, i)$ $(i = 1, 2, \ldots, p)$ and the neurons in the output layer; that is, in the second layer, are denoted by FN$(2, j)$ $(j = 1, 2, \ldots, m)$. Let the neuron FN$(1, i)$ in the first layer receive n input signals $x_1, x_2, \ldots, x_n \in [0,1]$, and deliver an output signal $x_i^{(1)}$. The outputs of all the neurons in the first layer are feedforwarded to every neuron in the second layer as input signals. Finally, FN$(2, j)$ $(j = 1, 2, \ldots, m)$ in the second layer generates an output signal y_j. Then, using the notations of the **T** and **S** operators, the input–output equations of the neurons in such a RFNN can be expressed as

$$\text{FN}(1,i) \quad : \quad \begin{cases} u_i^{(1)} = \mathbf{S}_{\ell=0}^{n}\left(w_{i\ell}^{(1)}\,\mathbf{T}\,x_\ell\right), & x_0 = 1 \\ \\ x_i^{(1)} = \sigma\left(u_i^{(1)}\right), & i = 1, 2, \ldots, p \end{cases} \tag{15.50}$$

$$\text{FN}(2,j) \quad : \quad \begin{cases} u_j^{(2)} = \mathbf{S}_{q=0}^{p}\left(w_{jq}^{(2)}\,\mathbf{T}\,x_q^{(1)}\right), & x_0^{(1)} = 1 \\ \\ y_j = \sigma\left(u_j^{(2)}\right), & j = 1, 2, \ldots, m \end{cases} \tag{15.51}$$

where $w_{i\ell}^{(1)}$ $(\ell = 0, 1, 2, \ldots, n)$ are the weights associated with FN$(1, i)$ and $w_{jq}^{(2)}$ $(q = 0, 1, 2, \ldots, p)$ are the weights of FN$(2, j)$. These equations are also called the *transfer functions* of the neurons.

15.4.2 Fuzzy Backpropagation (FBP) Learning

The learning procedure for the free parameters in such a neural network is considered on the basis of the elements of the set of the training patterns. Given a set of input and desired output pairs $(\boldsymbol{x}(k), \boldsymbol{y}^d(k))(k = 1, 2, \ldots, N)$, the adaptive weight learning rule performs an optimization process such that the output error function, defined as the summation of the square of the errors between the desired and the real outputs of the network, is minimized. To address this problem mathematically, an instantaneous error function for the network is defined as

$$\begin{aligned} E(k) &= \tfrac{1}{2}\sum_{j=1}^{m}\left[y_j^d(k) - y_j(k)\right]^2 \\ &= \tfrac{1}{2}\sum_{j=1}^{m} e_j^2(k) \end{aligned} \tag{15.52}$$

where the output error e_j describing the error between the jth desired output response and the jth neural network output at FN$(2,j)$ is defined by

$$e_j = y_j^d - y_j$$

In a manner similar to the gradient descent technique used in the conventional backpropagation (BP) network, the following updating formulations can be obtained

$$\begin{aligned} w_{i\ell}^{(1)}(k+1) &= sat\left(w_{i\ell}^{(1)}(k) + \Delta w_{i\ell}^{(1)}(k) \right) \\ & \qquad i = 0,1,2,\ldots,p; \quad \ell = 1,2,\ldots,n \qquad (15.53) \\ w_{jq}^{(2)}(k+1) &= sat\left(w_{jq}^{(2)}(k) + \Delta w_{jq}^{(2)}(k) \right) \\ & \qquad j = 0,1,2,\ldots,m; \quad q = 1,2,\ldots,p \qquad (15.54) \end{aligned}$$

where

$$\Delta w_{i\ell}^{(1)} = -\eta_1 \frac{\partial E}{\partial w_{i\ell}^{(1)}} \qquad (15.55)$$

and

$$\Delta w_{jq}^{(2)} = -\eta_2 \frac{\partial E}{\partial w_{jq}^{(2)}} \qquad (15.56)$$

and η_1 and η_2 are the learning rates associated with the weights in the hidden layer and the weights in the output layer, respectively. The choice of these learning rates will affect the convergence speed of the updating process. The detailed formulations of the partial derivatives in Eqns. (15.55) and (15.56) can be obtained using the method given in Section 15.3.

15.4.3 Some Limitations of Regular Fuzzy Neural Networks (RFNNs)

As learned in the previous subsection, a regular fuzzy neural network (RFNN) can be considered as a nonlinear mapping from an n-dimensional input hypercube $[0,1]^n$ to an m-dimensional output hypercube $[0,1]^m$. This nonlinear mapping is based on standard fuzzy arithmetic and fuzzy logic operations. The universal approximation capability of neural networks is one of the promising advantages for their applications to areas such as identification, control, and pattern recognition. How well does a neural network approximate an unknown function? This is an important question that is asked about all types of neural networks, including multilayered feedforward neural networks (MFNNs) and dynamic neural networks (DNNs). A neural network with an augmented neural input $\boldsymbol{x}_a$ and an augmented weight vector $\boldsymbol{w}_a$, and an input–output mapping $\boldsymbol{f}(\boldsymbol{w}_a, \boldsymbol{x}_a) : \Re^{n+1} \rightarrow \Re^m$, is a universal approximator for a given continuous vector-valued function $\boldsymbol{g} : \Re^{n+1} \rightarrow \Re^m$ if there exists a $\boldsymbol{w}_a$ such that $\boldsymbol{f}(\boldsymbol{w}_a, \boldsymbol{x}_a)$ can approximate $\boldsymbol{g}$ uniformly on an arbitrary compact set of $\Re^{n+1}$ to any degree of accuracy. We will show that the RFNNs developed above are not universal approximators in this context.

First, the two layered fuzzy network equations, Eqns. (15.50) and (15.51), can equivalently be represented as

(i) Output of the first layer:

$$
\begin{aligned}
x_i^{(1)} &= \sigma\left(u_i^{(1)}\right) = \sigma\left[\mathbf{S}_{\ell=0}^{n}(w_{i\ell}^{(1)}\ \mathbf{T}\ x_\ell)\right], \quad x_0 = 1 \\
&= \sigma\left(w_{i0}^{(1)}, w_{i1}^{(1)}, \ldots, w_{in}^{(1)}, x_0, x_1, \ldots, x_n\right) \\
&= \sigma\left(\boldsymbol{w}_{ai}^{(1)}, \boldsymbol{x}_a\right) \qquad (15.57)
\end{aligned}
$$

(ii) Output of the second layer:

$$
\begin{aligned}
y_j &= \sigma(u_j^{(2)}) = \sigma\left[\mathbf{S}_{q=0}^{p}\left(w_{jq}^{(2)}\mathbf{T}x_q^{(1)}\right)\right], \quad x_0^{(1)} = 1 \\
&= \sigma\left(w_{j0}^{(2)}, w_{j1}^{(2)}, \ldots, w_{jp}^{(2)}, x_0^{(1)}, x_1^{(1)}, \ldots, x_p^{(1)}\right) \\
&= \sigma\left(\boldsymbol{w}_{aj}^{(2)}, \boldsymbol{x}_a^{(1)}\right) \\
&\triangleq f_j\left(\boldsymbol{W}_a^{(1)}, \boldsymbol{w}_{aj}^{(2)}, \boldsymbol{x}_a\right) \qquad (15.58)
\end{aligned}
$$

or equivalently in a vector form, the mathematical expression of Eqns. (15.57) and (15.58) can be rewritten as

$$
\boldsymbol{y} = \boldsymbol{f}\left(\boldsymbol{W}_a^{(1)}, \boldsymbol{W}_a^{(2)}, \boldsymbol{x}_a\right) \qquad (15.59)
$$

where $\boldsymbol{x}_a = [x_0\ x_1\ \cdots\ x_n]^T$ is the augmented input vector, $\boldsymbol{x}^{(1)} = \left[x_1^{(1)}\ \cdots\ x_p^{(1)}\right]^T$ is the output vector of the first neural layer, $\boldsymbol{w}_{ai}^{(1)} = \left[w_{i0}^{(1)}\ w_{i1}^{(1)}\ \cdots\ w_{in}^{(1)}\right]^T$ is the augmented weight vector of the neuron FN$(1, i)$, $\boldsymbol{W}_a^{(1)} = \left[\boldsymbol{w}_{a1}^{(1)}\ \cdots\ \boldsymbol{w}_{ap}^{(1)}\right]$ represents the augmented weight matrix of all the weights in the first neural layer, $\boldsymbol{w}_{aj}^{(2)} = \left[w_{j0}^{(2)}\ w_{j1}^{(2)}\ \cdots\ w_{jp}^{(2)}\right]^T$ is the augmented weight vector associated with the neuron FN$(2, j)$ in the output neural layer, and $\boldsymbol{W}_a^{(2)} = \left[\boldsymbol{w}_{a1}^{(2)}\ \cdots\ \boldsymbol{w}_{am}^{(2)}\right]$ represents the augmented weight matrix of the weights in the output neural layer. Thus, Eqn. (15.59) describes the input–output relations of the RFNN by means of a nonlinear mapping $\boldsymbol{f} : [0,1]^n \rightarrow [0,1]^m$.

Noting the monotonicity of the **T** and **S** operators, and the sigmoidal function $\sigma(\cdot)$, thus, for an arbitrary input vectors $\boldsymbol{x} = [x_1\, x_2 \cdots x_n]^T$, $\overline{\boldsymbol{x}} = [\overline{x}_1\, \overline{x}_2\, \cdots\, \overline{x}_n]^T \in [0,1]^n$, with $x_i \leq \overline{x}_i$, it can be implied that

$$x_i^{(1)} = \sigma\left(\boldsymbol{w}_i^{(1)}, \boldsymbol{x}\right) \leq \overline{x}_i^{(1)} = \sigma\left(\boldsymbol{w}_i^{(1)}, \overline{\boldsymbol{x}}\right) \tag{15.60}$$

and

$$y_j = f_j\left(\boldsymbol{W}_a^{(1)}, \boldsymbol{w}_{aj}^{(2)}, \boldsymbol{x}_a\right) \leq \overline{y}_j = f_j\left(\boldsymbol{W}_a^{(1)}, \boldsymbol{w}_{aj}^{(2)}, \overline{\boldsymbol{x}}_a\right) \tag{15.61}$$

It can also be verified that the Jacobian of the output vector $\boldsymbol{y}$ with respect to the input vector $\boldsymbol{x}$ defined by

$$\frac{\partial \boldsymbol{y}}{\partial \boldsymbol{x}} = \frac{\partial \boldsymbol{f}}{\partial \boldsymbol{x}} = \begin{bmatrix} \dfrac{\partial f_1}{\partial x_1} & \dfrac{\partial f_2}{\partial x_1} & \cdots & \dfrac{\partial f_m}{\partial x_1} \\ \dfrac{\partial f_1}{\partial x_2} & \dfrac{\partial f_2}{\partial x_2} & \cdots & \dfrac{\partial f_m}{\partial x_2} \\ \vdots & \vdots & \ddots & \vdots \\ \dfrac{\partial f_1}{\partial x_n} & \dfrac{\partial f_2}{\partial x_n} & \cdots & \dfrac{\partial f_m}{\partial x_n} \end{bmatrix} \tag{15.62}$$

has only nonnegative elements:

$$\frac{\partial f_j}{\partial x_i} \geq 0; \quad \text{for all } i \text{ and } j, \quad i = 1, 2, \ldots, n; \quad j = 1, 2, \ldots, m \tag{15.63}$$

Therefore, it can be concluded that for fixed fuzzy weights on the unit interval [0,1], the nonlinear mapping realized by such a RFNN is a monotonically increasing function in terms of the fuzzy inputs. Assume that a vector inequality implies inequality for each component of the vector. For example, if $\boldsymbol{x} \in [0,1]^n \leq \overline{\boldsymbol{x}} \in [0,1]^n$, it implies that $x_i \leq \overline{x}_i, (i = 1, 2, \ldots, n)$. This analysis results can be summarized in the following theorem.

Theorem 15.1 (Monotonicity of RFNNs) *A regular fuzzy neural network (RFNN) with a neural input $\boldsymbol{x} \in [0,1]^n$, an output $y \in [0,1]^m$, and a network equation $\boldsymbol{y} = \boldsymbol{f}\left(\boldsymbol{W}_a^{(1)},\ \boldsymbol{W}_a^{(2)}, \boldsymbol{x}_a\right) : [0,1]^n \rightarrow [0,1]^m$ implements a* *monotonically increasing mapping from* $[0,1]^n$ *to* $[0,1]^m$*; that is, given two arbitrary vectors* $\boldsymbol{x} \in [0,1]^n$ *and* $\overline{\boldsymbol{x}} \in [0,1]^n$ *satisfying* $\boldsymbol{x} < \overline{\boldsymbol{x}}$*, then*

$$\boldsymbol{y} = \boldsymbol{f}\left(\boldsymbol{W}_a^{(1)}, \boldsymbol{W}_a^{(2)}, \boldsymbol{x}_a\right) \leq \overline{\boldsymbol{y}} = \boldsymbol{f}\left(\boldsymbol{W}_a^{(1)}, \boldsymbol{W}_a^{(2)}, \overline{\boldsymbol{x}}_a\right) \qquad \blacksquare$$

RFNNs can be used to implement a special class of fuzzy logic–based nonlinear functions which are monotonically increasing. In fact, this type of FNN can be used to approximate any fuzzy function that consists of only *AND* and *OR* operations. On the other hand, it will be seen in the following example that such a RFNN is incapable of implementing a simple binary two-variable *XOR* function that may be considered as a special nonlinear fuzzy logic function.

Example 15.3 The two-variable *XOR* (exclusive OR) logic function $y = x_1 \oplus x_2$ with binary input variables x_1 and x_2 that are either 0 or 1 may be considered as a special fuzzy logic function as shown in Fig. 15.12. Design a two-layered RFNN with the inputs x_1 and x_2, a single output y, two hidden fuzzy neurons, and a linear activation function $\sigma(x) = x$. It is easy to derive the input–output equations of such a network as follows:

(i) Input layer:

$$x_1^{(1)} = \max\left[\min\left(w_{11}^{(1)}, x_1\right), \min\left(w_{12}^{(1)}, x_2\right)\right]$$

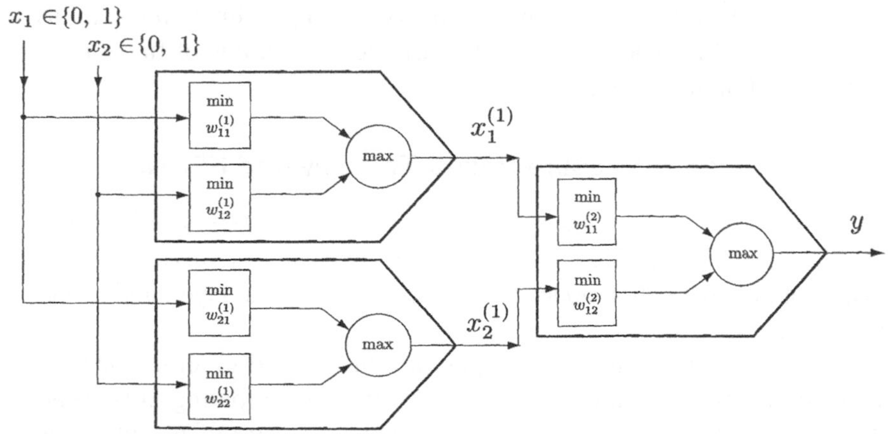

Figure 15.12 Example 15.3: a RFNN with two neurons in the input layer and one neuron in the output layer fails to implement a two-variable *XOR* function $y = x_1 \oplus x_2$.

$$x_2^{(1)} = \max\left[\min\left(w_{21}^{(1)}, x_1\right), \min\left(w_{22}^{(1)}, x_2\right)\right]$$

(ii) Output layer:

$$y = \max\left[\min(w_{11}^{(2)}, x_1^{(1)}), \min\left(w_{12}^{(2)}, x_2^{(1)}\right)\right]$$

Noting that $y = x_1 \oplus x_2$ is $0, 1, 1$, and 0, respectively, for the binary patterns $(0,0)$, $(0,1)$, $(1,0)$, and $(1,1)$, the output of the RFNN can be represented as

$$1 = \max\left[\min\left(w_{11}^{(2)}, w_{12}^{(1)}\right), \min\left(w_{12}^{(2)}, w_{22}^{(1)}\right)\right] \tag{15.64}$$

$$1 = \max\left[\min\left(w_{11}^{(2)}, w_{11}^{(1)}\right), \min\left(w_{12}^{(2)}, w_{21}^{(1)}\right)\right] \tag{15.65}$$

$$\begin{aligned} 0 = \max\Big[&\min\left(w_{11}^{(2)}, \max\left(w_{11}^{(1)}, w_{12}^{(1)}\right)\right), \\ &\min\left(w_{12}^{(2)}, \max\left(w_{21}^{(1)}, w_{22}^{(1)}\right)\right)\Big] \end{aligned} \tag{15.66}$$

The output given in Eqn. (15.64) contradicts the outputs given in Eqns. (15.65) and (15.66). Therefore, no solution exists for the weights for the implementation of the *XOR* logic, and the *XOR* function cannot be realized by such a RFNN. It can be verified that an increase in the number of the hidden units will not change this conclusion. ■

15.5 HYBRID FUZZY NEURAL NETWORKS (HFNNs)

To modify the fuzzy operations in the regular fuzzy neural network (RFNN) described in the last section so that the universal approximation capability of the fuzzy neural networks is ensured, some new structures of fuzzy neurons are discussed in this section.

15.5.1 Difference-Measure-Based Two-Layered HFNNs

A new architecture of a hybrid fuzzy neural network (HFNN) is shown in Fig. 15.13, where the HFNN has multiple inputs and a single output, and consists of an input neural node, one hidden fuzzy neural layer, and an output neural layer.

In the HFNN, all of the neural inputs are distributed to all the neurons in the hidden fuzzy neural layer. In such fuzzy neural computing, it is proposed that this operation be replaced by a *difference measure* of the input signal $x_i \in [0,1]$ and the weight $w_i \in [0,1]$ defined by

$$\boldsymbol{d}(x_i, w_i) \begin{cases} = 0, & \text{if} \quad x_i = w_i \\ > 0, & \text{otherwise} \end{cases} \tag{15.67}$$

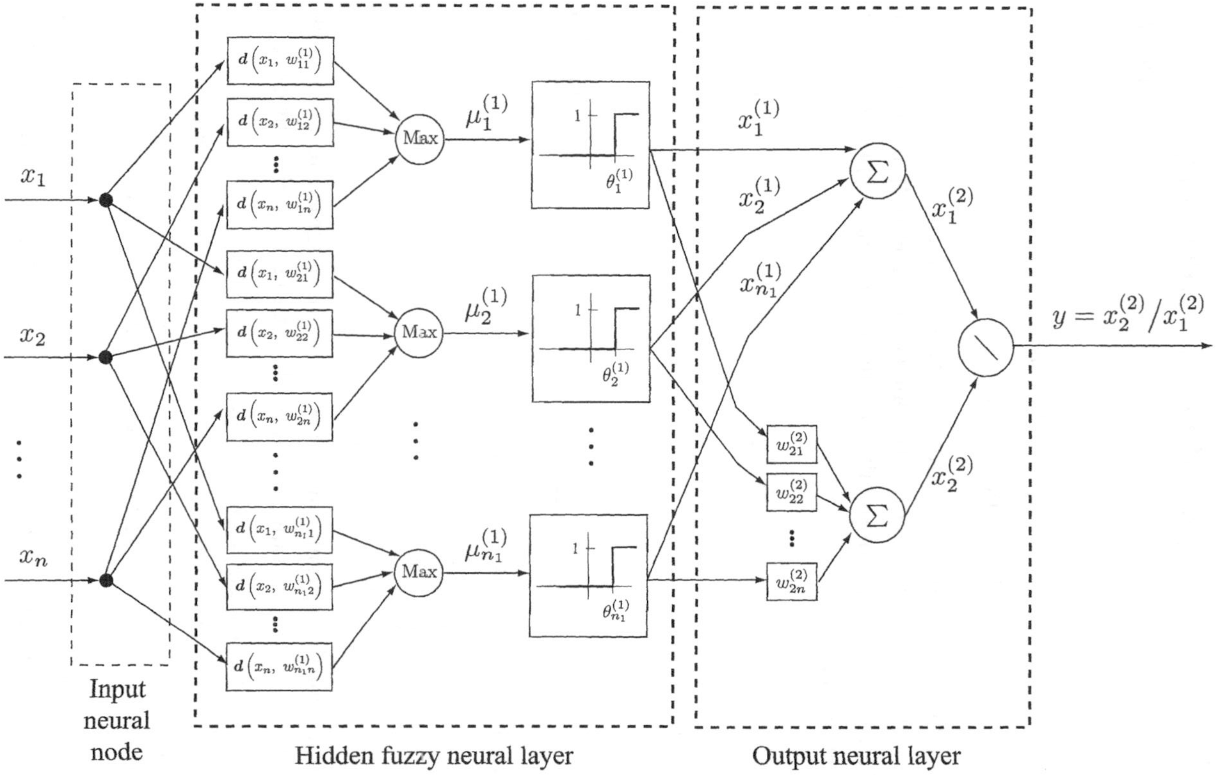

Figure 15.13 A difference-measure-based two-layered hybrid fuzzy neural network (HFNN).

Thus, the output of the neurons in the hidden fuzzy neural layer can be obtained as follows

$$\begin{aligned} u_i^{(1)} &= \max\left([\boldsymbol{d}(x_1, w_1), \boldsymbol{d}(x_2, w_2), \ldots, \boldsymbol{d}(x_n, w_n)]\right) \\ &= \max_{i=1}^{n}\left(\boldsymbol{d}(x_i, w_i) \right) \end{aligned} \tag{15.68}$$

and

$$x_i^{(i)} = \begin{cases} 1, & \text{if} \quad u_i^{(1)} > \theta_i^{(1)} \\ 0, & \text{otherwise} \end{cases} \tag{15.69}$$

where $\theta_i^{(1)}$ is a threshold associated with the neuron FN(1,i).

There are only two neurons in the output layer. The output of the first neuron in the output layer is simply the summation of the outputs of all the neurons in the first layer:

$$x_1^{(2)} = \sum_{j=1}^{n_1} x_j^{(1)} \tag{15.70}$$

The output of the second neuron in the output layer is a weighted summation of the form

$$x_2^{(2)} = \sum_{i=1}^{n_1} w_{2j}^{(2)} x_j^{(1)} \tag{15.71}$$

Finally, the output of the network is defined as

$$\begin{cases} \dfrac{x_2^{(2)}}{x_1^{(2)}}, & \text{if} \quad x_1^{(2)} > 0 \\ 0, & \text{otherwise} \end{cases} \tag{15.72}$$

In this definition all the weights and thresholds are assumed to be triangle fuzzy numbers. Thus, the operation from the hidden layer to the output layer deals with a *centroid defuzzifier*, where the input signals $x_1^{(1)}, x_2^{(1)}, \ldots, x_{n_1}^{(1)}$ are unipolar binary signals (Buckley and Hayashi 1993c, 1994a). These unipolar binary signals can easily be extended to bipolar binary signals as well as to some modified neural architectures and different types of fuzzy numbers.

It has been proved that the HFNN described above is a universal approximator (Buckley and Hayashi 1993c). However, no related learning algorithm has been reported to carry out such an approximation.

It is to be noted that the input–output mapping of such a HFNN is discontinuous since the max operation and hard-limiting functions are used in forming the input–output mapping. This may cause some difficulties with the learning phase.

15.5.2 Fuzzy Neurons and Hybrid Fuzzy Neural Networks (HFNNs)

As has been seen earlier, a conventional neuron involves a somatic operation, which is a confluence or similarity measure operation between the input signals and the corresponding synaptic weights. In the FN model discussed in Section 15.2, this operation was replaced by the **T** operator. This operation can also be replaced with a difference measure on the neural input signal $x_i \in [0,1]$ and the synaptic weight $w_i \in [0,1]$. This difference measure operation, as discussed in Section 15.5.1 on two-layered HFNNs and as seen in Eqn. (15.67), is denoted by $\boldsymbol{d}(x_i, w_i)$, which satisfies $0 \leq \boldsymbol{d}(x_i, w_i) \leq 1$. For example, $\boldsymbol{d}(x_i, w_i)$ can be selected as

$$\boldsymbol{d}(x_i, w_i) = |x_i, w_i|^n \tag{15.73}$$

In the following discussion, we assume that $\boldsymbol{d}(x_i, w_i)$ is of the quadratic form

$$\boldsymbol{d}(x_i, w_i) = (x_i - w_i)^2 \tag{15.74}$$

This difference measure operation is then used to replace the **T** operator in the fuzzy neuron introduced in Section 15.3. As shown in Fig. 15.14, all these difference measures between the inputs and the associate weights can be combined by means of the standard **S** operator.
Thus, the output of such a fuzzy neuron is given by

$$\begin{aligned} u &= \mathbf{S}_{i=1}^{n}\left(\, \boldsymbol{d}(x_i, w_i) \,\right) \\ &= \mathbf{S}\left(\, \boldsymbol{d}(x_1, w_1), \boldsymbol{d}(x_2, w_2), \ldots, \boldsymbol{d}(x_n, w_n) \,\right) \end{aligned} \tag{15.75}$$

and, finally, the neural output is given by

$$y = \sigma(u) \tag{15.76}$$

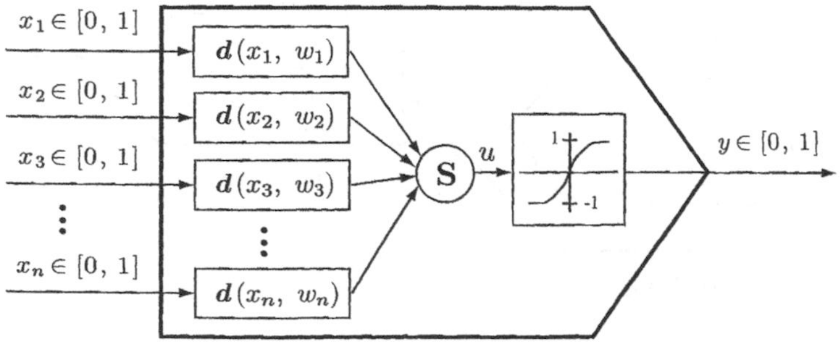

Figure 15.14 A fuzzy neuron with the difference measure and **S** operator, Eqns. (15.75) and (15.76).

Obviously, this type of fuzzy neuron is no longer monotonic in terms of its fuzzy inputs $x_1, x_2, \ldots, x_n$.

Using this type of fuzzy neuron, a two-layered fuzzy neural network, the *hybrid fuzzy neural network*, can easily be formed. The operational equations of such a HFNN are as follows:

$$\text{FN}(1,i): \begin{cases} u_1^{(1)} = \boldsymbol{S}_{\ell=1}^{n}\left(\boldsymbol{d}\left(w_{i\ell}^{(1)}, x_\ell\right)\right), & i = 1, 2, \ldots, p \\ x_1^{(1)} = \sigma\left(u_i^{(1)}\right), & i = 1, 2, \ldots, p \end{cases} \tag{15.77}$$

$$\text{FN}(2,j): \begin{cases} u_j^{(2)} = \boldsymbol{S}_{q=1}^{p}\left(\boldsymbol{d}\left(w_{jq}^{(2)}, x_q^{(1)}\right)\right), & i = 1, 2, \ldots, m \\ y_j = \sigma\left(u_j^{(2)}\right), & i = 1, 2, \ldots, m \end{cases} \tag{15.78}$$

It seems that this HFNN has a capability for approximation of functions, but no strict mathematical proof is currently available as to its universal approximation for this network. The following example will show that the HFNN is capable of solving the *XOR* problem.

Example 15.4 From this example, it will be seen that a two-variable binary *XOR* function $y = x_1 \oplus x_2$ can be implemented by a difference-measure-based two-layered HFNN with two neurons in the hidden layer and one in the output layer, as shown in Fig. 15.15. In fact, if the **S** operator is selected as a max operation, the input–output equation of such a network can be obtained

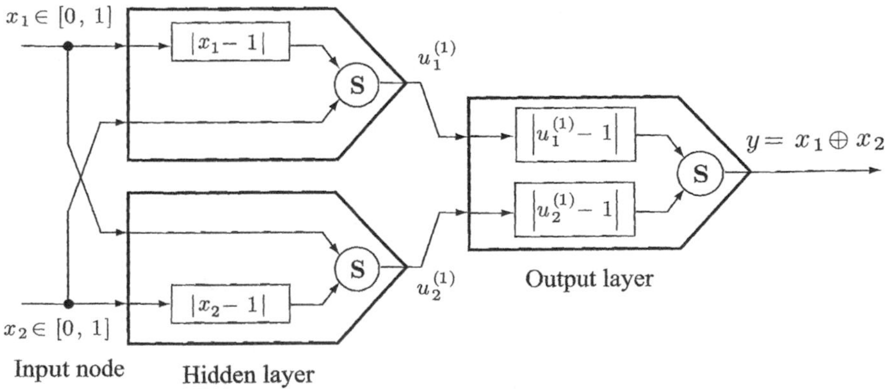

Figure 15.15 Example 15.4: a difference-measure-based HFNN with two neurons in the hidden layer and one neuron in the output layer for the implementation of a two-variable *XOR* function, $y = x_1 \oplus x_2$.

Table 15.6 **Example 15.4, fuzzy *XOR* operation**

x_1	x_2	$y = x_1 \oplus x_2$
0	0	0
0	1	1
1	0	1
1	1	0

as

$$\begin{aligned} u_1^{(1)} &= \max\{|x_1 - 1|,\ x_2\} \\ u_2^{(1)} &= \max\{x_1,\ |x_2 - 1|\} \\ y &= \max\left\{\left|u_1^{(1)} - 1\right|,\ \left|u_2^{(1)} - 1\right|\right\} \end{aligned}$$

The input–output relationship for this HFNN is given in Table 15.6, which clearly shows a *XOR* operation of this network.

It is to be noted that in this example, although we have used the **S**-operation as a max operation, other types of the **S**-operation, as tabulated in Table 15.2, can also be used. ■

15.5.3 Derivation of Backpropagation Algorithm for Hybrid Fuzzy Neural Networks

Given a set of desired data pairs $(\boldsymbol{x}(k), \boldsymbol{y}(k))$, an error index is defined as

$$E(k) = \tfrac{1}{2}\sum_{j=1}^{m}\left[y_j^d(k) - y_j(k)\right]^2 = \tfrac{1}{2}\sum_{j=1}^{m} e_j^2(k)$$

For a two-layered hybrid fuzzy neural network (HFNN) with the operational equations, Eqns. (15.77) and (15.78), the fuzzy backpropagation (FBP) algorithm is given by the following updating formulations

$$\begin{aligned} w_{i\ell}^{(1)}(k+1) &= sat\left(w_{i\ell}^{(1)}(k) + \Delta w_{i\ell}^{(1)}(k)\right) \\ & \qquad i = 1, 2, \ldots, p;\ \ \ell = 1, 2, \ldots, n \end{aligned} \tag{15.79}$$

$$\begin{aligned} w_{jq}^{(2)}(k+1) &= sat\left(w_{jq}^{(2)}(k) + \Delta w_{jq}^{(2)}(k)\right) \\ & \qquad j = 1, 2, \ldots, m;\ \ q = 1, 2, \ldots, p \end{aligned} \tag{15.80}$$

where

$$\Delta w_{i\ell}^{(1)} = -\eta_1 \frac{\partial E}{\partial w_{i\ell}^{(1)}} \tag{15.81}$$

$$\Delta w_{jq}^{(2)} = -\eta_2 \frac{\partial E}{\partial w_{jq}^{(2)}} \tag{15.82}$$

In order to derive these updating formulations, the concept of the error partial derivatives δs is introduced below. For such a two-layered fuzzy neural structure these intermediate variables are denoted as

$$\delta_i^{(1)} \triangleq -\frac{\partial E}{\partial u_i^{(1)}}, \quad i = 1, 2, \ldots, p \tag{15.83}$$

$$\delta_j^{(2)} \triangleq -\frac{\partial E}{\partial u_j^{(2)}}, \quad j = 1, 2, \ldots, m \tag{15.84}$$

where $\delta_i^{(1)}$ is the partial derivative of FN$(1, i)$ and $\delta_j^{(2)}$ is that of FN$(2, j)$. Therefore, Eqns. (15.81) and (15.82) can be represented as

$$\Delta w_{i\ell}^{(1)} = -\eta_1 \frac{\partial E}{\partial u_i^{(1)}} \frac{\partial u_i^{(1)}}{\partial w_{i\ell}^{(1)}} = -\eta_1 \delta_i^{(1)} \frac{\partial u_i^{(1)}}{\partial w_{i\ell}^{(1)}} \tag{15.85}$$

$$\Delta w_{jq}^{(2)} = -\eta_2 \frac{\partial E}{\partial u_j^{(2)}} \frac{\partial u_j^{(2)}}{\partial w_{jq}^{(2)}} = -\eta_2 \delta_j^{(2)} \frac{\partial u_j^{(2)}}{\partial w_{jq}^{(2)}} \tag{15.86}$$

It is seen that the definition of these partial derivatives not only keeps the derivation simple but also plays an important role in the final learning formulations. It is easy to derive the δs for the output neurons as follows:

$$\delta_j^{(2)} = e_j \sigma'\left(\delta_j^{(2)}\right) \tag{15.87}$$

For simplicity, assume that the **S** operator is defined as a max operation in the following derivation. Then

$$\frac{\partial u_j^{(2)}}{\partial w_{jq}^{(2)}} = \begin{cases} \left(w_{jq}^{(2)} - x_q^{(1)}\right), & \text{if } u_j^{(2)} = \left(w_{jq}^{(2)} - x_q^{(1)}\right)^2 \\ 0, & \text{otherwise} \end{cases} \tag{15.88}$$

Thus, the updating formulations for the weights in the output layer are obtained as follows:

$$w_{jq}^{(2)}(k+1) = \begin{cases} sat\left(w_{jq}^{(2)}(k) + \eta_2 \delta_j^{(2)} \left(w_{jq}^{(2)}(k) - x_q^{(1)}(k)\right)\right), \\ \qquad\qquad \text{if} \quad u_j^{(2)} = \left(w_{jq}^{(2)} - x_q^{(1)}\right)^2 \\ w_{jq}^{(2)}(k), \qquad \text{otherwise} \end{cases} \tag{15.89}$$

The next task is to derive the updating formulations for the weights associated with the hidden neurons. To do so, we first deal with the δs associated with the hidden neurons. By means of the chain law, Eqn. (15.83) can be represented as

$$\begin{aligned}\delta_i^{(1)} &= -\frac{\partial E}{\partial u_i^{(1)}} = -\sum_{j=1}^{m} \frac{\partial E}{\partial u_j^{(2)}} \frac{\partial u_j^{(2)}}{\partial u_i^{(1)}} = \sum_{j=1}^{m} \delta_j^{(2)} \frac{\partial u_j^{(2)}}{\partial u_i^{(1)}} \\ &= \sum_{j=1}^{m} \delta_j^{(2)} \frac{\partial u_j^{(2)}}{\partial x_i^{(1)}} \frac{\partial x_i^{(1)}}{\partial u_i^{(1)}} = \sum_{j=1}^{m} \delta_j^{(2)} \sigma'\left(u_i^{(1)}\right) \frac{\partial u_j^{(2)}}{\partial x_i^{(1)}} \end{aligned} \tag{15.90}$$

Noting the relationship between $u_j^{(2)}$ and $x_i^{(1)}$ given by Eqn. (15.88), the following partial derivative formulations can be obtained:

$$\frac{\partial u_j^{(2)}}{\partial x_i^{(1)}} = \begin{cases} \left(x_i^{(1)} - w_{ji}^{(2)}\right), & \text{if} \quad u_j^{(2)} = \left(w_{ji}^{(2)} - x_i^{(1)}\right)^2 \\ 0, & \text{otherwise} \end{cases} \tag{15.91}$$

Furthermore

$$\frac{\partial u_i^{(1)}}{\partial w_{i\ell}^{(1)}} = \begin{cases} \left(w_{i\ell}^{(1)} - x_i\right), & \text{if} \quad u_i^{(1)} = \left(w_{i\ell}^{(1)} - x_i\right)^2 \\ 0, & \text{otherwise} \end{cases} \tag{15.92}$$

In this case, the weight updating formulations are obtained as follows

$$w_{i\ell}^{(1)}(k+1) = \begin{cases} sat\left(w_{i\ell}^{(1)}(k) + \eta_1 \delta_i^{(1)} \left(w_{i\ell}^{(1)}(k) - x_\ell(k)\right)\right), \\ \qquad\qquad\qquad\qquad \text{if} \quad u_i^{(1)} = \left(w_{i\ell}^{(1)} - x_\ell\right)^2 \\ w_{i\ell}^{(1)}(k), \qquad\qquad\quad \text{otherwise} \end{cases} \tag{15.93}$$

The fuzzy backpropagation (FBP) algorithm obtained above has a two-way information transfer. First the input fuzzy signals are calculated in the feedforward path and then the error signals that are used for updating the process are produced in the backward path. In other words, the input signals are processed starting from the input layer to the output layer. The error signals are calculated in the output layer and then propagated to the lower neural layers. The term *backpropagation* is used here to reflect this interesting fact.

15.5.4 Summary of Fuzzy Backpropagation (FBP) Algorithm

The key distinguishing characteristic of a fuzzy neural network (FNN) with the fuzzy backpropagation (FBP) learning algorithm is that it forms a nonlinear mapping from a set of fuzzy input stimuli to a set of output units using features extracted from the input patterns. This network can be designed and trained to accomplish a wide variety of fuzzy mappings, some of which are very complex. This is because the units in the hidden layers of the network learn to respond to features found in the input stimuli. By applying the set of formulations of the FBP algorithm obtained in Section 15.5.3, a calculation procedure of such a learning process is summarized in Table 15.7. In this procedure, several learning factors such as the initial weights, the learning rate, and the number of hidden neurons may be reselected if the iterative learning process does not converge rapidly to the desired point.

Table 15.7 **The fuzzy backpropagation (FBP) learning algorithm for a two-layered FNN**

Given N desired input–output pairs $\left(\boldsymbol{x}(k), \boldsymbol{y}^d(k)\right)$ with $\boldsymbol{x}(k) \in [0,1]^n$ and $\boldsymbol{y}^d(k) \in [0,1]^m$:

Step 1: Select the number p of the hidden neurons, learning rate η_1 and η_2, error tolerance parameter $\epsilon > 0$, random initial values of the weights $w_{i\ell}^{(1)} \in [0,1]$ and $w_{jq}^{(2)} \in [0,1]$.

Step 2: Initialize $w_{i\ell}^{(1)} \leftarrow w_{i\ell}^{(1)}(0), w_{jq}^{(2)} \leftarrow w_{jq}^{(2)}(0), E \leftarrow 0$, and $k \leftarrow 1$.

Step 3: Calculate the neural outputs

$$\begin{cases} u_i^{(1)} &= \mathbf{S}_{\ell=1}^{n}\left(\boldsymbol{d}\left(w_{\ell i}^{(1)}, x_i\right)\right) \\ x_i^{(1)} &= \sigma\left(u_i^{(1)}\right) \end{cases}$$

and

$$\begin{cases} u_j^{(2)} &= \mathbf{S}_{q=1}^{p}\left(\boldsymbol{d}\left(w_{jq}^{(2)}, x_q^{(1)}\right)\right) \\ y_j &= \sigma\left(u_j^{(2)}\right) \end{cases}$$

Step 4: Calculate the partial derivatives $\partial u_i^{(1)}/\partial x_i^{(1)}, \partial u_j^{(2)}/\partial w_{jq}^{(2)}$, and $\partial u_j^{(2)}/\partial x_i^{(1)}$.

Step 5: Calculate the output error $e_j = y_j^d - y_j$.
Step 6: Calculate the output deltas $\delta_j^{(2)} = e_j \sigma' \left(u_j^{(2)} \right)$.
Step 7: Calculate the hidden neuronal deltas

$$\delta_i^{(1)} = \sum_{j=1}^{m} \delta_j^{(2)} \sigma' \left(u_i^{(1)} \right) \frac{\partial u_j^{(2)}}{\partial x_i^{(1)}}$$

Step 8: Update the weights

$$w_{i\ell}^{(1)} \quad \leftarrow \quad sat \left(w_{i\ell}^{(1)} + \eta_1 \delta_i^{(1)} \frac{\partial u_i^{(1)}}{\partial w_{i\ell}^{(1)}} \right)$$

$$w_{jq}^{(2)} \quad \leftarrow \quad sat \left(w_{jq}^{(2)} + \eta_2 \delta_j^{(2)} \frac{\partial u_j^{(2)}}{\partial w_{jq}^{(2)}} \right)$$

Step 9: Calculate the error function $E \leftarrow E + \frac{1}{2} \sum_{j=1}^{m} e_j^2$.
Step 10: If $k = N$ then go to Step 11. Otherwise, $k \rightarrow k + 1$ and go to Step 3.
Step 11: If $E \geq \varepsilon$ then go to Step 12. Otherwise go to Step 2.
Step 12: Learning is completed. Output the weights.

15.6 FUZZY BASIS FUNCTION NETWORKS (FBFNs)

As discussed in Section 15.1.3 and illustrated in Fig. 15.3, a fuzzy system is composed of four principal components: a fuzzifier, a fuzzy rule base, a fuzzy inference engine, and a defuzzifier, and it is an information processing machine. In such a machine, the crisp inputs are first converted into fuzzy quantities for the processing purposes. After some knowledge-based operations and processing on these fuzzy variables, the corresponding crisp outputs are obtained. The fuzzy neural network (FNN) structures discussed so far dealt only with the fuzzy input signals for a specified task as shown in Fig. 15.16. From the fuzzy systems point of view, this type of FNN is an important component and performs only a partial operation of a fuzzy system. A natural question raised here is how a FNN act as an entire fuzzy system for the purpose of information processing as shown in Fig. 15.17. In this section, some FNNs, namely, the *fuzzy basis function networks* (FBFNs), are

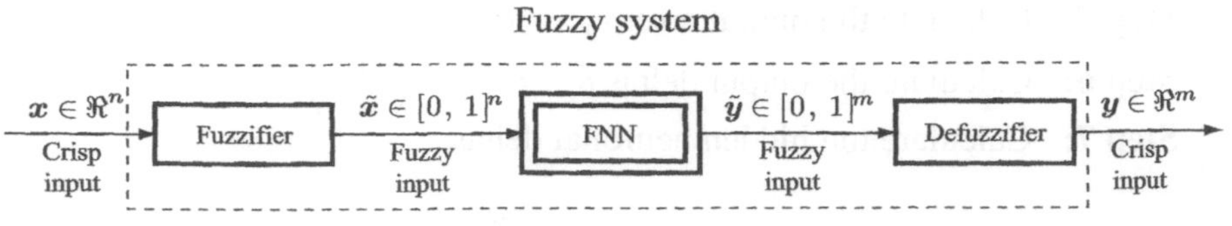

Figure 15.16 A fuzzy neural network (FNN) as a component of a fuzzy system.

Figure 15.17 A fuzzy neural network (FNN) implements an entire fuzzy system.

presented to implement an entire fuzzy system in the context of forming a desired input–output mapping function for crisp signals.

15.6.1 Gaussian Networks versus Fuzzy Systems

15.6.1.1 Single-Output Fuzzy System

Consider a fuzzy system with crisp inputs, $\boldsymbol{x} \in \Re^n$, M IF–THEN rules, the membership function $\mu_{A_i^j}$ for the jth rule ($j = 1, 2, \ldots, M$), and the ith component x_i of the input vector $\boldsymbol{x}$. If a singleton fuzzifier is used, the total result of the jth rule on the input vector $\boldsymbol{x}$ is given by

$$\begin{aligned} u_j(\boldsymbol{x}) &= \prod_{i=1}^{n} \mu_{A_i^j}(x_i) \\ &= \mu_{A_1^j}(x_1)\mu_{A_2^j}(x_2) \cdots \mu_{A_n^j}(x_n) \end{aligned} \tag{15.94}$$

A FNN can simply be constructed by means of the weighted summation of these quantities to form the output of the fuzzy system as follows

$$y = \sum_{j=1}^{M} w_j \left(\prod_{i=1}^{n} \mu_{A_i^j}(x_i) \right) \tag{15.95}$$

where $w_j \in \Re^n (j = 1, 2, \ldots, M)$ are the weight parameters. Since the membership functions are nonlinear parameterized functions, Eqn. (15.95) represents a nonlinear network with a nonfuzzy input vector $\boldsymbol{x}$, with membership functions (MFs) $\mu_{A_i^j}(x_i)$, weights w_j, and the nonfuzzy output $y \in \Re$. A schematic representation of this network is given in Fig. 15.18. It can be seen that such a fuzzy network structure can deal with not only some approximate

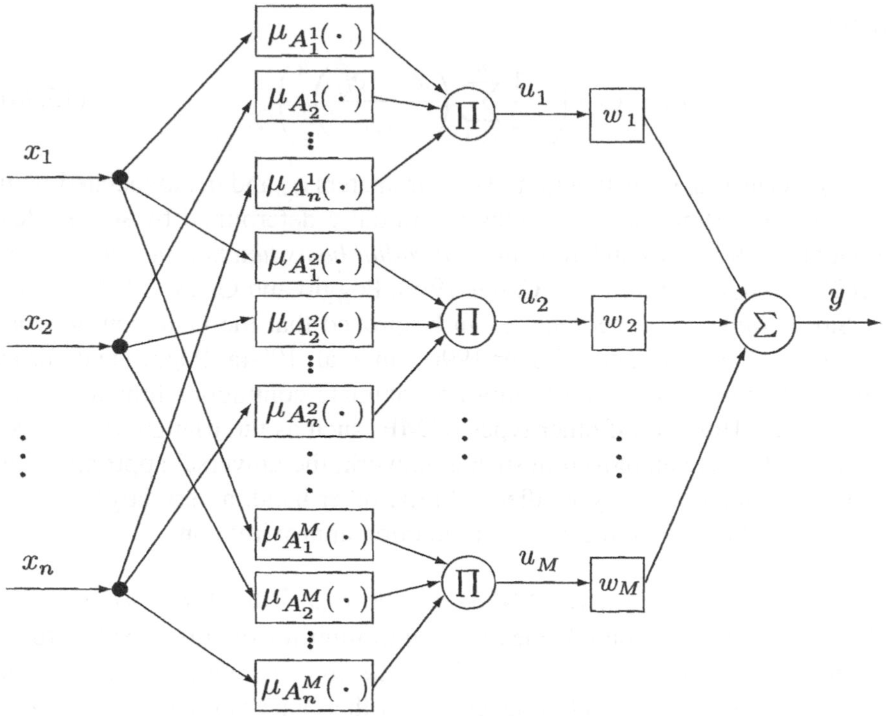

Figure 15.18 A fuzzy neural network as described in Eqns. (15.94) and (15.95).

reasoning that is involved in a fuzzy system but also a defuzzifier in a fuzzy system.

Furthermore, if a Gaussian radial membership function (GRMF)

$$\mu_{A_i^j}(x_i) = \exp\left(-\frac{1}{2}\left(\frac{x_i - c_{ij}}{\sigma_{ij}}\right)^2\right) \tag{15.96}$$

is employed, Eqn. (15.95) can be rewritten as follows

$$\begin{aligned} y &= \sum_{j=1}^{M} w_j \left(\prod_{i=1}^{n} \exp\left(-\frac{1}{2}\left(\frac{x_i - c_{ij}}{\sigma_{ij}}\right)^2\right)\right) \\ &= \sum_{j=1}^{M} w_j \exp\left(-\frac{1}{2}\sum_{i=1}^{n}\left(\frac{x_i - c_{ij}}{\sigma_{ij}}\right)^2\right) \\ &= \sum_{j=1}^{M} w_j u_j \end{aligned} \tag{15.97}$$

where

$$u_j = \exp\left(-\frac{1}{2}\sum_{i=1}^{n}\left(\frac{x_i - c_{ij}}{\sigma_{ij}}\right)^2\right) \tag{15.98}$$

is the jth Gaussian basis function. The parameters c_{ij} and σ_{ij} associated with the Gaussian membership functions are initially determined by some rules. Equation (15.97) is a standard *Gaussian radial basis function neural network* (GRBFNN) (Chen et al. 1991, Cotter 1990, Poggio and Girosi 1990). Using the Stone–Weierstrass theorem, it can be proved that the Gaussian network is a universal approximator (Cotter 1990, Jin et al. 1994a, Poggio and Girosi 1990) that can be used to uniformly approximate continuous functions on a compact set. However, if other types of MFs such as the triangular or trapezoidal function are employed in such a network, the universal approximation capability cannot be easily verified. On the other hand, a very large number of rules may be needed to carry out a function approximation.

15.6.1.2 Tuning Weights and Membership Functions (MFs)

Like the backpropagation (BP) learning algorithm for the membership function neural networks (MFNNs), if all of the free parameters, such as the weights w_j, centers c_{ij}, and variance σ_{ij} in the Gaussian network are considered as unknown, we may use the gradient descent method to form the updating equations for these parameters as shown in Fig. 15.19. Assume that the learning task is described by the input–output pairs $\{\boldsymbol{x}(k), \boldsymbol{y}(k)\}$. The number of such data sets might be finite or infinite. As seen in the previous sections, the first step for developing such a gradient descent technique-based supervised learning procedure is to define the instantaneous value of the cost function as follows

$$E = \tfrac{1}{2}\left(y^d(k) - y(k)\right)^2 = \tfrac{1}{2}e^2(k) \tag{15.99}$$

where

$$\begin{aligned} e &\triangleq y^d - y \\ &= y^d - \sum_{j=1}^{\ell} w_j \exp\left[-\tfrac{1}{2}\sum_{p=1}^{n}\left(\frac{x_k - c_{ip}}{\sigma_{ip}}\right)^2\right] \end{aligned} \tag{15.100}$$

Using the cost function relations given in Eqns. (15.99) and (15.100), and the network equations expressed in Eqns. (15.97) and (15.98), the following set of the updating equations for the parameters are obtained

$$w_j(k+1) = w_j(k) + \eta_1 u_j(k) e_j(k) \tag{15.101}$$

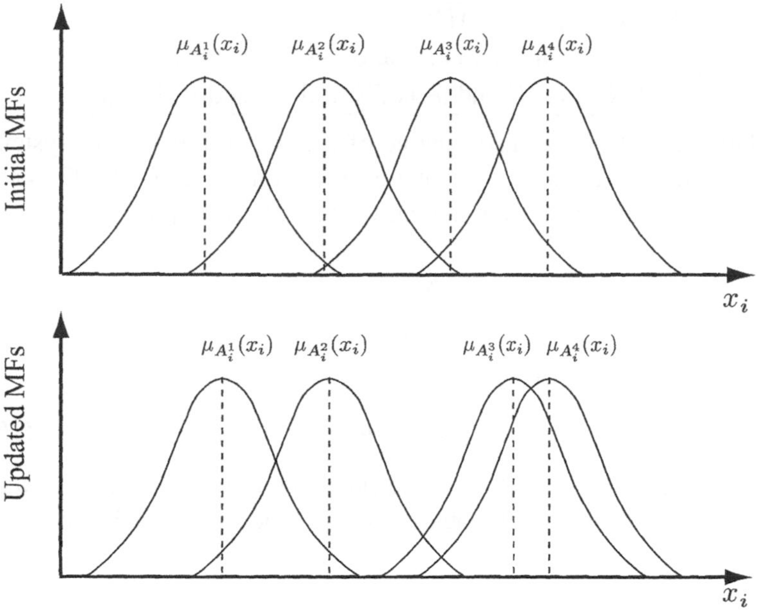

Figure 15.19 Adaptation and learning of Gaussian membership functions (GMFs).

$$c_{ij}(k+1) = c_{ij}(k) + \eta_2 \frac{(x_i(k) - c_{ij}(k))}{\sigma_{ij}^2(k)} y(k) e_j(k) \qquad (15.102)$$

$$\sigma_{ij}(k+1) = \sigma_{ij}(k) + \eta_3 \frac{(x_i(k) - c_{ij}(k))^2}{\sigma_{ij}^3(k)} y(k) e_j(k) \qquad (15.103)$$

$$1 \leq i \leq n; \quad 1 \leq j \leq M$$

where η_1, η_2, and η_3 are the learning rates associated with the weights, centers, and variance parameters, respectively. The iterative process goes repeatedly around the given learning data until the convergence values of the parameters of the membership functions (MFs) are updated for carrying out the task whose features are described by the known data.

15.6.1.3 Multiinput/Multioutput (MIMO) Fuzzy Systems

Fuzzy systems may have multiple outputs $y_1, y_2, \ldots, y_m$. To describe such a multiinput/multioutput (MIMO) fuzzy system, the fuzzy rule base, which is a set of fuzzy of the IF–THEN relationships between the inputs and outputs, may be modified to

R_j $(j = 1, 2, \ldots, M)$:
IF x_1 is A_1^j and x_2 is A_2^j and $\cdots$ and x_n is A_n^j,
THEN y_1 is B_1^j and y_2 is B_2^j and $\cdots$ and y_n is B_m^j .

A Gaussian network is also capable of implementing a fuzzy system with multiple outputs. In fact, a slight modification of Eqn. (15.97) gives the following equations for a Gaussian network with m outputs

$$y_p = \sum_{j=1}^{M} w_{pj} u_j \tag{15.104}$$

or equivalently in a vector form

$$\boldsymbol{y} = \boldsymbol{W}\boldsymbol{u} \tag{15.105}$$

where $\boldsymbol{y} = [y_1\ y_2\ \cdots\ y_m]^T$ is an output vector, $\boldsymbol{u} = [u_1\ u_2\ \cdots\ u_M]^T$ is a kernel vector consisting of Gaussian basis functions, and $\boldsymbol{W} = [u_{ij}]_{m \times M}$

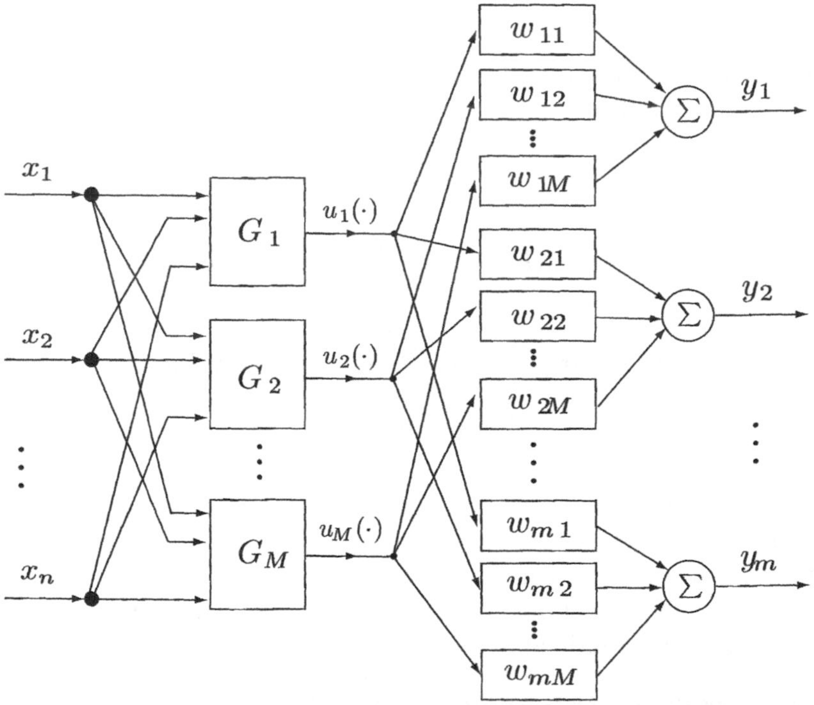

Figure 15.20 A Gaussian neural network with multiple inputs $\boldsymbol{x} \in \Re^n$ and multiple outputs $\boldsymbol{y} \in \Re^m$, G_i, $i = 1, \ldots, M$ represents the Gaussian operation as defined in Eqn. (15.98) and the output of the network as defined in Eqn. (15.104).

is the weight matrix. This network structure is shown in Fig. 15.20. Such a Gaussian network is capable of approximating uniformly a vector-valued continuous function on a compact set.

15.6.2 Fuzzy Basis Function Networks (FBFNs) Are Universal Approximators

15.6.2.1 Equations for Fuzzy Basis Function Networks (FBFNs)

As the last topic of this section, the approximation capabilities of FBFNs are now discussed (Mendel 1995, Wang and Mendel 1993, Wang 1993). Fuzzy systems, as fuzzy basis function expansions, can be represented as two-layered feedforward network structures. On the basis of this idea, the fuzzy systems may be trained to realize the desired input–output relationship using various learning algorithms such as the FBP algorithm. As pointed out by Wang and Mendel (1992a), the most important advantage of using fuzzy basis functions, rather than polynomials, radial basis functions, or other terms, is that a linguistic fuzzy IF–THEN rule is naturally related to a fuzzy basis function.

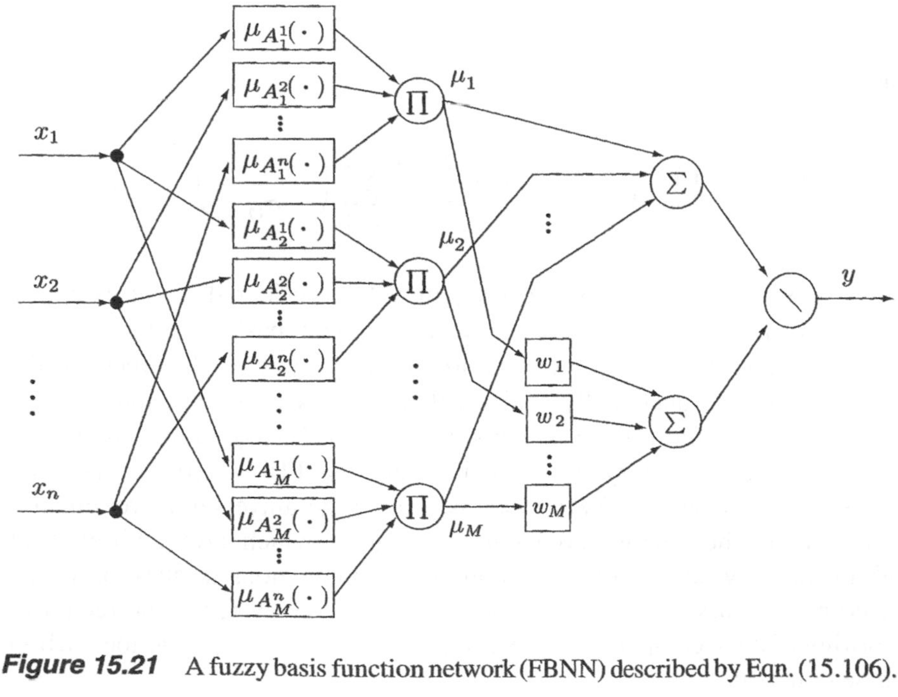

Figure 15.21 A fuzzy basis function network (FBNN) described by Eqn. (15.106).

It is known that the input–output equations of a fuzzy system with singleton fuzzifier, product inference, and centroid defuzzifier may be expressed as

$$y = \frac{\sum_{j=1}^{M} w_j \left(\prod_{i=1}^{n} \mu_{A_i^j}(x_i) \right)}{\sum_{j=1}^{M} \left(\prod_{i=1}^{n} \mu_{A_i^j}(x_i) \right)} = \sum_{j=1}^{M} w_j \phi_j(\boldsymbol{x}) \tag{15.106}$$

where

$$\phi_j(\boldsymbol{x}) = \frac{\prod_{i=1}^{n} \mu_{A_i^j}(x_i)}{\sum_{j=1}^{M} \left(\prod_{i=1}^{n} \mu_{A_i^j}(x_i) \right)} \tag{15.107}$$

are called the *fuzzy basis functions*. Equation (15.106) gives an expression for a fuzzy basis function as shown in Fig. 15.21.

In particular, if a Gaussian radial basis function is chosen as the membership function, then

$$\phi_j(\boldsymbol{x}) = \frac{u_i(\boldsymbol{x})}{\sum_{j=1}^{M} u_j(\boldsymbol{x})} \tag{15.108}$$

where

$$u_i(\boldsymbol{x}) = \left(\prod_{i=1}^{n} \mu_{A_i^j}(x_i) \right) = \exp\left(-\frac{1}{2} \sum_{i=1}^{n} \left(\frac{x_i - c_{ij}}{\sigma_{ij}} \right)^2 \right) \tag{15.109}$$

Fuzzy basis neural networks (FBNNs) may be considered as an extended version of the Gaussian network. However, a fuzzy basis function network (FBFN) represents directly a conventional fuzzy system. In other words, a fuzzy system is functionally equivalent to a fuzzy basis function network (FBFN) with the form given in Eqns. (15.106)–(15.109). From these two different aspects, the fuzzy basis function network (FBFN) rediscovers some interesting advantages of fuzzy systems; one is the universal approximation capability, and the other is learning and adaptation, which have not been dealt with in fuzzy systems. In fact, by applying the equations in question to the preceding network structures representing the fuzzy systems, the recursive algorithms for the computation of parameters of membership functions (MFs) can be obtained.

15.6.2.2 Universal Approximation Capability of Fuzzy Systems

In this case, let

$$\Omega_M = \left\{ f(\boldsymbol{x}) = \frac{\sum_{j=1}^{M} w_j u_j(\boldsymbol{X})}{\sum_{j=1}^{M} u_j(\boldsymbol{X})} : w_j \in \Re, \boldsymbol{x} \in S \right\} \tag{15.110}$$

$$\Omega = \bigcup_{M=1}^{\infty} \Omega_M \tag{15.111}$$

These results are summarized in the following theorem.

Theorem 15.2 *For an arbitrary continuous function* $g : S \subset \Re^n \rightarrow \Re$ *defined on the compact set* $S \subset \Re^n$ *and arbitrary* $\epsilon > 0$, *there exists a function* $f \in \Omega$ *such that max* $|g(\boldsymbol{x}) - f(\boldsymbol{x})| < \epsilon$ *for* $\boldsymbol{x} \in S$. ■

The proof of this theorem is based on the Stone–Weierstrass theorem. This result show that the fuzzy basis function network (FBFN) with the Gaussian membership function is a universal approximator. It might be noted that Eqns. (15.106)–(15.109) define only one type of FBFNs. Using the different definitions of a fuzzifier, fuzzy rule base, and defuzzifier, one may create other forms of FBFNs. In addition to carrying out such an input–output approximation process, learning algorithms such as the analog form of the backpropagation and orthogonal least square algorithms can be obtained (Funahashi 1989, Kosko 1992, Wang and Mendel 1992a).

15.7 CONCLUDING REMARKS

Fuzzy neural networks (FNNs) incorporate both neural networks and fuzzy mathematics. A neural network is a computational network that has some special characteristics such as learning, adaptation, and generalization. On the other hand, fuzzy mathematics has the capacity for processing the approximate reasoning and knowledge based information by using fuzzy logic operations. FNNs retain the advantages of both of these two structures and are capable of dealing with both numerically expressed and knowledge-based information. In practice, the learning and adaptation mechanisms of FNNs can enhance the approximate reasoning power of fuzzy systems.

Neural structures employing fuzzy logic operations, such as t-norm, t-conorm, and fuzzy implications, can be used for classification, approximation, and rule generation. Although the various definitions of t-norm and t-conorm could give different mathematical descriptions for a network mechanism, the final results of the mapping realized by the network are quite similar. This suggests that more attention to this type of FNN should be placed on hybrid fuzzy neural networks (HFNNs), which may have functional approximation capability. Also, fuzzy backpropagation (FBP) learning algorithms and genetic algorithms can be applied effectively to tune the parameters in such a fuzzy network using the data or online sensor measurements. On the other hand, fuzzy basis function networks (FBFNs) can be used to express fuzzy systems such that the learning and adaptation capabilities are easily enhanced for adapting both system parameters and membership functions. Both the gradient descent technique-based online learning schemes and clustering, and the generalized inverse approaches-based offline approaches can be employed in the learning of FBFNs to perform tasks such as modeling, control, and pattern recognition.

The purpose of this chapter is to help the reader learn not only the existing results in the field but also the state-of-the-art achievements. The topics studied in this chapter cover definition, structure, mathematical models, and learning and adaptation mechanisms of FNNs. The materials reported here form a basis for applications such as fuzzy modeling and control, pattern recognition, and fuzzy neural reasoning. Behind the foundations presented in this chapter, the advanced topics such as fuzzy genetic algorithms, dynamic fuzzy neural structures, and real-time implementations of FNNs have also been studied extensively since the mid-1990s. However, these topics are not discussed in this chapter. An extensive list of references at the end with this book will help the readers explore this field in more detail.

Problems

15.1 Assume $\boldsymbol{X} = \{a, b, c\}$ be a conventional set with generic elements $\{a, b, c\}$. Consider the following two fuzzy sets:

$$\begin{aligned} A &= \{0.3/a,\ 0.5/b,\ 1/c\} \\ B &= \{0.7/a,\ 0.2/b,\ 0/c\} \end{aligned}$$

Using the definition given in Table 15.1, obtain the *intersection* $A \cap B$, the *union* $A \cup B$, and the *complement* $\overline{A}$.

15.2 Consider a differnce-measure-based two-layered hibrid fuzzy neural network (HFNN) with two neurons in the hidden layer and one in the output layer. Using an **S** operation on the fuzzy variables x_1 and $x_2 \in [0,1]$ defined in Tables 15.2 and 15.3

$$\mathbf{S}(x_1, x_2) = x_1 + x_2 - x_1x_2$$

implement the two-variable binary *XOR* function $y = x_1 \oplus x_2$.

15.3 Let S be a fuzzy set on X that is either a discrete set with discrete elements or a continuous set with continuous elements. Show that there exists an operation in S, namely, addition and denoted by "(+)," for any x, y, and $z \in S$ such that

(a) $(\, x(+)y \,)(+)z = x(+)(\, y(+)z \,)$ (associative law)
(b) $x(+)y = y(+)x$ (commutability)
(c) $x(+)0 = x$ (zero element)

15.4 Following the previous problem, show that there exists a scalar multiplication operation $\otimes$ for any fuzzy scalars $a, b \in [0,1]$ and $a \otimes x \in S$ such that

(a) $a \otimes (\, b \otimes x \,) = (\, a \otimes b \,) \otimes x$ (associative law)
(b) $(\, a(+)b \,) \otimes x = a \otimes x \,(+)\, b \otimes x$ (distributive law)
(c) $a \otimes (\, x(+)y \,) = a \otimes x \,(+)\, a \otimes y$ (associative law)
(d) $x \otimes 0 = 0$ (zero element)

15.5 On the basis of the results obtained in Problems 15.3 and 15.4, compare similarities and differences between a fuzzy set and a conventional set.

15.6 List the basic building blocks of a fuzzy control system.

15.7 Human perception to daily temperature changes results in a typical fuzzy wording. Let the set X be defined as

$$X = \{VC, C, N, W, H, VH\}$$

where

$$\begin{cases} VC & \triangleq \text{ very cold} \\ C & \triangleq \text{ cold} \\ N & \triangleq \text{ normal} \\ W & \triangleq \text{ warm} \\ H & \triangleq \text{ hot} \\ VH & \triangleq \text{ very hot} \end{cases}$$

On the basis of your perception to the daily temperature changes, design a fuzzy membership function and use the fuzzy set theory to describe this fuzzy logic reasoning.

15.8 Let fuzzy sets A and B be defined by

$$\mu_A = \frac{1}{1+2x} \quad \text{and} \quad \mu_B = \sqrt{\frac{1}{1+2x}}$$

Calculate

(a) $\mu_{A \cup B}(x)$
(b) $\mu_{A \cap B}(x)$
(c) $\mu_{A \oplus B}(x)$
(d) $\mu_{\bar{A}}(x)$ and $\mu_{\bar{B}}(x)$

15.9 Let fuzzy sets A, B, and C be defined by

$$\begin{aligned}
\mu_A &= \begin{cases} (x-2)/3, & 2 \le x \le 5 \\ (8-x)/3, & 5 < x \le 8 \end{cases} \\
\mu_B &= \begin{cases} (x-3)/3, & 3 \le x \le 6 \\ (9-x)/3, & 6 < x \le 9 \end{cases} \\
\mu_C &= \begin{cases} (x-5)/3, & 5 \le x \le 8 \\ (11-x)/3, & 8 < x \le 11 \end{cases}
\end{aligned}$$

Calculate

(a) $\mu_{A \cup B \cup C}(x)$
(b) $\mu_{A \cap B \cap C}(x)$
(c) $\mu_{A \oplus B \oplus C}(x)$
(d) $\mu_{\bar{A}}(x)$, $\mu_{\bar{B}}(x)$, and $\mu_{\bar{C}}(x)$

15.10 Let $A_1, \ldots, A_n$ be fuzzy sets in the universes of discourse $X_1, \ldots, X_n = \Re$, characterized by Gaussian membership functions

$$\mu_{A_i}(x_i) = \exp\left(-\left[\frac{x_i - \bar{x}_i}{\sigma}\right]^2\right), \qquad i = 1, 2, \ldots, n$$

Show that the Cartesian product of the fuzzy sets $A_1, \ldots, A_n$ in the universe of discourse $X_1 \times \cdots \times X_n = \Re^n$, is a fuzzy set $A_1 \times \cdots \times A_n$ with the following membership function

$$\mu_{A_1 \times \cdots \times A_n}(x_1, \ldots, x_n) = \exp\left(-\frac{(\boldsymbol{x} - \bar{\boldsymbol{x}})^T(\boldsymbol{x} - \bar{\boldsymbol{x}})}{\sigma^2}\right)$$

where $\boldsymbol{x} = [x_1 \ \cdots \ x_n]^T \in X_1 \times \cdots \times X_n = \Re^n$
$\bar{\boldsymbol{x}} = [\bar{x}_1 \ \cdots \ \bar{x}_n]^T \in X_1 \times \cdots \times X_n = \Re^n$

15.11 Show that the various **T** and **S** operations given in Table 15.2 satisfy the following properties

(i)	$\mathbf{T}(x,y) = \mathbf{T}(y,x)$	(commutativity)
(ii)	$\mathbf{T}(\mathbf{T}(x,y),z) = \mathbf{T}(x,\mathbf{T}(y,z))$	(associativity)
(iii)	$\mathbf{T}(x_1,y_1) \geq \mathbf{T}(x_2,y_2)$ if $x_1 \geq x_2$ and $y_1 \geq y_2$	(monotonicity)
(iv)	$\mathbf{T}(x,1) = x$	(boundary condition)

and

(i')	$\mathbf{S}(x,y) = \mathbf{S}(y,x)$	(commutativity)
(ii')	$\mathbf{S}(\mathbf{S}(x,y),z) = \mathbf{S}(x,\mathbf{S}(y,z))$	(associativity)
(iii')	$\mathbf{S}(x_1,y_1) \geq \mathbf{S}(x_2,y_2)$ if $x_1 \geq x_2$ and $y_1 \geq y_2$	(monotonicity)
(iv')	$\mathbf{S}(x,0) = x$	(boundary condition)

15.12 If in Eqn. (15.19), the operation $\otimes$ is chosen as a min operation as shown in Eqn. (15.18), give the equation between the crisp input x and output y of the fuzzy system discussed in Section 15.1.

15.13 Prove the input and output equation of the fuzzy system given by Eqn. (15.95).

15.14 For the fuzzy system described by Eqn. (15.95), find a non-Gaussian membership function $\mu_{A_i^j}(x_i)$ such that the fuzzy system with singlet fuzzifier, product inference, and centroid defuzzifier is a universal approximator.

15.15 Consider a function that is a sine function in the interval $[0, \pi]$ and is zero elsewhere:

$$\phi(x) = \begin{cases} \sin(x), & \text{if } \ 0 \leq x \leq \pi \\ 0, & \text{otherwise} \end{cases}$$

A scaled sinusoidal membership function is defined as

$$\begin{aligned} \mu_{A_i^j}(x_i) &= d_{ji}\phi(a_{ji}x_i + b_{ji}) \\ &= \begin{cases} d_{ji}\sin(a_{ji}x_i + b_{ji}); & \text{if } -\dfrac{b_{ji}}{a_{ji}} \leq x_i \leq \left(\pi - \dfrac{b_{ji}}{a_{ji}}\right) \\ \\ 0, & \text{otherwise} \end{cases} \end{aligned}$$

where $0 \le d_{ji} \le 1$, a_{ji} and b_{ji} are the parameters associated with $\mu_{A_i^j}(x_i)$. Prove that

(a) The input–output equation of such a fuzzy system can be represented as

$$y = \frac{\sum_{j=1}^{m} v_j \phi\left(\sum_{i=1}^{n} q_{ji} x_i + \theta_{ji}\right)}{\sum_{j=1}^{m} d_j \phi\left(\sum_{i=1}^{n} q_{ji} x_i + \theta_{ji}\right)}$$

where the parameters m, v_j, q_{ji}, and θ_{ji} can be determined using the parameters d_{ji}, a_{ji}, and b_{ji};

(b) Prove that the above input–output equation is a universal approximator.

15.16 Consider a discrete-time nonlinear system of the form

$$y(k+1) = \frac{y^2(k) + y(k-1)y(k-2)}{1 + y^2(k) + y^2(k-1) + y^2(k-2)} + u(k)$$

(a) Design a fuzzy system to approximate such a nonlinear system;

(b) Give adaptation equations for updating such a fuzzy system;

(c) Give simulation results for such a nonlinear system identification problem.

15.17 Consider the fuzzy basis function network (FBFN) discussed in this chapter and the radial basis function network (RBFN) discussed in Chapter 6.

(a) State the similarities and differences both in structure and equation between the two networks;

(b) Can the FBFN as a universal approximator infer that the RBFN is also a universal approximator, and vice versa?

(c) Derive an orthogonal least squares learning algorithm of the FBFN.

15.18 For the fuzzy basis function network with a singleton fuzzifier and input–output equation

$$y = \sum_{j=1}^{m} w_j \left(\prod_{i=1}^{n} \mu_{A_i^j}(x_i) \right)$$

if the membership function $\mu_{A_i^j}(x_i)$ is chosen as a triangular function

$$\begin{aligned} \mu_{A_i^j}(x_i) &= \mu\left(x_i, a_i^j, b_i^j, c_i^j\right) \\ &= \max\left(\min\left(\frac{x_i - a_i^j}{b_i^j - a_i^j}, \frac{c_i^j - x_i}{c_i^j - b_i^j}\right), 0\right) \end{aligned}$$

where $a_i^j \neq b_i^j$ and $c_i^j \neq b_i^j$. Derive a training algorithm for updating the parameters of this FBFN.

15.19 Derive an input–output equation of a fuzzy basis function network of a non-singleton fuzzifier and discuss the universal approximation capability of this class of FBFNs.

*References and Bibliography**

[1] Al-Holou, N., Lahdhiri, T., Sung, J. D., Weaver, J., and Al-Abbas, F. (2002). "Sliding Mode Neural Network Inference Fuzzy Logic Control for Active Suspension Systems," *IEEE Trans. Fuzzy Syst.*, Vol. 10, No. 2, pp. 234–246.

[2] Abu-Mostafa, Y. and Jacques, J. St. (1985). "Information Capacity of the Hopfield Model," *IEEE Trans. Inf. Theory*, Vol. 7, pp. 1–11.

[3] Alahakoon, L. D., Halgamuge, S. K. and Srinivasan, B. (2000). "Dynamic Self Organizing Maps with Controlled Growth for Knowledge Discovery," *IEEE Trans. Neural Networks*, Vol. 11, No. 3, pp. 601–614.

[4] Amari, S. and Arbib, M. A. (eds.) (1982). "Competition and Cooperation in Neural Nets," *Lecture Notes in Biomathematics*, Springer-Verlag, New York, Vol. 45.

[5] Amit, D. J. (1989). *Modeling Brain Function: The World of Attractor Neural Networks*, Cambridge Univ. Press, Cambridge, UK.

[6] Anderberg, M. R. (1973). *Cluster Analysis for Applications*, Academic Press, New York.

[7] Anderson, D. (ed.) (1988). *Neural Information Processing Systems*, American Institute of Physics, New York.

*A classified extended bibliography is listed in Appendix B on the following ftp site: `ftp://ftp.wiley.com/public/sci_tech_med/neural_networks/`

[8] Aonishi, T. and Kurata, K. (2000). "Extension of Dynamic Link Matching by Introducing Local Linear Maps," *IEEE Trans. Neural Networks*, Vol. 11, No. 3, pp. 817–822.

[9] Arbib, M. A. (1987). *Brains, Machines and Mathematics*, 2nd ed., Springer-Verlag, New York.

[10] Asari, V. K. (2001). "Training of a Feedforward Multiple-Valued Neural Network by Error Backpropagation with a Multilevel Threshold Function," *IEEE Trans. Neural Networks*, Vol. 12, No. 6, pp. 1519–1520.

[11] Atiya, A. and Parlos, A. (2000). "New Results on Recurrent Network Training: Unifying the Algorithms and Accelerating Convergence," *IEEE Trans. Neural Networks*, Vol. 11, No. 3, pp. 697–709.

[12] Avitabile, G., Forti, M., Manetti, S., and Marini, M. (1992). "On a Class of Nonsymmetrical Neural Networks with Application to ADC," *IEEE Trans. Circuits Syst.*, Vol. 38, No. 2, (Feb.), pp. 202–209.

[13] Azimi-Sadjadi, M. R., Yao, D., Huang, Q., and Dobeck, G. J. (2000). "Underwater Target Classification Using Wavelet Packets and Neural Networks," *IEEE Trans. Neural Networks*, Vol. 11, No. 3, pp. 784–794.

[14] Bargiela, A. (2000). "Operational Decision Support through Confidence Limits Analysis and Pattern Classification," *Plenary Lecture, 5th Int. Conf. Computer Simulation and AI*, Mexico, Feb.

[15] Barmann, F. and Biegler-Konig, F. (1992). "On a Class of Efficient Learning Algorithms for Neural Networks," *Neural Networks*, Vol. 5, pp. 139–144.

[16] Battiti, R. (1992). "First and Second-Order Methods for Learning: Between Steepest Descent and Newton's Method," *Neural Comput.*, Vol. 4, pp. 141–166.

[17] Battiti, R. and Masulli F. (1990). "BFGS Optimization for Faster and Automated Supervised Learning," Proc. *INCC 90 Paris, Int. Neural Network Conf.*, pp. 757–760, Kluwer, Dordrecht, Germany.

[18] Bellman, R. E. and Zadeh, L. A. (1977). "Local and Fuzzy Logics," in *Modern Uses of Multiple-Valued Logic.*, Dunn, J. M. and Epstein, G. (eds.), Reidel, Dordrecht, Netherlands, pp. 103–165.

[19] Bengio, S. and Bengio, Y. (2000). "Taking on the Curse of Dimensionality in Joint Distribution Using Neural Networks," *IEEE Trans. Neural Networks*, Vol. 11, No. 3, pp. 550–557.

[20] Bianchini, M., Gori, M., and Scarselli, F. (2001a). "Theoretical Properties of Recursive Networks with Linear Neurons," *IEEE Trans. Neural Networks*, Vol. 12, No. 5, pp. 953–967.

[21] Bianchini, M., Gori, M., and Scarselli, F. (2001b). "Processing Directed Acyclic Graphs with Recursive Neural Networks," *IEEE Trans. Neural Networks*, Vol. 12, No. 6, pp. 1464–1470.

[22] Blum, E. K. and Li, L. K. (1991). "Approximation Theory and Feedforward Networks," *Neural Networks*, Vol. 4, No. 4, pp. 511–515.

[23] Brown, B. D. and Card, H. C. (2001). "Stochastic Neural Computation I and II," *IEEE Trans. Comput.*, Vol. 59 (Sept.).

[24] Bruck, J. (1990b). "On the Convergence Properties of the Hopfield Model," *Proc. IEEE*, Vol. 78, No. 10, pp. 1579–1585.

[25] Bryson, A. E. and Ho, Y.-C. (1969). *Applied Optimal Control*, Blaisdell.

[26] Buckley, J. J. and Hayashi, Y. (1993a). "Numerical Relationships between Neural Networks, Continuous Functions and Fuzzy Systems," *Fuzzy Sets Syst.*, Vol. 60, pp. 1–8.

[27] Buckley, J. J. and Hayashi, Y. (1993b). "Hybrid Neural Nets can be Fuzzy Controllers and Fuzzy Expert Systems," *Fuzzy Sets Syst.*, Vol. 60, pp. 135–142.

[28] Buckley, J. J. and Hayashi, Y. (1993c). "Can Fuzzy Neural Nets Approximate Continuous Fuzzy Functions," *Fuzzy Sets Syst.*, Vol. 61, pp. 43–52.

[29] Buckley, J. J. and Hayashi, Y. (1994a). "Fuzzy Genetic Algorithm and Applications" *Fuzzy Sets Syst.*, Vol. 61, pp. 129–136.

[30] Buckley, J. J. and Hayashi, Y. (1994b). "Fuzzy Neural Networks: A Survey," *Fuzzy Sets Syst.*, Vol. 66, No. 1, pp. 1–13.

[31] Buntine, W. and Weigend, A. S. (1994). "Computing Second Derivatives in Feed-forward Networks: A Review," *IEEE Trans. Neural Networks*, Vol. 5, No. 3, pp. 480–488.

[32] Burrascano, P. (1991). "A Norm Selection Criterion for the Generalized Delta Rule," *IEEE Trans. Neural Networks*, Vol. 2, No. 1, pp. 125–130.

[33] Cabrelli, C., Molter, U., and Shonkwiler, R. (2000). "A Constructive Algorithm to Solve 'Convex Recursive Deletion' (CoRD) Classification Problems via Two-Layer Perceptron Networks," *IEEE Trans. Neural Networks*, Vol. 11, No. 3, pp. 811–816.

[34] Card, H. C. (2001). "Compound Binomial Processes in Neural Integration," *IEEE Trans. Neural Networks*, Vol. 12, No. 6, pp. 1505–1512.

[35] Carroll, B. W. and Dickinson, B. D. (1989). "Construction of Neural Net Using The Radon Transform," *Proc. Int. Joint Conf. Neural Networks*, Vol. I, pp. 607–611.

[36] Castro, J. L., Delgado, M., and Mantas, C. J. (2000). "SEPARATE: A Machine Learning Method Based on Semi-Global Partitions," *IEEE Trans. Neural Networks*, Vol. 11, No. 3, pp. 710–720.

[37] Chauvin, Y. (1989). "A Back-propagation Algorithm with Optimal Use of Hidden Units," in *Advances in Neural Information Processing Systems*, Touretzky, D. S. (ed.), Vol. 1, Morgan Kaufmann, San Jose, CA.

[38] Chen, K. and Wang, D. L. (2001). "Perceiving Geometric Patterns: From Spirals to Inside-Outside Relations by a Neural Oscillator Network," *IEEE Trans. Neural Networks*, Vol. 12. pp. 1084–1102.

[39] Chen, S., Cowan, C. F. N., and Grant, P. M. (1991). "Orthogonal Least Squares Learning Algorithm for Radial Basis Function Networks," *IEEE Trans. Neural Networks*, Vol. 2 (Feb.), pp. 302–309.

[40] Chen, S., Gunn, S. R., and Harris, C. J. (2000). "Decision Feedback Equalizer Design Using Support Vector Machines," *Proc. Inst. Elect. Eng. Vision, Image, Signal Processing*, Vol. 147, No. 3, pp. 213–219.

[41] Chen, S., Gunn, S. R., and Harris, C. J. (2001a). "The Relevance Vector Machine Technique for Channel Equalization Application," *IEEE Trans. Neural Networks*, Vol. 12, No. 6, pp. 1529–1531.

[42] Chen, S., Samingan, A. K., and Hanzo, L. (2001b). "Support Vector Machine Multiuser Receiver for DS-CDMA Signals in Multipath Channels," *IEEE Trans. Neural Networks*, Vol. 12, pp. 604–611.

[43] Chen, T. (2001). "Global Convergence of Delayed Dynamical Systems," *IEEE Trans. Neural Networks*, Vol. 12, No. 6, pp. 1532–1535.

[44] Chen, T. P. and Amari, S. (2001a). "Exponential Convergence of Delayed Dynamical Systems?" *Neural Comput.*, Vol. 13, No. 3, pp. 621–636.

[45] Chen, T. P. and Amari, S. (2001b). "New Theorems on Global Convergence of Some Dynamical Systems," *Neural Networks*, Vol. 14, No. 3. pp. 251–255.

[46] Chen, T. P. and Amari, S. (2001c). "Stability of Asymmetric Hopfield Networks," *IEEE Trans. Neural Networks*, Vol. 12, pp. 159–163.

[47] Churchland, P. S. (1988). *Neurophilosophy*, MIT Press, Cambridge, MA.

[48] Churchland, P. S. and Sejnowski, T. J. (1988). "Perspectives on Cognitive Neuroscience," Science, Vol. 242, pp. 741–745.

[49] Churchland, P. S. and Sejnowski, T. J. (1992). *The Computational Brain*, MIT Press, Cambridge, MA.

[50] Cohen, M. A. and Grossberg, S. (1983). "Absolute Stability of Global Pattern Information and Parallel Memory Storage by Competitive Neural Networks," *IEEE Trans. Syst. Man Cybernet.*, Vol. 13, pp. 815–826.

[51] Cotter, N. (1990). "The Stone-Weierstrass Theorem and Its Application to Neural Networks," *IEEE Trans. Neural Networks*, Vol. 1, No. 4, pp. 290–295.

[52] Cristianini, N. and Shawe-Taylor, J. (2000). *An Introduction to Support Vector Machines and Other Kernel-Based Learning Methods*, Cambridge Univ. Press, Cambridge, UK.

[53] Cybenko, G. (1989). "Approximation by Superpositions of a Sigmoidal Function," *Math. Control Signal System*, Vol. 2, No. 3, pp. 303–314.

[54] Darken, C., Chang, J., and Moody, J. E. (1992). "Learning Rate Schedules for Faster Stochastic Gradient Search," *Proc. Neural Networks for Signal Processing* 2.

[55] Darken, C. and Moody, J. E. (1991). "Note on Learning Rate Schedules for Stochastic Optimization," in *Advances in Neural Information Processing Systems*, Lippmann, R. P., Moody, J.E., and Touretzky, D. S. (eds.), Vol. 3, Morgan Kaufmann, San Mateo, CA, pp. 832–838.

[56] Darken, C. and Moody, J. E. (1992). "Towards Faster Stochastic Gradient Search," in *Adcances in Neural Information Processing Systems*, Morgan Kaufmann, San Mateo, CA, Vol. 4, pp. 1009–1016.

[57] Dasgupta, S., Ghosh, A., and Cuykendall, R. (1989). "Convergence in Neural Memories (Corresp.)," *IEEE Trans. Inform. Theory*, Vol. 35, pp. 1069–1072.

[58] Datta, A., Pal, S., and Pal, N. R. (2000). "A Connectionist Model for Convex-Hull of a Planar Set," *Neural Networks*, Vol. 13, pp. 377–384.

[59] Deco, G. and Schürmann, B. (1997). "Dynamic Modelling Chaotic Time Series," *Computational Learning Theory and Neural Learning Systems*, Vol. 4 of series, Making Learning Systems Practical, MIT Press, Cambridge, MA, Chapter 9, pp. 137–153.

[60] Denker, J. S. (1986). "Neural Network Models of Learning and Adaptation," *Physica D*, Vol. 22, pp. 216–232.

[61] Ding, H. and Gupta, M. M. (2000). "Competitive and Cooperative Adaptive Reasoning with Fuzzy Causal Knowledge," *J. Intell. Fuzzy Syst.*, Vol. 3, No. 6, pp. 245–254.

[62] Douglas, S. C. and Meng, T. H. Y. (1991). "Linearized Least-Squares Training of Multilayer Feedforward Neural Networks," *Proc. IEEE IJCNN*, Vol. I, pp. 307–312, Seattle, WA, June.

[63] Dubois, D. and Prade, H. (1980). *Fuzzy Sets Syst.: Theory and Applications.*, Academic Press, Orlando, FL.

[64] Eichfeld, H., Kunemund, T., and Menke, M. (1996). "A 12b General-Purpose Fuzzy Logic Controller Chip," *IEEE Trans. Fuzzy Syst.*, Vol. 4, No. 4, pp. 460–475.

[65] Engelbrecht, A. P. (2001). "A New Pruning Heuristic Based on Variance Analysis of Sensitivity Information," *IEEE Trans. Neural Networks*, Vol. 12, No. 6, pp. 1386–1399.

[66] Fernandez de Canete, J., Barreiro, A., Garcia-Cerezo, A., and Garcia-Moral, I. (2001). "An Input-Output Based Robust Stabilization Criterion for Neural-Network Control of Nonlinear Systems," *IEEE Trans. Neural Networks*, Vol. 12, No. 6, pp. 1491–1497.

[67] Floréen, P. (1991). "Worst-Case Convergence Times for Hopfield Memories," *IEEE Trans. Neural Networks*, Vol. 2, No. 5, pp. 533–535.

[68] Fogelman-Soulie, F., Gallinari, P., LeCun, Y., and Thiria, S. (1987). "Automata Networks and Artificial Intelligence," in *Automata Networks in Computer Science: Theory and Applications*, Princeton Univ. Press, pp. 133–186.

[69] Franco, L. and Cannas, S. A. (2001). "Generalization Properties of Modular Networks: Implementing the Parity Function," *IEEE Trans. Neural Networks*, Vol. 12, No. 6, pp. 1306–1313.

[70] Fu, H. C., Lee, Y. P., Chiang, C. C., and Pao, H. T. (2001). "Divide-and-Conquer Learning and Modular Perceptron Networks," *IEEE Trans. Neural Networks*, Vol. 12, pp. 250–263.

[71] Fu, L. M. and Shortliffe, E. H. (2000). "The Application of Certainty Factors to Neural Computing for Rule Discovery," *IEEE Trans. Neural Networks*, Vol. 11, No. 3, pp. 647–657.

[72] Fujimori, A., Nikiforuk, P. N., and Gupta, M. M. (2001a). "A Flight Control Design of a Re-Entry Vehicle Using a Double-Loop Control System with Fuzzy Gain Scheduling," *Proc. Inst. Mech. Engineers*, Vol. 215, Part G, pp. 1–12.

[73] Fujimori, A., Teramoto, M., Nikiforuk, P. N., and Gupta, M. M. (2001b). "Cooperative Collision Avoidance between Multiple Mobile Robots," *J. Robotic Syst.*, Vol. 17, No. 7, pp. 347–363.

[74] Funahashi, K. (1989). "On the Approximate Realization of Continuous Mappings by Neural Networks," Vol. 2, No. 3, pp. 183–192.

[75] Gabrys, B. and Bargiela, A. (2000). "General Fuzzy Min-Max Neural Network for Clustering and Classification," *IEEE Trans. Neural Networks*, Vol. 11, No. 3, pp. 769–783.

[76] Gallant, A. R. and White, H. (1988). "There Exists a Neural Network that Do Not Make Avoidable Mistakes," *Proc. IEEE Conf Neural Networks*, San Diego, Vol. 1, pp. 657–664.

[77] Gers, F. A. and Schmidhuber, J. (2000). "Recurrent Nets that Time and Count," *Proc. Int. Joint Conf. Neural Networks*, Como, Italy.

[78] Gers, F. A. and Schmidhuber, J. (2001). "LSTM Recurrent Networks Learn Simple Context-Free and Context-Sensitive Languages," *IEEE Trans. Neural Networks*, Vol. 12, No. 6, pp. 1333–1380.

[79] Gers, F. A., Schmidhuber, J., and Cummins, F. (2000). "Learning to Forget: Continual Prediction with LSTM," *Neural Comput.*, Vol. 12, No. 10, pp. 2451–2471.

[80] Gerschgorin, S. (1931). "Uber die Abgrenzung der Eigenwerte Einer Matrix," *Izv. Akad. Nauk SSSR*, Ser. fiz.-mat., Vol. 6, pp. 749–754.

[81] Giles, C. L. and Maxwell, T. (1987). "Learning Invariance, and Generalization in Higher-Order Networks," *Appl. Optics*, Vol. 26, pp. 4972–4978.

[82] Girolami, M. (2001). "The Topographic Organization and Visualization of Binary Data Using Multivariate-Bernoulli Latent Variable Models," *IEEE Trans. Neural Networks*, Vol. 12, No. 6, pp. 1367–1374.

[83] Goles, E. (1986). "Antisymmetric Neural Networks," *Discrete Appl. Math.*, Vol. 13, pp. 97–100.

[84] Goles, E., Fogelman, F., and Pellegrin, D. (1985). "Decreasing Energy Functions as a Tool for Studying Threshold Networks," *Discrete Appl. Math.*, Vol. 12, pp. 261–277.

[85] Gori, M., Maggini, M., Martinelli, E., and Scarselli, F. (2000). "Learning User Profiles in NAUTILUS," *Proc. Int. Conf. Adaptive Hypermedia Adaptive Web-Based Systems-Lecture Notes Compututational Science, 1892*, Trento, Italy.

[86] Grossberg, S. (1990). "Content-addressable Memory Storage by Neural Networks: A General Model and Global Lyapunov Method," in *Computational Neuroscience*, Schwartz, E. L. (ed.), MIT Press, Cambridge, MA, pp. 56–68.

[87] Guez, A., Protopopsecu, V., and Bahren, J. (1988). "On the Stability, Storage Capacity, and Design of Continuous Nonlinear Neural Networks," *IEEE Trans. Syst. Man Cybernet.*, Vol. 18, No. 1, pp. 80–87.

[88] Gupta, M. M. (1994). "Fuzzy Logic and Neural Networks," in *Neuro Control*, Gupta, M. M. and Rao, D. H. (eds.), IEEE Press, New York, pp. 403–416.

[89] Gupta, M. M. (2001). "Fuzzy Sets, Fuzzy Logic and Fuzzy Systems," in *Encyclopedia of Physical Science and Technology*, Meyer, R. A. (ed.), Academic Press, San Diego.

[90] Gupta, M. M. and Knopf, G. K. (1992). "A Multitask Visual Information Processor with a Biologically Motivated Design," *J. Visual Commun. Image Represent.*, Vol. 3. No. 3 (Sept.), pp. 230–246.

[91] Gupta, M. M. and Knopf, G. K. (eds.) (1994). *Neuro-Vision Systems: Principles and Applications*, a volume of selected reprints, IEEE Neural Networks Council, IEEE Press, New York.

[92] Gupta, M. M. and Qi, J. (1991). "On Fuzzy Neuron Models," *Proc. 1991 IJCNN*, Vol. 1, July, pp. 431–456.

[93] Gupta, M. M. and Qi, J. (1992a). "On Fuzzy Neuron Models," in *Fuzzy Logic for the Management of Uncertainty*, Zadeh, L. and Kacprzyk, J. (eds.), Wiley, New York, pp. 479–491.

[94] Gupta, M. M. and Qi, J. (1992b). "Theory of T Nouns and Fuzzy Inference Method," *Fuzzy Sets Syst.*, Vol. 40, pp. 431–450.

[95] Gupta, M. M., Ragade, R. K., and Yager, R. R. (eds.) (1979). *Advances in Fuzzy Set Theory and Applications*, North-Holland Publishing, Oct.

[96] Gupta, M. M. and Rao, D. H. (eds.) (1994a). *Neuro-Control Systems: Theory and Applications*, a volume of selected reprints, IEEE Neural Networks Council, IEEE Press, New York.

[97] Gupta, M. M. and Rao, D. H. (1994b). "On the Principles of Fuzzy Neural Networks," *Fuzzy Sets Syst.*, Vol. 61, No. 1, pp. 1–18.

[98] Gupta, M. M. and Sinha, N. K. (eds.) (1995). *Intelligent Control Systems: Theory and Applications*, a volume of 29 invited chapters, Sponsor: IEEE Neural Networks Council and Co-sponsor: IEEE Control Systems Society, IEEE Press, New York (Revised 2nd ed., 1997).

[99] Gupta, M. M. and Yamakawa, T. (eds.) (1988a). *Fuzzy Computing: Theory Hardware and Applications*, North Holland.

[100] Gupta, M. M. and Yamakawa, T. (eds.) (1988b). *Fuzzy Logic in Knowledge-Based Systems, Decision and Control*, North Holland, Amsterdam, New York.

[101] Harston, C. T. (1990). "The Neurological Basis for Neural Computation," in *Handbook of Neural Computing Applications*, Maren, A. J., Harston, C. T., and Pap, R. M. (eds.), Academic Press, New York, pp. 29–44.

[102] Hassibi, B. and Stork, D. G. (1993). "Second-Order Derivatives for Network Pruning: Optimal Brain Surgeon," in *Advances in Neural Information Processing Systems*, Hanson, S. J., Cowan, J. D., and Giles, C. L. (eds.), Vol. 5, Morgan Kaufmann, San Jose, CA, pp. 164–172.

[103] Haykin, S. (1991). *Adaptive Filter Theory*, Prentice-Hall, Englewood Cliffs, NJ.

[104] Haykin, S. and Principe, J. (1998). "Making Sence of Complex World: Using Neural Networks to Dynamically Model Chaotic Events Such as Sea Clutter," *IEEE Signal Processing Magazine*, Vol. 15, No. 3, pp.66–81.

[105] Hebb, D. O. (1949). *The Organization of Behavior*, Wiley, New York.

[106] Hecht-Nielsen, R. (1987). "Kolmogorov's Mapping Neural Network Existence Theorem," *Proc. 1987 ICNN*, Vol. III, pp. 11–14.

[107] Hecht-Nielsen, R. (1989). "Theory of the Back-Propagation Neural Network," *Proc. Int. Joint Conf. Neural Networks*, Vol. I, pp. 593–605.

[108] Hecht-Nielsen, R. (1990). *Neurocomputing*, Addison-Wesley, Reading, MA.

[109] Heskes, T. (2001). "Self-Organizing Maps, Vector Quantization, and Mixture Modeling," *IEEE Trans. Neural Networks*, Vol. 12, No. 6, pp. 1299–1305.

[110] Hiramoto, M., Hiromi, Y., Giniger, E., and Hotta, Y. (2000). "The Drosophila Netrin Receptor Frazzled Guides Axons by Controlling Netrin Distribution," *Nature*, Vol. 406, No. 6798, pp. 886–888.

[111] Hirose, Y., Yamashita, K., and Hijiya, S. (1991). "Back-Propagation Algorithm which Varies the Number of Hidden Units," *Neural Networks*, Vol. 4, pp. 61–66.

[112] Hirsch, M. W. (1989). "Convergent Activation Dynamics in Continuous Time Networks," *Neural Networks*, Vol. 1 (May), pp. 331–349.

[113] Hirsch, M. W. and Smale, S. (1974). *Differential Equations, Dynamical Systems, and Linear Algebra*, Academic Press, New York.

[114] Homma, N. and Gupta, M. M. (2002a). "Superimposing Neural Learning by Dynamic and Spatial Changing Weights," *Proc. 7th Int. Symp. Artificial Life and Robotics*, Vol. 1, pp. 165–168.

[115] Homma, N. and Gupta, M. M. (2002b). "A General Second-order Neural Unit," *Bull. Coll. Med. Sci. Tohoku Univ.*, Vol. 11, No. 1, pp. 1–6.

[116] Homma, N., Sakai, M., Gupta, M. M., and Abe, K. (2001). "Stochastic Analysis of Chaos Dynamics in Recurrent Neural Networks," *Proc. Joint 9th IFSA World Congress and 20th NAFIPS Int. Conf.*, Vancouver, BC, Canada, July, pp. 1372–1376.

[117] Honma, N., Kamauchi, T., Abe, K., and Takeda, H. (1999a). "Auto-Learning by Dynamical Recognition Networks," *Proc. IEEE Int. Conf. Systems, Man, and Cybernetics*, Vol. III, pp. 211–216.

[118] Honma, N., Sakai, M., Abe, K., and Takeda, H. (1999b). "Control Method of the Lyapunov Exponents for Recurrent Neural Networks," *Proc. 14th IFAC World Congress*, Beijing, Vol. K, pp. 51–56.

[119] Hopfield, J. (1982). "Neural Networks and Physical Systems with Emergent Collective Computational Abilities," *Proc. Nat. Acad. Sci. USA*, Vol. 79, pp. 2554–2558.

[120] Hopfield, J. (1984). "Neurons with Graded Response Have Collective Computational Properties Like Those of Two-State Neurons," *Proc. Nat. Acad. Sci. USA*, Vol. 81, pp. 3088–3092.

[121] Hopfield, J. and Tank, D. W. (1986). "Computing with Neural Circuits: A Model," *Science*, Vol. 233, pp. 625–633.

[122] Hoppensteadt, F. C. and Izhikevich, (2000). "Pattern Recognition via Synchronization in Phase-Locked Loop Neural Networks," *IEEE Trans. Neural Networks*, Vol. 11, No. 3, pp. 734–738.

[123] Horn, R. A. and Johnson, C. R. (1985). *Matrix Analysis*, Cambridge Univ. Press.

[124] Hornik, K. (1991). "Some New Results on Neural Network Approximation," *Neural Networks*, Vol. 6, No. 8, pp. 1069–1072.

[125] Hornik, K., Stinchcombe, M., and White, H. (1989). "Multilayer Feedforward Networks Are Universal Approximators," *Neural Networks*, Vol. 2, No. 5, pp. 359–366.

[126] Hornik, K., Stinchcombe, M., and White, H. (1990). "Universal Approximation of an Unknown Mapping and Its Derivatives Using Multilayer Feedforward Networks," *Neural Networks*, Vol. 3, No. 6, pp. 551–560.

[127] Hoya, T. and Chambers, J. A. (2001). "Heuristic Pattern Correction Scheme Using Adaptively Trained Generalized Regression Neural Networks," *IEEE Trans. Neural Networks*, Vol. 12, pp. 91–100.

[128] Huang, G. B., Chen, Y. Q., and Babri, H. A. (2000). "Classification Ability of Single Hidden Layer Feedforward Neural Networks," *IEEE Trans. Neural Networks*, Vol. 11, No. 3, pp. 799–801.

[129] Hush, D. R. and Horne, B. G. (1993). "Progress in Supervised Neural Networks," *IEEE Signal Process. Mag.*, Vol. 10, No. 1 (Jan.), pp. 8–39.

[130] Hyvarinen, A. (2001). "Blind Source Separation by Nonstationarity of Variance: A Cumulant-Based Approach," *IEEE Trans. Neural Networks*, Vol. 12, No. 6, pp. 1471–1474.

[131] Hyvarinen, A., Karhunen, J., and Oja, E. (2001). *Independent Component Analysis*, Wiley, New York.

[132] Hyvarinen, A. and Oja, E. (1997). "A Fast Fixed-Point Algorithm for Independent Component Analysis," *Neural Comput.*, Vol. 9, No. 7, pp. 1483–1492.

[133] Indiveri, G. (2000). "Modeling Selective Attention Using a Neuromorphic Analog VLSI Device," *Neural Comput.*, Vol. 12, No. 12, pp. 2857–2880.

[134] Indiveri, G. (2001a). "A Current-Mode Analog Hysteretic Winner-Take-All Network, with Excitatory and Inhibitory Coupling," *J. Analog Integrated Circuits Signal Process.*, Vol. 28, pp. 279–291.

[135] Indiveri, G. (2001b). "A Neuromorphic VLSI Device for Implementing 2-D Selective Attention Systems," *IEEE Trans. Neural Networks*, Vol. 12, No. 6, pp. 1455–1463.

[136] Indiveri, G., Murer, R., and Kramer, J. (2001). "Active Vision Using an Analog VLSI Model of Selective Attention," *IEEE Trans. Circuits Syst. II*, Vol. 48, pp. 492–500.

[137] Isermann, R. (1989). "A Review on Detection and Diagnosis Illustrates that Process Faults Can Be Detected When Based on the Estimation of Unmeasurable Process Parameters and State Variables," *Automatica: IFAC J.*, Vol. 20, No. 4, pp. 387–404.

[138] Itti, L. and Koch, C. (2001). "Computational Modeling of Visual Attention," *Nature Neurosci. Rev.*, Vol. 2, pp. 194–204.

[139] Iyer, M. S. and Wunsch, I. I. (2001). "Dynamic Reoptimization of a Fed-Batch Fermentor Using Adaptive Critic Designs," *IEEE Trans. Neural Networks*, Vol. 12, No. 6, pp. 1433–1444.

[140] Jacobs, R. A. (1988). "Increased Rates of Convergence through Learning Rate Adaptation," *Neural Networks*, Vol. 1, No. 4, pp. 295–308.

[141] Jang, J. S. R. (1992). "Self-Learning Fuzzy Controllers Based on Temporal Back-Propagation," *IEEE Trans. Neural Networks*, Vol. 3 (Sept.), pp. 714–723.

[142] Jang, J. S. R. and Sun, C. T. (1990). "Neuro-Fuzzy Modeling and Control," *Proc. IEEE*, Vol. 83, No. 3 (March), pp. 378–406.

[143] Jang, J. S. R. and Sun, C. T. (1993). "Functional Equivalence between Radial Basis Function Networks and Fuzzy Inference Systems," *IEEE Trans. Neural Networks*, Vol. 4, No. 1 (Jan.), pp. 156–159.

[144] Jin, L. and Gupta, M. M. (1996a). "Equilibrium Capability of Analog Feedback Neural Networks," *IEEE Trans. Neural Networks*, Vol. 7, pp. 782–787.

[145] Jin, L. and Gupta, M. M. (1996b). "Globally Asymptotical Stability of Discrete-Time Analog Neural Networks," *IEEE Trans. Neural Networks*, Vol. 7, No. 4, pp. 1024–1031.

[146] Jin, L. and Gupta, M. M. (1999). "Stable Dynamic Backpropagation Learning in Recurrent Neural Networks," *IEEE Trans. Neural Networks*, Vol. 10, pp. 1321–1334.

[147] Jin, L., Gupta, M. M., and Nikiforuk, P. N. (1993a). "Computational Neural Architectures for Control Applications," in *Soft Computing: Fuzzy Logic, Neural Networks, and Distributed Artificial Intelligence*, Prentice-Hall, Englewood Cliffs, NJ, Chapter 6, pp. 121–152.

[148] Jin, L., Nikiforuk, P. N., and Gupta, M. M. (1993b). "Stable Fixed Point Learning Using Parallel Synaptic and Somatic Adaptation," *Proc. 1993 World Congress on Neural Networks*, Vol. II, pp. 945–950.

[149] Jin, L., Gupta, M. M., and Nikiforuk, P. N. (1994a). "Approximation Capabilities of Feedforward and Recurrent Neural Networks," in *Intelligent Control Systems*, Gupta M. M. and Sinha, N. K. (eds.), IEEE Press, Chapter 10, pp. 234–264.

[150] Jin, L., Nikiforuk, P. N., and Gupta, M. M. (1994b). "Absolute Stability Conditions for Discrete-time Recerrent Neural Networks," *IEEE Trans. Neural Networks*, Vol. 5, pp. 954–964.

[151] Jin, L., Gupta, M. M., and Nikiforuk, P. N. (1995). "Neural Networks and Fuzzy Basis Functions for Functional Approximation," in *Fuzzy Logic and Intelligent Control*, Li, H. and Gupta, M. M. (eds.), Kluwer Academic Publishers, Chapter 2, pp. 17–68.

[152] Jin, L., Nikiforuk, P. N., and Gupta, M. M. (1995). "Approximation of Discrete-time State-space Trajectories Using Dynamic Recurrent Neural Networks," *IEEE Trans. Automatic Control*, Vol. 40, pp. 1266–1270.

[153] Johansson, E. M., Dowla, F. U., and Goodman D. M. (1990). *Backpropagation Learning for Multi-Layer Feed-Forward Neural Networks Using the Conjugate Gradient Method*, Lawrence Livermore National Laboratory, Berkeley, CA, Preprint UCRL-JC-104850.

[154] Kahane, J. P. (1975). "Sur le Theoreme de Superposition de Kolmogorov," *J. Approx. Theory*, Vol. 13, pp. 229–234.

[155] Kalman, R. E. and Bertram, J. E. (1960). "Control System Analysis and Design via the Second Method of Lyapunov: II Discrete-time systems," *Trans. ASME J. Basic Eng.*, Vol. 82, pp. 394–400.

[156] Kandel, E. R. and Schwartz, J. H. (1985). *Principles of Neural Science*, New York, North-Holland.

[157] Karnin, E. D. (1990). "A Simple Procedure for Pruning Back-propagation Trained Neural Networks," *IEEE Trans. Neural Networks*, Vol. 1, No. 2, pp. 239–242.

[158] Kaszkurewicz, E. and Bhaya, A. (1993). "Robust Stability and Diagonal Liapunov Functions," *SIAM J. Matrix Analy. Appl.*, Vol. 14, No. 2, pp. 508–520.

[159] Kaufmann, A. and Gupta, M. M. (1985). *Introduction to Fuzzy Arithmetic, Theory and Applications*, 2nd ed., Van Nostrand Reinhold, New York (Japanese transl. by Atsuka, M., Ohmsha Ltd., Tokyo, 1991).

[160] Kaufmann, A. and Gupta, M. M. (1988). *Fuzzy Mathematical Models in Engineering and Management Science*, North Holland, Amsterdam (revised 1992; Japanese transl. by Matsuoka, H. and Tanaka, H., Ohmsha Ltd., Tokyo).

[161] Kelly, D. G. (1990). "Stability in Contractive Nonlinear Neural Networks," *IEEE Trans. Biomed. Eng.*, Vol. 37, pp. 231–242.

[162] Kelly, K. A., Caruso, M. J., and Austin, J. A. (1993). "Wind-forced Variations in Sea Surface Height in The Northeast Pacific Ocean," *J. Phys. Oceanogr.*, Vol. 23, pp. 2392–2411.

[163] Kewley, R., Embrechts, M., and Breneman, C. (2000). "Data Strip Mining for the Virtual Design of Pharmaceuticals with Neural Networks," *IEEE Trans. Neural Networks*, Vol. 11, No. 3, pp. 668–679.

[164] Khalil, H. (1992). *Nonlinear Systems*, Macmillan, New York.

[165] Kim, T., Kim, Y., Park, J., Ko, K., Choi, S., Kang, C., and Hong, D. (2000). "Performance of an MC-CDMA System with Frequency Offsets in Correlated Fading," *Proc. IEEE ICC 2000*, Vol. 2, pp. 1095–1099.

[166] Kiszka, J., Gupta, M. M., and Nikiforuk, P. N. (1985). "Energetistic Stability of Fuzzy Dynamic Systems," *IEEE Trans. Syst. Man Cybernet.*, Vol. 15, No. 5, pp. 783–792.

[167] Ko, K., Choi, S., and Hong, D. (2000a). "Multiuser Detector with an Ability of Channel Estimation Using an RBF Network in an MC-CDMA System," *Proc. IJCNN 2000*, Vol. 5, pp. 348–353.

[168] Ko, K., Choi, S., Kang, C., and Hong, D. (2000b). "RBF Multiuser Detector with Channel Estimation Capability in a Synchronous MC-CDMA System," *IEEE Trans. Neural Networks*, Vol. 12, No. 6, pp. 1536–1538.

[169] Kohara, K., Kitamura, A., Morishima, M., and Tsumoto, T. (2001). "Activity-Dependent Transfer of Brain-Derived Neurotrophic Factor to Postsynaptic Neurons," *Science*, Vol. 291 (March), pp. 2419–2423.

[170] Kohonen, T. (1988). "An Introduction to Neural Computing," *Neural Networks*, Vol. 1, No. 1, pp. 3–16.

[171] Kohonen, T., Kaski, S., Lagus, K., Salogarvi, J., Honkela, J, Paatero, V., and Sarrela, A. (2000). "Self-Organization of a Massive Document Collection," *IEEE Trans. Neural Networks*, Vol. 11, No. 3 (May), pp. 574–585.

[172] Kolmogorov, A. N. (1957). "On the Representation of Continuous Functions of Several Variables by Superposition of Continuous Functions of One Variable and Addition," *Dokl. Akad. Nauk USSR*, Vol. 114, pp. 953–956.

[173] Konig, A. (2000). "Interactive Visualization and Analysis of Hierarchical Neural Projections for Data Mining," *IEEE Trans. Neural Networks*, Vol. 11, No. 3 (May), pp. 615–624.

[174] Kosko, B. (1992). "Neural Networks and Fuzzy Systems," Prentice-Hall, Englewood Cliffs, NJ.

[175] Kosko, B. (1994). "Fuzzy Systems as Universal Approximators," *IEEE Trans. Comput.*, Vol. 43, No. 11, pp. 1329–1333.

[176] Krasovskii, N. N. (1963). *Stability of Motion*, Stanford Univ. Press.

[177] Kurkova, V. (1992). "Kolmogorov's Theorem and Multilayer Neural Networks," *Neural Networks*, Vol. 5, No. 3, pp. 501–506.

[178] Langari, R. and Berenji, H. R. (1992). "Fuzzy Logic in Control Engineering," in *Handbook of Intelligent Control.*, Van Nostrand, New York, pp. 93–140.

[179] Lapedes, A. and Farber, R. (1987). "How Neural Nets Work," in *Neural Information Processing Systems*, Anderson, D. Z. (ed.), American Institute of Physics, New York, pp. 442–456.

[180] LeCun, Y. (1987). *Modeles Connexionnistes de l'apprentissage* (*Connectionist Learning Models*), Ph.D. thesis, Universite' P. et M. Curie (Paris 6).

[181] LeCun, Y. (1988). "A Theoretical Framework for Back-Propagation," in *Proc. 1988, Connectionist Model Summer School*, Touretzky, D., Hinton C., and Sejnowski T. (eds.), June 17-26, Morgan Kaufmann, pp. 21–28.

[182] LeCun, Y., Boser, B., and Denker, J. S. (1989). "Backpropagation Applied to Handwritten Zip Code Recognition," *Neural Computation*, Vol. 1, pp. 541–551.

[183] LeCun, Y., Boser, B., and Solla, S. A. (1990). "Optimal Brain Damage," in *Advances in Neural Information Processing Systems*, Touretzky, D. S. (ed.), Vol. 2, Morgan Kaufmann, pp. 598–605.

[184] Lee, C. C. (1990a). "Fuzzy Logic in Control Systems: Fuzzy Logic Controller, Part I," *IEEE Trans. Syst. Man Cybernet.*, Vol. 20, No. 2, pp. 404–418.

[185] Lee, C. C. (1990b). "Fuzzy Logic in Control Systems: Fuzzy Logic Controller, Part II," *IEEE Trans. Syst. Man Cybernet.*, Vol. 20, No. 2, pp. 419–435.

[186] Lee, R. S. T. and Liu, J. N. K. (2000). "Tropical Cyclone Identification and Tracking System Using Integrated Neural Oscillatory Elastic Graph Matching and Hybrid RBF Network Track Mining Techniques," *IEEE Trans. Neural Networks*, Vol. 11, No. 3 (May), pp. 680–689.

[187] Lee, S. and Kil, R. M. (1991). "A Gaussian Potential Function Network with Hierarchically Self-organizing Learning," *Neural Networks*, Vol. 4, pp. 207–224.

[188] Lee, S. C. and Lee, E. T. (1974). "Fuzzy Sets and Neural Networks," *J. Cybernet.*, Vol. 4, pp. 83–101.

[189] Lehtokangas, M. (2000). "Cascade-Correlation Learning for Classification," *IEEE Trans. Neural Networks*, Vol. 11, No. 3 (May), pp. 784–794.

[190] Leistritz, L., Galicki, M., Witte, H., and Kochs, E. (2001). "Initial State Training Procedure Improves Dynamic Recurrent Networks with Time-Dependent Weights," *IEEE Trans. Neural Networks*, Vol. 12, No. 6 (Nov.), pp. 1513–1518.

[191] Leung, C. S., Tsoi, A.-C., and Chan, L. W. (2001). "Two Regularizers for Recursive Least Squared Algorithms in Feedforward Multilayered Neural Networks," *IEEE Trans. Neural Networks*, Vol. 12, No. 6 (Nov.), pp. 1314–1332.

[192] Li, J. H., Michel, A. N., and Porod, W. (1989). "Analysis and Synthesis of a Class of Neural Networks: Linear Systems Operating on a Closed Hypercube," *IEEE Trans. Circuits Syst.*, Vol. 36, pp. 1405–1422.

[193] Li, L.-H., Lin, I.-C., and Hwang, M.-S. (2001). "A Remote Password Authentication Scheme for Multiserver Architecture Using Neural Networks," *IEEE Trans. Neural Networks*, Vol. 12, No. 6 (Nov.), pp. 1498–1504.

[194] Li, L. K. (1992). "Fixed Point Analysis for Discrete-Time Recurrent Neural Networks," *Proc. Int. Joint Conf. Neural Networks*, June, Vol. IV, pp. 134–139.

[195] Li, W.-J. and Lee, T. (2001). "Hopfield Neural Networks for Affine Invariant Matching," *IEEE Trans. Neural Networks*, Vol. 12, No. 6 (Nov.), pp. 1400–1410.

[196] Liang, X. B. (2001a). "A Recurrent Neural Networks for Nonlinear Continuously Differentiable Optimization Over a Compact Convex Set," *IEEE Trans. Neural Networks*, Vol. 12, No. 6 (Nov.), pp. 1487–1490.

[197] Liang, X. B. (2001b). "Qualitative Analysis of a Recurrent Neural Network for Nonlinear Continuously Differentiable Convex Minimization over a Nonempty Closed Convex Subset Set," *IEEE Trans. Neural Networks*, Vol. 12, No. 6 (Nov.), pp. 1521–1524.

[198] Liang, X. B. and Wang, J. (2000). "A Recurrent Neural Network for Nonlinear Optimization with a Continuously Differentiable Objective Function and Bound Constraints," *IEEE Trans. Neural Networks*, Vol. 11 (Nov.), pp. 1251–1262.

[199] Light, W. A. (1992). "Some Aspects of Radial Basis Function Approximation," in *Approximation Theory, Spline Functions and Applications*, Singh, S. P. (ed.), Kluwer Academic, Boston, NATO ASI Series Vol. 256, pp. 163–190.

[200] Lim, T.-S., Loh, W.-Y., and Shih, Y.-S. (2000). "A Comparison of Prediction Accuracy, Complexity, and Training Time of 33 Old and New Classification Algorithms," *Machine Learning*, Vol. 40, pp. 203–228.

[201] Lin, C.-J. (2001). "On the Convergence of the Decomposition Method for Support Vector Machines," *IEEE Trans. Neural Networks*, Vol. 12, No. 6 (Nov.), pp. 1278–1287.

[202] Lorentz, G. G. (1962). "Metric Entropy, Widths, and Superposition of Functions," *Am. Math. Monthly*, Vol. 69, pp. 469–485.

[203] Lorentz, G. G. (1966). "Metric Entropy and Approximation," *Bull. Am. Math. Soc.*, Vol. 72 (Nov.), pp. 903–937.

[204] Lorentz, G. G. (1986). *Approximation of Functions*, Chelsea Publishing, New York.

[205] Lu, H. (2000). "On Stability of Nonlinear Continuous-Time Neural Networks with Delays," *Neural Networks*, Vol. 13, No. 10, pp. 1135–1144.

[206] Mackey, M. C. and Glass, L. (1977). "Oscillation and Chaos in Physiological Control Systems," *Science*, Vol. 197, pp. 287–289.

[207] Marcus, C. M. and Westervelt, R. M. (1989). "Dynamics of Iterated Map Neural Networks," *Phys. Rev. A*, Vol. 40, No. 1, pp. 577–587.

[208] Matsuoka, K. (1992). "Stability Conditions for Nonlinear Continuous Neural Networks with Asymmetric Connection Weights," *Neural Networks*, Vol. 5, pp. 495–500.

[209] Mays, C. H. (1963). *Adaptive Threshold Logic*, Ph.D. thesis, Technical Report 1557-1, Stanford Electron. Labs., Stanford, CA.

[210] McClelland, J. L. and Rumelhart, D. E. (1988). *Exportations in Parallel Distributed Processing*, MIT Press, Cambridge, MA.

[211] McCulloch, W. S. and Pitts, W. H. (1943). "A Logical Calculus of the Ideas Imminent in Nervous Activity," *Bull. Math. Biophys.*, Vol. 5, pp. 115–133.

[212] McEliece, R., Posner, E., Rodemich, E., and Venkatesh, S. (1987). "The Capacity of the Hopfield Associative Memory," *IEEE Trans. Inform. Theory*, Vol. 33, pp. 461–482.

[213] McLachlan, G. and Peel, D. (2000). *Finite Mixture Models*, Wiley series, Probability and Statistics, Wiley, New York.

[214] Mendel, J. M. (1995). "Fuzzy Logic Systems for Engineering: A Tutorial," *Proc. IEEE*, Vol. 83, No. 3 (March), pp. 345–377.

[215] Micchelli, C. A. (1986). "Interpolation of Scattered Data: Distance Matrices and Conditionally Positive Definite Functions," *Construct. Approx.*, Vol. 2, pp. 11–22.

[216] Michel, A. N. and Miller, R. K. (1977). *Qualitative Analysis of Large Scale Dynamical Systems*, Academic Press, New York.

[217] Mitra, S. and Hayashi, Y. (2000). "Neuro-Fuzzy Rule Generation: Survey in Soft Computing Framework," *IEEE Trans. Neural Networks*, Vol. 11, No. 3 (May), pp. 748–768.

[218] Moller, M. (1993). "A Scaled Conjugate Gradient Algorithm for Fast Supervised Learning," *Neural Networks*, Vol. 6, No. 4, pp. 525–534.

[219] Mozer, M. C. and Smolensky, P. (1989). "Skeletonization: A Technique for Trimming the Fat From a Network via Relevance Assessment," in *Advances in Neural Information Processing Systems*, Touretzky, D. S. (ed.), Vol. 1, Morgan Kaufmann, pp. 107–115.

[220] Mozer, M. C., Wolniewicz, R., Grimes, D. B., Johnson, E., and Kaushanksy, H. (2000). "Predicting Subscriber Dissatisfaction and Improving Retention in the Wireless Telecommunications Industry," *IEEE Trans. Neural Networks*, Vol. 11, No. 3 (May), pp. 690–696.

[221] Müller, B. and Reinhardt, J. (1991). *Neural Networks: An Introduction*, Springer-Verlag, Berlin.

[222] Muroga, S. (1971). *Threshold Logic and Its Application*, Wiley, New York.

[223] Musavi, M., Ahmed, W., Chan, K. H., Faris, K. B., and Hummels, D. M. (1992). "On the Training of Radial Basis Function Classifiers," *Neural Networks*, Vol. 5, pp. 595–603.

[224] Musilek, P. and Gupta, M. M. (2000). "Fuzzy Neural Models Based on Some New Fuzzy Arithmetic Operations," *J. Adv. Comput. Intell.*, Vol. 3, No. 6, pp. 245–254.

[225] Nabney, T. (1999). "Efficient Training of RBF Networks for Classification," *Proc. 9th ICANN*, Vol. 1, pp. 210–215.

[226] Nadeau, C. and Benjio, Y. (2000). "Inference for the Generalization Error," in *Advances in Neural Information Processing Systems*, Vol. 12, MIT Press, Cambridge, MA.

[227] Narendra, K. S. and Parthasarathy, K. (1990). "Identification and Control of Dynamical Systems Using Neural Networks," *IEEE Trans. Neural Networks*, Vol. 1, No. 1, pp. 4–27.

[228] Nicholls, J. G., Martin, A. R., Wallace, B. G., Fuchs, P. A. (2001). *From Neuron to Brain*, 4th ed., Sinauer Assoc., Sunderland, MA.

[229] Nishiyama, K. and Suzuki, K. (2001). "H_∞—Learning of Layered Neural Networks," *IEEE Trans. Neural Networks*, Vol. 12, No. 6 (Nov.), pp. 1265–1277.

[230] Pal, S. K., Datta, A., and Pal, N. R. (2001). "A Multilayer Self-Organizing Model for Convex-Hull," *IEEE Trans. Neural Networks*, Vol. 12, No. 6 (Nov.), pp. 1341–1347.

[231] Pao, Y. H. (1989). *Adaptive Pattern Recognition and Neural Networks*, Addison-Wesley, Reading, MA.

[232] Papadpopoulos, G., Edwards, P. J., and Murray, A. F. (2001). "Confidence Estimation Methods for Neural Networks: A Practical Comparison," *IEEE Trans. Neural Networks*, Vol. 12, No. 6 (Nov.), pp. 1278–1287.

[233] Parlos, A. G., Menton, S. K., and Atiya, A. F. (2001). "An Algorithmic Approach to Adaptive State Filtering Using Recurrent Neural Networks," *IEEE Trans. Neural Networks*, Vol. 12, No. 6 (Nov.), pp. 1411–1432.

[234] Pavlov, I. P. (1993). *Psychopathology and Psychiatry*, revised ed., Transaction Publishers, New Brunswick, Canada.

[235] Pedrycz, W. (1991a). "Neurocomputations in Relational Systems," *IEEE Trans. Pattern Anal. Machine Intell.*, Vol. 13, pp. 289–297.

[236] Pedrycz, W. (1991b). "A Referential Scheme of Fuzzy Decision Making and Its Neural Network Structure," *IEEE Trans. Syst. Man Cybernet.*, Vol. 21, pp. 1593–1604.

[237] Pedrycz, W. (1993). "Fuzzy Neural Networks and Neurocomputations," *Fuzzy Sets Syst.*, Vol. 56, No. 1, pp. 1–28.

[238] Pedrycz, W. (1995). "Genetic Algorithms for Learning in Fuzzy Relational Structures," *Fuzzy Sets Syst.*, Vol. 69, No. 1, pp. 37–52.

[239] Persidskii, S. K. (1969). "Problem of Absolute Stability," *Automation Remote Control*, Vol. 12, pp. 1889–1895.

[240] Personnaz, L., Guyon, I., and Dreyfus, G. (1986). "Collective Computational Properties of Neural Networks: New Learning Mechanisms," *Phys. Rev. A*, Vol. 34, pp. 4217–4228.

[241] Pham, D.-T. and Cardoso, J.-F. (2000). "Blind Separation of Instantaneous Mixtures of Nonstationary Sources," *Proc. Int. Workshop on Independent Component Analysis and Blind Signal Separation* (*ICA2000*), Helsinki, Finland, pp. 187–193.

[242] Pineda, F. J. (1987). "Generalization of Back-propagation to Recurrent Neural Networks," *Physical Rev. Lett.*, Vol. 59, No. 19, pp. 2229–2232.

[243] Pineda, F. J. (1988). "Dynamics and Architecture for Neural Computation," *J. Complexity*, Vol. 4, pp. 216–245.

[244] Poggio, T. and Girosi, F. (1989). "A Theory of Networks for Approximation and Learning," *AI Memo No. 1140*, July, CBIP Paper 31.

[245] Poggio, T. and Girosi, F. (1990). "Networks for Approximation and Learning," *Proc. IEEE*, Vol. 78, pp. 1481–1497.

[246] Principe, J. C. and Kuo, J. (1995). "Dynamic Modelling Chaotic Time Series with Neural Networks," in *Advances in Neural Information Processing System*, Tesauro, G., Touretzky, D., and Leen, T. (eds.), Vol. 7, MIT Press, Cambridge, MA, pp. 311–318.

[247] Psaltis, D., Sideris, A., and Yamamura, A. A. (1988). "A Multilayered Neural Network Controller," *IEEE Control Syst. Mag.*, Vol. 8, pp. 17–21.

[248] Rao, D. H., Gupta, M. M., and Sinha, N. K. (2000). "Dynamic Neural Networks: An Overview," *Int. Conf. Industrial Technology*, Gao, India, Jan., pp. 491–496.

[249] Ray, W. O. (1988). *Real Analysis*, Prentice-Hall, Englewood Cliffs, NJ.

[250] Reed, R. (1993). "Pruning Algorithms—A Survey," *IEEE Trans. Neural Networks*, Vol. 4, No. 5, pp. 740–747.

[251] Ridella, S. and Zunnio, R. (2001). "Empirical Measure of Multiclass Generalization Performance: The K-Winner Machine Class," *IEEE Trans. Neural Networks*, Vol. 12, No. 6 (Nov.), pp. 1525–1528.

[252] Rissanen, J. (1989). *Stochastic Complexity in Statistical Inquiry*, World Scientific, Singapore.

[253] Robinson, A. J. and Fallside, F. (1987). "Static and Dynamic Error Propagation Networks with Application to Speech Coding," *Proc. Neural Information Processing Systems*, Anderson, D. Z. (ed.), American Institute of Physics.

[254] Rumelhart, D. E., Hinton, G. E., and Williams, R. J. (1986). "Learning Internal Representations by Error Propagation," in *Parallel Distributed Processing: Explorations in the Microstructure of Cognition*, Rumelhart, D. E. and McClelland, J. L. (eds.), Vol. 1, MIT Press, Cambridge, MA, pp. 318–362.

[255] Rumelhart, D. E. and McClelland, J. L. (1986). *Parallel Distributed Processing: Explorations in the Microstructure of Cognition: Foundations*, Vol. 1, MIT Press, Cambridge, MA.

[256] Rosenblatt, F. (1958). "The Perceptron: A Probabilistic Model for Information Storage and Organization in the Brain," *Psychological Review*, Vol. 65, pp. 386–408.

[257] Saarinen, S., Bramley, R., and Cybenko, G. (1991). *The Numerical Solution of Neural Network Training Problems*, CRSD Report 1089, Center for Supercomputing Research and Development, Univ. Illinois, Urbana, IL.

[258] Saarinen, S., Bramley, R., and Cybenko, G. (1992). "Neural Networks, Backpropagation, and Automatic Differentiation," in *Automatic Differentiation of Algorithms: Theory, Implementation, and Application*, Griewank, A. and Corliss, G. F. (eds.), SIAM, Philadelphia, pp.31–42.

[259] Sakaguchi, H. (1988). "Oscillatory and Excitable Behaviours in a Population of Model Neuron," *Progress Theor. Phys.*, Vol. 79, No. 5, pp. 1061–1068.

[260] Scott, A. C. (1977). *Neurophysics*, Wiley, New York.

[261] Sebald, D. J. and Bucklew, J. A. (2000). "Support Vector Machine Techniques for Nonlinear Equalization," *IEEE Trans. Signal Process.*, Vol. 48 (Nov.), pp. 3217–3226.

[262] Segee, B. E. and Carter, M. J. (1991). "Fault Tolerance of Pruned Multilayer Networks," *Proc. Int. Joint Conf. Neural Networks*, Vol. II, Seattle, pp. 447–452.

[263] Shin, C. K., Yu, S. J., Yun, U. T., and Kim H. K. (2000). "A Hybrid Approach of Neural Network and Memory-Based Learning to Data Mining," *IEEE Trans. Neural Networks*, Vol. 11, No. 3 (May), pp. 637–646.

[264] Shin, Y. and Ghosh, J. (1991). "The Pi-sigma Network: An Efficient Higher-order Neural Network for Pattern Classification and Function Approximation," *Proc. Int. Joint Conf. on Neural Networks*, Vol. I, Seattle, WA, July, pp. 13–18.

[265] Sietsma, J. and Dow, R. J. F. (1991). "Creating Artificial Neural Networks that Generalize," *Neural Networks*, Vol. 4, pp. 67–79.

[266] Silva, F. M. and Almeida, L. B. (1990). "Speeding up Backpropagation," in *Advances of Neural Computers*, Eckmiller, R. (ed.), Elsevier Science Publishers B.V., North-Holland, pp. 151–158.

[267] Simmon, D. (2001). "Distributed Fault Tolerance in Optimal Interpolative Nets," *IEEE Trans. Neural Networks*, Vol. 12, No. 6 (Nov.), pp. 1348–1357.

[268] Simone, G. and Morabito, F. C. (2001). "RBFNN-Based Hole Identification System in Conducting Plates," *IEEE Trans. Neural Networks*, Vol. 12, No. 6 (Nov.), pp. 1445–1454.

[269] Singhal, S. and Wu, L. (1989). "Training Multilayer Perceptrons with the Extended Kalman Algorithm," in *Advances in Neural Information Processing Systems I*, Morgan Kaufmann, San Mateo, CA, pp. 133–140.

[270] Sinha, M., Gupta, M. M., and Nikiforuk, P. N. (2001). "A Compensatory Wavelet Neuron Model," *Joint 9th IFSA World Congress and 20th NAFIPS Int. Conf.*, Vancouver, BC, Canada, July 25–28, pp. 1372–1376.

[271] Sinha, N. K. and Gupta, M. M. and Zadeh, L. A. (1999). *Soft-Computing and Intelligent Control Systems, Theory and Applications*, Academic Press, New York.

[272] Skarda, C. A. and Freeman, W. J. (1987). "How Brains Make Chaos in Order to Make Sense of the World," *Behav. Brain Sci.*, Vol. 10, pp. 161–195.

[273] Smagt, P. (1994). "Minimisation Methods for Training Feedforward Neural Networks," *Neural Networks*, Vol. 7, No. 1, pp. 1–11.

[274] Softky, R. W. and Kammen, D. M. (1991). "Correlations in High Dimensional or Asymmetrical Data Sets: Hebbian Neuronal Processing," *Neural Networks*, Vol. 4, No. 3, pp. 337–347.

[275] Spath, H. (1980). *Cluster Analysis Algorithms for Data Reduction and Classification of Objects*, Ellis Horwood Ltd., Chichester, UK.

[276] Sprecher, D. A. (1965). "On the Structure of Continuous Functions of Several Variables," *Trans. Amer. Math. Soc.*, Vol. 115, pp. 340–355.

[277] Sprecher, D. A. (1993). "A Universal Mapping for Kolmogorov's Superposition Theorem," *Neural Networks*, Vol. 6, No. 8, pp. 1089–1094.

[278] Su, M. C. and Chang, H.-T. (2000). "Fast Self-Organizing Map Algorithm," *IEEE Trans. Neural Networks*, Vol. 11, No. 3 (May), pp. 721–733.

[279] Sudharsanan, S. I. and Sundareshan, M. K. (1991a). "Equilibrium Characterization of Dynamical Neural Networks and a Systematic Synthesis Procedure for Associative Memories," *IEEE Trans. Neural Networks*, Vol. 2, No. 5 (Sept.), pp. 509–521.

[280] Sudharsanan, S. I. and Sundareshan, M. K. (1991b). "Training of a Three-Layer Dynamical Recurrent Neural Network for Nonlinear Input-Output Mapping," *Proc. Int. Joint Conf. Neural Networks*, Nov., pp. III–115.

[281] Taylor, J. G. and Commbes, S. (1993). "Learning Higher Order Correlations," *Neural Networks*, Vol. 6, No. 3, pp. 423–428.

[282] Tipping, M. E. (2000). "The Relevance Vector Machine," in *Advances in Neural Information Processing Systems 12*, Solla, S. A., Leen, T. K., and Muller, K.-R. (eds.), MIT Press, Cambridge, MA.

[283] Tishby, N., Levin, E., and Solla, S. (1989). "Consistent Inference on Probabilities in Layered Networks, Predictions and Generalization," Proc. *Int. Joint Conf. Neural Networks*, Washington, DC, IEEE Press, pp. 403–410.

[284] Vesanto, J. and Alhoniemi, E. (2000). "Clustering of the Self-Organizing Map," *IEEE Trans. Neural Networks*, Vol. 11, No. 3 (May), pp. 586–600.

[285] Vogl, T. P., Mangis, J. K., Rigler, A. K., Zink, W. T., and Allcon, D. L. (1988). "Accelerating the Convergence of the Back-propagation Method," *Biol. Cybernet.*, Vol. 59, pp. 257–263.

[286] Wang, L. X. (1993). "Stable Adaptive Fuzzy Control of Nonlinear Systems," *IEEE Trans. Fuzzy Syst.*, Vol. 1 (Jan.), pp. 146–155.

[287] Wang, L. X. and Mendel, J. M. (1992a). "Fuzzy Basis Functions, Universal Approximation, and Orthogonal Least Square Learning," *IEEE Trans. Neural Networks*, Vol. 3, No. 5, pp. 807–814.

[288] Wang, L. X. and Mendel, J. M. (1992b). "Generating Fuzzy Rules from Numerical Data, with Applications," *IEEE Trans. Syst. Man Cybernet.*, Vol. 32, pp. 1414–1472.

[289] Wang, L. X. and Mendel, J. M. (1993). "Fuzzy Adaptive Filters, with Application to Nonlinear Channel Equalization," *IEEE Trans. Fuzzy Syst.*, Vol. 1 (March), pp. 161–170.

[290] Wang, Y. F., Luo, L., Freedman, M. T., and Kung, S.-Y. (2000). "Probabilistic Principal Component Subspaces: A Hierarchical Finite Mixture Model for Data Visualizations," *IEEE Trans. Neural Networks*, Vol. 11, No. 3 (May), pp. 625–636.

[291] Watanabe, S. (2001). "Learning Efficiency of Redundant Neural Networks in Bayesian Estimation," *IEEE Trans. Neural Networks*, Vol. 12, No. 6 (Nov.), pp. 1475–1486.

[292] Werbos, P. J. (1974). *Beyond Regression: New Tools for Prediction and Analysis in the Behavioral Sciences*, Ph.D. thesis, Applied Mathematics, Harvard Univ., Boston, MA, Nov.

[293] Weymaere, N. and Martens, J. P. (1991). "A Fast Robust Learning Algorithm for Feedforward Neural Networks," *Neural Networks*, Vol. 4, pp. 361–369.

[294] Widrow, B. (1962). "Generalization and Information Storage in Networks of Adaline Neurons," in *Self-Organizing Systems*, Yovitz, M., Jocobi, G., and Goldstein, C. (eds.), Spartan Books, Washington, DC, pp. 435–461.

[295] Widrow, B. and Hoff, M. E. (1960). "Adaptive Switching Circuits," in *IRE WESCON Convention Record*, Vol. 4, New York, pp. 96–104.

[296] Widrow, B. and Lehr, M. A. (1990). "30 Years of Adaptive Neural Networks: Perceptron, Madaline, and Backpropagation," Proc. *IEEE*, Vol. 78, No. 9, pp. 1415–1442.

[297] Williams, R. J. and Zipser, D. (1989). "A Learning Algorithm for Continually Running Fully Recurrent Neural Networks," *Neural Comput.*, Vol. 1, pp. 270–280.

[298] Williams, R. J. and Zipser, D. (1990). *Gradient-based Learning Algorithms for Recurrent Connectionist Networks*, Technical Report NU-CCS-90-9, Northeastern Univ., College of Computer Science, Boston.

[299] Xu, L., Oja, E., and Suen, C. Y. (1992). "Modified Hebbian Learning for Curve and Surface Fitting," *Neural Networks*, Vol. 5, No. 3, pp. 441–457.

[300] Xu, X., He, H. G., and Hu, D. (2002). "Efficient Reinforcement Learning Using Recursive Least-Squares Methods," *J. Artificial Intelligence Research*, Vol. 16, pp. 259–292.

[301] Yan, L. and Miller, D. J. (2000). "General Statistical Inference for Discrete and Mixed Spaces by an Approximate Application of the Maximum Entropy Principle," *IEEE Trans. Neural Networks*, Vol. 11, No. 3 (May), pp. 558–573.

[302] Yanai, H. and Sawada, Y. (1990). "Integrator Neurons for Analog Neural Networks," *IEEE Trans. Circuit Syst.*, Vol. 36, pp. 854–856.

[303] Yang, T.-N. and Wang, S.-D. (2000). "Fuzzy Auto-Associative Neural Networks for Principal Component Extraction of Noisy Data," *IEEE Trans. Neural Networks*, Vol. 11, No. 3 (May), pp. 799–801.

[304] Yidliz, O. T. (2001). "Omnivariate Decision Trees," *IEEE Trans. Neural Networks*, Vol. 12, No. 6 (Nov.), pp. 1539–1546

[305] Yidliz, O. T. and Alpaydin, E. (2000). "Linear Discriminant Trees," *Proc. 17th Int. Conf. Machine Learning*, Langely, P. (ed.), Morgan Kaufmann, San Mateo, CA, pp. 1175–1182.

[306] Yuan, C., Azimi-Sadjadi, M. R., Wilbur, J., and Dobeck, G. (2000). "Underwater Target Detection Using Multichannel Subb and Adaptive Filtering and High Order Correlation Schemes," *IEEE J. Ocean. Eng.*, Vol. 25 (Jan.), pp. 192–205.

[307] Zadeh, L. A. (1965). "Fuzzy Sets," *Inform. Control*, Vol. 8, pp. 338–353.

[308] Zadeh, L. A. (1968). "Probability Measures of Fuzzy Events," *J. Math. Anal. Appl.*, Vol. 23, pp. 421–427.

[309] Zadeh, L. A. (1972a). "A Fuzzy-Set – Theoretic Interpretation of Linguistic Hedges," *J. Cybernet.*, Vol. 2, pp. 4–34.

[310] Zadeh, L. A. (1972b). "A Rational for Fuzzy Control," *J. Dynamic Syst., Meas. Control*, Vol. 34, pp. 3–4.

[311] Zadeh, L. A. (1973). "Outline of a New Approach to the Analysis of Complex Systems and Decision Processes," *IEEE Trans. Syst. Man Cybernet.*, Vol. 3, pp. 28–44.

[312] Zadeh, L. A. (1984). "Making Computers Think Like People," *IEEE Spectrum*, Vol. 21, No. 8 (Aug.), pp. 26–32.

[313] Zadeh, L. A. (1986). "Outline of a Computational Approach to Meaning and Knowledge Representation Based on a Concept of a Generalized Assignment Statement," *Proc. Int. Seminar on Artificial Intelligence and Man-Machine Systems*, Thoma, M. and Wyner, A. (eds.), Springer-Verlag, Heidelberg, Germany, pp. 198–211.

[314] Zadeh, L. A. (1994). "Fuzzy Logic, Neural Networks, and Soft-computing," *Commun. ACM*, Vol. 37, pp. 77–84.

[315] Zadeh, L. A. (1996). "Fuzzy Logic = Computing with Words," *IEEE Trans. Fuzzy Systems*, Vol. 4, pp. 103–111.

[316] Zadeh, L. A. (1997). "Toward a Theory of Fuzzy Information Granulation and its Centrality in Human Reasoning and Fuzzy Logic," *Fuzzy Sets Syst.*, Vol. 90, pp. 111–127.

[317] Zadeh, L. A. (1999). "From Computing with Numbers to Computing with Words—from Manipulation of Measurements to Manipulation of Perceptions," *IEEE Trans. Circuits Syst.*, Vol. 45, pp. 105–119.

[318] Zeng, Z. and Yeung, D. S. (2001). "Sensitivity Analysis of Multilayer Perceptron to Input and Weight Perturbations," *IEEE Trans. Neural Networks*, Vol. 12, No. 6 (Nov.), pp. 1358–1366.

[319] Zhang, J. and Jin, X. (2000). "Global Stability Analysis in Delayed Hopfield Neural Models," *Neural Networks*, Vol. 13, No. 7, pp. 745–753.

[320] Zhang, Y. Q., Fraser, M. D., Gagliano, R. A., and Kandel, A. (2000). "Granular Neural Networks for Numerical-Linguistic Data Fusion and Knowledge Discovery," *IEEE Trans. Neural Networks*, Vol. 11, No. 3 (May), pp. 658–667.

[321] Zhao, L. and Macau, E. E. N. (2001). "A Network of Dynamically Coupled Chaotic Maps for Scene Segmentation," *IEEE Trans. Neural Networks*, Vol. 12, No. 6 (Nov.), pp. 1375–1385.

[322] Zhao, L., Macau, E. E. N., and Omar, N. (2000). "Scene Segmentation of the Chaotic Oscillator Network," *Int. J. Bifurcation Chaos*, Vol. 10, No. 7, pp. 1697–1708.

[323] Zurada, J. M. (1992). *Introduction to Artificial Neural Systems*, West Publishing Company, St. Paul, MN.

Appendix A

Current Bibliographic Sources on Neural Networks

SOCIETIES

- Canadian Society for Fuzzy Information and Neural Systems (CANS-FINS)
- Canadian Society for Computational Studies of Intelligence (CSCSI)
- Dutch Foundation for Neural Networks (SNN)
- European Neural Network Society (ENNS)
- IEEE Neural Networks for Signal Processing Committee
- International Fuzzy Systems Association (IFSA)
- Italian Neural Network Society (SIREN)
- Japanese Neural Network Society (JNNS)
- Neural Computing Applications Forum (NCAF)
- North American Fuzzy Information Processing Society (NAFIPS)
- Stimulation Initiative for European Neural Applications (SIENA)

- Swedish Neural Network Society (SNNS)
- The International Neural Network Society (INNS)

JOURNALS

- *Adaptive Behavior*
- *Behavioral and Brain Sciences*
- *Biological Cybernetics*
- *Biophysical Journal*
- *Connection Science*
- *Fuzzy Sets and Systems*
- *IEEE Transactions on Fuzzy Systems*
- *IEEE Transactions on Image Processing*
- *IEEE Transactions on Neural Networks*
- *IEEE Transactions on Signal Processing*
- *International Journal of Approximate Reasoning*
- *International Journal of Neural Systems*
- *Journal of Artificial Intelligence Research*
- *Journal of Cognitive Neuroscience*
- *Journal of Fuzzy Sets and Systems*
- *Journal of Uncertainty, Fuzziness and Knowledge-Based Systems*
- *Network: Computation in Neural Systems*
- *Neural Computation*
- *Neural Networks*
- *Neural Network World*
- *Neural Processing Letters*
- *Neurocomputing*

CONFERENCES

- Annual Conference on Evolutionary Programming
- Annual Meeting on Neural Control of Movement
- Artificial Neural Networks in Engineering (ANNIE)
- European Congress on Intelligent Techniques and Soft Computing (EUFIT)
- European Meeting on Cybernetics and Systems Research
- From Animals to Animate — International Conference on Simulation of Adaptive Behavior (SAB)
- Genetic Programming Conference

- IEEE International Conference on Fuzzy Systems (FUZZ IEEE)
- IEEE International Conference on Neural Networks (IEEE ICNN)
- IEEE International Conference on Systems, Man, and Cybernetics
- IEEE International Conference on Tools with Artificial Intelligence (ICTAI)
- IEEE Workshop on Neural Networks for Signal Processing
- IFAC Symposium on Intelligent Autonomous Vehicles
- Industrial Fuzzy control and Intelligent Systems Conference (IFIS)
- Intelligent Systems and Control (ISC)
- International Conference on Artificial Neural Networks (ICANN)
- International Conference on Evolutionary Computation
- International Conference on Evolvable Systems: From Biology to Hardware (ICES)
- International Conference on Intelligent Robots and Systems (IROS)
- International Conference on Neural Networks and Brain
- International Conference on Simulation of Adaptive Behavior
- International Fuzzy Systems and Intelligent Control Conference (IFSIC)
- International ICSC/IFAC Symposium on Neural Computation
- International Symposium on Intelligent Systems (AMSE-ISIS)
- International Symposium on Robotics with Applications (ISORA)
- International Symposium on Soft Computing (SOCO)
- International Workshop on Neural Networks for Identification, Control,
- Joint Conference on Information Sciences (JCIS)
- Neural Information Processing Systems - Natural and Synthetic (NIPS)
- Robotics, and Signal Image Processing (NICROSP)
- World Congress on Computational Intelligence (IJCNN, FUZZ-IEEE, ICEC)
- World Congress on Neural Networks (WCNN)

INTERNET RESOURCES

- IEEE Neural Network Council

  `http://engine.ieee.org/nnc/`
- Fuzzy Logic and Neurofuzzy Resources

  `http://www-isis.ecs.suton.ac.uk/research/nfinfo/fuzzy.html`
- Fuzzy Logic Entry at Yahoo

  `http://www.yahoo.com/Science/Computer_Science/`
  `Artificial_lntelligence/Fuzzy_logic`
- Neural Networks Entry at Yahoo

  `http://www.yahoo.com/Science/Engineering/Electrical_Engin`

- NeuroNet European Network of Excellence
  http://www.neuronet.ph.kcl.ac.uk
- North American Fuzzy Information Processing Society
  http://seraphim.csee.usf.edu/nafips.html
- Web Dictionary of Cybernetics and Systems
  http://pespmcl.vub.ac.be/ASC/indexASC.html
- Classified List of Bibliography on Neural Networks
  ftp://ftp.wiley.com/public/sci_tech_med/neural_networks/

Index

α-LMS algorithm, 71
α-perceptron learning rule, 66
μ-LMS, 77

A

Absolute stability, 445
Action potential, 24, 39, 317
Activation function, 80, 301, 470, 511
  linear —, 451
  nonlinear —, 451
  synapse-dependent nonlinear —, 448
Activation gain, 82, 470
Active state, 511
Adaline, 70
Adaptation, 4, 12, 63, 94, 431, 652
Adaptive algorithm, 64
Adaptive filter, 398
Adaptive weight learning rule, 113
Additive and shunting network, 305
Adjoint equation, 401
Affine coordinate transformation, 315
Algebraic closure, 240, 257
Algorithm, 64
  α-LMS —, 71
  μ-LMS —, 77
  adaptive —, 64
  backpropagation —, 83, 106, 118, 129
  BP —, 83
  modified relaxation —, 69
  momentum —, 144
Algorithm-based computing, 10
AND operation, 45
Associating learning rule, 623
Associative memory, 394–395, 436–437, 516, 580
Associativity, 647
Asymptotic stability, 333
Asymptotically stable, 474–475
  — equilibrium point, 311, 357
  — in large, 473
  globally —, 473
  locally —, 476
Asynchronous mode, 513
Asynchronous operating mode, 561
Asynchronous updating mode, 594
Attraction basin, 396
Attractive radius, 606
Attractive region, 606
Attractor, 514
Autoassociative memory, 398
Axon, 24, 28, 39, 581

B

Backpropagation, 83, 106, 118, 140, 172

— algorithm, 83, 129
— learning, 172
— through time, 411
Basin of attraction, 348
BFGS method, 199
Bias, 301
Bifurcation, 334
Binary logic, 14, 45
Block sequential mode, 513
Block sequential operating mode, 561
Boolean function, 511
Boundary condition, 647
Bounded measurable function, 257
BP, 83, 106, 118, 172
Brain, 4, 8, 10
Brouwer's fixed-point theorem, 332, 473
Broyden–Fletcher–Goldfarb–Shannon method, 199

C

CAM, 348, 359
Canonical form, 211
Carbon-based cognitive faculty, 10
Carbon-based computer, 4
Cartesian product, 275, 638
Central nervous system, 8, 22
CG, 200
CGL, 200
Chain rule, 89
Chaotic attractor, 396
Classification, 226
Closed set, 255
Closure, 255
Clustering algorithm, 242
CNS, 8, 22
Cognition, 4, 634
Cognitive computing machine, 5
Cognitive information, 7
Commutativity, 647
Compact, 255
Complement, 637
Complexity measure, 179
Complexity regularization, 179
Computational complexity, 246
Computational energy function, 357
Conjugate gradient method, 200
— with line search, 200
scaled —, 200
Content-addressable memory, 348, 359, 580, 598
Continuity, 383
Continuous-time, 346
— dynamic neural network, 346, 396, 421, 436
— dynamic neural unit, 399
— mapper, 398
— recurrent neural network, 380
Contraction mapping theorem, 489
Convergent K-means clustering algorithm, 244
Correlation coefficient, 610
Correlation matrix, 75
Cortex, 39
Cosig function, 263
Cosine squashing function, 263
Cost function, 113
Critical point, 365
Cross-layer connection, 346
CT-DNN, 421, 470
CT-DNU, 399
Cubic splines radial basis function, 229
Cycle length, 514

D

Davidson–Fletcher–Powell method, 199
DBP, 395
De Morgan's theorem, 648
Dead zone, 68
Deadbeat response, 212
Decaying-exponential network, 292
Decomposed extended Kalman filter, 205, 431
Defuzzifier, 641, 643
DEKF, 205, 431
Dendrite, 24, 27, 39
Dense set, 255
DFP method, 199
Diagonal Lyapunov equation, 483
Diagonal Lyapunov function, 483
Diagonal stability, 482
DIC, 211
Diffeomorphism, 388
Dirac's delta function, 582
Direct inverse control, 211
Discrete-time, 347
— binary neural network, 510
— dynamic neural network, 470
— dynamic neural structure, 347
— dynamic neural unit, 404
Dissipative property, 394
Dissipative system, 347
DNN, 351, 395, 436

DNN-S, 374
DNU, 18, 298, 395
DT-DNU, 404
Dynamic backpropagation, 395, 403
Dynamic memory, 624
Dynamic neural network, 18, 298, 351, 395, 436, 470
— with saturation, 374
continuous-time —, 346, 436
discrete-time —, 470
Hopfield —, 436
Dynamic neural unit, 18, 298, 338, 395

E

Effective Hamming distance, 591
Effective rise time, 26
Eigenvalue, 366, 439
EKF, 202, 204
Energy function, 357, 475, 519, 584
— method, 475
computational —, 357
Equilibrium memory, 338
Equilibrium point, 311, 331, 384, 394, 436, 473, 512, 584
— learning, 394
globally exponentially stable —, 334
saddle —, 476
stable —, 519
unstable —, 334
Error backpropagation, 431
Error measure index, 139
Error partial derivative, 138
Euclidean distance, 242
Euclidean norm, 225, 473, 622
Euclidean space, 588
Evolutionary theory, 316
Excitatory operation, 317
Excitatory–inhibitory neural model, 317
Exponential stability, 436, 452
Extended Kalman filter, 202, 204

F

Fault-tolerant system, 14
FBFN, 671
FBP, 667, 669
Feedback binary associative memory, 19, 580
Feedforward neural network, 18, 254
Finite impulse response, 346
FIR, 346
Firing state, 511
First-order pruning, 183
Fixed point, 473
Fixed-increment perceptron, 69
Fletcher–Reeves formulation, 201
FMF, 639
FN, 645
FNN, 634, 655
Fourier series, 258
Frequency modulation, 327
Function, 48
activation —, 80
hard-limiting —, 82
linearly separable —, 54
signum —, 82
step —, 48
threshold —, 54
Functional approximation, 18, 226, 254
Fundamental memory, 593
Fuzzifier, 641
Fuzzy, 8, 634
— addition, 645
— backpropagation, 667, 669
— basis function, 678
— basis function network, 671
— concept, 634
— IF–THEN rule, 634
— inference engine, 641, 643
— judgment, 634
— logic, 8, 14, 634
— logic operation, 646
— membership function, 639
— multiplication, 645
— neural network, 15, 19, 634, 655
— neuron, 635, 645
— reasoning, 634
— rule base, 641–642
— set, 636
— system, 641

G

Gain, 470
Gating term, 183
Gaussian density function, 224, 235
Gaussian neural network, 235
Gaussian radial basis function, 224, 229, 291
— neural network, 235, 674
Gaussian radial membership function, 673
Generalized delta rule, 113, 118, 172
Generalized inverse, 234
Generalized inverse method, 245
Generalized learning rule, 580, 620
Gerschgorin's theorem, 441, 483

Global asymptotic stability, 436, 444
Global exponential stability, 461
Global Lyapunov function, 475
Global minimum, 162, 369
Global stability theorem of Lyapunov, 475
Globally asymptotically stable, 473
Globally exponentially stable, 334, 474
Gradient descent method, 140, 245
Gradient steepest-descent method, 79
Gradient-like system, 365
Gram–Schmidt orthogonalization, 629
GRBFNN, 674
GRMF, 673
Gronwall's inequality, 490
Grossberg neuron model, 317

H

Habituation, 36–37
Hamming distance, 591
Hard-limiting quantizer, 517
Hebb's rule, 532
Hebbian learning rule, 580
Hessian, 191
Hessian matrix, 189
Hestenes–Stiefel formulation, 201
HFNN, 662
Hidden layer, 130
Higher-order neural network, 280
Higher-order neural unit, 280
Higher-order optimization, 198
Homeomorphism, 277
HONN, 280
HONU, 280
Hopfield neural network, 351, 479, 580
Hopfield neuron model, 317
Human cognition, 4
Human intelligence, 4
Human thinking, 634
Humanlike attribute, 4
Humanlike function, 4
Hybrid fuzzy neural network, 662, 666
Hyperbolic tangent function, 259

I

IC, 45
Identity function, 256
IIC, 213
IIR, 346
Inclusion, 637
Indirect inverse control, 213
Infimum, 255
Infinite impulse response, 346
Information capacity, 580
Information retrieval, 580, 597
Inhibitory operation, 317
Input layer, 130
Integrated circuit, 45
Intelligence, 4
Intelligent system, 7
Interlayer connection, 346
Internal state, 301
Interpolation condition, 228
Interpolation problem, 224, 227
Intersection, 637
Intralayer connection, 346
Inverse multiquadratic radial basis function, 229
Isolated DNU, 307
Isolated local minimum, 365

J

Jacobian, 366
Jacobian matrix, 203

K

K-means clustering, 242
Key pattern vector, 593
Kirchhoff's current law, 351
Kirchhoff's law, 309
Kolmogorov's mapping neural network existence theorem, 278
Kolmogorov's superposition theorem, 275
Kolmogorov's theorem, 254
Krasovskii's theorem, 464
Krönecker delta function, 427

L

L_2 norm, 172
Lagrange multiplier, 141, 400
Lagrangian, 141, 400
Large-scale system, 298
LaSalle's invariance principle, 475
Latency, 26
Lateral connection, 346
Lateral inhibition, 31, 39
— connection, 301
Lattice property, 256
Learning, 4, 12, 36, 63, 94, 431, 652
— algorithm, 394
— rate, 66
associative —, 36–37

supervised —, 38, 140, 242
unsupervised —, 38
Least mean square, 245
Least squares (LS), 172
— criterion, 172
— estimation, 202
— minimization, 203
Lebesgue-integrable function, 257
Li's norm stability condition, 486
Limit cycle, 519
Limit point, 255
Linear, 63
— activation function, 451
— combiner, 63, 119
— error, 69
— programming, 62
— splines radial basis function, 229
— subspace, 256
— term, 470
Linearized least squares learning, 202
Linearly separable function, 54
Linguistic input, 634
Linguistic output, 634
Linguistic variable, 636, 641
LLSL, 202
LMS, 245
Local asymptotic stability, 436–437
Local Lyapunov function, 474
Local minimum, 162, 365
Local stability theorem of Lyapunov, 474
Locally asymptotically stable, 476
Locomotion, 4
Logic, 44
— function, 284
binary —, 45
threshold —, 44, 51, 94
Logistic function, 259
Lotka–Volterra equation, 450
L_p norm, 172, 257
Lyapunov function, 310, 358, 519
Lyapunov function method, 333
Lyapunov stability, 333, 436
Lyapunov's first method, 368, 439, 476
Lyapunov's indirect method, 439, 476
Lyapunov's second method, 436

M

Max–min fuzzy neuron, 650
McCulloch–Pitts neuron, 85
Mc-P unit, 272
MDL, 179, 183
Mean square error, 75
Mean-value theorem, 448, 489
Measure of the relevance, 183
Memory, 4, 27
— matrix, 592
associative —, 35
long-term — (LTM), 27, 31, 33, 39
sensory — (SM), 32
short-term — (STM), 31, 33, 40
Metric space, 255
Metzler matrix, 449
MFNN, 18, 106, 172, 259
MIMO, 219
Min–max fuzzy neuron, 649
Minimal disturbance principle, 71
Minimum, 162
global —, 162
local —, 162
Minimum description length, 179, 183
Modified logistic neural network, 292
Modified relaxation, 69
Momentum constant, 145
Momentum term, 144
Monotonicity, 383, 647
Moore–Penrose pseudoinverse, 619
Multiinput/multioutput, 219
Multilayered feedforward neural network, 18, 106, 172, 259, 398
Multiple nonlinear feedback, 324
Multiquadratic radial basis function, 229

N

Natural language, 14, 636
NDEKF, 206
Nerve action potential, 25
Nerve impulse, 24–25
Neural filter, 396
Neural logic network, 272
Neural network, 5
discrete-time binary —, 510
dynamic —, 351
Hopfield —, 351
multilayered feedforward —, 106
static —, 106
two-layered —, 107
Neural population, 40
Neural state, 40, 470
Neurobiology, 316
Neurocontrol, 9
Neuron, 5, 9, 22, 39, 44, 85, 94
artificial —, 85

biologic —, 85
computational —, 85
excitatory —, 39
inhibitory —, 39
McCulloch–Pitts —, 85
Neuron-decoupled EKF, 206
Neuronal approximation, 13
Nominal point, 186
Nonactive state, 511
Nonlinear, 9, 286
— characteristics, 395
— mapping operation, 9
— sigmoidal function, 451
— surface fitting, 286
Nonorthogonal pattern vector, 608
Nonorthogonality, 614
Nonsigmoidal function, 261
Nonsingular, 283
Norm stability condition, 481
Normal fuzzy set, 637
NOT operation, 46

O

OBD, 186, 188
OBS, 186, 189
Ohm's law, 309
One-step prediction, 208
Operating region, 396
Operation, 29, 45
AND —, 45
NOT —, 46
OR —, 45
somatic —, 29, 85, 132
synaptic —, 29, 85, 132
XOR —, 47
Optimal brain damage, 186, 188
Optimal brain surgeon, 186, 189
Optimal control theory, 140
Optimal structure, 159
Optimality condition, 141
Optimization process, 113
OR operation, 45
Ordered partition, 562
Orthogonal pattern, 586
Orthogonal projection, 619
Orthogonal projection matrix, 619
Outer-product rule, 582
Output, 301
Output layer, 130

P

Pain reflex, 30
Parallel mode, 513
Parallel operating mode, 551
Parity function, 47
Partial parallel mode, 513
Pattern classification, 127
Pavlov's experiment, 37
Perceptron, 65
α —, 66
fixed-increment —, 69
Period, 513
Periodic point, 512
Pi–sigma network, 288
Piecewise-constant function, 267
Pitchfork bifurcation, 334
Plateau, 149
Point attractor, 396
Polak–Ribiere formulation, 201
Population biology, 316
Population effect, 395
Positivity, 383
Potential function network, 224
Probe vector, 593
Product–sum fuzzy neuron, 650
Projection learning rule, 580
Projection matrix, 235
Projection method, 234
Projection rule, 619
Propagation error, 116
Protoplasm, 24
Pruning, 183
first-order —, 183
second-order —, 183
Pseudoinverse, 284
Pseudoinverse rule, 619

Q

q-step prediction, 208
Quantizer error, 65
Quasi-Newton method, 199

R

Radial basis function, 18, 224–225
— network, 224
cubic splines —, 229
Gaussian —, 224, 229
inverse multiquadratic —, 229
linear splines —, 229
multiquadratic —, 229
thin plate splines —, 229
RAM, 625

Random access memory, 625
RBF, 18, 224
— network, 224
RBFN, 224
Recurrent connection, 346
Recurrent neural network, 298
Recursive least squares, 219, 431
Refractory period, 26, 40, 48, 317
absolute —, 27
Region of asymptotic stability, 437
Region of attraction, 437
Regular fuzzy neural network, 656
Rest state, 511
Retina, 40
RFNN, 656
Ridge function, 289
Ridge polynomial neural network, 289
Robust stability, 445
RPNN, 289

S

S operator, 647
Saddle, 439
— equilibrium point, 476
— point, 162
Saliency, 186
Saturating function, 262, 312, 652
Scaled conjugate gradient method, 200
SCG, 200
Schur stability, 482
Second-order pruning, 183
Self-feedback coefficient, 470
Self-feedback linear term, 470
Self-organization, 12
Self-recall, 580, 594
Self-recurrent connection, 301
Semilinear unit, 267
Sensitivity, 185
Sensitivity system, 413
Sensitization, 36–37
Sensor, 30
Separability, 256
Serial mode, 513
Shape matrix, 236
Sigma–pi network, 287
Sigmoidal activation function, 373
Sigmoidal cosine squashing function, 263
Sigmoidal function, 471
Signum function, 262, 517
Single-input/single-output, 211
Singular-value decomposition, 76, 235
Sink, 439, 476
SISO, 211
Skew–symmetric, 332, 465, 517, 556
Smoothness, 383
Soft computing, 4, 7
Solvability condition, 234
Soma, 9, 22, 24, 28, 40
Somatic operation, 29, 85, 132
Source, 439, 476
Speech, 4
Spike, 25
Spurious memory, 593
Spurious state, 369
Squashing function, 262
Stability analysis, 18, 436
Stable equilibrium point, 519
Stable state, 513
State attractor, 333
State feedback, 298
State space, 512
State trajectory, 311, 394, 396, 512
Static neural network, 18, 106
Statistical information, 7
Steady adjoint equation, 428
Steady state, 394, 512
Steady-state
— memory, 373
— solution, 348
Step function, 48
Stimulus, 40
Stone–Weierstrass theorem, 18, 239, 254, 256, 674
Sup–star composition, 643
Supervised learning, 140, 242
Supremum, 255
Switching algebra, 45
Symmetric, 479
Symmetry, 383
Synapse, 9, 24, 27, 40
Synapse-dependent nonlinear activation function, 448
Synaptic connection, 301
Synaptic operation, 29, 85, 132
Synaptic weight, 132, 301, 470, 580
Synchronous mode, 513
Synchronous operating mode, 561, 597, 600
Synchronous state mode, 548

T

T operator, 647
t-conorm, 635, 647

t-norm, 635, 647
Tapped delay line neural network, 208
Taylor series expansion, 186, 455
TDLNN, 208
Temporal learning, 398
Temporal learning process, 395
Temporal trajectory, 394
Thin plate splines radial basis function, 229
Thinking, 4
Threshold, 44, 301, 470
— function, 54
— logic, 44, 51, 94
Tolerance parameter, 127
TPBVP, 142, 402
Trajectory, 366
Transfer function, 110, 657
Transient activity, 331
Transient time, 514
Triangular inequality, 603
Triangular weighting matrix, 369
Trigonometric function, 258, 260
Two-layered neural network, 107
Two-point boundary-value problem, 142, 402

U

Undirected graph theory, 571
Uniform distribution, 175
Uniformly denseness, 257
Union, 637
Unipolar set, 45
Unipolar step function, 521
Universal approximation capability, 18, 254
Universal approximator, 324, 674
Unstable equilibrium point, 334

V

Variational principle, 140, 400
Vectorial norm, 450
Vision, 4
VLSI, 354

W

WDEKF, 207
Weight decay approach, 179
Weight elimination approach, 180
Weight matrix, 109
Weight-decoupled EKF, 207
Widrow's μ-LMS algorithm, 77
Widrow–Hoff delta rule, 72

X

XOR operation, 47
XOR problem, 231

Printed and bound by CPI Group (UK) Ltd, Croydon, CR0 4YY

27/10/2024

14580260-0004